P9-EEQ-903

JOHN JAY

THE MAKING OF A REVOLUTIONARY

1745–1780

A 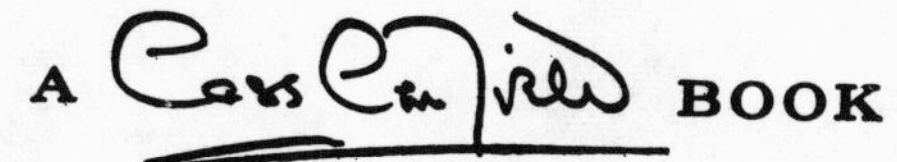 BOOK

BOOKS BY RICHARD B. MORRIS

John Jay: The Making of a Revolutionary 1745–1780 (1975)
Seven Who Shaped Our Destiny (1973)
Harper Encyclopedia of the Modern World (*with Graham W. Irwin*) (1970)
The Emerging Nations and the American Revolution (1970)
John Jay, the Nation, and the Court (1967)
The American Revolution Reconsidered (1967)
The Peacemakers (1965)
Great Presidential Decisions (1960)
The Spirit of 'Seventy-Six (*with Henry Steele Commager*) (1958, 1967)
Alexander Hamilton and the Founding of the Nation (1957)
The American Revolution: A Brief History (1955)
Encyclopedia of American History (*first edition*, 1953)
Fair Trial (1953)
A Treasury of Great Reporting (*with Louis L. Snyder*) (1949)
Government and Labor in Early America (1946)
The Era of the American Revolution (*editor*, 1939)
Studies in the History of American Law (1930)
A Guide to the Principal Sources for Early American History (*with Evarts Boutell Greene*) (1929)

(Volumes I and II of THE LIFE HISTORY OF THE UNITED STATES)

The New World (1963)
The Making of the Nation (1963)

John Jay

THE MAKING OF A REVOLUTIONARY

Unpublished Papers 1745–1780

EDITED BY

RICHARD B. MORRIS

ASSOCIATE EDITOR: *Floyd M. Shumway*

ASSISTANT EDITORS

Ene Sirvet

Elaine G. Brown

I

1817

HARPER & ROW, PUBLISHERS

NEW YORK, EVANSTON, SAN FRANCISCO, LONDON

 For information address Harper & Row, Publishers, Inc., 10 East 53rd Street, New York, N.Y. 10022. Published simultaneously in Canada by Fitzhenry & Whiteside Limited, Toronto.

FIRST EDITION

Designed by Sidney Feinberg

Library of Congress Cataloging in Publication Data

Jay, John, 1745–1829.
John Jay, the making of a revolutionary.
(A Cass Canfield book)
Consists chiefly of previously unpublished papers in the collections of Columbia University Libraries.
Bibliography: v. 1, p.
Includes index.
CONTENTS: v. 1 Unpublished papers, 1745–1780.
1. United States—Politics and government—Revolution, 1775–1783—Collected works. 2. Jay, John, 1745–1829. I. Morris, Richard Brandon, 1904– ed.
II. Title: The making of a revolutionary.
E302.J425 973.3'092'4 [B] ISBN 0-06-013080-6 75-6349

75 76 77 78 79 10 9 8 7 6 5 4 3 2 1

CONTENTS

INTRODUCTION

Tracking Down the Jay Papers 1
Publication Objectives 9
Mr. Jay Himself: A New Portrait 10
Editorial Guidelines 16
Transcription 16
Manuscript Designations 18
Textual Symbols 19
Sources 19
Short Titles of Works Frequently Cited 20
John Jay Chronology, 1745–1780 23

I
BOYHOOD, YOUTH, AND KING'S COLLEGE DAYS

The Jay Family 29
Parentage and Childhood 33
A Church Dispute 41
Entering Upon Law Studies 43
John Jay and the King's College Demonstration 55

II
JAY'S YEARS AS A LAWYER

Clerking for Benjamin Kissam 67
The Jay-Livingston Friendship 71
Sir James Jay, an Embarrassing Sibling 73
The Master's Degree 84

Legal and Personal Affairs 86
The Debating Society 87
License to Practice Law in New York 95
The Vermont Lands 102
A Confrontation with the Attorney General 106
The Social Club 112
The Dancing Assembly: An Invitation to a Duel 116
The New York–New Jersey Boundary Commission 118
Marriage 123

III

ON THE THRESHOLD OF REVOLUTION

Early Political Activism 129
Delegate to the First Continental Congress 133
Role in the First Congress 135
Organizing a Provisional Government 141
Jay's Draft of the "Olive Branch Petition" 147
Operating Under the Continental-Wide Boycott 162
Provincial Maneuvers 192
"Between Hawk and Buzzard"—Disclaiming Independence While Edging Toward Continentalism 194
Last Stand Against Independence 263
Rounding Up Subversives: The Hickey Plot 277

IV

THE DIE IS CAST: JAY AS A MILITANT PATRIOT

Endorsing Independence and Supporting Washington 287
Defending the Hudson 295
Detecting Conspiracies and Determining Loyalty 331
The Case of Peter Van Schaack 331
The Case of Enoch Crosby, Professedly Cooper's *Spy* 333
The Case of Beverly Robinson 345
The Case of Cadwallader Colden, Jr. 354

Jay's *An Address of the Convention of the Representatives of the State of New-York to their Constituents* Compared with Paine's *The Crisis Number 1* 359
Jay and the New York Constitution of 1777 389
Problems of the Northern Command 418
Jay's "A Hint to the Legislature of the State of New York" 461
Chief Justice of the State Supreme Court of Judicature 478

V

JAY'S PRESIDENCY OF THE CONGRESS 507

VI

JAY'S MISSION TO SPAIN

Jay's Mission to Spain 649
Jay's Use of Ciphers and Codes 660
Family Correspondence 675
The First Phase of the Spanish Mission 715
The Jay-Carmichael Relationship 769
The San Ildefonso Conference 824

Acknowledgments 836

Index 839

ILLUSTRATIONS

The following are grouped in a separate section after page 212:

Augustus Jay
Anna Maria Bayard Jay
Jay House, Rye
King's College in 1770
Samuel Johnson
Sir James Jay
Jay's license to practice law
Robert R. Livingston, Jr.
John Jay
Sarah Livingston Jay
Catharine W. Livingston
William Livingston
Montresor map of New York City in 1775
Queens Head (Fraunces) Tavern
Appointment of Jay as Colonel, 2d New York Regiment
Title page of *Extracts . . . from Congress*, 1774, containing Jay's "Address to the People of Great-Britain"
Richard Henry Lee
Signatories of the Continental Association
Alexander McDougall
James Duane
John Dickinson
Edward Rutledge
First page of Jay's draft of the Olive Branch Petition
The Great Fire in New York, September 1776
Beverly Robinson
Peter Van Schaack
General Philip Schuyler
Robert Troup

These are grouped in a separate section after page 564:

Independence Hall
"A Map of the Most Inhabited Part of New England," 1774
Silas Deane
Arthur Lee
Thomas Paine
Henry Laurens
General George Washington
The Marquis de Lafayette
General Horatio Gates
General John Sullivan
General Nathanael Greene
Gouverneur Morris and Robert Morris
The Continental Frigate *Confederacy*
Conrad Alexandre Gérard
William Carmichael
A sugar mill in Martinique
William Bingham
Passport to Madrid
The Harvesters
Brawling in Front of an Inn
Fighting on Stilts
Fiesta Outside the Summer Palace at Aranjuez
The Conde de Floridablanca
Samuel Huntington
Charles Thomson
The cipher portion of Jay's 6 November 1780 letter to Huntington

JOHN JAY

THE MAKING OF A REVOLUTIONARY

1745–1780

INTRODUCTION

Tracking Down the Jay Papers

If the commemoration of the American Revolution's bicentennial serves to remind the nation once again of the monumental achievements of America's first statesmen in winning independence against colossal odds and building not only a nation but an enduring constitutional structure to underpin it, so should it alert us to the ravages which two centuries have perpetrated upon the historic records of that era. Few if any need to be persuaded about the compelling obligation to preserve and collect the records of that notable epoch and to intensify our commitment to a reexploration of the creative ideas and audacious decisionmaking which made it so distinctive. No one, however, should have any illusions about the extraordinary complexity of the task. Indubitably, anyone venturing to edit the papers of a Founding Father needs to enlist the full resources of historical scholarship and command a team of professional sleuths. The leading statesmen of the Revolutionary and early National eras, as the magisterial editions of their writings currently sponsored by the National Historical Publications Commission attest, were both literate and articulate, conscious, even self-conscious, about the significance of the events in which they had participated. Professing a "decent respect to the opinions of mankind," they devoted what today would be deemed an inordinate amount of time to putting down on paper accounts of their own roles and to saving every scrap of correspondence that came to them.

Not one of the Founding Fathers, not even Thomas Jefferson or James Madison, was more meticulous in preserving his papers as essential sources for posterity than was John Jay, and in no case were a Founder's intentions more perversely frustrated by the passage of time, imprudent custodianship, and neglect. For a hundred and thirty years after Jay's death his papers were not generally available, a policy which did his reputation a disservice and withheld from the historians vital information about the great events with which he was associated.

A statesman whose life spanned a half-dozen eras in colonial and early national history, who was born when the colonies as part of the old British Empire were fighting King George's War against Spain and France and who lived to see Andrew Jackson become President of a nation transformed beyond the imaginings of an aged Federalist, captured on paper many if not most of the seminal events in that nation's early history. In his long and distinguished public career Jay held all the great posts of public service save the Presidency of the new republic—Chief Justice of the State of New York, President of the Continental Congress, minister plenipotentiary negotiating the peace with Great Britain which ended the American Revolution, Secretary for Foreign Affairs in the Confederation years and ad interim Secretary of State under Washington, co-author of *The Federalist* papers, first Chief Justice of the United States, and two-term governor of New York State. Last of the members of the First Continental Congress to pass away, Jay lived a full life of eighty-four years, one enriched by cherished friendships, ennobled by unimpeachable integrity, and distinguished by his advocacy of various humanitarian causes of which freedom for the blacks was perhaps the most noteworthy. He possessed, in addition, a special talent for stirring up controversy, and his role and judgments in diplomacy and adjudication earned him at least as many critics as they did advocates.

Despite the profound national interest in the issues and actions in which John Jay and his correspondents were deeply concerned, Jay's papers were retained in private hands down to the year 1957. Save for a few biographers and one editor, they were not generally accessible to scholars. Jay's son William brought out a brief selection of his letters in 1833, and Henry P. Johnston issued a four-volume edition, 1889–92. Neither collection proved free of serious errors of omission and transcription. Both signally failed to include some of the most significant papers associated with Jay's career. For the years covered by this volume Francis Wharton included in his *Revolutionary Diplomatic Correspondence of the United States* (6 vols., Washington, D.C., 1889), dispatches to and from Jay while serving in diplomatic posts in Spain and Paris, but he invariably omitted the unciphered sections of the dispatches without a caution to his readers. As a result, Wharton left out what the dispatch was really intended to convey.

Suddenly, the picture brightened. On 3 December 1957, Columbia University announced the acquisition of some two thousand papers of John Jay, a King's College (Columbia) alumnus, class of 1764. They had been purchased on 17 July 1957 from the estate of Mrs. Arthur Iselin, great-great-granddaughter of Jay. The collection included thirty-three letters from George Washington, of which a number had never been published, along with numerous letters from John Adams, Benjamin Franklin, Alexander Hamilton, Thomas Jefferson, Robert Morris, the Marquis de Lafayette, and Gouverneur Morris, among other notables. Perhaps most noteworthy was *The Federalist* No. 5, a draft of Jay's celebrated letter with many corrections and revisions. Of considerable historic interest also was the unpublished diary of Jay as Chief Justice riding the Northern circuit,[1] an item which no constitutional historian of the period has yet consulted.

Despite its riches, the collection on careful examination was manifestly incomplete. Jay's correspondents were abundantly represented; Jay's own letters or drafts thereof were meager. A letterbook containing the correspondence of Jay's wife, Sarah Livingston Jay, covering the years the couple spent in Spain, while listed in the inventory of sale, did not turn up among the items Columbia acquired. If the collection was truncated, it was soon discovered that the blame did not rest entirely with its twentieth-century custodians.

In his will dated 18 April 1829, John Jay made his wishes regarding his papers explicit. On this subject the will reads:

> I give all my manuscript books and papers other than such as respect my own estate or the estate of others, to my two sons Peter Augustus Jay and William Jay jointly and not to be divided. It is my will that after my death they do take possession of all my manuscript books and papers without exception, and without permiting them to be inspected by others. They are then to select and Seperate from them all title deeds books of accounts, and papers which concern my estate or the estate of others. These when so selected and Seperated ought of course to be in the hands of my Executors or of the persons entitled to them. Among the other manuscripts there are some which should, and some which should not be forthwith destroyed. I have greatly but not yet Sufficiently reduced their number. They must be kept together. The possession of them is to belong to Peter, during his life. But he may at his discretion deliver the possession of them to his brother William. Each of them is however at all reasonable times to have free access to them and permission to make extracts from or copies of them.[2]

[1] JJ's circuit court diary, 16 April 1790–4 Aug. 1792, JP.
[2] JJ, Last Will and Testament, 18 April 1829, JP.

In declining to grant the historian-editor Jared Sparks access to the Jay Papers, Peter Augustus Jay cited this will, adding, "until this selection shall be made I do not think we are permitted to shew them to others." As Jay explained his instructions to his eldest son, "he considered all private correspondence as confidential and that it was his duty to prevent the publication of any letter which he supposed the author would be unwilling to have published, and that this duty did not cease with the author's life."[3] William Jay took over the arrangement of the papers, and both brothers remained quite sticky about giving the persistent Mr. Sparks even a peek at them. As the distinguished president of Harvard was not only a less than objective critic of Mr. Jay but as editor of a series of bowdlerized versions of the papers of some of the Founding Fathers set American history back at least a generation and dismantled collections previously intact, the instincts of Jay's sons were sound. The John Jay Papers remained in the possession of William Jay, who used them in his edition of *The Life of John Jay,* and on the death of Peter Augustus, title vested in William as the survivor. Both brothers, however, had "carefully reviewed" the correspondence, according to William's son, John Jay II, with the result that "a large number" were "destroyed, those only being preserved that were deemed worthy of preservation."[4] Finally, in 1847 William Jay turned over to the New-York Historical Society a large collection of Jay manuscripts relating to the Treaty with Great Britain of 1794, of which Jay was the sole American negotiator.[5]

If the sons scrupulously followed their father's injunction to destroy what they thought the author "would be unwilling to have published," the grandson, John Jay II, a diplomat and historian in his own right, dipped into the manuscript till for an occasional munificent benefaction. When, in 1860, Albert Edward, Prince of Wales, much later to become Edward VII, visited the United States, he was entertained by Mr. Jay. As a parting gift Jay gave the prince fifty-seven of the choicest autographic items in the collection. Though a gift less suited to the tastes of Albert Edward could scarcely be imagined, his royal highness carefully preserved them, and they have since been on display at Windsor Castle. The efforts of Columbia University and the editor of the John Jay Papers to secure these originals as a special royal bequest having proved unavailing, Her

[3] Peter Augustus Jay to Jared Sparks, 12 Jan. 1830, dft in JP.

[4] John Jay II to Justin Winsor, 25 Aug. 1886, ALS in MHi: Justin Winsor Papers.

[5] NHi: Jay Papers.

Majesty Queen Elizabeth II donated a microfilm of these items to the United States Government, which in turn conveyed them to Columbia University. There, in Xerox form, they are now available for study in Special Collections, Columbia University Libraries.

John Jay II's generosity was only matched by his negligence. During the American Civil War Henry B. Dawson, who was engaged in bringing out an edition of *The Federalist* papers, prodded Jay for any drafts he might possess of his grandfather's contributions to that great work of collaboration. Going through a bundle of newspapers, Jay chanced upon an original draft of *Federalist* No. 64. Hoping that it would settle the question of proper attribution of authorship to that letter, which was indubitably by Jay, he sent it on to George H. Moore, the Secretary of the New-York Historical Society.[6] Dawson examined it and returned it to Moore, but the latter inadvertently failed to send it back to John Jay II. When Columbia acquired the Jay Papers from the Iselin Estate only a draft of *Federalist* No. 5 was among them. The absence of other drafts known to have been among Jay's papers spurred the search, which resulted in tracking down No. 64 in the manuscript files of the New-York Historical Society, an item not then known to be in the Society's possession.[7]

According to the late Frank Monaghan, a biographer of John Jay,[8] some members of the family were indifferent to the trust they had assumed as custodians of historic papers and participated in breaking up parts of the collection. Reputedly, when the Jay house at Rye was sold about 1906, the family converged, divided up the silver, portraits, and furniture, and shared the contents of a box of manuscripts. Those believed to have been present when the division took place were Laura Jay Welles, Mary Rutherford Jay, Pierre Jay, Mrs. Banyar Clarkson, John Clarkson Jay, and the two Misses Pierrepont of Brooklyn. John Clarkson Jay kept his Jay manuscripts in a hatbox. After he died and while the building in which he had lived was being demolished, the hatbox was tossed into a trashcan. Fortuitously, the item was retrieved by a court clerk, who secured whatever title could be acquired by slipping the building superintendent a five-dollar bill, and then sold the "find" to the New-York Historical Society. Under those extraordinary circumstances the Society acquired the correspondence of the American novelist James Fenimore Cooper with Peter Augustus Jay. Of the three tin containers of Jay correspondence

6 John Jay II to George H. Moore, 11 Dec. 1863, ALS, and *Federalist* 64, dft, n.d. [c. 5 March 1888], NHi.

7 *Federalist* 5, 10 Nov. 1787, dft in JP.

8 Notes in JP.

reputedly in the possession of Mary Rutherford Jay, two found their way to the New-York Historical Society; the third, according to report, was thrown away. At various times individuals disposed of Jay family papers through Forrest Sweet, a rare book and manuscript dealer of Battle Creek, Michigan, and numerous Jay items are found in Sweet's catalogues for the years of the 1930's and running down to the early fifties.

Furnishings and books from the Jay House were disposed of through various dealers. John Jay's personal library was even more cavalierly treated than his personal papers. A comparison of a list of books in John Jay's library at Katonah as located by Frank Monaghan in the early 1930's with a second list of Jay's books currently at the Jay Homestead as compiled by Lino S. Lipinsky de Orlov, the curator, reveals startling discrepancies. Among the prize items once in Jay's library was a copy of the *First Laws of the United States*, inscribed to John Jay by President Washington, an item acquired by a private Los Angeles collector, who donated it to the Henry E. Huntington Library and Art Gallery at San Marino, California. To compound the problem, bound manuscript volumes, considered by members of the family or by dealers to be books, managed to disappear from the Jay collection. Included among these items were Jay's letterbooks as governor of the State of New York, items acquired appropriately by the New York State Library at Albany, and as such immensely enriching the records of a period of New York State history, but which in large part perished in the Albany fire of 1911. Another example is a letterbook covering Jay's Spanish mission, unaccountably separated from his set of four letterbooks, and now owned by the Huntington Library.

While many of these facts explaining the lacunae in the Jay Papers were not generally known at the time Columbia University made its acquisition, it was evident, once the material was available for close analysis, that the utility of the collection for further study and possible publication would be enormously enhanced by undertaking an extensive search for missing papers which would fill out the details of John Jay's career. To complete the collection, whether by securing originals or photocopies, became the first objective of the John Jay Papers project, which, with a generous grant from the Avalon Foundation, launched a two-continent quest. The initial results were so promising that the project was able to continue and expand its operations as a result of the Avalon Foundation's further generosity, supplemented by a grant from the Rockefeller Foundation for an investigation of the documents relating to Jay's diplomatic career, notably his role in the peacemaking of 1782–83, and assistance from the American Council of Learned Societies. Calendaring was supported by a grant from the National Historical Publications Commission, while the major editorial work involved in preparing this first volume for the press has been made possible by grants from the National Endowment for the Humanities.

The quest for missing Jay items benefited immensely by the enthusiastic support of the late Roland Baughman, then head of Special Collections, and his successor, Kenneth A. Lohf, Librarian for Rare Books and Manuscripts, Columbia University Libraries. Members of the Jay family generously cooperated. Among the donors of extensive papers have been Mrs. Arthur M. R. Hughes of Rochester, New York, Jay's great-great-great-granddaughter, and other descendants, including Mrs. Pierre Jay and Miss Frances Jay of New York City and Mrs. Peter Augustus Jay of Washington, D.C. Mr. John Jay III of Williamstown, Massachusetts, made his collection of the Jay-Peloquin correspondence available for microfilming. Throughout Mrs. Dorothy Iselin Paschal and Mr. John Jay Iselin have been most generous of their time and effort on behalf of the project.

Supported in no small part by gifts from the classes of '23 and '25 of Columbia College and by such generous donors as Mr. and Mrs. Arthur C. Berol of Cross River, New York, and other devoted friends of the Columbia Libraries, Columbia over the last dozen years has acquired several thousand additional Jay papers. These include the bulk of the letters written by John Jay to correspondents whose letters to Jay were found in the original acquisition from the Iselin Estate, the missing letterbook of Sarah Livingston Jay, covering the years 1779–81, diary fragments for the summer of 1776 describing Jay's activities as a militant revolutionary shortly after the signing of the Declaration of Independence, Jay's diary during the peace negotiations of 1782, his notebook reporting conversations and anecdotes of Benjamin Franklin, Jay's draft of his letter to Hamilton enclosing the Proclamation of Neutrality of 1793, and other choice hitherto unknown items, which will be included in this and subsequent volumes. In addition the late Frank Monaghan kindly made available to the editor several batches of typewritten transcripts of Jay correspondence, to which he had access at one time.

When military events and political obligations conspired to compel John Jay to leave New York City, his law books and law papers proved a major casualty. They were presumably packed and shipped to his father's wartime residence at Fishkill, but many if not most of the papers relating to his law practice and almost all of his legal briefs are missing. Recently there has been discovered in the attic of the home of Mrs. Joseph C. Wilberding, the former Katherine Van Cortlandt of Mount Kisco, New York, the ledger kept by Augustus Van Cortlandt, clerk of the Mayor's Court of New York City, 1770–76, covering the very years for which the minute books of that court have long been missing from New York City's Hall of Records. This ledger, listing lawyers' fees, disclosed that over a period of less than six years John Jay litigated about three hundred cases in the Mayor's Court, a small number of them with his erstwhile law partner Robert R. Livingston, Jr. The fee book is on deposit at the Jay Homestead and a photocopy of the pages relating to Jay's lawsuits is in Special Collections, Columbia University Libraries. Since the sources available for reconstructing Jay's practice are more extensive than has hitherto been recognized, it is planned to publish Jay's law papers separately from his general correspondence, exceptions being made in the case of legal correspondence relating to Jay's training as a lawyer or illuminating his personality, ambitions, and views transcending the special concerns of his clients.

The John Jay Papers project supplemented the acquisition program by conducting an extensive search here and abroad to collect photocopies of papers to and from Jay, and concerning areas in which his role was of major significance—notably the peacemaking of 1782–83 and the negotiations culminating in the Jay Treaty. As the finding list appended indicates, many repositories in the United States contributed to the treasure trove of Jay items. The project especially benefited by the generous help of Dr. Philip M. Hamer, Dr. O. W. Holmes, and Dr. E. Berkeley Tompkins, in turn directors of the National Historical Publications Commission, and their highly competent staffs, in running down Jay items in the National Archives and in supporting the Jay program at every point in its development. A substantial number of Jay papers were located at such repositories abroad as the Archivo Histórico Nacional in Madrid, the Archivo General de Indías in Seville, and the Archivo General de Simancas, among the British Foreign Office records in the Public Record Office, London, and in the archives of the Ministère des Affaires Étrangères, at the Quai d'Orsay, in Paris. The Vatican's Archivio Segreto, and archives at The Hague, Vienna, Copenhagen, Stockholm, Venice, Florence, Turin, and Lisbon were searched for correspondence relating both to the peace negotiations of 1782–83 and to Jay's activities as Secretary for Foreign Affairs. The Lansdowne Papers, divided between the collection at the William L. Clements Library of the University of Michigan and Bowood, the private estate of the Marquess of Lansdowne, yielded rich ore on the subject of the peacemaking, as did such other private collections as the Grenville Papers, at the estate of the late George Fortescue, Boconnoc, Lostwithiel, Cornwall, among other private collections in Great Britain, acknowledged elsewhere.

The problems, time, and expense entailed in reassembling the John Jay Papers could doubtless be duplicated many times in the case of the papers of other statesmen of the Revolutionary and early National Periods save perhaps for the foresight of the Adams family which zealously preserved the papers of their distinguished forbears. Additionally, financial need as well as historical obligations motivated a few individuals or families, as in the cases of the Jefferson, Washington, Hamilton, and Madison Papers, to sell their collections to the Library of Congress. Even then some of these collections had already been seriously ravaged. As regards the rest, it seems obvious that families of eminent public figures have too often been unmindful of the stewardship they have assumed in acquiring documents in the national interest. Nor have the public laws been drawn with sufficient prudence or precision to distinguish between public papers prepared or acquired in the public service and at public expense and strictly personal papers. Seemingly, only the latter should be deemed private property subject to transferral by bequest, inheritance, or sale.

Publication Objectives

As a result of searching out and collecting papers relating to John Jay, the Columbia University Libraries now house some five thousand manuscript items comprising letters to or from John Jay or papers or memoranda by him (all of which have been Xeroxed for security reasons), along with some ten thousand photocopied items, including five thousand separately organized as a diplomatic series. Bearing in mind the fact that a single item such as the Records of the Commission for Settling the Boundary Line between New York and New Jersey, including the original journal kept by John Jay as Clerk of the Commissioners, July 1769–July 4, 1770,[9] runs to several thousand handwritten pages, it is obvious that any attempt to reproduce in a letter-press edition the totality of this formidable collection would prove not alone impractical but extravagant of editorial labor, time, and money. Hence, in publishing the Jay Papers the editors have ob-

9 NHi: New York–New Jersey Boundary Papers.

served the kind of selectivity which has governed the publication of *The Adams Papers,* for the publication of much that is routine or available in published form elsewhere seems clearly unwarranted.

This volume, as well as the others to come, has as its objective the publication of the significant papers to and from John Jay which have never before been published or, if printed elsewhere, to reproduce only those previously printed with substantial errors of omission or transliteration. Exception has been made in the case of a few state papers of immense significance, documents which have not hitherto been adequately annotated. Thus, the editorial guidelines, notes, and annotations seek to furnish the reader with the background needed to identify the persons and subjects treated in the correspondence and such other data essential to an understanding of its contents or to clarifying the relationship to previously published correspondence of the unpublished items herein printed for the first time.

The John Jay Papers project has not neglected its responsibility to the entire collection that has been assembled at considerable cost and labor. That collection has been calendared, each item having been abstracted for all essential data, and the calendar is to be separately published by the Columbia University Libraries. All papers, originals and photocopies, are to be permanently housed in Special Collections, Columbia University Libraries, and a chronological and subject name index serves to guide the reader seeking to locate particular items.

Mr. Jay Himself: A New Portrait

This volume, in essence a documented biography of Jay's early life, from his days as a King's College student to the climax of his mission to Spain, casts new light on his early triumphs, his agonizing decisions, his creative statesmanship, and his inevitable frustrations. It dispels the popular notion of Jay as an unbending, bloodless, overly prudent, and ever-inhibited lawyer, while it reinforces the evidence of his zest for controversy and his considerable self-esteem.

Jay's first recorded rebellion against the Establishment came when as a King's College student he stood up to the authorities and refused to inform on his classmates involved in rowdy behavior. He declined to give evidence against them, fully cognizant of the possible consequences to himself, but convinced of the moral and legal correctness of his position. As a youngish Secretary of the New York–New Jersey Boundary Commission he first demonstrated that rigid insistence on technicalities which would ever characterize his long public career. Pressing a claim for back pay for his services upon both New York and New Jersey, he stood out against both governors, the New York Assembly, and even the British Secretary of State for the Colonies in refusing to release a copy of the proceedings of the Commissioners, and obliged only after being so instructed by a directive from the Board of Trade and an act of the New York Assembly. What proved most important for Jay was not the accumulated irritations running over several years but the good grounding he had received in just how a mixed commission operated, a device that he himself was to innovate in the adjustment of international disputes at a much later time in his career.

Socially secure, a member of an affluent French Huguenot mercantile family, claiming Van Cortlandt blood on his mother's side, he was ever one to resent slights to his *amour propre*, slights which a person of lesser social standing could well afford to overlook. A fledgling lawyer, he had the presumption to excoriate John Tabor Kempe, the attorney general of the province, for not consulting him about a case where both were associated as counsel for the plaintiff. As a socialite he was prepared to fight a duel with Robert Randall, a candidate for membership in a dancing assembly whom Jay had rejected out of hand as not possessing the proper connections. "Your conduct at least represents me in an insignificant point of view," Jay noted, a course which one always took toward Jay at the actor's peril.

Conservative by both inclination and connections with affluent Tory families, Jay inched reluctantly toward revolution, as his letters and the correspondence of his disillusioned Tory associates reveal. Yet his grievances against the royal government mounted. His land petition was tabled; his interest in the Vermont claims, as with so many other prominent New Yorkers, seemed to be diminishing in value, and his bid for a royal judgeship, along with that of Robert R. Livingston, Jr., a quest which Jay had not yet abandoned when he attended the First Continental Congress, was finally rejected by the governor and Council.

Even were one to discount Jay's talents for ruffling the feathers of royal officials, along with his frustrations at their hands, his Whig ties proved on balance weightier than his Tory connections. His father and brothers were pronounced Whigs and he himself forged a tight bond to the Whig cause by marrying the daughter of the Whig lawyer-intellectual, William Livingston, soon to supplant Tory Governor William Franklin as the Revolutionary chief executive of New Jersey. Except for gossip, there is no documentary confirmation of his rumored prior courtship and rejection by two different daughters of Peter De Lancey. Jay's marriage to Sarah Livingston in 1774 served not only to elevate Jay in the esteem of the Whigs but proved, as the touching correspondence between the couple reveals, a love match rivaled among the Founding Fathers only by the long love affair between John Adams and Abigail Smith. To Sarah Livingston Jay, her husband, senior by eleven years, was a paragon, "virtue's own self." Jay was always miserable when separated from his "beloved" Sally. Alone of all the wives of foreign diplomats, Sally accompanied her husband to Spain and France, and her letters home published in this volume provide a refreshing sidelight on the rigors of foreign travel and the pomposities and frivolities of foreign courts.

Jay made his initial bow in provincial politics on the Committee of Fifty-One, a protest movement touched off by news of the closing of the port of Boston. On this committee the conservatives had a slight majority, Jay serving along with some nineteen future Tories. But by imperceptible stages he was drawn into a role of leadership of the Revolutionary movement in New York. At the start his talents were enlisted as a penman, and it was in that capacity that he served so conspicuously in the First Continental Congress. Rallying behind Joseph Galloway's Plan of Union, he earned thereby a "horrid opinion" in Patrick Henry's judgment. He signed the Continental Association, perhaps grudgingly, and then won the acclaim of Congress for his draft of an "Address to the People of Great Britain." That address propelled him at once into the front line of Whig propagandists, and the Tories, as this volume reveals, were now ready to write him off.

Back in New York he was elected to the Committee of Sixty, as well as to the Committee of Inspection appointed to police compliance with the Continental Association, an operation which he performed with zest. In a letter to the New Haven Committee of 17 April 1775, heretofore unpublished, Jay defended the New York committee's adherence to the Continental Association.

Associated in the Second Continental Congress with such moderates as John Dickinson and Edward Rutledge, Jay consented to prepare a "Letter to the Oppressed Inhabitants of Canada," but throughout the spring and summer of '75 he performed a neat balancing act. A shooting war had already broken out, but Jay's party made one last desperate stand. Jay moved for a second petition to the King (the first had been virtually ignored by Parliament). He wrote an early draft, herein included. That he was prepared to be much more conciliatory than his fellow committeemen is clear from comparing his draft with that of John Dickinson's, which was finally adopted. He still was an empire man, still loyal to the king, a state of mind borne out by a letter to Alexander McDougall dated 17 October 1775, and the draft of a paper, "Proofs that the Colonies Do Not Aim at Independence," written some time after 11 December 1775.

Even after the rejection of the Olive Branch Petition Jay continued vainly to hope for a conciliatory gesture from the crown. This did not foreclose his active cooperation with the Continentalists in Congress in insisting that both the war and peace powers should be left to the initiative of the Congress. Thus he served on such crucial committees as the Committee of Secret Correspondence to secure aid from abroad, and advocated the arrest of subversive persons, including the detention of those who voted against sending delegates to Congress, and the disarming of dissidents. While Jay edged toward independence, he was not present in Congress when some of the crucial decisions of the spring and summer of 1776 were made, serving instead in the New York Provincial Congress to which he had been elected a delegate.

On 11 June 1776, four days after Richard Henry Lee had offered in Congress his resolution affirming independence, Jay moved that it was the sense of the Provincial Congress "that the good people of this Colony have not, in the opinion of this Congress, authorized this Congress, or the delegates of this Colony in the Continental Congress, to declare this Colony to be and continue independent of the Crown of Great Britain." He was perhaps conveniently absent from Congress when the decisive vote on independence took place on 2 July. Not finding an opportunity to return to Congress for the rest of the year, his signature was never affixed to the Declaration of Independence. No longer did Jay entertain any doubts, however. On the afternoon of 9 July he reported to the Convention of the Representatives of the State of New York, a resolution of his own drafting, which was unanimously adopted, endorsing the Declaration of Independence and pledging "at the risk of our lives and fortunes," to "join with the other colonies in supporting it."

Among the most revealing documents published herein for the first time are the fragments from Jay's diary of July–August 1776 recording his strenuous activities for the Convention as a committeeman charged with obstructing the channel of the Hudson River and harassing the enemy's shipping. His trip to Connecticut to secure cannon and his return journey to Livingston Manor to acquire trucks and shot for transport across the Hudson to Fort Montgomery document a triumphantly breathless journey of a newly converted Revolutionary activist. Other documents portray him as a stern if fair-minded prosecutor of dissidents, as chairman of the Committee to Detect Conspiracies. In that capacity he had to deal not alone with the investigation of an alleged plot against the life of Washington but, in a reorganized committee operating out of Fishkill, with stamping out disaffection, calling out the militia to suppress counter-revolutionary activities, and making drafts on the state treasury. To ferret out hidden enemies Jay organized an intelligence operation, and his activities served as the germ of James Fenimore Cooper's *The Spy*. As Cooper acknowledged, Jay's reminiscences supplied the main outlines for his novel, even though the original for Harvey Birch remains a shadowy figure not positively identified. As the state's Chief Justice Jay was concerned not only with the suppression of disorders incident to revolution, but addressed the legislature criticizing the impressment of horses, teams, and carriages "by the military without the intervention of a civil magistrate" as violative of due process. As a member of the Council of Revision he wrote the veto of an excess profits tax levied upon war profiteers on the ground that it violated the equal protection of the law to which all citizens were entitled.

Jay, despite his reservations about preserving a climate of due process, had become a committed revolutionary, whose enthusiastic support for the cause was epitomized in his notable "Address of the Convention," written on 23 December 1776, at the nadir of the military hopes of the Patriots and before the heartening news of the Trenton victory. "We do not fight for a few acres of land," he declared, "but for freedom—for the freedom and happiness of millions yet unborn." The manuscript draft was in the original Iselin Collection[10] but has eluded search.

Jay has been traditionally credited with being the principal draftsman of that extraordinary constitution which the State of New York adopted in 1777. Exactly how much of Jay's thinking was finally embodied in that document will never be definitely established, since no draft in his hand has been located. Several drafts or fragments thereof have survived, including one by Abraham Yates. That constitution contained some extraordinary innovations in government, providing for a weak chief executive, who shared appointing power with a council of appointment and conferred a veto power upon a council of revision (a provision that Jay lived to regret as governor), while a court of impeachment and correction of errors assumed functions

[10] Frank Monaghan, *John Jay* (New York and Indianapolis, 1935), p. 443.

that had traditionally belonged to the legislature. Notably, the constitution embodied the broadest enunciation of the principles of religious liberty that had as yet been granted by any state of the modern world. While Jay proposed this section, he was unsuccessful in barring officeholders who would not publicly abjure the authority of the pope. With that deep-seated anti-Catholic prejudice explained by his Huguenot refugee background, Jay persuaded the Convention to bar ministers and priests from holding civil or military office and to withhold naturalization from persons who would not renounce "all allegiance" to "every foreign king, prince, potentate, and state, in all matters, ecclesiastical as well as civil."

Jay served as President of the Continental Congress from 10 December 1778 to 28 September 1779, when he resigned to undertake the mission to Spain. His most significant contribution during that period was the notable "Circular Letter" of September 1779, in which he exhorted the states to supply enough soldiers, money, and matériel to restore public credit and advance the common cause. Warning of an impending fiscal crisis, President Jay pledged that Congress would not increase its outstanding bills of credit, a pledge made to boost the public's fast eroding faith in the government's ability to redeem its bills. During his Presidency much correspondence passed over his desk. What is clearly routine and addressed to him in his official capacity has been calendared; what is clearly meant for Jay's eyes and influence or what contains especially significant and hitherto unpublished information about the conduct of the war has been included in this volume. In fact, some of the most revealing letters in this volume are those penned to Jay by such associates as Robert R. Livingston, Alexander McDougall, and Philip Schuyler, hitherto unpublished.

Jay's mission to Spain, his dramatic ocean crossing, his frustrations and meager triumphs have been recounted by the editor in his *The Peacemakers: The Great Powers and American Independence* (New York, 1965), but many of the letters relating to the mission have never been published, and this is notably true of the letters which have been deciphered through the valiant efforts of the staff of the Jay Papers. Of special significance is the portion of a letter in cipher from Jay to Samuel Huntington, the President of Congress, of 7 November 1780, reporting a crucial conference held on 23 September with the Conde de Floridablanca, Spain's principal minister. Jay's altercations with William Carmichael, the secretary of the mission, and at a later date with his young brother-in-law, Henry Brockholst Livingston, his personal secretary, and with his unacknowledged ward, Lewis Littlepage, reveal a special character trait. He got along extraordinarily well with his peers, with men like Franklin, Washington, and John Adams, but his subordinates could find him authoritarian, vain, and stuffy, a man who stiffened at slights deliberate or unintended. In extenuation of Jay's sensitivity, it is clear from correspondence herein included that Carmichael's devious past, perhaps suspected by Jay, properly put his superior on guard.

This first volume ends on a climactic note, the confrontation between Jay and Floridablanca. Whatever gains ensued from the interview Jay attributed "to the Exertions of America," to her need "to be formidable at home," if she expected "to be respectable any where." From the meeting Jay drew the further conclusion that nations never moved on purely disinterested principles. Accordingly he instructed Congress, "we should endeavor to be as Independent on the Charity of our friends, as on the Mercy of our Enemies." In short, "the way not to be in *Esau's* condition is to be prepared to meet with *Jacob's*." John Jay never forgot the lesson.

Thenceforward Jay's Spanish mission is a story of trifling gains and repeated humiliations. Not so Jay's career, however. Ahead lay his most notable achievement, his service as a principal negotiator of the peace with Great Britain, along with many more years of dedicated service to his nation and state.

EDITORIAL GUIDELINES

Transcription

The editorial aim in transcription was to combine authenticity with readability. Thus, spelling was retained as in the manuscripts; however, obvious slips of the pen were corrected without the use of brackets or explanatory footnotes. Capitalization was retained as in the manuscripts, with these exceptions: (1) all sentences begin with capital letters; (2) if it was impossible to tell whether the writer intended to use an upper- or lower-case letter, modern usage governed. Grammar and syntax were retained as in the originals, and the use of [*sic*] was avoided. But run-on sentences which were joined by commas have been separated by a period and capital letter. If run-on sentences were joined by a semicolon or colon, the original was retained if the sentence parts were related to each other.

Generally, punctuation has been inserted only when absolutely necessary. The author's salutation was retained, and no punctuation was added to supply the author's omission. But every sentence ends with a period or appropriate terminal puncuation mark. Where such a mark did not exist in the manuscript, it was inserted. Terminal dashes were replaced by periods when they were used to end a sentence; if used to fill up a line, they were silently omitted; if used to indicate a change of thought, they were retained. Where dashes connect clauses which, in modern usage, would be separated by a semicolon, that punctuation mark was substituted. Colons have been silently omitted or inserted for clarity. When words appear in a column or series in the manuscript, they have been printed in the text separated by commas. In printing dialogue passages, punctuation has been supplied to the extent necessary to insure intelligibility. In the case of sentences which, in the absence of punctuation, are ambiguous, no punctuation has been inserted when to do so would constitute an election on the part of the editors of one of the ambiguous meanings.

The place of writing and the date always appear at the head of the letter no matter where they have been entered by the author. When both the date and place of writing, or any part of them, have been omitted, this has been supplied, if possible, within square brackets. If either was abbreviated, they have been spelled out without brackets.

Generally, canceled matter was ignored unless it was of special significance. However, in draft letters, where possible, all canceled matter has been indicated. When canceled matter is included, it is set off by angle brackets and placed before the revised passage. Deletions within longer deletions have been set off by double angle brackets.

Where a portion of a word was missing from a manuscript and there was no doubt about the missing letters, the proper letters were inserted. If the number of letters supplied was less than five, this was done silently; if five or more letters were involved, the inserted letters appear within square brackets. Where missing matter consists of more than one word or must be supplied conjecturally, brackets were used regardless of the length of the insertion. If the missing portion of a word could not be supplied, it has been indicated by a long dash within square brackets.

All abbreviations were retained so long as they conformed to modern standard form. Thus, "Maj.," "Gen.," "Esq.," "inst.," "ult." were not changed. But "gent." is expanded to "gent[lemen]" and "come." becomes "com[mitte]e." In both cases, brackets were used in expanded abbreviations only if five or more letters were added; the exception is that all closings in a letter were expanded silently no matter how many letters were omitted. Archaic abbreviations have been expanded silently: (1) the thorn was rendered as "th"; (2) the "tailed P" was rendered as "per" or "pro"; (3) the ampersand used as an abbreviation for "and" will become "and," but "& Co." will be retained. The term "&c." has been rendered "etc." Abbreviations of verbs using raised letters were expanded silently. Thus, "sh^{d}" will be "should"; "rec^{g}" will be "receiving" (or, in the case of JJ, who always misspelled it, "recieving"). Archaic abbreviations followed by an apostrophe were spelled out. Thus "tho" would be retained, but "tho'" would become "though." Similarly, archaic use of the apostrophe in verbal contractions were eliminated. "Shoud" will remain, but "shou'd" becomes "should."

In many instances a document may be represented by an ALS, a Dft, an LbkC, etc. The most authentic is published, that is, the ALS, or if that does not exist, an LbkC takes precedence over a Dft, since it is the copy of the ALS. The existence of the variant copies is cited in the source note, and canceled matter, which usually appears in the draft, has been indicated within angle brackets.

Paragraphing has been introduced when necessary.

Cipher passages have been deciphered and are printed in small and large capital letters. The method of deciphering and special problems involved are explained in the source note; the general use by Jay of ciphers and codes is explained in the editorial note bearing that heading.

All manuscripts are located in the Papers of John Jay, Special Collections, Columbia University Libraries, unless otherwise noted. When reference is made to manuscripts in the Papers of John Jay which are not being published, the designation JP is used.

Manuscript Designations

AD	Autograph document
ADS	Autograph document signed
AL	Autograph letter
ALS	Autograph letter signed
AL[S]	Autograph letter, signature cropped
C	Contemporary copy
D	Document
DS	Document signed
Dft	Draft (in author's hand unless otherwise noted)
DftS	Draft signed
Dupl	Duplicate
E	Extract

FC	File copy (in author's hand unless otherwise noted)
L	Letter
LS	Letter signed
LbkC	Letterbook copy (not in author's hand unless so stated)
PrC	Press copy
PtD	Printed document
PtDS	Printed document signed
PtL	Printed letter
RC	Retained copy
Tr	Transcript (made at a much later date)
Tripl	Triplicate

Textual Symbols

[———]	words missing
[roman]	insertion, or conjectural reading, in roman brackets
<roman>	canceled matter in angle brackets

Sources

The bulk of the original material drawn on for this publication is in the Papers of John Jay in the Columbia University Libraries. The rest comes from various public and private collections here and abroad.

Public collections in the United States (with abbreviations as in the National Union Catalogue of the Library of Congress):

CSmH	Henry E. Huntington Library and Art Gallery
Ct	Connecticut State Library
CtY	Yale University
DLC	Library of Congress
DNA	National Archives
DNA:PCC	National Archives, Papers of the Continental Congress (microfilm)
FU	University of Florida, Gainesville
ICHi	Chicago Historical Society
MdAN	United States Naval Academy
MH	Harvard College Library
MHi	Massachusetts Historical Society
N	New York State Library

NcD	Duke University
NHi	New-York Historical Society
NHpR	Franklin D. Roosevelt Library
NjMoInd	Morristown National Historical Park
NjR	Rutgers University
NN	New York Public Library
NNC	Columbia University
NNebg	Newburgh Free Public Library
NNMus	Museum of the City of New York
NSchU	Union College
PEL	Lafayette College
PHi	Historical Society of Pennsylvania
PPAmP	American Philosophical Society
PPInd	Independence Hall
PPL	Library Company of Philadelphia
ViU	University of Virginia
WHi	State Historical Society of Wisconsin

Private collections in the United States:

Sol Feinstone, Washington Crossing, Pennsylvania
John Jay III, Williamstown, Massachusetts
Richard Maass, White Plains, New York
J. W. Redmond, Washington, D.C.

Foreign collections:

AHN	Archivo Histórico Nacional, Madrid
MAE:CP	Ministère des Affaires Étrangères, Correspondance politique, Paris
PRO:FO or CO	Public Record Office, Foreign Office or Colonial Office, London
RAWC	Royal Archives, Windsor Castle
SPG	Society for the Propagation of the Gospel, London

Short Titles of Works Frequently Cited

Becker, *N.Y. Political Parties*
Carl L. Becker, *The History of Political Parties in the Province of New York, 1760–1776* (Madison, 1909)

Cal. of Hist. Mss.

Calendar of Historical Manuscripts, Relating to the War of the Revolution, in the Office of the Secretary of State, Albany, N.Y. (2 vols., Albany, 1868)

Dangerfield, *Robert R. Livingston*

George Dangerfield, *Chancellor Robert R. Livingston of New York, 1746–1813* (New York, 1960)

Evans

Charles Evans *et al.*, comps., *American Bibliography: A Chronological Dictionary of All Books, Pamphlets and Periodical Publications Printed in the United States of America . . .* [*1639–1800*] (14 vols., Chicago and Worcester, 1903–1959)

FAA

Peter Force, ed., *American Archives: Fourth Series, Containing a Documentary History of the English Colonies in North America, from the King's Message to Parliament, of March 7, 1774, to the Declaration of Independence by the United States* (6 vols., Washington, D.C., 1837–1846)

GCP

Public Papers of George Clinton, First Governor of New York (10 vols., Albany, 1899–1914)

GWF

John C. Fitzpatrick, ed., *The Writings of George Washington from the Original Manuscript Sources, 1745–1799* (39 vols., Washington, D.C., 1931–1944)

HP

Harold C. Syrett *et al.*, eds., *The Papers of Alexander Hamilton* (New York, 1961–   )

HPJ

Henry P. Johnston, ed., *The Correspondence and Public Papers of John Jay* (4 vols., New York, 1893)

JCC

Worthington C. Ford *et al.*, eds., *Journals of the Continental Congress, 1774–1789* (34 vols., Washington, D.C., 1904–1937)

John Adams, *Diary*

Lyman H. Butterfield *et al.*, eds., *Diary and Autobiography of John Adams* (4 vols., Cambridge, Mass., 1961)

JPC

Journals of the Provincial Congress, Provincial Convention, Committee of Safety and Council of Safety of the State of New-York (2 vols., Albany, 1842)

Lincoln, *Constitutional Hist. of N.Y.*

Charles Z. Lincoln, *The Constitutional History of New York* (5 vols., Rochester, 1906)

LMCC

Edmund C. Burnett, ed., *Letters of Members of the Continental Congress* (8 vols., Washington, D.C., 1921–1936)

New York Civil List

Edgar A. Werner, *Civil List and Constitutional History of the Colony and State of New York* (Albany, 1889)

N.Y. Col. Docs.

E. B. O'Callaghan, ed., *Documents Relative to the Colonial History of the State of New-York* (15 vols., Albany, 1853–1887)

N.Y.G.B.R.

The New York Genealogical and Biographical Record (102 vols., New York, Jan. 1870–Oct. 1971)

N.Y.H.S., *Colls.*

New-York Historical Society, *Collections* (84 vols., New York, 1868–1973)

Peacemakers

Richard B. Morris, *The Peacemakers: The Great Powers and American Independence* (New York, 1965)

RDC

Francis Wharton, ed., *The Revolutionary Diplomatic Correspondence of the United States* (6 vols., Washington, D.C., 1889)

Reynolds, *Family History of So. N.Y.*

Cuyler Reynolds, *Genealogical and Family History of Southern New York and the Hudson River Valley* (3 vols., New York, 1914)

Sabine, *Biographical Sketches*

Lorenzo Sabine, *Biographical Sketches of Loyalists of the American Revolution* (2 vols., New York, 1864)

William Smith, *Memoirs*

William H.W. Sabine, ed., *Historical Memoirs, of William Smith, Historian of the Province of New York, Member of the Governor's Council and Last Chief Justice of that Province Under the Crown, Chief Justice of Quebec* (2 vols., New York, 1956–1958)

WJ

William Jay, ed., *The Life of John Jay: With Selections from his Correspondence and Miscellaneous Papers* (2 vols., New York, 1833)

JOHN JAY CHRONOLOGY, 1745–1780

1745	12	Dec. (N.S.). Born in New York City
1753–60		Studied at Latin grammar school in New Rochelle and was tutored at home in Rye
1760	29	Aug. Entered King's College
1764		April. "Dispute between Dr. Cooper and students abt. wooden horse"
	22	May. Graduated from King's College and was awarded the B.A. degree
	1	June. Began the study of the law with Benjamin Kissam in New York City
1767	19	May. Awarded the M.A. degree by King's College
1768	26	Oct. Granted license to practice law in New York
1768–Oct. 1771		Law partnership with Robert R. Livingston, Jr.
1769–4 July 1770		Clerk to Commission to Settle the Boundary Between New York and New Jersey
1773	17	Feb. Elected a member of the Corporation of New York Hospital
1774	28	April. Married Sarah Van Brugh Livingston
	16	May. Elected a member of the New York Committee of 51
	19	July. Elected a member of the Committee of 15
	28	July. Elected a delegate to the First Continental Congress
	5	Sept.–26 Oct. Attended Congress
	20	Oct. Adoption by Congress of JJ's "Address to the People of Great Britain"
	22	Nov. Elected a member of the New York Committee of 60
1775	15	March. Elected a delegate to the New York Provincial Convention
	21	April. Elected one of 12 delegates to the Second Continental Congress
	1	May. Elected a member of the New York Committee of 100

13 May–2 Aug. Attended Second Continental Congress

29 May. Congress adopted JJ's "Letter to the Oppressed Inhabitants of Canada"

3 June. Moved in Congress that the second petition be sent to the King

12 Sept.–3 Nov. Attended Continental Congress

3 Nov. Commissioned Colonel of the 2nd Regiment of New York Militia of Foot

23 Nov.–31 Dec. Attended Continental Congress

29 Nov. Elected to Committee of Secret Correspondence

1776 1–8 Jan. Attended Continental Congress

2 March–27 April. Attended Continental Congress

April. Elected a member of the New York Provincial Congress

24 May. Appointed a member of committee on the drafting of the state constitution

25 May–28 June. Attended New York Provincial Congress

11 June. Introduced resolution in Provincial Congress, unanimously carried, "that the people of this colony . . . have not authorized this Congress . . . to declare this Colony to be and continue independent of the Crown of Great Britain"

9 July–6 Dec. Attended 4th Provincial Congress, renamed "The Convention of the Representatives of the State of New York"

9 July. Drafted resolution endorsing the Declaration of Independence

16 July. Member of the secret committee for obstructing the Hudson

21 Sept. Appointed a member of committee for "inquiring into, detecting and defeating all conspiracies"

23 Dec. New York Convention adopted JJ's "An Address of the Convention of the Representatives of the State of New-York, to their Constituents"

1777 3 March–13 May. Attended New York Convention

20 April. Appointed a member of committee to report a plan for organizing the new government of New York State

3 May. Elected Chief Justice of the New York State Supreme Court of Judicature

14 May–9 Sept. Active member of New York Council of Safety

9 Sept. Opened first session of Supreme Court at Kingston, with address to the grand jury of Ulster County

1778 1–7 Jan. Attended New York State legislature; [c. 15 Jan.–2 April], JJ's "A Hint to the Legislature of New York," signed "A Freeholder"

4 Nov. Sent to Continental Congress by New York State to present its position on the Vermont lands

7–31 Dec. Attended Continental Congress

10 Dec. Elected President of the Continental Congress

1779 1 Jan.–28 Sept. Attended Continental Congress

28 Aug. Resigned Chief Justiceship of New York State Supreme Court of Judicature

13 Sept. Congress adopted JJ's Circular Letter "from the Congress of the United States of America to their Constituents" on finance

27 Sept. Elected Minister Plenipotentiary to Spain

28 Sept. Resigned the Presidency of Congress

20 Oct. The Jays sailed on the Continental frigate, *Confederacy*

18 Dec. *Confederacy* landed at St. Pierre, Martinique, for repairs

28 Dec. Sailed on the French frigate *Aurora* to Spain

1780 22 Jan. Arrived at Cádiz

31 March. First report to Continental Congress

4 April. Arrived in Madrid

21 April. Notified of election to membership in the American Philosophical Society
23 Sept. Third conference with Floridablanca, climax of the Spanish mission
6 Nov. Report to Continental Congress on prospects of negotiation

I

BOYHOOD, YOUTH, AND KING'S COLLEGE DAYS

The Jay Family

The Jay family in America was founded by JJ's grandfather, Auguste or Augustus Jay (1665–1751). According to a memorandum on the family's history prepared by JJ, Augustus came from a prominent Huguenot family in La Rochelle where his father, Pierre, was "an active and opulent merchant."[1] Augustus was trained to take his place in the Jay mercantile empire. At the age of twelve, he was sent to England for his further education. Six years later, he sailed to Africa for a lengthy visit. During Augustus's absence, the revocation of the Edict of Nantes forced his parents and brother and sister to flee to England in 1685. The young merchant returned to La Rochelle to find his family gone and their property confiscated. "Augustus," his grandson wrote, "very properly reflected that his parents had two younger children to provide for, and that it became him to depend on his own exertions."[2]

Those "exertions" took Augustus Jay to America. The young Protestant merchant slipped out of Catholic France and sailed to South Carolina. Within a year he had moved to New York where he found a congenial Huguenot community which worshipped at L'Église des Refugiés, the "French Church." On a trading voyage to Hamburg in 1692, Augustus's ship was captured and he, with the other passengers, was imprisoned at St. Malo. Making his escape at night, Jay found his way to England, where he was reunited with his father and sister, Françoise (d. 1742), the only surviving members of the family, before sailing back to New York.[3]

In New York, Augustus Jay soon acquired social position and financial security. The former came with his marriage to Anna Maria Bayard (1670–1756) in 1697.[4] Anna Bayard's father was the nephew of Governor Peter Stuyvesant and the descendant of French Protestants who found refuge in the Netherlands in the late sixteenth century.[5] Her mother was the second daughter of Govert Loockermans who, on his death in 1670, was perhaps the wealthiest man in the colony. On her mother's side, Augustus Jay's bride counted Van Cortlandts, Van Rensselaers, and Schuylers among her cousins.[6] Exploiting his wife's family connections and drawing upon his own talents, Augustus Jay built a respectable fortune. He became a freeman of the City of New York and a vestryman of Trinity Church.[7] His ships crossed the Atlantic and reached the West Indies on their trading voyages and, in business, he found a profitable correspondent in Stephen Peloquin (d. 1721), the Bristol widower who had married his sister Françoise.[8]

Augustus and Anna Bayard Jay saw four of their children live to adulthood. Their three daughters were Judith (1698–1757) who married Cornelius Van Horne (1694–1752), Marie (1700–62) who was the wife of Pierre or Peter Vallette (d. 1752), Françoise (1701–80), also known as Frances and Francena, who wed Frederick Van Cortlandt (1698–1750). Their only son, Peter (1704–82), was JJ's father.[9]

Peter Jay was as carefully trained for a mercantile career as had been his father. At the age of eighteen, Peter sailed to Europe where he spent much time in London and Amsterdam and visited such relatives as the Peloquins of Bristol and the Mouchards in Paris.[10] When he returned to New York, he again followed his father's example by making an advantageous marriage. On 31 January 1728, Peter Jay wed his mother's young second cousin, Mary Anna Van Cortlandt (1705–77), the daughter of Jacobus and Eve Philipse Van Cortlandt and the granddaughter of the first Lord of the Manor of Philipsburg.[11] On the day of his marriage, Peter Jay made the first entry in the record of his family, printed below.

1 *WJ*, I, 3.

2 *Ibid.*, 5. The most illuminating account of the Jays' history in France, tracing their ancestry to the sixteenth century, is found in Frank Monaghan, *John Jay* (New York and Indianapolis, 1935).

3 *WJ*, I, 6–7.

4 *N.Y.G.B.R.*, VII (July 1876), 112; VIII (Jan. 1877), 15.

5 *WJ*, I, 7–8; *N.Y.G.B.R.*, VIII, 15. James Grant Wilson's research into the ancestry of the Bayard family revealed that Anna Bayard Jay's great-grandfather was the Rev. Lazare Bayard and that the family line could be traced "to Nicholas Bayard, an eminent Huguenot clergyman who was in charge of the French church in Antwerp in 1592, and for several years previous to that date." James Grant Wilson, *The Memorial History of the City of New-York* (4 vols., New York, 1892–1893), I, 582n.; *N.Y.G.B.R.*, XXI (Jan., 1890), 46.

6 *N.Y.G.B.R.*, VIII, 12–14.

7 Wilson, *Memorial History of N.Y.*, IV, 546; Minutes of the Vestry of Trinity Church, 1732–38, JP.

8 The "Registers of the French Churches of Bristol, Stonehouse, Plymouth and Thorpe-le Soken" do not record the date of the marriage of Stephen Peloquin and Françoise Jay. However, Peloquin's first wife died 29 Nov. 1701, and the "Registers" place the date of birth of Stephen and Françoise's first child as 16 July 1704. Thus the Jay-Peloquin marriage probably took place in 1703. Huguenot Society of London, *Publications*, XX (London, 1912), 27, 52.

9 *N.Y.G.B.R.*, VII, 112–14.

10 A sister of Augustus Jay's mother married a M. Mouchard. Mme. Mouchard, although a Protestant, was able to remain in France after the revocation of the Edict of Nantes because her husband was a Catholic. *WJ*, I, 3; Laura Jay Wells, *The Jay Family of La Rochelle and New York* (New York, 1938), p. 7n.

11 *N.Y.G.B.R.*, VII, 114; Reynolds, *Family History of So. N.Y.*, III, 1398, 1405–06.

PETER AND MARY VAN CORTLANDT JAY'S FAMILY

New York. 20/31 January 1728. This day is solemnized the Marriage of Peter Jay and Mary Van Cortlandt, Daughter of Colln. Jacobus Van Cortlandt, by the Revd. Mr. Gualter Dubois.[1]

November 8th/19, N. Stile, 1728. On Fryday at 8 OClock in the morning is born my Daughter Eve Jay and Baptized on Wednesday the 13th/24 following by the Revd. Mr. Gualter Dubois having Colln. Jacobus Van Cortlandt and Mrs. Ann Jay for her Sureties.[2]

April 1st/12th, N. Stile, 1730. On Wednesday at 2 OClock in the morning is born my Son Augustus Jay and Baptized on Thursday the 9th/20th following by the Revd. Mr. William Vesey, having Messrs. Augustus Jay and Frederick Van Cortlandt and Mrs. Ann Jay for his Sureties.[3]

April 27th/May 8th, N. Stile, 1731. On Tuesday at 6 OClock in the morning is born my Second Son Jacobus Jay and Baptized the 13th/24th May following by the Revd. Mr. William Vesey, having Messrs. Peter Vallette, Abraham Depeyster Jr. and Mrs. Margaret Depeyster for his sureties.[4]

Deceased the 4/15 November 1731 and intered in the family Vault, Bowery.

October 16/27th, N. Stile, 1732. On Monday at 5 OClock in the morning is born my third Son James Jay and baptized on Wednesday the 1st/12th November following by the Revd. Mr. William Vesey, having Messrs. Adolph Philipse, Gerardus Stuyvesant and Mrs. Judith Jay for his sureties.[5]

December 8th/19, N.S., 1734. On Sunday at 2 OClock in the morning is born my fourth Son Peter Jay and baptized on Fryday the 27th/January 7 following by the Revd. Mr. William Vesey, having Messrs. Peter Vallete, Gulian Verplank and Mrs. Ann Van Cortlandt for his sureties.[6]

October 20th/31st, N.S., 1737. On Thursday at 3 OClock in the Afternoon is born my second Daughter Anna Maricka Jay, and baptized on Wednesday 26/November 6 following by the Revd. Mr. William Vesey, having Mr. Augustus Jay and Mesdselles Mary Vallete and Frances Van Cortlandt for her sureties.[7]

April 29th/May 10th, N.S., 1744. On Sunday at 6 OClock in the Morning is born my fifth Son Frederick Jay and baptized on Wednesday the 9th/20th May following by the Revd. Mr. William Vesey, having Messrs. Cornelius Van Horn, John Chambers and Mrs. Ann Chambers for his sureties.[8]

Deceased 24th June/5th July 1744. Intered in the family Vault, Bowery.

December 1st/12th N.S., 1745. On Sunday at ten OClock at night is born my sixth Son John Jay and baptized on Fryday the 6th/17 following by the Revd. Mr. William Vesey, having Messrs. Cornelius Van Horn, John Chambers and Mrs. Ann Chambers for his sureties.[9]

April 8th/19th, N.S., 1747. On Wednesday at seven OClock in the Evening is born my seventh Son Frederick Jay and baptized on Sunday the 3d/14th May following by the Revd. Mr. James Wettmore, having Messrs. John Livingston, James Van Cortlandt and Miss Eve Jay for his sureties.[10]

November 10th/21st, N.S., 1748. On Thursday at Eleven OClock at night is born my third Daughter Mary Jay and baptized the 4/15th December following by the Revd. Mr. James Wetmore, having Mr. Abraham Depeyster and Mesdselles Margaret Depeyster and Catherine Livingston for her sureties.[11]

Deceased 18th/29 April 1752, intered in family Vault, Bowery.

March 31st, 1766. This day was Solemnized the Marriage of my Daughter Eve Jay and the Revd. Mr. Harry Munro by the Revd. Mr. Ephraim Avery.[12]

January 10th, 1767. On Sunday about 5 OClock in the Afternoon was born Peter Jay Munro[13] my grand Son, and Son of my Daughter Eve and the Revd. Mr. Harry Munro and was baptized by his Father about the 16th day of the same month.

D. Undated.

1 Gaulterus Du Bois (c. 1680–1751), pastor of the Reformed Dutch Church in N.Y.C.

2 Sureties for Eve Jay (1728–1810) were her maternal grandfather, Jacobus Van Cortlandt (1648–1740) and her paternal grandmother, Anna Bayard Jay.

3 Augustus Jay (1730–1801) was baptized by William Vesey (1674–1746), the rector of Trinity Church in N.Y.C., with his uncle, Frederick Van Cortlandt, and his paternal grandparents as sureties.

4 Sureties for Jacobus Jay, who died in infancy, were his uncle, Peter Vallette, and his mother's sister and brother-in-law, Abraham (1696–1767), and Margaret Van Cortlandt De Peyster (c. 1700–70).

5 Sureties for James Jay (1732–1815) were Adolphus Philipse (1665–1750), the brother of his maternal grandmother, Gerardus Stuyvesant (b. 1691), the brother-in-law of Anna Bayard Jay, and his unmarried aunt, Judith Jay.

6 Sureties for Peter Jay (1734–1813) were his uncle, Peter Vallette, Gulian Ver Planck (1698–1751), a brother-in-law of Anna Bayard Jay, and Anne Van Cortlandt (c. 1715–74), his mother's younger sister.

7 Sureties for Anna Maricka Jay (1737–91) were her paternal grandfather and her father's sisters Marie Jay Vallette and Françoise Jay Van Cortlandt.

8 Sureties for Frederick Jay, who died in infancy, were his uncle Cornelius

Van Horne and his aunt Anne Van Cortlandt and her husband John Chambers (c. 1710–64).

[9] JJ's sureties were the same uncles and aunt who had been sureties for his deceased brother, Frederick.

[10] Frederick Jay (1747–99) was the first of the Jay children to be baptized in Rye, N.Y. James Wetmore (1695–1760) was the pastor of the Anglican mission at Rye. Frederick's sureties were John Livingston (1714–88), the husband of his cousin Catherine De Peyster, his cousin James Van Cortlandt (1727–81), and his elder sister, Eve.

[11] Sureties for Mary Jay (1748–52) were her uncle and aunt, Abraham and Margaret De Peyster, and the De Peysters' daughter, Catherine De Peyster Livingston (b. 1724).

[12] Harry Munro (1730–1801), a native of Scotland, came to America as chaplain to a Highland Regiment during the Seven Years' War. Munro left the Church of Scotland to take Anglican orders in 1765. He then returned to N.Y. where he served as missionary at Philipsburg Manor until 1768. Sabine, *Biographical Sketches*, II, 112; Society for the Propagation of the Gospel (London): *Journals*, XVI, 153, 286, 419, XVIII, 5–6; Franklin D. Dexter, *Biographical Sketches of the Graduates of Yale College* (New York, 1845), II, 685–86.

[13] Peter Jay Munro (1767–1833).

Parentage and Childhood

For many years, Peter and Mary Jay lived in prosperous ease in Manhattan. A freeman of the city and vestryman of Trinity Church, Peter traded with Europe and the Indies as had his father.[1] Eventually, however, family tragedy ended this comfortable pattern.

Of the ten children born to Peter and Mary Jay, seven lived to adulthood: Eve (1728–1810), Augustus (1730–1801), James (1732–1815), Peter (1734–1813), Anna Maricka (1737–91), JJ (1745–1829), and Frederick (1747–99). Of these, four suffered mental or physical handicaps. Eve displayed emotional problems in her girlhood, while Augustus was mentally retarded and could neither read nor write despite special tutoring by the Reverend Samuel Johnson.[2] Peter and Anna, the third son and second daughter, were blinded by smallpox in the epidemic of 1739.[3] For a few years the Jays tried to rear their afflicted children in Manhattan, but this proved impractical. During King George's War (1744–45), Peter Jay wrote that he had "in a great measure discontinued trade, being unwilling to risque much in precarious times Considering the helpless condition of part of my family."[4] A few months after JJ's birth in December 1745, the family moved to Rye, where "the little blind ones" would be safe from "the dangers and confusions of the city life."[5]

Largely retired from business after this point, Peter Jay supervised his farm and devoted himself to his family in their rambling house on Long Island Sound. While still at home, JJ learned "the rudiments of English, and the Latin grammar" before being sent to the New Rochelle grammar school operated by the Reverend Peter Stouppe, an eccentric Swiss pastor of the French and Anglican congregations. At the age of eleven, JJ returned to Rye for private tutoring with George Murray.[6]

We are indebted to JJ's father for the first extant accounts of JJ's childhood. These are found in Peter Jay's letters to his older son James, then a medical student in Britain, and to his aunt's stepsons, David (1699–1766) and John Peloquin (1700–54) of Bristol.[7] Peter Jay's letters, carefully recorded in three letterbook volumes at JP, taken with the letters written to the Jays by their cousins in Bristol, are an invaluable source. The Peloquin letters, now in the private collection of John Jay III of Williamstown, Massachusetts, span the years 1722–72, and the Jay-Peloquin correspondence furnishes a remarkable record of their commercial ventures as well as a revealing portrait of relationships within the Huguenot refugee family.[8]

[1] James Grant Wilson, *The Memorial History of the City of New-York* (4 vols., New York, 1892–1893), IV, 547; Minutes of the Vestry of Trinity Church, JP; Peter Jay's letterbooks and accounts in JP provide an outline of his business interests.

[2] See below, Peter Jay to James Jay, 3 July 1752; Samuel Johnson to Peter Jay, 19 June 1739, JP.

[3] Samuel Johnson to Peter Jay, 19 June 1739, JP.

[4] Peter Jay to David and John Peloquin, 9 Nov. 1745, Peter Jay Lbk., II.

[5] Laura Jay Wells, *The Jay Family of La Rochelle and New York* (New York, 1938), p. 13.

[6] *WJ*, I, 11–12; Pellew, *Jay*, p. 9.

[7] "Registers of the French Churches of Bristol," Huguenot Society of London, *Publications*, XX (1912), 15 and 18; David Peloquin to Peter Jay, 2 Oct. 1754, Coll. of John Jay III of Williamstown, Mass.

[8] Photocopies of the Peloquin letters are available in JP.

Peter Jay to James Jay

[*Rye*], 3 [*14 N.S.*] *July 1752*

My last was the 4 May by your Cousin James Van Cortlandt, who is gone in Capt. Bryant to London, where I hope he is now safe arrived.[1] I then acquainted you with our loss of your Uncle Van Horne, and of your little Sister Mary.[2]

I have lately received your letters of the 7 and 28th March last, and this day that of the 17th Aprill[3] per a Vessell from Leith, by the return of which I intend you shall hear from me again.

Your anxiety at the loss of several of our Relations of late and the ill state of health of Others, is a very commendable disposition. But am concerned at your growing weary of your long absence abroad, Occasioned, I believe, by these afflictions which you have been frequently acquainted with, and which should be considered only, as sent by the wise Dispenser of all things, without Suffering them to thwart your very ardent and Laudable pursute after Learning (the only and valuable motive that induced you to go hence) which you have given many testimonys of. I desire that nothing may discourage you from going on with chearfullness, and you'll find the remaining 21 Months to compleat your 5 years Plan will insensibly expire.

Your Mothers Rhumatick disorder continues as usual, but I thank God she seems now releaved of a Hectick Fever She was taken with last Fall, and also, in a great measure, of a Cough that attended it, which I believe is happily effected by regularly drinking Tar water ever since she was first taken.

Your Sister[4] had escaped the Hystericks about three months, but of late she has had them 2 or 3 times. If they continue I intend to consult Doctor Magrah about her.[5]

I hinted to you before that your Uncle Vallete was in a declining State of health, he is now very low and seems to be approaching very fast to a dissolution, where he is very sensible, and now feels the comfortable benefit of a well spent Religious life in a very surprizing tranquility of mind and a becoming resignation to the Will of God.[6]

Gustey[7] continues in his idle disposition, and it's a great grief to me that I can say nothing in commendation of his behaviour. The rest of the Children are well disposed. Johnny is of a very grave disposition and takes to learning exceeding well. He has lately gone through the five declensions etc. with much ease and is now in the Verbs. He will be soon fit to go to a Grammar School. Fady[8] is a little merry diverting Fellow, and begins to take to his Book, but I can't judge much of him Yet.

Your Letter I received yesterday came under a blank cover directed to your Uncle Chambers.[9] Had you wrote a line or two in it, it had been decent and respectfull, which I would have you be mindfull of hereafter.

We all assure you of our love, and it's my desire that you write oftener, haveing been without a line from you from about 1st January last[10] to the 1st instant, only 6 months. Your notice of this request will be agreeable to.

LbkC in the hand of Peter Jay. Peter Jay Lbk., III. Addressed "Mr. James Jay in Edinburgh, per Capt. Harmar to London. Copy per Capt. Rouchan to Leith." After serving a two-year apprenticeship to a physician in New York City, James Jay sailed to England in 1748 to continue his education. In 1749 he began studies in Edinburgh where he was admitted to the College of Physicians and Surgeons after preliminary work in mathematics and foreign languages. Peter Jay to David and John Peloquin, 1 Nov. 1748, Peter Jay Lbk., III; David and John Peloquin to Peter Jay, 30 March–3 May 1749, Coll. of John Jay III.

[1] Peter Jay to James Jay, 4 May 1752, Peter Jay Lbk., III. In this letter, Peter Jay wrote that his nephew James Van Cortlandt had decided to go abroad because of his "curiosity to see England." Van Cortlandt, the son of Peter Jay's sister Françoise Jay Van Cortlandt, was apprenticed to Jay for seven years in 1741. He returned to New York in Dec. 1752. Indenture of James Van Cortlandt to Peter Jay, 12 May 1741, JP; Peter Jay to David and John Peloquin, 13 Dec. 1752, Peter Jay Lbk., III.

[2] Cornelius Van Horne was the husband of Peter Jay's sister Judith. Mary (b. 1748), the youngest of Peter Jay's daughters, was described by her father as a "very fond and promising child" who died of "the Sore Throat" on 18 April 1752. *N.Y.G.B.R.*, VII (July, 1876), 115; Peter Jay to James Jay, 4 May 1752, Peter Jay Lbk., III.

[3] Letters not located.

[4] Eve, the Jays' eldest daughter.

[5] Dr. James Magra, an "eminent Physician" who died 13 April 1774, "in a very advanced Age." *N.Y. Mercury*, 18 April 1774.

[6] Peter Jay's brother-in-law, Peter Vallette, died 9 Dec. 1752 "after a very long declining state of health." Peter Jay to Augustus Vallette, 13 Dec. 1752, Peter Jay Lbk., III.

[7] Augustus, Peter Jay's eldest son.

[8] Frederick, Peter Jay's youngest son.

[9] John Chambers.

[10] James Jay to Peter Jay, Jan. 1752, not located.

Peter Jay to David and John Peloquin

[Rye], October 24th, 1753

My last was the 2nd July per Griffith to London. Have since received your favour of the 11th August, with its inclosed from Jemmy and the magazines, which I am heartily obliged to you for.[1]

I am highly obliged to you for your kind intentions of having Jemmy well recommended in Paris, where I hope he is now got safe, and that he will find the advantages to be reaped there a sufficient inducement to finish his Studyes in that City preferable to Gottingen, but altho it would be most agreeable to me, yet I am willing to leave it in his own choice.[2] I have sent him a Letter for Mr. Mouchard, who I was well acquainted with at his fathers, and I flatter my self that he will <be kind> take notice of him.[3]

I observe that Jemmy's last Draughts are earlyer than usual, and therefore I would willingly have sent you a Bill now, but Mr. Paul Richard,[4] to whom I applyed for one, can't draw till December, and then he will send you one on my account.

Having the greatest reason to be firmly perswaded of your good inclinations for me and mine, I can't forbear takeing the freedom of hinting to you that my Johnny also gives me a very pleasing prospect. He seems to be indowed with a very good capacity, is very reserved and quite of his Brother James's disposition for Books. He has made a beginning at the Latin and gives reason to expect that he will succeed very well.

I thank God, my Daughter Evey is bravely recovered of her long indisposition, and we relieved from great concern and anxiety about her.

I note with Surprize that you had not received a line from my Nephew Peter Vallete since he left your City, and indeed am greatly concerned at his remisness in point of gratitude and good Manners. You were exceeding kind to him, and he ought not to have neglected to acknowledge your favours in a Letter of thanks. The last letters from him were dated at Rome.[5]

Sir Danvers Osborne, our late new Governor, arrived lately here from England, and was received by the Inhabitants in general with the greatest rejoicing and marks of respect, that was ever known here before on the like occasion, but our Joy was very short lived, and succeeded by a general Sorrow for his very Shocking untimely Death within two days after the Publication of his Commission. The poor Gentleman seemed very unwell and his mind much disturbed, insomuch that he very unhappily committed a violence upon himself and was found in a melancholy situation fastened with his handkerchief. A very good Charecter was given him from England, and Every Body here was big with great expectations of much happiness under his Administration.[6]

Isaac Lattouch and Henry Lane are lately broke and in Goal, where it's very likely they will remain, and is a punishment not adequate to the many villanyes they have committed.[7] There already appears demands upon them for between 25 and £30,000; as a great part thereof is owing in this City, I wish it mayn't be of very bad consequence to some of the sufferers. I thank God for having happily escaped them.

My Mother and Sisters are very much obliged to you and the rest of my Cousins for your Notice, and join with me and mine in sincere assurances of Affection and Respects. I am,

P.S. I have passed Jemmy's £40 draught to your Credit.

LbkC in the hand of Peter Jay. Peter Jay Lbk., III. Addressed: "Messrs. David & John Peloquin in Bristl. per Capt. Bryant via London."

1 Peter Jay to David and John Peloquin, 2 July 1753, Peter Jay Lbk., III; David and John Peloquin to Peter Jay, 11 Aug. 1753, Coll. of John Jay III; James Jay to Peter Jay, c. Aug. 1753, not located.

2 During James Jay's stay in England and Scotland, the Peloquins aided him

with advice and letters of introduction. After James received his M.D. degree from the University of Edinburgh in 1753 (having written a dissertation entitled *De Fluore Albo*), his relatives in Bristol continued to help him. Apparently James's adviser at Edinburgh, a Dr. Sinclair, suggested that James continue his medical studies at Paris or Göttingen. David and John Peloquin to Peter Jay, 26 Jan. 1748, 30 March 1749, 11 Aug. 1753, and 22 Sept. 1753, Coll. of John Jay III.

3 Peter Jay to François Mouchard, 26 June 1753, Peter Jay Lbk., III. Mouchard was Peter Jay's second cousin. John Jay II, "The Jays of America and France: Notes and Queries," John Jay Homestead, Katonah, N.Y.

4 Paul Richard or Richards (c. 1697–1756), a former Mayor of New York, was a wealthy merchant. "Abstracts of Wills," N.Y.H.S., *Colls.*, XXIX (1896), 145.

5 Peter Vallette (1729–54) was the son of Peter Jay's sister Marie Jay Vallette. On 15 Aug. 1752, Peter Jay wrote his son James: "Your Cousin Peter Vallette is going to London about a month hence. He intends to see a great part of Europe upon an offer made him by his Uncle in Jamaica, who will be at the expence of it. He intends to see you next Spring, which will doubtless be very agreeable to you." Peter Jay to James Jay, 15 Aug. 1752, Peter Jay Lbk., III.

6 Sir Danvers Osborne, the brother-in-law of the Earl of Halifax, was appointed Governor of New York to succeed George Clinton. Although James De Lancey reported that Osborne was pleased by his reception in the city on 10 Oct. 1753, he "appeared with a sedate and melancholy Countenance, complaining of a great indisposition of body & disturbance of mind which could not be diverted." Osborne's suicide on 12 Oct. was commonly attributed to his grief over his wife's death. James De Lancey to the Board of Trade, 15 Oct. 1753, *N.Y. Col. Docs.*, VI, 803–04, 833n.

7 Henry Lane, Jr., merchant, became a freeman of the City of New York in 1738. Isaac Lattouche was the son of Jeremiah Lattouche, a New York merchant. A branch of the Lattouche family lived in Bristol. James Grant Wilson, *The Memorial History of the City of New-York* (4 vols., New York, 1892–1893), IV, 547; "Abstracts of Wills," N.Y.H.S., *Colls.*, XXVIII (1895), 491: "Registers of the French Churches of Bristol," Huguenot Society of London, *Publications*, XX (London, 1911), 21.

Peter Jay to David Peloquin

[Rye], 16 May 1762

I had the honour of writing to you the 12 December and 6 Feb. last, and have since received your favours of the 31st October and 17 November together with the Magazines.[1] It gives us a very sensible pleasure that you and my Cousins your Sisters[2] were well, and we wish you all a long continuance of perfect health.

In my last I acquainted you of my wife being on the recovery of a pretty severe indisposition, but this was soon after succeeded by another. She is now better again, though but in a lingering <condition> State, and wherein as well as in her long disabled Condition and great sufferings by the Rhumatism (which you <kindly> take notice of in your last) she always perseveres in a becoming submission to the Divine Will. A very long <long> Series of very affecting afflictions has, indeed, attended my Family, <but we are happy still in> and I pray God to continue to Us his support under these weighty Tryals, and <we are also blessed with> a firm <persuasion> belief that his Dispensations always tend to wise and good Ends.

My son James has long had an inclination to return to England, he says for two years only, and you will see him very unexpectedly the Bearer hereof.[3] I wish he could have been satisfyed to continue his Practice here, wherein he had great Success, and which was not inconsiderable. However, as he thinks his going abroad will be an advantage to him I ought to submit to it, notwithstanding I <am> shall be thereby deprived of a very great comfort I had in him near me.

My Son John has now been two years at College, <and> where he prosecutes his Studyes to satisfaction. He <has a very happy capacity> is indued with very good natural parts and is bent upon a learned Profession, I believe it will be the Law.[4] My youngest is Still with me, fitting him for his apprenticeship to a Merchant, which he is inclined to.[5] They both behave well and I shall be quite happy if I may live to see them also in a good way of doing well. You'll be kind enough to excuse my open freedom about my Boys, which indeed <I'm indued to> proceeds from a firm persuasion that you wish us very Well.

My poor Sister Vallete has laboured long under an ill State of health, and according to appearance we can't expect to see her long among us. Thus we are dropping off one after another, and God's Will be done![6]

An Expedition is now on foot here, said to be intended against St. Augustine, and is to be conducted by General Amherst.[7] My Wife and Children join with me in Compliments and our greatest regards to you and the rest of our dear Cousins.

I am

LbkC in the hand of Peter Jay. Peter Jay Lbk., III. Addressed: "David Peloquin Esqr. in Bristol per Doct. Jay." David Peloquin's younger brother, John, died 26 Sept. 1754. David Peloquin to Peter Jay, 2 Oct. 1754, Coll. of John Jay III.

1 Peter Jay to David Peloquin, 12 Dec. 1761 and 6 Feb. 1762, Peter Jay Lbk., III; Peloquin to Jay, 31 Oct. 1761, Coll. of John Jay III; Peloquin to Jay, 17 Nov. 1761, not located.

2 Five daughters were born to Stephen and Françoise Jay Peloquin. Only two of David Peloquin's half sisters, Marianne (1706–78) and Françoise (1707–64), were still alive in 1762. "Registers of the French Churches at Bristol," Huguenot Society of London, *Publications*, XX (London, 1912), 27, 28, 30–32; dates of death, correspondence in Coll. of John Jay III.

3 James Jay's plans for further study on the Continent were disrupted by the approach of the Seven Years' War. James served as a physician in a London infirmary after his graduation from the University of Edinburgh and was not able to leave for France until July 1755, remaining in Paris only until the end of November when the imminence of war made it prudent for him to return to England to await passage to America, to which he returned in 1756. James practiced medicine in New York City for several years. David and John Peloquin to Peter Jay, 4 Sept. 1754 and David Peloquin to Peter Jay, 11 Sept. and 18 Oct. 1755–23 March 1756, Coll. of John Jay III; Peter Jay to David Peloquin, 10 June 1756, Peter Jay Lbk., III.

4 JJ entered King's College in the fall of 1760. Matricula or Register of Admissions and Graduations and of Officers Employed in King's College at New York, p. 8, NNC: Columbiana Coll.

5 For Frederick Jay's apprenticeship, see below, Peter Jay to David Peloquin, 14 April 1763.

6 Marie Jay Vallette died 5 June 1762. Peter Jay to David Peloquin, 9 June [1762], Peter Jay Lbk., III.

7 As part of the British expedition against Havana in 1762, Lord Jeffery Amherst (1717–97), Governor General of North America, was instructed to dispatch 4,000 provincials and regular troops from New York City to the Caribbean. In his *Journal*, Amherst recorded that the soldiers were mustered and embarked for Cuba on 13, 15, and 18 May. The Americans reached Cuba just in time to take part in the final assault on Havana which capitulated on 13 Aug. 1762 after a two-month siege. David Syrett, ed., *The Siege and Capture of Havana* (London, 1970), pp. xiii-xxxv, 12–13, 293; J. Clarence Webster, ed., *The Journal of Jeffery Amherst* (Toronto, 1931), pp. 281–83, 291.

Samuel Johnson to Peter Jay

King's College, New York, September 24, 1762

Dear Sir,

In a Letter I had lately from the Archbishop of Canterbury, he expressed some Wonderment that the Church at Rye had never applied to the Society for another Minister since the Death of Mr. Wetmore.[1] This is indeed to be wondered at if they have not done it; at least to thank them for their past favour, and desire the Continuance of it, and l[e]ave to nominate one themselves, and to be looking out for one they may be pleased with. As your Son[2] is going home I thought I would write a line to you, and desire your Information that I might the better know what answer to make to his Grace.

On this Occasion I can't but express to you my Satisfaction in the proficiency and Conduct of your Son. I have good reason to hope, (as I pray God) he may be an Honour and Comfort both to you and me, as well as a Blessing to his Country. With our Complements to Mrs. Jay, I remain, Dear Sir, your affectionate Friend and humble Servant

SA. JOHNSON

ALS. Society for the Propagation of the Gospel (London): Letters, Series C. Samuel Johnson (1696–1772), an Anglican clergyman, was the President of King's College.

[1] Johnson's letter from Thomas Secker (1693–1768), Archbishop of Canterbury, has not been located. The death of James Wetmore, pastor of the Anglican mission at Rye for nearly thirty-four years, occasioned lengthy discord among his parishioners over the selection of a new minister. In a letter to the Society for the Propagation of the Gospel (which furnished partial support for the Rye church) of 5 Oct. 1762, the vestrymen and churchwardens of Rye explained that the parish had approached two clergymen as Wetmore's successor, but had neglected to inform the Society of these attempts to fill the pulpit. Franklin D. Dexter, *Biographical Sketches of the Graduates of Yale College* (New York, 1845), I, 133; Robert Bolton, Jr., *History of the County of Westchester* (New York, 1848), p. 68; Vestry and Churchwardens of Rye to Daniel Burton, 5 Oct. 1762, Society for the Propagation of the Gospel: Letters, Series C.

[2] JJ.

A Church Dispute

The document printed below is the first extant letter addressed to JJ. In this brief message to his son, Peter Jay revealed how much he had come to depend on the seventeen-year-old boy, then in his third year at King's College. Aside from the business and family problems committed to JJ's care by this letter, he was also entrusted with a role in a major Westchester church dispute, and Peter Jay's references to the controversy over rival claims to the Rye pastorate permit the dating of the manuscript.

After the death of James Wetmore, the Anglican congregation at Rye remained without a priest for more than two years. In September 1762, Ebenezer Punderson (1705–64), pastor of the Anglican mission at New Haven, preached at Rye and so impressed the parishioners that the vestrymen and churchwardens immediately invited him to take charge of the congregation.[1]

This apparently straightforward solution to the parish's problem was defeated by the actions of the Society for the Propagation of the Gospel in London. In April 1762, Samuel Johnson wrote the Society and recommended Solomon Palmer (1709–71), pastor of the church at Litchfield, Connecticut, for the Rye post. On 15 October 1762 the Society appointed Palmer to the vacancy at Rye.[2] Johnson did not receive word of the Society's choice for three months. On 27 January 1763 Johnson wrote the Society to acknowledge receipt of their letter announcing Palmer's appointment and to beg the Society to reconsider and place Punderson at Rye as the local congregation wished.[3]

It was at about this time that Peter Jay learned of Palmer's nomination. His letter to JJ was written before he "divulged" the news to his fellow parishioners at Rye. The Rye congregation learned of Palmer's appointment at some time before 21 February 1763 when the vestrymen and churchwardens prepared a sharp letter to the Litchfield clergyman in which they warned him that he would not be welcome at Rye if he attempted to take advantage of the Society's nomination.[4]

The dispute was settled amicably later that year when Samuel Johnson worked out a scheme by which Palmer would succeed Punderson in New Haven, and Punderson would move to Rye. The Society accepted this plan, and Punderson was inducted as pastor at Rye in November 1763.[5]

1 Franklin D. Dexter, *Biographical Sketches of the Graduates of Yale College* (New York, 1845), I, 336–38; Vestry and Churchwardens of Rye to Solomon Palmer, 21 Feb. 1763, Society for the Propagation of the Gospel: Letters, Series C.

2 Samuel Johnson to Daniel Burton, 25 April 1762, Society for the Propagation of the Gospel: Letters, Series B, II, 250; Society for the Propagation of the Gospel: Journals, XV, 257–58.

3 Johnson to Daniel Burton, 27 Jan. 1763, Society for the Propagation of the Gospel: Letters, Series B, II, 268.

4 *Ibid.*: Letters, Series C.

5 *Ibid.*: Journals, XV, 393; Charles W. Baird, *History of Rye* (New York, 1871), pp. 315–16.

From Peter Jay

[*Rye, 27 January–21 February 1763*]

Dear Johnny

You may send my Letter that covers this to your Aunts Depeyster and Chambers,[1] to prevent any exceptions at what we propose about Peter, and let them act therein as they think best.

Make my Compliments to Doctor Johnson and tell him that I'm very sorry for Mr. Punderson's and the Peoples dissappointment, and that I wish it mayn't prove unfortunate as the People are greatly prejudiced in favor of Mr. Punderson, and consequently Mr. Palmer will come here under great disadvantages, and I've not devulged his appointment to any Body, lest it should affect our Subscriptions now collecting to accommodate a Minister in a Confortable manner.

Order matters so that Fady may return back again a Wednesday Morning from Town, and take as much Rateen, the same as your Coat lining etc. as will make Peter a Coat and Send it by Fady.

Make my Compliments to Cousin Augustus VanCortland[2] and tell I forgot to desire him to pay you my Share of the money, when he received it, for the mile Lot at the Balts. I shall soon, if necessary, send you an order on Hays for a quarters rent. Let me know whether Mr. Holliwood has paid you.[3]

I am Dear Johnny, Yours

P. J.

If it should be necessary for Fady to take care of Peter in Town, he shall be sent with him. On receipt of my Letter desire leave of Mr. Johnson to go immediately to your Aunts and to provide for Peter's coat, that Fady may be dispatched back again as soon as possible.

Send the inclosed for your Brother per the Barker.[4]

ALS. Endorsed in an unidentified hand: "1764. P. Jay." Enclosure: Peter Jay to Margaret De Peyster and Anne Chambers, not located.

1 Margaret Van Cortlandt De Peyster and Anne Van Cortlandt Chambers, the sisters of JJ's mother.

2 Augustus Van Cortlandt (1728–1823), the son of Françoise Jay Van Cortlandt.

3 Judah Hays (1703–64), a well-known Jewish merchant, was Peter Jay's tenant in a building on the corner of Stone and Broad Streets. Holliwood, who has not been identified further, was apparently another Jay tenant. David De Sola Pool, *Portraits Etched in Stone: Early Jewish Settlers, 1682–1831* (New York, 1952), pp. 471–74.

4 Barker was probably a sea captain who commanded a vessel on the East River and Long Island Sound between Rye and New York City.

Entering Upon Law Studies

The legal profession in provincial New York was a closely controlled monopoly. An informal organization of the bar functioned in the province by the early eighteenth century, and from that time admissions to legal practice became increasingly restricted. In 1730 the Supreme Court ruled that no judge of the Court could recommend a candidate for admission to practice unless that person had served for seven years with an attorney of the Court or had completed an apprenticeship with an attorney at Westminster. In 1732 the bar association agreed to employ only its own members as assistant counsel in practice before the Supreme Court, while the Montgomerie Charter of 1731 had conferred a monopoly of practice in the Mayor's Court of New York City upon eight attorneys listed by name, with the governor empowered to fill vacancies on the list only when fewer than six of the original attorneys were still in practice. In 1756 the "gentlemen of the Law" in New York agreed to cease taking any clerks for a period of fourteen years, with the exception that each subscriber could take one of his sons. The agreement of 1756 further provided that when clerkships were reopened, clerks must possess college degrees and that attorneys could take only one clerk at a time and that a £200 fee and a minimum of five years' training would be required of clerks.[1] It was this agreement that stood in the way of JJ's plans for the study of law, and his father's determined efforts to provide his son with professional training are outlined, below, in Peter Jay to James Jay, 14 April 1763; to JJ, 23 Aug. 1763; and to David Peloquin, 15 Nov. 1763.

[1] Paul Hamlin, *Legal Education in Colonial New York* (New York, 1939), pp. 35–36, 103, 160–61, 163–64; Richard B. Morris, ed., *Select Cases of the Mayor's Court of New York City, 1674–1784* (Washington, D.C., 1935), pp. 52–54.

Peter Jay to James Jay

[*Rye*], *15th February 1763*

My last was the 15 ultimo, and have since received your letters of the 30 Sept., 5 Octob., and 6 November last.[1] Hearing so frequently from you is indeed a very great Satisfaction to us, and the more so, as it shews you are very sensible to our affection for you, and the pleasure it must consequently give us. It would be still greater if we could hear that your own affairs answer, at least in some measure, the intention of your going abroad.

This goes via Bristol, where, as per one of your Letters, you intended soon a visit to our Good Relations. I hope you've been mindfull of Fady if he can be of service there. I'm indeed ashamed to mention it My self to Cousin Peloquin, as his kindness to us is already beyond measure, altho I'm greatly at a loss for a proper Place for the Boy at York. He is greatly improved since you left us and I think him extremely well qualified for his apprenticeship. Johnny goes on bravely at College. He is still determined to Study the Law, so that I shall be greatly at a Loss about him, As, you know, the Attornyes at York have agreed among themselves to take no Clerks, that intend to Practice the Law, to write in their Offices, and therefore I should be very glad if you could get him to write in the Office of some Attorney, in full Business, Either in London or Bristol. The last I would chuse, as he would then be under the immediate care of Cousin Peloquin, and I suppose your stay in London will not be long enough to have him under yours. I intend to write some time this spring to Cousin Peloquin about it, and in the mean time, if you go to Bristol, it will not be amiss that you consult with him about it. Johnny will pass his Degrees at College about 15 months hence. His behaviour continues very good and discreet.

Blessed be God, we all continue tollerable well and remember our love to you. I am

LbkC in the hand of Peter Jay. Peter Jay Lbk., III. Addressed: "Doctr. James Jay in London."

[1] Letters not located.

PETER JAY TO JAMES JAY

[Rye], April 14th, 1763

Since my last of the 15th Feb., I have received your Letters of the 28 November and 8 January.[1] The good State of health you injoy and our kind Bristol Relation's attention for you, gives me great Satisfaction. I'm surprised you had received only two of the many Letters I've wrote you, which Johnny assures me he did put into the Ship's bags himself. He was lately here and when I told him you had received his Letter, he appeared concerned at his having received None from you. The greatest, and indeed almost only, comfort I can expect on this side the Grave is, from yourself and your two youngest Brothers, two very promising youths, and I pray God you may be a Blessing to each other, by an uninterrupted Brotherly intercourse always subsisting between you. Fady is now an apprentice to your Cousin James DPeyster,[2] and he lodges at your Uncle Chambers's, so that no application must be made about him, as hinted in my last Letter to you, wherein I also make mention of Johnny who continues determined to Study the Law, and finding that Nothing can be done for him here in that way I now request Cousin Peloquin to assist you[3] in getting him to write in the office of an Attorney in London or, much rather, in Bristol, where he'll be more immediately under Cousin Peloquin's Notice, and where I conceive it will be far less Expensive in regard to his Board etc., than in London, and where the End will be answered as Well. When he is well acquainted with the office of an attorney and the Practice in the Courts, he may then pass a year or two at the Temple. My great distance from England makes it necessary to look out Early, and if you succeed in getting a Place for him, i'll send him over this time twelve Month, immediately after he has passed his Degrees at the College.

About 4 weeks past your Uncle Chambers was seized with the Dead palsy, in so much that his life was despaired of. He is now something better, but its bad Effects in regard to his Memory etc. still remain. We all remember our love to you and I am

LbkC in the hand of Peter Jay. Peter Jay Lbk., III. Addressed: "Doctr. Js. Jay in London."

[1] James Jay to Peter Jay, 28 Nov. 1762 and 8 Jan. 1763, not located.

[2] James Abraham De Peyster (1726–99), the son of Abraham and Margaret Van Cortlandt De Peyster.

[3] See next letter.

Peter Jay to David Peloquin

[*Rye*], *14 April 1763*

My last was the 15th February and I have now before me your kind favours of the 18th November and 14th December last. At the same time I also received the magazines, which I'm obliged to you for.[1] The very many Testimonyes, I've received, of your regard for me, give me the greatest reason to hope for the favour of your assistance again, in forwarding another of my Sons in the prosecution of his Learning. I have been, indeed, already too troublesome, but yet I'll rely on your Friendship to plead an Excuse for my freedom. My Son John, now in our College, will pass his Degrees this time twelvemonth, and as he is determined to Study the Law, I'm under no inconsiderable difficulty to get him properly fitted here for the Practice of it in these Parts, where the Lawyers practice in the Capacity both of Attorney and Counsellor at Law, and it's therefore absolutely necessary for him to begin by writing, sometime, in the Office of an Attorney to get acquainted with that profession and what regards the Practice in the Courts. The advantage of acquiring this knowledge here, we are of late deprived of by our Practitioner's ingagement to Each other, for a Term of years, to take in their offices no clerks who intend to practice as Lawyers, in view to prevent an increase of their Number, which is the reason I am now necessitated to be troublesome to you again, in requesting the favour of your Assisting the Doctor, who I now write about it, with your good offices in getting his Brother in the office of an Attorney in London, or very much rather, in your City, as he will then be within your Notice, and the Doctor's continuance abroad being uncertain, tho I have hitherto no reason to doubt of his behaving Well, as he is a youth remarkably sedate, and is well disposed. But nevertheless it's prudent to gard, as much as possible, against the danger of bad Company he would be exposed to in London, where he might probably be under no restraint. My youngest Son[2] is now an Apprentice for 5 Years to his Cousin Mr. James Depeyster, who I account a compleat Merchant, is in full business and an extensive Trader, so that he is well placed for improvement.

Having recovered a small debt due to the Estate of late Mr. Samuel Piquenit[3] deceased, I beg the favour of you to pay to his Executors £8 9s 3-1/4d Sterling out of the inclosed Bill of £12 10 Sterling on Edward Pearsons in London, and pass the remainder to my Credit.

My Wife and Children join me in assurances of our greatest regard, to you and the Rest of our dear Cousins. I sincerely am

LbkC in the hand of Peter Jay. Peter Jay Lbk., III. Addressed: "David Peloquin Esqr. in Bristol."

1 Peter Jay to David Peloquin, 15 Feb. 1763, Peter Jay Lbk., III; Peloquin to Peter Jay, 18 Nov. and 14 Dec. 1762, Coll. of John Jay III.

2 Frederick Jay.

3 Piquenit was a Bristol merchant with whom Peter Jay had traded. See correspondence in Peter Jay Lbks., I, II, and III.

David Peloquin to Peter Jay

Bristol, 26 July–6 August 1763

Dear Cousin

I was duly favoured with yours of 14th of April last, with an inclosed for Sir James Jay[1] which I immediately forwarded to him and in about three weeks after being the 13th inst. I advised him of the result of the inquiry I had made here among the attorneys with regard to putting out Your Son Cousin John to one of them, which was that the Young Gentleman must engage himself for five Years and that two to three hundred pounds be paid down with him, to which I added that as it was apparently much more for his Brother's advantage to be placed at the temple or one of the inns of Court than at a private office here he would see on what conditions it might be brought to bear, but I have not yet heard from him, and find by the publick papers that on the 19 instant he was at Tunbridge. For my part mine acquaintance lies very little among the Lawyers, who are so thick set in this city that most people wonder in what manner many of em get their bread.

I will pay the Executors of the Late Mr. Samuel Piquenit £8 9s 3-1/4d on your account as soon as I hear of your remittance by bill of £12-10 on Edward Pearson being discharged.

Herewith you will receive the Magazines from April to June inclusive. My Sisters and Self join in Love and esteem for you and all Your family, and I am with affection, Dear Cousin, Your very Humble Servant

DAVID PELOQUIN

We are now at the 6 of August. Since what above written I have Your favours of 14 and 28 June, by the Latter of which I observe with concern that a fresh warr was breaking out in Your quarter of the Globe, which, unless nipt in its bud, might turn out a bad affair.[2] Sir James Jay arrived here yesterday and will write you by this opportunity. We are sorry to here of Cousin Evey's indisposition and hope Your next will inform us of her <indisposition> recovery.

I am at Supra

D. P.

ALS. Coll. of John Jay III. Addressed: "To Mr. Peter Jay, to be left with Mr. James Depeyster, mercht, New York, in Capt. Chambers." Endorsed.

[1] Dr. James Jay was knighted 25 March 1763 for his efforts in raising funds for King's College.

[2] Peter Jay to David Peloquin, 15 and 28 June 1763, Peter Jay Lbk., III. In his letter of 28 June, Jay wrote Peloquin concerning the outbreak of Pontiac's War (1763–64) and announced that hostilities had been "committed by the Indians at Forts Pit, Destroit etc. very many of our Indian Traders are kill'd and also abo't 70, its said, of the Regular Troops."

From Peter Jay

[*Rye*], *Tuesday, 9th August 1763*

Dear [Johnny][1]

It's very long since I've received any Letters from you. I received last Post a Letter from Doctor Johnson who remembers his Love to you and is desirous that you should write to him, and he would be glad to know how the College goes on now.[2] I would have you gratify him with a Letter next week per the Post, which he has a right to expect from you, and altho I believe things go on well in the College now, yet I would not have you write more than may be communicated out of College. We remember our love to you, and I always am, dear Johnny, Your Affectionate Father.

PETER JAY

ALS. Endorsed: ". . . P. Jay about writing Doct. Johnson."

[1] Name partly hidden by seal.

[2] Samuel Johnson retired as President of King's College 1 March 1763 and moved to Stratford, Conn. In his letter to Peter Jay of 4 Aug. 1763, Johnson wrote: "When you write give my Love to Mr. Johnny (of whom I have lately heard a good Account) and tell him to write to me how things go on at College. I most heartily give you Joy on Sir James's Success, and the Honour done him. The College now will undoubtedly Flourish." Society for the Propagation of the Gospel: Letters, Series C.

From Peter Jay

[*Rye*], *August 23rd, 1763*

Dear Johnny,

Your Letter and Box per Barker is received. Your Letter Per Alley was delivered me since Fady was here.[1] It's more safe to send your Letters etc. per Barker.

Your observation on the Study of the Law, I believe, is very just, and as it's your inclination to be of that Profession, I hope you'll closely attend to it with a firm Resolution that no difficultyes in prossecuting that Study shall discourage you from applying very close to it, and if possible, from taking a delight in it. The dictionary you've bought is doubtless necessary for you, but as to other Books, I suppose you have them in the College, or doubtless on application to your Uncle or Aunt Chambers, they would let you have the reading of such of his Books as you may want. It's paying very dear from them to buy them at York. I'm glad you've wrote to Doctor Johnson.[2] We all remember our love to you, and I always am dear Johnny.

[PETER JAY]

AL[S]. Addressed: "To Mr. John Jay in New-York." Endorsed. Signature cropped.

1 Neither letter of JJ to his father has been located.

2 JJ to Samuel Johnson, not located.

FROM SAMUEL JOHNSON

Stratford, 27 October 1763

Dear Mr. Jay

I should long since have answered your kind Letter[1] but heard you and Benson[2] intended me a Visit in the Vacation, which I should have been very glad of, and since that, I have been much engaged either in Company, riding, or writing. It was with much pleasure that I received your Letter and the Account you gave me of the good Condition of things at the College since I left it, for which I am no less solicitous that it may do well and flourish, than while I was there. I hope the Studiousness and good Conduct of all of you that are members of it, will be such, as will always be a Credit and Honour to it. I desire you to give my love to them all, and assure them that I retain the same affection and tenderness for them and concern for their best good and welfare, as I had while I was among them. I gave Brooks[3] a much better and more correct Copy of what I had added to Ossian's Address to the Sun, than what you had had before, from which I would wish you and all of them would exactly transcribe for the Future.[4] I give you Joy of the Honour done your Brother in England, and the great success he has had in collecting for the College, which must greatly contribute to make it flourish. If you write to him remember me to him very affectionately and tell him I heartily give him Joy. I thank God, I enjoy my self here in much Health and

Tranquility, and with my best prayers and wishes that you may continue to act a good part and prosper in the Course of your whole Life, etc., I remain your hearty Friend

S. JOHNSON

ALS. Addressed: "To Mr. John Jay at King's College. N.York." Endorsed in an unidentified hand.

1 JJ's letter to Johnson has not been located.

2 Egbert Benson (1746–1833), a member of the class of 1765 at King's College, later studied law in the office of John Morin Scott and became one of the leading attorneys in Dutchess County, N.Y., before the Revolution.

3 David Brooks (1744–1801) attended King's College, 1761–63, and later studied at Yale where he received his degree in 1768. Franklin D. Dexter, *Biographical Sketches of the Graduates of Yale College* (New York, 1845), III, 272–73.

4 The first of James MacPherson's "translations" of the nonexistent Gaelic bard, Ossian, were published in London in 1761. The "Address to the Sun" is the closing portion of the Ossianiac poem "Carthon," and the draft version of Johnson's notes "Added to Ossian's Address to the Sun" is in NNC: Samuel Johnson Correspondence, I, 15.

Peter Jay To David Peloquin

[*Rye*], *November 15, 1763*

Your kind favours of the 26 July, 6 and 10 August, together with the Magazines, are come to hand by Capt. Chambers.[1]

I'm much obliged to you for your information of the result of an enquiry you have favoured me with, about puting my Son John out to an Attorney, the Sum required to be paid down with him, and his engagement for 5 years, is a Consideration alone, exclusive of a farther necessary expence for his intertainment during that long Term, that inclines me to wait the result of Jemmy's enquiry in London, being informed that what is necessary for John to learn before he enters the Temple, to compleat his Studyes, is attainable in an Attorny's Office in less than too years, so that it would be learning too dear bought on your Attorny's Terms. I'm obliged to you for the payment you have made Mr. Piquenit, and you've Credit for it.

My daughter Evey is now better again, but is not altogether free from the bad Effects of her indisposition. She is still too frequently seized by a little lurking fever.

The Savages continue their cruel Ravages on the frontiers, and have hitherto been but faintly opposed. The General requires 1400 Men to be raised in and at the Expence of this Province, and is now under consideration of our Assembly.[2]

My wife and children join with me in sincere regard and affection for you and our dear Cousins your Sisters, and I always am

LbkC in the hand of Peter Jay. Peter Jay Lbk., III. Addressed: "Davd. Peloquin Esqr. in Bristol, per the Grace."

[1] 26 July 1763, above; Peloquin to Jay, 10 Aug. 1763, Coll. of John Jay III; letter of 6 Aug. 1763, not located.

[2] In a letter to Lieutenant Governor Cadwallader Colden of New York of 30 Oct. 1763, Jeffery Amherst asked that the province furnish 1400 troops for the spring campaign on the northern frontier. Colden presented this request to the Assembly on 9 November, but the legislature balked at furnishing such a large body of men when none were demanded of the New England colonies. Instead, the Assembly authorized the enlistment of 600 additional men for frontier defense; these, with the 173 already in the province's pay, brought New York's total of colonial soldiers to 773. Colden to the Earl of Halifax, 8 Dec. 1763, *N.Y. Col. Docs.*, VII, 586–87.

From Peter Jay

Rye, 16 January 1764

Dear Johnny

Your letter[1] and the Boy were immediately sent to Mr. Punderson, who I've not seen since but am informed that he is well pleased with him.

Seal the inclosed before you deliver it to Mr. Kissam, and you may conclude an agreement with him,[2] vizt:

To pay him £200 when the time of your being with him Commences, that is, immediately after the passing your Degrees at College in May next, tho perhaps he will not require the whole Sum to be then paid, and be satisfyed to have it in two payments, but leave that to himself to do therein as he chuses.

To engage for 5 years, if his agreement with the Lawyers don't allow less, but that you shall be at Liberty to apply the two last to the Study of the Law and attend the office occasionally so as to be no hindrance to the study and to which I believe Mr. Kissam can have no objection, considering the Sum he requires.

If you should immediately proceed to Articles of Agreement, it will be necessary to have it inserted that if either of you should dye before the time of your being with him commences, that in that Case the whole Agreement shall be void, as it would not be then reasonable that the money should be paid.

On the whole you must agree in the best manner you can, but I would observe that in case the Lawyers do soon come to another agreement (in consequence of some not approving the last made by Mr. Kissam and others) Whereby a less sum than £200 is to be required, it will then be reasonable that Mr. Kissam do lower his demand accordingly.

On receipt hereof you must require Mr. Hays's final answer, and if he leaves the house then immediately put up An Advertisement over the Door and also in Weymans and Gains papers. If Ernest or any other Person have a mind to take it, you must let me know what is offered for the whole house, and how much, if I reserve the Room over the Parlour for you and room in the yard for about 4 Cords of wood.[3] I am, Dear Johnny, Your Affectionate Father

PETER JAY

ALS. Addressed: "To Mr. John Jay at King's College, New York, per favr of Majr. Bloomer." Endorsed: "abt agreeing with Mr. Kissam." Enclosure not located.

[1] Not located.

[2] On 5 Jan. 1764, members of the New York City bar relaxed their rules on clerkship. Under the new agreement, law clerks were to possess at least two years' education at a college or university, were required to pay a £200 clerkship fee, and were compelled to serve at least five years as clerks. Attorneys were forbidden to take a second clerk until three years of service of the first clerk had expired, thus ensuring that no attorney would have more than two clerks at a time. Benjamin Kissam (c. 1730–82), one of the attorneys subscribing to this agreement, had apparently completed arrangements for taking JJ as his clerk in the brief time since the new rules had been worked out by the bar. No copy of the agreement signed by Kissam and JJ has been found, but Peter Jay's letter makes it clear that it corresponded with the rules outlined by the bar on 5 January. In one respect, however, JJ's clerkship conflicted with the new bar agreement: Kissam had taken Lindley Murray (1745–1826) as his clerk only a year before; strictly speaking, he should have waited until the end of 1764 before admitting another clerk to his office. Paul M. Hamlin, *Legal Education in Colonial New York* (New York, 1939), pp. 163–64; Herbert A. Johnson, "John Jay: Colonial Lawyer" (unpub. Ph.D. dissertation, Columbia Univ., 1965), p. 18.

[3] William Weyman published the *New-York Gazette*, while Hugh Gaine (1727–1807) published the *N.Y. Mercury*. The *Mercury* of 30 January 1764 carried this advertisement: "To be Let, the House and Store House now contained in the Tenure of Mr. Judah Hays, in Broad-Street. Enquire of John Jay at Abraham De Peyster's Esqr; in New York." "Ernest" was probably Matthew Earnest, a New York glassmaker.

From Ebenezer Punderson

Rye, 23 January 1764

Dear Sir

I have receivd the Boy and your kind Letter have executed and inclosd the Indenture you sent in yours.[1] Mrs. Punderson[2] joyns me in our Sincere thanks for the Kindness you have done us. Your whole Family seem to be raisd up by providence to be blessings and Comforts to [us]. You must let me know what the Cost of the [Inde]ntures my watch key and your trouble amount To and you shall be soon satisfied by Your very Affectionate Friend

E. PUNDERSON

P. Our most Sincere Regards To Mr. Chambers and Lady, and Compliments to all your Relations and Friends.

ALS. Addressed: "Mr. John Jay in New York per Mr. Fade Jay." Endorsed. Enclosure not located.

[1] Letter not located.

[2] Hannah Miner Punderson (c. 1712–92).

FROM PETER JAY

Rye, 28th February 1764

Dear Johnny.

I have received your Letter of last Friday.[1] I'm of your oppinion that Mr. Ernest's Terms are too high. I shall be well pleasd to have you lodged at Mrs. John Livingston's[2] or any other more private Family than I take D———n's to be, and with whom (between us) I apprehend it would not sute very well. If you can get suted near Mr. Kissam's or in that part of the Town,[3] it will be more convenient for you in regard to the Place our Boats commonly come at. I do however leave it to your own discretion to take your lodging agreeable to your own inclinations. I am Dear Johnny Your Affectionate Father

PETER JAY

P.S. You are desired to enquire of Mr. Punderson's Boy's Mother whether he has been Baptised.

ALS. Endorsed: ". . . abt. a Lodging." The problem of finding lodgings that would be suitable for JJ after his graduation from college is first discussed, above, Peter Jay to JJ, 16 Jan. 1764. During his first two years at King's, JJ had lived in the home of Lawrence Roomes at the Corner of Broadway and Verlettenbergh Hill (modern Exchange Place). In May 1762, JJ moved into rooms at the College, but these would not be appropriate after he received his degree in May 1764 and began his law clerkship. Peter Jay to JJ, [April–May 1762]; JJ: undated memoranda on vita, notes for 1762, JP.

[1] Not located.

[2] Probably the family of John Livingston, the husband of JJ's first cousin Catherine De Peyster.

[3] Benjamin Kissam's law offices on Golden Hill (modern John Street) were only a few blocks from the docks which lined the southeastern side of Manhattan.

Each Student pays 13/ a Week for his Diet, The Bill of Fare is as follows:

Bill of Fare

Breakfast { Tea & Coffee - Bread & Butter and Biscuit -

Dinner

Sunday: Roast Beef & Pudding -
Monday: Leg of Mutton & Roast Veal -
Tuesday: Corn'd Beef and Mutton Chops
Wednesday Peas Porridge & Beef Stakes
Thursday - Corn'd Beef and Mutton Pye
Friday - Leg of Mutton & Soup
Saturday - Fish, fresh & Salt in Season

Supper { Bread and Cheese, and the Remains of Dinner

Jay's College Diet—Bill of Fare at King's College, 1763–64
(*Columbiana Collection, Columbia University*)

John Jay and the King's College Demonstration

The document printed below relates to one of the few incidents which blemished JJ's reputation as "a youth remarkably sedate."[1] According to Jay family tradition, "a few weeks before he was to take his degree" in the spring of 1764, JJ was present in the college hall at King's when some of his fellow students "either through a silly spirit of mischief, or in revenge for some fault imputed to the steward, began to break the table." Myles Cooper (1737–85), Samuel Johnson's successor as President of King's, came to investigate. Cooper lined up the students and interrogated each in turn. None admitted any knowledge of the identity of the vandals until Cooper came to JJ. When asked who the culprits were, JJ replied: "I do not choose to tell you, sir." Cooper, the story went, "expostulated and threatened, but in vain."

When the students were called before a faculty committee, JJ presented their defense. Like all other students, JJ had been required to sign a promise of obedience to the college statutes, but he contended that his refusal to identify the students who had destroyed the table did not violate that oath "and that the president had no right to exact from him any thing not required by the statutes." The faculty disagreed, and JJ and his companions were "suspended and rusticated."

JJ was allowed to return to King's in time to receive his degree on 22 May 1764. Cooper, JJ's son recorded, "by the kindness of his reception, suffered him to perceive that he had not by his conduct forfeited any part of his good opinion." William Jay pointed out, with even greater satisfaction, that JJ had "retained among his papers to the day of his death a copy of the statutes, from which it appears that the conduct for which he was suspended was not even indirectly forbidden by them"[2] JJ's copy of those regulations, signed by him and Myles Cooper, bears out that interpretation.

[1] See above, Peter Jay to David Peloquin, 14 April 1763.

[2] *WJ*, I, 14–15; JJ's own record of the affair was limited to a note in his undated memoranda on vita: "April 1764 Dispute between Dr. Cooper & students abt. wooden Horse," JP.

Statutes of King's College in the City of New York

[adopted 2 March 1763]

Tit 1 Admission

1 Each person, to be admitted, shall be able to give a rational account of the Latin and Greek Grammers, to render Sallust, Caesar's Commentaries, or some part of Cicero's Works, into

English, the Gospels, at Least, from the Greek into Latin, and to translate correctly both English into Latin, and Latin into English. He shall be examined by the President, and, if admitted, shall subscribe to the Statutes of the College (having first carefully copied them) thereto Promissing all due Obedience, which Subscription shall be contersigned by the President.

2 Each person, admitted as above, shall have an Habitation in College, assigned him by the President, in which he shall be obliged to Lodge (unless by Special Leave obtained from the Governors or President) except at the Stated Vacations; under the penalty of five Shillings for the first Night of his absence, eight Shillings for the Second, twelve for the Third (or adequate Exercise) and expulsion for a Continuance of his Offence, or such other punishment as the Governors shall think necessary.

3 Each person also, admitted as above, shall procure within fourteen day's of his Entrance, a proper Academical Habit, in which he shall always appear (unless he have Leave of the President or Tutors) under the penalty of 2 Shillings for the first Offence (and so inproportion) or adequate Exercise.

4 No Student shall be admitted ad eundem from another College, without bringing proper Credentials of his Good Behaviour, and also satisfying the President and such of the Governors of the College as shall be appointed to regulate the Commencement, of his being properly qualified for such admission.

5 The Parent or Guardian of each Student at his Admission, shall give a Bond to the Corporation of the College, to pay all the dues to which the said Student shall thereby become Subject; as also to make good all Damages that the said Student shall willfully have been the Occasion of to his, or any other Apartments of the College.

Tit 2d. Attendance

1 Each Student shall attend Morning and evening Prayers in the College, and also Publick worship on the Lords Day, morning and evening at such places as his respective parents or Guardians shall appoint (unless in Case of Leave or Sickness) under the penalty of four pence for each Omission, or proportionate Exercise either for absence or Tardiness, of which an Account shall be taken by some of the Students and delivered weekly to

the President, and at such other Times as he, or any of the Tutors, shall think proper to demand it.

NB The prayers to be read by the President or Tutors, according to the form Perscribed.

2 The Students shall dine regularly in the Publick Hall: and such as are absent, without Leave, shall be subject to the same penalty as those that are absent Prayers.

3 The Students shall regularly and punctually attend upon their respective Tutors in the College, and at the Times, appointed and shall then and there perform such exercises, as have been ordered, and incase of neglects or absence, they shall be punished as the President and Tutors respectively shall think proper, either by pecuniary Muclt, not exceeding four pence for each offence, or by additional exercises, Proportioned to the Nature and frequency of it, And the President shall have Power to appoint what Books the Students are to read, what exercises they are regularly to perform, and the times of their Attendance.

4 If any of the Students shall be absent from their Chambers after nine o Clock at Night in Winter at ten in Summer (or at other times when the College Business requires their Attendance) they shall subject themselves to any fine not exceeding one Shilling for each time of their Delinquency or exercise adequate to the Offence.

5 Times of absence from Study shall be three Quarters of an Hour for Break fast an Hour and half for Dinner, and from evening Prayer till Bedtime (vide 4) and the Stated Vacations shall be one Month after Commencement, one Fortnight at Michaelmas, one Fortnight at Christmas and two days at Whitsentide.

NB Easter Week, viz from Good Friday till the Friday following being so near the time of Commencement, is to be considered only as a Vacation from Publick Exercise but not from Attendance at College, as at other Times.

Tit 3d Behaivour etc.

1 If any one of the Students wilfully and personally affront the President or Tutors, he shall be fined in any Sum not exceeding ten Shillings for the first Offence, or have proportionate Exercise set him and if he continues in his Fault, he shall subject himself to expulsion, or in Case of proper submission if the Nature of the Offence should require it, he shall be Obliged to compose,

and repeat in the publick Hall, a Modest Recantation of his Fault, in order to deter his Fellow Students from the Like practices.

2d None of the Students shall molest (by making unseasonable Noises, having Company at unseasonable hours or otherwise) either the President, Tutors, or their Fellow Students: Nor shall they entertain any Company in, or be themselves absent from their Chamber's, during studying Hours (except upon special Occasions, to be judged by the President or either of the Tutors) under the penalty of one Shilling for the first Offence, two for the Second, and so in proportion as the Nature and Continuance of the Fault shall require.

3 If any of the Students shall play at Cards Dice or any other Kind of Gaming within the apartments of the College, they shall be fined not exceeding five Shillings for the first Offence, ten for the Second, and so in proportion, or have adequate exercise set them and if they Persist, they shall subject themselves to expulsion.

4 If any of the Students shall be known to converse or have any Connections with persons of bad fame or such as are unsuitable Companions for them they shall be privately admonished for the first Offence, Publickly for the Second, and, if they persist, they shall subject themselves to Expulsion.

5 All Excesses, Indecencies, and Misdemeanours of an Inferior Nature (i.e. such as do not deserve expulsion) shall be punished by the President or Tutors, as they shall see Occasion, either by Pecuniary Mulct, not exceeding one Shilling for the first Offence and so inproportion, or by adequate Exercise, and in respect of Deportment and propriety of Behaviour the President and Tutors shall from time to time, prescribe such rules as they find necessary or think convenient.

6 The Students shall be examined publickly or privately, at such times, and in such manner, as the President shall appoint: and a visitation shall be held Quarterly by the Governors of the College, viz The Monday before Christmas, The Monday before Easter, the Second Monday in July, and the Second Monday in October.

7 The President and Tutors, or any of them, shall have power of visiting the Chambers of the Students, at whatever Hour they please, and of dismissing what ever Company they think proper,

and in Case Admission is refused, the Doors shall be forced open and the Student or Students fined in any Sum not exceeding ten Shillings for the first Offence (or adequate Exercise) and if the Fault is repeated He or they shall be subject to Expulsion.

8 The President and Tutors respectively shall have power in all Cases to augment the Exercises to which the Delinquents have subjected themselves if such Exercises are not properly finished, or not given in by the Time appointed; and also to confine such Delinquents to their respective Chambers (except at Times of Publick Attendance under what restrictions are thought proper, till they shall have compleated their Punishments or made proper Satisfaction.

9 No Student shall absent himself from College (except in Case of Sickness) without Leave obtained of the President or one of the Tutors, under the penalty of Such fine or Exercise as the Nature and Continuance of the Fault shall require, and the President only shall have power to give Leave of absence from [*sic*] more than one Day, unless he himself is absent, in which Case his Power shall devolve to the next in Authority.

10 The Junior Students shall pay such respect to the Seniors, and all of them to the President, Professors, Fellows and Tutors, as the President etc shall direct, and such penaltys as they shall think proper to Perscribe.

11 The Person who punishes shall have power also (if the Accounts are not passed) of remitting the Punishments.

12 If any dispute should arise concerning the due Proportion of Punishments, an Appeal shall lie (in this as well as in all other Cases) to the President and Tutors, and finally to the Governors of the College, agreeable to the Charter.

13 Obstinacy and Perseverance, in all Cases, may be punished by Expulsion.

14 During the Summer Season Morning Prayers shall begin between the Hours of five and Seven, and in Winter between the Hours of Six and Eight, as the President shall appoint; in the Evening also at what Hours he thinks proper.

15 The Steward's Accounts as also that of the fines, shall be passed Monthly, by the President and Quarterly by the Governors of the College, And the fines aforesaid shall be expended in Books

which shall be disposed of in the honorary and Publick manner, at the Quarterly meetings of the Governors, as Rewards to such of the Students as excell in the Course of their Studies, and the propriety of their Conduct, according as the President, Fellows, Professors and Tutors, or the major Part of them, shall direct.

Tit 4th. Graduation

The Examination of Candidates for the Degree of B.A. shall be held publickly in the College Hall, about six Weeks before Commencement, President, Fellows, Professors and Tutors, and such of the Governors as shall please to attend, and Such of the said Candidates as appear to be duly qualified (having fullfilled the Conditions Prescribed) shall, at the Commencement; be admitted to the aforesaid degree, and in three years more, if they have persued their Studies, and have otherwise behaved themselves soberly and decently, they shall be farther admitted (upon proper Application) to the Degree of M.A. To Neither of which Degrees aforesaid shall any Candidate be admitted without performing the Above Conditions, except in Cases of extraordinary Capacity and by a Particular Act of the Governors and President, *Honoris Causa.*

NB The regular Time for taking the Degree of B.A. is four Years from the Students Entrance and the fee for each Degree forty Shillings including the Presidents and Clerk's fees. Lastly. It is to be understood that the Greatest Punishments of expulsion, Suspension, Degradation and Publick Confession, be inflicted by the Governors of the College pursuant to the Charter, and that the Lesser Punishments herein mentioned be inflicted by the President, Fellows, Professors and Tutors, or any of them, according to the True Intent and meaning of these Laws.
Finis

JNO. JAY
MYLES COOPER PRES.

DS. These statutes were adopted by the trustees at a meeting of 2 March 1763. Columbia University, *Early Minutes of the Trustees,* I (New York, 1932).

Peter Jay to David Peloquin

[Rye], 15 May 1764

I have received your favour of the 2d Feb. together with the Magazines per the Minerva. My last was the 24 December,[1] and

The College, Hall and Library excluded, which if converted into Rooms would contain nine Students, is capable of receiving 48 Students allowing to each a private Study.

Salaries

President - - - - 150£ Ster: per Ann:

{Professor - - - - - 80£ Ster }
{Librarian - - - - -10£ Curr:} with the Priviledge of having as many Gent: under his private Tuition, as he can tend exclusive of College Business

Tutor - - - - - - - 80£ Ster. with the same Priviledges as the Professor

N:B: President, Professor, & Tutors pay no Room Rent.

Each Student pays 4£ pr. ann: for his Room, and 5£ for Tuition

The Salaries Jay's Teachers Were Paid in 1763
(Columbiana Collection, Columbia University)

Since which our Lawyers have dissolved their Contract, and engaged in another, under such restrictions as will greatly impede the lower Class of the People from Creeping in the Profession, which, they say, was their intention by the first. This has enabled me to place my Son, agreeable to his own choice and much to my own liking, with a gentleman Eminent in the Profession,[2] with whom he'll not only get perfectly acquainted with the Business of an Attorney and the Practice of our Courts, which he is at Liberty to attend every Sessions for his improvement, but he is also to Study the Law in a Regular manner under his Tuition, so that he will now have every necessary advantage to qualifye him for the Profession. He is to begin the 1st of next month, after the passing his Degrees in our College, where he has prosecuted his Studyes very much to his Credit. As you've been at great pains to get a Place for my Son in your City, I must now give you my thanks for your kind endeavours to serve me.

It gives me pleasure that you was well, and that my Cousins your Sisters were getting better of the Colds they had been troubled with. We beg our sincere regards may be acceptable to you and them. My Evey is not yet quite so well as I could wish. She is now among her kind relations in Town. Myself and the rest of my Family are middling well. I Sincerely am

LbkC in the hand of Peter Jay. Peter Jay Lbk., III. Addressed: "To David Peloquin Esqr. in Bristol per the Minerva."

1 David Peloquin to Peter Jay, 2 Feb. 1764, Coll. of John Jay III; Jay to Peloquin, 24 Dec. 1763, not located.

2 Benjamin Kissam.

King's College Commencement

[*New York, 22 May 1764*]

A publick Commencement was holden on Tuesday last, at St. George's Chapel,[1] in this City. The Procession from the College Library, was headed by the young Gentlemen of the Grammar School, to the Number of 50, with their Masters, and then the Students of the College, all uncovered. His Excellency General *Gage*,[2] was pleased to honour the Ceremony with his Presence, accompanied by several of the Members of his Majesty's Council, the Judges of the Supreme Court, the President and Governors of the College, and many of the Clergy and Gentlemen of the City and Country. The *President*[3] having offered up suitable Prayers, after relating the Occurrences of the preceeding Year, in an elegant Latin Speech, addressed a very pathetic and instructive Exhortation to the young Gentlemen who were to be graduated. Then followed a salutatory Oration, by Mr. *Richard Harrison*,[4] a young Gentleman of Seventeen; which was equally admired by the Audience, for Elegance and Purity of Diction, Propriety of Sentiment, and the graceful Elocution with which it was delivered. To this masterly Performance succeeded a spirited and sensible English Dissertation, on the Happiness and Advantages arising from a State of Peace, by Mr. *John Jay*. The Audience was next entertained with a Dispute in English, on the Subject of national Poverty, opposed to that of national Riches; masterly discussed, by Messrs. *Jay* and *Harrison*. A Syllogistic Dispute in Latin, on the Question,—*An Passiones sint indifferents*? was next handled by Messrs. *Van Dyck* and *Holland*,[5] with great Precision and Judgment. These Performances being ended, the President conferred on the Candidates their respective Degrees. Mr. *Van Dyck* then acquitted himself with great Honour, in an elegant and pathetic valedictory Oration, pronounced with very becoming Emphasis and Gestures. The Whole was concluded with a Prayer applicable to the Occasion.

The numerous and polite Audience expressed great Pleasure and Approbation at the Performance of the young Gentlemen, and the Order and Decency with which every Thing was conducted.

The Gentlemen who attended the Procession, returned in the same Order to the College-Hall, and dined together in Honour of the Day.

It would be injurious to the Reputation of the College, not to observe, that ample Amends were made for the Number of Candidates, by the Display of their Proficiency in the Elegance of their Performances.

N.Y. *Mercury*, 28 May 1764. Also printed in the *New-York Gazette; or, The Weekly Post-Boy*, 31 May 1764.

1 St. George's, the first "chapel of ease" in Trinity Parish, was opened in 1752. It was located on modern Beekman St., about half a mile from King's College.

2 Gen. Thomas Gage (1721–87), British Commander in Chief in America, 1763–75.

3 Myles Cooper.

4 Richard Harison (1747–1829).

5 Henry Van Dyck (1744–1804) and Henry Holland (d. 1806) were members of the Class of 1761 who received their M.A. degrees in 1767. Leonard F. Fuld, *King's College Alumni* (New York, 1913), p. 20; Milton H. Thomas, *Columbia University Officers and Alumni, 1754–1857* (New York, 1936), p. 98.

FROM PETER JAY

[Rye], Tuesday, 22d May 1764

Dear Johnny.

I've not received a line from you since I left Town. The Post told me this Morning the Commencement is this Day, so that I suppose you'll come up next Thursday with Barker, and you may go down with me again tomorrow Senight,[1] in order to settle with Mr. Kissam, acquaint him of it, and make my Compliments to him.

Bring with you 100 limes which I want.

As you are expected up, your Mother don't send your Linnon Now per the Boat. I am Dear Johnny Your Affectionate Father

PETER JAY

ALS.

1 Archaic for a week.

II

JAY'S YEARS AS A LAWYER

Clerking for Benjamin Kissam

On 1 June 1765, JJ entered Benjamin Kissam's law office on Golden Hill.[1] Such casual instruction in the law and legal practice as JJ may have received from his master was supplemented by contact with the senior clerk, Lindley Murray. Kissam's practice was a busy one, and even with the variety of printed forms available in New York in the 1760's, there was much laborious transcription left for his clerks. JJ's early years of clerkship were occupied largely with copying pleadings and judgment rolls, while Murray maintained Kissam's registers, billed clients, and performed duties involved in trial preparation.[2]

Reviewing his years in Benjamin Kissam's office, Lindley Murray remarked that as a clerk JJ was "remarkable for strong reasoning powers, comprehensive views, indefatigable application, and uncommon firmness of mind."[3] Such virtues were necessary in an era when a lawyer was largely self-educated, studying treatises and abridgments by himself with little or no guidance. JJ began the accumulation of legal treatises and law reports and, as was customary, drew up his own "Commonplace Book," entering therein a variety of legal forms, judicial precedents, and statutory references bearing directly on legal practice.[4]

Although JJ eventually assumed more and more responsibility for the management of Kissam's office,[5] his first years as a clerk gave him little opportunity to use any of the knowledge of legal theory and practice which he so arduously acquired. Instead, his duties were confined to matters such as the copying of the document printed below. The case is of more than routine interest since it involved members of JJ's family.

JJ copied the opinion given by Kissam on the will of Elizabeth De Peyster Hamilton (1694–1765), dated 3 December 1750. In her will, Mrs. Hamilton divided her estate among her brothers, Abraham and Pierre, her sister, Joanna De Peyster, and her nephew Pierre Van Cortlandt. Under a codicil of the same date, Mrs. Hamilton provided that her brother Abraham, who had been left two-sevenths of her property under the will, was to receive that portion of her estate that "may be entailed . . . and if it fall short [of two-sevenths of her estate] it is to be made up."[6] However, in the years following the signing of her will, Mrs. Hamilton had "docked" the entailed property or converted it into a fee simple estate. Thus, by the time her will was proved, there was no entailed property to go to her oldest brother.

Abraham DePeyster, the husband of JJ's aunt, Margaret Van Cortlandt, brought the problem to Kissam's office. Kissam's generous interpretation of Elizabeth Hamilton's will was concurred in by David Ogden (1707–98), a leader of the New Jersey bar who practiced in New York as well as in his own colony.

1 Frank Monaghan, *John Jay* (New York and Indianapolis, 1935), p. 32.

2 Sixteen judgment rolls covering Kissam's practice between June 1764 and November 1765 are in JJ's hand. Herbert A. Johnson, "John Jay: Colonial Lawyer" (unpub. Ph.D. dissertation, Columbia University, 1965), pp. 28–29.

3 Elizabeth Frank, ed., *Memoirs of the Life and Writings of Lindley Murray* (New York, 1827), p. 34.

4 The Commonplace Book is at N. JJ's surviving law books are in the Treasure Room of the Columbia University Law Library, some 100 titles predating 1776, and 150 legal titles for the period thereafter down to 1829.

5 See below, Benjamin Kissam to JJ, 26 April 1766 and 25 Aug. 1766.

6 "Abstracts of Wills," N.Y.H.S., *Colls.*, XXX (1897), 369–70.

Opinion on the Will of Elizabeth Hamilton

New York, 5 March 1765

Upon considering the last Will and Testament of Mrs. Elizabeth Hamilton, I am of Opinion

1st. That the Testatrix having Docked the Intail after making her Will, and thus become vested with the Inheritance in Fee Simple (unless the Deed to lead the Uses of the Recovery which I have not seen should be otherwise) that Part of her Estate must descend to the Treasurer[1] as her Heir at Law, provided she has not disposed of it by Deed or otherwise, which I am told has not been done.

2d. The next Question upon the Will is, what Interest the Treasurer has, in that Part of the Estate which she was seized of in Fee at the time of making her Will: And this may perhaps admit of some Dispute. For the Codicil and Will (which were both executed on the same Day) must be considered as one entire Instrument, and the Testatrix's Intention be collected from the whole together. Now tho she in the first part gives two sevenths of her Estate generally to the Treasurer; yet she afterwards says that she means it shall be *the Intailed part of her Estate, which would have descended to him, and no more;* provided that on a Valuation to be made of it, as a Fee simple Estate, it should be equal to two sevenths of the whole. Whence it might be argued that the Testatrix, designed the Treasurer should have no part of her Fee simple Estate. However from the

Tenor of both the Will and Codicil, its plain, she intended to make him equal with the Rest (including what would have descended to him). But, as she by Docking the Intail in her Life time, has cut off this Descent, so the Reason upon which that particular qualified Devise stood is taken away; and therefore the Will, it seems, should be considered as if the Circumstance of that Intail had not attended it; and then the two sevenths must necessarily extend to the Residue of the Estate. Besides unless the Treasurer is thus let in for a Proportion of the Residue, the Devise of the two sevenths becomes void, whereas every Devise by Law, being for the Benefit of the Devisee, shall be so construed as that he may if possible, take by it.

Suppose for Instance, That Mrs. Hamilton had conveyed away this Intailed Estate, after it was Docked as she might have done (by which it would have been lost to the Treasurer) how could he upon her Will as it now stands, have had any thing at all, unless the first general Devise be so construed, altho it is evident from the whole Will, that she intended he should have secured to him an equal Share with the Rest. Nor do I conceive the Estates descending to him, as Heir at Law, through a different Channel, can alter the Reason of this Construction, upon the first general Devise in the Will. In short, as the Treasurer's Proportion was limited by the after Devise, to the intailed Lands, that Limitation could exist no longer than the Intail did; when therefore the Common Recovery was suffered, which destroyed the Intail, the Limitation depending upon it was also destroyed and of Consequence the former part of the Will must be left to operate in its full Latitude, without any Restriction and hence altho the Point may admit of Dispute, I am <rath> of opinion, that the Treasurer must take the two sevenths of the Estate, exclusive of the Lands that were intailed, which now also descend to him in Fee Simple.

BENJN. KISSAM

July 12, 1766

I Join in Substance with Mr. Kissam in the above Opinion and further Ado

1st. That the alteration of the Estate which the Testatrix had at the time of making the Will and Codicill from a Tail to a Fee Simple in Docking the Estate Tail is an actual Revocation of the Will and Codicill as to the Intailed Estate.

2d. And that in Consequence thereof Abraham De Peyster, elder Brother and Heir to the Testatrix, will take by Discent the Real Estate docked by the Common Recovery unless afterwards disposed of by her, or the Deed to lead the Uses should be otherwise, and will also be intitled to two sevenths of the other Part of the Real Estate Either by the Will or Descent.

DAVID OGDEN

DS. NHi: Kempe Papers. Body of the ms. in the hand of JJ.

1 Abraham DePeyster served as Treasurer of New York, 1721–67.

From Peter Jay

Rye, 26th March 1765

Dear Johnny.

Yesterday I received your letter by the Boat, and another this Morning per the Post.[1] Your Brother's[2] not writing by Captain Montgomery may be owing to his not being in London when he sailed, but this will not altogether excuse him even if he had been then at Bath. If there be any news from him let me know it. I now enclose a bill of £5. Take 40/. for a Ticket and the Remainder you must give to Fady.

The sickness among my Negroes during these three last months, and which still continues, having from 3 to 5 always down at a time gives me more trouble and fatigue than I can well undergo. I believe our Hannah is very near her End, and Anthony and little Plat are both in a bad way with a constant fever which has hitherto baffled all the Doctor's Endeavours to relieve them. Susan and big Mary are also both unwell and London is just beginning to move about. In this distressed condition of my family I can't be spared from home to visit my Friends in Town, nor take any exercise abroad, which I stand in great need of, after a long Winter's confinement attended with great fatigue of Body and perplexity Mind. However, we must submit to the Will of Providence, and hope for more comfortable days hereafter.

I've sent your Letter to Strang.[3] Jotham Wright[4] who is bound with him in a Bond to your Aunt is looked upon here, to be in good Circumstances. I shall nevertheless endeavour to get the Bond Renewed with an additional Security.

We all remember our love to you and I always Am, Dear Johnny Your Affectionate Father

PETER JAY

ALS. Endorsed: ". . . abt. his Fatigue etc. occasioned by the Death of some and Indisposition of all his Servants."

1 Letter not located.

2 Sir James Jay.

3 Letter not located. Many members of the Strang family lived in the Rye area at this time. All were descendants of Daniel L'Estrange, a French Huguenot who settled in Rye in the late seventeenth century. Charles W. Baird, *History of Rye* (New York, 1871), p. 444.

4 A Rye ship-joiner. Baird, *History of Rye*, p. 450.

The Jay-Livingston Friendship

Robert R. Livingston, Jr. (1746–1813), who was to be one of JJ's closest friends and political allies for a quarter-century, was a member of the Clermont, or "Lower Manor," branch of the Livingston family. His great-grandfather, Robert Livingston I (1654–1722), the founder of the clan's fortunes in America, divided his landed holdings between his two sons, Philip and Robert. Philip, the elder, received the larger inheritance and succeeded his father as lord of Livingston Manor. Robert (1688–1775), the younger son, received the southwestern portion of the manor and named his estate "Clermont."

Robert R. Livingston, Jr., grandson of the first Robert of Clermont, graduated from King's College in 1765. He then studied law, first in the office of William Livingston, then under the direction of William Smith, Jr. After their admission to the bar in 1768, JJ and young Livingston formed a law partnership which was dissolved in 1771.[1]

1 Dangerfield, *Robert R. Livingston*, pp. 25–26, 45–48.

To Robert R. Livingston, Jr.

New York, April 2d, 1765

Dear Robert

After we parted last Saturday Evening I retired to my Room, and spent the remaining part of it in reflecting upon the Transactions of the Day, particularly such of them as emediately related to our present and future Connection. I always find myself greatly embarrassed, when I attempt to speak my Sentiments on a Subject that very nearly concerns me; it was this which prevented me from saying so much upon that head, during the time we were then together, as I could wish to have done and therefore think it necessary to have Recourse to this Method of making up the Deficiency. The remarkable Delicacy with which the Proposal was made, was to me a convincing argument of the Sincerity of your Intentions; and upon Recollection I find the whole of your late Behaveour towards me, speak the same agreable Language.

Convinced that Friendship was one of the greatest Blessings as well as advantages, this Life can boast, I have long since thought seriously of engageing in a Connection of this kind with one, whom I might have Reason to think qualified for such an Intimacy, by being not only of similar Profession and circumstance with myself, but one whose Disposition would concur with his Fidelity and good sense, in rendering that Tye firm and indissoluble, which once entered into, ought ever to be preserved inviolable. For [———][1] it my Business to know my Companions, and [———th] the different Degrees of Abilities honour and G[ood Nature of which] each was possessed. One in particular, (who had always before held the highest place in my Esteem) soon became the peculiar object of my Attention. Every Day afforded additional arguments to persuade me, that he possessed in a high Degree every social Qualification, every mental Endowment requisite to form a Person of this Caracter. One almost insuperable Obstacle constantly opposed my informing him of what, with no little Reluctance I concluded. I was in doubt whether he entertained the same Opinion of me that I did of him; I was not sure whether he had not entered into a connection of this kind already; and I thought it imprudent to make the Proposal, without having very good Reason to think it would meet with a favourable Reception.

You may easily concieve then what silent Satisfaction I must have felt, when he himself removed all these Difficulties, when he himself opened wide those Doors of Friendship, into which I had long desired to enter, and kindly offered to point out every Rock that might endanger my safety in our Voyage to Eternity.

These were my late and these are my present Sentiments respecting my Friend. We have now entered into a Connection of the most delicate nature, a Connection replete with Happiness and productive of very extensive advantages. It will heighten the Joys of each by adding to the Felicity of both, and the Misfortunes of either will by being devided become more tolerable. Let our kind spirits then unite in nourishing the encreasing Flame, let the Interest of one be the Interest of both, and, let us constantly reject with Disdain every maglignant Insinuation of insidious or malevolent Hearts. In a Word, let us maintain a virtuous Friendship while here below, and in the World to come we shall not be divided.

From your affectionate Friend

[JOHN JAY]

AL[S]. NHi: Robert R. Livingston Papers. Signature cropped.

[1] The mutilations of this ms. were caused by the cropping of the signature. In each case, about fifteen letters were removed in each line on the *verso* of the signature.

Sir James Jay, an Embarrassing Sibling

Ever torn by restlessness and ambition, James Jay found that provincial life did not come up to his expectations after his return from abroad. He approached the governors of King's College and secured their appointment as agent to raise funds in England, leaving for the Mother Country in May, 1762.[1] For the first year and a half his fund-raising mission had smooth sailing. Joining forces with the Reverend William Smith, abroad on a similar errand for the College of Philadelphia, Jay raised a substantial sum for King's College and, for his accomplishment, was knighted by George III in 1763. To the astonishment of the governors of King's College Sir James refused to turn over the funds, insisting on first deducting his expenses. The issue came to a head when Barlow Trecothick, another King's College agent in Britain, drew on Sir James for £1,000. As Sir James had neither authorized this draft nor received advance notice of the transaction, he "protested" the bills of the College and refused to honor them. At a meeting of 23 April 1765, the College governors heard two letters from Peter Jay concerning his son's dispute with the school. The board ordered a committee to prepare a letter of attorney to Trecothick authorizing the Englishman to settle the College's accounts with Sir James, but with the provision that the latter first pay the £1,000 in protested bills.[2] Sir James refused compliance on the ground that, once the accounts were settled, his expenses might reduce the balance in the College's favor to less than the disputed £1,000. When an attempt to arbitrate the matter in November 1766 failed, Trecothick brought a bill in chancery against Sir James.

The controversy was especially mortifying to the Jay family, whose relations with the first president of King's College had been on a footing of great intimacy. To young, sensitive, and prideful JJ, just two years out of college, the scandal was an acute embarrassment. Finally, after a controversy dragging out over a full decade, the issues were compromised, but not before protracted proceedings in chancery and the intercession of JJ's father as late as 1776.[3]

1 Columbia University, *Early Minutes of the Trustees,* I (New York, 1932), meetings of 6 and 15 April and 16 Nov. 1762.

2 *Ibid.,* meetings of 23 April, 14 May, 17 Dec. 1765.

3 Sir James Jay, *A Letter to the Governors of the College of New York . . .* (London, 1771); *A Letter to the Universities of Oxford and Cambridge . . .* (London, 1774). See below, Peter Jay to JJ, 15 April 1765, 18 April 1776. For an analysis of the curious sibling rivalry between Sir James and JJ, see Richard B. Morris, *Seven Who Shaped Our Destiny: The Founding Fathers as Revolutionaries* (New York, 1973), pp. 154–57.

FROM PETER JAY

Rye, 15th April 1765

Dear Johnny,

On receipt of this Letter, you must immediately deliver the inclosed to Mr. Auchmuty.[1] As much noise is made in Town about Jemmy's suffering the Bills of the Governors of the College to be returned protested, I send you the rough draught of my Letter to Mr. Auchmuty on that head. Jemmy is indeed very remiss in not sending Reasons to them for his Proceedings, and so are the Governors blamable for drawing without his orders for it. I suppose there may be about £1400 in Jemmy's hands, but this Sum will doubtless be reduced very low, when for his Services and the great Expences attending the transacting of their affairs is deducted therefrom. I would have you to peruse the rough draught carefully and make yourself master of the Affair, in order to vindicate your Brother's Character which I expect is now undeservedly pretty roughly handled. The truth of the whole matter I believe is, that Jemmy is determined to keep Sufficiently in his hands to pay for his trouble and Expenses and not be at the Mercy of the Governors to allow him what they shall think proper, but however we must be silent yet about these Matters, but you must acquaint your Aunt Chambers[2] of the whole, who will be also silent about it. You must send me the rough draught back again in the Box when it comes up.

I am, Dear Johnny Your Affectionate Father

PETER JAY

ALS. Endorsed: "Letter relatg. to the Docts. Dispute with the Govrs. of Coll." Enclosure: Peter Jay to Samuel Auchmuty, c. 15 April 1765, not located.

[1] Samuel Auchmuty (1722–77), the rector of Trinity Church, was a member of the Board of Governors of King's College.

[2] Anne Chambers's late husband, John, had been a member of the Board of Governors of King's College.

TO ROBERT R. LIVINGSTON, JR.

New York, April 19, 1765

Dear Robt:

It gives me pleasure to find the receipt of my letter[1] afforded you some satisfaction and am pleased to hear it was heightened by a mixture of self love, because I am persuaded your judgment would not have permitted self love to add anything to the pleasure, if a consciousness of merit had not attended the agreeable sensation. Sure I am therefore that my sentiments were not without foundation, particularly as they square with the testimony of your conscience, which I believe is seldom liable to deception.

You say when you recieved my letter, you expected to have been presented with a Chinese Glass, from which the views of the mind would have been reflected with as much exactness as the deformities of the person are from a common mirrour. Altho there are few, whose features are every way regular, and in whose form the nicest rules of proportion are observed, yet we meet with many so—unexceptionable in these particulars, that it is hard even for the most critical discernment, to point out their blemishes; and hence you must discover your expectations in this instance on that amount rather sanguine than well founded.

I should be inexcusable were I to omit answering the ensuing charge, which, tho perhaps not in express terms, yet virtually—impeaches that friendship, which you say you had reason to think I entertained for you, viz, that you expected from my good sense and sincere *friendship a remedy for every fault,* and are surprised to find *polite compliments* instead of *severe criticism* form the *greater* part of my letter. You doubtless with me are of opinion, that giving Physic to a healthy person by way of prevention, is for the most part rather an injury than an advantage to the constitution however strong, and that a Physician would hazard if not forfeit his reputation, were he to throw a man into a salivation in order to remove only a few pimples, which appear today and vanish tomorrow. Humanum est erare, and the *greatest* circumspection will hardly prevent our falling into such mistakes, as the infirmities of our nature generally lead us to commit. If in your conduct I observe willing deviations, from prudence, I think it no breach of friendship but rather for your advantage that I pass them over in silence. But rest assured that should any of consequence or any that I may think of consequence come within my notice, I shall not be backward (however disagreeable the task) to administer that severe criticism, of which you are surprised I am not more liberal—the same behaviour I expect from you, not in the least distrusting your readiness to pursue every measure that may contribute to my welfare.

As to the *greater part of my letters being made up of compliments* I would observe 1st, That compliments are expressive of our real sentiments, then I am under the necessity of pleading guilty to the charge, but if by compliments we are to understand nothing more or less than a designing adulation, I declare that there is not one compliment throughout the whole. You tell me, *you choose to put the most favourable construction on my actions, and imagine it was only a bate set for your vanity, which I having observed a prevailing foible has in that delicate way, either to discover to you, or convince myself of more fully.* If you suppose a bait laid for your vanity, by implication you must also suppose I had some ungenerous designs in view,—for every bait is supposed to cover a hook and the intent of concealing the hook is least the fish, by seeing, should avoid it as a dangerous consequence. If therefore I concealed my designs under the bait you mention, it must have been to prevent your seeing them, and why should I conceal them from you, unless I was conscious they were of pernicious tendency; now, knowingly to prejudice a person whom we profess our friend, is certainly to act upon ungenerous principles, to say no more of it. And is this my friend the most favourable construction that my actions will admit of? To this you will doubtless answer, that you did not intend such consequences should be drawn from your words; but only would have thus much deduced from them, viz: *That I, observing* Vanity to be your prevailing foible, either proposed in this way to discover it to you, or convince myself of more fully. To which I reply, 1st, That had I thereby intended to discover to you that I thought your vanity too great, friendship would have obliged me to express myself in a manner so free from ambiguity as to leave no doubts respecting my intention, and to avoid every expression that might lead you to mistake my meaning. This construction therefore as to the first point must entirely subside. 2nd. If vanity was your prevailing foible, and if I had observed it to be so, it would have been unnecessary (in order to convince myself of it) to have recourse to a method so extraordinary, as the one you suppose; my long acquaintance with you must have satisfied every doubt of that kind, and the difficulty of concealing a prevailing foible would have saved me the trouble at this late day, of concerting such schemes, as you suspect I have now been endeavouring to put in execution. Neither of these two constructions therefore are the true constructions. The words of the letter will best explain what I meant and what I intended you should understand by them; and I meant and intended you should understand, nothing more or less by them, than what the very words themselves import.

Your saying that you are not insensible to the advantages that must arise from a *correspondence* of this nature, looks as if you mistook the meaning of that part of my letter, to which you intended the above as an answer. If you turn over my letter, you will find I then spoke of the advantages resulting from a *Connection of this kind,* by which I meant the *advantages* inseparable from an unbounded unlimited friendship and not merely such as may attend this correspondence; which I look upon to be only an appendant to the connection before spoken of. Friendship in my opinion cannot be confined solely to any species of interview, but is of too extensive a nature,—to brook any restraint, or be satisfied within certain limits which it must not exceed. Tho I do not imagine so imperfect a friendship to have been the object of your intentions, yet I thought it necessary to make the above remarks least at any time we might mistake each other's meaning, and thereby be led to consider things in a different light, from what they ought to be considered. Your hearty concurrence in rejecting every malignant insinuation gives me great, tho not unexpected satisfaction; it is a measure highly necessary, tending greatly to strengthen the union which at present subsists between us, and which I shall ever be studious to preserve and maintain.

This then with what I propose to say, the first time I see you, will I believe remove every doubt in your letter, and I hope your next will consist of such *new* matter as you may think best calculated to answer the ends we have in view.

By the Postscript of your letter I am sorry to find you have been disappointed by those, who above all ought not to disappoint *you.* Fortune you know is none of the most settled beings in the world, however if she frowns today, you will know better how to value her smiles tomorrow, and when she begins to smile again, that she may ever after continue in a good humour with you, is the earnest wish of

Your sincere friend,

JOHN JAY

Tr. NcD: J. A. Chaloner MSS.

[1] See above, JJ to Robert R. Livingston, 2 April 1765. Livingston's reply has not been located.

To Robert R. Livingston, Jr.

[New York], Thursday night, 31 October 1765

Never my Dear Friend have I been more at a Loss in answering a Letter[1] than I now am, and never have I undertaken a Task more agreable or that has given me greater Satisfaction. Be not surprised that on *such* an Occasion, I should be at a Loss; for nothing that I can say, will be adequate to your Candour, and Generosity; nor can any Terms be fully expressive of my Sentiments on a Subject so singular and interesting. Neither think it a Contradiction, that I should notwithstanding, call it the most agreable Task I have undertaken; for if a bare assurance of Friendship from a Person whom we highly esteem gives us Pleasure, how happy must we be in an Opportunity of gratefully acknowledging our Obligations to him, for a Conduct, that must forever banish every Doubt of Sincerity; and fix our Friendship upon a Foundation able to resist the Waves of Envy, as well as protect it from the arrows of Detraction.

Suspect me not of Flattery, if I say your Ingenuousness has stood a Trial, that few, in our degenerate Days, are capable of undergoing; and that the Remonstrances of pride, to others the most insurmountable obstacles; only afforded a happy opportunity of evincing your Greatness of Mind. Such Principles, so directing your Actions, must render your private Caracter as much the Subject of Love as Admiration; and by diffusing their Influence through the more general Concerns of Life, make Your Reflections as pleasing to yourself, as the Causes of them beneficial to Society.

I forbear taking particular Notice of the several Reasons you mention for dropping the Correspondence; but this permit me to remark that in general they reflect more Honour on your Modesty, than Judgment, with respect to your Abilities. I think myself extremely happy in an assurance from you (whom I cant suspect of Dissimulation) that no other material Deficiency marks my Caracter than the one you mention; and I thankfully acknowledge your Endeavours to remove that. Agreable to your advice I shall keep a watchful Eye over my Conduct; and hope with your Assistance to preserve it fair and unspotted. The Method you take to prevent my suspecting You of Flattery, contains the most refined and delicate piece of Flattery I have hitherto met with, viz.: That I should impute your Inability to point out any other Faults, rather to Incapacity in the Critick than Perfection in the Subject. However, I am not displeased with it, as it tends to confirm me in the opinion I before entertained of your Genius and Invention.

I shall make one Observation more upon your Letter and then conclude. You say you was deterred from mentioning a Correspondence upon any other head, by a fear of not being able to support it properly. Don't decieve yourself; nor think that I am speaking other than my real Sentiments, when I tell you, that in my Opinion you are as capable of maintaining a Correspondence upon other Subjects, as the Person whom You honour with the Name of friend. Application is the only Requisite, for Nature has done her Part. But even admitting (since you will have it so) that you are not capable of supporting it *properly,* Yet let me ask, if that be the case, whether you dont wish and desire to become able? The Wish certainly is reasonable, and sure you wont refuse to gratify it. Begin then and try to make yourself capable; the Object undoubtedly is worth possessing especially as the attainment will cost you so little pains. Besides, between Persons who consider each other in the Light we do, no bad Consequences can attend a Discovery of our Defects; our Business being not to expose but remove them.

As it grows late, and the office will prevent my adding any thing in the morning, I shall defer saying any thing more till I see you, except that I am Your Friend

JOHN JAY

P.S. Pray think of our New England Frolick, and let no Objection prevent your adding to the Pleasure we expect to enjoy in that Excursion.

ALS. PHi: Gratz Collection.
1 Letter not located.

To Robert R. Livingston, Jr.

Rye, March the 4th, 1766

Dear Robert,

I received Yours of the 1st March Yesterday.[1] Altho I did not suspect any Part of my Letter to be misterious or unintelligable, I confess I imagind, you would hesitate in answering to every Part of it. There was a Hobby Horse in the Way.

You have it seems been highly entertained of late, and by your account of the Matter have attained every Qualification necessary to form a Buck, and entittle you to the appellation of a Man of Pleasure. Forgive me if [I] grow serious upon this Subject. As I am sure you dont think me capable of Flattering your Foibles, or mean enough to applaud what I disapprove, (especially in one to whom I profess to act with the greatest Candour, and Disinterestedness) so I hope Liberties of this kind will be taken in good Part, especially when dictated by Considerations, not necessary now to repeat. You are now in the Country, separated from Temptations, your Passions are reduced to their usual Calm, and your Spirits, like a silent Stream whose Woods defend it from the Winds that rage on Shoars more exposed to Storms, again unruffled flow and glide with Ease. Reason has resumed her Seat, you think cooly, and you reflect dispassionately.

Recollect for a Moment what time has elapsed since we have been Free from the Drudgery of Business—that such an opportunity will probably not again offer, and therefore that it was by no means to be neglected. Then ask yourself how that Leisure has been employed. Enquire minutely into the Success of every Enterprise, and see whether a better Plan of operations could not have been concerted. If I mistake not, and am allowed to judge from Appearances, you have lost by playing the Buck, and have gained nothing but a very uncertain Prospect of Advantage by pursuing some late Measures. Dont be surprized: I know my meaning here is hard to be understood, but necessity wont permit me to be less obscure. For my own Part, I dont consider these Irregularities or Inconsistancies as being the Result of your natural Disposition, and Turn of Inclinations. I think I can distinguish *the Scaffold, from the Pile*. I disapprove them only as they seem in my opinion inexpedient, and as they have not passed altogether uncensured. Their Propriety considered with Respect to right and wrong is another matter, but this is a tender Subject. I leave the whole to your own Reflections.

In your Letter is the following Passage, vizt.: "Nay, I will to fill up this Page go further, and tell without Fear, etc. how you pass your time, and show (*that tho your Fear of making your last Letter too long prevented your giving me any account*) that I am not wholly ignorant of the Happiness you enjoy, etc." Whence did you infer, that the fear of making my last Letter too long prevented my giving you an account how things went on with myself. I am sure there was nothing of this kind in my last Letter, at least of my inserting, and therefore cant concieve (unless some Tricks have been played with it) how you could think of making this observation. Look over my Letter again, for I should be glad to be satisfyed whether it contains any thing like this or not. I am Sorry you have given orders to have your Piece published before an answer thereto was prepared and agreed upon; it would be best you know, that the answer should be printed directly after the other, which cant now be done immediately, as your Removal to Cliermont will occasion Delays. I shall however desire Watt to defer the Publication till all things shall be ready, so that if he recieves my Letter before Thursday I hope everything will be well.[2]

Betsey Cruger going to be married! Alas poor Peter! indeed 'Tis a good Maxim which I have somewhere found vizt. Credere Pastores *levibus* nolite *Puellis*.[3]

When do you return to Town? I really long to see you, and had I recieved your Letter a little sooner should have met you at the Bridge.

I remain Dear Bob your sincere Friend

JOHN JAY

P.S. Pray present my Respects to your GrandPapa,[4] of whose Civilities while at Clermont I am far from b[———].[5]

ALS. NHi: Robert R. Livingston Papers. Endorsed.

1 Letter not located.

2 Livingston's biographer, George Dangerfield, was unable to establish Livingston's authorship of any political or other essays published before 1770. No letter from JJ to any member of the Watts family in March 1766 has been located, but the individual referred to was probably John Watts (1749–1836), later a colleague of JJ and Livingston in the Moot and the Social Club. Dangerfield, *Robert R. Livingston*, p. 49; Martha J. Lamb and Mrs. Burton Harrison, *History of the City of New York: Its Origin, Rise, and Progress* (3 vols., New York, 1896), II, 32; James Grant Wilson, *The Memorial History of the City of New-York* (4 vols., New York, 1892–1893), II, 474n.

3 Elizabeth Cruger (d. 1778) was the daughter of Henry Cruger, a New York merchant. In the fall of 1765, Elizabeth eloped with Peter Van Schaack (1747–1832), a student at King's College. Although Van Schaack's son and biographer states that Henry Cruger and the Van Schaacks were reconciled "shortly" after the marriage, it would appear from JJ's remark that the young couple kept their elopement secret for several months. Henry C. Van Schaack, *The Life of Peter Van Schaack, LL.D., Embracing Selections from his Correspondence and other Writings, During the American Revolution and his Exile in England* (New York, 1842), p. 5. The Latin maxim comes from a pastoral poem of the first century A.D.: "Shepherds, put not your trust in fickle maids." Calpurnius Siculus *Bucolica*, Loeb Classical Library (London [1935], 1954), Eclogue III, line 90, p. 243.

4 Robert Livingston of Clermont.

5 Ms. torn.

From Benjamin Kissam

New York, Saturday, 26th April 1766

Dear Jay,

We were last Night strangely deluded with a mistaken account of the Repeal of the Stamp Act; and all the Bells have been ringing since Break of Day. Upon Enquiry We find That the Intelligence amounts to no more than that the Bill had passed the House of Commons on the 28 of February and was to be sent up to the Lords on the 3rd March. There is indeed a Letter dated at Falmouth on the 5th of March which says the Stamp Act is repealed but this can be no more than its having passed the House of Commons, which we find they commonly call a Repeal.[1]

Fady tells me my horse is well. I intend to go to Philadelphia on

Tuesday next and would be glad to have my horse here by Monday Night. If he could be led down he would be better fit for the Journey the next day, but if he cannot be sent this way I would have him rid very moderately down. I refer You to my Letter of Yesterday.[2] I am Your humble Servant

BENJN: KISSAM

ALS: Addressed: "Mr. John Jay, at Rye." Endorsed.

1 It was not until 20 May that New Yorkers learned that the King had assented to the repeal of the Stamp Act on 18 March 1766.

2 Kissam had evidently allowed JJ to make a trip to Rye because of the dearth of legal business due to the Stamp Act. In his letter to JJ of 25 April, Kissam wrote that he planned to go to Philadelphia if "News of the Repeal of the Stamp Act should not arrive in the mean time" and asked that his horse be sent down to him. In the same letter, Kissam added that if the Stamp Act were repealed, "we shall doubtless have a Luxuriant Harvest of Law" and asked that JJ return to the city immediately to "be ready to secure all Business that offers." ALS, JP.

From Benjamin Kissam

Albany, the 25th of August 1766

Dear Sir,

I just now received your long Letter of the 12th Instant,[1] and am not a little pleased with the Humour and Freedom of Sentiment that Characterizes it. It would give me Pain, if I thought You could even suspect me capable of wishing to impose any Restraint upon You in this high and inestimable privilege of Friendship: Because I can see no Reason, why the Rights of one Relation in Life, should destroy those of another. I Detest that forbidding Pride, which, with formal Ceremony, can Stalk over the Social Rights of others, and elevate the Soul in a vain Conceit of its own Dignity and Importance; founded merely in some advantatious Circumstance of relative Superiority. Take this therefore, if you please, as a noli Prosoqui,[2] for the heinous Crime of writing a free and familiar Letter to me: with this further, That whenever You Transgress in the other Extreme, You must not expect to meet with the same Mercy.

I really Believe Jay, Your Pen was directed by the rapid Whirl of Imagination. Nay, I am convinced That this Whirl was begun continued and Ended with a strong Tide. I can't help conceiving it under the Idea of a Mill-Tide which keeps the wheels in a quick Rotation; save only, with this Difference, That the Motion of that is uniform; Yours irregular, an Irregularity however, that bespeaks the Grandeur, not the Meanness of the Intellectual Source from whence the Current flows. *Now,* You are racking your Brains for an explanation of my short Query; and after shifting the Question round and round again, You have at last Mistook my Meaning. *Then* Your Imagination takes a Flight, and gives Your Ideas a few Turns round the Wheels of human Life: From thence She Soars into the planetary Regions and moves in the Circuit of those larger Spheres. Down again she comes, and sweeps round the Confined Orbit of *our Little Selves*. And after opening the Ball, You give a Picture of the world, like Fairies *dancing to the Tunes in mystic Measures:* Till at last, the Musick, the Frolick and the Dance, all cease; and these busy Beings, breathing their last, in this little point of Time, fall asleep. To Sleep! Perchance to Dream! Etc.

So much for a Comment on the Freaks of your Imagination, and tho she has taken this wild and romantic Tour, I won't Condemn her Excursions: Because, like a Regent Queen, she sometimes will Govern in the Intellectual Realm, while Reason her Lord Paramount, stands aloof and admires the dextrous, varied Art, and Ease with which she Guides the Rein. Reason sometimes Checks her Progress, and sometimes suffers the Royal Dame to move unfettered. In the latter Case her Sallies are so bold, That *we know not with how much art the Windings turn, nor where the regular Confusion ends.*

I will now explain to You what I meant, by asking how Business went in the office. And first *Negatively* I did not want a List or the Number of the new Causes; neither was I anxious to know how often You visited the office. But as a Regard to your Modesty on the one hand, and your veracity on the other has induced you to evade an Answer to the last, I will nevertheless solve the Dilemma for You by saying That I believe You have too much Veracity to assume a false Modesty, and That You are too honest to declare an Untruth. And as You have left me between two Extremes, I shall take the Middle-Way, and do suppose, That upon the whole You attend the office as much as you ought to do: So that You see I save both Your Modesty and Veracity, and answer the Question, as you State it, into the Bargain.

But *affirmatively* I am to Tell You That I did mean to ask in general, whether my Business decreased much by my Absence; and whether my Returns at the last Term were pretty good, and whether Care has been taken to put that Business forward as much as possible. I conclude however, That tho You did not Take me, as the Irishman Says, Yet these Things have been properly attended to.

Here we are, and are likely to be so, I am afraid these Ten days.

There are no less than 47 Persons, charged all, upon three several Indictments, with the Murder of those persons, who lost their Lives in the Affray with the Sheriff. Four or five of them are in Gaol and will be tried this day. What their Fate will be God only knows; tis terrible to think that so many Lives should be at Stake upon the Principles of a constructive Murder: For I suppose that the immediate Agency of but a very few of the Party can be proved.[3]

I dont know when we shall have done, but hope at farthest to be at Home, in a Fortnight from this. It has been a tedious and perplexed piece of work, and I long to shake hands with, and be rid of it. Tell Mrs. Kissam,[4] That I wrote Yesterday by Capt. Van Alen a Skipper, who promised to deliver the Letter himself. I have not Time to write by the Post to her. Let as many Drafts of Declarations be drawn as can be.

I am Your affectionate Friend

BENJN: KISSAM

ALS. Addressed: "Mr. John Jay at Benjamin Kissams, Attorney at Law, Golden Hill at New York." Endorsed: ". . . containing Remarks on the romantick Turn of my Imagination."

1 In his letter of 12 Aug. 1766, JJ answered Kissam's request for " 'some account of the business of the office' " by reporting that affairs remained "pretty much in *statu quo*" in the city. "The ways of men, you know," JJ wrote, "are as circular as the orbit through which our planet moves, and the centre to which they gravitate is *self*." The letter reveals the informality of JJ's relations with Kissam, for he continued: "If I were writing to some folks, prudence would tell me to be more straight-laced: but I know upon what ground I stand; and professional pride shall give me no uneasiness, while you continue to turn it, with Satan behind your back." *HPJ*, I, 4–7.

2 An entry in court records when a plaintiff or prosecutor will proceed no further in the action.

3 The widespread dissatisfaction among New York tenant farmers reached a peak in 1766 with riots throughout the colony. On 26 June, Harmanus Schuyler, Albany County Sheriff, led a posse of 105 men to evict rebellious tenants of the Van Rensselaer family. In the skirmish that followed, Cornelis Ten Broeck was killed and seven other members of the Sheriff's party were wounded. Irving Mark, *Agrarian Conflicts in Colonial New York, 1711–1775* (New York, 1940), ch. V, *passim;* the incident in Albany County is mentioned on p. 142 of this study.

4 Catherine Rutgers Kissam.

The Master's Degree

Three years after JJ received his B.A., King's College awarded him a Master of Arts, a degree which was usually conferred after a perfunctory amount of extra study. JJ's diploma, dated 19 May 1767, is in JP.

King's College Commencement

[*New York, 19 May 1767*]

On Tuesday the 19th inst. was held our annual Commencement at St. Paul's Chapel in this City.[1] His Excellency the Governor,[2] the Members of his Majesty's Council, the Clergy of the City, and the neighbouring Governments, and a very numerous and splendid Audience, honoured the Day with their Presence.

The Procession was from the College to the Chapel. The Business of the Day began with solemn Prayers to Almighty God, suitable to the Occasion, and an elegant Latin Oration succeeded, by the Rev. Dr. Cooper, President of the College.

The Salutatory was delivered by Mr. Laight,[3] whose graceful Action, and correct Manner of Expression, were justly admired by every Gentleman of Learning present.

To this succeeded an excellent Discourse on the Usefulness of the Passions, by Mr. Jay, which for judicious Reasonings and Elegance of Stile, did great Honour to the Performer.

The next Performance was, an English forensick Dispute between Messrs. Jay and Harrison,[4] Wether a Man ought to engage in War without being persuaded of the Justness of his Cause? The masterly Sentiments that were exhibited on both sides of the Question, entertained the Audience with particular Pleasure.

The Exercise being finished, the President conferred upon the following young Gentlemen, the Degree of Batchelor of Arts, viz. Messrs. Laight and Tyler, also the Degree of Master of Arts upon Messrs. Jay and Harrison, and upon Doctor Glentworth, the Rev. Messrs. Neil, Avery and Ingliss. The Rev. Mr. Ogilvie, was admitted A.M. from Yale-College; and the Rev. Samuel Auchmuty and Thomas B. Chandler, *ad endum*, viz., D.D. from Oxford.[5]

The Audience were now entertained with an English Valedictory Oration, by Mr. Harrison, whose graceful Appearance and judicious Performance did him great Honour, and justly entitled him the general Applause.

The whole Ceremony concluded with solemn Prayers. It would be unpardonable not to observe that the Audience went away very much pleased with their Entertainment; the whole being conducted in the most decent and regular Manner.

N.Y. *Mercury*, 1 June 1767.

[1] St. Paul's, the second "chapel of ease" of Trinity Parish, was located at Broadway and Fulton St. and opened in Oct. 1766.

[2] Sir Henry Moore (c. 1700–69), Governor of New York, 1765–69.

[3] William Laight (1751–1804).

[4] Richard Harison.

[5] John Tyler (d. 1823) received an honorary B.A. Besides JJ and Harison, recipients of the M.A. degree in 1767 were: George Glentworth (d. 1792), later Surgeon General of Britain's Colonial Hospitals; Hugh Neil; Ephraim Avery, the Episcopalian missionary at Rye; and Charles Inglis (1733–1810) and John Ogilvie (1722–74), the assistant ministers of Trinity Parish. Samuel Auchmuty, the rector of Trinity, and Thomas Bradbury Chandler (1726–90), pastor of the Anglican church at Elizabeth, N.J., were granted D.D. degrees by Oxford in 1766. Milton H. Thomas, *Columbia University Officers and Alumni, 1754–1857* (New York, 1936), p. 280; Franklin D. Dexter, *Biographical Sketches of the Graduates of Yale College* (New York, 1845), II, 23–26, 685–86; Morgan Dix, *et al.*, eds., *A History of the Parish of Trinity Church in the City of New York* (6 vols., New York, 1898–1962), I, 246, 307, 310–11, 359–61, 405, 412, 446.

Legal and Personal Affairs

Admitted to the bar in October 1768, JJ entered at once into partnership with Robert R. Livingston, Jr., for three years, and thereafter operated his own law office until political involvements and military events made it necessary for him to forgo his practice. JJ represented litigants in the New York Supreme Court, Chancery, the Mayor's Court of New York City, and in the inferior courts in Queens, Westchester, Dutchess, Ulster, and Orange counties. While his relatives numbered some of his most valued clients, his practice included people of various political persuasions, who would later range from Tories to Whigs, and whose causes JJ defended with equal diligence during the six years he maintained a law office.

The close-knit Supreme Court bar, comprising a large contingent of graduates of King's College, Yale, and the College of New Jersey, systematically continued their legal education by organizing the Moot, a law society which met between 1770 and 1775 to debate points of law. JJ, a charter member, rarely missed a meeting and for a brief period served as secretary.[1] He and his fellow members debated such legal questions as to the manner an executor should plead to avoid payment of testator's book debts, various issues of intercolony comity and conflicts of laws, the precise words in a devise which constituted a fee tail, the authority of inferior courts of the province to grant new trials, and whether the English Statute of Frauds extended to the colony of New York, the subject of a learned opinion by a noted twentieth-century jurist.[2] Among more serious duties, members of the Moot agreed "to take notes of all questions of Law that may be agitated in the Supreme Court during the succeeding Term," and to "make Reports thereof, and produce them to the moot with all convenient speed."[3] Regrettably, these notes were not preserved in a formal series of law reports.

Toward the latter years of his brief practice a few cases brought JJ a certain *éclat* in Whig circles and stamped him as an antiadministration man. In April 1773, he defended Mayor Underhill of the borough town of Westchester in a contested election. The government, represented by Attorney General John Tabor Kempe, contended that unqualified voters had been permitted to vote in the election. JJ exploited a variety of procedural maneuvers to have the case postponed, in effect giving his client another three months of his term. Hard on the heels of the Underhill case was a mandamus issued against the officials of the town ordering them to admit Gilial Honeywell and Isaac Legget to the offices of aldermen to which, the government contended, they had been duly elected. By dilatory tactics, JJ succeeded in keeping them out of their posts from July 1773 to April 1774.[4] Although in the end the crown prevailed in each case, JJ's support of the local authorities against the royal government and of the broader suffrage in effect in the borough and town of Westchester elections, increased his popularity throughout the province and marked him as a potential leader of the dissident forces.[5]

1 Moot Cases argued at New York, 1770–74, NHi: BV Sec.; another version, covering the same years, but of different debates, also at NHi; The Moot, minutes and rules, 23 Nov. 1770–6 Jan. 1775, owned by John J. DuBois, on deposit, JP.

2 Cardozo, *C.J.*, in *Beers* v. *Hotchkiss*, 256 N.Y. 41 (1931).

3 Moot Minutes, 5 Feb. 1773. JJ was named with two others to attend the Supreme Court during the spring term, 1773, for that purpose. The Moot, minutes and rules, 5 March 1773.

4 See Minutes, Supreme Court of Judicature, 1772–76, pp. 101, 131, 153, Hall of Records, New York City.

5 See also Jared Sparks, *The Life of Gouverneur Morris* (3 vols., New York, 1832), I, 20; Henry B. Dawson, *Westchester-County, New York, During the American Revolution* (New York, 1886), p. 4.

The Debating Society

A group of young men, most of whom were King's College graduates, met on Thursday evenings during 1768 to engage in debates. The subjects selected for discussion generally concerned principles of government and how best the public welfare might be guaranteed. The members took turns presenting arguments and presiding over the four-hour meetings, which began at six o'clock.[1] Because discussions of this sort were particularly valuable training for lawyers, it is not surprising that the Debating Society of New York City was dominated by that profession or that JJ was an active participant. Notes on three of the debates appear below.

1 Paul M. Hamlin, *Legal Education in Colonial New York* (New York, 1939).

[*New York*], 22 *January* 1768

Whether in an absolute Monarchy it is better That the Crown should be elective than hereditary?

Kissam, Jay, Afft.; Van Schaick, De Lancey, Vardil,[1] Negt.; Benson President, Judgment given for the Affirmative.

[Kissam.][2] The Excellency of every political Institution determined by Expediency. Consider *absolute* as opposed to *limited* Monarchys. In the <limited> absolute Monarchys All depends upon the Wisdom of the Prince. Election gives good Princes, therefore most eligible.

[Speaker for Negative.] Elections occasion intestine Divisions. This Objection applies not to the first King. If the First has a Son of Merit, the Fathers Interest will secure him the Election and prevent Divisions, and so on ad infinitum.

[JJ.][2] But he may not have a Son fit to govern, and then a King must be chosen from among the Nobility etc. In all Monarchies the Nobility jealous of each other and unwilling to agrandize each other's Families. They have generally an equal Interest with the People. None therefore but Men of great Merit can obtain the Suffrages of the People, in this Case No Opposition. Five Kings of Rome.

Two of equal Merit may become Candidates. The civil Discord thence arising must be either *before* or *after* the Election. Not *before,* because impolitic and unnecessary. No Danger afterwards. 1. King of equal Talents. 2. Invested with the Powers of Government. 3. Elected in a *Constitutional* way. People will submit. 4. People wont risque by Rebellion their Lifes and Property to get rid of a good King.

Van Schaick. Admits that in Ab[solute] Monarchy's the Happiness of the People depends upon the wisdom of the Prince. Kingdom divided into a great Number of Factions. Bribery. *Disafection* in the losing Party. Not clear that the Prince will be a *wise* Man. Chosen by the Giddy People. *Poland* instanced. Choice may fall on a *Foreigner.*

Vardil. Barons and Nobles upon the Death of a Prince involved the State in faction.[3]

Kissam.[4]

[DeLancey.][5] The Subject before us opens so wide a Field of Argument and Declamation that I cannot help saying some thing on it, and however slight the Prospect may be of advancing any Thing conclusive in this Matter, yet some Observations may be not improper. The most probable Method of discovering the Truth in this Debate seems to be the estimating the Advantages and Disadvantages which will probably result from each of these Species of Government and those Gentlemen who have by proper Application made themselves Masters of the Principles of the Science of Government and of the Histories of different States and Nations, and the Causes of their Advancement and Declensions, will be able to give the most useful Hints on the Occasion. For my Part from a Conviction of the Blessings of order and Tranquility and of the pernicious Consequences of Faction and Riot, I cannot but prefer that Alternative in the present Debate which is most likely to secure the one and prevent the other, which I conceive to be an hereditary one.

Tis indeed a most plausible argument for the Gent[lemen] on the other Side of the Question that in all absolute Governments the Laws are supposed to be silent, except when they speak by the mouth of the Monarch, that this will however capricious when once signified being the Rule of Conduct for the Subject, is not to be gainsayed, consequently that the Happiness or Unhappiness of this People will depend on the Degree of Wisdom and Virtue with which the King is endued, that such being the Case that Species of Government which is most likely to secure such Qualities in the King must be preferable and finally that where the Election is free and the Elevation to the Throne unrestrained by fixt Rules and at their Disadvantages, thus it will be most likely to be effected. This which I believe includes all the Arguments that can be produced in favor of an elective Monarchy. I think it not sufficient to throw the Ballance against us. For let us but reflect on the Means by which this End is to be procured and we shall find that the State in all its Parts is to be convulsed with Faction and Disorder. A Crown being the Object what a Number of Candidates may be supposed at every Election, Each employing his Minions and engaging his <Retinue> Adherents. Bribery and Corruption circulated through the Nation to procure Friends to each Party, and Disaffection by the unsuccessful Parties to the prevailing one the natural Result. Nor can we suppose these will be dissipated by the actual Accession of the elected; nor a proper Harmony between the King and his Subjects, for how difficult will it prove for a People who have opposed and taken Arms against a man used every Means to oppose his accession afterwards to submit to his mere Will and Pleasure; and what Affection towards his Subjects can be hoped for from a King who is sensible How invidious his Success was to them. How natural to expect the same Disinclination rankling in their minds and a proportionate Degree of Resentment and Resolution to curb the Effects of it in his. In short as civil Wars were found necessary to procure his Accession so will a constant guard over the malcontents, and the disagreeable Effects of Jealousies and Suspicions be directed to prevent any ill Effects to the Government from them. How disadvantageous such Circumstances must be to all the good Effects of a civil Government.

'Tis I think worthy of Remark (And indeed 'tis a Fact founded on Experience) that the People will ever readily acquiesce in the Dispositions made by the Laws. Hence tho the Person of the Sovereign might be obnoxious to them, yet from a Sense of their conforming to the fixt Rules of the Constitution, they will with less Reluctance pay Allegiance to him than to a Person who has acquired his Accession merely through the Prevalence of a superior Faction, a Circumstance to which they will not be easily reconciled. But it is far from being evident that by an elective Government a Succession of more virtuous and wise Princes will be secured, for on what does this Supposition Rest? Why on the election and Judgment of a giddy Populace and even only the majority of them. A Populace never guided by Principles of Justice or Discernment, open to Corruption and led away by every Emotion of Passion. We have too many Instances every day of the Tumults of Elections and of how inconsistent with the Pretence of having the free Votes of People they are. Even an excellent Form of Laws calculated to support virtue and depress Vice cannot restrain the infamous Practices so destructive of these Views. That I may instance the fatal Consequences of an elective monarchy we need but cast our Eyes upon the History of Poland during the last Century; all the Disadvantages above mentioned were there experienced, and many more; Violence Contention Disorder Bloodshed and Assassination were there felt in the highest Degree, and felt as often as there was an Election.

It may be objected that its a great disadvantage in an hereditary Gov[ernmen]t that there frequently is a minority. But to this Chance which there undoubtedly is in all Gov[ernmen]ts of the hereditary kind We may oppose the inevitable Attendant of an election one namely an *Interregnum*. Besides in an hereditary Gov[ernmen]t there is in all Countries a Remedy applyed to this Objection namely the appointment of a Regency. There is this further Inconvenience attending an elective monarchy that as the Choice may fall on a Foreigner as We cannot expect from him so much Warmth of Affection as in [a native], or so well acquainted with the Genius of his People so, We may justly appreh[end] [———] will entail on his new Subjects all the Contentions of his antient [———] resolve them in all their Broils. This might be supported by many Instances and W[———] [———]d an Example where this Attachment to the *Natale Solum* [———] [———] Circumstances of the Accession of a foreign Prince has not produced [———].

The Roman Elections of Kings <and Consuls> cannot I think be opposed to what we have advanced and the Virtues of the first opposed to the Vices of the Emperors. We need but reflect on the Difference of the manners of that People in these different Periods. As all the Virtues flourished that exalt a national Character adorned the former So were the People in the other tinged with every Vice. [———] the Election of the Kings in Rome was chiefly directed by the Senate, that wise Body, so well calculated to discern Merit and with much Propriety empowered thus to reward it, and the Constitution of Rome moreover was a mixture of monarchy Aristocracy and Democracy.

D. NHi: Debating Society Papers.

1 Stephen De Lancey (1748–98) and John Vardill (1749–1811).

2 Another set of notes on this debate identifies the first and third speakers as Benjamin Kissam and JJ.

3 Up to this point the minutes are in the hand of JJ.

4 This version of the debate shows that Kissam took the floor at this point, but it omits his argument. The other set of notes indicates that he preferred an elected king, because selection by heredity was very unlikely to provide a wise one. He expressed his belief that the reward of a crown would cause many good candidates to present themselves, and he was equally confident that the best man would always win.

5 This unnamed debater must have been De Lancey, the only participant who had not yet presented his argument.

[*New York, 1768*]

Whether the Laws ought to compel a Subject to accept of a public Employment?

It was observed by the Gent[lemen] for the Affirmative that all Offices were either lucrative or honorary or 2 those that were neither of these. That the former had of themselves sufficient Temptation to the ambitious and avaricious and therefore could not come within the Circle of this Controversy that the latter Class therefore were to be considered, and only the inferior Offices to be regarded. They observed that a compulsory Power was good for these Reasons. 1 Because tis the Duty of every Man to serve the Gov[ernmen]t that protects him. 2 That the Execution of Justice might be obstructed for want of this. 3 That for Want of such Power many Inconsistencies would arise from the Refusal of Persons when appointed. 4 That the lower Sort of People are to be compelled to their Duty or they will neglect it.

The Gent[lemen] for Neg. observed that it is impolitic to make Laws for Inconsistencies unless such Inconsistencies actually have happened or from the Nature of Things may probably happen. He observed that a compulsory Power might produce these bad Effects 1 would render the Officers Slothful and inattentive. 2 That if these Employments were lucrative there would never be wanting Candidates. That therefore it would be best to make all Offices so by annexing to them certain Fees. That the Power of compelling Persons to accept Offices was often abused. That it was used to indulge Enmity and Spight. That it is common for a Minister to vent his Malice to set down the Object for the Office of Sheriff. Twas said by the Gent[lemen] for the aff[irmative] that a Sense of Duty and Fear of Punishment would incite Persons to accept Office tho disagreeable. To which it was answered that if such Virtue or Sense of Duty would be supposed that the compelling Power were unnecessary. That the Fear of Punishment certainly was not suff[icien]t.

Mr. J. for Aff[irmative] observed that all Offices were in the disposal of the Crown or particular Persons, that the latter had no Power to *compel*, therefore no Spite would be indulged, nor in the former because beneath the Attention etc.

Twas objected that in England twas necessary for Persons to take Oaths and the Sacrament, therefore improper to compel a Person to accept an Office, to which it was answered that as the taking the Sacrament and the filling the Offices were both Duties, it could be no Hardship.

D. NHi: Debating Society Papers.

[*New York, 1768*]

Was Virginius morally justified in putting his daughter, Virginia, to death to preserve her from violation by Appius?

Speakers: DeLancey, Kissam, Murray, Jay, Benson. In handwriting of Peter Van Schaack.

The matter was opened by Mr. D. L. who read the Story from the universal History. The Facts being agreed upon by the Gentlemen on both Sides of this Question, *Mr. Kissam,* on the Aff[irmative] began to observe upon them. He said that to form an adequate Judgment upon the Merits of this Question he thought it necessary to consider the Constitution of Rome at the Time this Act was committed, and particularly he urged that unlimited Power which the

Laws of the Republic gave to Parents; that even their Freedom and Liberty as well as the Lives of the Children were at their Disposal, for that they might *sell* Or *kill* them. He said that Virginius's Conduct was strictly agreeable to the Constitution of Rome. He observed upon the wisdom of this Power being vested in Parents. That each Family became a small republic and the Constitution of the State appeared in *miniature* in it, And when they entered upon the public Stage they were prepared to act their Parts. He observed that from the Sentiments cultivated at that Time, the *Honor* of Families was very much esteemed and that this was extremely proper as it inspired an Independence in each Breast. That in the Perpetration of this Act Appius was going to fix a lasting Stain on the Reputation of Virginius's Family. He was going to sacrifice his favorite, his beloved, Daughter an innocent Victim to his brutal Lust that should this have been effected as Appius admired her only for her Beauty it was probable that when Time had rendered the Object familiar, he would cast her off and She would have become a common Prostitute. That moved by this he threw off the Father and killed her. That had he suffered this Act of Violence he would have been detested by his Fellow Citizens, whereas all the contemporary Historians have agreed to commend him.

Mr. Murray for the Neg. observed that he conceived the Law of the Romans could not apply to this Question, That the Power vested in Parents was only to punish their Children for *Disobedience* or for their *Faults,* that it was absurd to extend a Punishment when there was no Crime. That even admitting that <Distress had followed> the Commission of the Crime would have produced much Unhappiness, We are not to get rid of their Distresses by unlawful Means, so that the Question again recurred to the previous Point was it consistent with *Morality*? He said it was not, That Morality among the Romans had reached a great Heigth, which plainly appeared from their laws against Murder. He observed that every Man had such a Right to Existence that he could not be deprived of it but through his own Crimes and by proper and lawful Means.

Mr. Jay supported Mr. Kissam's arguments and observed That *Error* was either *vincible* or *invincible,* That tho an Action might be in itself immoral yet, when it proceeded from an *invincible* Error the Agent was excusable and that this was the Case with Virginius. He observed that the Sense of a People with Respect to Morality and the Rules of Right and Wrong is best collected from the Laws and Institutions of that People, as they are generally composed by the wisest Persons in the State. That as these Laws are the best Interpreters of the Sense of the People so are they most commonly the Pattern after which the Consciences of Individuals are modelled. That according to the Informations people's Consciences at different Periods of Time receive, so are they to be judged, that Men at the Day of Judgment are to be judged according to the *Law written in their Heart.* He observed that whenever a man commits an immoral Act, he must be supposed to do it from sinister Views, that Virginius was a Man of *Probity* according to History, that he loved his Daughter, That in sacrificing her he wounded himself in the tenderest [point], That he could have no *sinister* Views; that the Honor and Reputation of his Family were his motives. That even supposing the Law did not apply to this Case that it was most probable <that> he was activated by Patriotism. He took Notice of the particular Situation of Rome at that Time. Appius's unlimited Power, that the Decemviri were become odious, that Appius exerted a most arbitrary Dominion, putting to Death all who opposed him. That he had even then *usurped* the Power of a Decemvir for as they were chosen for one Year only, he had continued himself after the War. That to destroy this extensive and unconstitutional Power it was necessary to raise a general Opposition, that this was best effected by the Step he took.

Mr. Benson. He insisted that the Spirit of the Law extended only to incorrigible Children, But admitted that it gave an arbitrary Power to Parents, yet he said as it was manifestly against Nature and Justice when applied to this Case no Man could be justified in Acting under it. However he conceived that could not have been the Law, Because, 1, The Laws about that Time were very imperfect, insomuch that the Code of the 12 Tables was compiled, That there was no future Instance referring to or acknowledging the Being of such a Law, but rather the contrary as he deduced from Cicero's oration for Milo. He observed that the Orator was there pleading for a man who had killed another. That he enumerated many Instances in which such a Conduct was justified but never mentioned the Case of a Parent's killing his Child, whence he concluded that in the introducing the Laws of the 12 Tables that one under Consideration here omitted, That as to his Ignorance being invincible, he could not agree to that, because it appeared that the Sentiments of the Romans as to Morality were very refined, And as to his Patriotism that could not have been the Motive, because if he meant to render his Country a Service if the Decemvirs were oppressive why did not Virginius lay the Ax to the Root and destroy the Evil at once. He rather concluded that Virginius was swayed by Passion, than Regard to his Country's Welfare, a Motive which he did not once avow but on the contrary told his Daughter that he killed her to preserve her Chastity. Mr. Benson further observed that even had Appius accomplished his brutal Purpose, as her Mind was *chaste* and *undefiled* she could not be said to have been *violated*. He also observed that Virginius was unjustifiable even supposing <him to have acted agains> the Laws of his Country to have been his proper Guides. The Decemvirs had an absolute Power from whence lay no Appeal. Appius in the Exercise of that Power adjudged Virginia to be not the Daughter of Virginius but the Slave of [———].[1] Now this Decree was a Law declared by the Supreme Authority and while that Decree was in Force Virginia was a Slave of another and therefore Virginius had no Right to kill her.

D. NHi: Debating Society Papers.

1 Virginia was decreed by Appius Claudius Crassus, decemvir, to be the slave of his retainer Marcus Claudius, an edict tantamount to appropriating Virginia for himself.

License to Practice Law in New York

New York, 26 October 1768

By His Excellency, Sir Henry Moore Baronet Captain General and Governor in Chief in and over the Province of New York and the Territories depending thereon in America Chancellor and Vice Admiral of the same.

To all to Whom these Presents shall come, or may concern Greeting.

Know Ye, That being well assured of the Ability, and Learning of John Jay Gentleman, I have thought fit to appoint him an Attorney at Law; hereby Authorizing him to appear in all his Majesty's Courts of Record within the Province of New York, and there to practise, as an Attorney at Law, according to the Laws and Customs of that part of Great Britain called England, and the Laws and Customs of the said Province. And all Judges, Justices, and others concerned, are hereby Required to Admit him Accordingly.

Given under my hand and Seal at Arms at Fort George in the City of New York the twenty sixth day of October, One thousand Seven hundred and Sixty Eight.

By His Excellency's Command

PH. LIVINGSTON JUNR.

H. MOORE

DS.

To Robert R. Livingston, Jr.

[New Yor]k, [Janua]ry, 1769

Dear Robert,

The Letter you mention to have wrote the Week before last, has never come to Hand and I cant account for the Miscarriage of two Letters I wrote you by the Post last Monday, in which I Informed You of the Dissolution, etc.[1] The Paper you inclosed will be printed to Night, and 100 shall be struck off and sent. Coll. Beekman[2] has either wrote or procured a Paper to be written, 60 of which you will recieve by this Opportunity. The Votes now sent are what can be found of those which the Printers Boy from Time to Time h[as thrown] into the Street Door. I applied to Gain[3] [for a] compleat Set, but was informed that [as the] Members were not yet supplyed the[re was] none to be disposed of. The Measures [which] the De-Lancey Gent[lemen] have adopted relative [to an] Act for dividing Beekman's Precinct h[ave given] offence to the Coll.[4] I suspect he begins to impute many things to Policy which he before considered as the Effect of publick Spirit.

All the News that I can write, will be but a Repetition of what you must have heard. Ph. Livingston shakes. He is said to have played a double Game. Appearances are against him. If true I hope he may lose his Election. No Presbeterian has given Place to no Lawyer, and no Churchman is substituted in the Room of no Bishop.[5] The Election here will be the Monday after the Court and at Westchester on the same Day. I hope you will give yourself no Concern about Matters here, nor leave the Country before it may be convenient. Be not sparing in your Commands. I shall always consider every Opportunity you give me of serving yourself or Family as an Instance of your Friendship. Present my Respects to your Family [and r]est assured that I am my Dear Robert, your affectionate Friend

John Jay

ALS. NHi: Livingston Papers.

[1] No other portions of the JJ-Livingston correspondence for Dec. 1768–Jan. 1769 have been located. The New York assembly met in October 1768. On 31 December the assembly passed a series of resolutions protesting British colonial policy which prompted Gov. Sir Henry Moore to dissolve the assembly two days later. Moore cited the "extraordinary nature of certain resolves lately entered on your journals; some flatly repugnant to the laws of Great Britain, and others, with an apparent tendency to give offence, where common prudence would avoid it. . . ." Becker, *N.Y. Political Parties,* pp. 53–74; the Assembly resolutions and Moore's statement of 2 Jan. 1769 dissolving the legislature are printed in *Journal of the Votes and Proceedings of the General Assembly of the Colony of New-*

York, from 1766 to 1776, Inclusive (Albany, 1820), Oct. 1768–Jan. 1769 session, pp. 70–72.

[2] Henry Beekman II (1688–1776), the proprietor of the great Beekman holdings in Dutchess County, was Robert R. Livingston, Jr.'s maternal grandfather.

[3] Hugh Gaine was appointed the colony's public printer 15 Jan. 1768. *Journal of the Votes and Proceedings of the General Assembly of the Colony of New-York, from 1766 to 1776, Inclusive* (Albany, 1820), Nov. 1767–Feb. 1768 session, p. 74.

[4] In November 1768, Dirck Brinckerhoff, an assemblyman from Dutchess County, introduced a bill entitled "an act to divide Beekman's precinct, in Dutchess county, into precincts, to be called Beekman's and Pauling's precinct." The Assembly and Council approved the bill, but it was vetoed by Governor Moore. On the last day of the Assembly session in January 1769, James De Lancey (1732–1800), the leader of his family's political faction, put through a resolution asking the Governor to reconsider the bill. *Ibid.*, Oct. 1768–Jan. 1769 session, pp. 21 and 74.

[5] Philip Livingston (1716–78), a prominent New York merchant, led the Livingston faction and had served as Speaker in the recently dissolved assembly. After the legislature's dissolution, Livingston declined to run for reelection on a ticket that listed him with the three other old assembly members from New York City. Instead, his name was placed on a ticket that included John Morin Scott (1730–84), the fiery leader of New York radicals. The Scott-Livingston slate was defeated after a campaign in which the De Lancey faction skillfully played upon fears of the legal profession and upon hostility toward Presbyterians. Livingston's place in the Assembly was taken by John Cruger. Becker, N.Y. *Political Parties*, pp. 74–75.

From Frederick Jay

Curracao, 23d March 1769
halfe past 12 in the morning

Dear Brother,

I have allready wrote you by this a few Lines, and as I have done writing my Letters on business (which amount to only twenty Six) and the Brigg[antin]e does not sail till the morning, have now a few moments to my selfe and as I think myselfe never happier than when I have an opportunity of writing to you, I am resolved to employ my Leisure hours that way; and for the present let it suffice, (for I am very sleepy) that I give you some account of this Country and the Inhabitants thereof; and First of the Harbour, which I can't pass over unnoticed, it being in my opinion the finest in the world, the entrance of which lies open to the sea, and but Narrow, and when you are once entered you are then Land Locked, on one side by the City, and on the other by the outerbanda, or City on the other side the River.[1]

To give a more plain insight into the matter I must tell you that the City lies on both sides the River, which is not a quarter of a mile wide, and is a most butifull prospect, the Houses being all painted white and the roofs of red pan tile, every House a Galliry supported by Large white Pillars. To return to my story, when you are entred the Harbour, you are then Surround with Land on each side, the water intirely calm and ships may Lay unhurt from all winds, except a So.W. which does not Visit this Island once in 10 yrs. In such case the Shipping are in danger, but even then they have a remidy. By carreing their Vessells to the Lagoune or spanish Harbour[2] about a mile up the River, where they may lay unhurt in the severest weather, it being sourrounded on all sides with high Land, the entrance narrow and the water very smoth. A vessell of the largest dimentions may anchor here, there being upwards of 16 Fathom water. Nothing more Common than to see 10 or 20 vessells Lay side and side, without the Least fear of danger, and I assure you it would make a Lawyers heart light to hear the musick these vessells gives us night and morning. I assure you its a medly: French, Spaniards, Dutch, English and all nations resort here. As I have not yet been in the Country, I cannot tell you much about the matter, only that it produces plenty of Vegetables, such as Beens, scallad, mellons and many others, that I can't at present think of. The People of this Country are in one word, mostly brutes getting drunk before sunsrise, frollicking, Whoaring and playing the Devil every night. Such a sett does not inhabit any other part of the world. The Ladies, as they are called, are the most ignorant, insignificant, foolish Devils in the world, fond of Englishmen and after you are once intimate with them, you receive many presents. But what is that to the purpose. When in Co[mpany] with them, you hardly find one that know their Right hand from their Left. I am absolutely so sleepy that I hardly know what Ive wrote, therefore must Conclude with telling you that I have sent you by Capn. Waldron 2 (Barrels marked F. Jay) of fine Limes which accept of from your Brother

F.J.

P.S. Have also given Waldron 1 small parcel, containing water and musk mellon seeds, which you'l not omit to send for. Had also a Letter for P.J.[3] in which are a few Jamaica news Papers. My best Respects to all my acquaintances of both Sexes, Bob and Benson in perticular, also the Doctor.[4]

ALS. Addressed: "To John Jay Esqr., Attorney at Law. New York. Per the Delancey. Capn. Waldron." Endorsed. Frederick Jay sailed to Curaçao some time in 1768. There he acted as an agent for his cousin, James Abraham De Peyster. The Dutch West Indies port was a favorite training ground for young New York merchants.

1 The western half of the modern city of Willemstad. At this time, Willemstad occupied only the eastern peninsula, formerly the site of Fort Andrew, while the western peninsula across the Anna Baai (St. Anna Bay) was known as the Otrabanda.

2 Probably the Waaigat, an elliptically shaped bay forming the northern shore of the Willemstad peninsula.

3 Frederick and JJ's father, Peter Jay.

4 Robert R. Livingston, Jr., Egbert Benson, and, probably, Samuel Kissam (b. 1745), a younger brother of Benjamin Kissam who was then completing his studies for the degree of Bachelor of Medicine at King's College.

FROM FREDERICK JAY

Curacao, 23 January 1770

Dear Johnny,

I wrote you a few Lines the 19 Inst.[1] per Capt. Sanders wherein I informed you that dePeyster was down with a fever. He is now perfectly recovered, but not well enough to do much business, and I have still the Burthen upon me, and which will prevent me from writing you fully per this opportunity.

Your letters of 15 November and 22 December have now before me, and note their Contents.[2]

I am much of your opinion, that if one of us was to go home it would be of service. It is what we intend doing, and one of us would have embraced this Opportunity, but as a Winter Passage is disagreeable, have Defered it till Spring.

Business is now much better, than when I wrote you last, the markets being now tollerable good, but we have little to do, our stores in a manner empty, and without a good deal of business, will never make a fortune here, unless we would get a House and Store upon the Same easy Terms, as yourselfe. I am much Surprised at not receiving a line from H. White, nor have I any news of him. A V. Horne wrote a few Lines, saying he would have Shipt per Houston, but thought flour too high, a very weak and foolish excuse. He has missed it this time, flour being very dear and Scarce here. Mr. J. Roosevelt was the only person who shipt any thing to us, and appears in every respect to have our Interest at heart, saying if he could do more he would.[3]

The fowls etc. are come safe to hand, and Mr. Cruger[4] is much pleased with them. The peace Tree, grows very well, and I make no doubt, we shall in a year or two have them in plenty.

I have given Bleeker[5] Credit in my books for calling that impudent Irishman to an Account. He behaved as a man of spirit, and ought to be commended for it.

I realy thought James D L[6] had more spirit, but am now convinced to the contrary. He deserves to be kicked out of every Gent[le-man']s Company, until such time as he had received that Satisfaction, which he demanded. Oh poor Jemmy

Let no wild fears of our hopes betray
Let no despair your courage pall
When Heaven so loudly does to Honour call
Fight my Boy fight though yo're sure to fall

I would have sent you some Limes or Oranges by Houston, but do assure you the great drougth which we have had for upward of 4 months has destroyed them all. The next opportunity you may expect Something. Have now only to send you, what perhaps you have plenty of, that is Simply, a Hogg, one of the greatest curiosities ever in New York. He must be kept in a pen, as he is wild. He came from the main a few Days ago, and I by my impudence prevailed upon the gent[le-man] to give him to me.

You say your desirous of knowing what became of the Quails I brought here. In one word I'll tell you. We made a fine pye of them two days after my arrival. The Island abounds with them, though not quite so Large as those from the Northward. I will Send you some in the Spring.

The Hog, mentioned on the other side, is not like other Hogs. I mean in one Respect, he has his navel upon his, or her back, whether it be a sow or a Boar I know not, as I have had no time to examine the premises.

I am extremely Sorry that Aunt Depeyster[7] was so ill, I sincerely wish her better. Make my love to her and all the Family.

If you chuse to have any more Water melon received, let me know it, and you should have as many as you wish. I wish my time would permit, I would write you a droll Story, but must leave that till another opportunity.

Tell Mr. Ceremony Alias Benson that I would have wrote him, but have not time at present.

We have now on board Houston near 6000 pounds 8/8, which I hope will open, some peoples Eyes. In haste Dear Brother your etc.

F. JAY

P.S. Would you believe that I have Received a Letter from [———][8] but do not intend to give it any other place but a little House.

ALS. Endorsed.
1 Letter not located.
2 Letters not located.

[3] Henry White (1732–85) was the husband of Frederick and JJ's cousin, Eva Van Cortlandt White. Augustus Van Horne (b. 1736), the son of their aunt, Judith Jay Van Horne, was a New York merchant. Since Frederick Jay used the same symbol for upper case "J" and upper case "I," it is not clear which Roosevelt is meant. At least three Roosevelts with these initials were active in New York commerce in 1770: the brothers Johannes (b. 1715) and Isaac (1726–97), and their cousin Jacobus (b. 1724). Isaac Roosevelt seems the most likely as his extensive interests in sugar refining required wide correspondence with agents in the West Indies.

[4] Tileman or Telemon Cruger, the son of Henry Cruger, a member of the New York Council, was a merchant in Curaçao.

[5] Probably Anthony Lispenard Bleecker (1741–1816), a New York merchant.

[6] This is probably a reference to James De Lancey (1746–1804), the son of Peter De Lancey, and not to his older cousin, James De Lancey (1732–1800), the New York political leader.

[7] Margaret Van Cortlandt De Peyster.

[8] This name has been carefully obliterated in the ms.

From Frederick Jay

London, 6th March 1771

Dear Jack

Since my last to you of the 10th ult.[1] per Capt. Winn am not favoured with any of yours.

You'l receive per this Conveyance a letter in print from Sir James to the Governors of Kings College,[2] which I make no doubt will not be pleasing to them. However, be that as it may, it is the Opinion of many here, that it will be of infinite service to the Author, of which, I shall be better enabled to inform you in my Next.

I make no doubt but that many of my Friends expect to see me in the spring. I hope I may have that pleasure, but am afraid it will not be in my power, being advised to stay 'till I am well recovered, and I think it would be imprudent in me to Sacrifice my Health to any other Consideration whatever.

In Order that you may form some Idea of my Complaint I will give you a short detail of it since my arrival here. About ten days before my arrival I was Seized with a pain and Stiffness in my shoulders, which I imagined might be owing to the wet weather we met with on the Coast, but I was soon convinced that it proceeded from a worse Cause. Some days after my landing the above Symptoms prevailed in every joint, and Limb, and became so severe that it was with the greatest difficulty I could walk. My Elbowes and wrists were so stiff that I could not shave nor Comb myself and with difficulty could raise my hand to my mouth. My Left Eye and that side of my face, were so effected that I could not Shut it for 4 weeks. I continued in this situation for two months and upwards. The use of my Limbs then returned, and every thing has since appeared in my favour, tho I am not yet free from pain and weakness in those parts that were so severely attacked. The Complaint in my Stomack has been Violent, but is now thank God much better than it has been since I left you, and I am in hopes to receive a perfect Cure, but time is required to remove so violent a Complaint. Were I to relate every Circumstance it would swell this Letter to a great Length. I shall stop here, and am confident that you and every other person must from this Short detail be convinced that my Disorder in no wise can be called the Hipp, as Dr. B. wrote Jemmy.

I am much Concerned in not receiving a line from D.P. since I left N.Y. (except one letter wrote in June last). Pray apply to N.D.P.[3] and enquire of him how affairs goes on. I have wrote him many letters but have had no answers. Therefore I am determined to drop all Correspondence with him, 'till he is pleased to favour me with a line.

I am not yet permitted to go out. The first Visit will be to Lady Drapens, who I am told has been very unwell since her arrival here. Jno. Watts and DeLancey[4] desires their Compliments. For News refer you to the papers now sent. Remember me to all who have the Compliments to enquire of your Affectionate Brother

FRED. JAY

ALS. Endorsed: ". . . Abt. his disorder." JJ wrote Samuel Kissam on 27 Aug. 1771: "My Brother Fade is just arrived from England; his Indisposition obliged him to go over abt. a year ago; thank God his health is now reestablished and he intends by the first opportunity to return to his Friends at Curacoa." Frank Monaghan, "Samuel Kissam and John Jay," *Columbia University Quarterly,* XXV (June, 1933), 130–31.

1 Letter not located.

2 Sir James Jay's *A Letter to the Governors of the College of New York . . .* was published in London in 1771 by G. Kearsley.

3 "D.P." is James Abraham De Peyster. "N.D.P." is his cousin, Nicholas De Peyster (b. 1740).

4 John Watts, Jr. and Oliver De Lancey, Jr. (1749–1822), the sons of prominent N.Y. families, were first cousins. De Lancey was serving in the British army.

The Vermont Lands

The petition printed below documents JJ's unsuccessful attempt to speculate in land in the disputed "Hampshire Grants" in what became the State of Vermont. Confusion over land titles in this area arose from a boundary dispute between New Hampshire and New York and was compounded by the eagerness of royal officials in the two provinces to grant patents, for which they pocketed the fees.

In the mid-eighteenth century, New York claimed territory as far east as the Connecticut River, thereby contesting New Hampshire's assertion that her own western boundary lay twenty miles east of Albany. While the boundary dispute was under adjudication by the crown, New Hampshire's governor Benning Wentworth made grants of three million acres in the disputed area. After the crown awarded jurisdiction over Vermont to New York in 1764, the latter's governors made almost equally generous grants, as well as issuing "confirmatory patents" to settlers who had held title from New Hampshire. Under a restraining order of the Privy Council of July 1767, New York was prohibited from making further grants in areas already granted by New Hampshire until the crown could render a final decision on the issue of land titles to the territory west of the Connecticut.

Each of the governors and the lieutenant governor who administered New York's affairs in the period 1767–75 interpreted this order differently. The most generous interpretation was made by John Murray, Earl of Dunmore (1732–1809), during his tenure as governor, October 1770–July 1771. Although Dunmore's instructions on land policy were even more restrictive than those given to his predecessors, he issued grants for 450,000 acres during his nine-month regime. One historian of Vermont has remarked: "Dunmore . . . adopted his own rule of action, which was apparently that a land patent should issue to any who would pay the fees, without regard to grants previously made by New Hampshire."[1]

Early in 1771, JJ and a group of other New Yorkers were granted the patent of "Socialborough" in the modern towns of Pittsford and Rutland, Vermont,[2] and JJ probably expected equal success with his petition of 12 June. However, this petition was not submitted until the last month of Dunmore's governorship and, as the endorsement shows, consideration of the petition was delayed when the Council demanded a map of the grant sought by JJ and his unidentified associates.[3] Governor William Tryon (1729–88), who assumed office from Dunmore on 9 July 1771, less than four weeks after the Council read JJ's petition, reversed his predecessor's policy of irresponsible grants in the Vermont area and, indeed, ceased making grants altogether in the autumn of 1772. Tryon issued no further grants until 1775 when he returned from London after conferences on the Hampshire Grants question.[4] Thus it is not surprising that the Land Office records of provincial New York do not record a grant in the town of Eugene to JJ.[5] The would-be speculators had waited too long to make their application, and they now had to deal with an unsympathetic governor.

1 Matt B. Jones, *Vermont in the Making, 1750–1777* (Cambridge, Mass., 1939), p. 226. For an analysis of the land policies of New Hampshire and New York in the "Grants," see *ibid.*, chs. II-VI and XI.

2 Edward Alexander, *A Revolutionary Conservative: James Duane of New York* (New York, 1938), pp. 72–73.

3 This request probably stemmed from the fact that the survey for one of the grants cited as boundaries for the land JJ sought, the Banks-Lubeken tract, had been returned to the Council only six days before JJ's petition was submitted. The Council doubtless felt that more precise information concerning the location of JJ's acreage would be necessary to insure that it did not conflict with other patents in the area.

4 Jones, *Vermont*, p. 235.

5 Grants made in the Hampshire territory by Dunmore and Tryon are listed *ibid.*, pp. 436–38.

Petition to the Earl of Dunmore

[New York], 12 June 1771

To his Excellency the Right honourable John Earl of Dunmore Captain General and Governor in Chief in and over the Province of New York and the Territories depending thereon in America Chancellor and Vice Admiral of the same In Council

The Petition of John Jay of the City of New York Esqr. Humbly Sheweth

That there are certain pieces of Vacant Land vested in the Crown on the East Side of Hudson's River in the County of Albany part of which lie within the Bounds of a Township lately erected under the Great Seal of the said Province by the Name of Eugene described and limitted as follows, to witt, bounded on the South by a due East Line drawn from the point where the South East Corner of the Tract granted to Lieutenant Farrant meets the East Bounds of the Tract granted to Alexander Turner and others on Batten Kill and terminating on the West Bounds of the Township of Chatham bounded on the East by the West Bounds of Chatham and the East Bounds of the Lands granted to Lieut. Josiah Banks Surgeon Albert Minert Lubkener and sundry Non Commission Officers and Soldiers in the Patent constituting the said Township named On the North by the North Bounds of the Lands so to the Commission and Non Commission Officers and Soldiers last mentioned granted and a West Line continued from the same until it is intersected by a North Line drawn from the North East Corner of the Tract granted to John Tabor Kempe Esqr. and others and on the West by the last mentioned Line and the East Bounds of the several Tracts granted to the said John Tabor Kempe Esqr. and others Quarter Master Monroe Lieutenant Mervin Perry and the said Alexander Turner and others part of which said Township not being granted to the Officers and Soldiers mentioned in the said Letters patent remain vested in the Crown. Other parcels of the said Vacant Land hereby petitioned for lie to the Southward of the said Township of Eugene and between the same and the Stream of Water called Batten Kill on the South the Tract granted to the said Alexander and others and sundry Soldiers on the West and the West Lands of the said Prince-Town on the East.[1]

Your Petitioner therefore most humbly prays that your Lordship will be pleased to grant unto him and his Associates to the Number of Twenty five each one thousand Acres of the said several pieces of Vacant Land so as the same shall not interfere with the Lands already petitioned for by sundry Officers and Soldiers by John Monier and John N. Blicker and by Doctor Thomas Clarke[2] and that the Lands so to be granted to your Petitioner and others and also the Lands which shall still remain Vacant to the Southward of the said Township Eugene to the Northward of Batten Kill to the Eastward of the Tract granted to Turner and others and to the Westward the said Prince Town may be erected into a Township with the usual Privileges.

And your Petitioner shall ever pray etc.

JOHN JAY for himself and his associates

DS. N: N.Y. Colonial Mss., Endorsed Land Papers. Endorsed: "To his Excellency the Right honourable John Earl of Dunmore Captain General and Governour in Chief in and over the Province of New York etc. In Council. The Petition of John Jay Esqr. and his Associates praying for a Tract of Vacant Land on the East Side of Hudson's River in the County of Albany. Presented June 12th 1771. N. 10. 1771 June 14 Read in Council & referred to a Committee. 1771 June 19. Read again and the Petitioners to exhibit a Map of the Vacancy."

1 The town of Eugene included portions of the modern towns of Pawlet, Danby, Rupert, and Dorset. In 1764, Henry Farrant, a retired lieutenant, received a grant on both sides of Batten Kill, bounded on the west by a grant made to Alexander Turner in the same year. A survey for the grant made to Lt. Banks and to Albert Lubeken, a former surgeon's mate, was returned to the New York Council 6 June 1771. The Banks-Lubeken tract lay in modern Rutland County, Vt. John Tabor Kempe (1735–95), the New York Attorney General, and his associates were granted 30,000 acres north of Batten Kill in 1762. William Munro's tract, adjoining Turner's and Kempe's, was granted in January 1764. The Perry grant has not been identified. Princetown was granted in 1765 to a group of associates who quickly conveyed the 26,000 acres in the Batten Kill valley to Kempe, James Duane, and Walter Rutherford. Edward P. Alexander, *A Revolutionary Conservative, James Duane of New York* (New York, 1938), p. 72 and map, facing p. 71; *Calendar of New York Colonial Manuscripts, Indorsed Land Papers in the Office of the Secretary of State, 1643–1803* (Albany, 1864), pp. 330, 337–38, 360, 535; Jones, *Vermont*, p. 98.

2 The land sought by Monier, John Bleecker, and Dr. Clarke has not been identified, although Monier and Bleecker apparently claimed 6,000 acres held by James Duane in the Camden Valley north of Batten Kill. Alexander, *James Duane*, p. 72n.

A Confrontation with the Attorney General

John Tabor Kempe, the province's attorney general, was considered an *arriviste* by socially secure young men like JJ. Between the two there appears to have been bad blood for some years. Almost a decade earlier Kempe had chaired the committee appointed by King's College to investigate James Jay's handling of the funds he had collected in England. The dealings of that committee with Jay's willful brother still rankled on both sides. The following exchange was initiated by JJ upon learning that Kempe, acting for the governor as attorney general, was engaged in Chancery in arguing a demurrer pleaded by the vestrymen of an Anglican parish in Jamaica who had withheld the salary of the Reverend Joshua Bloomer. As one of counsel to Bloomer, JJ felt that the interests of his client as well as common courtesy dictated consultation with all of Bloomer's attorneys. Considering the fact that JJ was in practice a bare three years, his overreaction to the incident speaks volumes for his concern about his reputation and his readiness to court the permanent enmity of a powerful royal official rather than suffer a slight to his self-esteem.

To John Tabor Kempe

New York, 27th December 1771

Sir

Your Doubts respecting Faulkners Declaration appear well founded, and the Remarks contained in your Letter judicious.[1] I concieve the Charge of his having robbed the Company imports no more than a Breach of Trust. If so, it would be hazardous to insert those Counts. If we recover Damages it will be on the other. I am therefore for resting the Cause upon them, and think the Partnership should not appear from the Declaration.

I must now Sir! call your Attention to another Subject.

Mr. Bloomer, you know, engaged me as Counsel with Mr. Duane and yourself in the Action you commenced for Recovery of his Salary. The Cause is now almost ripe for a Determination, and I have not been consulted in any one Stage of the Suit.[2] Had it been a mere matter of usual Compliment, I should have expected from the Attorney Generals Politeness. The Neglect however would then have produced no Complaint, for the Civility often gives Pleasure, a contrary Deportment is seldom of sufficient Importance to create Concern.

But Sir! in the present Case, as you was the Complainants Sollicitor I expected some little Attention, not from the Attorney

Generals Acquaintance with the Rules of Politeness, but the Rules of Business; and allow me to remark that a Deviation from the latter is sometimes a Violation of both. The Cause I confess would have recieved little Advantage from my Aid. It would nevertheless have been but decent to have gratified your Client, and treated the Person he retained as his Counsel, with common Respect.

Your Conduct at least represents me in an insignificant Point of View, and the more so, as your general Behaveour is deemed candid and polite; it therefore calls for an Explanation—to remain silent would argue little Spirit or little Regard for Reputation, Imputations which no Gentleman will either merit, or with Impunity permit.

I am Sir, your humble Servant

JOHN JAY

ALS. MHi: Sedgwick Papers. Endorsed.

1 Kempe's letter concerning the case of *Faulkner* v. *Rapalje* has not been located. On 20 June 1771, JJ was retained to defend Garret Rapalje against the suit of William D. Faulkner. Opposing counsel was John McKesson. N: JJ's Supreme Court Register, 1770–73.

2 In 1769, Governor Henry Moore named Joshua Bloomer (1735–90), an Anglican clergyman, to the vacant pulpit at Jamaica, N.Y. The churchwardens refused to pay Bloomer, and the minister retained JJ, Kempe, and James Duane (1733–97) to represent him in a suit to gain his salary. The first action recorded in the chancery suit of *Bloomer* v. *Hinchman* was that of 17 Oct. 1771 when Kempe moved that the defendants argue the demurrer they had entered "on this Day eight Days." However, John Morin Scott, the defense attorney, did not argue in support of the demurrer until 7 November when the Chancery Court accepted Kempe's request that he be given a "further day" on which to answer Scott. On 5 and 6 Dec. 1771 Bloomer's counsel completed "their Arguments" against the defendants' demurrer and the Court ordered that the defense counsel reply at "the next Court." JJ was mistaken in his belief that the case was "almost ripe for a Determination," for it was not until April 1772 that the Chancery Court ruled on the defense demurrer, and a decree in Bloomer's favor was not granted until 1774. This decree was appealed to the Privy Council, but the beginning of the Revolution precluded a royal decision on the matter. New York County Clerk's Office, Division of Old Records, Chancery Court Minutes, IV, 38, 43, 46, 64, 69, 151–53; Edward P. Alexander, *A Revolutionary Conservative: James Duane of New York* (New York, 1938), pp. 22–24. For a comment on the JJ–Kempe exchange and JJ's overreacting to this incident, see Richard B. Morris, *Seven Who Shaped Our Destiny* (New York, 1973), pp. 162–64.

From John Tabor Kempe

New York, 27 December 1771

Sir

I have delayed an Answer to your Letter for some Hours, least I should forget what I owe to myself, and catch from you a Warmth or Indelicacy of Expression, which I might on Reflection think blameable. This is the first Instance I ever met with of such an Address, and as I conceive it to be entirely without <Foundation> Provocation, I am the more astonished. I cannot charge myself with ever having intentionally given Offence to any Person living and esteem it incumbent on every Gentleman to explain his Conduct when it is misunderstood, and such Explanation is desired in proper Terms, the want of which on your part is the only Reason for my not doing it in the present Instance.

I must think that the warmth you have shewn should not have been excited by the Occasion which gave Rise to it, at least until you had been well assured of a Design in me to treat you with Disrespect.

I am Sir your humble servant.

J. T. KEMPE

ALS (FC). MHi: Sedgwick Papers. Endorsed.

To John Tabor Kempe

New York, 2d January 177[2][1]

Sir

The Receipt of your Letter should have been acknowledged before had I not been out of Town when it was delivered.

If by withholding an Explanation you mean to punish me for a <Defe> supposed Defect in Constitution, or Inaccuracy in Mode of Expression, you certainly Sir! fix your Resentment on Objects too triffling to merit serious Severity. To think with Freedom and to speak with Sincerity I knew often trespassed on Form and punctilious Refinement, but I did not apprehend it would have given Offence to a Gentleman who I imagined would attend more to Things than the Names by which they are called.

Your never having met with such an Address before, does not surprize me. I believe few of the Profession have. For however otherways divided, they have generally been uniform in Matters of Business. Another Hour devoted to Reflection would have reminded you, that whenever a Gentlemans Conduct is misunderstood, it is his Duty to explain it, not merely as a Compliment to those who may ask it, but as a piece of Justice to his own Reputation; nor should it be forgotten that Dignity can recieve no Support from Evasions, or be increased by Behaveour which renders Innocence suspected.

I cannot concur with you in thinking, that the Warmth I have shewn should not have been excited by the occasion which gave Rise to it. I deny not that I was warm, or, if you please, that I am warm still. Warmth excited by Attacks on Reputation, or inspired by a Sense of indelicate Treatment will never be blamed by those who are more under the Influence of Good Nature than a Desire of discovering Motes in a Neighbours Eye. Insensibility to Injuries never characterized an honest Man.

When you recollect that at the Time I first became engaged or rather retained in the Cause of the Parish of Jamaica, I was but just stepping into the World, a Season critical to a young man. That you was informed of my being concerned by Mr. DLancey[2] who was then your Clerk, that you nevertheless avoided all Conversation with me upon the Subject; that after the Bill was filed a Demurrer was put in, Hearings appointed, Consultations had, arguments framed, Objections considered without my being privy to or having Notice of either. That tho you was reminded by Mr. Duane of my being employed, you have never deigned to apologize for the omission, or correct the mistake, if a mistake it was. That these repeated Neglects tended to lessen me in the opinion of my Client and others, deprived me of an Opportunity of appearing in a Cause of great Consequence and much Expectation, from the merely being concerned in which a young man is often raised in the Estimation of the World. That all this was done and transacted deliberately unprovoked, nay while the very Smiles of Friendship appeared on your Countenance. I say when you recollect these Things I am astonished you should complain of a little Warmth, or expect I would rest satisfied with presenting you a little cold Remonstrance with humble Defference supplicating an Explanation.

You are amased at my acting as if I thought your Conduct proceeded from Design. I am really amased that you are. What other Construction does it bear? Upon what other Principles is it explicable?

A Rupture with you Sir! would be very disagreable to me; but I had rather reject the Friendship of the World than purchase it by Patience under Indignities offered by any Man in it. However I still hope to recieve that Satisfaction from an Explanation, which I should be sorry to seek from a less friendly Source.

I am Sir your humble Servant

JOHN JAY

ALS. MHi: Sedgwick Papers. Endorsed.

1 Misdated "1771" by JJ.

2 Probably John De Lancey (1741–1821).

To Peter W. Yates

New York, 23d March 1772

Dear Sir,

In the Case you put vizt. *A conveys his real Estate to B. C and D. and to their respective Heirs and assigns forever,* I am of opinion that the Grantees hold in *Joint-Tenancy.*[1]

I have filed the Declaration you inclosed,[2] and would have sent the writ before, had a good opportunity offered.

Politics have not given the assembly much Trouble this Session. Inclosed are three of the best written Papers against the majority. Though wrote with Poignancy they occasioned little noise, and by being left unanswered escaped that attention which opposition and Recrimination always excite.

The affair of Noyelles (like himself) made much Talk. Some Papers signed Brutus were dispersed through the Town, charging Noyelles with having been indicted some Years ago in orange County for stealing a Load of Hay, selling with false Weights and Measures and with having avoided being tryed on them, by some strokes of Finesse which do no Credit to the Parties concerned. Noyelle catched Fire, he complained to the House. They inquired into the Matter and by *their Verdict* he stands acquitted. The Fact I believe is that he was indicted, and there is also too much Reason to believe that those Indictments were not fairly obtained.[3]

The message sent by the House to the Sup. Court to stay Proceedings (during the Session) in an Action of Ejectment commenced against a Tenant of Noyelles, has been more the Topic of Conversation than any of their Manauvres. Noyelles informed the House that he was interested in the Lands in Question, therefore that serving a Declaration on his Tenant was a Breach of Priviledge. The House concurred with him in Sentiment, and the Message before mentioned was sent to the Judges. The Rule had been entered before the Message was recieved.[4] However I am told Mr. Livingston (who was then alone on the Bench) in a Letter to the Speaker informed the House that the Duty of his office and the Nature of his oath would not permit him to delay Justice. Here the Matter rested. The Exclusion of the Judge and the arguments for and against the measure have long since ceased to be the Objects of Novelty, and therefore occasioned little Attention.[5]

Most People think the Measure expedient, tho they condemn the manner of carrying it into Execution. Many admit his Right to a Seat who have no Objections to his losing it, and think the Wrong expiated by the advantages the Country derives from the Exclusion of Crown officers from offices in the Gift of the People.

The five pound act is passed much to the Satisfaction of the Country.[6]

We have had a great Deal of Snow. My Sleigh turns out well, it is strong and runs light. Pray what Lawyer brought the Writ of Error in the Cause of Bemus.[7] I have asked many without Success, nor is any Return to be found in the office. I assure you this Cause is a very critical one. Many of our best Lawyers doubt whether an action in one Province on a Judgment obtained in another can be supported. It is a Point that can apply only to the Colonies and therefore much Law respecting it cannot be expected. I have inquired whether actions in England can be brought on Judgments obtained in Ireland and find many Authorities against it. As to other Country, the Practice in several Instances has been to bring the Suit for the original Cause of Action, and give the Proceeding of the Court in Evidence. It is however a very important Point, and the Country is much interested in its Determination.

A Law is passed for the Revisal of our Law, and Mr. Van Schaack is employed for the Purpose.[8]

I shall be glad to hear from you often, and if I can at any Time render you any Services, believe me I shall be happy in doing it. I am Sir your Friend and very humble Servant

JOHN JAY

ALS. NHi: Misc. Mss. (Peter W. Yates). Endorsed: ". . . Fellows v. Bemus." In that case plaintiff, represented by Peter W. Yates (1747–1826), an Albany attorney, had been awarded a judgment in the Albany Mayor's Court on the basis of a prior judgment obtained in Massachusetts. Defendant Bemis appealed on a writ of error to the New York Supreme Court (20 May 1770), engaging John Morin Scott to represent him, while JJ was retained by the appellee. The Supreme Court held that the judgment in debt rendered in Massachusetts had not been proven as a fact, and for this reason sustained defendant's demurrer. Albany Mayor's Court Minutes, Albany County Clerk's Office, lib. 1768–1778, p. 65; parchment 136 G-1, Hall of Records, New York City. See also Minutes of the Moot, 23 Nov. 1770–13 May 1774, p. 34, NHi, wherein it appears that members of the N.Y. bar, JJ included, on several occasions argued the issues of interstate comity and conflict of laws between provinces. See also Herbert A. Johnson, "John Jay: Colonial Lawyer" (unpub. Ph.D. dissertation, Columbia Univ., 1965), pp. 155–57.

1 The Yates letter to which JJ is replying has not been located. JJ appears to mean that they hold as tenants in common.

2 Ms. not identified.

3 John De Noyelles (c. 1734–75) represented Orange County in the New York assembly. On 14 Jan. 1772, "Brutus" launched an attack on the De Lancey faction's efforts to challenge the qualifications of their political opponents elected

to the legislature in a broadside titled "To the Public." In a second publication, "When Vice Prevails . . . ," dated 28 Jan. 1772, "Brutus" pointed out that no one had questioned De Noyelles's qualifications even though he had been indicted in 1763 for theft and selling at false measure.

On 6 February De Noyelles asked the assembly to meet as a "grand committee for courts of justice" to investigate his case. The grand committee heard testimony on the matter on 14, 18, 25, and 26 February and reported on 27 February. The committee concluded that "undue means [had been] made use of in procuring the indictment against John De Noyelles" and "that the said paper contains a malicious aspersion of Mr. De Noyelles's character, and a scandalous reflection on the justice of the house." "Brutus," "To the Public," and "When Vice Prevails . . . ," Evans, 12335 and 12336; *Journal of the Votes and Proceedings of the General Assembly of the Colony of New-York, from 1766 to 1776, Inclusive* (Albany, 1820), Jan.–March 1772 session, pp. 42, 51, 53–54, 66, 68, 70.

[4] On 25 Jan. 1772, De Noyelles informed the assembly that an action had been brought against one of his tenants since the beginning of the assembly session. The assembly voted "That the judges of the supreme court be acquainted that a lease of ejectment has been served upon a tenant of John De Noyelles, Esq. . . . and that he is entitled to privilege both in his person and estate, during the sitting of the house; and that the proceedings thereon be stayed during the session." On 7 February, a committee was named "to search the journals of commons, for precedents where orders have been sent to stay the proceedings of the courts below, in matters where the privileges of the commons have been affected. . . ." This committee reported on 12 March 1772 and listed precedents appropriate to the De Noyelles case. *Journal of the Votes and Proceedings of the General Assembly of the Colony of New-York, from 1766 to 1776, Inclusive* (Albany, 1820), Jan.–March 1772 session, pp. 28, 42–43, 92–93.

[5] Judge Robert R. Livingston, Sr. (1718–75), a member of the provincial Supreme Court, was elected to the assembly from the Manor of Livingston in 1769 after his cousin, Philip Livingston, had been disqualified from this seat because of nonresidence. In December 1769, the De Lancey-dominated assembly disqualified Judge Livingston because of his judicial office. The voters of the Manor reelected the Judge again, and he was again disqualified in January 1771. He was chosen a third time and disqualified a third time by an assembly vote of 5 Feb. 1772. *Ibid.*, Nov. 1769–Jan. 1770 session, p. 46; Dec. 1770–March 1771 session, p. 51; Jan.–March 1772 session, p. 40.

[6] "An Act to impower Justices of the Peace, Mayors, recorders and Aldermen to try causes to the value of Five Pounds . . ." was passed by the New York assembly on 12 March 1772. *The Colonial Laws of New York* (5 vols., Albany, 1894), V, 304–14.

[7] *Fellows* v. *Bemus*. See above, source note.

[8] "An Act to Revise Digest and Print the Laws of this Colony" was passed by the assembly 24 March 1772. *Ibid.*, 355.

The Social Club

The "old *Club*" to which Samuel Kissam refers in the postscript to the following letter was the "Social Club," a well-entrenched institution by the eve of the Revolution, which held its entertainments in wintertime on Saturday evenings at Samuel Fraunces Tavern, corner of Broad and Dock

Streets, and in summer at Kip's Bay, where they had built a clubhouse. After its final gathering in December 1775, the club membership dispersed, never afterward to assemble under the name. John Moore, a Royal customs official, recorded a "List of Members of the Social Club," with his own commentary:

LIST OF MEMBERS OF THE SOCIAL CLUB

John Jay, disaffected, became a member of Congress, a President, Minister to Spain, commissioner to make Peace, Chief Justice, Minister to England, and on his return Governor of N. York—good and amiable man.

Gouverneur Morris, ditto, Member of Congress, Minister to France, etc.

Robert R. Livingston, ditto, Member Congress, Minister to France, Chancellor of New York, etc.

Egbert Benson, ditto, District Judge, N.Y., and in the Legislature—good Man.

Morgan Lewis, ditto, became Gov. of N.Y. and Gen. in War of 1812.

Gulian Verplanck, ditto, but in Europe till 1783, President, New York Bank.

John Livingston and his Brother Henry, ditto, but of no political importance.

James Seagrove, ditto, went to the Southward as a Merchant.

Francis Lewis, ditto, of no political importance.

John Watts, Doubtful, during the war—Recorder of N. York.

Leonard Lispenard and his Brother Anthony, ditto, but remained quiet at N. York.

Richard Harrison, Loyal, but has since been Recorder of N. York.

John Hay, ditto, An officer in British Army; killed in W. Indies.

Peter Van Schaick, ditto, A Lawyer, remained quiet at Kinderhook.

Daniel Ludlow, ditto, during the war; since President Manhattan Bank.

Dr. S. Bard, Loyal, though in 1775 doubtful, remained in N.Y.—good man.

George Ludlow, ditto, remained on Long Island in quiet—good man.

William, his Brother, ditto, or supposed to be so, remained on Long Island—inoffensive man.

William Imlay, ditto at first, but doubtful after 1777.

Edward Goold, ditto, at N.Y. all the war—a Merchant.

John Reade, Pro and Con, would have proved loyal no doubt, if his wife's family been otherwise.

J. Stevens, Disaffected.

Henry Kelly, Loyal, went to England and did not return.

Stephen Rapelje.

Jno. Moore, ditto, in public life all the war, and from the year 1765. May all his Sons be, as their Father was, good and obedient subjects to the Government wherever they may live.

AD. NHi. "Copied May 1857 by Tho. W. C. Moore," with the following notation: "Copy Of a Ms. found among my Father, John Moore's papers. Written during the Revolutionary War; with Explanatory remarks, made by him, in the Year 1820. List of members of the Social Club to which he belonged."

Gouverneur Morris (1752–1816) was a lawyer who graduated from King's College in 1768. Morgan Lewis (1754–1844), a 1773 graduate of the College of New Jersey, and Francis Lewis, Jr., were the sons of Francis Lewis (1713–1803), a retired merchant. Gulian Verplanck (1751–99) was JJ's second cousin. John Livingston (1749–1822) and his brother Hendrick (1752–1823) were sons of Robert Livingston (1708–90), third lord of Livingston Manor. Leonard and Anthony Lispenard (c. 1742–1806), graduates of King's College in 1762 and 1761, respectively, were merchants and owners of a brewery. John A. Scoville, *The Old Merchants of New York City* (4 vols., New York, 1885), II, 124–25; *N.Y.G.B.R.*, XXV, 132. Richard Harison, a lawyer, was the son-in-law of the Tory George Duncan Ludlow (1734–1808), provincial Justice of the Supreme Court. *N.Y.G.B.R.*, I, 41. The judge's younger half-brother, Daniel Ludlow (1750–1814), and Edward Goold were merchants who became partners after the Revolution. Dr. Samuel Bard (1742–1821) studied medicine at the University of Edinburgh after graduating from King's College in Gouverneur Morris's class. George (b. 1738) and William Ludlow (b. 1742), both merchants, were cousins of Daniel and George Duncan Ludlow. John Stevens (1749–1838), still another member of the class of 1768 of King's College and Robert R. Livingston's brother-in-law, later became an importer-developer of steam transportation and recipient of the first charter to build a railroad from New York City to Philadelphia. Stephen Rapalje (or Rapalye) was accused in 1777 of having acted as a guide for the British on Long Island, but he denied the charge and took the oath of allegiance. "Minutes of the Committee for Detecting Conspiracies," N.Y.H.S., *Colls.*, LVII, 122–23, 167–68.

From Samuel Kissam

Paramaribo, 22 July 1772

In the name of the Gods my Dear Jay! what can have made you the subject of Diseases?[1] I thought your Temperance might almost have baffled the unwholsom Blasts of Spring or Autumn, the Glowing heats of August or the nipping frosts of January. Or have you since my Departure indulged your self more freely in the use of Generous

Wine, adding to the pleasures of Sociability? Do your Friends use larger Glasses, or give more in number, do they give you Bumpers or offer the Lady next your Heart in Challenges, or have *you* in your Entertainments done all these? Or is it the India Spices to the palate so much pleasing added to your meats which have against your Health been so Rebellious? From what ever of these causes or if the cause you can divine, let it be your Study to oppose it. Let not the importunity of Business chain you to your Pen. Exercise tending to the restoration of your Health is of much more importance to you. Let your mind as little as possible with the disorder of your Body participate. They furnish food each for the other and without further nourishment Increase with absolute Dominion.

To me and not my Friends my absence proves Unfortunate, from pleasing Society being almost sequesterd, doubly do I feel its Influence. Custom tis true begets a property of Contentment, and sometimes to fate the Mind it Reconciles. But tis not always so; for of my Companions that I do the loss regret as much to day as the day on which we parted am I bold to testify.

Hence a month, or time a little more allowed, to leave this place is my Intention; and if report be true, my Situation for the better will be altered. Much for the worse it Cannot be, for since in this place I have held acquaintance, small have been my profits, and less my Satisfaction, with few people have I been able to converse, wanting fluency in the Language, and with Books as few, having no more than what I have my self Imported. Thus wanting the means not only of Improvement and Satisfaction but of adding to my fortune should I cast up my Account the Ballance Could be little more than ——[2] except indeed that the weakness and depravity of human nature to my view are more Conspicuous.

Should my Style somewhat Poetical appear, To astonishment let not a place be given; nor of my Sufficiency must you entertain a dubious thought, for to your understanding thus much shall be divulged, long in a Garret have I lived, and hence my Poetry its commencment took. But in this same Garret shall I not long Continue, and much to my Fear my Poetic Talents must thence depart, so health and happiness my Dear Jay. Write to me frequently I beseech you.

S. KISSAM

Please to give my most respectful Compliments to all my old *Club* Acquaintances. I would have wrote to Fade but suppose him to be in Coracao.

ALS. Addressed: "To John Jay Esqr In New York." Endorsed.

1 On 27 Aug. 1771 JJ had written Kissam: "I have not been well since last Fall, having from that time been attended by 3 Doctrs. A swelling in one of the Muscles of the Neck and a little lingering Fever last Spring have been the Complaints. I am now better but not well." Frank Monaghan, "Samuel Kissam and John Jay," *Columbia University Quarterly*, XXV (June, 1933), 130–31.

2 Blank line in letter.

The Dancing Assembly: An Invitation to a Duel

Dancing assemblies, which were generally held every two weeks during the fall and winter, had been a regular feature of the New York social season since as early as 1740. The city's most fashionable residents patronized these subscription parties, and JJ was naturally among those who attended. By 1772 he had become one of the three managers, along with John Reade and Robert R. Livingston, and he is known to have held the same post two years later.[1] The assemblies were discontinued during the Revolution, but they were revived later, and they continue to be held today. The present subscribers are for the most part members of families that were prominent during JJ's lifetime. The rigid social standards which JJ as a manager applied brought about another personal confrontation, as the following two communications to a rejected applicant reveal.

1 Esther Singleton, *Social New York Under the Georges, 1714–1776* (New York, 1902), pp. 301–05; Monaghan, *Jay*, p. 42; Martha J. Lamb and Mrs. Burton Harrison, *History of the City of New York: Its Origin, Rise, and Progress* (New York, 1896), III, 40.

To Robert Randall

New York, 2 February 1773

Sir

I have recieved and should have answered your Letter[1] immediately, had I not found myself more disposed to Violence, than might be justified on cool Reflection.

I believe the[re is no one] less dis[posed to in]jure or insult oth[ers than my]self, or more ready to give Satisfaction to such as have a Right [to] require it.

You speak of a Stab given your Honor this Morning. I have reflected deliberately on the Conversation which then passed between us, and cannot recollect any Thing that could offend the nicest Delicacy. I should have imagined, that the Motives which led me to a personal Conference with you, instead of causing Resentment, would have laid you under Obligations to me. You may remember I told you, this was the first Instance of my having ever explained the Reasons of my Conduct as a Manager; and I then acquainted you that my Reason for telling *you* the Real Objections I had to your Admission, was, in order to convince you that I had nothing personal against you, and to give you an Opportunity of removing those Objections. I repeatedly told you, that in point of Family you was unexceptionable, and that I knew Nothing to be censured in your Character or Behaveour but that notwithstanding you did not appear to me to be connected with the People who frequent the Assembly and as such Connection was in my Opinion necessary to intitle one to Admission, I objected to your Admission f[or the Pre]sent. I told [you] further [that y]ou might easily cultivate an Acquaintance with them, and that then I would readily vote for your becoming a Subscriber.

Now Sir! consider the <Tenor th> whole Tenor of my Conduct, and then determine dispassionately whether you had more Reason to think me your Friend than your Enemy. Instead of taking the precipitate Step you have, as my Objection arose from my Ignorance of your Acquaintance with the Subscribers, you should have requested some of them to recommend you to the Managers, in Consequence of which you would have instantly been admitted.

Tho acting with Spirit over Honor to a Man, yet that Spirit should be calm and reasonable. In short Sir! I desire to withhold Justice from no Man, and if any reasonable Person will say I have injured you or that you have a Right to Satisfaction, I will either ask your Pardon or <fyght> fight you.

I am Sir your humble Servant

JOHN JAY

ALS. Addressed: "To Mr. Robt. Randall." Probably Robert Richard Randall (1750–1801), the son of Thomas Randall, a prominent New York merchant, later founded the Sailor's Snug Harbor, a home for seamen, their widows, and orphans.

[1] Letter not located.

To Robert Randall

New York, 3 February 1773

Sir

Permit me to assure you, that you are exceedingly mistaken if you suppose me desirous of hushing up the Matter between us in a Way, that may be inconsistant either with your Honor or my own.

The Coolness with which I now act, and which I hope will never forsake me flows from another Principle, and will always lead me to behave with Decency and with Firmness.

I did not imagine that as you signified your Assent last Evening to a fair Determination of our Difference, that your Letter[1] required [no] an Answer. I have been expecting all the Morning that you would have mentioned, or conferred with me respecting the Persons we were to consult on the Occasion, and the Time and Place of doing it.

I am under an Engagement to go to Mr. Schuylers[2] at Second River Tomorrow on Matters of Business, and am ready to devote this Evening to the Purposes mentioned in your Letter. I am willing to Submit it to Mr. Watts, Mr. Bache, Mr. Ver Plank, or Mr. De Lancey or any of them.[3] Let me know your opinion of this Proposal, and let us appoint some Hour for the Purpose that may be convenient to us both. Any Time after five OClock will suit me.

I am Sir Your humble Servant

JOHN JAY

ALS. Addressed: "To Mr. Robt Randall, Prest."

1 Letter not located.

2 Arent Schuyler (1746–1803), a 1765 graduate of King's College, lived on an estate on the Passaic River opposite Second River or modern Belleville, N.J. The "Matters of Business" probably concerned the estate of Schuyler's father who had died 12 Jan. 1773. Cuyler Reynolds, *Hudson-Mohawk Genealogical and Family Memoirs* (4 vols., New York, 1911), I, 29.

3 The friends referred to here are probably John Watts, Jr., and Stephen DeLancey (1748–98), JJ's fellow members in the Moot, Theophylact Bache (1735–1807), a prominent New York merchant, and "Mr. Ver Planck" was either Samuel (1739–1820) or Gulian Ver Planck, JJ's second cousins. Martha J. Lamb and Mrs. Burton Harris, *History of the City of New York: Its Origin, Rise, and Progress* (3 vols., New York, 1896), II, 32, 683; *N.Y.G.B.R.*, XXIV (1893), 41–42.

The New York–New Jersey Boundary Commission

JJ filled the enforced leisure of his early days of relatively quiescent practice by serving as clerk to the Boundary Commission created to ascertain the location of the New York–New Jersey dividing line. He was appointed to that post on 21 July 1769, doubtless through the influence of Benjamin Kissam, one of the agents pleading New York's case before the Commission.[1]

Under a royal warrant of October 1767, the thirteen Commissioners, or any five of them, were to settle the boundary which had been in dispute since the creation of New Jersey as a separate colony in 1664. New York had not seriously contested a boundary line surveyed in 1719 until disagreements arose over the Minisink patent in 1755. In hearings before the Commission, New Jersey argued for the 1719 boundary which ran from 41° on the Hudson to 41° 40′ on the Delaware, while New York claimed a line from New York City to the site of Easton, Pennsylvania. To JJ and his assistant clerk fell the onerous task of copying land grants and marking evidence for future identification, then, once the proceedings began, of keeping the minutes and entering interrogatories and answers.

Meeting in New York during the height of the summer of 1769, the Commissioners received documents in evidence and heard testimony, adjourning on 22 September. On 30 September, the surveyors' reports were read and filed. The Commission, deliberating for five days, rendered a decision based upon the surveyors' findings: a compromise line substantially closer to New Jersey's claims than to New York's. Both sides entered appeals, and the Commission adjourned for two months to convene at Hartford for consideration of these appeals.

Beyond this point the Commission's operations became hopelessly confused. While JJ dutifully repaired to Hartford in December 1769, the Commissioners themselves could not muster a quorum, and the rival provinces did not file their promised appeals. JJ was ready for duty again at the Commission's next scheduled meeting in New York in July 1770, but only one Commissioner appeared and no provincial agents attended. In May 1771, only one Commissioner was present at the Commission's last meeting.

In the meantime, JJ had expended considerable time and money in behalf of the delinquent Commissioners. Besides the costs of his trip to Hartford, he had to employ six "writers" to prepare copies of the Commission's records when it was expected that the two provinces would appeal the Commission's findings. Some members of the New York Council, apprehensive that they might be held individually responsible for the costs of the Commission because of the unfavorable settlement, balked at settling accounts with the province's agents.[2] JJ hit upon the expedient of charging one-half of his salary and expenses to the agents of New Jersey, although it seems that he was not reimbursed by either province.

Even if his requests for compensation were ignored, JJ was not powerless, and he nearly frustrated the efforts of Governors William Franklin of New Jersey and William Tryon of New York to settle the troublesome dispute. In February 1772, the New York Assembly passed a statute accepting the Commission's line and recognizing land titles north of that line which originated from New Jersey grants. However, this act would not go into effect until New Jersey passed similar legislation and the Privy Council approved the laws of both colonies.[3] In April 1772, the Board of Trade considered the New York law and refused to report the act to the Privy Council until it was clear that neither colony still intended to appeal the boundary and until the commission under which the line had been determined was returned to England along with the proceedings of the Commissioners' hearings in 1769.[4]

At a conference with Franklin in September 1772, Tryon settled the first problem, that of New Jersey's accession to the boundary compromise.[5] Later that month, the New Jersey Assembly passed legislation endorsing the Commission's line and recognizing land titles south of the new boundary.[6] The only barrier to a settlement was the presentation of the Commission's records to the Board of Trade for review. Here JJ balked and refused to release a copy of the Commission's proceedings until he was directed to do so by an Order in Council or an act of the New York Assembly.[7] When the New York legislature met in January 1773, Tryon pushed through a bill directing JJ to turn over the records. Introduced on 3 February, it was enacted by the Assembly and approved by the Council in three days.[8]

On the evening of 6 February 1773, Andrew Elliot, one of the Boundary Commissioners, was able to deliver the proceedings to Tryon along with the certificate printed below. Tryon forwarded the records to London the next day and assigned the delay in dispatch to JJ's intransigence.[9] In acknowledging receipt of the Commission proceedings, the Secretary of State for the Colonies commented:

> I do not well see upon what ground it was, that Mr. Jay had his doubts as to the delivery of the Commission and the proceedings thereupon for running the boundary line between New York and New Jersey; I am to presume, however, from the step taken by the Legislature; that there was some foundation in Law for those doubts.[10]

In defense of JJ's obstinate course, it should be pointed out that, had he turned over the product of his labors before his own claims for back pay and other outlays were settled, he probably would have forfeited his chance of recovery. Complying only after being so instructed by an act of assembly, JJ may still not have received compensation for expenses as the Commission's clerk beyond fees paid for copying in the summer of 1769, absent affirmative evidence.[11] Thus early did JJ reveal that tenacity with regard to observing established procedures which was to stamp his entire career.

JJ's service as clerk of the Boundary Commission gave him good grounding in the operation of a mixed commission, a device that he himself was to innovate in the adjustment of international disputes, and it exposed him early in his career to the complicated relations between the different colonies on the one hand, and between the colonies and British colonial administrative agencies on the other.[12]

1 For JJ's experience as clerk to the Commission, see Herbert A. Johnson, "John Jay: Colonial Lawyer" (unpub. Ph.D. dissertation, Columbia Univ., 1965), pp. 100–116.

2 William Smith, *Memoirs*, I, 77–79.

3 *Laws of New York from the Year 1691, to 1773 inclusive* (New York, 1774), 29th Assembly, 3rd sess., ch. MCCCCLXXVI, pp. 602–06.

4 *Journals of the Commissioners for Trade and Plantations from January 1768 to December 1775* (London, 1937), p. 299.

5 Tryon to the Earl of Dartmouth, 7 Feb. 1773, *N.Y. Col. Docs.*, VIII, 349.

6 *Acts of the General Assembly of the Province of New-Jersey* (Burlington, N.J., 1776), 22nd Assembly, 1st sess., ch. DLXIV, pp. 368–73.

7 Tryon to Dartmouth, 7 Feb. 1773.

8 *N.Y. Assembly Journal, 1766–1776*, Jan.–March 1773 sess., pp. 44, 46, 47, 53.

9 Tryon to Dartmouth, 7 Feb. 1773.

10 Dartmouth to Tryon, 10 April 1773, *N.Y. Col. Docs.*, VIII, 358.

11 Johnson, "John Jay," pp. 115, 116.

12 Richard B. Morris, *John Jay, the Nation, and the Court* (Boston, 1967), pp. 5, 6; *Seven Who Shaped Our Destiny* (New York, 1973), pp. 160, 161.

John Jay: Certification of Proceedings

[*New York, c. 6 February 1773*]

I John Jay of the City of New York Esqr. Clerk of the Commissioners lately appointed under the Great Seal of Great Britain for settling and Determining the Boundary Line between the Colonies of New York and New Jersey do hereby Certify That all the Proceedings of the Commissioners upon his Majesty's said Commission which they directed <him> me to enter are contained in this Book and that all the Evidence given in the said Controversy (except what consisted of maps) is truly set forth therein. And I do further Certify That by the Request of the Agents for managing the Controversy for the said Colonies I delivered all the maps committed to my Care by the said Commissioners which were given in Evidence in the said Controversy, to Gerardus Bancker[1] of the City of New York to be Copied he having been frequently employed by the said Commissioners for that purpose while they were engaged in the Execution of the said Commission. And that the several maps hereunto annexed appear by the Oath of the said Gerardus Bancker to be Copies of the respective originals so Delivered to him and I do <Certify> further Certify That the said Copies of maps are Copies of all the maps so given in Evidence and committed to me by the said Commissioners except a map Intitled An accurate Map of North America describing and distinguishing the British Spanish and French Dominions on this great Continent according to the Definitive Treaty concluded at Paris 10th February 1763, also all the West India Islands belonging to and possessed by the several European Princes and States the whole laid down according to the latest and most authentic Improvements by

Eman Bowen,[2] Geographer to his majesty, which the Agents for both Colonies have agreed was unnecessary to be transmitted with the Proceedings, it having been given in Evidence only to shew how many miles were computed to a Degree at the time of making the said map.

AD. NHi: N.Y.-N.J. Boundary Papers.

1 Gerardus Bancker (1740–99) served on the commission appointed later in 1773 to settle the disputed New York–Massachusetts boundary.

2 Emanuel Bowen.

To The Earl of Dartmouth

New York, 25th March 1773

Tho a Stranger to your Lordship, I take the Liberty of troubling you with the inclosed Petition of the Inhabitants of New Britain, Settlement on the Frontier of this Province.

Principles of Humanity my Lord! have led me to interest myself in Behalf of these unhappy People; and I forbear paying an ill Compliment to a generous Mind, by endeavouring to apologize for giving it an opportunity, of supporting the Cause of Equity and Benevolence. If we may rest our Judgment on the Reports of Fame, your Lordship's Petitioners are happy in a Prospect of having the Matters of their Complaint, determined under the Directions of a Minister; who does not consider an Elevated Station as an asylum from the Plaints of Distress.

It gives me Pain my Lord! to observe that the prevailing monopoly of Lands in this Colony has become a Grievance to the lower Class of People in it; and confines the Bounty of our gracious Sovereign to mercenary Land-Jobbers, and Gentlemen who have already shared very largely in the royal Munificence.

My Lord! I have no Reason to suspect that these People have decieved me, and therefore, should further Inquiries be thought necessary to determine the merits of their Pretensions, I will readily be at the Trouble of making them.

I am my Lord, with the greatest Respect, your Lordships most obedient and most humble Servant

JOHN JAY

ALS. PRO: CO 5/1104. Enclosure: Petition of the Inhabitants of New-Britain, 25 March 1773, also in PRO: CO 5/1104. The petition traced the history of New Britain, a settlement in modern Columbia County, N.Y. just east of the Kinderhook patent. Settlers had come to the area in the early 1760's, and they were promised by Colonel John Van Rensselaer that if the crown recognized his claim to the area, he "would sell it to them as Waste Land for a low price." Should Van Rensselaer's claim be disallowed, the settlers at New Britain had expected they could easily receive grants directly from the crown. However, Van Rensselaer relinquished his claim to New Britain, and the settlers were alarmed at rumors that applications had been made for grants in their neighborhood. Their petition mentioned an earlier petition of January 1772 to Governor Tryon seeking grants for the lands they had cleared, but "nothing was done in Consequence thereof. . . ." William Legge, Earl of Dartmouth (1731–1801), served as British Secretary of State for Colonial Affairs, 1772–75.

Marriage

In the spring of 1774, JJ married and entered politics. At least one contemporary New Yorker, the Tory Thomas Jones, saw a link between the two. According to Jones, JJ was the rejected suitor of two daughters of Peter De Lancey, a member of the family which led conservative forces in New York politics. In retaliation, Jones claimed, JJ "took a wife in . . . the Livingston [family], a family ever opposed to the De Lanceys, turned Republican, espoused the Livingston interest, and ever after opposed all legal government."[1]

Whatever his earlier disappointments of the heart, JJ could hardly be described as settling for second best in marrying Sarah Van Brugh Livingston (1756–1802). Both as to family and personal charms, "Sally" seemed a prize worth winning. Her father, William Livingston (1723–90), was one of the sons of Philip Livingston, second lord of Livingston Manor. For two decades, William Livingston, with John Morin Scott and William Smith, Jr. (1728–93), formed the "triumvirate" of lawyers who kept the New York political kettle aboil by their opposition to crown measures. In 1772, Livingston moved his family to Elizabethtown, New Jersey, where he built his celebrated home, "Liberty Hall." Susannah French Livingston (1723–89), Sarah's mother, was the daughter of Philip French, a wealthy landowner of New Brunswick, New Jersey.[2]

Sarah Livingston's gaiety and high spirits were a perfect complement to JJ's sedate and reserved personality. The couple appear to have met in the winter of 1772–73 when Sarah came to New York City to visit relatives. Gouverneur Morris, a lifelong friend of the couple, described Sarah's conquest of New York society in a letter written to her older sister Catharine Wilhelmina Livingston (1751–1803).

> What do you think Kitty—I have adopted Sally for my Daughter. Believe me I will pay her the same Attention I would were I really a Father. To tell you a Secret I have a great many who pretend to the Honor of being my Son in Law. . . . I would make you laugh nay laughing would not serve the Turn you must do more. One bending forwards rolling up his Eyes and sighing most piteously. Another at a

> Distance setting Side long upon his Chair with melancholic and despondent Phiz prolongated unto the seventh button Hole of his Waistcoat. A third his Shoulders drawn up to his Ears his Elbows fastened to his short Ribs his Brow wrinkled and the Corners of his Mouth making over his Chin a most rueful Arch. In the Midst of all this sits Miss with seeming Unconsciousness of the whole. One would be led to imagine she is unconcerned. I shall dispose of her before the Winter is out I believe provided Mamma has no objections. . . .[3]

JJ's proposal of marriage was accepted by January 1774 when he informed his family in Rye of his betrothal. Peter Jay immediately wrote to his son's future father-in-law, assuring him that: "Tho we have not the Pleasure of knowing the young Lady, Yet the confidence we have in our Son's Prudence satisfies us of the Propriety of his choice. Give me leave Sir to assure you, that I will always readily adopt every measure that may conduce to their happiness, and tend to render the Connection between our Familyes agreeable to both."[4]

The young couple were married at Liberty Hall 28 April 1774.[5] Eight days later, Sarah Jay sent her mother this account of her wedding trip and her introduction to the Jay family.

1 Thomas Jones, *History of New York During the Revolutionary War*, ed. by Edward Floyd De Lancey (2 vols., New York, 1879), II, 223.

2 For summaries of William Livingston's pre-Revolutionary career, see Dorothy Rita Dillon, *The New York Triumvirate* (New York, 1949) and Milton H. Klein, "The American Whig: William Livingston of New York" (unpub. Ph.D. dissertation, Columbia University, 1954).

3 Gouverneur Morris to Catharine Livingston, 11 Jan. 1773, MHi: Ridley Papers.

4 Peter Jay to William Livingston, 31 Jan. 1774, JP.

5 According to a letter of JJ's to the Reverend Harry Munro, JJ's brother-in-law, in the possession of Edward Floyd De Lancey, maternally a great-grandson of the Munros and editor of Thomas Jones's *History of New York*, II, 475, JJ had asked Munro to officiate at his and Sarah Livingston's wedding ceremony.

Sarah Livingston Jay to Susannah French Livingston

Poughkeepsie, May 6th, [1774]

My dear Mamma,

This evening I had the pleasure of meeting Cousin Harry Livingston who informs that he is going to New York tomorrow and will be so obliging as to forward a Letter to you and as I know how generously you interest yourself in the Welfare of your children I shall take the liberty of troubling with an account of my little jaunt thus far. On Monday we left New York and arrived at Rye in the afternoon where we were received with a hearty welcome. I was not by any means so much affected at seeing the blind children[1] as I feared I should be. There was such an appearance of chearfulness and good humour in all they say that instead of depressing they raised my spirits which had been not a little damped at the sight of their afflicted Mother who we found extremely ill and who was amazingly affected at seeing me but after a little Chat she appeared much better and the next morning she was in very good spirits and wanted Mr. Jay exceedingly to leave me with her but since she could not obtain her request I am to spend a week with them on my return in which I have my Mamma's ease in view (though I am sorry to think how much trouble my dear Mamma will have at any rate.) Mrs. F. Jay is to meet me there and stay with me while Mr. Jay's business calls him at West Chester. On Tuesday We left Rye and lodged about twelve miles from Peekskill, Wednesday we went from thence to Cousin Robinson's where we were very politely received and did not leave them till to-day. She begd to be remembred to you and to tell you she would be amazingly glad to see you and sister Catesy or any of the family.[2] To day we met Judge Livingston[3] at Poughkeepsie. He goes home very early to let his family know that we drink tea with them to-morrow and spend a week with them. I do not go to Sopus,[4] Mr. Jay will be there very little while. The Land-Lady for this evening is waiting for this table to lay the cloth and I am obliged to conclude abruptly again but tell sisters I will write them from the Manor. I beg my dear Mamma not to be offended at these scrawls I assure you it is not my power to write well in this room where there is such a collection of country-men talking politicks. Good night my dear Mamma, God bless you and all your dear family. Believe me to be your ever grateful and affectionate daughter

SA. JAY

Mr. Jay joins with me in love to all. He begs Mamma will take care of her Cold. We have both been very uneasy about it. Likewise be pleased to remember us to Aunt Richards.[5]

ALS.

1 JJ's brother and sister, Peter and Anna Maricka.

2 Frederick Jay married Ann Margaret Barclay (1752–91) on 17 Nov. 1773. "Peggy" was the daughter of Andrew D. Barclay, a New York merchant. Susanna Philipse (Mrs. Beverly) Robinson (1727–1822) was Susannah French Livingston's cousin. "Catesy" was SLJ's older sister, Catharine.

3 Robert R. Livingston, Sr.

4 The town of Esopus near Kingston, N.Y.

5 There is no record of a relationship by blood or marriage between the Richard family and the Livingstons or Frenches. This reference may be to Esther (Mrs. Stephen) Richard (d. 1779), the wife of a prominent Elizabethtown landowner. "Abstracts of N.J. Wills," *N.J. Archives,* 1st ser., XXXIV, 420–21.

III

ON THE THRESHOLD OF REVOLUTION

Early Political Activism

Even had JJ not married the daughter of so able and active a political leader as William Livingston, it would have been difficult for him to avoid participation in public life by the spring of 1774. The repeal of the Townshend duties had brought comparative calm to the relations between New York and the British government, but the Tea Act of 10 May 1773 put an end to this peaceful interlude.

In New York, as in other ports, vocal opposition to the Tea Act resounded throughout the fall and winter of 1773, but not until the spring of 1774 did overt violence break out. In the third week of April 1774, the first ships bearing East India Company tea reached New York harbor. One of these ships, the *London,* was boarded and its cargo of tea dumped in the harbor, much as had happened in Boston the preceding December.

On 12 May, three weeks after the tea incident, word reached New York of the Boston Port Bill, the first of the "Intolerable Acts" passed by the British Parliament in retaliation for the Boston Tea Party and, in effect, closing the port of Boston until satisfaction was made for the damage done in the riots of November–December 1773.[1]

Seizing the initiative, New York's conservative faction called a meeting of merchants of 16 May when a slate of fifty names, including JJ's, was proposed for a committee to guide the protest movement in the city. Radicals, who had argued for a smaller, more efficient committee, drew up their own slate of twenty-five as an alternative to the list of fifty. On 19 May the rival tickets were considered by a meeting of "the inhabitants of the city and county." The conservatives' fifty nominees were approved, with the addition of Francis Lewis, to form the Committee of Fifty-One which was charged with "the important and salutary purposes of keeping up a correspondence with our sister Colonies." Isaac Low was elected to chair the committee, and JJ's public career was launched.[2]

Significantly, in reporting the activities of the "Fifty-One" in the letter to John Vardill printed below, JJ also confided his availability for a modest judicial post under the crown.

1 Text of the Boston Port Act is reprinted in 4 *FAA*, I, 61–66.

2 For readable and cogent accounts of the events in New York in 1773–74, see Becker, *N.Y. Political Parties*, chs. IV and V, and Bernard Mason, *The Road*

to Independence: The Revolutionary Movement in New York, 1773–1777 (Lexington, Ky., 1966), ch. I. Mason's study corrects Becker's error concerning the chronology of nominations of committees in May 1774. For documents relating to the formation of the Committee of Fifty-One, see 4 *FAA*, I, 293–96.

To John Vardill

New York, 23rd May 1774

Dear Vardil

In a Town filled with Politics, and with a Mind crouded with many indigested Ideas, I have taken up my Pen in order to acknowledge the Reciept of your very friendly Letter of the 5th April last.[1] It bears evident Marks of Attention and Attachment, for which recieve my Thanks. The several Topics you mention require more Thought than I can now bestow upon them. I returned from the northern Counties Yesterday, and found myself one of the Committee appointed by the City to take into Consideration the Measures of Parliament relative to Boston and consult upon the most effectual Methods to advance the Interest of the common Cause. We sat four Hours Per Day and have agreed to attempt a Congress of Deputies from all the Colonies, as the most probable Means of effecting a general Union and Consistency of Councils. Four (of which Number I am one) are appointed to prepare Dispatches for Boston.[2] I leave Town Tomorrow to attend the West Chester Court. Many collateral Matters will come before the Committee this Evening that require much thought and Circumspection. Judge therefore whether it is possible for me at this Juncture to think clearly, or write with that Precision which is necessary to do Justice to the Subjects you recommend. Upon some of them indeed I have bestowed much thought, and shall employ the first Leizure Hour I have in communicating my Sentiments fully.

As to the Office you mention, it is doubtless honorary, but my Circumstances will not admit of accepting it, unless it be rendered in some Degree lucrative in which Case I would chearfully resign the Toil of my Profession for *Otium cum Dignitate*.[3] Altho Governor Tryon has been civil to me, I have taken too little Pains to conciliate his particular good Graces, to expect his Recommendation to that Place. But there is another Matter which I believe he has at Heart and in which I fancy he would interest himself in my Favor. It is this.

In every County there is established by ordinance of the Governor and Council a Court, called an *inferiour* Court of Common Pleas authorized to try all Causes of five Pounds and upwards (the supreme Court being restricted to Causes above twenty pounds). In this Court actions are prosecuted at very little Expence, and are therefore very numerous. In each of these Courts there are three or four Judges. There being but few Gentlemen of Law or even liberal Education among us, and of those, very few indeed who reside in the Country; these Judges are taken from among the Farmers, who have no other Guide to direct them through the Mazes and Intricacies of the Law than the mere natural Sagacity they may happen to possess. Whence it happens that their Adjudications are constantly fluctuating and what is determined Law to Day, declared otherwise Tomorrow. Their Ignorance exposes them to the Neglect if not the Contempt of the Bar, and not knowing the Extent of, or when to exercise their Powers, find themselves incapable of supporting that Dignity of Office so necessary to render it respectable, and I may say useful. Add to this that the Judges and Justices are appointed by the Recommendation of the Representatives of the County, who are determined in their Choice less by Ability, than Attachment to particular Parties and Interest. These Considerations induced Mr. Livingston and myself to propose to Governor Tryon, that certain Gentlemen of the Law should be appointed to visit these Courts, and preside in Term time. The Judges of the Supreme Court recommended the Measure, and it would have taken Place had not the DeLancey Party in Council been against it. You know the Motives of their opposition. Gov. Tryon has promised Mr. Livingston to lay the Plan before the Ministry, and endeavour to interest them in its Favor. He also mentioned me as a proper Person to be one of the Number. 3 are sufficient. If the Government were to establish this Office and provide for its Support, it would evince an Attention to the Interest of the Colony that would not only be useful to the People, but place the Ministry in somewhat a more favorable point of View than they now appear to the Inhabitants of the Province. The due Distribution of Justice being of the highest Moment to any Country.[4]

These Hints may furnish you with Materials for further Measures. And whether they be productive of advantageous Consequences or not, I shall think myself equally indebted to the friendly Attention that called them forth.

Your Brethren of the Gown are quiet, and as yet no Schemes are forming among them disadvantageous to you. I will give you the earliest Notice of any Alarm. Since your absence I have laid such a Train for Intelligence that nothing meditated against you can long remain a Secret. The College Club exists, and my Endeavours shall not be wanting to support that or any other Institution of publick Utility.

Adieu my Dear Vardill, I am your Friend

JOHN JAY

ALS. PRO: AO 13/105. John Vardill graduated from King's College in 1766. After his graduation, Vardill became an active propagandist for the Anglican cause in New York and, in 1774, sailed to London for ordination as a priest. Despite his appointment as Regius Professor of Divinity at King's, Vardill remained in England throughout the Revolution. During this time, he was paid £200 annually by the crown, earning his pension by writing pamphlets and newspaper pieces and doing intelligence work among Americans and American sympathizers in London. In 1783 he submitted a petition to the Loyalist Commissioners, cataloging his services to the crown. Among his supposed accomplishments, according to this petition, was furnishing the "government with much and valuable Information, from an extensive Correspondence with Congress-Leaders," among them JJ. "One effect of this Correspondence," his petition continued, "was to secure to Government the interest of two Members of the Congress by the promise of the office of Judges in America. But the Negotiation was quashed by the unexpected Fray at Lexington in April 1775." In support of this assertion, Vardill submitted two letters from JJ, that published here and that of 24 Sept. 1774, below. These letters were filed with Vardill's petition of 16 Nov. 1783 in PRO: AO 13/105.

1 Letter not located.

2 The Committee of Fifty-One met for the first time at 10 A.M., 23 May 1774. JJ, Alexander McDougall, Isaac Low, and James Duane were named "a Committee to prepare and report a draft of an Answer to the Boston Committee at eight o'clock P.M." The Boston letter enclosed the resolutions of the Boston town meeting of 13 March which called for a nonimportation agreement by all the colonies until the repeal of the Boston Port Act. The reply drafted by the committee on which JJ served called for "a Congress of Deputies from the colonies in general" to enact "unanimous resolutions formed in this fatal emergency, not only respecting your deplorable circumstances, but for the security of our common rights." Although some historians have attempted to attribute this draft to JJ, it is clear from the notes kept by his fellow committee-member, Alexander McDougall, that JJ acted as "Scribe" when the committee discussed the contents of their report and that JJ's notes were taken home by James Duane who was to "furbish" them. Duane's polished version of the committee's joint efforts was presented to the Committee of Fifty-One on the evening of 23 May. Becker, *N.Y. Political Parties*, ch. V; 4 *FAA*, I, 295–98, 331; Alexander McDougall: "Political Memoranda relative to the Conduct of the Citizens on the Boston Port Bill," NHi: McDougall Papers.

3 Ease with dignity.

4 Although the law partnership of JJ and Robert R. Livingston, Jr. was virtually dissolved by 1771, the two young attorneys had continued to work together on a program of judiciary reform. A proposal to name JJ and Livingston as "advisors" of a sort to judges of the Courts of Common Pleas was apparently made to Governor William Tryon (1729–88) in 1772, for in November of that year Tryon submitted the proposal to the provincial Council. Livingston was to be "judge itinerant" for Tryon, Albany, Ulster, and Dutchess Counties; JJ, for Orange, Westchester, and Richmond. During Council discussions of the proposal

in December 1772, Tryon was less than ardent in defending the project. Even though JJ and Livingston offered to serve without pay, the measure was defeated in the Council and was never submitted to the Assembly. William Smith, *Memoirs*, I, 129–32.

Delegate to the First Continental Congress

New York was one of several provinces to react to the Boston Port Act with a call for an intercolonial congress.[1] Heartened by this response, the Massachusetts House of Representatives resolved on 17 June 1774 "that a meeting of Committees, from the several Colonies on this Continent is highly expedient and necessary," and proposed that the Congress be held in Philadelphia on 1 September.[2]

The election of delegates from New York to the First Continental Congress decisively split the extralegal Revolutionary movement in the province. On 4 July, the conservative faction on the Committee of Fifty-One gained the group's endorsement of its slate of Congressional nominees: Isaac Low, James Duane, Philip Livingston, John Alsop, and JJ. A day later, the Committee of Mechanics, the radical wing of the protest movement, named their own ticket, on which Duane and Alsop were replaced by Leonard Lispenard and Alexander McDougall.[3]

Soon the Fifty-One faced a rival platform as well as a rival ticket. On 6 July the Mechanics agreed to resolutions calling for a general nonimportation agreement. The Fifty-One had no choice but to formulate their own statement and named a subcommittee to draw up alternative resolves. However, preparation of these resolutions was delayed when eleven radical members of the Fifty-One, three of whom were on the subcommittee on drafting resolutions, resigned from the Fifty-One on 8 July. At a meeting of 13 July, the Fifty-One appointed a new subcommittee which included JJ, who had been absent from meetings since 10 June.[4]

The resolutions drafted by the new subcommittee were approved by the Fifty-One later in the session of 13 July. These proposals were far more conciliatory than those approved by the Mechanics a week earlier and their position on nonimportation was more ambiguous. They declined to give any explicit instructions to Congressional delegates on policy because, "as the wisdom of the Colonies will . . . be collected at the proposed Congress, it would be premature in any Colony to anticipate their conduct by resolving what ought to be done. . . ." Nonimportation was viewed only as a last resort in the resolutions of 13 July: "Nothing less than dire necessity can justify, or ought to induce the Colonies to unite in any measure that might materially injure our brethren, the manufacturers, traders, and merchants in Great Britain. . . ."[5]

On 19 July a public meeting at the Coffee House considered the resolutions of 13 July as well as the Fifty-One's slate of delegates to

Congress. The session proved a disaster for conservatives and moderates. While the conservative ticket for Congress was approved, the resolutions were roundly defeated after John Morin Scott, the fiery lawyer leader of New York's radicals, denounced these "pusillanimous Resolves."[6]

A new subcommittee of fifteen, with JJ as a member, was appointed to draw up new resolves after the conservative program was voted down, but JJ and other moderates refused to recognize the legality of any of the proceedings on 19 July. With three other appointees, JJ declined to serve on the subcommittee on the ground that their designation was "proposed and carried out without any previous notice of such design having been given to the inhabitants," thus making "our election too irregular to assume any authority."[7] In addition, JJ, Low, and Alsop declined to recognize their election to Congress by the Coffee House meeting and refused to serve "until the sentiments of the town are ascertained with great precision. . . ."[8] In a private letter to Scott, printed below, JJ was even more outspoken in his criticism of the radical-dominated meeting and of what JJ considered a personal attack upon himself and the other members of the subcommittee which had drafted the ill-fated resolutions of 13 July.

1 See above, JJ to John Vardill, 23 May 1774, editorial note.

2 4 *FAA*, I, 42.

3 For a summary of the factional strife connected with this election, see Becker, *N.Y. Political Parties*, ch. V, passim. Documents concerning the election are printed in 4 *FAA*, I, 307–22.

4 Becker, *N.Y. Political Parties*, 123–29, 129n.

5 The account of the meeting of 13 July as presented in the ms. minutes of the Committee of Fifty-One at NHi and printed in 4 *FAA*, I, 315, is incomplete. A fuller account of these proceedings was published in a contemporary broadside, "Proceedings of the Committee of Correspondence in New York . . . July 13, 1774," Evans, 13477. The resolutions of 13 July are printed in 4 *FAA*, I, 316–17.

6 William Smith, *Memoirs*, I, 189.

7 JJ *et al.*, "To the Respectable Public" (2nd address), 20 July 1774, 4 *FAA*, I, 317–18.

8 JJ *et al.*, "To the Respectable Public" (1st address), 20 July 1774, *ibid.*, 317.

To John Morin Scott

New York, [*20 July*] *1774*

Sir

I was much surprised last Evening on being informed that in your speech of yesterday at the Coffee house (the Conclusion of which only I heard) you charged the drawers of the resolves then under Consideration with a design of thereby disuniting the Colonies.

<On what Evidence you found an accusation . . . I am at a loss to conceive: but as it cannot be presumed you would wantonly sport with the reputation of persons whose attachment to the interest

of their Country has never yet been questioned, you doubtless rest your opinion on Reasons you judge sufficient to support it.>[1]

By the printed hand bill you will perceive Sir; that I was one of the Committee by whom these Resolves were formed,[2] and am therefore deeply interested in obtaining from you a Candid and open declaration of the reasons by which you mean to justify holding us up to publick view in a Point of Light which men of Common honesty and spirit can neither merit or permit. This is a piece of Justice which regard to my Character urges me to ask, and which I flatter myself you will have no objections to give.

I am Sir, Your humble Servant

JOHN JAY

Tr. NN: Bancroft, Samuel Adams. (All items from the New York Public Library, the Astor, Lenox, and Tilden Foundations, are from the Manuscripts and Archives Division.) The transcript, in the hand of J. M. Scott, the addressee's descendant, is dated "22nd June 1774," but in a letter to George Bancroft filed with the transcript, Scott confessed confusion over the dateline in the manuscript. Scott's "attempted . . . fac Simile" of the original date shows that JJ had written "July," even though Scott could not "make the word as written Stand for any thing but June." The "speech of yesterday" referred to in the letter was obviously that made at the Coffee House on 19 July 1774; the error in the day may have been JJ's or the transcriber's.

1 This paragraph in Scott's transcript was crossed out, probably by Scott, and recopied at the bottom of the page by George Bancroft. In copying the deleted material, Bancroft added the words "so black and so false" in the first phrase where J. M. Scott had indicated an elision by dots.

2 The handbill was probably the "Proceedings of the Committee of Correspondence in New-York . . . July 13, 1774," the only known contemporary publication which contains the names of the subcommittee appointed on 13 July 1774 to draft resolutions for the Committee of Fifty-One. Evans, 13477.

Role in the First Congress

Eventually the stalemate over New York's choice of Congressional delegates was broken, and on 27 July 1774 the Mechanics endorsed the slate which had been proposed by the Fifty-One more than three weeks earlier. Polls held in the city the next day brought the unanimous election of JJ, John Alsop, Philip Livingston, and James Duane—a resounding defeat for radical Whig John Morin Scott. Endorsement of these delegates by four rural counties followed, and the nominees were ready to proceed to the First Continental Congress.[1] JJ joined his father-in-law, William Livingston, a New Jersey delegate, for the journey to Philadelphia where both were present for the opening session on 5 September 1774.

The New York delegation allied itself with the moderate and conservative blocs in Congress on such preliminary issues as the choice of a meeting hall and of a secretary. Joseph Galloway, the speaker of the Pennsylvania Assembly, proposed the State House, which the New Yorkers preferred as "a piece of respect" due Galloway; but the prevailing view favored Carpenters' Hall as being "highly agreeable to the mechanics and citizens in general." JJ and his New York colleagues preferred Silas Deane as secretary to the more openly acknowledged radical Charles Thomson of Pennsylvania, but again they were defeated.

JJ's first victory was gained in contesting Patrick Henry's proposal that voting should be proportionate to population, slaves excluded from the count. Carried away by his own eloquence, Henry declared: "Government is at an End. All Distinctions are thrown out. All America is thrown into one Mass." In short, "We are in a State of Nature." In this first confrontation between a freshly converted nationalist ultimately to be the prototype of states-rights antifederalism, and JJ, one day to be a foremost nationalist and critic of state sovereignty, both parties played roles which they were later to repudiate. Mindful that in the Stamp Act Congress the vote had been by colonies and respectful of the decisions by which the delegates were bound, JJ injected a sobering note in his reply to Henry. "Could I suppose," he queried, "that We came to frame an American Constitution, instead of indeavouring to correct the faults in an old one—I cant yet think that all Government is at an End. The Measure of Arbitrary Power is not full, and I think it must run over, before We undertake to frame a new Constitution." JJ's supporters prevailed. It was agreed that each colony should have one vote, without the decision serving as a binding precedent. A binding precedent, however, it did become throughout the lifetime of this and the succeeding Second Congress.[2]

Consistent with JJ's conservative position on the three opening issues in contention, he supported the conservative plan of union proposed to Congress (28 September) by Joseph Galloway, a proposal defeated by a margin of one vote. JJ's moderate stance did not prevent him from signing the Continental Association of 22 October, which instituted a complicated system of nonimportation, nonexportation, and nonconsumption.[3]

Nor did JJ's hopes for reconciliation prevent him from preparing on his own a draft "Address to the People of Great Britain." Read to the Congress on 29 October by William Livingston, it evoked, as Jefferson recalled, "but one sentiment of admiration," and was substituted for the original draft prepared by Richard Henry Lee.[4] Notable both for the republican rhetoric which it voiced and the constitutional theories which it espoused, the "Address,"[5] despite JJ's known moderation, propelled him into the front line of Whig propagandists. Charging the British government with establishing "a system of slavery" at the restoration of peace in 1763, JJ reminded his fellow Englishmen that the colonists also claimed the rights of Englishmen, branded as "heresies" the assertion that Parliament could bind the colonists "in all cases without exception," and dispose of their property without their consent. To the contrary, JJ insisted "that no power on earth has the right to take our property from us without our consent," and coupled this right with the rights to trial by jury and a fair trial which guaranteed to the accused the right of adequate defense. It should be noted that JJ, the lawyer, in embracing both procedural and substantive due process as rights so fundamental as to go beyond government control anticipated a constitutional line that first emerged, in a guarded way, in the United States Supreme Court,[6] after JJ had vacated the Chief Justiceship, was more forcefully enunciated on the eve of the Civil War,[7] and emerged in full dress in the post–Civil War era.[8]

Questioning whether the dumping of tea in Boston harbor, a "trespass committed on some merchandise," was a proper ground to suspend the charter and change the constitution of Massachusetts Bay, JJ combined an appeal to the "justice" and "public spirit" of the British nation, with a warning: "We will never submit to be hewers of wood or drawers of water for any ministry or nation in the world." Strong words indeed from JJ, but his "Appeal" was a plea for the restoration of harmony and friendship, not a call to war, a conciliatory stand that JJ was to maintain through still more trying times.

1 Becker, *N.Y. Political Parties*, pp. 136–41.

2 John Adams, *Diary*, II, 124–26; Edmund C. Burnett, *The Continental Congress* (New York, 1941), pp. 37, 38.

3 *JCC*, I, 75–81.

4 Thomas Jefferson to William Wirt, 4 Aug. [1803], *LMCC*, I, 79.

5 *JCC*, I, 82–90.

6 Paterson, *J.*, in *Vanhorne's Lessee* v. *Dorrance*, 2 Dallas 304 (1795).

7 *Wynehamer* v. *N.Y.*, 13 N.Y. 378 (1856), and as dicta by Taney, *C.J.*, in *Dred Scott* v. *Sandford*, 19 Howard 393 (1857).

8 *Hepburn* v. *Griswold*, 8 Wallace 603 (1870).

To John Vardill

Philadelphia, 24 September 1774

Dear Vardell

The Receipt of your Letter (which Mr. Laight kindly forwarded to this Place) was exceedingly grateful to me.[1] I am so attached to my old friends that I feel myself interested in all that concerns them, and am always happy in hearing of their Welfare.

I am [much] obliged to you for the political Hints contained in your Letter: I wish they had as much Influence on others as they have upon me. The Indignation of all Ranks of People is very much roused by the Boston and Canada Bills.[2] God knows how the Contest will end. I sincerely wish it may terminate in a lasting Union with Great Britain. I am obliged to be very reserved on this Subject by the Injunction of Secrecy laid on all the Members of the Congress,[3] and tho I am aware of the Confidence I might repose in your Prudence, I must nevertheless submit to the Controul of Honour perhaps on this occasion too delicate. By the next opportunity I hope I shall be able to be more explicit. You may then expect my Sentiments at large.

I thank you for the Attention you pay to certain other matters. Nothing in your Letter pleases me more than the Circumstance of your returning to us in the Spring.

Pray inform me whether you ever see or hear of my Brother James. Where is he, what is he doing? We have recieved no Letters from him for some Time past. Be so kind as to forward the inclosed to him.[4]

Adieu my dear Vardell. I am your Friend

JOHN JAY

ALS. PRO: AO 13/105. Enclosure: JJ to Sir James Jay, c. 24 Sept. 1774, not located. For the circumstances under which this ALS came to be filed in the AO records, see above, JJ to Vardill, 23 May 1774, source note.

1 Vardill's letter has not been located. William Laight, a New York merchant, was to serve with JJ on the Committee of One Hundred later in 1774, but he remained loyal to the king and stayed in New York City during the British occupation. Becker, N.Y. *Political Parties*, p. 198; Leonard F. Fuld, *King's College Alumni* (New York, 1913), p. 36.

2 The Boston Port Act and the Quebec Act.

3 On 6 Sept. 1774, Congress resolved "That the doors be kept shut during the time of business, and that the members consider themselves under the strongest obligations of honour, to keep the proceedings secret, untill the majority shall direct them to be made public." *JCC*, I, 26.

4 Sir James Jay remained in England, practicing medicine in London until the outbreak of hostilities between Britain and the American colonies.

To Robert R. Livingston, Jr.

New York, January 1, 1775

Providence I confess has conferred Blessings upon me with a liberal hand and my days glide on thro this vale of Tears without Pain or sorrow. I thank God that (in spite of the Faculty) my Bones are not sore vexed neither do I mingle my Drink with continual Weeping. But there are many devious Paths from the common Road of Life, in which I must walk alone and be guided solely by my own Prudence and Discretion. In such circumstances particularly I feel the want of some Person in whom I could repose absolute confidence and from whose Counsel and attachment I could reap both Pleasure and Security. In short my dear Robert! I regret your absence.

When our friendship first commenced, or rather when it was

particularly professed to each other (the 29 March 1765)[1] and for some time after I took it into my head that our dispositions were in many respects similar. Afterwards I conceived a different opinion. It appeared to me that you had more vivacity. Bashfulness and Pride rendered me more Hard, both equally ambitious but pursuing it in different Roads. You flexible I pertinacious but equally sensible of Indignities, you less prone to sudden Resentment—both possessed of warm Passions, but you of more Self Possession, you formed for a citizen of the World I for a college or a Village, you fond of a large acquaintance, I careless of all but a few. You could forbid your countenance to tell tales, mine was a babler—You understood Men and Women early, I knew them not. You had talents and inclination for Intrigue, I had neither. Your mind (and body) received Pleasure from variety of objects, mine from few. You was naturally easy of Access and in advances, I in neither. Unbounded confidence kept us together—may it ever exist!

Within these few years we have been coming nearer to each other. Your vivacity is less, mine more. Though my Pride has suffered me Diminutive it has become less conspicuous, and therefore more on a Line with yours than formerly. You have become less flexible and I rather less pertinaceous. I find my Passions meliorated though strong I can command them, my Inattention to certain characters wears off and my countenance begins to keep secrets.

Thus you see I am thinking loud, and without adverting to connection, am merely committing to paper the present set of Ideas which are floating in my mind. I find pleasure in this negligence. I wish I could enjoy it fully—a social hour would afford it in perfection.

I ought to say something to you about politicks, but am sick of the subject. The enclosed pamphlets will give it you in gross. Provincial Politicks fluctuate—a year may give them quite another turn. After the assembly meets, I shall be able to give a better guess.

Were I in your situation, I would spend a few weeks of the winter in town. Exclusive of pleasure many good effects would follow it. To you I need not name them. Its pretty good sleighing—endeavor to prevail upon yourself (in the Language of New England) to *improve* it.

Tell Mrs. Livingston[2] that I heartily wish you both many happy years. Sally joins me in requesting you to present our respects and the compliments of the season to all the family.

I am my Dear Robert Your friend

JOHN JAY

Tr. American Art Association sale catalogue, 15 Jan. 1918; NN: Bancroft: Robert R. Livingston, item 19. The first three paragraphs are taken from the American Art Association tr.; the last four, from the Bancroft tr. Enclosures not located.

[1] See above, JJ to Livingston, 2 April 1765.

[2] Mary Stevens (1752–1814) married Livingston 9 Sept. 1770.

From Robert Morris

New Brunswick, January 26, 1775

Dear Sir

The contents of this letter may be unexpected, but I hope not disagreeable to you. Nothing, I assure you, is further from my wishes.

A Patent is lately granted, in which I am interested for 10,000 Acres of Land adjoining the Jersey line, and between that and the south bounds of the Chescoks Patent. On the first application for it, I proposed you as a partner, and went to York with intention to mention it to you; but was then informed by one of the partners that you was interested in the Chescoks patent under Mrs. Chambers Will,[1] and that the owners of that patent extended their claim to the Jersey line. The interest of a number of persons who had intrusted, and confided in me being at stake, I did not think I had a right to speak to you on the subject at that time; but as it was ever far from my intention to interfere with your interest, I then intended, and now propose, with your approbation, to intitle you to half my interest in the new patent, which, though not considerable, I am in hopes will be at least equal to what you would have been intitled to, if the lands had been actually contained within the bounds of Chescoks. I will, when next I have the pleasure to see you, inform the particular state of the matter, which is too long for the limits of this Letter; or you may speak to Mr. John DeLancey on the subject who is also interested. The desire of getting some little compensation for near £6000 loss, which my fathers estate unjustly sustained by the Laws for confirming the settlement of the Line, and quieting the Possessions, first put me on joining in this measure.

I am Dear Sir, Your very humble Servant

ROBT. MORRIS

ALS. Addressed: "To John Jay Esqr. New York." Endorsed. Dft in NjR. Robert Morris (1734–1815) of New Brunswick, N.J., the illegitimate son of Robert Hunter Morris (c. 1700–64), was admitted to the bar in 1770 and served as first Chief Justice of New Jersey.

[1] Anne Chambers, JJ's aunt, died on 14 April 1774. In her will she left all

her interest in the Cheesecock Patent in Orange County, N.Y., to JJ, Augustus Van Cortlandt, David Matthews, and John William Livingston. This land had been purchased by her husband, John Chambers, from Elizabeth Denn (or Dean) and willed to her. She also designated JJ as a co-executor of her will.

Organizing a Provisional Government

Following the adjournment of the First Continental Congress, the provincial movement of protest against imperial measures became noticeably transformed, while the individuals within that movement often seemed to their old friends altered beyond recognition. In a letter of 27 March 1775, William Laight, a New York conservative, remarked, "Greater contrariety of opinions no Country can produce than America, in its present State. The *Blues* [radicals] give that the name of moderate opposition, which the Protestants [conservatives] call unjustifiable resistance; the latter call Rebellion and Treason those Actions which the former say are rendered necessary from the spirit of the Times." As for JJ, Laight lamented "the loss of, that once steady, honest Protestant, *Jay*," who had "turned, in Politics, a rigid *Blue Skin*." Laight accounted for JJ's adoption of radical measures by "his too sudden elevation to a popular Character." Laight was convinced that "Popularity must be the Object at which Jay is aiming, and to please the Populace he must have thrown aside his *old principles*."[1]

JJ's "defection" lay in his posture toward the measures of the First Continental Congress. "The Interest of the Protestants made him [JJ] a Delegate for the Congress," Laight explained, but, he continued, "that Interest does not now *support* the measures which the Congress commended, altho it does not directly *counteract* them."[2] JJ, on the other hand, not only endorsed the resolutions of the First Congress, but acted to enforce Congress's nonimportation Association and to create the system by which delegates to the Second Congress were elected.

The Committee of Sixty was chosen in New York on 22 November 1774 to supervise observance of the Association in that port. JJ served on this committee, which had a distinctly more radical tone than its predecessor, the Fifty-One.[3] At the end of February 1775, the Committee was impelled to assume new responsibilities when it became obvious that the Provincial Assembly would neither confirm the Association nor vote to send delegates to the Second Continental Congress. The Sixty agreed that they had no authority to select Congressional delegates and, on 1 March, called a meeting of the city's freemen and freeholders to consider the best method of choosing representatives. Conservatives opposed this measure, and on 3 March John Thurman chaired a meeting at Montagnie's tavern which adopted resolutions urging delay in selecting delegates. Broadsides cautioning against precipitate action soon appeared in the city.[4] Conservative warnings failed, and the freemen and freeholders, meeting on 6 March, issued a formal call for the election of delegates from the city to a provincial convention which would name the colony's delegates to Congress. This poll was taken on 15 March, and JJ was elected to the convention along with the other members of a slate endorsed by the Sixty. The next day, the Committee issued a circular letter to the counties, drafted by JJ, which set 20 April as the day for the convention's meeting and called on the other counties to send representatives.[5]

News of the division of opinion in New York soon reached other colonies. On 20 March the New York Committee received a letter from the Committee in New Haven. Although the New Haven letter has not been located, it was described in some detail by Alexander McDougall, JJ's colleague on the Sixty:

> A Letter from the Committee of New Haven, inclosing an anonymous Letter from New York to the Assembly of Connecticut, purporting the weakness of the friends of Liberty, the defection of our Assembly, this Letter, the advertisement from the meeting at Hulls, to chuse the old five Delegates, and the advertisement of 6th March to call the People to the Liberty Pole, previous to their going to the exchange; which contained J Thurmans declaration against chusing or trusting delegates.[6]

A few days after the arrival of the New Haven letter, JJ began work on a reply. In that same week, William Laight reported with disdain, "The Blues trumpet his [JJ's] merits and Patriotism at every corner of the Streets. He now applauds the zeal of McD[ougal]l, who once could see, that Ambition and Popularity was a motive to all his Actions; he now joins in every measure with that *Set,* who he formerly was convinced was all absurdity!" While Laight held out the hope that "He may *and 'tis the prayer of his friends* that he should, see his error,"[7] the defense of the record of the Committee of Sixty printed below shows that JJ had lost none of his determination to fight for the colony's rights.

1 William Laight to John Vardill, 27 March 1775, PRO: AO 13/105.

2 *Ibid.*

3 For an insightful account of the history of the Committee of Sixty, see Carl L. Becker, *N.Y. Political Parties,* pp. 167–92.

4 *Ibid.*, pp. 181–82.

5 Alexander McDougall's notes of the Committee meetings show that on 15 March "Mr Jay was directed to bring in a draught of a Circular Letter to the Counties," and that on 16 March, "Mr. Jay reported the draught of the Circular letter to the Counties, which was approved." NHi: McDougall Papers; the circular is printed in 4 *FAA,* II, 148–49.

6 Notes of Committee meeting, 20 March 1775, NHi: McDougall Papers. The "advertisements" for meetings mentioned in McDougall's description of the New Haven letter have not been located. These meetings are not mentioned in the N.Y. press in March 1775.

7 Laight to Vardill, 27 March 1775.

[The New York Committee of Sixty to the New Haven Committee]

[*New York, 17 April 1775*]

Gent[lemen]

<We have recieved your friendly> Your Letter of the 6th March Inst.[1] has been laid before the Committee. They have directed us to return you their Thanks for the Candor diffused through it and to assure you that the association has hitherto been rigidly adhered to except in the Instance of landing some goods from the Beulah by the Messrs. Murray's whose Case has been published And all Dealings with them have accordingly ceased.[2]

Notwithstanding a small Majority of our House of Assembly have taken no notice of the Proceedings of the Congress, the People in general are zealous in the Cause. A provincial Convention for the Appointment of Delegates will be held <next month> this week and this City and <the City and county of Albany> County and indeed <all the> almost all the principal Counties in the Province have already chosen their Deputies.

The anonymous Letter you have recieved contains many Misrepresentations, and in Times like these <we must expect them> Misrepresentation is too common to cause Surprize. It is the Interest of our Enemies to sow Jealousies and Dissentions among us and Nothing but mutual Confidence and a free and candid Intercourse <between us> with each other can prevent it.

The Beulah has very probably gone to Halifax but this was not in our Power to hinder. All we could do was to prevent her unloading here. For this Purpose a Subcommittee was appointed to watch her, at a very considerable Expence, and <have Reasons to> believe proved very useful.

In short we have no Reason to apprehend a Defection of this Colony, whose Inhabitants are as sensible of the Blessings of Liberty as any People on the Continent and are <will never consent to yield them to the Disposal of any Ministry whatever> too well apprized of the Importance of the present Union <of the Colonies not> to violate or destroy it.

Men there are among us, and such there are in every Colony, to whom a Defection would be an agreable Event, but happily for us this is not the Case with the Bulk of the People. At present little more is to be feared from this Class of Individuals than impotent Invective and illiberal Calumny.

We are Gent[lemen] with the greatest Respect your most obedient and humble Servants

Dft. Endorsed: "Dr. Letter from New York Com[mitte]e I think to that of Boston. 1775." Alexander McDougall's notes of Committee meetings make it clear that the draft was composed in reply to a letter from the New Haven Committee; the McDougall notes for 17 April 1775 contain this information: "Mr Jay reported an Answer to the Letter from the Committee of Connecticut, which inclosed an Anonymous Letter from that Body. The answer was approved." Alterations in the ms. show that JJ first prepared the letter in the last week of March, immediately after the receipt of the New Haven letter; he then revised it in the third week of April and submitted the draft to the Committee of Sixty. His description of a convention that would meet "next month" was changed to "this week" in the revision. The election of delegates from New York City "and the city and county of Albany" became "almost all the principal Counties in the Province." Albany's slate was chosen 21 March; no other county elected delegates before 6 April. NHi: McDougall Papers; Becker, N.Y. *Political Parties,* p. 188.

1 Letter not located.

2 Robert (1721–86) and John (1737–1808) Murray were prominent New York merchants who made one of the few attempts to circumvent the nonimportation Association at that port. Their vessel, the *Beulah,* arrived at New York on 9 February. Under the terms of the Association, the Murray brothers were obliged to reship the *Beulah's* cargo. A subcommittee of the Committee of Sixty kept the vessel under constant surveillance and accompanied the *Beulah* when she set sail on 6 March 1775. The subcommittee's boat was forced to return to shore off Sandy Hook, and part of the ship's cargo was loaded onto a smaller vessel and carried to Elizabethtown, N.J. This deception was discovered immediately, and the Murrays admitted their violation of the Association in a letter to the Committee of Sixty of 13 March. On 16 March, the Committee voted to publish the facts in accordance with the eleventh article of the Association. This article instructed committees enforcing the Association to "forthwith cause the truth of the case to be published in the Gazette" when they learned of violations. 4 *FAA,* II, 48, 144–8, 284; *JCC,* I, 79.

From Frederick Jay

New York, 11th May 1775

Dear John

Your letter of the 9th Inst.[1] just came to hand. The one Directed for Papa will go to Morrow. The Money I have Received by Mr. B. Livingston[2] amounting to £703:17:4 will be paid as directed this Day. Inclosed you have the Names of the Committee and Deputies chosen for the County of West Chester, Gill Drake elected Chairman.[3] Last Night Some People in disguise assembled at Rivingtons and at the Colledge in order to lay hands upon Cooper and the former. The latter is gone in Cooper (if report is to be Credited) who sailed this Day.[4] Inclosed you have a letter from Sir James. I hope you may have his directions about the Medicine he has already sent you.

Strang[5] informs me you have left some papers of Consiquence with him, and begs you would give him timely advice to remove the Same in case you apprehend any danger.

I left Rye on Tuesday, the Old Folks as usual. Peter says if you can sell his Horse to advantge you may do it.

Shall write you more at large by next Conveyance being in great haste.

Your affectionate Brother

FRED. JAY

ALS. Endorsed. Enclosure: list of Westchester committee and county delegates, in JP. At this time, JJ was en route to Philadelphia to take part in the Second Continental Congress, to which he had been elected by the New York Convention in April.

1 Letter not located.

2 Probably JJ's brother-in-law, Henry Brockholst Livingston (1757–1823), who was known as Brockholst.

3 The extralegal committees of New York were forced to expand their functions after news of the Battle of Lexington reached the City on 23 April 1775. Royal government in the province collapsed as mob violence raged for a week. The Committee of Sixty called for the election of a new committee with authority to exercise governmental functions in the city. This body, the Committee of One Hundred, was chosen on 1 May with JJ as a member. The Sixty also sent circular letters to the counties to urge elections for delegates to a Provincial Congress which could administer the affairs of the colony. On 8 May, a meeting for this purpose was held at White Plains. A Westchester County committee was named with Gilbert Drake of Eastchester as chairman. This committee, in turn, proposed eleven delegates to represent Westchester at the Provincial Congress, and this slate was ratified by the White Plains meeting.

4 Myles Cooper was a staunch supporter of the Government. On 10 May 1775 a mob marched on King's College to seize Cooper. According to tradition, it was Alexander Hamilton, a student at the College, who helped Cooper make his escape through a back door. On 25 May 1775, Cooper sailed for England and never returned to America. For diverse accounts of Cooper's rescue, see Nathan Schachner, "Alexander Hamilton Viewed by His Friends: The Narratives of Robert Troup and Hercules Mulligan," *WMQ*, 3rd ser., IV (April 1947), 211, 219. James Rivington (1724–1802) arrived in the colonies in 1760 and established a chain of bookstores in New York, Boston, and Philadlephia. In 1773 he began publication of a newspaper, *Rivington's New York Gazeteer,* and his editorial stands on imperial issues soon incurred the wrath of Patriots throughout the colonies.

5 John Strang (1751–1829), JJ's law clerk.

To Sarah Livingston Jay

Schoolkill, 23 May 1775

My Dear Sally

Your kind Letter of the 16th Instant[1] was delivered to me last Evening, it relieved me from much Sollicitude, and I take the earliest opportunity of thanking you for it.

If I am not mistaken you promised to be chearful and in Spirits. How comes it then that pensive Contemplation has become a favourite Companion? Forbear my dear Sally to put yourself in the Power of Fortune. In the many Changes of this mortal Life occurrences unfriendly to our wishes must be expected, and that Philosophy is worth cultivating which teaches us to meet the Frowns of the fickle Goddess with Composure. The Sensibility however from whence these Anxieties result is amiable, and tho I can never discharge the obligations I am under to your Tenderness and Attention, I should be happy indeed were it in my Power to contribute as much to your Happiness as you do to mine. I am much obliged to you for being so mindful of my good Mother. It would give me pleasure to hear of the Family. I have recieved one Letter from Fady. I am anxious about them, and most sincerely wish I could be more instrumental than I am to their Prosperity and Ease.

Have you heard any Thing yet of Mrs. Lows going to Bristol? Sally! this State of Separation presses hard upon me. God grant it may be of short Duration. Remember me to all the Family, and believe that I am and always will be

Your affectionate

JOHN JAY

ALS. JJ wrote from Philadelphia where he had arrived on 12 May to attend the Second Continental Congress. JJ joined the Congress on 13 May. *JCC*, II, 44.

[1] Letter not located.

From Peter Jay

Rye, 30 May 1775

Dear Johnny.

I have received your letter of the 20th inst.[1] I could heartily wish that the meeting of the Congress were at a less distance from hence, that we might sometimes have the pleasure of seeing you among us. Nothing remarkable offers here to entertain you with, only of my being credibly informed that about 1700 Inhabitants of this County have signed the Association,[2] and that the Companies of Militia have weekly their Military Exercises.

Mama's Complaints continue much in the same way as when you was here last, and my daily head ach is very troublesome to me. Mama lately received a letter from Sally, which She takes extremely

Kind, and this day I write to her. We all remember our love to you, and I ever am your Affectionate Father.

PETER JAY

P.S. Fady is still in Town. He was hindered from going out so soon as he intended. You have a likely Mare Colt, folded about a fortnight ago.

ALS. Endorsed.

[1] Letter not located.

[2] On 29 April 1775, the Committee of Sixty issued its General Association, a statement pledging allegiance to the acts of the Continental Congress and of the projected New York Provincial Congress. At the Westchester County meeting at White Plains on 8 May, the County committee also "signed an Association similar to that which was signed in the City of *New-York*, and appointed Sub-committees to superintend the signing of the same throughout the County." 4 *FAA*, II, 471, 529.

Jay's Draft of the "Olive Branch Petition"

When the Second Continental Congress convened on 10 May 1775, JJ assumed a prominent role as a leader of the moderate faction. Here his legal training and literary skill made him a frequent choice for Congress's numerous committees. On 26 May he was appointed to the three-man committee charged with a major propaganda project: the preparation of a letter urging the Roman Catholics of Canada to join their Protestant neighbors against their mutual enemy. Although JJ had earlier played on anti-Catholic sentiment in his "Address to the People of Great-Britain," he now assumed a more ecumenical attitude and drafted the letter to the French Canadians.[1] There was perhaps less ambiguity in his work on the committee named to advise the Massachusetts convention on that province's affairs. JJ joined his fellow committeemen in urging the Bay Colony to repudiate the authority of her royal governor.[2]

Throughout these weeks, however, JJ opposed a final break with England. He demonstrated his commitment to keeping open channels for reconciliation by his fight for the adoption of a petition to the king from the Second Congress. By the spring of 1775, a number of conciliatory moves had been initiated in the form of petitions to the king and memorials to Lords and Commons. On 26 October 1774, the First Continental Congress had adopted a "loyal address" to his majesty to which the king declined to reply.[3] On 25 March 1775, the Tory-controlled New York Assembly petitioned the king and memorialized the two Houses of Parliament.[4]

Opinion was gaining ground that any further conciliatory moves would prove fruitless. On 11 May 1775 Congress heard reports from colonial agents in London that Parliament had not only virtually ignored Congress's petition, but that the ministry had announced its intention of enforcing Parliamentary acts in the colonies and had deployed troops to that end.[5] Thus it may have been with some sense of desperation that the conciliatory party in Congress, centering on JJ, James Duane, and John Dickinson (1732–1808) of Pennsylvania, pressed for one last petition to the king.

Since most of the proceedings of Congress in May 1775 were conducted as "the committee of the whole," there are no detailed official records of their debates on the question of submitting another petition. Most delegates observed the injunction of secrecy and left few informal notes of Congressional activities in the period. Contemporary records offer only a rough chronological outline of the events which led to the "Olive Branch Petition."

On 15 May the New York delegates submitted the New York Committee's request for guidance in case of a rumored British landing in the city. Congress advised the colonists to pursue defensive measures only, although conceding the need to "repel force by force" if a direct threat were offered.[6] JJ and his fellow New York delegates softened this injunction even further when they sent the resolutions home with a covering letter warning that the "Military Stores" which Congress suggested be removed were not to include crown property.[7] That same day a committee was named to consider what posts in New York should be occupied and what troops should be stationed in the province. The committee included George Washington, Thomas Lynch (1727–76) of South Carolina, Samuel Adams (1722–1803), and the New York delegation. The committee reported on 19 May, and this report was immediately referred to the committee of the whole.[8] On 25 May the committee of the whole reported its findings on the defense of New York to the Congress. After the resolutions had been read, the *JCC* records, "A motion being made for an addition to the foregoing Resolutions, [a debate arose thereon and] after some debate the same was referred till to Morrow, to which time Congress adjourned."[9]

On the morrow, 26 May, several crucial decisions were made. First, Congress received a letter from the New Jersey Assembly which enclosed a copy of Lord North's conciliation motion of 20 February. Debate then resumed on the "addition" to the resolutions on New York's defenses, and this "addition," as adopted, read: "Resolved, that it be recommended to the Congress aforesaid [New York] to persevere the more vigorously in preparing for their defence, as it is very uncertain whether the earnest endeavours of the Congress to accommodate the unhappy differences between G. Britain and the colonies by conciliatory Measures will be successful."[10] Congress then went into the committee of the whole and later resumed regular proceedings. Four resolutions were reported back to Congress: the first two recognized the need to put the provinces in a state of defense while the third authorized the adoption of a petition to the king, and the fourth expressed the colonists' readiness to negotiate the issue in dispute.[11]

On 3 June, a committee was named to draft the petition authorized on 26 May. JJ, Dickinson, Benjamin Franklin, Thomas Johnson (1732–1819) of Maryland, and John Rutledge (1739–1800) of South Carolina were appointed, giving the group a rather conservative coloration.[12] The committee submitted its draft report, the work of John Dickinson, on 19 June, and the petition was adopted by Congress on 5 July.[13]

JJ's part in persuading Congress to adopt this measure is universally acknowledged, but the substance of his contribution has hitherto remained obscure. George Bancroft linked JJ's role to the Congressional resolutions of 15 May which advised restraint to the inhabitants of New York in case of a British landing. Without citing sources, Bancroft concluded: "All parties tacitly agreed to avoid every decision which should invite attack or make reconciliation impossible. In conformity with this policy, Jay made the motion for a second petition to the king."[14] JJ's son and biographer, William Jay, who usually relied on his father's personal recollections for such assessments of JJ's career, stated: "This measure [the petition] originated with Mr. Jay, and was carried by him against a very strong opposition in Congress."[15] A later biographer asserts: "On June third Jay moved that a second petition be sent to the King; Dickinson seconded the motion."[16] The *JCC* does not identify the delegates who offered motions on the petition to the king in May and June 1775; while JJ obviously deserves credit for aiding in the fight to authorize the petition, it is impossible to pinpoint his specific contributions on the floor of Congress.

There is, however, new evidence concerning JJ's work in the committee appointed on 3 June to draft the petition to the king. Among the Dickinson Papers at the Library Company of Philadelphia there is a preliminary draft of that petition in JJ's hand.[17] Although the authorship of the final draft of what became known as the Olive Branch Petition is indisputably John Dickinson's, the presence of the JJ draft in the Dickinson Papers makes it clear that Dickinson examined JJ's version while preparing his own text. The remnant of Dickinson's first draft of the petition[18] reveals a concilitatory tone similar to JJ's. Both criticize the change in imperial administration since the Seven Years' War. JJ adverts to the colonial administration of the past dozen years while the Dickinson draft mentions "the new system of statutes and regulations." If all of Dickinson's first draft were extant, further similarities to JJ's draft might be found.

Such similarities are not surprising since many of the ideas embodied in JJ's draft had been bruited about for some time, and there are at least two specific sources which both JJ and Dickinson may have tapped. There was, for instance, the Petition to the King adopted by the New York

Assembly on 25 March 1775. Therein the Tory-controlled body professed inviolable attachment to the king, disavowed independence as an objective, denied Parliament's right of taxation without the consent of the colonists "or their lawful representatives," questioned the constitutionality of some of the laws passed since 1764, and sought the king's "merciful mediation and interposition." Significantly, the New York legislature, in a simultaneous petition to the Commons, demanded exemption from "internal taxation."[19] Another possible source of New York opinion which might well have influenced JJ and Dickinson was the neutralist William Smith, Jr., the colony's Chief Justice and member of the Provincial Council. On 5 June 1775, Smith sent a letter to Lewis Morris, a member of the New York delegation to the Continental Congress, advising that a conciliatory message be sent to the king.[20] Since the Dickinson draft was not reported from committee until 19 June, there would have been ample time to consider the suggestions embodied in the letter which Morris might well have brought to the attention of JJ, if not of Dickinson as well.

In terms of JJ's own draft, with its implicit concessions, it is perhaps significant that Smith's letter criticized the First Continental Congress for denying "the *whole Legislative* Authority of Great Britain," and asserted, "The Colonies *formerly,* and Ireland *now* give Proof from actual Experiment, that Great Britain may possess a useful Supremacy, without the Exercise of a Taxing Power." Taking exception to the Whig argument that the "*Taxing and Legislative Powers* are inseparable Concomitants," Smith refused to accept the logic of the conclusion that a refutation of a right to taxation implied denying a right of legislation. One may compare Smith's argument with JJ's concession to Parliament of the right to regulate commerce. One may also discover a few perhaps coincidental parallels of phraseology between the Smith letter and the final draft of the Olive Branch Petition. Smith admonished that not a word be said "about Rights."[21] Dickinson in a letter to Arthur Lee of 7 July stated: "You will perhaps at first be surpriz'd, that we made no *Claim,* and mention no *Right.*"[22]

Speculation over shared sources and similarities in phrasing is less useful, however, than an inspection of the differences between JJ's draft and Dickinson's final version of the Olive Branch Petition. Such differences far outnumber any similarities, and the nature of the dissimilarities is vital. JJ asked that "every irritating measure be suspended." Dickinson went beyond that and proposed the repeal of distasteful statutes.[23] JJ, with his fondness for commissions, proposed that George III "commission some good and great Men to enquire into the Grievances of her [England's] faithful subjects." Dickinson, sidestepping a concrete plan, asked only that "your Majesty be pleased to direct some mode by which the united application of your faithful colonists to the throne . . . be improved into a happy and permanent Reconciliation."[24] The final version carefully avoided that explicit disavowal of independence as an end which

JJ's draft incautiously includes, nor does one find in the former that admission of the legality of the acts of Parliament regulating trade that JJ was prepared to concede. Dickinson, with both prescience and prudence, chose not to follow JJ's lead in suggesting that negotiations might be conducted with the colonial assemblies should the royal government prefer not to deal with Congress. Nonetheless, Dickinson arranged that the petition be signed by the delegates as individuals, with even John Hancock signing as an individual rather than as President of Congress, to offset the fact that it was adopted in a general Congress. Retrospectively, Jefferson tells us that following the approval of the petition, Dickinson remarked: "There is but one word, Mr. President, in the paper which I disapprove, and that is the word *Congress.*" Benjamin Harrison (1740–91) of Virginia immediately retorted: "There is but one word in the paper, Mr. President, of which I approve, and that is the word *Congress.*"[25] Instead of incorporating JJ's proposal for a new compact of the empire, a far-reaching and advanced notion indeed, the final draft merely speaks of "a concord" on a firm basis.[26]

In short, Dickinson's final draft scrupulously avoided ruffling the sensibilities of Congress or making injudicious and even unnecessary admissions or concessions. In view of the heated opposition in Congress to so watered-down a version as the final Olive Branch Petition, it is obvious that JJ's draft would never have been adopted.[27]

1 "Address to the People of Great-Britain," 21 Oct. 1774, *JCC*, I, 82–90; for JJ's appointment to the committee on the letter to Canada and his draft, "To the oppressed Inhabitants of Canada," see *JCC*, II, 64, 68–70.

2 *JCC*, II, 79, 81, 83–85.

3 *Ibid.*, I, 115–21; see also Edwin Wolf 2nd, "The Authorship of the 1774 Petition to the King Restudied," *WMQ*, XXII (April, 1965), 189–224.

4 4 *FAA*, I, 1313–22.

5 *JCC*, II, 22–23.

6 *Ibid.*, 52.

7 N.Y. Delegates to the N.Y. Committee of Safety, 16 May 1775, *LMCC*, I, 91.

8 *JCC*, II, 53, 57.

9 *Ibid.*, 59–61.

10 *Ibid.*, 64.

11 *Ibid.*, 65–66.

12 *Ibid.*, 79–80.

13 *Ibid.*, 127.

14 George Bancroft, *History of the United States of America, From the Discovery of the Continent . . . the Author's Last Revision* (New York, 1892), IV, 192.

15 *WJ*, I, 45.

16 Frank Monaghan, *John Jay* (New York and Indianapolis, 1935), p. 70.

17 This undated draft, on four quarto pages, is now on deposit at PHi. The editors are grateful to the Library Company of Philadelphia and to the Historical Society of Pennsylvania for their permission to reproduce this draft, below.

18 This fragment of Dickinson's draft is in PHi: Robert R. Logan Papers.

19 4 *FAA*, I, 1313–16, 1319.

20 William Smith, *Memoirs,* I, 228–228c.
21 *Loc. cit.*
22 *LMCC,* I, 157.
23 *JCC,* II, 161.
24 *Ibid.,* 161.
25 *LMCC,* I, 158n.
26 *JCC,* II, 160.
27 For an account of the opposition to the petition, see John Adams, *Diary,* III, 313–21.

JOHN JAY: "TO THE KINGS MOST EXCELLENT MAJESTY"

[*Philadelphia, 3–19 June 1775*]

The <Peti Humb> Petition of the freeholders and Freemen of the Colonies of New Hampshire, Massachuset Bay, Rhode Island, Connecticut, New York, New Jersey, Pensylvania, the <Government of > <on> Delaware, Maryland, Virginia, North Carolina, South Carolina and the Parish of St. Johns in the Colony of Georgia by their Representatives convened in general Congress at the City of Philadelphia the Day of 1775

Most humbly sheweth

That your Majestys American Subjects bound to your Majesty by the strongest Ties of Allegiance and affection and attached to their Parent Country by every Bond that can unite Societies, deplore with the deepest Concern the continuance of that System of colonial Administration which <for twelve Years past has been drawing the Strength the Glory> for twelve Years past has <been drawing the British Empire to the Brink> Verge <of Desperation given so much has given Alarm and Disquiet to> filled the minds of the loyal Inhabitants of North America with <the most alarming> apprehensions of the most alarming Nature

That reposing the utmost Confidence in the <Justice of> paternal Care of their Prince and the Justice of the British Nation they were <compelled to by> urged by the perilous Situation of their Liberties to sollicit <by their late Peti> his Majestys Attention by their late Petition[1] to their real and unmerited Greivances, and to request his royal Interposition in their Behalf

That <deceived> tho disappointed in their Expectations of Relief they still remember their Duty to their Sovereign, and imputing the Rigour of their Treatment to <such> invidious Counsel and wicked Misrepresentation, they again beg Leave to entreat for Justice and to request only that Portion of Liberty to which God and the Constitution have given them Right.

<They> That nothing but the overruling Laws of self Preservation could ever have induced them to pursue any Measures which might <seem> be deemed offensive to their King or disrespectful to the British Nation, and that they ardently desire an opportunity of manifesting their Fidelity to the one and <th> evincing their Affection for the other.

That neither repeated Oppression nor all the miseries <of> which attend the sword or are threatened by Famine have yet weaned them from their Parent Country, and that they cannot yet cease to seek by every dutiful and peaceable Means in their Power to obtain a Restoration of that Harmony which Formerly gave union Wealth and Power to the Empire

That they most earnestly beseech his Majesty to commission some good and great Men to inquire into the Grievances and <examine the> of her faithful Subjects, and be pleased to devise some Means of accommodating those unhappy Dissentions which unless amicably terminated must endanger the safety of the whole Empire. And that, should his Majesty not be disposed to hear the Complaints of his American Subjects from their Representatives in Congress [they] most humbly beseech his Majesty to direct <that> Com[mitte]e from their different Assemblies <should assemble> to convene for the Purpose

That altho the People of North America are determined to be free they wish not to be independent and beg Leave again to assure his Majesty that they mean not to question the Right of the British Parliament to regulate the Commercial Concerns of the Empire in the Manner they have before declared as their Enemies have unkindly insinuated and to remove all Doubts upon this Head are ready to confirm these Declarations by Acts of their Legislatures in the different Colonies

That <to facilitate the Restoration of Union and Harmony> they <beg Leave to> most humbly submit it to his Majestys wisdom [whether] it would not tend to facilitate the Restoration of Union and Harmony th[at] <all> the further Effusion of Blood should <not> be preve[nted] and <that> every irritating <and> Measure <be> suspended and should his Majesty be graciously pleased by his royal Interposition to relieve his faithful Subjects from the Uneasiness and anxiety they feel from the several acts of the british Parliament <of> by which they think themselves so greatly agreived, they will with the utmost Gratitude and Chearfulness return to and resume that former Intercourse with <Great Britain> their parent State which Nothing but the most pressing Necessities could ever induce them to interrupt

They also take the Liberty of suggesting that when concord and mutual Confidence <and good will> shall then be re-established between his Majesty's British and American Subjects, their several Claims may be <adju> examined with <Candor> <more> Temper adjusted with Precision and the present unnatural Contest end in a Compact that may place the Union of the Empire on a firm and permanent Basis

Dft. PPL: John Dickinson Papers (at PHi).
[1] The petition of 26 Oct. 1774, *JCC*, I, 115–21.

To Sarah Livingston Jay

Philadelphia, 22 *June* 1775

At Length my dear Sally an opportunity offers of writing to You, and I assure you it gives me Pleasure to embrace it, not merely because every occasion of testifying my Affection conduces to my Happiness, but from the pleasing Reflection that it always affords you Satisfaction to hear of my Welfare.

I arrived here the Day after I left you, but in better Health than Spirits. The Anxiety you expressed at my Departure added to the disagreable Situation in which I left the Family at Rye, conspired with the Reflection of being absent from you, in diminishing that Chearfulness which I could wish ever to possess. However I am again reconciled or rather resigned to my Situation, and tho I cannot enjoy all I could wish, it is nevertheless no little Consolation to me to think that I enjoy abundantly more than I deserve, and that my Portion of Happiness far exceeds the common Lott of mankind.

I am anxious to hear from you. Pray omit no opportunity of favouring me with a Letter. In this however be entirely directed by your Convenience.

Let me entreat you to be careful of yourself, and endeavour to acquire that Tranquility and Composure so conducive to Health as well as Happiness.

Believe me my dear Sally, to be your very affectionate

JOHN JAY

ALS.

New York Provincial Congress to New York Delegates

In Provincial Congress, New York, June 29th, 1775

Gentlemen

Deeply impressed with the Importance, the Utility and necessity of an Accomodation with our Parent State and conscious that the best Service we can render to the present and all future Generations, must consist in promoting it; We have laboured without Intermission to point out such moderate Terms as may tend to reconcile the unhappy Difference which threaten the whole Empire with Destruction.

We now take the Liberty of inclosing to you the Result of our Deliberations,[1] and although we have not the presumption to suppose that our Weak Ideas on this momentuous Subject will be entirely approved of by you, much less by that august Body of which You are Members; Yet we take leave to observe that the breach hath been much widened since our first Dispute on the Subject of Taxation, and that as this was the Source of all our Grievances, so we have the hope, that the Temptations being taken away, our Civil and Religious and Political Rights will be easily adjusted and Confirmed.

You will observe Gentlemen that by a Resolution of the House subjoined to the Report of our Committee, We consider the whole as entirely subjected to your better Judgment, and each Article as far independent of every other, as You may think most proper or convenient.[2] We must now repeat to You, the common and just Observation that Contests for Liberty, fostered in their Infancy by the Virtuous and Wise, become Sources of Power to wicked and designing Men. From whence it follows that such Controversies as we are now engaged in frequently end in the Demolition of those Rights and Priviledges which they were instituted to defend. We pray You therefore to use every Effort for the Compromising of this unnatural Quarrel between the Parent and Child; and if such Terms as You may think best shall not be complied with, earnestly to labour, that at least some Terms may be held up, whereby a Treaty shall be set on foot, to restore Peace and Harmony to our Country, and spare the further Effusion of human Blood, So that if even at the last our well meant Endeavors shall fail to Effect, We may stand fair, and unreproachable by our own Consciences, in the last solemn Appeal to the God of Battles.

We are Gentlemen Your most Obedient and humble Servants

By order

P. V. B. LIVINGSTON PRESIDENT[3]

LS. NHi: Duane Papers. Addressed: "To the New York Delegates in Continental Congress." Enclosure: Plan of Accommodation of the New York Provincial Congress, 27 June 1775, printed in *JPC*, I, 58, under date of 28 June. A draft of this letter to the delegates was adopted on 28 June, and directions were given that two copies of the letter be signed by the President of the Provincial Congress; one copy was to be dispatched by express to Philadelphia on 29 June, while the other was to be carried to the Continental Congress by Francis Lewis, one of the colony's delegates. *Ibid.*, 59.

1 On 2 June 1775, the Provincial Congress named fourteen members to a committee to draft a "plan of accommodation" between Britain and the colonies. This committee reported its draft plan on 24 June, and debates on the proposal began that day and concluded on 27 June when the amended plan was adopted. For details of the revisions made in the draft during debate, see below, Gouverneur Morris to JJ, 30 June 1775. *JPC*, I, 26, 52–54, 58.

2 The concluding paragraph read: "*Resolved*, that no one article of the aforegoing report be considered preliminary to another, so as to preclude an accommodation without such article, and that no part of the said report be deemed binding or obligatory upon the Representatives of this Colony in Continental Congress."

3 Peter Van Brugh Livingston (1710–92), Sarah Livingston Jay's uncle, was a prominent New York merchant.

From Gouverneur Morris

New York, 30th June 1775

My dear Sir,

Our House are about to send you their Plan of Accomodation and I think Myself bound to say Something on the Subject for Reasons you will presently see. The second, third, fourth, sixth, seventh and eighth Articles form a short Plan which I drew in the Committee excepting that in the eighth the word Assemblies in the third Line was altered to Colonies.[1] The first Article was moved, debated, altered, amended and finally left as it is in the Committee. So was the fifth. The ninth foolish Religious Business I opposed untill I was weary. It was carried by a very small Majority and my Dissent entered.[2] The tenth I did not like but however it is in and the Resolution I moved and it was unanimously carried.[3] I forgot to mention that the second Article as I drew it stood thus: "That from the Necessity of the Case Britain ought to regulate the Trade of the whole Empire."[4] Now then my Reasons on this Occasion are these. The Article for triennial Assemblies, the first Article in the gross as it stands, and what relates to the Security of our own Legislature I think may work a Rejection of the Plan at Home. Particularly the last may raise an Idea that Britain has some Right to the Power of altering Colony Constitutions which is in American Politicks a most damnable Position. The Article about Religion is most arrant Nonsense and would do as well in a high Dutch Bible as the Place it now stands in. Our Letter to you on this Subject which tho drawn by myself was unanimously and literally assented to will shew you how strongly we are of Opinion that the Dispute ought to be simplified and every reasonable Man will be of Opinion that provided our essential Rights be secured on solid Foundations we may safely permit the British Parliament to use big sounding Words.

I drew a long Report for our Committee to which they could make no Objections excepting that none of them could understand it, one or two excepted who attacked it by Piece Meal but were afraid of the Principles because they could not meet them and the Mob of us were fearful of extensive Novelties. If I have time I will send you a Copy. But I was pleased at the Rejection because as I observed to you before I think the Question ought to be simplified. I address this Letter to you but I shall be glad you will send it to Livingston[5] for I intend it for both of you. Make my Compliments to him and tell him that I shall write to him when I have Leisure to write a good Letter. This is a damned bad one and would not exist if I did not think it a Duty to myself to shew my Friends that I had no Hand in that foolish religious Business.

I am as you well know, your Friend

GOUV. MORRIS

ALS. Addressed: "To John Jay Esqr. Philadelphia." Endorsed: ". . . abt. Plan of Reconciliation etc. answ." JJ's reply has not been located. Gouverneur Morris (1752–1816), a graduate of King's College (1768) and member of the New York Bar, was one of Westchester County's representatives in the First Provincial Congress.

1 Morris was a member of the committee which reported the draft plan of accommodation to the Provincial Congress on 24 June 1775. As printed in *JPC*, I, 58, the final version of the plan is divided into eight paragraphs followed by the explanatory resolution. The five articles to which Morris refers comprise the second, third, fifth, and sixth paragraphs as published in *JPC*. The second provided for British regulation of Empire trade for the "general benefit of the whole," while reserving the powers of taxation to the respective colonial legislatures. Subsequent paragraphs went on to avow the colonies' willingness to support civil government in the provinces and to "assist in the general defence of the Empire." The concluding articles suggested that the grants of such "general aids" from the colonies should be coordinated by a Continental Congress in consultation with a "President appointed by the Crown." This latter proposal, in article eight, had originally described "a Continental Congress deputed from the several Assemblies": the Congress voted to substitute "Colonies" for "Assemblies" in this phrase. *Ibid.*, 53.

2 The first article of the plan called for the repeal of the parliamentary statutes cited in the Continental Association of October 1774, as well as of any later statutes "restraining the trade and fishery of Colonies on this Continent." The fifth article (the fourth paragraph in the version printed in *JPC*) called for the triennial election of provincial legislatures.

The draft plan submitted by the committee on 24 June contained no article on religion. Melancton Smith of Dutchess County proposed an addition declaring: "And as the free enjoyment of the rights of conscience is, of all others the most valuable branch of human liberty, and the indulgence and establishment of Popery all along the interior confines of the old Protestant Colonies, tends not only to obstruct their growth, but to weaken their security; all concerns of a religious and ecclesiastical nature, so far as they may be under the cognizance and controul of civil authority, ought to remain exclusively with the respective Colony Legislatures as the most inestimable object of their internal police." The Congress approved Thomas Smith's suggestion that all of this article after "their security" be struck out and substituted Smith's addition: "That the Parliament of Great Britain cannot constitutionally or of right interfere or interpose in any wise howsoever in the religious and ecclesiastical concerns of the Colonies." Morris then proposed amendments which gave the second clause of the religious article its final wording: "that neither the Parliament of Great Britain, or any other earthly legislature or tribunal, ought or can interfere or interpose in any wise howsoever, in the religious and ecclesiastical concerns of the Colonies." The final text was adopted by a vote of 18 to 9, with Morris's dissent from the vote of Westchester County entered on the record. *Ibid.*, 53–54.

3 The tenth article (paragraph eight as published in *JPC*), was introduced by John Morin Scott on 27 June. It declared: "That the Colonies, respectively, are entitled to a free and exclusive power of legislation within themselves respectively, in all cases of internal polity whatsoever, subject only to the negative of their Sovereign in such manner as has been heretofore accustomed." The explanatory resolution is that quoted above, Provincial Congress to JJ, 29 June 1775, note 2. *Ibid.*, 58.

4 On 27 June, the Provincial Congress adopted John Morin Scott's proposed addition to Morris's original proviso on imperial taxation: "For the general benefit of the whole, and not for the separate interest of any particular part." *Ibid.*

5 Two members of the Livingston family, Philip and Robert R., Jr., served in the New York delegation to the Continental Congress in June 1775. This reference is to Robert R. Livingston, Jr., also a close friend of Morris.

From Robert R. Livingston, Jr

Bellvedere, 17th July 1775

Dear John

I take the opportunity of Bensons[1] going to New York to let you know what pleasure I should receive in hearing from [you] by the return of the Post, since Benson will return in a few days and deliver safely any Letter you may enclose him and I shall wait here till you think that it is necessary I should come to you.

I must confess that after breathing the pure air of the country I dread the Idea of a hot room at Philadelphia.

I am sorrey to say that the spirit of toryism is far far from being subdued in this province. One Liester is very active in Dutches County, and has got several signers to a counter Assotiation. How far it might be proper to apprehend him I leave to your judgment.[2] For my own part I dread a division among our selves infinitely more than the power of Great Britain. It may not however be improper to mention to you that there is one Volune[3] (or some such name) a young lad who pretends to have escaped from the Man of War. He is what they call a candidate for the ministry, and is now gone either to New York or Philadelphia to be ordained, he preaches both in high dutch and english the most violent Tory sermons, prays for success to the Kings Armies and has hyems [*sic*] composed for the purpose. As the Germans are extreamly ignorant and much attatched to him he will do an infinite deal of mischief if he is not prevented.

I told you some time before I left you that many of our Tenants have refused to sign the assotiation,[4] and resolved to stand by the King as they called it, in hopes that if he succeeded they should have their Lands. Since troops have been raised in the province and two of my Brothers have got comissions[5] they have been frighted and changed their battery in order to excuse themselves assert that they can not engage in the controversy since as their leases are for lives their families must want when they are killed. Tho this is common to them and every other man whose family is supported by his labour, yet to deprive them of all excuse, my father has declared to them that a new lease shall be given to the family of every man who is killed in the service and Mr. Livingston has come to the same resolution. Notwithstanding which the scoundrels have as we were informed sent in a petition to the congress replete with falsehoods and charges injurious to the memory of My Grandfather and Mr. Livingston.[6] I should be glad to hear the particulars. My father has made them a general offer that if any man of reputation appointed by the congress or any other way can shew a single instance of injustice he will repay it threefold. You who know the levity of his disposition and the extream low rents (not equal to one per Cent on the value) of the Lands, will take care to set this matter right if such petition should be presented you, and at the same time use some prety strong language to intimidate fellows who act on no principle but fear, and will if they meet with the least encouragement throw the whole country into confusion.

I wish exceedingly to hear what you are about, and how long you expect to stay at Philadelphia. For my own part I can not help thinking no place can be worse chosen on every account. Many advantages would attend your removal nearer to the scene of action the center of which would I conceive at present be Albany since the conduct of the Canada expedition[7] will be of the utmost importance and require your most constant attention. Besides that you will by that means be 180 nearer to Boston than you now are. But a reason that weighs much with me is one that we can not mention: the necessity of a serious regard to the affairs of our own province. I suppose you have by this time been applied to about giving leave to sell tea.[8] I wish something could be done in that matter to relieve some of the truest friends to liberty who will otherwise be ruined and the laws of the Congress brought into contempt by an open violation of them. And Pray let me hear from you immediately after this comes to hand for fear Benson should leave town before he receives your answer, and by that means my pleasure be delayed and I myself prevented from coming to you since I am resolved to wait for your answer to this. I am Dear John Yours most sincerely

ROBT R. LIVINGSTON JUNR.

ALS. Addressed: "To John Jay Esqr at Philadelphia." Endorsed. Livingston wrote from his country home, Belvedere, near Clermont. Livingston took his seat as a New York delegate to the Second Continental Congress on 15 May 1775 and attended as late as 8 July.

1 Egbert Benson.

2 On 26 May 1775 the New York Provincial Congress adopted a General Association based upon the Association promulgated by the New York Committee in April. On 29 May the Provincial Congress sent circular letters to the counties recommending the appointment of local committees and the circulation of the Association for signatures.

Several men in Dutchess County with names spelled variously Lester, Liester, and Luyster were Tory sympathizers who refused to sign the Association in June and July 1775. The Tory mentioned here may have been Mordecai Lester who was cited by the New York Committee of Safety in September 1775 on charges of having recruited men to fight for the crown and having purchased supplies for the British. *JPC*, I, 5, 18, 29, 138.

3 "Volune" has not been identified.

4 For the names of those who refused to sign the Association in Dutchess County, see *Cal. of Hist. Mss.*, I, 67–85.

5 John R. Livingston (1755–1851) and Henry Beekman Livingston (1750–1831) were appointed captains in the 4th New York Regiment at the end of June 1775. *Ibid.*, II, 41.

6 Livingston's grandfather, Robert Livingston of Clermont, was the uncle of "Mr. Livingston," Robert Livingston, the third lord of Livingston Manor. His father was Judge Robert R. Livingston, Sr. No petitions from the Livingston tenants to the Continental Congress have been located.

7 Maj. Gen. Philip Schuyler (1733–1804), commander of the Northern Department for the Continental troops, was instructed to invade Canada and to seize points required for the security of the colonies on 27 June 1775. Schuyler began his march from Ticonderoga to Canada on 28 Aug.

8 See below, Nathaniel Woodhull to New York Delegates in Congress, 1 Sept. 1775, editorial note.

FROM GOUVERNEUR MORRIS

New York, 28th July 1775

Dear Sir

What shall we do with our Westchester Causes.[1] I have not hitherto given you any Notices of Trial because the Uncertainty and Inquietude of the Times in some Measure prohibited me the Hope of trying them. Besides this I daily expected you in Town and wished for the Certainty of your Presence inasmuch as it would have been an improper Advantage over you while attending upon the public Business. It would give me Pleasure to hear from you on any Subject but especially on this as I must notice and try at least one of these Causes for Reasons which will certainly strike your Mind. At the same Time observe that I do not mean to be non suited for a Negligence which is only on my Word to be attributed to the Causes I have already declared to you. Nor do I expect that you will make use of the Advantage you have in my not giving you a Term's Notice. But you must send me an Answer on these Subjects and let me know whether you expect to be at Home or if not that you will write to Sam Jones[2] on the Subject. I am in immense Haste your Friend

GOUVR. MORRIS

ALS. Addressed: "John Jay Esqr. Philadelphia." Endorsed: ". . . answd."

1 Public responsibilities prevented both Gouverneur Morris and JJ from giving attention to their legal practices during the spring and early summer of 1775. Morris attended the Provincial Congress in New York City almost daily between 22 May and 28 July. JJ was preoccupied for an even longer time, busying himself in New York City with the affairs of the Committee of 100 from 1 May until he left for Philadelphia, when he sat in the Continental Congress from 12 May through 2 August.

2 Samuel Jones (1734–1819) was a Queens County lawyer.

TO GOUVERNEUR MORRIS

[*Elizabethtown, August 1775*]

Dear Morris

I have recieved your Letter of the 28th Ult. and taking the earliest opportunity which has offered of answering it. The Principles on which you account for having delayed Notices of Tryal on the WestChester Causes merit my Acknowledgment.

You need be under no Apprehension of non Suits in case you should prevail upon yourself to postpone the Tryal which I confess I cant forbear wishing may be the Case, tho it does not appear to me altogether reasonable to request it.

As to the omission of a Terms Notice, I beg you will be perfectly easy. Be assured that my Conduct towards you on this as well as all other occasions will be such as Friendship may dictate and approve.

The Person who is to be the bearer of this, is about setting off. I must therefore conclude without adding any Thing except to request that you will let me hear from you soon and often, and to assure you that I am etc.

J. J.

DftS.

Operating Under the Continental-Wide Boycott

By the late summer and early fall of 1775 the regulation of American trade under the Association of the previous year preempted a heavy share of debating time in Congress. According to the terms of the Association, imports from Great Britain and Ireland were to cease after 1 December 1774, while exportation of goods from the colonies was to end in September 1775.[1] The problems of establishing a system of enforcing nonexportation were complicated by the passage of Parliament's Restraining Acts in March and April 1775.[2] On 12 July 1775, JJ was named to the committee charged with devising "ways and means to protect the trade of the colonies." This committee reported on 21 July, but no action was taken on the problem before Congress adjourned for five weeks on 1 August.[3]

This adjournment delayed action on a trade issue of special interest to JJ's constituents in New York. While the Association had forbidden the importation of any English goods after 1 December 1774, the agreement placed special restrictions on East India tea. Tea belonging to the East India Company could neither be imported into the colonies nor used or purchased in the provinces after 1 December 1774. No tea whatever was to be sold or used in the American colonies after 1 March 1775.[4] Thus New York merchants trading with the Dutch were left with large quantities of tea which they could not sell under the terms of the Association.

At the end of July 1775, Congress received appeals to relax the prohibition on the tea trade. On 28 July, the New York Provincial Congress wrote the colony's delegates to propose a plan for new regulations on this commodity: merchants who had imported tea from Holland would be allowed to sell their stocks at a fixed price determined by the Provincial Congress, with a tax of one shilling per pound, to provide the province with revenue, give merchants relief, and allow those who traded with

Holland to use the proceeds of the sales to import military supplies from the United Provinces. An additional virtue of the proposal, as the Provincial Congress saw it, was that it would remove any "temptation to a clandestine trade."[5] On 31 July the Continental Congress heard petitions from the merchants of New York and Philadelphia who sought permission to sell their stores of tea.[6] No action was taken on this matter before the Congressional adjournment.

The New York Congress sat through August without any word on the question of tea. On 1 September, the day before the provincial body was to adjourn,[7] another appeal went out to the colony's delegation in Philadelphia, which is printed below. For the ultimate adverse response of Congress to the New York petition, see JJ to McDougall, 4 December.

The question of trade policy, left unsettled before the August adjournment, demanded Congress's attention when sessions resumed in September 1775. On 22 September, JJ was named to a new committee charged with considering American commerce. The committee report, in JJ's hand, was submitted on 2 October. Basically this report merely recommended continuing the "regulations respecting Imports and Exports" imposed by the First and Second Congresses. Some modifications were suggested for allowing trade that would bring scarce commodities like salt, and other sections looked toward the encouragement of "internal Commerce."[8] However, JJ's report did not touch on the central issue of whether those colonies not mentioned in the Restraining Acts should be allowed to carry on trade denied to the provinces cited by Parliament.

Debate on the trade resolutions ran from 2 to 5 October and was resumed a week later, continuing to the end of the month. Discussion eventually narrowed down to the question of shutting customs houses in all provinces to "remove jealousies and divisions" between those affected by the Restraining Acts and those which were still free of such restrictions.[9] The delegates weighed the wisdom of this procedure, which would have shut all provincial ports, as well as JJ's proposal that the colonies channel their trade through those ports which were still free of the Restraining Acts. JJ, opposing Richard Henry Lee's motion that all customs houses be shut down, reminded his colleagues that he had always opposed nonexportation and argued that closing the customs houses "should be the last business we undertake." He compared closing the available ports to "cutting the foot to the shoe, not making a shoe for the foot." "Let us," he urged, "establish a system first," and deemed it as foolhardy as making the right arm sore because the left arm was. Just "because the Enemy have burned Charleston," he queried sarcastically, "would Gentlemen have Us burn New York."[10]

While the provinces waited for the Congress to "establish a system," local trade problems multiplied. When the New York Provincial Congress reconvened on 4 October, there were still no "directions" from Congress on the sale of tea. That day a merchant presented a scheme "to load 500 barrels of flour to Hispaniola, and to bring in return five tons of gunpowder." This, too, prompted a request for "directions" from Philadelphia and a letter on the subject was dispatched.[11] New York, as one of the colonies which had not been affected by the Restraining Acts, was uncertain as to what trade should be undertaken in view of the limitations placed on other provinces. On 13 October the New York Provincial Congress asked Congress for still more "directions," this time as to "whether the inhabitants of this Colony ought to be prevented from exporting provisions or other articles to any places whatsoever, except those interdicted by the general association of the Congress."[12]

In the letter to McDougall, 17 October, below, JJ professed bewilderment at New York's confusion over Congress's interpretation of the Continental Association. However, the individual colonies had good ground to seek guidance on points that divided the Congress itself and were never fully resolved in the last winter before independence.[13]

To ward off the threat that in retaliation for New York's rumored violation of the Association, notably as regards tea imports, Philadelphia would do likewise, JJ proposed that the Philadelphia Committee purchase the quantity of goods at the price stated by the Association and see if they were to be had here at that price. His suggestion was followed. A committee was appointed to purchase £5,000 sterling worth of goods to be sent to the quartermaster and by him sold to the soldiers "at first cost and charges," plus a five percent commission for himself.[14]

[1] *JCC*, I, 75–80.

[2] The Restraining Act of 30 March 1775 forbade the New England colonies to trade with any nation except Great Britain and the British West Indies. The Restraining Act of 13 April 1775 extended this provision to New Jersey, Pennsylvania, Maryland, Virginia, and South Carolina. These five colonies were singled out when Parliament learned of their ratification of the Association.

[3] Other committee members were Benjamin Franklin, Christopher Gadsden, Silas Deane, and Richard Henry Lee. On 22 September a new committee, including JJ, but with somewhat altered membership, was named to consider the state of trade and report. *JCC*, II, 177, 200–01, 259.

[4] *JCC*, I, 76–77.

[5] *JPC*, I, 92.

[6] *JCC*, II, 235.

[7] *JPC*, I, 136.

[8] *JCC*, III, 259, 268–69.

[9] *Ibid.*, 490.

[10] *Ibid.*, 492; John Adams, *Diary*, II, 204–06, 12 October 1775.

[11] New York Provincial Congress to the Continental Congress, 4 Oct. 1775, *JPC*, I, 166. On 15 July 1775, Congress had adopted a resolution which allowed any vessels bringing in gunpowder and ammunition to "load and export the produce of these colonies, to the value of such powder and stores." The plan presented to the New York Congress would have involved shipping provisions to the Indies and bringing back powder and military stores on the return voyage. *JCC*, II, 184–85.

[12] *JPC*, I, 175.

[13] JJ to Alexander McDougall, 26 Oct. and 4 Dec. 1775.

[14] John Adams, *Diary*, II, 180.

New York Provincial Congress to New York Delegates

In Provincial Congress, New York,
1 September 1775

Gentlemen

It has been represented to us that there are very Considerable quantities of Tea in this Colony, which were ordered previous to the general Association and arrived here before the first of February last. As the Proprietors of that Article are now precluded from Selling it, and of course must suffer very great hardships by having so valuable a property lay useless on their hands, we earnestly recommend it to you, to endeavour to obtain from the Honorable Continental Congress some Indulgence with respect to that part of the Association, which prohibits the purchase and consumption of Tea. The equity of giving releif, in the present case cannot be denied, and the expediency of it will be admitted, when it is considered that the Importers of that Commodity whilst it remains unsold, are in a great measure deprived of the means of Introducing many other Articles such as Duck Oznabrigs and all kind of Ammunition, of which the Colonies are in the greatest want, and which are cheifly Imported by the Tea Traders. We should therefore think it adviseable to allow of the Sale of what Tea is now on the Continent, under such guards, as will prevent any Temptation to the Clandestine introduction of it in future; To effect which we presume that the following regulations might be adopted:

That every Person offering Tea for Sale, should previously obtain the permission of the Provincial Congress or of the Committee of the County in which he resides. That in order to obtain such permission, he should make it appear, that the Tea's were Imported before the first of February last, and should enter into Engagements, that he would neither import nor assist in the Importation of any more, during the Continuance of the present general Association. As we wish to give every reasonable Indulgence to our Constituents, that is consistant with the publick Safety, we hope that through your representation's the Honourable Continental Congress will take the matter into their Consideration, and grant such releif as in their Superior Wisdom they may think expedient.

By Order.

NATHL WOODHULL, PRESIDENT PRO TEMPORE

LS. Endorsed: "Lettr from N. York Convention about Tea 1 Septr 1775." Col. Nathaniel Woodhull (1722–76) of Suffolk County was elected President Pro Tempore of the New York Provincial Congress on 28 Aug. 1775. *JPC*, I, 123.

To Stephen Rapalje

Philadelphia, 15 September 1775

Sir

We are informed that a considerable Quantity of Drugs and medicines are in your Possession belonging to a Gent[leman] in England or Ireland. The Congress are desirous of purchasing such of them as may be of use to the Army, and I am desired to apply to you for that Purpose. Be so kind therefore as to inform me by the first opportunity whether you will dispose of them. Be assured that your Compliance will be very agreable to the Congress.[1]

I am Sir, your very humble Servant

J. JAY

DftS. Endorsed.

1 On 14 September JJ was appointed to a Congressional committee charged with procuring medicines for the army. On 23 September, Congress ordered the committee to purchase Rapalje's drugs. *JCC*, II, 250; III, 261.

To Sarah Livingston Jay

Philadelphia, 18th September 1775

My dear Sally

Accept my Thanks for your kind Letter of the 13th Inst.[1] It would have been cruel to have apologized for writing it. Excuses of this Kind You know pay ill Compliments.

Your Fathers Absence gave me Reason to suspect your Mama was still much indisposed.[2] I am sorry to find these Apprehensions confirmed, but still flatter myself you dont think her dangerous, or you would have mentioned it. I assure you her Illness gives me much Anxiety, and the more so as your Sensibility is as often awakened by the Apprehension as the Reality of misfortunes. Resist this Tendency in your Disposition, believe me it is unfriendly to human Happiness. I thank Heaven that you are well. May you never be otherwise. Again let me beg your never ceasing Attention to your Health. Reflect on its *Importance!*

This City is most intolerably wet and hot. We have not had a single fair or cool Day since my Arrival. It has however, thank God, had no Influence on my Health of which I am extremely careful.

To your great Joy and my Satisfaction, the Horse I bought of Mr. Troup[3] is sold and paid for. Claas[4] has a fever and sore Throat, but not very bad.

I hope your Sisters have regained their Spirits and Appetites. Remember me to them, and to your Mama. Your kind Attention to my Father gives me Pleasure. Forward the inclosed Letter to him. It might not be amiss to send it covered by one of your own. He will take it kind. But let me apprize of one Circumstance to be particularly attended to in writing to him, that should you be disposed to say civil Things, do it very tenderly; rather let them be implied than expressed. I have often heard him censure the Neglect of this Caution and inculcate this Rule to me when a Boy. Age indeed generally does away these Refinements. After a certain Period, People advance in Indelicacy as they advance in Years. This observation you know is not applicable to him, we both have Reason to think otherwise. Forgive my troubling you with Remarks so obvious to your Discernment. I always speak and write to you without that Circumspection which Prudence dictates in our common Converse with Mankind.

Adieu my dear Sally, I am your very affectionate

JOHN JAY

ALS. Addressed: "Mrs. Sarah Jay at Wm. Livingston's Esqr., Elizabeth Town." Enclosure not located.

1 Letter not located.

2 William Livingston, a New Jersey delegate to the Continental Congress, left Philadelphia before the summer adjournment, 2 Aug. 1775. He was not present when Congress resumed sessions on 5 September, but returned to Philadelphia in late September or early October and took his seat in Congress on 16 October.

3 Robert Troup (1757–1832) was JJ's law clerk.

4 JJ's Negro slave.

To Sarah Livingston Jay

Philadelphia, 29 September 1775

My dear Sally

My last to you was by Mr. Graham[1] which I hope you have recieved. It would give me Pleasure to have an opportunity of acknowledging the Reciept of one from you. I sometimes fear you are indisposed and that your Silence proceeds from a Desire of concealing it.

Your Papa is hearty and well. The Congress spent Yesterday in Festivity. The Com[mitte]e of Safety were so polite as to invite them to make a little Voyage in their Gondolas as far as the Fort which is about 12 Miles from the City. Each Galley had its Company and each Company entertained with Variety of Musick etc. etc. We proceeded six or Eight Miles down the River when the Tide being Spent and the wind unfavorable We tacked about and with a fine Breese returned, passed the City and landed six Miles above the town at a pretty little Place called Parr's Villa. It appears to have been the Property of a Gentleman of some Taste—a Garden, a close Walk, a Summer House etc. much out of order and partly in Ruins. I wished you and a few select Friends had been with me. This Idea tho admidst much noise and mirth, made me much alone.[2]

Adieu my beloved, I am most sincerely yours

JOHN JAY

ALS.

1 Possibly William Graham, a tavern keeper in Elizabethtown, N.J.

2 For other accounts of this outing, see *LMCC*, I, 209 and John Adams, *Diary*, II, 187–88.

From William Laight

London, 3 October 1775

Sir,

If my former acquaintance with you would not entitle me to take the Liberty of addressing you, The Interest of my <Country> America which calls upon every one of its Friends at this unhappy period to exert his endeavors in her behalf will sufficiently apologize for this <address> shor[t] Epistle.[1] A true State of the Situation of this Country cannot be uninteresting to one, who has been called on to take a part not inconsiderable in the Politicks of America. I have no interest in decieving you, and I call Heaven to witness, that I am influenced by no other motive than the best good of my native soil, which has too often been misled by false representations (I speak from Experience) from this side the Atlantic.

Since my Arrival in this Metropolis, (where you will readily confess that America has more Advocates than in any other part of England) I have sedulously endeavored to learn the sentiments of all Ranks of People with respect to the present Controversy with G. B. and her Colonies. Among the Mercantile Body with whom I am most conversant, there are many who say that they approve of the Principle upon Which the Americans first proceeded, but that having constantly changed the ground of opposition, and proceeded to unwarrantable lengths, they can no longer advocate the Cause. Many also from among the same Body hesitate not to declare, that the Americans are in a State of Rebellion, and that the most coercive measures ought to be used in order to bring them to a sense of their duty. Others, the most inconsiderable in number as well as Influence, speak in favor of America, in general Terms, but at the same time declare, that while the Colonies are protected by this Kingdom, they ought to contribute, in a constitutional manner their proportion of the Expenses of the Empire. From the first Class, no assistance can be expected, not even by Petition; The second use their whole influence in Support of the Ministry, and will, if necessary lend them any Sum of Money, which may be required. The last are not of sufficient weight, if they should exert themselves, to counterbalance those who are opposed to Them. Much has been said of the exertions of the Lord Mayor and Livery Men of the City of London in favor of America; but Time must already have convinced you, how feeble and ineffectual have been their efforts. It has indeed produced *an Address to Electors of G. B.* and instructions to the <Freeholders> Members of the County of Middlesex[2] but in opposition to these and of much greater weight are the many addresses which have been made to his Majesty, from Manufacturing as well as other Towns, assuring him that they highly approved of his Measures, and were willing with their Lives and Fortunes to support the Supremacy of <His> Parliament over every part of the Empire.[3] The Common People know but little of the dispute, and seem to care less. The Landed Interest are wholly in favor of Administration and during the last sessions of Parliament were warmer for Coercive measures than the Ministry. The Commerce of this Kingdom has as yet been very little if at all affected by the Nonimportation Agreement.[4] This is accounted for by the demand for British Manufactures from various parts of Europe. Provisions are plenty and cheap (the last crop of Grain being *very good*) and No voice of Complainting is to be heard in the Streets.

The strength, Riches and Grandeur of this Island has not I am afraid been sufficiently attended to by the Leaders of the Opposition in America or they would <with more caution have avoided> have been more careful to avoid its resentment, for well am I convinced that if its Power should be exerted against our Native Country that universal Desolation and Woe must inevitably be the unhappy Consequence. There are at all times Many Persons here who act in opposition to the Ministry, <tho> but it seems generally confessed that there never was a Period when, in an Affair of so much moment as the American Controversy, the opposition had less influence or were more disregarded. What then is to be done to save America from Ruin? Tis easier to answer the Question, What has brought it to the brink of Destruction? The remains of this Generation, and Posterity also will have Reason to curse the Authors of the unnatural Conflict. In this state of Imperfection, better most assuredly is it, to be contented with a moderate Share of Civil Liberty in enjoyment and well secured, than to be aiming at visionary Schemes of Perfect Freedom; the attainment of which must depend on Circumstances which are beyond the Reach of Human Prudence to foresee or human Power to Command.

At the meeting of Parliament, tis said, that overtures of a conciliatory nature will, once for all, be made to America. If these are not attended to, Fleets irresistable, and an Army of equal force will be sent out next Spring, <when> then distress and desolation of the deepest hue will undoubtedly cover the face of the *whole* Country. For this purpose Money Sufficient is already offered, and if Men are wanting Russia, tis said, has agreed to supply any Number.

God Grant however, that in the mean Time, the Phrenzy which has seized too many of my Countrymen may subside that they may be enabled to see the things which belong to their Peace. The Ministry here declare, that they want not the Power to tax the Americans *ad Libitum,* they desire only their Proportion of the Common expenses of the Empire, and with that a security of its being paid.[5] The Congress once said, "they were at all times ready and willing to contribute that Proportion." Where then is the cause of dispute? The Ministry adhere to the same declaration. Do the Congress adhere to theirs? But with *a Congress* I believe there will be held no Treaty. The Assemblies must resume their ancient Priviledges. <There must be no Repres of Represen> <They who only are the legal Rep. of the People will alone be attend[ed] to> <Do not object to Measures. If Peace the End why quarrel about Means>[6]

You will forgive the <Liberty> freedom with which I <communicate> convey to you my Opinion. In this Land of Slavery as tis stiled by some, there is one piece of Liberty which America cannot boast of—the Liberty of speaking your Sentiments, and without danger, of communication your opinions.

Adieu. Believe me to <be> remain with my most ardent Prayers for your and my Country's best good, your sincere friend

W L

Foreign Powers give Assurances of Peace.

DftS. NNMus: Jay Papers. Endorsed in an unidentified hand: "Copy of a Letter to J. Jay." Laight sailed for England on 2 Aug. 1775. Rivington's *N.Y. Gazeteer,* 3 Aug. 1775.

1 Laight did not actually cross out the word "address" when he added "shor[t] Epistle" above the line as a substitute. This peculiarity is repeated several times throughout the draft, and such incomplete deletions and substitutions have been transcribed as though the material to be omitted has been struck out.

2 On 6 April and 24 June 1775, the Lord Mayor and Livery of London adopted petitions to the king denouncing the government's colonial policy. When the king refused to receive their addresses, they published them in the press, and used the Commons to attack the architects of the American policy. The Continental Congress expressed its appreciation for the petition of 6 April in a letter to the Lord Mayor of 8 July. This letter was read at a meeting of the Lord Mayor and Livery on 29 September, and the same meeting issued an "Address to the Electors of Great Britain" which assailed preparations for war, denounced the ministry, and commended the colonists for their efforts toward reconciliation. The Freeholders of Middlesex County met on 25 Sept. 1775 and adopted instructions to their representatives in Parliament directing them to oppose the ministry and seek a rapid disengagement from the war. 4 *FAA*, II, 278–79, 1070–74; III, 829–33, 785–87; *JCC*, II, 170–71.

3 Many of the addresses to the king denouncing the colonies are reprinted in 4 *FAA*, III.

4 The Continental Association of October 1775.

5 The Continental Congress's "Address to the People of Great Britain," adopted 21 Oct. 1774, declared: "For the necessary support of government here, we ever were and ever shall be ready to provide. And whenever the exigencies of the state may require it, we shall, as we have heretofore done, chearfully contribute our full proportion of men and money." Lord North's motion of reconciliation, adopted in Parliament on 20 Feb. 1775, declared that when any of the American colonies agreed to "make provision . . . for contributing their proportion to the common defence" and "make provision for the support of the civil government, and the administration of Justice" in that province, the British government would "forbear" levying any taxes or duties in that colony except for those necessary "for the regulation of commerce." *JCC*, I, 85; II, 62–63.

6 Laight initially wrote the first bracketed phrase, "There must be no . . ." The second bracketed passage, "they who only . . . ," was added above the first, without deleting the original words. The third bracketed phrase, "Do not object . . . ," was added in the space between this paragraph and the one which follows.

To Alexander McDougall

Philadelphia, 17 October 1775

Dear Sir

I am much obliged to you for your friendly Letter by Mr. Fine. His Business will soon be determined.[1] The Hint you give is by no Means pleasing. I wish your apprehensions were without Foundation tho I have too good an opinion of your Discernment to entertain Hopes of your being mistaken. You will much oblige me by a few Lines now and then. I need not caution you to be careful by what Hands you send them.

Tho I lament your Absence from the Scene of Action It gives me Pleasure to find you on a Field which you should not quit with Precipitation. Prudence forbids my being explicit. Were I sure that this Letter would reach you unopened it would be a very long one.

Why you restrain Exports permitted by the association I know not. The Sacrifice tho well intended is expensive. Your Seamen will forsake you. I should not be surprized if Necessity should add them to the Number of your Enemies.[2]

No News yet as to the Effect of our Petition.[3] God grant it may be a Means of restoring the Peace and I may add the Prosperity of the Empire now rent by unnatural Convulsions. But we ought not to rely wholly on it, lest it prove a broken Reed and pierce us.

I am with great Sincerity, your Friend and humble Servant

JOHN JAY

ALS. NHi: McDougall Papers. Addressed: "Coll. Alexander McDougall in New York." Endorsed. McDougall (1732–86) was a New York merchant and former sea captain. Prior to the outbreak of hostilities, McDougall was a leading figure in the anti-British movement in New York. In May 1775 he was sent to the New York Provincial Congress as a delegate for New York City, and he quickly became one of its most active members. On 30 June 1775, he was appointed colonel of New York's 1st Regiment and participated actively in preparing the province for war.

1 Letter not located. Fine was the merchant who had approached the New York Provincial Congress with a plan for obtaining military supplies from Hispaniola. The Fine (or Fyn) family had settled in New Netherlands in the seventeenth century. The merchant mentioned here may have been Frederick Fyn (c. 1735–80) who was active in New York at this time.

2 A reference to the Provincial Congress's letter to Congress of 13 Oct. 1775 seeking "directions" on trade. JJ made a similar point concerning seamen in Congressional debates of October 1775. *JCC*, III, 493.

3 The "Olive Branch Petition" of July 1775; news of its rejection by the King did not reach Congress until 9 Nov. 1775. *JCC*, III, 343.

To Sarah Livingston Jay

Philadelphia, 26 October 1775

My dear Sally

I am much obliged to you for your kind Letter by the Stage.[1] The Bundle came safe to Hand, and Claas says he thanks you for it.

I was in Hopes you had recieved some of my Letters at the Time yours was written, and am at a Loss to account for their being so long on the way.

Since Mr. Ph. Livingston and Mr. Lewis left us, the Number of our Delegates here does not exceed that which is necessary to represent the Province, so that I shall not be able to leave this Town a Day till one of those Gentlemen return. Coll. Morris has not yet returned from Fort Pitt.[2] I saw Mrs. Laurence[3] the Day before Yesterday, she presents her Love etc. to you and your Sisters. The Weather thank God! grows cold, and from this Circumstance alone you may know that I am well. I shall be happy if it agrees as well with you, but cant help fearing it will prevent your having as much Exercise as I believe would be useful to you.

Mr. Fine who is to be the Bearer of this Letter has just called for it, and is now waiting.

Adieu my Dear Sally, believe me to be most affectionately Yours

JOHN JAY

ALS.

1 No letters from Sarah Jay to JJ for October 1775 have been located.

2 Under the terms of their appointment by the New York Convention, five of the twelve members of the province's delegation to the Second Continental Congress were required to be present to cast New York's vote. Delegates Philip Livingston and Francis Lewis had been absent from Congress since early October. Colonel Lewis Morris (1726–98), another delegate, was the eldest half-brother of JJ's friend Gouverneur Morris. Colonel Morris accompanied James Wilson, an Indian Commissioner, to Fort Pitt after Congress's adjournment on 2 August. On 14 September Morris was named to the Indian Commission in place of Benjamin Franklin (1706–90) of Pennsylvania, and he remained in western Pennsylvania to treat with the Indians. *JCC*, II, 15–16, 251; *LMCC*, I, liv-lv.

3 Mary Morris (1724–1805), Gouverneur Morris's half-sister, married Thomas Lawrence, Jr. (1720–75), who had been mayor of Philadelphia in 1758.

To Alexander McDougall

Philadelphia, 26 October 1775

Dear Sir

I have recieved your Letter by Mr. Clough and you may rely on my paying due Attention to your Recommendation.[1]

Mr. Fine has a Letter from us to your Convention enclosing a Resolve of Congress enabling them to ship on their Account Provisions etc. to the Foreign West Indies for the Purpose of purchasing Ammunition etc. Under this Resolve I apprehend you may avail yourself of Mr. Fine's Contract by taking it upon yourselves and allowing him such Com[mission]s as will be nearly adequate to the Proffits he expects from the Voyage. I have not informed him of the Purport of the Resolve, thinking it more prudent to refer him to the Convention.[2]

I am Sir, your Friend and humble Servant

JOHN JAY

ALS. NHi: McDougall Papers. Addressed: "To Coll. Alexr. McDougall at New York, By Mr Fine." Endorsed.

1 Letter not located. Clough has not been identified.

2 The Congressional resolution of 26 Oct. 1775 "recommended to the several provincial Assemblies, or councils of safety, of the United Colonies, to export to

the foreign West Indies . . . as much provision or any other produce . . . as they may deem necessary for the importation of arms, ammunition, sulphur, and salt petre." In their letter to the New York Congress which covered this resolution, the New York delegates pointed out "the propriety of keeping it [the proposed voyage to the West Indies] as secret as the nature of the business will admit." Upon receiving this letter and the resolve of 26 October, the Provincial Congress appointed a committee to negotiate with Fine and charged that "this letter and resolve . . . be kept secret." The delegates' letter to the New York Congress also promised that "it will not be long before you will be made acquainted with the sentiments of the Congress respecting the general state of trade." On 1 November Congress adopted resolutions forbidding exports until 1 March 1776 and decreeing that inhabitants of New York, Delaware, North Carolina, and Georgia "ought not to avail themselves of the benefit allowed to them by the late restraining act." These resolutions carried a proviso that they were not to interfere with Congress's resolves for the encouragement of the importation of arms and ammunition. *JCC*, III, 308; *JPC*, I, 190; *JCC*, III, 314–15.

From Alexander McDougall

New York, 30th October 1775

Dear Sir,

I have many matters of importance to communicate to you, respecting our own Safety and the Public Security, which time will not now permit to enumerate. Sufice it that the Tories are chearfal, and too many of the whigs make long Faces. Men of rank and Consideration refuse to accept of commissions as Field officers of the Militia; so that these commissions have gone a beging for six or seven weeks. This requires no comment to one of your disernment.

Our Congress wrote Some days since to your's, to replace the Powder you ordered from us for continental Service, and that we voluntarily spared it.[1] But we have not been favoured with an answer, altho we have not 300 pounds at our Command if it would save the Colony; and the inhabitants are very illey supplied, not a Quarter of a Pound per man in the Hands of half the Citizens; and the Country much worse. This is a deploreable State to be in for men who have their all at Stake, For God's sake *quicken the replacing of our Powder*.

The serving of Artillery require men of more Talents and greater Soberity than is requisite for Musketry; the former being more complex than the Latter. For this reason I got our Congress to write to yours for an order to enlist matrosses for the Fort on Hudsons River.[2] What detains it? Are the men for this part of the Service to be raised when the Guns are mounted; and thereby expose the Post to fall into the Hands of the Enemy from the unskilfulness of the matrosses. You may be assured infantry alone cannot defend such a Post; unless they have been long Trained to the Artillery. General Woster's corps, which you ordered for the Fort, is by this at St. John's in Consequence of orders he received from Genl. Schyler; before yours to the former to return hither reached him;[3] So that there are no Continental Forces nearer the Post on Hudsons river, than lake George, except two incompleat Companies in our Barracks; one of the first and the other of the Third Regiment. As it will be very dificult if not imposible, to procure the stores necessary for that Post, on the sea Coast, I wish the Continental Congress, would pass an order without delay to enable us to take Such Stores from Ticonderoga, as will be wanted for it; and also to enable this and the other Colonies to take from that Fort on Crown Point[4] Such Stores as may be requisite for the defence of the Colonies, especially lead of which there is a great abundance.

I have urged our Congress to dispatch a Sloop we were obliged to buy, for Powder; but as it is difficult to procure gold and Silver or Bills of exchange, it will be necessary to Send provission with her, which in Some of the Island will facilitate the geting that article.[5] But the Congress wait your determination on the Trade. To prevent excuses for those whose Parsimony is very Criminal, and pretexes for false Brethren, I think it would be advancive of the Public Service, were the Congress to pass a Resolution to enable us to send provissions for amunition if we shall Judge it Necessary.[6] For there is not a moment to be lost in procuring this necessary Article. Our all depend opon it. The Viper's Conduct detained a Sloop we had ready here to dispatch for Powder 15 days; and she is soon to return.[7] I therefore intreat you to get the *opinion of Congress on this matter without delay*, and if it should be *favourable* dispatch it by express that we may *expedite* that Vessel before the *return* of the Viper. The intelligence from St. John's is to the 13th Instant, by Captain Quackenboss of my Regiment who is returned Sick.[8] He say that he left it the 13th. That the next morning a Battery of 2 Twelve, 2 Nine and 2 Six pounders was to be opened on the East Side of the River[9] against John's which was to play on the Schoner and Galley of the Enemy. That the Ground on which the Battery is errected is much higher than that on which St. John's stand, in so much that the Battery would command the Parade of the Fort. That he Heard a very heavy cononade the 14th, which began at Sun rise and continued all the day, and commenced the next at sun rise; and ceased all at once about 10 oClock. That the Troops were healthier than they had been and in good spirits; That they had plenty of Provissions and latterly fresh. That one of our Bombs had fired a large House the Principal

Barrack in the Fort; but was extinguished. This intelligence is confirmed by another Person. From all I have been able to Collect, The Fort is compleatly invested, and so near, that the beseigers can hear the Garrison speak to each other. That they are not Strongh enough to make any sallies. So that if we do not Succeed, it must be for want of enginer's, and amunition. For if these were well supplied the place must have Surrender or been destroyed. Time will only permit me to add that I am with great Truth and regard Your Friend and very Humble Servant

ALEXR. McDOUGALL

ALS.

1 On 16 Oct. 1775 the Continental Congress directed the New York Congress to send to Maj. Gen. Philip Schuyler a ton of powder forwarded to New York the week before. The New York Congress received this directive on 18 October and immediately complied, but warned Congress that the province would be defenseless in case of invasion unless the powder were replaced. The Continental Congress responded on 8 November by directing that the powder recently sent to Schuyler from Philadelphia was to be "remanded, if it can be any ways spared, and left at the fortresses in the highlands." Further, the Philadelphia Committee of Safety was ordered to send 500 pounds of powder to New York. *JCC*, III, 296, 338–39; *JPC*, I, 178–79.

2 Pursuant to the instructions of Congress, construction began on the fort at West Point on the Hudson River in August 1775. On 17 October, the New York Congress wrote to the Continental Congress to request that four companies of matrosses, or artillery operators, be raised to man the fort and other points being fortified along the river. On 28 October, the Congress complied with this request in part by authorizing one such company. Notification of this did not reach the New York Congress until 2 Nov. 1775. *JPC*, I, 177, 191; *JCC*, III, 309.

3 Maj. Gen. David Wooster (1711–77) of Connecticut was ordered to the province of New York in June 1775. That summer he commanded troops on Long Island and at Harlem before being ordered northward in September. On 7 October Congress ordered Wooster to return to the Hudson highlands where he was to leave part of his men to help construct artillery batteries while he and the rest of his troops returned to New York. However, these orders were to take effect only if Wooster had "no orders to the contrary from General Schuyler." Wooster remained with the Canadian expedition through the fall and winter of 1775. He was present during the siege and capture of St. Johns, a fortified point twenty miles southeast of Montreal, which was invested in early September and which surrendered on 2 November. *JCC*, III, 282.

4 Crown Point, a post ten miles north of Fort Ticonderoga on Lake Champlain, fell to the Patriots on 12 May, two days after Ticonderoga's capture.

5 On 18 October, the Provincial Congress authorized the purchase of a pilot ship, the *Bishop of Landaff*. Six days later, McDougall and others notified the New York Congress that gunpowder could be procured in the West Indies, and a committee was delegated to plan a voyage for the vessel. On 3 November, the committee received orders to load the ship with flour, and dispatch her to the Indies to obtain ammunition and arms. *JPC*, I, 179, 184, 192.

6 For the Congressional resolve of 26 October on this point, see above, JJ to McDougall, 26 Oct. 1775. The New York Congress received notice of this resolution on 2 November. *JPC*, I, 190.

7 The *Viper*, a royal sloop of war, arrived in New York harbor from Rhode Island on 7 Oct. 1775. The vessel sailed for Boston on 19 October, but remained off Sandy Hook until 21 October. She carried with her four New York merchant vessels captured between the harbor and the Hook. *N.Y. Mercury*, 23 Oct. 1775.

8 John Quackenbos, captain of the 1st New York Regiment.

9 St. Johns was located on the Richelieu (or Sorel) River which connected Lake Champlain and the St. Lawrence.

From Robert Troup

New York, October 30th, 1775

Dear Sir

I was, this Day, informed by a Carman, that you had requested him to supply you with Wood sufficient for the subsequent Winter. Agreeable to your Desire he has engaged a large Quantity for your Use, and is desirous of knowing when it will be convenient for us to receive it. I answered, that in the present Situation of affairs, you would not choose to increase your Stock. My Opinion proceeded from a Supposition that you would reside a long Time at Philadelphia. Should this Conjecture prove true, I shall save considerable Expense. You have left, I believe, two Chaldron of Coals, and at least, eight Loads of Wood. Unless the Weather is uncommonly cold, we shall have more Fuel than is necessary for the office. To purchase more therefore when Wood is sold at 38/ per Cord, would be imprudent. In such Circumstances I could not, consistent with my Duty, suffer the Carman to bring any without your approbation. If you think proper, he will fulfil his Engagement; if not, he will sell it to other Persons. I beg you will give me your Directions by the first opportunity.

I hope, dear Sir, you have enjoyed much Health during your Absence. A continual Anxiety for the publick Welfare will, I fear, injure your Constitution. Persons of your Sensibility experience Pains unknown to the Generality of Mankind. These must be naturally heightened, when such important Deliberations employ your Attention.

When I reflect upon the present Business of the office, I am filled with the deepest Sorrrow. Formerly it was extensive, and attended with much Profit. Now it is confined within very narrow Bounds, and of Course accompanied with little Gain. Mr. Strang, with his usual Care and Regularity, does whatever is in his Power to promote your Interest. He acts as Council, I perform the office of Attorney. We are endeavouring to collect the Costs which have been long due. I am sorry to say the Calamity of the Times is a great Obstacle to our Success.

I know by Experience, that you wish the Improvement of those committed to your Tuition. Permit me, dear Sir, to confess that we feel the Want of your Counsel. [W]e cannot conveniently obtain a Solution of difficult Questions. Books are our only Informers, and these we peruse with as much Attention as the Disturbances in America, and this City in particular allow. I do not, however, mean to complain; [in] this Contest I am willing to be a common sufferer.

Pray, pardon the Length and Freedom of this Letter, and consider it as the genuine Production of Friendship. If it contains Impertinencies, I hope your Goodness will suffer them to sink into merited oblivion.

I am in Truth, and Sincerity your Friend.

ROB. TROUP

ALS. Addressed: "John Jay, Esqr, Philadelphia. favd. by Mr. Lewis." Endorsed.

From Samuel Kissam

Surinam, October 31, 1775

I was particularly happy my Dear Jay when I saw your name in the list of Deligates for the Continental Congress, not only because it favoured an opinion I had ever entertaind, that your Abilities would entitle you to the most distinguished honors; But because as I knew your Sentiments were favorable to Liberty and the public Good it convinced me that the Spirit of Freedom and not of Faction prevaild among those who confered on you their Suffrages.

It was ever my opinion, and agreeable to my affection and to my wish I have often foretold, that your Integrity, your knowledge of the Law, and the firmness with which you would maintain the Cause of your Clyent, would with rapidity advance your Reputation as a Lawyer; But little did I think that in the Course of so few years you could have opened your way to the first honors in the gift of a free People, and how you have been able to Stem the Current of those prejudices which formerly prevaild against your Profession in the City of New York, can only be accounted for from that Steady perseverence in Virtuous Actions which have ever been your peculiar Characteristics.

The distressed Situation of America has hitherto given me the greatest uneasiness; but by the almost divine Conduct of your Congress, the apprehension of danger begins to diminish, and I think it plain to be observed that *great Brittain has passed the meridian of her Glory:* and why should not America (like the Phenix) arise to A great Empire from the ashes of its mother. I have no more to say only that I wish you health and prosperity and am yours affectionately

SAML: KISSAM

Should an opportunity offer do dear Jay write to me.

ALS. Addressed: "To John Jay Esqr. <New York> Philade." New York was crossed out, and "Philade" added in another hand. Endorsed.

FROM ALEXANDER MCDOUGALL

New York, November 15th–16th, 1775

Dear Sir

Agreeable to my Promise to give you a memorandum of Severals acts and matters to be done relative to this Colony, I shall now mention them. The Troops at the Fort on Hudson's river, being of different Regiments, and the minute-men to be sent there as well as the former having no Surgeon; it will be absolutly necessary, that one should be provided; in order to take Care of them in ordinary, as well as Extraordinary Cases. For otherwise the Troops will not be easily kept there; nor will they defend the place in the Hour of danger so long when they reflect that even a wound may be as dangerous to them as immediate death. *The* Congress therefore should give orders to provide one without delay.[1] As there are Sundry Stores absolutly necessary for that post, which cannot be got in any of the Colonies on the seaboard, should not *the* Congress enable us, without delay to get such of them from Ticonderoga etc. as can be spared; as the want of those stores may defeat the end of Building the Fort. They may be sent down with the return of the Provission wagons.[2]

Altho you have directed us to raise a Company of Matrosses, yet you were Silent on the Subject of their pay. This ought to be determined, to encourage the enlisting, and to prevent any disputes after this is Compleated. The want of knowing in time the establishment of the Troops you first ordered us to raise, retarded the Levies; and was pruductive of discontents. This ought by all means to be prevented. If *the* Congress *intended* the Artillery Establishment for the Matrosses, they should inform us of it, and Transmit *a Copy* by the first Conveyance; for we have not been favoured with it.[3] The deputy Paymaster had the only one brought to this Colony, and carried it with him. You know we have no executive here, but the Militia; the calling upon them cant be secreet, and raises speculations and conjectures, which in many Cases may frustrate the end of the Call. But if we had continental Troops, they could be called out of the Barracks, at a Moments warning, and the business executed before it is known in the City; pray when the Citizens were in their Beds. It would therefore greatly contribute to the Public safety in particular as well General emergencies, to have Troops Quartered in this City. Why then are not some of those raised in Pen[nsylvani]a and Jersey sent here? There are good accommodations for a regiment of them in our Barracks. I hope *the* Congress will not delay the march of those of them, who are officered by Genteel or Sober discreet men. One of these is a necessary Qualification, for Troops Quartered in a Town. If this Flying Scrawl should be productive of any good, or not be disagreeable, it will be frequently repeated.

I am Dear Sir, Your affectionate Humble Servant

ALEXR. McDOUGALL

16th November 1775

I forgot before I closed this, to inform you that the Matrosses usualy have light muskets, and learn the discipline common to the Marching Regiments, to render them capable of assisting in the defence of the Army, if they should be deprived of the use of the Artillery. It will be next to impossible to get Matrosses with these or any other Muskets; and it would be unequal for our Colony, to be at the expence of them, which would cost from 65/ to 85/ each, and at the end of this Controversy, would not be worth above 30/ or 40/. *The* Congress therefore should order us to buy those arms, at Continental expence, or this Corps will not be raised, for we ought not to be left in a state of uncertainty, who should pay for those arms; as we are left with those of the first Artillery company raised by us, without which you would not have reduced the Post of St. John's. Twelve O' Clock, and but 10 Members of Congress appear, so that we shall not make one this day, which renders this communication the more necessary to expedite the public business.

I am Your affectionate as above

ALEXR. McDOUGALL

ALS. Addressed: "To Colonel John Jay, Delegate for the colony of New York in Congress, Philadelphia, Favoured by Silas Deane Esqr." Endorsed. JJ was designated a colonel of the New York City militia on 27 Oct. 1775; his signed commission, dated 3 Nov. 1775, is in JP, 4 *FAA*, III, 1206, and illustrated herein.

1 By a resolution of 8 Dec. 1775, the Continental Congress provided a surgeon for each regiment in the service of the United Colonies. *JCC*, III, 416.

2 Congress failed to follow McDougall's suggestion; no stores were dispatched from Ticonderoga to the Hudson highlands.

3 On 29 July 1775, Congress adopted pay scales for the Continental Army; matrosses in an artillery regiment were to be paid 6 5/6 dollars under this schedule. *JCC*, II, 220–21.

From Alexander McDougall

New York, November 26th, 1775

Dear Sir,

I am sorry to inform you, that the information I gave you, relative to the arrival of Powder, proved groundless.[1] The vessel arrived which gave rise to the report; but brought none of that Article. She waited 36 days at Barcalona, to gain advice from the neighbourhood, whether any could be purchased; but none could be procured. The Powder in Spain was all in the King's Magazines. To add to our distress, we have lost Judge Livingstons Mill,[2] by the Carelesness of two men, who fired off their Guns near some of Pans in which Powder was placed to dry. We have been informed, that there has been a Considerable arrival of Powder in Phi[ladelphi]a. If this be true, surely the Congress can borrow of them, to supply our pressing wants for what we have lent the Continent.

A Sufficient number of members have not yet appeared, to make a Congress;[3] so that we are without Power, or means to Crush with safety, those Machinations, which our restless Enemies are devising to destroy the Confederacy.

What detains the Continental Troops to the Southard? Last week I received intelligence, that a Captain Harris[4] of Dutchess County, had enlisted men for the Ministerial Army, and it was expected he would be on Monday Night on Long Island, at one of the Ferries. After searching 6 Houses at 11 at Night, I found him and two of his recruits, and brought them over, and Secured them under gard till they were upon evidence against each other, and the Confession of the Captain, found guilty by the Committee of Transgressing a resolution of our Congress. The next morning about 2 AM, the Captain and one of his men, made their escape, either by the Carelessness of the Militia Gard, or by their being bribed with money or Liquor, or disafection to the Common Cause; they are now Confined.

Our difficulties are increasing fast upon us. The Committee in enquiring into the exorbitant Sale of Goods, find that William Ludlow among many others will be a delinquent; and they have noticed

Robison and Price, in the same predicament with him, to be advertised; So that he must necessarily follow. From what you know of his connections, you will be at no loss to determine, that this necessary measure will decrease the Number of our Friends.[5] It will therefore be expedient, in order to strengthen our Hands, against the influence these measures will have on many; and to make the Principle of Fear, which now Causes many to look back, operate in our Favor to have Troops here without delay. Otherwise it is difficult to say what a Few weeks may bring forth in our Capitol, against the union. It is unnecessary to trouble you with a Particular detail. I am in great Haste Sir, Your affectionate Humble Servant

ALEXR. McDOUGALL

ALS. Endorsed.

[1] The letter to which McDougall refers has not been located.

[2] Judge Robert R. Livingston, Sr.'s powder mill at Rhinebeck, N.Y.

[3] The First New York Provincial Congress adjourned on 4 Nov. 1775. Elections for delegates to a Second Provincial Congress were held on 7 November, and the new Congress was to convene on 14 November. McDougall, a delegate to the Second Congress from New York City, seems to have attended sessions conscientiously in the last two weeks of November, but other Congressmen were less punctual, and no quorum could be formed until 6 December. *JPC*, I, 195–205.

[4] The *N.Y. Mercury* of 27 Nov. 1775 carried a colorful account of McDougall's pursuit of Captain Peter Harris. The Tory was found at Dagrushee's Ferry "in an upper Room in a Posture to defend himself, which appeared by two Pistols lying on his Bed, close by his Side, loaded and primed. . . ." Harris's activities were brought to the attention of the Provincial Congress on 2 December. *JPC*, I, 215.

[5] Robert Robinson and Michael Price, partners in a store on William Street, were examined by the Provincial Congress for selling overpriced druggets and blankets to the militia on 3 Nov. 1775. Notice of their violation of the Continental Association was published in the *N.Y. Mercury* of 27 Nov. 1775. *JPC*, I, 193.

William Ludlow was a dry-goods merchant in partnership with his brother George. No notice of profiteering by either Ludlow brother has been found in New York newspapers for the period. A "notice" of the Ludlows would have had serious political repercussions since William was then a member of the Committee of One Hundred and their cousin, George Duncan Ludlow, was a Justice of the Supreme Court of Judicature.

From Robert R. Livingston, Jr.

Fort George, 27th November 1775

Dear John

I am now on the borders of lake George where we have been detained this day and part of yesterday by a head wind and extream severe wheather. It is almost impossible to conceive the difference we found in the climate in half a miles riding. After we got over the mountain, within the reach of the winds that blew from the lake it was like leaping from October to December. We hope to leave this [place] tomorrow and have prepared tinder boxes and axes for an encapment on the shore, as we can hardly expect as they tell us to get over in one day and hope to experience the pleasure of laying on hemlock beds. They laugh at us here for having brought but one blanket with us, but we hope to make it up in fire.

This morning and part of yesterday I employed in going over the ground where the french received the first check from Sir Wm. Johnston, and this afternoon I went to see the remains of fort William Henry, and the french lines part of which are still visseable. No fort could have been more unfortunately scituated as it is commanded by almost all the ground about it, yet it appears that the defence must have been prety gallant, since the approaches were begun at a distance yet they held out till they got within twenty yards of the fort, every gun but one of which were dismounted. You remember how the capitulation was violated and the horrid Slaughter of those brave fellows by the Indians under the command of Lecorne.[1] I could hardly stir a step with immagining that I walked over the grave of some unfortunate victim to the ambition of princes. We have little hopes of getting farther than Ticanderoga, as the lake is already frozen to Crown point, and the cold of last night and this day has I dare say extended it not a little.[2]

We met upon the road great numbers of the Connecticut troops most of whom as we are informed have gone home. It give me great pleasure to find that Montgomerry[3] has contrived to gain the affection as well of the New England troops as our own. They speak of him in the highest terms. You can not conceive at the distance you are, the difficulties He and his troops have had to strugle with difficulties which I am amazed they should ever get over. By the last accounts we have from Montreal, we hear that Montgomerry had ordered a battery to be raised at the mouth of the sorrel and got a Gondola from the lake into the river St. Lawrance by which means he has stoped nine vessels loaded with Stores from going down, and I am in great hope they will be taken.[4] Carleton is said to have escaped by land to Quebeck, where we hear he has about 700 men chiefly of the Royal Emegrants (in which our Stephen Watts is enlisted) and they are employed below Quebeck in distressing the inhabitants who are favourable to us.[5] Arnold we hear is at point Levi waiting for assistance from Montgomerry who writes me that he will go down immediately if he can get his men to follow him in which we hear he is like to succeed.[6] He proposes to secure the channel below Quebeck and advises that some able general be sent to take the command, and recommends Lee[7] as he expects a pretty severe attack in the spring. I wish he would stay himself as I know [no] person of more prudence and conduct in our service, but I believe he finds that the provision made for a second in command, will not support one at the head of an army. He says nothing of this to me but express[es] a warm desire to return to his farm and mill. I hope you have seen Harry. I have great satisfaction in the commendation he receive[d] from all who have served with him. Both his Collonel and lieutenant Collonel have resigned, so that I hope he will receive the rank to which he was before entitled, and has now earned. If he is still with you I pray you to take him by the hand, you will find amidst his roughness, many good qualities.[8]

There is one subject on which I wished to speak to you had I had the pleasure of seeing you. They talk of sending the new levies to Boston. I think we should by no means consent to it, for many reasons that I dare not commit to paper but which will suggest themselves to you. If you are not tired of politicks I would just mention to you that under the notion of soldiers baggage there are two compleat suits of cloathing at Montreal for each Soldier, which have never yet be unpacked. Now I have great doubt whether by the capitulation they can be entitled to these? If they are, whether they may not be purchased of the soldiers for our Northern army at a cheap rate, indeed we may afford to pay well for them as the transportation will amount to nearly their value. If the congress should take any order with respect to this matter, I should be glad to if they would send off an express to stop them here.[9] Hitherto I have only asked your attention to those matters which your love of your country makes it your pleasure to attend to. I could wish to detain you by the less important concerns of private friendship, which I never feel so strongly as when absence and solitude acquaint me with the movements of my own heart, but Pain[10] already considers me as impolite. Let me hear from you, and direct to the care of Walter Livingston at Albany.[11] God bless you and remember me to any body you think fit. Farewell.

Yours Most Sincerely

ROBT R. LIVINGSTON JUNR

P.S. I just hear doubtful whether Carllton has escaped. His vessels have made too fruitless Attempts. Montgomerry has marched to join Arnold, most of our troops enlist. All those that Woster had with him stay amount to about 300.

ALS. Addressed: "John Jay Esqr., at Congress, Philadelphia, In care Walter Livingston Esqr. at Albany." Endorsed. Livingston, Robert Treat Paine (1731–1814) of Massachusetts, and John Langdon of New Hampshire were at Fort George en route to Ticonderoga as members of a committee named by Congress to confer with Philip Schuyler. Fort George, also known as Fort William Henry, was at the southern end of Lake George. *JCC*, III, 317, 339–42.

1 The ruins of the original Fort William Henry were about one mile from Fort George. William Johnson (1715–74) was knighted for his victory over the French at Lake George on 8 Sept. 1755. Fort William Henry, constructed by Johnson after this battle, was attacked and destroyed by General Montcalm in August 1757. France's Indian allies massacred approximately 800 of the British garrison in this engagement, and Pierre St. Luc de La Corne, a French-Canadian, was considered responsible for this outrage. La Corne was still alive in 1775 and had attempted to relieve the British forces at St. Johns earlier that fall.

2 Livingston's biographer, George Dangerfield, writes that the committee was supposed to proceed to Canada if possible. However, they did not reach Ticonderoga until 29 November, and Livingston returned to Albany on 6 December. Dangerfield, *Robert R. Livingston*, pp. 65–66.

3 Brig. Gen. Richard Montgomery (1738–75), Livingston's brother-in-law, was second in command of the Canadian expedition. Since Philip Schuyler was kept in the rear by illness during most of the campaign, the actual field command was left to Montgomery.

4 Montreal was captured 13 Nov. 1775. The Sorel (or Richelieu) River linked Lake Champlain and the St. Lawrence River.

5 Sir Guy Carleton (1724–1808), Governor of Canada, escaped from Montreal by boat as American forces approached. His small fleet was captured en route to Quebec, but Carleton eluded the Americans and made his way to the city. At Quebec, Carleton found the first battalion of Royal Highland Emigrants under the command of Colonel Allan Maclean. Recruitment for the regiment had begun earlier in 1775, and the troops included Scottish veterans living in Canada as well as less experienced provincial Loyalists. Stephen Watts (b. 1754) was the son of John Watts, a New York merchant.

6 Colonel Benedict Arnold (1741–1801) of Connecticut commanded an expedition which marched from Cambridge, Massachusetts, on 13 September. By 9 November Arnold and his men had reached Point Levis opposite Quebec, and on the nights of 13 and 14 November he took his troops across the St. Lawrence to the Plains of Abraham. On 19 November Arnold retreated to a point twenty miles up river to wait for Montgomery's forces who arrived on 2 December.

7 Major General Charles Lee (1731–82), then stationed at Boston with Washington, did not participate in the Canadian expedition.

8 Captain Henry Beekman Livingston participated in the first phase of the Canadian expedition as aide-de-camp to his brother-in-law, Richard Montgomery. In mid-November Captain Livingston left Canada with Montgomery's dispatches. On 12 Dec. 1775, Congress resolved to present him with a sword in recognition of his services and to "embrace the first opportunity of promoting him in the army." *JCC*, III, 424–25.

9 By the second article of the articles of capitulation under which the commander at St. Johns surrendered to Montgomery, the garrison at that fort was to enjoy "all the Honours of war, and suffered to proceed with their Baggage and Effects to the most Convenient port in America" from which they would sail for Britain. Livingston questioned whether the extra clothing ought to be considered part of that "Baggage." In this regard, he was at odds with Montgomery who had braved a "near mutiny" to insure that the clothing at Montreal was sent forward with the St. Johns prisoners. Montgomery declared to Schuyler: "I would not have sullied my own reputation, nor disgraced the Continental arms, by such a

breach of capitulation, for the universe; there was no driving it into their noddles [the American soldiers who demanded that the clothing be kept in Montreal] that the clothing was really the property of the soldier, that he had paid for it, and that every Regiment, in this country especially, saved a year's clothing, to have decent clothes to wear on particular occasions." "Articles of Capitulation . . . at St. John's," 2 Nov. 1775, DNA: PCC 161, 449–51; Montgomery to Schuyler, 13 Nov. 1775, 4 *FAA*, III, 1602–03.

10 Robert Treat Paine.

11 Walter Livingston (1740–97), the son of Robert Livingston, the lord of Livingston Manor, was Robert R. Livingston's second cousin. Walter Livingston was appointed "commisary of stores and provisions" for New York by the Continental Congress on 17 July 1775. *JCC*, II, 186.

From Alexander McDougall

New York, November 29th, 1775

Dear Sir,

It is now one P M, and Sixteen days, since the Congress was to have been convened; but we have not yet made a House; I think its probable we shall make one to morrow.[1]

It is an agreed point with all Civilized Nation[s], that a war is an appeal to God, as there can be none other to Judge between the Contending Parties. The Judge of all the Earth has determined in our favor, in the reduction of St. John's; we should therefore pay a sacred regard to the Articles of Capitulation, least we offend, that God to whom we profess to have appealed, in the awful and unnatural Contest. I am leed to these reflections by the opinion of two of the officers, taken there (now on parole in this City) "that we have violated the Articles of Surender by Seperating the Garrison," which they hint is designed (if the Seperation is continued) to debautch the Privates from their duty. From the Honorable treatment they have hitherto received, they ascribe the present seperate State of the Garrison, to inadvertence, but declare freely, if its not remedied they must consider it as a Violation. The bare mention of this to you, I doubt not will induce you to exert your self, to Correct whatever may have been done without design contrary to the stipulation with that Garrison.[2] For otherwise the war will be destitute of Honor, or Justice; and our Enemies will represent us as a sett of faithless banditti; which may provoke or entice many to enter into their Army, who now detest the Service. Besides the Garrison under the restaint of the Articles in a Colony remote from the Ministerial Army, will be less dangerous to us than seperated, under the Idea that the Capitulation is not obligatory, which will make them embrace the first favourable opportunity to

Join our conceald Enemies; and thereby give us no small trouble. The Post is on the point of departing and I have so many interruptions, that I have time only to add that I am Sir, Your affectionate Humble Servant

ALEXR. McDOUGALL

ALS. Addressed: "Col. John Jay Delegate for the Colony of New York, at Congress, Philadelphia." Endorsed: ". . . abt. Chambly Officers." For the repercussions of JJ's error in assuming this letter concerned the "Chambly Officers," see below, JJ to McDougall, 4 Dec. 1775 and McDougall to JJ, 14 Dec. 1775.

1 See above, McDougall to JJ, 26 Nov. 1775, n. 3.

2 Under the Articles of Capitulation agreed to at the surrender of St. Johns, "the garrison" was to be sent to Connecticut or any other place designated by the Continental Congress. On 17 Nov. 1775, Congress resolved that prisoners from St. Johns were to be sent to Reading, Lancaster, and York, Pa., while commissioned officers from that post were to be paroled and taken to Windham and Lebanon, Conn., "provided General Schuyler has not given his word for another disposition of them." Congress confirmed its decision to separate officers from privates on 16 Dec. 1775. "Articles of Capitulation . . . at St. John's," 2 Nov. 1775, DNA: PCC, 161, 449–51; *JCC*, III, 358–59, 434.

To Sarah Livingston Jay

Philadelphia, 4 December 1775

My dear Sally

When shall I have the Pleasure of acknowledging the Reciept of a Letter from You? I have been favoured only with one since I left you. Our Letters I fear often miscarry, and cant forbear suspecting that an idle and criminal Curiosity has proved fatal to several of them. It is really cruel thus to interrupt an Intercourse so innocent and interesting to us.

I begin to wish for the holy days as much as a School Boy ever did. I flatter myself with being able then to pay you a visit as it is very probable the Congress will then make a short Adjournment. My dear Sally! be attentive to your Health, and be assured that the most acceptable Office you can do me, is to ne[glect n]o means of rendering yourself chearful and happy. Adieu my beloved!

I am most sincerely yours

JOHN JAY

Remember me to your mama and all the Family.

ALS.

To Alexander McDougall

Philadelphia, 4 December 1775

Dear Sir

The Congress have at Length determined against the Tea holders,[1] a Measure in my opinion neither just or politic. The Objections offered to the Prayer of the Petition, were merely ostensible and consequently frivolous. I fancy you may easily discern the Hinge on which this strange Decision turned. There is no Tea southward of this Place but what has paid Duty. Etc. etc.

I mentioned to the Congress this Morning, the anxiety which some of the Chambly Officers expressed to you, relative to the Separation of that Garrison. On examining the Articles we find nothing to warrant their Construction, and consequently the Congress do not think proper to alter that arrangement.[2] If those Gent[lemen] had any assurances from the General that the Garrison should remain together or in any other Way were led to consider that as one of the Terms of Capitulation, I wish to be made acquainted with it. Your Observations on the Faith of Treaties are founded in Policy as well as Justice, and I am confident the Congress on being informed of any Errors of that Kind would most readily correct all Mistakes.

The late valorous Expedition against Rivington, gives me Pain.[3] I feel for the Honor of the Colony, and most sincerely hope they will upon this occasion act a Part that may do some little Credit to their Spirit as well as Prudence.

Would it be possible for you to furnish the Jersey Troops with any Arms?[4] Remember your Accounts. Several other Colonies are now pressing a Settlement of theirs. The sooner ours are liquidated the better.[5]

I hope your Convention will soon tell us whether they mean to make any and what Provision for us. Unless something of this Kind is soon done, I must return, my Finances being exhausted, and my Absence from Home putting it out of my Power to collect money.[6]

I am Dear Sir, Your Friend and humble Servant

JOHN JAY

Be so kind as to give the enclosed to young Hamilton.[7]

ALS. NHi: McDougall Papers. Addressed: "To Colonel Alexander McDougall in New York, free J. Jay." Endorsed. Enclosure not located.

1 On 13 Oct. 1775 Congress appointed a committee to consider the memo-

rials of New York and Philadelphia tea merchants which had been submitted the preceding summer. This committee made its report on 18 October, but Congress repeatedly postponed action on the report until 28 November when the committee's recommendations were defeated in a floor vote. The text of the committee report has not been located, but JJ's references make it clear that the report would have allowed some concessions to merchants who sought permission to sell their tea. *JCC*, III, 294, 298, 353, 370, 388–89.

[2] JJ had mistaken McDougall's concern for the British garrison which surrendered at St. Johns for a query concerning the troops who had surrendered at Chambly. Chambly, a small post ten miles north of St. Johns, capitulated on 18 Oct. 1775. The terms of surrender at Chambly were far vaguer than those agreed upon at St. Johns and contained no stipulation concerning the destination of the prisoners. For the articles of capitulation at Chambly, 18 Oct. 1775, see 4 *FAA*, III, 1133–34.

[3] On 23 November New York's radical leader, Isaac Sears (1730–86) rode into Westchester County with a band of men from New Haven, Conn. Joined by a group of local radicals, Sears's men seized a number of prominent Tories and destroyed the printing presses of James Rivington in New York City. JJ commented on the incident at length in a letter to Nathaniel Woodhull of 26 Nov. 1775. "The New England exploit," JJ told Woodhull, "is much talked of, and Conjectures are numerous as to the Part the Convention will take relative to it. Some consider it an ill Compliment to the Government of the Province, and prophesy that you have too much Christian meekness to take any notice of it." JJ made his own disapproval of the escapade clear, remarking that "it neither argues much Wisdom or much Bravery; at any Rate, If it was to have been done, I wish our own People and not Strangers had taken the Liberty of doing it. I confess I am not a little jealous of the Honor of the Province, and am persuaded that its Reputation cannot be maintained without some little Spirit being mingled with its Prudence." JJ to Woodhull, 26 Nov. 1775, ALS fragment in N: Provincial Congress Papers, printed in full, *JPC*, I, 219.

For the Provincial Congress's action on the Sears raid, see below, JJ to McDougall, 13 Dec. 1775, and McDougall to JJ, 14 and 18–19 Dec. 1775.

[4] In a letter of 27 Nov. 1775, the Continental Congress asked that New York send arms to troops in New Jersey, who were to aid in the defense of New York. This letter was received by the Provincial Congress on 1 December. When a quorum was formed on 6 December, the New York Congress appointed a committee to supply these arms, and a letter to the Continental Congress describing these measures was approved on 8 December. *JPC*, I, 202, 207, 208, 209.

[5] The Continental Congress created a Committee of Accounts to consider all claims against the Continental government on 25 Sept. 1775. *JCC*, III, 262.

[6] On 3 Nov. 1775 the New York delegates to Philadelphia wrote Nathaniel Woodhull concerning their appointment to the Continental Congress. They pointed out that no expiration date had been set for their terms in Congress and suggested that "a new appointment" would be appropriate. They went on to give a list of the allowances made to delegates by other colonies so that the New York Congress could establish some "compensation for our expenses and loss of time." *JPC*, II, 18; for the New York Congress's action on this matter, see below, JJ to McDougall, 13 Dec. 1775 and McDougall to JJ, 18–19 Dec. 1775.

[7] No letters from JJ to Alexander Hamilton (1755–1804) for 1775 have been located. In a letter of 26 Nov. 1775, Hamilton informed JJ of the Isaac Sears raid and suggested that the Continental Congress curb such escapades. Hamilton's letter to JJ of 31 Dec. 1775 reveals that JJ had replied to the November letter and had evidently asked Hamilton to keep him informed of affairs in New York. *HP*, I, 176–79.

From Robert R. Livingston, Jr.

Albany, 6th December 1775

Dear John

I wrote to you on my first arrival at lake George and hoped to have found a Line from you here on my return. My disappointment has not however so angered me as to prevent my appologizing for you, of which this second letter is a proof. I most sincerely congratulate you upon our amazing success in Canada. If you knew the Obstacles we have had to strugle with you would think it little short of a miracle. Though as you will find by the letters you will receive herewith the matter is far from being ended, as the base desertion of the troops in the hour of victory,[1] has left us much inferiour to the enemy and I could wish that no attemp was made upon Quebeck till the freezing of the lake admitted of our sending in a reinforcement, since there is no dependance to be placed upon the Canadians, and the first ill success will convert them into enemies, in which case with the assistance of Carleton we may be easily cut off. But the people that compose our army think so much for themselves that no general dare oppose their sentiments if he was so inclined. You can not conceive the trouble our generals have had, petition, mutinies and request to know the reason of every maneuver without a power to suspend or punish the offenders, the strongest proof of which is that Montgomerry was under a necessity to reinstate Mott[2] in order to quiet his men. Lamb is a good officer but so extreamly turbulent that he excites infinite mischief in the army. A few days ago he promoted a petition and remonstrance upon the subject of some indulgence that was shewn to one or two Officers who had families in Canada and were permitted to visit them on their parol. It was con[ceive]d in such terms that Montgomerry immediately resigned the command but on their making a proper appology reassumed it.[3]

You can form no judgment of the impositions on the publick by the Officers and troops of the New England Colonies. I speak this in confidence and without prejudice. A great number of troops have been raised but when ordered upon duty tho they had received pay the whole season for doing nothing they dwindled down to a handful whole companies falling sick at once and yet full muster rolls being returned. You ask why this is not punished? The <aggressors> Offenders form the court martial and tho it may seem incredible yet mutiny, disarming the centries and endeavouring to resque Offenders from the gaurd is punished only by a fine of 6/. Many of our own

Officers are little better. However I am pleased to find that our Troops have continued in Canada and have on all occasions behaved with spirit if we except the regiment raised in New York, who together with Waterburies regiment run away at the first landing of which you have had an account.[4] The rest of our Troops were not there accept one or two companies who behaved well. Contrive if possible to introduce Government into the army. Genl. Prescot is now here. He is the author of all the cruelties against Walker and Allen in Canada,[5] and even descended so low as to break the windows of the Barracks with his own cane. Montgomery resented his conduct so highly as to refuse to see him or any of the Officers of his party. The Officers taken at St. Johns we hear are gone with their men, notwithstanding an express direction to Capt. Mott of Connecticut who had the charge of them to separate them. This should by all means be done as they have it in idea to keep up the regiment which it would be very absurd to permit. You judging from the climate of Philadelphia may wonder we did not proceed to Canada but if I had been so inclined we should have met with many obstructions, besides that Canada is not yet in a state to negotiate, especially as we could derive no assistance from Montgomerry who was going down to Quebeck.

But my strongest objection was that your Committee[6] is by no means adapted to the manners of the people with whom they are to deal and I am persuaded would not greatly raise the reputation of the congress, nor answer any good purpose among that polished people.

You brought us into this scrape, pray get us out, chuse men who have the address to conciliate the affections of their fellow mortals, and send them up in February. I will accompany them in my private capacity, as I wish to make the jaunt. If it lays in your way to serve Harry I know you will do it.[7] Let me hear from you soon. The Express waits. Present my Compliments to Duane and Morris.[8] They both owe me a letter. Farewell.

Yours Most Affectionately,

ROBT. R. LIVINGSTON, JUNR

ALS. Addressed: "To John Jay Esqr. In Congress at Philadelphia." Endorsed.

1 Many enlisted men in the Canadian expedition returned to their homes after the victories at St. Johns and Montreal. For Richard Montgomery's complaints on this score, see his dispatches to Philip Schuyler, 13, 17, 19, and 24 Nov. 1775 in 4 *FAA*, III, 1603, 1633, 1683, 1684, 1694.

2 Capt. Edward Mott of the 6th Connecticut Regiment.

3 John Lamb (1735–1800), an original Son of Liberty and captain of the Independent Company of the New York Artillery, 17 July–31 Dec. 1775. The officers made their protest on 23 Nov. 1775 and offered their apology the next day. Richard Montgomery to Philip Schuyler, 24 Nov. 1775, 4 *FAA*, III, 1695.

4 Colonel David Waterbury commanded the 5th Connecticut Regiment, 1 May–13 Dec. 1775. An assault on the garrison at St. Johns on 10 and 11 September 1775 had failed when colonial troops panicked and fled.

5 Brigadier General Richard Prescott (1725–88), the British commander at Montreal, was captured by the Americans on 17 Nov. 1775. As commander, Prescott had earned a reputation for his harsh treatment of Patriots and Patriot-sympathizers. Ethan Allen (1738–89) was captured during an unauthorized advance on Montreal in September 1775, and Prescott placed Allen in irons and sent him to England for trial. Thomas Walker of Montreal, who had corresponded with the Continental Congress and been a vocal partisan of American rights, was seized at his home on 5 Oct. 1775. On Prescott's orders, Walker, too, was placed in irons, but he was freed by American troops after Prescott's own capture following the fall of Montreal. See Thomas Walker's statement, 24 April 1776, 4 *FAA*, IV, 1176–79.

6 The committee to which Livingston was appointed on 2 Nov. 1775 was instructed by Congress to "use their endeavours to procure an accession of the Canadians to a Union with these Colonies" as well as to confer with Gen. Schuyler on the Canadian expedition. *JCC*, III, 317.

7 Henry Beekman Livingston.

8 James Duane and Lewis Morris were members of the New York delegation in Congress in the winter of 1775–76.

Provincial Maneuvers

In December 1775 the extralegal Provincial Congress was the only effective governing body in New York. The royal assembly had been prorogued in April, and Governor William Tryon had been forced to take refuge on a British vessel at anchor in New York harbor, where he met periodically with his Council.[1] But, as the year drew to a close, New York Loyalists saw an opportunity to regain political control of the colony.

The first New York Congress was forced to adjourn frequently through the summer and fall because of absenteeism, and the Second Congress, elected on 14 November, could not muster a quorum until 6 December. Sensing a loss of momentum in the Revolutionary cause, conservative elements in the colony maneuvered to restore the authority of royal government. The plan, developed by Judge William Smith, envisioned persuading the Provincial Congress to request a meeting of the colony's royal assembly. The assembly, it was expected, would petition the king and Parliament and take up Lord North's proposal for reconciliation. Since North's overtures had been rejected by the Continental Congress in July,[2] the effect of Smith's strategem would have been to separate New York from the Continental Congress and her sister colonies as well as to reestablish Tryon's authority.

Smith convinced a reluctant Tryon to adopt his strategy, and on 4 December 1775 the governor published a letter to the inhabitants of New York lamenting the failure of the colony to express its objections to North's proposals in a constitutional manner.[3] The obvious inference to be drawn from this statement was that the assembly should be reconvened in order to determine the opinion of the populace.

In the letter printed below, JJ responded to a letter from Alexander McDougall of 6 December which obviously enclosed a copy of Tryon's public letter of 4 December. For McDougall's continuing chronicle of the results of the Tryon letter and Tory policy in the Provincial Congress in December 1775, see below, McDougall to JJ, 14 December and 18–19 December 1775.

1 *N.Y. Col. Docs.*, VIII, 641.

2 *JCC*, II, 224–34.

3 Tryon's letter is printed in 4 *FAA*, IV, 173. For a full account of Smith's plan and its fate in the Provincial Congress, see Bernard Mason, *The Road to Independence: The Revolutionary Movement in New York, 1773–1777* (Lexington, Ky., 1966), pp. 118–29.

TO ALEXANDER McDOUGALL

Philadelphia, 8 December 1775

Dear Sir

Accept my Thanks for your Letter of the 6th Inst.[1] which I recieved Yesterday. It gave me great Satisfaction to find you had at Length made a Convention,[2] my Apprehensions on that Head occasioned much anxiety, and am still grieved that the People of our Province have so little Firmness as to be duped by the Artifices of Men whose Views are obvious, and of the Rectitude of whose Intentions there has long been Reason to doubt.

The printed Paper inclosed in your Letter is alarming and that for the Reasons you suggest. It is a Piece of Finesse difficult to obviate, considering the Temper of the Province. The Conduct proper to observe on the occasion turns so much on Circumstances that it is difficult at this Distance to advise what would be best.

To declare absolutely against having any more Assemblies would be dangerous, because the People are too little informed to see the Propriety of such a Measure. And yet the Reasons you urge for supplying their Place by Conventions are very forceable.

If an Assembly of proper Members could be formed, it would give me little Uneasiness. For then should Lord North's[3] Proposition be laid before them, it would be in their Power to reduce Administration to a disagreable Dilemma. My Plan in that Case would be to assure the Governor of their Desire of seing Peace between Britain and the Colonies reestablished, and of their Readiness to declare their Sentiments respecting Lord North's Proposal, whenever his Majesty would be pleased to direct some Mode of hearing the joint Proposals and offers of his American Subjects; That hitherto the Petitions both of Assemblies and Congress had remained unanswered, and therefore that they must decline attempting to signify their Sentiments on the Subject till such Time a Way for their being heard was opened. That they had no Reason to expect that his Majesty would pay greater attention to their Desires when signified by a Governors Letter to a Secretary of State, than he had done to their Petitions, That the Faith of the Ministry had not be kept with the Colony, for that a former assembly had been invited to petition, and after being drawn into that Measure were neglected. That they were determined to share the Fate of their Neighbours, and tho disposed to Reconciliation, were determined to defend their Liberties.

The Jersey Troops are ordered to proceed to your Town as fast as they can procure Arms and Barack Necessaries.[4]

I hope Mr. Hamilton continues busy; I have not recieved Holts paper these 3 Months and therefore cannot Judge of the Progress he makes.[5]

Adieu. Yours most sincerely

JOHN JAY

ALS. NHi: McDougall Papers. Addressed: "Collonel Alexander McDougall in New York, free J. Jay." Endorsed.

1 Letter not located.

2 JJ referred to the New York Provincial Congress as the "convention." See also, below, JJ to McDougall, 13 Dec. 1775.

3 Frederick North (1732–92), Lord North, headed the British ministry from March 1770 to March 1782.

4 Congress ordered two battalions of New Jersey troops to march to New York City on 8 Dec. 1775. *JCC*, III, 416.

5 Alexander Hamilton's contributions to John Holt's (1721–84) *N.Y. Journal* in late 1775 have not been identified. For a discussion of the tracts which may have been involved, see Broadus Mitchell, *Alexander Hamilton* (2 vols., New York, 1962), I, 60–61.

"Between Hawk and Buzzard"—Disclaiming Independence While Edging Toward Continentalism

During the months between the adoption of the Olive Branch Petition and his draft of "Proofs that the Colonies Do Not Aim at Independence" JJ, like Congress itself, was in an increasingly ambivalent position, suspended, as John Adams impatiently described it, "between hawk and buzzard." By temperament an activist, a believer that government must be infused with energy and more and more inclined to adopt a continental approach to the exercise of war powers and the management of external relations, JJ demonstrated his nationalist-leaning sentiments by opposing initiatives stemming from the separate provinces aimed at conciliation. On 10 October he argued in favor of the appointment by Congress of officers in the battalions to be raised in New Jersey. His incipient nationalism emerges in the comment, "The Union depends much upon breaking down provincial Conventions." Two days later, in opposing the proposition that all custom houses be closed down, he remarked, "We are to consult the general Good of all America."[1]

By this time JJ was one of the most active committee men in Congress, serving on such crucial committees as the Committee to correspond "with our friends in Great Britain, Ireland, and other parts of the world,"[2] in fact, the secret committee of foreign affairs, which underwent numerous changes in personnel and function. When, in March 1776, the Congress's agent, Silas Deane, left for France under contract with the Secret Committee, JJ gave him a quantity of invisible ink which was an invention of his brother, Sir James, in order that confidential communications could be dispatched overseas in relative security.[3] On a committee of Congress to deal with disaffection in Queens County, New York, JJ participated in drafting a report urging that all persons who voted against sending deputies to the provincial convention "be put out of the protection of the United Colonies," that such persons may not leave the county without a certificate from the New York Congress, that they be debarred from courts of law, that their names be published in county newspapers for one month, and that they be disarmed—in all, strong medicine for a moderate.[4] By 23 December, as the letter to Alexander McDougall below reveals, JJ had become convinced of the expediency of the exercise of the taxing powers by provincial governments, a suggestion he would reiterate a few months later.

During the remainder of his attendance at sessions of the Second Congress JJ continued to press for vigorous measures of defense and against subversive activities. Already, on 3 November 1775, he had been commissioned as colonel of the Second Regiment of Militia of Foot of New York, and he vigorously supported the efforts of Congress not only to procure arms but to apprehend and imprison Tories, including "all Scotch and Roman Catholic solders" enlisted by a British Captain McDonald.[5] He assisted in drafting the preamble to the resolution of 23 March 1776 authorizing the commissioning of privateers.[6] In the latter part of April, before leaving Congress, he drafted a resolve setting up legal machinery in the colonies fixing liability for those assisting "enemies of the United Colonies" in the capture of Patriot vessels or goods. But the swift march of independence made this draft obsolete, and even sterner measures were adopted in July of 1776. Even before that, on 11 April, JJ conceded that "the Sword must decide the Controversy," and proposed that the first order of business was "to erect good and well ordered governments," thus anticipating in fact the Congressional resolution of 10 May, adopted after he had left Philadelphia.[7]

Concerned equally with the enhancement of governmental power in the war emergency and with clipping the wings of activist Tories, he was vigilant in seeing that the civilian government kept the upper hand. He joined with others on the New York delegation in Congress in protesting, 15 March 1776, the imposition by General Charles Lee of a test oath.[8] He was alarmed lest the enforcement of loyalty oaths be taken over by the army. "To impose a Test," he asserted, "is a sovereign act of Legislation, and when the army become our Legislators, the People that Moment become Slaves."[9]

Despite his activist role in the wartime emergency, JJ, back in the fall of 1775, had still maintained an anti-independence posture, though favoring united rather than separate colonial stands on that supreme issue. Since New Jersey and Pennsylvania both instructed their respective delegates in Congress "utterly to reject" any proposition for independence, Congress's hand was forced. On 13 November 1775 it named a committee to answer "the sundry illegal *ministerial* proclamations that have lately appeared in America."[10] Before this committee's report could be considered, Congress learned that the New Jersey Assembly planned to petition the king. Judging such an appeal "very dangerous to the liberties and welfare of America," Congress appointed John Jay, John Dickinson, and George Wythe (1726–1806) of Virginia to dissuade the colony from this measure.[11] On 5 December JJ, Dickinson, and Wythe addressed the New Jersey Assembly at Burlington. Governor William Franklin made these notes of JJ's speech:

> *Mr. Jay*—said We had nothing to expect from *the Mercy* or *Justice* of Britain—That *Petitions* were *now* not the *Means, Vigour & Unanimity* the only Means—That the *Petition of United America*[12] presented by Congress ought to be relied on,—others unnecessary—and Hoped the House would not think otherwise.[13]

The committee's arguments were persuasive, and the New Jersey Assembly voted against a separate address to George III.[14] On 6 December, the Continental Congress adopted the report of the committee on "ministerial proclamations" which indignantly denied the charge that the colonists were "forgetting the allegiance" they owed the crown.[15]

It was in this atmosphere that JJ drafted the paper printed below. It was composed at some time after 11 December 1775 when the edition of the *Journals* of Congress cited by JJ was published.[16] Although obviously intended for publication, no evidence has been found that the essay appeared in the New York or Pennsylvania press. This may indicate that JJ drafted the paragraphs in late December or early January, for the publication of Thomas Paine's *Common Sense* on 10 January 1776 would have persuaded JJ that publication of this defense of Congress would be ineffective. With Paine's historic pamphlet, the terms of debate on independence altered quickly. It no longer mattered whether Congress had "aimed" at independence in 1775; for JJ and other Americans the important question in 1776 was whether Congress should declare independence.

1 John Adams, *Diary*, II, 203, 204, 206. The issue of appointing officers was settled on 7 November, when Congress elected the identical officers nominated by the New Jersey Convention. *JCC*, III, 285–88, 335.

2 Elected 29 November. JJ originally served with Benjamin Harrison, Benjamin Thomson, Thomas Johnson, Jr., and John Dickinson.

3 See JJ to Robert Morris, 15 Sept. 1776. JJ also served on two other standing committees—Medicine (14 Sept. 1775) and Qualifications (or Applications) (8 December, replaced by Duane 16 Jan. 1776). *JCC*, II, 250; III, 417; IV, 61. He also was named, 2 Nov. 1775, to a committee to consider the admission of Nova Scotia to "the association of the North Americans." *Ibid.*, III, 316. For the committee report of 10 November to send a mission to Nova Scotia, see *ibid.*, p. 348. On 27 November JJ was added to the committee to consider the boundary dispute between Connecticut and Pennsylvania. *Ibid.*, p. 377. According to John Adams's later recollections (8 March 1805), JJ had expressed his dissatisfaction to Adams about the latter's omission from "the two great secret committees, of commerce and correspondence," attributing it to the partisan activities of Samuel Adams and Richard Henry Lee. JJ had won appointment to the secret committee of correspondence. *LMCC*, I, 265. For the unsubstantiated insinuations of Arthur Lee in London about JJ, spread either by his brother Richard Henry Lee or Samuel Adams, see *RDC*, II, 76–77.

4 *JCC*, III, 463; IV, 25–28.

5 See Thomas McKean, Thomas Lynch, and JJ to Schuyler, 1 Jan. 1776, in NN: Schuyler Papers.

6 *JCC*, IV, 213, 222–32; JJ to McDougall, 21, 27 March 1776, below. In the debates on this resolve JJ was reported to have declared that he was "for a War against such only of the British nation as are our enemies." Richard Smith Diary, 13 March 1776, *LMCC*, I, 386.

7 JJ to McDougall, 11 April 1776, below.

8 *JPC*, I, 379; 4 *FAA*, V, 1391. The protest bears two dates, 1 and 15 March for the postscript.

9 JJ to McDougall, 13 March 1776, below. For JJ's service on a committee appointed to examine the truth of a report that Governor Tryon had exacted an oath to persons embarking from New York, binding themselves not to disclose American affairs to anyone except the Ministry, and JJ's instructions to the New York Committee of Safety, 27 April 1776, to ascertain the facts by affidavits taken before the mayor or one of the judges of the "Superior Court," see 4 *FAA*, V, 1092; *JCC*, IV, 273; *LMCC*, I, 432.

10 *JCC*, III, 353.

11 *Ibid.*, p. 404.

12 The Olive Branch Petition of July 1775.

13 "Administration of Governor William Franklin," *N.J. Archives*, 1st ser., X, 691.

14 *Ibid.*, pp. 677–78.

15 *JCC*, III, 409–12.

16 The edition is that printed by William and Thomas Bradford of Philadelphia. Their *Journal of the Proceedings of the Congress, held at Philadelphia, May 10, 1775* was offered to the public in an announcement printed in the *Pennsylvania Packet* of 11 Dec. 1775.

John Jay: Proofs that the Colonies Do Not Aim at Independence

[*Philadelphia, after 11 December 1775*]

It has long been the Art of the Enemies of America to sow the Seeds of Dissentions among us and thereby weaken that Union on which our Salvation from Tyranny depends. For this Purpose Jealousies have been endeavoured to be excited, and false Reports, wicked Slanders and insidious misrepresentations <been so> industriously formed and propagated.

Well knowing that while the People reposed Confidence in the Congress, the Designs of the Ministry would probably be frustrated. No Pains have been spared to traduce <and> that respectable Assembly and misrepresent their Designs and Actions.

Among other Aspersions cast upon them, is an ungenerous and groundless Charge of their aiming at Independence, or a total Separation from G. Britain.

Whoever will be at the Trouble of reviewing their Journal will find ample Testimony against this Accusation, and for the Sake of those who may not have either Leisure or Opportunity to peruse it, I have selected the following Paragraphs which abundantly prove the Malice and Falsity of such a Charge.

Page 59. The Congress in giving orders for securing the Stores taken at Crown Point and Ticonderogah direct "That an Exact Inventory be taken of all such Cannon and Stores, in Order that they may be safely returned, *when the Restoration of the former Harmony between Great Britain and these Colonies, so ardently wished for by the latter* shall render it prudent and consistent with the *over-ruling Law of self Preservation*."[1]

Page 63. The Congress after resolving that the Colonies ought to be put in a State of Defence thus proceed: "But as *we most ardently wish* for a *Restoration of the Harmony* formerly subsisting between our Mother Country and these Colonies, the Interruption of which must, at all Events be exceedingly injurious to both Countries, *that with a sincere Design of contributing by all the means in our Power* (not incompatible with a just Regard for the undoubted Rights and true Interests of these Colonies) *to the Promotion of this most desireable Reconciliation,* an humble and dutiful Petition be presented to his Majesty Resolved That *Measures be entered into for opening a negotiation, in order to accommodate the unhappy Disputes subsisting between Great Britain and these Colonies,* and that *this* be made a *Part* of the *Petition to the King.*"[2]

Page 64. The Congress recommend to the Convention of New York "to persevere the more vigorously in preparing for their Defence, as it is very uncertain whether *the earnest Endeavours of the Congress to accommodate the unhappy Differences between Great Britain and the Colonies, by conciliatory Measures, will be successful.*"[3]

Page 84. The Congress in order to rescue the Province of Massachusets Bay from Anarchy, advise <them to> that their "Assembly or Council exercise the Powers of Government *untill a Governor of his Majestys Appointment* will consent *to govern <them> the Colony according to its Charter.*"[4]

Page 87. The Congress in their Vote for a general Fast <did> recommended that we should "offer up our joint Supplications to the all wise, omnipotent and merciful Disposer of all Events (among other Things) *To bless our rightful Sovereign King George the third.* That *a speedy End* may be put to the *civil Discord between great Britain and the american Colonies* without further Effusion of Blood. And that all America may soon behold a gracious Interposition of Heaven for the Redress of her many Grievances, the Restoration of her invaded Rights, *a Reconciliation with the parent State on Terms constitutional and honorable to both.*"[5]

Page 149. The Congress after declaring the Reasons which compelled them to recur to arms, thus express Themselves:

"Lest this Declaration should disquiet the Minds of our Friends and Fellow Subjects in any Part of the Empire, we assure Them that *we mean not to dissolve that Union which has so long and so happily subsisted between us,* and which we *sincerely wish* to see *restored. Necessity* has not yet *driven* us into that *desperate* Measure, or induced us to excite any other Nation to War against them. We *have not* raised Armies *with Ambitious Designs of separating from Great Britain, and establishing independent States.*"[6]

[Page] 150. "We most humbly implore the divine Goodness *to dispose our Adversaries to Reconciliation on reasonable Terms.*"[7]

Page 155. In the Petition to the King, every Line of which breaths affection for his Majesty and Great Britain, are these remarkable Sentences:

"Attached to your Majestys Person Family and Government, with all the Devotion that Principle and Affection can inspire, *connected with Great Britain by the strongest Ties that can unite Societies;* and *deploring every Event* that tends in *any Degree* to *weaken* them, we *solemnly assure* your Majesty, that we not only *most ardently desire* the former *Harmony* between her and these Colonies may be *restored,* but that a *Concord* may be *established between them* upon so *firm a Basis* as to perpetuate its Blessings uninterrupted *by any future* <Generations> *Dissentions to succeeding Generations in both Countries.* We beg Leave further to assure your Majesty that notwithstanding the *Sufferings* of your loyal Colonists during the Course of this present Controversy our Breasts retain *too tender a Regard for the Kingdom from which we derive our origin,* to request such a Reconciliation as might in *any Manner be inconsistent with her Dignity or Welfare.*"[8]

Page 163. In the last Address of the Congress to the People of Great Britain are the following Passages:

"*We are accused of aiming at Independence;* but *how* is this Accusation *supported?* By the *Allegations* of your *ministers* not by *our Actions. Abused insulted and contemned, what Steps have we pursued to obtain Redress? We have carried our dutiful Petitions to the Throne. We have applied to your Justice for Relief.*"

Page 165. "Give us Leave most solemnly to assure you, *That we have not yet lost Sight of the Object we have ever had in View, a Reconciliation with you on constitutional Principles, and a Restoration of that friendly Intercourse which to the Advantages of both, we till lately maintained.*"[9]

Page 172. In the address of the Congress to the Lord Mayor, Aldermen and Livery of London, there is this Paragraph, vizt.:

"*North America* My Lord! *wishes most ardently for a lasting Connection with Great Britain on Terms of just and equal Liberty.*"[10]

From these Testimonies it appears extremely evident that to charge the Congress with aiming at a Separation of these Colonies from great Britain is to charge them falsely and without a single Spark of Evidence to support the Accusation.

Many other Passages in their Journal might be mentioned, but as that would exceed the Limits of this Paper, I shall reserve them for some future Publication.

It is much to be wished that People would read the Proceedings of the Congress and <judge for themselves> consult their own Judgments and not suffer themselves to be *duped by Men who are paid for decieving them.*

AD. Sol Feinstone Collection (deposited at PPAmP). Endorsed in another hand: "Proofs that the colonies do not aim at independence. Probably in 1775." If it could be surmised that JJ was writing in reaction to George III's speech to Parliament of 26 Oct. 1775, in which the charge was made that Congress was striving for American independence, then the "Proofs" would have to be post-dated 7 Jan. 1776 because that is when a copy of the king's speech arrived in Philadelphia for the first time.

1 JJ gave page citations to the Bradford edition of the *Journal of Congress . . .* published in Philadelphia in December 1775. This reference corresponds to the entry of 18 May 1775 in *JCC*, II, 56. Editorial notes for later citations will give corresponding entries in the modern *JCC* series for the reader's convenience.

2 Entry for 26 May 1775, *JCC*, II, 65–66.

3 Entry for 26 May 1775, *JCC*, II, 64.

4 Entry for 9 June 1775, *JCC*, II, 84.

5 Entry for 12 June 1775. JJ omitted a catalogue of prayers and other sections of Congress's call for a general fast. *JCC*, II, 87–88.

6 Entry for 6 July 1775, *JCC*, II, 155.

7 Entry for 6 July 1775, *JCC*, II, 156–57.

8 In this selection from the Olive Branch Petition, JJ omitted several lines without indicating the elisions. *JCC*, II, 160.

9 Entry for 8 July 1775, *JCC*, II, 166, 167.

10 Entry for 8 July 1775, *JCC*, III, 171.

To Alexander McDougall

Philadelphia, 13 December 1775

Dear Sir

Your Letter of the 8th Inst.[1] is now before me. Did you know how much Satisfaction a Line from you gives me, you would not think of apologizing for the frequency of your Letters. I am much obliged to you for your Hints respecting the Command of a certain Post.[2] They are useful and will determine my Conduct, tho some Folks here may not coincide with me in opinion. I must confess that I think the Station might be better filled, and wished it consisted with the Interest of the Province to take you from the Convention etc. but as I am sure such a Measure would be highly impolitic and imprudent, it must be declined.

I am very glad to hear that the Convention begins to think of us, and am in daily Expectation of hearing from them on the Subject. I wish they would lessen the Number of Delegates; it would diminish the Expence, without injuring the Interest of the Colony. As I cant confer with you on this Subject, the Matter must be entirely submitted to your Discretion; it is too delicate to trust to the uncertain Fate of a Letter.[3]

Pray does the Convention mean to take up the New England Expedition? I really think they should thank Connecticut for the Aid they afforded West Chester, and complain loudly of the late improper Incursion. The Honor of the Colony is at Stake and the Convention is now the only Guardian of it.[4]

Adieu. I am with great Sincerity, your Friend

JOHN JAY

You forget your Accounts!

ALS. NHi: McDougall Papers. Addressed: "To Collonel Alexander McDougall in New York. free J. Jay." Endorsed.

1 Letter not located.

2 On 9 Nov. 1775 the New York delegates at Philadelphia informed the Provincial Congress that a commander would be named for the fort under construction in the Hudson Highlands. The delegates asked the New York Congress to propose "three or four gentlemen who are competent for the trust." The Provincial Congress did not reply to this letter until 8 December when they wrote the delegates recommending SLJ's second cousin, Gilbert Livingston (1742–1806) of Dutchess County, William Bedlow, Thomas Grenell, and Jonathan Lawrence (1737–1812) of New York City as candidates for the command. *JPC*, I, 209; II, 107.

3 See above, JJ to McDougall, 4 Dec. 1775. For the Provincial Congress's resolutions on their delegates to the Continental Congress, see below, McDougall to JJ, 18–19 Dec. 1775.

4 For the Provincial Congress's action on the Sears expedition, see below, McDougall to JJ, 14 and 18–19 Dec. 1775.

From Alexander McDougall

New York, December 14th, 1775

Dear Sir,

Your favors of the 4th and 8th instant I received this moment. It was the St John's officers, and not those of Chamblee, who were apprehensive that the Capitulation, would not be maintained; but if my information of the destination of that Corps be true, their suspicions must be groundless.[1]

You are fully acquainted of my opinion on the subject of the Tea. Sure I am their determination is very impolitic.

The Convention have wrote to Governor Trumbul on the subject of the expedition against Mr Rivington, and expressed it in such Terms, as will not be prejudicial to the Virtuous Union, and the Committee who drafted this Letter, are charged with reporting another to Your Congress, to pass a Resolution to prevent the inhabitants of one Colony's coming into another in a Hostile manner, without the orders of the Continental or provincal Congress, the

Committee of the County, or Safety, or the orders of one of the Continental Generals.[2]

A Committee has been appointed to state and report the Continental disbursments, and I hope in a few days they will be ready.[3] To morrow I shall move, that the Provission for our Continental delegates be determined.[4]

We have ordered that 100 <Arms> Muskets be procured for the Jersey Troops, which will be ready in a few days. But this is the last that our neighbour can expect from us. For we want all we can make for our selves; the Colony is already too much striped of its Arms, both Public and private, to Arm the Continental Troops, while we have reason to beleive, that some of our neighbours are too tenacious of their provincial Security to spare their Arms to the Confederated Colonies.[5] Have the Jersies taken their public Arms to arm the Troops. Last Summer they were very illiberal on our poor Colony, for not expediting the march of our Troops detained Soley for the want of Arms, vaunting if they had orders to raise forces, they would be <filled> Compleated and appointed in a very short time. Why dont they take the 80 Stand of Fire Arms, in the Tory County of Bergen, that belong to it? Must New York already too much abused, be Striped of all; and Subject to further abuses, if for want of Arms and amunition they fall an easey prey to envaders?

Mr. Thomas Smith has brought the consideration of Governor Tryons Letter, before Congress in an ill Judged manner. But the mischief of it will be defeated. They have determined opon resolutions approving of Assemblies and the ancient form of our excellent Constitution; but avoid an approbation of calling of Such a Body, at present; for the reasons hinted to you, and many others, which time will alow me to mention.[6]

The Bearrer hereof Capt. John Hazard has been master of a Vessel out of this port; and inclines entering into the Sea Service, of the Colonies. From the recommendations I have received of him, he will be fit to fill some important office, in that department, above petty officers. I therefore think you may with safety recommend him.[7] My Nephew John McDougall[8] is Gone to your City; to enter into the same service. He is Capable to serve, as first mate of a Vessel having served his time regularly to the Sea in the London Trade and well instructed in Letters for a Sea officer. I shall direct him to apply to you. If there should be such a vacancy, he may be relied on for his sobriety and integrity.

I am Dear Sir in Haste Your Humble Servant

ALEXR. McDOUGALL

ALS. Addressed: "Col. John Jay delegate for the Colony of New York in Congress, Phia., by Capt. Hazard." Endorsed.

[1] For the confusion over the prisoners from Chambly and St. Johns, see McDougall to JJ, 29 Nov. 1775 and JJ to McDougall, 4 Dec. 1775.

[2] On 12 Dec. 1775 the Provincial Congress approved a letter to Jonathan Trumbull, Sr. (1710–85), governor of Connecticut, 1769–84. The Congress asked that Connecticut see to it that no such unauthorized raids would be repeated. Later in that session, the Congress voted resolutions which expressed thanks to "the inhabitants of the Colony of Connecticut, who so cheerfully gave their aid at the request of the Committee of Westchester county, in the late suppression of the insurgents in that county against the cause of liberty" and which authorized local committees to call for assistance from committees in other provinces in emergencies. The Provincial Congress's letter to its delegates on this subject, dated 18 December, is omitted from *JPC* but is printed in 4 *FAA*, IV, 422–23. *JPC*, I, 214.

[3] This committee was named on 6 Dec. 1775. No report is entered in the *JPC*, and on 16 December, when the Provincial Congress listed the powers of a Committee of Safety that would sit during its adjournment, the Congress empowered the Committee "to carry into execution a settlement of accounts with the Continental Congress." *JPC*, I, 206, 223.

[4] On 15 December McDougall moved that delegates to the First and Second Continental Congresses be allowed $5.00 for each day of their attendance. *JPC*, I, 220.

[5] For New York's supply of arms to New Jersey troops, see above, JJ to McDougall, 4 Dec. 1775, n. 4.

[6] Thomas Smith (1734–c. 1800), Judge William Smith's brother, was a N.Y. City delegate to the Second Provincial Congress. As part of the Loyalist strategy developed by Judge Smith, his brother introduced four resolutions in the New York Congress on 8 December. These resolutions reaffirmed the province's loyalty to the crown and declared the necessity of the colony's expressing its views on Lord North's reconciliation plan in "such a way as His Excellency [Governor Tryon] may conceive to be most constitutional." Debate on these resolutions was interrupted on 8 December and did not resume until five days later. On 13 December John Sloss Hobart offered substitute resolutions which gave explicit approval to an assembly session, but included a sharp rebuke to the British ministry for its "arbitrary and tyrannical encroachments" upon provincial rights. On the morning of 14 December McDougall and John Morin Scott led radical delegates in amending the resolutions offered the day before. By the noon recess that day, the resolutions had been altered to include an indictment of Parliament as well as the ministry, and the call for an Assembly session was deleted. McDougall probably wrote to JJ during the midday break in the proceedings since he does not discuss the afternoon debates which resulted in resolutions declaring that "nothing of a salutary nature" would result from a "separate declaration" of New York on North's plan and that the province was "fully and effectually represented in the Continental Congress" and that Congress had already "Fully and dispassionately expressed the sense" of the province in their July resolutions on the North reconciliation proposal. *JPC*, I, 210–11, 217–20.

[7] John Hazard did not receive a Continental naval commission during the Revolution.

[8] John McDougall was appointed a second lieutenant in the Navy on 22 Dec. 1775. *JCC*, III, 443.

FROM PETER JAY

Rye, 18 December 1775

Dear Johnny

My last was of the 1st inst., which in Fady's absence to Albany, was delivered to Garrit Van Horne to be forwarded to you per the Post. I am surprised that neither of my letters had reached your hands. Yours of the 4 and 8 inst.[1] I just now received, and am very glad that you and Sally were both well. Remember our love to her. Mama continues as well as can be expected, and we shall be very happy if her Pains don't considerably increase when the Season grows more severe.

It gives me pain that there is no prospect yet of an accommodation with the Mother Country. God grant that a happy reconciliation may soon take place upon Equitable terms, instead of a long bloody struggle we are threatened with. I once expected to pass the remainder of my life in the injoyment of happy days with my Family, which to my inexpressible grief I've now no prospect of, but hope it will please God to enable me to be Resigned in every condition in Life with a commendable Spirit.

Although your presence always gives me great pleasure, I am nevertheless too Anxious about your welfare to desire your coming in this dangerous Season of the year.

Peter promises to take good Care of your Colt, which as well as the Mare is in very good Order. We have hitherto had good Pasture, and they have always taken care to find out the best.

We all remember our love to you, and I always am Your Very Affectionate Father,

PETER JAY

P.S. Let me hear often from you.

ALS.

[1] Peter Jay to JJ, 1 Dec. 1775 and JJ to Peter Jay, 4 Dec. and 8 Dec. 1775, not located. Garret Van Horne was JJ's first cousin.

FROM ALEXANDER MCDOUGALL

New York, December 18th–19th, 1775

Dear Sir,

Your two late favors by post came duly to Hand and note their Contents.[1] You will see by Gaines Paper what our Convention have done on the subject of Governor Tryon's Letter; I hope it will please the Friends of the common Cause, and avoid the difficulties, that Paper was designed to put us into. Mr. Smith brought on the Consideration of the Letter by motion, followed by a string of resolutions, purporting, that we had not withdrawn our allegiance, that this and protection was reciprocal, that we considered his Excellency's Letter, as a mark of his affection for this Colony; wished he might know the sense of the Colony, on Lord North's Motion, in a constitutional way.

Mr. Scott and Mr. Hobart[2] consulted a sett of resolves, in order to cast them out, but they contained an approbation of Calling an Assembly. Here you may easily conceive the difficulty that must have ensued. The Friends of the cause agreeing in what I feared, might ruine us. After much Debate the Congress was convinced, that while on the one hand we did not interdict, the Calling an Assembly, but approved of that part of Constitution, yet it would be dangerous on the other to approve of the calling of one, as we could not be certain but they might divide the Colonies. If an Assembly should meet, we gave it as our opinion they ought not to treat seperatly, and that the Colony had already by its Delegates, declared their sense on the Motion of Lord North. These sentiments produced the resolves. Thus the Tories have lost an opportunity of dividing the People by new, and ill grounded fears, of a design to become independent, and the Whigs run no risque of a disunion of this, from the other Colonies of which I think there might have been some danger, if an assembly had been called, by our approbation, as was intended. The particular grounds of this apprehension I shall communicate to you, when I have the pleasure of seeing you. Suffice it now, that no prudent marriner should put his Vessel to sea in a storm out of a sure and safe Haven.

Since I began this, your favor of the 13th was handed to me. It gives me great pleasure, that any of my hasty communications give you satisfaction. This will convince you of my determination to continue it. I think I have mentioned to you, that the Parsimonious Spirit of the Colony, is very manefest in its Conventions. Attending to this, I Judged it most likely to succeed, in my intended motion for a provision to the Delegates, by confining it to near the Connecticut allowance;[3] and knowing, that they despised being paid for their Time, and expected only a reimburstment of their expences, and that what was given by that Colony under this denomination would not be adequate for yours; I moved that you should be allowed five dollars per day cash for your expences for every day, you were absent from your Families on the Public business. Suffolk by instruction moved for an amendment that it be three Dollars; but they lost it 11 County Votes by 10. Tryon moved another amendment for 4 dollars. Fearing, that this would be carried, New York and Albany offered to compromise for a Guinea, and enter it Nem. Con.; but they were too certain of carrying it to agree to this proposal. And carried it was: New York and Albany only against it, so that the provission is now fixed. It goes to the Delegates of the last as well [as] this Congress.[4] The Treasurer is ordered, upon certificate from the Convention or the Committee of Safety, of the Number of days; the delegates were on the Public Service in *quality* of Delegates to pay the money. Whenever you furnish this, the former will issue, and the payment will be made, as soon as we receive the first money from Phi[ladelphi]a. Two Members of Congress are appointed to go for the 50,000 Dollars.[5] The Convention wait for the New Counties, appearing by their Deputies, to make the representation fuller, before they enter on the Choice of the Delegates. The Number will certainly be lessened, to Three or Five, I am inclined to think the latter will be the number.[6]

What you wished to have done, on the New England expedition, is the very thing done. The Letter to the Governor complaining of the Incursion, inclosed a Vote of Thanks for their ready assistance in queling the West Chester insurrection. And a Letter was this day agreed upon, to Delegates, to obtain a resolution of Congress to prevent incursions of that kind for the future.

The favourable opinion you are pleased to express of placeing me at a Certain post is very obliging. Altho I suffer here by the Public business, harrassed almost to death, Yet I fear I should not suffer less there from apprehensions, that would arise from the State of the Colony. I have much to say to you and but little time to do it. What is done, or to be done, with the Arms taken at St. John's and Chamblee? They are greatly wanted in the Southermost part of this Colony, where no Price can purchase a sufficient quantity. If all the Arms we could collect here, to remove Carlton's Yoke from Canada, are to remain there, as well as those taken from the instruments of his Tyranny; I fear the next Year, will put one on us, as grievious to be borne as that we took of, from our Neighbour's. I suppose the Army was sent to Canada to enable the inhabitants to speak out, if they Chose it, and join the Virtuous Confederacy; And to secure amunition; the first of these is effected, But it was utterly improbable, that any officer of deserment would Suffer you to obtain the Last. If they dont join the confederacy, before the opening of the Spring, will it answer any Valuable end, for the united colonies to maintain a large army there to compel them? Will not the continental army, in this case, if they are at Quebec, be exposed to have their communication cut off with Montreal, by the Enemy's landing Troops and intrenching between those places, as they will have the command of the Navigation by their Navy. These are questions that should be well and early considered, least our success's there should weaken, instead of strengthening the Confederacy. If *the* Congress mean to maintain any of the sea ports, they ought to leave no stone unturned to procure Heavy cannon; these mounted in Fachine Batteries, and Bomb's are the only instruments, which terify and destroy ships of the Greatest Force. The materials for these, are in Great abundance to be had in our own Country. Why then have we not errected large furnaces capable to cast such ordinance?

19th December

The News of the day. Mr. Curson's Son a merchant in St. Eustacia,[7] writes his Father that a fleet had arrived at Martinico, with great quantities of military stores; and two Batallions of Troops, part of Eight destined for that Island; to be ready for the call of the Continent. Be the end, what it may, certain it is, that nation never keep such a Force in the Island in times of peace or ordinary speculation. God grant that our Nation may attend to the things, which make for her Peace and safety, before they are eternally out of her Power.

I am Dear Sir, Your affectionate Humble Servant

ALEXR. McDOUGALL

ALS. Endorsed.

1 JJ's letter to Nathaniel Woodhull, 26 Nov. 1775, was not "read & filed" in the New York Congress until 14 Dec. 1775. The second letter has not been identified. *JPC*, I, 218–19.

2 John Sloss Hobart (1738–1805) was a Suffolk County delegate in the New York Congress.

3 Connecticut delegates to the Continental Congress were paid $3.00 a day plus expenses. *JPC*, II, 19.

4 For the debates in the New York Congress on the delegates' pay, see *JPC*, I, 220.

5 On 18 Dec. 1775, the New York Congress directed Abraham Brasher and Thomas Palmer to proceed to Philadelphia to receive $50,000 granted to the province by the Continental Congress on 11 Nov. The Continental Congress had ordered the Pennsylvania delegates to "count and forward the said sums under a guard of three," but the New York Congress sent Brasher and Palmer to save the expense of a guard. *JCC*, III, 352; *JPC*, I, 224.

6 On 21 Dec. 1775, the Provincial Congress resolved that five members of its delegation could represent the colony in the Continental Congress and "that in case of the necessary absence of any one or two . . . that three or four of them be a quorum." *JPC*, I, 231.

[7] Richard Curson (1726–1805) was a New York merchant and shipowner. His eldest son, Samuel (c. 1753–86), represented the family firm of Curson & Seton on the Dutch island of St. Eustatius.

To Robert R. Livingston

Philadelphia, 19 [December] 1775

Dear Robert

How it came to pass I know not, but so the Fact is, that neither of your Letters to me came to Hand till the Day before Yesterday, when they were delivered to the President[1] by Gen. Schuylers last Express.

Mr. Duane just now accidentally told me that your Brother[2] was about to leave this Town, and I am now retired to the Lobby, in a Hurry to say a Word or two to you.

I confess I was a little hurt at not being favoured with a Line from you, especially as your writing to others convinced me that it was in your Power. The Matter is now explained and I have only to regret the accident by which the Letter was detained.

I most sincerely condole with you on the Loss of your good Father[3] and my good Friend. The many Instances of Friendship and Attention recieved from him and the Family will always command my Gratitude and interest me in every Thing that concerns them.

Something hangs about Harry that I dont understand and probably never shall unless you and I should hereafter confer upon the Subject. On hearing of his being in town I took Ph. Livingston[4] with and went to his Lodgings to pay him a Visit Intending unless preengaged to take him Home to dine with me. I asked him whether he dined out that Day—he told me he should dine with Mr. Duane and at Smiths, on which I replied that I would do myself the Pleasure of dining with him, which I accordingly did. From that Day to this I have not seen his Face except in the Street or at some Gentlemans House.

I am not without my suspicions relative to his Behaviour which you will easily guess and which shall in due Time be explained to you. Lest this Letter should miss him I must conclude—though I have much to say.

Adieu my dear Robert, I am your affectionate Friend

JOHN JAY

ALS. N. Endorsed.

[1] John Hancock (1737–93) had been elected president of the Continental Congress on 24 May 1775.

2 Henry Beekman Livingston. See above, Livingston to JJ, 27 Nov. 1775.

3 Judge Robert R. Livingston, Sr., died on 9 Dec. 1775.

4 Philip Livingston represented New York in the Continental Congress, 1774–78.

To Alexander McDougall

Philadelphia, 22nd December 1775

Dear Sir

Few Things have for some time past given me more Pleasure than the address with which you managed the Governors Letter on the Subject of Lord North's motion. It occasions however both Surprize and Concern that the *Sin of Fear* (as Lewis Morris calls it) should operate so powerfully on some of your Patriots, as it seems to do.

The Provision for the Delegates I imagined Would be similar to that of Connecticut. However as the Convention has thought proper to move on other Principles, I am determined that pecuniary Considerations shall never induce me to quit the Field so long as my Constituents will keep me whole. The Allowance they have agreed upon will, if I retrench a little, about do that.

It must be obvious that keeping much Company, is necessary to obtain a personal Influence with the Members, and that the Colony is interested in their Delegates possessing such Influence. Should we ever converse upon this Subject I will mention some important Instances of its Use.

I am glad you think of reducing our Number. Five is certainly sufficient, 3 of them to be a Quorum.

The Congress I am persuaded will not make the Loan you ask.[1]

Your Conduct relative to Sears Expedition so far as it respects Connecticut is certainly proper. But I suspect this will be the first Instance of censuring the Followers without reprehending the Leaders. It is time that your Government should acquire a firmer Tone.[2]

Tomorrow I shall go to Elizabeth Town, for a Week, and shall devote the first Leizure Hour I have to telling you twenty things about which Want of Time compels me now to be silent.

Mr. Duane complains to me that you have taken no Notice of a Letter he wrote you some time ago. He says it was friendly and expected you would treat it as such. It respected some Observations made on your Detention from the Army, and his Remarks on that Subject which were just.[3]

Coll. Morris was very useful at the Indian Treaty and had he not, by being accidentally at Pittsburgh, given the Congress an opportunity of supplying Dr. Franklins absence, by appointing him Com[missione]r pro Tempore, there is Reason to believe our affairs in that Quarter might have suffered.[4]

As to Arms, I think you should take Care how you strip yourselves to cover your Neighbours Nakedness, Neighbours too who have no Reason to expect. It is Time that you should look to your own Necessities. New York never stood better with Congress than now. Your Alacrity in raising and arming your Troops last Summer etc. is compared with the Tediousness and slow moving of others.

Some Powder has arrived here, but the Fleet will consume it. More has arrived to the Eastward, and the Congress will take that.[5] For the future remember that Charity should begin at Home.

God bless you. Yours etc.

JOHN JAY

ALS. NHi: McDougall Papers. Addressed: "To Collonel Alexander McDougall at New York. free J. Jay." Endorsed.

1 On 9 Dec. 1775 the Provincial Congress instructed New York's delegates in Philadelphia to seek a loan of £45,000. The New York Congress explained that it feared that a provincial emission of paper money for this amount might depreciate, while Continental currency would prove sound. However, on 23 December, the Continental Congress voted against such a loan. When the Committee of Safety of the New York Congress learned of this action, it passed a resolution of 6 Jan. 1776 which provided for an issue of N.Y. currency. 4 *FAA*, IV, 397, 1025–27; *JCC*, III, 452.

2 The New York Provincial Congress did not single out the leaders of the raid for reprimand in the various letters and resolutions passed on this subject.

3 On 15 Nov. 1775 James Duane wrote McDougall concerning criticism of the latter's decision not to join his regiment on active duty in Canada. Duane explained: "Upon an Occasion which I shall be at Liberty to mention when we meet, a member took notice in Congress of your not having Joind your Regiment when it was in actual Service and which he conceived to have been your indispensible Duty. I recalled that in August you told me you proposed to proceed with the last Detachment and that your Stay so long was necessary to forward the Business. I afterwards understood, but undistinctly, that you had been requested to remain in New York by the provincial Convention as it was thought your presence was useful. I mentioned these Circumstances adding that there could be no doubt but that you would be able to explain the Reason for not proceding with the Regiment to the Satisfaction of the most Scrupulous. After informing you of the fact advice must be superfluous as you must immediately see the propriety of asking General Schuyler at a convenient time to report to the Congress the motives of your remaining in Convention instead of taking the Field. I would not wish this to be done by way of Excuse but in the ordinary Course of Business when the Returns are forwarded." NHi: McDougall Papers.

4 See above, JJ to Sarah Livingston Jay, 26 Oct. 1775, n. 2.

5 The Continental Navy was created under the "Rules for the Regulation of the Navy" passed in Congress 28 Nov. 1775. *JCC*, III, 378–87.

To Sarah Livingston Jay

Philadelphia, 23 December 1775

My dear Wife

I have now the Pleasure of informing you that the New York Convention has at Length made some Provision for their Delegates vizt. 4 Dollars per Day for their Attendance on the last, and this Congress, so that I shall not be so great a Sufferer as I once apprehended. The Allowance indeed does by no Means equal the Loss I have sustained by the Appointment, but the Convention I suppose consider the Honor as an Equivalent for the Residue.

The Congress this Day refused to give me Leave of absence for next Week. There are but five New York Delegates here Coll. Morris and Mr. Lewis being absent, so that should either of us leave the Town, the Province would be unrepresented. We expect however soon to adjourn, and your Papa has engaged Mr. Hooper[1] to accompany him to Elizabeth Town, where I hope we shall soon be all very happy. My Horses were new shod, Wheels greased, Cloaths put up and every thing ready to set off early in the Morning, when on going to Congress this Morning all my pleasing Expectations of seeing you on Christmas Day were disappointed. Dont you pity me my Dear Sally? It is however some Consolation that should the Congress not adjourn in less than ten Days, I am determined to stay with you till ———.[2] And depend upon it nothing but actual Imprisonment will be able to keep me from you.

At present I find the Objections of the Congress so reasonable, that I am sure you would blame me, were I to attempt leaving them without Permission. I must endeavour to resign my self to my Fate, and am sure you have too much good Sence and too much Regard for ———[3] to permit the Disappointment to occasion unavailing Anxiety. Tomorrow or on Tuesday next the Congress will I believe determine the Time of Adjournment so that it is probable I shall have the Happiness of wishing you a happy New Year.

Adieu my beloved. I am most sincerely, Your affectionate

JOHN JAY

P.S. I have recieved a Letter from Rye of an old Date. They were as well as usual. I dined with your Papa to Day. He was very well. Once more let me intreat you to be chearful and keep up your Spirits. I know by my own Feelings that these kind of Disappointments are disagreable but when I reflect how much more happy were [*sic*] are

FOUNDERS OF A DYNASTY
John Jay's Paternal Grandparents

Augustus Jay. Copy after Gerret Duyckinck. (*Courtesy of The New-York Historical Society, New York City*)

nna Maria Bayard Jay. By Gerret uyckinck. (*Courtesy of The New-ork Historical Society, New York ity*)

Jay House, Rye. American School, nineteenth century. (*Courtesy of the New York State Office of Parks and Recreation*)

King's College in 1770. (*Columbiana Collection, Columbia University*)

Samuel Johnson, first President of King's College, New York, 1754–1764, and an intimate friend of the Jays. By John Smibert. (*Columbiana Collection, Columbia University*)

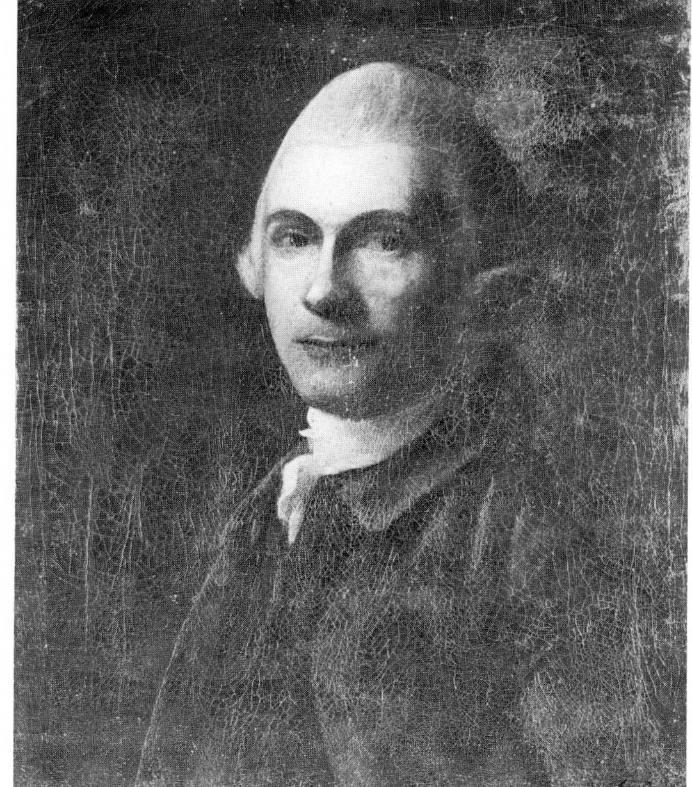

Sir James Jay, an embarrassing sibling. English School, eighteenth century. (*Courtesy of Alfred Thayer Mahan, Blauvelt, New York, and the Frick Art Reference Library*)

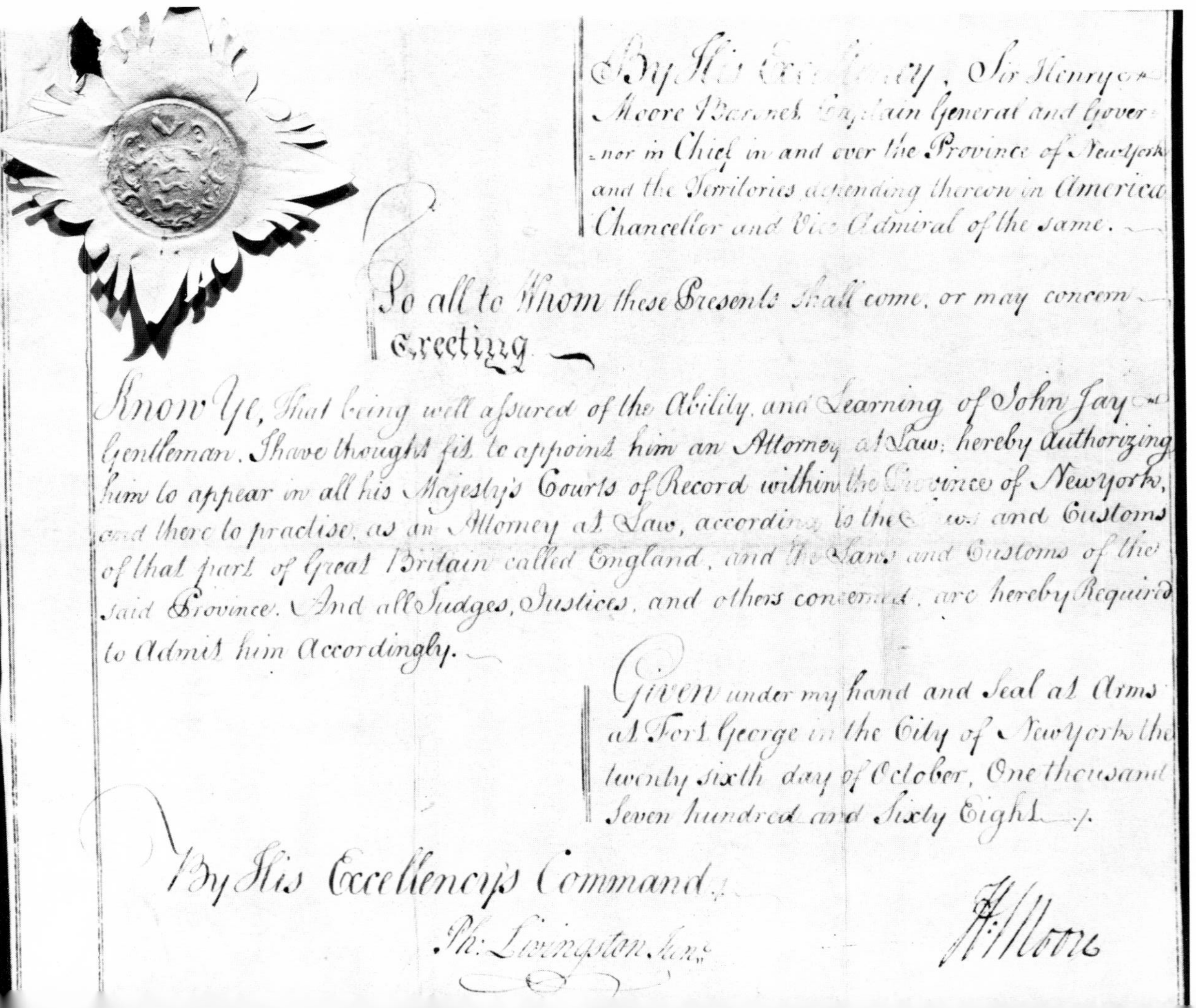

By His Excellency, Sir Henry Moore Baronet Captain General and Governor in Chief in and over the Province of New York and the Territories depending thereon in America Chancellor and Vice Admiral of the same.

To all to Whom these Presents shall come, or may concern Greeting

Know Ye, That being well assured of the Ability, and Learning of John Jay Gentleman. I have thought fit to appoint him an Attorney at Law; hereby Authorizing him to appear in all his Majesty's Courts of Record within the Province of New York, and there to practise, as an Attorney at Law, according to the Laws and Customs of that part of Great Britain called England, and the Laws and Customs of the said Province. And all Judges, Justices, and others concerned, are hereby Required to Admit him Accordingly.

Given under my hand and Seal at Arms at Fort George in the City of New York the twenty sixth day of October, One thousand Seven hundred and Sixty Eight.

By His Excellency's Command
Ph: Livingston Jun.

H Moore

Jay's license to practice law. (*Jay Papers, Special Collections, Columbia University Libraries*)

Jay's early law partner and intimate friend, Robert R. Livingston, Jr. By Ezra Ames. (*Collection of the Albany Institute of History and Art*)

A LOVE-STARRED COUPLE

John Jay at thirty-eight. Mixed stipple and line engraving by artist "B.B.E.," London, 1783. (*Courtesy of the New York State Office of Parks and Recreation*)

Sarah Livingston Jay. From an original pastel by James Sharpless. (*Courtesy of the New York State Office of Parks and Recreation and the Frick Art Reference Library*)

JAY IN-LAWS

Catharine W. Livingston. American School, eighteenth century. (*Courtesy of Mrs. Paul Hammond, New York City*)

William Livingston. By John Wollaston the Younger. (*Historic Fraunces Tavern and the Frick Art Reference Library*)

THE WORLD OF JOHN JAY ON THE EVE OF THE REVOLUTION

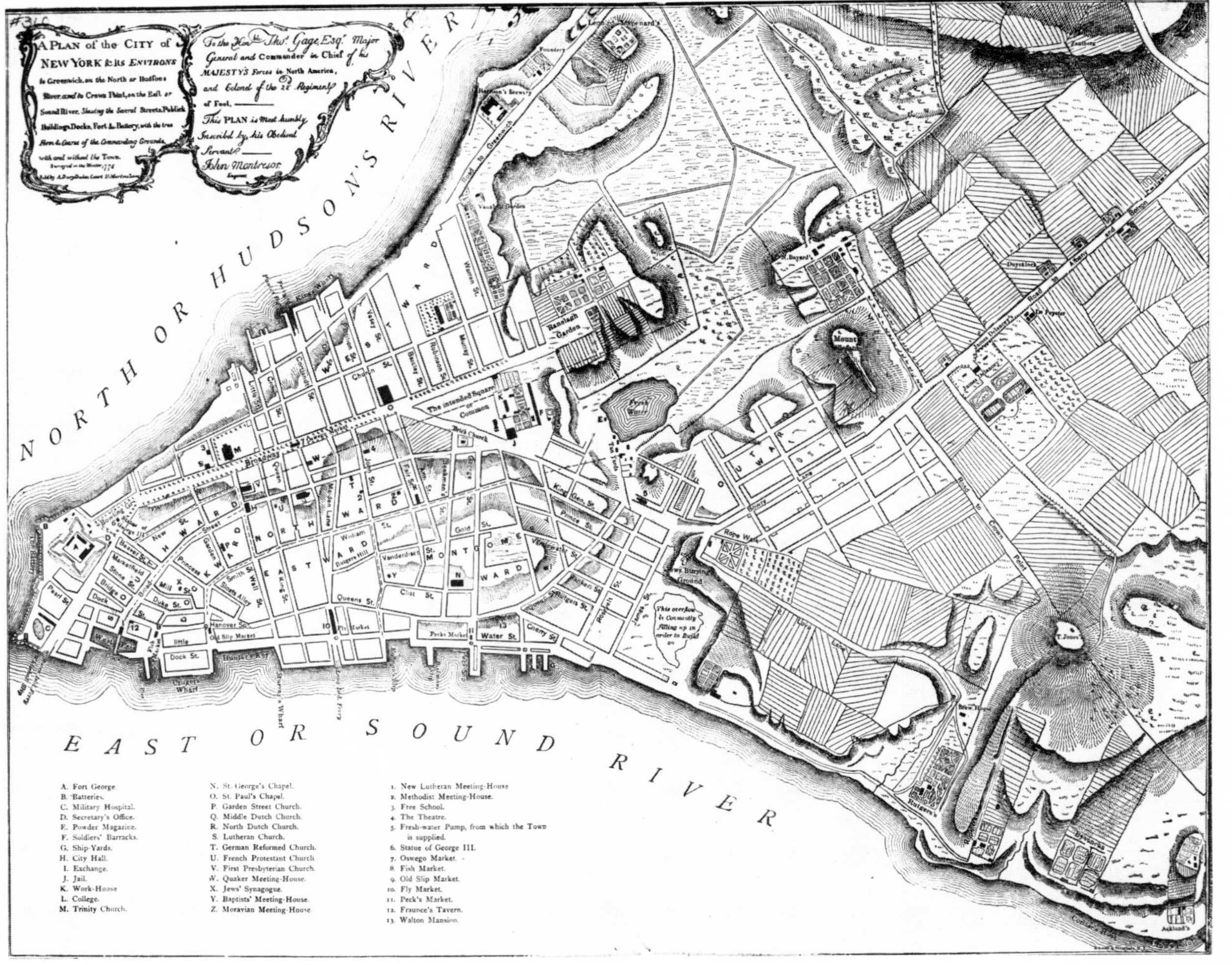

Montresor map of New York City, 1775. (*Courtesy of The New-York Historical Society,*

Queens Head (Fraunces) Tavern: Meeting place of the Dancing Assembly and the Social Club over which Jay presided. View in 1777. (*Historic Fraunces Tavern*)

FROM SOCIAL ARBITER TO MILITIA OFFICER

Appointment of John Jay as Colonel, 2d N.Y. Regiment, 3 November 1775. (*Jay Papers, Special Collections, Columbia University Libraries*)

In PROVINCIAL CONGRESS for the Colony of *New-York*, the *Third* Day of *November* 1775.

To *John Jay of the City of New York Esquire* Greeting:

BY Virtue of the Authority repoſed in us We do hereby nominate, authorize, conſtitute and appoint you *the said John Jay to be Colonel of the second Regiment of Militia of Foot* of the *City of New York* hereby requiring you, before you enter into the Exerciſe of your ſaid Office, to make in Writing, and ſubſcribe in Preſence of the Chairman of the Committee of the City, Town, Diſtrict, or Precinct wherein you reſide, the Declaration appointed and directed by the Eleventh Section of the Seventh Reſolve contained in the Rules and Orders for regulating the Militia of the Colony of New-York, recommended by this Congreſs on the 22d Day of Auguſt 1775, and authorizing you fully to execute all the Powers belonging to your ſaid Office, by Virtue of the ſaid Rules and Orders, and the ſaid Declaration: And we do hereby require all Perſons under your Command, to pay due Obedience to you, according to the ſaid Rules and Orders, and ſuch further Rules and Orders as ſhall be made and recommended for the Militia of this Colony, by the preſent, or any future Continental Congreſs, or Provincial Congreſs of this Colony.

Atteſt, *John McKesson Secry.*

By Order, *Abm. Yates Jun President*

AT THE FIRST CONTINENTAL CONGRESS

EXTRACTS

FROM THE

VOTES and PROCEEDINGS

Of the AMERICAN CONTINENTAL

CONGRESS,

Held at PHILADELPHIA on the

5th of *September* 1774.

CONTAINING

An *Aſſociation*, an *Addreſs* to the PEOPLE of GREAT-BRITAIN, and a *Memorial* to the INHABITANTS of the BRITISH AMERICAN COLONIES.

Publiſhed by order of the CONGRESS.

PHILADELPHIA:

Printed by WILLIAM and THOMAS BRADFORD;

October 24th, M,DCC,LXXIV.

Jay's debut as a republican polemicist: "Address to the People of Great-Britain," issued by the First Congress. (*Rare Book Division, The New York Public Library, Astor, Lenox and Tilden Foundations*)

Richard Henry Lee, delegate from Virginia, drafter of the "Memorial," who came off second best in a confrontation with Jay. By Charles Willson Peale. (*The National Archives*)

JAY SIGNS THE CONTINENTAL ASSOCIATION

foreign paper, glass and painters colours imported into America, and extend the powers of the admiralty courts beyond their ancient limits, deprive the American subjects of trial by jury, authorise the judges certificate to indemnify the prosecutor from damages that he might otherwise be liable to from a trial by his peers, require oppressive security from a claimant of ships or goods seized, before he shall be allowed to defend his property, are repealed — And until that part of the Act of the 12 G. 3. ch. 24 entitled an Act, for the better securing his Majesty's Dock yards, magazines, ships ammunition and stores" by which any person charged with committing any of the offences therein described, in America, may be tried in any shire or county within the realm is repealed. And until the four acts passed in the last session of Parliament, viz. that for stopping the port and blocking up the harbour of Boston — that for altering the charter and government of the Massachusetts Bay — and that which is entitled an act for the better administration of Justice &c., and that for extending the limits of Quebec &c. are repealed. And we recommend it to the provincial conventions and to the committees in the respective colonies to establish such farther regulations as they may think proper for carrying into execution this association. —

The foregoing association being determined upon by the Congress, was ordered to be subscribed by the several Members thereof and thereupon we have hereunto set our respective names accordingly.

In Congress, Philadelphia October 20th 1774. —

Peyton Randolph President

Jno. Sullivan
Nathl. Folsom

Thomas Cushing
Saml. Adams
John Adams
Robt. Treat Paine

Step. Hopkins
Sam: Ward

Eliphet Dyer
Roger Sherman
Silas Deane

Isaac Low
John Alsop
John Jay
Jas. Duane
Phil. Livingston
Wm. Floyd
Henry Wisner
S. Boerum

Wil: Livingston
Stepn. Crane
Richd. Smith
John De Hart

Pensylvania
Jos. Galloway
John Dickinson
Chas. Humphreys
Thomas Mifflin
E. Biddle
John Morton
Geo: Ross

The Lower Counties New Castle &c.
Cæsar Rodney
Tho McKean
Geo. Read

Maryland
Mat. Tilghman
Ths. Johnson Junr.
Wm. Paca
Samuel Chase

Virginia
Richard Henry Lee
G^o Washington
P. Henry Jr.
Richard Bland
Benj. Harrison
Edmd. Pendleton

North Carolina
Will Hooper
Joseph Hewes
R. Caswell

South Carolina
Henry Middleton
Tho Lynch
Christ Gadsden
J. Rutledge
Edward Rutledge

(*Papers of the Continental Congress, National Archives*)

Alexander McDougall. By John Ramage. (*Courtesy of The New-York Historical Society, New York City*)

James Duane. By John Ramage. (*Muse of the City of New York*)

JAY'S POLITICAL COLLABORATORS

John Dickinson. By Charles Willson Peale. (*Historical Society of Pennsylvania and the Frick Art Reference Library*)

Edward Rutledge. By James Earl. (C *tesy of Edward Rutledge Moore, Atla Georgia, and the Frick Art Reference brary*)

JOHN JAY'S DRAFT OF THE OLIVE BRANCH PETITION

To the Kings most excellent Majesty

The Petition of the Freeholders & Freemen of the Colonies of New Hampshire Massachusetts Bay Rhode Island, Connecticut, New York, New Jersey, Pensylvania, the Delaware, Maryland Virginia North Carolina South Carolina & the Parish of St. Johns in the Colony of Georgia, by their Representatives convened in general Congress at the City of Philadelphia the Day of 1775

humbly sheweth

That your Majestys american Subjects bound to your Majesty by the strongest Ties of Allegiance & affection and attached to their Parent Country by every Bond that can unite Societies, deplore with the deepest Concern the continuance of that System of colonial Administration which for twelve Years past has filled the minds of the loyal Inhabitants of North America with apprehensions of the most alarming Nature

That reposing the utmost Confidence in the Wisdom care of their Prince and the Justice of the British Nation they were urged by the perilous Situation of their Liberties to solicit his Majesty's Attention by their late

The first page. (*Courtesy, The Library Company of Philadelphia; now located in the Historical Society of Pennsylvania*)

THE GREAT FIRE IN NEW YORK, 20–21 SEPTEMBER 1776

An event that John Jay retrospectively applauded as an advocate of a scorched-earth policy. Washington attributed the conflagration to "Providence, or to some good, honest fellow." Print by André Bas-

Beverly Robinson, a double-dealing Tory. By Matthew Pratt. (*Museum of the City of New York*)

eter Van Schaack, victim f conscience. Oil on wood anel, artist unknown, cop-d *c.* 1820–1840 from lost riginal by John Trumbull. *Courtesy of The New-York istorical Society, New York ity*)

IMPORTUNATE CORRESPONDENTS

General Philip Schuyler, whose bruised feelings proved a trying burden to his friend John Jay. By John Trumbull. *(Courtesy of The New-York Historical Society, New York City)*

Robert Troup, whose so ing ambitions were harc commensurate with his m est talents. By Ralph Ea *(Courtesy of James D. I land, Cleveland, Ohio, a the Frick Art Reference brary)*

than thousands of our Fellow Mortals my Uneasiness is lost in Gratitude.

ALS. N. Addressed: "To Mrs. Sarah Jay at Wm. Livingstons Esqr Elizabeth Town. free J. Jay." Endorsed in an unidentified hand.

1 William Hooper (1742–90), a North Carolina delegate to the Congress.

2 Line drawn in ms.

3 Line drawn in ms.

To Alexander McDougall

Philadelphia, 23 December 1775

Dear Sir

Since writing my last to You, I find the Congress will not adjourn even for the Holydays. They have not indeed so *determined* but that seems to be the opinion of the majority of the members.[1]

Where does Mr. Alsop[2] stay? Should any Thing happen to one of us the Colony would be unrepresented. For my Part I wish some of the absent Gent[lemen] would return. We but just make a Quorum. Did not this Circumstance forbid my leaving the Congress I would pay you a short Visit during the Session of the Convention. What has become of Queens and Richmond?[3] Rival Governments or Governors are Solecisms in Politics.

It appears to me prudent that you should begin to impose light Taxes, rather with a View to *Precedent* than Profit. Suppose salt Petre, Wool or Yarn should be recieved in Payment. I think such a measure would tend to encourage Manufactures. They are essential to the Support of the Poor, and Care should be taken to encrease materials for them. The People of this Place are amazingly attentive to this Object; it keeps People easy and Quiet. By being employed they gain Bread. And when our Fellow Mortals are busy and well fed, they forget to complain. I hope your Convention will leave a Com[mitte]e of Safety.

Adieu. Yours most sincerely

JOHN JAY

ALS. NHi: McDougall Papers. Addressed: "To Coll. Alexander McDougall in New York. free J. Jay."

1 On 23 Dec. 1775 a committee on which JJ served submitted a report which listed the pending business before Congress. Congress adjourned until the day after Christmas, but a regular session was held on New Year's Day. *JCC*, III, 454–56; IV, 13.

2 John Alsop (d. 1794) represented New York in the First and Second Continental Congresses. He was absent from Philadelphia from the first week of November 1775 until early January 1776. *LMCC*, I, lii.

3 These counties sent no delegates to the Second Provincial Congress.

From Alexander McDougall

New York, December 24th, 1775

Dear Sir,

As this day has given me some respite, from the Hurry of Public Business, I embrace the favorable moment to give you some intelligence on our common Concern. The Convention who Elected our Continental Delegates, being unanimous in that choice, and the last Congress having in a full House recognized that act, it was Judged inexpedient by the Present convention (as they are not a full representation of the Colony) to alter the Delegates, but to lessen the expence to the Colony, they have determined, that Five of the Delegates do represent it; and that no more than this number, be on the Public Service at one time from the first of January next; and that they make such an arangement among themselves, as will answer the end of that resolution. But if one or two of the Delegates, thus appointed for a Fixed time to represent the Colony, should be sick, or by any other unavoidable accident prevented from attending for time appointed, in that case, the other Three or Four, who do attend are authorised to represent the Colony. Many other reasons suggested this measure in preference to a New Election, which I beleive will occur to you, without enumerating them. The secretaries are ordered to Transmit the Vote to our Delegates, and the act of the last Congress above mentioned.[1] The Congress adjourned the day before yesterday, till the first of February; and appointed a Committee of safety, consisting of thirteen members, with very ample powers. I wish they had the means of Carrying them into execution.[2]

If *the* Congress should take any other measures with Queens County, than those we have taken, they should have security for their object; for altho the majority of the County are not against the Public measures, Yet a majority of those who are active are against them; and therefore if Delegates should be sent by these, if the measures are to have this for their end, they would only be spies on our Conduct; without any security of the County's abiding by Congressional Determinations. I know of no steps that have not many objections. If you suffer them to continue in their present state, Kings will follow their example as Richmond has done; and whenever a Considerable number of Troops arrive, the Mal-Contents in Queens will join them.[3] If you disarm the latter, and take their chiefs as Hostages, it will raise their passions, and when the Troops arrive, if they have spare arms (which they probably will have) the mal-Contents will receive them, to be revenged of their Country men. But notwithstanding these difficulties, the latter mode offers itself in preference to the former. For I take it for granted, they will oppose us with arms, when they have it their Power, and by dissarming them now, we shall have their arms, to put in the Hands of our Friends; and our Enemies in the other Counties will be taught by our treatment to Queens, not to oppose the measures of the Continent. But if we passivly suffer them to declare against the Confederacy, they will have their arms, to use against us, which we want, and the defection in the Colony will be increased by their conduct, passing with impunity.

Should *the* Congress adopt the measure of dissarming Queens, the farther distant from it the Persons come, who are to execute the work, the safer it will be for them, and the Friends of the Cause in the County; for should it be done by Suffolk, and those attached to the Cause in Queens, the mal-contents would be tempted to wreak their Vengance on those neighbours. For these reasons, and those mentioned by the Convention to you, I think it will be safest for the confederacy to have our Friends in New-England deal with Queens. As many of the Jersey Vessels, which bring wood, hay, and provisions of all kinds to the City, are under the Denomination of Richmond's, will it not be prudent to let them alone for some time, till it is seen how they will relish the treatment to Queens?

I am well informed, that Colonel Dalrymple[4] is on board the Phenix. As there are no Vessels here bound to England, I suspect his business here is to examine and reconitre the state of this Colony, to enable the ministry or the General[5] to form the operations against it in the spring, or to head the adherents of the ministeral party, if they should dare to hold up their heads, or to command the Regiment And the Three Companies of Light Horse lately embarked at Boston, probably destined for Queens County, for the purpose of securing fresh provissions for the army at Boston. For as Nassau Island[6] is so distant from the main, but where they command, they may think, and with too much reason, that the experiment may be tried without any great risque in that County. If they succeed in any degree, it will amply pay them in their disstressed state for fresh provisions, if not as they command at sea, they can easily embark in the sound under the Protection of three or Four Frigates. It is Probable, the fears of their Creatures in that county, has induced them to promise them more sucess, that they can secure to them, in order to tempt the army there for their protection. We shall do the best we can, to prepare our Friends in that county and Suffolk against such an event. But a certain necessary article is long a coming. Should not that part of

New England, near to that county, have some intimation to be ready to give aid, if the Troops should land in Queens?

I am very anxious to hear what is determined in your cabinet, with respect to Canada, for the next Campaign. Colonel Ritzema and Captain Goforth,[7] both write me from Montreal that 10,000 men will be necessary to secure the Colony and engage the Canadians heartily in the Cause. They also urge very much, the sending the Troops from hence on the Ice, over the iakes to be ready in the spring. This does not indicate any Zeal in the Canadians. If my memory serves me, General Murray gave it as his opinion, that it would require 6,000 men to man the works of Quebec, which he assigned as the reason for Hazarding the Battle of April 1760.[8] I think this has been the received opinion. As our Enemies have the command of the sea, and very little Provissions are salted in Canada, suppose Quebec now in our possession, how is it to be furnished with salt Provissions during the next Summer, in case it should be Blockaded by sea, and by Land? Remember that ships of the Line got by Quebec in the seige of 1759; and some of the Frigates went a Considerable distance up above it.

We are in suspence here about the destination of your Fleet. If they go to Virginia, I fear they will be ruffly handled, as some ships of war, have been dispatched there from Boston. The Americans individuly considered, know the use of a musket better than the best of the Kings Troops; to this in a great degree is to be ascribed the advantages, the former have gained over the Latter, when secured against their descipline. By the saylors we have picked up for our Vessels, do not understand the use of Cannon, equal to those who are continually exercised with them on board the Kings Ships, nor are they so attached to the Country, from connextions as our soldiers are, besides many of the saylors have been taught the superiority of the British Navy officers, to all others in world. Sir, there is no entrenching or covering behind Trees at sea. Superior Force or address only must determine the Victory, if the engagement once commences. You are not to measure your expectations of the success of this Fleet, against the men of war, by the success of our Troops against the King's, or the success of our Cruisers against Transports.

You may be now ready to ask me, are we then never to send out armed Vessels against the men of war, because they have been superior to all the world with equal Force at sea. Yes. But the first experiment should not be made where there is danger of the force being near equal, before your officers and men are practised in sea engagments. If it is, our american Fleet I fear will not be long in our

Possesion. I know that so much depends on address and preparation founded on experience, that I tremble for the Consequences. A small omition determines the fate of a sea engagment. I speak with confidence, because it is from experience. It has been the business of my life.[9] A superiour force at sea, divided in different Bottoms, is not equal to two thirds of it in fewer, because if one or two of the small vessels, on which the force is estimated should be disabled, the disparity against that side becomes instantly great. I have seen this Position exemplified at the age of 14, when one Million of Dollars was depending and since cast about for the principle.

Three things must be attended to in equiping this Fleet, if they are designed to act against the Enemy on this Coast, at this stormy season. They must be able to carry a stiff sail. This does not depend so much on their being deep loaded, as on the Center of Gravity being properly placed, in stowing them, for they may be deep in the water and yet carry but a small sail, owing to the Center of gravity being too high. They must not be loaded deep, for if they are, they will not be able to come up with a weak Enemy, in good sailing Trim, nor escape from a stronger one. The officers, marriners, and marines should be exercised in their stations, with the Cannon and musketry with Powder before they quit the river, as they may soon expect the enemy, and stormy weather may deprive them of that advantage, before they engage. One Ton of Powder however scarce it may be, properly expended in this way will save Five in an engagment, if not save the Fleet. New and hasty sea armaments meet cruizing ships, of near their Force on very unequal ground. The former is generally all confusion and not properly aranged; the Latter in order and ready for action. Hence it was that the Privateers fitted out of France the last warr fell so easy a Prey to our Frigates, altho the ships of the Former were superior in size, men and Guns to ours. The same thing frequently happened to their Cruizers in the West Indies, when they came out of Port Expressly to take ours Cruizing within their sight. I have wrote you in the confidence of Friendship, and from an anxiety for the Cause of our bleeding Country; and not with any intention the lessen the merit of any of the Gentlemen who command those Vessels.

I am in Haste your affectionate Friend

ALEXR. McDOUGALL

ALS.

1 The New York delegates presented a copy of the resolutions on the province's representation to the Continental Congress on 1 Jan. 1776. *JCC*, IV, 14.

2 On 16 Dec. 1775 the Provincial Congress named a Committee of Safety

which was to sit during Congress's adjournment. McDougall was a member of this Committee which was empowered to issue militia commissions, summon Congress in case of emergency, conduct correspondence in the Congress's name, discipline opponents of the Patriot cause, and maintain contact with the Continental Congress. *JPC*, I, 222–23.

3 "Disaffection" in the counties on Long Island and in Richmond (Staten Island) became more pronounced in the winter of 1775. Although elections for the second Provincial Congress were held in Queens and Richmond on 7 November and 15 December, respectively, inhabitants voted not to send delegates. No more than two delegates from Kings County attended the New York Congress, and even they made no appearance after 19 Dec. 1775. On 13 December the Congress acted on reports that Loyalists in Queens were being armed by the British. The Congress summoned Queens leaders to appear, but the Queens Tories ignored this demand. On 21 December the Congress resolved that there be no communication between Patriots and the Loyalists in Queens and Richmond. Names of these Loyalists were published in the local press, and the New York Congress dispatched a letter to the colony's delegation in Philadelphia describing the action that had been taken and explaining that more stringent measures could not be adopted lest British vessels in New York harbor bombard the city. *JPC*, I, 215–16, 227, 229–30.

4 Col. William Dalrymple (d. 1807) commanded the British garrison at Boston, 1768–72.

5 In September 1775 General Thomas Gage was recalled to England, ostensibly to confer on the spring campaign. In his absence, Sir William Howe (1729–1814) was to be acting commander in North America. Gage was removed from command in April 1776 and Howe assumed permanent command.

6 Long Island.

7 Lieutenant Colonel Rudolphus Ritzema (c. 1740–1803) and Captain William Goforth (d. 1807) were officers in McDougall's 1st New York Regiment. *Cal. of Hist. Mss.*, I, 117; II, 29.

8 Brigadier General James Murray (1721–94) commanded British forces at Quebec after Wolfe's death in 1759. When the French attempted to retake Quebec in April 1760, Murray led a desperate attack from the city and was forced to fall back to the fortress where he and his men were besieged until mid-May.

9 McDougall had been a sea captain before he retired to New York City in 1764 to become a merchant.

From Robert R. Livingston

Clare Mount, 29th December 1775

Dear John

I Snatch a moment from grief, from the melancholy attention I owe to widowed parent, and from the Duties a deing [*sic*] Grandfather has a right to claim to answer your friendly letter.[1] Tho you knew my father and shared his friendship yet you can hardly feel till death deprives you at one stroke of the warmest friend, the tenderest parent, and the most instructive and agreeable companion the extent of my loss, a loss greatly agravated by my not having been with Him at the awful hour of his disolution, or received his last commands say rather instructions for he never said anything to me that would carry with it the Idea of command. It gives me great consolation to think however that death carried with it no terrors, though he had had a slow fever for some time, yet he felt no pain, not five minutes before his death he was in the parlour retired to his bed, and expired with a pious ejaculation uttered with his usual serenity without any apparent pang; his countenance in death retained its usual composure and persuade me that his thoughts were intent on that blessed immortality which he now enjoys.

He had heard some time before that he was removed from his office,[2] at which he expressed the greatest satisfaction, he observed that he was growing old that it was time for him to be at peace. I should have thought him intirely weaned from the things of this world, had not an unfinished essay that he left behind him, convinced me that he still retained his warm attatchment to his country and the great cause in which we are now engaged. I find myself too much moved, I can write no more on this subject nor am I disposed to think of any other, perhaps I should appologize for this, but my sorrows are poured into the bosom of a friend who has long known and will excuse my weakness, A friend who may drop a tear upon what I have already blotted. O' John you can hardly conceive how much my grieve is agravated by the necessity I am under of concealing it from my mother sisters, and even from my wife, whose health has suffered by the rude shock it has sustained.

John[3] is tired of Idleness and wishes to be employed, begs I would write to you. I bid him write himself, he is greatly improved and bids fair to make a shining figure, if you can assist him I know I need not ask your aid. The bearer of this will return immediately, dont let him come back empty handed; let me hear much and often from you. My friendship is now more drawn to a point than ever. Let it meet with equal returns and afford me the comfort and satisfaction I expect from it. You shall hear from me again shortly on a less melancholy subject.

I congratulate you on the good news from Canada and the fair prospect we now have of the reduction of Quebeck from his unhoped for accession to Montgomerrys strength.[4] By the blessing of heaven all may be well yet, God bless you may long soon enjoy that freedom and ease which your labours have already earned. Let me again press you to write to me.

Yours most Affectionately and sincerely

ROBT R. LIVINGSTON

ALS. Addressed: "To John Jay Esqr In Congress at Philadelphia." Endorsed.

1 JJ to Livingston, 19 Dec. 1775.

2 Robert R. Livingston, Sr., had been named a puisne judge of the New York Supreme Court of Judicature in 1763. His name was omitted from the Commission of Oyer and Terminer in the fall of 1775, but this amounted to a suspension from his duties, not removal from the bench. Dangerfield, *Robert R. Livingston,* p. 59.

3 Livingston's brother.

4 On 2 Dec. 1775 Richard Montgomery joined forces with Benedict Arnold for an attack on Quebec.

From Henry Beekman Livingston

Clare Mont, January 2d, 1776

Dear Sir,

I arrived here on Thursday and found the Family much distressed on account of the irreparable Loss they have sustained, my Brother Robert unwell, and my Grandfather takeing leave of this troublesome World.[1]

I am verry sorry the Necessity for my sudden Departure from Philadelphia deprived me of the Pleasure of seeing some of my best Freinds: Some Days before I came away I did myself the Honour to wait on You but was not so fortunate as to find you at home.

Before I arrived here, Mrs. Montgomery[2] received a Letter from General Montgomery in which he informs her that there is a Vacant Majority for me, in the Regiment to which I belong, if I think proper to accept it.

This I wrote him word I would do, till the Congress settle the Appointment. Since the Date of his Letter my Colonel has also resigned, so that of course if I am not superseded (which I flatter myself You Sir, and the rest of the Gentlemen who have befreinded in Congress, will take care to prevent) I must be Lt. Colonel of the 4th Regiment.[3]

Since my Arrival here Mrs. Montgomery received another Letter from the General dated 5th December who writes, that he is now before Quebeck, with 4,000 Men, and that the Garrison are far from being sufficient in Number to man their Works.[4] When You look at the Length of this Letter be so Obliging as to excuse it as it was protracted merely from a desire to please.

My best Respects to Mr. Wm. Livingston and Coll. Morris.[5] I promised myself Honour of visiteing them before I left Philadelphia but was disapointed. My compliments to Mr. Rutlage, Mr. Lynch, Mr.

Jefferson, Mr. Nelson and Mr. Phl. Livingston[6] when You see them.

I am sir with the greatest respect Your most Obedient and Humble Servant

HENRY B. LIVINGSTON

ALS. Addressed: "To John Jay Esqr. a Member of the Honble the Congress Philadelphia." Endorsed. For the contents of the *verso* of this letter, see below, JJ to James Duane, 6 Jan. 1776.

1 Henry Beekman, the Livingston brothers' maternal grandfather, died at Rhinebeck 3 Jan. 1776.

2 Livingston's sister Janet (1743–1838) married Richard Montgomery in 1773.

3 Henry Livingston was appointed lieutenant colonel in one of the four battalions raised in New York by the Continental Congress in March, 1776. *JCC*, IV, 190.

4 Montgomery's campaign to capture Quebec ended in disaster, the General himself dying in the assault on the Plains of Abraham, 31 Dec. 1775.

5 Lewis Morris.

6 JJ's colleagues in the Continental Congress: Edward Rutledge (1749–1800) and Thomas Lynch, Sr., of South Carolina, Thomas Jefferson and Thomas Nelson (1738–89) of Virginia, and Philip Livingston of New York.

To James Duane

Philadelphia, 6 January 1776

Dear Sir,

As I intend to leave this City Tomorrow I take the Liberty of sending you the inclosed.

I have just recieved a Letter from H. B. Livingston and his Brother John.[1] Harry informs me that his major has quitted the Service and that his Colonel has also resigned. These Places being vacant I think Harry should be made a Lieut. Colonel immediately, for as the Lieut. Colonel continues in the Service he certainly [ought] to have the Regiment.

John it seems had heard that the Congress were about employing a Person to purchase Goods at Montreal and is desirous of that Appointment.[2]

By attending to these Matters you will have the Satisfaction of obliging a worthy Family as well as your Friend and humble Servant

J. J.

DftS. This letter is written on the *verso* of the address page of Henry Beekman Livingston to JJ, 2 Jan. 1776, with this explanatory note by JJ: "On recieving this Letter [from Livingston], being about leaving said Town I wrote the following Lines to James Duane Esquire inclosing some public Papers." Enclosures not identified.

1 The letter from John R. Livingston has not been located.

2 There is no record of John R. Livingston's receiving such an appointment from Congress in 1776.

To Robert R. Livingston

Philadelphia, 6 January 1776

Dear Robert

<Your Letter and those from your Brothers were delivered to me this Afternoon just as I was about setting off for Elizabeth Town. I shall leave this Place in the Morning and probably be absent near a Month.>[1]

Amid the various Sources of Consolation in Seasons of poignant Distress which the wise have long amused themselves and the World with, the little Share of Observation and Experience which has fallen to my Lott convinces me that Resignation to the Dispensations of a benevolent as well as omnipotent Being can alone administer Relief.

The Sensations which the first Paragraph of your Letter has occasioned mock the Force of Philosophy, and I confess have rendered me the Sport of Feelings which You can more easily concieve than I express. Grief if a Weakness, is nevertheless on certain occasion amiable and recommends itself by being in the Train of Passions which follow Virtue.

But remember my Friend that your Country bleeds and calls for your Exertions. The Fate of those very Friends whose Misfortune so justly afflicts You is linked with the Common Cause and cannot have a separate Issue. Rouse therefore and after vigorously discharging the duties you owe your Country, return to Your peaceful Shades, and supply the Place of your former Joys, by the Reflection that they are only removed to a more Kindred Soil (like Flowers from a thorny Wilderness, by a friendly Florist) under whose Care they will flourish and bloom and court your Embraces forever.

Accept my warmest thanks for the ardor with which you wish a Continuance and Increase of that Friendship to which I have long been much indebted. Be assured that its Duration will always be among the first objects of my Care; let us unite in proving by our Example that the Rule, which declares juvenile Friendships, like vernal Flowers to be of short continuance, is not without Exception, even in our degenerate Days.

I wish something could be done for John. At present I know of nothing except in the military Line. The first opportunity of serving him in some other Department which offers shall engage my attention. Mr. Deane[2] has this moment come in, so that I must conclude as I hope to conclude every Letter to you with an Assurance that I am your affectionate Friend

J.J.

P.S. 50 Tons of Salt Petre arrived this Day.

DftS. Endorsed by JJ.

1 Robert R. Livingston to JJ, 29 Dec. 1775, and Henry Beekman Livingston to JJ, 2 Jan. 1776. JJ returned to Philadelphia on 2 March.

2 Silas Deane (1737–89), a lawyer and merchant, was a member of the Connecticut delegation to Congress.

To Robert R. Livingston

Elizabeth Town, 26 January 1776

Dear Robert

The Concern occasioned by the many misfortunes lately attending your Family, is greatly augmented by a Report which has for some Days prevailed of your being much indisposed. Did not Mrs. Jays Illness forbid my leaving her I should most certainly pay you a Visit. She was the Day before Yesterday delivered of a Boy,[1] and tho there is no Reason to apprehend Danger at present, yet the precarious Situation of Life in such Circumstances makes me the Subject of many Fears and much anxiety.

As I suspect that your present ill State of Health proceeds from Sollicitude and Distress, let me entreat you, by Change of Place and Change of Objects to avoid that settled Dejection, to which I fear your too great Sensibility may incline you.

Endeavour to write me a few Lines. They will find me here for 3 weeks yet to come. Tell me how you do, and whether all your good Family are in Health. I fear to inquire about Mrs. Montgomery—but this is a Subject on which you will readily percieve the Propriety of Silence—it is too tender. God be with you my dear Robert.

Your Friend

JOHN JAY

ALS. Coll. of J. W. Redmond, on deposit at NHpR. Addressed: "Majr. Robert R. Livingston at Clermont Manor of Livingston. free J. Jay." Endorsed: ". . . answd."

1 Peter Augustus Jay (1776–1843), JJ's eldest son.

FROM ALEXANDER McDOUGALL

New York, February 13th, 1776

Dear Sir

Yesterday we made a Convention. I have the pleasure to inform you it will be a full one in a day or two.[1] They have such a spirit as will maintain the reputation of the Colony and the Common Union.

When Mr. Deane was here in the Course of the winter,[2] on the business of the Navey, I suggested to him the Propriety of geting a Copy of Lieut. OBrien's Naval evolutions, to be reprinted. He approved of it, but I could not then obtain a Copy.[3] I have since procured one and sent it this morning by Col Morris to Congress which I beg them to accept. As this is the only tract on this Subject, in our language, and but one other Copy of it in this City, I think it should be reprinted at Public expence. If this should be the opinion of Congress, great care ought to be observed in the work. The Copy should be corrected, by the Errata before its begun; for if the work is not clear, as those for whose use it is designed are not the most intelligent, the end of the republication will not be answered.

From the diminss[ions] transmitted to New York for the building the ships in our Colony, I fear the Construction of them will be improper for the force designated for them.[4] All the modern Frigates, English as well as French, which carry Nine or Twelve Pounders, have their Ports seven feet distant in the Clear from sill to sill of the Ports, and each Port from 2 feet to 2 feet three inches clear, and the Bow gun standing in its proper Place not farther forward than the scarf that is mat over the strait part of the Keel. And the aftermost Gun is generally the distance of one port, from the scag, that is from the aftermost part of Keel. From whence it will necessarily Follow, that the whole length of the Keel should be equally to the dimenssions of the Ports and their distance for the number of the Guns a ship is intended to Carry, on the Lower Deck. This will be clearly understood by the ruff Diagram, on the other side. My solicitude for the reputation of the united Colonies, is the motive that induced me to make this hasty address in Convention, which I hope will plead my excuse.

I am with great truth and regard in Haste Sir Your affectionate Humble Servant

ALEXR. McDOUGALL

ALS. MdAN. Addressed: "To John Jay Esquire Delegate for the Colony of New York in Congress, and in his absence to be opened by James Duane Esqr Delegate for the said Colony Phia." Enclosure: diagram captioned: "Keel for a

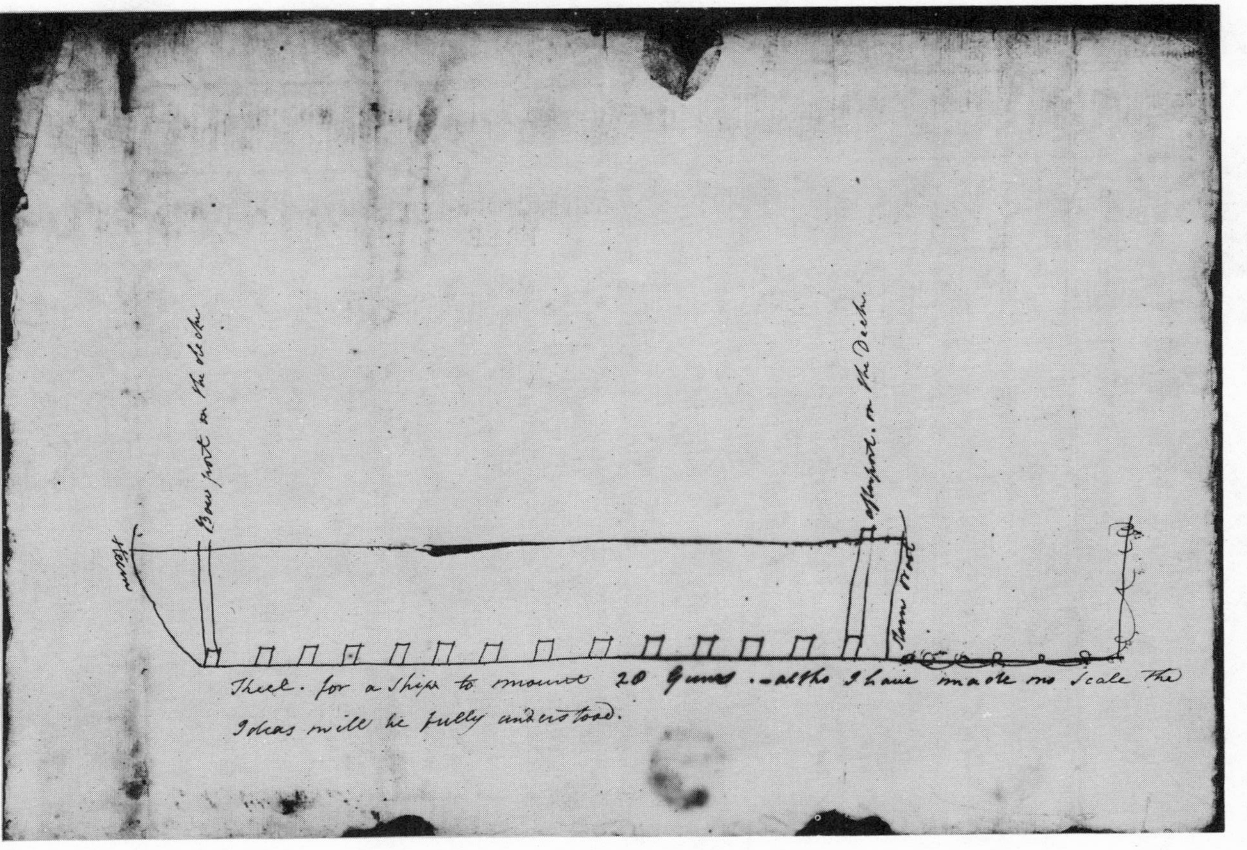

McDougall's Diagram in 1776 of "Keel for a Ship to Mount 28 Guns"

ship to mount 28 Guns, altho I have made no scale the Ideas will be fully understood." Endorsed.

[1] On the morning of 12 Feb. 1776 the New York Provincial Congress resumed sessions with all counties except Richmond and Queens represented. Richmond had elected two delegates, Adrian Bancker and Richard Lawrence, on 19 January, and Bancker began attendance at the Congress on 26 February. Queens, however, remained unrepresented throughout the session. *JPC*, I, 263, 310, 324.

[2] In the third week of November 1775 Silas Deane visited New York on a mission for the committee named by Congress to obtain ships for the American cause. Deane was to arrange for the purchase of two vessels for the Continental service in New York. *JCC*, III, 311–12; "The Deane Papers," N.Y.H.S., *Colls.*, XXIX (1886), 90–94.

[3] Christopher O'Bryen's book, in large part a translation of Paul Hoste's work, was *Naval Evolutions: or, A system of sea-discipline; extracted from the celebrated treatise of L'Hoste . . . with copper plates; and adapted to the use of the British navy to which are added, an Abstract of the Theory of Shipbuildng; An Essay on Naval Discipline by a Late Experienced Sea Commander; A General Idea of the Armament of the French Navy; with Some Practical Observations by Christopher O'Bryen* (London, 1762). The book was not printed in America during the Revolution.

[4] On 13 Dec. 1775 Congress adopted a report calling for the construction of thirteen frigates, two of which were to be built in New York. The *JPC* for December 1775–February 1776 does not record the receipt of these orders by the New York authorities, but the instructions were probably conveyed verbally by Francis Lewis, New York's representative on the Continental Marine Committee, when he visited his home colony in January 1776 to make arrangements for the construction of the Continental vessels. *JCC*, III, 425–26; *JPC*, I, 255.

From Robert R. Livingston

Clare Mount, 15th February 1776

Dear John

I received your truly affectionate Letter, And most sincerely congratulate you upon an event which the share I take in your happiness makes me rejoice it though it deprived me of what I should think my greatest happiness the pleasure of seeing you here. May the extension of your tender connections give you as much pleasure as the narrowing of mine has given me pain.

You rightly judge that I severely feel the reiterated misfortunes which have clouded my prospect of happiness and abriged if not anihilated all that felicity with which rural ease and the converse of such dear and tender friends flattered me; yet I have had philosophy enough to bear it with patience, to submit with resignation to the wise degrees of the supreme disposer of all events, and to acknowledge that it is infinitely better to die in the full carreer of glory when our reputation is at the hight, to be followed to the grave by the sorrows of the wise and good than to out live our enjoyments, and be forgotten before we die. And yet even in this view some years might have been added to the life of my tender father and many to that of my Dear friend;[1] his loss affects me the more as from him I had vainly hoped to derive some consolation, some assistance in the discharge of those duties which (with a numerous family) have devolved upon me. It is still more agravated by his solemn resolutions to quit the army and enjoy that rural ease for which he so eagerly panthed. He assures me in his last letter that he had lost those ambitious hopes which were the spring of action in his youthful days; that a sense of duty alone had called him forth, that our affairs were too prosperous to make him longer necessary, and he was resolved to retire at the end of this campaign and concludes with this ominous exclamation "O Rus quam de te asspicium."[2] But enough of this. Gods will be done.

You do not tell me whether you received a letter which I sent to Philadelphia to you some time since; it was melancholy enough to make you conclude that my illness arises from the source you mention, but though that may perhaps have in some measure increased it, yet it is an old complaint that has been lurking in my veins for some time, and for ought I see bids fair to undermine my constitution. I am not so much in love with life as to be very uneasy on my own account, but I think myself necessary to my family, and I should be sorrey to add to the affliction of those who have already felt as much as their constitution will bear. A similarity between my disorder and that which deprived them of a father alarms their fears;[3] And in compliance with their requests, and the directions of my Phisicians I am nursing myself here instead of attending to those publick duties which demand my attention.

I congratulate you on the success of your election. It is no small pleasure to me that we meet in all our walks, heaven seems to regard our friendship, and by puting it in our power to be useful to each other cements it.[4] Let us my Dear John acknowledge the omen though our first object is, and I hope ever will be the Interest of our country yet let us not lose sight of the second but endeavour to improve and serve each other. I do not imagine that the assembly will proceed to business, if it should pray let me hear what they are about. If they should not, let me hear that also. You have not given me a word of politicks since I left you, in which I have been greatly disappointed for nothing will ever render me inattentive to events that affect my country and if I do not hear more I shall be obliged in spite of every thing to come to you. General Schuyler has wrote for a committee to set at Albany in case the whole congress can not remove;[5] I am fully convinced of its necessity from what passed under my own observation while I was there, and indeed to the want of it I attribute all our miscariages there this campaign, and the grosist and most palpable impositions on the public. I think I can demonstrate that every man in Canada cost us at least £6 a month and that instead of an army of between 5 and 6000 men we had at no time above 2000 and that too very late in the season. If a Committee should be sent to superintend the operation of the Canada expedition I should like to be one of the number. I can not go far from home in my present state of ill health without exciting great uneasiness here nor can my attendance on the affairs of this family be dispenced with altogether, and yet I can not bear to be entirely useless to those who have thought proper to honour me with a publick trust. This if it should take place will rid me of my uneasiness on these several accounts. You will manage this matter.

I have been some what hurt at a story I had from Nich. Hoffman[6] not on account of the thing itself but because I did not hear it from you, since from his relation I thought it could not have escaped you. I mean a suspicion of my having betrayed the secrets of the congress to Mr. Tryon. The report itself gave me no pain because whatever my own character may be the little contemptible resentment which Mr. Tryon discovered in suspending my father from his office, shews that he did not think he had many friends in this family; nor do I believe that the most credulous could have found any thing in my conduct which should induce them to think that I would belie the acknoledged principles of my father, and two Brothers, both of whom through my means were armed, in defence of those rights which I am not less interested in the defence of, than any other person at congress, or elswere. But I am asshamed of having said that much upon the subject, if my conduct needs a justification I should not be trusted. I am only hurt that my friends should be silent on a subject in which I was so deeply interested.

I would be obliged to you if you would draw for my wages for my attendance on Congress 162 days which amounts to 648 dollars. You can pay off my bond in your hands and deliver the remainder to John[7] who will wait upon I have like wise given him an order to receive it least you should not be in town.

I have been alarmed on Mrs. Jays account. Dr. Bard who called to see told me that she was not quite free from danger when he left her. Mr. Ketteltas[8] who is here tells me she is better; present my affectionate compliments [to] her and the rest of your good family and congratulate them upon its increase. Farewell God bless you.

Your sincere friend etc.

ROBT R. LIVINGSTON

Mrs. Livingston joins in my compliments and wishes to you and yours.

ALS. Addressed: "To John Jay Esqr at William Livingston's Elizabeth Town pr favor of Mr. Kettletas." Endorsed.

1 Richard Montgomery.

2 "Oh, the Countryside, how I think of you."

3 Livingston suffered from a low fever as had his father during his last illness in December 1775. Dangerfield, *Robert R. Livingston*, pp. 66–67.

4 On 2 Jan. 1776 Governor Tryon dissolved the existing assembly and called for new elections. In the resulting polls, JJ was returned to the assembly from New York City, and Livingston from Dutchess County. 4 *FAA*, IV, 542.

5 Gen. Philip Schuyler wrote the Continental Congress from Albany on 13 Jan. 1776: "Congress undoubtedly conceives it to be advantageous to the Cause of America to sit at Philadelphia; but they will be good enough to permit me to suggest the Necessity of a full-empowered Committee immediately to repair to this place." DNA: PCC, 153, I, 396.

6 Nicholas Hoffman, a New York merchant and a member of the Committee of One Hundred.

7 John R. Livingston.

8 The Reverend Abraham Keteltas (1732–98), a Queens County delegate to the Second New York Provincial Congress.

To Robert R. Livingston

Elizabeth Town, 25 February 1776

Dear Robert

Your Letter of the 15th Inst. informs me that you continue indisposed and that you are nursing yourself at Home. I am sorry for both. The first alarms me, on account of your Health and the second forebodes your being long sick. Amusement and Exercise ought to be your Objects. At Home you can have little of either. Domestic Concerns, Variety of Business and twenty things going wrong for want of that Care and Attention which a sick Man should not think of, agitate your mind and prevent that even Flow of Spirits and that Calm throughout the whole Man, so necessary to invite the Return of Health. This would be my Case were I in your Situation. If it be yours, get rid of it. The Spring advances fast and as soon as the Roads will permit you, go to the Camp, to Philadelphia, in short anywhere, so that you are but moving. You must however leave off riding Post—no more 60 and 70 Miles a Day. Travel like a Citizen of the World who thinks himself at Home at every Inn, and leave it as you would your House when you are about to take an Airing. If I can with any tolerable Propriety leave the Congress I will accompany you, and as I have often done Save your Horse from many a Sweat.

I am happy to find your Letters evince so much firmness and Resignation; they bespeak a sound Mind and God Grant it may soon dwell in a sound Body. Two Days only have I spent in New York since I left Philadelphia. Mrs. Jays Illness has detained me here almost the whole time except ten Days spent at Rye, so that I can tell you but little of Politics. With occurrences generally known the Papers have and will continue to inform you, and as to Matters more private the uncertain Fate of Letters forbids me to commit them to Paper. The Letter you mention to have sent to me at Philadelphia came safe to Hand late in the Day and just as I was setting off for this Place, but being desirous of answering it by the Bearer I determined to postpone my Journey till the next Day. In the Evening as I was writing Dean came in, I broke off and copied what I had written and enclosed it together with Letters for your Brothers to Mr. Duane to be forwarded by the Express. I acquainted him particularly with the Contents of Harry and John's Letter and desired his Attention to them. It being then late and intending to set off early in the Morning I gave the Packet to Dean who promised to deliver it to Mr. Duane. I am surprized you never recieved it. The enclosed are Copies of those several Letters.

The ridiculous Story of your having been concerned in giving Intelligence to Governor Tryon I once or twice heard, but as I never met with a single Person who gave the least Credit to it, and as it occasioned general Disgust and Indignation, I did not think it worthy of Notice and therefore treated it with the Contempt it deserved.

A Report of this kind relative to Mr. Duane has long been extensive and serious. It has given him much Concern, and tho I believe him to be innocent every Body doees not.[1] He told me I was coupled with him and that the Report was against us both. A few Days Inquiry however made me perfectly easy, for neither myself or my Friends could find the least Trace of such Report respecting me. Mr. Duanes Author for it never appeared. Some of our Delegates and others indeed heard it but they assured me, from no other Person but Mr. Duane. It is natural for Men to desire Company in Distress, and it sometimes happens that improper Means are used to gratify that as well as other Desires.

I would readily recieve the Money due to you from the Province, but am now at Eliz[abeth] Town and shall set off tomorrow or next

Day for Philadelphia. Be under no Concern about the Bond. It is of no Consequence whether it be paid now or some Years hence.

Whether the Governor will call the Assembly is at present very uncertain and I am told the knowing ones in New York are divided in opinion about it. It gives me Pleasure to hear that Dutchess has acted with Propriety and I assure you I shall be happy to meet you in all my Walks both here and hereafter.[2] I think with you that our proceeding hand in Hand *pari Passu* through the many ups and downs of this topsy turvy world is not a little singular. It is a happy Presage and I heartily join with you in obeying its Dictates.

Mrs. Jay who is now almost recovered joins me in thanking you for the friendly Sollicitude you express for her Health, and to present our Compliments and best Wishes to Mrs. Livingston, your Mama and all the Family.

I am and will be, Your Friend

J.J.

P.S. I shall remember the Albany Com[mitte]e.[3]

DftS. Enclosures: JJ to James Duane, 6 Jan. 1776, and JJ to Robert R. Livingston, 6 Jan. 1776, printed above; JJ to Henry Beekman Livingston and to John R. Livingston, *c.*, 6 Jan. 1776, not located.

1 Governor Tryon's information concerning the proceedings in the Continental Congress came from James Brattle, a servant in James Duane's household. Becker, *N.Y. Political Parties,* p. 243, n.

2 Although writs for the Assembly election were returned 14 Feb. 1776, Tryon repeatedly prorogued the new legislature and it never functioned as a law-making body. Becker, *N.Y. Political Parties,* pp. 241–42.

3 The committee which General Schuyler had asked Congress to appoint for conferences at Albany.

To Robert R. Livingston

Philadelphia, 4 March 1776

My dear Friend

The Evening before the last I arrived here after a most disagreable Journey thro intolerable bad Roads. I heard by the Way that your Brother[1] had been here and was returning. How we missed each other is a mystery to me. I wish I had seen him. He would have told me twenty things about you that I am anxious to know. Fame says you are still much indisposed. I pray God she may on this, as she does on many other occasions prove a Lyar. I wrote you last Week from Elizabeth Town. Tell me whether you have recieved that and which other of my Letters. I was in Hopes of finding a Letter from you here for me, and the Disapointment is the greater as the State of your Health for some time past has given me much anxiety. The Prospect of being soon deprived of a Father and a Mother whom you know I tenderly love,[2] the unhappy Situation of some of my Family, added to the Distress I feel for the late Misfortunes and Sickness of my Friend, have occasioned more gloomy Ideas in my mind than it has ever before been the Subject of. Despondency however ill becomes a man. I hope I shall meet every severe Stroke of Fate with Firmness and Resignation, tho not with sullen Indifference. It gives me Consolation to reflect that the human Race are immortal, that my Parents and Frends will be divided from me only by a Curtain which will soon be drawn up, and that our great and benevolent Creator will (if I please) be my Guide thro this Vale of Tears to our eternal and blessed Habitation.

Notwithstanding your Letter, I still suspect that your Disorder is to be ascribed more to your Solicitude, than Constitution. I well remember that though to appearance not robust, you could endure great Fatigue and few of our Contemporaries have enjoyed more Health than yourself. I possess a kind of *Confidence* that Exercise, Temperance and Chearfulness would be as friendly to you as they were to old *Cornaro*.[3] I wish you could get away from Home and pursue no other objects. Try, if it be only for a Month or two and give up all Kind of Business of what nature soever. Dont permit any Body to say a Word to you about your Causes, your Rents, your Farm, nay for the present avoid even politics; defer joining the Congress, the Assembly or any other Body of Men whose Object is Business. Suppose, when the Season becomes more mild you were to take Lodgings at Bristol? The Waters would probably be useful to you; they have kept Mr. Verplank alive for some Years past. You would see as much and as little Company as you pleased, and I promise to go to Church with you every Sunday. Tell Mrs. Livingston I beg she will join her Persuasions to mine; such a little Journey would be useful to you both and I should think the middle of April would not be too early for it.

The Committee for Canada was appointed before I reached this Place; it consists of Doctr. Franklin, Mr. Chase and a Mr. Carryl from Maryland.[4] Had I been here I should have proposed you, tho I must confess I think you can employ your Time more to the advantage of your Health in many other Ways. Your Country has no Demands upon you till that be reestablished. Let me entreat you therefore to confine your Attention to it.

Mr. Lynch[5] continues very ill, tho better than he has been. 27 Tons of Powder, some Salt petre and 300 Arms arrived here Yesterday; and we hear from good Authority that 5 tons of Powder has arrived safe at N. Carolina. This is all the News I have heard since I have been in Town. As to Politics, you know the Letters of Congress People should be silent on that Subject in these Times, when Letters often miscarry etc.

God bless you and give you Health. I am etc.

Dft. Endorsed by JJ.

1 Henry Beekman Livingston.

2 For Peter Jay's illness, see below, Frederick Jay to JJ, 6 March 1776.

3 Many of Luigi Cornaro's tracts on the relationship between temperance and longevity had been translated into English during the third quarter of the eighteenth century.

4 On 15 February Congress appointed Benjamin Franklin of Pennsylvania and Samuel Chase (1741–1811) and Charles Carroll (1737–1832) of Maryland to a committee "to proceed to Canada, there to pursue such instructions as shall be given them by Congress." *JCC*, IV, 151–52.

5 Thomas Lynch, Sr., suffered a paralytic stroke on 18 February. *LMCC*, II, lxviii.

From Frederick Jay

New York, 6th March 1776

Dear Jack

I came to Town last Saturday, Since which have received Your several Letters of the 7th, 9th, 23 and 27 Inst.[1] and note there Contents.

I left Papa but very unwell, I am affraid (unless a speedy restoration for the better) that he will not see this month out. What a Scene I shall have before me if that should be the case which I pray God to prevent. However we must be content and not Murmer at the Will of Heaven. They seem to be happy to have me with them. I shall take care of them.

I am happy to find that Sally is so well recovered. The old People would give half their Estate to see her and the Colt.[2]

I shall embrace every opportunity of writing to You. At present I am much hurried having some goods now landing from Curacao.

The Bl[ac]k Sheep[3] is still in the Neighbourhood, but I have full Liberty from the Master of the Flock to Sett the Dogs at him. I shall be on my Guard and do m[y bes]t. Peggy Joins me in Love to you.

F. JAY

I wish You would let me know what I am to do with Your Money. Hallet[4] has applied to me for the Ballance of your Account.

Mr. ———[5] to whom You paid the Minister and poor Tax, left with me a piece of Gold which you paid him for £5 ult. He says you know the affair. Give me your directions about the Matter.

Our People are very busy in fortifying the Broad way and the ferry on Long Island—have stopt up Flatenbergh Hill—all in good Spirits.

F. JAY

11 at Night.

If you could get a piece of Common linnen for Gusey, I *wish* you *will* send it me by the Stage. I *cannot get* an *Inch* here. He is *much* in *want of them.*

ALS. Addressed: "Jno. Jay Esqr, in Philadelphia per Post." Endorsed.

1 Letters not located.

2 Peter Augustus Jay.

3 Sir James Jay.

4 Probably Joseph Hallet, a member of the Provincial Congress.

5 Left blank in ms.

From Alexander McDougall

Head Quarters, New York, 7th March 1776

Dear Sir,

While I am waiting for General Lee, Just at the Point of his departure, I am induced to put a few incoherent thought together. I fear the Confederacy will Suffer by altering General Lee's destination, from Canada.[1] The officer who is to command there should speak french, if such an officer can be procured; a frenchman's eyes sparkles when he is addressed in that Language. Many reasons might be urged in favor of his taking that command. The Confidence the well affected canadians would have in his experience, as well as our Troops loudly, proclaim him to be the man. The advantage of his acquaintence with the manners of the people of that Nation among the many motives that designate him for that Colony. The object of the Enemy there will be more fixed than in Virginia, which renders it more necessary the Officer should be a man of experience.

In Virginia the attacks of the Enemy must from the nature of the Country be irregular, and may therefore be more easily repulsed by an officer of less Experience, than those made on Quebec, in the Spring. For you may rest assured the Ministry will pay particular attention to the relief of that Town and Colony, for there they have some prospect with a tolerable force to Secure the Province, not only from the Confederacy, but to gain some strengths by aiding the inhabitants to take up arms in their favor. Such an Event would greatly increased our embarassment. If these reasons have any weight Pray reconsider the expediency of sending the General to the Southard.

The Sloop we are fitting out is ready, but wait to know from Congress what pay you alow the officers and Saylors on board the Smalest Continental Vessel, and the description of the Continental Colours.[2] *I beg you to furnish me with a Copy of these, without delay as the Publick Service* Suffers, without regarding at whose expense the armament is to be. Send me also a Sample of the Pikes made at Phi[ladelphia] I am in Great Haste. Your affectionate

ALEXR. McDOUGALL

ALS. Addressed: "To John Jay Esquire at Philadelphia." Endorsed.

1 On 4 Feb. 1776 Gen. Charles Lee arrived in New York to prepare the city's defenses for the expected British invasion. Thirteen days later he was ordered to Canada to succeed Schuyler as commander of troops in that province. However, on 28 February, Congress countermanded Lee's orders, instructing him not to depart for Canada until further notice, and on 1 March Lee was ordered to assume command of Continental forces in the southern colonies. *JCC*, IV, 157, 175, 180, 196.

2 The *Schuyler*, described variously as a sloop and as a schooner in the *JPC*, had been fitted out by the New York Congress and was ordered into service 9 March 1776. Salary scales for the Continental naval officers and seamen had been adopted in November and December 1775; no provisions for a Continental flag had been made. *JPC*, I, 349; *JCC*, III, 384, 417.

To ALEXANDER McDOUGALL

Philadelphia, 13 March 1776

Dear Sir

Had your Letter[1] been sent by the Post it would ere this have come to my Hands. I am now retired to the Lobby to answer it without Delay. I have many things to say to you and upon many Subjects. The enclosed Articles will furnish Answers to the Questions you ask relative to Seamans Wages etc. A Model of a Pike shall be sent you.[2] The Resolution of Congress restraining military officers from offering oaths by Way of Test to the Inhabitants I hope has reached you. I cant account for your Convention's submitting to this usurpation on the Rights of their Constituents—to impose a Test is a sovereign act of Legislation—and when the army become our Legislators, the People that Moment become Slaves.[3] I must conclude And am Dear Sir Your Friend and humble Servant

JOHN JAY

ALS. NSchU: W. Wright Hawkes Coll. Addressed: "To Coll. Alexander McDougall in New York free J. Jay." Enclosure: *Rules for the Regulation of the Navy of the United Colonies of North America* (Philadelphia, 1775); the *Rules* were adopted by Congress 28 Nov. 1775 and are entered in *JCC*, III, 378–87.

[1] McDougall to JJ, 7 March 1776.

[2] On 20 March 1776 the Continental Congress directed Colonel Robert Magaw to prepare "a pike or spear" and to present it to Congress with a statement of its cost. *JCC*, IV, 215.

[3] In New York on 5 March General Charles Lee directed Colonel Isaac Sears to present a test oath to persons whose names appeared on a list prepared by Lee. "Their refusal," Lee pointed out to Sears, "might be considered an avowal of their hostile intentions. You are therefore to secure their persons, and, without loss of time, to send them up as irreclaimable enemies to their country, to close custody in *Connecticut*." On 9 March the Continental Congress resolved that no military officer could demand loyalty oaths and tests of the civilian population. 4 *FAA*, V, 75; *JCC*, IV, 195.

From Peter Jay

Rye, the 18th March 1776

Dear Johnny

I wrote to you the 12 inst. and have since received yours of the 4th and also one from Sally, to whom I write to day.[1]

By an advertizement in the Paper I observe the death of D[a]vid Ross,[2] who was Security in a Bond with Mr. Grant to your Brother Jemmy. It may require your attention in order the better to Secure that money for your Brother. When Fady went lately to Town, I gave him money to discharge and take up Jemmy's Bond to the College.

I am in great want of Jesuit's Bark,[3] and Fady can't get any in N. York, it being all bought up for the Army. Endeavor to get 2 lb. for me at Philadelphia and bring it with you when you come this way.

I am still weak, the weather has hitherto prevented me from taking an Airing in the Carriage, and I fear the troubles we are threatened with by an invasion, will be another impediment. Fady wrote me last Friday or Saturday that 7 Tons of Powder safely got in at N. York the day before.[4]

We all remember our love to you And I always am Your Very Affectionate Father.

PETER JAY

ALS. Addressed: "To John Jay Esqr. in Philadelphia." Endorsed.

[1] Peter Jay to JJ, 12 March 1776, and to SLJ, 18 March 1776, JP; JJ to Peter Jay, 4 March 1776, and SLJ to Peter Jay, *c.* March 1776, not located.

[2] The *N.Y. Mercury* of 11 and 18 March 1776 carried a notice from John Byvanck, the administrator of David Post's estate, desiring Post's creditors to submit their claims.

[3] A popular medicine.

[4] Frederick Jay to Peter Jay, 15 or 16 March 1776, not located.

FROM ALEXANDER McDOUGALL

New York, 20th March 1776

Dear Sir,

I received your favor of the 13th, and am greatly pleased with the resolution of Congress interdicting the military to impose Tests.[1] General Lee sent Col. Sears on that extraordinary business without consulting the Convention, as he was near departing and the Colony is so much suspected they Judged it best to pass the matter over; but I am perswaded it will be the last instance of their pasivity on a point of so much importance to the Liberty of a freeman.

The inclosure you sent me was no answer to my Letter. It was only the regulations for the Government of the Navy.

I want the *Pay Establishment* and the *description* of the Continental Colours, And I beg you once more to send them to me.[2]

The man of warr's tender is either gone or goeing to egg Harbour to intercept our amunition. It is some time since I put my thoughts together, for the security of that place, which were Communicated to our Delegates by the Committee of Safety.[3] For Gods sake attend to the *securing* that Post. I see the want of Government, in many instances. I fear Liberty is in danger from the Licentiousness of the people on the one Hand, and the army on the other. The former feel their own Liberty in the extreme, and we are too fond from our Zeal to encourage the latter, for the advancement of the Public Safety, to connive at many undue exertions of their Power, which may in the end be fatal to us. For ought we know we are but in the begining of a long warr. God save our Poor Country. Your convention are Virtuous, but they want wisdom and knowledge as a Body. They are adjourned to the first monday in may, subject to be called by the Committee of Safety.[4]

Governor Tryon is not Idle. The works for our defence are carrying on with tolerable dispatch. Our Citizens are more alert at them, than the Soldiers. Altho my Lord Sterling is a much Younger Field officer than I am, I find he is appointed a Brigadier General.[5] I wish to know if you can inform me, on what principle this partiality took place. Rank is a matter of no moment to me when it is unacompanied with marks of disgrace. But when it is, every man of sensibility must be affected with it. Conscious that I had not merited any mark of Contempt from Congress, and that my Lord Stirling had done nothing to intitle him to being promoted over others, I ascribed this appointment of Congress to a design to give Jersey their due weight in the army, as they had raised three Battalions; Under the influence of this opinion, I told him when his promotion was announced at head Quarters, I would give him all the assistance in my Power. Indeed my dear sir, as the Enemy has been momently expected, for some time, and I was not in the field last Year, I had determined, if Congress had put one of my Serjants over me, to serve this Campaign. But I find a determination to submit to persons being advanced over me, will not be sufficient to retain me in the army.

I must submit to take rank in the Continental army after all the Field officers, who have been appointed Eight months after me. The Congress have dated the Commissons of the Field officers of our four Regiments the 8th march, those of the officers who have not been promoted as well as those who have. The Consequence of which is, that Col Clinton now the Second in Command before Quebec will be commanded by every Colonel in chief who go from Pen[nsylvani]a, Jersey and Connecticut and were appointed long after him; and Lieut Col Cortlandt of the fourth, last Year and continued in that Regiment, will be commanded by three field officers of our four Regiments whom he commanded the last Year.[6] This arangement can never advance the service of any Country. Altho I had not the Honorable part of the service last Year I was a slave to the Service and submitted to many drudgeries which I cannot do for the future. If the Congress mean those four regiments or the old field officers are to take rank in the Continental army from the 8th March and not from their first Commissions, I consider it as a gentell way of saying we dont want your services. I do not consider my appointment as a favor, because courts only proceed on the principle of favor in their appointments, but the representatives of a free people upon a very different one. And however willing I am to serve the Country even under the disadvantages I first mentioned, I will not serve the Angel Gabriel on terms dishonorable to my reputation. I must therefore beg you to get the sense of Congress, on the Question whether the officers in the new york departement are to take rank in the army according to the dates of their first Commissions, for their respective offices, or according to the dates of their commissions renewed.

I wish no arguments to be used that may have the most distant relation to me. I wish the General tendency and expedincy of the principle only to be considered. If they shall Judge it Necessary from any reasons, which I cannot be acquainted with, to adhere to the last dates of the Commissions as the rule of rank, I doubt not but the Colony will put it in my power to serve them Consistent with my Honor. Whatever may be the determination of Congress, whether favorable or unfavorable to my sentiments, I shall take the Necessary care of the Regiment, till a Colonel in Chief is appointed if unfavorable, and Continue in the City as long as any friend to the Country will dare to show his face in it.

I am in great Haste, Your affectionate Humble Servant

ALEXR. McDOUGALL

ALS. Addressed: "Col John Jay." Endorsed.

1 See above, JJ to McDougall, 13 March 1776.

2 While the pay scales for naval officers and sailors were entered on the *Journals* of Congress as part of the "Rules for the Regulation of the Navy," they were omitted from the published *Rules* which JJ forwarded to McDougall on 13 March. *JCC*, III, 378–87.

3 On 22 Jan. 1776 the New York Committee of Safety wrote the province's delegates in Congress to urge the construction of a redoubt at Egg Harbor. *JPC*, I, 261.

4 The New York Provincial Congress adjourned 16 March 1776 and resumed sessions on 8 May. A Committee of Safety was appointed to sit during this adjournment. *JPC*, I, 368, 435.

5 William Alexander (1726–83), a native New Yorker who settled in New Jersey in 1762, was the husband of SLJ's aunt, Sarah Livingston. A wealthy landowner and powerful political figure, Alexander claimed the earldom of Stirling, and though his claim was never recognized in Britain, he was known in America as "Lord Stirling." On 7 Nov. 1775, Alexander was commissioned a colonel in the 1st New Jersey Regiment, four months after McDougall was appointed colonel of the 1st New York. When Congress elected general officers on 1 March 1776, Alexander was appointed a brigadier general. *JCC*, III, 181.

6 On 19 Jan. 1776 the Continental Congress voted to raise four battalions in New York and asked that the Provincial Congress submit lists of proposed field officers, "at least two for each command," from which a final selection could be made. The New York Congress prepared these slates, offering eight candidates for the four colonelcies, lieutenant colonelcies, and majorities. The lists of nominees, together with "a state of the former regiments" raised in the province in June 1775, were sent to the New York delegates in Philadelphia on 28 Feb. 1776. The appointments made by the Continental Congress from these lists on 8 March caused much discontent among the New York officers who had served in the four New York regiments of 1775.

McDougall, James Clinton (1736–1812), the brother of Congressman George Clinton, and Philip Van Cortlandt (1749–1831) were recommended for appointments as colonels in the New York Congress's lists of 28 February. McDougall was named colonel of the new 1st New York Battalion, the same rank he had held in the 1st New York Regiment of 1775. Clinton, a colonel in the 3rd New York Regiment of 1775, was named colonel of the new 2nd New York Battalion. Since his commission in the 2nd New York was dated 8 March 1776, Clinton was considered junior to colonels in the various battalions raised by Congress in other provinces in late 1775 and early 1776. Van Cortlandt, a lieutenant colonel in the 4th New York Regiment of 1775, was given the same rank in the new 4th New York Battalion in 1776. However, under the rules of seniority in the Continental Army, Van Cortlandt was considered junior not only to men of higher rank, but also to men with the same rank whose names were entered in the *Journals* of Congress prior to the day of his commission. Thus, by the resolutions of 8 March 1776, Van Cortlandt was junior to Lieutenant Colonel Frederick Van Weissenfels of the new 3rd New York Battalion, a captain in the 1775 establishment; to Colonel Cornelius Wyncoop of the new 4th New York Battalion, a major in the 3rd New York Regiment of 1775; to Lieutenant Colonel Herman Zedwitz of the new 1st New York Battalion who had served as a major in the 1st New York in 1775; and to Lieutenant Colonel Henry Beekman Livingston of the new 2nd New York Battalion, a captain in the old 4th New York Regiment. *JCC*, IV, 69, 190; *JPC*, I, 62, 328; *Cal. of Hist. Mss.*, I, 105, 117; II, 41, 45.

From Alexander McDougall

New York, 20th March 1776

Dear Sir,

I wrote you this morning pretty fully. I then forgot to inform you, that I got Mr. Nichol's provided for, in the Second Company of first Regiment; I wish he may retrieve his Character.[1] There is great want of Artillery officers and men in Canad[a]; none are Yet gone to that important Service. A Captain Romain, who speaks French, is appointed to an Artillery Company in the Continental Service, and has raised his Company in Pensylvania.[2] He is to be in a few days with you at Phi[ladelphi]a. As he speaks French he is the fitest in that department to go to Canad[a]. It is to little Purpose to send Heavy ordinance to that Country without men to use them. The Ministerial Troops destined for Virginia, can be easier repul[s]ed, without artillery officers, than the Strong Hold of Quebec can be taken without them. It will therefore be most advancive of the Service to Send them to Canada than to Virginia. Without a Spirit of Prophecy, I forsee that unless Quebec Surrenders, for want of Provissions, the Continent will repent that General Lee was not sent there. I beg you to view these crude and incoherent thoughts with an indulgent Eye, and beleive me to be

Your affectionate Humble Servant

ALEXR. McDOUGALL

My best wishes wait on you and your brother Delegates. The times are exceding Critical, and important, pregnant with some very interesting event to this Country. God direct you. Adieu.

ALS. Addressed: "To Colonel John Jay Delegate for the Colony of New York in Congress Philadelphia." Endorsed.

1 Edward Nicoll (1741–1809), a 1766 graduate of King's College, wrote JJ early in February 1776 to request a commission in one of the New York regiments. On 17 February JJ wrote McDougall to ask him to use his influence to obtain a military appointment for Nicoll despite "his Behavior [which] for many Years has been reprehensable." Nicoll was commissioned a lieutenant in the 1st New York Regiment in 1776. Nicoll to JJ, [n.d., Feb. 1776], and JJ to McDougall, 17 Feb. 1776, JP; *Cal. of Hist. Mss.*, I, 223.

2 Bernard Romans aided the New York Provincial Congress in constructing fortifications on the Hudson in the fall of 1775. In February 1776, he was appointed captain of the Independent Pennsylvania Artillery Company, and on 1 April the Continental Congress provided funds for Romans and his company at Albany. *JPC*, I, 159–61, 174, 179, 189; *JCC*, IV, 243.

To Alexander McDougall

[*Philadelphia*], *21 March 1776*

Dear Sir

I have at Length procured a Pike for you which will be sent by the Stage.[1] Your fitting out an armed Vessel on the Colony account does you Honor. I am at Liberty to inform you that the Congress have passed a Vote for privateering, by which I hope the Losses of some of our Friends will be repaired.[2]

It is expected that vigorous measures will be taken in preventing such as may be inimical to the Cause from injuring its Friends. Future Subscriptions to associations must be ridiculous and was inserted in the Resolve of Congress merely to accommodate it to those Colonies who have hitherto had no associations among them. Fear and motives of Interest and Convenience would doubtless induce many to sign it who are our Enemies in their Hearts and whose uniform Conduct has hitherto been very suspicious if not unfriendly.[3]

This Subject recalls to my Mind a little Report which I am told some Tories on long Island were pleased to form and propagate respecting me, Vizt. That I should have said they were misrepresented to Congress. This Is not true, and to be ranked with many other False Reports which there is Reason to believe originated with that order of Men.

Would it not be well to remove such as are notoriously disaffected to Places where their arts and Influence will do us no Harm. Where are your Accounts?

It is suspected that certain People on Staten Island daily afford Supplies to the Enemy. Ought not the watering Place[4] to be guarded and would not the Troops which might be designed for that Purpose be useful in other Respects. I should think your Army sufficiently numerous to admit of such a Detachment.

I hope you are careful of provincial Powder. The Continent are able to supply a Sufficiency of that article for continental Purposes. This Colony[5] takes Care to keep their own Stock good, and I think act wisely. I wish your Convention would pass a Place Bill, and direct their Delegates to promote such a Measure here; one or two other

Colonies have done it, and it would redound much to your Honor to patronize such a Measure.[6]

Adieu for the present. I am your Friend

JOHN JAY

ALS. NHi: McDougall Papers. Addressed: "Coll. Alexander McDoug[all] in [New York]. free J. Jay." Endorsed.

[1] On 21 March two samples of pikes were presented to Congress. *JCC*, IV, 224.

[2] On 19 March the Continental Congress adopted a report empowering colonists to arm their vessels and prey on enemy shipping. JJ, James Wilson (1742–98) of Pennsylvania, and George Wythe (1726–1806) of Virginia were then named to prepare a prefatory declaration to accompany these resolves. The declaration, which was adopted 23 March, justified privateering on the grounds that petitions by the United Colonies for the redress of grievances had been rejected and that Britain had declared an unjust war and was preparing to seize colonial ships and cargoes at sea. It was hoped, the declaration concluded, that English friends would understand the necessity for self-defense and retaliation. Congress ordered 23 March that the declaration and resolves be published. *JCC*, IV, 213–14, 229–32; for JJ's part in the phrasing of the draft preamble, see *LMCC*, I, 404–05.

[3] By a resolution of 14 March Congress recommended that local authorities disarm "all persons notoriously disaffected to the cause of America, or who have not associated, and shall refuse to associate, to defend, by arms, these United Colonies. . . ." *JCC*, IV, 205.

[4] A large spring on eastern Staten Island used by ships to take on water before putting out to sea.

[5] Pennsylvania.

[6] On 15 June 1776 the New York Congress passed a bill barring military officers in the Continental or Provincial service from sitting in the Provincial Congress. *JPC*, I, 495.

To Alexander McDougall

Philadelphia, March 23, 1776

Dear Collonel

When the Clerk of the Congress gave me the printed Papers which I inclosed you, he told me they contained the Navy Establishment. Whatever Deficiencies there may be in them as to that Matter will I hope be supplied by the Extract now enclosed.

As to continental Colors, the Congress have made no order as yet respecting them, and I believe the Captains of their armed Vessels have in that particular been directed by their own Fancies and Inclinations. I remember to have seen a Flag designed for one of them on which was extremely well painted a Rattle Snake rearing his Crest and shaking his Rattles, with this Motto, "*Dont tread on me.*" But whether this Device was generally adopted by the Fleet, I am not able to say. I rather think it was not.[1]

The Inlet you allude to certainly deserves Attention, and the Hints you gave me respecting it have not been forgotten. Something of that Kind is now under Consideration. A Distinction however will always be made between continental and provincial objects, and how far this may affect that Matter is as yet uncertain.[2]

I am by no means without my Apprehensions of Danger from that Licentiousness which in your Situation is not uncommon. Nothing will contribute more to its Suppression than a vigorous Exertion of the Powers vested in your Convention and Committee of Safety, at least till more regular Forms can be introduced. The Tenderness shewn to some wild People on Account of their supposed attachment to the Cause has been of Disservice. Their eccentric Behaviour, has by passing unreproved gained Countenance, lessened your Authority and diminished that Dignity so essential to give weight and Respect your ordinances. Some of your People are daily (if not employed) yet, instigated to calumniate and abuse the whole Province and misrepresent all their actions and Intentions. One in particular has had the Impudence to intimate to certain Persons that your Regiments[3] last Campaign were not half full and that Van Schaacks Regiment[4] had more officers than Privates. Others insinuate[5] that you have all along supplied the Men of War with whatever they pleased to have, and through them, our Enemies in Boston. By Tales like these they pay their Court to People who have more ostensible Consequence than real Honesty, and more Cunning than Wisdom.

I am happy to find that our intermedling in the Affairs of the Test is agreable to you. For Gods Sake resist all such attempts for the future.

Your own Discernment has pointed out to you the Principle of Lord Sterlings Advancement. Had the age of a Collonels Commission been a proper Rule, it would have determined in Favor of some Coll. at Cambridge, many of whose Commissions were prior in Date to any in New York. The Spirit you betray on this occasion becomes a Soldier.

The inclosed Copy of a Resolve of Congress will I hope settle all Doubts relative to Rank, which may arise from your new Commission.

The Consequence you drew from that Circumstance was more ingenious than solid, for I can assure You that the Congress were not disposed to do any thing wrong or uncivil. And I can also add that your not having joined your Regiment last Summer has been explained to their Satisfaction as far as I am able to judge. With Respect to this however as well as some other Matters I shall defer particulars till we meet. In a word with some Men in these as in other Times, a Man must either be their Tool and be dispised, or act a firm disinterested Part and be abused. The latter has in one or two matters been your Fate as well as that of many other good Men. The Attack was insidious not open or effectual.[6]

Adieu. I am Dear Sir your Friend

JOHN JAY

ALS. NHi: McDougall Papers. Endorsed. Enclosures: "The Pay of the officers & Men . . ." for the Navy, AD in JJ's hand; resolution of Congress, 22 March 1776, *JCC*, IV, 226. The resolution of Congress provided that the rank of Continental officers who had earlier commissions in the service would be determined by the date of their first commissions, not by their most recent appointments. DftS in JP.

[1] This flag was designed by Colonel Christopher Gadsden (1723–1805; South Carolina), a delegate to the Continental Congress and a member of the Marine Committee, and was presented to Congress on 8 Feb. 1776. It reputedly was flown on the flagship *Alfred* as the personal standard of Commodore Esek Hopkins, commander of the Continental Navy. Alverda S. Beck, ed., *The Correspondence of Esek Hopkins, Commander-in-Chief of the United States Navy* (Providence, R.I., 1933), pp. 9, 12–13.

[2] For McDougall's concern over fortifications at Egg Harbor, see above, McDougall to JJ, 20 March 1776 (first letter). Not until June 1776 did a committee of the Continental Congress recommend that the harbor be patrolled by two vessels at Continental expense. *JCC*, V, 476.

[3] "Batalions" in draft.

[4] Colonel Goose Van Schaick (1736–89) commanded the 2d New York Regiment in 1775.

[5] "Report" in draft.

[6] In the draft JJ continued with this passage which was deleted before the ALS was copied: "If you should happen to see Mr. Sears, be so kind as to remind him of the Bond he gave Congress and that his not having taken it up by settling his Account has been talked of." Captain Isaac Sears had forwarded 7,000 barrels of flour to Cambridge at the request of Commissary General Joseph Trumbull, but Trumbull was unable to pay Sears. On 19 Oct. 1775 Congress resolved that Sears be paid $30,000 "on account of the above flour, he giving bond to account for the same with Mr. Trumbull. . . ." *JCC*, III, 299–300.

To Alexander McDougall

Philadelphia, 27 March 1776

Dear Sir

As Mr. Willet leaves this Place in the Morning, I shall commit these few Lines to his Care, and tho they contain nothing important will nevertheless tend to manifest my constant Attention to the

Province as well as to the Person for whom they are designed. I am sorry no Provision has been made for Mr. Willet. From every thing I can learn, he has Merit, and I hope when we shall be informed of the Arrangements in Canada, that a Place will be found for him.[1]

How do your People like the Design of privateering? In the year 1757 [*sic*] they had thirty nine Sail and no less than 4060 Men employed in that Business. I feel so much for the Honor of our calumniated Colony, that it would give me Pleasure to see them distinguished by vigorous Exertion. Indeed had it not been for the Slanders of some of our own Citizens, Fame would have done us Justice. However she has been detected in so many dirty Misrepresentations to vilify New York that I can assure you the Province stands well with the Congress and has at least its due Weight. It gives me great Satisfaction that your military Appointment will probably admit of your continuing in the City, where I cant but think your Presence extremely necessary, and the more so as many among you observe no medium, and are either all Flame or all Frost.

It is said Boyd has not fulfilled his Contract and has only delivered six or seven Musquets. I suspect all is not right in this Business, and that there are more Reasons for the Delay than ostensible ones.[2] If so he ought to feel the Indignation of the Public.

That no Salt Petre is making in the Province is a sad Tale. I wish we could contradict it. A Work at public Expence should be erected, if it were only for the Honor of the Colony.[3] I hear you have emitted more Money.[4] Will you never think of Taxes? The Ice must be broken, the sooner it is begun and more insensibly performed the better. I Tremble for this Delay. There is much Money in the Province, the Produce of the Country retains its Price and a moderate Tax would be born without Murmur especially and its Payment can be enforced and the Necessity obvious.

The Tories at Boston are left to the Mercy of their incensed Countrymen.[5] I hope our wise ones will draw proper Inferences from this Circumstance, and not seek for Protection from those who never think of their Friends longer than Interest may dictate Attention. Mr. Willet is waiting.

Adieu. I am your Friend

JOHN JAY

ALS. NHi: McDougall Papers. Endorsed.

[1] Marinus Willett (1740–1830), a New York merchant and Son of Liberty, served as captain in the 1st New York Regiment in 1775. Willett participated in the Canadian expedition of that year and commanded St. Johns after its surrender to the Americans.

[2] Robert Boyd of New Windsor contracted with the New York Provincial Congress to manufacture muskets in June 1775. Boyd was to be allowed six months to fulfill his contract, and, in February 1776, the New York Congress wrote Boyd to request him to forward all such guns as he had made and to press completion of the contract. In his reply of 23 February Boyd agreed to deliver the arms for which he had been paid, but indicated that he would not proceed under the contract because of the shortage of labor. *JPC*, I, 41, 51, 294, 328.

[3] By a resolution of 23 Feb. 1776 the Continental Congress recommended that local authorities erect works for the manufacture of saltpeter at public expense. New York's Congress responded on 16 March by directing the Committee of Safety to negotiate with suitable persons for this purpose. On 17 April the Committee resolved that county committees be appointed to supervise the manufacture and purchase of saltpeter in the province. *JCC*, IV, 170; *JPC*, I, 366, 409–10.

[4] On 5 March the New York Provincial Congress voted to emit $137,500 in bills of credit. *JPC*, I, 338.

[5] American forces entered Boston on 17 March 1776, one day after the British garrison withdrew at the conclusion of an eleven-month siege.

To Sarah Livingston Jay

Philadelphia, 31st March 1776

My dear Sally

I have recieved your complimentary Letter of the 24th March Inst.[1] and I should be happy to merit half the civil Things you say of your Husband.

How does our little Boy do? Have your apprehensions of his getting the Dow Worm proved groundless? By your Silence for these Eight or ten Days I fear all is not well. It gives me Pleasure to hear of your being in perfect Health, though I confess your continuing so thin is an unpleasing Circumstance. Perhaps being a Nurse disagrees with You. If so, I hope you will decline it. Let no Consideration induce you to injure your Consitution.

I suspect your Attention to your Son and too much Industry renders you negligent of Exercise. The Roads will now admit of riding. The Weather is often pleasant, and I am sure frequent Airings would do you more good than a Physician. Have you played Battledore and Shuttlecock since I left you? God bless you, and give you Grace to take Care of the Health of your *Body* as well as your Soul.

With my Love to all the Family I am my Dear Sally, your affectionate Husband

JOHN JAY

ALS. Endorsed.

[1] Letter not located.

John Jay's Draft of a Letter from the Continental Congress to George Washington

Philadelphia, April 2nd, 1776

Sir

It gives me the most sensible Pleasure to convey to you by order of Congress the only Tribute which a free People will ever consent to pay, the Tribute of Thanks and Gratitude to their Friends and Benefactors.

The disinterested and patriotic Principles which led you to the Field, have also led you to Glory, and it affords no little Consolation to your Countrymen to reflect, that as a peculiar Greatness of Mind induced you to decline any Compensation for serving them except the Pleasure of promoting their Happiness, they may without your Permission bestow upon you the largest Share of their Affections and Esteem.

Those Pages in the Annals of America will record your Title to a conspicuous Place in the Temple of Fame, which shall inform Posterity that under your Direction an undisciplined Band of Husbandmen in the Course of a few Months became Soldiers, And that the Desolation meditated against the Country by a brave Army of Veterans commanded by the most experienced Generals, but employed by bad Men in the worst of Causes, was by the Fortitude of your Troops and the Address of their Officers next to the kind Interposition of Providence, confined for near a Year within such narrow Limits as scarce to admit more Room than was necessary for the Encampments and Fortifications they lately abandoned.

Accept therefore Sir the Thanks of the united Colonies unanimously declared by their Delegates to be due to you and the brave Officers and Troops under your Command; and be pleased to communicate to them this distinguished Mark of the Approbation of their Country.

The Congress have ordered a golden Medal adapted to the occasion to be struck and when finished, to be presented to You.[1]

<I am etc.>

I have the honour to be with every Sentiment of Esteem, Sir, Your most obedient and very humble servant.

Dft. PHi: Conarroe Coll. The heading and complimentary closing are not in JJ's hand. Endorsed in another hand. On 25 March 1776, JJ, John Adams and Stephen Hopkins (1707–85) of Rhode Island were named a committee of Congress responsible for drafting a letter of thanks to Washington who had commanded the American forces since June 1775 on the occasion of the end of the siege of Boston and for preparing a "proper device" for a gold medal to be presented to the Commander. Their report was made on 2 April and the draft letter was accepted by Congress that day and dispatched to Washington over the signature of John Hancock. As Adams complained bitterly in his *Autobiography* some twenty-nine years later: "But the Letter a great part of the Compliment of which would have lain in the Insertion of it in the Journal, was carefully secluded. Perhaps the Secretary or the President or both, chose rather to conceal the Compliment to the General than make one to the Member who made the motion [Adams] and the Committee who prepared it." The version of the letter printed in the modern *JCC*, IV, 248–49, is taken from the LS version in DLC: Washington Papers, not from earlier editions of the *Journals* or the ms. minutes in DNA: PCC. *JCC*, IV, 234; John Adams, *Diary*, III, 377.

1 The designs for this medal are reproduced in John Adams, *Diary*, III, facing p. 257. The artist was Pierre Eugène Du Simitière (1736–84), a native of Geneva who resided in Philadelphia during the Revolution and executed portraits of many leading political and military figures, including JJ.

From William Goforth

Three Rivers in Canada, April the 8th, 1776[1]

Honoured Sir

I haveing been ordered by his Excellency General Wooster[2] on the 3d Feb. with a Small party to take the Command of this place I have thereby had an Opportunity to take an Exact account of all the Fresh Forces which have passd this place Since the defeat at Quebec which I make Bold to transmit you as also what I Supposed a few days ago to have been the number of our Army at the Camp before that place.

Fresh Forces, officers included which past this Post Since the defeat, 1772; I Imagined those which moved from the Garrisson at Montreal before I arrived here to be 400; and that the Number of well, Sick and wounded after the defeat to be 500; and the new Recruited Canadians to be according to the best accounts I could get to be 500; Total, 3172.

But on receiving a Letter from a Brother Captain a few days ago I was obliged to Conclude I was wrong Somewhere or Else that great Numbers must have died an Extract of which I send also and is as follows. You'll please to observe says he that by the Generale Return of the army, Canadians Included, we have 2475, 786 of them Sick, Six hundred and odd present fit for duty, the Remainder at different out Posts, Some of them 30 and 40 miles Distant.[3] This is the State of our Army, Officers included, and after mentioning Some other things he Says To insure Certain Ruin, the officers of the Different Provinces, are Continually Stygmatizeing Each other. And again

Seventy odd men less this day fit for duty than there was two days ago. I mean not to Reflect and was I disposed so to do I know not on whom I Should lay the Reflection but Cant help Saying I am Extremely Sorry this department had not had greater attention paid to it and been better Supplyd with men. Had we had the number of Men which it was reported we had last Summer the Business would have been finisht. But instead of the talked of thousands I believe Colonel Fleming the D. A. G.[4] Can tell you that when he wanted men he could not Sometimes Call on more than Eight hundred fit for duty.

Had we been properly succored this Spring the Town of Quebec might have been Stormd without Risque of great Loss. However we have heard Ten Batalions are Comeing for this place and Perhaps by this time you may have heard they are arrived. But where they Stay I know not. It may be you ask where are the Pensylvania men, the Jersey men and the three thousand Green Mountain Boys.[5] Thats a question I Cant answer but this I Can tell you that on the sixth Instant young Mr. Maccord[6] on his way from Camp to Montreal Calld to See me and told me a return was made of the Green Mountain men under Command of Colonel Warner[7] and that only 92 were Returned fit for Service. Upon a Supposition that Quebec Should not be taken before the arrival of the Ships of War, I Should on that Score be much Concerned for our little Army and for the poor Canadians who have taken part with the United Colonies, for in my Opinion there would be great Danger of the Communication being Cut of[f] between the Southern Colonies and this, in Consequence of which our little neglected army must fall in to the hands of our inveterate Enemies and if so the Poor Canadians must by a Natural Consequence fall a Victim to Ministerial Vengence of which they are greatly affraid. But upon the Supposition that Quebec Should be taken (which I would rather Choose to beleive) I hope you will not then Conclude that all is over and that this Country is then fully Secured.

I well know that Quebec is Generally looked upon to be a place of Such Strength as to make it a Barrier Sufficient to prevent any Vessells Passing by it but it Should be rememberd that it has been passed by Vessells of war and may be again. And Should one Single twenty-Gun Ship Get up the River it would be in the power of the Commander to destroy the Towns of three Rivers and Montreal, together with most of the Vilages on both sides the River Saint Laurance for one hundred and Eighty miles. On the one hand the Towns and Vilages must be destroyed or on the other the People must Subject to any Contributions Either of men or Money that might be

Called for, not a Single Battery being Erected for the defence of any [of] the Towns or Vilages.

At Montreal a Battery might in my Opinion be Constructed for its own defence. The Channel Before the Town of three Rivers puts down on both Sides of the River but at Cape Magdline about one League and a half below ther[e] the[y] Unite and Channel Sets Close in with the North Shore where a Battery might be So Constructed as to prevent any thing perhaps from Passing. But the best place in the River is at Richleiu Rappids about 45 miles below this place. There the Tide never Sets up, at most only Swells. The Channel is narrow and near the Shore and is so difficult that they must have a good Pilot and day light or a very Clear night to pass it and what would make that place more advantegeous is that the Rapids Lets down So Strong that it requires a Breeze from 6 to 8 Knotts to Stem the Current. If a Battery was well Constructed at this place of about 20 peices of heavy Cannon and put under the Command of a good Officer and men Sufficient to defend the works I allow it would answer Every purpose for all places above it and in my opinion be a greater Security to the upper parts of the Country than Quebec.

Again if Quebec is taken of other things Will immediate Call for your attention [to] a printing office is much wanting which if put under the direction a prudent man that understands French and English and orderd to publish Every thing in both Languages would I doubt not be of great use to the Cause of Liberty. The different Posts for Indians trade will for your direction also, and Cant help thinking the Supplieng the Indians this Summer is a Matter that deserves Serious Consideration. On the one hand if they are Served with Amunition they may Use it against us. On the other if they have it not, they have been so long out of the Use of Bows and Arrows that they must Starve which doubtless they will try in time to prevent in time and if Possible Something ought to be done to divert the trade of the merchants in Canada for altho the most of them are as fond of freedom as you are below and have Petitioned against the Quebec Bill[8] yet they be Easily taught to Sacrifice their trade as our friends below have done and you may depend on it one great Reason why we have so many Tories is because the[y] dread to Shut their Stores. The Establishing Regular Courts of Justice is much wanted and ardantly Calld for by many of the best People.

It may be you might be willing to have my candid opinion Respecting the takeing Quebec. I beleive we Shall take it and I as Candidly must tell you that I beleive we Shall as Soon lose it if we are not better Reinforced with men. If we do not take it it will be for want of men and if we do not keep it will be for want of Secureing the Passes of the River.

I had the Honour to Spend part of the Evening of the 29th March with General Worster and in my turn was Calld upon to give my Toast which was that the General might Speedily Enter the Gates of Quebec with Tryumph. With this he did not Seem fully to agree and said for his part he determined to go over the Walls. Seemd in high Spirits and on being informd of the Rumpos with the Tories below. Seemed not to regard it and gave me Express orders if any difficulty Should arise in this district to Stop as many men as I thought proper Saying he was affraid of haveing too many men below. I have Stop none yet, neither Shall I till he is better Supplied unless the necessity Should be very Pressing, this District Laying between the army of Quebec and Montreal I Conceive to be the Quietest part of Canada at present. On the fourth Instant Leiutenant Witcom arrived here from Chomble by the way of the Parish of St Ours[9] and acquainted me that the Captain of malitia of Said Parish desired him to leave a Small party of men there, that he was endangerd by Executeing orders in favour of the Congress. That was Confirmd by an Ensign who arrived last night with another party with this addition that the Tories were as privately so they Could inlisting men in order to fall in with the Tories. If we faild at Quebec this parish of St Ours Laying in Colonel Hazens[10] District I Immediately Sent a letter to inform thereof who I doubt not will Soon give a good account of them.

The Minds of the Canadians Seems to be freted and wavering and begin to think our hand full of men not Sufficient to protect them from Ministerial Vengence. As to fighting for us we need [not] Expect them any farther than they think we dont Stand in need of th[em]. If we should miss takeing Quebec depend upon it they will be pan[ic] Struck and to Save Appearances, Secure their Estates and prevent their [fami]lies from being Butcherd Join in helping to drive us out of the Country.

I hope you will Excuse Every freedom I have taken. I only mean to Give you a true State of facts. I hope also you will not cons[i]ter anything I have said as intended to Discourage the Carr[y]ing on the war in this province. So far from any thing of that Sort that I am of Opinion it would be better for the back Settlers in the Lower Colonies to Support the war in this province by a Special tax on themselves than to lose it as a Barrier. I hope Quebec will Soon be ours, that I may get permission on[c]e more in an honourable way to Return to my family. I[n] the meantime beg Leave to Subscribe myself as in Reality I am your most obedient and most humble Servant

WILLIAM GOFORTH Captain in the first Batalion of the 1st New York Force

One thing I beg as a favour of the Congress and that is that as Soon as the season is proper they would Issue forth a decree ordering all the Doctors in America to prepare to Newangland and Anoculate all its inhabitants for the Small Pox, the want of which being done has almost Broke up our Army and Cost many a brave man his life. Otherwise the Camp is tolerablee Healthy.[11]

ALS. Addressed: "To John Jay Esquire Member of the Continental Congress." Endorsed. Enclosure not located. Tr. in NN: Bancroft, Amer. Rev., I, 37.

1 Three Rivers was located on the north side of the St. Lawrence, halfway between Montreal and Quebec.

2 On 1 Jan. 1776, Brigadier General David Wooster succeeded Richard Montgomery as American commander in Canada.

3 Goforth's unidentified informant seems to have had more reliable reports than did Goforth. Modern authorities estimate American forces before Quebec in early April as about 2,000. Christopher Ward, *The War of the Revolution* (2 vols., New York, 1952), I, 196.

4 Colonel Edward Fleming served as Deputy Adjutant General for the Continental Army, 29 Aug. 1775–20 June 1776. *JPC*, I, 126. 500.

5 On 19 Jan. 1776 the Congress resolved to reinforce the troops in Canada and urged Pennsylvania and New Jersey to increase their efforts to raise troops for this theater. Additional men were also to be drawn from Washington's army at Boston and from New Hampshire, Connecticut, and New York. *JCC*, IV, 70–71.

6 Probably John McCord, Jr., the son of a Quebec merchant who had long opposed the British administration in Canada and had fled Quebec in November 1775 after refusing to accept Governor Carleton's ultimatum to join the militia. Justin H. Smith, *Our Struggle for the Fourteenth Colony* (2 vols., New York, 1907), I, 56; II, 95; George M. Wrong, *Canada and the American Revolution* (New York, 1935), p. 229.

7 Lieutenant Colonel Seth Warner (1743–84) of the Vermont militia.

8 The Quebec Act of 1774.

9 Probably either Second Lieutenant Benjamin Whitcomb or First Lieutenant Elisha Whitcomb of Bedel's New Hampshire Rangers. St. Ours was located at the junction of the Richelieu and St. Lawrence Rivers. Chambly was on the Richelieu.

10 Colonel Moses Hazen (1733–1803), a Massachusetts native, was a resident of St. Johns, Quebec, at the outbreak of the Revolution. Hazen joined the American troops in 1775 and participated in the assaults on Quebec and Montreal. He was commissioned a colonel in the 2nd Canadian Regiment on 22 Jan. 1776.

11 Official requests for improved medical care for the troops in Canada reached Congress in May 1776. On 22 May, a Congressional committee recommended the appointment of a second surgeon to the hospital staff in Canada, and Dr. Jonathan Potts was named to this post the next month. *JCC*, IV, 343–44, 358, 378; V, 424, 661.

To Alexander McDougall

Philadelphia, 11 April 1776

Whether my last Letter has reached you or not is uncertain. From your Silence I sometimes suspect it has not. However as I know you must be perpetually engaged in Matters of more Consequence, I cannot expect to hear from you so often as when you enjoyed more Leizure.

I wuld wish to be informed of the number of Troops now employed in New York, how your Levies go on, and whether there is a Prospect of your Battalions soon being compleated.

From a late York Paper there is reason to apprehend a disagreable Dispute between some of the Citizens and the Convention relative to the Mode of Appointing Delegates to the Congress. I esteem every Controversey of this kind as a misfortune to the Colony and cannot but think the mode proposed by the Mechanicks useless as well as unseasonable. All the Delegates who now compose this Congress were chosen either by provincial Assemblies or Convention and I really can see no good Reason for deviating from it in one Colony.

As it is intended that the next Convention should be expresly authorized by their Constituents to appoint Delegates, I cannot percieve how the Right of Election will be injured by their exerting a Power so publickly and openly given them by the People, from whom I readily admit all civil Authority must originate.[1]

The making of Gun Locks, Arms and Salt petre goes on rapidly in this Colony, and from the Accounts recieved lately from Virginia they will soon manufacture as much Powder as they may want.

A very rich mine of Sulphur lying just under the Surface of the Earth has been discovered in Jersey, and a Man who understands preparing or refining the Ore has been found and employed, so that in all Probability [we sh]all never after this Year be indebted to [Forei]gners for ammunition.

As the Sound is now pretty well secured against the Incursions of the Enemy, would it not be prudent for the Convention to cause Salt Works to be erected. I fear the Scarcity of that Commodity will in the Course of another Year distress our People exceedingly.[2]

I hope to see you sometime next Month unless the Arrival of the Commissioners[3] or some other extraordinary Event should detain me. As to those Gentlemen, I sometimes think their coming questionable, and should they arrive, I suspect their Powers will be too limited, to promise us much from Negotiation.

From the present Appearance of Things it is natural to suppose that the Sword must decide the Controversy. And with a View to that Object our measures should in a great Degree be taken. The first Thing therefore in my Opinion to be done is to erect good and well ordered Governments in all the Colonies, and thereby exclude that Anarchy which already too much prevails. This is a Step which it is probable will not be taken by the Conventions till the Business of the Commissioners is over, but it is a Matter which ought nevertheless to be attended to, and inculcated.[4]

I am Dear Sir, Your Friend and humble Servant

JOHN JAY

ALS. NHi: McDougall Papers. Endorsed.

[1] Before its adjournment on 16 March 1776 the Second New York Provincial Congress enacted resolutions for the election of a Third Congress in mid-April. In the campaign for the Third Provincial Congress, the method of selecting delegates to the Continental Congress became a major issue. The Committee of Mechanics issued a statement of 1 April 1776 advocating the future selection of Continental delegates by popular elections rather than by the Provincial Congress. The Mechanics' statement appeared in the *N.Y. Mercury* of 8 April 1776. For a discussion of this issue in the April 1776 campaign, see Becker, *N.Y. Political Parties*, pp. 255–58.

[2] On 16 March 1776 the Provincial Congress resolved to offer loans and premiums to encourage the extraction of salt from sea water, and the Committee of Safety which sat after the Congress's adjournment was empowered to publish accounts of methods for processing salt. *JPC*, I, 366.

[3] As early as mid-February 1776 rumors circulated in the colonies to the effect that Parliament had appointed commissioners to negotiate provincial grievances. However, in the third week of March, the Congress received a copy of the Act of Parliament of 19 Dec. 1775 which interdicted trade with the colonies and provided for commissioners who would have only the powers of granting pardons and accepting oaths of allegiance to the crown, not any power to negotiate with the Congress. *LMCC*, I, 355, 401; 4 *FAA*, IV, 439–41.

[4] JJ's proposal anticipated the momentous resolution of Congress of 10 May 1776 calling on the people of the colonies to institute new state governments. John Adams had advocated such a move back in June of '75. *JCC*, IV, 342, 351, 357–58; John Adams, *Diary*, III, 351–52.

John Jay's Draft Resolution in Congress

[*15 April–4 May*] *1776*

Whereas it is unjust as well as impolitic that Americans should afford aid to the Enemies of their Country, and particularly in the Seizure of Vessels or other Property belonging to Inhabitants of these Colonies or by purchasing of the Enemy any of their Property so seized.

Resolved That all Americans who shall be guilty of the said Offences ought to be liable for the Damages which the Persons injured by such Seizure may sustain thereby.

Resolved therefore that it be recommended to all the Legislatures and Conventions in these united Colonies to enact Laws or Ordinances for the Purposes aforesaid where Courts competent to the Cognizance of such Cause, do not already exist to erect them and to the End That the said Laws or Ordinances in the different Colonies may the better correspond, and their objects obtained with the greater Facility and Justice.

Resolved That the Party injured as af[oresai]d ought to commence his Action against the offender who ought to be entitled to Bail in the Court so erected or to be erected in the Colony where the Offender <shall happen, be committed, and where the same shall happen on the high Seas then in these Colonies next that he may think proper> can or shall be taken, and that the Proceedings in the said Action ought to be according to the Modes of Proceeding used in the said Colony in Civil Causes. And that appeals ought to be admitted and prosecuted as in other civil action, except in Colonies where the Governors or others appointed by the King were heretofore Judges in Error, In which Colonies the Conventions ought to appoint proper persons to recieve and determine such Appeals provided the Parties demanding the same shall and give reasonable Security for prosecuting the same in which all further Proceedings ought to be stayed till the said Appeal be determined.

And whereas it may happen that the Estate or Effects of the Def[endan]t may not be in the Colony in which such Cause may be tryed but in some other whereby in case Judgment should pass against the Def[endan]t the Damages cannot be levied Resolved that in all such Cases a Transcript of the Record certified by the Judge or Judges of the said Court ought on the Request of the Pl[ain]t[iff] to be transmitted to the Judge or Judges of the Court erected or to be erected as af[oresai]d in the Colony where the Estate or Effects of such Def]endan]t may be which Judge or Judges on Reciept thereof ought to award and cause Execution of the said Judgment to be had.

Resolved further that Costs agreable to the Laws and usage of the Colony in which such Actions may be commenced and prosecuted ought to be allowed in these as in other civil actions.

And the better to prevent any vexatious Suits being commenced under Color of the said Laws or Ordinances Resolved that the Pl[ain]-t[iff] ought previous to the commencement of the said action to make Aff[idavi]t of the Cause of Action and file the same with the Clerk of the Court, and further give Bond with Security to the said Clerk to prosecute the said Action to Judgment and in Case Judgment should pass on the appeal (in case there should be one *determination*) against him to pay the Def[endan]t his Costs, and such Clerk ought in Case the said Action should be finally determined against the Pl[ain]t[iff] to assign the said Bond to the Def[endan]t.

Dft. Endorsed: "Dr. Resolutions in Congress agt. purchasg the Enemy's Prizes &c." Additional endorsement in another hand: "by J. Jay 1776." On 15 April 1776, JJ, Carter Braxton (1736–97), and George Wythe of Virginia were appointed to prepare a resolution "whereby persons resident, having property in America, who assist any of the enemies of these United Colonies in the captures of vessels or goods, may be made liable to make good the damages to the sufferers." These resolutions were drafted by JJ before he left Philadelphia to visit his wife's family in Elizabeth Town en route to New York. JJ's last letter dated at Philadelphia was written on 27 April, while he wrote from Elizabeth as early as 5 May 1776. *JCC*, IV, 284; *LMCC*, I, liv; JJ to Philip Schuyler, 5 May 1776, NN: Schuyler Papers.

The carefully prepared resolutions were never considered by Congress, since the debates on independence placed supporters of the British cause in a legal position completely different from that envisioned by JJ's proposed statutes. Indeed, the Declaration of Independence forced Congress to reconsider and revise all earlier resolutions on privateering and the confiscation of British goods in a series of resolutions beginning in July 1776. *JCC*, V, 605–06; VI, 885, 986.

From Alexander McDougall

New York, April 16th, 1776

Dear Sir,

Your four last favors are now before me. My long Silence was owing to what you ascribed it. I have however Stole a moment, to peruse your Letters, and to return you some answer.

We have two sloops and a peteauger armed on account of the Colony, ready to Saile on a Cruze. They have been detained for want of a regulation for the Seamen's pay. One of the Sloops carries Six four pounders, and the other four of the best Guns of their Denominations I ever saw; and the largest Sloop is very well calculated for the Service. The Peteauger mounts Swivels on the Combing of the Hatches, as she is decked; carries about twenty men, Designed to Secure inland Navigation.[1]

You will be informed by the Pamphlets which accompanys this, what encouragement the Convention have given for errecting Powder Mills, making of arms, and diffused the Knowledge of making Salt Peter through the Colony. Experiments are pursued by Sundry Persons on private account in the Colony, with Success, and in a few days the Committee of Safety will errect works on Colony accounts.[2] There is no foundation for Boyed's disappointing us from any motive unfriendly to the Country; but from necessity. His forge man was drownded, a short time before he errected his works for boring the muskets, and the call has been so great in the neighbouring Colonies, for workmen in the Gun Smiths branch, that he has not been able after much traveling to procure a proper and Sufficient number of Hands. And so great a part of the time Contracted elapsed before he finished his works, that he was discouraged from hiring men on great encouragement, as it was optional in us whether we would take the arms made after the time limited. But as he has his works ready, I think he will Soon be of Service to himself and the Public, in making arms. A Contract we made with one Attherton[3] in Dutches County for 250 arms to be made by the first instant, is in some forwardness, about 100 of the barrels and Locks are made. Powder Mills there will be a Sufficient Number. The Pike you Promised is not come to Hand. We have a Committee continually on our accounts; but as there are So many works carrying on, which continually incurs expence, the accounts by this and pay to the minute men we left incomplete.[4] But no time nor attention will be lost. You know that Egg Harbour is not in our Colony, but it is frequented by the Trade of Pen[nsylvani]a, New Jersey and New York and Should therefore be Secured.

I have long been of your opinion on the Subject of Taxing, but I confess there are weighty difficulties in the way. The great Stagnation of Commerce, and the removal of the inhabitants out of this City, were important reasons, which induced my assent to delay that measure. If we had taxed, where Should the Rich men of this Capital who have taken their flight be taxed? And how is the Poor freeholder of it, to pay his, when he can receive no rent? I was determined to delayed the tax for these difficulties, as the Country members Seem bent on Sadling us, with one third of the Colony expence. The Public Service calls upon me, and must therefore defer the answer to the other parts of Yours till another oppertunity.

I am Dear Sir Your affectionate Humble Servant

ALEXR. McDOUGALL

Your Brother delivered me the message relative to your House, which has been attended to, and its Secured.

ALS. Endorsed: ". . . answd. 27 Inst." Enclosures: *Essays upon the Making of Salt-Petre and Gun Powder. Published by Order of the Committee of Safety of the Colony of New York* (New York, 1776); *Resolutions of the Provincial Congress of the Colony of New York for the Encouragement of Manufacturies of Gun-*

Powder, Musket Barrels, Musket Locks and Salt (New York, 1776). Tr. in NN: Bancroft, Amer. Rev., I, 53.

[1] On 10 Dec. 1775 the New York Provincial Congress named a committee to "plan a voyage, or voyages, for at least two more vessels . . ." to procure military stores and other supplies. By March 1776 the colony had fitted out the *Schuyler* and was arming the sloop *Bishop*, and the sloop *Montgomerie* was purchased on 19 March so that it could be armed for the colony's defense. *JPC*, I, 212, 349, 372, 408.

[2] Resolutions offering various premiums to encourage the construction of powder mills and works for the manufacture of bayonets, gunlocks, and musket barrels were passed by the New York Congress on 16 March. During the recess of Congress, the Committee of Safety was empowered to contract for stands of arms and to negotiate with contractors for the manufacture of saltpeter. *JPC*, I, 365–66.

[3] For the Provincial Congress's contract with Cornelius Atherton of Amenia, Dutchess County, see *JPC*, I, 221.

[4] Various new committees were regularly appointed to audit and settle the accounts in early 1776. *JPC*, I, 316, 325, 351.

John Alsop, John Jay, George Clinton, and Lewis Morris to Walter Livingston

Philadelphia, 17th April 1776

Sir,

We received your Favour of the 8th Inst.[1] The Office of Commissary is extreamly embarassed. The Commissary General (who it was expected would have continued in the Eastern Department) is now by the Removal of the Army from Boston in New York,[2] tho it was originally intended (as we understood) that you as Deputy Commissary General shoud have the sole Management of that Office in the Northern Department. The Provincial Congress of New York by the Directions of this Congress entered into a Contract with Mr. Abraham Livingston to supply the Army stationed at New York with Provissions at the Price you mention per Ration.[3] When the Pensylvania Batallions were raised (Part of which are now at New York) a certain Mr. Wharton[4] was appointed by Congress Commissary for those Levies who contracted to supply them at the Rate of 7d. Pensylvania Currency per Ration, which you will perceive interferes with Mr. Abraham Livingston's Contract. But it is probable Mr. Wharton who was lately at New York and is returned here will relinquish his Contract. The Congress have lately appointed Mr. Price[5] Commissary for the Troops in Canada but have not made any particular Contract with him for furnishing the Provissions for that Part of the Army. He is to consult General Schuyler as to the Mode of supplying those Troops and is to be furnished With Money by Congress for that

Purpose. Flour and Bread he expects to procure in Canada, but no other Part of the Provissions.

These being the Facts we have but little if any Prospect of procuring any Contract or Appointment for you that we think may be worth your accepting. It is not thought that any of the above Contracts interfere with your Office of Deputy Commissary General which it is likely will continue to be a necessary Office in Albany. Perhaps on Mr. Price's consulting with General Schuyler on the most proper Method of suppling the Army in Canada something may turn up worth your Attention; should this be the Case be assured we will not forget you as we consider you as having served the Public in your present Office without an adequate Compensation for your extraordinary Trouble.

We are your Most Obedient Servants

JOHN ALSOP,
JOHN JAY,
GEO. CLINTON,
LEWIS MORRIS

LS. NHi: Misc. Mss. (Livingston). Body of the letter in the hand of George Clinton (1739–1812) who rejoined the New York delegation in Congress in early April 1776 after an absence of eight months.

1 Letter not located.

2 Joseph Trumbull (1738–78) of Connecticut was named Continental Commissary General 19 July 1775. After the British evacuation of Boston, Washington began to dispatch troops to New York and arrived in the city himself on 13 April 1776.

3 On 17 Feb. 1776 the Continental Congress advanced New York $35,000 to supply the troops ordered to defend the colony and directed the Provincial Congress to make contracts for provisioning these soldiers. On 14 March the New York Congress accepted the proposals of Walter Livingston's cousin Abraham (1754–c. 1781) for supplying Continental troops in New York City, and this contract was confirmed by the Continental Congress on 6 April. *JCC*, IV, 159–60, 260; *JPC*, I, 360.

4 Carpenter Wharton contracted to supply the battalion raised in Pennsylvania in 1775. His responsibility for provisioning Pennsylvania units was confirmed by the Continental Congress in January and March 1776 when these troops were sent to New York. *JCC*, III, 419; IV, 87, 210.

5 James Price, a Montreal merchant who had aided American forces in Canada, was appointed deputy commissary on 29 March 1776. *JCC*, IV, 240–41.

FROM PETER JAY

Rye, 18th April 1776

Dear Johnny,

Since I wrote to you last I've had the pleasure of receiving several of your Letters. The Jesuits Bark came to hand very Opportunely, but am at a loss how to send you the Money it Cost, And fear I must wait till you come here.[1]

It's a doubt, I think, whether the defeat of the Scotch and Tories in North Carolina will settle the internal Peace of that Colony. Clinton's arrival there and being joind, as it's said, by a Number of regular Troops, may probably Spirit them to take up Arms Again, And in that Case there may be warm work.[2] N. York I'm told is put in a good posture of defence. God grant that all attempts of the Ministerial Troops may be frustrated, and be the means of a happy reconciliation.

Your Mother continues as usual, And as to myself I now feel better and my Strength comes on slow, Which can only be expected at my advanced Age.

I have discharged Jemmy's Bond to the College and is delivered up to me. We all remember our love to you. I am Dear Johnny your Affectionate Father.

PETER JAY

P.S. When you are about coming to Rye with Sally, if you can let me know about what time you will be at N. York, i'll send the Chariot down, which I believe will gard her better against the Cold than an open Carriage. When you come to N. York you may send Claas up immediately for the Carriage. Be carefull to come over at Powles Creek and run no risk.

ALS. Addressed: "To John Jay Esqr. in Philadelphia." Endorsed.

1 Peter Jay to JJ, 18 March 1776; JJ's reply and succeeding letters to his father of March and April 1776 have not been located.

2 General Sir Henry Clinton (1738–95), second in command at Boston, sailed on a military expedition to the southern colonies in January 1776, but did not reach Cape Fear, N.C., until 12 March. Clinton was disappointed in his expectation of reinforcement by local Loyalists because of Patriot victories like that at Moore's Creek Bridge on 27 February 1776 where Tories, marching to the coast to join Clinton, were cut down, captured, or forced to flee in confusion. Clinton's campaign was hampered further when ships bringing reinforcements from Ireland were delayed in their Atlantic passages, and the full complement of naval and military forces promised for his Southern campaign did not assemble until 31 May.

From Marinus Willett

[*New York, before 27 April 1776*]

Sir

I should have troubled you with this letter before now, had it not been for an indissposition that seized me immediately after my return from Philedelphia which tied me to my bed till two days ago. The reason of my sending *you* the Inclosed is your asking me in the first conversation I had with you when at Philedelphia, whether I had seen Gen. Schuyler on my way from Canada, which by the manner and time of its being introduced appeared to me to convey an expectation of a recommendation from him if I merited it. Whether this Conjecture is true or not is not very material, tho it has been a Spur to prompt me to trouble you with the inclosed Certified copy of a letter from Gen. Schuyler to our Provincial Congress. I acknowledge I do not leave myself intirly out of the Question in this affair, yet if this was realy the case I should count it my duty for the good of such as may come after me to endeavour by every means in my power to prevent [th]em from receiving the like severe treatment that I have. For, to be superceeded in the way I have been I cant help thinking upon your being asked seriously to reflect upon must appear to be an unnescesary as well as dissagreable evil. I, for my part, have you will Naturly suppose thought something about it. I have considered the reasons you gave for the Appointment of Mr. Schuyler to a Majority and however insufficient the cause of that appointment may appear to me, yet inasmuch as it was thought weighty enough by the Honorable Gentlemen into whose hands the right of communicating power is deposited I am dissposed to leave any farther consideration of that matter.

But how it came to pass that I should be superceeded by Captain Benidect is truly Strange to me, nor can I conceive the Shadow of a cause for it from any part of that Gentlemans conduct which I have been able to come at. On the contrary the more I aim at investigating it, the more obscure it appears.[1]

I am no way uneasy about your being disspleased at the incroachment I have made on your patience in this Tedious Harangue inacurate as it is, because I think I know enough of your candor, to convince me that you will rather be inclined to put a favourable, than an unfavourable construction on my intentions in it. I have only to add that if you should have an opportunity and think it right to grant me any futer appointment I shall not be willing to serve in any Military <appo[intment]> Capacity where I shall rank under the present Major Benedict. I am Sir most affectionatly Your's

MARINUS WILLETT

P.S. Believe me Sir we have a Number of Officers who are indeed Men of Approved Perserverance and Courage, who must be now on their way from Canada, who it will be the highth of ungenerousity not to provide for. I am Sorry there is reason to say that Gentlemen in office here are too much taken up about themselves to think of those wirthies abroad.

ALS. Endorsed: "Marinus Willett—recd. Ap. 1776 answd. 27th. Inst." Enclosure: Philip Schuyler to the New York Provincial Congress, 27 Feb. 1776, *JPC*, II, 121. Schuyler's letter of recommendation for Willett remarked that: "When an officer has acted with remarkable attention and propriety, it becomes a duty in his commander to give public testimony of it. Such has been the conduct of Capt. Willets during the last campaign. . . ." In his reply to Willett of 27 April 1776 JJ conceded: "General Schuyler's letter does you honor, and had it been made known to the members of Congress a few months sooner, I am confident it would have had all the influence you would have wished." *HPJ*, I, 56; mutilated dftS in JP.

[1] For the problems created by the Continental Congress's appointment of field officers for the four New York battalions in March 1776, see above, McDougall to JJ, 20 March 1776, n. 6 (first letter). Willett, one of the New York Congress's eight nominees for a majority, was not given any commission by the Continental Congress's resolves of 8 March 1776, while Peter P. Schuyler, whom the New York Congress had suggested as a lieutenant colonel, and Joseph Benedict, one of the New York Congress's nominees for Major, were named Majors of the 2nd and 1st New York Battalions, respectively. Schuyler served as major of the 5th Albany Regiment of militia in 1775. Benedict had been named a "Jr." captain of the 4th New York Regiment 27 July 1775, nearly a month after Willett had received his commission as Captain of the 1st New York Regiment. *JCC*, IV, 69, 190; *JPC*, I, 328; *Cal. of Hist. Mss.*, I, 105, 171, 246; II, 410.

Angered by the action of the Continental Congress, Willett wrote to the New York Committee of Safety on 20 April 1776 and returned the warrant issued to him for raising troops in the province. He explained: "I can by no means submit to the indignity of being superseded." *JPC*, II, 190.

To Alexander McDougall

Philadelphia, 27 April 1776

Dear Collonel

Accept my Thanks for your friendly Letter of the 16th Inst. and its Inclosures, which contain useful as well as agreable Information. I am glad to see New York doing something in the naval Way, and think the Encouragement given by the Convention to the Manufacture of arms, Powder, Salt Petre and Sea Salt, does them Honor.

Many of the Reasons you alledge for delaying Taxation are weighty, and I confess did not occur to me. It is certainly unreasonable to impose on the City, in its present Circumstances, so great a Share of the public Expences.[1]

The late Election, so far as it respects yourself, has taken a Turn I did not expect, and am at a Loss to account for, except on the Principles of your holding a military Commission,[2] or of that Mutability which from various Causes, often strongly marks popular Opinions of men and measures in Times like these. But whatever may have been the Reason, I am persuaded that the Zeal you have shewn[3] and the Sacrifices you have made in this great Cause, will always afford You the most pleasing Reflections, and will one Day, not only merit, but recieve the Gratitude of your Fellow Citizens. Posterity you know always does Justice. Let no Circumstance of this Kind diminish your Ardors but by persevering in a firm uniform Course of Conduct, silence Detraction and compel Approbation.

I am much obliged to You for your kind Attention to my House, and be assured that I shall omit no Opportunity of evincing the Esteem and Sincerity with which I am your Friend and humble Servant

JOHN JAY

ALS. NHi: McDougall Papers. Addressed: "To Collonel Alexander McDougall at New York. Favd. by Mr. Clinton." Endorsed. Dft. in JP.

1 "Burden" in dft.

2 "Office" in dft. McDougall was defeated for a seat in the Third New York Provincial Congress in the elections of 16 April 1776.

3 In the draft "your own Reflections" was deleted and replaced by the phrase "the Zeal you have shewn."

Last Stand Against Independence

The serious illnesses of his wife and both parents prompted JJ to quit Philadelphia toward the end of April 1776. In his absence from Congress James Duane and other conservatives kept prodding him about the radical bent of Congress, about the resolution for the setting up of state governments, which JJ himself had anticipated, and the rising tide of pro-independence sentiment. Come back, we need you, Duane and South Carolinian Edward Rutledge urged, the latter beseeching him to support "the Sensible part of the House" opposing independence.

JJ did not come back. Instead, elected to the Third New York Provincial Congress, he began to attend its sessions the last week of May. At once he was placed on one committee to draft a law relating to the perils to which the colony was exposed by "its intestine enemies" and on another to act on the congressional mandate to form a new government.[1] Subversive as both these actions were in fact, JJ was still not reconciled to independence. On 11 June, four days after Richard Henry Lee's Congressional resolution affirming that the United Colonies "are, and of right ought to be, free and independent states," JJ moved in his province's Congress "that the good people of this Colony have not, in the opinion of this Congress, authorized this Congress, or the Delegates of this Colony, in the Continental Congress, to declare this Colony to be and continue independent of the Crown of Great Britain."[2] Ostensibly, he remained in New York where his presence was urgently needed, and thus was, perhaps conveniently, absent on 2 July when the decisive vote on independence took place in Congress. As he explained in a letter to Rutledge, he was engaged by "plots, conspiracies, and chimeras dire." State business came first. "We have a government, you know, to form; and God only knows what it will resemble."[3] In fact, the resolution he had sponsored inhibited the New York delegation from voting on the issue of independence, even if the delegates had been inclined to cast their votes in the affirmative.

1 *JPC*, I, 461.
2 *Ibid.*, 490.
3 JJ to Edward Rutledge, 6 July 1776, *HPJ*, I, 68–70.

From James Duane

Philadelphia, 11 May 1776

I received, my dear Sir, your favour of the 8 Instant[1] and really feel for you in the double distress which attends you. I sincerely wish that in both Instances you may be speedily relieved by the Recovery of Persons so near and dear to you.[2]

The Report you mention of the Arrival of Commissioners is not founded on any authority nor Credited. A Resolution has passed a Committee of the whole Congress recommending it to the Colonies to assume All the powers of Government. It waits only for a preface and will then be usherd into the world.[3] This in Confidence as *res infecta*.[4] A Business of still greater moment is on the Carpet.[5] You may Judge of my Situation when our Representation is so Slender. I hope my Friend Bob is on the way.[6] I will do the best I can.

The enclosed Note I have Just received from Mr. Lynch.[7] It speaks his Sentiments fully with respect to this Horse or rather Mare he wishes you to purchase.

The enclosed Letters I have taken up for you. I wish you'd send the Note enclosed to Mr. Jones; it relates to a Sum of money he owes our Friend Dick Peters[8] for Land.

I am with great Regard Your affectionate and most Obedient Servant

JAS. DUANE

ALS. RAWC. All letters from Windsor Castle are published with the kind permission of Her Majesty Queen Elizabeth II. Endorsed. Tr versions in JP and

NN: Bancroft, Amer. Rev., I, 65. Enclosures: Thomas Lynch, Sr. or Jr. to JJ, *c.* 11 May 1776, and "Mr. Jones" to Richard Peters, *c.* 11 May 1776, not located.

1 Letter not located.

2 JJ left Philadelphia between 27 April and 4 May 1776 to visit his ailing wife at her father's home in New Jersey. JJ's parents were also in ill health at this time. JJ to Philip Schuyler, 5 May 1776, NN: Schuyler Papers; JJ to Robert R. Livingston, 29 May 1776, below.

3 On 10 May 1776 Congress resolved: "That it be recommended to the respective assemblies and conventions of the United Colonies, where no government sufficient to the exigencies of their affairs have been hitherto established, to adopt such government as shall, in the opinion of the representatives of the people, best conduce to the happiness and safety of their constituents in particular, and America in general." After this resolution was adopted, John Adams, Edward Rutledge, and Richard Henry Lee (1732–94) of Virginia were named a committee to draft a preamble for the resolution. *JCC*, IV, 342.

4 Unfinished business.

5 The resolution of 10 May recommending that provinces establish new forms of government was, as Duane realized, intimately connected with the greater question of independence for the colonies as a whole.

6 At the end of April 1776, JJ, John Alsop, and George Clinton departed from Philadelphia, leaving only Duane, William Floyd, and Lewis Morris to represent the province. Three delegates were the minimum number capable of casting the colony's vote in Congress. Robert R. Livingston had not attended Congress since Nov. 1775. *JPC*, I, 231; *LMCC*, I, liii-lvii.

7 Thomas Lynch, Jr. (1749–79), joined Congress in April 1776 as a South Carolina delegate to aid his father, Thomas Lynch, Sr., who had been disabled by a paralytic stroke in January 1776. *LMCC*, I, lxii-lxiii.

8 Richard Peters (1744–1828), a Philadelphia attorney and militia captain, was named Secretary to the Board of War by Congress on 13 June 1776.

From James Duane

Philadelphia, 16 May 1776

Yesterday, my dear Friend, was an important day, productive of the Resolutions of which I enclose you a Copy. I shall not enter into particulars; the Resolution itself first passed and then a Committee was appointed to fit it with a preamble. Compare them with each other and it will probably lead you into Reflections which I dare not point out.[1] I hope you will relieve me soon as I am impatient to visit my Friends, and look upon Business here to be in such a Train that I can well be spared.

My Friend Robert is arrived here better in health than I expected. I like his and your plan for a Summer Residence very well as I take it for granted that you will both give your Attention here and leave me in Case I should be reelected at large.[2]

I beg you'l make my Compliments acceptable to Mrs. Jay and the rest of our Friends.

And am with the utmost Regard My dear Sir your affectionate and most obedient servant

JAS. DUANE

ALS. Endorsed. Enclosures: Resolution of Congress, 10 May 1776, with preamble adopted 15 May 1776, *JCC*, IV, 342, 357–58. The preamble to the 10 May resolution was much more far-reaching than the resolution it introduced, for it declared that "it is necessary that the exercise of every kind of authority under the said crown [of Great Britain] should be totally suppressed, and all the powers of government exerted, under the authority of the people of the colonies. . . ."

[1] Duane led the opposition to the preamble, and after the preamble was accepted, John Adams recounted: "Mr. Duane called it, to me, a Machine for the fabrication of Independence. I said, smiling, I thought it was independence itself: but We must have it with more formality yet." John Adams, *Diary*, III, 386.

[2] For JJ's and Robert R. Livingston's plans to rent summer homes for their families in Bristol, Pa., while they sat in Congress, see below, JJ to Livingston, 29 May 1776, n. 1. The commissions for New York's delegates to the Second Continental Congress placed no expiration dates on their appointments, but it was expected that the Third New York Provincial Congress would elect a new slate of Congressmen. *JCC*, II, 15.

From James Duane

Philadelphia, 18th May 1776

I wrote you, my dear Sir, a hasty Scrawl by the post on a most important Subject. You know the Maryland Instructions and those of Pensylvania.[1] I am greatly in doubt whether either of their Assemblies or Conventions will listen to a Recommendation the preamble of which so openly avows Independance and Seperation. The lower Counties[2] will probably adhere to Pensylvania—New Jersey you can form a good Judgement of from the Reception this important Resolution has met with.[3] The orators of Virginia with Col. Henry at their Head are against a Change of Government. The Body of the People, Col. Nelson, on whose Authority you have this Hint, thinks are for it.[4] The late Election of Deputies for the Convention of New York sufficiently proves that those who assumed a Controling power and gave Laws to the Convention and Committees were unsupported by the people.[5] There seems therefore no Reason that our Colony should be too precipitate in changing the present mode of Government. I woud wish first to be well assured of the Opinion of the Inhabitants at large. Let them be rather followed than driven on an Occasion of such momentuous Concern. But, above all, let us see the Conduct of the middle Colonies before we come to a decision. It cannot injure us to wait a few weeks. The Advantage will be great, for this trying

Question will clearly discover the true principles and the Extent of the union of the Colonies. This, my dear Sir, is a delicate Subject on which I cannot enlarge at present—If I coud be relievd I woud immediately set out and give you a meeting. Pray hasten the Return of one of the Gentlemen. I know *you ought* to be at the Convention who are too uninformed of the State and Temper of their Neighbours, and want, at least in this Respect, some Assistance.

I am pleased with the Situation Mr. Livingston has found for your Saturday's Retreat on the Banks of the Shemmony.[6] Nothing could have been more convenient. Present my Compliments to Mrs. Jay and believe me to be with great Regard, Dear Sir, Your Affectionate and most Obedient Servant

JAS. DUANE

ALS. Endorsed. Tr in NN: Bancroft, Amer. Rev., I, 77.

[1] In January 1776, Maryland's Provincial Convention instructed the colony's delegates to Congress to work toward the original goals for which the provinces had united, "the redress of American grievances, and securing the rights of the Colonists," The delegates were explicitly instructed to vote against any resolutions declaring the colonies independent or against any foreign alliances which might lead to a separation from England unless such actions were "absolutely necessary for the preservation of the liberties of the United Colonies." Further, the delegates were ordered to call the Maryland Convention should such resolutions pass Congress and to present the resolutions to the Convention for its consideration; only with the Convention's assent would Maryland consider herself bound by any measures for independence adopted by Congress. 4, *FAA*, IV, 653–54.

The Pennsylvania Assembly drew up similar instructions for that province's delegates to Congress in November 1775. The Pennsylvania Congressmen were enjoined to "dissent from and utterly reject any propositions, should such be made, that may cause or lead to a separation from our Mother Country, or a change of the form of this Government." 4 *FAA*, III, 1793.

[2] Delaware.

[3] The Congressional resolutions of 10 May 1776, published on 15 May with a preamble of that date.

[4] Patrick Henry (1736–99) served in the First Congress and had been a Virginia delegate to the Second Congress until the end of July 1775 when he returned to his home province where he commanded the Virginia militia. Thomas Nelson represented Virginia in the Congress, September 1775–February 1776. Both Henry and Nelson were members of the Virginia Convention which met at Williamsburg 6 May 1776. On 15 May the Convention voted to instruct the province's delegates in Congress "to propose to that respectable body to declare the United Colonies free and independent States . . ." and appointed a committee to prepare a "plan of government" for the colony. 4 *FAA*, VI, 1509, 1524.

[5] The elections for the Third New York Provincial Congress in April 1776 represented far more widespread political participation than had been seen in the polls for the earlier Provincial Congresses. For the first time, all fourteen counties in the colony elected representatives, and 101 delegates were chosen, twenty-one more than had been sent to the Second New York Congress. Thirty-two members of the Second Congress failed to be reelected to the Third Congress, and Carl

Becker detected a "probable . . . conservative victory" in the polling of April 1776. Becker, N.Y. *Political Parties*, pp. 258–60.

6 Neshaminy Creek flowed into the Delaware River just south of Bristol, Pa.

From James Duane

Philadelphia, 25 May 1776

I conclude, my dear Sir, that the late Resolution of Congress recommending the assumption of Government will induce you to give your Attendance for a few days at our own Convention.[1] If this should be the Case it will [be] of Advantage to you to be informed of the Temper and proceedings of the Neighbouring Colonies on this great Resolution.

You recollect the Maryland Instructions which, upon any Measure of Congress to this Effect, required the Delegates of that Colony to repair to their provincial Convention. These Gent[lemen] accordingly declared that they should consider their Colony as unrepresented untill they received the directions of their principals who were then sitting at Annapolis. Yesterday the sense of that Convention was made publick; they approve of the Conduct of their delegates in dissenting from the preamble and the Resolution. They repeat [and] enforce their former Instructions, declare that they have not lost sight of a Reconciliation with Great Britain, and that they will adhere to the Common Cause and support it on the principles of the Union as explained at the time of entering on the War. So much for Maryland.[2]

The General Assembly of Pensylvania is averse to any Change. The People of this Town assembled last monday in the State house yard and agreed to a set of Resolutions in favour of a Change. Another body are signing a Remonstrance against the Acts of that meeting and in support of the Assembly. The Committee for the County of Philadelphia have unanimously supported the Assembly and protested against any Change.[3] It is supposed the other Counties will follow the Example and take a part in the dispute. Is it not to be feared that this spirit of Dissention will spread itself into the adjoining Colonies? But I intend to make no Reflections. The facts I have hinted at will be published—what relates to this City and the County of Phil[adelphi]a already are—and the Maryland Delegates have express directions to submit their Acts to the publick View. It may be some days before they come to your Knowledge through the channel of the Press. I coud say a great deal to you on this interesting subject, but you are master of my Sentiments which are not altered since you left me here.

I expect Mr. Alsop this Evening and shall in that Case set out on monday to visit my Family. It is more than 9 months since I have seen my Children. I have spent but about ten days in that time with Mrs. Duane.

I am my dear Sir, with the greatest Respect, Your affectionate and most Obedient Servant

JAS. DUANE

ALS. Endorsed. Tr in NN: Bancroft, Amer. Rev., I, 85.

1 The Third New York Provincial Congress met on 14 May 1776, although there was no quorum until 18 May. JJ did not take his seat in the New York Congress until 25 May. *JPC*, I, 443–61.

2 When the Maryland delegates informed their colony's Convention of Congress's resolutions calling for the formation of new governments, the Convention reaffirmed its commitment to reconciliation and ordered the delegates to adhere to their earlier instructions. In these resolutions of 21 May, the Maryland Convention declared that "it is not necessary that the exercise of every kind of authority under the . . . Crown should be now totally suppressed in this Province, and all the powers of government exerted under the authority of the People." This clause specifically repudiated the controversial preamble to the resolutions adopted by Congress on 15 May. 4 *FAA*, V, 1588–89.

3 The Pennsylvania Assembly convened on Monday, 20 May 1776. That same day, a radical rally summoned by the Philadelphia Committee of Inspection drew up "A Protest . . ." hailing Congress's call for new governments and demanding that the Philadelphia committee convene a joint meeting with other Pennsylvania county committees to plan a provincial convention which could create a new government for Pennsylvania. The present Assembly, the subscribers to "A Protest" declared, could not be entrusted with this task since its authority derived from a Crown charter and since many Assemblymen were bound by personal interest to Crown officers. The "Protest" was presented to the Assembly on 21 May, and was soon followed by declarations from more conservative groups.

The Committee for the County of Philadelphia submitted its own remonstrance to the assembly on 23 May 1776, disavowing the "Protest" and urging reconciliation with Britain and adherence to the delegates' instructions of November 1775. Six days later, the assembly was favored with a petition signed by local conservatives denouncing the "Protest" and supporting the existing Assembly. 4 *FAA*, IV, 846–48, 852–53.

To James Duane

New York, 29 May 1776

Dear Sir

Since my last I have had the Pleasure of recieving your Letter of the 25th Inst.[1] and am obliged to You for the Intelligence contained in it. So great are the Inconveniences resulting from the present Mode of Government, that I believe our Convention will almost unanimously agree to institute a better, to continue till a Peace with Great Britain shall render it unnecessary.

The Proceedings of Maryland etc. will probably check the Ardor of some People. I fear that the Divisions of Pennsylvania will injure the common Cause.

Mrs. Jay is so much better as to quit her Room. When I shall return is uncertain, the Convention having directed me not to leave till further order.

Be so kind as to inform Mr. Lynch that I have not yet been able to procure a Horse for him. The fine Mares fit for riding, have in Consequence of the Resolve of Congress forbidding Races, been put to Breeding; and I believe it will be difficult to get a handsome Gelding. I shall however continue my Inquiries, and should I meet with any Thing very clever, shall perhaps be rather lavish of his Guineas. Be pleased to present my Compliments to him and Mr. Rutledge, and dont forget either Merkle or White Eyes.[2]

I am Dear Sir, Your most obedient Servant

JOHN JAY

ALS in NHi: Duane Papers. Addressed: "James Duane Esqr. A member of the Continental Congress at <Philadelphia> New York." "New York" entered in an unidentified hand. DftS in JP.

[1] In his letter of 11 May 1776, Duane mentions a letter from JJ of 8 May; neither this letter nor any others from JJ to Duane for May 1776 have been located. Duane's letters of 11 and 25 May 1776 are printed above. The *Journals* of the Third Provincial Congress first record JJ's attendance on 25 May, but he may have been present the day before since he was appointed to a committee on 24 May. JJ remained in constant attendance at the 3rd New York Congress until 29 June. *JPC*, I, 460–511.

[2] JJ furnished Johann Philip Merkle, a Dutch adventurer, with a letter of introduction which was read in Congress 29 May 1776. Merkle was directed to confer with the Secret Committee, and was entrusted with a mission for Congress at the end of July. Merkle sailed on the *Despatch*, a brig in the U.S. service, and was empowered to sell the *Despatch*'s cargo and to use the proceeds to purchase "merchandise, arms, and ammunition" in France or Holland for shipment to the U.S. on the *Despatch*'s return voyage. However, Merkle apparently did nothing to implement his orders after landing in Bordeaux in December 1776 and, in the fall of 1777, America's commissioners in France complained to Congress: "We were obliged to discharge a debt of Myrtle's [Merkle's] at Bordeaux, amounting to about five thousand livres, and he now duns us at every post for between four and five thousand pounds sterling, to disengage him in Holland, where he has purchased arms for you." *JCC*, IV, 403; 5 *FAA*, I, 156, 670–71; *RDC*, II, 278, 405.

Captain White Eyes, a chief of the Delaware tribe, visited Congress 16 Dec. 1775. In a speech to the chief, the President of Congress promised that the Delawares would receive "a minister and a schoolmaster" so that the tribe could "embrace Christianity and a more civilized Way of Life." A petition from the chief was read in Congress on 16 March 1776, and on 10 April a committee report was adopted which provided for implementation of the oral promises made in Dec. 1775. Congress's address to White Eyes of 10 April 1776 also asked the chief to inform neighboring tribes of "what you have seen and heard among us, and exhort them to keep fast hold of the covenant chain of friendship, which we have so lately repaired and strengthened." *LMCC*, I, 278; *JCC*, III, 433; IV, 208, 267–70.

To Robert R. Livingston

New York, 29 May 1776

Dear Robert,

The Pleasure I expected from a Junction of our little Families at Bristol has vanished. Doctor Bard tells me the Waters there would be injurious to Mrs. Jays Complaints, so that I shall again take a solitary Ride to Philadelphia whenever the Convention who have directed me to abide here till their further Order, shall think proper to dismiss me.

I wish it had been in my power to have met you at Bristol at the time you mentioned,[1] but Mrs. Jay was then so ill that Doctor Bard was sent for. She is now thank God so much better as to leave her Room, and unless some unfortunate Relapse should happen is I hope in a fair way of recovering her former Health.

Messrs. Alsop and Lewis set out next Saturday for Philadelphia. Mr. Duane informs me that he is about to return home, and considering how long he has been absent from his Family I think him intitled to that Indulgence. I pray God that your Health may enable you to attend constantly, at least till it may be in my Power to relieve you.[2] Is Mr. Clinton returned?

Our Convention will I believe institute a better Government than the present which in my opinion will no longer work any Thing but Mischief; and Although the Measure of obtaining Authority by Instructions may have its Advocates, I have Reason to think that such a Resolution will be taken as will open a Door to the Election of new or additional Members. But be the Resolution what it may, you shall have the earliest Advice of it. And should my Conjectures prove right, I shall inform the Members of Dutches of your Readiness to serve, and advise them to elect you.[3]

Benson is not yet come to Town. Your <Caution on> Attention to this Subject was proper, and I will second it.

Dont be uneasy at recieving so few Letters from me. I have been so distressed by the Ill Health of my Wife and Parents, that I have scarce written any Thing.

I am Dear Robert, Your affectionate Friend

J. J.

DftS. Endorsed by JJ.

1 The mineral springs at Bristol, Pa., twenty miles northeast of Philadelphia, had been popularly used for medicinal purposes since the first quarter of the eighteenth century. On 17 May 1776 Livingston wrote to JJ that he had rented "three Bedrooms & a large parlour in a retired country house, about two miles from Bristol. . . . The lodgings are to be entered upon next Wednesday [22 May], by which time I hope to see you & Mrs. Jay there. . . ." *HPJ*, I, 59.

2 In his letter of 17 May Livingston appealed to JJ: "I wish to God you could be here. If you do not get this length [to Philadelphia] meet me at least at Bristol next week from whence you may return in a few days & send some of our delegates along as the province will otherwise be often unrepresented, since I find it inconsistant with my health to be close in my attendance in Congress." *HPJ*, I, 60.

3 On 24 May JJ was named to a committee of the New York Congress entrusted with consideration of the Continental Congress's resolutions calling for the establishment of new governments. This committee reported 27 May and concluded that: "it hath become absolutely necessary for the good people of this Colony to institute a new and regular form of internal government and police." The report acknowledged that "some doubts existed" as to whether the Third Provincial Congress was authorized to frame a new form of government, and concluded with a recommendation that the inhabitants of the province be polled "either to confirm their present representatives" in the New York Congress "in their present powers, and with express authority . . . to institute a new internal form of government and police for the province . . . or elect new members for that purpose. . . ."

The procedure for forming a new government had divided the Third Congress. Radicals, led by John Morin Scott, contended that the present Congress was competent to draw up a new constitution for New York as well as to conduct legislative business, while conservatives like Gouverneur Morris held that a special convention must be chosen with explicit power to draft a form of government.

The committee report of 27 May was adopted by the Congress, and JJ, Scott, and John Haring were named a committee "to take the said report and frame it into resolutions to be published." Although this committee did not submit its report to the Congress until 31 May, JJ's letter to Livingston indicates that the committee had already decided that some form of new elections would be necessary. The resolutions adopted by the New York Congress on 31 May stated that electors were "either to authorize (in addition to the powers vested in this Congress) their present Deputies or others . . . or either of them" to consider the necessity of instituting a new government. If a majority of this newly constituted group agreed on the need for a new government, they were then "to institute and establish such a government." *JPC*, I, 462–63, 468–69; Bernard Mason, *The Road to Independence* (Lexington, Ky., 1967), pp. 150–52.

From Robert R. Livingston

Philadelphia, 4th June 1776

Dear John

I own I was very much mortified at not hearing from you nor can I yet quite forgive your neglect since it takes but little time to write when the pen is only copying from the heart. I am very sorrey that we are not to have the pleasure of Mrs. Jay's company but greatly rejoyced at the prospect of her recovery about which from your Letter to Duane I had some uneasy apprehentions.

We have been for some days past occupied in settling a plan of defence. The attatchment which some people have for Canada has left us very defenceless. However I have contrived to lessten the number after much altercation and settle our own quota much to my satisfaction at 3750 men who are to be drafted from the militia, 3000 of them to serve at New York.[1] This I hope will not prove very burthensome as a large proportion may be taken from the City where I suppose many of the Citizens are unemployed. What I want you particularly to attend to is to endeavour to get volunteers for Canada if possible from the Green Mountain boys, by offering higher pay than the Continent allows, the expence of which will be very triffling to the Colony. What makes me wish it most is in order to frustrate the schemes of some people here who affect to consider them as no part of our Colony, and to assert that they never did nor ever will act under our convention. They even introduced a motion founded on this supposition. However I treated them so roughly as prevented their proceeding and has silenced them for the present.[2] The force ordered for our defence at New York is 25000, so that I hope we shall be able to give an enimy a pretty warm reception.[3] I wrote to you about Gallis but I have got the Congress to take it upon themselves and the General has power to build as many as he thinks proper.[4] We have received an answer of the King to the livery of London, which I hope will be productive of very good effects since it takes away all hopes of acommodation and shows that nothing less will do than absolute submission.[5] It comes in very happy time for this place, in which the people were very unfortunately divided between the advocates for the old and new government.

I learn from the paper the steps you have taken to collect the sentiments of the people. I wish to be with you a while, but do not know whether it is absolutely necessary, and I am unwilling to leave this till it is. I hope you are laying the foundation for a better form than I have yet seen, and inculcating the proper principles. You can not begin too early to point out both men and measures.

Morris they tell me flourishes as much as ever. As you are either too lazy or too cautious engage him to write with as much freedom as he speaks. I have heard Mr. S———[6] does he not look very high. Clinton is not come. Send him on if you see him. I am, Dear John, Your Affectionate Friend

ROBT. R. LIVINGSTON

ALS. RAWC. Addressed: "To Coll. John Jay New York, pr favour of Majr. Genl. Gates." Endorsed. Tr in JP.

1 Livingston was intimately acquainted with Continental defense plans because of his appointment to a committee of conference on 25 May 1776. This committee consulted with General Washington, Brigadier General Thomas Mifflin (1744–1800), the Continental Quartermaster, and with Major General Horatio Gates (1727–1806), Washington's Adjutant General. The committee's report of 29 May called on New York to supply 1,500 troops for reinforcements in Canada, but when Congress acted on this report, New York's quota for the Canadian expedition was reduced to 750. On 3 June, Congress considered the committee's recommendations on general strategy for the coming campaign and ordered that forces in New York be reinforced by 13,800 militiamen, of whom 3,000 were to be New Yorkers. *JCC*, IV, 391, 399–400, 410–12.

2 On 8 May 1776 the Congress read a petition from a committee appointed by residents of the New Hampshire Grants. This petition, dated 17 Jan. 1776, recited the history of land disputes in the region and summarized the contributions of settlers in the Grants to the Continental struggle against the crown. However, the petitioners stated firmly: "Yet while Your Petitioners are . . . entirely willing to do all in our Power in the General Cause under the Continental Congress and have been ever since the taking of Ticonderoga &c. . . . but are not willing to put ourselves under the Honorable provincial Congress of New York in such a manner as might in future be detrimental to our private property. . . ."

The committee named to consider this petition reported on 30 May and recommended that the "petitioners, for the present . . . submit to the government of New York, and contribute their assistance . . . in the contest between Great Britain and the united colonies. . . ." The committee report went on to promise "that such submission ought not to prejudice the right of them or others to the land in controversy . . . nor be construed to affirm or admit the jurisdiction of New York in and over that country" and concluded with the statement that "when the present Troubles are at an End" the jurisdictional dispute would be determined by "proper Judges." This report was not acted upon and was endorsed: "Ordered to lie on the table." Since Vermonters refused to accept the sovereignty of New York over them, the continuing dispute was to be a source of concern to leading New Yorkers, among them JJ, in the years ahead. *JCC*, IV, 334–35, 405; DNA: PCC, 40, I, 7.

3 The report of the committee of conference of 29 May estimated that "the Continental force now at N. York for the defence of that place and the communication with Albany does not exceed 10,000 Men . . ." and recommended that the force be brought up to 25,000 by the dispatch of the 13,800 militiamen and 1,200 members of the Pennsylvania line. *JCC*, IV, 400.

4 Livingston wrote JJ on 21 May: "If your Congress have any spirit, they will at least build fourteen or fifteen light boats capable of carrying a twelve-pounder, to secure Hudson River, which is to be the chief scene of action." The committee of conference recommended to Congress that General Washington be authorized to "direct the building as many Fire rafts and Gallies as may be necessary and suitable for the immediate defence of the port at N. York and Hudsons river." Congress adopted this section of the committee's report on 30 May. *HPJ*, I, 62; *JCC*, IV, 401, 406–07.

5 The Address and Petition of the City of London of 22 March 1776 was printed in the American press in June 1776 along with George III's reply. The London Petition expressed concern at the "exposed state" of the British Isles should the government implement its plans for military operations in North America and called the crown's treaties for foreign mercenaries a "dangerous disgrace." The petitioners asked that "the most solemn, clear, distinct and

unambiguous specification of those just and honorable terms" which the king and Parliament "meant to grant to the colonies, may precede the dreadful operations of your armament." The king's brief reply to the London officials read: "I Deplore with the deepest concern, the miseries which a great part of my subjects in North America have brought upon themselves by an unjustifiable resistance to the constitutional authority of this kingdom; and I shall be ready and happy to alleviate those miseries, by acts of mercy and clemency, whenever that authority is established, and the now existing rebellion is at an end. To obtain those salutary principles I will invariably pursue the most proper and effectual means." *N.Y. Mercury,* 10 June 1776.

[6] John Morin Scott.

From Edward Rutledge

Philadelphia, Saturday Evening 10 o'clock [*8 June 1776*]

My dear Jay

I am much obliged to you for your Introduction of Mr. Merckle. He will tell you what has been done in Consequence of it. I have shewn him all the Civility in my Power. I fear in the present Situation of Affairs we will not be able to give the Dutch much Security as will induce so cautious a Power to part with that which they consider the first Blessing.

The Congress sat till 7 o'clock this Evening in Consequence of a Motion of R. H. Lee's resolving ourselves free and independent States.[1] The Sensible part of the House opposed the Motion. They had no Objection to forming a Scheme of a Treaty which they would send to France by proper Persons, and uniting this Continent by a Confedracy. They saw no Wisdom in a *Declaration* of Independence, nor any other Purpose to be answered by it, but placing ourselves in the Power of those with whom we mean to treat, giving our Enemy Notice of our Intentions before we had taken any Steps to execute them and there by enabling them to counteract in our Intentions and rendering ourselves ridiculous in the Eyes of foreign Powers by attempting to bring them into an Union with us before we had united with each other. For daily experience evinces that the Inhabitants of every Colony consider themselves at Liberty to do as they please upon almost every occasion. And a Man must have the Impudence of a New Englander to propose in our present disjointed State any Treaty (honourable to us) to a Nation now at Peace. No Reason could be assigned for pressing into this Measure, but the Reason of every Madman a Shew of our Spirit. The Event however was that the Question was postponed. It is to be renewed on Monday when I mean to move that it should be postponed for 3 Weeks or a Month. In the mean Time the plan of Confederation and the Scheme of Treaty may go on.

I don't know whether I shall succeed in this Motion; I *think not*. It is at least Doubtful.[2] However I must do what is right in my own Eyes and Consequences must take Care of themselves. I wish you had been here. The whole Argument was sustained on one side by R. Livingston, Wilson, Dickinson and myself, and by the Power of all N. England, Virginia and Georgia on the other.[3]

Remember me to Morris affectionately. I would have wrote to him, but did not know of this Conveyance until a few Minutes ago, and am as you will see by this incorrect Letter too fatigued to hold my pen any longer than whilst I fell you how sincerely I esteem and love you.

Yours affectionately

E. RUTLEDGE

ALS. Endorsed: "Edw. Rutledge June 1776." The substance of Rutledge's letter permits assigning the date of 8 June. Tr in NN: Bancroft, Amer. Rev., I, 97.

1 On Friday, 7 June, Richard Henry Lee introduced a motion declaring that "these United Colonies are, and of right ought to be, free and independent States . . . and that all political connection between them and the State of Great Britain is, and ought to be totally dissolved." Lee introduced two other resolutions at the same time, one declaring the expediency of forming "foreign Alliances" and the other recommending that "a plan of confederation" be prepared and submitted to the provinces for ratification. *JCC*, V, 425.

2 The undated endorsement on Lee's resolutions in DNA: PCC, 23, 11, reads: "Resolved that it is the Opinion of this Com that the first Resolution be postponed to this day three weeks, and that in the mean time, least any time shd be lost in case the Congress agree to this resolution, a committee be appointed to prepare a Declaration to the effect of the said first resolution." On Monday, 10 June, Congress resolved: "That the consideration of the first resolution [on independence] be postponed to this day, three weeks [1 July], and in the mean while, that no time be lost, in case the Congress agree thereto, that a committee be appointed to prepare a declaration to the effect of the said first resolution. . . ." *JCC*, V, 428–29. The following day, Thomas Jefferson, John Adams, Benjamin Franklin, Roger Sherman (1721–93) of Connecticut, and Robert R. Livingston were named to this committee. *JCC*, V, 428–29, 431.

3 For the part played by Robert R. Livingston, James Wilson (1742–98), and John Dickinson of Pennsylvania, see Thomas Jefferson's notes on the debates of 7 and 8 June 1776, *TJP*, I, 309–13.

To Robert R. Livingston

New York, 11th June 1776

Dear Robert.

. . . Caution I confess grows upon me, and Prudence, which you know I used to consider as a little virtue, daily appears more estimable. But my good friend, I shall never forget that where caution encroaches on the rights of friendship, it becomes criminal. Without mutual and full confidence it must cease. And as I sincerely wish Permanence and Stability to our connection, believe me its support will always be among the first of my cares. Of this however, I shall say more when we meet.

The late resolution of the Congress relative to obtaining authority from the people to institute a form of Government you have seen. On this occasion I was desirous you should be returned a member. For that purpose I have so far settled matters with James Livingston, that if no other of the present members from Dutchess should resign, he will in order to make room for you, and I have written to Benson on the subject. . . .[1]

Tr. (incomplete). NN: Bancroft, Robert R. Livingston, I, 187.

[1] JJ's letter to Egbert Benson has not been located. James Livingston (b. 1728), a cousin of Robert R. Livingston's father, was a Dutchess County delegate to the Third Provincial Congress. In the elections held for the Fourth Provincial Congress, Robert R. Livingston was named a Dutchess delegate, and he took his seat in the New York Congress 15 July 1776. *JPC*, I, 523, 526.

Rounding Up Subversives: The Hickey Plot

JJ played an early and central role in the effort to identify and apprehend enemies of the State of New York and the new nation of which it was a part. He first became involved in this program in June 1776, and his activities produced prompt and sensational results.

On 17 June the Provincial Congress directed him, along with Philip Livingston and Gouverneur Morris "to confer with Genl. Washington relative to certain secret intelligence communicated to this Congress, and take such examinations relative thereto as they shall think proper." There was much to discuss and considerable need for action, because Isaac Ketchum, a Tory prisoner in the New York City jail, had just made an alarming revelation, reporting that two of his fellow inmates named Thomas Hickey and Michael Lynch had boasted of belonging to a "corps" being paid by the British fleet. Hickey and Lynch were privates in the Commander-in-Chief's security guard who had been arrested for trying to pass counterfeit currency, but they now appeared involved in much more serious crimes.[1]

The appointment of JJ to investigate what became known as the Hickey Plot was logical, because he had already shown concern about how to deal with subversives and had suggested in a 21 March letter to Alexander McDougall that "such as are notoriously disaffected" should be removed to some area where the enemy's army was not apt to penetrate.

Ketchum's 8 June written offer to turn informer was addressed to JJ, and perhaps this explains why JJ's name was added five days later to a list of men picked earlier in June to concern themselves with "persons dangerous and disaffected to the American cause, and to persons of equivocal character." The three-man task force of JJ, Livingston, and Morris functioned in effect as a subcommittee of this larger group.[2]

Once the Provincial Congress heard Isaac Ketchum's testimony, events moved rapidly. JJ and his two associates began examining suspects on 18 June, and they soon learned that Governor William Tryon had attempted to enlist men to aid the British fleet when it landed in New York. More than a dozen men were implicated in the plot and arrested for their part in the conspiracy. The most important of these malefactors, David Matthews,[3] the Mayor of New York City, was arrested 22 June and examined the next day. He was found guilty of "treasonable practices" and in fairly short order was sent off to jail in Litchfield, Conn., a remote community highly unlikely to be invaded by the British.[4]

Meanwhile the cases of Thomas Hickey and Michael Lynch were transferred to the army by the civil authorities, who decided that courts deriving their original authority from the crown were incompetent to try members of the rebel army. Thus Hickey, a soldier, paid the extreme penalty for criminal involvement, of "mutiny and sedition," and of treacherous correspondence with and receiving pay "from the Enemies of the united American colonies" in the plot as distinguished from Matthews, a civilian. Hickey was tried by court martial, 26 June 1776, convicted, and hanged two days later; Matthews was jailed for "Treasonable practices against the States of America."[5] JJ believed that this disparity between military and civil law should be corrected, and on 16 July the Provincial Convention passed a motion proposed by him prescribing the death penalty for treason.[6]

The documents reproduced below provide insight into how the investigation was conducted. When the original committee was created on 5 June, it was empowered to employ Continental troops to make arrests, because calling out the militia for that purpose would be both expensive and so conspicuous that it would warn individuals about to be apprehended.[7] When JJ and his fellow investigators wanted to arrest Matthews, therefore, they asked Washington to act for them. JJ expressed fear in his 1 July letter to Robert R. Livingston that prosecution of Matthews and the other suspects would be unreasonably delayed by the sudden adjournment of the Provincial Congress. He was unduly pessimistic on this score, because the task was completed by 18 July when a report was issued on the disposition of all cases.[8]

1 *JPC*, I, 495–97.

2 JJ to Alexander McDougall, 21 March 1776, NHi: McDougall Papers; *JPC*, I, 476–78, 492; II, 201.

3 David Matthews, appointed Mayor in 1776 after having held other crown offices in New York, removed after the war to the island of Cape Breton where he

served as President of the Council and Commander-in-Chief. Sabine, *Biographical Sketches*, II, 51–52.

[4] *JPC*, I, 498, 500, 509, 530; 4 *FAA*, VI, 1158, 1164–66.

[5] *JPC*, I, 530.

[6] *JPC*, I, 496–97, 527; 4 *FAA*, VI, 1084–88, 1118–20. For the impact of the Hickey Plot on the evolution of the law of treason on the part of the Continental Congress, see Richard B. Morris, "The Forging of the Union Reconsidered," *Columbia Law Review*, LXXIV (1974), 1083–85. For the further resolution of Congress, 21 Aug. 1776, see *JCC*, V, 693.

[7] *JPC*, I, 477.

[8] Sixteen others were sentenced, and jailed, along with Matthews, for treasonable practices, disaffection, counterfeiting, and aiding the enemy.

Philip Livingston, John Jay, and Gouverneur Morris to George Washington

[New York], 21 June 1776

Sir

Whereas David Matthews, Esquire, stands charged with dangerous designs and treasonable conspiracies against the rights and liberties of the United Colonies of America: We do, in pursuance of a certain resolve of the Congress of the Colony of the 20th of June instant, authorize and request you to cause the said David Matthews to be, with all his papers, forthwith apprehended and secured, and that return be made to us of the manner in which the warrant shall be executed, in order that the same may be made known to the said Congress.

Given under our hands, this 21st day of June, 1776.

PHILIP LIVINGSTON
JOHN JAY
GOUVERNEUR MORRIS

PtD. 4 *FAA*, VI, 1158.

George Washington to Nathanael Greene

[New York], Friday afternoon, June 21, 1776

General Greene is desired to have the within warrant executed with precision, and exactly by one o'clock the ensuing morning, by a careful officer.

GEORGE WASHINGTON

PtD. 4 *FAA* VI, 1158.

Nathanael Greene to George Washington

Long-Island, June 22, 1776

In obedience to the within order and warrant, I sent a detachment of my brigade, under the command of Colonel Vernon, to the house of the within-named David Matthews, Esq., at Flatbush, who surrounded his house and seized his person precisely at the hour of one this morning. After having made him a prisoner, diligent search was made after his papers, but none could be found, notwithstanding great care was taken that none of the family should have the least opportunity to remove or destroy them.

NATHANAEL GREENE

PtD. 4 *FAA*, VI, 1158.

From Edward Rutledge

Philadelphia, June 29, 1776

My dear Jay

I write this for the express Purpose of requesting that if possible you will give your Attendance in Congress on Monday next. I know full well that your Presence must be useful at New York, but I am sincerely convinced that it will be absolutely necessary in this City during the whole of the ensuing Week. A Declaration of Independence, the Form of a Confederation of these Colonies, and a Scheme for a Treaty with foreign Powers will be laid before the House on Monday. Whether we shall be able effectually to oppose the first, and infuse Wisdom into the others will depend in a great Measure upon the Exertions of the Honest and sensible part of the Members. I trust you will contribute in a considerable degree to effect the Business and therefore I wish you to be with us. Recollect the manner in which your Colony is at this Time unpresented. Clinton has Abilities but is silent in general, and wants (when he does speak) that Influence to which he is intitled. Floyd, Wisner, Lewis and Alsop[1] though good Men, never quit their Chairs. You must know the Importance of these Questions too well not to wish to [be] present whilst they are debating and therefore I shall say no more upon the Subject.

I have been much engaged lately upon a plan of a Confederation which Dickenson has drawn. It has the Vice of all his Productions to a considerable Degree; I mean the Vice of Refining too much. Unless it is greatly curtailed it never can pass, as it is to be submitted to Men in the respective Provinces who will not be led or rather driven into Measures which may lay the Foundation of their Ruin. If the Plan now proposed should be adopted nothing less than Ruin to some Colonies will be the Consequence of it. The Idea of destroying all Provincial Distinctions and making every thing of the most minute kind bend to what they call the good of the whole, is in other Terms to say that these Colonies must be subject to the Government of the Eastern Provinces. The Force of their Arms I hold exceeding Cheap, but I confess I dread their over-ruling Influence in Council, I dread their low Cunning, and those levelling Principles which Men without Character and without Fortune in general Possess, which are so captivating to the lower Class of Mankind, and which will occasion such a fluctuation of Property as to introduce the greatest disorder. I am resolved to vest the Congress with no more Power than what is absolutely necessary, and to use a familiar Expression to keep the Staff in our own Hands, for I am confident if surrendered into the Hands of others a most pernicious use will be made of it.

If you can't come let me hear from you by the Return of the Post.[2] Compliments to Livingston and G. Morris. God bless you. With Esteem and affection, Yours

E. RUTLEDGE

ALS. Addressed: "John Jay Esquire at New York, E. Rutledge." Endorsed. Tr in NN: Bancroft, American Revolution Series, I, 105; printed in *HPJ*, I, 66–68, missing several crucial words.

[1] New York delegates to Congress: William Floyd (1734–1821), Henry Wisner (1720–90), Joseph Alsop (d. 1794).

[2] JJ answered Rutledge on 6 July (*HPJ*, I, 68–70; ALS listed in Kenneth W. Rendell sale catalogue no. 75 [June, 1792]), regretting that he had been "so engaged by plots, conspiracies, and chimeras dire" that he could not consider going to Philadelphia. He remarked that "your ideas of men and things (to speak mathematically) run, for the most part, parallel with my own." JJ was in fact too deeply involved in the activities of the New York Provincial Congress to consider leaving New York City, having been appointed to no less than fourteen of its committees during the six-week period between 15 May and 29 June 1776. *JPC*, I, 460–98.

To Robert R. Livingston

[New York], Monday, 1 July 1776

Dear Robert,

I returned to this City about Noon this Day from Eliz[abeth] Town, and to my great mortification am informed that our Convention influenced by one of G. Morris vagrant Plans have adjourned to the White Plains to meet there Tomorrow.[1] This precipitate ill advised Retreat I fear will be not a little injurious to the publick. The Prosecution of the Late Discoveries of Governor Tryons Plot will be delayed, and may it not by our Enemies be imputed to a Design of keeping the Necks of some of our Citizens out of the Halter? The Business of some other Com[mittee]s of Importance is at a Stand. I begin to loose Pati[e]nce. This Stroke of Morrisania Politics quite confounds me. They tell me too that a Resolve has passed granting certain Powers to the Gen.[2] God knows what they are. I think of it with Fear and Trembling. I wish Mr. Ph. Livingston could have been prevailed upon to stay here a little longer.[3] I exhausted all my Rhetorick on the occasion but in vain. Nor Did he assign a better Reason for leaving the Province, than that he *would* go to Philadelphia. The ways of some Men like Solomons Serpent on a Rock, are past finding out. I am too much out of Humour to add any Thing except that I a[m you]r Friend

JOHN JAY

ALS. DLC: Keane Coll. Addressed: "To Majr. Robt. R. Livingston Esqr, a member of the Continental Congress Philadelphia, free J. Jay." Endorsed.

1 The British fleet began to arrive in New York harbor on the morning of 29 June 1776. The same day, JJ received leave from the Third Provincial Congress to "go to Elizabeth Town, and . . . to return on Monday Morning [1 July]." On 30 June, the New York Congress, fearful of an attack by the British, adjourned from the city to reconvene at White Plains on 2 July. However, the Third Congress never met again. and provincial government was in a state of limbo until the Fourth Provincial Congress made a quorum at White Plains on 9 July. *JPC*, I, 511, 512, 515.

2 During JJ's absence, on 30 June, the New York Congress resolved that Washington be authorized to "apply to the brigadier-generals" of the province "for any proportion of the militia under their respective commands" and also "to take such measures for apprehending and securing dangerous and disaffected persons as he shall think necessary for the security of this Colony and the liberties of America." *JPC*, I, 512.

3 On Wednesday, 26 June, the New York Congress gave Livingston leave to attend the Continental Congress "after next Saturday." *JPC*, I, 506.

From Robert R. Livingston

[*Philadelphia*, c. 6 *July 1776*]

Dear John

I have but a moments time to answer your letter. I am mortified at the removal of our convention. I think as you do on the subject. If my fears on account of your health would permit I should request you never to leave that volatile politician[1] a moment. I have wished to be with you when I knew your situation.

The Congress have done me the honour to refuse to let me go. I will however apply again to day.[2] I thank God I have been the happy Means of falling on a expedient which will call out the whole militia of this country in a few days. Though the Congress had lost hopes of it from an unhappy dispute and other causes with which I will acquaint you in a few days. We have desired a General to take the Command. I wish Mifflin may be sent for very obvious reasons.[3] If you see [him] tell [him] so from me. I have much to say to you but not a moment to say it in. God be with you.

Yours etc.

ROBT R LIVINGSTON

ALS. Addressed: "To Coll. John Jay New York, free Robt R. Livingston." Endorsed: "R. R. Livingston 1776." The postmaster's stamp, "Phila. July 6," permits the dating of the letter.

1 Gouverneur Morris.

2 Livingston left Philadelphia the next day to join the New York Provincial Congress. Dangerfield, *Robert R. Livingston,* p. 80.

3 On 4 July, the delegates from New York, New Jersey, and Pennsylvania were named a committee to confer with the Pennsylvania committee of safety and the Philadelphia committee of inspection "on the best means of defending the colonies of New Jersey and Pennsylvania." Defense of the middle colonies had been endangered by the delays in collecting the "flying camp" of 10,000 Delaware, Maryland, and Pennsylvania militiamen authorized by Congress on 3 June. This corps was never fully completed, and the solution worked out by the committees which met on 4 July was an agreement that all the Pennsylvania militia (except for units from the westernmost counties) would be sent to Trenton, N.J., and continue in Continental service until the flying camp had been recruited and could relieve the militia units. This agreement was agreed to by Congress on 5 July. Despite Livingston's efforts, Mifflin was not given command of the Pennsylvania militiamen. *JCC,* V, 516, 519.

IV

THE DIE IS CAST: JAY AS A MILITANT PATRIOT

Endorsing Independence and Supporting Washington

By the time the Fourth Congress made a quorum at White Plains on 9 July, the Continental Congress had already acted on independence, and the first order of business for the New York legislature was consideration of a letter from their delegates in Philadelphia enclosing a copy of the Declaration of Independence. JJ drafted the committee report on the Declaration which was adopted on the afternoon of 9 July. "While we lament the cruel necessity which has rendered that measure unavoidable," his report asserted, "we approve the same, and will, at the risk of our lives and fortunes, join with the other colonies in supporting it."[1] The next day the Provincial Congress changed its name to "the Convention of the Representatives of the State of New-York," and the business of administering a state threatened by enemy invasion succeeded debates on loyalty to the crown or the wisdom of precipitate action in declaring independence.

Military exigencies occupied JJ and the Convention for much of the last six months of 1776, and there was little time that year for the Convention's avowed purpose of perfecting a new "frame of government" for New York. The Third Congress's committee on "disaffected persons" and the committee which had aided Washington in uncovering the "Hickey Plot" were combined on 9 July. JJ served on the new committee which bore responsibility not only for the disposal of prisoners but also for the "execution [of] all such necessary resolves" and compliance "with all such necessary requisitions of the General as require so much despatch as to render an application to this Congress impracticable or attended with dangerous delay."[2]

Such committees played a vital part in the Convention since the state legislators found it almost impossible to convene regularly. Their place of meeting was changed twice in the first eight months of the Convention's existence; on 29 August 1776 sessions were moved to Fishkill, while on 19 February 1777 the seat of government was transferred to the west side of the Hudson at Kingston. Indeed the body met as a "Convention," rather than as a Committee of Safety appointed during Convention adjournments, for less than three months in the period July 1776–March 1777. The duration of full convention sessions were 9 July–28 August, 5 September–7 October, 15 October, and 6 December 1776. Thus, after the end of August 1776, JJ's most important work was done in special committees of the Convention: the Secret Committee responsible for fortifying the Hudson and the Committee for Detecting Conspiracies.[3] At the same time, his personal concerns lay with his family and his wife's parents, whose homes were threatened by the British advance.[4]

Perhaps the change in JJ's attitude can best be judged by the undated resolution printed below. On 1 July he had written Robert R. Livingston of the "Fear and Trembling" with which he awaited details of a resolution "granting certain Powers to the General."[5] But after working closely with Washington on the problems of New York's defense, JJ prepared this resolution, probably in July or August 1776, which would have committed New York to allowing the commander complete tactical freedom in order to liberate Washington from "Plans drawn by or Consultations with large Assemblies of Politicians unpracticed in the Art of War."

[1] *JPC*, I, 517, 518; *WJ*, I, 45.
[2] *JPC*, I, 518.
[3] See editorial notes, documents, and letters below.
[4] See below, JJ to SLJ, 17, 21, and 29 July 1776; Frederick Jay to JJ, 1 Oct. 1776; and JJ to Catharine W. Livingston, 8 Nov. 1776.
[5] See above, JJ to Livingston, 1 July 1776.

John Jay's Motion for an Instruction to the Delegates

[*New York, after 9 July 1776*]

In Convention etc.

Whereas it is no less consonant to Reason than confirmed by the Experience of almost all Nations, that military Operations whose Success often depends on the proper Use of critical Moments and Contingencies not [to] be foreseen, should never be encumbered delayed or perplexed by Plans drawn by or Consultations with large Assemblies of Politicians unpracticed in the Art of War

And whereas the Command of the American Armies has been wisely committed to a General who has given abundant Proofs of Ability as well as Virtue

Resolved that the Delegates of this State in the honorable the General Congress of the united States of America, be, and they hereby are instructed and enjoined <to use their best endeavours> to give the Vote of this State against any Resolutions which may be proposed in Congress for directing the military operations of the Army immediately under the Command of his Excellency General Washington, To the End that the said General as far as the Vote of this State in Congress will avail may be at perfect Liberty to Station and direct the Movements of his Army, in such Manner as he in his Discretion may think proper.

Dft. Endorsed: "Dr. Mr. Jay's Motion for an Instruction to the Delegates &c." The resolution was probably drafted during the late summer of 1776 when Washington's military operations still centered in the state of New York. JJ attended the "Convention" (as opposed to sessions of the Committee of Safety) during the periods 9–16 July, 14–28 August, 6–19 September, 28 September–5 October, and 15 Oct. 1776. The resolution may have been drafted 9–16 July since the Continental Congress resolved, on 23 July: "That General Washington be informed that Congress have such an entire confidence in his judgment, that they will give him no particular directions about the disposition of the troops, but desire that he will dispose of those at New York, the flying camp and Ticonderoga, as to him shall seem most conducive to the public good." This resolution answered the purpose for which JJ had drafted his resolution; *JPC* carry no record of the resolution having been submitted or adopted by the Convention. *JCC*, V, 602.

New York Convention to John Hancock

[*New York, 10 July*] *1776*

In Pursuance of a Resolution of your honorable House of the 17th June last we passed a Resolve to authorize the Commander in Chief to call out all or any Part of our Militia whenever he might think it necessary. Of this Resolve the Inclosure No. 1 is a Copy.[1]

We have also taken into Consideration the Recommendation of the Congress relative to providing Cloathing for the Troops, and thereupon passed a Resolution of which the Inclosure No. 2 is a Copy.[2]

On the Reciept of the Resolution of Congress relative to making Provision for the officers who had served in Canada by raising a Regiment in this Colony, we referred it to a Com[mitte]e in order that such an arrangement might be made as by avoiding all clashing of Rank, would not be followed by Disgust and Resignations—We being of Opinion that young officers should not be raised over the Heads of elder ones except in Cases of extraordinary and distinguished Merit. And we intended to have complyed with the Request of Congress by nominating Mr. Dubois for one of the Field officers, tho we would not forbear observing that such Recommendations tend not a little to destroy that Liberty of nomination so essential to constitute it a Priviledge.

While we were engaged in settling that Arrangement we were surprized as well as hurt at rec[ievin]g a Resolution of Congress of the 26 June, by which it appears that your Honorable House had taken from us the Right of nominating not only the Field Officers but also the Captains and Lieutenants of that Regiment contrary to the common Usage hitherto observed and practiced in all similar Cases, and making a Discrimination invidious to this Colony.

The three Reasons assigned for this extraordinary Proceedure are by no means satisfactory to us.

The *first* is That the Congress were furnished with a List of the Officers who had served in Canada and therefore were enabled to appoint without our Interposition.

That the Congress were in this and in all Cases adequate to the Task of such of Appointments is a Proposition which we readily admit to be true, but with all Submission we beg Leave to observe that Ability to do an Act was never supposed to involve a Right to do it. We consider those appointments as appertaining to us, and cannot be vested in any Body of Men however able to make them, without our Consent.

The second Reason assigned is "That the Congress have appointed only such officers as were originally appointed and recommended by us, and that we should probably have fixed our Choice on the same Persons."

It is true that the greater Part of the Officers were appointed and recommended by us the last Year but not to the same Rank and Commissions now given them <and we can assure the Congress that they were exceedingly mistaken in apprehending that we should have classed them in the Manner they now are, for the Arrangement we had prepared is widely different from the one they have made> and it is also true that we have never recommended or appointed or know Evans Wherry, Henry Van DenBurgh, Nathaniel Concklin, Henry Dodge, John Coats or Henry DuBois[3]—all of whom we find on the List of Officers and we are really at a Loss to concieve how our having nominated certain Persons to Offices in a Regiment which was disbanded on the Expiration of the Term of its Inlistment should on the raising of a New Regiment either confine our Nomination to the same Persons or vest the Right of Nomination in the Congress. Respect doubtless ought and would have been had to the Merit of those who by their Services deserved well of their Country, but we consider that merit, as giving them only a Recommendation not a Title to Preference, and therefore <we should have been permitted> our Right of Nomination remained just as complete and as competent to this as to other Cases.

As to the Probability of our fixing our Choice on the same Persons, we cannot not think that Conjecture even if well founded, can justify the Conclusions drawn from it because if the Right of choosing be in us, no other Body can claim a Right of choosing for us from a mere Apprehension that their Choice would be similar to ours. But the Fact really is that the Arrangement made by your honorable House is materially and widely different from the one we had prepared.

The third Reason given for depriving us in this Instance of the Right of Nomination, is the good of the Service the Danger of Delay.

The *necessity of the Case* has in all Ages and Nations of the World been a fruitful tho dangerous Source of Power. <on that Foundation many Despotisms have been reared> It has often sown Tares in the fair Fields of Liberty and like a malignant Blast destroyed the Fruits of Patriotism and public Spirit. The whole History of Mankind bears Testimony against the Propriety of considering this Principle as the Parent of civil Rights, and a People jealous of their Liberties will ever reprobate it. <But from this we would not be understood to be tenacious of this Right, and we are content that it be vested in the Congress, provided the other Colonies do the like.>

We believe the Congress went into this Measure with pure Intentions and with no other Design than that of serving their Country—<but Sir good Things may be done in a Manner not to be approved and particularly> and we entertain too high an opinion of their Virtue and Integrity to apologize for a Plainess of Speech becoming Freemen and which we know can give Offence only to that counterfiet and adulterated Dignity which swells the Pride of those who instead of lending borrow Consequence from their Offices. And Sir we beg Leave to assure the Congress that tho we shall always complain and oppose their Resolutions when they injure our Rights we shall ever be ready (however callumniated by Individuals whose Censure we consider as Praises) to risque our Lives and Fortunes in supporting the American Cause.

But on percieving the Interference and clashing of Rank which marks the List of Officers sent us—and the Disgust it has given to many who deserved better we cannot think of intermeddling with it, and must therefore beg of the Congress to make the few remaining appointments wanting to compleat the Complement of Officers necessary for that Battalion. We have recieved so many Complaints and Applications on that Head and think many of them so well founded, that we wish to avoid all Interference with it. It cannot be necessary to point out its several Deviations from the Line of Rank—a Comparison of the present Arrangement with the last Years Rank Roll will discover them.

The Enclosure No. 3 is a Copy of a Letter we have recieved from William Goforth a very good Man and we are informed a good Officer who served the last Campaign in Canada, containing the Reasons of his quitting the Service.[4]

The Enclosure No. 4 is a Copy of a Letter from Coll. Fleming on the same Subject.[5]

We daily expect other Resignations, and we think the Case of Lieutenant Collonel Cortlandt[6] singularly hard. He entered the Service last Year as Lieutenant Collonel, in which Capacity he continues still and is now made an inferior Officer to Mr. DuBois who entered the Service last year as a Captain.

Mr. Pell and other spirited good Officers have been wholly laid aside, and younger Officers promoted.[7]

If by such Neglect many respectable Inhabitants among us should with their numerous and extensive Connections be disgusted and rendered inactive, we flatter ourselves that this Colony will not be censured for any Ill Consequences which may result from it.

Yesterday we took into Consideration the Declaration of your Honorable House proclaiming the united Colonies free and independent States, and thereupon unanimously came to a Resolution of which the Enclosure No. 5 is a Copy.

Governor Tryon has enlisted into the Kings Service certain disaffected Persons belonging to this Colony New Jersey etc. some of whom are now in our Custody. We are greatly at a Loss what to do with them, there being no Laws according to which they can be tryed and punished, and ex post Facto Laws are liable to many Objections. We unanimously join in requesting the Favor of your Honorable House to advise us what would be proper to do in this Case.

We take the Liberty of suggesting to your Consideration also the Propriety of taking some Measures for expunging from the Book of Common Prayer, such Parts as interfere with the Interest of the American Cause, and whether a Convention of the Clergy would not be proper for that Purpose. It is a Subject we are afraid to meddle with. The Enemies of America having taken great Pains to insinuate into the Minds of the Episcopalians that the Church was in Danger. We could wish the Congress would pass some Resolve to quiet these Fears, and we are confident it would do essential Service to the Cause of America, at least in this Colony.

Dft in JJ's hand. Endorsed by JJ: "Dr. Letter of Convention to Congress 1776." LS version, as approved by the New York Convention, in DNA: PCC, 67, I, 232–48 with enclosures as listed in JJ's draft. Enclosures: (1) Resolutions of the New York Congress, 22 and 30 June 1776, *JPC*, I, 503–04, 512; (2) resolution of the New York Congress, 24 June 1776, *JPC*, I, 505; (3) William Goforth to the New York Congress, 6 July 1776, *JPC*, II, 313; (4) Edward Fleming to the

New York Congress, 21 June 1776, 4 *FAA*, VI, 1013–14; (5) resolution of the New York Congress, 9 July 1776, *JPC*, I, 518.

1 On 17 June the Continental Congress ordered that letters be written to the New Jersey, New York, and Connecticut governments asking them to "authorize the commander in chief in the colony of New York, to call to the assistance of that colony, when necessity shall require it, such of the militia of those colonies as may be necessary; and to afford him such assistance as the situation of affairs may require." John Hancock's letter of 18 June recommending this measure was read in the New York Congress on 21 June 1776. The next day, the Provincial Congress adopted a resolution promising, "upon application" from Washington, to "call to his assistance . . . such part of the militia . . . as the said Commander-in-Chief shall think necessary. . . ." On 30 June, before adjourning to White Plains, the New York Congress passed a second resolution which allowed Washington to apply directly to militia commanders for reinforcements. *JCC*, V, 452; *JPC*, I, 501–02, 503–04, 512; Hancock to the New York Congress, 18 June 1776, 4 *FAA*, VI, 949–50.

2 The Continental Congress's resolution of 19 June required that the colonial assemblies provide "a suit of cloaths for each soldier enlisted in the province in the present campaign." Hancock's letter of 21 June enclosing this measure was read in the New York Congress 24 June, and resolutions were adopted later that day for the purchase of "all the coarse woolen cloth that is for sale in and about this city," as well as of deerskins, blankets, hats, shirts, hose, and shoes. *JCC*, V, 466–67; Hancock to the New York Congress, 21 June 1776, 4 *FAA*, VI, 1009; *JPC*, I, 505.

3 Wherry, Conklin, and Dodge were sergeants in the 3rd New York at the beginning of the Canadian expedition; Vandenburgh was a corporal in the same unit. During the campaign, Montgomery promoted the four non-commissioned officers to the rank of second lieutenant. The nomination of "John Coats" as surgeon by the Continental Congress was probably a clerical error. Samuel Cooke, who served as surgeon in the 3rd New York in the 1775–76 campaign, was listed as surgeon of the regiment under DuBois later in 1776. Henry DuBois, Lewis DuBois's younger brother, was appointed adjutant of the Canadian regiment in June 1776. *Cal. of Hist. Mss.*, II, 30, 36, 41; *New York in the Revolution as Colony and State* (2 vols., Albany, 1904), I, 55.

4 In his letter of 6 July 1776 Goforth resigned after being notified that he had been commissioned a major in the battalion to be raised by Lewis DuBois. In 1775, Goforth, DuBois, and Jacobus Bruyn had been named captains in the four regiments raised in New York for the Canadian expedition. Goforth, as fourth captain of the 1st Regiment, was then considered senior to DuBois and Bruyn, the fourth and seventh captains of the 3rd New York. In the arrangement of 26 June 1776, Goforth was to serve under DuBois as colonel and under Bruyn as lieutenant colonel. Goforth remarked acidly: "I view my appointment as speaking two things: first, that you have found men of greater merit than myself, and men who are better qualified for the public service, of which I am extremely glad; and secondly, that your now appointing me to serve under two junior officers, is no more than taking the most genteel way of discharging me from the public service as an officer."

5 Fleming, First Deputy Adjutant of the Army during the Canadian campaign, submitted his resignation on 21 June 1776 when he learned that Joseph Reed had been named to succeed Horatio Gates as Adjutant General. "As first Deputy," Fleming declared, "I naturally expected to succeed to the adjutant Generalship when it became vacant."

6 Philip Van Cortlandt. See above, Alexander McDougall to JJ, 20 March 1776 (first letter), n. 6.

7 Samuel Treadwell Pell (1755–86) served as a first lieutenant in the 4th

New York Regiment in Canada in 1775, but was omitted from appointments of officers for the five New York regiments authorized by Congress in 1776. On 6 July, JJ wrote to John Hancock to endorse Pell's memorial concerning his past services and remarked: "He is a fine, spirited, young Gentleman, of one or two and twenty, of an ancient and once oppulent Family in this Colony. His Connections are extensive in the County, and he seems to possess that generous kind of Ambition so essential to the Character of a good officer. What renders his Case the more unfortunate is, that he is almost the only one of his Family, who has discovered any great Degree of Ardor in the American Cause. His Promotion would have contributed as much to increase their Zeal, as his being laid aside may tend to diminish it." DNA: PCC, 78, XIII, 27–30.

To Sarah Livingston Jay

Rye, 17 July 1776

My dear good Wife

The Convention has done me the Honor of appointing me one of a Committee who are to set out in the morning for Albany.[1] This Jaunt will give me what I have long wanted vizt. Exercise, and as I shall be out of the Way of all Danger, will I dare say not be disagreable to you. We shall be gone a Fortnight or three Weeks but as opportunities of writing will doubtless offer, you may expect to recieve Letters from me before my Return.

I Yesterday attended the Funeral of our Friend Mrs. Lawrence. You may easily judge of my Feelings on that melancholy occasion. She was a fine as well as a good Woman. Tom is most sincerely to be pitied. I remember when I thought I was in eminent Danger of being in a similar Situation, and I remember too that I was extremely miserable.[2] My dear Sally Providence has been kind to us, and let us manifest our Gratitude by acquiescing in all its Dispensations. Kiss our dear little Boy for me. Let me again and again intreat and beseech you to attend to the Recovery of your Health. Let no Considerations whatever induce you to neglect it. Consider how much my Happiness as well as yours depends upon it.

My Father and Mother present their kind Regards to You. Direct for me at Rye. My Compliments to all the Family.

I am my dearest Sally your very affectionate Husband

JOHN JAY

ALS. MHi: Livingston Papers. Addressed: "To Mrs. Sarah Jay at General Livingstons Elizabeth Town, free J. Jay." Endorsed: "Mrs. Lawrence's passing." SLJ spent the summer of 1776 with her parents in New Jersey. Earlier in July JJ had been alarmed by an erroneous report that British forces had landed in that province and had seized the American barracks at Elizabeth. JJ to SLJ, 12 July 1776, JP.

[1] See below, Secret Committee, 19 July–7 August 1776.

[2] Mary Morris Lawrence, a daughter of Lewis Morris, the Lord of the Manor of Morrisania, married her first cousin, Thomas Lawrence, Jr. (1745–1823) of Philadelphia in 1775. Mrs. Morris died shortly after the birth of her first child, Thomas John Lawrence (1776–98), on 4 July 1776.

Defending the Hudson

Deeming it crucial to hold New York City against the British, Washington disposed most of the Continental troops in Manhattan and Long Island during the early summer of 1776. However, even as extensive military defenses were being erected on the two islands, enemy troops began to converge. On 29 June the first warships arrived with troops from Halifax under General William Howe (1729–1814), who had been named British commander in April. Within a few days a fleet of eighty-two ships filled New York Bay. On 12 July two British vessels, the *Phoenix* and the *Rose,* sailed past American batteries on the Hudson and anchored at Tappan Zee, four miles upriver. The same day the *Eagle* arrived at New York with General Howe's brother, Vice Admiral Viscount Richard Howe (1726–99), who had sailed from England at the head of a fleet whose strength was rumored to be 150 ships with 15,000 British and Hessian soldiers.

On 16 July the New York Convention established a "secret committee . . . to devise and carry into execution such measures as to them shall appear most effectual for obstructing the channel of Hudson's river, or annoying the enemy's ships in their navigation up the said river. . . ." JJ, Robert Yates (1738–1801) of Albany, Christopher Tappen of Ulster, Robert R. Livingston and Gilbert Livingston of Dutchess, and William Paulding of Westchester were named to the committee.[1] The next day the Convention amplified the committee's powers: JJ and his colleagues were authorized to take over the materials being used for the construction of vessels at Poughkeepsie, impress "boats, Vessels, Teams, Waggons, Horses, and Drivers," and even "call out the militia" to fulfill their mission.[2] The Committee left White Plains to meet on 19 July at Fort Montgomery on the west bank of the Hudson near Bear Mountain. In addition to authorizing the manufacture of a chain to be run across the river,[3] the Committee voted to augment the armament of all forts along the Hudson. At a meeting at Poughkeepsie on 22 July JJ was instructed to travel to the Salisbury, Connecticut, ironworks to procure heavy cannon, shot, and trucks for fortification of the vital waterway. The documents printed below, including minutes and correspondence of the Secret Committee, a diary record kept by JJ covering 22–24 July, supplemented by his report to the Committee, and a letter from Robert R. Livingston, record his mission of July 1776.

[1] *JPC,* I, 526–27. Although JJ accepted this assignment and worked energetically to carry it out, he believed that a serious mistake had been made which complicated the defense of the area. In a letter written several months later, JJ

described what he thought should have been done: "Had I been vested with absolute power in this State, I have often said and still think that I would last spring have desolated all Long Island, Staten-Island, the City and County of New York, and all that part of the County of Westchester which lies below the mountains. I would then have stationed the main body of the army in the mountains on the east, and eight or ten thousand men in the highlands on the west side of the river." JJ to Robert Morris, 6 Oct. 1776, printed in *American Book Prices* catalogue, 16 Jan. 1917.

2 *Ibid.*, 528.

3 The committee appointed Jacobus Van Zandt, Augustine Laurence, and Samuel Tudor to superintend "the making a Chain to fix across Hudson's River at the most convenient place near fort Montgomery. . . ." JJ *et al.:* commission to Van Zandt, Laurence, and Tudor, 22 July 1776, N.

Document I: Minutes of the Secret Committee

19–20 July 1776

At a meeting of the Secret Committee from the Convention of the state of New York. Present Mr. Jay, Mr. R. Livingston, Mr. Tappen, Mr. G. Livingston, Mr. Yates—Committee. General Clinton, Coll. Clinton, Capt. Bedlow.[1]

It is proposed and agreed to that in order to obstruct the navigation of Hudson's River so as to prevent any of the Ships of the King of Great Britain from coming up the same it will be necessary to throw across the River at or near Fort Montgomery a Boom, and below it to anchor Frames of Timber the points or ends whereof to be shod with Iron so as to answer the double purpose of founding any Ships who may sail up to it, and if that should fail, to Lessen the Shocke of those Vessels when they come at the Boom. Such frames to be made in the following manner ———[2] the pointed Beams to be of about the Length of ———[3] foot, and to be made about 16 foot apart, and two cross beams worked in and bolted.

At a meeting July 20

Agreed to have 200 Iron Trucks cast at the furnace in the high lands and gave orders to Mr. Boyd to have moulds made for the purpose.[4]

Also wrote a Letter to General Washington, apprizing him of our proceeding and requesting him to send to the Forts in the highlands a number of Artilery Men. [Insert the Letter].[5]

<Also wrote a Letter to the proprietors of the Iron Furnace at Salsbury requesting them to send to the Landing at Coll. Hoffman, all 20 of the Heavy Cannon they may have cast, for the use of the Shipping at Poughkeepsing. [Insert the letter].[6]>

Agreed that Rober[t ———] Cas[tle] be appointed and [is]

hereby appointed Commander of the Sloop Cambden and to be subject to such orders as he may receive from this Committee of the Convention of the State of New York, and receive such pay, as the said Convention or the Continental Congress shall or may have regulated.[7]

Agreed that Henry Benson be appointed and he is hereby appointed Commander of the Sloop Hudson under the Regulations as above.

Also wrote a Letter to Charles Giles[8] at Kingston requesting his attendance here immediately, as the Committee intended to offer him an employ in which he could serve his Country.

It is farther resolved and agreed to that one of the above Commanders do immediately proceed to New York in order to procure Gunmen and Sailors for navigating the said Vessels.

Messrs. G. Smart, Jas Van Deusen and Theople. Anthony, James Odill in Consequence of a Request from the Committee writed on them, and the Committee Proposing to them to consider at what Price they could make up the remainder of a Chain to be drawn across the River, they gave for answer that they would make it in the same manner of the other chain at the rate of 6 pen. P and render neat for gross weight after your ag[reeing] on the Subject they at Last agreed to make it 5 pen. P.[9]

The Committee agreed to the above Proposal, and ordered them to Proceed to the making of it immediately.

It was also Proposed to them to know at what rate they would make up Bolts for the floats.

It is farther agre[ed] [th]at the Chairman of this Committee write to the Comm[ittee] of Albany for to Purchase 2.60 Saw Logs [and] to send them down immediately to [Poug]hkeepsie.[10]

D. NNebg: Washington's Headquarters.

1 Brigadier General George Clinton of the Ulster County militia set up his headquarters at Fort Montgomery after the *Rose* and *Phoenix* sailed upriver. Captain William Bedlow was a commissioner "for erecting fortifications in the Highlands" in August 1775, and was named supervisor of construction of obstructions in the Hudson near New Windsor in early 1777. *PPGC,* I, 617, 832, 851–52.

2 Frames drawn in manuscript.

3 Space left blank in manuscript.

4 The Committee's letter to Robert Boyd has not been located. In the margin next to this paragraph is written "Omit."

5 See below, Document II.

6 Secret Committee to Joshua Porter and Hezekiah Fitch, 20 July 1776, in Ct. The ironworks at Salisbury, Conn., sixty-three miles northwest of Hartford, were owned by a Loyalist before their confiscation by the Connecticut government. Colonel Joshua Porter (1730–1825) was named overseer of the Salisbury

works 18 March 1776. Louis F. Middlebrook, *Salisbury, Connecticut Cannon, Revolutionary War* (Salem, Mass., 1935), pp. 7–8.

7 On 14 Jan. 1777 the New York Committee of Safety ordered the State Treasurer to advance Captain Robert Castle eighty pounds for himself and his crew on the *Camden*, "fitted out by order of the secret committee for obstructing Hudson's river." *JPC*, I, 171.

8 Charles Giles was a member of the 2nd Ulster militia regiment. *New York in the Revolution* (2 vols., Albany, 1904), I, 192.

9 George Smart and James Odell were members of the Dutchess County militia. Ja[me]s Van Deusen and Theop[hi]le Anthony have not been identified. *Ibid.*, 153.

10 Robert Yates's letter to the Albany Committee has not been located.

Document II: Secret Committee to George Washington

Fort Montgomery, [20] *July 1776*

Sir

We informed your Excellency of our appointment, in consequence of which we took a Survey of the Fortresses in the Highlands.[1] We are extreamly sorry to say that notwithstanding their importance and advantageous situation they are by no means in a proper posture of Defence, part of the few Cannon at Fort Constitution were sent away, and the whole Number now there, and at Fort Montgomery are not sufficient, this want we suppose your Excellency will be unable to supply, we have therefore sent for those that were designed for the Ships that are building at Poughkeepsie. But if we should Obtain them they will be of little use unless some Mattrosses can be spared from New York since there are only 14 at both Forts. If your Excellency could spare a few Howitzers they might be of singular use at this place. A skilful Engineer could be at no place more serviceable than here, as many small Posts which command this ought to be Fortified. We cannot think the Garrisons by any means, proportioned to the Extent of the Works or the Importance of the Places. We know the Difficultys that your Excellency will find in supplying these wants yet we cannot but suggest them, since we are satisfied that even if the Enemy should be defeated at New-York they might take such Posts here as we should find it impossible to dispossess them of.

We remain with the greatest respect Your Excellency's most Obedient Humble Servants

ROBERT YATES
JOHN JAY
ROBT R LIVINGSTON
CHRISTR. TAPPEN
GILBERT LIVINGSTON

Since writing the above we have been informed that the Salisbury Furnace, at which place the Cannon are Cast is under the Direction of the Government of Connecticut so that we have some doubt whether we can procure those for which we wrote, unless your Excellency will be pleased to lend us your Assistance by writing to Governor Trumbull on the Subject.

LS. DLC: Washington Papers, Series 4. Addressed: "On the Public Service To His Excellency George Washington Esqr. at New York." Misdated "18th" July; date of 20 July supplied from entry in the Minutes of the Secret Committee, 19–20 July 1776, Document I, above.

1 The Committee announced their appointment to Washington in a letter dated White Plains, 17 July. DLC: Washington Papers, Series 4.

Document III: Minutes of the Secret Committee

Poughkeepsie, 22 July 1776

Poghkeepsy, 22 July 1776, The said Committee met according to Agreement at the House of Van Kleeck. Present: Mr. Robert Yates, Chairman, Mr. Jay, Major Tappen, Mr. Robert R. Livingston, Mr. Gilbert Livingston.

It appearing to the said Committee that a number of Cannon were absolutely necessary and wanting for the Defence of Hudsons River, as well at the Forts erected on its Shores, as for the armed vessels ordered to be prepared for its Defence.

Resolved unanimously That Mr. Jay forthwith repair to Salisbury Iron Works and endeavour to procure there Twenty of the heaviest Cannon which can be had there, Eight Cannon, six pounders, and Eight four pounders. Also a proper Quantity of Shot and Trux for the said Cannon. The whole to be sent to Collonel Hoffman's Landing, And that he take with him Davis Hunt a Carpenter to take the Dimensions of the said Trux in order that Carriages may immediately be made for the said Cannon.

Resolved unanimously also, That Mr. Jay be authorized to apply to Governor Trumbull, and in Behalf of the Convention of the State of New York, to request his Aid and Influence in the Premisses. And further that Mr. Jay be and he hereby is authorized and empowered to impress Carriages, Teems, Sloops and Horses and to call out Detachments of the Militia, and generally to do or cause to be done at his Discretion all such Matters and Things as he may deem necessary or expedient to forward and complete the aforesaid Business committed to his Care.

AD. Enclosure in JJ to Jonathan Trumbull, Lebanon, 27 July 1776. In his covering draft note to Trumbull JJ wrote: "The above is a true Copy of my Instructions from the Com[mitte]e therin mentioned and in pursuance thereof I request the favor of his Excellency Governor Trumbull to furnish the Convention of the State on N York with as many Cannon for the Defence of Hudsons River as the State of Connecticut can conveniently supply." Tr in NN: Bancroft Amer. Series.

Document IV: Notes on Mission to Connecticut for the Secret Committee

[*Salisbury*], 22–24 *July* [1776]

22 July. Set off from Pogkeepsie this afternoon and lodged at John Carpenters.

23d. Reached Salisbury this afternoon. Saw Messrs. Fitch and Norton the Superintendants of the Iron Works, informed them of my Business and requested them to meet me at Doctor Wheelers Tomorrow Morning.[1] The weather being too bad to inspect the State of the Works etc.

24. Those Gent[lemen] met me acc[ordin]g to Appointment. We visited the Works. They furnished me with a Return of the Cannon shot etc. there and told me that they could not deliver me any without Orders from Governor Trumbul or Gen. Washington. I determined therefore as the former was nearer than the other to set out for Lebanon.

Wrote to Gilb. Livingston advising him of the above ment[ionin]g the getting Trux and Shot cast at Mr. Livingstons, and that Benson's Ferry here would expedite getting the Cannon down, and that he meet me here next saturday or Sunday etc.[2]

AD.

[1] Lot Norton and Dr. Lemuel Wheeler were prominent Salisbury patriots. Both served with Hezekiah Fitch and Joshua Porter on the town committee appointed to enforce the Continental Association in December 1774. *Historical Collections relating to the Town of Salisbury* (2 vols., Salisbury, 1913), I, 141, 143.

[2] In his letter to Gilbert Livingston, misdated 24 "June," JJ reported: "The Superintendants . . . cannot part with them [the twelve-pound Cannon] without orders from Govr. Trumbul. I shall set out for Lebanon immediately. There are no Trux at the Works. They advise me to get them made at Mr. Livingstons, but say if directed by Govr. Trumbull they will set about it. Write to him on the Subject. I shall most certainly I think get some of these Cannon and [his] being here would expedite getting them down. Tell him so, and if convenient let him meet me here next Saturday or Sunday by which Time I expect to return. . . . There a few Ton of Shot here. It would be proper to get a Quantity made by Mr. Livingston. They will not have Time here. The Ships in Connecticut ready are yet to be supplied." Colonel Robert Livingston, the lord of Livingston Manor, operated

ironworks and a foundry on his estate. Colonel Livingston was a first cousin of Gilbert Livingston's father. JJ to Gilbert Livingston, 24 [July] 1776, JP; see also Gilbert Livingston to Robert Livingston, 25 July 1776, NHpR: Livingston-Redmond Papers.

Document V: To the Secret Committee

Poghkeepsie, 7th August 1776

To the secret Committee of the Convention of the State of New York, appointed to devise and carry into Execution such measures as to them should appear most effectual for obstructing the Channel of Hudsons River or annoying the Enemies Ships in their Navigation up the said River.

Gentlemen

In Pursuance of your Instructions given me at this Place on the 22d Day of July last,[1] I immediately repaired to Salisbury Furnace, and applied to Messrs. Fitch and Norton, two of the Superintendents of the Furnace (Collonel Porter the other Superintendant being absent) for the Cannon and other Articles mentioned in the said Instructions.

They informed me that there were several Cannon, and a considerable Quantity of Shot ready, but that they were not authorized to dispose of, or part with, any of them, without Licence from Governor Trumbull; That they had no Trux made, and could not order any to be made without his Direction. They furnished me with a State of the ordinance Stores they had prepared, and I forthwith proceeded to Govr. Trumbull's at Lebanon.

I gave the Governor a Copy of my Instructions,[2] and requested the Favor of him to furnish the Convention of the State of New York with as many Cannon for the Defence of Hudsons River as the State of Connecticut could conveniently spare, not exceeding the number mentioned, in my Instructions, together with a proportionable Quantity of Shot. I also desired him to give Directions for the casting Trux for the said Cannon, and intimated to him, that Messrs. Fitch and Norton had informed me it might be done without delaying the making of Cannon.

Governor Trumbull expressed his Readiness to contribute all in his Power towards the Good of the American Cause and the Safety of this State, but thought it most prudent to summon his Council, [and sub]mit my Request to their Consideration.

When the Council convened, they concurred with the Governor

in an order for "lending ten twelve pounders and ten six pounders then at the Furnace at Salisbury, to the State of New York, also a suitable Proportion of Shot for said Cannon. Said Cannon to be replaced and said Shot returned or accounted for by said State when requested, and the overseers of said Furnace were required to cast a sufficient Number, or as many as could be of Iron Trux or Carriage Wheels for said Cannon to be loaned to said State and returned or accounted for with the Cannon aforesaid, All to be delivered to me or my order by said overseers, taking proper Reciepts for the same." Of this order they gave me the certified Copy which is annexed to this Report.

On my Return to Salisbury I found Collonel Porter there, and the overseers of the Furnace agreed to prepare the Cannon mentioned in the above order, with the greatest Expedition; several of them not being as yet bored or drilled. As to the Trux, Coll. Porter was averse to entering on that Branch of Business, objecting that it would impede the casting of Cannon, and gave me very satisfactory Reasons for his being of that opinion, and on the same account, expressed a Desire that Salisbury Furnace might be confined to the making of Cannon, and Coll. Livingston's employed in casting Shot and other ordinance Stores, adding that he would furnish the Coll. with some sand-moulders and give him every other Assistance in his Power. For these Reasons I did not think it either reasonable or prudent to insist on a Compliance with the Governor's order respecting the Trux.

I then hired Teems to carry four twelve Pounders which were soon made ready, together with fifty rounds of Shot for each of them to Coll. Hoffmans Landing at 35/ lawful Money of Connecticut per Ton, and requested Hezekiah Fitch Esqr. to forward the Remainder as they became ready, with fifty rounds of Shot for each Cannon to the same Place, and engaged to make him a reasonable Compensation for his Trouble. He consented to undertake the Business, and I left with him twenty Eight pounds, four Shillings lawful Money of Connecticut to defray the Expences attending it, and to pay the Teemsmen then employed in transporting the four twelve pounders and Shot aforesaid, for which Money I took his Reciept and have annexed it to this Report.

Being of opinion that Application should immediately be made to Coll. Livingston for Trux and Shot, and it being uncertain whether he was at Ancram or the manor, I went to Ancram, and not finding him there proceeded to the Manor. At my Request he has undertaken to furnish the Convention of the State of New York with proper Trux for ten twelve, and ten six pounders, together with Cannon Shot of various sizes.[3]

On my Way to this Place, I overtook the four Cannon and Shot aforesaid going to Coll. Hoffmans Landing, and being informed that a Sloop was there ready to sail to Fort Montgomery, I ordered the said Cannon and Shot to be put on Board and carried to the said Fort.

JOHN JAY

ALS. NNebg: Washington's Headquarters. Endorsed: "Mr. Jay's Report to the Committee of the Convention of New York respecting his proceedings in procuring Cannon Shot etc. Received and approved of by the Committee. 13 Augt. 1776. Rob. Yates Ch[airm]an." Enclosures: Extract from the Minutes of a meeting of the Governor and Council of Safety, Lebanon, Conn., 27 July 1776, copy in the hand of Benjamin Huntington, signed by Jonathan Trumbull with a pass for JJ signed by Trumbull; receipt from Hezekiah Fitch for £28/4 paid by JJ "on acct. of Expences which will attend the sending Cannon and Shot . . . ," Salisbury, 3 Aug. 1776. Draft of covering letter in JP endorsed: "Dt. of my Rept. to secret Com. 1776 23 July"; Tr in NN: Bancroft: Amer. Series, II, 60, dated "July 1776."

1 See above, Document III.

2 These instructions, with a brief covering note from JJ to Trumbull, 27 July 1776, are in Ct.

3 See above, Document IV.

From Robert R. Livingston

Manor Livingston, 12 August 1776

Dear Sir

I wrote Colonel Porter by Express, desiring him to Spare me two of his moulders to assist my hands, in Casting doubleheaded Shott, and the Trux you desired me to cast for the Convention of the State of New York.[1] He wrote me immeadiately that he Could not possibly fulfill the orders he had from his Honor The Governour if he Spared one of his hands; upon which I went out to Speak with him my Self and endeavour to prevail on him for one of his Moulders but without Success. Indeed he told me he had Sent an Express to his Honor requesting that his Furnace might be Excused from Casting Shott, but had no answer back, in that case he told me I might have his two Moulders. Now Sir this being so very uncertain I cant think it Safe for either of us to depend on, and as we cannot cast the trux without this help, must advise you to apply else where for my hands cannot do it.

I have orderd Moulds to be made to cast Shott, at which we will do all we can, to Supply General Schuyler, but this fear will not be able to do in time for want of Moulders so that its not yet in my power to Supply you even with that article, however desirous and anxious I am to oblige my Country which hope will plead my Excuse.

Am with respect Dear Sir, Your Most Humble Servant

ROBT. LIVINGSTON

ALS. NNebg: Washington's Headquarters. Addressed: "For John Jay Esqr at Pouchkepsie." Endorsed.

1 Colonel Livingston to Joshua Porter [August 1776], not located.

From Edward Rutledge

Philadelphia, July 20th, 1776

My dear Jay

I am most obliged to you for your friendly Letter of the 6th[1] which did not come to Hand until a few Days ago, and I have been so much engaged since that I really had no time to acknowledge the Receipt of it. But I can no longer delay it, when I have it in my Power to communicate a piece of Intelligence which I am sure must afford you (who are interested in the Happiness of my Countrymen) the highest Satisfaction. By Express which arrived Yesterday we learn that the British Fleet has been repulsed with very considerable Loss.[2] Two 50 Gun Ships have received so much Damage that it is thought they will never be able to go to Sea again; ano[the]r the Actdon of 28 blown up,[3] the remainder considerably injured; the Captain of the Experiment killed, the Captain of the Bristol lost his Arm, Sir Peter Parker wounded,[4] 104 Seamen and inferior Officers killed and about 64 wounded, Several of whom have since died of the wounds. The Loss of our side is 12 killed and 24 wounded, all privates. The Battle lasted near 12 Hours during the whole of which time General Lee says our Men were as cool and as determined as ever he saw Men in his Life. This is the more to be wondered at when I tell you, that their Number was but 500 and that but one of that Number had ever seen a battle. At the Time that the Ships lay before the Fort, General Clynton attempted to land about 2000 of his Forces at another part of the Island; they were in 35 Flat Bottom Boats, but they were twice repulsed by Colonel Thompson of our Rangers,[5] commanding 300 Men with considerable Loss on their Side, but none on ours.

It is thought that they would make another Attack with their Land Forces, but Lee says they may do in that as they please; he is confident we shall repulse them as often as they attack with as much Honour to ourselves as we have done already. Remember me to

Morris.[6] I am in very great Haste. Shall answer some Queries in your Letter in a day or two.

God bless you, my dear Friend. I am truly and affectionately yours

E. RUTLEDGE

ALS. Addressed: "Free, John Jay Esquire at the Congress at New York." Endorsed. Tr in NN: Bancroft, Amer. Rev., I, 117.

1 JJ to Rutledge, 6 July 1776, *HPJ*, I, 68–70; *WJ*, I, 62–64.

2 British forces under General Henry Clinton attacked Charleston, S.C., on 28 June 1776. American troops under General Charles Lee turned back the amphibious assault.

3 The *Actaeon*, a twenty-eight gun vessel, ran aground during the battle and was fired by her crew when they abandoned the ship. The *Bristol* and *Experiment*, both fifty-gun ships, were also damaged in the engagement.

4 Sir Peter Parker (1721–1811), commander of the British squadron which had sailed from Dublin to participate in the Charleston campaign, suffered minor injuries. Captain Alexander Scott of the *Experiment* lost his right arm in this action.

5 Lieutenant Colonel William Thompson of the South Carolina Rangers.

6 This may be a reference either to Lewis Morris, then Rutledge's colleague in the Continental Congress, or to his half-brother Gouverneur. In a letter to JJ of 29 June 1776, above, Rutledge had written, "Compliments to Livingston and G. Morris."

To Sarah Livingston Jay

Poghkeepsy, 21 July 1776

My dear Sally

In a hot little Room, in Spite of Importunities to hear the pompous Chauncey Graham[1] preach, and in Defiance of the God of Sleep whom the Bugs and Fleas banished from my Pillow last night, am I set down to write a few Lines to my good little Wife.

On leaving Rye, I informed you of my intended Journey, which Letter you have doubtless ere this recieved.[2] We have paid a Visit to the Forts in the Highlands, and after a Jaunt of three Days which afforded us Pleasure as well as Exercise, I arrived here about an hour ago in perfect Health. Should I continue this kind of Life for three Weeks or a Month by Cloaths would be too narrow for me.

I have recieved no Letter from you since the one by Dyckman. Have you recieved mine from the White Plains?[3] Direct for me at Rye. I am impatient to hear of your Health. My Sollicitude on that Head however was abated by Kitty's telling me at Morrissania that Doctor Bard had seen and left you better. May God of his infinite mercy perfect your Recovery! I am happy in a kind of Confidence or PreSentiment that we shall yet enjoy many good Days together, and I indulge myself in imaginary Scenes of Happiness which I expect in a few Years to be realized. If it be a Delusion, it is a pleasing one, and therefore I embrace it. Should it like a Bubble vanish into Air, Resignation will blunt the Edge of Disappointment, and a firm Persuasion of after Bliss give me Consolation. Then my dear Wife shall we fear no Tyrants Power, neither shall we know Anxiety any more, and, if ———,[4] I cant fill up the blank, we shall again join Hands and Hearts and continue our virtuous Connection forever.

My Return is uncertain. I hope our Boy is well. God bless and keep you both. My Compliments to all the Family.

I am my dear Sally, your very affectionate Husband

JOHN JAY

ALS. MHi: Sedgwick Coll. Addressed: "To Mrs. Sarah Jay at General Livingston's Elizabeth Town, free J. Jay."

1 Chauncey Graham (1731–84), a Presbyterian minister who preached in Fishkill and Poughkeepsie, N.Y.

2 See above, JJ to SLJ, 17 July 1776.

3 JJ probably referred to his letter of 12 July in which he wrote SLJ that he had sent Samson Dyckman, a messenger for the New York Congress, to Elizabeth Town to help her should the rumors of British invasion prove true. JP.

4 Left blank in ms.

To Sarah Livingston Jay

Salisbury, 29 July 1776

My dear Sally

I am now returning to Poghkeepsey, where I am to meet some Members of the Convention on the 7th of August. How long I may stay there is entirely uncertain. Unless some unforeseen Business should intervene I purpose returning to the White Plains by the Way of Elizabeth Town.

The Journey will be long and fatiguing, but as all the Inconveniences of it will be amply compensated by the Pleasure of spending a Day or two with you, I consider it with Satisfaction, and shall pursue it with Chearfulness.

Dont however depend on it lest you be disappointed. In these Days of Uncertainty we can be certain only of the present; the future must be the object rather of Hope than Expectation. I have not heard of you since your Letter by Dyckman. You have doubtless written but I have lately been so far out of the Course of your Letters, that none of them have come to Hand. My dear Sally! Are you yet provided with a secure Retreat in Case Elizabeth Town should cease to be a Place of Safety? I shall not be at Ease till this be done. You know my Happiness depends on your Welfare, and therefore I flatter myself your Affection for me has before this will reach you, induced to attend to that necessary Object.

I daily please myself with an Expectation of finding our Boy in Health and much grown, and my good Wife perfectly recovered and in good Spirits. I always endeavour to anticipate good instead of ill Fortune, and find it turns to good Account. Were this Practice more general, I fancy Mankind would experience more Happiness than they usually do.

The only Danger attending it is, that by being too sanguine in our Expectations, Disappointment often punishes our Confidence and renders the Sensations occasioned by Mortification and Chagrin more painful, than those arising from anticipated and imaginary Enjoyments were pleasing. These however are Inconveniences which a little Prudence will easily obviate. A Person must possess no great Share of Sagacity who in this Whirl of human Affairs, would account that certain, which in the Nature of things cannot be so. But this looks more like writing an Essay than a Letter. I was thinking *loud* my dear Wife, which you know is a Species of Enjoyment which never falls to my Lott but when in your Company. May I long and often Enjoy it.

My Compliments to all the Family. I am my dear Sally and always will be your very affectionate Husband

JOHN JAY

ALS. Coll. of Richard Maass. Addressed: "To Mrs. Sarah Jay at General Livingston's Elizabeth Town New Jersey, free J. Jay."

From Gouverneur Morris

Harlem Church, 3d August 1776

Dear Jay

If you play Truant thus, *Le tout est perdue.* How do you expect that your unruly Horses can be kept in Order by a Whip and a Spur. They want the Reins. On Tuesday next it is to be determined as to the Seat of our General.[1] Unless etc. etc. I would not give a Fig for your Resolution. This is not the worst of it. Make haste.

Yours

GOUVR. MORRIS

ALS. Address mutilated. Endorsed.

[1] John Morin Scott, a member of the Third Provincial Congress, was commissioned a brigadier general in the New York militia on 9 June 1776, six days

before the New York Congress resolved "That no military officer in the pay of the Continental Congress or the Congress of this Colony, ought to be eligible to a seat in the Congress of this Colony." Scott was returned to the New York Convention as a delegate from New York City, and on 31 July Morris challenged Scott's eligibility to his seat. Scott claimed his seat "on behalf of his constituents." The issue of Scott's qualifications for membership in the Convention was postponed several times and subsequently dropped. *JPC*, I, 488, 495, 551.

From Augustus Van Cortlandt

Flat Bush, Wednesday Morning, 7th of August 1776

My dear Sir,

Sunday last, I went from hence to Yonkers on a Visit to my mother, who was then Very ill, and at the Same time to remove the Anxiety I had on my mind with respect to the Insecurity of the publick Records under my Care. Since when I have Secured them in Such manner (over the arch of my brothers family Vault) as Will Effectually preserve them from fire Water and Vermin.[1]

Having finished that part of Business, I returned to flat Bush the Tuesday following and in the Evening of the Same day, I was Called out of Bed by Abraham Skinner and a party he Commanded to repair to New York, that on Seeing General Greens[2] orders for that purpose, I Agreed to go with him, and fully intended so to do. After first putting up a few Cloths, but when done, he informed me I must first go to Jamaica. I told him his orders were to remove me to New York; he however insisted on my Going with him. I Sollicited him to let me Stay with my family until the morning (not Chosing to be Carried from County to County like a Vagabond or felon) and Gave him my honour to meet him at such place as he Should appoint, but without Effect. I then determined within my self to Avoid Going, but nevertheless ordered my horse and Chair to be Got ready, at seeing which, he went off Saying he had Some other Business in the Neighbourhood he must first Execute, leaving two of his party with me. I took Occasion to Go into a Side Room, and as I made no Engagement or promise to Go with him, I walked off into the Neighbourhood, and Shall this Evening take my self into Queens or Suffolk County, I believe the latter, and there remain, unless I Can Obtain the protection of the Congress to Continue here. I flatter my self I have a right to Expect it, as I dont know, of my having been in any instance unfriendly to their measures, but on the Contrary Very friendly. It is Verifyed in my ready Compliance with their requisition, relative to the removal of the publick records out of the City, for which I had the honor of their thanks; also my ready loan of Cash without Interest, and furnishing Some of their Officers with all the Muskets I then had, tho unsollicited for by them.

If the Congress will permit me to Continue with my family at flat Bush, until the British Troops Shall land there, I will, and you may also engage for me in any penalty they may reasonably require, that I will at Such time remove my self Immediately into Queens or Suffolk County with my family, and that in the Meantime or at any time thereafter will not directly nor indirectly Counteract the measures pursuing by the Congress. This or any other favor you'l be pleased to do for me herein, Will be Gratefully remembred by, Dear Sir, Your most Obedient Servant

AUGT. V CORTLANDT

P.S. Please to favor me with a line, whether my Caption was in Consequence of an order of the Congress, or by What Other Authority as also an answer to the above. Robin has directions to wait for that purpose.[3]

ALS. Addressed: "John Jay Esqr. if in his Absence to Governieur Morris Esqr. at Harlem." Endorsed. Van Cortlandt, JJ's first cousin, was clerk of the City and County of New York and a reputed Loyalist.

1 On 2 Sept. 1775 the Provincial Congress directed Van Cortlandt to secure the town and county records in his care. Three days later he informed the Committee of Safety that these records had been placed in a dry cellar and would be moved to his brother's home in Yonkers, Westchester County, if the city were invaded. In February 1776 he notified the Committee that he had transferred the records to Westchester. Some of these "publick records" are still in the possession of Van Cortlandt's descendants; the family has recently deposited the Mayor's Court Fee Book at the Jay Homestead, Bedford, N.Y.

2 Abraham Skinner (d. 1826) was an ensign in the 1st Continental Infantry. Brigadier General Nathanael Greene (1742–86) of Rhode Island commanded American troops on Long Island.

3 No reply from JJ has been located.

From Frederick Jay

Rye, 27th August 1776

Dear John

It is with great difficulty that we can get the Militia together and many of them without either Arms or Amunition. I think it necessary to apply to Congress for Capt. Sam. Townsends Company now at Kings bridge and as many more men as the Congress thinks necessary to guard the Coast.[1] Last Night (before we had any Information of the men of warr) Severall Canoes went off from this place. Pray attend to this business. Send us a supply of men and we will then bid defiance to the Sheep Stealers.

I am etc. etc. in haste.

FREDR JAY

P.S. If the Militia should be obliged to attend for any time it will be of great Damage to the Country and therefore request that a sufficient Number of Continental troops should be sent to guard the Coast.

ALS. Addressed: "On the Service of the State to Jno. Jay Esqr at Harlem." Endorsed. On 27 July the New York Convention adjourned from White Plains to meet at Harlem. Sessions of the Convention and its Committees of Safety continued at the Harlem Church until 29 Aug. *JPC*, I, 548, 601.

1 King's Bridge, at the northern end of Manhattan, linked the island to the mainland. Samuel Townsend of Westchester was promoted to captain of a county militia company 16 Aug. 1776.

John Morin Scott to the New York Convention

New York, September 6th, 1776

Dear Sir

I recieved your Letter about half an hour ago by the Messenger of the honorable Convention, in which you inform me that they are anxious to be informed of any Transactions at this Place that may be of use to the State, or otherwise of Importance.[1] My Duty would have directed me to execute this Task before the Reciept of your Letter, had I been possessed of the Means of Conveyance. I shall do it now as far as the Want of good pen and Ink, as scarce as almost every other necessary Article will permit.

I shall begin with our Retreat from Long Island. For previous to that Event the Convention was so near the Scene of Action, that they must have been acquainted with every occurrence.[2] I was summoned to a Council of War at Mr. Philip Livingstons House on Thursday 29th Ult.[3] never having had Reason to expect a Proposition for a Retreat till it was mentioned. Upon my Arrival at the Lines on the Tuesday Morning before, and just after the Enemy, by beating General Sullivan and Lord Stirling had gained the Heights[4] *which in their Nature appear to have been more defensible than the Lines were*. It was obvious to me we could not maintain them for any long Time, should the Enemy approach us regularly. *They were unfinished in several Places when I arrived there*, and we were obliged hastily to finish them, and you may imagine with very little Perfection, particularly across the main Road, the most likely for the Approach of the

Enemys heavy Artillery. *In this place, three of my Battalions* were placed, the Traverse of the Line in Ground so low, that the rising Ground immediately without it, would have put it in the Power of a Man at 40 Yards Distance *to fire under my Horses Belly* whenever he pleased.

You may judge of our Situation, subject to almost incessant Rains without Baggage or Tents and almost without Victuals or Drink, and in some Part of the Lines the Men standing up to their Middles in Water. The Enemy were evidently incircling us from Water to Water with Intent to hem us in upon a small Neck of Land. In this Situation they had as perfect a Command of the Island except the small neck on which we were posted as they now have.

Thus Things stood when the Retreat was proposed. As it was suddenly proposed *I as suddenly objected to it* from an aversion to giving the Enemy a single Inch of Ground. *But was soon convinced by the unanswerable Reasons for it.* They were these. Invested by an Enemy of above double our Number from Water to Water, scant in almost every necessary of Life and without Covering and liable every Moment to have the Communication between us and the City cut off by the Entrance of the Frigates into the East River between (late) Governor's Island and Long Island, which General McDougal[5] assured us from his own nautic Experience was very feazible. In such a Situation we should have been reduced to the Alternative of desperately attempting to cut our way a vastly superior Enemy with the certain Loss of a valuable Stock of Artillery and Artillery Stores which the Continent had been collecting with great Pains; or by Famine and Fatigue been made an easy Prey to the Enemy. In either Case the Campaign would have ended in the total Ruin of our army.

The Resolution therefore to retreat was unanimous and tho formed late in the Day was executed the following Night with unexpected Success. We how'er lost some of our heavy Cannon on the Forts at a Distance from the Water, the Softness of the Ground occasioned by the Rains having rendered it impossible to remove them in so short a Time. Almost every Thing else valuable was saved; and not a Dozen Men lost in the Retreat.

The Consequence of our Retreat was the Loss of (late Governors) Island which is perfectly commanded by the Fort on Red Hook. The Enemy however from Fear or other Reasons, indulged with the Opportunity of two Nights to carry off all except some heavy Cannon. The Garrison was drawn off in the Afternoon after our Retreat under the Fire of the Shipping who are now drawn up just behind (late) Governors Island, and the Fire of some Cannon from Long Island

Shore; but with no other Loss than that of one Mans Arm. What our Loss on Long Island was I am not able to estimate. I think the Hills might have been well maintained with 5,000 Men.

I fear their natural Strength was our Bane by lulling us into a State of Security and enabling the Enemy to steal a March upon us. I think from the best Accounts we must have killed many of the Enemy. We are sure that late Coll. and afterwards General Grant who was so bitter against us in Parliament, is among the Slain.[6] General Parsons late Coll. and promoted to the Rank of a General Officer[7] escaped from the Action and Pursuit as by a Miracle. I believe him to be a brave Man. He is a Connecticut Lawyer. He told me that in the Action he commanded a Party of about 250 Men, with orders from Lord Stirling to cover his Flank; and that when the Enemy gave Way, he threw into a Heap about thirty of the Enemies dead, and that in advancing a little farther he found a Heap made by the Enemy at least as large as that which he had collected. Lord Sitrling had ordered him to maintain his Ground till Receipt of his orders to retreat. However finding that no such orders came; and finding the Enemy by rallying to increase on his Hands, he flew to the Place where Lord Stirling was posted, leaving his Party on the Ground with strict Orders to maintain it till his Return; but he found his Lordship and his whole Body of Troops gone. There can be no Doubt but Lord Stirling behaved bravely; but I wish that he had retreated sooner. He would have saved himself, and a great Number of Troops from Captivity; but he refused to retreat for Want of orders. We miss him much; he was a very active Officer. General Sullivan who was also made a Prisoner in the Action on the Heights went some days ago on Parole to Congress to endeavour to procure his Exchange for Prescot.[8] I have not heard of his Return.

Two or three Days ago the Rose Frigate went up between the Islands and took Shelter, after a severe Cannonade from us, behind Blackwells Island. She retreated Yesterday as far as opposite Corlear's Hook, where she was briskly cannonaded till Night. I have not heard of her this Morning.

By the Loss on Long Island and the running away of our Militia *especially those of Connecticut*, to their respective Homes our Army is much diminished, and I am sure is vastly inferior to that of the Enemy. *The Troops are vastly dispirited, publickly say but I believe without Reason that they are sold. In short they have great Diffidence of Head Quarters and the Officers of all Ranks suspect two certain Persons near the General, whom I believe to be a good Man, to have more Influence than their Abilities entitle them to. I seldom go to*

Head Quarters; because I think my Visits there not ever acceptable. I content myself with doing my Duty which is very severe, as for some time past I *have been Brigadier of the Day every other Day*—The more severe as the Hardships to which I was reduced on Long Island, *without Bedding* almost without *Food* and exposed to the Rain have much impaired my Health.

The Army is continually praying most ardently for the Arrival of General Lee as their Guardian Angel. He is daily expected. His Arrival will probably *revive their Spirits.*[9] The Number of the Army I do not know, probably not so many by one half as the Congress intended. Its present Disposition is this. It is divided into three Divisions, one in the City where I am with my Brigade under the Command of Major General Putnam;[10] the other two under the respective Commands of Majors General Spencer and Heath,[11] one between Haerlem and us, the other at and about Kings Bridge.

What the Enemy intend we cannot yet discover. I am inclined to think to choose to avoid a Cannonade and Bombardment of the City and an Attempt to land in it. I imagine by their filing off to the Eastward they intend an Attempt on WestChester County, should they make it and succeed the Consequences are obvious. We shall be totally confined to this Island and cut off from all Communication with the Continent.

With a View to this Danger *I wrote a few Days ago to the General,* giving it as *my opinion* that we should abandon the City, make a strong post in the Heights of Kings Bridge and dispose of the Bulk of the Army in WestChester County and support the Communication between both, by placing the armed Vessels in the Mouth of Spuyten Devil on the East River.[12] *I have recieved no Answer.*

The Vessels lie in parade before Head Quarters, but some of the Artillery and Stores are removing. God knows what will be the Event of this Campaign; but I beg Leave to assure the honorable Convention that *I will never bring Disgrace on their Appointment.* Poor General Woodhull with a Lieutenant and four Men were made Prisoners on Long Island.[13] I had a Letter from him dated the 1st Inst. but not dated from any Place, nor does he tell me how he was taken. He has lost all his Baggage and requested of me two Shirts and two Pairs of Stockings, which I should have sent him had not the Flag of Truce been gone before I recieved the Letter. I shall comply with his Request by the first opportunity. Commend me with all possible Devotion to the Honorable Convention.

I am Sir Your most obedient Servant

JNO. MORIN SCOTT

P.S. *The Army badly paid and wretchedly fed.* 1100 men arrived from the Southward. A Deserter tells me but 3,000 *foreign Troops on Staten Island. I know not what the flying Camp is doing.* He says the Enemy on Long Island are 26,000. I believe this much exagerated, and 1000 in the Shipping.

C in JJ's hand. Endorsed by JJ: "Genl. Scotts Letter to Convention 6 Sept. 1776. Copy." Tr in NN: Bancroft, Amer. Rev., I, 191. JJ was privy to this letter as a member of the Committee of Safety appointed on 7 September by the New York Convention to conduct business during the Convention's adjournment. *JPC*, I, 614–15.

1 The Convention's letter to Scott has not been located. When Scott's letter of 6 September was read in the Committee of Safety his dispatch was described as "in pursuance of the request of the Convention on the —— instant." *JPC*, I, 615.

2 American forces on Long Island were routed on 27 August. Evacuation of the defeated Continental troops took place on the night of 29–30 August. The Convention sat at Harlem until 29 August. On 30 and 31 August the Committee of Safety held sessions at King's Bridge and Philipse Manor in Westchester. On 2 September the Committee of Safety met at Fishkill, Dutchess County, where sessions of the Committee and the Convention continued through 1776. *JPC*, I, 600–04.

3 Minutes of the Council of General Officers held on 29 Aug. 1776 are printed in 5 *FAA*, I, 1246.

4 In taking Brooklyn Heights on 27 August the British captured Brigadier General William Alexander, who had succeeded Charles Lee as commander in New York in March 1776 and Major General John Sullivan (1740–95) of New Hampshire, who joined the Continental Army in New York in July 1776 and succeeded Nathanael Greene as commander on Long Island 20 August when Greene was incapacitated by illness.

5 Alexander McDougall was named a brigadier general in August 1776.

6 Brigadier General James Grant (1720–1806) of the British Army served in North America during the French and Indian War and was governor of Florida, 1763–71. As a member of Parliament, 1773–75, Grant betrayed an anti-American bias. On Long Island Grant commanded the troops which defeated Alexander. A Lieutenant Colonel James Grant was a casualty on 27 Aug. 1776, and he has been confused with General Grant.

7 Samuel Holden Parsons (1737–89) of Connecticut was promoted to brigadier general on 9 Aug. 1776 and commanded forces in Alexander's wing on 27 August.

8 Brigadier General Richard Prescott was exchanged for Sullivan later in September 1776.

9 Charles Lee returned from his successful defense of Charleston, S.C., the next month and joined Washington's army 28 Oct. 1776.

10 Major General Israel Putnam (1718–90) of Connecticut succeeded Sullivan as U.S. commander on Long Island 24 Aug. 1776.

11 Major General Joseph Spencer (1714–89) of Connecticut and William Heath (1737–1814) of Massachusetts.

12 See Scott to Washington, 31 Aug. 1776, DLC: Washington Papers, Series 4.

13 Brigadier General Nathaniel Woodhull, President of the New York Convention, was ordered to lead Suffolk County militiamen to Queens on 24 Aug. 1776. Woodhull was captured at Jamaica on 28 August and died of battle wounds 20 Sept. 1776.

From Lewis Morris

Philadelphia, September 8, 1776

My Dear friend

I am very anxious about our Situation at N. York. I should have gone off this day but Mr. Lewis[1] has taken flight towards <N York> that Place in quest of his family, that were on Long Island, and there remains only three of us. I wish you would let me know how matters stand and at what Place our convention are. Genl Sullivan brought a Message from Lord Howe to Congress in consequence of which they have Sent Doctor Franklin, John Adams and Ned Rutledge.[2] I doubt in my own mind any good effect that it can have, as he was desirous to meet them in their private Characters. I will inclose you the resolve of Congress. Sullivan Says that Howe Said he was ever against taxing of us, and that they had no right to interfere with our internal Police, and that he was very sure America could not be conquered, and that it was a great pitty so brave a Nation Should be cutting one another to pieces.

Mr. Linch yesterday asked me if you would part with your Chesnut Horse. I told him I did know I thought I had heard you Say once in this Place that if you did Sel[l] him you would have Seventy pounds. He beged of me to write to you and get your answer.[3] Poor Mr. Lawrence remains very unwell.[4] He joins me in our best regards to you and all friends. Yours Most Sincerely

LEWIS MORRIS

ALS. Addressed: "To Coll. John Jay Esqr. New York, favd. by E. Rutledge Esqr." Endorsed. Tr in NN: Bancroft, Amer. Rev., I, 211.

1 Francis Lewis, Morris's colleague on the New York delegation at Philadelphia.

2 After his capture at the battle of Long Island, John Sullivan was sent to Philadelphia with a proposal for peace negotiations from Lord Richard Howe. Congress named Franklin, Adams, and Rutledge to meet with Howe, and the first conference between the American commissioners and the British commander took place on Staten Island on 11 Sept. *JCC*, V, 730–31, 737–38, 765–66.

3 See above, James Duane to JJ, 11 May 1776.

4 Morris's recently widowed son-in-law, Thomas Lawrence, Jr.

To Robert Morris

Fishkill, 15 September 1776

Dear Sir

When Mr. Deane went to France I communicated to him a Mode of invisible writing unknown to any but the Inventor and myself.[1]

The inclosed Letter will explain it. On opening his Letter to me Yesterday and finding one directed to you inclosed in it, I without thought gave it to a Gentleman of your Light Horse who had been to Ticonderoga with Money from the Congress. I dont recollect his Name. I had not at that Time the Materials with me for rendering Deans Letter visible. But I from reading it, I now find the Letter directed to you is nothing more than a Continuation of the Intelligence begun in mine, and designed to prevent any Suspicion that might arise from his inclosing so much (seemingly) blank paper.[2] Be so kind therefore as to send me the Letter by the return of the Express together with the one I now inclose. You will be pleased to communicate such of the Contents as are of a public Nature to the Committee of Intelligence. And by all Means conceal from them and as well as every body else, the Discovery now made to you.

I am Sir, with great Respect and Esteem, Your very humble Servant

JOHN JAY

I shall on recieving the Letter abovementioned immediately transcribe and send you a Copy of it.

ALS. NN: Jay, 25d. Addressed: "To Robert Morris Esqr a Member of the General Congress Philadelphia." Endorsed. Enclosure: unidentified document explaining the use of invisible ink. Morris (1734–1806), a wealthy Philadelphia merchant, was JJ's colleague in the Continental Congress, November 1775–May 1776. After JJ's departure for New York Morris remained in the Congress until October 1778.

1 In March 1776 Silas Deane sailed to Europe as an agent of the Continental Congress. Under a contract with the Secret Committee (better known by its later title, the Commercial Committee), Deane was to obtain goods in France "suitable for the Indians." However, this mission was secondary to that given him by the Committee of Secret Correspondence (which eventually evolved into the Committee for Foreign Affairs) of which JJ and Robert Morris were members in the winter and spring of 1775–76. Deane's instructions from this committee made it clear that the contract for "the Indian trade" would merely give Deane "good countenance to . . . appearing in the character of a merchant . . . it being probable that the court of France may not like it should be known publicly that any agent from the Colonies is in that country." Under his instructions from the Committee of Secret Correspondence Deane was to seek an agreement with the French government for "clothing and arms for twenty-five thousand men, with a suitable quantity of ammunition, and one hundred field pieces" for which the Congress would pay "as soon as our navigation can be protected by ourselves or friends." The invisible ink used by Deane and JJ in their correspondence was the invention of JJ's brother Sir James. *LMCC*, I, 372–77; Frank Monaghan, *John Jay* (New York and Indianapolis, 1935), pp. 89–90.

2 The letter to Morris is that of 23 June 1776. This is the only letter from Deane which Morris acknowledged receiving between 12 Sept. 1776 and 23 Oct. 1776. "The Deane Papers," N.Y.H.S. *Colls.*, XIX, 141–42, 305, 331–32.

From Robert Morris

Philadelphia, September 23d, 1776

Dear Sir

Altho your express delivered me your favour last Wednesday or Thursday yet I did not receive the letter from Mr. Deane untill this day and shall now send after the Express that he may Convey this safe to your hands. Should he be gone I must find some other safe conveyance. You will find enclosed both Mr. D[ea]ne's letters as you desired and I shall thank you for the Copy of the Invisible part. He had Communicated so much of this Secret to me, before his departure, as to let me know he had fixed with you a mode of writing that would be invisible to the rest of the World. He also promised to ask you to make a full Communication to me, but in this use your pleasure. The Secret so farr as I do or shall know it, will remain so to all other persons.[1]

It appears clear to me that we may very soon Involve all Europe in a Warr by managing properly the apparent forwardness of the Court of France. Its a horrid consideration that our own Safety should call on us to involve other Nations in the Calamities of Warr. Can this be morally right or have morality and Policy nothing to do with each other? Perhaps it may not be good Policy to investigate the Question at this time. I will therefore only ask you whether General Howe will give us time to cause a diversion favourable to us in Europe. I confess as things now appear to me the prospect is gloomy Indeed. Therefore if you can administer Comfort do it. Why are we so long deprived of your abilitys in Congress? Perhaps they are more usefully exerted where you are. That may be the case, but such Men as You, in times like these, should be every where.

I am with true sentiments of respect and esteem, Dear Sir, Your obedient humble Servant.

ROBT MORRIS

ALS. Addressed: "To John Jay Esqr." Endorsed. Enclosure: portion of Silas Deane to Morris, 23 June 1776. For the background of the enclosure, see above, JJ to Morris, 15 Sept. 1776.

[1] In his reply of 6 Oct. 1776 JJ forwarded the decoded portions of Deane's letter of 23 June and explained to Morris: "Had Mr Deane mentioned to me his having conversed with you relative to the mode of writing I communicated to him, I should most certainly have spoken to you on the subject, and will when we meet give you the same information respecting it that I did to him." *HPJ*, I, 85–89.

From Frederick Jay

Harrisons Purchase, 1st October 1776

Dear Jack

Your letter of the 16th ultimo[1] I have received and would have made a reply thereto ere this had you not informed me of your going to the Jersey to fetch your *Ribb.*[2] I am extremely happy that you are so well provided for where you are. I could wish that the Old People[3] would retire to the place you have provided for them. They seem very uneasy with their present Situation. I have endeavored to persuade them to go up immediately, but in vain. I am very confident that they cannot with any degree of Comfort remove to Rye, the House and Barn being now occupied with NE. Troops, and if the Army continues at the Bridge this winter, Rye will be no place for Papa and Mama. I could wish you would give them your advice respecting this matter.[4]

I could wish with you that I had Better reason to be reconciled to my Lodgings. My Landlady is such a Devil that it will be impossible for me to stay with her this winter.

I think it would be needless to Order Generall Morris to join his Brigade, as few of them are to be depended upon.[5] I at present apprehend no danger from the Tories nor from the Enemy in this Quarter, as the whole Coast is lined with New England Men. (However they are not to be depended upon.)

As for Jemmy's Mare I think it would be best to procure a *flag* to send for her. She is gone to the Devil; Lewis left her upon long Island. Your Horse Morris has sent with his own to Philadelphia; your Colt at Bedford is well and the blue Colt has lost one of his Nutmegs. I shall go to Jersey to morrow on business.

Attend to what follows. At the last General Meeting of the Committee for this County, I was unanimously elected Treasurer to the said Committee in the Room of Colonel Thomas (their late Treasurer) now in the Service. I acquainted Colonel Thomas of my appointment, also that Messrs Tom Miller and Phillip Pell Junior were appointed to inspect into the settlement of the Accounts. Colonel Thomas on the receipt of my letter wrote to his Brother John Thomas Junior informing him that he was chosen Treasurer for one Year (an absolute falshood) (he was only chosen for the time he acted) and that if any money was wanted the Committee should call *upon his Wife*.[6]

This Matter as you may suppose did by no means please me, not upon Account of my not holding the Office to which I was appointed (for I desire no reward) but on this account that the Colonel who is not One of the Committee should take upon himself to sett aside a Resolve that was made and passed by the whole Committee of West Chester County, I for my part can not, nor will not, put up with such an insult. I have left the Committee and will not return to it till this matter is fairly settled by the Congress.

Col. Thomas's motives for not coming to a settlement are obvious to me. The money is spent and he does not chuse to undergo an examination. I have sufficient reason to think this to be the case. I would therefore request of you to lay this Matter before the Congress and have an Order made out to this Committee or to the Committee of safety, that Colonel Thomas does in consequence of my appointment deliver into my hands his account fairly stated with all the Vouchers and the ballance that may be due from him to the Committee. I could wish it might be done as soon as possible; if you are not active in this Matter, the Colonel and that party will rejoice and bid defiance to us. Consider this matter well, and I am sure you will not then be inactive.[7]

Papa has for severall days been very unwell and I am affraid that unless there is a speedy change for the better, that he will not be long with us. God grant it may be otherwise.

Adieu my Dear Jack. Remember me to Sally. Peggys love to her and the little Boy, and beleive me to be with Sincerity Your Affectionate Brother

FRED JAY

P.S. Papa and Mama seem anxious to see you.

ALS. Addressed: "To John Jay Esqr. at Fish Kills." Endorsed.

[1] Letter not located.

[2] SLJ.

[3] JJ's parents.

[4] At this time Peter Jay and his wife were at Harrison's Purchase, a few miles north of their farm at Rye. On 22 September Peter Jay wrote to approve JJ's plan to rent a farm at Fishkill belonging to Dr. Theodorus Van Wyck (1730–89) for the family's use. In this same letter Peter Jay expressed a desire to move to Fishkill as soon as possible. On 19 October JJ informed SLJ that he would travel to Rye the next day "in order to remove the Family," and the same day Frederick Jay wrote from Harrison's Purchase to tell JJ that "Papa has directed me to have all the stock removed from Rye to Fish Kills." Peter Jay to JJ, 22 Sept. 1776; JJ to SLJ, and Frederick Jay to JJ, 19 Oct. 1776 in JP.

[5] On 16 September the Provincial Congress ordered Lewis Morris to leave the Continental Congress and return to his brigade in Westchester County. *JPC*, I, 626–27.

[6] On 16 July 1776 the Provincial Convention named Thomas Thomas

(1745–1824) of Rye colonel of a militia regiment which was "to go into immediate service." Colonel Thomas's older brother, John Thomas, Jr. (b. 1732), and Frederick Jay represented Rye on the Westchester County Committee. *JPC*, I, 526; Charles W. Baird, *History of Rye* (New York, 1871), pp. 492–93.

7 *JPC* reveal no action in this matter.

TO CATHARINE W. LIVINGSTON

Fish Kill, 8th November 1776

My much respected and very *respectful* Sister

Your Letter dated on some Wednesday in October last came to Hand when I was so engaged as to be deprived of the Pleasure of acknowledging the Reciept of it.[1] My Fathers Family with such of their Effects as have escaped the Ruin to which the Property of the Whigs in that Part of the Country was exposed, are now here. Sally returned two Days ago from the Manor in much better Health than she went. Her appetite is as good as any Body's. The Rheumatism still *vexes her Bones,* tho less than formerly.

How shall we contrive to remove your little Friend to the Arms of his Mother? I am sure my Father and Mother are desirous of seeing him, tho they appear unwilling that he should be exposed to the Fatigue and Trouble of the Journey. If I could have three or four Leisure Day's I should certainly fetch him, and I am not certain that it will not be in my Power before the End of the Month. It will however not be without Reluctance, for I am so well convinced of the kind Attention paid him by his Grandmama and Aunts, that I am persuaded it is impossible to change his Situation for the better.

The Cravat you was so kind as to purchase (for which accept my Thanks) came safe. I wish Sally's Fur Gown may be as fortunate, but that continues uncertain, as the Movements of military People often depend as much on adventitious Circumstances as more uniform Principles.

The Enemy's Army is retreating to I know not where. Perhaps to a *less mountainous* Country. Some suspect they are going into Winter Quarters which I think improbable.

Brockholst was at the Manor before Sally left it in exceeding good Health and much improved. He is a fine young Fellow, and will do Honor to the Family.[2]

Sally took so little *Thought for the Morrow* as to bring only one pair of Shoes with her. They are almost worn out, and Shoemakers are as scarce here as Saints were in Sodom. Be so obliging as to get a

Copple of neat Pair, at any Price, made for her, and send them by the first good opportunity.

Thank Mama for th Rice etc. she sent us.

Our Love to all the Family.

I am Dear Cate, or Catherine or Kitty your affectionate Brother

JOHN JAY

P.S. Sally has read this Letter. She directs me to subjoin the following explanatory note vizt "The Rheumatism is now only in her Right Hand. Her Bone Waistcoat, and purple and white Calico Gown and the Cuffs thereunto belonging would be very acceptable to her."

ALS. MHi: Ridley Papers. Endorsed.

[1] Letter not located.

[2] In the spring of 1776 Henry Brockholst Livingston joined the Army at Albany as Philip Schuyler's aide-de-camp with the rank of major.

To Robert Morris

Fish Kill, 19 November 1776

Dear Sir

The late unfortunate Miscarriage of General Washingtons Letters to the Congress makes me anxious about the Fate of a Letter I wrote you the 6th Ultimo enclosing Copies of two I had recieved from Mr. Dean.[1] My Letter was sent to Head Quarters to go with the Generals Dispatches. Be so kind as to inform me whether you ever recieved it.

I am Dear Sir, Your most obedient Servant

JOHN JAY

P.S. Colonel Williams passed through this Place Yesterday and reported that your firm and stable Body were not a little alarmed at the Apprehensions of Gen. How's paying them a Visit.[2] These Tales make bad Impressions on vulgar Minds.

ALS NjMoInd: Lloyd Smith Coll. Addressed: "Free, Robert Morris Esqr. General Congress Philadelphia." Endorsed.

[1] For the interception of Washington's letters, see John Hancock to Washington, 9 Nov. 1776, *LMCC*, II, 136–37. For a summary of Morris's letter of 6 Oct. 1776, see above, Morris to JJ, 23 Sept. 1776, n. 2.

[2] Colonel William Williams (1731–1811) of Connecticut began his journey home from the Continental Congress in the second week of November 1776. A report had spread through Philadelphia that a fleet of British vessels had sailed from New York bound for Philadelphia, and the Congress adjourned to Baltimore on 9 December. *LMCC*, II, xl, 156–57; *JCC*, VI, 1015.

FROM EDWARD RUTLEDGE

Philadelphia, November 24th, 1776

My dear Jay

I expected long e'er this to have been seated quietly at Home; but the Progress which the Enemy had made and seemed likely to make into your Country, induced me to suspend my Resolution which I came to several Months ago, and assist with the whole of my Power (little enough God knows) a State which appeared to be marked for Destruction. The Storm however has past over you; and (though I have Reason to dread its bursting upon the Heads of my Countrymen) I cannot but most sincerely congratulate you upon the Event.[1] I wish you may improve the Time, and if you concur with me in Sentiment it will be improved in the following Manner.

Let Schuyler whose Reputation has been deeply wounded by the Malevolence of party Spirit immediately repair to Congress, and after establishing himself in the good Opinion of his Countrymen, by a fair and open Enquiry into his Conduct, concert with the House such a Plan as he shall think will effectually secure *all* the upper Country of New York against the Attacks of the Enemy, which Plan being agreed to by the House, give him full Powers to effect it and send him off with all possible Dispatch to carry it into Execution.[2] Let Steps be taken to place *real* Obstructions in the North River at least in that part of it which can be commanded by Fort Montgomery and the other Fort in the High Lands.[3] If these things be done and that soon, your Country I think will be safe, provided you establish, a good Government, with a strong Executive. A pure Democracy may possibly do when patriotism is the ruling Passion, but when a State abounds in Rascals (as is the case with too many at this day) you must suppress a little of that Popular Spirit, vest the executive Powers of Government in an individual that they may have Vigor, and let them be as ample as is consistent with the great Outlines of Freedom.

As several of the Reasons which operated against you, or Livingstons quitting your State are now removed, I think you would be of vast Service in Congress. You know that Body possesses its Share of human Weakness, and that it is not impossible for the Members of that House to have their Attention engrossed by Subjects which might as well be postponed for the present, whilst such as require Dispatch have been,—I had almost said,—neglected. This may be the case with the Measures which should be taken for the Defence of your State. It is therefore your Interest and your Duty, if you are not prevented by some superior public Concern, to attend the House, and that soon; You have a Right to demand their Attention, and I think they will give you early Assistance.

Every Intelligence from New York for the last ten Days convincing me that the Enemy are preparing to attack my State with a large Body of Troops.[4] I shall take the Wings of the Morning, and hasten to my native Home; where I shall endeavour to render my Country more Service in the Field than I have been able to render her in the Cabinet. I have therefore very little Time to write, and none to lengthen this Letter. I could not however think of quitting this part of the Continent without writing you what appeared to me of Consequence, especially when I consider that it is probable, or at least possible, that this may be the last Time I may have it in my Power to give you any Evidence of my Affection. I shall add no more than that you have my best Wishes, for your Happiness and that if I fall in the Defence of my Country it will alleviate my Misfortune to think that it is in support of the best of Causes, and that I am esteemed by one of the best of Men. God bless you. Adieu my Friend.

Yours Sincerely

E. RUTLEDGE

ALS. Endorsed. Tr in NN: Bancroft, Amer. Rev., I, 277.

[1] Following the Battle of Long Island the British landed on Manhattan, where they were temporarily repulsed by the Americans at the Battle of Harlem Heights in mid-September. Lord Howe outflanked the Continental forces by landing on the mainland, and the Americans were forced to withdraw to Westchester County where the opposing armies clashed at White Plains on 25 October. Following Washington's withdrawal from positions there, Howe wheeled southward to attack Fort Washington at the northern end of Manhattan. The fall of that fortress on 16 November was a serious setback for the American cause, and forced Washington's withdrawal across New Jersey.

[2] American forces in Canada were in continual retreat after May 1776 when a British fleet arrived in the St. Lawrence. Schuyler, the commander of the Northern Department, was subjected to harsh criticism and submitted his resignation to Congress on 14 September. While Congress refused to accept Schuyler's resignation in a vote taken on 2 October, the New York commander was exposed to even more bitter attacks later that month when a squadron assembled by Benedict Arnold was destroyed in an engagement with the British on Lake Champlain. Schuyler to President of Congress, 14 Sept. 1776, DNA: PCC, 153, III, 368–71; *JCC*, V, 841; Don R. Gerlach, *Philip Schuyler and the American Revolution in New York, 1733–1777* (Lincoln, Neb., 1964), p. 288.

[3] Forts Montgomery and Clinton guarded the Hudson Highlands.

[4] Rutledge's fears were unfounded. After the British defeat at Charleston in June 1776, the enemy did not undertake major military operations in the South again until late 1778.

FROM ALEXANDER McDOUGALL

Peeks Kill, December 2d, 1776

My dear Sir,

I have much to say to you, which the moveable State of the army prevented and still prevents. General Lee in Consequence of Positive orders from General Washington, is to Cross the north river to Jersey to morrow, with about three small Brigades of the Continental army,[1] illy cloathed, many of the men without Blankets, Shirts or Shoes. Mine is the most wanting in those articles. Those troops have been so fatigued in marching from the Plains[2] by rains and deep roads that they are almost beat out; and to continue a forced march of near 100 Miles will ruine them. In the present low and dissolved State of the army, its Idle to attempt an attack on the Enemy. All that should be aimed at, with any tolerable prospect of Success, ought to be to take Strong Posts to Stop the progress of the Enemy, and bend our utmost attention to recruiting our army. Instead of this we are carr[y]ing the most of the officers who are to effect it out of the Country where alone it can be done; and harrassing the Troops the last moment of the Campaign, to deter them, by Severe toil and Service from reenlisting.

Sir I tremble for the Consequences. The levi[e]s will be greatly retarded by this mov[e]ment. God grant this may be the worst Consequence of this moment. General Spincer[3] with a few Militia is the only force now below Crotten river, except about 400 men General Woster[4] has about Mamarinek, And these a Squadron of light Horse and three Companies of light Troops would frighten out of the County, which will soon below that be all under the command of the Enemy. The High lands Should be better guarded than I fear they will be in the Course of the winter. The Northern expedition cost me my eldest Son; and the other Ranald S. McDougall was made a Prisoner in Canada.[5] He is now on his Parole to Governor Carlton; and is extreamly uneasey, least he should be called opon to deliver himself up. As he was at the taking of the Prisoners, taken at St Johns, whenever they are released, he is entituled to the Benefit of them in preference to those, who were not there; and who have been prisoners for a much less time than he has. I have therefore to beg you, to write to Congress in his behalf, least he should in the exchange of those prisoners be forgot; the sooner you do it, the more you will oblige me.[6] He was a Second Lieut. in my old Regiment. If I should do otherwise than well I pray remember this boy. Mr John Laurence, my son in Law is now Paymaster to my old Regiment; but as it will soon be dissolved, I spoke to Col Livingston of the 4th[7] to get him appointed for his. He assured me he would write to convention on the Subject. If he has, I should be glad you would Speak to the members, if it should be judged Necessary. May God bless you, and Save my bleeding distressed Country.

I am your affectionate

ALEXR. McDOUGALL

ALS. Addressed: "To John Jay Esquire Member of Convention Fish Kills." Endorsed. Tr in NN: Bancroft, Amer. Rev., I, 289. In October McDougall's brigade became a part of the division commanded by Charles Lee after Lee's return from South Carolina. This unit fought at the Battle of White Plains, 28 October, and remained with Lee at Peekskill after Washington and the main army left for New Jersey.

1 As early as 20 November Washington had urged Lee to bring his troops to the west bank of the Hudson, but Lee ignored his commander's urgent requests and did not begin his leisurely move south until December.

2 White Plains.

3 Joseph Spencer.

4 Brigadier General David Wooster was recalled from Canada in June 1776. Because of his proven incompetence in that command, Wooster was given no new assignment in the Continental Army, but was reappointed a major general in the Connecticut militia and commanded state troops on that border in the winter of 1776.

5 First Lieutenant John McDougall of the 1st New York Reg. died near St. Johns in 1775. His younger brother, Ronald, a second lieutenant in the same regiment, was captured at Quebec on 31 Dec. 1775.

6 No letters from JJ to the Congress on the subject of Ronald T. McDougall's exchange have been found. On 28 Dec. 1776 Washington wrote Alexander McDougall: "Your Son was mentioned among the first of our Prisoners that I demanded in Exchange, but Genl. Howe (or Mr. Loring in his absence) sent out others than those I demanded. I have remonstrated to him upon this head, and have assured him that I will send in no more prisoners till he sends out the Paroles of the Officers taken in Canada." *GWF*, VI, 449.

7 John Laurance (1750–1810), the husband of McDougall's daughter Elizabeth, was named paymaster of the 1st New York on 15 Aug. 1776. Henry Beekman Livingston was named colonel of the 4th New York in November 1776 when the New York Convention reorganized the state's regiments under new regulations for the Continental line.

FROM SILAS DEANE

Paris, December 3d, 1776

Dear Jay

If my Letters arrive safe they will give you some Idea of my situation, without Intelligence, without Orders, and without remittances, yet boldly plunging into Contracts, Engagements, and Negotiations, hourly hoping that something will arrive from America.[1] By General *Coudry* I send 30.000 Fusils, 200 pieces of Brass Cannon,

Thirty Mortars, 4000 Tents, and Cloathing for 30.000 Men, with 200 Tons of Gun powder, Lead, Balls etc, etc; by which you may judge we have some friends here.[2]

A War in Europe is inevitable. The Eyes of all are on you, and the fear of your giving up or Accommodating is the greatest Obstacle I have to Contend with. Mons Beaumarchais has been my Minister in effect, as this Court is extreme cautious, and I now Advise you to Attend Carefully to the Articles sent you. I could not examine them here. I was promised they should be good and at the lowest prices, and that from persons in such station that had I hesitated it might have ruined my affairs. But as in so large a Contract there is room for imposition, my Advice is that you send back to me samples of the Articles sent you—Cannon, Powder, etc Mortars etc are Articles known, but of the Cloths the Fusils etc by which any imposition may be detected.

Large remittances are Necessary for your Credit and The enormous price of Tobacco, of Rice, of Flour and many other Articles, gives you an Opportunity of making Your remittances to very great Advantage. 20.000 Hogs Heads of Tobacco are wanted immediately for this Kingdom, and more for other parts of Europe.

I have wrote you on several subjects some of which I will Attempt briefly to recapitulate Tho I have but a Drop of Ink having received none from your Brother. The destruction of the Newfoundland Fishery, may be effected, by Two or Three of your Frigates, sent there early in February, and by that means a fatal blow given to G Britain I mean by destroying the Stages, Boats etc and bringing away the People left there as Prisoners. Glasgow in Scotland, may be plundered and burnt with ease, as may Liverpool, by two or three stout Frigates, which may find a shelter and protection in the ports of France and Spain afterwards. Blank Commissions are wanted here to cruise under your Flag against the British Commerce. This is a Capital Stroke and must bring on a War. Hasten them out I pray you. France, and Spain, are Freindly, and you will greatly oblige the Latter, by seizing the Portuguese Commerce, Wherever it is found. I have had overtures from the King of Prussia in the Commercial Way and have sent a person of great Confidence [to][3] his Court in person, with Letters of Introduction from his Agent here with whom I am on the best terms.[4] A Loan may be Obtained, if you make punctual remittances for the sum[5] now Advanced, for any Sum at five Per Cent Interest perhaps for less. The Western Lands ought to be held up to View as an encouragement for your soldiers, especially Foreigners and are a good fund to raise Mony on. You may if you judge proper, have any number of German, and Swiss Troops. They have been Offered me but you know I have no power to treat. A Number of Frigates may be purchased at Leghorn, The Great Duke of Tuskany being zealously in favor of America, and doing all in his power to encourage its Commerce. Troubles are rising in Ireland and with a little Assistance, much work may be cut out for G Britain there, by sending from hence a few Preists, a little Money, and plenty of Arms. *Omnia Tentanda* is my Motto, Therefore I hint they[6] playing their own Game on them by spiriting up the Caribbs in St. Vincents, and the Negroes in Jamaica to revolt.

On all These Subjects I have wrote to you—also on Various particulars of Commerce. Our Vessels have more Liberty in the ports of France, and Spain, and Tuscany, than the Vessels of any other Nations and that Openly.

I presented the Declaration of independancy to this Court after it had indeed become an Old Storey in every part of Europe. It was well received, but as you say you have Articles for Alliance under Consideration any resolution must be deferred untill We know what they are.[7] The want of Intelligence has more than once well nigh ruined my affairs. Pray be more Attentive to this important subject, or drop at once all Thoughts of a Foreign Connection. I must mention some Trifles. The Queen is fond of parade, and I believe wishes a War, and is our Friend. She loves riding on horseback, could you send me a fine Narragansett Horse or Two. The present might be Money exceedingly well laid out. Rittenhouses Orrery, or Arnolds Collection of Insects,[8] a Phaeton of American make and a pair of Bay Horses, A few barrells of Apples, of Walnutts, of Butter Nutts etc would be great Curiosities here where everything American is gazed at and where the American Contest engrosses the Attention of all Ages, Rank and Sexes.

Had I Ten Ships here I could fill them all with passengers for America. I hope the Officers sent will be Agreeable. They were recommended by the Ministry here, and are at this instant really in their Army but this must be a secret. Do you want heavy Iron Cannon, Sea Officers of distinction or ships your special Orders will enable me to procure them. For the situation of Affairs, in England refer you to Mr. Rogers Aid De Camp to Mons du Coudry.[9]

I have presented a Number of Memorials[10] which have been very favorably received, and the last by his Majesty, but my being wholly destitute of other than Accidental and gratuitous Assistance will not permit my sending you Copies as they are lengthy. Indeed I was obliged to make them so to explain the rise, the Nature, and the progress of the dispute. I have been assured from the Ministers that I have thrown much light on the subject and have Obviated many Difficulties. But his Majesty is not of the Disposition of his Great Grand Father Louis 14th. If he was, England would soon be ruined. Do not forget, or omit, sending me blank Commissions for Privateers, under these, infinite damage may be done, to the British Commerce, and as the prizes must be sent to you, for Condemnation, the eventual profits, will remain with you.

Tell Mrs Trist that her Husband, and Capt. Fowler, were well, the 16th instant I had a Letter from the latter.[11] Pray be careful who You trust in Europe. One Williamson a Native of Pennsylvania is here as a spy, yet I believe he Corresponds with very good People on your side of the Water.[12] The Villain returns to London once in about six Weeks to discharge his Budget.

Doctr. Bancroft has been of very great service to Me. No Man has better Intelligence in England in my Opinion but it costs something.[13]

The following Articles have been shewn to me. They have been seen by both the Courts of France, and Spain, and I send them to you for speculation.[14]

1st. The Thirteen United Colonies now known by [the Name of][15] the Thirteen United States of North America shall be acknowledged, by France, and Spain, and treated with as Independant States and as such shall be guarantead in the possession of all that part of the Continent of North America, which by the last Treaty of Peace was ceded, and Confirmed, to the Crown of Great Britain.

2d The United States shall guaranty, and Confirm To the Crowns of France, and Spain, all, and Singular, their Possessions, and Claims, in every other part of America, whither North, or South of the Equater, and of the Islands, possessed by them in the American Seas.

3d Should France, or Spain, either, or both of them, possess themselves of the Islands in the West Indies now in possession of the Crown of Great Britain (as an indemnity for the Injuries sustained in the last War in Consiquence of its being Commenced on the part of Great Britain in Violation of the Laws of Nations The United Colonies shall assist The said powers in Obtaining such satisfaction, and Guaranty and Confirm to them the possession of such Acquisition.

4. The Fisheries on the Banks of Newfoundland, of Cape Breton, and parts adjacent commonly known, and called by the Name of the Cod Fishery shall be equally Free to the Subjects of France,

Spain, and the United states[16] of North America and to the subjects of no other State, or Nation. And the Islands of Newfoundland and Cape Breton, equally free to either for curing, and carrying on such Fisherys, under such regulation as may prevent the utmost possibility of any Misunderstanding on the subject.

5. There shall be free Liberty of Commerce, between the subjects of France, and Spain, and the United states respectively, and they shall mutually engage, to protect and Defend each other in such Commerce.

6 The more effectually to preserve this Alliance and to Obtain the great Objection Viz it shall be Agreed, and any and every British ship or Vessel found, or met with, on the Coasts of North America, of South America, or of the Islands, adjacent, and belonging thereto, within a Certain Degree or Distance to be agreed on, shall be for ever hereafter considered as Lawfull prize, to any of the subjects, of France, Spain or the United Colonies, and treated as such as Well in Peace as in War. Nor shall France, Spain, or The United [Colonies][17] ever after admit British Ships into any of their Ports in America North or South, or the Islands Adjacent. This Article never to be altered, or dispenced with, but only by and with The Consent of each of the Three Contracting States.

7 During the Present War, between The United states, and Great Britain, France and Spain shall send into North America and support there a Fleet to defend, and protect The Coasts, and the Commerce of the United states in Consequence of which; if the Possessions of France or Spain shall be Attacked in America by Great Britain, or her Allies, The United Colonies,[18] will Afford them all that Aid and Assistance in their Power.

8 No Peace or Accomodation shall be made with Great Britain, to the infringment or Violation of any one of These Articles.

I have sent you this in secret hand, and am with the utmost impatience to hear from you Dear Sir Your's

S DEANE

ALS (Copy A). Endorsed. Second ALS (Copy B) in JP. Tr in NN: Bancroft, Amer. Rev., I, 297, based largely on Copy A.

1 No other letters from Deane to JJ in 1776 have been located. Deane assumed that JJ was still privy to his dispatches to the Committee of Secret Correspondence.

2 Jean Baptiste Tronson du Coudray (1738–77) was selected to supervise the shipment of arms to the U.S. in late 1776. Deane agreed to commission du Coudray a major general in the Continental Army before du Coudray's voyage from France.

[3] Supplied from Copy B.

[4] In October 1776 William Carmichael (c. 1750–95) of Maryland traveled to the court of Frederick II at Deane's request. Carmichael was "to give the necessary information of the state of the American dispute, and to endeavour to open a correspondence and commerce from thence for the benefit of the United States." Carmichael returned to Paris in December 1776. "The Deane Papers," N.Y.H.S., *Colls.*, XXI, 158.

[5] "Sums" in Copy B.

[6] "The" in Copy B; "they" in Copy A.

[7] Deane presented a copy of the Declaration of Independence to Charles Gravier, comte de Vergennes (1717–87), the French foreign secretary, on 20 Nov. 1776. "The Deane Papers," XIX, 358–59.

[8] David Rittenhouse (1732–96), the Philadelphia clockmaker and astronomer, built his first orrery or mechanical planetarium in 1767. "Arnold" has not been identified. The only American whose entomological collection bore a reputation similar to that of Rittenhouse's orreries was Dr. Alexander Garden (1730–91) of South Carolina. Raymond P. Stearns, *Science in the British Colonies of America* (Urbana, Ill., 1970), pp. 599–619.

[9] Nicholas Rogers, du Coudray's aide, was given the rank of major in the U.S. Army in 1777 and promoted to lieutenant colonel in 1778. According to du Coudray, Rogers was an American recommended to him by Deane. André Lasseray, *Les François sous les treize Étoiles, 1775–1783* (2 vols., Paris, 1935), II, 391–92.

[10] "Memoirs" in Copy B. For examples of the memorials presented by Deane to the French government, see "The Deane Papers," XIX, 184–95, 223–26, 252–85, 361–64.

[11] Mrs. Trist was the daughter-in-law of Mrs. House, Deane's landlady in Philadelphia in 1775 and early 1776. "The Deane Papers," XIX, 25, 45.

[12] For the background of Deane's suspicions concerning Hugh Williamson, see Julian P. Boyd, "Silas Deane: Death by a Kindly Teacher of Treason?" *WMQ*, XVI (April 1959), 186.

[13] Edward Bancroft (1745–1820) was Deane's pupil shortly after Deane's graduation from Yale in 1758. Young Bancroft left Connecticut in 1763 and traveled in the West Indies before settling in Britain in 1766. Bancroft had studied medicine in Connecticut, pursued his studies in Britain, and was awarded an M.D. by the University of Aberdeen in 1774. Bancroft acted as an unofficial agent for Benjamin Franklin during Franklin's stay in London in the 1770's, and Deane's instructions from the Committee of Secret Correspondence urged him "to procure a meeting with Mr. Bancroft." Deane and Bancroft met in Paris in the summer of 1776, and Deane quickly came to rely on Bancroft's advice, unaware that Bancroft was in the pay of the British government and dutifully reported the details of his conversations to the ministry in London long before Deane's dispatches could reach America. For the background of the Deane-Bancroft relationship, see Julian P. Boyd, "Silas Deane: Death by a Kindly Teacher of Treason?," *WMQ*, XVI (April–Oct. 1959), 165–87, 319–42, 515–50.

[14] These articles, purportedly "shewn to" Deane, were actually the same "Articles of a Treaty between France and Spain and the United States" which Deane himself had presented to Conrad Gérard of the French Foreign Office on 23 Nov. 1776. These articles are reprinted in "The Deane Papers," XIX, 361–64.

[15] Supplied from Copy B.

[16] At this point in Copy B, the rest of article 4 is omitted, and the last portion of article 5 is miscopied as the conclusion of the fourth proviso.

[17] Supplied from Copy B.

[18] "States" in Copy B.

Detecting Conspiracies and Determining Loyalty

On 21 September 1776 the New York Convention created a committee "for the express purpose of enquiring into, detecting and defeating all conspiracies which may be formed in this State, against the liberties of America."[1] JJ, William Duer (1747–99) of Charlotte County, Charles De Witt (1727–87) of Ulster, Leonard Gansevoort (1751–1810) of Albany, and Zephaniah Platt (1740–1807) and Nathaniel Sackett of Dutchess County assumed their duties as members of the committee on 28 September.[2] On 11 February 1777 this committee was dissolved and was succeeded by a special commission which fulfilled the same functions.

During the four and a half months in which JJ served on the Committee for Detecting Conspiracies, Nathaniel Sackett supervised an intelligence system of local agents who alerted the Committee to the activities of Loyalist sympathizers and recruiters for the British army. The Committee learned about possible "conspiracies" from these secret agents and from various other sources, and it pursued each report with care, examining witnesses, committing suspects to jail, and weighing the wisdom of paroles and deportation for the prisoners in its custody. These activities are recorded in the minutes of the Committee and its successor Commission, which have been published by the New-York Historical Society.[3]

1 *JPC*, I, 638.

2 Seven more members were added to the committee before the end of January 1777.

3 "Minutes of the Committee and of the First Commission for Detecting and Defeating Conspiracies in the State of New York December 11, 1776–September 23, 1778," N.Y.H.S., *Colls.*, LVII and LVIII. The introduction to this series offers a good summary of the history of the Committee and Commission. The oaths administered involved a pledge of allegiance to the State of New York and an avowal of support for the "General Congress of the United States of America" and the "American States in General." See R. B. Morris, "The Forging of the Union Reconsidered," *Columbia Law Review*, LXXIV (1974), 1087.

The Case of Peter Van Schaack

JJ was one of the four members present on 21 December 1776 when the Committee for Detecting Conspiracies ordered the local authorities in Albany to examine four men presumed to be disloyal. Participating in this first action taken against Peter Van Schaack because of his political beliefs was an unhappy duty for JJ, for the two had been close friends since they studied together at King's College and then became rising young New York City lawyers. Although his public responsibilities forced JJ to play an important role in the series of proceedings that led eventually to Van Schaack's banishment to England, their friendship survived the crisis of the war years. Much later, after Van Schaack had been allowed to come home and had regained his citizenship, he gave strong support to JJ's campaign for the governorship.[1]

Some men feigned neutrality to mask pro-British inclinations, but Van Schaack was so genuinely impartial that he was utterly immobilized. "Although he decidedly condemned the conduct of the Home government," his son reported, "he was yet opposed to taking up arms in opposition to it." When forced to travel from Kinderhook, to which he had moved in 1775, to make his appearance in Albany, his conscience would not permit him to swear allegiance to the State of New York. He suffered thereafter much the same fate as if he had been an aggressive and scheming Tory. He was sent to Boston, where many men found guilty of disloyalty were being held. From there he was called back for a hearing before the Provincial Convention in Kingston and was then paroled to Kinderhook. He remained there over two years until the Banishing Act of 13 June 1778 forced him to leave the part of New York State that was held by the Patriots. He journeyed to England and did not return to his native land until after the war ended.[2]

During this difficult period in Peter Van Schaack's life, he remained in occasional contact with JJ. In 1776 JJ helped him by forwarding a copy of the instructions to return from Boston, the original having gone astray, but two years later he was unable to oblige when Van Schaack sought permission to take his sick wife to New York City. The men were out of touch with one another between 1778, when Van Schaack left the country, and 1782, when the exile wrote a cautious letter to JJ in Paris. JJ's prompt and warm reply was the beginning of regular correspondence, and they were reunited when JJ made his 1783 visit to London. When Peter Van Schaack returned to the United States in 1785, JJ came aboard his ship in New York harbor to welcome him home.[3]

1 Henry C. Van Schaack, *The Life of Peter Van Schaack, LL.D.* (New York, 1842), pp. 6, 14, 15, 402, 437.

2 *Ibid.*, pp. 51, 54–58, 63, 70–71, 85, 109, 134, 257.

3 *Ibid.*, pp. 77, 95–97, 301–13, 390.

Minutes of the Committee for Detecting Conspiracies

[*Fishkill*], *21 December 1776*

Present: Leonard Gansevoort, Chairman; Zephaniah Platt, John Jay, William Duer, Esqrs.

. . . Whereas this Committee have been credibly informed and have good Reason to believe that David Van Schaack[1] and Peter Van

Schaack Esqrs., Messrs. John Stevenson,[2] Cornelius Glen[3] of the City and County of Albany have long maintained an equivocal Neutrality in the present Struggles and are in General supposed unfriendly to the American Cause and from their Influence are enabled to do it essential Injury

Resolved that the Committee of the City and County of Albany be requested to summon the said Persons to appear before them to ask them whether they respectively consider themselves as Subjects of the State of New York, or of the King of Great Brittain, if they answer that they consider themselves as Subjects of the State of New York, then to tender to them the Oath of Allegiance and on their taking and subscribing the same to Discharge them; but if they should Answer that they consider themselves as Subjects of the King of Great Brittain or refuse to take the Oath aforesaid then to remove them, under the Care of some discreet Officer to the Town of Boston at their own Expence and there to remain on their Parole of Honour 'till the further Order of this Committee or the Convention or future Legislature of this State—and that Copy of their parole be sent to the Select Men of the said Town of Boston.

Resolved that a Copy of the Oath of Allegiance and the Parole aforesaid be sent to the Committee of the City and County of Albany.

Ordered that the Chairman write to the said Committee and inclose the above.

D. NHi.

1 David Van Schaack refused to take the oath of loyalty at Albany in September 1778. He was held under arrest there and in Fishkill and Goshen before being turned over to the British in an exchange of prisoners. He was allowed to return to New York in 1784. *GCP*, IV, 58; VI, 142–43, 232–34, 514, 517–19; Lorenzo Sabine, *Biographical Sketches*, II, 381.

2 The name of John Stevenson, merchant, appears on a 4 Aug. 1778 list of men who had refused to take the oath in Albany. He was apparently banished, because there is a record of his being allowed back into the state in 1784. *GCP*, III, 605; Sabine, *Biographical Sketches*, II, 582.

3 Cornelius Glen, another Albany merchant, was cited on 4 Aug. 1778 for refusing to take the oath. *GCP*, III, 605.

The Case of Enoch Crosby, Professedly Cooper's *Spy*

Readers of historical novels are bound to speculate about the extent to which plot and character development are based on actual people and events, and this was notably true after James Fenimore Cooper's *The Spy: A Tale of the Neutral Ground* was published in 1821. Suspecting that the patriot secret agent Harvey Birch was not completely a product of Cooper's imagination, the curious public sought to uncover the real person whom the author had selected as his model.[1] Several claimants were brought forward, but the one whose credentials seemed most authentic was Enoch Crosby (1750–1835), a resident of Carmel in Putnam County who had posed as a Tory during the Revolution in order to collect information about persons suspected of aiding the British in and near Westchester County, the area in which the action of the book took place. In this capacity he had worked under the Committee and later the Commission for Detecting Conspiracies. Crosby himself felt that he had been the inspiration for Harvey Birch, and this theory was advanced with great vigor by H. L. Barnum in *The Spy Unmasked; or, Memoirs of Enoch Crosby; alias Harvey Birch, the Hero of Mr. Cooper's Tale of the Neutral Ground,* appearing in 1828.[2]

Cooper's introduction to the 1831 edition of *The Spy* revealed that the idea for his protagonist had in fact been suggested by an anecdote told to him years previously by "an illustrious man, who had been employed in various situations of high trust during the darkest days of the American revolution."[3] While acting as chairman of a secret committee to root out pockets of subversion, this gentleman had employed a shrewd, fearless secret agent who gave the impression of being a Loyalist in order to learn as many secrets of the enemy as possible. Although the novelist did not identify the storyteller, the description of the man's wartime activities makes it clear that he was JJ, who was one of Cooper's close friends.[4] JJ in his turn declined to reveal the name of his spy, but it is logical to conclude that Enoch Crosby was that person.

Although James Fenimore Cooper was willing to confess his debt to JJ for suggesting the character called Birch, he could never see any possible connection between Birch and Crosby. Writing to an unknown correspondent on 21 August 1850, he stated that "I know nothing of such a man as Enoch Crosby, never having heard his name, until I saw it coupled with the character of the Spy, after my return from Europe."[5] Writing in later years, Susan Cooper, the novelist's daughter, conceded that "the conversation with Governor Jay was the sole foundation of the character of Harvey Birch," but she maintained that her father had invented "every incident in the book" except for the use he made of JJ's brief anecdote, and she stated flatly that Mr. Cooper "never for a moment believed that Enoch Crosby was the man."[6]

Most people, including historians of Westchester County, remained satisfied that H. L. Barnum had unmasked the true spy, but denials by the Cooper family gave rise to some feeling that Crosby might have been an impostor.[7] In two magazine articles in 1887, Guy Hatfield attacked the notion that there could have been a connection between Crosby and Birch, and he rested a good deal of his case on the position Susan Cooper had taken.[8] A prompt refutation came from James Deane, who had just republished Barnum's book. He pointed out that James Fenimore Cooper admitted getting the basic idea for his secret agent from JJ and that the latter's chairmanship of the Committee for Detecting Conspiracies had indubitably provided him with a reason to have intimate contact with Enoch Crosby. Granted that some other spy employed by the committee might possibly have provided the model, Crosby looked like the logical candidate because many of his experiences were similar to occurrences related by JJ. Crosby considered himself the original of Cooper's hero, and so did knowledgeable contemporaries. Finally, Deane emphasized, JJ appears never to have questioned Barnum's claims for Crosby.[9]

A sophisticated attack on the belief that Enoch Crosby's career influenced James Fenimore Cooper was mounted by Tremaine McDowell in 1930. Conceding that the claim for Crosby might possibly contain merit, McDowell cast serious doubt on it by a detailed analysis of the available facts. Crosby had been only one of eleven men functioning as agents for the Revolutionary government in Westchester, and there was no conclusive resemblance between any one of them and the man JJ described to Cooper. McDowell demonstrated that Barnum had added so many fictitious details to Crosby's story as to make all of it suspect. Cooper did not follow the story as he received it from JJ. Harvey Birch and Enoch Crosby were much more dissimilar than they were similar, and thus the latter was not at all likely to have been the prototype for the former.[10]

Another way to discredit Enoch Crosby's claim is to identify somebody else as the true model for Harvey Birch, and Warren S. Walker offered not just one model but two in "The Prototype of Harvey Birch." This article called attention to two Long Islanders, Abraham Woodhull of Setauket and Robert Townsend of Oyster Bay, who worked together as spies under the direction of Major Benjamin Tallmadge and who both used the alias Samuel Culper. Tallmadge married Mary Floyd, who was a cousin of Mrs. James Fenimore Cooper, and it was Walker's not unreasonable presumption that this relationship should have made the novelist familiar with the wartime exploits of this team of spies. There are some convincing parallels between what happened to them and events in *The Spy*. Townsend's occupation as an itinerant merchant made it possible for him to move around constantly without attracting suspicion; Harvey Birch derived the same advantage from being a peddler. Woodhull operated in predominantly Loyalist territory, as did Birch, and his friends, the Floyds, had much in common with the Whartons in *The Spy*. Cooper's secret agent refused reimbursement for his services; Townsend was never paid. There are other suggestive similarities, but there are also some serious weaknesses in Walker's argument. The twin agents did their work on Long Island, not in Westchester. They never posed as royal agents. Townsend may never have been paid, but Woodhull was. Taken altogether, Walker's thesis is provocative but not really convincing.[11]

In *Turncoats, Traitors and Heroes* John Bakeless gave unqualified support to Enoch Crosby, calling attention to the specific details about his wartime service contained in his 1832 application for a federal pension and the extent to which experiences described in that document are confirmed by entries in *Minutes of the Committee and First Commission for Detecting and Defeating Conspiracies in the State of New York.*[12]

The argument about the origin of James Fenimore Cooper's spy will never be resolved, because two vital points cannot be clarified. Only JJ could have said whether or not he was thinking of Enoch Crosby when he told Cooper about the secret agent he had employed, and this he never did. Only Cooper could have confessed the extent to which he was obliged to JJ for the character of Harvey Birch. Although the debate will continue, there are some aspects of it about which there can be agreement. Enoch Crosby described his activities as a spy very clearly in his 1832 deposition, and many of his claims are confirmed by the minutes of the Committee for Detecting Conspiracies. These committee records were not published until 1924, and Crosby could have had no access to them in their unpublished form, so we can be certain that he was in fact the spy he claimed to be. These same minutes also establish that JJ knew a good deal about Crosby and his wartime espionage activities. Finally, there is no question that the novelist got at least the germ of the idea of Harvey Birch from JJ, as both Cooper and his daughter admitted.

Given these facts and considering what has been said both for and against Enoch Crosby, it does not seem imprudent to suggest that JJ described Crosby to Cooper, who built on that description to create the hero of *The Spy.* The author necessarily added depth to the personality of his protagonist and invented a plot sufficiently complex to sustain reader interest through a full-length novel, but the idea for Harvey Birch came from JJ. Knowing what we do, the argument that Birch was made up out of thin air seems specious. It is equally unsatisfactory to look elsewhere for Cooper's inspiration, as for example to the Long Islanders Townsend and Woodhull. The logical conclusion is that JJ made an important contribution to American literature by supplying the nation's first successful novelist with the concept for the hero of his first successful book.

Regardless of his connection, if any, with Cooper's famous protagonist, Enoch Crosby was unquestionably the most effective of the secret agents employed by the Committee for Detecting Conspiracies. We find him, in the excerpt from the minutes of that body reproduced below, being ordered to break up a Tory recruiting ring. He did this successfully several times, as his 1832 application for a veteran's pension relates. This sworn testimony describes his service in 1775 in a Connecticut regiment in the invasion of Canada and three enlistments in New York units in 1776, 1779, and 1780. His career as a spy, which was an accidental by-product of his 1776 enlistment, appears below.

[1] William Howard Garrison's review of the novel in *The North American Review,* XV (July 1822), 259, described Harvey Birch as "not wholly without historical foundation" but did not attempt to name the person on whom he was based.

[2] (New York, 1828).

[3] (London), pp. vii–x.

4 Susan Cooper, "Small Family Memories," ed. by James Fenimore Cooper, *Correspondence of James Fenimore-Cooper* (2 vols., New Haven, 1922), I, 40.

5 *Ibid.*, II, 684.

6 Susan Cooper, "A Glance Backward," *Atlantic Monthly,* LIX (February 1881), 204; Susan Cooper, "Small Family Memories," ed. by Cooper, *James Fenimore-Cooper,* I, 42; Guy Hatfield, "Harvey Birch Not Enoch Crosby," *Magazine of American History,* XVIII (Oct., 1887), 341.

7 Local historians accepted H. L. Barnum without question and thus uniformly celebrated Enoch Crosby as the inspiration for Cooper's hero. Among these were William S. Pelletreau, whose genealogy of the Crosby family appeared in the 1887 edition of Barnum's book; Harry Edward Miller, "The Spy of the Neutral Ground," *New England Magazine,* XVIII (May, 1898), 307–19. Frederic Shonnard and W. W. Spooner, *History of Westchester County, New York* (New York, 1900), p. 420; Robert Bolton, *A History of the County of Westchester* (2 vols., New York, 1905), I, 75.

8 "Harvey Birch and the Myth of Enoch Crosby," *Magazine of American History,* XVII (May 1887), 431–43; "Harvey Birch Not Enoch Crosby," *Magazine of American History,* XVIII (Oct., 1887), 341.

9 "Enoch Crosby Not a Myth," *Magazine of American History,* XVIII (July 1887), 73–75.

10 The Identity of Harvey Birch," *American Literature,* II (May 1930), 111–20.

11 *New York History,* CIV (October 1956), 399–413. See also his foreword in *The Spy* (New York, 1960), pp. 10–11. The identity of the two Samuel Culpers had been previously established by Morton Pennypacker in *The Two Spies, Nathan Hale and Robert Townsend* (Boston, 1930).

12 (Philadelphia, 1959), pp. 136–40; (2 vols., New York, 1924–25), I, 27, 47, 48, 80, 93–94, 158–59, 160, 165, 265; II, 420. Crosby's deposition was published in its entirety in James H. Pickering, "Enoch Crosby, Secret Agent of the Neutral Ground: His Own Story," *New York History,* XLVII (January 1966), 61–73, and it shows that the old man had retained a surprisingly accurate recollection of events and the order in which they occurred, although he was understandably off a bit with respect to dates.

Minutes of the Committee for Detecting Conspiracies

[Fishkill], December 23rd, 1776

Present: Leonard Gansevoort Esqr. Chairman; John Jay, Zephaniah Platt, Nathaniel Sacket, Esqrs.

Resolved that Enoch Crosby assuming the Name of [———][1] do forthwith repair to Mount Ephraim and use his utmost Art to discover the designs, Places of Resort, and Route, of certain disaffected Persons in that Quarter, who have formed a Design of Joining the Enemy, and that for that Purpose the said Enoch be made acquainted with all the Information received by this Committee concerning this Plan, and that he be furnished with such Passes as will enable him to pass there without interruption, and with such others as will enable him to pass as an Emissary of the Enemy amongst Persons disaffected to the American Cause.

Resolved that Enoch Crosby be furnished with an Horse, and the Sum of Thirty Dollars in order to enable him to execute the above Resolution.

Resolved that Mr. Nathaniel Sackett be requested to give such Instructions to Enoch Crosby as he shall think best calculated to defeat the Designs of the Persons above mentioned.

Ordered that the Treasurer pay Enoch Crosby Thirty Dollars for secret Services. . . .

Resolved that Nathaniel Sacket Esqr. be requested to furnish Mr. Enoch Crosby with such Cloathing as he may stand in Need of.

D. NHi.
[1] Blank space in manuscript.

Enoch Crosby Describes His Career as a Spy

Southeast, Putnam County, 15 October 1832

In the latter part of the month of August in the year 1776 he enlisted into the regiment commanded by Col Sworthaut[1] in Fredericksburgh now Carmel in the County of Putnam and started to join the army at Kingsbridge. The company had left Fredericksburgh before declarent started, and he started alone after his said enlistment and on his way at a place in Westchester County about two miles from Pines bridge he fell in company with a stranger, who accosted the deponent and asked him if he was going *down.* Declarent replied he was. The stranger then asked if declarent was not afraid to venture alone, and said there were many rebels *below* and he would meet with difficulty in *getting down.* The declarent perceived from the observations of the stranger that he supposed the declarent intended to go to the British and willing to encourage that misapprehension and turn it to the best advantage, he asked if there was any mode which he the stranger could point out by which the declarent could *get through* safely. The stranger after being satisfied that declarent was wishing to join the British army, told him that there was a company raising in that vicinity to join the British army, that it was nearly complete and in a few days would be ready to go *down* and that declarent had better join that company and *go down* with them. The stranger finally gave to the declarent his name, it was Bunker, and told the declarent where and showed the house in which he lived and also told him that ——— Fowler[2] was to be the captain of the company then raising and ——— Kipp[3] Lieutenant. After having learned this much from Bunker the declarent told him that he was unwilling to wait until the company could be ready to march and would try to get *through alone* and parted from him on his way down and continued until night when he stopped at the house of a man who was called Esquire Young,[4] and put up there for the night. In the course of conversation with Esquire Young in the evening declarent learned that he was a member of the committee of safety for the county of Westchester and then communicated to him the information he had obtained from Mr. Bunker, Esqr. Young requested the declarent to accompany him the next morning to the White plains in Westchester County as the committee of safety for the County were on that day to meet at the Court house in that place. The next morning the declarent in company with Esqr. Young went to the White plains and found the Committee there sitting. After Esqr. Young had had an interview with the committee, the declarent was sent for, and went before the committee, then sitting in the Court room, and there communicated the information he had obtained from Bunker. The committee after learning the situation of declarent, that he was a soldier enlisted in Col. Swortwauts regiment and on his way to join it engaged to write to the Colonel and explain the reason why he did not join it if he would consent to aid in the apprehension of the company then raising. It was by all thought best, that he should not join the regiment, but should act in a different character as he could thus be more useful to his country.

He was accordingly announced to Capt. Townsend[5] who then was at the White plains commanding a company of rangers as a prisoner, and the Captain was directed to keep him until further orders. In the evening after he was placed as a prisoner under Capt. Townsend, he made an excuse to go out and was accompanied by a soldier. His excuse led him over a fence into a field of corn then nearly or quite full grown. As soon as he was out of sight of the soldier he made the best of his way from the soldier and when the soldier hailed him to return he was allmost beyond hearing. An alarm gun was fired but declarent was far from danger. In the course of the night the declarent reached the house of said Bunker, who got up and let him in. Declarent then related to Bunker the circumstance of his having been taken prisoner, of his going before the committee at the Court house, of being put under the charge of Capt. Townsend and of his escape, that he had concluded to avail himself of the protection of the company raising in his neighborhood to get down. The next morning Bunker went with declarent and introduced him as a good loyalist to several of the company. Declarent remained some days with different individuals of the company and until it was about to go down, when declarent went one night to the house of Esqr. Young to give information of the state and progress of the company. The distance was four or five miles from Bunkers. At the house of Esqr. Young declarent found Capt. Townsend with a great part of his company and after giving the information he returned to the neighborhood of Bunkers and that night declarent with a great part of the company which was preparing to go down were made prisoners. The next day all of them about thirty in number were marched to the White plains, and remained there several days, a part of the time locked up in jail with the other prisoners, the residue of the time he was with the committee. The prisoners were finally ordered to Fishkill in the County of Dutchess where the State Convention was then sitting. The declarent went as a prisoner to Fishkill. Capt. Townsend with his company of rangers took charge of the company. At Fishkill a committee for detecting conspiracies was sitting composed of John Jay, afterwards Governor of N York, Zepeniah Platt afterwards first judge of Dutchess County, Colonel Duer of the County of Albany, & a Mr. Sackett. The declarent was called before that committee, who understood the character of declarent and the nature of his services, this the committee must have learned either from Capt. Townsend or from the Committee at White plains. The declarent was examined under oath and his examination reduced to writing.[6] The prisoners with the declarent were kept whilst declarent remained at Fishkill in a building which had been occupied as a Hatters shop and they were guarded by a company of rangers commanded by Capt. Clark.[7] The declarent remained about a week at Fishkill when he was bailed by Jonathan Hopkins. This was done to cover the character in which declarent acted.

Before the declarent was bailed the Fishkill committee had requested him to continue in this service, and on declarent mentioning the fact of his having enlisted in Col. Swortwauts company and the necessity there was of his joining it, he was informed that he should be indemnified from that enlistment, that they would write to the Colonel and inform him that declarent was in their service The committee then wished declarent to undertake a secret service over the river. He was furnished with a secret pass, which was a writing signed by the committee which is now lost and directed to go to the house of Nicholas Brawer[8] near the mouth of the Wappingers creek who would take him across the river, and then to proceed to the house of John Russell about ten miles from the river, and make such inquiries & discoveries as he could. He proceeded according to his directions to said Brawers, and from thence to John Russells, and there hired himself to said Russell to work for him but for no definite time. This was a neighborhood of Loyalists and it was expected that a company was there raising for the British army. The declarent remained about ten days in Russells employment and during that time ascertained that a company was then raising but was not completed. Before declarent left Fishkill on this service a time was fixed for him to recross the river and give information to some one of the committee who was to meet him. This time having arrived and the company not being completed the declarent recrossed the river and met Zepeniah Platt one of the committee and gave him all the information he had then obtained. Declarent was directed to recross the river to the neighborhood of Russells and on a time then fixed, again to meet the committee on the east side of the river. Declarent returned to Russells neighborhood, soon became intimate with the Loyalists, was introduced to Capt Robinson said to be an English officer and who was to command the company then raising. Capt. Robinson occupied a cave in the mountains and deponent having agreed to go with the company was invited and accepted of the invitation to lodge with Robinson in the cave. They slept together nearly a week in the cave and the time for the company to start having been fixed and the rout designated to pass Severns, to Bush Carricks where they were to stop the first night. This time for starting having arrived before the appointed time to meet the committee on the east side of the river, the declarent in order to get an opportunity to convey information to Fishkill, recommended that each man should the night before they started sleep where he chose and that each should be by himself for if they should be discovered that night together all would be taken which would be avoided if they were separated. This proposition was acceded to, and when they separated declarent not having time to go to Fishkill, and as the only and as it appeared to him the best means of giving the information, was to go to a Mr. Purdy who was a stranger to declarent and all he knew of him was that the Tories called him a wicked rebel and said that he ought to die. Declarent went and found Purdy informed him of the situation of affairs, of the time the company was to start and the place at which they were to stop the first night, and requested him to go to Fishkill and give the information to the committee. Purdy assured the declarent that the information should be given. Declarent returned to Russells and lodged in his house. The following evening the company assembled consisting of about thirty men and started from Russells house which was in the Town of Marlborough and County of Ulster for New York and in the course of the night arrived at Bush Carricks and went into the barn to lodge after taking refreshments. Before morning the barn was surrounded by American troops and the whole company including Capt. Robinson were made prisoners. The troops who took the company prisoners were commanded by Capt. Melancton Smith, who commanded a company of rangers at Fishkill. His company crossed the river to perform this service. Col. Duer was with Capt. Smiths Company on this expedition.

The prisoners including the declarent were marched to Fishkill and confined in the stone church in which there was near two hundred prisoners.[9] After remaining one night in the church the Committee sent for declarent and told him that it was unsafe for him to remain with the prisoners, as the least suspicion of the course he had pursued would prove fatal to him, and advised him to leave the village of Fishkill but to remain where they could call upon him if his services should be wanted. Declarent went to the house of a Dutchman a farmer whose name is forgotten about five miles from the Village of Fishkill and there went to work at making shoes. After declarent had made arrangements for working at shoes he informed Mr. Sacket one of the committee where he could be found if he should be wanted. In about a week declarent received a letter from the committee requesting him to meet some one of the Committee at the house of Doct. Osborn[10] about one mile from Fishkill. Declarent according to the request went to the house of Doct. Osborn and soon after John Jay came there, inquired for the Doctor, who was absent, inquired for medicine but found none that he wanted. He came out of the house, and went to his horse near which declarent stood and as he passed he said in a low voice it wont do, there are too many around, return to your work. Declarent went back and went to work at shoes but within a day or two was again notified and a horse sent to him, requiring him to go to Bennington in Vermont and from thence westerly to a place called Maloonscack,[11] and there call on one Hazard Wilcox, a tory of much notoriety and ascertain if anything was going on there injurious to the american cause. Declarent followed his instructions, found Wilcox but could not learn that any secret measure was then projected against the interest of the country at that place, but learned from Wilcox a list of persons friendly to the British cause who could be safely trusted, from that place quite down to the south part of Dutchess County. Declarent followed the directions of said Wilcox and called on the different individuals by him mentioned but could discover nothing of importance until he reached the town of Pawling in Dutchess County where he called upon a

Doctor, whose name he thinks was Prosser, and informed him that he wished to go below, but was fearful of some trouble. The Doctor informed him that there was a company raising in that vicinity to go to New York to join the British Army, that the Captains name was Shelden,[12] that he had been down and got a commission, that he Prosser was doctoring the Lieutenant, whose name was Chase, that if declarent would wait a few days he could safely go down with that company, that he could stay about the neighborhood, and should be informed when the company was ready. That declarent remained in that vicinity, became acquainted with several of the persons who were going with that company, was acquainted with the Lieut. Chase, but never saw the Captain to form any acquaintance with him. The season had got so far advanced that the company were about to start to join the enemy to be ready for an early commencement of the campaign in 1777. It was about the last of February of that year, when a place was fixed and also a time for meeting. It was at a house situated half a mile from the road and about three miles from a house then occupied by Col Morehause[13] a militia Colonel. After the time was fixed for the marching of Capt. Sheldens company the deponent went in the night to Col. Morehause and informed him of the situation of the company of the time appointed for meeting of the place etc. And Morehause informed declarent that they should be attended to. The declarent remained about one month in this neighborhood, and once in the time met Mr. Sackett one of the Committee at Col. Ludingtons,[14] and apprised him of what was then going on, and was to have given the committee inteligence when the company was to march but the shortness of the time between the final arrangement and the time of starting was that declarent was obliged to give the information to Col Morehause.

The company consisting of about thirty met at the time and place appointed and after they had been there an hour or two two young men of the company came in and said there was a gathering under arms at old Morehauses. The inquirey became general, what could it mean, was there any traitors in the company. The captain soon called one or two of the company out the door for the purpose of private conversation about the situation, and very soon declarent heard the cry of stand, stand. Those out the door ran but were soon met by a company coming from a different direction. They were taken the house surrounded and the company all made prisoners. The Colonel then ordered them to be tied together, two and two. They came to declarent and he beged to be excused from going as he was lame and could not travel. The Colonel replied, you shall go dead or alive and if in no other way you shall be carried on the horse with me. The rest were marched off and declarent put onto the horse with Col. Morehause. All went to the house of Col. Morehause and when the prisoners were marched into the house declarent with the permission of Morehause left them and made the best of his way to Col. Ludingtons and there informed him of the operations of the night. He reached Col. Ludingtons about day light in the morning, from thence he went to Fishkill to the house of Doct. Van Wyck[15] where John Jay boarded and there informed him of all the occurrences on that northern expedition. Said Jay requested the declarent to come before the committee the next night when they would be ready to receive him. He accordingly went before the committee where he declared under his oath all that had occurred since he had seen them.[16] The committee then directed him to go to the house of Col. Van Ness in Albany County[17] and there take directions from him. He went to Van Ness's house and was directed by him to go to the North but declarent cannot tell the place the duty was performed, but nothing material discovered, further than that the confiscation of the personal property of the Tories and leasing of their lands had a great tendency to discourage them from joining the British Army. Declarent then returned to Pokeepsie, where Egbert Benson and Melancton Smith acted in the room of the Fishkill committee There was no more business at that time in which they wished to employ declarent, and he being somewhat apprehensive that a longer continuance in that employment would be dangerous, and the time for which he enlisted in Col Swartwauts regiment having expired he came home with the approbation of the committee. This was about the last of May 1777, and in the course of the fall after, the declarent saw Col. Swortwaut at his house in Fishkill and there talked over the subject of the employment of the declarent by the committee and the Colonel told declarent that he had drawn his pay the same as if he had been with the regiment, that the Paymaster of the Regiment lived in the town of Hurley in Ulster County. Declarent went to the paymaster and received his pay for nine months service or for the term for which the regiment was raised. The declarent was employed in the secret service for a period of full nine months.

D. DNA: Records of the Veterans' Bureau, Pension File S-10505.

1 Col. Jacobus Swartwout (d.1826), commander of the 2d Dutchess County Regiment of Minute Men.

2 Jonathan Fowler.

3 James Kipp.

4 Joseph Young, one of the Westchester County Commissioners of Public Safety, lived in the southeastern corner of the town of Mount Pleasant, approxi-

mately six miles from Tarrytown, where the road from Pines Bridge crossed the road linking White Plains and Tarrytown.

5 Captain Micah Townsend of Westchester, commander of a unit known as Townsend's Rangers, which was frequently utilized to arrest local Tories.

6 These minutes do not exist.

7 Captain William Clark, 5th regiment, Dutchess County militia, whose unit often carried out orders issued by the Committee. A letter from Nathaniel Sackett to Peter Van Gaasbeck dated Fishkill, 10 Jan. 1777, connects Captain Clark and Enoch Crosby in a most intriguing manner. "Minutes of the Committee for Detecting Conspiracies," N.Y.H.S., *Colls.*, LVIII, 420:

> I had almost forgot to give you directions to Give our friend an opertunity of making his Escape Upon our plan you will Take him prisoner with his partie you are now wateing for his Name is Enoch Crosby Alias John Brown I could wish that he may escape before you bring him Two miles on your way to Committee you will be pleased to advise with Messrs Cornwill and Capt Clark on this Subject and form such plan of conduct as your wisdom may direct but by no means neglect this friend of ours.

8 Nicholas Brewer, or Brower (d. 1787), a Patriot who reported to the Committee on 30 Dec. 1776 about the suspicious activities of some of his Dutchess County neighbors. See "Minutes of the Committee for Detecting Conspiracies," LVII, 56.

9 The minutes of the Committee for 15 Dec. 1776 report the arrival at Fishkill of Tories arrested for "treasonable Conspiracy."

10 Dr. Cornelius Osborn (1723–82) lived half a mile north of Fishkill village and served as surgeon with Colonel Jacobus Swartwout's regiment.

11 Walloomsac.

12 Enoch Crosby's first meeting with Sheldon is described in "Minutes of the Committee for Detecting Conspiracies," LVII, 164.

13 Colonel Andrew Morehouse, 3d regiment, Dutchess County militia.

14 Colonel Henry Ludington (1739–1817), of the Dutchess County militia.

15 Doubtless Dr. Theodorus Van Wyck, a member of Fishkill's Vigilance Committee.

16 Crosby first reported to the Committee on 8 Jan. 1777 about the subversive activities of Dr. Prosser and his associates. Morehouse arrested them more than a month later, on 26 February. The examination of Joseph Sheldon by the Committee occurred on 28 February, and Crosby testified at the same meeting about the whole episode. "Minutes of the Committee for Detecting Conspiracies," LVII, 93–94, 160–61, 163–64.

17 Probably Colonel Peter Van Ness, 9th regiment, 2d Claverack battalion, of the Albany County militia. He had notified the Committee on 15 Jan. 1777 that there was a plot to rescue prisoners held at Claverack, and Crosby may have been sent to Albany to see what he could learn about the situation. "Minutes of the Committee for Detecting Conspiracies," LVII, 100.

The Case of Beverly Robinson

The appearance of Beverly Robinson before the Committee for Detecting Conspiracies is of particular interest, demonstrating as it does JJ's tact and restraint in dealing with an important man suspected of Tory leanings. JJ knew that Robinson's oldest son had left to join the British, and while not making any effort to conceal his own knowledge, he refrained from cajoling or threatening the witness. Instead, he granted him a generous amount of time to clarify his position.[1]

Born into a prominent Virginia family in 1721, Beverly Robinson had settled by about 1749 in New York City, where he became a merchant in partnership with Oliver De Lancey.[2] His marriage to Susanna Philipse, a cousin of SLJ's mother, made him a member of New York's aristocracy and put him in possession of a considerable fortune. About 1764 he and his family removed to a part of Dutchess County that is now in Putnam County. He lived thereafter at Beverly, the mansion he built across the Hudson River from West Point, cultivating a large farm and operating a grist and saw mill and potash works on a 60,000-acre estate on which there were 146 tenants. His wealth and his services as militia colonel, judge, and founder and principal benefactor of St. Philip's Church in the Highlands established him without a rival as the leading personage in the area.[3]

On 22 February 1777 in his testimony before the Committee Beverly Robinson appeared anxious to remain neutral, but it is difficult to believe that he could have ended up as anything except an active Loyalist. His zealous Anglicanism gave him a predisposition to favor the crown, and several of the people closest to him became avowed Tories. Both of his brothers-in-law, Frederick Philipse and Roger Morris, rejected the American cause, and so did his former business partner, Oliver De Lancey.[4] Beverly Robinson opposed sending Dutchess County delegates to the Provincial Congress in 1777, and he remained inactive and publicly uncommitted as long as possible after the Revolution started.

Robinson was still maintaining his neutralist posture when the Committee examined him, but very shortly thereafter he began to espouse his true position. On 4 March he wrote JJ that he was going down to Colonel Philipse's to discuss the state of the country and that he might or might not return. Upon receipt of that letter, which was forwarded to him by Egbert Benson, JJ wrote the 21 March letter to Robinson's wife that appears below. In it he shows his unwillingness to lose so respected a man to the enemy without one last attempt to persuade him to reconsider.

JJ's friendly warning arrived too late to have any effect, because Beverly Robinson had already started to raise the Loyal American Regiment in New York City. He served as its colonel during the balance of the conflict and played a role in the negotiation between Major André and Benedict Arnold. Robinson's entire estate, valued at £79,980, was forfeited under the terms of the Act of Attainder dated 22 October 1779, and he and his wife arrived in England in 1783 as penniless political refugees. They remained there permanently, and ultimately the British government awarded him £17,000 as partial reimbursement for his losses.

1 JJ had learned from a report received by the Committee 15 Feb. 1777 that Beverly Robinson, Jr., had gone to New York City. Later that year the young man

became a captain in his father's Loyalist regiment, eventually achieving a lieutenant colonelcy. "Minutes of the Committee for Detecting Conspiracies," N.Y.H.S. *Colls.*, LVII, 123, 283; Catherine S. Crary, *The Price of Loyalty* (New York, 1973), pp. 149–50. See Enoch Crosby's description of his career as a spy 15 Oct. 1832, above, for an explanation of the manner in which Crosby broke up Robinson's attempt in 1777 to recruit soldiers for the Loyal American Regiment.

2 Oliver De Lancey (1718–85) enjoyed a successful career as a merchant until June 1776, when he joined General Howe on Staten Island. He raised three Loyalist regiments, was commissioned a brigadier general, and served as commanding officer on Long Island. All of his estates were confiscated, and he died in England. Margherita Hamm, *Famous Families of New York* (2 vols., New York, 1901), I, 94–95.

3 NN: American Loyalists' Claims Transcripts, XLIII, 203–07. An excellent biography of Beverly Robinson will be found in E. Clowes Chorley, *History of St. Philip's Church in the Highlands, Garrison, New York* (New York, 1912), pp. 117–154. Edwin R. Purple, *Contributions to the History of Ancient Families of New Amsterdam and New York* (New York, 1881), pp. 93–98, provides genealogical information about the Robinson and Philipse families.

4 Roger Morris (1727–94), a British officer who had served in the Braddock campaign, married Mary Philipse, with whom he lived at what is now known as the Morris-Jumel Mansion in New York City. Before her marriage she had caught the eye of George Washington when he paid two visits to New York in 1756, staying both times with his friend Beverly Robinson. The Morris properties were all confiscated in 1779, and Colonel Morris and his wife spent their last years in England. Colonel Frederick Philipse (1720–85) was the proprietor of Philipse Manor. In August 1776 Washington ordered him removed to Connecticut because of his dubious loyalty, and Philipse was not allowed to return to his home until December 1776. Purple, *Ancient Families*, pp. 96–97; Thomas Jones, *History of New York During the Revolutionary War*, Edward F. De Lancey, ed. (2 vols., New York, 1879), II, 531.

Minutes of the Committee for Detecting Conspiracies

[Fishkill], February 22, 1777

Beverly Robinson Esqr. appeared before the Committee appointed by the Convention of the State of New York for inquiring into Detecting and Defeating all conspiracies that may be formed against the Liberties of the Same and the Board of Commissioners appointed By the Convention for the Same purpose.

John Jay Esqr. Chairman, Judge Graham,[1] Nathaniel Sackett, Members of the Committee. Colonel Swartwout, Egbert Benson, Malancton Smith, Commissioners.

He was interigated in the following manner Vizt. Mr. Jay. Sir you having observed an Equivocal Neutrality through the Course of your conduct the Committee is at a Loss to know how to Rank you.

Mr. Robinson. Sir it is True, at first I offered my Servis to the publick but they Did not think proper to Chuse me Since which Time

I have made my Self Prisoner on my farm in order to keep myself from a necessity of Expressing my Sentiments.

Mr. Jay. Sir your Son has gone to New York to the enemy.

Mr. Robinson. No Sir he is gone to Long Island.

Mr. Jay. Sir this Committee is informed that when your Son was about Taking a Commission you was much Displeased at it.

Mr. Robinson. I was not Sir, but I believe that committees through their Severity have made a Great many Tories, for it is Natural when a man is hurt to kick.

Mr. Jay. Sir we have passed the Rubicon and it is now necessary every man Take his part, Cast off all alliegiance to the King of Great Britain and take an oath of Alliegiance to the States of america or Go over to the Enemy for we have Declared our Selves Independent.

Mr. Robinson. Sir I cannot Take the Oath but should be exceeding Glad to Stay in the Country, to Inable me to Stay in the Country, and Expecting that there wold be a great Deal of Trouble about the forts in the Spring have already Sent Some of my Goods farther Back in the Country to patersons and I Should be extreemly unhappy in being obliged to go over to the enemy for I have no way to mentain my familey there but I have here. If I go to the enemy can I carry with me any of my effects. It is very uncertain who will Rule yet for the matter is not Determined.

Mr. Jay. Yes Sir undoubtedly you can carry your effects but we Don't Desire you Sir to give your answer now. We would Chuse that you Should take Time to Consider the matter before you give your answer for I can assure you Sir without flattery we Should be exceeding happy to have you with us.

(Mr. Benson then Laboured much to Shew Mr. Robinson the propriety of the measures and the great pleasure it would give us to have him with us.)

Mr. Robinson. How Long before I must give my answer, a Day or Two.

Mr. Jay. No Sir you need not hurry your Self. You can Take a month or Six weeks.

Mr. Robinson. You Gentlemen are not Ingaged on Sundays. Will you come and See me one Sunday.

Mr. Jay. I am obliged to you Sir. I don't Expect to be Long here.

Mr. Benson. I am much obiged to you Sir and will Do myself the Pleasure of Coming to See you one Sunday.

Mr. Robinson then Retired.

D. NNebg: Washington's Headquarters.

1 Lewis Graham (d. 1793) served as a representative from Westchester in the New York Convention, was a lieutenant colonel in the army, and was appointed judge of the Court of Admiralty of New York State in August 1776. *JPC*, I, 302, 556, 566.

From Beverly Robinson

Highlands, March 4th, 1777

Dear Sir

The Information you gave me when I was before the Committee of the Resolution of the Convention, that every person without Exception, must take an Oath of Allegiance to the States of America, or go with their families to the King's Army has given me the greatest concern.[1] I cannot as yet think of forfeiting my Allegiance to the King, and I am as unwilling to remove myself or family, from this Place, or at least out of this Country; under my Anxiety and the perplexity of mind that I am in at present, I am determined to take a Step, that I may be condemned for by Warm and unthinking Persons, but I hope you and every reasonable man will put a more favourable construction on my Conduct.

I have come to the resolution of going down to Col. Philip's in Order to have an opportunity to Conferring with my Friends on the unhappy and distracted State of my poor Bleeding Country and if I am Convinced that a Reconciliation cannot be had upon Just and reasonable Terms, I will return, and content myself to share the same fate with my Country. For you may be assured, that nothing shall ever tempt or force me to do any thing, that I think or have the least reason to believe will be prejudicial to my Country, I may Err for want of better judgment but never will knowingly or designedly. And now Sir as I have wrote so freely to you, I must build some hopes upon our former acquaintance and friendship, as well as on your known good and humane disposition, and desire you will use your Influence, that Mrs. Robinson and the Children may be used with Humanity and tenderness, they would be glad to continue here, but if it should finally be determined that they must be removed, let me intreat that Mrs. Robinson may be allowed to take her necessary furniture and provision for the family and to go by Water.

The man who engages in any part from cool Consideration and weighs Matters Well without Pique or prejudice, and Acts from a real belief that he is doing his Duty to his Country and Posterity is an honest Man, and if such a Man should be in the wrong is more to be

Pitied than Blamed, but if he Acts ever so much from conviction that he is right in the Part he takes, I can see no reason why he should be divested of all humanity or the Duties of a Christian. A Cause that obliges People to banish those Virtues can never prosper nor succeed. I can't say at present when or whether I shall return or not, as it is uncertain; but the Concern and Anxious Care I have for my dear family makes me write so freely to you about them. I will only further Ask the favour of you to come here to see Mrs. Robinson, she will give you a true Account of what Personable Estate will be left behind us, that it may be taken proper Care of.

I am, Dear Sir, Your most humble Servant

BEV. ROBINSON

We both desire to be remembered to Mrs. Jay.

C. Addressed: "Directed To John Jay Esqr. one of the Convent. for the State of New York at Fish Kill." Endorsed by JJ: "Copy of Bev. Robinson's Letter 4 March 1777 to JJ."

[1] This "information" merely anticipated the action of the New York Convention three days after Robinson wrote JJ. On 7 March the Convention resolved that those of the disaffected who had "been sent into some or one of the neighbouring States, or confined within this State by parol or otherwise" would be required to take an oath of allegiance to the state of New York and, failing to take this oath, would "receive a pass and be directed to repair, with their families, apparel and household furniture, to the city of New-York, or some other place in the possession of the enemy." *JPC*, I, 827; for the oath presented to Robinson on 22 Feb. 1777, see "Minutes of the Committee for Detecting Conspiracies," N.Y.H.S., *Colls.*, LVIII, 427–28.

From Egbert Benson

Fish Kill, March 19th, 1777

Dear Sir

We have this day wrote to Convention that Persons going to New York might be prohibited from taking *all* their Apparel and Furniture and You doubtless will hear the Letter read. We have not subjoined our Reasons as We proposed only to suggest the Matter and leave it entirely to be determined by Convention as they shall think best without an Attempt to influence their Judgment. It appeared however worth while to send an Express, as We expect the Gentry daily and if the Measure should be approved of the sooner the better, and We should like to have the Resolution before they have an Opportunity of applying for a Pass.[1]

Mr. Robinson (as You will perceive by his Letter of which We sent You a Copy) is gone off and most of the others are determined to go likewise.[2] Is this right? Have We nothing to fear from this Spirit and such Examples? May not the former become more universal than We wish and the latter render going to the Enemy *honorable*, and may not the Enemy from the Effect of both receive a considerable Accession of Strength before We are aware of it? These People have taken a decisive part and consequently will become desperate. Can they not by Means of Emissaries do more Mischief while out of Reach than when at Home in Your Power and under the Fear of being punished if detected?

To me I must own it appears in numberless respects very unwise. I do not like to see our Councils versatile and fluctuating. It argues Weakness, and therefore do not wish to see an entire *new* System adopted, but if the present could be helped by way of *Amendment* it might be well. However We do not mean to dictate, and shall [be] satisfied with the Determination of Convention be it what it will, and though possible not quite agreeable to our own private Sentiments, be assured You will not find Us upon that Score the least remiss. We are determined to persevere and as the Resolutions are so they *shall* be executed.

From the inclosed Paper You will see a Clause in our Original Draft of the Letter, but which upon Reflection We omitted, it being out of our Department and might carry with it the Air of being forward and meddlesome. Is there not the same Reason why the Families of those *already with* the Enemy should be sent them and as that these who are *going* should be obliged to take theirs with them.

This will be delivered to You by Mr. Robinson's Servant who calls on You for an Answer to his Letter. We have sent a Copy of the Letter to the Com[missio]n of Sequestration.[3]

Least the Copy We have sent You might have miscarried We have sent You the Original. You will please to return it to [us] again.

Yours etc.

E. BENSON

ALS. Endorsed: ". . . abt. Mr Robinson etc." Enclosure: dft of Benson, *et al.*, to the New York Convention, 19 March 1777, not located. Benson, Melancton Smith, and Jacobus Swartwout were named to the Commission for Detecting Conspiracies on 11 Feb. 1777. "Minutes of the Committee for Detecting Conspiracies," N.Y.H.S., *Colls.*, LVII, xiv–xv.

1 For the resolution of 7 March 1777 providing for the expulsion of Loyalists who declined to take the oath of allegiance to the State of New York, see above, Beverly Robinson to JJ, 4 March, n. 1. In their letter to the Convention of 19 March Benson, Smith, and Swartwout pointed out: "By the terms of the resolution they [the nonsubscribers] are to be permitted to take with them their

apparel and furniture. We could wish they were restricted to such only as is necessary, and leave us to determine that from the particular circumstances of each person. . . . The obstinate and inveterate spirit indicated by such a conduct, we conceive has precluded these people from all indulgence, and numbers of them have clothing and bedding more than is requisite for their immediate use, and much wanted in the present exigencies of the country." Upon receiving this letter on 21 March the Convention resolved that the Commissioners be "instructed to use a discretionary power in granting the indulgences" to those who chose to go behind British lines and that those who left "be not suffered to carry with them more apparel and household furniture than are necessary for their comfortable accommodation." *JPC*, I, 844; II, 398.

2 See above, Beverly Robinson to JJ, 4 March. The Commission minutes of 18 March 1777 record this action: "A Letter from Beverly Robinson Esqr of the 4th Inst to John Jay Esqr. . . . Ordered that a Copy thereof be sent to the Com. of Sequestration in Dutchess County."

On 5 March 1777 Robinson crossed British lines to join his eldest son in New York City. Nine days later he was granted a warrant to raise a Loyalist regiment in New York and, before the end of the month, had aided British military intelligence operations. NN: American Loyalists' Claims Transcripts, XLIII, 203–07; "Minutes of the Committee for Detecting Conspiracies," LVII, 204–05, 283; Robert Troup to JJ, 29 March, below.

3 On 6 March 1777 the New York Convention created local committees of sequestration throughout the state to supervise the seizure and sale of the personal property of Loyalists who had joined the British. *JPC*, I, 826.

To Susanna Philipse Robinson

Kingston, 21st March 1777

Dear Madam

Mr. Robinson's Letter directed to me as one of the late Committee at Fish Kills, was delivered to the Commissioners appointed for the like Purpose at the Place; from whom I have recieved a Copy of it.[1] As I presume you cannot be unacquainted with its Contents, many Reasons conspire in persuading me to take the Liberty of troubling you with a few Remarks on that Subject.

Among the various Exertions of Power dictated by self Preservation in the Course of the present War, few give me more Pain than those which involve whole Families without Distinction of age or Sex in Calamity, and among the Number of Families threatened with these Calamities, permit me to assure you Madam that I feel for none more sensibly than for yours.

When your Friends reflect, that not only Mr. Robinsons Estate, but the Reputation and Influence he has justly acquired, would become the Inheritance of Children who promise to do Honor to their Parents, they can entertain few Ideas more painful, than those which arise from the Danger of your Family's being deprived of Expectations so well founded and so valuable; and of a Ladys being subjected to all the anguish of misfortune and Disappointment, who hath so uniformly promoted the Happiness and Prosperity of others. Pardon my calling your Attention to Subjects so delicate, though interesting. Mr. Robinson has put his own and the Happiness of his Family and Posterity at Hazard, and for what? For the Sake of a fanciful Regard to an Ideal Obligation to a Prince, who on his Part disdains to be fettered by any obligations, a Prince who with his Parliament, arrogating the Attributes of Omnipotence, claim a Right to bind you and your Children in all Cases whatsoever. Persuaded that all former Oaths of Allegiance were dissolved by his usurpations, does he not daily attempt to bind the Inhabitants of this Country by new ones? If he deemed the former Oaths valid, why this Exaction of new Obligations of Allegiance?[2]

Can you on such Principles think of quitting a People who respect you, a Habitation and a Country which afford you every Necessary every Convenience? Remember that should you carry your numerous Family to New York, Famine may meet you and incessant anxiety banish your Peace. The Fortune or Policy of War may induce and oblige your Protectors to remove from that Place to some other Part of the Continent, perhaps to Europe. Picture to your Imagination a City beseiged, yourself and Children mixt with contending Armies —Should it be evacuated, where, with whom and in what Manner are you next to fly? Can you think of living under the restless wings of an Army? Should Heaven determine that America shall be free, In what Country are you prepared to spend the Remainder of your Days and how provide for your Children?

These Things it is true may not happen, but dont forget that they *may*—Admit they should not—suppose Heaven unjust, Britain victorious, and the Americans bound in all Cases whatsoever, will you ever Madam be able to reconcile yourself to the mortifying Reflection of being the Mother of Slaves? For who are Slaves but those, who in all Cases without Exception are bound to obey the uncontroulable Mandates of a Man—whether stiled King or called Peasant. Slaves Madam! can have no Property—they toil not for themselves, but live mere Pensioners on the Bounty of their Masters. And how contracted will be the Bounty of those Masters, who know but too well, that Poverty will be necessary to ensure Subjection.

For the Sake then of every Thing dear to you Madam! be persuaded to prevail on Mr. Robinson to return, and advise him to take an open decisive Part with his Country. His Attention to Subjects in which Honor as well as Duty may be concerned merits Commendation; and I still flatter myself that the same Attention to Honor as well as Duty will yet render his Character as distinguished by an Attachment to the Interest and Rights of his Country, as it has hitherto been eminent for other Virtues. Be pleased to assure him that I shall always think myself happy in being useful to him in every occasion consistant with the Duties I owe to that important Cause, to which, after the most mature Consideration, I have chearfully devoted myself, Family and Fortune.

I am my dear Madam with perfect Esteem and Respect Your Friend and obedient Servant

JOHN JAY

ALS. PRO: AO/105.

[1] See above, Beverly Robinson to JJ, 4 March, and Egbert Benson to JJ, 19 March.

[2] In a proclamation dated 30 Nov. 1776 General Howe and Lord Howe prescribed an oath of allegiance to be taken within the next sixty days by all seeking pardon from the crown. The following month Governor William Tryon administered his own "oath of allegiance and fidelity" to Suffolk County militiamen and, in January 1777, Tryon began a campaign to administer the same oath to all the residents of British-occupied New York. By 11 Feb. 1777, 5,600 citizens had taken Tryon's oath in Manhattan, Staten Island, Long Island, and Westchester County. 5 *FAA*, III, 927–28; *N.Y. Col. Docs.*, VIII, 693–94, 696–97.

The Case of Cadwallader Colden, Jr.

One of the most influential and articulate Loyalists imprisoned by the New York authorities was Cadwallader Colden, Jr., son of the former lieutenant governor. Although he repeatedly insisted that he be classified as a neutral, he felt himself bound by his oath to the king and was openly hostile to the notion of independence. If left at large he could have become a focal point for disaffection or even an active counterrevolutionary. Colden was so accustomed to deference that he felt free to complain and demand special consideration even when confined in jail. Some of his requests were directed to JJ, who treated Colden with respect but who was unprepared to offer him anything beyond very minor concessions.[1]

Colden's difficulties began on 4 July 1776 when the Ulster County Committee of Safety charged him with disloyalty and jailed him for a time. Later that year the Committee for Detecting Conspiracies arrested and examined him and decided that he was too dangerous to be left at large. He was held at Fort Montgomery until Governor George Clinton moved him on 2 May 1777 to the Kingston prison. From there he was transferred late in the month to the Fleet Prison in Rondout Creek at Esopus, where he stayed until he was paroled in October and allowed to go to nearby Hurley. Finally, in September 1777, he obtained a pass permitting him to take his family to New York City. He left Cadwallader III behind at Coldenham, their Ulster County farm. This son's patriot leanings saved the property from confiscation, and the Coldens were able to return there after the war.[2]

The documents printed below all date from mid-1777. The first letter, written almost immediately after Cadwallader Colden, Jr., was sent from Fort Montgomery to Kingston, is an unsuccessful plea for the lives of two fellow-prisoners. The 31 May complaint about being ordered to the Fleet Prison is surprising, considering the fact that Colden himself had originally requested the transfer, fearing that a change of jailers in Kingston would result in poor treatment.[3] JJ arranged that day for Colden to have a one-day furlough at home, and when he saw the prisoner again at Esopus on 27 July, he suggested the possibility of parole, but on neither occasion did he show any willingness to discuss complete freedom.

1 D: NHi: Minutes of the Committee for Detecting Conspiracies, for 30 Dec. 1776, 4 and 6 Jan. 1777, 19 March 1777. JJ served as committee chairman in December and January, but he was not on the board on 19 March. See also *JPC*, I, 768, 784–85, 829; II, 306, 468.

2 Minutes of the Committee for Detecting Conspiracies, 28 Nov. 1776; *JPC*, I, 762–63, 1071–72; *GCP*, I, 784–85; Catherine S. Crary, *The Price of Loyalty* (New York, 1973), pp. 203–05.

3 *JPC*, II, 448.

From Cadwallader Colden, Jr.

Kingston jail, May 12th, 1777

Sir

You are not Unacquainted with my Sentiment in Regard to this Unhappy affair, that has allready Cost so Much Blood and treasure, and Likely Yet to Cost a Vast Deal More, And notwithstanding my Determined Resolution to keep a Clear Conscience by takeing no Active Part on Either Side of the Contraversey, Yet it Seems I have a full Share of Punishment. But it is not on My own Account that I am goeing to trouble you at this time. No, it is on a Matter that gives me much More Concern, both on Your Accounts, and that of a Number of Fellow Prisoners, I hear You have Condemned to Die.[1]

Oh! My Dear Sir, Consider the Consequences that Must attend Such a Scene, both in this World and the Next. Coolly and Deliberately to take the Life of our fellow Creatures, Must Add much to the account of those who have been instrumental in Bringing Publick affairs to this Pass. But I fear this argument will have but Little Weight. I would therefore Endeavour to Perswade You Upon the Principles of good Pollicy to Delay putting in Execution this Sentence of Death, (At Least for Some Days) for Depend upon it, the hanging of these Men Will not Make one Man Change his Sentements in Your favour, but the Very Reverse, And though it may prevent Some Exposeing themselves as foolishly as these poor Men did, Yet the time may be Drawing Near When they will not have that Risque to Run, and When Many a One who now is forced to Pretend to be fighting your Cause will prove not to be so honest as these poor men you are goeing to hang. Besides the President [sic] may have awfull Effects, should the other Party take the Example.

I found myself Constrained to say this Much to You, As an old friend and Acquaintance for Whome I have had a perticular Regard. God Grant it May have the Desired affect, is the Prayer of, Sir Your Most Humble and Obydient Servant

CADWALLADER COLDEN

ALS. Addressed: "To John Jay Esqr of the Honble Convention Kingston." Endorsed. LbkCS, in Colden's hand, in CSmH: Cadwallader Colden, Jr., Journal, HM 607.

1 Jacobus Rose (or Roosa), Jacob Midagh, and others had been found guilty of treason for recruiting in Ulster County for the British army. Rose and Midagh were executed, and their associates served prison terms. *GCP*, I, 783–84; Marius Schoonmaker, *The History of Kingston, New York* (New York, 1888), pp. 254–55.

FROM CADWALLADER COLDEN, JR.

Kingston, May 31st, 1777

Dear Sir

I had Desired Doctr. Jones[1] to Speak to You and some other Gentlemen of the Council of Safety Concerning a Report I had heard, that I with some other Gentlemen now at Lodgings was to be Confined on bord a Vessel. The Doctr Told me Yesterday that You was so kind as to Propose to Call to See me on that Account; But this Moment the Sherriff Sent a Man to inform Mr Cumming[2] and Myself to hold Ourselves in Readyness to go on bord a Vessel in an hours time.

Though I have not been informd of any Perticular Charges against me, Yet While I thought it might be to Answer Some Political View, that the Convention thought Proper not to Let me Remain at my own house I Readly Acquiesed. But while any View or End of that kind might as Well be answered by Allowing me to Remain Where I am I Can't but think it Exceeding hard that My Situation Should be Renderd Still more Disagreable. I shall take it very kind if you take this under Consideration And any the Least Services Shall ever be thankfully Rememberd by Sir Your Most Humble Servant

CADWALLADER COLDEN

LbkCS, in Colden's hand, in CSmH: Cadwallader Colden, Jr., Journal, HM 607.

[1] Dr. Jones was a resident of Kingston, whose house and barn were burned when the British attacked the town on 16 Oct. 1777. Marius Schoonmaker, *The History of Kingston, New York* (New York, 1888), p. 524.

[2] John Cumming or Cummins, a Loyalist who lived in Catskill, Greene County. *GCP*, IX, 242.

Cadwallader Colden, Jr.: Notes of a Conference with John Jay

[*Kingston, May 31st, 1777*]

I Sent my Son with the forgoing Letter to Mr Jay who was then in Council and he bid him tell me that he would wait on me Emediately. He accordingly soon Came. When he informed me that he had Laid my Letter before the Council, and that they had bid him to tell me that their former Resolution must take Place, I only Replyed that I thought it exceeding hard, and asked him what was the Charge against me. He Said that he know of None but Surmised that wanted foundation of My haveing Given Directions to an officer Charged with Dispatches from Canada to Gen How, who had been with Rosses Party how to pass the Guards and that I had Stimulated Rosse when in Jayl to behave as he did telling him that they Dare not put him to Death.[1] I told him that I had had no acquaintance with Rosse till I See him in the Jayl the Day before he was Executed, And so far from giveing him any Encouragement that he would not Die I had Done all in my Power to Prepare him for it as I thought he appeard to be too Litle Concerned about it himself, which he Said was so far well done. I then told him that My Wife had great Concern to see me and it would be a great Stroke to her to have me sent away from her so Sudenly and Said that if I might be indulged to Stay with her another Day I should take it kind. He answered, that that was so Reasonable that he thought it would not be Denied me and said he Would go and Propose it to the Council. He Accordingly Went to the Council and Returnd Emediately and told me that the Council had agreed to Postpone their order for going bord the Vessel till Tuesday, for which I thanked him. He then Desired to See my Wife. I took him into the Room to her where he Satt a Quarter of an hour and when indeed some part of the Conversation that I have already Related Passed.

LbkC, in Colden's hand, in CSmH: Cadwallader Colden, Jr., Journal, HM 607. This note in Colden's Journal is entered immediately after his letter to JJ of 31 May and before an entry for 2 June.

[1] Jacobus Rose (or Roosa) is here doubtless referred to as Rosse.

Cadwallader Colden, Jr.: Notes of a Conference with John Jay

[*Esopus*, 27 *July* 1777]

Sunday Morning soon after Breakfast Mr. Jay Called in. I told him I was Sorry to have given him that trouble, that I had Desired Mr Sleght to ask Leave for me to have Waited on him. He answered that he Should have been glad to See me at his Lodgeings, however it was no trouble to him to Wait on Me. I then told him that what I wanted to see him for was to know if no Method Could be fallen upon that I might get to my own house, that I had Left my Wife and Family very unwell, had Lost one of my Best Negroes, that No hands was to be hierd and that all my farm affairs must go to Rack if I Could not be allowed to Look after them. That, as no Charge was Laid against me but my avowed Disaffection, I thought it hard to be thus Confind, When I thought that if they Confined every Man, who Disaproved of Measures as well as I did they Would have More Prisoners then they would know what to Do With.

He answerd that he Did not know of any Gentlemen of Distinction who had avowed these Sentiments as I had Done, that was left at Liberty. That it was known that Mr Banyar, was not with them,[1] Yet he had behaved so Cautious and prudent as to give no handle against him. That Mr. Smith had Lately talked a Litle freely, upon hearing of Whičh the Council of Safety had Sent for him, and that they had Let him go home again upon his Parole and Promise not to talk so freely any more.[2] That as to me though there was no Charge against me of Late but Disaffection, Yet there was Strong Suspicions, And that there Was so many Instances of Gentlemen of My Disposition who had Broke throo their Promises and Paroles and taken up Arms against the Country (as he Called it) that there was no Confidence to be had in any one any more and that he Suposed they thought No faith or Promise was to be kept with the Rebels. That though they Could not Charge me with the Least Disinginuity, Yet if I thought my fate was harder then I Deserved, I must Charge it to the Conduct of Others.

I told him that My Wifes Uneasyness was Encreased by a Report in the Country (upon what grounds I Could not tell,) that the

Prisoners were to be Removed to Some Distant Province, and that we in that Case Might be kept Prisoners Dureing the War. He Said no Such thing had been moved in Councill. Yet he acknowledged that should the Kings troops, approach this Way, in all Probability we would be Removed. He then added that he thought it would not be Safe for me to be at home, that they had allowed one or two to go home to take Care of their Harvests, and that they were made so uneasy by their Neighbours, that they were glad to Come back again. But that if I would Choose to be at Vanduesen at Hurley, he believed the Council would agree to that.[3]

I answerd that If I had but a Permitt from the Council to Return home, I should be very Easy about the Conduct of my Neighbours, that I did not Doubt I Could get three fourths of them to joyn in application for my Return, that I thought it impossible a Man Should be in Danger of Loseing his Life by his Neighbours who had Never Done a Private Injury to one of them. That if I was not allowed to Return home, it was Matter of indifference to me where I was, If I was not Carryd farther from my family and where I Could not hear from them.

Some Company Comeing in Stoped our Discourse and he soon Rose to go away. I waited on him to the Door, where he stoped and told me he would Propose it to the Council to have me Lodged at Vanduesen, I just thanked him not Being then Determined in my own Mind wether to Accept of the Offer or no.

LbkC, in Colden's hand, in CSmH: Cadwallader Colden, Jr., Journal, HM 607.

1 Goldsbrow Banyar (1727–1815), British-born Loyalist, New York City officeholder, who lived in Rhinebeck during the Revolution and later settled in Albany. Sabine, *Biographical Sketches*, I, 206.

2 William Smith, Jr., the Chief Justice.

3 Doubtless Captain Jan Van Deusen, at whose home in Hurley the Council of Safety met between 18 Nov. and 17 Dec. 1777. Nathaniel B. Sylvester, *History of Ulster County, New York* (Philadelphia, 1880), p. 200.

Jay's *An Address of the Convention of the Representatives of the State of New-York to Their Constituents* Compared with Paine's *The Crisis Number 1*

[*Fishkill, 23 December 1776*]

Lord Cornwallis took Fort Lee on 20 November 1776, and for the next five weeks the Continental Army retreated across New Jersey closely pursued by an enemy seemingly on the verge of final victory. In that dark hour two major spokesmen for the American cause, Thomas Paine and JJ, published inspirational essays rallying disheartened Patriots to the defense of the nation. Both documents were widely read, and both received official recognition; General Washington had *The Crisis Number 1* read to the troops before they crossed the Delaware River,[1] and the Continental Congress was so impressed by JJ's tract that arrangements were made to have it translated, printed, and distributed in the German-speaking sections of New Jersey and Pennsylvania, where the enemy was apt to penetrate.[2] Although Paine and JJ were arguing the same case, their minds worked in different ways, and their tracts were consequently very dissimilar.

The two publications appeared almost simultaneously, so it is very unlikely that either author could have been inspired or influenced by the other. Tom Paine was a witness to the military disasters of the late autumn, being then aide-de-camp to Nathanael Greene, and he is known to have begun work on his piece between 22 and 28 November, while the army was encamped at Newark.[3] As soon as he finished it, he went to Philadelphia to arrange for publication, and *The Crisis Number 1* appeared in the *Pennsylvania Journal* on 19 December.[4] The chronology of JJ's labor is known in less detail, but the essential facts are clear. *An Address of the Convention of the Representatives of the State of New-York to their Constituents,* signed by Abraham Ten Broeck as president of that body, was printed by Samuel Loudon in Fishkill carrying the date 23 December.[5] While the publication may not have come off the press that day, the Provincial Convention clearly had given the Address its imprimatur by that date. Considering the length of the *Address* and the evident care with which it was reasoned and written, its production might well have consumed several days. Only four days elapsed between the appearance of Paine's essay and the acceptance for publication of JJ's. The only way a copy of the *Pennsylvania Journal* could have reached Fishkill while JJ was still completing his manuscript would have been if it were carried from Philadelphia by someone traveling in haste who had the good fortune not to be delayed or intercepted by the British army. One may not rule out the possibility, therefore, that JJ could have seen Paine's writing before he finished his own but the probabilities are against that hypothesis.

Both Paine's *Crisis* and JJ's *Address* ring with patriotic fervor, contain many passages of genuine eloquence, and end by calling their readers to action, but it is difficult to find much else that they have in common. Both authors point out that Howe avoided a general engagement until expiring enlistments eroded Washington's army toward the end of 1776, and both argue that the loss of Philadelphia would not be a fatal blow; but either of these sentiments might have been heard in any tavern patronized by Patriots, and they certainly do not suggest that one of the authors borrowed ideas from the other.

The first of the several *Crisis* papers opens with the electrifying declaration that "these are the times that try men's souls," and it addresses itself directly to believers in the American cause, urging them to recognize that "by perseverance and fortitude we have the prospect of a glorious issue." At the same time, the author gives much of his attention to the problem of how to deal with the disaffected. He suggests trying to persuade them that "separation must some time or other finally take place." Should logic not convince them and should they persist in aiding the British, the necessary response must be the confiscation of their estates. The paper also contains a vivid firsthand account of the campaign, from Fort Lee to the Delaware, emphasizing that both officers and men "bore it with a manly and martial spirit" and that their military effectiveness was not destroyed. Paine's uncomplicated logic and his superb journalistic style make this a propaganda piece of extraordinary force and enduring vitality.

JJ's purpose in the *Address* is the same as Tom Paine's in *The Crisis:* to insure victory by instilling courage. His method, however, is very different, for, where Paine relies on simple exhortation, JJ offers a lawyer's brief in which he explains past failure, warns against listening to insincere peace feelers, and demonstrates the inevitability of final triumph if only the people will rise to the occasion. He blames recent military disasters on the overconfidence that followed the British evacuation of Boston, adding that "we ascribed that to our own prowess which was only to be attributed to the great Guardian of the innocent." The enemy is beset by weaknesses, which include problems relating to supply and finance as well as growing discontent at home. America, conversely, enjoys great advantages, particularly an improving supply system and the prospect of European support. The United Netherlands once prevailed over tyranny, and so can the United States. JJ's argument rests throughout on Lockean logic, and his appeal is much more intellectual than Paine's. His clarity of expression, however, makes his writing comprehensible to a mass audience, and his polished prose contains many memorable passages. "We believe," he concludes, "and are persuaded, that you will do your duty like men, and cheerfully refer your cause to the great and righteous Judge. If success crown your efforts, all the blessings of Freedom will be your reward. If you fail in the contest, you will be happy with God and Liberty in Heaven."

1 Philip S. Foner, ed., *The Complete Writings of Thomas Paine* (2 vols., New York, 1945), I, 49.

2 *JCC*, VII, 42; the translation by Lewis Weiss, "printed at the expense of the Continent," appeared in an edition of 1,000 copies. Evans, 15468.

3 Foner, ed., *Thomas Paine*, I, xv–xvi; for details of the retreat across New Jersey, see Christopher Ward, *The War of the Revolution* (2 vols., New York, 1952), I, 275–90.

4 This was a special edition, because regular publication of the *Pennsylvania Journal* was suspended between 27 Nov. 1776 and 29 Jan. 1777. *The Crisis Number 1* was published at Philadelphia as a pamphlet by Steiner and Cist on 23 Dec. 1776. Evans, 14953.

5 *HPJ*, I, 102–20; DNA: PCC, 67, I, 372–92; Samuel Loudon (1727–1813) suspended publication of the *New York Packet* at New York City on 29 Aug.

1776 and removed to Fishkill, resuming publication at the latter place in January 1777 after being voted a £200-a-year subsidy by the Committee of Safety on 12 Dec. 1776 for publishing occasional articles. Clarence S. Brigham, *History and Bibliography of American Newspapers, 1690–1820* (2 vols., Worcester, Mass., 1947), I, 675; *JPC*, I, 750.

FROM WILLIAM DUER

Peeks Kill, January 3d, 177[7]

Dear Jay,

Two Men, who have enlisted with Rogers[1] were taken two or three Days ago, who declare that they deserted in consequence of a Report, which Prevails in the Enemy's Camp, that the Convention had issued a Proclamation of Pardon to those who had joind the Enemy. From the Character of these Men there is little Doubt but they speak Truth. I would therefore earnestly recommend it to you to publish immediately a Proclamation of Pardon under such Restrictions as you think consistent with sound Policy. Our Friend Gouverneur Morris had made a Draft of one, which appears to me one of his hasty Productions, and is in my opinion by no means dignified enough for a Public Body. I have therefore to request that you will pay attention to this Matter, which I doubt not will be productive of good Consequences, particularly at this Crisis.[2]

I have received Intelligence that one Peter Clements who lives near Staatsborough, and Charity French are now raising Companies for the Enemies Service. Thomas Tobias has not yet joined the Enemy, and if proper measures are taken may probably be secured.[3]

General Washington in a Letter to Major General Heath gives a very favorable account of our affairs in Jersey. The Enemy are retreating towards South Amboy, and General Washington and the other Detachments of our Army in Jersey persuing.[4]

To morrow I shall set out for North Castle,[5] but I am apprehensive from the weakness of our Force at the different Posts that we shall not be able to strike any very decisive Stroke. Only Part of two Regiments of the Massachusets Militia consisting of about 600 Men are as yet come in, and from [*what*] I can learn will come in very slowly. I think however it will be good Policy to put on a bold Face, and by harassing the Enemy with Scouting Parties in the lower Parts of Westchester County prevent them if possible from knowing our real Strength, or from benefiting of the Forage.

Rogers has had Intelligence that an attack has been meditated against him, in Consequence of which he and his Men have for some Nights past slept in Mount Washington.[6] Persevere, my dear Friend, in the Department you are engaged in, and be assured that my Endeavors as an Individual will not be wanting in this Quarter to protect our Friends, and to harass the Enemy.

Yours very sincerely

W. DUER

Tr. Note on transcript: "The date on the manuscript is 1776, but Jay's note on the back of the letter is 1777. Probably it is Duer's error." Duer wrote as JJ's colleague on the Committee for Detecting Conspiracies.

1 Robert Rogers.

2 On 7 March Morris presented to the New York Convention a report on "the resolutions as an act of grace to such of the inhabitants who are gone, or sent out of the State, or confined as disaffected persons." Morris's report, as adopted by the Convention, prescribed an oath to be taken by those who had been banished from the state or confined within the state for their disaffection. Those who refused to subscribe to the oath were to be sent behind British lines. However, the March resolutions did not extend the offer of pardon to those who were "charged with taking up arms against the United States, with enlisting men for the service of the enemy, accepting a warrant or commission for that purpose, supplying them with provisions, or conveying intelligence to them. . . ." Two months later, Morris and JJ were named to a new committee charged with preparing "an act of grace for such of the inhabitants of this State as have been guilty of treasonable practices against the State. . . ," and their report, presented by JJ and adopted on 10 May, offered pardon to those who took an oath of allegiance. *JPC*, I, 827, 920–21.

3 Peter Clements rose to the rank of captain in the King's American Regiment and emigrated to Canada after the Revolution. Thomas Tobias's activities had been reported to the Committee for Detecting Conspiracies on several occasions, and on 31 Dec. 1776, the Committee was notified that he was on his way to New York City to join the British Army. Charity French has not been identified. "Minutes of the Committee for Detecting Conspiracies," N.Y.H.S., *Colls.*, LVII, 31–32, 58–59, 63–64.

4 On 12 Nov. 1776 Major General William Heath was left in command of the Hudson Highlands when Washington and the main army withdrew to New Jersey. Washington's letters to Heath of 27 and 28 Dec. 1776 described the American raid on Trenton on Christmas Eve and the ensuing retreat to South Amboy. *GWF*, V, 275–78, 444–45, 447–48.

5 A post in northern Westchester.

6 The site of Fort Washington in northern Manhattan.

From Robert Morris

Philadelphia, January 12th, 1777

Dear Sir

I have been possessed of your obliging favor of the 2d Ulto[1] a considerable time, but being too much pressed with Public and private business to permit my being a regular correspondent it is needless to apologize. You undoubtedly must have been well acquainted with the rapid progress made by our Enemies through the

Jerseys and the danger to which this City has been exposed for some Weeks past, and you will have heard of the removal of Congress to Baltimore in the midst of the pannic.[2] This step has been highly censured by many of their Friends and undoubtedly lost them the confidence of some valueable Men.

I confess for my own part I am not amongst the Number of those that Censure them for this hasty measure, for when it is considered that the Enemys Troops were within a very few miles of us and no apparent Force sufficient to oppose their progress, it surely was time for a Public body on which the support of the american cause so much depended to provide for their safety. Meer personal safety I suppose would not have induced many of them to fly, but their Security as a body was the object. Had any Number of them fallen into the Enemies hands so as to break up the Congress America might have been ruined before another Choice of Delegates could be had, and in such an event they would have been deemed criminal and rash to the last degree. Most of them dislike their present Station and complain horridly, particularly those you esteem, but it seems, some others who generally carry their points, like their quarters and are for staying. I suppose it answers some of their purposes and I have but one objection in the World. They have appointed Mr. Walton of Georgia, Mr. Clymer and myself a Committee to transact all Continental business that may be necessary and proper in this place.[3] The business of this Committee engrosses my whole time and increases daily, so that I am now the veriest Slave you ever saw and wish them back to be relieved.

I wish to Heaven they had removed from hence last Winter. If they had, Pensylvania would long since have had a wholesome constitution, its Strength might have been drawn into proper exertion and her Capital would never have been made to trouble. What has happened is the fruits of that winters Cabals, our Constitution is disliked, the People divided, unhappy, and consequently weak. The Power if any there be, is placed in improper hands and in short the People seem to loose one day, the Confidence they placed in leaders of the day before.[4]

Where it will end God only knows. Dickenson and A. Allen have given mortal Stabs to their own Characters and pity it is the wounds should penetrate any further, but they were men of property, Men of fair private characters and what they have done, seems to pierce through their sides into the Vitals of <their Contemporarys> those who have similar pretentions to Fortune and good Character. The defection of these men is supposed to originate in a desire to preserve their Estates and consequently glances a suspicion on all that have Estates to loose. I pity them both exceedingly. Dickensons Nerves gave way and his fears dictated a letter to his Brother advising him not to receive Continental Money.[5] His Judgement and his Virtue should have prevented this Act of Folly. I call it such because I believe his Heart to be good and regret much that his exalted character <must> should be degraded, by what <can> could hardly be called a Crime at the time he did it, but he thought the Game was up. A. Allen deserves a better fate than he will meet with. Aimiable in private character and deserving of the Felicity he has heretofore enjoyed he has rashly sacrificed it by a <temerity> hasty resolution. He has long thought it impossible for us to withstand the power of Great Britain and he complained of that Conduct amongst ourselves which has been loudly censured by America's Warmest advocates and frequently exposed by the keen sentences of Mr. Jay. However nothing can justify the Step he has taken and it seems wrong to paliate it. I will therefore only say, I am most sincerely sorry for him.

I removed my Family and some of my effects in the heat of our Fright but determined to stay by the City to the last moment. Very happy have I been since, in this determination, as it is fallen in m[y w]ay to be very usefull on many occasions, both to this State and to the Continent and in every instance I have exerted myself to the utmost. Congress are Sensible of it and have approved all my doings, altho I acted for a considerable time without their Authority. I join in all your Sentiments respecting our good Friend Duane and if I had not been well convinced how Ill used he was by that Cursed piece of Slander I should not have troubled him with it, nor should I have sent it when I did, but having heard he was coming to Congress, I thought it my duty to prepare him. I have a letter from him on the Subject and think he treats it very properly by despising the report and its Author or Authors.[6] I wish to heaven the affairs of your State would permit both your attendance at Congress. Believe me You and others are wanted there. There is a leader there that you do not like and as I understand they have the rule of the roost totally since their removal to the Southward. Pray shew this to Mr. Duane and tell him the next bit of leisure I get shall be devoted to answer his two letters.

I do not pretend to give you any account of Military operations as I suppose you get them from day to day. What a glorious change in our prospects; pray heaven Continue our Success and grant me an opportunity of Congratulating you on regaining the City of New York. I have not heard from Mr. Deane for sometime past and fear he will complain for want of remittances and Intelligence. Those Damnd Men of War plague us exceedingly and have taken many of our Vessells, but we must persevere untill we gain success. I am Dear Sir Your affectionate Friend and Servant

ROBT. MORRIS

ALS. Addressed: "The Honorable John Jay Esqr Member of Convention at the Fish Kills." Endorsed.

[1] JJ to Morris, 2 Dec. 1776, not located.

[2] Fearing a British advance on Philadelphia, Congress adjourned to Baltimore on 12 Dec. 1776. Sessions were held there 20 Dec. 1776–March 1777. *JCC*, VI, 1027, 1028.

[3] Morris, George Walton (1741–1804) of Georgia, and George Clymer (1739–1813) of Pennsylvania were appointed "a committee with powers to execute such continental business as may be proper and necessary to be done at Philadelphia" on 21 Dec. 1776. *JCC*, VI, 1032.

[4] On 28 Sept. 1776 the Pennsylvania Convention adopted a radical state constitution which provided a unicameral legislature and an Executive Council presided over by a President. Conservative opponents of the new constitution mobilized forces for the assembly campaign which followed. Anti-Constitutionalists won one-third of the seats in the legislature, enough to prevent the assembly from organizing when it met on 28 November. John Dickinson, Anti-Constitutionalist leader in the assembly, proposed that his followers would agree to elect a Speaker and cooperate in routine business if the assembly consented to call a new constitutional convention in January 1777, but this compromise was not adopted, and the assembly adjourned until January 1777 when conservative forces again prevented the organization of the new state government. Allan Nevins, *The American States During and After the Revolution, 1775–1789* (New York, 1924), pp. 150–56; Robert L. Brunhouse, *The Counter-Revolution in Pennsylvania, 1776–1790* (New York, 1971).

[5] Andrew Allen (1740–1825), a Pennsylvania delegate to the Continental Congress, did not attend sessions of Congress after May 1776. In December 1776 Allen fled to the British lines at Trenton.

John Dickinson was left out of the Pennsylvania delegation chosen in July 1776. Despite his opposition to the adoption of the Declaration of Independence, Dickinson saw military service against the British in the late summer of 1776. Dickinson's dissatisfaction with the political situation in Pennsylvania, along with the anticipated British march on Philadelphia, prompted him to make arrangements to move his family to his estate in Delaware in late 1776. His political standing in both Pennsylvania and Delaware was harmed by the interception of a note written to his brother on 14 December from Newcastle, Del.: "Receive no more continental money on your bonds and mortgages—The British have conquered the Jerseys, and your being in camp, are sufficient reasons—Be sure you remember this—It will end better for you." When Dickinson's servant applied to the Council of Safety for a pass, the Council assumed that Dickinson's compromising note was intended for the Council and opened the letter. The servant was jailed, and Dickinson's new home in Philadelphia seized for use as a hospital. Despite Dickinson's efforts to explain the circumstances of the letter, the Council published part of the note and refused to discuss the matter with him.

Delaware had elected him to the Continental Congress in November, but he declined the office in January 1777. After resigning his seat as a Delaware Congressman, Dickinson withdrew to private life and did not hold public office again for two years. For Dickinson's account of the circumstances of his note to his brother, see Charles J. Stillé, *The Life and Times of John Dickinson, 1732–1808* (Philadelphia, 1891), pp. 400–07.

[6] Letter not located.

From Charles DeWitt

Green Hill, January 22nd, 1777

Dear Sir

Many favourable accounts of Importance, respecting our Army to the Southward have reached our Ears here, for sometime past, some of which have been sufficiently authenticated, and others (I suppose) some clean Hands at the fashionable Vice of Lying have invented. However such as it is my Heart has exulted and even leaped for Joy in my Breast; my Ideas of Conquest run so High at present that nothing short of the Possession of New York the Destruction of the British Fleet at the Docks seem to satisfy. But you may say it could be easily done provided every one could stay at his own fire side; and I confess I should Blush with Guilt if my reasons for so long Absence were not sufficient which in order to exculpate myself from the Expected charge of Neglect, I must take the Liberty to give you, and if necessary to communicate them to Convention. When I left Fish Kiles my Son[1] (who is the only Superintendant of my affairs) had Marched with the Militia to Jersey. He was out almost one Month. When he returned home he fell sick and is still in a Critical Situation tho I hope he will soon recover. While he was absent my Miller was Sick and is not yet entirely recovered, so that I have been closely confined to this spot. You may be assured Sir that I shall give my Attandance as soon as the situation of my Family will admit of it, which I hope will be soon, for I never have longed more to be at Convention than at present, as I expect I should know the Grand Councils of State now held for the entire Dismission of those troublesom fellows from our happy Shores. I am intirely in the Dark surrounded only with Rocks and Trees which afford me no more information than that the Beneficent maker has granted them for our Convenience and not to be destroyed by a Band of wicked men, should be exceedingly obliged to you to favor me with the news of the Season. Have expected you here once since the snow fall. Cannot you and Mr Duer spend a few days with me.

The Pamphlets distributed by the Convention are much liked; they are calculated to draw the attention of the Meanest capacity, seriously to consider our present situation.[2] I have read it once, I wish I had one of them.

A Resolve for the exemption of Coopers for two Months had Passed when I was at Convention, since which I understand another is Published which varies from the first. I have been told that printed exemptions are handed to Millers to Issue to such as furnish a proper Quantity of Casks. As I expect the Army will be in want of Flour, and though we cannot supply the country for want of Water, yet as soon as a thaw comes on, I shall want a Quantity to put flour in, which I shall be puzzled to get unless some Coopers stick to their Business, and as I cannot find that the officers here know of such Resolve, I shall take it as a favor of you to furnish me with Materials to accomplish this necessary work.[3]

The Committee of Kingston I suppose will apply to you for a Guard to watch the Tories in their Goal. It will in my opinion be very necessary.[4] I have but just room to say that I am with great esteem Sir, Your most obedient and Humble Servant

CH. D. WITT

Tr.

1 John C. DeWitt (1755–1833), an officer in the Marbletown militia. *Cal. of Hist. Mss.*, I, 151.

2 *An Address of the Convention of the Representatives of the State of New-York, to their Constituents.*

3 On 17 Sept. 1776 the New York Convention named DeWitt an agent to purchase flour in Ulster County and arrange for its shipment by water to Joseph Trumbull, the Continental Commissary. Two resolutions were passed by the Convention's Committee of Safety the following month concerning the exemption of coopers from the militia draft: the first, passed 24 October, provided that coopers and other workmen employed in transporting and processing flour for the Convention at Croton River and Peekskill "be exempted from military duty of any kind whatsoever"; the second, of 29 October, is not printed in *JPC* but is described merely as a resolution "to exempt coopers for two months from military duty." DeWitt is not recorded as present at sessions of the Committee of Safety, 7–27 Oct. 1776, and he was probably familiar only with the resolution of 29 October granting a two-month exemption to coopers. In addition, several resolutions on militia duty were passed in the Committee of Safety during the period 1–14 Dec. 1776 for which *JPC* is incomplete. A copy of one of these resolves is preserved in DNA: PCC, 67, I, 395 and provides for the appointment of a committee "empowered to discharge from the Militia such Mechanicks as the public Service, or the Necessity of the Inhabitants may render expedient." No separately published copies of these resolutions have survived. *JPC*, I, 629, 689, 693.

4 On 1 Feb. 1777 the New York Committee of Safety acted on an application from the Kingston committee of January 1777 and approved the action of a subcommittee which had ordered the posting of a guard at the Kingston jail and provided funds for the payments of the guard. *JPC*, I, 794.

To Lewis Morris

[Fishkill], *3 February 1777*

Dear Sir

I am informed that the Congress have taken the place of Director general of the Hospital from Dr. Morgan. As he has not recieved a Copy of their Resolution for that purpose, I have promised him to write to you for it.[1] Be so kind therefore as to obtain and send it to me without Delay. Let it be certified.

What Reasons may have induced the Congress to dismiss this Gent[leman] from the service I know not. I suppose they are contained in a preamble to the Resolution, and therefore I am the more desirous of seeing it.

I shall in a Day or two write to you more fully.

Present my Compliments to all my Friends.

I am Dear Sir your Friend and humble Servant

Dft. Endorsed by JJ: "Gen. Morris."

[1] Dr. John Morgan (1735–89) succeeded Dr. Benjamin Church as Director General of hospitals and physician-in-chief of the army on 17 Oct. 1775. In October 1776 Morgan was ordered to "provide and superintend a hospital . . . for the army posted on the east side of Hudson's river," and on 9 Jan. 1777 was dismissed by Congress as Director General and physician-in-chief without explanation. When Congress's medical committee reported on 9 Aug. 1777 on Morgan's dismissal, "general complaints of persons of all ranks in the army" were cited for his removal and the committee conceded that there had been "no particular charges against him." *JCC*, III, 297; V, 460, 568–71; VII, 24; VIII, 626.

From Robert Morris

Philadelphia, February 4th, 1777

Dear Sir

Your favour of the 7th Ultimo came safe to hand.[1]

Timothy Jones is certainly a very entertaining agreable Man. One would not judge so from any thing contained in his cold insipid letter of the 7th September unless you take pains to find the Concealed beauties therein.[2] The Cursory observation of a Sea Captain would never *discover* them, but transferred from his hand to the penetrating Eye of a *Jay* the Diamonds Stand Confessed at once. It puts me in mind of a Search after the Philosophers Stone, but I believe not one of the followers of that Phantom have come so near the Mark as you my Good Friend.

I handed a Copy of your discoverys to the Committee which now

Consists of Harrison, R. H. Lee, Hooper, Doctor Witherspoon, Johnson, you, and myself[3] and honestly told them who it was from because, *measures* are necessary in Consequence of it, but I have not received any directions yet. I should never doubt the success of measures Conducted by such able heads as those that take the leads in your Convention. I hate to pay Compliments and would avoid the appearance of doing it, but I cannot refrain from saying I love Duane, admire Mr. Livingston and have an Epithet for you if I had been writing to another.

I am stationed here with Mr. Walton of Georgia and my Colleague Mr. Clymer as a Committee of Congress for transacting all Continental business that may be proper and necessary at this place. Abundance of it we have and I believe we dispatch about 7/8ths of that damned trash that used to take up 3/4ths of the debates in Congress; and give them no trouble about the matter, but we have this day wrote them pressingly to come back.[4] Whether they will or not is uncertain as I am told some of them are attached to the place; others execrate it. I do not Condemn their flight from hence as I should have done had I been at the distance you are, but I cannot spare time to explain myself for I write in haste and proceed to unfold a little business I want to trouble you with.

Major West the Nephew of my Friend Will West was taken Prisoner at Fort Washington. He had made a kind of bargain with Mr. Elliot late Collector of New York to get exchanged for Mr. Jauncey junior and I represented the matter to Congress, who very *wisely* passed the inclosed Resolve.[5] The agreement was that if Major West could evoke interest with Congress, Mr. Elliot would do the needfull with General Howe to effect this exchange, at least so I understand it. West is an active good Officer, and has great interest in our back Country that would enable him to recruit fast. Mr. Jauncey I fancy may as well be in N York as Connecticut and I wish you would forward this business of Exchange if you think it right. My Compliments to Mr. Duane and Mr. Livingston and I hope they will join you in it.

I wish you had done with your convention. You are really wanted exceedingly in Congress; they are very thin, Hooper gone of with a Fever, Tom Nelson with an appoplectic complaint, when I say gone off I dont mean to the other World, only to another part of this, one for Virginia and tother for N Carolina. Harrison has barely weathered it, but he is mending. T. Johnson passed through here a few days ago a General for the Camp.[6] Maryland is not represented,

Jersey and Delaware seldom are, your state and this not so fully as they ought. We shall have a New appointment here soon. I wish it may do honor to us, but much I fear the reverse from the Names now talked off. Adieu my Dear Sir. God Bless you and grant Success to America in the present Contest, with Wisdom and Virtue to Secure Peace and happiness to her Sons in all future ages. I am with true regard Your most Obedient Servant,

ROBT. MORRIS

ALS. Endorsed. Enclosure: resolution of Congress, 21 Jan. 1777 concerning the exchange of William West, Jr., for James Jauncey, Jr., *JCC*, VII, 52–53.

1 JJ to Morris, 7 Jan. 1777, not located.

2 "Timothy Jones" was a name used by Silas Deane in his secret correspondence with JJ in 1776. The note from "Jones" to JJ, 17 Sept. 1776, is reprinted in *WJ*, I, 67. This brief and innocuous message was written in ordinary ink at the top of a sheet of paper while the apparently blank remainder of the page contained Deane's letter to Morris of 17 Sept. 1776 written in invisible ink. In his letter to Morris, Deane advised him that a shipment of clothing, powder, cannon, and ammunition would be sent from France in October and urged Congress to "give commissions to seize Portugese ships." "The Deane Papers," N.Y.H.S., *Colls.*, XIX (1886), 247.

3 Benjamin Harrison, Richard Henry Lee, William Hooper, Dr. John Witherspoon (1723–94) of New Jersey, and Thomas Johnson were JJ's and Morris's colleagues on the Committee of Secret Correspondence. Harrison, Johnson, and JJ were named to the Committee 29 Nov. 1775; Morris was appointed 30 Jan. 1776; and Lee, Witherspoon, and Hooper were added to the Committee on 11 Oct. 1776. *JCC*, III, 392; IV, 104; VI, 867.

4 Committee at Philadelphia to Congress, 4 Feb. 1777, DNA: PCC, 137, Appendix, 137.

5 Major William West, Jr., of the 3d Pennsylvania Battalion was captured at Fort Washington, 16 Nov. 1776. James Jauncey, Jr., the son-in-law of Andrew Elliott, the royal Collector of Customs at New York, was seized by the New York Convention in the summer of 1776 and sent to Connecticut. On 21 Jan. 1777 the Continental Congress resolved to permit the exchange of West for Jauncey subject to the approval of the New York authorities. *JPC*, II, 233.

6 Thomas Johnson, as first brigadier general of the Maryland militia, led 1800 men to Washington's headquarters at Morristown, N.J., at the end of January 1777.

From Lewis Morris

Philadelphia, February 15th, 1777

Dear Sir

I yesterday received your Letter of the 3d instant.[1] When I came to this place, Bob Morris told me he had wrote very pressing to Congress to come here, and from the necessity of affairs at present he had not the least doubt but that they would come, and therefore advised me not to set off untill he got an answer to his Letter, which last night was not come.[2] As Soon as it does, if they should be determined not to remove I shall immediately set out for Baltimore. Until then it will not be in my power to write you fully relative to Doctor Morgan, but whenever it is you may rest assured I shall do it.

Some time ago I Saw Coll Livingston at Prussia.[3] He Says that the Leut Coll is vacant in his Regiment, and expressed a desire that Lewis or Jacob should be appointed. However the Committee are the best judges, and I am sure if they can consistent with their duty they will.[4] My Son Jacob at the request of Mr West, begs of me to write to you for your interest in bringing about an exchange of James Jancey Junior for Major West. He is a good Officer, and I think the exchange must be in our favor. Morris has wrote you on this Subject.

The great resort of People to this Place has raised the Markets to a most enormous price, Beef at 1/ to 1/6 mutton 1/ to 1/6 Turkes from 10/ to 15/ Ducks 6/ to 8/ fowls 3/ to 4/.

I had the pleasure a few nights ago to Spend the Evening with Governor Livingston; we were very merry, as he was in high Spirrits. He is now at a place called Hattenfield with his Assembly;[5] it is within Six Miles of this Town. Mrs Morris[6] joins me in our best regards to Mrs. Jay and all friends at Fish Kills. Believe me Dear Sir Yours Most Sincerely

LEWIS MORRIS

ALS. Endorsed in an unidentified hand.

[1] See above, JJ to Lewis Morris, 3 Feb. 1777.

[2] See above, Robert Morris to JJ, 4 Feb. 1777.

[3] King of Prussia, a town near Valley Forge, Pa.

[4] John Hulbert was named lieutenant colonel of Henry Beekman Livingston's 4th New York Regiment in the plan submitted to the Convention by the committee on arrangements in November 1776. Hulbert resigned his commission the following month. General Morris's sons, Lewis, Jr. (1752–1824) and Jacob (1755–1844), were commissioned majors in the New York militia in 1776 and 1775, respectively. Lewis, Jr., became General John Sullivan's aide-de-camp in August 1776 and continued in this post until June 1779. Jacob Morris joined Charles Lee's staff in the late spring of 1776 and served at Charleston before accompanying the General back to New York in the fall. In December 1776 Jacob Morris was offered the post of major in the newly organized 5th New York, but he declined this appointment. Neither of the Morris brothers was appointed to the vacant colonelcy in Livingston's regiment. *Cal. of Hist. Mss.*, II, 4, 35.

[5] JJ's father-in-law, William Livingston, was elected the first governor of the State of New Jersey in August 1776. As British forces advanced into New Jersey in the fall and winter of 1776, the legislature sat, successively, at Princeton, Trenton, and Burlington. When the assembly reconvened on 22 Jan. 1777 sessions were held for two days at Pitts Town before adjournment to Haddonfield in Gloucester County.

[6] Mary Walton Morris (1727–94).

FROM HENRY G. LIVINGSTON

Rhinebeck, 23 February 1777

Sir

Would esteem it a favor, when you write Gen. Washington, you'd assure him from me that my intentions were not inimical to my country going in York, but thought I could have been of service, and was in hopes to have returned immediately, which I could have done, had not the treachery of Wallace prevented. Am in hopes my future conduct will convince the world I ever did and do now love my country equal to any person existing, and as a further testimony of which, if agreeable to Gen. Washington, will immediately join the army in his department, as a Volunteer or any other capacity most agreable to him, for I think I can be of singular service there by encouraging the soldiery [and] acquainting them with facts which I know [by] experience. This is the advice of some of my best friends, particularly Mr. Duer whose friendship I've often experienced. I want my zeal in this cause to be as conspicuous and held in the esteem it formerly was, and no pains or risque shall be wanting to accomplish it. I make no doubt but *your* friendship will readily be given to restore a person to the love of his country who has undeservedly lost it.

Your humble servant,

H. G. LIVINGSTON

Tr. In late January 1777 the Committee for Detecting Conspiracies received reports that Henry Gilbert Livingston (1754–1817) had been seen in British-occupied New York City earlier that month. On 15 February Livingston, who had served as brigade major and aide to General William Alexander during the Long Island campaign in August 1776, appeared before the committee. Livingston explained that in December 1776 he had traveled to Connecticut, where he met Hugh Wallace, a member of New York's royal council, who had advised him to go behind British lines since the Americans would soon be defeated "and that the sooner this Deponent [Livingston] took the Benefit of Lord and General Howes proclamation [of pardon] the better. . . ." On 25 Dec. 1776 Livingston subscribed to Lord Howe's oath of allegiance, but he claimed that he had done this only to avoid suspicion that he was an American spy. Livingston asserted that after taking the oath he had tried to leave the city, but had been turned back at his first attempt. Six days prior to his hearing before the Committee, Livingston appeared before General George Clinton, surrendered his copy of the oath taken in New York, and took an oath of allegiance to the "United States of America." In a further effort to clear himself of suspicion, Livingston gave the Committee information concerning British troop movements and the reports of conversations with people whom he had encountered behind British lines.

Livingston may have been all the more ready to follow Wallace's advice since he had been recently disappointed in a bid for a place in the New York line. On 7 Nov. 1776 Alexander McDougall urged the New York Convention to name Livingston lieutenant colonel in the reorganized 1st New York Regiment.

Shortly thereafter McDougall was forced to write the Convention that Livingston's name should be withdrawn since conversations with members of the regiment had shown that "those officers who are worth retaining in the service will not continue" should Livingston be appointed. "Minutes of the Committee for Detecting Conspiracies," N.Y.H.S., *Colls.*, LVII, 108, 115, 119–25; *Cal. of Hist. Mss.*, II, 15; 5 *FAA*, III, 558; *GCP*, I, 594–95.

From Thomas Johnson

Basking Ridge, 24 February 1777

My dear Sir

I am much obliged by your Favor which reached me in the Jerseys; in my Way, at philadelphia, I had the pleasure of reading the Address which you kindly inclosed me.[1] I had in my own Mind given you the Credit of having a principal Hand in it. When I left Home I had no Expectation of crossing the Delaware. I imagined our utmost Exertions would scarce save philadelphia; our people like all other Militia are tired and had I not received a Summons Yesterday to take on me a Civil Office my Generalship would have ended in a few Days. No Matter you'll say for the Skill I had in that Way; I think so too but I felt a strong Desire to do the little I could when Things were at the worst. The Americans are almost daily pecking at our Enemies and if it is continued we shall, I believe, make and kill a good many Soldiers.

By the Express which came to me Yesterday I understand the Congress intend to remove soon to phil[adelphi]a. It will give me no Inquietude though I fancy the most democratical Gent[lemen] find they have at least as much Democracy at Home as Mankind can bear. In Maryland we have more than I wish because I think we have too much for the Quiet and Happiness of my Countrymen. I have been so strongly impressed with this Idea that it was my Wish and more than half my Resolution not to have any thing to do in an Executive whose powers are much inadequate to the Ends of it's Institution. Perhaps if others are convinced on Experience of what I am satisfied in Theory we may in Time get Things to rights. I have not been at Congress for a long Time past; it was pretty enough at first. Amongst the Acquisitions I made there there is none I re[me]mber with greater pleasure than the Acquaintance I gained with you, Mr. Duaine and a few others. You know I do not love to write Letters which must be my Excuse for not writing to him at present yet am I desirous of being thought of by him wherefore put him in Mind of me and tell him I am well.

I am my dear Sir With great Sincerity and Affection Your Friend and Servant

TH. JOHNSON

ALS. Addressed erroneously: "James Jay Esqr. at The FishKilns." Endorsed by JJ: "Govr. Johnson of Maryland, 24 Feb. 1777." Earlier in February 1777 Johnson had been elected the first governor of the State of Maryland; he was inaugurated 21 March 1777.

1 Letter not located. *Address of the Convention of . . . New-York, to their Constituents.*

FROM WILLIAM LIVINGSTON

Haddonfield, 3d March 1777

Dear Sir

Mrs. Livingston informs me that Master Peter is now really gone; and one of his Grandfathers can inform you that he will go home with a Heavy Heart upon account of his being gone.

General Howe is lately arived at Brunswick and the Enemy's Army reinforced with between 3000 and 4000 men. They now doubtless intend to make some last Push to retrieve their late Disgraces. And though We have for some time past kept them at Bay, and so stuck to them that they could scarcely stirr for the purpose of foraging without being drove into their Quarters with loss and infamy, I fear that we are not sufficiently strong to resist, if they should all move in a Body, and I am not sure that they have yet given over their Project of visiting at Philadelphia. Our Assembly, after having spent as much time in framing a Militia Bill, as Alexander would have required to subdue Persia, will at last make such a ridiculous Bussiness of it, as not to oblige a single man to turn out who can only bring him to consume three gallons of spirits in Toddy Per Annum less than he does at present.[1]

Please accept of the inclosed, and believe me to be Your most humble servant

WIL. LIVINGSTON

ALS. Addressed: "To John Jay Esqr, Kingston, Ulster County, State of New York." Endorsed. Enclosure: Livingston's speech to the New Jersey Council and Assembly, 28 Feb. 1777. In this address Livingston presented his "Sentiments on the present Situation of Affairs; and the eventful Contest between *Great-Britain* and *America*"; the speech is found in Evans, 15464 (misdated 25 Feb.), and in the *Votes and Proceedings of the General Assembly of the State of New-Jersey . . .* (Burlington, 1777), pp. 85 ff.

1 On 24 Jan. 1777 Governor Livingston sent a message to the assembly

urging a new and more effective militia law. He repeated his plea on 3 February but no militia bill was reported in the assembly until 19 February. The bill passed the assembly three days later, but met opposition in the council. On 1 March a committee of conference from the two houses was formed to prepare a compromise bill and the committee's report was presented to the Assembly on 7 March. After further debate in the assembly acceptable provisions were adopted on 13 March and the statute received Livingston's signature on 15 March 1777. The Militia Law of 1777 provided for a sliding scale of fines, from £5 to £40, to be imposed on enlisted men or officers who refused to march in time of "Invasion or Alarm," while citizens exempted from militia duty by reason of age, physical disability, or occupation were to be taxed in lieu of military service. *Votes and Proceedings of the General Assembly of the State of New-Jersey . . .*, pp. 52, 56, 73–74, 76, 90, 94–95, 103–04, 105; *Acts of the General Assembly of the State of New-Jersey At a Session Begun . . . on the 27th Day of August 1776 . . .* (Burlington, 1777), ch. XX, pp. 26–36.

FROM LEWIS MORRIS

Philadelphia, March 8th, 1777

Dear Sir

A Mr. Jackson[1] that will hand you this goes to our state in order to fix on some person or persons to make Sale of the States Lottery Tickets. I have wrote to Gou[verneu]r on the Subject, but least he should not be there, I have Troubled you with this.[2]

The Congress meets to day for the first time since their flight.[3] I wish to God we had more men in jersey. You may be assured from the best Authority Howe has not more than Seven Thousand Eight hundred Sick and well, shamefull to the Continent that they do not drive him out. However let us hope for the best; they go on very Sloly with recruiting in this State. The man waits for this I mean Jacksons Servant, So must conclude with mine and the family's best regards to Mrs Jay and believe me Dear Sir Yours Most Sincerely

LEWIS MORRIS

ALS. Addressed: "John Jay Esq. at Esopus. In Convention. Mr. Jackson." Endorsed erroneously: ". . . 3d March 1777."

1 Dr. David Jackson (1747?–1801), a Philadelphia physician, was a Pennsylvania delegate to the Continental Congress. On 26 Nov. 1776 Jackson was elected a manager of the Continental lottery established on 1 November "for defraying the expences of the next campaign. . . ." On 30 November Congress resolved that the lottery managers "be authorized to appoint agents for the sale of tickets in the several states," and on 14 Feb. 1777 Congress ordered the managers to send tickets to the states. *JCC*, VI, 917, 968, 981–82, 994, 1007; VII, 119.

2 Lewis Morris to Gouverneur Morris, not located.

3 Congress was unable to make a quorum at Philadelphia until 12 March 1777. *JCC*, VII, 169.

From Alexander McDougall

Head Quarters, Peeks Kill, 9th March 1777

Sir

General Sullivan arrived here to To-day from Head Quarters in Jersey. He had it in charge from General Washington to communicate to me, a matter of the utmost importance in Condfidence.[1] It is of Such a Nature and of Such moment that it must not be commited to Paper. I cannot Posibly Quit this post, or I would have mounted my Horse the moment he left me, (in his way to Connecticut) to converse with you on the Subject, in order that the Convention might be made acquainted with it, in a way the most advansive of the Public Security. Colonel Livingston[2] informed me this evening, that you intended to Set off tomorrow morning for Kingston, induced me to Send you this by express. I have therefore to beg of you to come down to this post, as soon as Posible. You must not think of goeing up before I see you; more depends upon it, than you can conceive. It cannot be let off to convention without previous deliberation; nor will it be Safe to risque it on Paper; and the Subject requires dispatch.[3] I flatter my Self you have so much Condfidence in my Judgment, that I would not urge you to this Journey without necessity Called for it. Adieu.

ALEXR. McDOUGALL

ALS. Endorsed: ". . . Desiring me to come to Peeks Kill." On 21 Dec. 1776 McDougall was ordered to return to the Highlands from New Jersey to command at Peekskill "in Conjunction with" George Clinton. *GWF*, VI, 419.

1 Major General John Sullivan apparently delivered to McDougall Washington's letter of 6 March 1777 in which the commander ordered McDougall to compile "exact returns" of all the troops in New York "except those which are gone to Ticonderoga," and to call these forces to Peekskill, "there to hold themselves in perfect readiness to march at a moment's warning." Expecting a spring offensive against Philadelphia, Washington planned to use Peekskill as an assembly point for forces from New England as well as from New York, so that troops could easily be moved to the south in case of a British attack. On 9 March Sullivan reported to Washington: "I have called on General McDougale & Informed him Confidentially of the State of our Army—he Says there is about 600 Continental Troops here with two Massa. Militia Regts—he is of opinion that the Continental Troops here Should be Sent forward & that this State Should Garrison this post, for which purpose he will call on Mr Jay to consult with him about the most effectual Measures to Bring it About." Washington to McDougall, 6 March 1777, *GWF*, VII, 257–58; Sullivan to Washington, 9 March 1777, "Letters and Papers of Major-General John Sullivan, Continental Army," N.H.H.S., *Colls.*, XIII (1930), 326–27.

2 Henry Beekman Livingston.

3 On 12 March McDougall wrote Washington: "I sent for Mr. Jay and . . .

we were both of Opinion, that Draughts must immediately be made out of the Militia, to fill up the Regiments. He is gone to Convention, to endeavour to accomplish it. I think he will effect it." JJ did not join the New York Convention until 17 March. While the Convention made some provisions for strengthening the armaments of the Highland forts in the next week, no resolutions for calling out the militia to Peekskill and other strongholds were passed until 24 March, when news of the British raid on Peekskill made reinforcement of the Highlands imperative. McDougall to Washington, 12 March 1777, DLC: Washington Papers, Series 4; *JPC*, 838, 847–48.

From Robert Troup

Peeks Kill, March 22, 1777

Dear Sir,

I thought it would be best to defer writing to the Com[mittee] of Arrangement about my late Appointment 'till Col. Livingston accepted of my Resignation. He, so far from being displeased, approved of my Conduct. I shall therefore not meet with the least Difficulty. By Dyckman I sent a Letter to the Committee. You will see it. I endeavoured to be as decent as possible.[1] Tomorrow I shall set off for Jersey. I have not seen my Sisters for this twelve month past. Unless I embrace the present Opportunity I shall probably not have another during the ensuing Campaign. I wish I could see Mrs. Jay and Sister[2] before I went. I shall make it my Business to visit the Governor's[3] Family.

We have little News here. Last Night I had a long Conversation with one of my old Fellow Prisoners who came from the City the Day before Yesterday. He says the Enemy is vastly distressed for fresh Provisions. Beef sells for 2/6, Mutton 3/ and a Turkey 6 Dollars. The Tories are still insolent and abusive. They flatter themselves with an Idea of a speedy Conquest of America. The Prisoners were removed some Time ago to L Island. They are billeted upon the Inhabitants of Flat-Bush, New Utrecht and Graves-End. They indulge themselfes in Pleasures of every Kind. Dancing they are particularly fond of. A Night seldom passes without a Hop. The Behaviour of the Girls on these Occasions is truly Spirited and noble. Col. Ed. Fanning's Regiment[4] is stationed on that Part of the Island. His officers several Times engaged a Room, and made every Preparation for a splendid Ball; but the Ladies disappointed them. They declared they would not associate with them, while they could be honored with the Company of the handsome, genteel, sensible and virtuous Sons of America.

When I reflect upon this Circumstance I almost regret I was so soon exchanged. It would have given me the highest Satisfaction to have tormented them. He also says they have fared much better in every Respect since the Trenton and Princeton Actions. They have now the best Feather Beds and the best Provisions the Country can produce. He says Nothing of any Preparations to leave N York. From the best Accounts he could collect the Enemy intended to co-operate by Sea and Land in an Attempt upon Philadelphia. This Opinion is confirmed by a Letter I received yesterday from Col. Hamilton.[5] It is generally believed at Head Quarters that Phil[adelphia] will be the object of their subsequent operations. I wish our Men were raised. If our Army was properly collected in Jersey, their Maneuvers might be attended with their Ruin.

Yours etc. in Haste

R. TROUP

ALS. Endorsed. While serving as a captain in the New York militia, Troup was captured at the Battle of Long Island in August 1776 and was exchanged 9 Dec. 1776. During his imprisonment Troup was named first lieutenant in Colonel Henry Beekman Livingston's 4th New York Regiment.

1 The committee on arrangements was appointed by the New York Convention on 30 Sept. 1776 to implement the resolutions of Congress authorizing the establishment of four Continental battalions from New York for the duration of the war. The committee's report, listing the officers for four battalions and recommending the creation of a 5th regiment, was adopted by the Committee of Safety in November 1776. After the Continental Congress approved the "arrangements" of November, including a 5th regiment, the committee continued in existence through the winter of 1776–77, resolving disputes over rank and providing for new commissions when officers resigned their posts. Troup wrote the committee on 21 March 1777 to resign his commission in Livingston's unit to accept a captain lieutenancy in a Continental artillery corps. *JPC*, I, 712–14, 715, 747; *Cal. of Hist. Mss.*, II, 3–54; Livingston to the committee, 21 March 1777, *JPC*, II, 414.

2 SLJ and Catharine W. Livingston.

3 William Livingston.

4 Colonel Edmund Fanning (1737–1818) of the Associated Refugees or King's American Regiment of Foot, a Loyalist unit.

5 Alexander Hamilton to Troup, not located. Troup and Hamilton had shared rooms at King's College. On 1 March 1777 Hamilton was named lieutenant colonel and aide-de-camp to Washington.

From Sarah Livingston Jay

Fish Kill, March 23d–24, [1777]

The happiness of my dear Mr. Jay is so nearly connected with my own that it is impossible for mine to be intire when I have reason to apprehend that yours is in any-wise diminished, which I fear has been the case when I wrote you that I was unwell with a cold.[1] It is in order to remove any anxiety you may feel on that account that I again trouble you with another letter, as I am perfectly recovered.

Your father and mother still continue very much indisposed. They desire to be affectionately remembered to you.

Accept my thanks for your last letter.[2] I assure you I felt a secret pleasure when I observed that in sending those letters to the Post-office (which I did the day after your departure) and in sometimes visiting and often inquiring about your horse I had been beforehand with your wishes. Thinking of your horse reminds me of an odd accident that happened yesterday to Claas, who I had sent to your father's for grain in the morning. He returned at noon without his bag, and in tears, inquiring for the doctor,[3] at which I was alarmed, and asked him the cause of his uneasiness; after a few sobs he replied that in his way home being asleep, he was awakened by a couple of men who were holding his horse, and insisted upon having his whip to rouse him, which accordingly they wrested from him and after awaking him sufficiently, they took his bag of grain, and bid adieu. The Doctor not being at home he returned alone in pursuit of the men who had so unpolitely disturbed his rest, and overtook them at Mr. Wickoff's, to whom he related his story, but to the surprise of Claas they absolutely denied there having ever seen him before, and insisted upon it that if he had been asleep he had likewise dreamt; but the whipping was too recent in his memory to admit that thought, and he returned without receiving any satisfaction, or obtaining any intelligence from them about his bag, but near the place that they had stoped him he found it hanging on the fence; the impatience With which he had pursued the men had prevented his percieving it before.

Our dear little boy is well and in fine spirits, he has been setting on my lap playing with the pen, by which means he interupted me till Fady came in, and informed me that General Scott was going to Esopus to morrow. I shall trouble with this letter.

I have heard this afternoon that there are transports in the north river,[4] about 4 miles below Croton ferry. It's thought forage is the object they have in view, in consequence of which I hear it's ordered to be removed. This very instant the Doctor came into the room, his look bespeaking the utmost discomposure. Bad news Mrs. Jay, aye Doctor what now? The regulars madam are landed at Peekskill,[5] my own and other waggons are presed to go instantly down to remove the Stores. Wherever I am, I think there are alarms. However I am determined to remember your maxim, prepare for the worst and hope the best. The Doctor is now going to Fish-kill. I leave my letter unsealed till he returns.

Sister Caty gives her Compliments to you. She intends writing a letter to be inclosed in this for mamma and begs you'll forward it as soon as possible. May the blessings of peace be soon restored to us! And that health and safety may ever attend you is the sincere prayer of your affectionate Wife

SARAH JAY

Monday Morning, [24 *March*]

The Doctor returned at midnight; he says that Mr. Duer is come to Fish-Kill and that he says not less than twelve hundred of the Enemy landed at Peekskill, that General McDougal with the men under his command (a small number) were upon the high hill near the place where the regu[lars had] landed and that they had been firing sometime. I wish I kn[ew what i]s to be done with your white chest. It is not perhaps safe [or a]t least the stores being all ordered from Fish Kill make me think not. All the forrage and other Stores (except ammunition) are burnt at Peeks Kill. The Militia are all order[ed] down. This morning Frank was here. He tells me Peter came home last night, and that Mamma is very Ill. A line from you by the first opportunity to advise me in what manner to proceed will much oblige your Affectionate Wife

SARAH JAY

ALS. Addressed: "To The Honble John Jay Esqr. at Esopus." Endorsed.

1 SLJ discussed her illness in a letter to JJ of 21 March 1777, JP.

2 Letter not located.

3 The Jays' landlord, Dr. Theodorus Van Wyck.

4 The Hudson.

5 For the British raid on Peekskill, see below, Robert Troup to JJ, 29 March 1777.

To Sarah Livingston Jay

Kingston, 25 *March* 1777

My dear Sally

Accept my thanks for your affectionate Letters of the 17th and 21st Inst.[1] I am happy to hear of the Health of yourself and Son and am pleased with your Candor and Sincerity on that Subject.

I have received a Letter from Susan. She appears to have been in high Spirits and well pleased with her Situation. As the Chearfulness diffused through it may give you Pleasure, and the *divine* Stroke contained in it, excite agreable Sensations in Cate, I inclose it. I hope however its Influence will not be so great as to induce her to regret her Journey to FishKill.

We have lately recieved an uncertain tho unpleasant account of the Enemys landing at Peeks Kill.[2] How did your Nerves bear the Shock? My Father and Mother I apprehend were very uneasy. I should be happy were [it] in my Power to bear all their as well as all your Misfortunes. The Infirmities of Age added to the Terrors and Calamities of War conspire in depriving them of Ease and Enjoyment. I most sensibly feel for and pity them. God grant them the only Remedy against the Evils inseparable from Humanity, Fortitude founded on Resignation. The moment I may suspect you to be exposed to Danger I shall set out for Fish Kill. As Yet I think you very safe, for if the Report we have heard be true, the Enemys Force is not sufficient to penetrate the Country.

I congratulate Peter on his Recovery and Return. Remind him of sending to Capt. Platts for the Barley. Let not the Fear of the Enemy deter him from pursuing the Business of the Farm. The same Providence which enables us to sow, may enable us to reap.

Present my Compliments to our good Friend the Doctor and Mrs. V. Wycke. My Love to Cate. I am my dear Wife your very affectionate

JOHN JAY

ALS. Enclosure: Susan Livingston to JJ, *c.* March 1777, not located. Susan Livingston (b. 1748) was SLJ's sister.

[1] SLJ to JJ, 17 and 21 March 1777 in JP.

[2] On Monday, 24 March, the New York Convention was notified of the 23 March raid on Peekskill. *JPC*, I, 847.

From Robert Troup

Fish Kill, March 29, 1777

My dear Sir,

Had I not been prevented by Business, I should have informed you earlier of what has happened below.[1] But having not yet seen any Account altogether true, I have taken the Liberty of sending you the following Particulars, of which I was a Spectator. On Sunday the 23d ultimo, about 11 o'Clock in the Morning, the Brune Frigate, with the two Gallies taken from us last Fall, and four Transports anchored in Peeks-Kill Bay. At 1 PM. the 15th, 23d, 44th and 64th Regiments, with 50 of the Train of Artillery, under the Command of Major Hutchinson, landed at Lent's Cove, the South Side of the Bay, (under cover of the Gallies,) about a Mile and a half from the Town; they immediately formed and advanced with 4 Field Pieces, to Kronk's

Hill, on the South East of the Town. Before they landed, several Boats, [fille]d with Men, rowed towards the North Landing, as if they intended [to ma]ke a Descent at that Place, with a View of flanking us, or getting in our Rear. From the Number of Boats employed in landing the Troops, Gen. McDougall and every discerning officer were clearly of Opinion that the Enemy's Force far exceeded ours; but the General determined to have the fullest Evidence, before he quitted the Post, and therefore waited for them in a Position, from which our Retreat was secured, till they came within Muskit Shot. At this Distance, we had a full View of the Enemy, who were at least treble our Force. As they advanced they cannonaded us, by which we had one Man mortally wounded. The Rum, and Flour being destroyed and the heavy Artillery sent off (except one Iron 12 Pounder, which was left for Want of Horses,) the Gen. ordered the Troops to retire, which they did in good Order, to Barrack No. 2, about two Miles and a half from the Town, the Enemy not daring to disturb us in our Retreat. Here we took Post to secure the Pass of the Mountains and some Mills, containing a Quantity of Flour and Grain, belonging to the Continent.

The next Day they placed a Piquet Guard, consisting of upwards 100 Men, a Mile from our Front. At 4 o'Clock in the afternoon, Lt Col. Willett with about 70 of Gansevoort's Regiment,[2] got undiscovered, to a Hill in their Front, and immediately detached Cap. Swarthout[3] with a few of his Men, with Orders to attack them in Front, and make a regular Retreat, in Case the Enemy should advance. This Manouvre was intended to draw them from the Height, which they occupied, and give the other Part of the Detachment, an Opportunity of falling in upon their Rear, while Cap. Riker, of Col. Cortlandt's Regiment,[4] with 10 Men, advanced along a Creek on their left, with a View of flanking them. But Col. Willett's Party were discovered, before this could possibly be effected, and a very smart Skirmish ensued, which lasted about 15 Minutes; the Col. apprehending that their Main Body would advance to sustain their Piquet, ordered his Men to fix Bayonets, and rush upon the Enemy, which they perceiving fled with the greatest Precipitation.

We had two Men wounded, one dangerously; the Inhabitants say the Enemy had nine killed and wounded. Their Main Body were drawn up in View of the Field, where the Skirmish happened; they appeared to be Panic struck, and immediately prepared to reimbark, which they did, the same Evening, leaving behind a large Quantity of nails and other Stores, which from the Precipitancy of their Flight they had not time to send off to their Ships. The next Morning we took Possession of the Town, and the Day following, the Ships fell down below Croton's River. These Maroders (according to their usual Practice) plundered, and abused some Houses and burnt several others, carried off a few Cattle, and Sheep and some light Articles from the public Stores. Our principal Loss is in Rum, Molasses, and Flour which we destroyed, and a Quantity of Sugar burnt by the Enemy in the Commissary's Store. The Militia on the first Alarm turned out with the greatest Alacrity, and marched to our Assistance, and if these British Heroes had staid a Day longer, we should have had the Pleasure of paying them for their Trouble. A Sufficient Number of flat bottomed Boats, and the large Scow are preserved, so that the Ferry will be carried on as formerly.

I have the Pleasure of observing to you that the Conduct of our Officers and Men on this Occasion would have done Honor to the oldest Veterans. The Spirit, Zeal, and Activity they discovered give me sufficient Reason to believe that we shall end the War the ensuing Campaign, if the Continental Regiments are properly filled. I wish the Convention would adopt some other Mode of raising their Quota.[5] It is really an object of Importance, and till it is done, we shall have the lower Parts of the State continually exposed to the Ravages of the Enemy.

One Circumstance, however, I have omitted which perhaps will astonish you. It is this. *That vile, infamous, rascally, hypocritical Friend to America* [*Beverly Robinson*][6] *was their principal Guide and assistant at P. Kill.* I think it may be depended on, because several of the Inhabitants say they saw him on the Spot. As it is somewhat material to know the Certainty of this ma[tter] Gen. McDougall intends to make particular Inquiries about it. This Fray prevented my going to Morris Town according to Expectation. I shall though without fail set out next Wednesday. This Morning I waited upon Mrs. Jay and Katy and desired them to prepare their Letters which I shall deliver in Person. I found the Family well. Little Peter has had another Cold since you saw him; but it has left him. The Rogue looks as healthy and lively as any Child I ever saw.

The French Ship has certainly arrived at the Eastward and two at the Southward, with Arms, Ammunition, Clothing etc. A fifty Gun Ship with many Pieces of artillery and twenty odd Vessels with other Necessaries under her Convoy are hourly expected in Boston.[7] Pilots are already sent to bring them safely in.

Yours etc.

R. TROUP

ALS. Addressed: "The Honble John Jay, at Kingston." Endorsed. Tr. in NN: Bancroft American Series, I, 128-1/2.

[1] The American post at Peekskill lay about twelve miles down the Hudson from Fishkill Landing.

[2] Lieutenant Colonel Marinus Willett headed a detachment at Fort Independence a few miles from Peekskill. McDougall summoned Willett's men on the morning of 23 March when he first received warning of a possible British attack. Willett and his troops were part of the 3d New York Regiment commanded by Colonel Peter Gansevoort (1749–1812).

[3] Captain Abraham Swartwout of the 3d New York.

[4] Captain Abraham Riker of Colonel Philip Van Cortlandt's 2d New York.

[5] The New York Convention had named a committee to devise improved methods of recruiting for the Continental regiments on 3 March. This committee's report was considered on 27 March and recommitted. On 3 April the Convention adopted an amended report which provided for a system by which exemption from militia drafts could be obtained by any man who furnished an enlistee in the state's Continental units. *JPC*, I, 822, 829, 853, 863–64.

[6] Name partially obliterated in ms.

[7] The first vessel bearing military supplies from France docked at Portsmouth, N.H., on 17 March 1777. A week later, a second vessel from France arrived at Philadelphia. *JCC*, VII, 197; *LMCC*, II, 310, 352–53n.

From Lewis Morris

Philadelphia, April 14th–17th, 1777

Dear Jay

I did not until this day receive yours of 12 March.[1] I have wrote by almost every opportunity and shall continue so to do as long as I remain at this Place. Just now we had an alarm that the Enemy where coming up the river.[2] I hope and wish the People of this State may act like men. A few days ago I made a Motion in Congress that the Congress should direct to be immediately made an Elegant Standard, and on the approach of the Enemy they should Erect it, and that the Motto should be Conquer or Die. However they did not Seem to like it, in my opinion it would have had a good effect.[3]

I am Sorry and Say our Army is exceeding weak And I was some time ago for establishing a general and indiscriminate Ballote throughout all the States without any Respect to Rank Sect of Religion or Profession whatsoever. They seem now to be about doing Something of the kind.[4]

I hope when peace comes we shall not have our farms far apart. I am Sure we shall be happy and be good neibours. Aurora did not prove with foale and Mr. Lawrence has Sold her for two hundred pounds. I think you have made Capt. Platt[5] a present of the half of your horse. I am sure he would fetch £150 or more if he was here. Bay Richmond is much admired and I have been offered one thousand pounds. I saw my Price was two. He covers here at 20 Dollars the Season, and if Howe does not drive us away he will have a great many Mares.

April 17th. Nine Sail of men of war now in this river. Yesterday an account came up that they had burnt a large Ship belonging to Some Merchants bound out. Last night Livingston and Duane[6] came here. I shall Set of Soon for Esopus. Inclosed you have a Letter I wrote you Some time ago. It was a long time at Morristown and come back again. I Send to Shew that I have not neglected to write. My best regards to all friends. Yours most Sincerely

LEWIS MORRIS

ALS. Addressed: "The Honbl. John Jay Esquire, Kingston. favor of Saml Tudor Esqr." Endorsed. Enclosure: probably Morris to JJ, 15 Feb. 1777, printed above.

1 Letter not located.

2 Such reports had been current in Philadelphia for several days. James Sykes to George Read, 10 April 1777, and Thomas Burke to Richard Caswell, 15 April 1777, *LMCC*, II, 323–24, 325–26.

3 No record of such a motion appears in *JCC* for April 1777.

4 On 12 April 1777 Congress named a committee "to devise ways and means of aiding the recruiting service and preventing abuses therein." However, the committee's report, submitted 14 April, included no provision for creating a "ballot" or lottery for military service. *JCC*, VII, 257, 261–63.

5 Zephaniah Platt.

6 Philip Livingston and James Duane.

James Duane to Robert R. Livingston, John Jay, Gouverneur Morris, Robert Yates

Philadelphia, 19th April 1777

My dear Sirs

We arrived in this City on Wednesday afternoon. If you talk seriously to its Inhabitants you'l find them full of the Expectation of a Visit from General Howe; but examine their Conduct and the Appearance of everything about you, and you cannot but conclude that they are in a State of the most perfect Tranquility and Security. Talk to them about the scandalous depreciation of the continental and other paper money, and the extravagant Prices of all Commodities, they may go so far as to express their Concern; but they afect to consider it as an irremediable misfortune and nothing is farther from their Thoughts than to provide a Plan for Reformation.

Their Supreme executive have *adjourned themselves for a month—Executive* adjourned, say you, how is that possible? Sirs they *have* adjourned; not for want of Business, for surely no Country ever cried more loudly for a vigilant active and decisive Government. They have adjourned because—faith I cannot tell you why—perhaps for the Want of Authority to save their Country under their new Constitution, perhaps for want of Resolution to exercise the power they have. Under these Circumstances, the civil Governours having in effect abdicated for a month, Congress has interposed and supplied an executive as you'l observe by the Resolution enclosed.[1] With the free Consent of the *sleeping* executive Congress might have taken the whole power of the State into their Hands and provided for it's Safety as they pleasd. It is evident that this same supreme executive are under Apprehensions that must incumber and defeat all Business. They must not make themselves *Odious!* The People may not be satisfied with such a Measure! They wish Congress woud direct what they think best! They will chearfully submit every thing to our superior Wisdom etc. etc. I am of Opinion that Congress will recommend the Arrival of the Committees of Inspection etc. as essential to the Salvation of the State. It is truly the only System which can give sufficient Vigour Unanimity and Stability to publick Measures. These refined Speculative Plans may amuse: in times of peace they may produce Happiness: But Stagrante bello they afford no Hope of Success, no Prospect of Advantage.

The Reputation of our State stands high though on the floor we are surrounded with Strangers. This is an evil which will be cured by good manners and Sociability. It is in our power to be *civil,* as we keep House, and shall always have company when we dine at Home. I say we keep House, as we have taken a boarding House for our exclusive Use.

We have got a Committee appointed of one Member from each State to examine into General Schuyler's Conduct: but not without great difficulty and objections from our Neighbours. It was pretended that there was no Complaint against him; no Accusor and that therefore an Enquiry was absurd. This subtle Evasion did not pass. I am confident that Schuyler will be acquitted with Honour.[2]

Doctor Young formerly of our State has published an address to our Mountaineers advising them to be firm in their Revolt; and expresly assuring them that this is the opinion and wish of many leading members of Congress.[3] Col. Floyd[4] informed us that he had not been able, though he livd with Roger Sharman to make the least discovery of such a disposition.

I have only time now to add that I am with Compliments to all our Friends, and the utmost Regard to yourselves Dear Gentlemen, Your most Obedient humble Servant

JAS. DUANE

ALS. Enclosure: Resolution of Congress concerning the government of Pennsylvania, 15 April 1777, *JCC*, VII, 268–69. Duane's reasons for addressing his letter to these members of the New York Convention are not clear. While the four had been associated on many committees of the Convention, *JPC* does not record their appointment to any committee responsible for corresponding with New York's delegates in Congress in the spring of 1777.

[1] The governmental crisis in Pennsylvania under the state constitution ended after new assembly elections in February 1777. On 4 March the legislature was able to organize, and the first President of Pennsylvania's Supreme Executive Council, Thomas Wharton, was elected. However, on 21 March the assembly adjourned until 12 May, leaving the President and council to act in cases of emergency. The council met only until 9 April when members of the executive body were granted payment for their attendance and left for their homes until council sessions resumed on 6 May.

On the last day of council meetings a Congressional committee conferred with Pennsylvania officials on measures to be taken "for opposing the enemy, if they should attempt to penetrate through New Jersey, or to attack Philadelphia." Five days later Congress adopted the Committee's recommendations that a committee of three be named to "confer" with the President of Pennsylvania, the state Board of War, and Pennsylvania delegates in Congress "concerning the mode of authority which they shall conceive most eligible to be exercised, during the recess of the house of assembly and council. . . ." On 15 April this committee submitted its report which, as adopted by Congress, provided that the President of Pennsylvania with "as many members of" the Executive Council "as can be convened," and the Board of War and Navy Board of the state should "exercise every authority to promote the safety of the State, till such time as the legislative and executive authorities of the commonwealth of Pennsylvania can be convened." *Journals and Proceedings of the General Assembly of the Common-Wealth of Pennsylvania* (Philadelphia, 1777), I, 56; "Minutes of the Supreme Executive Council of Pennsylvania," *Pennsylvania Colonial Records* (16 vols., Philadelphia and Harrisburg, 1851–53), XI (1852), 204–06; *JCC*, VII, 246, 263–64, 268–69.

[2] The need to defend Philip Schuyler's professional and personal reputation had not ended when Congress declined to accept his resignation in October 1776. Indeed, the exoneration of the general's character was one of the major duties of the New York delegation in Philadelphia in the spring of 1777. Schuyler's position in the army was threatened at the end of March 1777 when Congress named Horatio Gates to command the American troops at Ticonderoga without stating explicitly whether Schuyler or Gates was to be in charge of the Northern Department. Schuyler himself took his seat in Congress for the first time since 1775 on 7 April 1777, and on 18 April a Congressional committee was named "to enquire into the conduct of Major General Schuyler, since he has held a command in the army of the United States." For Schuyler's threatened resignation in 1776, see above, Edward Rutledge to JJ, 24 Nov. 1776, n. 2; Don R. Gerlach, *Philip Schuyler and the American Revolution in New York, 1733–1777* (Lincoln, Neb., 1964), pp. 287–90; *JCC*, VII, 202, 279–80; *LMCC*, II, lx.

[3] Dr. Thomas Young (1732–77) published his letter "To the Inhabitants of Vermont, a free and independent State . . ." on 11 April 1777. The inhabitants of the Hampshire Grants had formed a separate state, to be called Vermont, on 15 Jan. 1777, and their "Declaration and Petition" seeking Congressional

support for their "freedom and independence" was read in Congress on 8 April 1777. "To the Inhabitants of Vermont . . . ," Evans, 15649; Declaration and Petition, 15 Jan. 1777, DNA: PCC, 40, I, 135–72; *JCC*, VII, 239; for the early intrusion of Vermont into New York and Congressional politics, see above, JJ and the Vermont Lands and Petition to the Earl of Dunmore, 12 June 1771; and Robert R. Livingston to JJ, 4 June 1776, n. 2.

4 William Floyd (1734–1821) was JJ's colleague on the New York delegation to the first Continental Congress and served intermittently in the second Congress, May 1775–December 1776.

Jay and the New York Constitution of 1777

Although the Fourth New York Congress was elected with an implied mandate to create a new state government, no constitution was approved for more than nine months after the Congress declared itself a "Convention" in July 1776. On 1 August 1776 the Convention named JJ to a committee to draft a plan of government, but members of the committee served simultaneously on such Convention bodies as the secret committee on fortification of the Hudson whose operations were given priority over that of drafting a constitution.[1] Two deadlines, 24 August and 4 September 1776, passed with no report from the committee and, at length, on 28 September the Convention ordered the committee to present a draft "on or before 12 October and to sit, if necessary, every afternoon till they shall be ready to report."[2] Although a draft was prepared by 18 October it was apparently unsatisfactory, and the committee resumed its work in November.[3] In the course of the next month presentation of the report was deferred twice.[4] While two committee members, Abraham Yates, Jr. (1724–96) of Albany, the chairman, and William Duer insisted that the draft was completed in February 1777, the draft constitution was not reported to the Convention until 12 March.[5] Five weeks of debate ensued before final approval of the constitution on 20 April 1777.

Traditionally JJ has received credit for having "written" the version of the constitution laid before the Convention in March 1777. His son William asserted that the plan reported by the committee "is in Mr. Jay's handwriting."[6] This claim was supported by Robert R. Livingston and by the pseudonymous writer "Schuyler" who stated in 1821 that the final draft was "chiefly or wholly drawn up by Mr. Jay, and is in his handwriting. There were annexed to it," Schuyler continued, " 'Addenda'. . . . These amendments and alterations were mostly introduced and supported by Mr. Jay, Mr. Duane, Mr. G. Morris, Mr. R. R. Livingston, and a few others; but the most considerable part of the constitution now stands as it came from the hands of Mr. Jay." It is clear, too, that the constitution represented a compromise between these well-known conservative leaders and more radical Whigs like Robert Yates of Albany and Henry Wisner and Charles De Witt of Ulster.[7]

But, if it is agreed that JJ's role in drafting the constitution was a significant one, the precise nature of his contribution is elusive. Much of the evidence pertaining to the preparation of the draft of March 1777 is confused or missing. The actual draft report considered by the Convention in March and April 1777 was not printed in *JPC* and has never been located by later scholars. Charles Z. Lincoln published two preliminary drafts, designated "A" (prepared in December 1776) and "B" (apparently dating from February 1777) in his *Constitutional History of New York.*[8] In addition, an intermediate draft, in fragmentary form, survives in the Yates Papers of the New York Public Library.

Bernard Mason, a recent student of the Convention's proceedings, concluded that until the completion of draft "B" in February 1777 "it seems clear that the constitution was the product of the joint labors of the committee," but that this was not the version submitted to the Convention in March. Instead, another version, "very likely Jay's handiwork," formed the basis for Convention debates.[9] Mason infers, from a reconstruction of that final report, as revealed in motions and amendments recorded in *JPC*, that JJ followed draft "B" closely and retained the topical order of its paragraphs, although he appears to have eliminated two sections, one describing territorial boundaries and another prescribing oaths of office. As well, JJ seems to have cut much extraneous detail from the section in draft "B" on Assembly elections. On the whole, Mason concludes, "Jay seems principally to have contributed clarity and economy of language" to the constitution in his final revision of the committee's drafts.[10]

All political thinkers draw on one another for ideas, and evidence exists that JJ's contribution to the New York constitution was consciously influenced by the theories of John Adams. When JJ left Philadelphia to take his place in the New York Provincial Congress, he carried with him a copy of "Thoughts on Government," a pamphlet published in January 1776, in which Adams described the type of government he recommended for adoption by the several states. James Duane reported this fact to Adams, who recalled it in a letter written to Thomas Jefferson nearly half a century later.[11] The brochure became, according to Duane, JJ's "Model and foundation," and there are in fact many similarities between what Adams advised and what JJ incorporated in his draft. If JJ did adopt some of these ideas, it has also to be said that Adams in turn owed debts to other political theorists. In "Thoughts on Government" he acknowledged the influence on his thinking of such seventeenth-century English aficionados of republicanism as James Harrington, John Locke, and John Milton.[12] From them he gained respect for the British constitution and faith in popular government responsive to the will of the people. He also shared their conviction that good administration depended on fixed, impartial laws and that only a careful separation and balance of powers could assure order and stability.

If Robert R. Livingston was thoroughly fatigued by theoretical speculations and declared that he would not "give one scene in Shakespeare for

1000 Harringtons, Lockes and [John] Adams,"[13] JJ was temperamentally less inclined to ignore authorities supporting his side. As Abraham Yates, Jr., pointed out retrospectively, the "diversity of opinion" that existed was not over whether the republican form of government should embody mixed elements of "monarchy, aristocracy, and democracy." Rather, the issue was "what proportion of the ingredients out of each should make up the components."[14]

The plan submitted to the Convention in March 1777 provided for a balanced state government, both innovative and relatively conservative. The assembly and Senate composed the bicameral legislature, with assemblymen chosen from counties and Senators from "four great Districts" in the state. Assemblymen, drawn from freeholders, were to be chosen annually by taxpaying freeholders in their respective counties, while Senators, also subject to freehold qualifications, were to be elected for four-year terms by £100 freeholders in their districts. The Governor, with limited executive powers, was to be a freeholder elected by Senatorial electors. The provincial judicial system, with a Supreme Court and Court of Chancery, was to be retained.

By the time the constitution was approved on 20 April 1777 this plan was modified considerably. The colonial £40 freehold qualification for voting for the assembly was lowered to a £20 freehold or "renting a tenement to the yearly value of 40 shillings," such qualification not to bar freeholders of Albany and New York City made freemen before 14 October 1775. On the other hand, in elections for governor and senators the old £40 freehold was raised to £100. Thus the state electorate was somewhat larger than the provincial, but only half the voters could vote for the higher offices.[15] As a gesture to more responsive government, assembly elections were made annual, instead of at four-year intervals as the conservatives desired, the number of representatives in the assembly increased from thirty-one to seventy, the three manor seats were abolished, and both the executive and legislative powers curbed. The executive structure was altered by the creation of two councils, one of Revision, the other of Appointment. The Council of Revision, in which the Governor was joined by the Chancellor and justices of the Supreme Court, could disallow bills passed by the legislature; the council's veto, in turn, could be overridden by a two-thirds vote of the senate and assembly. The Council of Appointment, consisting of the Governor and four Senators chosen by the Assembly, was to pass on nominees for state offices not otherwise provided for in the Constitution.

The pages of *JPC* show that JJ was as active as any member of the Convention in revising the draft constitution he had prepared. It is clear that the plan of government reported to the Convention in March 1777 did not represent JJ's ideal for state government, but was merely intended as a practical base for debate. On the floor of the convention JJ was quite ready to propose several items which it had seemed inadvisable to include in the committee draft.

There was, for example, his proposal for voting by ballot, as contrasted to *viva voce* methods. On 6 April JJ won adoption of an amendment which provided that "a fair experiment be made" of ballots in Senate and Assembly elections "as soon as may be after the termination of the present war." This amendment may have represented a compromise, for it provided that if the "experiment" proved unsuccessful, the legislature might reinstitute *viva voce* voting.[16] This provision could have been included to make the amendment more palatable to such Convention members as Gouverneur Morris who opposed ballot voting altogether, while other colleagues, notably Abraham Yates, Jr., a strong advocate of voting by ballot, sought to strike out the provision for legislative reinstatement of voice voting, and JJ apparently acted as mediator in the dispute.[17]

JJ also exerted his influence in Convention debates on behalf of his own views of religious freedom. The draft report submitted to the Convention provided for "the free toleration of religious profession and worship,"[18] but JJ attempted to modify his own draft proposal in a series of amendments introduced on 20 and 21 March. First JJ proposed that the religious toleration offered in New York would not "be construed to extend the toleration of any sect or denomination of Christians, or others . . . who inculcate and hold for true doctrines, principles inconsistent with the safety of civil society, of and concerning which the Legislature of this State shall from time to time judge and determine."[19] Debate on this amendment apparently convinced JJ that the proposal had little chance of success, and he withdrew it in favor of a second amendment which would have excluded from the general toleration "the professors of the religion of the church of Rome" who would be barred from owning land or enjoying civil rights until they had appeared before the state Supreme Court to swear that "no pope, priest or foreign authority on earth, hath power to absolve the subjects of this State from their allegiance to the same" and to renounce "the dangerous and damnable doctrine, that the pope, or any other earthly authority, have power to absolve men from sins . . . and particularly, that no pope, priest or foreign authority on earth, hath power to absolve them from the obligation of this oath."[20] This second amendment, with its explicit anti-Catholic bias, was defeated two to one.[21]

On 21 March JJ continued his fight against the Catholic Church. He then introduced a third amendment on religious toleration, this one providing that "the liberty of conscience hereby granted, shall not be construed to encourage licentiousness, or be used in such manner as to disturb or endanger the safety of the State."[22] This amendment, later modified further by the Convention, was adopted. Subsequently, JJ also succeeded in making special provisions for Catholics in the Constitution's article on the naturalization of foreigners. Under JJ's amendment aliens were not only required to take an oath of allegiance to the state, but to renounce any obligations "to all and every foreign king, prince potentate and state, in all matters ecclesiastical as well as civil."[23]

Despite the central role he had played, JJ was unable to remain at the

Convention until debates on the constitution were completed. On 17 April he was called away to attend his dying mother at Fishkill. Paradoxically, it was that very absence of JJ during the last three days of consideration of the new state government that gave him a subsequent opportunity to spell out his views on the New York constitution, views which have been recorded. After approving the final version of the constitution on 20 April, the Convention named a committee to prepare a "plan for organizing and establishing the government agreed to by this Convention." JJ, Robert R. Livingston, John Morin Scott, Gouverneur Morris, Abraham Yates, Jr., and John Sloss Hobart were named to this panel. At the same time the Convention ordered one of its secretaries to travel to Fishkill to arrange for the printing of three thousand copies of the new constitution.[24]

John McKesson (c. 1735–98), the secretary designated to supervise the printing, and John Sloss Hobart of the committee on the plan for organizing the government, arrived in Fishkill shortly after completion of work on the constitution and both conferred with JJ. JJ's reactions to the final version of the constitution were quickly reported to the Convention in letters from McKesson and his fellow secretary, Robert Benson (1739–1823). JJ's criticisms centered on important details in the organization of the state court system and on the method of electing Senators. On 19 April Abraham Yates, Robert R. Livingston, and Gouverneur Morris had joined in moving and seconding a series of motions which altered the judiciary plan as it had stood when JJ left Kingston. After their amendments had been adopted the right of designating the clerks of state courts was removed from the Council of Appointment and placed in the hands of the judges of the respective courts. Further, attorneys were required to "be appointed by the court and licensed by the first judge of the court in which they shall respectively plead or practise, and be regulated by the rules and orders of the said courts."[25]

John Sloss Hobart reported JJ's objections to the twenty-seventh article on the appointment of clerks in a letter from Fishkill dated 24 April 1777:

> Mr. Jay is Exceedingly unhappy about the 27th paragraph of the form of Government which puts the appointment of the Clerks of Courts in the power of the respective Judges. I do not recollect to have seen [him] so much dissatisfied about any other part of it. He alledges that 'tis puting in the power of the respective Judges to provide for Sons, Brothers, creatures, Dependants, &ca. That it will prevent obtaining Evidence against the most wicked Judge should such be appointed. Corrupt Bargains may be made for appointments to those offices. If the Tenor of the office should render it too precarious to be purchased yet the grantee may appoint upon conditions to receive part of the profits. By the second sentence of the paragraph every attorney & councellor must be licensed in every court in the state in which he may incline to practice. . . . As Mr. Jay from the state of the Family

cannot go to convention immediately & says he will give notice and move for the reconsideration of the 27th paragraph as soon as he shall arive at Kingston that the Records may at least bear his Testimony against it. Would it not be best to reconsider the paragraph immediately & if any amendment should be made it might arrive here on Saturday. . . .[26]

JJ's objections to the rules for licensing attorneys and his displeasure with the constitution's provisions for the election of Senators were apparently outlined in a letter from John McKesson to Robert Benson, which has not been located but which is described in detail below.

The first letter printed below is the response of JJ's friends and colleagues, Robert R. Livingston and Gouverneur Morris, to reports from Hobart and McKesson of JJ's criticisms of the Convention's handiwork. Here, and in JJ's reply, modern readers have an unusual opportunity to glimpse the workings of New York's Convention of 1777 and to sense the conflicts which arose among even such close friends and allies as JJ, Morris, and Livingston.

Privately JJ, recognizing how delicately balanced the constitution was, retrospectively observed that "another turn of the winch would have cracked the cord."[27] Despite these reservations about details JJ's public position was one of enthusiastic endorsement of the constitution. He had been elected Chief Justice of the New York State Supreme Court of Judicature by the Provincial Convention on 3 May 1777, defeating his old antagonist John Morin Scott by four votes. (On the same day JJ's friend Robert R. Livingston defeated Scott in the race for Chancellor by six votes.)[28] Sitting in that post, he informed the Grand Jury of Ulster County on 9 September 1777, when the first court under the new constitution convened, of the solid merits of that document, comparing it favorably to the old governmental structure that it replaced. He singled out its respect for "those great and equal rights of human nature, which should forever remain inviolate in every society," for the "adequate security" given "to the rights of conscience and private judgment" (and this in the face of his own anti-Catholic proposals), but described as wise the provision which would not construe liberty of conscience so as "to excuse acts of licentiousness, or justify practices inconsistent with the peace or safety of the State."[29]

1 *JPC*, I, 552, 568. JJ's colleagues on the committee on the constitution were: Abraham Yates, Jr. (1724–96), the chairman, Gouverneur Morris, Robert R. Livingston, William Duer, John Sloss Hobart, John Morin Scott, Robert Yates, Henry Wisner, William Smith of Suffolk County, John Broome, and Samuel Townsend.

2 *JPC*, I, 594, 625, 649, 651.

3 Bernard Mason, *The Road to Independence: The Revolutionary Movement in New York, 1773–1777* (Lexington, Ky., 1966), p. 221.

4 Lincoln, *Constitutional Hist. of N.Y.*, I, 494.

5 *JPC*, I, 833.

6 *WJ*, I, 69.

7 Nathaniel Carter and William Stone, eds., *Reports of the Proceedings and Debates of the Convention of 1821* (Albany, 1821), p. 692. See also Alfred F. Young, *The Democratic Republicans of New York* (Chapel Hill, N.C., 1967), pp. 17, 18.

8 Lincoln, *Constitutional Hist. of N.Y.*, I, 501 ff.

9 Mason, *Road to Independence*, p. 227.

10 *Ibid.*, p. 228.

11 Lester J. Cappon, ed., *The Adams-Jefferson Letters: The Complete Correspondence Between Thomas Jefferson and Abigail and John Adams* (2 vols., Chapel Hill, N.C., 1959), II, 596–99; Charles Francis Adams, ed., *The Works of John Adams, Second President of the United States* (10 vols., Freeport, N.Y., 1969), IV, 191.

12 The genesis of Adams's ideas about state governments is described in John Adams, *Diary*, III, 351–59. Comprehensive analyses of his political thought will be found in John R. Howe, Jr., *The Changing Political Thought of John Adams* (Princeton, 1966) and Zoltán Haraszti, *John Adams and the Prophets of Progress* (Cambridge, Mass., 1952).

13 Livingston to Philip Schuyler, 2 Oct. 1776, NN: Philip Schuyler Papers.

14 Abraham Yates, Jr., 23 Feb. 1789, NN: "Rough Hewers."

15 For an analysis of this point, see Young, *The Democratic Republicans*, p. 19.

16 *JPC*, I, 866–67.

17 *Ibid.*

18 *Ibid.*, 844.

19 *Ibid.*; see also Evarts B. Greene, *Religion and the State, The Making and Testing of an American Tradition* (Ithaca, 1959), p. 81.

20 *Ibid.*

21 *Ibid.*

22 *Ibid.*, 845–46.

23 *Ibid.*, 846.

24 *Ibid.*, 898.

25 *Ibid.*, 889–90.

26 Misdated 24 "March," *Cal. of Hist. Mss.*, I, 678–79.

27 Cited by George Pellew, *John Jay* (Boston and New York, 1894), quoting William Jay.

28 *JPC*, I, 910.

29 *HPJ*, I, 158–65.

From Robert R. Livingston and Gouverneur Morris

Kingston, 26 April 1777

Dear Sir,

We were much surprized at your Letter to Mr. Hobart as we could not perceive the Danger which would result from permitting the several Courts to appoint their own Clerks while on the other Hand great Inconveniences must arise from suffering them to be independent of such Courts and of Consequence frequently ignorant always inattentive. Neither had we the most distant Idea that a Clause of this Sort could meet with your Disapprobation since you was so fully of Opinion to appoint by Judges of the supreme Court not only Clerks but all other civil officers in the Government.

As to what you mention about the Licensing of Attornies there might perhaps be a Propriety in permitting one Court to do this Drudgery for the Rest if we could agree upon the proper Court but as the Gentlemen who preside in each may think themselves qualified to determine as well upon the Abilities of the several Advocates as upon the Merits of the Causes advocated it will not be quite easy to perswade them that they have not an equal Right with others to say who shall and who shall not be entitled to practice.[1]

The Division of the State into Districts was in your own Opinion as you wi[ll w]ell remember improper as a Part of the Constitution and only to be taken up by the Legislature. If this Opinion was well founded there can be no great Evil in the Omission. Neither had you any Ground to suppose that we would go into the Connecticut Plan of holding up which we have declared to be in our Opinion inconvenient and by Reason of the rotatory Mode of electing entirely useless.[2]

But if we had been so fortunate as to agree in all or any of your Ideas yet as the Government was not only agreed to but solemnly published it would have been highly improper to attempt any Reconsideration. Besides this the Difficulties we were obliged to wade thro in Order to get any Government at all meerly by Reason of Reconsiderations were so great and by us so highly reprobated that no Persons could have stood in a more awkward Situation to propose them.

Judge then our Amazement at reading a Letter from Mr. McKesson to his Fellow Secretary[3] in which your Sentiments against the Power vested in the Courts are blazoned in glowing Colours and consider how far your Reputation may or may not contribute to make this Constitution a living Law or a dead Letter according to the Scale in which you shall choose to place it.

For many Reasons we could have wished that upon perusing this Clause you had written to us upon the Subject without sporting your Sentiments to the Secretary. They are now public and may perhaps produce no very agreable Consequences and such as certainly cannot be pleasing to you should you be convinced as we are and expect you will be that the Clause complained of stands right.

We wish you could get here soon as many Matters of considerable Importance are on the Carpet.

We are yours etc.

ROBT. R. LIVINGSTON
GOUVR. MORRIS

LS in the hand of Gouverneur Morris. Addressed: "John Jay Esqr. Fish Kill." Endorsed.

[1] JJ's letter to Hobart has not been located. For Hobart's account of JJ's objections to the twenty-seventh article on court clerkships and licensing of attorneys, see above, editorial note.

[2] The New York Convention debated the provisions of the constitution on the State Senate on 20 March and 6 April. As adopted by the Convention, and as they stood when JJ left the Convention, these articles provided for a twenty-four member Senate, of which a quarter were to be chosen from each of four "great districts" for four-year terms. The constitution also provided for a census to be taken seven years after the end of the Revolution to guide redrawing of the districts' lines should shifts in population dictate. The Assistants, or members of the upper house in Connecticut, were chosen at large throughout the state in yearly elections. *JPC*, I, 843, 868, 895.

[3] Not located.

To Robert R. Livingston and Gouverneur Morris

Fish Kill, 29 April 1777

Gentlemen

Your Letter of the 26 Instant was this Evening delivered to me. When I was called last from Convention, a Clause in the Report of the Form of Government had been by a very great Majority agreed to, instituting a Council for the appointment of military and many civil Officers, *including Clerks of Courts;* and though I publicly advocated and voted for that Clause, you express much Surprize at my disapproving a material alteration of it.[1] Had you retained the most distant Idea of the part I took relative to the various modes proposed for the appointment of officers, I am confident you would not have asserted *"that I was fully of opinion to appoint by Judges of the Sup. Court, not only Clerks, but all other civil Officers in the Government."* Had such a Representation of my opinion relative to the best mode of appointing those officers, fallen from some Persons whom I could name, I should have called it very disengenuous and uncandid.

The Fact was thus. The Clause directing the Governor to *nominate* officers to the Legislature for their approbation being read and debated, was generally disapproved. Many other methods were devised by different Members, and mentioned to the House merely for Consideration. I mentioned several myself, and told the Convention at the Time, that however I might then incline to adopt them, I was not certain but that after considering them, I should vote for their Rejection. While the Minds of the members were thus fluctuating between various opinions, Capt. Platt moved for the only amendment which was proposed to the House for introducing the Judges. I told the House I preferred the amendment to the original Clause in the

Report, but that I thought a better mode might be devised. I finally opposed the adoption of Capt. Platts amendment, and well remember that I spent the Evening of that Day with Mr Morris at your Lodgings, in the Course of which I proposed the Plan for the Institution of the Council as it now stands, and after conversing on the Subject, we agreed to bring it into the House the next Day. It was moved and debated and carried with this only amendment, that the Speaker of the General Assembly for the Time being was then (to avoid the Governors having frequent opportunities of a casting Vote) added to the Council.[2]

As to the Alteration in question, vizt. transferring the appointment of Clerks etc of Courts from the Council to the respective Judges, I dislike it for many Reasons which the Limits of a Letter will not admit of being fully enumerated and discussed.

You say that *"great Inconveniencies must arise from suffering Clerks to be independent of such Courts, and of Consequence* frequently ignorant, always inattentive." If Ignorance and Inattention would by some necessary Consequence unknown to me, characterize all such Clerks as the Council (of which the Governor is President, and consisting of the Speaker of the General assembly and four Senators elected in that House) Should appoint, I grant that the appointment ought to be in other Hands. But I am at a Loss and unable to Conjecture by what subtle Refinement or new Improvement in the Science of Politics it should be discovered, that a Council acknowledged to be competent to the Choice and appointment of the first Judges of the Land, was insufficient to the nomination of clerks of Courts; or from whence it is to be inferred that they, by where will and pleasure the Duration of many other offices is limited by the Constitution, would either appoint or continue in office ignorant or inattentive Clerks more than ignorant or inattentive Judges Sherifs or Justices of the peace. Nor can I percieve why the clerks in chancery appointed by the Council, should be more ignorant and inattentive than the Examiners, who you are content should still be appointed by that Body; unless Ignorance and Inattention be supposed less dangerous and important in the one than the other.

That Clerks should be *dependent* is agreed on all Hands, on whom? is the only question. I think not on the Judges Because

The chancellor, and the Judges of the Sup. Court holding permanent Commissions, will be *tempted* not only to give these appointments to their Children Brothers Relatives and Favorites, but to continue them in Office against the public Good. You I dare say, know

Men of too little Probity Abilities and Industry to fill an office well, and yet of sufficient art and attention to avoid such gross Misbehaveour, as might justify loud Clamors against them.

Besides, Men who appoint others to offices, generally have a Partiality for them, and are often disposed, on Principles of Pride as well as Interest, to support them. By the Clerks of Courts being dependent on the Judges Collusion becomes more easy to be practiced, and more difficult to be detected, and instead of publishing and punishing each others Transgressions, will combine in concealing palliating or excusing their mutual Defects or misdemeanours.

From the Clerks, etc. being appointed by the Council, these advantages would result.

The Council might avail themselves of the advice of the Judges without being bound by their Prejudices or interested in their Designs.

Should the Council promote their Favorites at the Expence of the public, that Body, having a new Set of members every Year, a bad officer thus appointed would lose his office on his Patrons being removed from the Council.

It would avoid that odium to which that part of the Constitution will now be exposed vizt. that it was framed by Lawyers, and done with Design to favor the Profession.

The new Clause respecting the licensing of attornies, to speake plain, is in my opinion the most whimsical crude and indigested Thing I have met with.

There will be between thirty and forty Courts in this State, and as that Clause now stands, an Attorney (however well qualified, and licensed by the Sup. Court) must before he can issue a writ in a little Borough or Mayors Court, obtain their Licence also. The Reasons assigned for this, seem to be

That it would be improper for one Court to do this *Drudgery* for the Rest.

That it would be difficult to distinguish which Court it would be most proper to impose it upon.

That the Judges of the inferior Courts might be offended at being relieved from this *Drudgery,* thinking themselves as capable of judging of the Merits of an Attorney as of a Cause; and that they had equal Right with others to say who shall and who shall not be entitled to Practice.

To say that it would be improper for one to do this *Drudgery* for the Rest, is begging the Question. Other Courts than the Sup. Court *never* had this *Drudgery* to do; and I believe never will have in any part of the World, except in the State and by the Constitution of New York.

Why the Examination and licensing of Attornies should with more Propriety be stiled *a Drudgery*, than striking a Jury, or any other Business incident to the office of Judge, I know not. If it be, I should think it ought not to be multiplied by thirty or forty, and then imposed on all in the State, and compelling an Attorney to sollicit, and pay fees for admission to thirty or forty Courts, when one would have sufficed.

How it should be difficult to distinguish the proper Court for the Purpose, is to me misterious.

The Sup. Court controuls all the Courts in the State which proceed according to the Course of the common Law, and its Jurisdiction is bounded only by the Limits of the State. An Attorney is an officer of a common Law Court. That Court therefore which by the Constitution is made superior to the others, must be supposed most competent not only to the Determination of Causes, but of the Qualification of the attornies who manage them. The lesser Courts cannot be deemed equally qualified for either; and being dependent and inferior in every other Respect, ought not to have *concurrent, independent* or *equal* Authority in this. Justice as well as Decency forbids that a Mayor and four Alderman should constitutionally have a Right to refuse Admission to Attornies licensed by the Sup. Court.

Whence is it to be inferred that the Judges of the inferior Courts, unless gratified with this novel unprecedented power, would *complain*? It is not to be found among the Rights enjoyed by them prior to the Revolution; and I much doubt whether, unless within this Fortnight or three Weeks, there was a single man in the State who ever thought of such a Thing.

It would be arrogance in them to expect to be endulged in a Right to examine question and reject the Judgment of the Sup. Court respecting the Qualifications of Attornies, when that very Court is appointed among other Things to correct their Errors in all other Cases, nay in this Case the mere will of these little courts is to be the Law; and an Attorney of Reputation and Eminence in the Sup. Court is without Remedy in Case an inferior Court should unjustly refuse to admit him.

According to the present System an Attorney must, if he chuses to have *general* Licence, obtain admission into the Sup. Court, three Mayors Courts, thirteen inferior Courts of common pleas for Counties, fourteen Courts of Sessions for the peace, and the Lord knows how often, or in how many Courts of oyer and Terminer and Goal Delivery.

Remember that I now predict, that this same Clause which thus gives inferiour Courts uncontrouled and unlimited authority to admit as many Attornies as they please, will fill every County in the State with a Swarm of designing cheating litigious Pettifoggers, who like Leaches and Spiders will fatten on the Spoils of the Poor the Ignorant the Feeble and the unwary.

The Division of the State into Districts for the purpose of facilitating Elections I well remember was agreed to be referred to the Legislature, and I well remember too, several members as well as myself were of Opinion that a short Clause should be inserted in the Constitution, which should give the People a <Right> Claim on the Legislature for it.

The Connecticut Plan of nominating or holding up Senators, I ever warmly espoused. I thought it bore strong marks of Wisdom and sound Policy. Nor have I forgot that others opposed it; or that I undertook with the Leave of the House, to reduce it to Writing and offer it to their Consideration. The opinion that the rotatory mode of electing renders it entirely useless, I have neither heard nor can I percieve any Reason for.

The Difficulty of getting any Government at all, you know has long been an apprehension of little Influence on my mind; and always appeared to be founded less in Fact, than in a Design of quickning the Pace of the House.

What the Secretary may have written to Mr. Benson, I know not. I expressed the same Sentiments to him that were inserted in my Letter to Mr Hobart, and no others.

The other parts of the Constitution I approve, and only regret that like a Harvest cut before it was all ripe, some of the Grains have shrunk. Exclusive of the Clauses which I have mentioned, and which I wish had been added; another material one has been omitted, vizt. a Direction that all Persons holding Offices under the Government should swear allegiance to it, and renounce all allegiance and Subjection to foreign Kings Princes and States in all matters ecclesiastical as well as civil.[3] I should also have been for a Clause against the Continuation of domestic Slavery,[4] and the Support and Encouragement of Literature; as well as some other Matters though perhaps of less Consequence.

Though the Birth of the Constitution is in my opinion premature, I shall nevertheless do all in my power to nurse and keep it alive, being far from approving the spartan Law which encouraged

Parents to destroy such of their Children as perhaps by some cross accident, might come into the World defective or misshapen.

I am etc.

Dft. Coll. of Richard Maass. Endorsed by JJ: "Dr. Letter To R. R. Livingston and Gouverneur Morris Esqrs. In answr. to their's of 26 Instant 29 April 1777." For Livingston's and Morris's letter to JJ, see above.

[1] Article XXIII, creating the Council of Appointment, had been adopted on 12 April. As this article stood when JJ left the Convention on 17 April, a Council composed of the Governor, the Speaker of the Assembly, and four Senators chosen by the Assembly, was to appoint "all officers other than those who by this constitution are directed to be otherwise appointed. . . ." On 19 April the Convention removed the appointment of court clerkships from the Council and eliminated the Speaker from the Council. *JPC*, I, 877, 889–90.

[2] Article XXIII (referred to as paragraph "twenty-two" in the Convention debates) was read in Convention on 10 April. Its original provisions were similar to those of draft "B" as reprinted by Charles Z. Lincoln: ". . . all other civil officers in this State not heretofore eligible by the people shall be appointed in the manner following, viz.: The Governor . . . shall name to the Legislature such persons as he may deem qualified for the same and the Legislature if they think proper may appoint them, if not the Governor shall continue to name others till he shall name such as may be agreeable to the Legislature. And in case none of the first four persons whom the Governor may name shall be agreeable to the Legislature for any of the said offices, that then the Legislature shall proceed to appoint without waiting for his further nomination." After the original article had been given a second reading, Zephaniah Platt moved for an amendment under which such appointments would be made "by the Governor for the time being, by and with the advice and consent of the judges of the supreme court." The next day, 11 April, JJ introduced an amendment creating a Council of Appointment consisting of the Governor and four Senators to be chosen by the Assembly in which the Governor would "have a casting vote, but no other vote." The Speaker's addition to the Council was moved by JJ and seconded by Gouverneur Morris on 11 April, and this version of Article XXIII was adopted on 12 April. Lincoln, *Constitutional Hist. of N.Y.*, I, 531–32; *JPC*, I, 873–75.

[3] JJ did succeed in inserting this phrase into the Constitution's provisions for oaths of naturalization to be taken by aliens in an amendment to the constitution adopted on 21 March 1777. *JPC*, I, 846.

[4] On the evening of 17 April, a few hours after JJ had left the Convention, Gouverneur Morris introduced a motion that the constitution include a recommendation "to the future Legislatures of the State of New-York, to take the most effectual measures consistent with the public safety, and the private property of individuals, for abolishing domestic slavery within the same. . . ." Morris's resolution was defeated on 19 April. *JPC*, I, 887, 889.

To Richard Morris

Kingston, 10th May 1777

Dear Sir

The enclosed is a Copy of the Constitution of this State, which I am persuaded you will read with Pleasure.

By the Section, the appointment of Clerks of Courts is vested in their respective chief Judges.[1] The Convention having appointed me to the first Place on the Bench, affords me an opportunity of acknowledging the friendly Obligations you have often conferred on me; particularly the first Court after I was licenced.

What the Emoluments of Clerk of the Sup. Court and Circuits may amount to, I am at a Loss to determine. They will probably be considerable. Your Acceptance of these Places would open a Way to others, and I may add that should you hereafter be disposed to resign them in favor of your Son[2] when qualified for them, you will meet with no Obstacles.

Be pleased to favor me with your Answer without Delay.

I am Dear Sir Your obliged and obedient Servant

JOHN JAY

ALS. DLC: Morris-Popham Papers. Enclosure: Constitution of the State of New York. Richard Morris (1730–1810), the younger brother of General Lewis Morris and a half brother of JJ's contemporary, Gouverneur Morris, had been a prominent member of the New York provincial bar and served as an admiralty judge, 1762–75.

1 Left blank in ms. For a discussion of Article XXVII of the constitution, referred to in this passage, see above, Robert R. Livingston and Gouverneur Morris to JJ, 26 April 1777, and editorial note; and JJ to Livingston and Morris, 29 April 1777.

2 Lewis Richard Morris (1760–1825).

From Robert Troup

Albany, May 15, 1777

My dear Sir,

The Day after I arrived your Letter to the General came safe to Hand. He is pleased with the Contents, and doubts not you will do every thing in your Power to promote the Good of the service.[1]

Our Remoteness from Continental Congress will frequently oblige us to ask the Assistance of your Legislature. This, I am confident, will be readily granted if they possess that Spirit which marked the Proceedings of your late Convention.

The General has read your Constitution with Care and Attention. He really venerates it, and thinks it preserves a proper Line between Aristocracy on the one Hand, and Democracy on the other.

Since I saw you we have received an Account that Cap Whitcomb, who commands three Companies of Rangers, and who last Year killed Brig Gen Gordon, has brought to Ticonderoga one Captain and thirteen British soldiers and Tories. The Officer is expected here every Hour. After he is examined shall communicate the Particulars.[2]

Matters in this Quarter, I think, wear a favorable aspect. We have near 8000 Men at Ticonderoga, and a Surgeon of the Hospital there, who came to Town a few Days ago, says there are only 14 sick. There is no Prospect of the Enemys attacking us very soon, for it Appears they are as much, if not more embarrassed than the Army under General Howe.

I congratulate you on the Intelligence a French officer brings, who lately passed thro Fish-Kill on his Way to Congress. We are led to place some Confidence in it from the Declaration of a Number of Gentlemen who conversed with him. They say he left a Fleet with 12000 Men on Board, near the Mouth of the River St. Lawrence, which was to proceed to Quebec with all Expedition, and that another was to sail from Brest, shortly after he left it, with 8000, but its Destination was not known. Should this be the Case G Britain must and will fall like Lucifer, never to rise again.

Yesterday I went to Dr. Livingstons[3] to beg the Favor of his dining with the General; but he excused himself because Mrs Livingston had been riding, was somewhat fatigued, and had a slight Fever. She, I understand, is in a fair Way of recovering her Health, tho at present she is rather weak and low.

I cannot conclude without returning you my sincerest Thanks for the great and many Favors you have from Time to Time conferred upon me. Be assured I shall always retain the most grateful Sense of them, and never shall lose an Opportunity of making every Return in My Power.

Be so kind as to present my best Respects to Mrs. Jay and Miss Katy. Tell the former to kiss her little son for me the first time she sees him, and the latter, I shall mention in my next the Success I have met with in getting her the striped Cambrick she desired.

I am, my dear Sir, your much obliged and humble Servant

ROB. TROUP

ALS. Addressed: "The Honorable John Jay Esq Kingston." Endorsed. Shortly after resigning his commission in the 4th New York in March 1777, Troup was named an aide-de-camp to Horatio Gates, newly appointed commander at Ticonderoga. In April Troup joined Gates at Albany and, in the first week of May 1777, was sent to Fishkill to seek supplies for the Northern Army. Frustrated by the destruction of stores at Peekskill by British raiders, Troup then journeyed to Washington's headquarters at Morristown, N.J., on the same mission. He returned to Albany on the evening of 12 May. Wendell Tripp, "Robert Troup: A Quest for Order and Security, 1757–1832" (unpubl. Ph.D. dissertation, Columbia University, 1973), pp. 22–23; Gates to Washington, 13 May 1777, DNA: PCC, 154, I, 193–96.

1 Gates's letter to the New York Convention of 9 May 1777 was referred to JJ and Gouverneur Morris the following day. Their draft reply was approved by the Convention on 12 May and dispatched the same day. *JPC*, I, 921, 927.

2 Capt. Benjamin Whitcomb of Bedel's New Hampshire Rangers was at Gates's headquarters as late as 24 May 1777, but Gates's dispatches contain no further details of Whitcomb's capture of the British troops and Tories. Patrick Gordon, a lieutenant colonel of the British 108th Foot, held the rank of brigadier general in America. Gordon was fatally wounded in an ambush near St. John's by an American party from Ticonderoga in the summer of 1776. *GWF*, V, 466 n.

3 John Henry Livingston (1746–1825), who held a divinity degree from the University of Utrecht.

To Abraham Yates, Jr.

[Kingston], *16 May 1777*

Dear Sir

From the Information you was pleased to give me before you left this place <of a Danger> I would be proposed in the County of Albany to hold me as a Candidate for the Office of Governor, I think it necessary to be very explicit on that Subject.

That the Office of first Magistrate of this State will be more respectable as well as more lucrative and consequently more desirable than the Place I now fill, is very apparent. But Sir! my Object in the Course of the present Great Contest neither has been nor will be, either Rank or Money. I am persuaded that I can be more useful to the State in the office I now hold, than in the one alluded to, and therefore think it my Duty to continue in it. You are acquainted with the Reasons which induce me to be of this opinion, and altho I entertain a high Sense of the Honor which my Friends are disposed to confer upon me, I must request the Favor of them not to encourage my being named as a Candidate for that Office, but to endeavour to unite the Votes of the Electors in that County of Albany in favor of some other Gentleman.

I am Dear Sir Your most Obedient and humble Servant

J. J.

DftS. Endorsed by JJ: "To Ab. Yates Junr Esqr Dr Letter 16 May 1777." Yates was an Albany representative in the three Provincial Congresses and the New York Convention, 1775–77. In the Convention he chaired the committee which drafted the state constitution. On 3 May Yates and JJ were named to the fifteen-man Council of Safety which was to hold "all the powers necessary for the safety and preservation of the State until a meeting of the Legislature," and was to act jointly with the governor as soon as he should be elected. The Convention was dissolved on 13 May and Yates sat on the Council through 15 May. *JPC*, I, 910, 916, 934.

FROM WILLIAM DUER

[*Philadelphia*], *May 28th, 1777*

My dear Sir,

You have been undoubtedly surprised at my long Silence, but when I assure you what is Fact, that my principal Reasons for not writing have been want of Time, and of Satisfactory Matter, I flatter myself I shall stand acquitted, (if not with honor) at least as a Wilful Offender against the Laws of Friendship.

As General Schuyler expects me to deliver this Letter in Person I shall refer you to him for the particular Manavres [*sic*] respecting his own Affairs, and for the political Complexion of Affairs in Congress. From a very low Ebb at which our Affairs were when we arrived here we have recovered surprisingly; and I may venture to Say that the Eyes of all those who are not willfully blind are open, and that we may expect Justice to take Place with respect to our State.[1]

I congratulate you on the Completion of the Task of forming and Organising our New Government. I think it upon the maturest Reflection the best System which has as yet been adopted, and possibly as good as the Temper of the Times would admit of. If it is well administered, and some Wise and Vigorous Laws passed at the Opening of the Sessions for watching, and defeating the Machinations of the Enemy and their Abettors, and for Supporting by Taxes, and other Means the Credit of the Circulating Money, it will be a formidable Engine of Opposition to the Designs of our Tyrannical Enemies; but I assure you I am not without my Fears concerning the Choice which will be made of those who are to set the Machine in Motion.

Our All Depends on it. It is very observable that in almost every other State where Government has been formed and established either from the Contention of Parties, or from a Want of proper Powers being vested in the Executive Branches, Disaffection has encreased prodigiously, and an unhappy langour has prevailed in the whole Political System. I sincerely wish that this may not be the Case with us, but that the new Government may continue to act with that Spirit, Integrity, and Wisdom which animated the Councils of the Old!

In this State Toryism (or rather Treason) stalks triumphant; the Credit of our Money is sapped by the Arts, and Avarice of the

Malignants, and Monopolisers, and such is the desperate Situation of Affairs, that nothing but desperate Remedies can restore these People to Reason, and Virtue.

The Assembly is now convened, but I am afraid will not dare to lay a Tax to call in part of the large Sums of Money circulating in this State, or to pass vigorous Laws to crush the disaffected; all my hope is that the Spirit of Whiggism will at length break forth in some of the Populace, which (if well directed) may effect by Quackery a Cure which the regular State Physicians are either not adequate to, or unwilling to attempt.

A Spirit of this kind under the Name of Joyce Junr. has made his Appearance in Boston.[2] I should not be surprised if he was to travel Westward. It would be attended with these good Effects: it would either supply the Want of Vigor in the present Government, or it would induce those whose duty it is to act with Spirit and Vigor. What think you of an Episcopalian Clergyman in this City praying last Sunday for the Lords Spiritual and Temporal, or rather what think you of the Congregation which heard him with Patience?

If in the midst of your Political Business you can now and then drop me a Line I will esteem it as a favor, and (if not regularly) I will by Starts when there is any thing worth communicating write to you.

A Word in the Ear of a Friend. When I was sent here I had some Idea that I was entering into the Temple of Public Virtue. I am disappointed and Chagrined. General Schuyler will communicate my Sentiments and his own at large.

The *Chaste* Colonel Lee will I am credibly informed be left out of the next Delagation for Virginia which is now in Agitation.[3] The mere Contemplation of this Event gives me Pleasure. My Mind is full, and I wish to unburthen it; but Prudence forbids me.

I condole with you on the Loss of your Aged Mother; or rather should I not congratulate you that she is arrived in a secure and pleasant Haven, from a Storm, which she was little calculated to bear? This Reflection I beleive has alleviated your Distress. May we be as Virtuous as your Parents should we live to be as old! From the rapid Increase of Villainy both Moral and Political, it is to be feared that we shall not increase in Virtue, as we may in Years. Remember me to all my Friends, particularly to my Fellow-Labourers in the Council of *Conspiracy*. Adieu, and beleive me Yours with much Esteem and Affection.

W. DUER

I have delivered General Schuyler a Letter from your Friend Mr. Dean in France.[4] I have had it some Time by me, but waited a Safe Mode of Conveyance.

ALS. Addressed: "To the Honble. John Jay Esqr Cheif Justice of the State of New York." Endorsed. On 29 March 1777 Duer had been added to the New York delegation to Congress. When the New York Convention elected a new slate of delegates on 13 May, Duer was named along with Philip Schuyler, Philip Livingston, James Duane, and Gouverneur Morris. *JPC*, I, 855, 931.

1 On 15 May the Board of War submitted to Congress a report recommending that Schuyler "be directed forthwith to proceed to the Northern Department, and take upon him the Command there." The report continued with a recommendation that the President of Congress inform Horatio Gates of this decision and notify Gates "that Congress are desirous that Major General Gates should make his own choice, either to continue in the Command in the Northern Department, under Major General Schuyler; or to take upon him the Office of Adjutant General in the Grand Army immediately under the Commander in Chief, with the rank he now holds. . . ." On 22 May Congress directed Schuyler to take his command in New York. *JCC*, VII, 364; VIII, 375.

2 "Joyce, Junior," whose true identity is unknown to this day, was a leader of the Boston mobs in 1774. During the British occupation he disappeared from Boston and did not reappear until early 1777 when he announced that his mission was the disciplining of Tories. In April he led a mob which removed five Loyalists from Boston and threatened them with death should they return. R. S. Longley, "Mob Activities in Revolutionary Massachusetts," *New England Quarterly*, VI (1933), 126–28.

3 Richard Henry Lee of Virginia had voted against Philip Schuyler's reinstatement as Commander of the Northern Department. To Duer's disappointment, Lee was returned to Congress in June 1777. *LMCC*, II, lxxi, 377, 410.

4 Silas Deane's letter to JJ has not been identified. This may have been a copy of Deane's letter of 3 Dec. 1776, above.

From Robert Troup

Albany, June 2, 1777

My dear Sir

I beg you will not form any unfavorable Opinion of my long Silence. Nothing would give me more Pleasure than to have it in my Power to write you a daily Account of every Thing that passes in this Department. But it is impossible. So far from being idle, I have scarcely a Moment to attend to my Friends. Ever Since my last I have been upon a tedious Command. The General[1] desired I would superintend the Removal of some Cannon from this Place to Fort-George.[2] With the Greatest Difficulty I returned this Day. What occasioned such a long Delay was the extreme Badness of the Road which has been, and is still almost impassable.

I have the Satisfaction of informing you that the General has several Times returned me his particular Thanks for my Vigilance in executing his Commands. In my Opinion, I could live with him upon the best Terms of Friendship. I say "could live with him," because there is little Probability of his having a *military Family* much longer. The Congress have superseded him by a late Resolve in Favor of Gen Schuyler, who is expected in Town every Moment. As soon as he arrives we shall proceed in Haste to Philadelphia, where Gen Gates will resign his Commission.

This Resolution, tho passed by one of the most *august Bodies* in the World, astonishes me beyond Measure. It betrays a Fickleness and Inconstancy which necessarily relaxe the Springs of Government. Thus, my dearest Sir, I shall soon be reduced from a public, to a private Capacity. The Consequences of this Change, I shall mention in my next.

By an Express, just arrived from Ticonderoga, we learn the Enemy's Vessels, which for some Days past, have been hovering round Split-Rock, have returned.[3] Near this Place six Tories were taken who were going to them. One was dangerously wounded, and is since dead.

I see no Prospect of a speedy Attack upon Ticonderoga. The Situation of the Enemy will not admit of such a movement. I would be more particular but the Post-Rider is now waiting for this. Therefore beg you will present my best Regards to Mrs. Jay, and Miss Katy. You may expect to hear from me soon. Adieu!

ROB. TROUP

ALS. Addressed: "The Honorable John Jay Esq, Kingston, per Post." Endorsed.

1 Horatio Gates.

2 Fort George stood at the southern end of Lake George.

3 On 29 May Gates received a dispatch from Brigadier General Enoch Poor at Ticonderoga giving a scout's detailed account of British ships at Split Rock, a post on the western shore of Lake Champlain, approximately thirty miles north of Ticonderoga. On 31 May Poor sent a second dispatch which showed that the British had withdrawn all but one of their ships from the vicinity of Split Rock and reported the capture of six British soldiers. Poor to Gates, 27 May and 31 May 1777; Gates to Washington, 30 May and 2 June 1777, DLC: Washington Papers, Series 4.

From Nicholas Rogers

Philadelphia, June 4th, 1777

Sir

I think it my duty to trouble you with these few lines concerning the papers that Mr. Deane has committed to my Charge and which I promised to deliver into your hands, had I found you in the Congress as Mr. Deane informed Me. You will use certain liquid (that Mr. Deane told me you had) upon the Margin of the printed Sheets so as to make legible what Mr. Deane has wrote. Should it not have it's proper effect which I am afraid of as the Letters were put into a Tin Box in a Barrel of Rum which was eat through and I am afraid has damaged them, the enclosed Letter is of the same Contents and I hope will make up whatever deficiencies may be in the margins.

According to Mr. Deane's orders you will please to seal up the printed papers and send them to Mrs. Deane[1] after you have read and considered them with Attention.

I lived at Paris in the same house with Mr. Deane and had the Pleasure of being particularly intimate with him so that I became in some measure his Confident. Could I flatter myself with the hopes of your Correspondence I should be happy to inform you or answer you any Questions concerning the most of Mr. Deane's transactions the last summer which he performed with the Warmth of the most zealous of Patriots. My coming by the Way of West indies is the reason of the date of your Letter being so old. I was taken with General Du Coudray within fifteen Leagues of Cape Ann by the Greyhound frigate but made a most singular escape from them.

I shall go off for the Camp in a few days where I hope to have the pleasure of a letter from you directed to the Care of Mr. Clemt. Biddle deputy Quarter Master.[2] 'Till then I remain your sincerest humble servant

NICHOLAS ROGERS

N.B. The enclosed Letter from Mr. Deane I will send by another Opportunity as I dont think it prudent to hazard them by the same post.

ALS. Endorsed: ". . . inclg Papers from Mr. Deane." Enclosures: Silas Deane to JJ, 3 Dec. 1776 (see above); unidentified printed papers bearing messages in secret ink.

[1] Elizabeth Saltonstall Deane.

[2] Lieutenant Colonel Clement Biddle (1740–1814), Deputy Commissary General for the Flying Camp.

From Philip Schuyler

Albany, June 4, 1777

Dear Sir

Inclose you Copy of the letter You requested. I wish you to well Consider the propriety of publishing It before you order It to be done.

Mr. Yates has agreed to accept the office convention has been pleased to bestow on him, but such is the distracted Situation of affairs here that I have Intreated him to remain a day or two longer. I mention this least the Hon. Council of Safety Should Consider his nonattendance in an unfavourable point of view.[1]

The Account of the Enemy's Approach to Tyonderoga,[2] was Groundless or If not they were returned before our Scouts got to the place where they were supposeed to be seen.

Pardon my vanity when I tell you that my return to this place has given Almost universal Satisfaction to my Country men. The County Committee Intend me the honor of a formal visit this Afternoon.

I have been spoken to on the Subject You mentioned at Kingston,[3] and know I shall probably be Able to give you some Information on that head. Adieu and Believe me, Dear Sir with Every friendly wish your Obedient and humble Servant

PHI. SCHUYLER

ALS. Endorsed. Enclosures not identified.

1 On 3 May 1777 Robert Yates and John Sloss Hobart were elected puisne justices of the New York Supreme Court. On 27 May the Council of Safety ordered that expresses be sent to the two justices-elect, "commanding their immediate attendance at this Council, to take the oaths and proceed to the execution of their offices." *JPC*, I, 946.

2 Schuyler habitually misspelled Ticonderoga.

3 On his journey from Philadelphia to reassume his command at Albany, Schuyler conferred with the Council of Safety at Kingston on the evening of 1 June. On 2 June 1777 JJ, heading a five-man committee of the Committee of Safety, transmitted to Egbert Benson at New Windsor a resolution "unanimously" endorsing Schuyler for governor and Clinton for lieutenant governor, both of whom were praised as "respectable abroad," their attachment to the cause "confessed" and "their Abilities unquestionable," and urging Benson to "exert" himself in behalf of their respective candidacies at the forthcoming meeting of the Orange, Ulster, and Dutchess County committees to be convened "for the Important Purpose of agreeing on the men proper to fill the great offices of Government." Their appeal for unanimity fell on deaf ears. In fact, among a plethora of candidates for the two top statewide posts JJ himself, already elected Chief Justice, his own candidacy expressly and repeatedly disavowed, received 367 votes for governor in the June 1777 election out of a total of 3,786 votes, with an additional 108 votes in a field of nineteen candidates for the lieutenant governorship. For the gubernatorial post George Clinton defeated his closest rival, Philip Schuyler, and also captured the lieutenant governorship. On 1 September the legislature chose Pierre Van Cortlandt (1721–1814) for the latter office which Clinton had declined to accept. Council to Benson, 2 June 1777, printed without name of addressee, *GCP*, I, 855–56; copy with full address at NNebg: Washington's Headquarters; *Cal. of Hist. Mss.*, II, 242.

FROM PETER W. YATES

Albany, 5 June 1777

Dear Sir

As the Election for Governor and Lieut. Govr. draws near I would be glad to know how Matters Respecting this stand below, and whom the lower Counties will be disposed to chuse.

Your Name is mentioned here and so is Genl. Schuylers. As I am disposed to render you all the Service I can on this Occasion, please to favour me with a few Lines on the Subject and who is held up at Esopus for Lieut. Govr. that we may know how to conduct ourselves here.[1] Your Answer by the Bearer will oblidge in great Haste your most Humble Servant

PETER W. YATES

ALS. Addressed: "To John Jay Esqr Kingston." Endorsed.

[1] No reply from JJ to Yates has been located, but see the following letter.

TO JOHN TEN BROECK

Kingston, 6th June 1777

Dear Sir:

Having understood that I was named as one of the candidates for the office of Governor, by some of my friends in Albany; and being desirous that as much unanimity as possible should prevail on this occasion, I take the liberty of informing you, that in my opinion it will be most for the common good that I should remain in the office I now hold.

I am very sensible of the honor intended to be conferred upon me by my friends and am extremely obliged to them for this instance of their attention and confidence, but the same principles which have actuated my conduct through the course of this great contest, influence me to decline this promotion. When I consider how well General Schuyler is qualified for that important office, I think he ought in justice to the public to be preferred to Your most obedient humble servant[1]

JOHN JAY

Tr. NN: Bancroft, Schuyler Papers. Ten Broeck (1740–1822), an Albany delegate in the last Provincial Assembly, had been JJ's colleague in the Third Provincial Congress and in the New York Convention.

[1] On 5 June JJ had written Leonard Gansevoort of Albany to ask that he not

be considered for the governorship by his "friends in your county." JJ closed his letter to Gansevoort with this remark: "For my own part, I know of no person at present whom I would prefer to General Schuyler." *WJ*, II, 12–13.

From Sarah Livingston Jay

Troy,[1] *June 17th, 1777*

My dear Mr. Jay,

I have just heard that Mr. Ogden[2] knows of an opportunity to send a letter to Esopus. I shall therefore embrace it with pleasure to assure my dear Mr. Jay of my confirmed health, and of the welfare of our family. Little Peter continues active and well. I dare not trust myself to say more of him lest I should say too much. Suffice it therefore that I tell you he speaks a few words, and that every acquisition in way of tricks etc. have from us the approbation that should be bestowed upon real merit.

Our situation here, although retired is by no means unpleasant, and if my friend who is now absent could make one of our party, I should even pronounce it happy. When Mr. Morris was here he desired Mrs. Ogden to supply us with any books from his library that were most agreable to us,[3] which, together with those we had before, make quite a clever collection. Since I have been at Troy we have entertained ourselves with reading from breakfast time 'till noon, and when alone of an afternoon a play of Shakespears furnishes an elegant amusement. The history of Madame de Maintenon was my yesterday's study,[4] and I intend to continue it 'till I have finished it. Were a person inclined to be dissatisfied with a private life, such a sketch of the inside of a court, as is presented to us by those Memoirs, I should think sufficient to hush impatience, and raise us

far above
Those little cares, and visionary joys,
That so perplex the fond impassioned heart
Of ever-cheated, ever-trusting man.

After having given you an account of the manner in which we pass our time, you'll readily percieve (or if you would not any one else would) the great advantages that our little party might derive from the observations of my dear sage friend.

I believe I omitted telling you in my last that Grand Papa French[5] had left this confused world of ours. I hope that the exchange which he has made is an happy one.

Papa returned from Haddonfield a saturday and the Council of safety are to meet on tuesday at Morris Town.[6] Papa, mamma and sisters unite in desiring to be remembered to you and our other friends where you are.

I am my dear Mr. Jay, with unalterable affection Yours

SARAH JAY

turn over

P.S. Please to direct your letters to me to the care of Coll. Sam. Ogden. Hannah[7] begs to be remembered to you.

ALS. Addressed: "John Jay Esqr. at Kingston. To the care of Mr. Morris." Endorsed.

1 Troy, N.J., was a village on the Parsippany seven miles northeast of Morristown.

2 Samuel Ogden (1746–1810) a New Jersey businessman with interests in the ironworks at Boonton, a few miles from Troy.

3 Gouverneur Morris's younger sister, Euphemia (1754–1818), was the wife of Samuel Ogden.

4 Several translations of Laurent Angliviel de la Beaumelle's *Mémoires pour servir à l'histoire de Madame de Maintenon* were published in London before the Revolution. SLJ was probably referring to *Memoirs for the History of Madame de Maintenon, and of the Last Age* (5 vols., London, 1757).

5 Philip French of New Brunswick.

6 The New Jersey Assembly and Council adjourned on Saturday, 7 June 1777. *Votes and Proceedings of the General Assembly of the State of New-Jersey* . . . (Burlington, 1777), p. 147.

7 Hannah Benjamin, Peter Augustus Jay's nurse.

To Sarah Livingston Jay

Kingston, 25 June 1777

My dear Sally

Yesterday afternoon Mr. Morris delivered to me your Letter of the 17th Instant.[1] I have written two Letters to you lately. They were sent to Col. Hamilton,[2] by our weekly Express; but as you dont mention having recieved either of them, I fear they are still on the Way.

I am happy to find that in speaking of your Health you can make use of so strong an Expression as *confirmed,* but beware lest you be decieved in your Strength, and by thinking yourself hardy hazard your Health. Bathing and riding will I am persuaded be of great Service to You, and I hope your abode at Troy will continue as pleasant as you say it has hitherto been. Your Opinion of Madame de Maintenon corresponds with my own. A Lady of her wit, good Humour and Discretion must be an agreable Guest every where, Do you think she would have been one of a Party to Elizabeth Town? The Rider I am just informed sets out immediately. I must therefore conclude this Letter as I hope to conclude my Life in assuring you that I am with great Sincerity Your affectionate Husband

JOHN JAY

ALS.

1 See above.

2 Letters not located. In March 1777 Lieutenant Colonel Alexander Hamilton became the New York Convention's semiofficial correspondent at Washington's headquarters in New Jersey. *HP*, I, 209.

FROM SARAH LIVINGSTON JAY

Persipiney, 27th June 1777

My dear Mr. Jay,

Your letter of the 25 Inst.[1] afforded me at once pleasure and surprise. Upon my word I had no idea of danger when mamma and I went to Eliz[abeth] Town, but since it has been the cause of uneasiness to you, I regret that I have ever been, though it was a very agreable jaunt and I don't doubt but that it contributed to confirm my health. Had it not been for the circumstance of your anxiety I doubt it would be difficult to suppress vanity when we find that our manouvres occasion almost as much speculation as those of General Howe and his army.[2] Thus, my dear, you see if we will but attend even common occurrences in a proper manner we should seldom find opportunities for negligence but on the contrary we should often observe that those very things which upon a superficial view may appear to be cause for vanity, if inspected more attentively, are only admonitions to greater circumspection.

The genteel manner in which you reprimand me for my imprudence (as you think it) charms me, and is I am sure much more effectual than the most lofty censure. Why don't every one that wishes to be happy study your example?

I am sorry I suffered you to remain in suspense about the fate of those letters, as they are come safe to hand, and have afforded me great satisfaction.

Don't, my dear, indulge an anxious thought about my health. The near connection you are so kind as to make between that and your own happiness would be sufficient reason, were there no other motive, to induce me to attend to whatever was necessary to preserve it.

The rapid, and at present, unaccountable movements of the

Enemy occasion numberless conjectures. You'll no doubt have more particular accounts of there conduct by the return of your Express than it's in my power to give you.

There is not any writing paper to be bought here. I think you had better get one or two Quires more of Gasharee.

Continue, my dear Mr. Jay to indulge me with the pleasure of hearing often from you. You can't imagine how much satisfaction your Letters afford your affectionate Wife

SA. JAY

Please to give our Compliments to Mr. Morris.[3]

ALS. Addressed: "John Jay Esqr Kingston."

[1] See above.

[2] In June 1777 General Howe engaged in a series of maneuvers in New Jersey near Washington's camp while Burgoyne prepared his invasion of northern New York.

[3] Gouverneur Morris, JJ's colleague on the New York Council of Safety.

FROM PHILIP SCHUYLER

Albany, June 30th, 1777

Dear Sir

Your favor of the 20th Instant I received on the 26th and I have not been Able to Snatch a moment to give you a line in Answer.[1]

General Scott I am Informed has a majority of votes for the Chair.[2] If so he has played his Cards better than was Expected.

The Enemy have opened the Ball in every Quarter. It is pretty Certain that they will pay us a visit from the westward as well as from the North.[3] I am in much pain about Tyonderoga. Little or nothing has been done there this Spring however. If the Garrison Escapes, or If It does not and we get a reinforcement from below and are Spiritedly seconded by the Militia we Shall prevent them from penetrating on this Side of the Lakes.

It would greatly Inspire the people with Confidence to see the whole Council of Safety here. As I shall be to the northward somebody ought to be here to give advice and Assistance to Our people In the western Quarter. I therefore earnestly wish to see You and your Brethern.

My Compliments to all friends. I am Dear Sir Very sincerely Your Most obedient Humble Servant

PH. SCHUYLER

ALS. Endorsed.

1 JJ to Schuyler, 20 June 1777, *HPJ*, I, 142–43.

2 John Morin Scott was one of Schuyler's rivals in the New York gubernatorial race in 1777.

3 Major General John Burgoyne (1722–92) returned to America in the spring of 1777 with authorization for an offensive in New York. Burgoyne reached Quebec in May and began his advance from St. Johns to Lake Champlain in the third week of June. Burgoyne's aim was to seize control of the Lake Champlain-Hudson River route to Albany. The western prong of this offensive, under the command of Lieutenant Colonel Barry St. Leger (1737–89), did not begin until the end of July.

To Sarah Livingston Jay

Kingston, 3d July 1777

My dear Sally

The last Evening I had the Pleasure of recieving your kind Letters of the 25 and 27 June last.[1] My anxiety occasioned by your Excursion to Eliz[abeth] Town, has I assure You been amply compensated by the Benefit and Pleasure you recieved from it. One of the first Reports which reached us after the Evacuation of Brunswick,[2] was that when the Enemy arrived at Bonum Town[3] they separated, and that one Division filing off towards Springfield marched to Staten Island through Elizabeth Town. This Manoeuvre it was said was occasioned by a strong Post taken by Gen. Maxwell[4] at bonum Town where we had before heard he was stationed. On comparing the time when you went to Eliz[abeth] Town with the Time of this March, they corresponded so nearly that I was not a little uneasy at the Prospect of your being much terrified and perhaps made Captive by them.

I am much obliged to you for the gloves and druget. The former fit me very well. The Express delivered them to me. We were disappointed in the Expectation of seeing Coll. Ogden,[5] to whom be pleased to present my Compliments. Mrs. Jones has a Boy—both well. My next will contain less blank Paper. Adieu my dear Sally.

I am your very affectionate Husband

JOHN JAY

Remember me to all the Family.

ALS. WHi.

1 SLJ's ALS of the 25th is in JP; that of the 27th is printed above.

2 The British retreated from New Brunswick on 22 June.

[3] A small town situated northeast of Piscataway near present-day Metuchen, N.J.

[4] Brigadier General William Maxwell (c. 1733–96), military commander active in New Jersey.

[5] Matthias Ogden (1755–91), colonel of the 1st New Jersey Line.

Problems of the Northern Command

Yankee-Yorker antagonisms were a constant source of Congressional frictions during 1777–1778. As one of New York's leaders, both politically and socially, JJ continually found himself involved in these struggles, perhaps best epitomized in the Gates-Schuyler contest for control of the Northern Department. Although this appeared to be primarily a military affair, it was part of the same battle between New York and New England, with New England favoring Horatio Gates, and New York championing the cause of Philip Schuyler, Washington's choice. JJ gave Schuyler his personal support and whatever political influence he could in order to aid Schuyler in this factional dispute.

The sectional jealousies led to seesaw conditions in the Northern Department during the early part of 1777, with Gates replacing Schuyler at Ticonderoga in March and then seeing Schuyler reinstated one month later. The problem of shifts in command, compounded by supply shortages, the unwillingness of many New England soldiers to serve under the autocratic Schuyler, and the exposed location of the fort combined to render Ticonderoga vulnerable to Burgoyne's massive offensive.

When Arthur St. Clair, whom Schuyler had appointed to command the post in June 1777, awoke on the morning of 5 July to discover that the British had mounted and fortified Sugar Loaf Mountain (Mount Defiance), he considered his position untenable and gave the order to evacuate the fort, thereby hoping to save his troops for later battle.

Thus Ticonderoga fell to the British without a single shot being fired, and Schuyler's enemies were provided with the perfect ammunition to reopen their attack on the New York general. Facts flavored with malicious rumors served to discredit Schuyler. In a sour mood, Congress dismissed him on 4 August 1777, and appointed Gates to succeed him in the command of the Northern Department.

After the debacle, JJ proved Schuyler's staunch friend and defender. He supported the general during the long months he pressed Congress for a court-martial in an effort to clear his name. JJ encouraged Schuyler to maintain his useful contacts with the Indians and always assured him that time would vindicate him. From among the numerous letters between the two New Yorkers, only the most revealing are printed herein.

To PHILIP SCHUYLER

Kingston, 11 July 1777

Copy of a Letter from the Council of Safety to Major Gen. Putnam.[1]

Sir

The Council have directed me to transmit to you by Express the enclosed Extracts of a Letter from General Schuyler.[2] They think it of Importance that you should from time to time be apprized of the Situation of Affairs in the Northern Department, and will omit no opportunity of communicating to you whatever Intelligence they may recieve from that Quarter.

The Evacuation of Ticonderoga appears to the Council highly reprehensible, and it gives them great Pain to find that a Measure so absurd and probably criminal should be imputed to the Direction of General Schuyler in whose Zeal, vigilance, and Integrity the Council repose the highest Confidence.

I have the Honor to be etc.

P. V. C.[3]

Kingston, 11 July, 1777

Dear Sir

As the Contents of the above Letter may be agreable to You, I take this opportunity of transmitting to You a Copy of it. Let not the hasty Suspicions of the ignorant or the malicious Insinuations of the wicked discompose You. The best and greatest Men in all Ages have met with the like Fate, and gloriously risen superior to Calumny.

I wont detain You longer than to assure you how sincerely I am your Friend

JOHN JAY

N.B. The Extracts sent to Putnam contain nothing of your Letter to Gen. Washington.[4]

ALS. Addressed: "The Honble Major General Schuyler, Fort Edward." Endorsed. Tr in NN: Bancroft, Schuyler Papers, 1776–88.

1 Israel Putnam, commander of the fortifications in the Hudson Highlands since May 1777. Letter to Putnam is published in *JPC*, I, 992.

2 In the letter of 9 July to the Council of Safety Schuyler denied rumors that he had ordered the retreat from Fort Ticonderoga and angrily stated, "What could induce General St. Clair and the general officers with him, to evacuate Ticonderoga, God only knows." He also commented on widespread desertions in the

militia, and asserted he hoped to halt the enemy before they reached Albany. *JPC*, I, 992; II, 514.

3 Pierre Van Cortlandt from Westchester County, President of the Council of Safety.

4 In the letter of 9 July to the Council, Schuyler also included two letters of 7 July to George Washington, to be forwarded to the Commander as soon as the Council had read them. In these letters, one written from Stillwater and the other from Saratoga, Schuyler related Lieutenant Colonel A. Hawks Hay's account of the evacuation of Fort Ticonderoga and Mount Independence. DLC: Washington Papers, Series 4.

From Richard Morris

Claverack, July 12th, 1777

Good Sir,

Three days ago going through the constitution and makeing Marginal notes for my own convenience I was greatly Surprized when I came to the 23d Section to find that the Judges and the Chancellor did not make a part of the Councill for the Appointment of Officers which I always thought they did and I must Confess I neither see the propriety or Necessity for their App[ointmen]t by the Convention unless they had been by Office named of that Councill. With Submission to your Better Judgment I much Doubt the Validity of the Appointments by the 24th Section. The Governor is to Commission. The Commission will declare the Tenure. Will the Governor Commission Contrary to the Constitution? If he will not, is it not necessary that the Appointment of the Judges Should be Conformable to the 23d. Section? It may be Answered the Necessity of the times Called for Judges. Admitt it, but will they not be Considered as Judges pro tempore, and will not the Councill for App[ointmen]t appoint de Novo? I make no doubt the Appointment will amount to an Approbation of the present Appointment.[1]

Since I last saw you by Conversation with some of my friends and yours, I find they are Averse to putting the Secretary and Clerk into one Hand. I also find that the tenure of the Secretarys Office will depend upon the Councill of Appointment. (And as it is not to be presumed they would Lessen their Own importance,) I am Inclined to think it will be Annual at most Triennual.[2] In the present state of things I can by no Means think of Embarrassing myself with the care of the publick Records. I find my Budgets with the Necessarys for myself and family Quite Unweildy Enough.

From these Several Considerations I am Come to the Determination of Adhereing to my first Resolution of Holding no Office Whatever which I informed the Congress of the Last year at Harlem with my Reasons.[3] I am much Obliged to you for your particular Attention to me and my family in this instance and Shall Remember it with pleasure and Gratitude. I am Assured our Affairs to the North have been very Ill Conducted and I much fear I shall be Obliged to move again. My son is up at fort Edward with our Militia which makes my Attendance at Home Absolutely Necessary. Otherways I should have seen you at Esopus and have talked this Matter Over.

My best Respects to Mrs. Jay and all friends that [are] with you. I sincerely wish you and them Health and Success and am Sir with Real Esteem your Most Obedient Humble Servant

RID MORRIS

ALS.

1 Actually, the chancellor and judges of the Supreme Court, along with the governor, made up the Council of Revision, article 3 of the constitution. Article 23 provided for a Council of Appointment, consisting of the governor, and 4 senators elected annually by the assembly, for appointing officers not otherwise provided for in the constitution. Section 24 states that the governor "commissioned officers," both civil and military. Control of appointments to office, as well as duration in office if not specified was, therefore, lodged with the Council of Appointment, wherein the governor could only vote in the event of a tie. When JJ was governor he found that the council handcuffed him considerably. Lincoln, *Constitutional Hist. of N.Y.*, I, 167, 178, 180; see also JJ and the Constitution of 1777, above.

2 The Provincial Convention adjourned on 13 May 1777, leaving government temporarily in the hands of the Council of Safety, with Pierre Van Cortlandt as its president and Robert Benson and John McKesson continuing as secretaries (they had held the same posts in the Convention). When the new legislature convened in September, they were elected clerks of the Senate and Assembly, respectively. Any danger that might have resulted from multiple officeholding was avoided by the creation of a new Council of Safety on 7 October that did not include either Benson or McKesson. Lincoln, *Constitutional Hist. of N.Y.*, I, 571, 574–75, 582.

3 The Provincial Convention resolved unanimously on 31 July 1776 that Morris be appointed judge of the high court of admiralty of New York State. Morris appeared before the Convention, meeting in Harlem, on 2 Aug. 1776 and declined, the *JPC* stating that "from the situation of his family and property, the remainder of his life was necessary for attention to his own affairs." *JPC*, I, 550, 553, 554.

From Henry Brockholst Livingston

Fort Edward, July 17th, 1777

Dear Sir,

Inclose You two Letters which I must trouble You to forward.[1] It gives me pain that Necessity has so long obliged me to neglect Dr. Van Wyck. On my way up I made but a day or two's stay at Albany and am now but just returned from Tyonderoga. In this situation it was next to impossible to purchase a horse and send it down. As this may continue to be the case the whole Campaign will it not be best to send him an equivalent in Money. If You agree with me I will transmit him the Cash immediately.

You have heard of our retreat from Tyonderoga and Mount Independance.[2] Great as the Loss of those important Fortresses may be, I cannot but think the evacuation of them a very necessary Step. Genl. St. Clair had with him only two-thousand, and eighty nine effectives, including two regiments of Militia, and a Company of Artificers—these were most of them raw and undisciplined. Yet with these he had to defend works of a League in extent against an Army of Six thousand Men, aided by a very respectable fleet. His Stores of Provisions were small and very inadequate for even a short Siege. The Enemy's Batteries which were nearly ready to open, commanded every Part of the Camp. Our Communication was nearly cut off in which case there would have been no hopes of releif. You must be sensible it would have been a miracle for Militia to have raised the Siege, And before any other aid could have arrived a Capitulation must have taken place. Under these Circumstances a Council of General Officers judged a retreat necessary. As many of the Stores and Cannon, were removed as was possible in one Night, though these also unfortunately fell into the Enemy's hands at Skenesborough. We had a very severe and circuitous march to this place.[3]

Burgoyne finding it impracticable to come by the way of Wood Creek, (the Passage of which we had obstructed by falling trees into it) has returned to Tyonderoga to come by Fort George.[4] For this purpose they are carrying their Batteaus from Lake Champlain into Lake George. We have been so fortunate as to get off all our Stores from Fort George which were very considerable, with the loss of only two Waggons cut off by the Indians. Yesterday the Garrison left it after setting fire to the Fort Hospital, Barrack and other buildings. A Stand is to be made three miles below this at Moses' Creek,[5] there being some advantageous heights to fortify. For my own part I trust more to the Woods for Security than any Forts we can raise. The Enemy seldom attack us in our works, when they do they generally succeed.

Genl. Burgoyne has sent a Summons to the People of the Grants, to meet Gov. Skene[6] at Castletown to be there acquainted with the terms on which they are to hold their property, And threatening with immediate death all who refuse their attendance. Genl. Schuyler in answer to this has sent a Proclamation thither declaring that those who comply with Burgoyne's Summons shall be punished as Traitors.

Many have taken Protection, Those who are discovered are committed to Gaol.

With my best Love to Mrs. Jay I am Dear Sir Your Affectionate Humble Servant

HENRY B. LIVINGSTON

ALS in NN: Bancroft American Series, II, p. 84-1/2.

1 Letters not located.

2 The Americans evacuated Fort Ticonderoga and Mount Independence on 5 July.

3 The Americans retreated to Skenesboro, N.Y., on 6 July.

4 Also known as Fort William Henry, a British base during Burgoyne's offensive.

5 The Americans did not make a stand at Moses Creek but retreated to Stillwater, twelve miles farther south.

6 Philip Skene (1725–1810), a Tory landowner, imprisoned for Loyalist sympathies but released in October 1776, induced Burgoyne to continue by an overland route from Skenesboro to Ford Edward, a march of twenty-three miles through a tractless wilderness, which consumed twenty-four days. James J. Hadden, *A Journal Kept in Canada and Upon Burgoyne's Campaign in 1776 and 1777* (Albany, 1884), pp. 93–95.

To Gouverneur Morris

Kingston, 21 July 1777

Dear Morris,

The Situation of Tryon County is both shameful and deplorable. Such abject Dejection and Despondency as mark the Letters we have recieved from thence disgrace human Nature. God knows what to do with or for them. Were they alone interested in their Fate, I should be for leaving their Cart in the Slough till they would put their Shoulders to the Wheel.[1]

Be more cautious in your Letters to the Council. It was imprudent to say that the Gen. offered <you> two N England for one York Soldier, or that Sinclair alone of the 4 Gen. was worth a Crown.[2] Schuyler has his Enemies here, and they use these things to his Disadvantage. Suspicions of his having been privy to the Evacuation of Tycond. spread wide, and twenty little Circumstances which perhaps are false are tromped up to give Colour to the Conjecture.

We could wish that Your Letters <would> might contain Paragraphs for the Public. We are silent because we have Nothing to say, and the People suspect <every thing> the worst because we say Nothing. Their Curiosity must be constantly gratified, or they will be <restless and> uneasy. Indeed I dont wonder at their Impatience, The late northern Events having been such as to have given occasion to Alarm and Suspicion.

I have not Liesure to add any Thing more than that I am etc.

Dft. Endorsed by JJ: "Dt. Letter to G Morris 21 July 1777." E in NN: Bancroft American Series, II, 112-1/2.

1 On 21 July the Council of Safety received a letter from the Committee of Tryon County, dated 18 July, warning of the likelihood of invasion by the British, Tories, and Indians, without prospects of protection from Continental troops; the morale of the militia was so low that desertions could be expected. *JPC*, II, 518.

2 On 16 July Morris wrote to the Council of Safety, addressed to its President, Pierre Van Cortlandt, from Fort Edward: "Excepting the General [Schuyler] and Genl. Sinclair, you have not a general officer here worth a crown" and "it would give him [Schuyler] great pleasure to command the troops of this State; so much that he offers to give two men for one." *JPC*, II, 511.

From Robert Troup

Philadelphia, July 22nd, 1777

My dear Sir,

I have written to you repeatedly, since I have been here, but not having received an Answer to either of my Letters, I conclude they have not reached you.[1] To the Disgrace of Human Nature, it has become a common Practice to betray the Confidence we repose in each other either by opening Letters, or not sending them to the Persons to whom they are directed. I have seen so many Instances of such Behaviour that I am determined to use more Caution hereafter. This Letter therefore, is directed to the Care of Col. Hamilton, who will send it by the first Express.

Yours of the 5 Ulto.[2] I received at Esopus on my Way to this City. I am greatly obliged to you for the Friendship it contains. You always was my Benefactor, and I hope will continue so, as long as I walk in the Line of Prudence, and prove myself a Lover of American Liberty.

I have the Satisfaction of informing you that the Suspicions I mentioned to you some Time ago, are entirely removed. Gen. Gates will not leave the Service; he is indulged with the Allowance given to a Commander of a separate Department, and will join the Army when the Enemy make a Movement.[3]

I cannot help reminding you of the Joy I feel on this Occasion. I confess I was much chagrined at the thoughts of leaving the Army at a Period when *a rich Harvest of Laurels was to be reaped*. Whether I shall ever be *one of the fortunate* is uncertain. I promise myself no Great Reputation as a Soldier, and shall be content if I am not an Object for Scorn, and Derision to point their Fingers at.

I congratulate you, most sincerely, on the Success which has lately attended our Arms in Jersey.[4] The precipitate Retreats of the Enemy are convincing Proofs, with me, that they fear *a general Action on equal Terms*. The Idea they entertained of the Cowardice and Irregularity of our Troops has now vanished, *and they hope to effect by fine spun Generalship, what they cannot do with all their boasted British Valor*. This and this only, I believe, is the Ground on which they build their Expectations of Conquest. Gloomy Prospect indeed! If we may judge of Futurity by the past, they have not *those supernatural Talents so constantly celebrated by the Tories*.

But let us for a Moment, shift the Scene from the Southward to the Northward. How striking the Contrast! We have lost Ticonderoga, together with the Cannon, and military Stores of every Kind. This is doubtless an unfortunate Blow, but I do not conceive it will be so severely felt as is generally imagined. By taking Post at Fort Edward[5] we can stop the Progress of the Goths, Huns and Vandals and confine their Ravages within very narrow Bounds. What vexes me most, is the Disgrace, which the Evacuation of such a strong Post will fix upon our Arms, in Europe.

I wish I could see Burgoyne's Letter to Ld. Germaine[6] on this Subject. His Proclamation shews more Profound Depth, in the Knowledge of Composition, than I ever discovered in the Works of the celebrated Martinus Scriblerus.[7]

Inclosed I send you the News Paper of this Day. I have Nothing more of Importance to communicate.

Be so kind as to give my Regards to Mrs. Jay, your Brother, and all my Friends you are acquainted with. I am affectionately Yours.

ROB. TROUP

ALS. Endorsed. Enclosure not located.

1 No letters from Troup to JJ have been located for the period between 2 June and 22 July.

2 Not located.

3 Troup, an aide to Gates, had written JJ on 2 June (above) that Gates was going to resign his commission in protest against Schuyler's elevation to the command of the Northern Department. Evidently Gates had a change of heart, as Congress on 8 July ordered him to report to Washington's headquarters. *JCC*, VIII, 540.

4 During June the American and British forces, commanded respectively by Washington and Howe, sparred with each other in New Jersey, meeting in various brief engagements. At the end of the month Howe withdrew entirely

from New Jersey. Christopher Ward, *The War of the Revolution* (2 vols., New York, 1952), I, 325–28.

[5] Decrepit and indefensible, Fort Edward was situated on the Hudson River south of Lake Champlain, on Burgoyne's line of march southward. Schuyler abandoned it at the end of July. Ward, I, 391, 415–20.

[6] George Sackville, Lord Germain (1716–85) was Secretary of State for the American Colonies, 1775–82.

[7] On 20 June 1777 Burgoyne issued an overblown proclamation warning civilians against assisting the enemy and threatening resisters with "the vengeance of the state." For the text, see Hoffman Nickerson, *The Turning Point of the Revolution, Or Burgoyne in America* (Boston, 1928), pp. 120–22, and a Whig parody attributed to Francis Hopkinson (1731–91), in Henry Steele Commager and Richard B. Morris, eds., *The Spirit of '76* (New York, 1967), pp. 548–50.

From Philip Schuyler

Moses Creek four Miles below Fort Edward,
July 24th 1777. 8 O'Clock P.M.

My dear Sir

Half an Hour ago I was favored with your's of the 21st Instant.[1] That Variety of Distress and Difficulty which surrounds me is greatly encreased by the Information contained in your Letter. It is however a Consolation that I have a Friend, who has given me so great a proof of his Regard as not to hide from me any of the Calumny which so unjustly and cruelly attempts to ruin my Reputation, and that I have not only the happy Reflection that every part of it is undeserved, but that I can most fully refute it, and clearly convince the World that my Conduct has been upright proper, and that I have done every Thing that an Officer in my Situation could do to save a Fortress, the Evacuation of which has given such universal Disatisfaction.

General St. Clair and all the other General Officers that were at that post have publicly declared that I never have given an Order for its Evacuation, that if the Measure were culpable they only are guilty, and that if I experience any Censure it is most unjustly. That if the Measure was wise, I am not entitled to share in the Credit of it. The Letter from General St. Clair I hope will be convincing on that Head,[2] and the Orders I have given and the Measures I have taken to secure that post, which claimed my Attention even before the End of last Campaign will I trust wipe away the Charges of Want of Integrity and evince that I took the most timely and proper Measures for the Security of Tyonderoga. These Orders are at Albany. I shall cause them to be extracted and transmit them to you, but as they will form a small Volume, it will take some Time to do it.[3]

Nothing less than the strictest Scrutiny into my Conduct will wipe away the Odium which I am loaded with and that I shall immediately apply for, and confident I am, that the Result will be much to my Honor, and that the candid and honest will be convinced. But as this must necessarily be a Matter of Time, I shall immediately dispatch my Secretary to Albany for the Orders I have given since I returned to the Command of the Northern Department, until the Evacuation took place and then transmit the Council of Safety an authentic State of Facts.

The Report that a Number of heavy Cannon were by my order dismounted and laid aside, and small ones placed in their Room is equally false with the others.[4]

A Number of heavy Cannon were laying unmounted on the Bank of the Lake and on the Tyonderoga Side. They had never been mounted because there never had been, nor were there then any Carriages for them. These I ordered to be collected and carried to Mount Independance, after the Council of General Officers called by me on the 20th and 21st of June, had resolved "that both Tyonderoga and Mount Independance should be defended as long as possible, but that if it was necessary to abandon either, it should be the Tyonderoga Side." It was therefore prudent to remove useless Cannon to that post which was strongest and was to be defended in Case both could not be kept.

Those that draw unfavorable Conclusions from my Absence from Tyonderoga ought to know that I hastened from it, in order to provide for its Safety, to throw in a greater Quantity of provisions, and those Reinforcements of Men which I had applied for, That I had every Thing to do, Nothing, literally Nothing having been done whilst the Department was committed to General Gates's Direction.

The certain Gentleman you mention, if I am not mistaken who you mean, has a very bad Heart, and I have Reason to think would do me an ill Turn. I thank my God, it is not in his power and he will have the Mortification to see me fully justify myself.[5]

I wish the Council of Safety to depute a Committee to repair hither and enquire into my Conduct, for although I am not properly accountable to any, but Congress or General Washington, yet I will, with pleasure, consent to such an Enquiry, and the rather as my Fellow Citizens will then be more generally informed of my Conduct.

I wish you to send me the original or a certified Copy of General St. Clair's Letter to you. If the former pray keep a Copy of it, and advise me by the first Opportunity whether the Council does not believe that Tyonderoga was left without my Direction, Advice or Knowledge. Would it not be proper to publish part of General St. Clair's Letter?[6] I am Dear Sir Your Friend and much obliged humble Servant

PH. SCHUYLER

ALS. Endorsed. LbkC in NN: Philip Schuyler Papers, Schuyler Lbk.

[1] JJ's letter of 21 July reported that Schuyler was being charged with responsibility for the loss of Ticonderoga. *WJ*, I, 74–77; *HPJ*, I, 148–51; dft. in JP.

[2] See below, St. Clair to JJ, 25 July.

[3] Schuyler wrote JJ on 6 August, enclosing copies of all his orders relating to Ticonderoga's provisioning and defense. ALS in MH; LbkC in NN: Philip Schuyler Papers, Schuyler Lbk.

[4] JJ had relayed this rumor to Schuyler in his letter of 21 July.

[5] JJ had written on 21 July that "a certain gentleman at that board [the New York Council of Safety], whom I need not name, and from whom I do *not* desire this information should be concealed, it is my opinion your secret enemy." *HPJ*, I, 151. JJ is probably referring to John Morin Scott.

[6] See below, JJ to Schuyler, 26 July.

From Arthur St. Clair

Moses's Creek, July 25th, 1777

Sir

General Schuyler was good enough to read to me part of a letter he received last night from you.[1] I can not recollect that any of my officers ever asked my reasons for leaving Ticonderoga; but, as I have found the measure much decried, I have often expressed myself in this manner: "That as to myself I was perfectly easy; I was conscious of the uprightness and propriety of my conduct, and despised the vague censure of an uninformed populace;" but had no allusion to an order from General Schuyler for my justification, because no such order existed.[2]

The calumny thrown on General Schuyler, on account of that matter, has given me great uneasiness. I assure you, Sir, there never was any thing more cruel and unjust, for he knew nothing of the matter until it was over, more than you did at Kingston. It was done in consequence of a consultation with the other general officers, without the possibility of General Schuyler's concurrence; and had the opinion of that council been contrary to what it was, it would nevertheless have taken place, because I knew it to be impossible to defend the post with our numbers.

In my letter to Congress from Fort Edward, in which I gave them an account of the retreat, is this paragraph: "It was my original design to retreat to this place, that I might be betwixt General Burgoyne and the inhabitants, and that militia might have something in this quarter to collect to. It is now effected, and the militia are coming in, so that I have the most sanguine hopes that the progress of the enemy will be checked, and I may have the satisfaction to experience that, *although I have lost a post, I have eventually saved a State.*"[3]

Whether my conjecture is right or not, is uncertain; but, had our army been made prisoners, which it certainly would have been, the State of New York would have been much more exposed at present.

I proposed to General Schuyler, on my arrival at Fort Edward, to have sent a note to the printer to assure the people he had no part in abandoning what they considered their strongholds. He thought it was not so proper at that time, but it is no more than what I owe to truth and to him to declare that he was totally unacquainted with the matter; and I should be very glad that this letter, or any part of it you may think proper to communicate, may convince the unbelieving.[4] Simple unbelief is easily and soon convinced, but, when malice or envy occasions it, it is needless to attempt conviction.[5]

PtdL: William Henry Smith, ed., *The St. Clair Papers. The Life and Public Services of Arthur St. Clair* (2 vols., Cincinnati, 1882), I, 433–34.

1 JJ to Schuyler, 21 July, dft. in JP.

2 JJ had written on 21 July: "It is said, but I know not with what truth, that St. Clair, on being asked by some of his officers why the fort was evacuated, replied generally, that he knew what he did; that on his own account he was very easy about the matter, and that he had it in his power to justify himself. From hence some inferred that he must have alluded to orders from you [Schuyler]." *HPJ*, I, 149.

3 See St. Clair to John Hancock, President of the Continental Congress, 14 July, in Smith, ed., *St. Clair Papers*, I, 426–29.

4 JJ sent this letter to the press on the 26th July. It was published in the *New York Journal*, at Kingston, 28 July 1777, with this introduction by JJ to John Holt, its printer: "Be pleased to give the enclosed letter, which I have just received from Brigadier General St. Clair, a place in your next paper. With the candour and ingenuity becoming a man of honour, he acquits Major-General Schuyler of having ordered or been privy to the evacuation of Ticonderoga—a charge which it seems has gained credit without proof, and found zealous advocates though unsupported by truth."

5 JJ's reply to St. Clair, 28 July, is in JP.

To Philip Schuyler

Kingston, 26–28 July 1777

Dear Sir

Your Favor of the 24th Inst. covering a Letter from General St. Clair was delivered to me this Evening. I have sent the latter to the

Press. It will be printed entire. Extracts might be followed by Suspicions. The malicious might remark that Parts were consealed which if made known would probably give a different Color to the whole. A Number of Holts Papers shall be sent You; and Care taken to transmit others to Congress, to Head Quarters, Peeks Kill etc. I shall also request Loudon[1] to reprint it.

This <imprudent> Attack on your Reputation will I hope do you only a temporary Injury. The honest tho credulous Multitude when undecieved will regret <the Part they have acted and be happy in making amends for the Injustice they were incautiously> their giving Way to Suspicions which have led them to do You Injustice. <Like other Attempts of your Enemies it will terminate in their Shame. After being thus repeatedly foiled they will probably cease Hostilities.>

I have <not the least> Reason to suspect that the Council of Safety believed Tyconderogah was left by your Direction or Advice, or with your Knowledge. They appear fully satisfied of the contrary[2] and in my Opinion St. Clairs Letter will remove <the> all Doubts <of every honest Man> on that Head.

The Propriety of appointing a Committee to inquire into your Conduct appears to me very questionable. Supposing it unexceptionable in point of Delicacy with Respect to You (which I by no Means think it) yet <it is not clear that the Object or View could be fully obtained> as The Council <as well as> and the late Convention, <as it is well known>, have on certain occasions made your Cause their own; <and> your Enemies would not fail to insinuate that the proposed Inquiry, was a mere Contrivance to give a favorable Complection to your Conduct.[3]

Your Readiness to submit to such an Inquiry is no Doubt a strong argument of Innocence and conscious Rectitude; but whether it would not be assuming in the Council to propose it, and inconsistant with the Dignity of your Station to accede to it, are Questions of Importance. Besides, a Proposition so apparently officious, and out of their Line, might perhaps be maliciously ascribed to their Apprehensions of Mismanagement, and consequently <would> cast Weight in the Scale against You.

A temperate State of Facts formed from the Materials you mention <will> would doubtless <answer valuable Purposes and> set your Conduct in its true Point of View. <I wish it may be so communicated to the Council. . . .>

Altho a strict Scrutiny <into Your Conduct> may be eligible, yet how far it would be proper to *press* Congress to adopt that

Measure is worth Consideration. <Inquiries of that Kind are at best unpleasant, and> The Affairs of the northern Department have lately engaged much of their Time and Attention.[4] <To hint at a general Inquiry, and to furnish them with every Fact necessary to form a Judgment of your Proceedings, I should think would be sufficient for the <<Purpose>> present.> The Evacuation of Tyconderogah will *naturally* bring about an Inquiry. The Country will not be satisfied without it. You will then have a fair Opportunity of vindicating your Conduct.

The Manner in which you account for the Removal of the Cannon mentioned in my Letter is very satisfactory <and proper use shall be made of it.>

Mr. Morris returned this Afternoon. The Council were displeased with the last Letter from him and Mr. Yates. They have passed a Resolution Declaring it disrespectful and unsatisfactory and dissolved that Com[mitte]e.[5] They have nevertheless <appointed> joined Mr. Morris with me <com[mitte]e> and directed us to repair to Head Quarters to confer with his Excellency on the State of your Army, the Means of reinforcing it etc. We set out Tomorrow.[6]

<Monday 28 July>

Holt has published a Piece immediately under St. Clair's Letter, which I wish had been suppressed.[7] As it contained Extracts of Papers transmitted to the Council by You, and not ordered to be made public, I moved that Inquiry be made for the Author, and the Manner in which he obtained these Extracts. Mr. R. Harpur[8] confessed himself to be the Author and <made some sham> endeavoured to apologize for it. I then moved for the Sense of the Board on this Question, whether any Member had a Right to publish any Papers or Extracts from any Papers belonging to the Council, unless by their express Order or Consent. It was carried Nem. Con. that no Member had such Right. I mention these Facts as that Performance will doubtless excite your Attention.

With the best Wishes for your Health and Prosperity I am Dear Sir your Friend and Obedient Servant

JOHN JAY

DftS. Endorsed by JJ: "Dr. to Gen. Schuyler <28> & 26 July 1777." Tr in NN: Bancroft, Schuyler Papers, 1776–88.

1 Samuel Loudon published the *New York Packet* at Fishkill. No copies of this paper for July 1777 (except for 3 July) survive.

[2] Pierre Van Cortlandt, the President of the Council of Safety, had already openly defended Schuyler's conduct in the Fort Ticonderoga affair.

[3] Schuyler's conduct was under heavy fire from members of the Continental Congress. Martin H. Bush, *Revolutionary Enigma, A Re-Appraisal of General Philip Schuyler of New York* (Port Washington, N.Y., 1969), pp. 124–25.

[4] Schuyler explained the removal of the cannon in his letter to JJ of 24 July 1777, above.

[5] Gouverneur Morris and Abraham Yates had been appointed by the Council of Safety to visit Schuyler at his headquarters and report on the causes of the evacuation. Instead, Morris and Yates had dispatched to the Council a letter warning both of Loyalist agents active in Tryon County and of British agents working for the state of Vermont. The legislature, displeased, ordered Morris and Yates to submit a report that could be made public explaining the reasons for the loss of Ticonderoga. This communication irked Morris, who replied that even Schuyler could not explain this defeat. They wrote to the Council on 23 July, which, on a motion made by JJ, was considered "disrespectful and unsatisfactory," and the Council "dissolved" the committee. *JPC*, I, 989, 991, 1004, 1016, 1017; see also Max M. Mintz, *Gouverneur Morris and the American Revolution* (Norman, Okla., 1970), pp. 79–82.

[6] JJ and Morris departed on this mission to General Washington on 29 July. Washington informed them he could only spare the two brigades that he had already authorized to aid Schuyler. *JPC*, I, 1019; *GCP*, II, 146, 235–36.

[7] Holt published this piece in the *New York Journal*, 28 July 1777, under the initial "T." "T" demanded an explanation for St. Clair's conduct at Ticonderoga. It contained excerpts from a letter of St. Clair expressing confidence that Ticonderoga could be held.

[8] Robert Harpur (c. 1731–1825), formerly a professor of mathematics at King's College, had tutored JJ. He was a member of the Provincial Congress, and subsequently served on the Council of Safety.

From Philip Schuyler

Moses Creek, July 27th, 1777

Dear Sir

General Arnold who is Advanced with two Brigades of continental troops and the Militia of the County of Albany about two miles In our front has Just Informed me that the Enemy have appeared on the heights above fort Edward In Considerable force and that from their movements he Judges an Attack will be made to day, loth as I am that a General Engagement Should Ensue And that I will take Every prudent measure to prevent It. It is not Impossible but It may take place, and as the fate of Every person engaged In It is uncertain, as I Shall certainly be there, and, In order to Inspirit my troops shall Expose myself more than It is prudent for a Commanding officer to do. I may possibly get rid of the Cares of this life or fall Into their hands, in Either case I Intreat you to Rescue my memory from that load of Calumny that Ever follows the unfortunate. My papers will furnish you with Sufficient Materials and I trust that the Goodness of

Your heart will Induce you to devote a part of Your time to It. I leave this with my Secretary to be sent to you If I shall not return. I am this moment going to mount.

Adieu. Yours Sincerely

PH. SCHUYLER

ALS. Addressed: "To The Honorable John Jay Esqr at Kingston to be sent him If an Incident should happen to me." Endorsed.

From James Duane

Philadelphia, 3rd August 1777

Dear Sir

I enclose you a Letter from France for yourself and another to Mr. Platt[1] which last you'l be pleased to forward with my respectful Compliments.

General Howe and his grand fleet to the utter Astonishment and Vexation of the People here have disappeared as every necessary preparation for his Reception was made. He has left us to guess at his next Attempt.[2]

General Schuyler to humour the Eastern people who declare that their Militia will not fight under his command is recalled.[3] As is St. Clair for surrendering Ticonderoga and in order to take his Trial which he has demanded.[4] Congress have left it to General Washington to name the Commander of the Northern Department. On whom that arduous Task will fall is yet unknown?[5]

Is it possible, my dear Sir, that Burgoine at the head of not more than 6000 men can dare to penetrate into the Country in defiance of the numberless Enemies he must have to encounter. Two years ago such an attempt would have been thought fortunate for America, and now it terrifies. Oh New England are thou so fallen, so lost to publick Virtue!

The Accounts from France are flattering. Our Ambassadors have negotiated very considerable Loans of money and Supplies of Ammunition and Goods; and assure us that all Europe except England are our Friends.[6]

I have no time to add. To say the Truth I can hardly perswade myself to write thus much. Since two long Letters to you and Mr. Livingston I remain totally disregarded![7] Present my respectful Compliments to Mrs. Jay and believe me to be with great Respect Dear Sir Your most obedient and very humble Servant

JAS. DUANE

ALS. Endorsed. Enclosures not located.

1 Zephaniah Platt was serving as "second in command of corps of associated exempts in Dutchess County." *JPC*, I, 987.

2 Howe gathered a large fleet at New York and sailed from there on 23 July, but the American forces could not determine his destination. On 30 July the vessels appeared off Delaware Bay in a feint, vanishing, and heading toward the Chesapeake, leaving the American leadership thoroughly confused until the British fleet was sighted in the Chesapeake 22 August. Christopher Ward, *The War of the Revolution* (2 vols., New York, 1952), I, 328–31.

3 New York's delegates in the Continental Congress wrote on 29 July to the New York Council of Safety that "the Eastern States [New England] openly affirm that their Troops have no Confidence in General Schuyler and assign this as the Reason that they have not marched to his Assistance." On 1 August Congress ordered Schuyler to return to headquarters, leaving the Northern command. *LMCC*, II, 429; *JCC*, VIII, 596.

4 By a resolution of 30 July St. Clair was ordered to report immediately to headquarters. On 3 August Congress received his letter of 27 July, in which he asked for a trial. *JCC*, VIII, 590, 600; PCC, 161, 509.

5 Congress issued this directive to Washington on 1 August and repeated it on 3 August. *JCC*, VIII, 596, 600.

6 Lee, Deane, and Franklin had recently sent optimistic reports to the Committee of Foreign Affairs on the prospects of a French loan, the purchase of a large quantity of supplies, and of England's difficulty in raising troops. *RDC*, II, 319–20, 322–25, 342–43.

7 Duane had written to JJ, Robert R. Livingston *et al.* on 2 May (ALS in JP), and to Livingston, 24 June–8 July, ALS in NHi: Robert R. Livingston Papers.

From Philip Schuyler

Stilwater, August 4th, 1777

Dear Sir

Your Favor inclosing Holt's papers of the 28th July I received on my Way down from Moses Creek, and you will readily excuse my not having acknowledged it sooner, when you reflect that with a retreating army an officer that commands has seldom a Moment's Time to himself.[1] I have not one.

I am much obliged by the Measure you have taken to exculpate me, at least, from the Charge of having ordered the Retreat. As soon as I can have an Hour or two, which, I hope, will be to Morrow, I shall send you Extracts of all my orders relative to Tyonderoga, since my Return from Philadelphia, and a short account, from Memory, of what Measures I took as early as the Beginning of November last, for the Security of that post. The Letters I have written and the Orders I have issued for that purpose, previous to my Departure for Philadelphia, would make a little Volume; and, I trust redound much to my Credit.[2]

If we should be enabled to force Burgoyne at this post and he meet with a Check it must be fatal to him; but unhappily such a Langor prevails, especially in the Eastern States, that they seem to have given up the Cause for lost. If they would pour forth part of those Thousands which they still have at Home (for not one in ten, Boys, Negroes and old Men excepted, of the Troops raised in their States are Natives) we should still not only save our Country, but give a deadly Blow to the Enemy, for if Burgoyne was obliged to retreat the whole of the six Nations, I believe would join us, and we should have Nothing more to fear in this Quarter.[3]

Adieu. I am Dear Sir with every friendly Wish Your affectionate humble Servant

PH. SCHUYLER

ALS. Also LbkC, NN: Philip Schuyler Papers.

[1] Schuyler retreated down the Hudson River from Fort Edward to Moses Creek and then to Stillwater, twelve miles below Saratoga.

[2] Schuyler sent this material to JJ in a letter dated 6 Aug. LS is at MH; LbkC at NN: Philip Schuyler Papers.

[3] Schuyler was overoptimistic. Only the Tuscaroras and Oneidas, of the Six Nations, supported the colonists. Barbara Graymont, *The Iroquois in the American Revolution* (Syracuse, 1972).

FROM PHILIP SCHUYLER

Albany, August 17th, 1777

Dear Sir

This morning I had the pleasure to recieve your favor of the 12th Instant.[1]

Mr. Duane has acknowledged the receipt of my letter to you Inclosing the orders etc. I am happy that he thinks my "Conduct needs no Apology." He also Informed me that the motives for my removal were the same as you gave. They were certainly sufficient to Induce Congress to the measure but they might have done me the Justice to have advised me thereof.[2] In making my defence against any Charges that may be brought against me, I propose to lay before the Court all my letters to Congress, Gen. Washington, and Every public body, with their Answers, and Every order I have given since the Close of last Campaign that they may become part of the proceedings of the Court, by which means I can procure a Copy of the whole, and deliver It to the Public who will then be Enabled to Judge whence the Misfortunes to the Northward have Originated, and hope Every Candid reader will Exculpate me.

Gen. Gates left Van Schaicks Island and the other posts which the Army occupyed when he took the Command in the fullest Intention to proceed in pursuit of Gen. Burgoyn whom he declared would not dare to risk a battle. I wish things had turned out as he flattered himself they would.[3] They have not and he is halted three miles above Still water, and Occupys ground that I do not think very Advantageous. There is better In the vicinity but It lays at a little distance In his rear and I suppose he dare not retire to It least It should damp the Spirits of his troops, which are high. So far He may be right, but I cannot concive he was so In detatching so Capital a part of his Army as that Corps under the Command of Gen. Lincoln is to so great a distance.[4] It is certain that he is at Skensborough and has detatched two thousand more from thence to Tycnderoga and Mount Independance.[5] Of what Consequence is either of those places If we should be beat at Still water? I believe he sees his Error for he has called on all the Militia of this County to March and reinforce him. Before I left the Army I had ordered Lincoln to the North part of Cambridge which is about fourteen miles East of Saratoga from thence to try and make an Impression on some of the Enemies posts. And If that was not practicable to move down keeping on their flank. By this means I concived he would be Always at hand to Assist when a General Engagement should take place. Perhaps It was a sufficient reason to change this disposition because I had made it.

A Gentleman In the army observes that when Gen. Gates was coming up to take the Command the British Army by his Account did not Exceed five or six thousand men, but that now It is made to be ten or twelve thousand. What must It have been before the Bennington Affair.[6] If he really believes It is so numerous he is Inexcusable for dividing his army. If not, he ought not to hazard the Effect such an account may have on his troops. God Grant him success; our all depends upon It, but If he has It I can never Impute It to his Military abilities, for altho he may have Courage I am sure he has nothing Else. Before I left the Army I offered him my services and beged he would call on me whenever he had Occasion. I suppose he has had none, for he has never advised with me, nor given me the least Intimation of his Intentions. Perhaps I might have been of Some Service.

The Oneidas Tuscarros and such part of the Onandagas as are here have taken the Hatchet about fifty or Sixty will Join our Army to day.

I am anxious to hear from the Southward. I wish the Enemy had Stuck to their Original plan and had Attempted to penetrate by

Delewar river, where they are they will have a great Accession of Tories.[7]

Adieu My Dear Sir I am most Sincerely Your obedient and Humble Servant

PH. SCHUYLER

ALS.

1 Not located.

2 The Continental Congress did not inform Schuyler directly of his removal. Gates was simply ordered to replace Schuyler as soon as possible. *JCC*, VIII, 604.

3 Gates had hoped to drive the British into Canada. Samuel W. Patterson, *Horatio Gates* (New York, 1941), p. 149.

4 Benjamin Lincoln (1733–1810), a Continental major general from Massachusetts, was in Vermont with about 500 militia, ready to move against Burgoyne's rear. Christopher Ward, *The War of the Revolution* (2 vols., New York, 1952), II, 500.

5 In fact, troops were not dispatched to Skenesboro and Ticonderoga until the middle of September. Ward, II, 523.

6 The British suffered severe losses at the Battle of Bennington (14–16 August), 207 dead and 700 prisoners.

7 Howe had abandoned his plan to sail up the Delaware River and was heading south around Cape Charles towards the Chesapeake. Ward, *The War of the Revolution,* I, 331–33.

Sarah Livingston Jay to Henry Brockholst Livingston

Persipiney, 18th August 1777

Will you not be surprised my dear brother when you find I venture to tax you with a little piece of cruelty which I could not forbear taking notice of in one of your letters to Susan? For what else can I term a suspicion of our love, which upon a long silence on our part you had permitted to steal into your bosam? And yet by allowing it to have been an intruder (perhaps in guise of friendship) do I not acquit you of the very charge which I had alledged against you?

The truth is, that being conscious of my own demerits, I had a mind by challenging, to draw you upon the defensive and so to escape with my own faults unobserved; but considering you are not to be amused by such trifling manouvres I think it more prudent to surrender at discretion.

The ravages and destructive cruelties which appear to be the inevitable lot of poor New York and the sufferings which many of our hapless friends have already experienced, together with the more immediate dangers to which a beloved brother is exposed, are circumstances sufficient to erase from a mind even less susceptible of anxious forethought, the very traces of joy and gaiety that used to mark my converse and my conduct. May the sad prospect which we have in view introduce those more useful Guests, I mean fortitude and resignation, which alone can support us in these changing scenes.

Poor Clarkson's[1] disagreable situation is not singly regretted; we all joined in lamenting the chance of war which had so soon signalized him by misfortunes. Please to present our united Compliments to him.

Yesterday Mr. Jay bid us adieu in order to attend the convention;[2] how long it will be before he returns depends upon the limits you army gentlemen prescribe for General Burgoyne.[3] Is it not a mortification to us who disclaim the tyranny of the King of England, that even the most interesting actions of our lives are controuled by his minions.

My little dear boy grows finely, and every day presents him to his partial mother still more lovely—it will be some time yet before he'll be able to amuse us with his innocent prattle, but when he does, be assured it shall not be long before he'll endeavor to express his gratitude to his kind uncle.

Can you my dear Harry pardon me for not telling you before, that when Mr. Jay was at Philadelphia he had the felicity of seeing your fair friend and that he left her in health and spirits so I find my very sly brother that the reward which you very humbly propose to yourself for all your dangers and toil is no less than would have been esteemed a sufficient prize for the victorious arms of either Greece or Troy.

But I forget that while I am amusing myself with scribling, I am perhaps intruding upon your hours of business. I will therefore only beg your partial reception of these few lines, and conclude with assuring you of the esteem of Your affectionate Sister

SA. JAY

ALS.

[1] Matthew Clarkson (1758–1825), SLJ's cousin, then a major in Schuyler's army. He was wounded in an encounter at Fort Edward. Reynolds, *Family Hist. of So. N.Y.*, III, 1026.

[2] On 21 and 22 August Jay was in attendance at the Council of Safety. *JPC*, I, 1046.

[3] Burgoyne at that date was marching toward Albany.

To Robert Morris

Kingston, 23 August 1777

Dear Sir

Mr. Deane in a Letter of the 28 May last,[1] after recommending an attack on the Greenland Fishery and Hudsons Bay Trade, desired me to communicate the following Plan to Congress vizt. "To send three Frigates loaded with Tobacco to Nantz or Bordeaux, equipped in the best Manner and on their arrival hide the chief of their Guns and appear as Cruzers. Intelligence may be had every week what the Station of the British Fleet is, and how the Coast is defended, and a sudden Blow may be struck which will alarm and shake Great Britain to the Center. This Plan will appear bold and extravagant—so much the more likely to succeed as it will be unexpected, and the plundering and burning of Liverpool and Glascow would be a most glorious Revenge. And believe me it is very easily effected. I dare put my Life on the Issue of it, if left to my Management, and I can get good Men to execute."

This was a favourite Plan of Mr. Dean before he left Philadelphia, and I confess I wish the Experiment may be tryed.[2] The greatest Difficulty I fear would be to get the Frigates well manned etc. safe to France.

I am Sir very sincerely Yours etc.

JOHN JAY

ALS. Addressed: "The Hon'ble Robert Morris Esqr Congress Philadelphia." Endorsed.

1 Not located.

2 George L. Clark, Deane's biographer, notes that as early as October 1776 Deane had proposed to the Committee of Secret Correspondence that frigates bringing supplies to France could be refitted and used "as cruisers to prey on British commerce and pillage the west coast of England and Scotland." See Clark, *Silas Deane, A Connecticut Leader in the American Revolution* (New York, 1913), pp. 87–88.

From Robert Troup

Head Quarters, August 29, 1777

My dear Sir,

In my last[1] I informed you of the Enemy's Retreat from Fort Stanwix. Gen. Arnold upon, the earliest Notice of this fortunate Event, made a forced March to the Fort, with a View of harassing their Rear.

In a Letter of the 24, he says Col. Gansevoort had anticipated his Design, by sending out a Party, which took 4 Royals, and a considerable Number of Prisoners.[2] He adds that he shall, that Evening, detach some faithful Oneidas, and the next Morning, 500 regular Troops, to go as far as the Oneida Lake. When they return he will use all possible Dispatch to join the Army at this Post.[3]

As he brings with him a formidable Body of Oneidas, and Tuskororas, I think we shall be able to cope with Burgoyne upon equal Ground. These, added to Col. Morgan's Riflemen, will teach his murderers to pay a little Respect to the Laws of Humanity.[4]

We still remain on the Islands. It would be impolitic to change our Situation before our Reinforcements come in. These are hourly looked for, and when they are collected, we shall not lose the present Opportunity of doing Some thing pretty decisive.[5]

Prisoners and Deserters say that Burgoyne has posted one Regiment at Fort George, another at Fort Edward, and three at Skeensborough. That his Main Body, of between 4 and 5000, lies at Fort Miller, and his advanced Guard at Saratoga; That he seems to be preparing rather for a defensive, than an offensive Campaign; That he has thrown a Bridge across the North River, at Mt. Niels, one Mile and a half back of Saratoga. That the Troops are sickly, and badly paid; that fresh Provisions are scarce; that there is a Misunderstanding between the English and Germans; that Burgoyne gives 20 Dollars for a Prisoner, and 10 for a Scalp; that he buoys up their Spirits by saying he will soon be joined by 15,000 Men; that many would desert if they were not fearful of the Indians, who are ordered to treat them as Rebels, if they are caught out of the Lines.

I am, dear Sir, Yours,

R. TROUP

My best Respects to Mrs. Jay and your Brother.

ALS. Addressed: "The Honorable John Jay Esqr. Kingston." Endorsed.

1 Robert Troup to JJ, 25 August 1777, in JP.

2 Colonel Peter Gansevoort routed the British, utilizing the successful ploy of the halfwit Hon Yost Schuyler. Christopher Ward, *The War of the Revolution* (2 vols., New York, 1952), II, 490–91; Barbara Graymont, *The Iroquois in the American Revolution* (Syracuse, 1972), p. 144.

3 Leaving 700 men at Fort Stanwix, Arnold departed with 1,200 others for the main camp.

4 Colonel Daniel Morgan (1736–1802) had been dispatched to join Gates as Burgoyne's offensive developed.

5 Washington, then west of Wilmington, was reinforced by the Pennsylvania militia.

MARINUS WILLETT TO JAMES DUANE AND JOHN JAY

Fort Schuyler, September 1st, 1777

Honored Sirs,

In times like these when the most horrid Murders and Affecting carnage are taking place all around us, and when the cruel and inveterate enemies we have to deal with are sticking at nothing to bring about their Diabolical purposses every genuine friend to our injured countrey (among which number I have the most powerfull reason to be convinced you are) will undoubtedly use all their influence to fix in offices of importance men who are most likely to fill these offices to the Advantage of the publick, for tho it is possible there may be times when interested connections may sway even the Patriot, Yet this is by no means one of those times; our very oppressed and bleeding Countrey demands from the Patriot a Pure and most disinterested disstribution of offices to be Lodged into the hands only of those Men who appear most likly to serve there countrey. It is from a firm faith of your integrity in the cause of your Countrey that I now Address you on a Subject of more importance then is perhaps generally conceived.

The Indians appear to me to be a people who can hardly restrain themselves from fighting in time of war. I have endeavoured much to Study there dissposition and think this is truly the case. If then they will fight is it not better that they fight for us then against us? For however trifleing we may view them they are not without there brave Actions, and their barbarities frequently fill their enemies with Terror: (I have seen too much of this) but the manner of <acquiring> employing them is curious and appears to require much art, and it is plain to me that before this time we might have a large Majority of the six Nations fighting for us if proper steps had been taken for that purpose, and it is as plain that the Conduct of the Commissioners[1] has had a quite contrary tendency. It is not my intention to Attempt to point out the steps Necessary to be taken in order to procure the Indians to take up the Hatchet in our favour, I only beg leave to mention that I am prety clear it may be done, and that it would be an Advantage to us in the present war to have it done, and at the same time to give it as my opinion that the person to be employed in this business ought to be a man who has Virtue, has evidenced himself a friend to our cause, and is well acquanted with the manners and customs of the Indians, who will be willing to lay himself out in the business and if it should be necessary as I think it will be, he must be ready to encounter danger and endure much hardness in performing the Arduous task.

I have had this affair in Contemplation for some time, and thought about a person who appeared to me to be Adequate to the task. It was a certain Mr. Spencer[2] who lived among the Oneidas, but he has died the Death of a Hero! in the late battle with General Harkaman.[3] The situation of this man's famaly (who if I am rightly informed live at Cherry Valley) is penurious. I hope our countrey will not let them suffer for want. At present I can think of no person who is likly to perform this business, without it is Mr. Dean[4] an Indian interpreter, who is well known to the Commissioners of Indian affairs, and who at least might be consulted upon this business. I shall only add that it appears to me that the person employed will require good encouragment, that his duty and interest may be united.

I shall make no apology for troubeling you upon this business. I have only done my duty in mentioning to Gentlemen in your Situation, a matter that appears to me to be of importance to my Countrey.

I am Gentlemen Your Very Humble Servant

MARINUS WILLETT

ALS. Endorsed by JJ.

1 The Commissioners for Indian Affairs in the Northern Department (which included the Six Nations and all tribes north of this group). The Commissioners were reluctant to seek outright alliance with the tribes because of the expense necessary to maintain such friendship. They were willing to settle, if possible, for declarations of Indian neutrality during the British-American conflict. Barbara Graymont, *The Iroquois in the American Revolution* (Syracuse, 1972), pp. 65, 66, 89, 90.

2 Thomas Spencer (d. 1777), an Oneida half-breed blacksmith who had undertaken a secret mission to Canada for the Americans. Spencer fell at the Battle of Oriskany, 6 Aug. 1777. *Ibid.*, pp. 112, 134, 135.

3 General Nicholas Herkimer (1728–77).

4 James Dean, an interpreter for the Oneidas. Dean, with the renowned missionary to the Oneidas Samuel Kirkland, did much to retain the loyalty of that tribe for the Americans. *Ibid.*, pp. 37, 38, 59, 65, *passim*.

FROM SARAH LIVINGSTON JAY

Persipiney, September 3d, 1777

My dear Mr. Jay,

No less then three weeks have already elapsed, and not a single line from my beloved friend. Lord Chesterfield tells his son that women never frame any excuse arising from business, or any other circumstance to apologize for the silence of a correspondant, but always make a point of attributing it to neglect; how much his Lordship was mistaken I leave you to judge, when I assure you, That the suspension of a pleasure which I have frequently told you was the prime satisfaction I enjoyed in your absence, is attributed by me to the negligence of some person or other to whom you have intrusted the care of your letters, or perhaps to the want of a safe conveyance, occasioned it may be by your absence from Kingston, and in short to anything but a diminished affection.[1]

Should you be at Fishkill pray let me know how your Father's family are and present the united compliments of our family to them. Tell sister Jay, her friends Mrs. and Miss Banker are well. Cousin David Clarkson[2] had the pleasure of seeing them at the north branch of Raritan where they still reside. Mrs. Cortlandt informs me that she has heard that Mr. Munro was dead, I should be glad to know whether the report be true or not. If it is, I don't think his widow has reason to be very disconsolate; there are few men whose death deserves less to be deplored by their families.[3]

I long to know my destination next winter, and yet I could wish not to wait so long as winter neither before your abode is mine. I am the more earnest to be with you upon our sons account. The dear child has been very fractious these two or three weeks, and I know not whether to impute it to Ill health or impatience of temper. If the latter be the only cause I need not tell you how effectually your presence would obviate any difficulty on that score since his implicit obedience to whatever appeared to be your pleasure is too recent not to be recollected. Mamma, Cousin Nancy, and Sisters present you with their esteem, and if you'll write me soon, you may assure yourself of the love of your Ever affectionate Wife

SARAH JAY

ALS. Addressed: "John Jay Esqr. Kingston per Express." Endorsed.

1 Philip Dormer Stanhope, fourth Earl of Chesterfield (1694–1773), maintained correspondence for over thirty years with his son Philip, advising him, among other matters, on how men of fashion behaved toward women. An edition of his letters appears to have been published in 1775.

2 David Clarkson (1751–1825), SLJ's cousin. Reynolds, *Family Hist. of So. N.Y.*, III, 1025.

3 Reverend Dr. Harry Munro, Eve Jay's husband, became a Loyalist and served as chaplain to British prisoners at Fort Albany, where he himself was later imprisoned. Rumors of his death were unfounded. In October 1777 he escaped from prison and joined the British army at Ticonderoga. In 1778 he went back to England. *N.Y.G.B.R.*, IV, 113–124.

To PHILIP SCHUYLER

Kingston, 12 September 1777

Dear Sir

Your Letters should not have remained so long unanswered, had I not daily expected the Pleasure of seeing you here but Coll. Renselaer a few Days ago informed me that the Business of the Public would detain you sometime longer yet at Albany.[1]

The several Copies of Orders etc., I recieved on the Way from Philadelphia, and immediately inclosed them together with Your Letter to Mr. Duane. It was committed to the Care of Govr. Livingston, and I make no Doubt Mr. Duane has recieved it, tho I have not heard from him since.[2]

The Letter inclosing one for Mr. Duer arrived in my Absence and was given to me after my Return. Mr. Duer's Letter was immediately forwarded by Express to Head Quarters.

I exceedingly regret that Train of cross Accidents, as well as those Effects of Malevolence and Envy which seem thus incessantly to pursue you, but I hope the Day will yet arrive when the important Services you have rendered your Country will, appear in their proper Light, and the desire of diminishing, will give way to a Disposition of acknowledging and rewarding them. Truth must and will triumph.

General Washington and Congress were assured that unless another General presided in the northern Department the Militia of New England could not be brought into the Field. The Congress under this apprehension exchanged their General for this Militia, a Bargain which can recieve no Justification but from the supposed Necessity of the Times.

Permit me to hint that Care should be take lest Prosperity be influenced in their opinions of your Character and Conduct by the Tales and Prejudices of the present Day.

I am Dear General Your Friend and Obedient Servant

JOHN JAY

ALS. Endorsed.

[1] After Gates assumed command of the Northern Department on 20 August Schuyler went to his home in Albany. There, in his capacity as a commissioner of Indian Affairs for the Northern Department, he was heavily involved in conferences with the Six Nations. The commission's responsibility was to hold a large segment of the Six Nations in a neutral posture. According to a recent scholar, Schuyler had "emerged as a leading member of this commission." Schuyler, Volkert P. Douw, Oliver Wolcott (1726–97) of Connecticut, Major Joseph Hawley (1723–88) of Massachusetts, and Colonel Turbot Francies of Philadelphia were

appointed Indian Commissioners on 13 July 1775. Timothy Edwards (1738–1813) of Massachusetts, a son of Jonathan, was added to the Commission on 24 Nov. 1775. Martin H. Bush, *Revolutionary Enigma, A Re-appraisal of General Philip Schuyler of New York* (Port Washington, N.Y., 1969), p. 134; Barbara Graymont, *The Iroquois in the American Revolution* (Syracuse, 1972), p. 66; *JCC*, II, 183; III, 368.

2 Duane's having received the letter and enclosure is mentioned in Schuyler to JJ, 17 Aug. 1777, ALS in JP.

Susan Livingston to Sarah Livingston Jay

Morris County, November 1st, 1777

Dearly beloved Sarah

I am in expectation of the arrival of the Post every moment, he usually comes in on Fryday Evening, and returns next Morning as he goes no farther than Morris Town—last Evening he did not come. Mama received a Letter, but the Post did not deliver it till his return from Morris Town which deprived me of the pleasure of acknowledging it at that time, the things you mentioned were already taken care of. I hope to receive one when the Post arrives, he told us last Saturday, that he saw Mr. F. Jay, at Loudons who told him you were all moving at your Fathers; so that I do not know where to direct to you; we are afraid Mr. Jay has lost all his Clothes that were at Kingston. Mama says if your warm Petticoat is lost, she can spare you one, rather than you should suffer for want of it.

Papa has been home since Sunday Evening, the Accounts he brought are old now, and not worth writing, on the 23d Inst. 5 or 6 Men of War, warped through an opening they had made in the lower Cheveaux de Frieze,[1] and came up to attack our Fort and Ships and Gallies but they found the Navigation so difficult, that they set Fire to the Augusta of 64, and the Apollo of 32 Guns, and the rest made the best of their way back again.[2] A few days before 2500 of the Enemy (most of them Hessians) under the command of Count Donolp, attacked Fort Mercer, or Red Bank, and were soon obliged to retreat in a most shameful and confused manner, leaving behind them killed and wounded 1500. The Count is a Prisoner—they also left 12 pieces of Artillery.[3]

The 22d our Troops attempted a stroke upon a Detachment of six Regiments lying at Grays Ferry where they had thrown a Bridge over the River. They marched all night and reached the Ground about Sunrise, but the Birds were flown, they had suddenly the preceding night deserted the Post, left all their works unfinished and broke up the Bridge. To day Sen'night there was a very warm Engagement, but reports respecting it are so vague, and contradictory, I cannot pretend to give you any account of it.

The Articles of Capitulation that appeared in Loudons last Paper are not relished this way, neither by Whigs, nor Tories, the latter say if Mr. Burgoyne was in a Situation to obtain such Terms he ought to have fought, the Former say if Burgoyne was obliged to surrender at all, Gates might have brought him to what Terms he pleased, so that it looks as if the two Generals wished to avoid fighting. The Troops will go home and Garrison the Forts abroad, and let those Garrisons come to America—so it will be only an exchange of Men.[4]

The Doctor proposes to Inoculate our little Fellow next week. He is now a Fit subject for it, his blood is well purified, he has pretended to inoculate him often, so he will not be afraid of it.[5] You know old Woodruff, that carts for us, his Son that lived next door to Dr. Darby, died a few days ago of the Small pox the natural way, and now his Widow and Child have it, the old Man has never had it, he stayed in the same House with his Son till a day or two before he expired, they are not entitled to much pity, for they say the Avarice of the old Man prevented their being inoculated. The Child will perish with it, it is thought.

A few days after you left us Mama went down with Johnny[6] to Eliz[abeth] T[own] to see about some Business. John was taken Ill, and Mama was obliged to come back the very next Morning. Our House is a Barrack there was a whole Artillery Company in it, so I expect every thing will be destroyed.[7]

We have not heard from B[rockhol]st since the last Action to the Northward,[8] (I have no doubt but his Letters have miscarried) but Mama has allmost persuaded herself he is among the Slain, and if there was any mourning to be purchased, I do not know but she would exhibit a dismal Spectacle of bombazeen and crape. Where can Gates stay with his Army? I wish he would quicken his Diligence to join Gen. Washington.[9]

We have had the Taylor here (that you engaged) these 3 weeks, which has kept Kitty tightly employed. She is his Journey-woman. Mr. Jay's green suit is turned. Papa has brought home a Cargo of broken things, so that we have not eat the bread of Idleness since you left us.

Mr. Jay's Letter is this instant brought in, it mentions a former that has never reached us.[10] We want to know whether your Fathers Family is removed to Kent. Kitty desires me to leave a little blank Paper that she may reply to said Letter.[11] I think this, scrawl as it is, with the first I wrote, entitles me to a few Lines from your fair hand. This I submit to you and whether you write or not, I am yours most Affectionately.

AL. Addressed: "To The Honble. John Jay Esqr. At the Revd. Mr. Bordwell's In Kent Connecticut." Endorsed by JJ.

1 An obstacle of heavy timber and spikes which, when it was sunk, could rip the hull of a vessel.

2 The Americans opened fire on the *Augusta* after the unsuccessful British attack on Fort Mercer on the Delaware. The *Augusta* was set on fire and blew up, as did the *Merlin*, which is probably confused in this account with the *Apollo*. William Bradford to President Wharton, Oct. 27, 1777, *Pa. Archives*, 1st ser., V (1853), 207–09. This "Battle of the Kegs" was the subject of a witty ballad by Francis Hopkinson, in Henry Steele Commager and Richard B. Morris, eds., *The Spirit of '76* (New York, 1958), pp. 635–37.

3 The attack on Fort Mercer on 21 and 22 October was a complete failure, the Hessian troops suffering 371 killed, wounded, and captured. Colonel Carl von Donop (1740–77) was fatally wounded during the attack and died three days later.

4 The Articles of Capitulation appeared in the *N.Y. Packet* on 23 October. The generous terms Gates offered Burgoyne were the target of criticism by Patriots. The key provision of the Articles was Article II which provided for "A free passage to be granted to the army under Lieut. Gen. Burgoyne to Great Britain, upon condition of their not serving again in North America, during the present contest; and the port of Boston to be assigned for the entry of transports to receive the troops, whenever General Howe shall order." Thus British troops were not to be taken as prisoners of war but were to be permitted to return to Great Britain. In addition, Canadian troops were allowed to return to Canada. There was nothing in the Articles to prevent other British troops being dispatched to America to replace Burgoyne's soldiers. *N.Y. Packet*, 23 and 30 October 1777; Hoffman Nickerson, *The Turning Point of the Revolution, Or Burgoyne in America* (Boston, 1928), pp. 369–403.

5 Peter Augustus Jay was staying with the Livingstons. Smallpox proved more fatal than battle casualties in the army during the war. Before Jenner's discovery of vaccination in 1796, inoculation was performed with pus from a skin lesion of another human who had contracted smallpox. Dr. John Darby, a physician and occasional Presbyterian preacher, settled in Parsippany about 1772. W. W. Munsell, *History of Morris County* (New York, 1882), p. 220.

6 John Lawrence Livingston (1762–81), the youngest son of Governor William Livingston. Reynolds, *Family Hist. of So. N.Y.*, III, 1335.

7 The Livingstons had a 120-acre estate at Elizabethtown named Liberty Hall. The Americans had recaptured Elizabethtown at the end of the New Jersey campaign.

8 Henry Brockholst Livingston was a lieutenant colonel and aide-de-camp to General St. Clair in 1776 and 1777.

9 Gates stayed at his Albany headquarters. The troops Washington sent north to Saratoga eventually returned to Valley Forge.

10 Not located.

11 Catharine W. Livingston wrote on or after 1 November that Peter had been inoculated "this morning." Undated AL in JP.

CATHARINE W. LIVINGSTON TO JOHN JAY AND SARAH LIVINGSTON JAY

Persippiney, November 21st, 1777

My Dear Sister and Brother

It is with very great pleasure I announce to you, the recovery of your little Boy from the Small Pox; please to accept of the Congratulations of the Family on the happy event. No person ever was more favored in that disorder, he had only one pustle, and scarce a days illness. The Doctor bid me tell you that he had behaved Manfully thro the whole. He intends sharing the Thousand pounds with Hannah.[1] If Sally you have at any time felt a regret at having left him least he should be spoiled, be assured there never was a better Child, I have my doubts if ever any equaled him in goodness. I have but one Complaint to lodge against him, and that is, that we cannot make him talk; it is something very extraordinary in our Family; but I flatter myself he will prattle every thing before he leaves us. I have more than one reason for wishing that to be the case.

I hope to morrow's Post will bring some tidings of your return to Fish Kill; only two Letters, one from each of you, since your absence has come to hand, this is the fifth from Persippiney.[2] I hope this and those already sent will share a better fate than yours I am convinced have. This Evening we received a Letter from Pappa, informing us that we have lost Fort Mifflin,[3] with about thirty Men killed, before our Troops evacuated the Garrison, and seventy wounded. The wounded with the rest of the Troops made their escape before the Enemy took possession;[4] Our Men were so galled by the grape shot of a large India Man who came within one hundred yards of the Fort, that it was impossible to stand it; they removed, all the Stores and fired the Barracks, when they found the place no longer tenable.

Gen. Washington is reinforced with two Thousand Troops from the Southward, and Five from the Northward, and some hundreds from this State, of the Militia, of the Pensylvania Militia only twelve hundred have lent him their assistance.[5] The Philadelphians have lent Gen. Howe twenty thousand pound sterling and He has given the Old Money of Pensylvania, New Jersey, and New York a Currency.[6] The Quakers mount guard and do all Military duty that is required of them.[7] Billy Allen is full Col. in the Enemys service, and is to raise his Regiment in his native State.[8] Young Nat Phillips died in Philadelphia of the wound received at Brandy-Wine. They write from our Camp that the Philadelphians come out in shoals, that some of them had not bread for several days before they left the City. Gen. Clinton[9] did not Sail with the fleet, he has been seen very lately at New York, and on Staten Island. Lord Petershem is gone with Burgoyne dispatches.[10] He has said that if he should lose them he would not be believed in England. He intends joining the Minority as he is convinced of the impossibility of their conquering us. I hope our successes to the Southward will be yet more favorable than those to the Northward, but I fear something serious will happen before the close of the Campaign tho it is late in the Season. I wish I had Duche's Letter[11] to Gen. Washington to send to you, the like I believe you never saw, it is a most insolent performance.

Yesterday I returned from Elizabeth. Gen. Dickenson is at that Post with between eight hundred and a Thousand Troops. My Fathers House for six weeks was made a Guard House, for a Bullock Guard, the first instance I believe of a Governors House being so degraded. I do not exaggerate In telling you the Guards have done ten times the Mischief to the House that the Hessians did; they have left only two locks in the House, taken off many pains of glass, left about a third of the paper hanging, burnt up some Mahogany banisters, a Quantity of timber, striped the roof of all the lead; one of the Men was heard to boast that he had at one heat taken 30 pounds of Lead off. The furniture that Mamma left there when Sally and myself was last down is stolen except a few things of which there is only some fragments. It is as in the time of Pharoah what the Canker worm dont eat the Locusts destroy.

Mr. Hood of Brunswick and Uncle Ph. French and many others have Petitioned Gen. Dickinson[12] to let them return to this State. Cousin Clarkson[13] has at length obtained a permit to go in to New York. Aunt Van Horne and Uncle Clarkson[14] have differed, the Consequence she is removed to a House formerly belonging to Mr. Cruger. I feel much Compassion for her, and the girls, tho I can't approve their conduct. They have now thrown themselves out of the Protection of all their Friends. David called on us in his way to the Southard, he passed thro Kent, and was extremely sorry he did not know of your being there. He gave us a horrid description of the Place. In my last I informed you that we had not in a long time heard of, nor from, Brother B. no Letters from him, or Matt have since that come to hand. B. we are told has had a Duel on hand and acquited himself with honor, and is now in Boston.[15] I wish he would return to us, we are quite lon[ely in] Billy's absence.[16] Governeur is at present in the neighbourhood and has paid us several Friendly visits. His sudden Gravity I am at a loss to account for. I have imperceptibly got to the last side of my paper, you can't complain of postage for blank paper, perhaps more would be agreable. The least intimation of which will be carefully observed by your truly Affectionate Sister.

The Family join with me in offering respects to your Worthy Father and his Family, and their Affectionate regards to your-selves.

AL. Addressed: "Honble. John Jay Esqr. To the Care of Mr. Louden Fish Kill." Endorsed by JJ.

[1] The figure of £1,000 for inoculating young Peter, even considering inflation, is not possible. In fact, John Adams records in his *Diary* that he paid £2:0:0 to be inoculated in Philadelphia in mid-1775. In addition, members of his family were inoculated in the Boston area in mid-1776 at an approximate cost of a little over £1 apiece. Hannah Benjamin was Peter's nurse. John Adams, *Diary*, II, 167; L. H. Butterfield *et al.*, eds., *Adams Family Correspondence* (2 vols., Cambridge, Mass., 1963), II, 37.

[2] The other extant letters from Catharine W. Livingston are to SLJ, 1 Nov. and n.d. Nov. 1777, both AL's in JP; from the Jays, the only letter in 1777 is from JJ to Catharine W. Livingston, dated 20 Jan.

[3] Fort Mifflin on Port (or Mud) Island in the Schuylkill River was evacuated on 16 November.

[4] Actually, the Americans suffered 250 wounded and killed; the British suffered only twelve casualties. Christopher Ward, *The War of the Revolution* (2 vols., New York, 1952), I, 377.

[5] Washington had issued a call for reinforcements in order to concentrate his forces against Sir William Howe. See Washington to Major General Putnam, 4 Nov. 1777, *GWF*, X, 2–3.

[6] Because paper money issued by the Continental Congress had greatly depreciated in Pennsylvania, hard money and British-backed currency were preferred in financial transactions. See Anne Bezanson, *Prices and Inflation During the American Revolution* (Philadelphia, 1951).

[7] The Quakers in Philadelphia were generally suspected of Loyalist sympathies. Before evacuating Philadelphia the Continental Congress had ordered a number of Friends arrested on the "general charge of opposing and discouraging the American cause." John Russell Young, ed., *Memorial History of the City of Philadelphia, From Its First Settlement to the Year 1895* (2 vols., New York, 1895–98), I, 347.

[8] William Allen of Pennsylvania had served in the Continental army (1775–76) before defecting to Howe. In 1778 he raised and commanded a Pennsylvania Loyalist corps. Sabine, *Biographical Sketches*, I, 157.

[9] General Sir Henry Clinton, second in command of the Burgoyne army in America.

[10] Charles Stanhope, Viscount Petersham (1753–1829), aide-de-camp to Burgoyne, returned to England in December 1777 with news of the surrender at Saratoga, and was a principal witness in the inquiry about the disaster. He voted against the Administration on 3 March 1779 on a motion of censure against the Admiralty. Sir Lewis Namier and John Brooke, *The House of Commons, 1754–1790* (3 vols., New York, 1964), III, 462–63.

[11] Reverend Jacob Duché (1738–98), formerly chaplain of the Continental Congress turned Loyalist. On 3 Oct. 1777 he wrote Washington a long letter urging him to give up his command of the army or, as its head, to force Congress to stop hostilities and revoke the Declaration of Independence. If this were not done, Washington could, as the head of the army, begin negotiations for peace with Britain. Jared Sparks, ed., *Correspondence of the American Revolution;*

Being Letters of Eminent Men to George Washington (4 vols., Boston, 1853), I, 458.

12 Brigadier General Philemon Dickinson of the New Jersey militia.

13 Matthew Clarkson was then aide-de-camp to General Benedict Arnold. Reynolds, *Family Hist. of So. N.Y.*, III, 1026.

14 Ann French Van Horne, widow of David Van Horne of New York, was Catharine Livingston's and SLJ's aunt. David Clarkson (1726–82), merchant, married Elizabeth French, sister of Mrs. Ann French Van Horne and Mrs. Susannah French Livingston (SLJ's mother). In the summer of 1776 the Clarksons, with Mrs. Van Horne and her five daughters, fled from New York to New Brunswick, N.J. In the spring of 1777 Clarkson, although a Whig, was permitted to go to his summer home in Flatbush, accompanied by the Van Hornes. Reynolds, *Family Hist. of So. N.Y.*, III, 1025.

15 "Brother B" is Brockholst Livingston, who was involved in a duel with Major Chester, which, however, had no serious consequences. Edwin B. Livingston, *The Livingstons of Livingston Manor* (New York, 1910), p. 251.

16 William Livingston (1754–1817), SLJ's brother.

From James Duane

York Town, Pennsylvania, 2d December 1777

Dear Sir

I have had so much Publick Business on my hands that I have been unavoidably deprived of paying that Attention to my Friends which always gives me Pleasure.[1] As one of the Number I have the Honour of considering yourself; and of you I have not been entirely unmindful. At the same time that I cannot boast of much Encouragement, or any great Merit.

To the Governour and Council of Safety I have communicated every Occurrence of Moment and doubt not from your publick Station that you have had an Opportunity of Information.

Since my last publick dispatches the Confederacy, and an address to the Legislatures, and a System for supporting the publick Credit have received the Sanction of Congress and are now forwarded to each State. The Confederacy I presume will please. If it is objected to I shall despair of the Happiness of this Country, notwithstanding the bright prospect of our Affairs.[2]

Fort Mercer at Redbank soon followed the Example of Fort Mifflin having been evacuated on the approach of Lord Cornwallis, who meant to besiege instead of storming it; And the Troops sent to support the Garrison, under Genl. Green, coming up too late.[3] In Consequence several of our Vessels of War were burnt by our own People to prevent their falling into the hands of the Enemy. General Howe will of Course be master of the Delaware and enable his brother to bring up the British Fleet to the City. After all this Success they must feel their debility; having no Army to pursue those vast projects of Conquest which they contemplated. Burgoine's total defeat must work the Ruin of their affairs, as the whole Strength of the united States will be now centered in one Object, to watch and defeat the Designs of these ill fated Brothers. What will be the plan of Winter Operations I cannot yet tell you. Our Troops are ill clad and the Weather is uncommonly severe for this Climate. This day we have a deep Snow. Whether they will be able to keep the Field and act offensively I cannot decide.

I have leave of Absence at last, I shall set out as soon as Mr. Morris or Mr. Lewis arrives after a painful Service of more than eight months.[4]

The enclosed Letter for you from Europe I have the pleasure of forwarding.

And am with Compliments to our friendly Circle Dear Sir Your Affectionate and Obedient Servant

JAS. DUANE

ALS. Endorsed. Enclosure not located.

1 Duane was a delegate to the Continental Congress. He had been reelected 3 Oct. 1777. *LMCC*, II, lviii.

2 The Continental Congress on 22 Nov. 1777 approved a scheme to raise $5,000,000 from the states. *JCC*, IX, 955–58.

3 Colonel Christopher Greene (1737–81), a distant relative of General Nathanael Greene, and under his general command, directed the defenses of Fort Mercer, N.J., on the Delaware River, against an unsuccessful British attack in October 1777. However, the evacuation on 15–16 November of Fort Mifflin, a post on the river opposite Fort Mercer, made the latter post untenable, and it was evacuated 20–21 November.

4 Francis Lewis and Gouverneur Morris were two members in the New York delegation to the Continental Congress. Both had been reelected 3 Oct. 1777. *LMCC*, II, lviii, lix.

To PHILIP SCHUYLER

[*Fishkill*], *11 December 1777*

Dear General

Your very friendly Letter of the 6th Ult.[1] was this moment delivered. In what careless Hands it has lain so long I cannot concieve. An Expectation of being speedily sent to Albany induced me to defer answering your Favor of the 7th October[2] till I should have the Pleasure of a personal Interview. Our wise ones however for certain Reasons have suffered the Constitution to lay dormant, and Efforts have been made to postpone its organization.[3]

Your Sentiments respecting The Preparations for another campaign and the obstructing Hudsons River are just, and I should have Hopes of their being properly carried into Execution if under your Directions. These important Objects have been neglected, and the People begin to grow sensible of it.[4] They must feel it seems before they can percieve.

I am happy to find your Firmness unimpaired, and your Attachment to your Country unabated by its Ingratitude. Justice will yet take place, and I do not despair of seeing the Time when it will be confessed that <you laid> the Foundation of our Success in the northern Department was lain by the present Commanders Predecessor. I am nevertheless anxious that such authentic Evidence of the Propriety of your Conduct should be transmitted to Posterity as may contradict the many <Falsehoods as they will hear of You> Lies which will be told them by Writers under Impressions and under an Influence unfriendly to your Reputation. This Subject <I think> merits Attention. Facts and not <a civil tho just> a Single Resolution of Congress will in my opinion be <sufficient> effectual <to do the Business>. I have thought much of this Matter but more of this when we meet.

Your Offer of a Farm etc. is very obliging. Be pleased to accept my Thanks for it. I am at present at a Loss how to determine. Let not my Delays however be injurious to You. This Place at which all the Family now reside[5] is by no means agreable or convenient if secure, which is also doubtful. I purpose doing myself the Pleasure of seeing you this winter and shall then avail myself of your Advice.

The Rapidity with which the Desolation of your seat at Saraghtoga is repairing does not surprize me.[6] I remember <the Expedition> the Dispatch with which the Preparations for our first Expedition into Canada were compleated. I wish the Repair of our Forts etc. on the River was in the same Train.

As to your Loss of Influence among a certain Body, it is less so than you may imagine. The virtuous and sensible still retain their former Sentiments. The Residue ever will be directed by accident and Circumstances. Few possess Honesty or Spirit enough openly to defend unpopular Merit, and by their Silence permit Calumny to gain Strength. These however are temporary Evils and you do well to despise them.

I am my dear Sir very sincerely your Friend and obedient Servant

J. J.

DftS. Endorsed by JJ. Tr in NN: Bancroft, Schuyler Papers, 1776–88.

1 Schuyler to JJ, 6 November, in JP.

2 Not located.

3 When the New York legislature fled Kingston in October 1777 as the British advanced on that town, the Council of Safety held the reins of government. The legislature did not meet again until January 1778. *JPC*, I, 1111.

4 In his letter of 6 November Schuyler recommended blockading the Hudson River.

5 The farm had been abandoned by Tory tenants.

6 Schuyler's home just outside Saratoga had been damaged during the battle of Saratoga. Burgoyne ordered it burned in October 1777. Don R. Gerlach, *Philip Schuyler and the American Revolution in New York, 1733–1777* (Lincoln, Neb., 1964), p. 307.

To James Duane

Fish Kill, 14 December 1777

Dear Sir

Your obliging Letter of the 2d Inst.[1] did not reach me till two Days ago. I am very sensible that Your Time must have been greatly engrossed at Congress, and the more so as the Treasury Department was I believe almost wholly under your particular Inspection. I ardently wish to see the Time when Matters of general Importance will cease to deny us Leisure for regular Correspondence; and be assured that I am not insensible, and shall never be unmindful, of the Attention with which from my Youth You have been pleased to honor me.

I am happy to hear the Confederacy accords with your Sentiments. That Circumstance *augurs* well. I hope some omissions in the former Draft are supplied in this. An indifferent one however is better than none; upon this Principle I mean for my own Part to act.

Your long Absence from your Family has doubtless been painful, but it has nevertheless been mixed with the Pleasure of rendering Services to your Country, which I believe have contributed not a little to your Good and the common Interest.

I purpose e're long to do myself the Pleasure of a Visit to our Friends at the Manor, when I flatter myself with an Opportunity of conversing with You on many interesting Subjects. Be pleased to present my Respects to Coll. and Mrs. Livingston, Mrs. Duane,[2] and my other Friends at the Manor.

I am Dear Sir Your obliged and obedient Servant

JOHN JAY

ALS: CtY, The Pequot Library, deposited in the Beinecke Rare Book and Manuscript Library. DftS in JP.

1 See above, Duane to JJ.

2 Maria Livingston Duane (1739–1821) was the oldest daughter of Colonel Robert Livingston, Jr., third lord of the manor. See genealogical chart in Dangerfield, *Robert R. Livingston.*

FROM MARINUS WILLETT

Danbury, December 17th, 1777

Honored Sir

Hitherto hath the Lord helped us, is an acknowledgment as honorable as it is ancient, but never more properly adapted to the situation of any people then it is at present to the inhabitants of this Continent, for never where a people more remarkable blessed with signal interpositions of divine favour; how suddenly have we beheld our most gloomy prospects to brighten? and how conspicuous has the hand of Heaven appeared in disspeling the darkest clouds we have had reason to fear?

From the begining of our present controversy our affairs have not perhaps had so pleasing an appearance as they have at present; the forces of our enemies may truly be called trifling to what they have been, whilst we have become stronger by means of our sufferings; but still is our situation so criticle as to require all the watchfull sagacity power and spirit that can be employed in our behalf; it is not only all the armed force which Briton and her emissaries can bring against us we have to encounter, but the secret machinations and villainous traffick of persons who dwell or trade among us that we have to struggle with. What watchfull diligence then is required in this day of our countreys distress, from men into whose hands the power of preserving her is committed!

A person can hardly turn his eyes about him without discovering some malady or other which wants a remedy. With pleasure I have observed the late restrictions laid upon trade by our council of safty, on the exportation of Flower,[1] as there is no doubt but a considerable supply of that article sent from our State has been received by our enemies. The same kind of villainy however that has been hitherto practiced with Flower is now carrying on with some other articles, esspecially Pork, which is constantly passing from the State of New York, to Norwalk and some other sea-port Towns in Connecticut, the most of which articles there is too much reason to apprehend go to supply our enemies; it is true that the people in general who carry there Pork etc. receive pay for them in Salt, an article so essential that the want of it must be accompanied with severe distress, but the trade which is carried on in this way is so infamous, that every thinking persons breast must rise with indignation against it. 100 lbs. of Pork or twenty two dollars must be paid per bushell for Salt. Mind the consequence—one bushel of Salt is worth 22 dollars and so is 100 lbs. of Pork; consequently the quantity of Pork and Salt necessary to fill a Barrell will amount to about *Fifty Dollars,* and thus the barrell of Pork becomes worth that sum. But there is reason, strong reason to believe that this very Pork 100 lbs. of which we give for a Busshell of Salt goes to the enemy. The Salt is said to come from Nantucket, for which place it is said the Pork is designed, (and a dangerous place it is to trust it as we all know,) so that the matter appears to stand thus, we receive from the enemy one bushell of Salt for which we give them 100 lbs. of Pork but the Salt received from the enemy cost them about one quarter of a Dollar per bushell, the consequence then is that the enemy can supply themselves with Pork and pay all the Charges attending at less then *three Dollars per Barrell,* whilst our Pork must cost us *Fifty Dollars per Barrell,* surly this is a dissorder that wants a remedy.

I am not unaware of that common argument that trade will regulate itself, nor do I presume to deney its force, it is I believe a general truth, but in some casses liable to exceptions, and may require the interference of the Publick authority. A virtuous private trader appears to me as rare in this day as the Phoenix; trade is got into the hands of I dont know who, but am sure it is not in the hands of men of public virtue; the instance of the Salt is one out of many of the evils which threaten us with destruction more then all the armed force of Britton, and does undoubtedly require the Publick Attention.

In short when I reflect on the horrid extortions which have taken place amongst us they appear so big with inevitable destruction, that I am ready to draw the sad conclusion, that we *bleed in vain.*

But powerfull as these evils may appear, methinks I can look forward to see them all vanish before the determined exertions of a labourious people into whose hands Providence has amply stored every requisite for that important purpose; it is but for us to look around and what a fund of resorces present themselves to our view, such as have a manifest tendency to make us grow stronger, and stronger, in proportion as our disstresses increase. So many and great do our internal resorces appear, that I am at times on the point of concluding that if we had no sort of foreign traffick we would be better off then we are at present. Necessaty in that case that great Mother of inventions, would instruct us how to make a proper use of the many materials we have among ourselves, and call forth our most vigorous exertions into execution; at any rate I am inclined to believe that with proper encouragment from the Publick, we might make a more respectable internal appearance then we do in many respects.

Suppose for instance the State of New York, was to appropriate a Township in the County of Cumberland for a Manufacturing Town, and give proper encouragment for carrying on all kinds of Manufactories in it; the security of the situation, and largness of the encouragment, (for that must be great) would induce many to repair to it for employ; and though many articles may come much higher then they might be procured otherways, they would not affect us in the same manner the Salt does, because everything would continue among ourselves. But the Busshell of Salt received being by no means eaqual to the 100 lbs. of Pork expended, forms an unreasonable ballence against us, and looks very much like the "big fish eating up the little ones." But in this case of encouraging Arts, and Industrey, among ourselves let our articles cost what they will, we must be the gainers in the end, and I am inclined to think that besides the internal increase of our strength, which must grow in proportion as the interiour parts of our Countrey becomes filled with inhabitants, we will be able in a short time to supply both our armey and the inhabitants, in such a manner as to prevent them from suffering, and surly this must be preferable to the uncertain dependance of any foreign power in our present situation. But with respect to the article of Salt, I think the publick must fall upon some other way to supply the inhabitants with that article, as the want of it is such a disstress that the people will stick at nothing to procure it.

But I have been too tedious, and must therefore finish, with hopeing soon to see some mode adopted among ourselves to insure the conveniences of life for our inhabitants, and esspecially necessaries for our Armey; I cant help pleasing myself with the view of sufficient supplys, from Manufactories among ourselves, without looking to Asia, Africa, or Europe, we undoubtedly have sufficient materials for this important purpose, and we must learn to make use of them, but great vigilance and exertions are necessary for this end.

I have mentioned the County of Cumberland not only because of its internal situation, but on account of its contiguousness to New England, from whence by means of the populacness of that place we may receive some Assistance, as well as its being some security to us. And the County of Cumberland being large and fertile we may hope that it will increase faster in agriculture, by means of the extensive demands for grain etc. which it will have within itself, all of which will tend to increase our internal power.

To you Sir, as to a person of large penetration and influence, I have thought proper to address these thoughts, with confidence that if a scheme of this kind is proper and practicable, you are a very likly person to promote it, but if it should appear to you either improper or impracticable, I have but had the trouble of writing them, and dont doubt but your candor will overlook my giving you the trouble of reading them.[2]

I am Honored Sir your Very Humble Servant

MARINUS WILLETT

ALS. Endorsed: ". . . ansd. 2 Jan. 1778."

[1] The Council of Safety exercised general control over trade in New York State. On 21 November the Council passed extensive regulations over trading in flour and meal. Anyone exporting flour was required to be licensed, to swear not to export any flour or meal to the enemy, and to promise to export no more than thirty barrels of flour or meal by virtue of any one license. *JPC*, I, 1084–85.

[2] On 2 Jan. 1778 JJ replied briefly (dftS in JP): "Your favor of the 17 ultimo was lately delivered to me. The Information and Hints contained in it are important, and I shall take the Liberty of mentioning them to some of the Members of the Legislature.

"The Confusion occasioned by the Want of regular Government has given Birth to many Evils which I hope will be removed as soon as our Constitution shall be organized, and begin to operate.

"You will oblige me by communicating from Time to Time such Intelligence and Observations as you may think useful. Opportunities of rendering Services to my Country and its Friends will always give me Pleasure."

FROM JAMES DUANE

Manour Livingston, 23d December 1777

My dear Sir

I did not receive your very obliging Favour of the 14th[1] Untill this morning. It gave a double pleasure as we have your promise of a Visit at the Manshion. Mr. Livingston, and indeed the whole Family, Join me in requesting that Mrs. Jay will be so kind as to accompany you. When the Legislature assembles you will be confind, and by that Time I shall be caled on Business to Albany, with which Congress has charged me in a measure quite suficient for the winter's Amusement.[2] Can you not then hasten your Visit so as to pass the Holydays at the Manour? In spite of our Enemies you will find us chearful and Sociable. The last sessions of Congress has, with respect to me, been a Campaign. I have had many dificulties to encounter From the particular Views and Instructions of our own State, the progress and issue of which, in detail, will aford you some Amusement.

The Confederacy is upon a liberal Plan, calculated to establish general Security, and Social Intercourse, among the States; and to extinguish All territorial Disputes.[3] There are only two points that can admit of much Debate—The *Equality* of each State in Congress; and the Ratio, for assessing their respective Quotas of the publick charges. Both are copious Themes and have, and will, occasion much Controversy. When I see you I shall explain the different Principles on which the latter point depends. Much may be said on either side. To regulate the comparative Value of and ability of each State by one fixed and permanent Medium is exceedingly dificult. The Estimate of Landed property; and of the number of People, were opposed to each other. To both there are strong Objections, and perhaps All *visible Property* would have given a preferable Rule. With the Confederacy is a Short address from Congress to each of the Legislatures; which fully explains the dificulties they encountered in forming any System which could be reconciled to the prejudices, the policy, and the Interest, of so many independent States. If it has it's Weight the States will come to a Conclusion to endeavour to obtain Improvements which they conceive important, but to consent to the present Plan rather than delay a Measure essential to their Safety.

When I got home I had the Afliction to find Mrs. Duane's Health greatly impaird, her spirits exhausted and a nervous disorder making Havock of her Constitution. My long absence for which she was not prepard, and the Approach and Ravages of the Enemy overcame the Fortitude with which she had been blessed. She flatters me that she is getting better; and I am sure I shall have your best Wishes for her Recovery; the more especially as she has literally suffered for the Sake of her Country; for had she not conceald from me the declining State of her Health no earthly consideration coud have induced me to continue so long at Congress. She Joins me in afectionate Compliments to yourself and Mrs. Jay as do Col. and Mrs. Livingston and my Daughter.[4]

I am with great Regard Dear Sir Your most Obedient most humble Servant

JAS. DUANE

ALS. Endorsed.

1 See above.

2 The Continental Congress on 3 Dec. 1777 requested Duane "to confer with the commissioners for Indian affairs in the northern department." *JCC*, IX, 999.

3 The Articles of Confederation were forwarded to the states on 17 November. *JCC*, IX, 935.

4 Maria Duane (1761–1813).

To Robert Morris

Fish Kill, 26 December 1777

Dear Sir

About a Fortnight ago I recieved three Letters from France, one dated at Dunkirk 2d June, another at Passy near Paris the 8th June, and the third at Havre the 10th June, 1777.[1] All of the same Import and nearly in the same words; an exact Copy of the first is enclosed for the Committee.[2]

I should have immediately on the Reciept of them have sent you Copies, but the necessary Materials for rendering them visible, were in the Neighbourhood of Kingston, and the Ice on the River prevented my getting them till within a few Days past.

Military Matters with us are strangely managed. Gates is playing with his Laurels at Albany, and Putnam catching oysters on the Shores of the Sound. In my opinion the Resolutions of Congress respecting the Forts and Navigation of Hudsons River, will not be executed properly, if at all, unless under other Directors.[3] Pray hasten the Inquiry into the Causes to which the Loss of the Forts etc. is to be ascribed. A fair Opportunity will then offer of redressing one of the Evils we suffer.

I hear Deane is recalled. Greece over again. Nothing like the ostracism.[4] Your Confederation, if I am not mistaken will be ratified by our Legislature. Is there any Probability of a French War?

How has the little Temple you erected to Hospitality at the Hills fared?[5] Polluted I suppose. God bless You.

I am Dear Sir with great Regard and Esteem your obedient Servant

JOHN JAY

ALS. NN: Robert Morris Papers. Dft in JP.

1 The copy of the letter of 2 June 1777 from Dunkirk, in the hand of JJ, with the signatures of Franklin and Deane (not in JJ's hand), is in DNA: PCC, 85, pp. 65–66, with this postscript: "N.B. The Words scored in the aforegoing Copy are inserted from a Letter of the 8 June of the like & no other Import, that part of the original being too indistinct to be read with Certainty—J.J." The letter is endorsed in an unidentified hand. The originals of the letters of 2, 8, and 10 June have not been located.

2 The Continental Congress's Committee of Secret Correspondence, on which Morris sat, and of which JJ had been a member in 1775–76. The Committee became that of Foreign Affairs on 17 April 1777. *JCC*, VII, 274.

3 The Continental Congress on 5 Nov. 1777 had directed Generals Gates and Putnam "to regain the possession of the forts and passes of the North or Hudson's River." *JCC*, IX, 865.

4 The Continental Congress on 21 November recalled Silas Deane from France. *JCC*, IX, 946.

5 Morris's town house was referred to as The Hills.

Jay's "A Hint to the Legislature of the State of New York"

This draft paper may be reliably attributed to the period between 15 January 1778, when the first session of the New York State Legislature reconvened at Poughkeepsie, and 2 April 1778, when the legislature enacted a law entitled "An Act for regulating Impresses of forage and Carriages, and for billeting Troops within the State."[1] It lays down a procedure for impressment along the precise lines of JJ's "Hints." Section XI forbade impressment of teams, horses, carriages, or drivers for same, without a warrant from the justice of the peace, and Section XII instructs the justice of the peace, upon due application, to draw up a list of the people "he judges able to furnish the necessary items and designate the amount, length of time, or distance to be exacted, the justice to receive 2 s. for each team procured." Section XIII provides for compensation by the quartermaster for teams, horses, or carriages impressed, with penalties for noncompliance provided by section XIV. Finally, section XV permits the act to be suspended in case of emergency. It should be noted that the issue of impressment plagued civil-military relations throughout the Revolution and commanded considerable attention from General Washington himself.[2] Publication of JJ's letter has not been located.[3]

1 Laws of the State of New York, 1st Sess., ch. xxix.

2 See, e.g., *GWF*, IX, 420–41; XI, 490 *passim*.

3 Holt's *New York Journal* had suspended publication during this period, and this item has not turned up in the extra issues of the [Fishkill] *New York Packet*, covering February to April 1778.

A Hint to the Legislature of the State of New York

[*15 January–2 April 1778*]

Under Governments which have just and equal Liberty for their Foundation, every Subject has a Right to give his Sentiments on all Matters of public Concern; provided it be done with Modesty and Decency. I shall therefore take the Liberty of calling the Attention of my Countrymen to a Subject, which however important seems to have passed without due Notice; I mean *the Practice of impressing Horses,*

Teems, and Carriages by the military, without the Intervention of a civil Magistrate, and without any Authority from the Law of the Land.

It is the undoubted Right and unalienable Priviledge of a Freeman not to be divested, or interrupted in the <use> innocent use, of Life Liberty or Property, but by Laws to which he has assented, either personally or by his Representatives. This is the Corner Stone of every free Constitution, and to defend it from the Iron Hand of the Tyrant of Britain, all America is now in arms; every Man in America being most deeply interested in its Preservation. Violations of this inestimable Right, by the King of Great Britain, or by an American Quarter Master; are of the same Nature, equally partaking of Injustice; and differing only in the Degree and Continuance of the Injury.

That the Army either stationed in, or passing through, this State should be accommodated with Carriages etc. is not to be denied; and that it may often be necessary to impress them is equally true. The only Question is, whether the Army shall at their mere *Will and Pleasure* furnish themselves, and that *at the Point of the Bayonet;* or whether they shall be furnished under the civil Authority of the State; and that in a Manner consistant with Reason, Liberty, and the Rights of Freemen.

It is neither my Desire or Design, to dwell on the *licencious* manner, in which this unconstitutional Power has been exercised <on the Freemen of> in this State, by the little Officers belonging to the Quarter masters Department. Few among us require any Information on that Head. Nor would I be thought to impute it to the Directors of that Department <in this State>; several of whom deserve Credit for Humanity, Prudence, and Love of Liberty. They cannot be present on every occasion, and are often obliged to employ Persons, who are ignorant of the Circumstances of the Inhabitants, and more sollicitous to shew their Power than Discretion.

It is against the Principle, not the Manner of its Exercise, that I contend. It would equally be an Insult to our Government, which ought to be a Government of Laws, as well as a Violation of the Rights of its Subjects; for the wisest and most discreet Man in the World, with a Party of armed Men at his Heels, without any Law, but that of *the necessity of the Case,* which cloaks as many Sins in Politics, as Charity is said to do in Religion; arbitrarily and by Force, to take the Property of a free Inhabitant, for the Use of the Army.

Nor does this extraordinary Exertion of Power admit of any other Excuse, than that the Legislature of this State have passed no Laws on the Subject, but have left the Quarter Master and his Agents

<to do that which should> without any other Rule for their Conduct than what should seem right in their own Eyes. In my Opinion such Laws ought no longer to be delayed. We cannot foresee to what Lengths this dangerous Practice may extend, or where a Line can be drawn. The army may want Blankets, Shoes and many other articles besides Horses and Carriages, and there certainly is as much Propriety in deducing a Right in them to impress the one as the other, from *the necessity of the Case.* In short, it is difficult to concieve of any arbitrary Act, which that prolific Mother of Tyranny may not breed, and when in Conjunction with Power, has not bred. There is scarce a Page in the History of any Nation, which does not exhibit a black account of some of her Progeny, or which does not represent her as a common Prostitute to all the Tyrants in the World, from Great Tyrants on Thrones, down to <little> Petty Tyrants in Village Schools.

These Impresses may I think easily be so regulated by Laws, as to relieve the Inhabitants from reasonable Cause of Complaint, and yet not, retard or embarrass the Service. It may not be improper to observe that it is no less the Interest <of the People at large than> of the Quarter Master and their agents than of the People at large that such Laws should take Place. The Time may come when Law and Justice will again pervade the State, and many who now <feel this> severely feel this kind of oppression, may then bring Actions and recover Damages. This is true Doctrine, however questionable the Policy of declaring it at this Time may be. For my own Part I think it ought to be declared and sounded from one End of the State to the other. Let such oppressive Evils be examined not concealed. Let them be remedied and not permitted silently to fester in the Hearts of Freemen. In an ensuing Paper I shall communicate my Ideas of the Remedy.

A FREEHOLDER

Dft.

FROM PHILIP SCHUYLER

Albany, February 1, 177[8]

Dear Sir

It is whispered here that an Expedition into Canada is to take place under the Command of the Marquis Fayette, Gen. Conway and Gen. Starke with 3000 men.[1] Entre nous I may venture my Opinion, which Is that the body is Insufficient, should they be able to penetrate

Into Canada, which I much doubt, as nothing (as far as I can learn) has been prepared. The men are In want of the proper Cloathing to bear up against the rigour of the season in that Severe Climate. There is not a sufficient quantity of provision in that part of the Country whence It be Conveyed In Sleds. No forrage Is Collected, no snow Shoes are prepared, no hatchetts, no Ice spurs or crupers, no Carriages fixed for transporting the Cannons, besides a variety of other articles Indispensably necessary for Such an Enterprize; but should we be able to Obviate every difficulty, I fear the plundering spirit of the people who are Chiefly to be Militia will Injure us In the Opinion of the Canadians. I hear Mr. Duer is to be of the party.[2]

People here are very uneasy and much Alarmed at the profusion with which the public Money is Expended and I think not without reason. The Expences of the last Year are, I guess, In this department only at least five times as much as they amounted to In the most Expensive Year last war, when we had an Army of Sixteen thousand men and went Into Canada, the whole of that years Expenditure which was 1759, In the Quarter Masters, Barrack Masters and forrage Masters departments, which Included all transportation did not Exceed £145,000 Currency. I Sincerely wish Congress would adopt Measures that had a tendency to Induce Oeconomy Into the Military Departments. If they do not we shall Surely Conquer ourselves.

It is said that Abraham Yates will be put Into nomination for the office of Lieut. Governor.[3]

I hope soon to have the pleasure of a visit from You. Compliments to the Chancellor.

I am Dear Sir Affectionately Your's etc. etc. etc.

PHI. SCHUYLER

ALS. Endorsed: ". . . ansd. 6 Feb." Erroneously dated 1777 by Schuyler.

1 Marquis de Lafayette (1757–1834), came to America in 1777 and was commissioned a major general by Congress in July of that year after offering to serve at his own expense. Thomas Conway (1733–1800?), an Irish-Catholic raised and educated in France, in whose army he had served until coming to America in December 1776, was commissioned a major general in May 1777 on Washington's recommendation. John Stark (1728–1822), a veteran of Rogers' Rangers in the French and Indian Wars, having been passed over for promotion in the Continental Army in 1777, had resigned his position, but he received a commission as brigadier general in October 1777 after his victory at the head of the militia over a detachment from Burgoyne's army at the Battle of Bennington, August 1777.

2 In January 1778 the new Board of War, contrary to Washington's advice, planned an invasion of Canada, which Congress authorized, electing Lafayette, Conway, and Stark to conduct the operation. However, Schuyler's pessimism was well grounded, and at Washington's urging the campaign was eventually called

off. See below, JJ to Lafayette, 3 Jan. 1779 and Washington to JJ, 14 April 1779, *JCC*, X, 84–86.

[3] Abraham Yates, Jr., apparently sought the lieutenant-governorship, following Clinton's resignation from that post.

To Philip Schuyler

Poghkeepsie, 6 February 1778

Dear Sir

Your Favors of the 26 Ult. and 1st Inst.[1] have reached me. Mr. Yates has delivered to me the Loan Office Bill.[2] Accept my Thanks for your Attention to it.

The Council of Revision and the Indisposition of my Father forbid my being at a greater Distance from Fish Kill at present. God knows how long the latter Reason may exist or in what Manner cease. Of all Evils those of the domestic kind give most Pain. Be assured however that I shall be happy in an opportunity of accepting your friendly Invitation. The Members of Albany are applying for a Commission of Oyer and Terminer. If they succeed I shall of Course obtain Leave of Absence from the Council of Revision.[3]

The unmilitary Arrangement like other Affairs of the northern Department, has no Marks of Wisdom or Attention. I hear the Congress has ordered one of its Members to repair to Albany and inquire into the State of the Hospital there. If great Confusion generally terminates in order, we may soon expect to see our Affairs in a glorious Way.

Expeditions into Canada have heretofore been determined upon with as few Preparations as the present, and those Obstacles gave Way to Care and Industry. I wish the like might be expected of this. If it succeeds it will conduce greatly to the Interest of the American Cause, if not Congress will be taught a useful Lesson. When the Expense of preceding Campaigns are compared with the Profusions of the last, People will begin to Reason and make Comparisons.

I wish I could know the Amount of the last and preceding, in such a Way as that I might with Propriety make it an Article in a Gazette.

The Wheels of Gov[ernment] like those of a new Carriage do not yet go easy. Affairs however are in a better Train than they have been. If a certain gent[leman] should push into Nomination for the Office you mention, it is not probable he will hold any.[4]

I am Dear General Your obedient Servant

JOHN JAY

ALS. N. Endorsed.

[1] See Schuyler to JJ, 26 Jan. 1778, JP, and 1 Feb. 1778, above.

[2] The loan office bills were interest-bearing government bonds intended to raise revenue by functioning as investment securities rather than a circulating medium. Their issuance by state loan officers was authorized by Congress on 11 June 1777 following the receipt of assurances from the American commissioners in Paris of their ability to borrow enough specie to pay interest on all such certificates. *JCC*, VIII, 456–57; E. James Ferguson, *The Power of the Purse, A History of American Public Finance, 1776–1790* (Chapel Hill, 1961), pp. 35–36.

[3] A Commission of Oyer and Terminer was appointed. For the report see below, 19 May 1778.

[4] Refers to Abraham Yates, Jr.

To Philip Schuyler

Poghkeepsie, 12 February 1778

Dear General

The assembly are preparing a Tax Bill and Debates run high on the Question whether unimproved located Lands shall be taxed. They have ordered a separate Bill for that Purpose to be prepared, and seem determined that it shall proceed pari Passu with the other.[1]

I hope you will seriously determine to serve your Country, at least in a legislative Capacity. Class yourself with those great men of antiquity who, unmoved by the Ingratitude of their Country, omitted no Opportunities of promoting the public Weal. In this Field Malice cannot prevent your reaping Laurels, and remember that the present State of our Affairs offer you a plentiful Harvest. Set about it then my dear Sir in earnest.

I know not who will be the Bearer of this Letter, and therefore forbear enlarging.

I am Dear Sir Your most obedient Servant

JOHN JAY

ALS. Endorsed. DftS in JP.

[1] The Tax Bill was passed 28 March 1778. It included a three-pence tax on unimproved lands. *Votes and Proceedings of the Senate of New York . . .* (1777–[79]), pp. 99–100.

John Jay and Sarah Livingston Jay to Susannah Livingston

Fish Kill, 16th March 1778

Dear Susan

Sally returned from Rhinebeck about ten Days ago in good Health, and except now and then a short Visit from her old acquaintance, the Rheumatism, has continued so ever since. You cant concieve how easy she is about You all, and is quite content to live the ensuing Summer without her Son. Indeed there is no great Prospect of her committing her delicate Frame to the rough Treatment which Travellers thru your Roads meet with. The nine Partners[1] will probably be our abiding Place this Summer, and it is not altogether certain that we shall not request the Favor of Master Peter's Company. His mother expects that by the Time she sees him his Education will be considerably advanced, and that he will by that Time have been taught to d—n the King and say the Westminster Confession of Faith. However the first may be the Case, I tell her she will be disappointed as to the latter, for you may remember you promised before Parson Charlton[2] to make a Churchman of him.

Sally says if I write such things she wishes I would conclude my Letter, so that as I always mean to be a very civil Husband I have concluded to write no more at present except to desire you to present my Compliments to all the Family and to assure you that I am your affectionate Brother

JOHN JAY

What a critical situation, my dear Susan, is that of your sister at present, to contradict the assertions of my Lord and Master may for ought I know be esteemed Petty Treason in the eye of every man who has the *honor* of being a husband, and to let the above assertions pass in silence would by the ladies at Persepone be thought an indication of insensibility in a mother that is blest with so lovely a son I will only therefore submit it to your own Judgment. I am my dear Susan your's affectionately

SARAH JAY

P.S. Mrs. Montgomery offers to let you have a clever little Yellow Boy about seven Years old provided you will keep him till he is 18 or 21 Years old. I think he would be a great Relief to Belle, and a Convenience to the whole Family. What adds to his Value in Sally's Estimation is, his being the Son of a Wench brought up in your Family, as to the Residue of his Parentage I know not.

ALS. MHi: Livingston II. Addressed: "Miss Susan W. Livingston Governor Livingston's Persipeney New Jersey." Endorsed.

1 The Nine Partners was originally the name used to refer to a Dutch land grant to nine partners in the seventeenth century encompassing the area around Poughkeepsie, N.Y.

2 Richard Charlton, assistant minister of Trinity Church, New York City, 1732–47, and thereafter a pastor on Staten Island until his death in 1777. Morgan Dix *et al.*, eds., *A History of the Parish of Trinity Church in the City of New York* (6 vols., New York, 1898–1962), I, 210, 231, 243–44 n.

To Gouverneur Morris

[Fishkill], 17 March 1778

Dear Morris

Your Favor of the 1st February came to Hand last week. It gives me Pleasure to hear you was then at Head Quarters especially on Business so important and perplexed.[1] It is Time that Inquiries as well as Punishments should become more frequent. I wish better, or rather more use was made of Courts Martial. Why is the Inquiry directed to be made into the Causes to which we are to ascribe the Loss of Fort Montgomery etc. so long delayed.[2] Had it been made immediately after that Event took place, the River would now have been well fortified and a General at the Head of the Troops, in the Southern part of the State.

Pennsylvania I believe is sick unto Death. It will nevertheless recover, tho perhaps not soon. Weak and bad Constitutions incline to chronical Disorders.

Were I sure that this Letter would reach you uninspected I should commit many things to Paper worth your knowing but which would give you little pleasure or surprize. But as it is uncertain who will be the Bearer, they must be reserved for the present. God bless and give you Diligence and Patience. Where you are, both are necessary.

I am etc.

Dft.

1 In Morris's letter dated Camp Valley Forge, 1 February (ALS in JP), he informed JJ of his appointment by Congress to a committee to reorganize the Army's battalion structure. *JCC*, X, 40, 67.

2 The courts martial of General Putnam and Governor George Clinton over the loss of Forts Montgomery and Clinton on 6 Oct. 1777 to Sir Henry Clinton were concluded 17 Aug. 1778. See below, JJ to Gouverneur Morris, 13 Sept. 1778.

To Gouverneur Morris

Poughkeepsie, 14 April 1778

Dear Morris

Your Favor of the 16th Ulto. was delivered to me two Days ago by Majr. Morris.[1] It makes the third I have had the Pleasure of recieving from you since your Departure, altho the Letters I have written to you amount to double that Number.

The Session of the Legislature is at an End, a weak perplexed wrangling one it has been. No wonder. Little applications within or without Doors, but you know these Things as well as I do.

Livingston[2] was to have told me the Amount of certain *Sums* you set him, but I have not seen or heard from him these three Weeks.

The Errata of a certain Gentleman, to whom your long Letter was directed,[3] are I believe imputable to other Causes than those you hint at. A vacant Majority was to be filled. The Concurrence of the Council of App[ointmen]t was supposed necessary and effectual. The prevailing Influence at that Board was therefore to be soothed by every Species of Compliance and Attention. I am not certain this was the Case but I firmly believe it. The Part was too much overacted to have been occasioned by Carelessness on the one Hand or Pique on the other. This is writing freely, but you have long seen my Heart, and I dont find myself disposed to veil anything that passes in it from your View. I wish you would write and publish a few civil Things on our Constitution, censuring however an omission in not restraining the Council of Appointment from granting Offices to themselves, with Remarks on the Danger of that Practice. Send the Paper in which it may be printed to me.

Effectual Measures should be taken to prevent Staff Officers from Trading. The Forage Department is mismanaged. The Governor has Power to interpose, and I hope will.

A considerable Detachment of the Troops at the High Lands are under marching orders to Head Quarters. This Measure may be right, but a similar one last Fall proved otherwise.

Think of Vermont. The Governor has written on that Subject to Congress.[4] Let them be decisive.

Ought not the Tryals of Schuyler, St. Claire and Putnam[5] to be expedited? Adieu.

Remember me to Duer.

I am your Friend

JOHN JAY

Dft. Endorsed.

1 Probably Major Jacob Morris, son of Lewis Morris, who was an aide-de-camp to Charles Lee at this time.

2 Robert R. Livingston.

3 Gouverneur Morris to Robert R. Livingston, 10 March 1778, ALS in NHi, in cipher variation of James Lovell's cipher, on Congressional affairs and Pennsylvania politics. Robert R. Livingston's deciphered transcript filed therein.

4 George Clinton to Henry Laurens, President of Congress, 7 April 1778, in *GCP*, III, 144–46. Clinton urged Congress to state its disapproval of the Vermont separatists and warned that New York's aid to the common cause might be depleted by the need to deal with them.

5 Schuyler's court-martial was held in October 1778; Arthur St. Clair's in August 1778.

To Peter Van Schaack

Poughkeepsie, 18 April 1778

Dear Sir

Your Favor of the 15 Inst. came to Hand last Evening. I <feel very sensibly for your unfortunate> am fully impressed with a sense of your unfortunate Situation and should be <very> happy were it in my Power to alleviate the Pain and Anxiety it must give You.[1]

I delivered your Petition and read your Letter to me, to his Ex[cellenc]y the Governor this Morning. He regrets the Necessity which opposes a Compliance with Your Request, but still thinks it his indispensable Duty to <cut off all possible> prevent all Intercourse <with the Enemy> between the Inhabitants and the Enemy except such as Reasons of State may dictate. The Objections do not in this Instance arise from Distrust, he means to make it a general Rule that no Citizen shall with his Permission go to the Enemy on private Business and return. He desires me to assure You that there is no Gentleman in this State to whom he would grant the Indulgence <you wish> in Question but that he will nevertheless be always ready to do you any kind Office which may not contravene the Principles <on> by which his administration is directed.

<Thus my dear Sir> Endeavour to Prevail then my Dear Sir upon Mrs. Van Schaack to suspend a fruitless Anxiety to visit her former Habitation. The Time may yet come and perhaps is not far distant when that natural Desire may be gratified, and when she may again partake of those social Enjoyments of which these turbulent Times have deprived so many.

I should have <enlarged on this Subject> enlarged, but Company this moment <arrived> comes in, and constrains me to conclude this Letter.

I am Dear Sir with every friendly wish <for Mrs. Van Schaacks Recovery and Happiness and person> Yours etc.

J. J.

Dft. Endorsed by JJ.

1 See above, "The Case of Peter Van Schaack."

FROM GOUVERNEUR MORRIS

York Town, 28th April 1778

Dear Jay,

This Letter is to be handed to you by General Gates.[1] Let me recommend him to your particular Attention. Vermont you will say prevents this. Policy may have induced him to flatter those People when he wanted their Assistance.[2] Let us take it up on that Ground. In his present Command he will want the Assistance of our State the cordial Assistance of its Rulers. I have promised this. I write to you to Livingston and jointly with Duer to the Governor.[3] This is sufficient and you will all three I am confident exert yourselves whenever Necessity shall [require it].

I am Yours etc.

GOUVR. MORRIS

ALS. Addressed: "Honle. John Jay Esqr. Chief Justice of the State of N York Fish Kill or elsewhere. By the honle. Majr. Genl. H. Gates." Endorsed: ". . . answd. 3 June." Tr: MH.

1 On 15 April Gates had been ordered by Congress to Fishkill to "take the command of [the] . . . northern department; and immediately take effectual measures to secure the communication with the eastern states, by maintaining the possession of Hudson's river; and for that purpose, . . . Gates be authorized to call for militia and artificers from the states of New York, Connecticut, Massachusetts bay, and New Hampshire." *JCC*, X, 354.

2 Gates had alienated many leading New Yorkers in 1776 when he had applied to the Bennington Committee of Safety, a body not recognized as lawful by New York, for supplies for the army. Hiland Hall, *The History of Vermont* (Albany, 1868), pp. 222–23.

3 Gouverneur Morris and William Duer were New York delegates to the Continental Congress. *LMCC*, II, lviii, lix; III, lvi, lvii.

FROM GOUVERNEUR MORRIS

York Town, 29th April 1778

Dear Jay.

I wont dispute who has written most. I have written more than twice what you acknowlege to have received but this is of no Consequence.

I am sorry for your Session but I wish you had marked out what Taxes have been laid, what Salaries given and a few more striking out Lines of Legislation; these with what I know of your Men would have enabled me to imagine proper Lights and Shades.

My *Arithmetical* Friend will not find much from the Sum you mention worth casting up. Remember my Love to him.[1]

I chuse that my Friends should write freely and those who know me must know that such Freedoms need no Apology. I never thought the Person you allude to so steady as could be wished.[2] We have all of us our weak Sides. Would to God that were the worst.

What you mention relative to our Plan of Rights shall be attended to.[3] I am a busy Man tho as heretofore a pleasurable one.

Let your Governor cleanse the Augean Stable in his State which no public Body would do tho it stink under their Noses. I am laboring at Arrangements of various Kinds; God prosper me and give me Patience and Industry. It was a good Wish from one who knew my Wants.

We have ordered Troops from the Highlands but we still send thither a General who shall be impowered to call forth the Swarms of the Eastern Hive.[4] Men were necessary at the Vallye Forge. I have a good Knack at Guessing; I guess the Enemy won't Attempt Hudson's River.

I do think of Vermont and unless I mistake Matters shall be managed to Effect without bellowing in the Forum which I beleive hath been a little too much the Case. But why should I blame impetuous Vivacity; hath it never led me into an Error?

Putnam will soon be tried.[5] The Affair of Schuyler and St. Clair laboured under aukward Circumstances. Their Friends and their Enemies appear to me to have been equally blind. I enclose Extracts from the Minutes made the other Night to possess myself of the real State of Facts. There are some other Entries from Time to Time. It was erroneous to order a Committee simply to collect Facts; they should have been directed to state Charges. This Morning my Colleague being absent I got a Committee appointed for the latter Purpose. Sherman, Dana (Massachusetts) and Drayton (South Carolina).[6] This was unanimous and yet I would have undertaken to argue for it in a Stile which would absolutely have ruined the Measure. You know it would have been easy to say *Justice to these injured Gentlemen* instead of *Justice to an injured Country* requires etc.

Great Britain seriously means to treat.[7] Our Affairs are most critical tho not dangerously so. If the Minister from France were present as well as him from England I am a blind Politician if the Thirteen States (with their extended Territory) would not be in peaceable Possession of their Independency three Months from this Day. As it is, expect a long War. I believe it will not require such astonishing Efforts after this Campaign to keep the Enemy at Bay.

Probably a Treaty is signed with the House of Bourbon ere this;[8] if so a Spark hath fallen upon the Train which is to fire the World. Ye Gods what Havock does Ambition make among your Works.

My dear Friend Adieu. My Love to your Wife. Remember me to all my Friends of every Rank and Sex. I am your

GOUV. MORRIS

P.S. I meant to have said the present is within the Spirit of our Constitution *a special Occasion*. The foregoing is in Answer to yours of the 14th.

ALS. Addressed: "Honle. John Jay Esqr. Chief Justice of the State of New York at Poughkeepsie or elsewhere. Free Gouvr. Morris." Endorsed: ". . . ansd. 3 June." The date on this letter is smudged. In filing his copy JJ dated it 28 April, but comparison with *JCC* entries shows it was written on the 29th.

1 Robert R. Livingston.

2 See above, JJ to Morris, 14 April, n. 4.

3 See JJ's request to Morris, above, 14 April, to "write and publish a few civil things on our Constitution."

4 General Gates.

5 General Israel Putnam. See below, JJ to Gouverneur Morris, 13 Sept. 1778, for the outcome of the inquiry.

6 An earlier Congressional commission, appointed 28 Aug. 1777, had limited itself to gathering facts about the evacuation of Ticonderoga. That secured by Morris on 29 April 1778, which consisted of Roger Sherman, Francis Dana (1743–1811), and William Henry Drayton (1742–79), was instructed "to examine the evidence collected and state charges against the general officers who were in the northern department when Ticonderoga and Mount Independence were evacuated." *JCC*, VIII, 688; X, 403.

7 Copies of bills introduced in Parliament in February which sought reconciliation with America and appointed a peace commission were received in New York in mid-April. See next letter.

8 See next letter.

FROM GEORGE CLINTON

Poughkeepsie, 29th April 1778

Dear Sir

A few Days since Mr. Benson enclosed Lord Norths famous Speech (in the English House of Commons) to Mr. McKesson for the perusal of the Court and I now enclose you Copies of the two Bills aluded to therein.[1] His Lordship is two years too late with this political Maneuvre. This at the Time of his former Conciliatory Proposition (as he calls it) woud have divided and ruined us. At this Day it will have a very different Effect; it gives Spirit to our Friends and divides and disheartens our Enemies. The Tories (as Brasher[2] would express it) are all aback.

The Account of these Measures and of his *Majesty's most Gracious Disposition towards us* had hardly reached us before we were enabled to Account for the great Change. Capt. Deane Brother to Silas arrived Day before yesterday at Fishkill (on his Way to Congress) in forty Days from France.[3] He came in a French Ship encharged with Dispatches from that Court to Congress of great Importance. He travelled with an Escort of Light Horse. Particulars have not yet been said. This much I may venture to tell you as a Truth—a Treaty is concluded between that Court and our Embassadors,[4] these very favourable to these States (of which Capt. Deane was charged with the Counterpart). I believe I may farther venture to say it is more so than could have been expected. A Sensible Friend of ours who has had an Opportunity of learning the particulars writes me so. Should not Lord Norths Speech and the two Bills be published with some strictures on them?[5] I think it woud have a good effect and I wish you coud spare a little Time to prepare them for the press.

By a Letter enclosing some Resolutions of Congress[6] I learn Genl. Gates is to Command in this Department including what was formerly the Northern Department. Genl. Starke is to be employed under him to the Northward at his particular Request. Genl. McDougal[7] on Gates's Arrival which is daily expected is to Join the Grand Army. Our good Fortune not our Wise Management must save us. Instability and Folly cant ruin us or it would have been effected ere now.

You must accept this Uncorrect Scroll or nothing. I am not able even to read it over there is a Crowd about me that I am not likely to get rid of soon and Mrs. Clinton is very Sick.

Adieu. Believe me yours Sincerely

GEO. CLINTON

ALS. RAWC. E in NN: Bancroft American Series, III, 164-1/2.

1 Letter of Robert Benson to John McKesson not located. McKesson was then Clerk of the Supreme Court; Benson was Clinton's secretary. On 19 February Lord North had proposed conciliatory measures with America, in hopes of preventing the Franco-American Alliance. He moved that two bills be passed: one, to establish a peace commission to treat with Congress; the second, to enable the commissioners to suspend or abolish taxation and to "treat, discuss, and conclude upon every point whatsoever." *The Parliamentary History of England, From the Earliest Period to the Year 1803*, printed by T. C. Hammond (36 vols., London, 1806–20), XIX, 762–870.

2 Abraham Brasher was a member of the Committee of One Hundred, and served in the New York Provincial Congress and the New York Legislature. *NYGBR*, XXVII, 37.

3 Captain Simeon Deane.

4 On 6 Feb. 1778 a Treaty of Amity and Commerce and a Treaty of Alliance were signed at Paris by American Commissioners Benjamin Franklin, Silas Deane, and Arthur Lee, and the French Minister Plenipotentiary, Conrad Alexandre Gérard (1729–90). Both treaties were read and ratified by Congress on 4 May 1778. David Hunter Miller, ed., *Treaties and Other International Acts* (8 vols., Washington, 1831–48), II, 3, 35.

5 Lord North's speech and bills, together with the 22 April resolutions of Congress, were published in the *Pennsylvania Gazette*, 24 April 1778.

6 Henry Laurens to George Clinton, 20 April 1778, enclosing the Congressional resolution of 15 April, in *GCP*, III, 197–200.

7 On 16 March 1778 General Alexander McDougall was ordered by Washington to replace Israel Putnam as commander of the Continental forces in the Hudson Highlands. *GWF*, XI, 90–91, 95–96.

To Gouverneur Morris

Albany, April 29, 1778

Dear Morris

My last to you was written about a Week ago.[1] I am now engaged in the most disagreable part of my Duty—trying Criminals.[2] They multiply exceedingly; Robberies become frequent. The Woods afford them Shelter and the Tories Food. Punishments must of Course become certain, and Mercy dormant, a harsh System repugnant to my Feelings, but nevertheless necessary. In such Circumstances Levity would be Cruelty, and Severity is found on the Side of Humanity.

The Influence of Lord North's Conciliatory Plan is happily counter balanced by the Intelligence from France. There was danger of its creating Division. A Desire of Peace is natural to an harrassed People and the Mass of Mankind prefer present Ease to the arduous Exertions often necessary to ensure permanent Tranquility.

What the french Treaty may be I know not. If Britain would acknowledge our Independence and enter into a liberal Alliance with us, I should prefer a Connection with her, to a League with any Power on Earth. Whether those Objects be attainable Experience only can determine. I suspect the Com[missione]rs will have Instructions to exceed their Powers if necessary.[3] Peace at all Events is in my Opinion the Wish of the Minister. <If they will consent to withdraw their Armies and give us a two Years Truce, I would boast> I hope the <and actually> present favorable aspect of our Affairs will neither make us arrogant or careless. Moderation in Prosperity marks great Minds and denotes a generous People. Your game is now in a delicate Situation and the least bad Play may ruin it. I view a Return to the

Domination of Britain with Horror, and would risque all for Independence but that Point ceded, I would give them advantageous commercial Terms. The Destruction of old England would hurt me. I wish it well; it afforded my Ancestors an Assylum from Persecution.

Parties here are still in a Ferment. I hope it will be the Means of purging off much Scum and Dross. I cant be particular. This Letter may never reach You.

I expect in a few Days to see Gen. Schuyler and my Importunities shall not be wanting to urge him to join you without Delay.[4] The People grow more reconciled to him.

The military Departments here I believe are well managed. The Commissary deserves Credit. Handsome Things are said of the Quarter Master, and there is one at the Head of the Artillery who appears to me to have much Merit.[5] The Park, Elaboratory, and Stores are in high Order. There is the appearance of Regularity, Care and Attention in all the public Works. As to the hospital I can say little not being as yet well informed. Conway is pleased with Schuyler and manages the Vermont Troop properly, but of this say nothing. I fancy he does not well understand the Views of his Patron.[6] Neither of them ought to know this.

The Clothier General once the Duke of Boltons Butler is an aide [to] Washington. An ignorant Butcher is issuing Commissary.[7] Let me again hint to you the Propriety of restraining the Staff from Trade. Besides general Reasons there are particular ones. Many good Cannon remain yet at Ticonderogah, strange Neglect. Remember Vermont. Why do the marine Com[mitte]e keep Tudor in Pay, I cant hear that he does anything for it.[8]

I am and will be your Friend

JOHN JAY

Dft.

1 Letter not located.

2 JJ was then sitting at a Court of Oyer and Terminer held at Albany.

3 On 16 March Parliament authorized the Carlisle Peace Commission to negotiate with Congress. The members of the Commission were William Eden, George Johnstone, and the Howe brothers. The latter two were already in America in their military capacities.

4 Schuyler took his seat as a member of the New York delegation to the Continental Congress on 19 Nov. 1778. *JCC*, XII, 1145.

5 The Deputy Commissary General of Purchases serving the Northern Army was Jacob Cuyler, who held the post from June 1777 to July 1782. Ebenezer Stevens of Rhode Island, in command of the artillery of the Northern Army, was promoted to brevet lieutenant colonel on 30 April 1778 "in consideration of his services and the strict attention with which he discharged his duty as command-

ing officer of artillery in the northern department during two campaigns." *JCC*, X, 410.

6 Conway's "patron" was General Horatio Gates.

7 The Clothier General of the Continental Army from January 1776 to July 1779 was James Mease of Pennsylvania. The reference to the Commissary is probably Colonel Charles Stewart of New Jersey, who served the army as Commissary of Issues from 18 June 1777 to 24 July 1782.

8 William Tudor of Massachusetts served as judge advocate of the Continental Army from 29 July 1775, holding the rank of lieutenant colonel as of 10 Aug. 1776. He was also named lieutenant colonel of Henty's Additional Continental Regiment in January 1777. He had, at the time of JJ's letter, already resigned all his posts on 9 April 1778.

From Gouverneur Morris

York Town, 3d May 1778

Dear Jay

I shall plague you with very few Words. I congratulate you on our Alliance with France; for Particulars I refer you to our Friend Robert. I enclose you a News Paper containing a Report I drew on North's Bills which were sent us by the General.[1] I have marked in the Margin two Clauses inserted by the House; you may find perhaps some Difficulty to discover how they shew the Wickedness or Insincerity of the Enemy. The following Clause (the Reason of which you will see) was struck out. "Your Committee etc. that in the present Conjuncture of Affairs when the unalienable Rights of human Nature may probably become the Subject of Negotiation the Wisdom of America should be as far as possible collected and therefore that the States be called upon to send a full and adequate Representation to Congress upon the present *special Occasion*."[2]

Sundry small Alterations were made as is the Case in Matrimony for better for worse. We have recommended an Act of Grace with Exceptions. How to make these Exceptions will be a nice Card if Gentlemen have *particular* Friends in the Legislature. A Word to the Wise. I do not chuse to be explicit but I shall set some Sums to our numerical Correspondent when I have Time etc.

Love to Sally. Adieu. Yours

GOUVR. MORRIS

ALS, RAWC. Tr in MH: Jared Sparks Collection; E in NN: Bancroft American Series, 180-1/2.

1 On 20 April 1778 Congress received from Washington a letter enclosing a copy of Lord North's bill providing for the appointment of peace commissioners. Both Washington and Congress were suspicious of the proposal

and Morris prepared a report, adopted and published by Congress, rejecting the British terms. *JCC*, X, 374–80; Max M. Mintz, *Gouverneur Morris and the American Revolution* (Norman, Okla., 1970), p. 101.

2 According to Burnett, "The original of the report on Lord North's measures has not been found among the Papers of the Continental Congress, therefore it cannot be determined just what changes were made by the house." *LMCC*, III, 219 n.

Chief Justice of the State Supreme Court of Judicature

As Chief Justice JJ was exposed to the realities of New York's political and military situation; as an *ex officio* member of the Council of Revision he was required to participate in the legislative process;[1] and as a presiding judge he was called upon to administer justice in a state where outlawry and murder were as often as not associated with men's political loyalties.

JJ's role in this situation must be determined from isolated documents like the report printed below. Although he did not resign from the Court until 18 August 1779,[2] his actual participation in state government ended on 6 November 1778 when he last sat on the Council of Revision. His service on the state bench began on 9 September 1777 when he presided over the first session of the Supreme Court at Kingston. The records of his activities as a presiding judge are incomplete, since there is a gap in the Minutes of the Supreme Court of Judicature for the twelve months after that first session. The proceedings resume with the session of October 1778 at which Robert Yates presided in JJ's absence.[3]

The surviving records demonstrate little if any change between the causes of action which came before the Court during JJ's service and those brought after his departure from New York in November 1778. At the September 1777 session, JJ and the puisne justices considered cases involving murder, assault, attempted rape, counterfeiting, and grand larceny. In Supreme Court sessions for 1778 and 1779 over half the indictments were brought for robbery and assault. Cases of counterfeiting, riot, and receiving stolen goods accounted for most of the other actions, while the only civil cases heard by the Court in 1778–79 were actions of ejectment.[4]

This concern for the prosecution of acts of violence against persons or property is even more marked when one considers the frequency with which JJ and his associates were called upon to preside at courts of oyer and terminer. In the judicial system of provincial New York "oyer and terminer" referred to specially commissioned courts called to try serious offenses which required adjudication before the next sitting of the local Supreme Court circuit.[5] This usage continued under the new state government. Although justices of the Supreme Court presided at these sessions, courts of oyer and terminer were not considered sessions of the Court proper, and their minutes were not included in the records of the Supreme Court. Instead, such minutes were considered part of the judicial records of the counties in which courts of oyer and terminer were held. The fragmentary nature of New York county court records for this period makes it impossible to determine the number of special oyer and terminer sessions the Supreme Court justices were commissioned to hold. However, existing documents do place JJ at oyer and terminer sessions at Kingston in April 1778 and at Albany in September 1778, as well as at the Albany session reported below.[6]

The backgrounds of the prisoners tried at Albany in May 1778 are revealing of law enforcement problems during this period. The *New-York Journal* described the felons convicted at that session as "tory criminals," and reported "Their thefts and robberies they justified, under the pretense of the goods being lawful prizes, forfeited to the King."[7] A visitor to Albany who witnessed the proceedings at the City Hall in May 1778 recalled that JJ "pronounced the awful sentence of death, and addressed them in a very solemn and affecting manner, calculated to rouse them to a sense of their dreadful condition, and in a moving and pathetic strain, enjoined it on them to prepare to meet their God."[8] To a devout Christian and firm patriot like JJ, the "dreadful condition" of the ten men whom he sentenced to the gallows was the more affecting since they were not only convicted murderers and thieves, but the political enemies of a state which was threatened by British regulars, Loyalist volunteers, and hostile Indians. In cases like these, it was impossible to draw the line between banditry and treason.

1 See above, "A Hint to the Legislature," 15 Jan.–2 April 1778.

2 See below, JJ to George Clinton, 18 Aug. 1779.

3 New York County Clerk's Office, Division of Old Records: Minutes of the Supreme Court of Judicature, 1776–81. The minutes for the opening session of September 1777 cover pp. 107–16. Five blank, numbered pages follow in the volume, and entries for the October 1778 session begin on p. 123. The minutes for 23 April 1779 refer to a session of the Court for April 1778. It is probable that the clerk left pp. 117–22 blank with the intention of adding minutes for the April 1778 session from his loose notes. *The New-York Journal and the General Advertiser,* 10 Aug. 1778, refers to "the Supreme Court held at Albany in July term," and this session also went unrecorded in the official Minutes.

4 Supreme Court sessions for October 1778 and January, April, and July 1779, Minutes of the Supreme Court, pp. 122–32.

5 Paul M. Hamlin and Charles E. Baker, *Supreme Court of Judicature of the Province of New York, 1691–1704* (3 vols., New York, 1952–59 [NYHS *Colls.,* LXXVIII–LXXX]), I, 295–309.

6 *GCP,* III, 180–83; IV, 121.

7 *New York Journal and the General Advertiser,* 15 June 1778.

8 James Thacher, *A Military Journal during the American Revolutionary War, from 1775–1783* (2nd ed., Boston, 1827), p. 130.

John Jay et al., Report of the Judges of Oyer and Terminer to Governor George Clinton

Albany, 19th May 1778

Sir,

On this Day the Commission for holding a Court of Oyer and Terminer and Goal Delivery in and for the County of Albany expires. At this Court the following persons have been convicted of capital offences. They will have this Day Judgment of Death and we have agreed to order their execution on fryday the fifth day of June next.

David Dick. Robbery. On Sufficient Evidence.

James Esmond, Robert Ferguson. Murder. They were of the party who robbed Van Ness. Jacob Korpinder one of that party at the time of the robbery murdered Abraham Van Ness—full Evidence. Robbery, of Van Alstyne, sufficient Evidence.

Christopher Galer. Murder of Abraham Van Ness in Like manner with Esmond and Ferguson.[1]

Carel Muller. Horse stealing. He plead Guilty.

Daniel Shaver, Francis Deboe. Horse stealing. Full Evidence.

William Rogers. Horse stealing on two Indictments, full Evidence in one, Very slender in the other.

James Hart. Horse stealing. On the direct and distinct Testimony of Frederick Reemer a sensible Lad of 16 Years, from whose immediate possession the Horse was taken.[2]

Benjamin Rogers. Horse stealing, very slender Evidence indeed.

Of these Convicts we think it our duty to recommend the following to your Excellency for pardon, for the following Reasons.

David Dick. Because his Character heretofore was uniformly that of a domestic inoffensive man, because he appears to have had very little agency in the Robbery, and that with a degree of reluctance which indicates his being a young Sinner, and because in our opinion he is one of the most ignorant uninformed men we ever met with.

Francis DeBoe. A Young Canadian. Because we are well informed that he rendered essential service to the American Army when in Canada and retreated with it. He is very penitent and his character heretofore good.

Benjamin Rogers. Because in our opinion the Evidence against him was insufficient, and that the offence he committed, so far as it respected the taking the Horse, amounted not to Horse stealing, but trespass. He is a Lad of about 18, and under the influence of his father William Rogers one of the Convicts aforesaid.[3]

With respect to the other Convicts nothing appeared to us in the course of their tryals or otherwise sufficient to induce us to think them objects of mercy. Circumstances favourable to them may however be made known to your Excellency in the Course of the applications they will probably make to you, with which we are at present unacquainted. We have the Honour to be with the greatest respect and esteem Your Excellency's most obedient humble Servants.

JOHN JAY
ROBERT YATES
JOHN BARCLAY
ABM. TEN BROECK
WM. YATES JUNR.[4]

P.S. Mr. Hobart is Absent.

ALS. NN: Emmet, 11632. Addressed: "To his Excellency George Clinton Esqr. Governor of the State of New York etc. Poughkeepsie." Endorsed: ". . . Report of Judges of Oyer and Terminer held at Albany." The body of the report is in JJ's hand.

1 In August 1777, a band of Tories looted the farm of John Van Ness at Kinderhook (near the modern village of Malden in Columbia County), killing his son Abraham, a soldier home on furlough. On the same raid, the outlaws robbed the home of Abraham Van Alstyne, a patriot farmer at nearby Chatham. Franklin Ellis, *History of Columbia County, New York* (Philadelphia, 1878), pp. 30–31, 220; "Minutes of the Committee for Detecting Conspiracies," N.Y.H.S. *Colls.*, LVIII, 361–62, 372–73; *Minutes of the Albany Committee of Correspondence, 1775–1778* (2 vols., Albany, 1923–24), I, 860, 867, 948; *Minutes of the Commissioners for Detecting and Defeating Conspiracies in the State of New York, Albany County Sessions, 1778–1781* (3 vols., Albany, 1909–10), I, 87, 129.

2 The *New York Journal and the General Advertiser* of 15 June 1778 described Hart and Rogers as "the most noted" of the criminals tried at this court. The records of the Albany Commissioners for Detecting Conspiracies for 18 April 1778 list the two among those who had been "some time since Confined by the Committee of the County of Albany for being Persons disaffected to the Cause of America." *Minutes of the Albany Commissioners*, I, 89, James Thacher, *A Military Journal during the American Revolutionary War, from 1775 to 1783* (2nd. ed., Boston, 1827), p. 130.

3 Although Clinton's reply to this report is no longer extant, it is clear that he acted affirmatively on the judges' recommendations for clemency for David Dick, Francis Deboe, and Benjamin Rogers. The *New-York Journal and the General Advertiser*, 15 June 1778.

4 Robert Yates was a puisne justice of the State Supreme Court. John Barclay (d. 1779) was the Mayor of Albany and chairman of the Albany Committee of Correspondence. Brigadier General Abraham Ten Broeck (1734–1810) commanded the Albany County Militia. William Yates, Jr., a prominent Albany attorney, served in the State Senate, 1777–90.

To Gouverneur Morris

Albany, 20th May 1778

Dear Morris

Accept my thanks for the last letter I received from you, and the papers inclosed in it.[1]

The report of Congress on the subject of Lord North's Bills was too strikingly marked with Morris not to be known by his friends to have been produced by his pen. Your history of that business gives me pleasure, as it acquits you of certain paragraphs which I could not understand the propriety of, especially considering the influence they were intended to have in illustrating the propositions meant to be supported.

Our friend Livingston is with his wife in Jersey. When he will return I have not learned, nor can conjecture. Gov. [*sic*] Schuyler will be returned a senator and Ab. Yates with him.[2] It will not be long before the former will join you; and, as he will be able to give you a true idea of our state and Politics, I forbear committing them to paper. It is sufficient for me to say that our friends have been and always will be too sanguine and too lazy. Adieu.

John Jay

Copy. MH: Jared Sparks. Addressed: "GM, a delegate from the State of New York, Congress, York Town."

1 See above, Gouverneur Morris to JJ, 3 May 1778.

2 There was a dispute over Philip Schuyler's election when the Senate met 13 Oct. 1778. It was never settled during that session and there is no record of Schuyler's having attended. *N.Y. Civil List*, p. 371; *Votes and Proceedings of the Senate of the State of* N.Y. . . . (Fishkill, 1777 [1779]), p. 123.

To Gouverneur Morris

Fish Kill, 3d June 1778

Dear Morris,

Your two letters of the 28th April were delivered a few days ago on my return from Albany; another of the 23d of May came to hand last night.[1]

On the future conduct of a certain General towards this State, will depend the countenance he may meet with in it.[2] My endeavours shall not be wanting to render his situation as happy and agreeable as his behaviour may merit; and I am with you of opinion, that it will be more wise to prevent the repetition of past ill offices, than promote their continuation.

A history of the last session would be a history of blunders, arbitrary exactions of legislative powers, and unconstitutional measures for perpetuating committees and retarding the full organization and vigorous execution of government.

The Senate have not published their votes; a copy of those of the Assembly shall be sent you by some private conveyance; they are too voluminous to go by the Post.

The salary of the Governor is £2,000. Scot labored to reduce it to £1,000. The Chancellor, £300; Chief Justice, £300; P[uisne] Justices, £200; Treasurer, £300; Members of senate and assembly, 16/ per day. The other allowances are in the same stile, that is, some proportioned to the present and others to the former value of money, influenced apparently by no other rule or distinction than party purposes. G. Bancker is Treasurer; £10,000 security was demanded and given. Scot is Secretary. He was at the Council and made up the necessary number of members when appointed, but did not Vote, of which at his instance an entry was made in their minutes.[3]

The operation of the measures of the legislature on the minds of their constituents, the systems they have produced, and the aspect they have on private influence and public reputation, are improper to be trusted to the uncertain fate of a letter. Here is field for guessing. The supineness of certain persons in amazing. Like the austere man, they wish to reap what they sowed not. Yates and Schuyler are returned for the western district. An opposition was made to the former; it was feeble and has given him strength: feeble, because those who conducted it were sure of success, and too indolent to ensure it or deserve it.

The Augean stable will not for some time yet be cleansed in the way you mention.

The extracts you sent me relative to the proceedings against Schuyler and St. Clair are calculated more to make a noise than decide: perhaps that was their object; if so, you have spoiled the plan. Your stating of charges is liable to one danger; possibly some of them may be such as, if supported, imply neither neglect nor criminality, and therefore will mislead. For instance, supposing one of the charges against General Schuyler should be his absence from Ticonderoga at the time of its seige. Was it his business to be there? I think not. A commander in chief putting himself for six or eight weeks in salva et arca custodia is to me a new way of extending his care and superintendance to a whole department.[4] Suppose, further, that this charge should be found true. What will be the next thing to be done? To say he is not to be censured for it! That won't do, because it would be saying that the charge was futile, or it would be telling the People you gave him mercy instead of justice.

The affair of Vermont doubtless requires more delicacy and address than Wit and sarcasm: but take care that while Rome consults Saguntum be not lost.[5]

The address of Congress is much liked, and has its use. I have not yet met with a single Whig in this State willing to accept peace on Lord North's terms. A happy circumstance.

I am glad that arrangments employ so much of your time: nothing else can save us. Press the business of taxation, and assign days for the payment of Quotas; provide also, in time, for the payment of interest money. Delays ruin your funds.

The Quarter Master's department at Albany is in very good order, and Lewis has and deserves credit for it.[6]

The Forage Master's department here is not rightly managed; and, in my opinion, never will be, till in other hands. Bostwick never took care of his own business etc. etc.

Johannes Christopher Hartwick is alive.[7] I saw him lately at Albany. I have known him these twelve years, and never otherwise than poor. A copy of that part of your letter which respects him shall be transmitted to him. I am persuaded he is the person intended by it.

However desirous I may at all times be to see you, and however useful you would be at the ensuing session, I still doubt the propriety of your leaving Congress at present. I think I know the strength of your body, and I would not wish to diminish it, especially at a time when your task is so great and extensive.

The words "special occasion" if agitated here, would produce great contention; for though our hero has lost much influence, he still retains sufficient to create divisions. We may say of our friend Robert as somebody did of Homer "Aliquando nodit."[8]

I this moment received your letter, without date, enclosing a Baltimore paper. In return I shall send you the first from this way that may equally deserve your notice.

I expect our friend P. Livingston would leave the world, as his Wit does him in a crack.[9] He is one of the last men whom I ever expected to see fine drawn by a Hectic. I am sorry for him, and wish most sincerely that he may live, at least to enjoy the first fruits of our great contest.

Duer, I am told, is fairly worn down.[10] He deserves much of his country. Present my compliments to him.

Adieu. Yours sincerely,

JOHN JAY

Tr: MH. This and subsequent letters from MH are included by permission of the Harvard College Library.

1 See above, Gouverneur Morris to JJ, 28 April 1778. Gouverneur Morris to JJ, 23 May in JP.

2 Horatio Gates.

3 Gerardus Bancker (1740–99) was appointed Treasurer of New York 1 April 1778. John Morin Scott, appointed to the Council of Appointment 16 Sept. 1777, was appointed Secretary of State 13 March 1778. *New York Civil List*, pp. 173, 175, 367.

4 *In Salva et arca custodia*—in a place of safety and confinement.

5 Saguntum (Sagunto since 1877) is an Iberian town associated with Rome. Hannibal's attack on it precipitated the Second Punic War.

6 Francis Lewis.

7 Johannes Christopher Hartwig (Hartwick) (1714–96), Lutheran clergyman from Saxe-Gotha sent to America as a missionary, who preached at congregations in the Hudson Valley, Pennsylvania, Maryland, and Virginia before the Revolution. See Gouverneur Morris to JJ, 23 May 1778 in JP.

8 *Aliquando nadit*—sometimes he ties himself up.

9 Philip Livingston died 12 June 1778.

10 William Duer, delegate to Congress 1777–78, member of the Board of War and other committees. *LMCC*, III, lvi.

From Robert Troup

Peeks Kill, June 29, 1778,
½ after 9 o'Clock, P.M.

My dear Sir,

By a Letter received a few Hours ago, from Major Armstrong,[1] we learn that our Army were, the Night before last, at English Town,[2] in New-Jersey between six and seven Miles from Monmouth Court House, where the main Body of the Enemy were posted; that they were then marching, it is presumed, in Order to cut off their Communication entirely with South Amboy and the other possible Places of Embarkation; that Gen. Lee[3] commanded 4000 Men which were constantly harassing their Flanks; that the Militia of N. Jersey were in the highest Spirits, and almost to a Man in Arms; that 500, British and German Soldiers, had deserted, and more were hourly coming in.

We shall move at 2 o'Clock in the Morning for the White Plains. Our Object is to make a Shew of attacking N. York, to prevent their throwing a Force into N. Jersey to operate in Favor of Sir Henry Clinton. We have a pretty respectable Army.

I am sorry we can't grant Miss Bayard's Request, and the more so because you have applied for her.[4] But, my dear Sir, we shall be Putnamised, to all Intents and Purposes, if we suffer any Persons to go into New York.[5] This Consideration induced me, to prevail upon the General,[6] to shut the Door, immediately after I left you at Fish-

Kill. I do not think that a Single Flag will be granted, during the whole Campaign, unless for public Purposes.

When I receive any further Intelligence that may be depended on I shall communicate it to you without the least Delay.

My best Respects to all my Friends at Poughkeepsie.

In the greatest Hurry, I am, My dear Sir, Your obliged humble Servant

ROB. TROUP

ALS. Addressed: "Hon'ble Mr. Chief Justice Jay, Poughkeepsie." Endorsed.

1 Probably Major John Armstrong, Jr., of Pennsylvania, serving as aide-de-camp to Gates.

2 A part of Freehold township, Monmouth County, N.J.

3 Major General Charles Lee. Lee's handling of his troops at the 28 June Battle of Monmouth resulted in his court-martial 4 July, and suspension from service. See below, Robert Troup to JJ, 16 Aug. 1778.

4 By a letter dated 28 June 1778 Rebecca Bayard requested JJ to intercede with General Gates to obtain permission to proceed down the Hudson to seek relief for her brother in New York City. Rebecca Bayard was a daughter of Colonel William Bayard, merchant, of the firm of Bayard & Co., who sided with the British in 1776. Sabine, *Biographical Sketches*, I, 217. Rebecca Bayard to JJ, 28 June 1778 in JP.

5 The reference is presumably to Israel Putnam, who by this time had lost the respect of Washington. After Forts Montgomery and Clinton fell to the British 6 Oct. 1777, Putnam reputedly gave permits to various persons who later turned out to be Loyalists to go within the British lines. W. F. Livingston, *Israel Putnam* (N.Y., 1901), p. 368.

6 Horatio Gates.

From Gouverneur Morris

Philadelphia, 23d July 1778

Dear Jay,

I received yours of the 4th some Days ago but I was in so unsettled a Situation that I could not answer it.[1] At present I must be short for I have Company waiting. I have no Apprehension that these Money Matters can affect *me*. I have not taken nor would I on any Consideration have taken the Agency of the Business. Duer I trust will do what is right. Your Caution however is useful and proper and I thank you for it. On no Occasion do I wish to give Room for the Exercise of Slanderous Tongues much less where money Matters are in Question for they are indeed delicate very delicate.

As to the Malevolence of Individuals It is what I have to expect. It is by no Means a Matter of Surprize that I should be hated by some Men but I will have my Revenge. By laboring in the public Service so as to gain the Applause of those whose Applause is worth gaining I will punish them severely. You will see another American to another

Letter of the Commissioners.[2] I mention this to convince you I am not quite idle.

The Letter you refer to was one enclosing me a Libel against myself. I think I have answered it but am not sure as I was then in a moving State. My Servant being sick also hath prevented me in some Degree from the Worship of the Regularities. Let me hear from you often. My Love to all Friends. Remember me to Lewis and when you see him Richard who by this Time has no small Reason to lament his non Acceptance of a certain Office.[3]

Adieu. Believe me with Sincerity your Friend

GOUV. MORRIS

I hear by Accident of the Arrival of your Brother.[4] I congratulate you on it. Again Adieu.

ALS. Endorsed.

1 JJ to Gouverneur Morris, 4 July 1778, not located.

2 On 13 June 1778 Congress received Lord North's proposals for conciliation, which had been delivered to Philadelphia by the Earl of Carlisle, William Eden, and George Johnstone, the British commissioners sent to undertake peace negotiations. Gouverneur Morris wrote the reply rejecting this overture, but in order to make it acceptable to the other delegates he had to make it blander than he wanted it to be. Consequently he also produced a much stronger anonymous statement, which the *Pennsylvania Gazette* published on 20 June and to which he refers above. Max M. Mintz, *Gouverneur Morris and the American Revolution* (Norman, Okla., 1970), pp. 104–05.

3 Lewis Morris and Richard Morris, half-brothers of Gouverneur Morris. The office refused by Richard Morris might be the clerkship of the New York State Supreme Court. See above, Richard Morris to JJ, 12 July 1777.

4 SLJ to JJ, 8 April 1778 in JP, mentions the possible arrival of Sir James.

FROM GOUVERNEUR MORRIS

Philadelphia, 16th August 1778

Dear Jay,

We are at Length fairly setting about our Finances and our foreign Affairs. For the latter particularly I much wish you were here. Many Persons whom you know are very liberal of Illiberality. Your Friend Deane who hath rendered the most essential Services stands as one accused. The Storm increases and I think some one of the tall Trees must be torn up by the Roots.

I have not heard from you in a long Time. I did expect a letter by your Brother James but was disappointed. I am informed that he brought Letters from you to Nobody here. How happened that? A propos I will give you a little History.

Just before his Arrival, I saw a Letter from Arthur Lee speaking of him most disrespectfully. I was informed and induced to beleive that he was come to Congress charged with Lee's Information and to promote his Designs. The Length of my Acquaintance with him required Nothing. But it was my Duty to take Care that your Brother did not render himself ridiculous. I felt more than I can tell at the Idea of a Connection between him and some Persons who I am confident you do from your Soul despise and abhor. In Consequence I waited of [*sic*] him. I told him candidly that I suspected him to be charged with Matter which was to militate much in favor of Mr. Lee, that Mr. Lee had in a Letter which would then shortly become public tradused him. I had forgot to tell you that the Letter was to Mr. Carmichael who (being accused before Congress by Mr. Lee) shewed it in his own Defense to a Committee of which I was a Member.[1] And I stated the Ridicule which falls from being *instrumental* in forwarding the Views of a Man who had said of him that he was a Vilain.

He was as you may well suppose much obliged by this Instance of my Friendship and so far all was Right. So far I had saved him out of bad Hands. As the Devil would have it I was appointed one Member of a Committee to superintend an Entertainment given by the Congress to Monsieur Gerard.[2] Unfortunately the Line which by the general Sense of the Members of Congress had been drawn for Invitations excluded him. He was offended. He made Inquiries into the Reasons. You may readily imagine what some Folks would say on the Occasion. He inquired of me in a Stile which really put it out of my Power to give him satisfactory Answers. It is a Pity for his own Sake that he appeared to feel the Omission. To you the Reasons need not be assigned. I fear he is now in the Possession of those Gentlemen. I would dilate upon the Consequences but the Idea is painful to me and cannot be pleasant to you. I have only to add on this Chapter that I will save him if I can even from himself. The Mischeif he is now in is such Dudgeon that any Advances from me would produce the direct contrary Effect from what they ought.

Adieu my Friend. Remember me to our Friends. To your Wife particularly. Write to me oftener. In all Cases beleive me most sincerely yours

GOUV. MORRIS

ALS. Tr in MH: Jared Sparks Coll.

1 William Carmichael was secretary to the American Commissioners in Paris.

2 Conrad Alexandre Gérard, the recently-appointed French minister to the United States, who had arrived in Philadelphia in July 1778.

FROM ROBERT TROUP

Camp, at White Plains, August 16, 1778
6 o'Clock P.M.

My dear Sir,

Our Army is still encamped on the Heights near the White Plains. We shall move as soon as the Event of the Rhode Island Expedition is known. The last Accounts from that Quarter are: that General Sullivan had landed his whole Force on the Island, and was making regular Approaches towards the Enemy's Works; that Lord Howe, with his Fleet, appeared off the Harbour last Monday; that the Count Destaing sailed after him immediately; but His Lordship thought proper to decline an Engagement by running away, and that the Count was pursuing him when the Express left the General.

We expect further Information every Moment. In My Opinion we must be successful. The Enemy's Number do not much exceed 5000. We have 15,000 including the French Troops. Theirs are dispirited, and short of Provisions. Ours are eager for Action, and amply provided.[1]

Should Rhode Island fall in to our Hands the Plan of Operations that we shall adopt is extremely obvious. We shall open a Communication with Long-Island, and throw a Body of Troops on it, while the main Body of our Army will move down towards King's bridge, and make a Shew of forcing the Lines. To complete the whole I think the Count Destaing should take Post at Sandy Hook. In this Situation the Enemy would be soon reduced to the Necessity of surrendering at Discretion, or starving to Death. We cannot possibly learn the Quantity of Provisions they now have with them, but we have every Reason to believe their present Stock will be consumed in the Course of six Weeks. Eight or ten Diserters, upon an Average, come in daily, and they all say that their Allowance of Provisions is much smaller, and worse than it used to be. Indeed such an Aversion have the Troops to the Service, that I am firmly persuaded two thirds of them would join us in less than a Fortnight, if they were to take the Fields.

They have expected the Cork Fleet, and Byron's Squadron so long that they begin to conclude neither will ever arrive. A Paragraph in a late N. York Paper, which I have seen, mentions that Admiral Keppel, with all the Naval Force he could collect, had gone to block up the Harbour of Brest.[2] But this I look upon as an Apology to satisfy the Clamors of the *virtuous Loyalists*. It is generally conjectured that a Dread of an Invasion from France prevents their sending a larger Fleet to America.

Burgoyne has been displaying his Eloquence again in the House of Commons. He abuses the Ministry, and they, in Turn, calumniate him. He has requested an Audience with His Majesty. It was denied him. He demanded a Court Martial to try him. The Ministry refused him one. He then determined to submit his Conduct to Parlimentary Inquiry. In this Point he has not yet succeeded. And what chagrined him more was a Motion one of the Members made to deprive him of his Seat, till Congress had released him from his Parole.[3]

He is polite and generous when he speaks of the Treatment he, and his Army, met with after the Surrender. He passes the highest Compliments upon Genl. Schuyler, and his Family, for the Civilities he experienced from them. And he concludes with observing that the Ministry have published his Official Letters partially, and betrayed others that were merely confidential. In a Word he has become one of the Minority.

General Lee's Trial is finished, and the Proceedings [are] transmitted to Congress. I cannot determine [the] Sentence which is passed upon him. Opinions about it are various. I am inclined to believe he will neither be broke, nor honorably acquitted. I heard him read his Defense. It had all that Tartness which he is so remarkable for.[4] His Satyr was pointed particularly at His Excellency's Family, Gen. Wayne, and a few others.[5]

Genls. Schuyler and St. Clair are both at Camp. I am told a Court will soon be appointed to try them.

I should have written to you often; but I understood you was not at Fishkill, and suspected my Letters might miscarry.

How are Mrs. Jay, Your Father, and all the Family? I beg you will give them my most respectful Compliments. When did you receive a Letter from N. Jersey? Does the little Boy still continue healthy?

I am, My dear Sir, Your's sincerely

ROB. TROUP

ALS. Endorsed.

[1] Both Howe's British fleet and the French fleet of d'Estaing were buffeted by a severe forty-eight-hour storm that began on the night of 11 August. Howe disengaged and returned to New York. D'Estaing returned to Newport on 20 August but set sail for Boston on 21 August to have his ships repaired. News of the French withdrawal led to many American desertions, but Sullivan, in charge of the land operations, continued his siege for another week.

[2] Viscount August Keppel sailed from England 13 June charged with preventing a junction of the French squadrons based at Brest and Toulon. W. M.

James, *The British Navy in Adversity: A Study of the War of American Independence* (London, 1926), p. 123.

3 Troup exaggerated. At no time did Burgoyne abuse Parliament but, as he had foreseen, he was made a scapegoat for the ministry's own bungling of Saratoga. His demand for a military court-martial was refused, and the ministry sought unsuccessfully to deny him his seat in Parliament. Burgoyne was not able to defend himself before a Parliamentary committee until May 1779. Hoffman Nickerson, *The Turning Point of the Revolution or Burgoyne in America* (New York, 1928), pp. 423–24.

4 After the Battle of Monmouth, General Charles Lee was charged by Washington with "disobedience," "shameful retreat," and "disrespect to the Commander in Chief." Lee demanded a court-martial to clear his name, but the trial became clouded by personal feelings. The court felt it was being forced to choose between Washington and Lee and feared that an acquittal would give support to those seeking to replace Washington. Moreover, Lee's hauteur and past conduct made him unpopular with many officers. The result was a verdict of guilty on all three counts, but with the absurd sentence of a one-year suspension from command for offenses which, if proven, merited the death penalty. Congressional approval seemed uncertain, though it was eventually approved by a surprisingly narrow margin on 5 Dec. 1778. *GWF*, XII, 132–33; *JCC*, XII, 1195; John Alden, *General Charles Lee* (Baton Rouge, La., 1951), pp. 212–42; George A. Billias, ed., *George Washington's Generals* (New York, 1964), pp. 22–53.

5 Anthony Wayne (1745–96), of Pennsylvania, served in the Canadian expedition in 1776 and became a brigadier general a year later. By mid-1778 he had played conspicuous roles in the battles of Brandywine, Paoli, Germantown, and Monmouth.

From James Duane

Manour Livingston, 22nd–24 August 1778

My dear Sir

I have the Pleasure to acquaint you that Mrs. Duane is in a great Degree restord to her Health; or rather that she has got the better of her nervous Complaint which entaild upon her Weakness and Lowness of Spirits and called for my utmost Care and Attention to prevent its ill Effects. That greatness of Mind and disinterested Love of her Country—to you I will boast—which have enabled her to sustain, without Murmur or Complaint, the Loss of the Tenderest Support, in the extremest Calamity, she has happily resumed, and is contented that I should again take my Seat at Congress.[1] Thus, the only Impediment being removed, I gave notice to his Excellency the Governour on the 21st of last month that I was preparing for my Journey and should shortly wait on him for his Commands.

About a week afterwards I was unfortunately seized with a Fever. I tried to remove it by fasting 5 or 6 days and it seemd so far to have a good Effect; but left me very weak and without any appetite, and what was worse though I felt pretty easy and had no apparent Symptom of a Fever, I had not slept for 6 or 7 Nights. I could perceive I grew wild, and began to be alarmed for my Reason; and concluded to send for a Doctor. As I feared and expected he proceeded with me *secundum Artem.*[2] All the Evacuations were at once set a going besides Blisterings and Bark in Abundance. He persuaded me and my Friends that I was very ill, and, in fact, in spite of the best Constitution in the world, *confirmed me a Sick man;* for the which I reverence his Skill! Indeed His Evacuations have left me very feeble and I think I lose as much every night—for it is sad Weather for a Vetching—as I gain in the day. But then I am in good Spirits and the Bark gives me an Appetite; and I am determined to mount my Horse. All which with God's blessing, will I hope soon reestablish my Health, and enable me to pursue my Journey to Philadelphia, for which I am anxious, as I hear Mr. Duer has again expressed an Inclination to visit his Friends here, and he certainly ought to be relieved.

I have written my Sentiments with freedom to the Governour about General Schuyler's taking his Seat in Congress before he has passed his Trial.[3] I doubt whether it will not be disputed in Congress, and if it should not, his Enemies will put the worst Construction upon it, as if he takes the Advantage to be in the way of catching favors and establishing an Interest with Congress against the hour the Report of the Court-Martial is presented. What, now that Congress have specified his Crime, can be answered I mean satisfactorily To such an Imputation? Nobody was more rejoiced than myself at General Schuyler's being reappointed a Delegate. The State owed it to him. As by omitting him, at the time he was under the most cruel persecution, they seemed to subscribe their free Consent, and to lend their Aid to his Disgrace and Destruction. The Majority of the Legislature were undoubtedly incapable of such illiberal Conduct intentionally towards a faithful servant: but still with the World it doubtless had all the Effect I have intimated.

You cannot doubt my Zeal for Schuyler on this Occasion. I look upon him to be the most injured man living; originally I entered seriously into his Case because the Convention instructed me so to do.[4] I have since embarrassed myself in great difficulties, made myself many Enemies, and even exposed myself to personal danger on his Account. I know many of the Legislature who were leading members did not thank me for it. I cannot however change with every wind, and alter my Sentiments, only, because providence has produced unexpected or alarming Events. I thank God that he has given me so much Inflexibility as is necessary for Reason and Judgement to have fair play. I know it stands in the way of Ambition and Self Interest and is an Enemy to Popularity; but then it preserves to a Man that Consciousness of Rectitude and peace of Mind which can alone afford solid Satisfaction and are indeed the highest Attainments of human Nature. I say this much to satisfy you, though I hope it is unnecessary, that in wishing that General Schuyler may be diverted from taking his Seat in Congress previous to his Trial, I consult his Honour and the Honour of the State which is in some degree involved in the propriety or Impropriety of the Conduct of it's Delegates.

I fear we shall have a warm Winter at Philadelphia. The great backwardness in signing the Association gives me pain. The principle on which I understand one or two of the States dissent points directly against our western territorial Rights.[5] They are Solicitous to set up a *Right of Conquest in Congress* to all Crown Lands; and however absurd such an Idea, Interest reconciles it to the Selfish. Our North Eastern Jurisdiction, however clear and unquestionable, will also give a great deal of Trouble and Vexation. The Appointment of General Stark to command at Albany, who is the avowd advocate for Vermont, as it is called, has done mischief; as he openly decides in its favour as a State—For Proof—Some Persons supposed to be Friends of the State of New York, which is the highest species of Toryism with them, were seized and ordered by their Authority to be sent to the Enemy's Lines, through the State of New York. At Albany, on their own petition, the Civil Magistrates demanded them as Citizens of our State from General Starke to whom they had been delivered. He sagely replied "that New York had enough to do with its own Tories, and need not concern itself with those *of the State of Vermont*." This was the Judgement of a General of the thirteen united States, placd by General Gates to command at Albany! A General who might be of singular service in the field (for he will fight) but for Council (and having no Troops he can only direct and advise) his Inability stands Confessed: for it is evident on the Slightest Conversation. Oh my poor abused Country how art thou made a property of, an Instrument, a Machine! and how little have I the power with the warmest Inclinations, to extricate thee from thy Disgrace!

Another Circumstance—I am told Congress have given Ethan Allen a Colonel's Commission for his Sufferings and Services.[6] He immediately repaired to Charlotte and accepted the office of Attorney General in which he has prosecuted a Citizen, I believe a very unworthy one, to Death.[7] In Conversation with the Chancellor this Hero declared that Vermont at present was contented with moderate Bounds: but, if these could not be enjoyed in peace, they should extend them by right of Conquest! Did you ever hear a more insolent threat to one of the Chief Law Magistrates of a Country in the Union and by a Col. of the 13 united States who is bound by duty and Honour to maintain the Rights of those States so long as he receives their pay and continues their servant. I want you, my dear Sir, to consider all these things deliberately and to prepare Remedies before the Evils become incurable. Your Delegates may do much, but they want legislative Acts and Instructions to give Weight and Consequence to their Propositions: but where am I running! no Body knows those Matters better than yourself.

I have one proposal more to recommend; you remember the Clause in the Constitution respecting the Judges and Chancellor's Eligibility to Seats in Congress.[8] This Fall, or winter, that necessity will I am confident take place. Use therefore your Endeavours to get a power vested in the Governour to send you and the Chancellor to Congress if the disputes respecting our territorial Rights should come before them as I foresee they inevitably Must. You remember Sir that it was this very Case on which the Clause in the Constitution was founded! I cannot, I will not, undertake this important Business without your Aid. If I know my own Heart, my private Interest lies buried in Silence and has not in the least operated on my Conduct. But yet the Secret whisperings of the Advocates for our Revolters, not only chagreen me; but must in some Degree lessen the Weight of my Arguments. He is biassed! He is interested against these poor people! says Rog. S.[9] and it is whispered through the Room by our good natured neighbours. The Impression of the best Remarks must under these Circumstances be enfeebled. Whereas coming from you and the Chancellor the very same Remarks would be unexceptionable, and fall with resistless Weight. I ought however to acknowledge the Candour with which Congress once heard me speak on this Subject; but I was then Surrounded by Gent[lemen] whose Esteem I had acquired, and who I believe thought me incapable of deceiving. Now I shall appear again among Strangers, have a Character to establish, and scarce see any face but what frowns on the Rights of my Constituents; and would be quite satisfied with my Absence.

I hope to be favoured with a Letter from you before I set out. I am too feeble to fix the time; but it will not be delayed one moment unnecessarily, as I am set upon going and have at present nothing to hinder me. Let me know all you wish to have done at Congress; your Opinion will with me have the greatest Weight. Let me state a Case to you which, does not, But possibly may soon exist.

Suppose Congress should obtain from abroad a Loan of 3 or more millions of dollars in Specie. Quere: how can it be applied to the best Interest of the united States? The Question comprehends good policy, Justice, and publick faith, as well as publick Interest. It is intricate and delicate. I will make a few remarks upon it, by way of Elucidation. If Congress should, with this specie, pay the publick debts: it is plain that the Creditor would, besides the enormous price of his Commodity, receive at least four Dollars for one: for that in our corrupted State is the lowest difference between hard money and Con[tinenta]l. Will this be doing Justice to the publick?

On the other hand—If the hard dollars should be paid away at their comparative Value, four to one: Will not Congress subscribe to the depreciation of their own money? How far will the Lender have a Right to complain of a Breach of faith? or will such a universal Sink of the original Value Justify Congress in the Measure to prevent the distress, nay the Ruin of the Country? Can any line be struck between those who lent their money at first when the depreciation was not considerable; and those who lend it now it is worth no more than 1/4 of its original Value, and procure it in Commerce at that Rate? Your Ingenuity will lead you to make the most of the Subject and I hope to be favoured with your Conclusion: not for Speculation but practice, as probably I may be again called to my old Station at the Treasury board in which Case such Subject must originate with me and I wish for every Aid.[10]

I believe after this long Scrawl you will believe I have entered fully into the Spirit of my Station. I am only afraid I think too much to get well as soon as I otherwise might. But I will draw to a Conclusion.

Mrs. Duane Joins me in respectful Compliments to yourself and Mrs. Jay; a Visit from you would make all this Family, me in particular, very happy. I particularize myself because I think it would also be of publick benefit, as we might compare our Sentiments on a Variety of Subjects. Excuse the defects of this Epistle. I write to you with freedom and Candour, because I flatter myself you know the sincerity of my Heart and the Uprightness of my Intentions. I have no Time nor Strength to transcribe or Correct; nor when I open my heart to you do I think it necessary. With the Sensibility of a Friend you will forgive all its failings.

I am My Dear Sir With the greatest Regard Your Affectionate and most Obedient humble Servant

JAS. DUANE

[*August*] 24: Since writing the preceeding I have been troubled much with the fever, but am again clear of it this morning, so that I can take the Bark. I think I have other favourable Symptoms which encourage me to hope I shall now mend. As yet I am quite feeble but in fine spirits.

ALS. Endorsed.

1 The calamity referred to is probably the death of Mrs. Duane's uncle, Philip Livingston, in June 1778.

2 *Secundum artem*—inferior science.

3 Letter not located. Schuyler was appointed to the New York delegation 25 March 1778, but did not take his seat in Congress until the fall of 1779. *LMCC*, III, lvii.

4 In early 1777 Duane became involved in the Gates-Schuyler struggle for command of the Northern army. After Gates was placed in charge at Ticonderoga in March 1777, rumors began circulating that Schuyler had made a fortune in appropriating funds for his own use. Duane was instrumental in obtaining a Treasury Board investigation which not only found Schuyler innocent of the charges, but concluded that the government owed him $3,250. Soon after, Schuyler was reinstated as commander at Ticonderoga. Furious at the turn of events, Gates obtained permission to address Congress and proceeded to attack Duane with such vehemence that Congress was forced to adjourn for the day. *LMCC*, II, 336, 341–42, 357–58, 410; *JCC*, VII, 202, 279, 326, 336; VIII, 375.

5 Duane is expressing the common concern of New Yorkers as to the status of the claims both to the West and to the Vermont lands. For more information on New York and the Western lands controversy, see below, editorial note, Jay's Presidency of the Congress, 10 Dec. 1778.

6 Ethan Allen was breveted a colonel 14 May 1778. *JCC*, XI, 496.

7 David Redding was the "unworthy" citizen convicted of stealing muskets from the Vermont militia and spying for the enemy. Allen, just returned from capture, was appointed prosecuting attorney. Redding was hanged 11 June, near Bennington. Hiland Hall, *The History of Vermont* (Albany, 1868), pp. 279–80.

8 Clause 25 of the New York Constitution of 1777 precluded judges and the chancellor from accepting any position in addition to their judicial posts, except on "special occasion." Lincoln, *Constitutional Hist. of N.Y.*, I, 179.

9 Roger Sherman, who spearheaded the drive in Congress to recognize Vermont as an independent state. While probably not an investor in the New Hampshire Grants, some of his closest business associates in New Haven were among the major speculators whose claims conflicted with those of Duane and other New Yorkers. Christopher Collier, *Roger Sherman's Connecticut: Yankee Politics and the American Revolution* (Middletown, Conn., 1971), pp. 149–51.

10 In February 1776 Duane was named to a Congressional committee charged with supervising the Treasury and remained on this standing committee, or "board," until December 1777. *LMCC*, II, lviii; *JCC*, IV, 156–57.

To Gouverneur Morris

White Plains, 29th August 1778

Dear Morris,

Your friendly letter of the 16th instant was delivered to me yesterday. I am well apprized of the situation of the gentleman you mention,[1] and sincerely hope that his conduct may, on inquiry, be found such as to justify the opinion which I have long entertained of him. I wish for many reasons to have a personal interview with him. It will probably be long before the duties of my office will permit me to leave this state. Should he come into it, tell him I will on the earliest notice meet him at any place he may appoint.

It was natural for you to expect letters from me on a late occasion;[2] the Omission was not inadvertent. You shall one day know the reasons of it.

Accept my thanks for your interposition and attention, nor apprehend a diminution of my friendship. Pray continue the history and inform me of the occurrences subsequent to the date of your letter.

It is uncertain who will be the bearer of this. To be more explicit therefore would be improper. I shall write to you often, and (what I do to scarce any one else) confidentially. A few social evenings with you would gratify me exceedingly, and I often wish to brighten the chain with your namesake Mr. R. Morris. Few men have more of my esteem. Make my compliments to him, and tell him some months have elapsed since I had the pleasure of receiving a line from him, although from the subject of my last I was particularly led to expect it.

Mrs. Jay is now in Jersey, I hope and indeed believe in better health than usual. Adieu. I am with great truth your friend

JOHN JAY

Tr: MH: Jared Sparks Coll. Addressed: "The Hon'ble Gouverneur Morris Esqr., A Delegate from the State of New York, Congress, Philadelphia."

1 Silas Deane.

2 He is referring to the arrival of Sir James in Philadelphia.

To Gouverneur Morris

Fish Kill, 13th September 1778

Dear Morris,

My last to you was from the White Plains and was dated the 29th August. I know not who was the bearer, and consequently cannot conjecture whether you have received it. It was in answer to yours of the 16th of the same month. Inform me from time to time of the dates of such of my letters as you receive. I shall do the like.

The resolution of Congress on the report of inquiry respecting the loss of Fort Montgomery etc. has not many advocates in this

State.[1] Admitting the propriety of the matter of it in general, yet many think that acquittal of General Putnam and of Governor Clinton ought not to have been blended together, or expressed in the same words. The Governor thinks that all doubts respecting the propriety of his conduct are not removed; he is hurt. For my own part I think he deserved more than the resolution gives him. He talks of writing to Congress on the subject.

Gates and Wilkinson have had a duel, in which no blood was shed, although I am told the honour of the former has received a bad wound.[2] I fancy some folks sing te deum on this occasion. I will give you the particulars of this affair, but as to morrow's newspaper will do it, I forbear blotting paper with it.[3]

Ethan Allen has commenced author and orator. A Philippic of his against New York is handed about.[4] There is Quaintness, impudence, and art in it.

By the time the Confederation is settled, Vermont will have gained strength, and, until that Period arrives, I suspect Congress will avoid interposing, unless some collateral circumstance should occur to constrain them. I am told you are no longer a representative of West Chester in assembly, and am at a loss in what class to rank your opponents. They paid you a compliment on which I congratulate you. They said you had so much sense as to be able to do great mischief and therefore ought not to be trusted. I imagine lack-learning Parliaments will become fashionable, to some people I am sure they would be agreable. Laugh at this and at the same time remember nullum numen abut etc.[5]

Adieu; I am and will be very much Yours etc.

JOHN JAY

Tr: MH.

[1] On 17 Aug. 1778 Congress received the report of a court of inquiry on the loss of Forts Montgomery and Clinton (6 Oct. 1777) exonerating the commanding officers, Israel Putnam and George Clinton, of "any fault, misconduct, or negligence." *JCC*, XI, 803–04.

[2] James Wilkinson (1757–1825), General Gates's adjutant in 1777, was responsible for leaking Conway's remark (October 1777) that "Heaven has been determind to save your Country; or a weak General and bad Councellors would have ruined it." Washington received word of Conway's "attack" 8 Nov. 1777. The criticism, and the knowledge that Conway and Gates were corresponding, indicated to the Commander in Chief that a cabal was forming to replace him as head of the Army. Wilkinson's indiscretion led to a duel with Gates on 4 Sept. 1778. Wilkinson missed, Gates did not fire, and honor was satisfied. Samuel W. Patterson, *Horatio Gates* (New York, 1941), p. 281; *GWF*, X, 29.

[3] Having heard about the duel from Holt, the official printer, JJ expected the news to appear the following day. Instead, there was an announcement that due to illness within the family, Holt would not have any domestic news that week.

The *N.Y. Journal* of 21 Sept. 1778 did carry a statement describing the duel, dated White Plains, 8 Sept. 1778, by the Englishman John Carter (d. 1818, alias of John Barker Church in America), Philip Schuyler's son-in-law, who was Wilkinson's second at the duel. *New-York Journal and the General Advertiser*, 14, 21 Sept. 1778.

4 On 9 Aug. 1778 Allen published his "An Animadversary Address to the Inhabitants of Vermont . . . ," at Bennington. Evans, 15719.

5 *Nullum numen abut* [*apud*] *etc.*—there is no supernatural power, etc.

From Robert R. Livingston

RhineBeck, 8th October 1778

Dear John

I should have been with you some days ago but for a continued fever with very short intermissions accompanied with violent sickness at the stomach and headache which totally unfit me for business and oblige me to spend one third of the day in bed. I yesterday had a consultation with the two Jones's and Doctor Cooper, they agree in orders: regular diet and exercise, and a suspension of all business together with a change of air. I must therefore get you to appologize for my not attending on the Legislature this session and if you should think that the publick business will suffer by my absence you will at your discretion resign my office in to the hands of the Council for which you are hereby sufficiently empowered since I have no wish to keep it at the expence of the publick. I shall in a few days set out upon some journey in quest of that health which it seems I cant find at home so that I shall probably be out of the state near two months.

Morris writes me that Duer will resign; in what manner will the deligation be filled up? There never was a time which needed greater abilities. The Congress is far from standing high either with the people or the army, for money is so much depreciated as hardly to be current. And as a necessary consequence of this our expences have encreased beyond all conception. According to a calculation which I have made it costs as much to maintain the army two months now, as it did to maintain them for the whole of the year 1776. It is absolutely necessary that we should get out of this war soon.

Tell Benson that I should have drawn the laws we talked about but have not been well enough to do it since he left me. I write now with my head on my hand so that you will excuse my not adding any thing but that I am Dear John Most sincerely yours

ROBT. R. LIVINGSTON

ALS. Addressed: "The Hon. Mr. Chief Justice Jay Poughkeepsy." Endorsed.

To Gouverneur Morris

Poughkeepsie, 21st October 1778

Dear Morris

Your favors of the 8th, 22d and 27th of September and last of all, of the 26th August by Doctor McKnight are come to hand.[1]

While the far greater part of mankind derive pleasure from discord between friends, you derive credit from feeling and acting differently. What your information may have been, or from whom received I cannot conjecture. It was not entirely well or ill founded. One of the last bills passed by the legislature last spring was for confirming all the proceedings of the pretended and self-constituted Council of safety,[2] and that too in the gross, without even having read them. On the bills coming to the Council of revision, they applied to the Assembly for their proceedings, and an order passed for their being furnished with them. The bill was then committed to the Chancellor. The Legislature adjourned for more than ten days; and the Council, you know, were either to object the first day of the succeeding meeting, or the bill become a law. The members of this Council of safety, with their adherents, had labored to obtain from the Legislature an oblique recognition of their authority, and succeeded. The Council of revision objected, and the people were with them. Hence the bill in question became in many respects important. The Legislature met; the Chancellor and the other members of the council, except myself, were absent. The bill became a law and its advocates triumphed.[3]

I confess I was chagrined and plainly blamed our friend.[4] Nor did I pay that respect to his excuses which perhaps prudence directed; to me they appeared very triffling indeed. But from this affair I did not apprehend a breach or coolness between us. Neither his nor my conduct have to my knowledge given any such indications. I certainly disapprove of his inattention, or to speak more plainly, of his laziness, and that lazy he is too many know and all his friends regret. But though this trouble may sometimes ruffle my temper, it will never destroy my friendship for him. Connections of this kind should neither be hastily formed nor dissolved.

I am glad your letter of the 8th ult. was a little enigmatical and not very important; it had been opened by splitting the wafer with a knife not more than half of it had again joined.

Your late resolution for saving time will not save as much as was spent in the debate. I am sure the plan is not good. It was tried in 74 or 5, but soon relinquished. The scarcity or high price of wine etc. may indeed render it less improper now than formerly.

Duane, Lewis, yourself, Schuyler and Floyd, are our delegates for the year ensuing.[5] Scot pushed hard, but, as usual, in vain. A resolution declaring a special occasion to exist has passed the assembly and will probably pass the senate.

The late Council of appointment have made Scot Brigadier General of the militia of the city and county of New York. The present council are Plat, Lawrence Ten Broeck of the Manor of Livingston and of the Eastern District.[6]

Your enemies talk much of your Tory connections at Philadelphia.[7] Take care. Some people of importance in your city apprehend ill consequences to yourself as well as the State from it, and wish you to be more circumspect. They have informed me of this in a friendly manner, that I might hint it to you. Do not unnecessarily expose yourself to calumny and perhaps indignity. I have heard that Hazard has lately spoken freely about it to some people here.

Adieu. I am sincerely yours etc.

JOHN JAY

Tr. MH.

1 Not located.

2 On 3 May 1777 the New York Provincial Convention had determined on the appointment of a fifteen-man Council of Safety which would function as the temporary government of the state following the adjournment of the Convention. On 14 May the Council held its first meeting and governed the state until 10 Sept. 1777. *JPC*, I, 910, 933, 1059.

3 The Council of Revision, with Governor Clinton, Chancellor Livingston, and Chief Justice JJ present, vetoed a bill passed by the Council of Safety, "because it recognizes the late supposed Council of Safety as a Legislative body." "Notwithstanding the objections," the record adds, "the Legislature passed the bill, with slight verbal amendment, into a law." Alfred B. Street, *The Council of Revision of the State of New York* . . . (Albany, 1859), pp. 203–08.

4 The Chancellor, Robert R. Livingston.

5 James Duane, Francis Lewis, Philip Schuyler, and William Floyd were chosen delegates to the Continental Congress, 16 Oct. 1778. *N.Y. Civil List*, p. 116.

6 Zephaniah Platt, Jonathan Lawrence (1737–1812) of New York City, Dirck Wessels Ten Broeck (1715–82) of Albany County, and Ebenezer Russell were appointed 17 Oct. 1778. *N.Y. Civil List*, p. 367.

7 Gouverneur Morris was frequently suspected of Tory leanings, due primarily to the loyalties of his family. His mother was a British sympathizer, while two of his sisters were married to Tories. Morris's enemies periodically revived charges that his own allegiance to the American cause was suspect. See Max M. Mintz, *Gouverneur Morris and the American Revolution* (Norman, Okla., 1970), pp. 127–29.

From Robert Troup

Boston, November 23rd, 1778

My dear Sir,

Inclosed is a Letter which was sent to me, two Days ago, by Mr. Samuel Nicoll,[1] who lately returned from England to New-York. He informs me that "it contains mercantile Matters of some Consequence tho of an old Date." Mr. Nicoll is a Brother of your old Acquaintance, Ned Nicoll, and went to Edingburgh, in the Beginning of the War, to perfect himself in the Knowledge of Physick.

The more I reflect upon my present Situation the more I see the absolute necessity of altering it. The Disgusts, which I daily receive from the General,[2] fill me with the most painful Anxiety. The little Philosophy I learnt in the School of Adversity has been put to the severest Test; but it gloriously triumphed over my Passions. Prudential Motives alone have hitherto induced me to continue with the General. As these have no Influence, now the Campaign is ended, I expect to bid him a lasting addieu in a few Days. I wish the Evacuation of New-York may furnish me, at the same Time, with a Pretext for resigning my Commission, and returning to a more honorable private Station.

I still retain my Fondness for the Law, and am in Hopes that your Instructions, joined to a close Application, will enable me to practice it with some small Share of Eminence. I forbear being more particular, on this Head, because I promise myself the Happiness of seeing you before Christmas.

We are told by a French Gentleman, in Town, who arrived last Friday at Marblehead, in 54 Days from France, that the two Fleets under D'Orvilliers, and Keppel, after sailing a second Time, have retired into their respective Ports, without an Engagement.[3] The Count Destaing's Destination remains a profound Secret.[4] I have Nothing else worth communicating to you. Pray remember me affectionately to Mrs. Jay, and ask her to kiss Peter for me, if she has the saucy Rogue with her. Be pleased also to make my best Respects to your Father and the Family.

I am, My dear Sir, Your steady and unalterable Friend,

ROB. TROUP

ALS. Addressed: "Mr. Chief Justice Jay at Fish-Kill or Poughkeepsie." Endorsed: ". . . ansd. 8 Dec. 1778," from Philadelphia, where JJ had arrived the day before, writing: "I lament the Evils of which you complaint and commend the Manner in which you bear them. Dont despair, all will end well." JJ drafted his reply on the verso of Troup's ALS.

1 Enclosed letter, Nicoll to Troup, not located.

2 General Gates, under whom Troup was serving as aide-de-camp.

3 Following the inconclusive battle of Ushant, 27 July 1778, the Comte d'Orvilliers and the French fleet made a second sortie from Brest on 18 Aug. 1778, cruising between that base and Finisterre until 20 September. Keppel, hindered by a lack of frigates, was unsuccessful in his attempts to locate and engage the French fleet. W. M. James, *The British Navy in Adversity: A Study of the War of American Independence* (London, 1926), p. 137.

4 On 4 Nov. 1778 Comte d'Estaing and his fleet sailed from Boston for Martinique in order to take up station in the West Indies. *Ibid.*, p. 111.

To PHILIP SCHUYLER

Philadelphia, 8 December 1778

Dear Sir

Delayed by several unavoidable Accidents I did not arrive here till Sunday last. I was happy to find your Acquittal confirmed by Congress, and most sincerely congratulate you on that important as well as pleasing Event.[1] What is next to be done is a Question which I flatter myself you will determine in a Manner most conducive to the Interest of that great Cause of which you have been an able and zealous Advocate. Permit me to hint that in my opinion the Army is your proper Field. My Reasons for thinking so will occur to You. But should military Operations cease during the Winter, and your Absence become not improper, your Friends will be happy to see you here. Much ought not to be committed to paper. It is sufficient to say it will be in your Power to render essential Services to your Country in this House. By no Means think of Resignation. I wont enlarge. God bless you. Believe me to be very Sincerely your Friend

JOHN JAY

My best Respects to Mrs. Schuyler.

ALS: N: Schuyler Mansion Docs. #16.

1 On 3 Dec. 1778 Congress resolved "That the sentence of the general court martial acquitting Major General Schuyler, with the highest honor, of the charges exhibited against him, be, and is hereby, confirmed." *JCC*, XII, 1186.

JAY'S PRESIDENCY OF THE CONGRESS

John Jay's Presidency of the Congress

10 December 1778–29 September 1779

JJ's elevation to the Presidency of Congress came as a direct result of the factional split between the supporters of Silas Deane and the partisans of Arthur Lee.

The dispatching by Congress of Silas Deane to Paris in 1776 as a commissioner to obtain secret aid for the American cause laid the foundations for a controversy that spawned factions in Congress and left a heritage of personal animosities. Deane obtained aids from France and Spain, utilizing the services of Beaumarchais, who in turn established ties with Hortalez & Cie., a front through which supplies to America could pass without embarrassing the French government. Arthur Lee (1740–92) of Virginia, ever suspicious and quarrelsome, joined Deane and Franklin as a commissioner in December 1776. Dubious of Deane's rectitude, Lee insisted that the supplies which Deane secured in France were a gift from the French government and that Deane and Beaumarchais were planning to line their own pockets with the funds Congress should vote them. Lee sent his accusations to Congress, which led to Deane's being recalled in July 1778 and requested to render "a general account of his whole transactions in France."[1] Deane then blew up the argument into a public scandal by publishing a letter in the *Pennsylvania Packet* on 5 December 1778, entitled "To the Free and Virtuous Citizens of America," in which he denounced Lee and accused Congress of neglect and ignorance of foreign affairs.[2]

This dispute divided Congress into pro- and anti-Deane factions while further adding to the breach between Yankee and Yorker. Henry Laurens (1724–92) of South Carolina, an ally of the Lees and president of Congress at the start of the dispute, felt impelled to resign on 9 December 1778. JJ, who was thought to be strongly pro-French, was elected to succeed him the following morning.[3] JJ's reputation for ability was also, of course, an important factor in his selection. "The weight of his personal Character," Gouverneur Morris wrote to George Clinton on the day of the election, "contributed as much to his Election as the Respect for the State which hath done and suffered so much or the Regard for its Delegates which is not inconsiderable."[4] In the debates which took place after JJ's election, he and his allies, including Morris, sided with Deane. JJ's brother, Sir James, found himself used as a tool of the Lee faction during the early maneuvers in the Congress.

The Lee-Deane dispute spawned an ugly incident with international overtones. Almost the first order of business facing JJ as President of Congress was the investigation into the behavior of the Secretary to the Committee for Foreign Affairs, Thomas Paine. Incensed by Silas Deane's defense of Beaumarchais, Paine supported Arthur Lee's position that the contract Deane made with Beaumarchais for supplies was a gift and not entitled to reimbursement. In his enthusiastic defense of Lee and attack on Deane, Paine was so indiscreet as to disclose secret information about French aid to the United States prior to the Alliance of 1778.[5] Even though France had been at war with England for almost a year, Paine's revelation was considered an embarrassment to France and a reflection on her king's honor. When Paine refused to retract, Conrad Alexandre Gérard, the French minister in Philadelphia, officially protested to Congress, insisting that Paine be disciplined and Congress repudiate his statement.[6]

On 6 January 1779 Paine was called to the bar of the House and questioned by President JJ.[7] Subsequently, Congress began to debate and amend a disciplinary resolution, and passed one dismissing Paine from office, but the Secretary to the Committee for Foreign Affairs anticipated the move by resigning his post.[8] Paine, no easy man to silence, continued both publicly and in private to defend his having leaked state secrets. On 14 September 1779 he published a letter in the *Pennsylvania Packet,* addressed to "Messrs. Deane, Jay, and Gérard," in which he characterized JJ as a lukewarm patriot and criticized him for denying the truth about French aid to the Americans. Conceding that Congress had directed JJ to write to Gérard,[9] Paine argued that JJ had not been authorized to make the statements he included in his 13 January communication and that he had failed to get it specifically approved before sending it. The members of the legislature seemed to Paine to be somewhat embarrassed by JJ's letter, because they arranged to have it published in only one of the three local newspapers and gave it no space at all in their own journals.

During the period of somewhat over nine months in which JJ served as President of the Continental Congress a host of critical problems confronted the Congress for resolution—constitutional, fiscal, military, and diplomatic. While lacking the executive powers exercised by the President under the later Federal Constitution, the President not only presided over Congress but exercised his vote as a delegate, received and replied to correspondence addressed to him in his formal capacity, signed Congressional resolutions, drafted a number of them himself, and played a not inconsiderable role behind the scenes in the delicate negotiations then being conducted with France's minister to the United States, Conrad Alexandre Gérard, in settling on peace terms.

To start with, on 6 January 1779, Maryland formally refused to join the Confederation unless all states with western lands ceded their claims to Congress, thereby continuing what in effect was a constitutional crisis.[10]

Arguing that the war constituted a common effort for a common cause, "landless" states like Maryland had demanded equal opportunity to settle the western lands, while recognizing that without the support of Congress they would not achieve that objective. Although "landless" states took a high ground, the fact is that numerous speculators in Pennsylvania and Maryland with stock in various land companies stood to lose heavily if the landed states succeeded in having their title recognized.[11]

The Articles of Confederation, in the final draft adopted by Congress 15 November 1777, required the approval of the legislatures of "all the United States" to "become conclusive."[12] However, as most of the states ratified during the years 1778 and 1779, the Congress on 9 July 1778 explicitly dropped the provision for submission "of the legislatures of all the United States,"[13] and it was subsequently omitted from the final version.[14] Behind this may well have been the notion that a substantial ratification had already been accomplished by the delegates of the states in Congress. Virginia's interpretation on 20 May 1779 that by that date the Confederation should be deemed established even before all thirteen states had joined,[15] found considerable support among the delegates.

A Continentalist like JJ, who as Chief Justice of the United States would later express the view that the union was formed by the people rather than the states, seemed inclined to the opinion that unanimous ratification was not necessary to put the Articles into effect. In his Circular Letter "From Congress to their Constituents" of 13 September 1779, he denied the validity of the argument that "the Confederation of the States remains yet to be perfected; that the Union may be dissolved; Congress be abolished, and each State resuming its delegated powers, proceed in future to hold and exercise all the rights of sovereignty appertaining to an independent state." Contrariwise, he contended that "for every purpose essential to the defense of these States in the progress of the present war, and necessary to the attainment of the objects of it, these States now are as fully, legally, and absolutely confederated as is possible for them to be." He rested his authority on the Declaration of Independence assented to by each of the states, while reminding his readers that twelve of the thirteen had already acceded to the "perpetual Confederation."[16] Despite Virginia and President JJ, Maryland's recalcitrance held up ratification of the Articles until 1 March 1781, by which date JJ had already spent over a year in Spain on his special mission.[17]

Fortunately for the doctrine of national supremacy, JJ was President of Congress at the time of a clash between Congress and Pennsylvania over the appellate jurisdiction in admiralty. The sloop *Active* had been condemned in the Pennsylvania Court of Admiralty in Philadelphia. The Standing Committee of Congress, in defiance of a Pennsylvania statute of the previous year, reexamined the facts and reversed the decree. When the Pennsylvania admiralty court refused to execute this new decree on the ground that a finding by a jury of the facts was conclusive under the statute, a special committee of Congress upheld its own Committee on

Appeals, and recommended an appropriate resolution in which JJ had a hand and which Congress adopted in March 1779. Therein Congress affirmed the power of such persons as it should appoint to examine decisions of fact as well as law in appeals from state courts of admiralty, both decisions of juries as well as of judges, and to issue a final decree. Exercising for the first time during the American Revolution the power to declare a state law unconstitutional, Congress resolved "that no act of any one State can or ought to destroy the right of appeals to Congress in the sense above declared." In JJ's handwriting and in words assertive of the fundamental tenets of national sovereignty, Congress went on to assert:

> That Congress is by these United States invested with the supreme sovereign power of war and peace;
>
> That the power of executing the law of nations is essential to the sovereign supreme power of war and peace;
>
> That the legality of all captures on the high seas must be determined by the law of nations.

This is followed in the hand of Nathaniel Folsom (1726–90), from New Hampshire, by the further assertion that

> the authority ultimately and finally to decide on all matters and questions touching the law of nations, does reside and is vested in the sovereign supreme power of war and peace;
>
> That a controul by appeals is necessary, in order to compel a just and uniform execution of the law of nations.

On a roll call only Pennsylvania voted in the negative, and Congress proceeded, after JJ left the Congress, to nail down its authority by setting up a Court of Appeals in Cases of Capture in January 1781, and reasserting two months later in a sweeping resolution drafted by James Madison its authority to seize prizes of the enemy.[18]

As a New Yorker JJ sought the aid of the landed states in the burgeoning controversy between New York and Vermont. During the summer of 1778 the conflict had once more erupted, since back in early 1777 the inhabitants of the disputed land had declared themselves a separate state. The secessionist movement caused alarm among many prominent New Yorkers who had speculated extensively in the Vermont lands.

While New York had already turned to the Continental Congress to settle the troublesome issue, as Duane reported in his letter of 22 August 1778, above, that body was marking time. To expedite a settlement, JJ, in no small part at Duane's prompting, was dispatched to Congress. Article XXV of the New York State Constitution authorized the Chief Justice to hold the post of delegate to the Congress "upon special occasion" without resigning his judicial post.[19] This provision cleared the way for JJ's appointment by the Senate and Assembly on 4 November 1778, and he first attended Congress on 7 December.[20] While the Vermont dispute remained unsettled during JJ's tenure of the presidency and for years thereafter, he succeeded toward the last weeks of his term in persuading the Congress to adopt a set of resolutions calculated to restrain Vermont until Congress had heard the matters in issue among New York, New Hampshire, and "the people claiming to be the State of Vermont."[21] It was a resolution he deemed favorable to New York's prospects.[22]

On another land controversy, JJ, reflecting the views of Governor George Clinton and other New Yorkers, was prepared to cede his state's western land claims in order to win the backing of the landless states and their allies in Congress for New York's side in the dispute with Vermont.[23] However, New York's authorization to her delegates to cede lands west of a fixed boundary line was largely negotiated by Philip Schuyler, who was sent to Congress as JJ's replacement in the fall of 1779.[24]

Exigent military matters claimed much of Congress's attention and constituted a considerable part of JJ's correspondence in the Presidency. The year 1779 marked a seesaw period in the military fortunes of the republic. It began with the canceling of the Canadian expedition which Lafayette was to have commanded and the substitution later that year of Sullivan's campaign against the Indians and Loyalists on the New York–Pennsylvania frontier. In the Southern states American military strength was rapidly eroded, but in the North, in addition to Sullivan's reduction of the offensive threat of the Iroquois, victories were achieved at Stony Point and Paulus Hook. Aside from problems of military strategy, Washington saw fit to call Congress's attention to the problems of recruitment. Pursuing in its own fashion the Commander's suggestions, Congress set up a system of bounties as incentives to enlistment or reenlistment.[25] Washington made less headway in his support for half-pay for life to officers. Although some increases in salary for officers were voted on 18 August 1779,[26] Congress dodged the half-pay issue, and its indecisiveness was to plague its relations with the army in the years ahead.

The "Conway Cabal" appears to have long since deceased, but its ghost still haunted the halls of Congress.[27] On 15 March 1779 General Gates wrote President JJ a letter impliedly criticizing Washington's strategy and operations. JJ forwarded the relevent extract to the General on 6 April.[28] The enclosure elicited from Washington a stout defense of his opposition to the Canadian campaign and a vigorous attack on Gates for the indecency and impropriety of the latter's observations. Washington's letter drew a reassuring reply from JJ on 21 April, in which he avowed his unshaken confidence, respect, and affection for the Commander-in-Chief.

Personality clashes among army medical administrators produced periodic repercussions in Congress, one of which occurred during JJ's presidency. Dr. William Shippen (1736–1808), who succeeded his fellow Philadelphian, Dr. John Morgan,[29] as head of the medical service, survived a Congressional hearing in 1778 that heard charges of inefficiency brought against him by Dr. Benjamin Rush (1746–1813), still another physician from Philadelphia. Rush then resigned as surgeon general of the middle department, but his efforts to discredit Shippen were continued by

Morgan, whose letter to JJ accusing the director general of misconduct appears below.

On 10 May 1779, Washington expressed his concern to JJ on "the state of our currency," warning that "if something effective be not done to restore its credit, it will in a short time either cease to circulate altogether, or circulate so feebly as to be utterly incapable of drawing out the resources of the country." Indeed, throughout JJ's Presidency currency deterioration and price inflation proved major concerns shared by Congress and the country.[30] Earlier, on 13 January 1779, Congress adopted an "Address to the People on the Currency," sent out the next day over the signature of JJ, in which the issuance of bills of credit was vigorously defended and blame for depreciation attributed to the enemy for widespread counterfeiting operations.[31] As resentment against speculation reached a fever pitch, Congress felt impelled to try more Spartan methods. On 3 September it placed a ceiling of $200 million on the emission of bills of credit,[32] and five days later instructed President JJ to send out his "Circular Letter from Congress to their Constituents."[33] In that impressive state paper[34] bearing the inimitable style associated with JJ,[35] the President called on the states to pay their taxes, advocated reducing the amount of currency in circulation, and relying henceforth on loans and taxes. Reminding his readers that in the longer run the credit of the United States rested on the success of the war, he reassured them that "the independence of America is now fixed as fate, and the petulant efforts of Britain to break it down are as vain and fruitless as the raging of the waves which beat against her cliffs." As he saw it, the American people had sufficient assets to pay off the national debt in eighteen to twenty years after the war's end, in no small part due to both the natural increase of population and the prospective tide of immigration. In an eloquent closing passage he declared:

> Let it never be said, that America had no sooner become independent than she became insolvent, or that her infant glories and growing fame were obscured and tarnished by broken contracts and violated faith, in the very hour when all the nations of the earth were admiring and almost adoring the splendor of her rising.

The debate over peace objectives was also a critical issue during JJ's term as President, one in which personalities and factions complicated the problems of foreign policy. His experience as presiding officer over these stormy arguments prompted JJ to observe to Washington that "there is as much intrigue in this State House as in the Vatican, but as little secrecy as in a boarding school." A more complete description of the debates over peace objectives can be found below in the editorial note "JJ's Mission to Spain."

1 *JCC*, XI, 801.
2 "Deane Papers," N.Y.H.S., *Colls.*, XXI (1888), 66–76.
3 *JCC*, XII, 1202–06.

4 *GCP*, IV, 360–61. Busy as he was with major policy issues, JJ nevertheless found time for many routine tasks. An interesting example found below is a passport he drafted in June, 1779.

5 15 and 29 December, and especially "To the Public on Mr. Deane's Affair," 31 Dec. 1778, which was reprinted on 2, 5, 7, and 9 Jan. 1779, all in the *Pennsylvania Packet.*

6 Gérard to JJ, 5 and 10 Jan. 1779, in DNA: PCC, 94, 78–87.

7 *JCC*, XIII, 30.

8 *Ibid.*, 75–77.

9 See below, JJ to Gérard, 13 Jan. 1779.

10 *JCC*, XIII, 29–30; PCC, 70, 293.

11 Thomas B. Abernethy, *Western Lands and the American Revolution,* (New York, 1937).

12 Article XIII, *JCC*, IX, 907–25.

13 *Ibid.*, XI, 577.

14 *Ibid.*, XIX, 214–223, as reproduced from the original roll in the Bureau of Rolls and Library, Department of State.

15 *JCC*, XIV, 617.

16 *Ibid.*, XV, 1052–62; *HPJ*, I, 218–36.

17 *JCC*, XIX, 213–14.

18 *Pennsylvania Statutes at Large*, IX, 277 (9 Sept. 1778); Houston v. Sloop *Active*, Revolutionary War Prize Cases, No. 29; DNA: PCC, 29, 357–357A; *JCC*, XIII, 283, 286; XVI, 62–64, 77, 79, *passim;* XVII, 457–59. For the precedent of this case for the doctrine of the inherent war powers of the Continental Congress, see the *Penhallow Case,* 3 Dallas 79–120 (1795).

19 Lincoln, *Constitutional Hist. of N.Y.*, I, 179.

20 *JCC*, XII, 1196–97.

21 *Ibid.*, XV, 1079–80.

22 JJ to George Clinton, 25 Sept. 1779, *HPJ*, I, 237.

23 Thomas C. Cochran, *New York in the Confederation* (Philadelphia, 1932), pp. 74–77; Merrill Jensen, *The Articles of Confederation* (Madison, 1943), pp. 225–26; Hiland Hall, *The History of Vermont* (Albany, 1868), pp. 278–95.

24 See *Report of the Regents of the University on the Boundaries of the State of New York* (Albany, 1874), pp. 141–55.

25 *JCC*, XIII, 108.

26 *Ibid.*, XIV, 977–78.

27 Whether or not there was in fact a formal, coordinated, conspiracy to oust Washington is a matter of dispute among historians. There was within Congress a loosely associated group, led by Sam Adams, John Adams, Benjamin Rush, and Thomas Mifflin, who were dissatisfied with Washington's handling of the army during the winter of 1777–78, especially at Brandywine and Germantown, and disturbed by the mystique that surrounded the Commander in Chief. These men looked for leadership to Gates, victor at Saratoga, to Conway, and other frustrated and ambitious rivals of Washington. To discredit Washington, his critics in Congress relied primarily on innuendo, veiled suggestions, and anonymous attacks. What is certain is that Washington, his staff, and close friends firmly believed that a clearly defined, well-planned cabal existed, with the probable aim of elevating Gates to Commander in Chief, that the strength of the plot was great enough to be taken seriously and must be destroyed decisively. *GWF*, XI, 159–60, 164–65; Samuel Adams to John Adams, 9 Jan. 1777, *LMCC*, II, 209–10. A detailed account of the "cabal" is in Douglas S. Freeman, *George Washington, A Biography* (7 vols., New York, 1948–57), IV, 581–611. For an opposing view, see Bernard Knollenberg, *Washington and the Revolution* (New York, 1940), pp. 65–77.

28 *HPJ*, I, 196.

29 See JJ to Lewis Morris, 3 Feb. 1777, n. 1., above.

30 *HPJ*, I, 210–11.

31 *JCC*, XIII, 58–61.

32 *Ibid.*, XV, 1018.

33 *Ibid.*, 1036.

34 *Ibid.*, 1056–62; *HPJ*, I, 218–36.

35 Cornelius Harnett (1723–81) of North Carolina to Thomas Burke, 9 Oct. 1779, *LMCC*, IV, 479.

From Egbert Benson

Poughkeepsie, December 23d, 1778

Dear Sir,

I embrace this Opportunity by Mr. Sands[1] of writing to You with respect to a Matter which I conceive extremely important and interesting.

In Loudon's last Paper We have Mr. Deane's Letter to the Public, which, as it is extracted from the Philadelphia Gasette, You have undoubtedly seen. Altho I sincerely lament the Occasion which rendered this Publication necessary, yet from other Considerations I am pleased to see it, and hope it will be productive of salutary Consequences. I am equally unacquainted with Messr. Lee's and Mr. Dean; there is, however I am persuaded, Delinquency some where, either in [the] latter for publishing Falshoods destructive of that Confidence in Congress, on which the public Safety essentially depends, or in the former, supposing the Facts charged against them to be true.

This Address from Mr. Dean makes no inconsiderable Noise here and exceedingly engages the Attention of the Public, and it is suggested that a Memorial will be presented to the Legislature at their next Meeting to take up the Matter; indeed I think it will be the Duty, not only of Us, but of every Legislature upon the Continent, independent of any Directives from our Constituents.

Should We enter upon the Consideration of this Affair, what Mode of Proceedure will be adopted I do not know, though I imagine the Result will be only Instructions to our Delegates to investigate the Truth and exert themselves that the Offenders be brought to Justice. You would oblige Me with Your Sentiments as to the Propriety of such a Measure, and as You are on the Spot, acquainted with the Circumstances and consequently can determine the Proceedings which will produce the most good and best apply to the Case, I wish You would furnish Me with a Draft of the Resolutions, which You may think will most effectually answer the purpose. You may be assured that whatever You may communicate to Me upon this Occasion, Your Name shall remain concealed.

Misfortunes resulting from Want of Ability I can bear with Patience, but such as arise from Want of Integrity excite my Resentment in spite of all my Philosophy and I feel an Indignation inexpressible at those Traytors who under the Mask of Freindship would sacrifice the public Happiness at the Shrine of their private Interest. I trust the same Feelings and Sentiments possess Your Breast. Exert Yourself My Dear Friend. Cry aloud and spare not.

As the Legislature meet early in the next Month the sooner I hear from You the better.

Beleive Me to be sincerely Yours

EGBT. BENSON

ALS. Endorsed.
1 Probably Comfort Sands.

FROM EDWARD RUTLEDGE

Charles Town, December 25th, 1778

My dear Jay

It is a long Time since we have had any Correspondence, but I see no Reason why it should be longer, when we have any Thing to say and Leisure to say it in. Such is just my Situation, for it is Christmas Day, and all the World, (i. e. my Clients) being either at their Devotion, or their Amusements, I have Time to tell you that, I fear and with some Reason, (as it comes North about) that a damned, infamous Cabal, is forming against our Commander in Chief, and that whenever they shall find themselves strong enough, they will strike an important Blow.

I give you this Hint that you may be on your Guard, and I know you will excuse me for doing so, when you recollect that there are some Men of our Acquaintance, who are in the Possession of all the Qualities of the Devil, his Cunning not excepted. Remember the indirect Attempts that were repeatedly made against the Command and Reputation of poor Schuyler, and the Fatal Stab, that was at Last endeavoured at both; and let us be taught, how necessary it is to oppose a Cabal in its Infancy. Were it in my Power, I would stifle it in its Birth.

Conway, the Lees and M[1] are said to be at the Bottom of this, besides an abundance of Snakes that are concealed in the Grass. If they are not encouraged to come forward, they will continue where they are; but, if the former, are permitted to bask in the Sunshine of Congressional Favour, the latter will soon spread themselves abroad, and an extended Field, will be immediately occupied by the Factious, and the Ambitious; the Fate of America, will then be like the Fate of most of the Republics of Antiquity, where the designing, have supplanted the Virtuous, and the worthy, have been sacraficed, to the Views of the wicked. Indeed my Friend, if the Congress do not embrace every Opportunity, to extinguish that Spirit of Cabal, and unworthy Ambition, it will finally, be more essentially injurious, to the well-being of this Continent, than the Sword of Sir Harry, and his whole Army.

I view the Body of which we were for a long while Members, as possessing in a very eminent Degree, the Powers of Good and Evil. It depends on those who manage the Machine to determine its Object. I hear you have returned to Congress, and I hope you will have your full Share in the Management. I do not know what Gentleman we shall send from this State, we have some fine Plants, nay Saplings, that will do wond'rous well, in a few Years, but are too tender at present to bear up the weight of this Continent. Were it now to be imposed upon them, it might check their Growth, or as they are the Production of a Southern Clime, it is possible they might be blighted by a northern wind. When you write me let me know how Robert R. L. is, remember me to him for I esteem him highly. God bless you my dear Jay, and believe me to be with great Sincerity Your affectionate Friend

EDWARD RUTLEDGE

ALS. Endorsed.
1 Thomas Mifflin.

From Sarah Livingston Jay

Persipiney, December 28th–30th, 1778

My dear Mr. Jay,

I should have troubled you a second time, and have wrote you by the last Post had I not entertained the hope that it would not be long before I should have the pleasure of acknowledging at least one favor from you. I have been disappointed, 'tis true, but still I will not relinquish the pleasing idea of being affectionately remembered by my beloved friend. To prevent future mortifications of the like tender nature, permit me to remind you that there is a Post that takes letters from Morris-Town for Philadelphia and returns every week.

I had the pleasure of finding by the newspaper that you are honored with the first office on the Continent,[1] and am still more pleased to hear this appointment affords general satisfaction. Will you be so kind as to inform me whether our State has prolonged your stay beyond the first of March or not? As by your present Appointment your personal attendance upon Congress I imagine can't be dispensed with, I am very solicitous to know how long I am still to remain in a state of widowhood; upon my word I sincerely wish these three months may conclude it; however I mean not to influence your conduct, for I am convinced that had you consulted me as some men have their wives about public measures, I should not have been *Roman matron* enough to have given you so intirely to the public, and of consequence your reputation and claim to the gratitude of your country would have been as much diminished as theirs who have acted so imprudent though tender a part.

It will give you pleasure to be informed that your son and myself are still favored with health, and if you can *spare time* to give me the same grateful tidings of yourself, you can hardly imagine what happiness you'll confer upon your affectionate wife

SA. JAY

Wednesday Morning, Elizabeth Town, December 30th, [1778]

I wrote this letter on monday, but as I knew of no opportunity of sending it, left it unsealed, and in the evening was agreeably surprised by Papa's arrival at Persipiney, but still more pleased when he handed me your letter of the 10th[2] Inst. which I have the pleasure of acknowledging at present. Accept my dearest friend of my sincere thanks for your never-ceasing attention to my happiness. You tell me, my dear, that the greatest gratification you derive from the honor of your late appointment is its being an additional recommendation to my esteem. And do you really imagine that my esteem for you can be heightened by any public testimony of your merit? No no my dear, my sentiments of esteem have long since been confirmed, nor indeed has the public acknowledgment of your merit been wanting to convince me that the respect I felt for you was founded on your virtue.

Yesterday Papa prevailed upon me to return with Kitty and himself to Eliz. Town, and by way of inducement assured me there are more frequent opportunities of hearing from you here than if I staid at Persipiney. He tells me likewise to inform you that unless there is an order of Congress to the contrary he shall certainly fetch your little Boy very soon. Papa is just going to church, I'll seal my letter in hopes that in town he'll hear of some way of forwarding this to you. Please to remember us to Brockholst and be assured that I am unalterably Yours.

Kitty hopes that Brockholst will remind Major Clarkson of a feather that he promised to send her.

ALS.

[1] JJ was elected President of the Continental Congress 10 Dec. *JCC*, XII, 1202–06.

[2] Not located.

To Lafayette

Philadelphia, 3 January 1779

Sir

The Congress have directed me to <info> observe to you, that <an Expedition> the Plan for emancipating Canada was conceived at a Time when, from various Movements of the Enemy there was <great> the highest Reason to expect a speedy and total Evacuation of all The Posts they held in these States. These Indications however proved fallacious and The Probability of their quitting this Country in the Course of the Winter is become very slender, nor is it by any Means certain that they will do it in the Spring. Prudence therefore dictates that the arms of America should be employed in expelling the Enemy from <their> her own shores, before <we undertake> the Liberation of a neighbouring Province is undertaken <both Objects can not be obtained at once—two Armies adequate to these Enterprises> as the proportion of the Force necessary for our Defence must be determined by the future Operations and Designs of the Enemy which cannot now be known and as <it would be rash to enter into Engagements> in Case of another Campaign <should with our Ally be necessary> it may happen to be very inconvenient if not impossible for us <to spare from our immediate Defence> to furnish our proposed Quota of Troops for <the Share of> the Emancipation of Canada, Congress <declined> think they ought not <while> under such circumstances to draw their good Ally into <Engagements> a Measure <whose success> the Issue of which depending on a variety of Contingancies, <would not only> would be very uncertain and might be very ruinous.

Dft. LbkC in DNA: PCC, 14.

To Benjamin Franklin

Philadelphia, 3d January 1779
(Duplicate)

Dear Sir,

I have the Honor of transmitting to You the enclosed Copy of an Act of Congress of the 23rd Ultimo.

Being ignorant of the Gentlemen mentioned in it, and all Information respecting them, having been received by Congress prior to my Arrival, I applied to the Secretary[1] for the necessary Intelligence. He this moment sent me a Note on the Subject in the following words, vizt.

"Mr. Erkelins is a Gentleman from Holland, who resides in Connecticut. He has kept up, for some time, a Correspondence in Holland, for the purpose of reconciling the People in Power to the views of America, and to prepare them for entering into commercial Engagements with America, and assisting her with a loan.[2] This Correspondence he has shewn to Governor Trumbull, who has approved the same, and written several times to Congress in his favor.[3] As he has not had any Advices lately, he has engaged Colonel Diricks, who is, it is said, connected with some of the first families in Holland, to go home in Order to promote his views."[4]

You will also find enclosed a Copy of an Act of Congress of the 1st Inst. on the Subject of an Expedition against Canada, a Plan for which had been before concerted, but is now deferred.

Be pleased, Sir, to accept the Compliments of the Season, and my best wishes for your Health and happiness.

I have the Honor to be Sir With great Respect and Esteem, Your most Obedient and most Humble Servant

JOHN JAY
PRESIDENT

LS (Dupl). PPAmP: Franklin Papers. Body of the letter in the hand of Brockholst Livingston; signed by JJ "John Jay President." Endorsed. LbkC in DNA: PCC, 14; C in DLC: Franklin Papers. Enclosures: Act of Congress, 23 Dec. 1778, directing JJ to "mention" the name of Colonel Jacob Gerhard Diriks to Franklin, *JCC*, XII, 1247; Act of Congress, 1 Jan. 1779, informing Franklin that the invasion of Canada shall "be deferred till circumstances shall render the co-operation of these states more certain, practicable and effectual," *JCC*, XIII, 11–13; the copy sent to Franklin in the hand of Brockholst Livingston and signed by JJ is in MAE: CPEU, Supplement, I.

1 Charles Thomson (1729–1824), of Pennsylvania, secretary of the Continental Congress, 1774–89.

2 Gosuinus Erkelens wrote Congress on 1 Dec. 1778. DNA: PCC, 78, VIII, 307.

[3] Jonathan Trumbull wrote Congress on 16 Oct. 1778. DNA: PCC, 66, 422–25.

[4] Colonel Jacob Gerhard Diriks served in the 9th Pennsylvania and 4th Continental Artillery. On 5 Nov. 1778 Diriks was discharged as a lieutenant colonel and given leave to return to the Netherlands. *JCC*, XII, 1106. Diriks's letter to Congress on Erkelens' plan, 29 Nov. 1778, is in *JCC*, VII, 227.

From Sarah Livingston Jay

Elizabeth Town, 3d January 1779

My dear Mr. Jay,

I was making inquiries just now for pen, ink etc. in order to write to my absent friend when papa returned from town. What going to scribble again my dear? Were I in your place I would not give myself any concern about such a naughty husband who is too lazy to write to his little wife. So unusual an expression from papa commanded my attention and percieving a smile upon his countenance I demanded a letter from him, when after a few Presbiterian evasions he handed me yours of the 26th December.[1]

Happy should I be, were it in my power to make suitable returns to my inestimable friend for the favors he has conferred and still continues to bestow upon me, but since it is my fortune (and sure it's a happy one) to be so much obliged, I have additional motives for gratitude in the delicacy as well as generosity of my benefactor. If I may form a Judgment of other persons of worth by the knowledge I have of my most intimate friend I may indeed conclude that modesty is inseperable from real merit, and how conspicuous is that charming virtue in your very agreeable letters as well as in every other circumstance that relates to the best of men.

You justly conclude that I have not been unmindful of you, for I have wrote several times purposely to prevent any anxious thoughts from possessing a mind which is I fear but too much harassed with unavoidable cares.

Sister Kitty is much obliged to you for your polite invitation, and already anticipates the pleasure of being with us. Papa too has made her happy by his acquiescence with your request, though it's my opinion you could not make a request with which he would not chearfully comply. As to me, you know that the pleasure of your company is my prime enjoyment and therefore your proposal to send for me is very agreeable. If you think it probable that accomodations will be provided by the 1st February let that be the time for the Colonel[2] to attend us. I think it will not be amiss if Jacob should come with the waggen for our baggage, unless Brockholst can procure a continental one, but be that as it will, order your Sec[retar]y to inform us of your determination previous to his leaving Philadelphia.

The company of your dear little boy proved a great consolation to me since you've been absent, and I should not have forsaken him for Eliz[abeth] Town had I not found my spirits a key too low, which I thought a ride would contribute to enliven. As soon as a convenient opportunity offers Kitty and I shall return to Persipiney and wait there the Colonels arrival. Adieu my dear Mr. Jay. I dare not ask you to write frequently, if the time to be so employed, must be deducted from sleep, for certain I am, that if a sufficient portion of time is not alotted for repose, your too intense application to business will inevitably impair your health.

Accept the Compliments of the season from our little circle, and may we repeat the same to each other fifty years hence. Once more my beloved Adieu. Yours affectionately

SA. JAY

ALS. Endorsed.
[1] Not located.
[2] Henry Brockholst Livingston.

GÉRARD TO CONGRESS

Philadelphia, January 5, 1779

The Minister Plenipotentiary of France can not dispense referring to the Congress of the United States the Passages under lined in the two News Papers hereunto annexed of the 3 and 5th of this Month,[1] he does not doubt but Congress has been offended at the indiscreet assertions those passages Contain which expose Equally the Dignity and the Reputation of the King my Master and that of the United States. Those assertions will become a more dangerous and Powerful Weapon in the hands of the Common Ennemy in as much as the Author is an Officer of Congress and values himself of his Station to give Credit to his opinions and assertions.

The above mentioned Minister relies intirely on the Prudence of Congress to take measures agreable to the Circumstance, he could not prevail on the Author to answer the Evil which he had committed, tho the Minister Plenipotentiary endeavoured to make him sensible of his Error as soon as the first of those Papers were Published.

GÉRARD

ALS in French. DNA: PCC, 94, 78–82. (Gérard customarily did not use the *é* in his signature.) Endorsed: "Read 5." Enclosures: 2 and 5 Jan. editions of the *Pennsylvania Gazette*. Trans. in DNA: *PCC*, 94, 81–82; trans. varying much in detail but little in substance appears in *RDC*, III, 11–12.

[1] The marked copies of the newspapers enclosed with this letter have not been located. It is certain, however, that they must have been the 2 and 5 January editions of the *Pennsylvania Gazette*, because Paine's article appeared on those dates rather than on 3 and 5 January as Gérard claimed. In a passage particularly sure to have attracted the Frenchman's unfavorable attention, Paine offered to show a confidential document assigned to his care to anyone permitted by Congress to read it.

Thomas Paine to Congress

Philadelphia, January 6th, 1779

Honored Sirs

Understanding that exceptions have been taken at some parts of my Conduct, which exceptions as I am unacquainted with I can make no reply to. I therefore humbly beg leave to submit every part of my Conduct public and private, so far as relate to public measures to the judgment of this Honorable House, to be by them approved or censured as they shall judge proper, at the same time reserving to myself that conscious Satisfaction of having ever intended well and to the best of my abilities executed these instructions.

The Honorable Congress in April 1777 were pleased, not only unsolicited on my part, but wholly unknown to me, to appoint me unanimously Secretary to the Commitee for foreign Affairs, which mode of appointment I conceive to be the most honorable that can take place. The Salary they were pleased to affix to it was 70 dollars per Month. It has remained at the same rate ever Since, and is not at this time equal to the most moderate expences I can live at; yet I have never complained; and always conceiving it my duty to bear a Share of the inconveniences of the Country have ever chearfully submitted to them. This being my Situation, I am at this time conscious of no error unless the cheapness of my Services, and the Generosity with which I have endeavored to do good in other respects, can be imputed to me as a Crime, by such individuals as may have acted otherwise.

As my appointment was honorable, therefore whenever it shall appear to Congress that I have not fulfilled their expectations, I shall, though with Concern at any misapprehension that might lead to such an opinion, surrender up the Books and papers entrusted to my Care.

Were my appointment an Office of Profit it might become me to resign it, but as it is otherwise, I conceive that such a Step in me, might imply a dissatisfaction on account of the Smallness of the Pay. Therefore I think it my duty to wait the orders of this Honorable House; at the same time begging leave to assure them, that whatever may be their determination respecting me, that my disposition to serve in so Honorable a Cause, and in any character in which I can best do it, will suffer no Alteration.

I am with profound respect your Honors Dutiful and Obedient Humble Servant

THOMAS PAINE

ALS. DNA: PCC, 55, 1–4. Addressed: "To The Honble. John Jay Esqr. President of Congress." Endorsed by Charles Thomson: ". . . Read the same day."

Thomas Paine to Congress

Philadelphia, January 7th, 1779

Honored Sirs

From the manner in which I was called before this House yesterday, I have reason to suspect an unfavorable disposition in them, towards some parts in my late publications. What the parts are against which they object, or what these objections are, are wholly unknown to me. If any Gentleman has presented any Memorial to this House, which contains any Charge against me, or any ways allude in a censurable manner, to my character or interest, so as to become the ground of any such charge, I request, as a Servant under your Authority, an attested Copy of that charge, and in my personal character as a freeman of this Country, I demand it. I attended at the *bar* of this House yesterday, as their Servant, though the warrant did not express my official Station, which I conceive it ought to have done otherwise it could not be compulsive unless backed by a Magistrate. My hopes were, that I should be made acquainted with the Charges, and admitted to my defence, which I am all times ready to make either in writing or personally.

I cannot in duty to my Character as a freeman, submit to be censured unheard. I have evidence which I presume will justify me. And I entreat this House to Consider how great their reproach will be, <when> should it <shall> be told, that they passed a Sentence upon me without hearing me and that a Copy of the charge against was refused to <be> me; and likewise, how much that reproach will be aggravated should I afterwards prove the Censure of this

House to be a Libel, grounded upon a mistake which <this House> they refused to enquire fully into.

I make my application to the heart of every Gentleman in this House, that he, before he decides on a point that may affect my Reputation, will duly consider his own. Did I covet popular praise I should not <send this> send this letter. My wish is, that by thus Stating my Situation to the House, that they may not commit an Act they cannot Justify.

I have obtained Fame Honor and Credit in this Country. I am Proud of those honors. And as they can be taken from me by any unjust Censure, grounded on a concealed Charge, therefore it will become my duty afterwards to do Justice to myself. I have no favor to ask more than to be candidly and honorably dealt by, and such being my right, I ought to have no doubt but this House will proceed accordingly. Should Congress be disposed to hear me, I have to request that they will give me sufficient Time to prepare.

I am Honorable Sirs your honors most Obedient and dutiful Humble Servant

THOS. PAINE

ALS. DNA: PCC, 55, 5–8. Addressed: "To The Honorable John Jay Esqr. President of Congress." Endorsed by Charles Thomson: ". . . Read the same day."

Thomas Paine to Congress

Philadelphia, January 8th, 1779

Honorable Sirs

Finding by the Journals of this House, of yesterday, that I am not to be heard,[1] and having in my letter of the same day, prior to that resolution, declared that I could not *"in duty to my Character as a freeman submit to be censured unheard,"* therefore consistent with that declaration, and to maintain that Right, I think it my duty to resign the Office of Secretary <for foreign> to the Committee for foreign Affairs and I do hereby resign the same day. The Papers and documents in my charge, I shall faithfully deliver up to the Committee, either on Honor or oath as they, or this House shall direct.

Considering myself now no longer a Servant of Congress, I conceive it convenient that I should declare what have been the motives for my Conduct.

On the appearance of Mr. Deane's Address to the Public of the

5th of December, in which he said, that, "the case of the Representatives were shut against him," the honor and Justice of this House <was> were impeached, and its Reputation sunk to the lowest ebb in the opinions of the People. The Expressions of Suspicion and degradation which have been uttered in my hearing and are too indecent to be related in this letter, first induced me to set the Public right; but so grounded were they, almost without exception, in their Ill opinion of this House, that instead of succeeding as I wished in my first address, I fell under the same reproach, and was frequently told, that I was defending Congress in their bad designs. This obliged me to go farther into the matter, and I have now reason to believe, that my endeavors have been, and will be effectual.

My wish and my <endeavor> intentions in all my late Publications, were, to preserve the Public from Error and Imposition, to support as far as laid in my Power, the *Just* Authority of the Representatives of the People, and to cordiallize and cement the Union, that has so happily taken place between this Country and France.

I have betrayed no Trust, because I have constantly employed that trust to the Public good. I have revealed no Secrets, because I have told nothing that was, or, I conceive, ought to be a Secret. <It is to the> I have convicted Mr. Deane of Error, and in so doing, I hope I have done my duty.

It is to the Interest of the Alliance, that the People should know, that before America had any Agent in Europe, the *"Public Spirited Gentlemen"* in that Quarter of the World were her warm friends. And I hope <that> this Honorable House will receive it from me, as a further Testimony of my Affection for that Alliance, and of my attention to the duty of my Office, that I mention, That the Duplicates of the dispatches of October 6th and 7th, 1777 from the *Commissioners*, the Originals of which are in the Enemy's possession, seem to require, on *that Account* a reconsideration.

His Excellency the Minister of France is well acquainted with the liberality of my Sentiments, and I have had the pleasure of receiving repeated Testimonies of his esteem for me. I am concerned that he should in any Instance <misunderstand> misconceive me. I beg likewise to <be> have it understood, that my appeal to this Honorable House for a hearing yesterday, was as a matter of Right in the character of a Freeman; which Right I ought to yield up to no Power whatever. I return my utmost thanks to the Honorable Members of this House, who endeavored to support me in that Right so sacred to themselves and to their Constituents; and I have the pleasure of reflecting and saying, that as I came into office, an honest Man, I go out of it with the same Character.

I am Honorable Sirs your Honors Obedient Humble Servant

THOS. PAINE

ALS. DNA: PCC 55, 9–14. Addressed: "To the Honble. John Jay Esquire President of Congress." Endorsed by Charles Thomson: ". . . Read the same day."

[1] This statement, implying that Paine had been allowed to examine the confidential Journals of the Continental Congress, created consternation in that body when the letter was read. Called on for an explanation, Charles Thomson reported that he had taken the Journals home the previous evening, making it impossible for Paine to have seen them. Henry Laurens thereupon confessed that he had disclosed the information during a talk with the Secretary to the Committee for Foreign Affairs. *JCC*, XIII, 36–38.

From Gérard

Philadelphia, 10 January 1779

Sir

I cannot forbear to present to Congress the forceful observations which are prompted by the response to my representation made at the beginning of this month. Already the enemies of the common cause point to it as proof of the divergence of opinion which governs the Congress, for if such could exist on so simple and clear an issue, casting doubts about it would have the effect of compromising at the same time the solidarity and even the existence of the alliance.

No one in the world, Sir, least of all myself, would venture to accept suspicions that would be so fatal to the common cause, but I have had the honor to set forth the motives which should impel Congress to give to this subject a prompt, formal, and categorical declaration. It is well known how erroneous and devious opinions are more difficult to destroy when they have had time to implant themselves in the minds. One would wish then to remedy this ailment, but it stands unrepudiated.

The greater part of these reflections is applicable equally to the communication I have had the honor of making to Congress the fifth of this month, and I await with impatience some replies which can quiet a court despite the efforts that her enemies put forth, replies which will distinguish the facts from the false inferences against the Allies and the Alliance. Only Congress can obviate such dangers.

My zeal and my respect will not permit me to dissimulate my fears which appear only too well founded, and hence merit its attention.

I have the honor to be, with respect and devotion, Your very humble and very obedient Servant

GERARD

Transl. by the editors of the LS in French in DNA: PCC, 94, 83–86. Endorsed by Charles Thomson: ". . . Read. Entered." Transl. (so wooden as to be at times almost incomprehensible) in DNA: PCC, 94, 87. C in French in MAE: CP, États-Unis, suppl., vol. I; C in DNA: PCC, misc., roll 5.

To Gérard

Philadelphia, 10 January 1779

Sir,

I shall do myself the honor of communicating your Letter this day to Congress in the morning;[1] and permit me to assure You of my sincere desire as well as Expectation of your speedily receiving an explicit and satisfactory answer to the Important Requisition contained in it.

I shall consider every Occurence as unfortunate which may deprive me of the pleasure of your Company, and particularly such as arise from want of Health. May that great Blessing be soon restored to You. The same cause has confined me to the house today. Unless the weather should be very bad in the morning I promise myself the pleasure of paying my Respects to You.

I have the Honor to be with perfect Respect and Esteem, Your Most obedient and most Humble Servant,

J. J.

LbkC. DNA: PCC, 14.

[1] Gérard to JJ, 5 and 10 Jan. 1779, in DNA: PCC, 94, 78–87.

To George Clinton

Philadelphia, 10 January 1779

Dear Sir

Had I more Leisure I should send you less blank Paper. Intelligence of Importance we have none. The News Papers will tell you little. I wish they said less. If I am not greatly decieved the Vermont Affair will end well. Send us the Papers.[1] If my Brothers are with you request them to write to me. My Compliments to those about you whom you know I esteem, particularly Livingston, Benson and Platt.[2] My best Respects to Mrs. Clinton.

I am Dear Sir very much Yours etc.

J. JAY

ALS. MHi: Washburn. Endorsed.

1 The "papers" requested by JJ were maps and documents relating to the New York–Vermont dispute. After Vermont's declaration of independence from New Hampshire and New York in January 1777, the Vermonters petitioned Congress for recognition. Congress responded by asking Vermont to desist from their separation and submit themselves to New York's jurisdiction, so the matter had remained unresolved. *JCC*, VIII, 509, 513; DNA: PCC, 47, 143–56.

2 Sir James Jay and Zephaniah Platt, who were then members of the State Senate; Frederick Jay and Egbert Benson, who served in the Assembly; Robert R. Livingston.

From Frederick Jay

Fish Kill, 12th January 1779

Dear Jack

Your letter of the 8th ultimo came to hand the 7th Inst., also those to Papa and Sir James by Barclay.[1] Papa is much pleased with the papers you sent him, and begs you'l favour him with a continuance of them.

You may rest assured that my attention to the Famely is the Same as it ever was, and when Occasion requires my assistance I shall not be wanting to make them as happy as Circumstances will admit of.

As nothing appears to me like an accommodation between the States and Great Britain, I think it high time to endeavour to do something for myself, being compleatly tired of my situation. I think too much ought not to be expected. I have spent much time and expence in the Cause, and have never had the offer of even the lowest Commission in the State. It now becomes necessary for me to put myself in Commission if possible, my endeavours shall not be wanting. I have already wrote to my Friend Mr. J. Broome,[2] who has returned me a very polite answer and offered me every assistance in his power. He observes at the same time that the only business he would advise me to engage in is the speculating Branch in one of the Eastern Ports. But as every article has advanced greatly in that Quarter, I have deferred going there, till I could be informed of the Situation of Trade at Philad[elphi]a for which purpose I must beg the favour of you to make enquiry. I would have you advise with Mr. Rob. Morris, who I make no doubt will be very candid on the Subject. He is well acquainted with me, and as he is a man of great fortune, he may perhaps give me some assistance. I did intend to have paid Philad[elphi]a a visit, but as you are on the spot, it may be a means of saving the expence of such a journey for the present.

I make no doubt you'l pay attention to what I have wrote, my situation realy requires it. You must be sensible that I have no prospect of getting into any public business in this State, that my time decreases as well as my fortune, and that without some post of profitt in some of the States, or entering into some kind of business I shall in a short time be in a situation not the most agreable.

You tell me that Generals Lee's and Schuylers Sentences are confirmed by Congress, but give me leave to tell you, that you have been very careful not to inform me what those Sentences are.[3] Gen. Schuyler's I have seen and believe it to be a just one, the other I am still ignorant of.

I have been informed that Congress have published their proceedings from their Commencement till [———].[4] If you can conveniently send them to me I should be glad to have them.

Baxter[5] has not yet fetched your Mare and Colt, the latter strayed away a few days ago. Care shall be taken to recover it. I think there will be too much risque in sending the Mare to Bedford. I shall therefore only send the Colt when Baxter calls.

Nancey[6] desires to remind you of the Castor Oyle. When you write to Sally give the Love of the Family to her. Tom Carman is well and makes a fine figure. Blamed here by many, it is said he has treated in a manner very unbecoming a Gentleman. I shall suspend my judgement till I hear more of the Matter. Our Legislature was to meet this Day. I shall go to Poughkeepsiee in a day or two. Your speedy answer to this letter will greatly oblidge your Affectionate Brother

FRED. JAY

ALS. Addressed: "His Excellency John Jay Esqr. President of Congress Philadelphia." Endorsed.

1 None of these letters have been located.

2 John Broome.

3 At Major General Charles Lee's court-martial, 4 July 1778, he was suspended from command in the army for one year. Congress confirmed the sentence of the court-martial on 5 Dec. 1778. The court-martial investigating Major General Philip Schuyler, convened 1 Oct. 1778, found him not guilty of "Any Neglect of duty in not being at Ticonderoga." Congress confirmed the court-martial's acquittal on 3 Dec. 1778. *GWF*, XIII, 448–50; *JCC*, XII, 1186, 1195; see above, Robert Troup to JJ, 16 Aug. 1778, n. 3.

4 Blank space in the letter.

5 Baxter was a tenant on Frederick Jay's property.

6 Anna Maricka Jay, JJ's sister.

To Gérard

Philadelphia, 13th January 1779

Sir,

It is with real Satisfaction that I execute the Order of Congress for transmitting to you the enclosed Copy of an Act of the 12th Inst. on a Subject rendered important, by affecting the dignity of Congress, the Honor of their great Ally, and the Interest of both Nations.

The explicit disavowal and high disapprobation of Congress, relative to the Publications referred to in this Act, will, I flatter myself be no less satisfactory to his most Christian Majesty, than pleasing to the people of these States. Nor have I the least doubt but that every Attempt to injure the Reputation of either, or impair their mutual confidence, will meet with the Indignation and Resentment of both.

I have the Honor to be Sir, with Great Respect and Esteem, Your most Obedient and most Humble Servant,

JOHN JAY
PRESIDENT

LS. MAE: CP: États-Unis Supplement, vol. 7. LbkC in DNA: PCC, 14; C in hand of Charles Thomson in MAE: CP, États-Unis, vol. 7; printed in the *Pennsylvania Packet,* 16 Jan. 1779.

"Copy of a Resolution of Congress"

[Philadelphia], January 12, 1779

Congress took into consideration the publication in the Pensylvania packet of the 2d and 5th instant under the title of common sense to the public on M. Deane's affair, of which M. Thomas Paine Secretary to the Committee for foreign affairs has acknowledged himself to be the author; and also the memorials of the Minister Plenipotentiary of France of the 5th and 10th instant respecting the said publications, and Thereupon.

Resolved unanimously that in answer to the Memorials of the honorable Sieur Gerard Minister Plenipotentiary of his most Christian Majesty of the 5th and 10th instant, the President be directed to assure the said Minister that Congress do fully in the clearest and most explicit manner disavow the publications referred to in the said Memorials, and as they are convinced by indisputable evidence that the supplies shipped in the Amphitrite, Seine and Mercury were not a present, and that his most Christian Majesty the great and generous ally of these United States did not preface his alliance with any supplies whatever sent to America, so they have not authorized the writer of the said publications to make any such assertions as are contained therein, but on the contrary do highly disapprove of the same.

ADS. Extracted from the minutes by Charles Thomson. MAE: CP: États-Unis, vol. 7. LbkC, with minor variations, in DNA: PCC, 14, in hand of Gouverneur Morris.

From Gérard

Philadelphia, 14th January 1779

Sir,

I have received the Letter with which you honored me the 13th instant inclosing me the resolve of Congress in answer to the representations I had the honor to make them on the 5th and 10th.

I intreat you to receive and to express to Congress the great sensibility with which I feel their frank, noble and Categorical manner of distroying these false and dangerous actions which might mislead Ignorant People and put arms into the hands of the Common Enemy.

To the King my Master Sir no proofs are necessary for the foundation of a confidence in the firm and constant adherence of Congress to the principles of the Alliance. But his Majesty will always behold with pleasure the measures which Congress may take to preserve inviolate its reputation, and it is from the same consideration, I flatter myself You will find my representations on the 7th of December equally worthy of his Attention.

I am with respect and Consideration, Sir, your most Humble and most Obedient Servant

GERARD

Transl. DNA: PCC, 94, 91–92; ALS, in French, in DNA: PCC, 94, 89. C in French in MAE: CP, États-Unis, vol. 7 and in DNA: PCC, misc. roll 5.

To Beaumarchais

Philadelphia, 15th January 1779

Sir,

The Congress of the United States of America sensible of your Exertions in their favor present you with their thanks and assure you of their Regard.

They lament the Inconveiences you have suffered, by the great Advances made in support of these States. Circumstances have prevented a compliance with their wishes, but they will take the most effectual measures in their power to discharge the debt due to you.

The liberal Sentiments and extensive views which alone could dictate a Conduct like yours, are conspicuous in your Actions and adorn your Character. While with great Talents you served your Prince, you have gained the Esteem of this Infant Republic, and will receive the merited Applause of a new world.

By Order of Congress

JOHN JAY
PRESIDENT

LbkC. DNA: PCC, 14.

To PHILLIP SCHUYLER

Philadelphia, 15th January, 1779

Dear General,

As the Secretary has neglected to furnish me (as usual) with the dates of your late Letters to Congress, and your Express sets out early in the Morning I must describe them by the Subject-Matter.

The one on the Subject of your Resignation still remains under consideration. The one respecting the Request of the Oneidas is referred to a Committee appointed to confer with General Washington who are directed, without the further Intervention of Congress to determine and give order relative to it. The third, which, If I mistake not, states the Embarrassments you have been subjected to by General Gates' having forbid the Quarter Master to pay certain Notes you gave while in command, is referred to a special Committee who are ordered to report without delay.[1] As the Act of Congress, of which the enclosed is a copy, was intended to accommodate the Resolutions on Finances to the convenience of the Army, I take the Opportunity of transmitting it to you. It may be proper also to inform you that Congress have accepted the Resignations of Colonel Henry Beekman Livingston, and Lieutenant Houghkirk.[2] I have written you two private Letters since my arrival,[3] which, by your silence respecting them, I fear have miscarried. Expect another by the next Express.

I have the Honor to be Sir, with great Respect and Esteem Your most Obedient and most Humble Servant

J. J.

LbkC. DNA: PCC, 14. Enclosure: Resolution of Congress, 12 Jan. 1779, providing that officers and soldiers who had received part of their pay for September–November 1778 in the Continental emissions of 20 May 1777 and 11 April 1778 could exchange such currency through the paymasters of their respective departments. *JCC*, XIII, 52–53.

[1] Schuyler's letter to the President of Congress, 27 Dec. 1778, tendering his resignation is in DNA: PCC, 153, III. Two letters from Schuyler of 3 and 5 Jan. 1779 were read in Congress on 14 January and referred to committees. Reports on these letters were deferred until 30 January, after which they were not mentioned again. Neither letter has been located in DNA: PCC. *JCC*, XIII, 63.

[2] The resignations of Colonel Henry Beekman Livingston and Lieutenant John Hooghkirk of New York were accepted by Congress on 13 Jan. 1779. *JCC*, XIII, 56, 58.

[3] No private letters from JJ to Schuyler dated December 1778 or January 1779 have been located.

From Nathanael Greene

Philadelphia, 18th January 1779

Sir

It cannot be unknown to Congress that in the different Departments of the Army there are many Persons employed in the Character of Officers who have no other Commission than a kind of Warrant or Appointment from the Head of the Department in which they serve. They consequently have no Rank in the Army, but are left on the Footing of private Soldiers as to Arrests, and Modes of Trial. Amongst these there are many who from their Abilities and good Conduct are respectable Characters; their Feelings are therefore sensibly touched by being placed in a Situation which subjects them to Confinement in the common Guard House at the Will of even the lowest commissioned Officer in the Army for an Offence of a trivial Nature, or perhaps for a supposed Offence.

The present Situation of Affairs affords so many Opportunities of acquiring Money in a private Capacity, and the publick Service requires the Employment of so great a Number of Men of Abilities for Business, that with all the Encouragement in our Power to give, it is found not a little difficult to fill the different Stations in the Staff Departments with Men of suitable Talents; it therefore seems requisite to remove from their View every Discouragement which can be laid aside without injuring the Publick in a greater Degree in some other Way. If Congress would be pleased, by a publick Resolution, to put these Warrant Officers on the same Footing with the Officers in the Line of the Army with respect to Arrests, Trials, and Punishment, it would probably have a good Effect on their Minds without working any Injury to the commissioned Officers or to the Publick.[1]

I have the Honour to be, with great Respect, Sir your most obedient and most humble Servant

NATHEL. GREENE QMG

ALS. DNA: PCC, 155. Addressed: "Honble. John Jay Esqr. President of Congress." Endorsed by Charles Thomson: ". . . Read Jany 19, Referd to Board of war respecting Arrests & Tryals of Officers of the Staff." Nathanael Greene was Quartermaster General, 2 March 1778–3 Aug. 1780.

[1] The Board's report of 5 February agreed "entirely" with Greene's letter; the report was read and passed by Congress on 16 March. JJ acknowledged receipt of Greene's letter on 22 Jan. 1779. *JCC*, XIII, 321–22; DNA: PCC, 33, 305.

To Sarah Livingston Jay

Philadelphia, 18 January 1779

My dear Sally

Yesterday I had the Pleasure to hear of you tho not *from* you. Your Brother recieved a Letter from Caty, who was then at Elizabeth Town.[1] I imagine from her Letter that you must have returned to Persipiney. This Letter will nevertheless go to Elizabeth Town. I suppose there is a constant Communication between the two Families.

No Home yet. About the Middle of February we shall have one. But that will be so near the 1st of March, when my Delegation will expire, that unless it should be prolonged I doubt whether I ought to put you to so much Trouble, for the Sake of spending only a Week in Philadelphia. But more of this hereafter. Whether our Legislature will think proper to leave me here longer, is uncertain. I expect soon to be informed, and shall give you the earliest Intelligence of their Determination whatever it may [be]. At any Rate I hope they will not keep me here in the summer Months; until May or the first of June I should be content, but no longer. God bless you my dear Sally. I am your very affectionate Husband

JOHN JAY

ALS. N. Addressed: "Mrs. Sarah Jay Governor Livingston's Elizabeth Town."

[1] Catharine W. Livingston to Henry Brockholst Livingston, above.

From Philip Schuyler

Saratoga, January 18th, 1779

Dear Sir

I had not the pleasure to receive Your favor of the 8th ult. until last night. Pray accept my best thanks for your Congratulations on my Acquital.[1]

I did myself the pleasure to write you some time ago from this place and Since that from Albany were I passed the holidays.[2] In the first of these letters I advised you of my Intention to resign, In the last that I had, and In both gave the reasons that led me to It. I hope they were Satisfactory. Yesterday I received a line from General Washington of the 31st December. You will see by the turn of the following paragraph that he Expected something like a resignation.

"In a letter which I had the pleasure of writing you the 18th Instant I requested you to take the direction of the Magazines etc. etc. which were to be prepared towards a Certain Expedition. I should have Extended the Idea to your taking the full Command in the Northern Department but I was restrained by a doubt how far the measure might be agreable to your own views and Intentions. The same doubt Still remains but as It is very much my desire you should resume that Command I take Occassion to Signify It to you. At the Same time If you have any Material Objections against It, I would not wish to preclude their Operation. If you have not You will be pleased to Consider this as an order for the purpose."[3]

You will readily See my Dear Sir that I cannot with any degree of propriety take the Command he wishes or Indeed any other. I have long since Justifyed Congress for depriving me of the Command in 1777 convinced that It was their duty to Sacrifice the feelings of an Individual to the Safety of the States when the people who only could defend the Country refused to Serve under him. But who is capable of finding an apology for their Subsequent Conduct? for leaving me in a Situation which naturally Induced Mankind to believe that I was not to be trusted, which had a most Evident tendency to Continue nay to Increase the Clamour against me. But they were not Content to deprive me of a Command In the army; they Resolved that Council learned In the law, Should assist the Judge Advocate In the prosecution.[4] This held up to the public that my crime was of a henious nature, and thousands have by that very resolution been made to believe so. I believe It is not unbecoming the most August body that ever existed to make reparation for Injuries. It is not presuming In an Individual to Expect It. If the first refuses to afford It, there is danger In serving them; If the latter can tamely Submit to the most flagrant Injustice he is unworthy of a public trust.

These My dear Sir are my Sentiments. I hope they are neither Erroneous or Intemperate. I will however add that If my services Are deemed necessary to the public weal, I shall never decline giving them as a Servant of the public when reparation has been made, but wether that takes place or not, as a Citizen they shall never be witheld. Of this I shall give a most Convincing proof. If any Operations are prosecuted from this quarter, such unequivocal testimony as will Induce honest men to revere my principles and cause my Enemies to blush If they are Susceptible of the sentiment of Shame.

Adieu. God bless you and give you felicity. I am with Esteem, affection and the warmest friendship Dear Sir Your obedient Humble Servant

PH. SCHUYLER

ALS. Endorsed.

1 See JJ to Schuyler, 8 Dec. 1778.

2 The letters from Saratoga and Albany have not been located.

3 Washington's letters to Schuyler of 18 and 31 Dec. 1778 are in *GWF*, XIII, 429–33, 469–70.

4 On 5 Feb. 1778 Congress resolved that "two counsellors, learned in the law, be appointed to assist and co-operate with the judge advocate in conducting the trial." Jonathan D. Sergeant, attorney general of Pennsylvania, and William Paterson, attorney general of New Jersey, were chosen. *JCC*, X, 125.

From Robert Troup

Camp, Middle Brook, January 21st, 1779

My dear Sir,

I wrote to you from Boston, some Time in November, and inclosed a Letter for you, which was sent to my Care, by Mr. Sam. Nicoll in New York.[1] In my Letter I informed you that General Gates's ungenerous Conduct to me had determined me to leave his Family, as soon as the Army had taken Winter Quarters. After writing this Letter he gave me a fresh Proof of his inveterate Prejudice against me, and his passive Obedience to the Tyranny of Petticoat Government.[2] Being persuaded that every Moment of your Time is devoted to the important Duties of your Office, I will not remind you of the Reasons why General Gates has treated me with so little Candor, or rather with so much Injustice. I wish you therefore, my dear Sir, to reflect on the short Conversation, I had with you, at Poughkeepsie in October. You will then find that my Reverence for particular Persons, who had done me repeated and infinite Favors, was the most henous of all my Crimes. This I solemnly assure you was the Source of those sarcastical Sneers, and those malicious Reflections, which forced me to leave him about six Weeks ago. I travelled in Company with Madam De Riedesel,[3] and did not arrive in New Jersey till the 9th Instant.

You may easily conceive, my dear Sir, that my Feelings at parting with General Gates, were extremely delicate. I am happy to add that he discovered the most affectionate Concern for my Welfare, asked me to write to him often, and put into my Hands a very flattering Certificate of my Services.

Could I have been base enough to have sold my Judgement and my Friends to purchase the Smile of Vanity, I should now be a Young Fellow of the utmost Probity, as well as the most remarkable military Genius in the Army. And it is more than probable that he would have recommended me to Congress, in the strongest Terms, for the Rank of B[rigadier] General.

Thus, my dear Sir, I am faced from the most insupportable Misery I ever indured. I mean the Misery occasioned to a liberal Mind, by hearing Nothing but Invective uttered against deserving Characters.

I have been waiting here for these eight Days past for the Return of Col. Hamilton who has always been my sincere Friend. I propose spending the Winter in this State, and think it would be best to know what the Enemy will do, before I form any Resolutions respecting my future Conduct.[4]

I beg you to present my best Respects to Col. Hamilton, and your Brother, Col. Livingston.

I am, My dear Sir, With all possible Sincerity, Your Friend.

ROB. TROUP

ALS. Endorsed.

[1] See Robert Troup to JJ, 23 Nov. 1778.

[2] The tyranny to which Troup referred was Gates's wife Elizabeth who, as Charles Lee opined, "governed her husband with a rod of scorpions." Samuel W. Patterson, *Horatio Gates* (New York, 1941), p. 330.

[3] Frederike Charlotte Luise, Baroness von Riedesel (1745–1808) was the wife of the commander of the Hessian troops who surrendered at Saratoga. Troup was assigned to escort the General's party to Virginia.

[4] After receiving this letter, JJ sent word by way of Alexander Hamilton that he felt Troup should not leave the military service. The young man acknowledged that "many Advantages will result from my staying in the Army till the War is ended," but he wondered how, under the existing circumstances, he could expect to be assigned to useful duty. Robert Troup to JJ, 15 Feb. 1779, in JP.

To William Phillips

Philadelphia, 23 January 1779

Sir,

Your Favor of the 6th Inst. was this morning delivered to me and communicated to Congress.[1] The enclosed Copy of their Resolution on the Subject matter of it, specifies the Reason which restrains them from complying with your Request.

<As the Humanity which distinguishes the manner in> Permit me to assure You that my Endeavours shall never be wanting to render Humanity a national Characteristic of these States, and I am persuaded that nothing but a contrary Conduct on the Part of their Enemies will ever reconcile Congress to the exercise of a greater Degree of Rigor than the necessary and immediate Objects of War may demand.

Whenever the present Objections cease, I shall be happy Sir to join in giving you higher Evidence of this Disposition than Professions, and in the mean Time will chearfully promote every reasonable Measure for rendering your Situation as agreable and Happy as the Nature of it will admit.

I am Sir Your most obedient and humble Servant

Dft. Enclosure: Resolution of Congress, 23 Jan. 1779, denying Phillips's request that he be given leave to visit New York City for six weeks. C of covering letter and enclosure in NN; C also in DNA: PCC, 14.

Captured at Saratoga, Major General William Phillips (1731?–81) was held prisoner in Massachusetts until early 1779, when he was moved to Virginia. While there, he lived at Blenheim, Edward Carter's home, and became acquainted with Jefferson. He went to New York on parole at the end of 1779 and was exchanged a year later. After returning to active service, he died of typhoid fever in May 1781 while commanding troops in Virginia.

[1] William Phillips to the President of Congress, 6 Jan. 1779, DNA: PCC, 57, 345.

From Donadieu De Fleury

Saint Hypolite, January 24, 1779

Sir

The respectable Body of which you are a part presents itself to the Eyes of Europe as an Assemblage of all the Vertues. This Reputation emboldens me to importune your Humanity and the Goodness of which you are capable. I am going to seek to touch your generous Bosom by presenting to you the picture of an Heart of Sensibility under affliction from the Feelings of Nature. I am deprived of a Son, Sir, named Fleuri who has the good Fortune of being in your Service, and who has also had that of distinguishing himself therein and of meriting the Suffrage of Congress, as I have learnt by the public Intelligence.[1] Permit me in quality of an Anxious and weeping Mother, but, at the same time, of one proud of having an Ofspring who has been able to make himself useful among you, to presume so far as to intreat you to relieve me from the cruel uncertainty I am in respecting the Situation of my Son. You must perceive, Sir, that the more he renders himself worthy of your Favor and that of the Congress in general, the more dear he becomes to me; but my Self Love in that respect is only gratified at the Expence of maternal tranquility. I have groaned and wasted myself during the whole absence of my Son; nor have I been so fortunate, in all the Time that he hath been in your Country, as to receive any letters from him. I have written to him twenty at the least, without answer. I am certain his Letters are intercepted. Allow me therefore Sir to ask of you, in the name of that Esteem and Glory which my Son is solicitous of acquiring among your People, as a Recompense to him and to me, that you would condescend to furnish him with the means of sending to my hand with certainty Intelligence of his Situation.[2] I should be greatly flattered Sir would you yourself be pleased to grant that precious Favor to my Son and to me, which would unite us in the desire of convincing you of our Gratitude and the respectful Sentiments with which

I have the Honor to be Sir Your most humble And most obedient Servant

DONADIEU DE FLEURY

ALS. NN: Emmet. Marguerite Donadieu was the wife of François Teissèdre, Seigneur de Fleury.

1 Lieutenant Colonel François Louis Teissèdre de Fleury (1749–?) was one of the most distinguished French officers who served the American cause. On 13 Sept. 1777 Congress voted to present Fleury with a horse to replace the mount killed under him at the battle of Brandywine "as a testimonial of the sense the Congress have of the said Mons. de Fleury's merit." *JCC*, VIII, 739.

2 On 27 Sept. 1779 Congress granted Fleury leave to return to France. *JCC*, XV, 1111.

From Horatio Gates

Boston, January 29th, 1779

Sir

Since I had the Honour to write to Your Excellency upon the [——] Instant,[1] I have received the inclosed intelligence from General Bayley, and Colonel Bedel, Copies of which are also transmitted to General Washington.[2] I am confident the Enemy's Magazines of Provisions are exhausting very fast. Admiral Gambier, sent from New-York to New London, in Three Vessels with Flags of Truce, 367 Prisoners; Admiral Byron sent 144 to General Sullivan from Rhode Island; Admiral Hughes, in a Cartel Ship just arrived at this port from Hallifax, sent 115; in all 626 Prisoners.[3] For these, no other return have been made than about one half the Crew of the

Somerset Ship of War, the rest having enlisted in The Privateers of this, and the Neighbouring States.

General Heath acquaints me He has long ago made Application to Congress, respecting Ensign John Brown, under Sentence of Death, in the Jail of this City.[4] I wish to receive their Commands in regard to this unhappy Convict. I can say nothing as to the Merit or Demerit of the Man, as he was tried and Condemned, long before my Arrival here. General Heath likewise informs me, that Ten Thousand Dollars in Hard Money have been paid into his Hands by The Paymaster of the Convention Troops, for the disposal of which he is desirous to receive Orders.

I must again entreat the Honourable Congress to take the immediate Supply of Flower [*sic*] for the Magazines in this Department, into their most serious consideration. The Inhabitants of this City, and the Surrounding Districts, are in great Want of it, insomuch that I have lately had a very Earnest application to lend Flower out of The Continental Magazine, to Supply the pressing wants of the poor; but if I had thought myself authorized to Comply with this request, the Magazine here was in too low a State to admit of it; I was therefore reluctantly Obliged to decline Granting the request of a Committee deputed to me in a Town Meeting which was called for that purpose. If the Time between this, and the First of May, is not made the best use of to fill the Magazines in the Eastern Department with Flower, the Consequences may be fatal to our Cause.

I am, Sir, Your Excellency's Most Obedient Servant

HORATIO GATES

ALS. DNA: PCC, 154, I–II, 53–60. Endorsed by Charles Thomson: "(read Feby. 11th) referred to the Board of War." Enclosures: Jacob Bayley to Horatio Gates, 2 Jan. 1779 and Timothy Bedel to Gates, 13 Jan. 1779. Bayley wrote that Canada expected an imminent invasion by American forces. Bedel, writing from Newberry, complained of shortages of ammunition and blankets and wrote that an American invasion would be well received by Canadians. E in DNA: PCC, 154, I–II, 61–62.

1 Date left blank in letter. Gates wrote JJ on 15 January congratulating him on his election as President. DNA: PCC, 154.

2 Gates enclosed copies of the Bedel and Bayley reports in his letter to Washington, 26 Jan. 1779. Brigadier General Timothy Bedel (d. 1787) of New Hampshire was then serving in the Vermont militia, and Jacob Bayley was his quartermaster. DLC: Washington Papers, Series IV.

3 Vice Admiral John Byron (1723–86) succeeded Lord Richard Howe as commander of British naval forces in America in the summer of 1778. Rear Admiral James Gambier (1723–89) served as second in command to Howe and Byron. Admiral Sir Richard Hughes (1729?–1812) was the resident commissioner of the British Navy at Halifax.

4 A general court-martial had sentenced Brown to die on 8 July 1778 for

fraudulently accepting bounty payments. Heath began his correspondence with Congress about Brown on 9 May 1778 when he forwarded petitions for clemency from Brown and his wife. Heath had also postponed Brown's execution to permit filing of further petitions. On 20 July 1778 Congress appointed a committee to review Brown's case; Brown was finally pardoned on 9 March 1779. *JCC*, XI, 690, 704; XII, 1053, 1174, 1184; XIII, 296; DNA: PCC, 157.

To George Washington

Philadelphia, 31st January 1779

Sir

Congress, agreeable to your Excellency's Recommendation, have directed the Commissary and Quarter Master General to pay such of the Accounts mentioned in Governor Clinton's Letter as he shall certify. And by their Act of the 30th Inst., of which the enclosed is a copy, have consented to your Excellency's Return to Camp.[1]

The Opinion of Congress, respecting the continuation of the Committee of Conference, is as yet undetermined. To me it appears proper, as well as necessary, that, until they become dissolved by making a Report on the several Matters committed to them, they should consider an Epistolary Correspondence with your Excellency on those Subjects to be as much within the line of their Appointment as personal conferences.[2]

There are several Acts of Congress, of which I ought to have sent you Copies, and application has several times been made to the Secretary's Office for them. I am now informed that the Clerks, instead of delivering them to me have left them with your Excellency. Those Irregularities will, I hope, be in future avoided.

I have the Honor to be with the greatest Respect and Esteem Your Excellency's most Obedient and Humble Servant

J. JAY

LbkC. DNA: PCC, 14. Enclosure: Resolution of Congress, 30 Jan. 1779. This resolution authorized the quartermaster and commissary generals to pay accounts certified by Governor George Clinton for provisions and forage taken from private citizens following the loss of forts in the New York highlands. *JCC*, XIII, 124–125.

1 The resolution of 30 January was passed after reading a letter by Washington, 29 January, which outlined the circumstances of the seizure of private property for the use of Clinton's command. Washington enclosed a letter from Clinton of 28 Dec. 1778. Washington's covering letter is reprinted in *GWF*, XIV, 52. The ALS of the Washington letter and a copy of Clinton's letter of 28 Dec. 1778 are in DNA: PCC, 152, VII.

2 On 24 Dec. 1778 a committee of conference was appointed to discuss "the operations of the next campaign" with Washington, who was then visiting Philadelphia. In a letter to JJ of 29 January 1779 Washington remarked: "There are

several matters which have been the subjects of conference between the Committee and myself that are yet undecided, and which, with other points that may occur occasionally, may be proper objects for an intercourse of letters, if it should be the pleasure of Congress to continue the Committee for this purpose; the expedience and propriety of which they will judge. . . ." *GWF*, XIV, 54; *JCC*, XII, 1250.

From Nathanael Greene

Philadelphia, 1st February 1779

Sir,

In the different Movements of the Army it frequently happens that the Inhabitants of the Country unavoidably suffer damages of various kinds for which Justice seems to demand that they should receive a Compensation from the publick. There are two ways in which these damages usually happen one of which is the taking of such Articles on sudden Emergencies as the Army may stand in need of, which political Necessity will justify, and which reasonable Men will acquiesce in; the other is that kind of Trespass on private property which Armies in all Countries commit, partly from Necessity and partly from Accident and other Causes which even the best discipline does not wholly guard against.

Such Articles as are taken for the use of the Army are usually paid for by the Quarter Master or Commissary; but the common Mode of ascertaining the Sums to be paid, by the Appraisement of Persons chosen in the Neighbourhood, is not unexceptionable, Experience having shewn that it admits of great diversity and Partiality in the Assessments; and though in many Instances the Parties receive more than may be justly due, they are frequently dissatisfied. The incidental Damages which happen to Buildings, Gardens, Fields, etc., whether necessary or not, are equally injurious to the Owner, and it may be no less politick than just, to establish some Mode for ascertaining Damages of this kind, and fixing how far Satisfaction ought to be made to the Sufferers.

Great Mischiefs of this kind have already happened in many parts of the Country and the People call loudly for Redress. They do not expect in all Cases a full Compensation for their Damages, but they wish to see a Systematick Plan formed for the Distribution of Justice in such Cases by some known Rule, that they may know what to rely on, and to whom they may apply for a common Measure of Redress. The want of such a Regulation leaves Business in a state of Confusion and Difficulty. It creates discontent and an Unwillingness in the people to furnish Supplies for the Army. Some obtain pay at a higher rate than perhaps they are entitled to, while common Justice is withheld from others, the Resolutions of Congress on this Subject being not sufficiently explicit to direct the conduct of the Quarter Masters in one steady Line.

I would therefore beg leave to suggest to Congress the propriety of appointing certain Commissioners of proper Character and Abilities to hear and determine upon all Claims of this kind, subject to the Instructions of the Board of War, or such other Board as Congress shall be pleased to appoint, and to whom they shall report all their Proceedings; That the Commissioners be instructed to certify to the Quarter Master General or to his Deputy such Assessments as are proper for him to pay, and in like manner to other Officers such as it may be proper for them to pay. There may be some Instances in which the Damages are so necessarily involved in the common Calamities of War that the Public cannot with propriety make any Compensation for them; and in others it may be doubtful by whom they ought to be paid: In every such Case a Certificate may be given to the party injured, setting forth his Name, place of Abode, the Amount of his Damages and how they arose, a Duplicate of which may be lodged in the War-Office as a Record to be recurred to when it shall be determined what farther Steps shall be taken respecting it. The Principles on which they are to be determined should, however, be previously settled as clearly and explicitly as may be, and the Commissioners instructed accordingly. In order to avoid Expence it may be well to appoint Officers of the Army to this Commission, as suitable Men may doubtless be found amongst them, who for some additional pay would execute the Trust with Fidelity. The Appointment of Officers might also be attended with a farther good Effect, especially if a set of Commissioners were to attend every separate Command or considerable Detachment of the Army, as they would be Witnesses of the Transactions and of course afford a constant Caution to the Officers in Command against permitting wanton Destruction, or the unnecessary Invasion of private property.

If Congress should think proper to adopt the Measure herein recommended, or any other that will be likely to effect the desired purpose, either myself or one of my Assistants will wait on such Committee or Board as they shall be pleased to appoint, to give such farther Information as shall be required.[1]

I have the Honour to be, with the utmost Respect, Sir, Your most obedient humble Servant

NATHEAL. GREENE, QMG

ALS. DNA: PCC, 155. Endorsed by Charles Thomson: ". . . Read 2 [Feb.]. Referred to the comm. appointed to supperintend the qr. master and Comy. genl. departments."

1 The committee appointed to superintend the quartermaster's and commissary's departments considered this letter and made their report on 2 February, recommending that articles taken "for the use of the Army . . . be paid for at the rate which such articles are really worth, at the time and place when taken." The committee felt it would be "improper" to make any further allowance "for wanton devastations," as in such cases "remedy may be had against the Commanding Officer, whose duty it is to prevent such mischiefs." *JCC*, XIII, 133.

From Anthony Benezet

Chesnut Street, the 2nd February 1779

With affectionate respect, I hereby salute thee, and take the freedom to send thee the inclosed Pamphlet, containing Some Thoughts on War, Slavery etc. of which I earnestly request thy serious perusal. Indeed the subject is of the greatest weight of All, even as Human-Beings; but much more so to those who, indeed believe the great truths of the Christian Religion, God becoming man, and dying for Mankind, even for his Enemies, "Leaving us," says the Apostle, "*an example, that we should follow his footsteps*." This and other arguments therein deduced, from the doctrines and nature of the Gospel, will I trust tend to soften, if not remove, any offence which *The Friends'* refusal to take part in matters of a military nature may have raised in thy mind; and induce thee to distinguish between such who are active in opposition, and those who have been restrained from an apprehension of duty, and a persuasion that our common beneficent Father, who has the hearts of all men in his power, and has in former times so eminently displayed his goodness in favour of these countries, if properly sought unto, would, in his love and mercy, have averted the evil effects of any attempt which might have been made to impede our real welfare.

By the deplorable effects which attends on these dreadful contests, it is evident, that it cannot be agreable to God who the Apostles denominates under the appelation of Love, as thereby every noxious passions of the human mind, instead of being calmed by the benign influences of Grace, the end and aim of Christianity, are thereby inflamed into greater wrath and evil of every kind, as has been verified in that destruction of morals, that waste of substance; but more particularly in the hasty death of so vast a number of our Fellow-men hurried into eternity; many it is to be feared in that distracted frame of mind which generally attends on war.

These are considerations which cannot but strike every thoughtful mind with awe, and which, from the kindness and considerateness of thy disposition, will, I trust, incite thee to advocate the cause of a number of innocent people, of different Religions Persuasions, who from the above mentioned view of things, have not dared to give life or support to military operations; yet at the same time are, indeed, friends to, and really concerned for the true welfare of America, but willing to sacrifice their all, rather than do that whereby they apprehend they may offend that great and good Being, from whom alone, they look for any permanent happiness for themselves or their afflicted country.

With affectionate desires, that the blessing of the Peace-Maker, the peculiar favorite of heaven may be thine I remain, thy friend[1]

ANTHY. BENEZET

ALS. Addressed: "John Jay President of Congress." Endorsed. Enclosure: Anthony Benezet's "Serious Considerations on several important subjects; viz. On war and its inconsistency with the Gospel. Observations on Slavery. And Remarks on the nature and bad effects of spirituous liquors," (Philadelphia, 1778). Evans, 15737.

Anthony Benezet (1713–84) was the son of French Huguenots who emigrated to England, where Benezet became a Quaker. In 1731 the family removed to Philadelphia, where Benezet established himself as a teacher and antislavery crusader. His activities included aid to Acadian exiles in Philadelphia, agitation against the slave trade, and the founding of a school for Negroes.

1 Encouraged by JJ's 5 March 1779 reply to his letter, Benezet wrote again, probably in the spring of that year. The enclosures in that communication were: William Law, *The Spirit of Prayer,* first published in 1749 (Evans, 16817), sent for JJ's "wisdom and comfort," and Benezet's edited version of Daniel Defoe's *The Dreadful Visitation, in a short account of the progress and effects of the plague, the last time it spread in the city of London, in the year 1665*, printed by Joseph Cruikshank, Philadelphia, 1774 (Evans, 16817, 13145), which, it was suggested, JJ would find "agreably solemn, and instructive." Benezet to JJ [c. March?], 1779, JP.

FROM GEORGE CLINTON

Poukeepsie, 2nd February 1779

Dear Sir

I wrote you on the 10th Ultimo in Answer to your Letters prior to that Date; Since which I have had the Pleasure of receiving yours of the 10th and 13th. Mr. Yates has not yet favoured me with an Answer to my Letter requesting the Papers and Maps respecting our Boundaries.[1] You may depend upon their being forwarded the Moment they are received.

A sufficient Number of Members to form a Legislature did not meet until the 27th so that they are now only entring upon Business. A Tax and Confiscation Bill have been read in the Assembly[2] and are in some forwardness.

The General[3] I am informed has announced this to be a Session of Politics and has introduced this Tune in the Senate by moving for a Bill for regulating the Council of Revision, founded on Doubts (which I am persuaded never existed except in his own Mind) whether the Lieutenant Governor or President of the Senate administring the Government are by the Constitution Members of the Council of Revision; And whether the Members of the Council are amenable to the Laws of the Land for Mal or Corrupt Conduct in the Council as Governor, Chancellor etc. and containing a Clause obliging the Council to publish their Minutes as well past as future. You will readilly perceive that the Intention of this Bill is to hold up the Members of the Council of Revision to the Public on an obnoxious Point of View as having already been guilty of Corrupt Conduct which is concealed from the Public Eye.

The Chancellor has not yet appeared or either of the Judges so that I am deprived of their Aid in warding off a wicked factious Measure[4] which might perhaps be more easilly defeated now than at later Period. I flatter myself however I shall be able to render the present Attempt abortive.

The People of this State warmly interest themselves in the Controversey between Mr. Deane and the Lees and without knowing more than the Gazette informs them pretty generally espouse the Cause of the former.

I send you the Papers continued from the Date of my last. They are scarcely worth your perusal. The Author of the Farmer is unknown to me. The Language as well as Sentiment will discover the Author of the Real Farmer.[5] Your Brothers are here and well. I have mentioned to them Your Desire that they should write you frequently. Mrs. Clinton beggs to be remembered to you. I am my Dear Sir with the most perfect Regard and Esteem, Yours Sincerely

GEO. CLINTON

P.S. Mr. McKesson[6] who is just arrived from Albany informs me that the Maps and Papers wanted are not in Mr. Yates Possession or in his (McKesson's) and he cannot tell me where it is likely to find them.

ALS. Endorsed.

1 Clinton to JJ, 10 Jan. 1779, not located. JJ to Clinton, 10 Jan. 1779; JJ to Clinton, 13 Jan. 1779, *GCP*, VI, 482. The "Papers and Maps respecting our Boundaries" refers to the New York–Vermont dispute. "Mr. Yates" is Robert Yates.

2 On 2 February "A Bill to lay a Duty of Excise on strong liquors, to appropriate the Monies arising thereon . . ." was read. On 4 February the Assembly passed a resolution strengthening an act providing for seizure of all flour, meal, and wheat. Evans, 16408, 51 and 53.

3 John Morin Scott.

4 The 1777 New York State Constitution provided that the veto power was to be exercised by the governor, chancellor, and the "Judges of the Supreme Court, or any two of them," sitting as the Council of Revision. Robert R. Livingston was chancellor; JJ was still chief justice; the two associate justices were Robert Yates and John Sloss Hobart. Lincoln, *Constitutional Hist. of N.Y.* I, 167; *N.Y. Civil List*, p. 343.

5 A reference to Samuel Seabury, who wrote under the name of "A. W. Farmer." Bruce E. Steiner, *Samuel Seabury, 1729–1796* (Athens, Ohio, 1971), pp. 129–31.

6 Clerk of the State Senate.

From William Bingham

St. Pierre, Martinique, February 3d, 1779

Dear Sir

I did myself the honor of writing to you on my arrival here, Since which have not had the pleasure of hearing from you. I imagine my Letter must have miscarried, or perhaps found you so busily engaged in public affairs as to prevent your paying any Attention to private Correspondence.

Various Revolutions and Changes have happened Since I last Saw you. Your being chosen President of the Honorable the Continental Congress is to me not the least agreable. Tis the highest Station you can arrive at, and the greatest honor your Country could confer on you, and is only a gratefull Return for your unwearied Efforts in her Service.

It is the prevailing Opinion that through the powerfull Mediation of Spain (who has 50 Ships of the Line ready to enforce her Arguments) there will be a general Peace take place in the Spring; that G. Britain will acknowledge the Independence of America and withdraw her Troops from the Continent. It is certainly the wisest plan She can pursue. But Should the Same Folly and Infatuation on her part that produced the War Still operate in rejecting the mediatory Influence of the Court of Madrid, I am afraid that the War will become more general, and that Peace, however desireable, will be far distant.

G. Britain, exhausted as She is, cannot alone and unassisted, continue a War that requires Such immense Resources to Support it; and if other Powers in Alliance with her Should interfere, it will Still become more difficult to Satisfy Such a Variety of Pretensions as will be formed, and to adjust Such a Number of clashing Interests.

What induces your Friends abroad more particularly and most earnestly to wish for Peace on principles of Independence, is the daily Accounts received from America of the Depreciation of the Continental Currency,[1] which Seems to be a growing Evil of a most alarming Nature. It prevents Foreigners entirely from entering into commercial Speculations for the Continent, for as there are no Remittances can be procured from thence, their Funds must remain exposed to the unfavorable Vicissitudes that have hitherto attended the declining State of our Paper Money.

The Person who could discover the Means of raising its Credit or of Stopping the progressive Evil, Should be regarded as the Saviour of his Country.

I take the liberty of requesting your Attention to the Delivery of Sundry Letters enclosed for the Several Committees of Congress.[2]

I have the honor to be with due Respect Dear Sir Your obedient humble servant

WM. BINGHAM

ALS. Enclosures: William Bingham to the Continental Congress, 2 Feb. 1779; William Bingham's accounts with the Committee of Foreign Affairs, 19 Jan. 1779. DNA: PCC, 90.

William Bingham (1752–1804), a Philadelphia merchant, served as American commissioner in Martinique, 1776–80. For a discussion of Bingham's role as U.S. representative on the island and his private financial dealings with Robert Morris at the time, see Margaret Brown, "William Bingham, Agent of the Continental Congress in Martinique," *Pennsylvania Magazine of History and Biography*, LVI (1937), 54–87; and Robert C. Alberts, *The Golden Voyage: The Life and Times of William Bingham, 1752–1804* (Boston, 1969).

1 The depreciation of continental currency began in 1776 and continued at a moderate but steady rate until the autumn of 1779 when it began to increase quite sharply. Based on figures in E. James Ferguson, *The Power of the Purse, A History of American Public Finance, 1776–1790* (Chapel Hill, 1961), p. 32.

2 When Bingham's letters were read in Congress on 22 February, his letter of 2 February was referred to the Marine Committee and his accounts were referred to the Committee of Foreign Affairs. *JCC*, XIII, 218–219.

To George Clinton

Philadelphia, 3d February 1779

Sir

Major General Arnold has it in Contemplation to establish a Settlement of Officers and Soldiers who have served with him in the present War, and to lay the necessary Foundation without Loss of Time.[1] From a Desire to become a Citizen of New York he gives our State the Preferrence and now visits your Excellency to make the necessary Enquiries, it being out of our Power to give him any Information. The Necessity of strengthning our Frontiers is as obvious, as the Policy of drawing the Attention of the People to that Quarter in Season. Virginia we learn has taken the Lead and already passed Laws for laying out a district of Country for Settlement, and assigning Farms for their own Soldiers, as well as those of Maryland, Delaware and New Jersey.[2] A Strong Predilection, however, prevails in favour of our State, on Account of its' Situation for Trade, the acknowledged Excellency of its' Constitution, and the steady and vigorous Exertions of its' Government; Nothing, we are persuaded, will be wanting for it's rapid Settlement and Cultivation but a wise and liberal System for the distribution of the publick Land.

To you, Sir, or to our State, General Arnold can require no Recommendation. A Series of distinguished Services entitle him to Respect and Favour.

To him, We beg leave to refer your Excellency for the Intelligence from the Southward and from the West Indies; from Europe we have none.

We have the Honour to be with the highest Respect Sir your Excellency's most Obedient humble Servants

FRA. LEWIS
WM. FLOYD
JOHN JAY
JAS. DUANE

LS. MH. Body of the letter in the hand of James Duane.

1 Benedict Arnold, who had taken command of Philadelphia in May 1778, developed this scheme in late 1778. He set out for New York early in February 1779 to present his plan to the New York government. Shortly after he left the city, however, he received word of the misconduct charges drawn up against him by the Philadelphia council. He returned immediately to defend himself against these charges and his plans for a land grant in western New York were never presented to the state government at Poughkeepsie.

2 On 19 December 1778, the Virginia Senate approved a resolution "to more fully enable Congress to comply with the promise of a bounty in lands to the officers and soldiers of the army on the continental establishment . . . to furnish out of its territory between the rivers Ohio and Mississippi . . . without any purchase money, to the troops on continental establishment of such of the United States. . . ." *Journal of the Senate* (Williamsburg, 1779), p. 55.

From Robert R. Livingston

Poughkeepsie, 3d February 177[9]

Dear John

The pleasure I felt from your Letter of the 13th Ult. which I just now received was great in proportion to the pain I experienced from your neglect, and your friendly penitance has disarmed my resentment, and convinced me that there is no impropriety in supposing (at least if Angels resemble men) that there may be "more joy in heaven over one repentant sinner, than over 90 just that need no repentance."

Our Legislature have been convened near three weeks but have not proceeded upon business till within these few days. I shall attend regularly, and endeavour to render them all the little services in my power, not with a view to increase my own interest, or popularity, which I learn every day more and more to despise. From habit and passion I love and pity my fellow creatures, would to god I could esteem. My spirits never failed while our necessities called for great exertions, or while I was impelled by love for my country to contribute to the establishment of a government which was to be the basis of its future happiness. But I feel myself light in the scale of little party politicks. I can not combat a knave with calumnies, and to manage fools (to which I have some times submitted) disgusts me when it is no longer justified by any important end. I regard the present period as a blank in my time. I cannot enjoy the tranquil pleasures of a rural life. I converse with men I cant esteem, And I am engaged in a round of little politicks to which I feel myself superior. A happier hour may come, till when with hope for my companion I will endeavour to jog on.

You ask me whether any considerations would induce me to vissit another quarter of the globe? Those considerations must be weighty. The direction I go in must be respectable, my companion, if I have one, must be so too, And my appointments must be so far equal to my station that I may not break in upon my private fortune, for I have no Idea of being a great man abroad to be a little one all my life after at home. I would not have you conclude from this, that I have any eager desire to begin my travels, but merely to leave to you, if any thing of this kind should be proposed to act as you thought best for the interest of the community and your friend. You know my strong and my weak sides well enough to save my modesty the pain of saying how far I might be useful, and my vanity the mortification of hearing in how many more points I am disqualified.

Some folks here have thought it might lessten my popularity to report that I was concerned with Hake in some goods that he brought out from New York, and he was scoundrel enough to encourage the report, in hopes that it might contribute to save them after they were seized. As this report may have possibly reached you, I enclose you a certificate, which when closely pressed he was compelled to give, and an affidavit of Johns who was concerned with him in the goods.[1] With these you may contradict any calumnies that may have reached you. I declined any publication as I thought it rather beneath the character I have endeavoured to maintain to take any notice of it. You will find by the Governor's Letter which accompanies this,[2] that you are continued in the delegation, a measure which will I hope be agreeable to you. Remember me to Morris who seems to have forgot me. I am Dear John Affectionately your friend and Humble Servant

ROBT. R. LIVINGSTON

ALS. Endorsed: ". . . with Hake's Certificate." Livingston misdated his letter 1778 and JJ endorsed the letter with the same erroneous date. Enclosures: Certificate of Samuel Hake and affidavit of John R. Livingston. Neither document has been located.

1 Samuel Hake, the husband of Livingston's second cousin Helen Livingston, was a New York merchant. In January 1776 Hake left for England; two years later while returning to New York he was taken prisoner. However, in September 1778, Hake obtained a pass from Washington and, with George Clinton's consent, traveled to New York City to remove his books, papers, and other personal property. When he returned from behind enemy lines in October, Hake brought merchandise to be sold in American-held territory. He was promptly arrested and remained on parole until the end of the war. John R. Livingston (1755–1851), Chancellor Livingston's younger brother, had entered into an agreement with Hake on 12 Aug. 1778 which provided that the two were to be equal partners in the purchase and sale of "whatever Goods he [Hake] may purchase in the City of N. York." After his arrest, Hake complained that John Livingston had assured him that Robert Livingston had obtained Washington's approval of the plan to bring merchandise out of New York City. *GCP*, IV, 232–33, 265–66; V, 297–300.

2 Clinton did not write JJ concerning his continuance as a delegate until 9 February, ALS in JP.

FROM ROBERT TROUP

Middle Brook, February 7th, 1779

My dear Sir,

In the Conclusion of my last Letter to you I intimated that I should wait for Intelligence from England before I resolved either to leave the Army or to continue in it. I think it idle to form Conjectures about the future Measures the Ministry will adopt. To me, who am a Child in the Science of Politics, it would appear Madness in them to prosecute the War against us and the House of Bourbon. But there are so many of them, quibus Bellum utile est,[1] that I should not be surprised if the same ruinous Councils should still prevail. If they cannot reinforce their Army so as to enable it to take the Field with a Prospect of important Success they may carry on a partisan War and endeavour to deprive us of the Pleasure of eating *Poultry*.

In this Situation of Affairs I should be at a Loss to know what to do. The Motives which led me into the Army would in great Measure cease. This time Peace would not be restored; but the Independence and with it the Freedom of America would be fixed on a sure and permanent Basis. Ought I then to resign, and return to my Studies? I believe I ought. My Reasons will be the Subject of another Letter.

I enclose for your Perusal a Copy of the Certificate General Gates gave me. It paints his Inconsistency in striking Colours. Hence you will see the Futility, to say Nothing of the Cruelty, of all his Charges against me.

Before I got this Certificate I was extremely uneasy for I foresaw the Benefit I should derive from it. I trusted some Time to his Generosity; but was deceived. At length I embraced a favorable Opportunity, when he was alone, of addressing him in the following Manner. "Sir, I have already apprised you of my serious Intention to leave you. I have now one Request to make which probably will be the last I shall ever trouble you with. Sir, as I have only a Brevet Commission I request of you a Certificate of my Services since I have been in your Family. Do not imagine, Sir, that by granting me one you will oblige me. Upon this Footing I disdain it. Sir, I demand it as a Matter of Right, because I am conscious of the Uprightness of my Conduct." He said, "sit down—write one to please yourself—and I will sign it." I replied, "Sir, You are very polite; but sooner than my Right Hand should be guilty of an Act so dishonorable I would cut it off." He then directed his Secretary, Mr. Clajon,[2] to draw one: and after the Original of the inclosed was finished he signed it with Reluctance, observing "it might have been more respectful."

I can apoligise for sending you a Copy of it, in no other Manner, than by assuring you of my Desire to be favored with the indulgent Opinion your Goodness has long entertained of me. When I become a Toole to designing Ambition, When I stoop to the vile Arts of Adulation to secure a temporary Interest, And when I lose the grateful Remembrance of your many Kindnesses to me may I be despised by you as much as I shall be hated by myself.

I offer my Compliments to Col. Livingston, and Major Clarkson, and am, My dear Sir, With the purest Affection, Your Friend

ROB. TROUP

ALS. Endorsed. Enclosure: copy in Troup's hand of Horatio Gates' certificate on behalf of Robert Troup, 27 Nov. 1777, stating that Gates ". . . had many Proofs of Lieutenant Colonel Troup's Bravery, Integrity and watchful Zeal. . . ."

1 "For whom war is useful."

2 William Clajon, a Frenchman, was Gates's secretary.

FROM JOHN MCKESSON

Poughkeepsie, February 8th 1779

Sir

I have the Pleasure to inform you that in pursuance of a Resolution of the Assembly on the second, and a concurrent Resolution of Senate on the 4th Instant, (in both cases without a dissenting voice) your appointment as a Delegate to Congress is to be continued until thirty Days after the next meeting of the Legislature.[1]

Mr. Allen in A late publication[2] asserts, that all the Members of Congress, except those from New York, are of opinion, that the three disaffected Counties (alias the State of Vermont) ought to be erected into a Separate State. If this is true, which I do not believe, the sooner the matter is determined the better. But even in that Case, care should be taken to make it an express Condition that the other Inhabitants of this State should be secured in the Lands they hold in those Counties, by Title derived from both the former Governments of New Hampshire and New York, or under the former Government of New York, where there was not any prior Grant to the New York Title. Senate and Assembly have appointed a joint Committee to report a Letter to the Delegates of this State on the Subject of those three Counties. Nothing is yet done towards forming the draft of that Letter, but I imagine it will be in general Terms, not containing any particular directions.

The Assembly have agreed to a Tax Bill which is ordered to be engrossed; the Tax is to be one Shilling in the pound on real Estates, as valued in the year 1775, and Six pence in the pound on personal Estates at their present value.[3]

The Resolutions of Congress as to their two Emissions of Bills of Credit to be called in, have entirely struck those Bills out of Circulation here.[4] If some marks or Criterions to distinguish the true Bills of those Emissions from the False, which are in the Hands of a few here, be right, we have more of the Counterfeit than the true Bills. And in that Case unless Congress redeem the Counterfeit Bills, either our State and County Treasurers are ruined, or the State itself immensly burthened to bear the Loss. In general we distinguished and stopped the many Copperplated Counterfeits of those two Emissions, and also the Copperplated Counterfeits dated at Baltimore on the 26th February but until lately had not any Apprehension of Counterfeits printed with the Same Types, and on paper which cannot be distinguished from that of the true Bills, except by certain private marks in the printing. And I may at least say, that the Credit of all Continental Currency suffers so much, that the Bills of Credit of our own State is the most acceptable circulating paper Medium amongst us.

Notwithstanding the Law of this State empowering Commissaries in certain Cases to seize Flour, meal and Wheat for the use of the Army,[5] the Legislature is now obliged to very serious Exertions to feed (and preserve from disbanding) the little Army in and about the Highlands.

An Expedition to Canada is not much relished in this State, nor any Advantages expected from the Measure. It is said that Considering how indian Affairs have been managed, a Western Expedition to humble the Indians, and keep their Country in Possession or put it out of their Power to do further mischief, would be the only beneficial inland Measure.

My Situation does not allow me time to Copy anything I write in this way, you will therefore excuse sending you the Draft; and if any Hints I can communicate of matters here can be of any use to you, no one will more cheerfully embrace every opportunity, than Sir your most obedient humble servant

JOHN MCKESSON

ALS. Addressed: "The Honorable John Jay Esquire President of Congress Philadelphia pr Mr. Barclay." Endorsed: ". . . ackd 16 Inst." JJ's reply of 16 Feb. 1779 has not been located.

1 *Votes and Proceedings of the Assembly of the State of New York* . . . (Fishkill, 1777 [1779]), p. 49. *Votes and Proceedings of the Senate of the State of New York* . . . (Fishkill, 1777 [1779]), p. 163.

2 Ethan Allen, "An Animadversory Address to the Inhabitants of the State of Vermont . . . ," at Bennington, 9 Aug. 1778. Evans, 15719.

3 "An Act for raising monies to be applied towards the public Exigencies of this State," passed by the Assembly on 6 Feb. 1779. *Votes and Proceedings of the Assembly of the State of New York* . . . (Fishkill, 1777 [1779]), p. 57.

4 The emissions of 20 May 1777 and 11 April 1778. See *LMCC*, III, 542–43, for debates on the recall of these issues.

5 "An Act more effectually to provide supplies of Flour, Meal and Wheat for the Army," passed 31 Oct. 1778 and strengthened by the Assembly on 4 Feb. 1779. *Votes and Proceedings of the Assembly of the State of New York* . . . (Fishkill, 1777 [1779]), p. 53.

From Sarah Livingston Jay

Persipiney, February 12th, 1779

My dear Mr. Jay,

I am utterly at a loss to account for the miscarriages of my letters, having frequently wrote and sent my letters by what I then thought safe conveyances, and I am more surprised still that neither you nor your brother[1] have received those which Susan and I wrote by Mrs. Ferguson who promised Susan to send them as soon as she arrived at Philadelphia. I will not trouble you with repetition of my anxiety to see you. Permit me however to transcribe a couple of lines that Mason gives us from the lips of his amiable Elfrida as very expressive of my own impatience.

> With what a tedious and retarding weight
> Does Expectation load the wing of Time.[2]

Poor Kit is very anxious to know her fate as she calls it whether she shall spend the months of march and april agreably at Philadelphia or waste them in obscurity and dullness. We last evening received invitations from General Knox[3] to celebrate the Alliance with France at his Quarters the 18th inst. As Brockholst dropt a hint in his letter to the girls of being at Camp at that time if business would admit, I am very solicitous that Kitty should be there, especially as there has been several dances at which she has been invitated but been present at none.

I wrote to sister Jay[4] some time ago desiring she would send me the gloves she had of mine and in an answer to my letter she informs me that she has sent them to you. Pray, my dear, have you received them?

Our dear little boy has had two severe fits of illness occasioned by worms. During his indisposition my suffering I think was little inferior to his as he was only affected by immediate pain and not by any apprehension of future consequences, happy negligence of disposition that attends the state of child-hood!

I have been blessed with a great share of health the whole winter. The weather is very dull at present. Perhaps the transition from such lovely weather as we have been accustomed to lately may effect my spirits. Whatever it is, they are not as I would wish when with you. I will therefore bid you adieu. Perhaps when Montanie returns he will bring me a letter from you which (should the depression of my spirits continue till then) will effectually chear the gloom and for the time banish every disagreeable sensation. Once more my Love, adieu. Believe me to be most affectionately your

SA. JAY

My love to Brockholst.

ALS.

1 Frederick Jay.

2 A quote from *Elfrida,* written in 1753 by the British poet William Mason (1725–97).

3 Brigadier General Henry Knox (1750–1806) of Massachusetts commanded the Continental Army's artillery.

4 Margaret Barclay Jay.

To Robert Morris

Philadelphia, 15th February 1779

Sir

When Characters, rendered amiable by Virtues, and important by talents, are exposed to suspicions and become Subjects of Investigation, the Sensibility of Individuals, as well as the Interest of the Public are concerned in the Event of the Enquiry.

It gives me particular pleasure therefore to transmit to You an unanimous Act of Congress of the 11th Inst. not only acquitting your Conduct in the transaction it relates to, of blame, but giving it that express Approbation which Patriotism in the public, and Integrity in every walk of Life always merit and seldom fail ultimately to receive.

I am Sir with great Respect and Esteem Your most Obedient Servant

J. J.

LbkC. DNA: PCC, 14. Enclosure: Resolution of Congress, 11 Feb. 1779, in *JCC,* XIII, 164–67. Dft. in JP; Tr in NN: Bancroft American Series, vol. 1, p. 194.

In December 1778 Thomas Paine, a partisan in the Deane-Lee controversy, published a series of articles hinting at improprieties on the part of Robert Morris and other men who had business relationships with Silas Deane. In January 1779 Henry Laurens accused Morris of mishandling the accounts of the secret commercial committee of Congress as well as the tobacco consignment. After a week of charges and countercharges, Congress appointed a committee "to enquire into the facts." Its report adopted by Congress 11 February completely vindicating Morris was forwarded to him by President JJ. *LMCC,* IV, 20; *JCC,* XIII, 46–47, 49–50, 79–86, 158–59, 164–67.

To Robert R. Livingston

Philadelphia, 16 February 1779

Dear Robert

Your Favor of the 3d Inst. came to Hand this morning. The Satisfaction my Letter afforded you flatters as well as pleases me. It argues a Remembrance of former Times; for which and other Reasons I shall give you no more opportunities of joining the assembly of angels in rejoicing over penitent Mortals. Not that I mean, on the one Hand, to enter the State of Reprobation and become a hardned Sinner, or on the other enlist with those Saints who *slip not with their Feet.* This Letter, written on the very Day I recieved Yours, will be some Evidence of my having gone thro the whole Process of Amendment. Divines you know describe it as consisting of Conviction, Contrition, and Conversion. Whether I shall persevere or not, is a Subject on which Time will utter the surest Prophecies.

The Complections of Resignation, soft Complaint, and joyless Sensibility, are so blended in your Letter, that (if anonymous) one would suppose it written by a wayworn Traveller through this Vale of Tears, who journeying towards his distant Heaven, thro sultry Heats and dreary Paths, at Length lays his languid Limbs under some friendly Shade, and permits the Effusions of his Soul to escape in words. My Friend a mind unbraced and Nerves relaxed are not fit Company for each other. It was not a Man whom the Poet tells us "pined in Thought and sat like Patience on a monument smiling at Grief." In such rugged Times as these other Sensations are to be cherished. Rural Scenes, domestic Bliss, and the charming Group of Pleasures found in the Train of Peace, fly at the approach of War, and are seldom to be found in Fields stained with Blood, or Habitations polluted by outrage and Desolation. I admire your Sensibility, nor would I wish to see less Milk in your Veins—you would be less amiable. In my Opinion however your Reasoning is not quite just. I think a Mans Happiness requires that he should Condescend to keep himself free from Fleas and Wasps, as well as Thiefs and Robbers.

When the present Session of your Legislature is ended, take a Ride and see us. You will find many here happy to see you. Morris[1] has not forgotten you, and I will answer for his Memory on that Subject. He is busy and useful, more busy indeed than most others, for besides the Affairs of Congress, he is daily employed in making Oblations to Venus and Sacrifices to Asculapius. Remember this is to be translated in the best Sense, and not so construed as to mean Vice or Pox.

The Report arising from Hakes Importations has no Currency here. If it should, I shall put your Mark of Counterfiet upon it. I have heard Nothing of that Business since I left you, except Capt. Banckers[2] telling me that some of the goods had been discovered and seized. If Hake deserved half the Censure bestowed upon him by those, who ought to have known him, he had a Right only to that

Species of Politeness which Gentlemen practice to keep Men of that Character at a Distance.

I have something, tho not very interesting, to say to you on the Subject of Politics, but as it is now very late, and I have been writing Letters ever since Dinner, I am really too much fatigued to proceed. Make my Compliments to Mrs. Livingston, who I presume is with You. Adieu.

I am your Friend and Servant

JOHN JAY

P.S. You say Nothing of Edward.[3]

ALS. NHi: Robert R. Livingston Papers. Dft in JP.

[1] Gouverneur Morris was a member of New York's delegation to the Continental Congress. *LMCC*, VI, lix.

[2] Probably Captain Johannes, or John, Bancker (b. 1738), a descendant of the Albany family who lived in New York. *N.Y.G.B.R.*, II, 69.

[3] Edward Livingston (1764–1836), the youngest child of Robert R., Sr., and Margaret Beekman Livingston (c. 1724–1800).

From William Bingham

[St. Pierre, Martinique], February 17th, 1779
Duplicate

Dear Sir,

Above is Copy of my last Respects, since writing of which the Continental Frigate the Deane, and the armed Brig[antin]e the General Gates have arrived here in order to careen and refit.

I am sensible I shall expose myself to innumerable Difficulties in undertaking to supply these Vessels with what they stand in need of. Nothing but the Pain I must feel at seeing the Service suffer could induce me to do it. Perhaps you may be surprized at my making these Observations to you in your private Capacity, but I am inclined to do it from the Hopes that you will use your Influence in removing the Cause of Complaint, which is the want of sufficient permanent Funds for the Payment of the various incidental Expences of the Service. Deprived of Remittances from the Continent, and not having Liberty to draw upon France, I have no Resources that can enable me to do Honor to the Engagements that it is necessary to enter into for the Public Account, for Disbursements on Continental Vessels and Expences attending the Maintenance of Prisoners, their Exchange, etc., etc.[1]

The Balance of Account due to me from Congress Amounts to an enormous Sum, and that I should be again called upon to make fresh Advances is a peculiar and grievous Hardship.

Perhaps I am the only Person that without Public Money, has supplied the Public Necessities, and whilst the Continent laboured under a Difficulty of establishing Funds abroad, I chearfully ventured as far as my Credit and my Personal Safety would admit. But at present, when they have such Resources in France I cannot see the Propriety or Justice of being called upon to sacrifice my Credit, and torment my Feelings, by entering into Engagements on the Public Account, which I am not able to fulfil. It is a partial, and I cannot but think an unmerited Distinction, operating greatly to my Disadvantage.

I must request that you would use your Influence with Congress for establishing Funds to reimburse me for the Advances that I have already made, and shall be again under the Necessity of making; in doing which you will greatly oblige me, and you may be well assured that I shall always entertain a grateful Sense of the Faver. My Letters on this Subject to the respective Committees of Congress have been treated with a peculiar Inattention.[2]

I have the Honor to be with Sentiments of perfect Esteem Dear Sir your obedient humble Servant

WM. BINGHAM

ALS. TriplC also in JP. Enclosure: C of William Bingham to JJ, [3] Feb. 1779, misdated "5 February." This letter is printed above under the correct date.

[1] Under his instructions of 3 June 1776 Bingham was permitted as a private citizen to carry on personal business affairs while commercial agent in Martinique. Congress, however, exhibited a reluctance to pay the debts contracted by Bingham in his official capacity. In the emergency created by the arrival of the *Deane* and the *General Gates,* whose commanders expected Bingham to pay for repairs, he borrowed 90,910 livres Martinique from the government of Martinique. In turn, Bingham drew on Benjamin Franklin for 100,000 livres tournois for this and other charges which Franklin refused to honor because of the many financial demands on him. Robert C. Alberts, *The Golden Voyage: The Life and Times of William Bingham, 1752–1804* (Boston, 1969), pp. 72–73, 78; for a discussion of Bingham's public and private accounts, see E. James Ferguson, *The Power of the Purse: A History of American Public Finance, 1776–1790* (Chapel Hill, 1961), pp. 78–80, 134–35, 193, 199.

[2] In a letter to the Commercial Committee of 24 January Bingham sent a copy of current accounts showing that Congress owed him 247,000 *livres.* Bingham's letter of 2 February was read in Congress on 22 February and referred to the Marine Committee and the Committee of Foreign Affairs. William Bingham to the Commercial Commitee, 27 Jan. 1779, DNA: PCC, Miscellany, CIV; *JCC,* XIII, 218–19.

FROM SARAH LIVINGSTON JAY

Persipiney, February 18th, 1779

I thank you my dear Mr. Jay, for your kind letters of the 31st of January and 5th of February.[1] Be assured the advice contained in them was as welcome as indeed it was requisite. Continue I beseech you your friendly admonitions, for really no one ever required that aid from friendship more than I do in my present circumstances. For am I not prevented from indulging the pleasing prospect of the re-union of my family lest the frowns of disappointment check my innocent expectations? And if I contract my views to my present situation, what consideration can compensate for the loss I suffer by the absence of my friend, and that for God knows how long a time, since who can tell when this unhappy war shall cease. But avaunt painful reflections! Pardon my dear these emotions of discontent. I know they are wrong and discourage as much as possible sentiments of despondency.

Sister Kitty and brother Jack are at Pluckemin.[2] They dine to-day at General Knox's quarters where he has prepared splendid entertainments of Fireworks, Balls etc. We had an invitation from the ladies at Baskenridge to take their house in our way. Several reasons induced me to decline making one of the party. I hope Kitty will not be disappointed in her expectation of meeting Brockholst at Pluckemin.

Why enjoin me my dear so frequently to be particular about my health? I remember Papa once told William when at school that he would always take it for granted that he was well, provided William mentioned nothing to the contrary. Will not that be a sufficient assurance likewise for you if I promise to inform you when I am indisposed.

You can't imagine what satisfaction I receive from the increasing fondness of my little boy who frequently inquires where his papa stays so long and if you never intend to return. In telling him stories and teaching him to spell I deceive many hours that would otherwise linger on unamused and sometimes unemployed.

Mamma and William desire to be remembred to you and your Sec[retar]y. Susan and Judy are at Eliz[abeth] Town with Papa. Mr. W[3] urges his suit with great ardour; I fancy I will be prevailed upon to resign her hand and liberty to his guardianship next autumn. He pleads for that happiness in the spring but prudential reasons incline her to wait till fall. Dr. Darby can't be prevailed upon to part with the boy. I have examined the trunks, but found no moth in them.

Adieu my dear. May providence smile upon your endeavour's for the public weal and reward your constancy. I am most affectionately Yours

SA. JAY

ALS. Endorsed.

1 JJ to SLJ, 31 Jan. and 5 Feb. 1779 have not been located.

2 Pluckemin, N.J., is in Somerset County, about thirty-nine miles from Trenton.

3 John Watkyn Watkins, Jr., of New York served as a major in the Continental Army and aide-de-camp to SLJ's uncle by marriage, William Alexander, Lord Stirling. He married SLJ's younger sister Judith Livingston (1758–1843) on 6 April 1780.

To George Clinton

Philadelphia, 19 February 1779

Dear Sir

Your very friendly Letters of the 10th Ulto. and 2d and 9th Inst.[1] by Mr. Barclay, gave me Pleasure. Accept my Thanks for these Instances of Attention, and be so obliging as now and then to tell me how you do, and what political operations distress or promote the public Weal.

The Bill respecting the Council of Revision is a most insidious Measure. I always wished to see their Proceedings published, and think the Circumstance will afford full Justification to that Step. The real Farmers Plan of Finance is so abominably wicked as well as unpolitic, that it ought to be exposed, and the Eyes of the public turned to the Author.[2]

We have no late accounts from Georgia. There is little Reason however to doubt of the Enemy's being in full possession of it. Large Reinforcements are ordered and probably gone to Gen. Lincoln.[3] What his Force will on their arrival amount to is uncertain; nor can We be certain that they will be equal to the Recovery of that State. Besides you know militia cannot be kept long in the Field. We are under no great apprehensions for South Carolina, tho several Circumstances render it vulnerable. The Enemy possess St. Lucia. What further Events have happened in the W. Indies is a Subject on which we have no Information.

Mr Duane promises to prepare a joint Letter for the Delegates to you, and I imagine it will be ready in the Morning.[4] Lest it should not, it may be proper to inform you that all the Departments are placed under the immediate Direction of Gen. Washington, and therefore that Provision for the Security of the Frontiers fall within the Line of his Duty and Authority. Pennsylvania is under similar Circumstances with you, and will equally demand and be referred to his Care and Protection. His Respect for New York, and the personal Regard he assures me, he entertains for its Governor, will I am persuaded unite with other more general Considerations in drawing his Attention to your Exegences and affording the State all the Security in his Power to give.

The Scarcity of Bread in the East and South is become a serious Subject, and I hope Care will be taken to prevent so great a Calamity in New York. Give while you have to spare, but Regard to self Preservation ought to set Bounds even to Acts of Benevolence.

One of our Frigates has sent a fine armed Vessel of 16 Guns into Boston. The Coast from Delaware to Chesspeake is extremely infested by Privateers from the City of New York. The Merchants here are preparing to protect their Trade by fitting out armed Vessels for the Purpose.

This State is immersed in politics and Perplexity, the opposition to the Constitution is respectable and formidable. The Presidents want of Temper and Prudence has injured him. The public Papers will give you more Information on this Subject. Arnold is hard run by them.[5]

Be pleased to make my Compliments to Mrs. Clinton, and to the two Bensons and Lush.[6]

I am Dear Sir Your friend and Servant[7]

JOHN JAY

ALS. NjMoInd: Lloyd W. Smith Coll. Endorsed. Dft in JP; E in NN: Bancroft American Series, I, 197.

[1] Clinton's letter of 10 Jan. 1779 has not been located. The 2 February letter is printed above; for Clinton to JJ, 9 Feb. 1779, see *GCP*, IV, 554–55.

[2] See Clinton to JJ, 2 Feb. 1779, above, and 9 Feb. 1779 in *GCP*, IV, 554–55.

[3] Major General Benjamin Lincoln was named commander of the Southern Department in September 1778. *JCC*, XII, 951.

[4] Joint letter of the New York delegates to Clinton, 19 Feb. 1779, *GCP*, IV, 580–82.

[5] Joseph Reed (1741–85) of New Jersey, the President of the Supreme Executive Council of Pennsylvania, presented the Continental Congress with eight charges against Benedict Arnold on 15 Feb. 1779. Arnold had been indicted in January by the Pennsylvania Council for alleged abuses of his command in Philadelphia. Congress directed that Arnold be tried by a court-martial. *JCC*, XIII, 184.

6 Egbert and Robert Benson. Major Stephen Lush was Governor Clinton's aide.

7 JJ's closing sentence in the draft, which is omitted from the ALS: "Let all your private Letters to me be rendered *private*—God bless you."

FROM CATHARINE W. LIVINGSTON

Quarters of the Artillery,
New Jersey, February 20th, 1779

Its with pleasure I acquies in the request Sister Jay made of my sending you a bill of health from this place. I wish I could say as much for her spirits as health, the latter she has enjoyed all winter, and deserves credit for her Chearfullness, but her spirits have of late flagd. I believe if the good Company, Fire-Works and the rest of the entertainment, could they have induced her, or I have influenced her to have been of the party, would have concured to have raised her spirits. Its to her influence and the expectation I had of seeing my brother that I partook of the entertainment, and was not a little mortified at my disappointment, but that was not the greatest I met with.

I wont now take up your attention with what, as its less interesting to you than the welfare of your sweet dear Boy, who every day presents more and more pleasing to his partial Relations. Do not suspect his being a hot bed plant, he eludes every wish of his Grand Mothers to keep him with her, and is almost altogether in the Wood yard. He observed to his Grand-Mother the other day when puting in his shoes a little wool to make them smaller, that she did not do well his Pappa would not like it. Mamma was indisposed when I left home; she has not enjoyed her usual share of health this winter. The rest of the Family were well. I came out an invalid, and am very anxious to return, least I should be absent when B.[1] comes for Sister. I sent to the Post office for Letters. If there was any for me they are in the packet for Morris Town and are gone on. B. is very punctual and he has I hope received two long letters from me. I began this one at General Knox's quarters, but the incessant interruptions from the Ladies to the toilet, and the shower of Continental powder on my paper obliged me to defered it till today. Yesterday I had the pleasure of dining at head quarters, and was quite delighted with Mrs. Washington. The General and some other General Officers expressed their satisfaction at your continuance in your office.

A few days ago we were made happy by the receipt of some Letters from long Island. Cousins Sally Browne, and Peggy Clarkson, are very desireous to pay us a visit, and have solicited our influence for a pass for them. Colonel Webb who is at present at Philadelphia is an humble Servant of Peggy's. I have not had the pleasure of seeing him but have heard civil things of him.[2]

One of your favorite Beauties, Miss Helena Morris is seting by me and desires her Compliments to B. I am afraid it will make the creature vain if he sets out in the course of this week. I wish he would call at head quarters, he will find me there or in the neighbourhood. Next week Mr. Duer is to escort me home, by the way of Elizabeth Town. Its very gay at Camp at present, the Troy, the Prince Ton, and the Baskenridge Belles are all here. Colonel Tilgman[3] who is to forward this to you desires his Compliments may accompany it. As there will not be any enquirys none will be necessary from me. My Love to Brock. and accept the same from your Affectionate Friend and Sister

AL.

1 Henry Brockholst Livingston.

2 Sarah Browne (b. 1745), the stepdaughter of SLJ's aunt, Mary French (Mrs. William) Browne, was the daughter of William Browne of Salem, Mass., and his first wife, Mary Burnet Browne. Ann Margaret Clarkson (1761–84) was the daughter of SLJ's aunt, Elizabeth French (Mrs. Matthew) Clarkson. Colonel Webb was probably Colonel Samuel Blatchley Webb (1753–1807), Silas Deane's stepson. He had been captured by the British during a raid on Long Island in December 1777 and exchanged a year later.

3 Helena Morris (1762–1840), the daughter of Lewis and Mary Walton Morris of New York, married John Rutherford in 1782. Colonel Tench Tilghman (1744–86) was an aide-de-camp and military secretary to George Washington.

From Charles Lee

Philadelphia, February the 27th, 1779

Sir

The negative put by Congress on my request to avail myself of Capt. Tolty's friendship and Sir Henry Clintons kindness throws me into the most serious distress. When I wrote from Elizabeth Town to Colonel Butler on this subject supposing him to be at N. York, I had reason to believe that the only difficulty I shoud have to combat with woud arise from Sir Henry Clinton, not from Congress, as I coud have no notion that the drawing hard money from New York coud be prejudicial to this Continent. Indeed the greater the portion of my property I coud procure the greater I thought woud be the advantage to America who are bound by their Representatives in Congress to indemnify me for my fortune according to the estimate I gave in, (which is several thousand pounds less than what it at present really

AT THE SECOND CONTINENTAL CONGRESS

Pennsylvania State House ("Independence Hall"), site of the sessions of the Second Continental Congress. Serving as a prison for captured American soldiers during the British occupation of Philadelphia, the edifice was remodeled and refurbished by 1779, the period of Jay's Presidency. (*Independence National Historical Park Collection*)

VERMONT: THE ISSUE THAT PROMPTED JAY'S RETURN TO CONGRESS

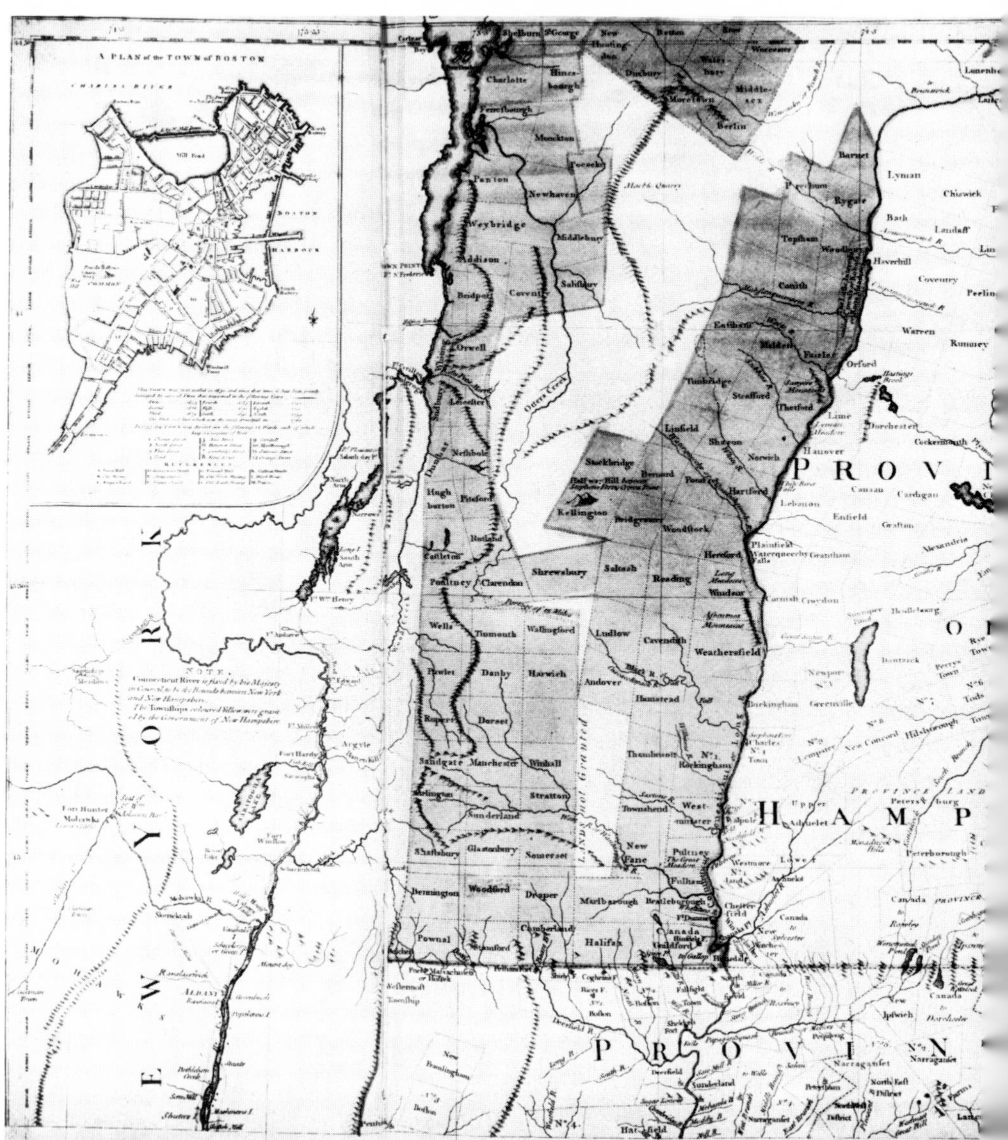

"A Map of the Most Inhabited Part of New England," depicting the New Hampshire Grants, 1774. By Thomas Jefferys. (*Vermont Historical Society*)

Silas Deane. Attributed to Charles Willson Peale. (*Connecticut Historical Society*)

Arthur Lee. By Charles Willson Peale. (*Independence National Historical Park Collection*)

Thomas Paine. By John Wesley Jarvis. (*National Gallery of Art, Washington, D.C.*)

Henry Laurens. By John Singleton Copley. (*National Portrait Gallery, Smithsonian Institution, Washington, D.C., Gift of Andrew Mellon*)

WASHINGTON WINS THE BACKING OF CONGRESS'S NEW PRESIDENT

General George Washington. By Charles Willson Peale. (*The Pennsylvania Academy of the Fine Arts*)

THE MILITARY THEATER DURING JAY'S PRESIDENCY: THE NORTHERN CAMPAIGN

The Marquis de Lafayette, whose Canadian campaign was countermanded. After an original by Charles Willson Peale. (*Independence National Historical Park Collection*)

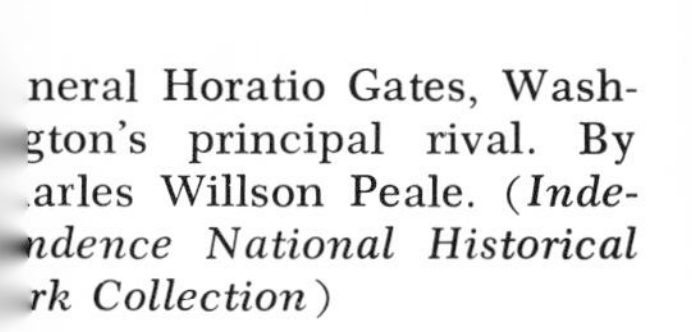

neral Horatio Gates, Washgton's principal rival. By .arles Willson Peale. (*Indendence National Historical rk Collection*)

General John Sullivan, who brought terror and devastation to the Indian country. By Charles Willson Peale. (*Independence National Historical Park Collection*)

General Nathanael Greene, Quartermaster-General during Jay's Presidency. After an original by Charles Willson Peale. (*Independence National Historical Park Collection*)

LEADERS IN THE EFFORT TO CURB RUNAWAY INFLATION AND FISCAL IRRESPONSIBILITY

Gouverneur Morris and Robert Morris. By Charles Willson Peale. (*Pennsylvania Academy of the Fine Arts*)

THE JAY PARTY SAILS FOR SPAIN

The Continental Frigate *Confederacy*. By Nowland Van Powell. (*Courtesy of the Bruce Gallery, Memphis, Tennessee*)

SHIPBOARD COMPANIONS

Conrad Alexandre Gérard, retiring minister from France to the United States. By Charles Willson Peale. (*Independence National Historical Park Collection*)

William Carmichael, Secretary of Jay's Mission to Spain. American School, Maryland, eighteenth century. (*Courtesy of Mrs. Frederick Ewing, Fall City, Washington, and the Frick Art Reference Library*)

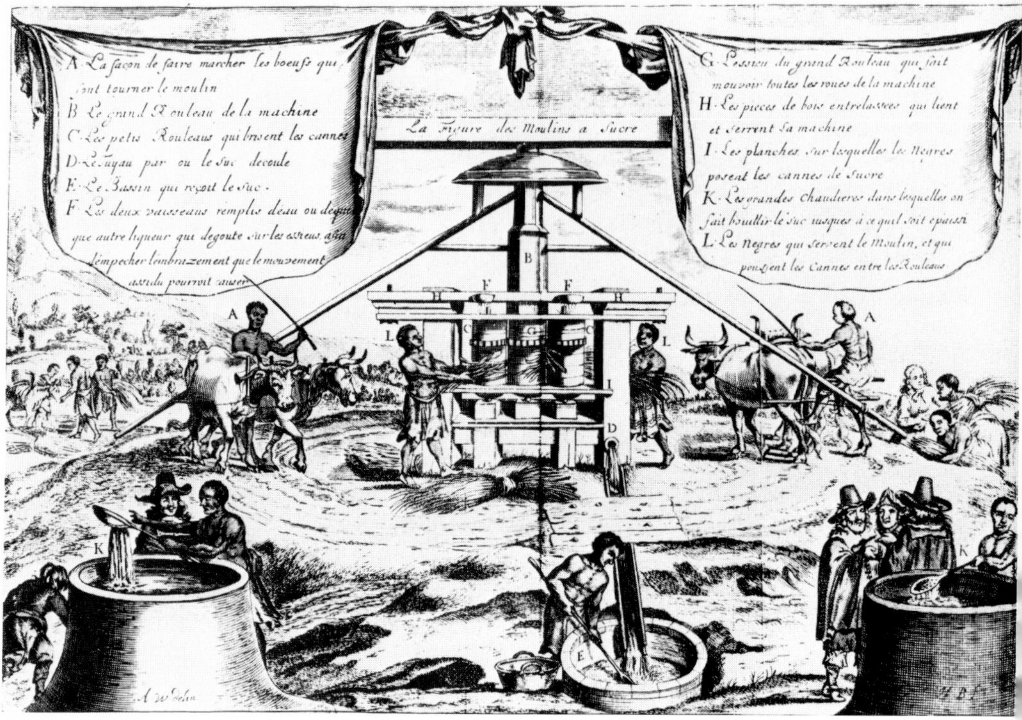

A FORCED LAY-OVER IN MARTINIQUE

A sugar mill in Martinique of the type described by Sarah Jay. Engraving from P. Du Tertre, *Histoire Naturelle et morale des îles Antilles de l'Amerique.* (*Rotterdam, 1665*)

William Bingham, Congressional agent in Martinique and trading partner of Robert Morris. Bingham was host to the Jays on their visit. By Charles Willson Peale. (*Museum of Art, Carnegie Institute*)

PASSPORT TO MADRID

D. ALEXANDRO O REILLY, CONDE DE O REILLY,
CABALLERO COMENDADOR DE BENFAYAN EN LA ORDEN DE ALCANTARA
Consejero Nato en el Supremo de Guerra, Theniente General de los Reales Exercitos, Inspector General de la Infanteria, Governador, y Capitan General del Exercito, y Reynos de Andalucia, y de las Costas del Mar Occeano, &c.

POR quanto Dn Juan Jay con su familia criados, y Armas para resguardo de su Persona, para à Madrid. Las Justicias le facilitaràn todos los auxilios que pidiere

Ordeno, y mando á las Justicias sugetas à mi Jurisdiccion, y à las que no lo son pido, y encargo no le pongan impedimento alguno en su viage, antes sì le dèn el favor, y auxilio que necesitare, el Aloxamiento, Carros, y Bagages que pidiere, pagandolos à los precios reglados, sin que passen de un transito à otro, por convenir assi al Real Servicio. Puerto de Santa Maria, y Marzo a 20 de 1780

(*Jay Papers, Special Collections, Columbia University Libraries*)

The Harvesters. By Goya. (*Museo del Prado, Madrid*)

Brawling in Front of an Inn. By Goya. (*Museo del Prado, Madrid*)

►

Fiesta Outside the Summer Palace at Aranjuez, "Parejas reales." Painting by Louis Paret y Alcázar. (*Museo del Prado, Madrid*)

Fighting on Stilts. By Goya. (*Museo del Prado, Madrid*)

JAY'S PRINCIPAL ANTAGONIST IN SPAIN

The Conde de Floridablanca, Spain's Principal Minister. Attributed to Raphael Mengs. (*Courtesy of Señor D. Estobán Hernández, Madrid*)

ımuel Huntington, President Congress during Jay's Span- Mission. By Charles Will- n Peale. (*Independence Na- nal Historical Park Collec- n*)

arles Thomson, Philadelphia lical and Congress's Perma- t Secretary. By Charles llson Peale. (*Independence tional Historical Park Col- tion*)

JAY'S CRUCIAL CONFERENCE WITH FLORIDABLANCA, 23 SEPTEMBER 1780

The count here interrupted Mr. Jay by saying that the interest of France and Spain with respect to America were so distinct as necessarily different Treaties necessary Mr. Jay answered that admitting this to be the case, the Treaty with France might be made the basis, and they might go on Mutatis Mutandis— The Count

that his Majesty would never consent make Treaty
replied 509.23, 269.14, 336.27, 557.24, 363.19, 118.17, to 336.13, that 520.36,

the basis of one between him and that Treaty
510.40, 44.13, 371.12, 373.22, 551.7, 269.30 24.18 the United States, that 509.23 520.36

concluded by French without the knowledge of without
had been 115.33 79.17 the 227.12 555.11 510.40, 313.21 371.12 the King and 555.11

having made him the offer of party to it That the
261.11 g 335.20, 269.30, 570.40, 371.25, 371.12, being a 386.11, 514.13 307.29. 509.23 510.40

Kings resentment so much excited by this conduct as nigh to have
311.39 437.12 had been 477.12, 357.22, 102.31, 79.17, 511.13 116.34 32.15 well 564.15, 514.13, 261.11

occasioned a rupture that on the secret article
317.35 614 448.16 551.7 between the two Courts, and 509.23 372.12 510.40 458.12 31.25

being made known to him he answered that when he
511.2, 335.20, 313.19, 514.13, 269.30, 262.22 had 25.25, 509.23, 551.17, 262.22, found it

enter into Treaty with the colonies he would take care
convenient to 186.17, 302.18, 520.36, 555.38, 510.40, 107.18, 262.22; 557.24, 504.12, 84.11,

of his interest without consulting any one
371.12, 269.14, 301.15, 555.11, 120.29, 26.11 373.11 Hence he observed it would

not be proper to mention any thing of the French
366.14, 45.13, 414.27, 514.13, 344.27, 514.13. 346.27, 26.11, 570.43, 371.12, 570.40. 227.12,

Treaty but to form new
520.36, 78.11 514.13 224.21 one of a 363.33, Mr. Jay assured his Excellency

first time he had ever heard of this anecdote
that this was the 213.15 513.13 262.22 255.30, 190.11, 263.24, 371.12, 511.13, 25.34,

and expressed some surprize at it— keep it
24.18, 196.16, 479.11, 500.12, 34.12, 307.29. The count desired him to 309.14, 307.29

secret adding that the French ambassador knew very well
458.12, 131.6, 509.23, 510.40, 227.12, 184.40, 312.13, it 525.33, 550.14—

Deciphered portion of Jay's report to President Huntington, 6 November 1780. (*Courtesy of the Henry E. Huntington Library and Art Gallery, San Marino, California*.)

is) shoud it be confiscated. In this idea instead of three hundred pounds I shoud have drawn for three thousand, if I had thought there had been any chance of obtaining it.[1] This was likewise the idea of Mr. Morris and I think one or two more members of Congress to whom I mentioned my intention, and I confess I was agreeably surprized when General Leslie[2] informd me by a note that Sir H. Clinton consented to it particularly as I remember when I was Prisoner[3] at N. York I was not sufferd to send out £50 to an Aid de Camp of mine who happened at that time to be in great necessity. But be this as it may, I thought that if I coud obtain this sum or a greater I at least coud not disserve the Continent and certainly very essentially serve myself.

I did it in the openest manner, the bills were drawn in the presence of General Maxwell and the letter accompanying these bills read by that Gentleman. As my distress is therefore very serious from the want of means to furnish my farm I once more entreat Congress to grant me this indulgence, but if They possibly cannot consent consistently with any rules They may have laid down, that They will advance me that sum in hard money and make me an accountant for it to be repayd in the same species at a future day. For to confess the truth if I am put under the necessity of purchasing the necessary hands for my farm at this instant in continental money as it at present goes, which I am confident must be good in the end, I shoud be ruind, and on the other hand without the necessary hands, as I observd before, I have no means of subsistance.

I hope on this occasion there can be no impropriety in mentioning my circumstances. When from an ardent zeal for the rights of America, and as I thought of mankind, I embarked in this cause, I was possesd if not of an ample, at least of a very easy fortune for a private Gentleman. Give me leave enter into the detail of it. 1stly I had £480 pr annum on a mortgage in Jamaica which was punctually paid. 2dly an estate in Middlesex of £200 pr annum for another Person's life but which was insurd against my own. 3dly one thousand pounds on a County turnpike security at four pr cent. 4thly £1500 at five pr cent on bond. 5thly my half pay £136 pr annum. Besides this about twelve hundred pounds in my Agents and in different debts. In all my clear income besides this money at command was about nine hundred and forty pounds pr annum. I had likewise ten thousand acres of land in the Island of St. Johns which had been settled and located at the expence of seven or eight hundred pounds, a mandamus for twenty thousand more in East Florida and a claim as half pay field Officer who had servd the last War in America, in any part of the new lands either on the Ohio, Missisippi or West Florida. Lastly eight hundred Ducats pr annum my table lodging and provisions for my horses as Aid de Camp General to his Majesty of Poland whenever I chose to reside in that Country. Thus such was the fortune and income which I staked on the die of American Liberty, and I playd a losing game for I might lost all and had no prospect or wish to better it.

What is my present situation? In the first place I was struck off the half pay list. My Jamaican Mortgagee who is a Creature of the Ministry has protested my bills. It is not certain whether my Agent has received any rents from the Middlesex estate; this is the reason I woud not chuse to draw upon him unless my bills are endorsd as Capt. Tolty now at N. York offers to do. He knows that He can be no sufferer as my Sister who is rich will at any rate indemnify him. £1500 has indeed been remitted to this Country and put out to interest in S. Carolina.[4] But of interest of this I have never yet receivd one farthing and if I was to receive it at present it woud be of little or no value. So that in fact from near a thousand pounds a year clear income (an income which coud not have been impaird had the tyrannical schemes of the Ministry succeeded, so that my predicament is singular), from an income of near one thousand pound a year from my zeal for this Country I am reducd to nothing at all, to absolute beggary.

It is true the Congress advancd me a sum for the purchase of my farm,[5] but unless I am furnishd with the means of putting this farm in some order, I had better or at least should be full as well without it. I therefore most earnestly intreat Congress either to permit to draw this money from N. York whilst it is in my power or to give me an order for that sum in hard money. Tho in my opinion the former woud be the more advantageous, and if there is any objection from the precedent, I hope the great peculiarity of my case may obbiate it.

I am, Sir, with the greatest respect Your most obedient humble Servant

CHARLES LEE

Tr. NN: Bancroft, American Revolution Series, III, 457–59. Addressed: "His Excelly the Honble Mr Jay President of Congress." Endorsed: ". . . Read."

1 On 26 Feb. 1779 Congress disapproved Lee's arrangements with his British friends in New York to negotiate his bills there. However, on the 27th, after this letter was read in Congress, a motion was made that the Board of Treasury "be directed to advance General Lee 300 pounds sterling in gold and silver, the sum he requests in his letter, and take his bills therefor. . . ." This letter was one of many requests for money made by Lee; Congress had promised to compensate

him for his British estates confiscated when he accepted his commission in the Continental Army on 17 June 1775. *JCC*, XIII, 253, 259.

2 Alexander Leslie (c. 1740–94), a British brigadier general.

3 Lee was captured at the battle of Basking Ridge on 13 Dec. 1776 and remained a prisoner in New York until he was exchanged in April 1778. His activities during this period have led historians to accuse Lee of treason, a view challenged by John R. Alden's *General Charles Lee, Traitor or Patriot?* (Baton Rouge, La., 1951).

4 Sidney Lee (1726–88) was Lee's oldest sister. Congress advanced Lee $1,000 on 28 Feb. 1778, which he invested in South Carolina. *JCC*, XII, 1171.

5 Lee purchased his Virginia estate in 1775 and in October of 1776 Congress had to advance him $30,000 as purchase money for the estate. *JCC*, V, 851.

To Catharine W. Livingston

Philadelphia, 27–28 February 1779

Dear Kitty

Accept my Thanks for your friendly Letter of the 20th Inst. I am happy to hear that Sally has enjoyed so great a Share of Health during the Winter. It is a Blessing which has been sparingly dispensed to her for these three Years past, tho I still flatter myself that by Care and Attention it may yet be re-established. Her Want of Spirits is an unfortunate Circumstance, and I lament it the more, as it results from a Cause in which I am nearly concerned.

I have been from Time to Time decieved in my Expectations of getting a House. We hired Mr. Gurney's[1] in January. He promised to move the 10th February. About that Time Mrs. Gurney fell sick, and still continues so. When her Health will permit her to quit the House is uncertain, tho I hope it will not be long, especially as the Approach of Spring will invite her to the Country, where she was very averse to spending any Part of the Winter. Assure Sally that the Moment this Obstacle ceases, she may expect Brockholst, and you will oblige me by favoring us with your Company.

The Fire Works and Entertainment at the Camp are said to have been well concerted and well executed. The Number of Ladies who were present must have added greatly to what Johnson calls, the *Celebrity* of the Occasion. To this I am persuaded my Correspondent contributed not a little, at least if one may judge from her Intimacy with the Graces, who generally display Taste in the Choice of their Company. That You should be a little mortified at not meeting with your Brother, I can concieve and account for, but what those other more important Mortifications should be, I cannot so easily divine or comprehend. But this is a Subject we will reserve till we meet.

Your Account of your Nephew pleases me, particularly that part of it which relates to his Excursions. More Attention you know, is due to his Health and Constitution, than to his Caprices or Complection. Unfortunately this Doctrine is treated as heritical by too many of your Sex. I regret your Mama's Indisposition as well on her own Account as that of the Family; but as mild Weather and dry Roads will soon enable her to partake of the Benefit of Air and Exercise, I hope her Health will mend.

Since when have you been an Invalid? You appeared to be very well when I left you. I fancy Philadelphia will agree better with you than Persipiney. I'll tell you why, when I have the Pleasure of seeing you. I have seen the Colonel, and heard of the Attachment you mention, but as I seldom write a Letter without adverting to the Possibility of its miscarrying, Prudence bids me postpone a Discussion of this Subject.

Two Years have elapsed since I have seen the Beauty you mention. In that Interval you know Changes for the better or worse may have happened.

This City has been and indeed still is very gay: no appearance of War or Want. Many Circumstances deprive me of partaking largely of these Pleasures. Business on the one Hand, and Sallys Absence on the other, allow me little Time or Inclination for them.

A Report has just reached us that the Enemy have visited Elizabeth Town, and burnt your Fathers Home.[2] This if True is a Misfortune to the Family, which I hope they will bear with Fortitude and Dignity. Similar Losses have been my Lott. They never have, and hope never will cost me an Hours Sleep. Perseverance in doing what we think Right, and Resignation to the Dispensations of the great Governor of the World, offer a Shield against the Darts of these Afflictions, to every body that will use it.

I am Dear Kitty Your affectionate Friend and Brother

JOHN JAY

Sunday

An express from General Washington delivered me a letter from him this Morning on the Subject of the Enemys Excursion to Elizabeth Town. From the Account sent him by Gen. Maxwell it appears to have been nothing very formidable. He mentions the burning of two or three Homes, but does not mention yours as being one of the Number. From this Circumstance I presume it is still standing.

I dined today with Mrs. Lawrence at the Plantation. They are as hospitable and agreable as ever, and desire me to say twenty civil things to you and Sally. The younger Daughter has grown a fine Girl.[3] I think she has more Beauty than any Young Lady of her Age that I have seen in Philadelphia.

Adieu.

ALS. MHi: Ridley. Dft in JP.

[1] Francis Gurney (1738–1815) was a wealthy Philadelphia merchant who was active in the Revolutionary movement in Pennsylvania.

[2] This rumor was unfounded. However, on the next day, 28 February, a British raiding party did reach Liberty Hall. See SLJ to JJ, 5 March 1779 and n.

[3] Mary Morris Lawrence's youngest daughter, Mary, was fourteen years old at the time.

To George Washington

Philadelphia, 2d March 1779

Dear Sir

Accept my Thanks for your obliging Favor of the 23rd Ult.,[1] and be pleased to add to the obligation by a Repetition of them.

The arrival of a Reinforcement from Rhode Island at New York[2] seems to indicate, either another Embarkation to the Southward, or offensive operations in your Quarter, but of military Matters I have too little Knowledge to hazard Conjectures, especially to Persons familiar with that Science.

In one of the English Papers I have the Honor to enclose, is a Copy of the Family Compact between the Branches of the House of Bourbon.[3] As it explains the political Connection between France and Spain, I think it interesting.

We hear nothing from General Lincoln. A little Vessel with military Stores, which lately sailed from hence bound to South Carolina, is taken.

My best Respects to Mrs. Washington.

I am Dear Sir with perfect Esteem and personal Regard your most obedient Servant

JOHN JAY

ALS. DLC: Washington Papers, Series IV. Endorsed. Dft in JP; E in NN: Bancroft American Series, I, 251. This letter was acknowledged by Washington on 10 March. *GWF*, XIV, 218.

[1] Letter from Washington of 23 February has not been located; JJ probably referred to the General's letter of 4 Feb. 1779. *GWF*, XIV, 141.

[2] Washington scoffed at rumors of troop movements from Rhode Island to New York. Washington to JJ, 6 March 1779, *GWF*, XIV, 206–07.

[3] The French and Spanish Houses of Bourbon concluded three treaties by

which the Family Compact was strengthened and the two monarchies offered a united front against their enemies. The first two, of 1733 and 1743, were directed against the Hapsburgs as well as Britain. The last, of 15 Aug. 1761, was ostensibly general in character, but the Spanish, in a separate convention, promised to join the French in hostilities against Britain if peace was not established by May 1762. Significantly, in April 1779, Spain and France entered into a secret alliance at Aranjuez.

From Robert R. Livingston

Poughkeepsie, 4th March 1779

Dear John

Your Letter and one I lately received from Morris have given me pain.[1] They have represented me to myself as negligent of the duties of a man, and a citizen, as buried in indolence, or lost in the pursuit of enervating pleasures. When I consider these charges as coming from those who should, and do, know me better than I do myself, and who see my faults with the eye of friendship, through the narrow end of the perspective, I fear that their censures are too well founded. When on the other hand I look back upon my past life and compare my age with the several important stations which I have held, as I hope without discredit, when I reflect upon the weighty business in which I have been engaged, and above all when I consult my own heart, I am ready to cry out with the petulant Marcus.

"Whene'er did Juba, or did Portius, shew an ardour that has thrown me out in the pursuit of virtue."[2] I persuade myself that that sensibility which gives me a relish for social and refined enjoyments, makes me feel more keenly those that affect the body of which I am a member, and impels me to labour its preservation, with the same warmth with which, in tranquil hours, I engage in more pleasing toils. Whether I am deficient in political courage, and firmness, you who have seen me in trying situations, alike oppressed by restricted private, and publick evils, are best able to judge.

That I am weary of the little paltry party politicks of this place I confess, but I am not however conscious that I neglect them: though as your own experience has taught you, my present situation is by no means adapted for carrying them on to advantage. I will allow you to draw no arguments against me from my last letter. You possess my inmost soul, and it discovers to you disgusts and uneasinesses which it conceals from all the world besides. Nor shall you argue from what I have now written, that I am impatient of censure. I offer you an India painting of myself, it consists of out lines, and contours, 'tis yours to finish the picture by a just distribution of shades. I will promise, rather to trust to your judgment for the likeness, than to my own glass. Thus much for myself; it is well egotizms are allowable between friends.

Now for a State of our politicks, which go on as usual except that the complection of both houses is daily mending. Yet the old leaven of party still works, though less briskly than before. A bill, "for facilitating the impeachment of members of the Council of revision in their Legislative capacity etc." (I give you the design I have forgot the title) was put to sleep in *Senate* after the first reading; other little squibs of a similar nature have been thrown without effect. However several batteries are playing off out of doors, chiefly designed to make a change in the Delegation and for that purpose, as well as some others too long to mention here, instructions have been drawn *here* and subscribed in Orange and Ulster Counties; one of the complaints is that you are not sufficiently communicative to the *Assembly*.

Your brother, Sir James, has an unlucky list against Dean, and Frankling, which has produced a motion that may possibly give you trouble if the Assembly should concur in it,[3] which however I have reason to believe they will not. The Assembly have passed a confiscation bill which takes in two hundred and eighty persons by name; the Senate are divided about it, and have made some amendments, which will probably indanger the Law and excite a flame out of doors. Thus you have a summary of our politicks, in return for which I expect some from you upon a more enlarged scale.

You say nothing further upon a subject that you mentioned to me in your first letter.[4] I should wish to know whether such an event was probable or remote. Remember me to Morris, and Duane, from whom I am in daily expectation of hearing. Tell the first, to purchase for me a genteel suit of Cloaths, and keep them by him till I send for or fetch them. If I send my measure let him get them made up so as to be ready to try on, without finishing them for fear of mistakes. I have some thoughts of visiting you next month. In the mean time let me hear from you often. I am Dear John, Most sincerely Yours etc.

R. R. LIVINGSTON

ALS. Addressed: "To His Excellency John Jay Esqr Congress." Endorsed. Dft, dated 2 February in NHi: Robert R. Livingston.

[1] JJ to Livingston, 16 Feb. 1779; Gouverneur Morris to Livingston, most likely 21 Jan. 1779, cited in Dangerfield, *Robert R. Livingston*, p. 109.

[2] Livingston was referring to Joseph Addison's *Cato*, act 1, scene 1, where Portius, Cato's son, indirectly admonishes his brother Marcus by praising Juba, a Numidian prince who was fiercely loyal to Cato.

3 On 1 March the Senate resolved that the delegates to the Continental Congress render a full report on the conduct of Arthur and William Lee and Silas Deane in Europe. The resolution was read in the Assembly on 2 March but its consideration was postponed. Evans, 16408.

4 On 13 Jan. 1779 JJ wrote Livingston asking if he would be willing to accept a diplomatic assignment: "Will any Consideration induce you to visit another Quarter of the Globe? I dont know that you will be called up, but am not sure that you may not. My Conduct will be greatly influenced by your Inclination." ALS in NHi: Robert R. Livingston; dft in JP. See Livingston's reply, 3 February, page 549.

To Anthony Benezet

Philadelphia, 5 March 1779

Sir

Agreable to the Request contained in your favor of the 2d Ult. I have perused the Pamphlet you was so obliging as to send me. The Benevolence by which the Author appears to have been influenced, does him Credit, and tho I cannot subscribe to all his opinions, many of his Sentiments are liberal and merit Commendation.

Civil and religious Liberty is a Blessing which I sincerely wish to all mankind; and I hope it will ever be the policy of these States so to extend and secure it to all their Citizens, as that none may have Reason to complain of Partiality or Oppression.

Your favorable Opinion of me, and kind wishes for my welfare demand my Acknowledgement.

I am Sir your Friend and Servant

Dft.

From Sarah Livingston Jay

Persipiney, March 5th, 1779

You may recollect my dear, that I informed you in my last that I had not received a line from you since the 5th of February. I did not then know that I had been deprived of that pleasure by a British Officer, who Susan writes me to her (and I am sure equally to my) great regret had taken two letters of yours from the mantle-piece.[1] From the loss of them I suffered great solicitude about your welfare 'till happily for me Montanie's arrival dispeled my anxiety. In yours you flatter me with the expectation of shortly seeing my friend.[2] Pray my love, when and where are we to be restored to each other? To a person, who like me has been agitated with suspense near the fourth part of a year, the information that will banish doubt and introduce certainty in it's place you'll readily believe will be very acceptable.

Sister Kitty returned from Camp last monday; she desires her compliments to you and Brockholst. The family are all well. If the roads were dry enough for me to walk I believe I should be heartier but confinement makes me feel feeble. Adieu my love. Yours sincerely

SA. JAY

ALS. Endorsed: ". . . answd. 14 Inst."; this has not been located.

1 The letter from Susan Livingston to SLJ reporting the loss of these letters has not been located. On 28 February a British raiding party from New York landed at Elizabeth Town. That evening a detachment entered the Livingston mansion, Liberty Hall, searching for the "damned rebel Governor." The commanding officer demanded that Susan Livingston surrender the Governor's papers, after learning that the Governor himself was absent. She persuaded the British to ignore a box containing her father's official correspondence with Washington and state and continental officials, and surrendered instead insignificant papers which the British took back to New York. Theodore Sedgwick, *William Livingston* (New York, 1883), pp. 322–23.

2 JJ's letter to his wife has not been located. JJ wanted Sally to join him in Philadelphia.

From Philip Schuyler

Albany, March 5th, 1779

Sir

As more than two Months are elapsed since my Resignation was laid before Congress I hope I shall not be deemed too importunate if I entreat that respectable Body to a speedy Compliance with my Request. Were it necessary, I might adduce other Reasons to point out the Necessity of my retiring from public Life, but I concieve those I gave in my Letter of the 27th December last[1] will be thought sufficient especially if I add, that my Constitution, which never was a hale one, is so much shaken by a late severe Fit of the Gout on my Stomach that it requires more Care and Attention than the Military Life would permit me to bestow on it.

In my Letter of the 27th January,[2] I advised Congress that part of the Onondagas intended to seperate from those who were Enemies to us. This has lately taken place, as you will percieve by the inclosed.

A Legacy of one thousand pounds Currency is due from me to Miss Elizabeth Bradstreet, a Daughter of the late General Bradstreet's

Wife by her first Husband.[3] As I have to pay it in Specie with the Interest due on it since September 1774, and as I advanced about as much as that will amount to, whilst our Troops were in Canada, for which I took paper Money, and as I have no Means of paying off the Legacy in Specie, without the Aid of Congress, I should be exceedingly obliged if Bills on France to that Amount could be afforded me. If so, I shall entreat the Favor of one of the Gentlemen of the Committee of Foreign Correspondence to cause our Agent in France to pay the Money to Miss Bradstreet's order, and I will either repay it in paper Currency or, if that is not acceptable, in Specie as soon as I can collect it.

March 8th. I have this Moment received an Application from Oneidas for an additional Supply of provisions for the Indians who have very little left to subsist on and will in the Course of twenty Days have Nothing as the Onondagas that are come to reside amongst them have brought no provisions with them. This has added to their Distress and as neither the one or the other can go to hunt they must inevitably starve or remove to the interior part of the Country, and if they do that, the Frontiers will be still more exposed than they are at present. I therefore entreat the Direction of Congress on this Subject, with all the Dispatch possible, It being a Matter of too great importance for me to venture a Decision upon, and yet, such is my Idea of the Necessity of supporting those people, expensive as it may be, that I shall direct the commanding Officer at Fort Schuyler not to let them suffer but in giving them Assistance to do it as from himself, until I can have the pleasure of Congress communicated.[4]

I have the Honor to be with the greatest respect and Esteem Your Excellencys Most Obedient Humble Servant

PH. SCHUYLER

ALS. DNA: PCC, 153, III, 426–29.

1 Schuyler to the President of Congress, 27 Dec. 1778, DNA: PCC, 153, III, 396–98.

2 *Ibid.*

3 General John Bradstreet (1711–74) enjoyed a twenty-year relationship with Schuyler in which Bradstreet was always, albeit occasionally a secret partner, in Schuyler's business ventures. Bradstreet's will named Schuyler executor of the estate. The General's stepdaughter Elizabeth (d. 1794) married a "Mr. Livius." Bradstreet's will is reprinted in the *New England Historical and Genealogical Register* (Boston, 1847–1971), XVI, 315; Don R. Gerlach, *Philip Schuyler and the American Revolution in New York* (Lincoln, Neb., 1964).

4 This letter was read in Congress on 18 March. Congress refused to accept Schuyler's resignation and referred the section of the letter concerning the Oneidas and Onondagas to the Board of War. The Board reported to Congress on

24 March and Congress empowered the Commissioners for Indian Affairs in the Northern Department to supply their "faithful friends the Oneidas and other friendly Indians." *JCC*, XIII, 332–35, 363.

To Robert R. Livingston

Philadelphia, 14 March 1779

Dear Robert

Mr. Sands delivered me your Favor of the 4th Inst.[1] Yesterday. It gave me much Pleasure. The Length, the Subjects and the Spirit of it pleased me. Dont apologize for Egotisms, for I would much rather recieve them than not. Unless the Pain my last occasioned was severe, I dont regret it. That You have deserved well of your Country is agreed, and that you became latterly a little relaxed, is not disputable. You have never been thrown out or distanced in the Pursuit of Virtue, but like some Game Horses, you sometimes want a Whip. This is a coarse Simile—Friendship will pardon it.

That full Confidence which enduced You to think loud, flatters me; the like Return is due and shall be paid. But Letters in our Days are dangerous Conveyances of our Sentiments on many Subjects. I seldom write without adverting to the Consequences of a miscarriage, and hence the Reserve and Caution which mark all such of mine, as are trusted to common Carriers or doubtful Bearers.

The State of your Politics is much as I expected. I fear some of your Measures are more severe than Wisdom or Humanity will justify. Posterity will think dispassionately and probably condemn, especially when informed, that they were hastened, lest the Influence of Resentment should be lost.

My Silence on a certain Subject arose from reflecting that an Explanation ought not to be on Paper. The Probability of it turns on an Event not yet determined. If I discern right, there will be Room.

A Genteel Suit of Cloaths, will cost a noble Price. We shall be exceedingly happy to see you. I hope your Visit will not be delayed longer than the Roads may render it necessary. Manage matters so as to stay at least a Month. My best Respects to your Mama, Mrs. Livingston and the Rest of the Family.

I am Dear Robert Your Friend and Servant

JOHN JAY

ALS. NHi: Robert R. Livingston. Endorsed. Dft in JP; E in NN: Bancroft American Series, II, 60.

[1] On 8 March Clinton sent Comfort Sands to Philadelphia to deliver papers to JJ and give him a "satisfactory acc't of the Debates and Proceedings" of the New York legislature. *GCP*, IV, 624.

From Horatio Gates

Boston, March 15th, 1779

Sir,

Persuaded that your Excellency punctually attends to every Thing which may respect the Eastern Department, as you declared in the first Letter I have been honoured with from you, since you are in the Chair. I hope all my Letters, since my Arrival in Boston, will be answered as far as it may be necessary for my Conduct.

I do not yet know what Congress intend to do towards fortifying this City and Harbour, the Necessity of which I urged in my Letter of the 30th of November last, inclosing General Duportail's Memorial on that Subject. The Season advances rapidly, and we may be attacked before we have Troops, a Magazine to feed them, or proper Batteries to keep off the Enemy. What the British Generals will attempt, I know not; but the Advantages we throw in their Laps are really alarming to us. The Invitation which the State of this City now presents to them is so tempting, that I believe, if they were ordered to return to Europe, they would visit us here, before their Departure, even though they had no other Prospect than that of exalting their own military Fame, and diminishing the Opinion which our Friends entertain of our Wisdom.[1]

The most opulent Families of this City are without Bread, and the Poor almost in a State of Desperation. The public Magazine being guarded by, and consequently at the Mercy of the Militia of this State, I fear with more Reason than it is prudent to publish, that Violence will take away the few Barrels of Flower which are left. It cannot be expected that the People of New England will submit to the Horrors of an artificial Famine, with that Tameness which distinguished, Five or Six Years ago, the People of Bengal, in a similar Case. Men of the most extensive Reading have already observed, that such Patience is not recorded in the historical Page of any other Nation. If Outrages of this kind begin here, their Progress may extend further than we can imagine; for, to stop it, without Troops, is impossible; and with American Troops, the most enterprizing General, if a systematic Republican, or a Man acquainted with human Nature, will act Cautiously in Stopping the Disorder.

The inclosed Copy of my Letter to General Washington of the 4th Instant, in Answer to his of the 14th Ultimo from Middlebrook, will give Congress a true Idea of my Opinion, respecting our entering Canada, and the only Route which we can take with reasonable

Hopes of Success. Individuals, and not the Public, will be benefitted by an Expedition into Canada, by either of the Routes from Albany. That of co'os[2] alone is practicable, in our Situation, but not without the Co-operation of the Allied Fleet.[3]

If Congress intend that John Brown be executed, their Resolution should be known very soon; or the only Advantage which the United States may reap from avenging Justice, will be lost. He is in a melancholy Situation, and cannot live long, unless set at full Liberty. Clemency itself would scarcely be an Act of Beneficence, if retarded.

The Ten Thousand Dollars in Specie, now in the Hands of General Heath, seem to demand the Attention of Congress. I wrote on that Head, the 29th of January, but have not yet received any Instructions. In Justice to General Heath, I entreat your Excellency will inform Congress, that he is very solicitous of being eased of that Burden.

Captain Banck, the respectable German Officer I mentioned in my Letter of the 3rd of December inclosing his Memorial, is needlessly maintained at great Expence, without doing any Service. He might be usefully employed in Count Pulaski's Corps, or otherwise.[4] Not to countenance him, would be cruel; for he deserves well of us.

General Washington's Letter of the 14th of February is inclosed. It being the only Letter I have received from his Excellency since December, Congress will immediately judge of the Extent, or Limitation which it is proper to Observe in their Instructions to me.

I am Sir Your Excellencys most Obedient Servant

HORATIO GATES

ALS. DNA: PCC, 154, II, 63–66. Endorsed by Charles Thomson: ". . . Read April 5. Referred to the board of War." Enclosures: Washington to Gates, 14 Feb. 1779 (printed in *GWF*, XIV, 108–10); Gates to Washington, 4 March 1779, dft in NHi: Gates.

1 Gates's letter of 30 Nov. 1778, with its enclosed memorial from Brigadier General Louis Le Bégue de Presle Duportail (1743–1802), has not been located. Duportail, a French officer, was commandant of the Corps of Engineers in the Continental Army. The documents were read in Congress, 31 Dec. 1778, and referred to the Marine Committee. JJ's reply to Gates's letter of 30 November simply stated: "I am not authorized to say anything of the Intention of Congress relative to the proposed Fortification at Boston." *JCC*, XII, 1265; JJ to Gates, 4 April 1779, NHi: Gates.

2 Cohoes was General Schuyler's retreat in New York State.

3 This paragraph and the concluding paragraph of the letter were copied and sent to Washington in a letter from JJ, 6 April 1779. JJ characterized the letter from which they were extracted as being "in a certain degree interesting." Washington replied: "Conscious that it is the aim of my actions to promote the public good, and that no part of my conduct is influenced by personal enmity to individuals, I cannot be insensible to the artifice, employed by some men to

prejudice me in the public esteem. The circumstance of which you have obliged me with a communication, is among a number of other instances of the unfriendly views which have governed a certain gentleman from a very early period." JJ to Washington, 6 April 1779, DLC: Washington Papers, I, 102–14; Washington to JJ, 14 April, in JP.

4 General Gates's letter of 3 Dec. 1778 and the memorial of Captain Bancke have not been located. On 10 July 1779 Congress voted to reimburse Bancke for his services to enable him to return to Germany. Count Casimir Pulaski (1749–79), a Polish refugee, served as a dragoon leader until March 1778, when he received Congressional approval to raise an independent body of cavalry.

To Sarah Livingston Jay

Philadelphia, 21 March 1779

My dear Sally

It gives me Pleasure to inform you that Mrs. Gurney appears now to be moving in earnest. I have got Possession of the Cellar and Stables, and unless some cross Accident should again happen, the House will be ready for me by Thursday next. In this Case your Brother[1] will set out the Day after. Do not however be too sanguine in your Expectations; another Disappointment tho not very probable, may take Place. It is with great Reluctance that Mrs. Gurney can prevail on herself to go to the Country, and perhaps this Disinclination may occasion further Delay. Believe me My Love, my sollicitude for the Pleasure of seeing you is such that not a Moment shall be lost; and it is not without Difficulty I can persuade myself not to let your Brother go for you, till I see the House free from its present Inhabitants.

My Love to all the family.

I am my dear Sally very affectionately Yours

JOHN JAY

ALS.

1 Henry Brockholst Livingston.

From Alexander McDougall

Head Quarters, Peeks Kill, March 21st, 1779

My Dear Sir

This will be delivered to you by Mr. Elijah Hunter whom I suppose you know, as a Friend to the common Cause of America. He goes to Philadelphia on a Matter of importance, which he will communicate to you.[1] It is of a very important and delicate Nature,

And I have my Doubts on the Expediency of it's being divulged to any other Person whatsoever. If it is, there is Danger, that the Object of the Plan will be frustrated. It is already unavoidably into many Hands. The Lives of four Citizens depend on it's remaining a secret; besides the great Utility intended by the System <proving abortive>.

I am my Dear Sir Your affectionate humble Servant

ALEXR. McDOUGALL

ALS. Endorsed: ". . . my Ans. 28 Inst. By Capt. Hunter."

1 Elijah Hunter, who had been a captain in the New York militia and had retired from the army in 1776, now wanted to rejoin the service as a double agent. McDougall suggested a conference with Washington, which took place on 25 March. Although impressed by Hunter's abilities, Washington advised McDougall "to trust him with caution and to watch his conduct with a jealous eye." Washington to McDougall, 25 March 1779, *GWF*, XIV, 291–92.

To PHILIP SCHUYLER

Philadelphia, 21 March 1779

Dear Sir

So uncertain has been the Fate of Letters during the Course of this War, that I very seldom write one without adverting to the Possibility and Consequences of its Miscarriage and Publication. This Caution has on a late occasion given me much Consolation. Two of my Letters to Mrs. Jay fell into the Enemy's Hands at Elizabeth Town. They contained nothing that would give me Uneasiness if published. Prudential Considerations of this Kind, have since my arrival here restrained me from writing several confidential Letters to You; and I should now be equally cautious, had I not full Confidence in the Bearer and under little Apprehension of Danger from accidents on the Road.

Congress has refused to accept your Resignation. Twelve States were represented. New England and Pennsylvania against you. The Delegates of the Latter are new Men, and not free from the Influence of the former. From New York South you have fast Friends. Mr. Laurens' Disposition indeed is at least questionable. Deleware was unrepresented.[1]

What is now to be done? You best can answer this Question. Were I in your Situation I should not hesitate a Moment to continue in the Service. I have the best Authority to assure you that the Commander in Chief wishes you to retain your Commission. The

Propriety of your Resignation is now out of Question. Those Laws of Honor which might have required it are satisfied. Are you certain they do not demand contrary Conduct. You have Talents to render you conspicuous in the Field, and Address to conciliate the affections of those who may now wish you ill. Both these Circumstances are of worth to your Family and independent of public Considerations argue forceably for your joining the Army. Gather Laurels for the Sake of your Country and your Children. You can leave them a sufficient Share of Property. Leave them also the Reputation of being descended from an incontestably great Man, a Man who uninfluenced by the Ingratitude of his Country was unremitted in his Exertions to promote her Happiness. You have hitherto been no Stranger to these Sentiments, and therefore I forbear to enlarge. Would it not do you Honor to inform Congress that while in their opinion your Services ought not to be withheld from your Country, neither the Derangement of your private affairs, the Severities you have experienced, or Regard to your Health already impaired in their Service, shall restrain you from devoting yourself to the Execution of their Commands. But that whenever the Situation of public Affairs may cease to call you to the Field, you hope they will permit you to retire and attend to the Duties you owe your Family.

Should this be your Determination, would not the main army be your proper Object? There you may be best known and there best acquire military Influence. Consider, this Campaign will in all human Probability be decisive and the last. Can you therefore employ six or Eight Months better?

I will not apologize for the Freedom with which I write, being persuaded that although our opinions may vary, you will consider this Letter as some Evidence of the Sincerity with which I am Your Friend and Servant

JOHN JAY

My best Respects to Mrs. Schuyler

ALS. N: Schuyler Mansion Documents. Addressed: "Major General Schuyler Albany." Endorsed. Dft in JP.

[1] By a resolution of 18 March Congress directed JJ "to acquaint Major General Schuyler, that the situation of the army renders it inconvenient to accept his resignation, and therefore Congress cannot comply with his request." The membership of the Pennsylvania delegation changed completely between December 1778 and March 1779. The "questionable" conduct of Henry Laurens was his opposition to the resolution passed on the 18th and his apparent support of another resolution which would have accepted Schuyler's resignation. *JCC*, XIII, 332–33.

To John Dickinson

Philadelphia, 22d March 1779

Dear Sir

Your Election to a Seat in Congress is an Event for many Reasons pleasing to me. I have for some time past flattered myself with soon having the Pleasure of again seeing you in a Place which you formerly filled with advantage to your Country and Reputation to yourself.

Permit me to hint that your State is unrepresented and that were you apprized of the very important Affairs now under Consideration, you would think with me that your Attendance ought not to be longer delayed.

I am Dear Sir with great Respect Your most obedient and humble Servant

JOHN JAY

ALS. PHi: M. O. Logan. Endorsed by a member of the Dickinson family: "My father took his seat in Congress in April 1779." Dickinson was elected to Congress from the State of Delaware on 18 Jan. 1779. *LMCC*, IV, 1.

To Alexander McDougall

Philadelphia, 28 March 1779

Dear Sir

I have the Pleasure of acknowledging the Reciept of your Favor of the 21st Instant.

Your Sentiments on the Subject of it coincide perfectly with my own. Great Prudence is necessary and Care should be taken in what is committed to Paper. Discoveries often arise from Letters meeting with Accidents which the wisest could not have forseen or the most wary have suspected. The fewer Parties the better.

I am Dear Sir with Esteem and personal Regard Your obedient Servant

Dft.

From George Bascome

Bermuda, April 5th 1779

Dear Sir,

On the Score of the Acquaintance which I had the Honor some Years past, during my Residence at New York, to have with you, I take the Liberty to solicit your Attention to the application now about to be made to the Honorable the Congress of the American States, through you as President thereof, for the Necessaries of Life. On its Success depend the Lives of near fifteen thousand People. And as the Bermudians are indebted to the Benevolence of Congress for their Support for upward of three Years past, they presume to hope that the like Relief will not now, in the Hour of their direst Distress, be refused them. Captain Leonard Albuoy,[1] who will have the Honor to hand you this, is of a very reputable Family among us; and, so far as his Knowledge may extend, will give just and satisfactory Answers to any Questions you may be pleased to ask him.

I am, Dear Sir, with the highest Deference Your most obedient humble Servant

GEO. BASCOME

ALS. Endorsed. Addressed: "His excellency John Jay Esquire President of the Congress of the United States of America, Philadelphia." Enclosure: inhabitants of Bermuda to the President of Congress, 28 March 1779, in DNA: PCC, 41, I, 176–83.

George Bascome, a leading Bermuda lawyer, was a member of that group of prominent pro-American Bermuda families seeking special trading privileges from the Continental Congress, even at the risk of offending Great Britain. That permission was necessary because Congress, in retaliation for naval action against American vessels, had withdrawn its exemption to Bermuda from the general embargo, leaving the island hard-pressed for food. The 28 March letter, signed by 20 of the leading citizens of Bermuda, appealed for trading privileges with America. It was read in Congress on 19 April and referred to a committee (Ellery, Fell, Laurens; directed to report with "all convenient Speed"), which reported unfavorably on 23 April that "sound policy and the duty they owe to their constituents, will constrain them to refuse a compliance with the request of the memorialists." The vote taken on this ended in a tie, and the report and appeal were recommitted. The committee reported again on 5 May but Congress adjourned without taking any action. In the 7 May report the committee had a change of heart, stating "that it be recommended to the executive powers of the states of Pensylvania, Delaware, Maryland, Virginia and North Carolina, respectively to permit 1000 bushels of Indian corn to be exported from each of the said states for the relief of the distressed inhabitants of those islands." However, before a vote could be taken, a substitute motion was made by Thomas Burke, seconded by Gouverneur Morris, "that Congress deem it highly inexpedient to grant" their request. It passed in the affirmative.

Washington was alert to the Bermuda problem, and wrote JJ from Middlebrook on [23] April asking whether Congress would provision Bermuda's ships with flour in exchange for salt. He went on to say that, besides the need of this staple by America (to export it would be "injurious" to the country), privateers in Bermuda waters would confiscate the cargo. But in addition to "these considerations," Washington felt that "by withholding a supply, we throw many additional mouths upon the enemy's magazines, and increase proportionably their distress. They will not and cannot let their people starve." *JCC*, XIII, 471; XIV, 501–02, 553, 555; see Wilfred B. Kerr, *Bermuda and the American Revolution, 1760–1783* (Princeton, 1936); Washington's ALS in JP.

1 Leonard Albouy, along with two other Bermuda mariners, Joseph Basden and Nathaniel Prudden, came to Philadelphia to deliver the petition. Kerr, *Bermuda and the American Revolution*, pp. 89–90.

FROM ROBERT R. LIVINGSTON

ClerMount, 21st April 1779

Dear John

A fortnight has already elapsed since I received yours of the 14th Ult. I feel my self ashamed of my neglect, though as far as business and company may plead my excuse I am excusable, since I have Opened my court at Albany, transacted some business for Duer there, and been ever since crowded with company. But I am more willing to own my fault than to offer an appology which you will too often have it your power to return, to make it politick in me to admit.

I can not as I at first proposed be with you this month, being detained here till the middle of May in order to see my sister Gitty[1] married, after which I shall hope to have the pleasure of seeing you at Philadelphia. I hardly know how to admit your excuse for the reserve and caution which (to use your own phraze) mark your Letter since safe conveyances are very frequently afforded and I do not find that one of our Letters have miscarried. I long for that free and open communication of sentiment that make the soul of friendship. Politicks you may communicate or not as you please, not that I would have you suppose me indifferent to them. On the contrary I am very desirous of knowing what passes, and speak according to knowledge on the present subjects of every conversation.

Your grand secret begins here to be considered by many as a political term, tho from what I can learn of it, it is not exactly what I wish.[2] Yet I am so desirous of peace and see so manifestly the impossibility of carrying on another campaign without some thing better than a paper exchequer. Or even with specie if the enimy should remove the seat of war far eastward, from the difficulty of collecting, and transporting provissions, that I am willing to make the most of it. And I do not know whether upon the whole in our present tumultuous situation Congress should seem rather to *acquiess* in the terms that may be offered from attention to its allies, than agree to them.

Never was the spirit of discontent more alive among us than at present. The people are uneasy and know not to what object to direct their complaints; they see things go wrong but know not how to mend them. This will produce many changes in our legislature, among others I believe Benson will lose his seat.[3] You have I suppose heard the history of our last sessions. You rightly judge of the spirit that actuated it. Never was there a greater compound of folly, avarice, and injustice, than our confiscation bill, to which Bensons compromising genious not a little contributed. Many preparetory steps were taken to produce a change in the delegation, which will take place shortly. Morris and Schuyler will I think undoubtedly be left out the first opportunity.[4] I have freequently wrote to the first to entreat him to break out and shew himself here, to remove prejudices that accumulate during a man's absence. You can mention this matter to him. I should write to him but I am unwilling to expose myself to further neglects, since I can ascribe them to no motives that do not lessten him in my esteem.

I wrote to Mr. Duane about Mr. Tetard who has been with me the whole winter. He is entitled to some provission from Congress; he promissed to procure for him the place of chaplain in the Highlands or interpreter to Congress, since which I have heard nothing from him, though I have written twice pressingly to him upon the subject. You would do a charitable deed, and oblige me, by providing for him in some way or other. His memorial lays before congress and his poverty is extream.[5] Present my compliments to Mrs. Jay and believe me Dear John Most sinsirely Your's

ROBT. R. LIVINGSTON

How goes the Vermont business. I am fearful that you will be blamed for not procuring some settlement of it.

ALS. Dft, dated 20 April, in NHi: Robert R. Livingston.

1 Gertrude Livingston (1749–1823) married Colonel Morgan Lewis 11 May 1779.

2 The "grand secret" apparently refers to secret negotiations over peace terms. In earlier letters JJ had hinted at such matters, but his extreme caution when writing did little to satisfy Livingston's curiosity. Russia and Austria had, independently of one another, begun to sponsor the idea of a negotiated peace, and in May 1779 both nations volunteered to play the role of mediator. France rejected both offers at that time, but the services of the two neutral powers remained available, and the stage was set for future progress.

3 At this time, Egbert Benson was a representative from Dutchess County to the New York Assembly. Livingston apparently felt that the troubled economic conditions of 1779 would lead many small and tenant farmers to vent their anger by turning out of office representatives such as Benson. However, Benson was reelected to the Assembly. Dangerfield, *Robert R. Livingston,* pp. 116–17; *Votes and proceedings of the Assembly of the State of New York . . .* (Fishkill, 1777 [1779]), 3d sess., entry for 18 Aug. 1779, p. 3.

4 Livingston was half right: Gouverneur Morris's enemies in the Assembly were able to defeat him, but Philip Schuyler was appointed on 18 Oct. 1779 to

replace Jay as a delegate from New York. Max M. Mintz, *Gouverneur Morris and the American Revolution* (Norman, Okla., 1970), pp. 135–37; *Votes and Proceedings of the Senate of the State of New York . . .* (Fishkill, 1777 [1779]), 13 Oct. 1779, p. 47.

[5] John Peter Tetard (1722–87), Swiss-born Protestant clergyman, had served as chaplain to the regiment commanded by Brigadier General Richard Montgomery. Tetard's memorial, enclosed in a letter to Congress from General Washington, 4 Sept. 1778, was referred to a committee on 8 Sept. 1778. There is no record of any action taken during JJ's term as President. *GWF*, XII, 401 n.; *JCC*, XII, 891.

To George Washington

Philadelphia, 21 April 1779

Dear Sir

<The Friendship of the Wise and Virtuous, marks of Confidence in View> Accept my Thanks for the long and friendly Letter of the 14th Inst which I have had the Pleasure of recieving from you.[1] <The Friendship of the wise and virtuous is among those Objects which I value most, and therefore the kind Expressions of mark of Confidence and Regard is particularly grateful and has my warmest Acknowledgements.> It was for many Reasons grateful to me. I value <and am happy to possess> the Esteem and Regard of the wise and virtuous, and <confess that I had not been without> had wished to know the Particulars of Transactions respecting which only vague and unsatisfactory Reports had come to my Knowledge. Delicacy forbids my breaking the Subject to you when here. I was sure of your Politeness but not certain of <your> a more than usual Degree of Confidence. The latter <is unequivocal> has now become manifest and permit me to assure you it shall be mutual. The Impression attempted to be made <on Congress has been without Eff> has not taken. <It produced a contrary Effect in the minds of a large Majority> It passed without a single Remark. Your Friends thought it merited nothing but Silence and neglect <nor does my answer to it take the least Notice of those Paragraphs> The same Reason induced me to take no Notice of it in my Answer.

I have perused the several Papers with which <accompanied the Letter <<were enclosed>>> you favored me. The Delicacy Candor and Temper diffused thro your Letters form a strong Contrast to the Evasions and Design observable in some others. Gratitude ought to have attached a Certain Gentleman <to you> to the Friend who raised him. A spurious Ambition however has it seems made him your Enemy.[2] This is not uncommon. To the Dishonor of human Nature the History of Mankind has many Pages filled with similar

Instances, and we have little Reason to expect that the Annals of the present or future Times will present us with fewer Characters of this Class. On the contrary there is Reason to expect that they will multiply in the Course of this Revolution.

<The same steady Magnanimity <<Envy delights to walk in the Shade of Merit and like the Serpent of old, to bite its Heel.>> Seasons of general Heat Tumult and Fermentation <a Leaven friendly to the> favor the production and growth of some great Virtues and of many Great and little Vices which will predominate is < not determined, and depends upon> [a] Question which Events not yet produced nor now to be discerned can alone determine. What Parties and Factions will arise, to what Objects be directed, <is not within the Reach <<Sphere>> of human Prevision> what Sacrifices they will require, and who will be the victims are matters beyond the sphere of human Prevision. New <fashioned Governments> Modes of Governments, not generally understood, nor in certain Instances <generally> approved, Want of moderation <and perhaps Wisdom> and Information in the People, and <of both a greater> Want of Abilities and Rectitude in some of their Rule[r]s, a wide Field open for the <Exertion> operations of Ambition. Men raised from low Degrees to high Stations and <grown> rendered giddy <with Exaltation> by Elevation, and the Extent of their Views, a Revolution in private Property, in <political> national Attachments. <The Silence of the> Laws dictated by the Spirit of the Times not the Spirit of Justice and liberal Policy, Latitude in Principles as well as Commerce, Suspension of Education, Fluctuation in Manners and public Counsels <and I may add> and moral obligations Indifference to Religion etc etc <in greater or lesser Degrees may be rationally emputed to Circumstances within the Laws of Probability of which Times like the present are usually fertile They are however rather Objects calculated to excite caution and vigilance than Dismay and Despair. A few Years more will make us> are Circumstances that portend Evils which much prudence Vigour and Circumspection are necessary to prevent or controul. To me there appears Reason to expect a long Storm, and difficult Navigation, calm Repose and the Success of undisturbed Retirement appear more distant than a Peace with Britain. It gives me Pleasure however to reflect that the period is approaching when we shall become Citizens of a better ordered State and the spending <thirty or forty> a few troublesome Years of our Eternity in doing good to this and future Generations is not to be avoided or regretted. Things will come right

and these States will be great and flourishing. The Dissolution of our Governments threw us into a political Chaos. Time wisdom and perseverance will reduce it into form and give it streng[th] order and Harmony. In this Work you are to [speak] in the Stile of one of your Professions a master builder, and <to speak in the Stile of one of your professions> God grant that you may long continue <to be> a *free* and *accepted* Mason.

Thus my dear Sir I have endulged myself in thinking loud in your Hearing, it would be an Hybernicism to say in your *Sight*, tho <more litterally> in one Sense true. <Thus nature or Habit has given me a Propensity to Reserve> It is more than probable I shall frequently do the like. Your Letter shall be my apology, and the Pleasure resulting from Converse with those we esteem, my Motive.

I am Dear Sir <very sincerely> with perfect Esteem and Regard Your <Friend and> most obedient Servant

Dft. Endorsed by JJ. ALS in DLC: Washington Papers, Ser. 4.

1 Washington to JJ, 14 April 1779, marked "private." ALS in JP; dft in DLC: Washington Papers, ser. 4, 12.

2 General Horatio Gates.

To George Washington

Philadelphia, 26 April 1779

Dear Sir

The Questions contained in your Favor of the [23][1] April Inst. are as important, as the Manner of introducing them is delicate.

While the maritime affairs of the Continent continue under the Direction of a Committee, they will be exposed to all the Consequences of want of System, Attention and Knowledge. The marine Committee consists of a Delegate from each State. It fluctuates, new Members constantly coming in and old ones going out; three or 4 indeed have remained in it from the Beginning and have a proportionate Influence or more properly *Interest* in it.[2] Very few of the members understand even the state of our naval affairs, or have Time or Inclination to attend to them. <Committees cannot easily be made responsible.> But why is not this System changed? It is in my opinion convenient to the Family Compact.[3] The Commercial Committee is equally useless. A Proposition was made to appoint a commercial agent for the States, <pay him generously and restrain him from doing other Business> under certain Regulations. Opposition was made. The ostensible objections were various. The true Reason was its Interference with a certain commercial agent in <France> Europe, and his Connections.[4]

You will if I am not greatly mistaken find Mr. Gerard disposed to be open and communicative.[5] He has acquired an extensive knowledge of our affairs. I have no Reason to believe he will use it to our Prejudice. There is as much Intrigue in this State House as in the Vatican, but as little secrecy as in a boarding School. It mortifies me on this Occasion to reflect that the Rules of Congress on the Subject of Secrecy which are far too general and perhaps for that Reason more frequently violated, <from Inadvertence or Design>, restrain me from saying twenty things to You, which have ceased to be private. <There appears to me an important Relation between the civil Polity and military operations of every Country.>

The State of our Currency is really serious; when or by what means the Progress of its Depreciation will be prevented is uncertain. The Subject is delicate, but the Conduct of some men really indicate at least great Indifference about it. <There is either much Weakness or much Wickedness at the Bottom.> It will not be many Days before measures having a great tho not immediate Influence on this Subject will be either adopted or rejected. I shall then have an opportunity of being more particular.

I am my dear Sir with perfect Esteem and Regard Your obedient Servant

Dft. Endorsed by JJ. ALS in DLC: Washington Papers, Series IV.

[1] Date left blank in ms. Letter to which JJ refers is in JP.

[2] The Marine Committee was established 14 Dec. 1775. Its members to whom JJ referred were probably Samuel Adams, William Whipple, William Ellery, and Richard Henry Lee. This was in reply to Washington's query to JJ of [23] April as to what the reasons were for keeping the continental frigates idle and useless in port. Washington suggested that Congress "lend them" to "Commanders of known bravery" for a limited time, after which the ships would revert to the states. *JCC*, III, 428; VI, 1062–66; Washington to JJ, [23] April, in JP.

[3] The Family Compact to which JJ alludes is the Adams-Lee alliance in Congress.

[4] The objection to a commercial agent presumably came from the Lees and their allies, for it would have interfered with, if not curtailed, the European activities of William (1739–95) and Arthur Lee. William Lee was appointed in early December 1776 to join Thomas Morris as a commercial agent in Nantes. Lee's commission was enclosed in a letter from Robert Morris to Franklin, Deane, and Arthur Lee, 18 Feb. 1777. "Deane Papers," N.Y. Hist. Soc., *Colls.*, XIX (1886), 491.

[5] Gérard arrived at Washington's camp on 1 May 1779. *GWF*, XIV, 455, n. 18.

FROM PHILIP SCHUYLER

Albany, April 29th, 1779

Sir

Yesterday I was honored with your Excellency's Letter of the 20th covering the Act of Congress permitting my Resignation. I embrace the Opportunity of an Express to his Excellency General Washington to acknowledge the Receipt of it.[1]

The Distance at which Messrs. Wolcott and Edwards reside from this place will not often permit those Gentlemen to afford Mr. Dow their Aid on the Business of the Indian Department and as the late Event at Onondaga will probably occasion a Meeting with the Indians,[2] it seems therefore necessary that the Board should be strengthened by a person residing in this City or its Vicinity. In the present critical Conjuncture I shall continue to act in order to give Time for the Appointment of another, lest an Injury should arise to the public by my immediately declining the Business.

Be pleased Sir, to assure Congress that, although unjustly calumniated, persecuted and deeply injured in public Life, I retire with the solid Consolation which is inseperable from a clear Conviction of my Consciousness that I have on all Occasions endeavored to serve my Country with Integrity, Zeal and Alacrity, and as the Weal of my Country is the first Wish of my Heart, that I stand ready to promote its Interest as a private Citizen and will with Chearfulness execute any Commands conducive to that great End.[3]

I have the Honor to be with perfect Respect and Esteem Your Excellency's most obedient humble Servant

PH. SCHUYLER

Since writing the above Lt. Colonel Willett is arrived from Fort Schuyler.[4] He informs me that a considerable Body of Indians will soon repair to this place. He wishes me to mention that in the Copy which Colonel Van Schaick sent me of the proceedings against Onondaga, *Afternoon* was, by Mistake inserted in Every Instance where it ought to be *Forenoon,* and so vice versa.

ALS. DNA: PCC, 152. Endorsed by Charles Thomson: ". . . Read May 10. Referred to the Come. on indian Affairs."

[1] JJ to Schuyler, 20 April 1779, in DNA: PCC, 14. Enclosed in that letter was the 19 April resolution of Congress accepting Schuyler's resignation. *JCC,* XIII, 473.

[2] The Onondagas, one of the Six Nations of the Iroquois, suffered destruc-

tion of their villages in April 1779 by Colonel Goose Van Shaick (1736–89). This raid preceded Sullivan's expedition.

[3] In the autumn of 1779 Schuyler returned to Congress as a delegate from New York State. *JCC*, XV, 1272.

[4] Lieutenant Colonel Marinus Willett was especially aware of the Indian movements in the area, having just taken part in the raid against the Onondagas.

From Frederick Jay

Fish Kill, 10 May 1779

Dear Brother

I did myself the pleasure of writing you the 7 Inst. per Post covering a letter from Mr. John Bancker to yourself. He requests that you'l use your interest in his behalf.[1]

Since my last Baxter has been and paid his last Years Rent. He has given his Obligation to pay for the next Years Rent 110 bushells of wheat or the Value thereof at the time it becomes due. Papa agreed with Deane early in the Spring (which I knew nothing of till lately) to pay 50£ for the next year, which in my opinion is triffling, but it is now too late to alter it.

I have been fortunate enough to exchange all the money Papa had (of my owne I had none) of the Emissions of 77 and 78 without trouble or expence;[2] overlooking his money some time ago, I found about forty pounds in Connecticut Bills, which Colonel Lamb[3] was kind enough to take with him to N. England and has exchanged it, though for the Emissions above mentioned; I am in hopes to get rid of it.

The Tories are again troublesome in this Quarter. Mr. Annin (son in Law to Mr. W. V. W.[4]) was robbed of everything he had a Thursday Evening last, by six Villians, one of them a Mr. Keel, who told Annin that he had Stole Your Mare and Mr. V. W. two Horses. They treated Mrs. Annin very ill, tyed a rope about his Neck, hoisted him up, and after letting him hang for several minutes cut him down; he is like to do well. The Same party shot a man last night near the Same place. I am informed that Search is making after those Hell hounds.

Peggy's indisposition has prevented my doing any thing for myself, I have not been absent from home Since Sir James left this. Farming goes on well considering all things.

The Family's love to you and Sally.

I am your Affectionate Brother

FRED. JAY

P.S. You have forgot the Lottery Ticket of Haskins.[5]

ALS. Endorsed.

[1] Not located.

[2] The Continental currency issued on 20 May 1777 and 11 April 1778 was declared void by Congress on 2 Jan. 1779 because of widespread counterfeiting of these emissions. Anyone who held bills of those dates was given the option of exchanging them for other bills or converting them into loan certificates. *JCC*, XIII, 21–22.

[3] John Lamb held a commission as colonel in the 2nd Continental Artillery at this time, and commanded the artillery at West Point, 1779–80.

[4] Daniel Annin married Lavinia Van Wyck (b. 1753), who was the daughter of William Van Wyck (1727–93) and the niece of Dr. Theodorus Van Wyck.

[5] The Continental lottery was authorized by Congressional resolution, 18 Nov. 1776. *JCC*, VI, 957–60.

FROM GUSTAVUS RISBERG

Philadelphia, May 10, 1779

Sir

This morning I waited on the Honorable Governeur Morris Esqr. one of the Committee for our Department, to know if the Alteration proposed by Col. Stewart Commissary General of Issues had passed the Approbation of Congress, when I was informed they had been reported but nothing further done.[1]

As Col. Stewart is at Camp I beg leave to trouble you with these lines, and report, that for this four Months past I have with the greatest difficulty been able to prevail on the different Assistant Commissaries in my Department, not to resign, in hopes that your Honorable Body would adopt Such measures as would answer their Expectations and services; Their Patience is now exhausted and Letters from every Quarter mention their leaving me, which I am sensible will be a great Injury to the Cause we are engaged in; And in Order the service may not Suffer, I pray Sir, you will represent to the Honorable Congress the necessity of having the Department immediately arranged on Such a footing as will induce them to Continue.

I beg further leave to represent, that the Clerks employed in the late Deputy Commissary General's Office have left us on Account of the Pay of Eighty Dollars proposed by Col. Stewart is deemed very insufficient for their Support these times. I pray therefore to have Liberty to engage them on the best Terms I can; otherwise the Business required from me must inevitably suffer.[2]

I am with respect Sir Your most Obedient Servant

GUSTAVUS RISBERG
D.C.G. OF ISSUE DEPT.

ALS. DNA: PCC, XIX, 219–22. Endorsed in an unidentified hand: ". . . Read May 11." Addressed: "Honorable John Jay Esquire, President of Congress." Risberg, a resident of Maryland, had previously served as assistant quartermaster-general of the Flying Camp, 17 Aug.–1 Dec. 1776.

1 Charles Stewart, a colonel in the New Jersey militia, served as Commissary General of Issues, June 1777–July 1782. Stewart's letter of 1 May 1779 concerning salaries to employees in the Commissary Department has not been located. It was enclosed with one of the same date from the Board of War to JJ. The Board remarked that Stewart's letter "is but a Repitition of the Complaints we hear from that and all other Departments wherein there are Officers on Sallaries. We are at Loss what farther to say to these officers having exhausted all our stack of Excuses. . . . [W]e must take the Freedom to observe that unless something is speedily done for the Relief of the Officers in the civil departments of the Army all Kind of Business therein must inevitably stop." The letters were read in Congress on 3 May and ordered "To lie on the table." DNA: PCC, 147, III, 297; *JCC*, XIV, 540–41.

2 After Risberg's letter was read on 11 May, Congress proceeded to consider a report of the Board of War dated 15 April 1779 concerning pay scales for officers in the Department of the Commissary General of Issues. The recommended salary schedule was adopted by Congress on the same day. *JCC*, XIV, 571–73.

Circular Letter

Philadelphia, 22 May 1779

Sir,

You will receive herewith enclosed a Copy of an Act of Congress of the 21st Inst. calling on the States for forty five Millions of Dollars.[1]

The late rapid depreciation of the Currency demanded a speedy and effectual Remedy.[2] While the great purposes for which the money was originally issued are remembered there can be no doubt that every measure calculated to support it's credit and preserve the public faith will be readily adopted.

I have the honor to be With great Respect Your Excellency's Most Obedient Servant

LbkC. DNA: PCC, 14. Enclosure: *JCC*, XIV, 626.

1 On 21 May 1779 Congress passed a resolution that the states add to a previous requisition of 2 Jan. 1779 an additional $45,000,000 to be paid into the Continental treasury before 1 Jan. 1780. As was customary by 1779, each state was assigned a definite quota of this sum: New Hampshire, $1,500,000; Massachusetts, $6,000,000; Rhode Island, $750,000; Connecticut, $5,100,000; New York, $2,400,000; New Jersey, $2,400,000; Pennsylvania, $5,700,000; Delaware, $450,000; Maryland, $4,680,000; Virginia, $7,200,000; North Carolina, $3,270,000; South Carolina, $5,500,000. Georgia, then under attack, was to raise her quota later. According to the Articles of Confederation, the quotas were to be based on land values, but since it was impossible to assess them during the war, the quotas were based on population. *JCC*, XIV, 626; E. James Ferguson, *The Power of the Purse, A History of American Public Finance, 1776–1790* (Chapel Hill, 1961), p. 33.

2 Continental currency had depreciated rapidly in 1779. In January 1778 the exchange rate of currency for specie was 4:1. By January 1779 the rate was 8:1, and by April of that year the rate was 16:1. Anne Bezanson, *Prices and Inflation During the American Revolution* (Philadelphia, 1951), p. 65.

From Robert Troup

Camp at Middle Brook, May 22nd, 1779

My dear Sir

After mature Reflection I think it best for me to continue in the Army till the War is ended. You say an Officer who resigns at present will lose the Eclat his Services have given him. I thank you for your Advice, and have already improved it to Advantage, as you will find in the Subsequent Part of this Letter. Besides I feel my Happiness so intimately connected with the Prosperity of my Country that I cannot desert her in the Hour of Danger. And surely we are not free from Danger when the alarming Depreciation of our Money, and the unfortunate Dissentions amongst our Rulers afford the Enemy such a flattering Prospect of Success.

How I shall be employed this Campaign is a Source of little Uneasiness to me. It is in public as in private Life a Person disposed to do Good will never want Occasions for the Exercise of his Abilities. I shall therefore content myself with serving as a Volunteer, which I hope you will consider as a Mark of my extreme Modesty especially as I saw the Surrender of General Burgoyne and his whole Army.

The Hint I just mentioned has Reference to an Affair which I endeavoured to manage with all the Address of a modern Speculator. I will tell you the Particulars of it. My Brother's Part of a Farm in Morris County was advertised for Sale pursuant to a Law of this State.[1] Persuaded that my Part would be rendered less valuable if I did not purchase his I attended the Vendue for that Purpose. When it was set up the Commissioners indulged me with the Liberty of speaking to the People. I informed them of my Situation, my Services, my Sufferings in the Cause—and entreated them not to bid against me. I offered 500£ for it, not much more than enough to discharge my Brother's Debts, and it was struck off to me. This purchase entitled me to one Half of the Farm which I afterwards sold for 3500£ Proceeds. I paid the Commissioners, kept a Trifle for a few Necessaries, and have put between 28 and 2900£ of the Money into the Continental Funds. Have I acted right? Hamilton thinks I have. I apply to Money as well as Knowledge that excellent Maxim of Horace, "Condo et repono Quid mox depromere possum."[2] The principal Reason which influenced me to take this Step, was a Conviction, in my own Mind, that the Money will regain a proper Credit in three Years at most. Does it not stand on the Broad Bottom of our Independence?

I was at Persippany a few Days ago with Mr. Watkins, who, I presume has waited upon you since he has been in Philadelphia. The little Boy and the Family were well. I am happy to hear that Mrs. Jay and Miss Katy are so agreeably situated in Philadelphia. I beg my best Respects to them and Brockhost. I promised to pay them a Visit; but have counted the Cost, and find, even if I had a Super-abundancy of Cash, that my Servant's Horse is too poor to carry enough to bear my Expences.

I am, My dear Sir, Your affectionate Friend,

ROB. TROUP

ALS. Endorsed.

1 John Troup (d. 1781), elder brother of Robert, was a member of a Loyalist unit at Howe's headquarters on Staten Island just before the battle of Long Island, 1776. He was arrested in 1777 by American troops while recruiting for the British in lower New Jersey. Wendell Tripp, "Robert Troup" (unpub. Ph.D. dissertation, Columbia University, 1973), p. 12; Lorenzo Sabine, *The American Loyalists* (Boston, 1847), p. 651; W. W. Munsell, *History of Morris County* (New York, 1882), p. 220.

2 "I put away and store up what I may soon be able to draw upon."

From Thomas Pitcairn

Reading, May 27th, 1779

Sir

In Justice to my Brother officers and myself on Parole at this Place, my Duty directs me to adress you. To sett forth the insult and abuse of some persons Inhabitants of Reading; Of which I beg leave to trouble you with a Short naration founded on facts. On Saturday last the 23rd Inst. Lieut. Dunlop[1] in Company with some ladies of the Place, were walking the Streets, he received several rotten Eggs, thrown by some boys standing a Short distance from him, That was often repeated. He found it necessary to correct the offenders, whose fathers with a mob immediatly interferd, and beat the Said Lieut. Dunlop in most Inhuman manner, insomuch I find his life was in danger.

Lieut. Dunlop was in that condition committed to Jail, under the same rooff with the common Felons. This is a treatment (as British Officers) we cannot look over. We therefor presume to hope the Congress will take this affair into consideration, that the offenders may be brought to Punishment. Lieut. Dunlop is still Confined and required to give bail and appear at the Quarter Sessions to answer Just Conduct. This is a requisition I presume Congress will by no means think necessary, but on the contrary will consider a Parole sufficient for a Man of honor. Also the imposibility of his getting bail being totally unknown to any body here and every man being equally his Enemy.[2]

I have the Honor to be, Sir, your most obedient Servant

T. PITCAIRN
CAPTAIN 82ND REGIMENT

ALS. DNA: PCC, 78, XVIII, 223. Endorsed by Charles Thomson: ". . . Read 29. Referred to the board of war, who are directed to take order thereon. Acted upon." (No action on this is recorded in the journals of Congress.)

1 James Dunlop (d. 1832), of Dunlop, Ayrshire. In the spring of 1779 Lieutenant Dunlop, 82nd Hamilton foot, was with flank companies en route to New York when their ship was wrecked off the coast of New Jersey. Four-fifths of the company to which he belonged was drowned, the remainder taken prisoner by the Americans. Dunlop was later exchanged and accompanied the 80th foot from New York to Virginia.

2 Captain Pitcairn wrote JJ on 7 July 1779 and again complained of the treatment received by his officers at Reading. This letter was also referred to the Board of War; its report does not appear in the journals. *JCC*, XIV, 815; DNA: PCC, 78, VIII, 231.

From Jeremiah Wadsworth

Philadelphia, June 5th, 1779

Sir

Before any considerable Evils had happened in my Department as early as September last I asked liberty of Congress to resign my office of Commissary General of Purchases and gave some reasons which induced me to ask a dessmission. In October I repeated my earnest desire to be desmissed, when the Year shoud end. A Committee from Congress confered with me and I believe made a report which has never been acted on.[1]

I have now some new reasons to offer Congress which appear to me to be so just that I can not doubt but they will readily consent to my dissmission. Many objections have been made to the mode of doing business by commission. Last Winter Congress appointed a Committee who made some efforts to alter the System, with those Gentlemen, I had several conferences,[2] and though I had not altered my opinion respecting the mode, I freely offered to attempt executeing any thing they shoud Point out, but after waiting here a long time, I found it necessary to attend to the business of my Department in the Eastern States where I had not been for more than half a Year, and where the boundless expenditur of Provisions seemed ready to swallow up the whole produce of the United States. When I went from hence I had reason to believe the Committee would form some new System which they believed would better answer the Purpose than the present one, which has suffered so much by General Attacks and unsupported complaints that it has lost its force. Thus Sir is the old System destroyed and nothing substituted in its place.

The State of Mayreland have taken the business into their own hands and some of my Purchasers have been imployed by that State at 5 Per Cent Commissions, and the whole flour of the State is out of my controul. The report of the Treasury Board and the Resolutions of Congress, have abated if not destroyed the influence of the purchaseing Commissaries.

I have some Vacancies which I cant fill in the present State of uncertainty for these with many other reasons. I now once more ask permission of Congress to retire and resign my office. This I should not have done at this critical season if I had any prospect of feeding the Army.

Conscious of haveing acted faithfully I shall not trouble Congress with remarks on the unmerritted abuse and slander indiscriminately heaped on my Department by every petty scribler in the United States, nor would their Malice have pained me if I had no reason to believe they were supported by men of influence, who would have better served their Country by Assisting to detect the Guilty than helping to Slander the innocent.

I wish not to multiply the troubles of Congress or involve them in any new difficulties. I have an earnest desire to render every possible service to my Country but I must part with my peace of mind and good Name, or my Office! Under these circumstances uninfluenced by Passion, or resentment for any real, or supposed injuries, or neglect, I am constrained to resign my office, and request you will signify this my resignation to Congress.[3]

I am with the greatest respect Your Excellency most Obedient Servant,

JEREH. WADSWORTH

ALS. DNA: PCC, 78, XXIV, 41–44. Endorsed by Charles Thomson: ". . . Read 7." Jeremiah Wadsworth (1743–1804), Connecticut-born Revolutionary soldier and congressman, since April 1778 commissary general.

[1] On two previous occasions Wadsworth tendered his resignation which

Congress declined to accept. DNA: PCC, 78, XXIII, 551, 573, 577; *JCC*, XII, 968, 1024–25.

2 On 10 Nov. 1778 a committee of three, comprising Nathaniel Scudder (1759–1836) of New Jersey, William Whipple (1730–85) of New Hampshire, and Gouverneur Morris had been appointed to supervise the commissary and quartermaster departments. *JCC*, XII, 1115.

3 On 29 Nov. 1779 Congress agreed to Wadsworth's resignation as of 1 Jan. 1780. On 4 Dec. 1779 Congress announced that Ephraim Blaine had been elected to succeed Wadsworth, but that Wadsworth continue until Blaine accepted and could take over the duties of the office. *JCC*, XV, 1326, 1349.

From Lafayette

St. Jean d'angely Near Rochefort, 12th–13th June 1779

Sir

How happy I shall think Myself whenever a Safe opportunity of writing to Congress will be offered, I Cannot Better any way express But in Reminding them of that unbounded Affection and Gratitude I Shall ever feel for them. So deeply are those Sentiments Engraved in my heart, that I every day lament upon that distance which Separates me from them, and that never any thing was so warmly and passionately wished for, as I desire to Return again to that Country of which I shall ever Consider myself as a Citizen. There is no pleasure to be enjoyed which Might Equal this of finding Myself among that free liberal Nation By whose affection and Confidence I am so highly honored, to fight again with those Brother Soldiers of Mine to whom I am So much indebted. But Congress know that former plans have been altered By themselves, that other ones have been thought impossible, as they were asked too late in the year. I therefore will Make use of the leave of absence they were pleased to Grant me, and Serve the Common Cause among My Countrymen theyr allies, till happy Circumstances May Conduct me to the American shores in such a way as would Make that Return More useful to the United States.

The affairs of America I shall ever look upon as My first Business while I am in Europe. Any Confidence from the king and ministers, any popularity I May have among My Countrymen, any mean [*sic*] in My power, shall be to the Best of My skill, and till the end of My life erected in Behalf of an interest I have so much at heart. What I have hitherto done or Said Relating to America, I think Needless to Mention, as my ardent zeal for her is, I hope, well known to Congress. But I want to let them know that, if in my proposals in My repeated warm instances for Getting ships, Monney, Supplies of Any kind, I have found the Ministry not alwais So much in Earnest as I was

Myself. I was then Stopped By theyr *Natural fear* of inconveniences which might arise for Both, or By theyr Conviction that Such a thing was impossible for the present, But I never could question theyr Ardent good will towards America. In Case Congress Believe My influence May any way Serve them, I wish they would direct such orders to me, that I might more certainly and properly employ the knowledge I have of this Court and Country for obtaining a peace to which my heart Shall be So much interested.

His Excellency Doctor Franklin, will, no doubt, inform you, Sir, of the situation of Europe and Respective State of our affairs. The Chevalier de La Luzerne[1] will also add intelligences which will be intrusted to him in the time of his departure. By the doctor you will learn what has been Said or thought of on account of finances. Germany, Prussia, Turkey and Russia have Made Such a peace as the French have desired. All the Northern Kingdoms, the Dutch themselves Seem Rather disgusted with English pride and vexations. They put themselves in situation of protecting theyr trade of Any kind with France. Irish intelligences You will be fully and particularly Acquainted of. What Concerns Spain will also be laid Before you. To that I have Nothing to Add but telling you that our Affairs Seem Going very fast towards a Speedy and honorable end. England is Now Making her last efforts and I hope a great Stroke will before long abate theyr fantastik swelled appearance, and Shew the Narrow Bounds of theyr actual true power.

Since we have taken Senegal I don't know of any Military event which I Might Mention. There has been a privateering expedition against Jersay island which has been Stopped by the dificulty of getting a shore. That little attempt Made by Some far private Volunteers, England honored with the Name of a public French expedition, and very unwisely employed their Admiral Arbuthnot[2] which will put a great delay to his Spoken of departure. Congress will hear of an expedition against our friends of Liverpool and other parts of the English Coast, for to Shew there French troops under American Colours, which on account of Raising Contributions, my Concern for American finances, had at lenght Brought into My head. But the plan was afterwards Reduced to So Small a Scale, that they thought the Command would no More fitt me, and the expedition itself has been delayed till more important operations are to take place. There I hope to be employed, and if Any thing important is the Matter I Shall as a faithfull American officer Give an accurate account thereof to Congress and General Washington.[3]

That So flattering affection Congress and the American Nation are pleased to honor me with, Make me very desirous of letting them know, and if I dare Speack So friendly enjoy my private Situation, happy in the Sight of My friends and family, after I was By Your attentive goodness, Safely Brought Again to My Native Shore, I Met there with Such an honorable Reception, with Such kind Sentiments as By far exceed any wishes I durst have Conceived. That unexpressible Satisfaction which the Good will of My Countrymen toward me affords to My heart, I feel indebted for to theyr ardent love for America, for the Cause of freedom, and its defenders theyr new allies, and to the idea they entertain that I had the happiness to Serve the United States. To those very Motives, Sir, and to the letter Congress were pleased to write on My Account, I owe the Many favors the king has Conferred upon me. There was no Time lost in appointing me to the Command of his own Regiment of dragoons, and Any thing he Might have done, any thing I Might have wished I have Received on account of your kind Reccommendations.

Since Some days I am in this Small town, Near Rochefort harbor where I have joined the King's Regiment, and where other troops which I for the Moment Command are Stationed. But I hope leaving Before long this place for to play a more active part and Come Nearer the Common ennemy. Before My departure from Paris, I Sent to the Minister of foreign affairs who, by the bye, is one of our Best friends, an intelligence Concerning a loan in Holland which I want France to Make or answer for in Behalf of America. But I din't hear yet any thing on that head.[4] Monsieur le chev[alier] de la Luzerne will Carry you longer and fresher News as he is particularly ordered to do So, and he directly Setts of from Versailles. That New plenipotentiary Minister I beg leave to Recommend most instantly to Congress, not only as a public but also as a private Gentleman. By the acquaintance I have Made with him, I Conceive he is a Sensible, modest, well meaning man, a Man truly worthy of enjoying the Sight of American freedom. I hope that By his Natural temper as well as By his abilities he will obtain Both public Confidence and private friendship.

As whenever the interests of Beloved friends are Seriously Concerned, Candid and warm affection don't know how to Calculate and throws a way all Considerations, I shall frankly tell you, Sir, that Nothing may more effectually hurt theyr interests, Consequences and Reputation in Europe, than to hear of Some thing like dispute or division between Whigs. Nothing Could urge My touching this delicate Matter, but the unhappy experience I every day Make on that head, Since I May hear Myself what is Said on this Side of the Atlantic, and the Arguments I am to fight against.

Let me, Sir, finish this So long letter in Begging you Would present once more to the Congress of the United States, that tribute of an endless, unbounded, zeal and affection, of the highest Respect, and most sincere gratitude, I shall profess and deeply feel for them till the last moment of My life.

With the Most perfect Regard I have the honor to be, Sir, Your excellency's Most obedient humble Servant

LAFAYETTE

The 13th June

In the very time I was going to write to My friends in Congress and the Several States, I Receive the king's order for to Repair immediately to Versailles where I am to Meet the Lieutenant General Count de Vaux[5] who will Command the French troop in Normandy. There I am to be employed in the Most agreable Manner, and I shall Certainly have the honor to Acquaint you of any thing which Might be put in execution. As I have no time to spare and I fear the frigatte Might be gone I Am obliged to wait for an other occasion, and to lead to a more Convenient Moment the pleasure I had promised Myself of writing to all My American particular friends.

ALS. DNA: PCC, 156. Endorsed by Charles Thomson: ". . . Read Sept. 13." On 21 Oct. 1778 Congress had granted Lafayette a leave of absence to return to France. He arrived at Brest 12 Feb. 1779. *JCC*, XII, 1034, 1054.

1 Chevalier Anne-César de la Luzerne (1741–91) succeeded Gérard as French minister to the U.S. in 1779.

2 Appointed commander of the American station, Admiral Marriot Arbuthnot (1711–94) sailed from England on 1 May 1779 and reached New York on 25 August.

3 Lafayette hoped to distinguish himself in the European theater by an attack on English seaports. Preliminary plans were drawn up for a combined operation with John Paul Jones (1747–92), but in mid-May Lafayette received orders to proceed to his newly appointed post as commander of a regiment of the king's dragoons. The plans for coastal raids had been discarded by the king in favor of a massive naval attack against England, predicated on the expectation that Spain was about to enter the war. Not even Lafayette understood the importance of the change in orders until 13 June, as is indicated in the postscript. Louis Gottschalk, *Lafayette and the Close of the American Revolution* (Chicago, 1942), pp. 9–16; Samuel Eliot Morison, *John Paul Jones: A Sailor's Biography* (Boston, 1959), p. 188; *Peacemakers*, pp. 28, 35–36, 42.

4 When Lafayette heard that an English effort to borrow from Dutch bankers had failed, he hoped that a Dutch loan might be available for the Americans and wrote to Vergennes about the possibility. Necker, however, was not enthusiastic. America was unable to secure a Dutch loan until 1782. Louis Gottschalk, *Lafayette and the Close of the American Revolution*, pp. 19–20.

5 Noël de Jourda, comte de Vaux (1705–88), a lieutenant-general of the king's forces in Brittany and Normandy, was to command the invasion of England. Lafayette was to serve on his staff as lieutenant to M. de Joucourt, one of the three quartermaster-generals. The expedition was abandoned in the fall of 1779. Gottschalk, *op cit.*, pp. 29–30; *Peacemakers*, p. 37.

FROM JOHN MORGAN

Philadelphia, June 15, 1779

Sir

Congress having been pleased by its resolve of the 12th Inst.,[1] on the full and weighty evidence before them, to restore me, in the most ample Manner, to my former fair and unsullied reputation, I thankfully acknowledge the honourable approbation which it has been pleased, in consequence thereof, to bestow on my Conduct in the service of my Country. I consider it as a proof of the disposition of the house to render Justice to all Men, and to give me adequate reparation for the Injuries I have sustained from a faithful discharge of the truly difficult and important trust reposed in me by Congress.

As, in the execution of my Duty in the station of Director General and Physician in Chief, the public good was my only pursuit, the prosecuting it now continues to be my favorite Object and on that Object I still purpose to keep my Views invariably fixed. Conscious I am, that it is incumbent on me, on every Servant of the Public, and on every free Citizen, to prosecute to Conviction all persons in commission, who are guilty of misconduct in Office and have abused the public trust. Being further stirred up to this needful Measure by the loud and repeated Calls and exhortations of Congress, particularly by its resolve of June 20, 1778 and its late earnest Address to the Inhabitants of the united States of America, May 1779; Assured moreover that it is the Intention of Congress vigorously to execute a Resolve of that Consequence, so warmly enforced on their Constituents, without respect of persons, and that it will therefore give immediate orders for a Trial, free from the embarrassments of any tedious delay from which innocent Men sometimes suffer inconcievable hardships and distress, and the guilty are enabled to elude and baffle the testimony of Witnesses wearied out in a fruitless Attempt to bring them to Justice, I do hereby charge Dr. William Shippen junior, in the service of the united states with Malpractices and Misconduct in Office. And, whereas Congress, by a resolve of the House, has subjected a Director of the General Hospital on any Accusation of Malconduct, to be tried by a Court Martial I therefore now declare my readiness to give before the proper Court having Jurisdiction the necessary Evidence in the premisses against the said Dr. Wm. Shippen.[2]

I remain, with warm devotion to my Countries Liberties and Wellfare, Sir, and Your faithful obedient Servant

JOHN MORGAN

ALS. DNA: PCC, 63, 129–30. Addressed: "To His Excellency John Jay Esq. President of the Congress of the united States of America." Endorsed by Charles Thomson: ". . . read the same day." Dft in Kewaunee County Museum, Kewaunee, Wisc. Endorsed by Morgan: "To the Presidt. of Congress, June 15, 1779, from which the fair Copy was sent for the Impeachmt. of Dr. Shippen."

[1] At Dr. Morgan's request Congress conducted an inquiry into his administration as director general and physician in chief and resolved that it was satisfied with his record. *JCC*, XIV, 724.

[2] The word "impeachment" appears in Dr. Morgan's endorsement, but this was a misuse of terminology. Being under the jurisdiction of the army, Shippen could be tried only by a court-martial, and Morgan understood this, as he makes clear in this paragraph. Congress transmitted Morgan's letter with a covering note of the same day to George Washington, directing him to act promptly to see that justice was done. The commander did not seem in any hurry, but in October he agreed to try Shippen after the current campaign ended. The court-martial, which began in March 1780 and continued until 27 June, acquitted the accused man on all five charges but reprimanded him for speculating in hospital stores. *JCC*, XIV, 733–34; David Freeman Hawke, *Benjamin Rush: Revolutionary Gadfly* (Indianapolis, 1971), pp. 237–44.

From Jonathan Trumbull

State of Connecticut, Lebanon, 22nd June 1779

Sir

The General Assembly of this State, at its sessions in January last ordered taxes to be levied to collect their quota assigned for the 15,000,000 Dollars requested by Congress in their Resolve of 5th January last. At their May Sessions further taxes are granted to collect the quota assigned this State of 45,000,000 Dollars.[1] They are payable at different periods, none exceed the 1st January next. The tax bills are ordered to be made out together, with intention that such who are able, may have opportunity to pay the whole at the first payment.

At the time the Enemy moved up North river, the three Brigades west of Connecticut River were ordered to be in readiness to march, equipped, and furnished with six days provisions. One quarter to march forthwith, these turned out with alacrity, but were soon dismissed. In consequence of intelligence from Horseneck in Greenwich, of the appearance of the Enemy, and damages done by plundering Cattle, Corn Houses etc. a Regiment of 500 Men was immediately sent, in addition to the Guards, which were already on the ground for their defence. It was likewise judged necessary to raise two Regiments of 500 Men each by voluntary inlistments, or if not filled by 15th July next, to be drafted peremptorily, to serve till January next, for defence of New London, Groton, and the Western Frontiers.[2]

This State being frequently called upon, and under necessity to furnish, either for its own immediate defence, or the security of the other United States, large drafts of Militia, which have been at various times chearfully sent into the Field, and the same being at this time necessary, and requisitions for that purpose complied with in the last Assembly, I am directed to request that Congress will be pleased to order, that the Troops raised for Defence, and also whenever the Militia of this State is drawn into service, that Continental Pay, Rations, and Allowances be given said drafts of Militia, such as are allowed and given to other States under like circumstances.

At a Session of Assembly in April last it was ordered that Eight hundred men, being the quota of this State to recruit the Continental Army should be raised, and in May Session this order was fully enforced.[3] The Recruits will be soon furnished; such as do not inlist by the 10th of July next are to be filled by Drafts, to serve to the 15th January next. The encouragements given the men to inlist during the war, it is hoped, will induce them to engage.

On Request of the Delegates of this State, Congress advanced to its use, for payment of the Troops belonging thereto, £45,000, to be on Account.[4] This Sum is received. Before its arrival other ways were found to effect the payment, and the sum actually forwarded for the purpose intended. But as orders for recruiting our Quota of the deficiency of the Continental Army are already issued, and no money is forwarded for said purpose from Congress, the money abovementioned, not being needed for the purpose first designed, the Assembly of this State have ordered, that with the approbation of Congress, the £45,000 shall be used to recruit our said quota of deficiences, and request that the said sum be charged to this State, not as a Sum loaned, as first intended, but as part of a sum to be furnished them towards raising, recruiting, and filling their deficiency of the Continental Army paying bounties, procuring cloathing etc. without any charge of interest.

Agreeable to a Resolution of Congress, recommending some measures to be adopted for procuring a supply of cloathing for the

Continental Troops of this State, Our General Assembly, at their last session have recommended to the several towns in said State, and injoined upon them, to furnish certain specified articles of cloathing, amounting to considerable part of the necessary cloathing for Troops of this State, for one year, which is to be received and forwarded by a suitable person thereunto appointed, to the Sub or State Cloathier, appointed for this State with the Army.[5] For the purpose of procuring and paying for such cloathing, a large Sum of money will be wanted, which I must beg may be immediately furnished, either by supply from the Continental Treasury or by Draft on the Treasurer of this State, to be paid out of monies in his hands, collected for Continental Service.

I am, with Esteem and Regard Sir Your Obedient humble Servant

JONTH. TRUMBULL

ALS. DNA: PCC, 66, 23–26. Endorsed by Charles Thomson: ". . . Read July 1. Referred to the board of treasury." Tr in DLC: Trumbull Papers, XX, Force Transcripts.

1 "An Act, in addition to, and alteration of an Act, entitled, An Act for the direction of Listers in their Office and Duty," Jan. 1779 sess., Evans, 16231; "An Act for the direction of Listers in their Office and Duty," May 1779 sess., Evans, 16233.

2 In July 1779 Sir Henry Clinton began a large-scale punitive expedition against Connecticut towns on Long Island Sound for interfering with British shipping. In preparation, Clinton assembled 2,600 troops at Whitestone at the end of June 1779.

3 "An Act for repealing a Part of a Law of this State, made and passed in May, A.D. 1777, entitled, An Act for raising and compleating the Quota of the continental Army to be ratified in this State," April 1779 sess., Evans, 16232; "An Act, in Addition to a Law of this State, entitled, An Act for forming and regulating the Militia . . . ," May 1779 sess., Evans, 16233.

4 On 22 May 1779 Congress granted a warrant issue for $150,000 to Connecticut delegates to be repaid with 6 percent interest to the Commissioner of the Continental Loan Office by August 1780. *JCC*, XIV, 629–30.

5 On 1 June 1779 the Connecticut Assembly ordered the clothier to issue clothing in accordance with the resolve of Congress of 23 March 1779. A broadside on the appointment of Elijah Hubbard (1745–1808) as clothier, urging cooperation by citizens and local governments, is in Evans, 16239. *JCC*, XIII, 353–56.

From Egbert Benson

Poughkeepsie, June 23d, 1779

Dear Sir

I have frequently of late determined to write to You and have been as often interrupted; indeed this disagreeable Business, in which I am engaged, though it is not sufficient to furnish Me with constant Employment, yet is of such a Nature as to leave Me scarce a Moment which I can call my own, or in which I am free from Interruption.[1] We were flattered that when our Government was established the Powers of the ordinary civil Magistrate would be adequate to preserving the Peace of the State; We have however been disappointed, and I am apprehensive Commissioners will be necessary, if not during the War at least while the Enemy possess any part of the State and as I can procure no Substitute it is more than probable that I shall be obliged to attend the Board.

Your Brother has doubtless given You a History of the last Sessions of the Legislature. I think upon the whole it was tolerably peacable and harmonious. The Confiscation Bill as it was the most important Matter occupied the most of our time, and after a safe passage through both Houses to the Council of Revision and on it's Return, having [passed] the Assembly, suffered Ship-wreck in the Senate. The Bill was far from being unexceptionable, but, considering the Diversity of Sentiment in the Members upon the Subject, I am doubtful if We ever obtain any whether it will be more perfect, and therefore wish the Last had passed, and as We hereafter perceived it's Defects amended. The Loss of it has occasioned some Clamor and Uneasiness.

Congress have at length taken up the Vermont Business; their Proceedings however are not pleasing to some of our Friends; I beleive they expected more and are rather disappointed. If my Opinion is of any Importance I must candidly own I approve of the Measure of Your Embassy, as I would not only wish to take from the Inhabitants of Vermont every Pretext for Complaint, but We really stand in need of Information ourselves with respect to the Claims of these People and the State of the Country. You may recollect the Difficulties that flowed from this Source in our Deliberations last fall. The Information We shall receive from Your Committee will certainly be the best, for I trust they are Men of Integrity and Discernment and will doubtless have a free Communication with the principal Characters in Vermont. I scarcely supposed myself authorized to exercise any Judgment respecting the Propriety of this Proceedure unless it had been flagrantly wrong. You are on the Spot and have the various Views and Tempers of the Members and I have the fullest Confidence that You and Your Colleagues will do the best You can.[2]

Great Changes throughout the State for Representatives at the last Election, whether for the better or the worse is not yet determined. If I am rightly informed at least two thirds of the Members of the next House will be new and it is said that only two of the old Members are elected in Albany County, Messers Whiting and Gordon.[3] This is by no means unexpected to Me. Such a Love of Money or Ease and Retirement and such a Loathing of public Business has prevailed of late among our Men of Substance and Importance that I should not have been surprized at greater Changes; and I hope the People will always possess a Spirit not to elect as their Representative any Person who appears insensible of the Honor and does not accept the Office with Chearfulness and Alacrity. One would imagine this Revolution had purified our Manners, We are become so wonderfully disinterested disdaining to make an Interest or accept an Office. I can distinguish between mean Sollicitations, and a Conduct discovering that You wish to be appointed to public Employments only because You wish to serve Your Country and that You conceive this Service Your highest Honor. If all our Freinds would make this Distinction and pursue this Conduct our Legislature would be more respectable than I fear it otherwise will. There was a considerable Opposition made to Me in this County but without Success. It proceeded from the worst of Principles namely because [I was] an Advocate for Taxation.

This will be delivered to You by my Brother. He has a Letter relative to his Business from the Governor to Mr. Lewis and he would wish if possible to have an Opportunity of communicating his Errand to You. I need not introduce him to Your Acquaintance and only take the Liberty of recommending him to Your Notice.

I remain Yours most sincerely

EGBT. BENSON

ALS. Endorsed. Addressed: "The Honble John Jay Esqr. Philadelphia."

1 In addition to his position as attorney general for New York State (elected 1777), which would involve him in any litigation claims for the state, Benson seems to have served as a liaison between the Assembly (of which he was a member) and Governor Clinton, in keeping the government informed of the status of the Vermont claims. *GCP*, V, 52, 113–16; *JPC*, I, 910.

2 On 1 June 1779 Congress resolved to send a committee to the New Hampshire Grants to "confer with the said inhabitants" and to "take every prudent measure to promote an amicable settlement." The following day, Oliver Ellsworth (1745–88) of Connecticut, Timothy Edwards of Massachusetts, John Witherspoon, Samuel Atlee (1738–86) of Pennsylvania, and Jesse Root (1736–1822) of Connecticut were appointed, "any three . . . to be empowered to act." Ellsworth's and Root's letter of 4 July was read in Congress on the 12th. They had gotten to the Grants after Atlee and Witherspoon, and stated that more people wanted to make their case heard before Congress. Atlee and Witherspoon reported to Congress on 13 July that the inhabitants, if they could represent their case, would "submit themselves and finally . . . abide by the Decision of the

United States in Congress assembled." *JCC*, XIV, 674, 676, 823–24; DNA: PCC, 59, III, 15–18.

3 William B. Whiting and James Gordon. *New York Civil List*, p. 410.

FROM NATHANAEL GREENE

Smith's Clove, June 24th, 1779

Sir

A late law has been passed by the legislature of the state of New Jersey for the express purpose of taxing the assistant and Deputy Quarter Masters General, which I am afraid will be productive of the most disagreeable consequences.[1] This law appears so arbitrary and unprecedented upon any free principles of taxation, that I am surprized it ever had the sanction of a deliberative body.

Such a resolution might have been justified in a Committee, appointed from necessity, with powers to act at discression; who conceived themselves bound, neither by the constitution of the State, or by antient customs or usages, but by no other body of men, and who were at liberty to take their measures from conveniency, and not from a principle of equal Justice. This Law seems to be leveled at the staff departments, and appears to be such a stretch of power, under the sanction of law, as neither the constitution, good policy or common Justice can warrant. Should it be submitted to, it will establish a precedent, dangerous to the people, as well as the privilege of your Officers. Had it been confined to the officers of that state, its absurdity might have been less obvious, yet both dangerous and unjust. From persons discribed by the law, it appears to be designed to tax continental officers, who as such, have no more connection with that state, than any other, and may with equal justice be taxed by every other, as by that. Colonel John Cox and Mr. Charles Pettit seem to have been in contemplation in framing the law as assistants Quarter Masters General.[2] These Gentlemen cannot be described in that state in a taxable light, from their official characters, although they may reside there as common Citizens. This being the case, who will serve in the department subject to the tax of every State, not from any equal principles with other citizens, but wholly under the influence of popular prejudice on private views.

Are staff officers necessary to the operations of the Army? If they are, why are these embarrasments thrown in the way? If they are not why is the public burthened with an unnecessary expense? If the conditions upon which they are employed are exceptionable, let there be a change, but let not those employed in the staff be subject to arbitrary impositions which cannot fail to drive every man out of the department that is worthy of trust, or capable of conducting the business.

Mr. Furman D.Q.M.General for the State of New Jersey, has already resigned his Commission,[3] and Colonel Cox and Mr. Pettit only wait to know the issue of a memorial presented to congress.[4] If this mode of taxation takes place in the other States, it is not difficult to foresee the dreadful convulsion that resignations in the staff department will produce. Let them be answerable for the consequences who cause the necessity. The business of my department is attended with so many obstructions, that it is with the utmost difficulty I can keep the wheels in motion, owing to the great scarcity of supplies, and the present depreciated state of the money. However strong the prejudices of the people may operate, with respect to the emolument of staff officers, I am persuaded you can make few alterations wherein the public interest will be benefited.

Should Mr. Pettit and Colonel Cox resign, I cannot be answerable for the consequences at this critical Juncture and in the present embarrassed state that things are in. I shall continue to do my utmost to execute the duties of the department, but will not be held responsible for debts contracted or monies disbursed, as I am confident it will throw every thing into confusion and to free myself from this incumbrance, I will take no fee or reward for any services I render in the department after their resignation.

I have the honor to be Sir, your very humble Servant

NATH. GREENE QMG

ALS. DNA: PCC, 155, 139–42. Endorsed by Charles Thomson: ". . . Read July 1. Referred to Mr. Duane, Mr. McKean, Mr. Burke."

1 "An Act to raise the Sum of One Million of Pounds in the State of New Jersey," passed 8 June 1779. On 8 July the committee which had considered the 7 July memorial from Cox and Pettit, recommended that the New Jersey legislature revise the 8 June law so that "the sum assessed upon" their offices would not be "so much taken from the whole States for the benefit of a particular state," thus reducing the allowance by Congress far below "what was intended and engaged." Therefore they urged that the tax on account of their office be repealed and restitution made for any back taxes paid. *Acts of the General Assembly of the State of New Jersey* (Trenton, 1779); *JCC*, XIV, 807–08.

2 John Cox (1731–93) of Philadelphia and Charles Pettit (1737–1806), former secretary of the province of New Jersey, were appointed Assistant Quartermasters General on 2 March 1778. *JCC*, X, 210.

3 Moore Furman (1728–1808), was named Deputy Quartermaster General and Forage Master of New Jersey on 2 March 1778. On 24 June 1779 he submitted his resignation to Greene and thereafter acted "by his particular desire as a volunteer in the Department until the cause of my resignation be removed or

another is appointed." Furman remained in the post on this basis until 19 Sept. 1780. Furman to Cox and Pettit, 29 June 1779, DNA: PCC, 78, V, 376.

4 The memorial of Cox and Pettit was read in Congress on 18 June 1779 and referred to a committee comprising Thomas McKean, James Lovell, and William Paca. Ten days later the committee reported that "Congress cannot in any manner controul the legislature of New Jersey in the internal police of the said State," and suggested that Cox and Pettit seek redress from the New Jersey legislature if they felt themselves unjustly taxed. DNA: PCC, 41, VIII, 72; 19, V, 109; *JCC*, XIV, 744–45, 779–80.

Passport Issued to Joseph Deane

Philadelphia, June 1779

By his Excellency John Jay Esquire President of the Congress of the united States of America.

To All Governors Generals, Admirals, and other officers, civil and military, of the said united States and of his most Christian majesty etc., etc. and others whom it may concern.

Be it known That by a certain Act of the said Congress, made and passed on the thirty first Day of May in the Year of our Lord one thousand seven hundred and seventy nine; reciting That "Whereas Timothy Penny now an Inhabitant of Massachusets Bay but formerly of the Island of Jamaica, where his Estate lies, had represented the Necessity he was under of sending a Person to purchase a Vessel in that Island, and load her with Produce for the Support of his numerous Family." And reciting further that "Whereas it appeared that the Character and Circumstances of the said Timothy Penny rendered such Indulgence proper" the said Congress Resolved that Letters of safe Conduct be granted to the said Timothy Penny for any one Vessel, which may be purchased and loaded as above mentioned and sent to any Port or Place in any of the united States not in Possession of the Enemy, and for the Person of Captain Joseph Deane who is to be employed by the said Penny on that Business." Wherefore in Pursuance of the said Resolution, Passport and Safe Conduct is hereby granted to the said Captain Joseph Deane to go in the Employ and under the Direction of the said Timothy Penny to the Island of Jamaica, and return from thence to any Port or Place in these united States, not in Possession of the Enemy, with any one Vessel which shall be purchased and laden in the said Island as aforesaid, by or on account of the said Timothy Penny Uninterrupted so that neither the said Joseph Deane shall on account thereof be liable to Detention or molestation nor the said Vessel or her Cargoe to

Seizure or Confiscation. Given under my Hand and Seal at Philadelphia the Day of June in the Year of our Lord one thousand seven hundred and seventy nine and in the third Year of our Independence.

Dft. DNA: PCC, 49, 501–02. Endorsed by Charles Thomson: "Draft of a Passport to [*sic*] 31 May 1779, Copied Jan. 16th 1780." Formerly of Jamaica, Timothy Penny was a resident of Massachusetts who, in his own words, "steadily adhered to the Cause of these United States in the present Contest for their Rights." He owned a plantation on the island of Jamaica, about which he had had no news for the past three years, and therefore petitioned the President of Congress for permission to dispatch Joseph Deane, a sea captain, to retrieve "at least a Portion" of his estate and for clearance upon Deane's return voyage to dock at a port in America held by the Patriots. Penny's letter, dated February 1779, was read in Congress on 20 February and referred to a committee; at the committee's recommendation on 31 May Congress complied with his request. JJ drew up Deane's passport on the basis of Penny's letter and the Congressional resolution. *JCC*, XIII, 217; XIV, 671–72. Penny's ALS is in DNA: PCC, 78, XVIII, 207–10; the resolution of Congress is also in DNA: PCC, 19, V, 75–76; a copy of the passport, in an unidentified hand, is in DNA: PCC, 177, 1–2.

From Frederick Jay

Fish Kill, 7th July 1779

Dear Sir

On Saturday last I returned from Red Hook and found here your favour of the 22d, also the last post brought me letters from you.

Yesterday came on the Arbitration between yourself and Carman. The Arbitrators could not agree, and they have accordingly chosen Jonathan Lawrence Esq. (a very good Man) Umpire. They are to meet the 20th of this month.[1]

I hope by this time your Horse is Safe with you. Montangnie took him down last week and promised to take great care of him. It was impossible to send him any other way. I could not hire a man for the purpose. I am confident I shall not have halfe the trouble with my own Children, as I have had with Mr. Lath, however I shall be satisfied if I do but get the better of Carman, and I think there is not the least reason to doubt it.

Sir James is with us, but intends in a few days to set off for your place, his business I am a stranger to, and I am of opinion that he himself is not perfectly acquainted with it.

I shall return to Red Hook in a few days. Peggy is now there and is better than when she left this. I also intend to procure one or two Rooms in Some good Farmers House in this County, and then set off for Boston and endeavour to do for myself. I am sorry that necessity oblidges me to leave the Family in its present Situation but it is high time I should be doing something. No one can with reason blame me. I have been here too long. I have Suffered too much. I would with pleasure undergo ten times more than I have done on account of the Family but reason tells me its high time to take care of myself. Had it not been on their Account I might have done as well as others. I shall say no more. The very thoughts of Seperating from the Family gives me pain; I wish it could be avoided, but it is not in my power.

Never was there finer Crops of Grain seen than at present. I am afraid we shall not be able to get ours in in due time. As Papa will not hire a man, I dread the Consequence, however I mean to stay with him till harvest is over and do the best I can. Masters are now become Servants and Servants Masters, this is the case here. I shall thank you for a line by the next post. The Family all join me in our sincerest affection for Sally and yourself and I am with great regard Your Affectionate Brother

FRED. JAY

P.S. Have you procured a Certificate for Mr. Haskin. You make no mention of it, though the Ticket was sent you many months ago.

ALS. Endorsed.
1 No further records have been uncovered about this arbitration.

FROM NATHANAEL GREENE

New Windsor, July 14th, 1779

Sir

The enclosed is a letter from Col. Chace DQMG at Boston. The representation it contains, and the consequences that will follow, point out the necessity of some mode being adopted for the security of the Barracks.

For the present, I have directed Col. Chace to enter into contract with the proprietors of the soil on which the Barracks stand, to make them a reasonable compensation for the use thereof; and have instructed him to consult the principal characters in Boston, with respect to the mode and conditions of the contract; but as these Contracts are of a temporary nature, and from the Advantages the owners have, the public may be subject to very hard and unreasonable conditions, it will be highly necessary therefore that a more effectual mode be adopted, not only for the remedy of the present evil, but to establish a more permanent security for public property under simular circumstances.

It is a melancholy truth that Continental Interest in different States, finds too little protection to secure it from unjust invaders, either from the force of law, or the attention of the people. It being a received opinion among many, that whatever public property, shall by accident, or otherwise, fall in their way, they have a right to apply to their own use. Thousands of arms and all kinds of public Stores have been conveyed away upon this principle.

It is not uncommon for people who live in some obscure place, to take up public Horses astray and keep them for a year together.

The prodigious quantities of public stores, that are constantly upon the roads, and the various accidents that attend them, give many opportunities to the people, to apply them to their own use.

Waggons often break, and loads prove too heavy in one part of the country, that was light and easy in another, owing to the state of the roads and change of weather. This renders it necessary to deposit the stores with the inhabitants; but they frequently refuse to receive them or be accountable, by which many losses are sustained.

In remedying all these evils, I would beg leave to propose, that each state pass a law that whatever grounds are wanted for erecting public buildings, or to determine the rents or value of Lands on which public buildings now stand, that those persons be appointed by the Quarter Master General, or any of his Deputies, in whatever state the lands are wanted; and that they fix the rent and value thereof, which shall be binding upon both parties, this to take place only in such cases, as the proprietors and public agent cannot agree.

I would beg leave also to propose, that it be recommended to each state, to pass a law, subjecting all persons to a large fine, who has public property in possession, either by accident or otherwise, and do not report it in writing to the nearest public agent in ten days after it comes into their hands. Such a law being passed in each state, will be a legal declaration of the light in which these crimes are viewed, and leave the people no excuse, and therefore will operate as a check. A large fine added to this, may in a great measure prevent the mischief; and in order to make the people watch over one another, I would recommend that the fines recovered be given to the informers, as well for a reward for their information, as to make people afraid of concealing public property, least their Neighbours should report them.

I have taken the liberty to throw out those hints. The Congress will improve upon them, or reject them altogether, as they shall think proper; but something is necessary to be done to remedy the mischiefs that now prevail, and I believe I may say with truth, are constantly encreasing.

I have the honor to be, with great respect, your Excellency's most obedient, humble Servant

NATHL. GREENE, QMG.

ALS. DNA: PCC, 155.

THOMAS CHASE TO NATHANAEL GREENE

Boston, July 1st, 1779

Sir,

Your favor of the 16th June I have receivd,[1] Shall send on my Accounts and returns as Soon as I possibly can, which will be in a few days.

A Certain Tuffts of Charlstown, who owns the Land the Continental Barracks Stand on, Has taken down one of the Barracks and converted it to his own use, and threatens to take down all the rest.

The Guard who are at Cambridge Guarding the Barracks and Magazine, confined said Tuffts for about an hour under Guard. He has Sued the Soldiers for puting him under Guard.

I have petitioned the General Court concerning the Barracks.[2] They have risen without doing any thing, beg you would give me instructions which way to secure the Barracks from total Destruction, 50,000 Dollars will not make good the Dammage they have already sustained by the people of Charlstown and Cambridge. The Guard are not able to do their duty, if they do, they are liable to a Civil prosecution.

If Congress does not do something the Barracks will be totally destroyed on his Land, every body will do the same, and every body who owns the Land where any Fort is, will have a right to Dismantle it when he pleases.

I am Sir with Great respect your Obedient Servant

THOS. CHASE

ALS. DNA: PCC, 155, 147–54. Endorsed by Charles Thomson: ". . . Read July 19, 1779. Referred to board of war." Enclosure: C of Thomas Chase to Nathanael Greene 1 July 1779, C in NjP. On 23 July, based on the Board's report, Congress "resolved that it be recommended to the legislatures of the respective states, to make effectual provision by laws for the preservation of the buildings belonging to the United States. . . ." *JCC*, XIV, 868–69.

1 Greene to Thomas Chase, 16 June 1779, has not been located.

[2] On 28 June 1779 the Massachusetts General Court considered Chase's petition against "one Tufts, of Charlestown, [who] had taken down a barrack belonging to the United States." The petition was referred to a committee, but its report has not been located. *Journal of the Honorable House of Representatives of the State of Massachusetts Bay* (Boston, 1779), p. 67.

From Anne Conyngham

Philadelphia, July 17, 1779

Honored Sir

I beg leave to trouble your Excellency and the Honorable Congress, with the perusal of the inclosed letter from my Husband, Capt. Gustavus Conyngham, late Commador of the Cutter Revenge, now a Prisoner and in Irons on board a British Packet, bound to England.[1]

As these Extraordinary and in the present Stage of the War between Britain and America, Singular Cruelties exercised upon the Person of my Husband, have been inflicted, in consequence of his Zeal and Successfull exertions against the common Enemy, in the English Channell, where he first hoisted the American Flag.[2] I take the liberty of calling the attention of Congress, to his distressed Situation and of requesting that thay would be pleased to take such Steps for his relief as have in Similar instances prevented the execution of the bloody and vindictive purposes of the enemy upon the Officers and Citizens of these States. I hope it is unnecessary to say any thing to the Honorable Congress of my distress upon this Occasion. To have lost a worthy and beloved Husband in Battle fighting for the honour and liberties of his Country would have been a light Affliction.

But to hear of a Person thus dearly connected being chained to the hold of a ship in vain looking back towards the beloved Country for whom he had fought, wasting his Health and Spirits in hopeless grief and at last Compleating the measure of his Sufferings by an ignominious Death under a [———].[3] Good God my heart Shudders at the thought. Forbid it Heaven. Forbid it Honorable Gentlemen the Guardians of the lives and Happiness of the good People of these States that a freeman and a Soldier of America should even fear or feel a moments distress or pain from the hands of Englishmen Unrevenged.

The Delay of a single Hour may fix my Husband's fate for ever. Pardon me therefore whilst I once more intreate your immediate attention to his case, consider Sirs the safety of your numerous Officers and Soldiers by Sea and land is connected with that of my

Husband. This I presume will be a sufficient motive with you to procure Justice for him and to afford some consolation to Honorable Sirs and Gentleman.[4] Your most obedient and most devoted

ANNE CONYNGHAM

ALS. DNA: PCC, 78, V, 371–72. Endorsed by Charles Thomson: ". . . Read." Anne Hockly married Gustavus Conyngham (1747–1819), an Irish-born sea captain, in 1773. Mrs. Conyngham's petition was presented to Congress on 17 July, along with a memorial of "a number of the inhabitants of Philadelphia" in the captain's behalf, and referred to a committee. Later that day Gouverneur Morris, John Dickinson, and William Whipple brought in a letter to be written by the secretary of Congress "to the admiral or other commanding officer of the fleets or ships of his Britannic Majesty" in New York harbor. It stated that Congress had received evidence that Conyngham, "a citizen of America," had been mistreated by the British and, in the name of Congress, demanded "that good and sufficient reasons be given for this conduct" or that Conyngham be immediately released. A reply, 23 July, came from John Marr, secretary of the British Commander-in-Chief, which was read in Congress on 29 July. It denied charges of mistreatment and informed them that Conyngham was to be sent to England, "to receive that punishment from his injured country which his crimes shall be found to deserve." *JCC*, XIV, 844, 849, 895.

1 In 1777 and 1778 Conyngham, authorized by the American commissioners in Paris, commanded the *Revenge*, then a continental frigate, in a series of daring raids on British shipping in the North and Irish seas, as well as the Azores and the Atlantic. Conyngham sailed in 1779 with the *Revenge*, at that time a privateer owned by a group of Philadelphia merchants. His ship was captured 27 April by the British frigate *Galatea*. Samuel Eliot Morison, *John Paul Jones: A Sailor's Biography* (Boston, 1959), p. 259.

2 Without disputing Mrs. Conyngham's claim as to the first hoisting of the American flag in the English Channel, the probabilities are that the Stars and Stripes adopted as the official flag by Congress on 14 June 1777 was first raised by John Paul Jones on the *Ranger* shortly thereafter. Gordon Walker, *A Naval History of the American Revolution*, 2 vols. (New York, 1913), I, 194; Nowland Van Powell, *The American Navies of the Revolutionary War* (New York, 1974), p. 70.

3 Appears as a blank in the manuscript.

4 Captain Conyngham did not wait for congressional action to end his imprisonment. In November 1779 he tunneled his way out of Mill Prison, Plymouth, and escaped to the Texel, Holland. Unfortunately, the ship on which he returned to America was captured by the British and Conyngham was returned to confinement until his exchange in 1781.

From John Sullivan

Head Quarters, Wyoming, July 21st, 1779

Sir,

I have hitherto delayed troubling congress with any accounts from this quarter, from a hope, that before this time I should have been able to have given them more favourable accounts from this quarter than is now in my power. My duty to the publick and regard to my own reputation, compel me to state to congress the reasons of the army under my command being so long delayed at this post, without advancing into the enemy's country.[1]

In order to which I must beg leave to observe that in April last it was agreed, the army should be put in motion the fifteenth of May and rendevous at Easton on the twentieth, and to proceed immediately on the expedition.[2] The necessary preparations were to be made in the Quarter Master and Commissary departments by the time prefixed, so that no delay should take place in carrying on an expedition, the success of which seemed in a great measure to depend on secrecy and dispatch. I immediately detached parties to clear a road from Easton to Wyoming which was done in season and might have been done sooner, had not the backwardness of affairs in other quarters obliged me to hold great part of the army at Easton to prevent the unnecessary consumption of stores destined for the expedition.

I must here observe that the plan for carrying on the expedition was not agreeable to my mind nor were the number of men destined for it, sufficient in my opinion to ensure success. This Congress will see by the enclosed copies of my letters to General Washington. Number 1 and 2 which eventually had no other effect than to alter the rout of General Clinton's detachment from Mohawk river to Susquehannah.[3]

I had early in April enquired from the heads of the quarter Master and Commissary department, and received every possible assurance that every thing would be in a perfect state of readiness upon my arrival at this post. But on my arrival at Easton I was informed by General Hand[4] who then commanded here, that there was not the least prospect of the booty or stores being in readiness in season; upon which I halved the army at Easton, sending forward only such corps as were necessary to defend this post and to assist in forwarding the stores. I remained at Easton until I was ashamed, and then receiving some flattering letters proceeded on to this post, where I have remained without having it in my power to advance toward the enemy.

To prove this clearly to Congress I enclose a return of provisions (Number 3) made me in April, which were said to be deposited on the Susquehannah and would be at Kelso's ferry so as to be transported here by the time prefixed (the notes at the bottom of the return will shew what we now have on hand and of what quality), and here permit me to observe that near one half the flour and more than two thirds of the live stock mentioned, I have caused to be procured from Easton, fearing to meet with those dissapointments I have too often experienced. The Inspector of provision is now on the ground by order of the board of war inspecting the provisions and his regard to truth must oblige him on his return to report to Congress that of the salted meat on hand, there is not a single pound fit to be eaten, even at this day thou every measure has been taken to preserve it that possibly could be devised.

I also enclose Congress a list of articles in the Quarter-Master department (Number 4) which were to have been procured, with notes thereon of what have been received; upon examining which returns, Congress will be at no loss to account for the delay of this army. I requested Commissary Blaine[5] to forward a thousand head of cattle; some few more than Two hundred arrived and about One hundred and fifty more having arrived at Sunbury were left, being too poor to walk and many of them unable to stand. Three hundred of our horses came in with Colonel Copperthwait[6] on the 20th Instant and there is not a sufficiency of those and no packsaddles for one half we have. I enclose a letter from Major Clayburn of the 19th of May to shew that the boats were then unbuilt which were to have brought the provision to this post by the 20th, and to shew that the first boats were upon the presumption of others being procured, ordered not to return, but the small number of boats which have been procured has occasioned those boats to be sent down the river four times since.

The other copies of letters numbered from 5 to 10 inclusively, shew the steps which have been taken to procure provisions, will point out the deficiencies and shew the mortifying necessity I have been under of remaining in a state of inactivity at this post, and will shew that we are now bringing on pack horses from Carlisle, flour destined for the use of this army, and which ought to have been here the 20th of May last. I beg leave to assure Congress that those deficiences did not arise from want of proper and repeated application, nor has a single step been left untried, which was possible for me or the army under my command to take for procuring and forwarding the store. Having been taught by repeated dissapointments to be cautious I early gave orders to General Clinton to supply his troops with three months provisions, and wrote Governor Clinton for his assistance in April last, this has been done and they are supplied. I have procured provision from Easton and other places, which, with what is now on its way from Sunbury (which will be here on Sunday) will enable us to move the beginning of next week. But in order to avoid censure in case of misfortune, I must beg Congress to recur to the reasonings in my letters to General Washington respecting the numbers necessary to ensure success and then to examine the enclosed return of the forces here. They now stand at Two thousand three hundred and twelve rank and file only.

General Washington in consequence of my letters wrote the Executive council of Pennsylvania for rangers and riflemen; they engaged seven hundred and twenty and the president frequently wrote me that they would be ready in season.[7] Not a man of them has joined us, nor are any about to do it; the reason assigned by them, is, that the Quarter-master gave such extravagant prices to boatmen, that they all enlisted into the boat service. But this is evidently a mistake for we have not a hundred boatmen engaged for the army and but forty two pack horses and men, so that I must Draughted for boatmen and pack horsemen, near nine hundred. This will reduce my numbers to fourteen hundred and twelve, then I must deduct for drivers of cattle and for the artillery, one hundred and fifty, for the garrison one hundred, which leaves me eleven hundred and sixty two. From these I deduct the officers waiters and managers of Bat-horses Two hundred and twenty four; this reduces me to nine hundred and thirty eight, and more than a third of them without a shirt to their backs. This is a force with which I am to advance against an enemy allowed to be Two thousand strong and who have certainly been lately reinforced with seven hundred British troops from Canada.

I need not mention to Congress that it is easy for the enemy to act with their whole force against either party of our army before the junction is formed and that common prudence will direct to it. I have therefore nothing to rely on but the ardour and well known bravery of my troops which I trust will surmount all opposition. But should a defeat take place and the ruin of the army be the consequence, whether I do or do not perish in the action, I call upon the members of Congress to witness to the world that I early foresaw and foretold the danger and used every means in my power, to procure a force sufficient to ensure success but failed to obtain it.

I have the honour to be with the highest respect, sir, Your most obedient and very humble servant,

JNO. SULLIVAN

ALS. DNA: PCC, 160, 249–54; enclosures, pp. 255–93. Endorsed by Charles Thomson: ". . . Read 26. Copies ordered for Genl. Washington"; by a clerk: "(Copied)." Enclosures: Sullivan to Washington, 16 April 1779, DLC: Washington Papers, Series IV, and 29 April 1779; return to provisions, April 1779, not located; list of articles to be procured by the Quartermaster, 2 March 1779; list of stores received at Wyoming, 21 July 1779; Major Richard Claiborne to Edward Hand, 19 May 1779; ranks of troops at Wyoming, 22 July 1779; Lieutenant Colonel Adam Hudley to Sullivan, 2 July 1779; Edward Hand to Sullivan, 6 June, 13 July, and 14 July 1779; Alexander Steel to Sullivan, 15 July 1779. LbkC of covering letter in MHi: Sullivan Papers.

As endorsed, copies were sent to Washington; that part concerning troops promised by Pennsylvania was to be sent to the president and council of Pennsylvania. *JCC*, XIV, 887.

1 In order to end Indian raids on the northern frontier, Major General Sullivan was put in charge of a campaign against the Indians. He joined the main body of the expedition at Easton, Pa., on 7 May 1779, but he did not get his troops under way until 18 June, and it was 10 August before they reached Tioga, Pa., where they joined Brigadier General James Clinton's smaller force. This sluggish progress annoyed Washington and provoked a round of correspondence, of which the above is an example. The expedition, however, did eventually accomplish its purpose, because the combined army routed the Indians and their Tory allies at Newtown on 29 August and then burned towns, destroyed crops, and seriously impaired the military capability of the Iroquois.

2 No record of such orders has been located. Sullivan's biographer writes that "a decision came some time in April that the army move on May 15," but he cites only this, 21 July, letter as his source for the statement. Charles Whittemore, *A General of the Revolution* (New York, 1961), p. 121.

3 James Clinton, by now a brigadier general, led a 1,500-man column south from the Mohawk Valley and joined Sullivan at Tioga.

4 Brigadier General Edward Hand (1744–1802) of Pennsylvania.

5 Ephraim Blaine, Deputy Commissary General of Purchases for the Continental Army.

6 Colonel Joseph Cowperthwait of Philadelphia, 2d brigade of the Pennsylvania militia. *Pa. Archives*, 5th Series, V (1853), 32.

7 Washington addressed the Pennsylvania government on this subject in a letter of 20 May 1779 and informed Sullivan about this on 28 May. *GWF*, XV, 109–10, 171–73.

From William A. Atlee

Lancaster, July the 23d, 1779

Sir

As the Convention Troops passed through this County, many of them, especially of the Germans, left the Corps they belonged to, and have remained among the Inhabitants, as Labourers and Tradesmen.[1] It was then said that the Officers who conducted them, permitted them thus to leave their Parties, and they have therefore remained unmolested; but as it is now currently reported, that many of these Troops have lately passed along on their way from Virginia to the Eastward, I think it my duty to mention this matter to Congress, as these people may have left their Stations by consent of their own officers and are perhaps endeavouring to join the Enemy. Four of them have been taken up here to day belonging to the 9th Regiment,[2] and are secured in Gaol by the Town-Major; they are just from Virginia, and upon the Town Major's consulting me, we thought it best to secure them, till Congress should give orders concerning them, especially as Mr. Boyd of Wright's Ferry at Susquahanna by a Letter of this date, to a Gentleman here, mentions, that scarce a Day passes, but some of those Troops cross at that Ferry, and many may cross the River at other places.

I have never received any directions, as Commissary of Prisoners, respecting these Troops and have therefore never before interfered with them; but as the reports of such numbers coming this way gives reason to believe their design is to join the Army under General Clinton, I have ventured, with Mr. Wirtz[3] the Town Major, to have these Fellows secured and we shall think it our duty to detain such others as we may be informed of, taking this rout, unless Congress shall please to order otherwise.

Permit me, Sir, to trouble you for directions respecting these People, and if they properly fall under my notice as Commissary of Prisoners, shall be glad of instructions in what manner and quantity, they are to be supplied with provisions etc.

I am, Sir, with the greatest respect Your most obedient Servant

WILL A. ATLEE

ALS. DNA: PCC, 78, I, 215–16, 218. Addressed: "His Excellency John Jay Esquire President of Congress." Endorsed in an unidentified hand: ". . . respecting Convention troops. Referred to the Board of War." William Augustus Atlee (1735–93), a Judge of the Supreme Court of Pennsylvania, had become President Judge of the 2d judicial district. *Pennsylvania Magazine of History and Biography*, XLIII (1937), 246–47.

1 The "Convention troops" had been surrendered by Burgoyne after his defeat at Saratoga. They were quartered in Massachusetts until January and February 1779, when the prisoners of war were marched south to Charlottesville, Va.

2 The Ninth Foot Regiment.

3 Christian Wirtz was a merchant with interests in Philadelphia and Lancaster, Pa.

To George Washington

Philadelphia, 27th July 1779

Sir

The Success of the Enterprize against Stony-Point was splendid and important.[1] It has added another Laurel to your wreath, and given a grateful Country a fresh opportunity of presenting You their thanks for the vigilance, Wisdom, and Magnanimity, with which their Arms have been conducted. I have now the Honor of conveying them expressed in the enclosed Act of Congress. Prudence forbids me to indulge my feelings or my Pen on this interesting Occasion lest in their warmth too little attention might be paid to the delicacy blended with the virtues they wish to celebrate. Permit me however most sincerely to assure You that I am With the greatest Respect and Esteem Your Excellency's most Obedient and Humble Servant

LbkC. DNA: PCC, 14. This letter was dispatched to Washington in accordance with the unanimous resolution of Congress, 26 July 1779, to thank him for the "vigilance, wisdom and magnanimity, with which he hath conducted the military operations . . ." *JCC*, XIV, 887.

1 On 16 July 1779 General Anthony Wayne recaptured Stony Point on the west bank of the Hudson, twelve miles below West Point.

To Anthony Wayne

Philadelphia, 27th July 1779

Sir

Your late glorious Atchievements have merited, and now recieve the Approbation and Thanks of your Country. They are contained in the enclosed Act of Congress which I have the Honor to transmit.

This brilliant Action adds fresh Lustre to our Arms, and will teach the Enemy to respect our Power if not to imitate our Humanity. You have nobly reaped Laurels in the Cause of your Country, and in Fields of Danger and Death. May these prove the earnest of more, and may Victory ever bear your Standard, and Providence be your Shield.

I have the Honor to be Sir with great Respect and Esteem your most obedient and humble Servant

JOHN JAY
PRESIDENT

ALS. PHi: Wayne, vol. 7, p. 70. Enclosure: unanimous resolution of Congress, 26 July 1779, ordering "that the thanks of Congress be presented to Brigadier General Wayne, for his brave, prudent and soldierly conduct in the spirited and well conducted attack on Stoney Point." *JCC*, XIV, 887. LbkC in DNA: PCC, 14.

From Timothy Pickering

War office, Philadelphia, August 4th, 1779

Sir

Maj. Gen. Sullivan having in a way of complaint informed Congress that notwithstanding his repeated applications, the board had not supplied the necessary clothing for the troops under his command; and his letter on the subject being referred to the board, We beg leave to state the mode of his application, and what supplies we have sent him. On the 11th of May[1] we received a letter from General Sullivan requesting us to supply Col. Spencer's and Malcoms combined regiment[2] with clothing agreeable to the returns he transmitted. We the same day gave orders for that purpose. In the same letter he expresses his hope that a proper supply of clothing of all kinds may be sent on by the Susquehannah, with a proper person to deal them out, a very considerable quantity of shoes will be wanting, and also plenty of light clothing.

The same day we wrote an answer to him[3] informing him that we had no light clothing on hand (having just sent the whole to camp) but had given orders for the purchase of linen requisite for Spencer's regiment, which should be made and forwarded without delay, adding that such regiments as we knew were going on the expedition had been furnished with necessary clothing. When we considered the nature of the expedition, and the general terms of this application, we did not know how to answer the demand, we could not see the necessity or propriety of encumbering his army with a general clothing store. On the 23rd of May General Washington desired us to send 2000 pairs of overalls to General Sullivans army; and on the 9th of June they were dispatched accordingly, as the materials were only then making up it was not possible to send them sooner. Before this his Excellency had desired that 8 or 10,000 pairs of shoes might be prepared for this Expedition.[4] Orders were immediately given for the purpose. In consequence whereof 7420 pairs were sent (of which we informed the Commander in Chief in due time) for that Army at large; besides which, more than 600 pairs were delivered out to Colonel Proctor's and the 11th Pennsylvania Regiment, after the expedition was formed. These shoes and overalls were all the articles in the clothing department which the Commander in Chief has ever desired us to send to General Sullivans Army. Nevertheless receiving afterwards his farther (the Generals) complaints of the distress of the troops under his command for want of clothing and especially shirts (without mentioning any quantity) we ordered a further supply to be sent him of 1000 pairs of overalls, 1000 hunting shirts, and 2000 body shirts, these were sent off the 20th ultimo and could not have arrived when General Sullivan wrote the before mentioned letter to Congress.

He has now made a demand of 1000 blankets and 5000 shirts which at present 'tis not possible to comply with.[5] Could we have formed any certain judgement of the quantity of clothing requisite for General Sullivans Army, we should have spared no pains to supply it, but all his information was very general; we had complied with every requisition from the Commander in Chief, and were for a long time utterly ignorant of the corps destined for the Indian expedition, excepting those three before named. Moreover, General Sullivans demands being usually on a large scale we deemed some caution necessary in granting him supplies. He asked for 1000 spare muskets at a time we had but a single one in store. We communicated the matter to General Washington, at the same time informing him that we had some time before ordered 200 stands of spare arms and accoutrements complete for the troops under General Sullivan; and these his Excellency in his answer judged adequate to the service. From this view of the matter we humbly conceive it will appear that the board were not in fault if General Sullivan has not been supplied with the necessary clothing for the troops under his command.

We have the honor to be with the greatest esteem Your Excellency's most obedient servants

TIM PICKERING
BY ORDER

P.S. We have since ordered 1000 body shirts to be sent to Easton and if possible sent on to General Sullivan's army.

C in MHi: Pickering, 33, 249–51.

1 Not located.

2 Colonel William Malcolm's (d. 1792) regiment "at large," one of sixteen "additional continental regiments" authorized by congressional resolution, had been consolidated with Colonel Oliver Spencer's (d. 1811) like regiment on 22 April 1779.

3 Not located.

4 Washington to the Board of War, 22 April and 23 May 1779. *GWF*, XIV, 430–31; XV, 131–32.

5 Sullivan made this request in a letter to Congress on 26 July 1779. DNA: PCC, 160, 294.

To Jeremiah Wadsworth

Philadelphia, 16 August 1779

Sir

The Reasons which at present induce many good men to avoid holding Places in the Staff Departments, ought in my opinion to stimulate them to accept them. These Departments are important.

The Public suffers from the Clamors which prevail against them, and perhaps no measure would tend more to restore them to the Confidence of the People, than for Men of known and established Reputation in each State to take Employments in them.

These Considerations have induced me to press my Brother to offer you his Service. Tho bred a merchant, he has since the Evacuation of New York declined Commerce; and tho constantly engaged in public Business, has hitherto declined those Places in which a mans Reputation is often exposed to little Jealousies and unmerited Censures.

I am Sir with Esteem and Regard your most obedient and humble Servant.

JOHN JAY

ALS. PPAmP: Feinstone Coll.

To George Clinton

Philadelphia, 18th August 1779

Dear Sir

I send you two Sets of the Journals of Congress, two acts of the Legislature of Virginia one for establishing a Land office and the other laying of Tax payable in Certain enumerated Commodities,[1] four news Papers from the 5 to the 17th Inst. inclusive, 3 Parcel's of German ones, and an Essay on Trade and Finance by Pelatiah Webster.[2] There are also enclosed with this Letter, two for my Brother Frederick and one for the Chancellor, which I take the Liberty of committing to your Care.

Mr. Duane, who set out from hence <Yesterday> last Monday, will give you <satisfactory Information on every Subject of public Importance here> much interesting Information. Mr. Morris will also be with you soon. I should have written by Mr. Duane but Want of Leisure as well as Want of Health prevented me.

Mr. Morris will explain to you very fully the Steps which in our Opinion are necessary to be pursued respecting the Grants. I therefore forbear saying any Thing on that Subject now.[3]

The Exertions of our State have placed her in a very respectable point of View, and permit me to tell you that your March to the Highlands has given occasion to many handsome things being said and written of you here.[4]

In my Letter to the Chancellor is enclosed a Resignation of my office; say nothing of it till you see him.[5] You will find no Reasons assigned for this Measure; to you they would be unnecessary. <Altho> I shall <soon> return to private Life <it will be with a Determination (<<as long as>> during this Conflict) <<lasts>>, to quit it whenever my Country shall call me from it, <<and afford>> and while out of it afford me Subsistence, and that in any Place or Station except the Senate.> <I shall by no means> It will be with a Determination not to shrink from the Duties of a Citizen <but shall be ready to serve the People of New York>. During the continuance of the present Contest I <have always> consider the public as entitled to my Time and Services.

My best Respects to Mrs. Clinton. I am dear Sir very sincerely Yours etc.

J. J.

DftS. Endorsed. Enclosures: unspecified issues of the *Journals of Congress,* probably part of the weekly series of publication undertaken by the Continental Congress in April 1779; either Pelatiah Webster's "An Essay on Free Trade and Finance . . ." or "A Second Essay on Free Trade and Finance . . . By a Citizen of Philadelphia," both of which were published in 1779. ALS printed in *GCP,* V, 198–99. JJ to Frederick Jay, not located; JJ to Robert R. Livingston, 18 Aug. 1779, dft in JP, ALS in NHi: Livingston Papers.

[1] On 13 May 1779 the General Assembly of Virginia passed an act entitled "An Act, for establishing a Land Office, and ascertaining the terms and manner of granting waste and unappropriated lands. On 18 May it passed "An act for laying a tax, payable in certain enumerated commodities." W. W. Hening, *The statutes at large; being a collection of all the laws of Virginia from the first session of the legislature, in the year 1619,* 13 vols. (Richmond, 1819–23), X, 50–65, 79–81.

[2] Pelatiah Webster (1726–95), a Yale-educated clergyman, was a prominent Philadelphia merchant who contributed a series of articles to the *Pennsylvania Evening Post,* signed "a Financier" and "A Citizen of Philadelphia," in which he argued for support of the war by taxation rather than by loans, free trade, and the curtailment of paper money issues.

[3] The New York delegation of course did not support the application of the Vermonters, but neither Duane's nor Morris's accounts of New York's policy in Congress have been located. However, on 27 August JJ wrote to Clinton: "If New York and New Hampshire by Acts of their respective Legislatures will authorize Congress to settle the Line between them, and if New York will farther by Act of their Legislature empower Congress to adjust the Disputes with the People of the Grants on equitable and liberal Principles, I am well persuaded it will conduce to the Interest and Happiness of the State." Dft in JP.

[4] The battle of Stony Point.

[5] JJ's letter of resignation was addressed to Governor Clinton and the Council of Appointment but sent to Livingston, 18 Aug. 1779: "I do hereby resign the office of Chief Justice of the Supream Court of Judicature for the State of New York." ALS in IChi; dft in JP.

To George Washington

Philadelphia, 24 August 1779

Dear Sir

I have had the Pleasure of recieving your Favor of the 16th Instant.[1]

Britain refused the Mediation of Spain[2] at a Time when their Spirits were elated by their Successes in the West Indies, and the Southern States, and by the accounts they recieved of Discord in Congress, Discontent among the People and a Prospect of the Evils with which we were threatened by the Depreciation of our Currency. <How far it was to be influenced by these Considerations is another Question, most certainly it was not> Decieved by these illusory Gleams of Hope they permitted their Counsels to be <easily determined> guided by their Pride. What Reasons they may have to expect Succor from other Powers is as yet a Secret. Mr. Gerard is decided in his Opinion that they will obtain none.

The Conduct of France in establishing Peace between Russia and the Porte has won the Heart of the Empress, and the Influence of Versailles <with the Turk> at Constantiniple will probably <render his Aff> give Duration to her Gratitude.[3] The Emperor and Prussia are under similar obligations. The latter wishes us well, and the Finances of the former are too much exhausted to support the Expences of War without Subsidies from Britain who at present cannot afford them. There is no Reason to suspect that the Peace of Germany will soon be interrupted. Britain may hire some Troops there, but it is not probable she will be able to do more. <As to> Portugal and the Dutch <we can hardly suppose they will be so imprudent as to risque their own Safety by aiding a Nation running to Ruin, and unable to defend their own Territories> while <like other Nations will be> directed by their Interest <and that Inducement will not on this occasion persuade them and therefore in the Contest> will not rashly raise their Hands to support a Nation, which like a Tower in an Earthquake sliding from its Base will crush every slender Prop that may be raised to prevent its Fall. <This is a pleasing Prospect to us, but with a fine Sky may soon change, <<and>> in all our Determinations the mutability of human affairs should have a certain Degree of Influence.>

General Waynes Letter has been referred to the Committee of Intelligence for Publication.[4]

<We have lately recieved a Letter from Gen. Sullivan. If I have

time to obtain a Copy, it will accompany this. It is not very interesting.>[5]

<In a Letter I recieved> You may remember Sir to have recieved a Letter from me last winter recommending the Person who carried it as an honest Man and who in my opinion would <faithfully> with great Fidelity do the Business you wished, and I <persuaded> advised him to undertake.[6]

In May last I recieved a Letter from him <containing important Intelligence> informing me of his having written to you at the same Time, and mentioning a matter of very delicate Nature, which I believe was <not mentioned> omitted in your letter. As he gave me Reason to expect he would soon be here, I avoided Particulars in my Reply, not choosing to risque more on Paper than was necessary. He has not however been here, nor have I <heard> had a Line from him for some Time past. From this Circumstance I have been apprehensive of his having relinquished that Business, and the more so as <when here last> he intimated <to me that it would not be> to me his Doubts of its being well conducted <with Propriety but> unless under your immediate Direction, <for> that the Views of the Gentleman with whom he first <applied> conversed[7] on the Subject were <not sufficiently extensive. It seems that Gentleman was cautious of <<rather too contracted to produce much>>> not very extensive and his attention to Expence too great. The opinion I have of this mans usefulness leads me to mention these matters, that if he has left the Business I might if you think proper <endeavor urge> press him to resume it. If he <has> still perseveres, I <wish> do not wish to be informed of any other Particulars.[8]

Dft. ALS in DLC: Washington Papers, Series IV, dated 25 August, marked "private."

1 *GWF*, XVI, 115–16.

2 See below, editorial note, "Jay's Mission to Spain."

3 A reference to the Treaty of Kuchuk Kainarji, 21 July 1774.

4 Wayne's letter of 10 Aug. 1779 was enclosed in one from Washington to Congress, 15 Aug. 1779, and referred to the Committee of Intelligence on the 23rd. *JCC*, XIV, 989; Washington letter in DNA: PCC, 152, VII, 573; Wayne letter in DNA: PCC, 161, p. 221.

5 Sullivan's letter, 15 August, was read on the 23rd. *JCC*, XIV, 988.

6 JJ to Washington, 28 March 1779, recommending Elijah Hunter, an espionage agent. Dft in JP; ALS in DLC: Washington Papers, Series IV.

7 This is obviously a reference to Alexander McDougall. See above, 21 March 1779, McDougall to JJ.

8 Hunter's letter to JJ, May 1779, not located. Washington wrote JJ assuring him of the agent's good faith and ability, but pointing out that Hunter's usefulness was limited since he did not reside within the British lines. Washington to JJ, 7 Sept. 1779, ALS in RAWC.

FROM JOHN PENN

Colonel Pendletons, [Edmundsbury], [August] 27th, 1779

Dear Sir

I am thus far on my way home, I got to Annapolis as soon as Doctor Burke and Mr. Randolp.[1] I have the pleasure to tell you that I never saw such a prospect for Corn as the present crop, it is thought that there will be much more made than has been for many years past.

Mr. William Lee[2] has directed his Brother to pay all the Gentleman in Virginia to whom he was indebted for Tobacco shipped to him at the rate of 33 1/3 per Cent. Colonel Mason has a Bill protested for about £1000, all Mr. Lee's shifts, his hiding himself to prevent being seen, and the manner in which the French Gentleman pursued him, the questions put to Lee's Servants their answers, and the assistance they gave in having him discovered are mentioned at length in the protest. When Lee could retreat no farther he denied he was the man; he directly went to Nanty and wrote Colonel Mason that he had directed his Brother to pay him, but antedates his letter three or four months. This Mr. Mason says he can prove. The above is what I have been told by several Gentlemen that have conversed with Mr. Mason and has seen the papers. Something ought to be done relative to this Man, if the above is true and nobody here doubts it. Mr. Lee ought not to be employed any longer in the service of the united States.

If my prayers or wishes are of any consequence, you are restored to health long before this. Pray Remember me to Sir James, Colonel Livingston, Mrs. Jay, and Lady Kitty and believe me to be with great truth Your sincere Friend etc.

J. PENN

ALS. Addressed: "His Excellency John Jay Esqr. Philada. John Penn." Endorsed: ". . . ansd. 21 Sept." Jay endorsed the letter as having been written in August rather than in September; indeed, Penn was on his way to the South at the end of August, as JJ wrote about 1 September to Pendleton. John Penn (1741–88), a relative of Pendleton's, was a native of Virginia, who had moved to North Carolina in 1774. He represented the latter state in the Continental Congress, 1775–80.

1 Thomas Burke (c. 1747–83) represented North Carolina in the Continental Congress, 1777–81. Edmund Randolph (1753–1813) was elected from Virginia in 1779.

2 Prior to his appointment as commercial agent at Nantes in 1777, William Lee had been engaged in business ventures in London, receiving consignments of tobacco from several Virginia planters, among them George Mason (1725–92), framer of the Virginia Constitution. Mason wrote Lee on at least two occasions

complaining of the low price he had received for the tobacco shipment. Lee answered that he had obtained the highest possible price, especially since some of the crop had arrived in England decayed. ViU:Lee Family Papers, 1742–1795.

From Alexander Gillon

Nantes, 29 August 1779

Sir

I flatter myself with the hopes that you have enjoyed a perfect State of health Since I had the pleasure of Seeing you at Philadelphia, and that you will very Soon Reap the Reward due to your perserverance and labour, as a little Success of the united fleet must I Conceive produce next Spring that inestimable blessing.

I have been 7 months in this Kingdom labouring to execute the business I was Sent on, by the State of South Carolina, but the losses said State experienced in their Remittances to Europe with the denials to my Requests to those in power, and no inclination to facilitate and support my applications by him, that your honorable body sent to France to aid evry American particularly officers on Public Business, has Retarded my Success hitherto.

I will not trouble your Excellency with a Recital of them here, as enclosed is a packet for the honorable the delegates of South Carolina, wherein is one for his Excellency John Rutledge Esquire[1] which contains the particulars of my Conduct and observations, part of which may not be Amiss to be known, have therefore Requested those Gentlemen to open Said packet, and to Communicate its Contents to you.

The Affair of the fleet fitted out at L'orient I particularly attended to, by their Conduct there and the pains that was taken in other places to have them thought Continental Caused me to believe they was, in that Supposition I did no more than my duty and what I owe to America by Stating to Mr. Franklin the use Such a fleet would be of to America in general if it was immediately sent to South Carolina and Virginia, at either of which places I presume there was no Superiour british naval force whereby their Sea and Land forces must have experiencd Burgoigns fate. I did not wish to interfere in the command, as I had formerly proposed, so I then Repeated that with all my officers I would go as Volunteers in this Fleet. Please observe Mr. Franklins Reply thereto, And Capt. Jones's Conduct Since, but admit me to Remark that at Same time Capt. Landais of the Alliance was orderd by Mr. Franklin to put himself under the Orders of Capt. Jones[2] who's ship the bon homme Richard was private property, and under the publick management of Mr. Chaumont, Mr. Franklin's Landlord and Oracle.[3] They are again Saild and I hope on a plan of Serving their Country, I do not mean Injury to any of those partys but I Concieve I am Right in saying what is come to my knowledge thereon, and that as your honorable body has formed Rules for to guide your naval officers and men So they will be pleased to Cause an enquiery to be made wether the different Courts that have been held at L'orient by Capt. Jones's order are not Repugnant to those Rules, thus very prejudicial to a young Service, that Cries aloud for Stability to enforce its Consequence, the orders for an enquiery into Capt. Landais Conduct and his officers was so inconsistant in my humble opinion that I Requested Capt. Robeson[4] in the South Carolina Service, who was president of that Curious Court to withdraw, their proceedings will be known to you no doubt on Capt. Landais arrival.

I am now in hopes of building in Prussia for when Set off in a few days on the encouragement mentioned in my enclosed letters, if I can there, or whilst in Europe be of any Service, I shall deem myself honored to Receive your Commands, in Such Case please to order my letters to be under Cover to any of your ministers that will Carefully order it to be forwarded to me. It gives me pleasure to assure you I Receivd evry Aid from the honorable Messers Lee and Izard,[5] but their endeavors to Serve their Country Could avail very little when underhand opposition was made to evry proposal that was made by them and me, I truly wish for America's Sake in particular that Mr. Adams may in this be amongst you.[6]

Sincerely do I wish your Excellency evry blessing and am with all due Respect

Your Excellency's Most obedient Servant

A. GILLON

ALS. DNA: PCC, 78, X, 171–74. Endorsed by Charles Thomson: ". . . received July 31st, 1780." Enclosures not located. This letter never reached JJ while he was President of Congress, but is included for its illuminating account of American naval operations carried on in foreign waters under the direction of Benjamin Franklin. Alexander Gillon (d. 1794) was a Dutch-born merchant and naval officer from Charleston, S.C. In 1778 he was named commodore of the South Carolina navy and in August sailed on an abortive mission to obtain three frigates in Europe for the state fleet.

1 John Rutledge (1739–1800), then Governor of South Carolina.

2 Pierre Landais (1731–1818), former French naval captain, was named commander of the *Alliance* in June 1778 by the Continental Congress. Landais was emotionally unstable and his crew was on the point of mutiny when the *Alliance* finally reached France in 1779.

Franklin put Landais under the command of John Paul Jones, who led the

Bonhomme Richard from L'Orient on 14 Aug. 1779 on a raiding expedition on the British coast. The campaign was climaxed by engagement with the *Serapis* on 23 Sept. During the battle, the unstable Landais opened fire on the *Bonhomme Richard*, quite possibly on purpose, so as to emerge the victor in this battle. Samuel Eliot Morison, *John Paul Jones: A Sailor's Biography* (Boston, 1959), pp. 189–90, 226–40; Richard B. Morris, "The Revolution's Caine Mutiny," *American Heritage*, XI (April, 1960), 3, pp. 10–13, 88–91; *JCC*, XI, 625.

3 Jacques Donatien Le Ray de Chaumont, a partisan of the American cause, was the owner of the Hôtel Valentinois, on whose premises the American commissioners had their quarters.

4 Probably Captain William Robertson, who accompanied Gillon on the voyage to Europe.

5 Arthur Lee. Ralph Izard (1742–1804), of South Carolina, was appointed Commissioner to the Grand Duchy of Tuscany in July, 1777. His commission was revoked in June 1779. *JCC*, VII, 334; XIV, 700–03.

6 Gillon doubtless refers here to John Adams, who sailed from France 22 March 1779 and reached Boston on 2 August.

PETER JAY TO JOHN JAY AND JAMES JAY

Fish Kill, 1st September 1779

Dear James and Johnny,

It's with extreme difficulty that I now put Pen to paper to acknowledge the recipt of your Letters of the 15 and 17th ultimo.[1] I wish it were in my power to give you some agreeable information of our present Situation, which, indeed, grows daily more and more very distressing. I am unfortunately too much reduced to attend Effectually to Business, Peter does as much and more than could be expected from a Person in his Condition, but I am nevertheless destitute of necessary Assistance. My Hay is now almost all cut, I've imployed Several Mowers and payed the exorbitant wages of 15 Dollars per day to each Man, and I pay in proportion for every thing Else I want to have done. I've not yet got an inch of ground plowed for wheat. The two Plats are faithfull in their work. Frank and Fady's Boy are got to the Enemy, and are sold to the Officers by a white Man who carryed them off. This we hear from deserters at different times, come away from the British Army.

Last week Baxter brought here Johnny's Mare; there is so much Stealing of Horses, etc. at Bedford that he thought her not safe with him, and indeed I doubt whether She is more so here. I have her stabled every night. The screw hopples Jeommy had made here are not sufficient, the horses have lost two of them already.

I've not heard from Fady since he left us. I suppose he's still at Esopus. I have no prospect yet of Getting any Salt for salting my Beef or Pork this Fall, nor have I any Body to look out for me, hard Times!

God grant us speedily more happy Times. Jemmy's handkerchief is not yet found and I suppose it never will.

We all remember our love to Sally and to you and I remain most affectionately,

PETER JAY

P.S. I've two small bundles of Tobacco made up for Johnny, shall send them if the Express can take them both, or one only when he calls here. I've just now received Jemmy's Letter of the 26 ulto. and congratulate you both on the good news it contains.

ALS.
[1] Not located.

FROM EGBERT BENSON

Kingston, September 4th, 1779

My Dear Sir:

I have stolen a Moment from the Business of the House to write You by Mr. Phelps, who is dispatched some Hours sooner than I was apprised of or I should have wrote You more fully.

He is the Bearer of our peremptory Instructions to the Delegates relative to the Affair of Vermont.[1] This Business I must entreat Your utmost Endeavors to dispatch, for You will observe We are to continue sitting til We receive an Answer. We are now at our Ne plus, as I mentioned to You in my last, and We are every day growing worse and worse. By a Change in the Legislature several new Members are come in who are, (as I firmly beleive) more attached to Vermont than New York. Others are become fearful.

In short from a Variety of Circumstances I am fully convinced that our Proceedings in this Session will decide the Question whether We are to relinquish or to reduce by force of Arms that part of the Country. Should the former Alternative happen I foresee the inevitable Ruin of the State. One Proof of this is the following fact, that in April a Tenant in the Manor of Rensselaer and whose Farm is in the second Tier of Lots from the North-Eastern Boundary of the Manor, and of which he has been in quiet Possession for upwards of thirty Year, was sued in an Action of Trespass for £2000 by Process out of the Court of Vermont and the Trespass was charged to be committed on the above Farm. This is a fact for the Defendant applied to Me for Advice and Direction.

The Army here has only Three Weeks Flour and to save them

from starving We have upon the Application of the Commissary General[2] compelled the Farmers to thresh out one sixteenth within Eight and the other Sixteenth within Twenty days of their last Crop of Wheat beyond the annual necessary Consumption of their respective Families at 20 Dollars Per Bushel. Can We have no Compensation for these Exertions and Losses? It would be some if Congress would order a Quantity of Salt into the State.

Mr. Phelps waits and as Lord Chesterfield concludes some of his Letters with *the Graces, the Graces, the Graces,* so I conclude mine with Vermont, Vermont, Vermont.

Yours sincerely,

EGBT. BENSON

ALS. Addressed: "His Excellency John Jay Esqr. Philadelphia." Endorsed.

1 Charles Phelps of Cumberland County delivered the instructions of 27 Aug. 1779, which presented a plan for settling the question of land titles in the New Hampshire Grants. Should Congress fail to act on the proposal, the New York legislature directed JJ "to whom we have in a special manner committed this Business immediately to withdraw and attend us at this Place [Kingston]." E. B. O'Callaghan, ed., "Controversy between New York and New Hampshire respecting the Territory now the State of Vermont," *The Documentary History of the State of New York* . . . (4 vols., Albany, 1850–51), IV, 531–1034.

2 Wadsworth wrote Washington from West Point on 27 Aug. 1779 about the shortage of flour in the state. Washington enclosed copies of Wadsworth's letter in a circular to the governors on the 28th. Gov. Clinton presented them to the legislature on 1 Sept. Wadsworth to Washington, 27 Aug. 1779, *GCP*, V, 218–19; Washington, Circular to the States, 28 Aug., *GWF*, XVI, 188–89; Clinton to the legislature, 1 Sept., *GCP*, V, 259.

FROM BENJAMIN LINCOLN

Charles Town, September 5th, 1779

Sir,

I have the pleasure to congratulate Congress on the arrival of Count D'Estaing's Fleet off Savannah, but am sorry to inform them that his stay on this coast will be but short, and the aid we can afford him very inconsiderable. The Count has sent one of his Officers on shore to establish a plan of operations. He returns immediately with Dispatches on that head.[1]

All the Troops are ordered to take the field. I expect there will be assembled at Ebenezer[2] or in it's vicinity by the 11th Instant one thousand men. It has been proposed to the Count to land three thousand troops. I hope he will do it, and have the highest reasons to believe, if in his power, he will. Every exertion will be made to cooperate with him, and I hope the necessity of his speedy return, or any other cause, will not render abortive that plan from the execution of which so much good will result to the common Cause.

I have the honor to be with the highest respect Your Excellency's most obedient humble servant

DNA: PCC, 158, II, 275–76. Endorsed by Charles Thomson: ". . . Read Oct. 1." LbkC in MH and in MB.

[1] Savannah was captured by the British 29 Dec. 1778. When Admiral d'Estaing returned in the early fall from the West Indies he disregarded Washington's plans for combined operations in the north and sailed to Georgia in response to an appeal from General Lincoln. So unexpected was the French commander's appearance that he easily captured four British vessels off the Georgia coast. Lincoln and d'Estaing undertook a brief siege of the British post at Savannah, ending in an attack on the town on 9 October in which the British repulsed the French and American forces. D'Estaing and Lincoln retreated; Savannah remained in British hands until July, 1782.

[2] A town north of Savannah on the west bank of the Savannah River.

From Frederick Jay

Fish Kill, 7th September 1779

Dear Sir

The 1st Inst. I was made happy in receiving yours of the 16th ultimo inclosing a daught on G.B. [Gerard Banker, Treasurer][1] for three hundred pounds, which is received and passed to the Credit of your Accompt.[2]

It gives me real satisfaction to find that you like the award. I think the Umpire has done you Justice. The trouble that business gave me is amply compensated by your approval of its termination.

I have seen Colonel Wadsworth to whom I delivered your letter. He seems disposed to serve me, but from the Conversation that passed between us, I am confident that it will be out of his power to serve me in the way I would chuse. He has however promised to write me fully very soon; you shall be made acquainted with the results. I give you my sincere thanks for the trouble you have taken on my account.

I have wrote to Montangnie and desired him to send the Bundle to Governor Livingstons, I have not the least doubt but that you'l receive it soon.

I am just returned from the Nine Partners. I have been there to take a View of a Farm formerly James Harris, who it is said, is gone off to the Enemy; should that be the case, I shall take it. Dr. Van Wycke has given me his Consent, I shall apply to Mr. Livingston the other Commissioner to Morrow on my Return to Kingston.[3]

This will go by Post; by the same Conveyance you'l receive some of P.'s Tobacco. Mrs. Munro is gone to Albany, her Husbands Name will not be inserted in the Confiscation Bill.[4]

Farming business goes on as you may imagine. I am Sorry its not in my power to carry the business on more to my inclination. Things Suffer, but there is no Remedy.

Baxter has returned your Mare; many Horses are stolen in that Quarter, which is the reason of his returning her. I do not think her safe here, your directions on this head is requested.

Gussey is well and *has every thing* that makes him satisfied.

I could wish to say much to you, but most be deprived of that pleasure 'till a more favourable opportunity presents itself. Tell Sir James that the Legislature agree well, and are determined to pass such Laws as they think will be for the Honour and safety of the State. I could wish that he was present. I shall write him Soon.

Adieu and believe me to be Yours most Affectionately

FRED. JAY

P.S. The news papers you sent me gave *Satisfaction to the whole House.*

ALS. Endorsed.

1 Addition of name in JJ's hand.

2 JJ to Frederick Jay, 16 Aug. 1779, not located.

3 Robert R. Livingston, Theodorus Van Wyck, and a Mr. Sheldon were the Commissioners of Sequestration for Dutchess County.

4 After the Reverend Harry Munro's departure for England in 1778, Eve Jay Munro and her son Peter remained in New York State. The family was never reunited.

To George Clinton

Philadelphia, 16 September 1779

Dear Sir

Your Favor by Mr. Phelps has arrived. I approve much of your Resolutions respecting Vermont. It is a Pity they had not taken Place two Years ago. They were committed; a Report I <am told will> believe will be made To Day or Tomorrow <whether it will be sufficiently explicit or pass in its present Form> is uncertain. My Endeavours [to] render it proper neither have or shall be wanting.[1]

<I am now in Congress and a very extraordinary Vote has this moment passed. The Proprietors of Indiana and Vandalia, claiming a Right to the Sovereignty and Soil of a Tract of country <<claimed by>> which Virginia <<have petitioned Congress to interfere,

asserting they had a Right to become a>> says is within her Lines petitioned Congress to interpose in their Behalf. On reading the Petition seperate Independent Government by Virtue of certain Acts of the British King and Council previous to our Independency.[2]>

My Resolution to resign the Office of Chief Justice was taken after much Deliberation and Thought on the Subject. I have since frequently examined the Reasons which influenced me to that Measure, and still remain perfectly satisfied <of their Propriety, that> with them, as there is therefore no probability of a Change in my Opinion, <and therefore> it will be unnecessary to detain my Resignation any longer from the Council of Appointment. The Legislature may perhaps in Consequence of this Step incline to keep me here. On this Head I must inform you that the Situation of my Fathers Family is such that I cannot longer reconcile it to my Ideas of filial Duty to be absent from them unless my Brother should be so circumstanced as to pay them necessary Attention. The enclosed Letter to him is on that Subject, and I have desired him in Case he cannot undertake to have his Father and Family almost constantly under his Eye, to prevent my Election. The Determination therefore on this Point will govern mine <on the other>. Should he not be at Kingston be pleased to send the Bearer with it to him.

Dft. Endorsed. The "6" in the date has been written over a "4." The proceedings described in the second, deleted, paragraph affirm that the letter was drafted on the 14th, then revised and redated. Enclosure: JJ to Frederick Jay, 16 Sept. 1779.

[1] Clinton's letter to JJ, 1 Sept. 1779 (ALS in JP), was delivered by Charles Phelps. On 8 September the New York delegation laid these documents before Congress, which referred them to a committee composed of Thomas McKean, William Paca (1740–99), Samuel Huntington, Meriwether Smith (1730–90), and Samuel Holten (1738–1816). In its report on 17 September the committee "recommended to the people claiming to be the state of Vermont, to cease and desist from the exercise of any authority or power whatsoever over any person or persons, or their property, who acknowledge the jurisdiction of New York, New Hampshire, or Massachusetts Bay, until the beforementioned controversy shall be heard and determined by Congress." *JCC*, XV, 1078–80.

[2] On 14 September a memorial signed by George Morgan for "the proprietors of a tract of land called Indiana" and one by William Trent for "Thomas Walpole and his associates, claiming a right to the tract of land called Vandalia" were read in Congress. By a vote of 6–5 (with New York's delegation divided, JJ in the negative) Congress referred Morgan's memorial to committee. Trent's petition was sent to the same committee on 8 October. On the thirtieth of that month the committee's final report recommended that Virginia and "all other states similarly circumstanced . . . forbear settling or issuing warrants for unappropriated lands, or granting the same during the continuance of the present war." The report was then entered in the *JCC*. *JCC*, XV, 1063–64, 1155, 1213, 1223–24, 1226–30; see also Thomas B. Abernethy, *Western Lands and the American Revolution* (New York, 1937).

To Frederick Jay

Philadelphia, 16 September 1779

Dear Fady

Your obliging Letter with the Parcel of Tobacco which came with it arrived Yesterday.

I am now to inform you that I have resigned the Office of Chief Justice, and that if the State should incline to keep me here, I shall consent to stay, provided either you or Sir James will <be in Circumstances> undertake to attend constantly to our good old Father and his unfortunate Family. Otherwise I shall at all Events return for that Purpose.[1] Sir James has his Doubts respecting his future Destination. <where your Objects may lead you is uncertain and> Therefore his Return is precarious at present but this he would not chuse to have known. I wish to know without Delay the Result of your Reflections on this Subject. Should you succeed with Wadsworth, I think you would then be in Capacity to serve them as well [as] ever. If you live on Harris's Farm you will not make up your Mind on this matter. If you find you cannot pay necessary Attention to Fish Kill, prevent my Election, and let me know your Inclination by the first opportunity.

<Sally joins with me in Love and Compliments to Peggy and you> Thank Peter for the Tobacco. Sally joins me in our Love to you all. I am Dear Fady Your affectionate Brother

Dft. Endorsed by JJ.

1 JJ discussed this subject in a letter (dft in JP) written the same day to Robert R. Livingston. "If my Brother will be so circumstanced as to be able to pay constant Attention to my Father and Family," he said, "I have no objections to remaining here, but should that not be the Case, my Feelings will not permit me to be longer from him."

From Nathanael Greene

West Point, 19th September 1779

Sir,

His Excellency, General Washington, has shewn me a Letter of General Sullivan's to Congress, wherein he exclaims against the force and preparations for the Expedition he is sent upon; particularly against the preparations in the Quarter Master's Department.

It was the 2nd of March before His Excellency, General Washington determined upon the plan of operation. This was owing to the difficulty of obtaining the necessary information, whether to carry on the expedition by the way of the Susquehannah, or Fort Schuyler. Had it gone on by the way of Fort Schuyler, the preparation in that quarter had been so liberal, with respect to Boats for another expedition which had been in contemplation, that few, if any, would have been wanted more than was on hand; therefore it was unnecessary to give an order for any early preparations in that quarter.[1] But upon the most diligent enquiry, and from the best information of the state of the Magazine of Flour and other provisions at Albany, together with the difficulty of entering the Indian Country to advantage upon that route, determined the General to make his approaches by the way of the Susquahannah. But, as I said before, it was late in the season before he was decided upon this point.

After I received the General's Instructions upon this business, every measure was taken to collect men and materials for executing the work. The Men were to be collected from different Governments, even as far as Albany; and the materials were mostly growing in the Woods. Major Eyre was appointed to superintend the building of the Boats.[2] His knowledge, activity and zeal are so well known to the Board of War, that I think it unnecessary to say anything upon this head. His orders were positive and pressing; and I believe no Man could have made greater exertions than he did to accomplish the business.

My orders were to build 150 two-ton Batteaus, and to provide eight or ten Boats, already built, of a larger size. Upon examining the navagation of the River, the Batteaus were found unsuitable for the service: the stream was too rapid, and too many rocks were interspersed in the River for such flat-bottom craft, and of so slender a make, to endure the hardships incident to the transportation. We were obliged therefore to change the construction of the Boats, and build them with keels and round futtocks. This was necessary, as well to give them strength, as to prevent their sticking upon the rocks; but this unavoidably took up more time than was sufficient to build three times the number of Batteaus. I did not understand the plan of the expedition as rendering it necessary to have all the Boats completed at the same time: I had been taught to believe, from the nature of the expedition, that there would be several Posts established as the troops moved forward into the Indian Country; from which a communication would be kept up with the place of deposit for the Stores; and therefore I thought, if the whole of the Boats had not been completed by the arrival of the Troops at Wyoming, such as were deficient, might, as soon as they were completed, to be employed in transporting Stores from Post to Post. And I believe, if the expedition had not been rendered too unwieldy by the vast quantity of Stores taken along, there would have been little, if any, deficiency of tonage necessary for the transportation by the arrival of the Troops at that place. However, whether there was or was not, it was not owing to either a want of attention, or exertion to expedite the business. There was no particular time set for having the Boats completed in the General's instructions; but the business was to be accomplished as soon as possible, and we completed nearly the tonage demanded within a few days after the arrival of the Troops at Wyoming. The number of Boats, ordered for the expedition, was thought to be a very large provision, and notwithstanding the number made did not come up to the order given, yet the size was so much larger as more than make up the deficiency.

You will see by the inclosed order of His Excellency, that the Stores which we had deposited at Estherton,[3] (asserted in the remarks, and can be proved by Colonel Cox's Return) were there seasonably for the expedition at the most early period; and was abundantly sufficient for all the purposes thereof. The whole quantity deposited at Estherton was by no means intended as a supply for that expedition; and had General Sullivan consulted his real wants instead of grasping at every thing he could get, he must have been sensible of it. I believe there never were greater exertions, or more ample provision made for any expedition whatever; and I was so far from expecting censure for any imaginary deficiency's, that I really expected his warmest acknowledgement.

I was so anxious to have every thing put in a proper train upon the Susquahannah, that I sent up Major Claiborne, the 30th of April, to expedite the business, although I could illy spare him from the duties of the Office in Camp, being pressed on every side at that time in the necessary preparations to put the Army in motion at Middlebrook. Notwithstanding the inconveniencies I felt from his absence, I never recalled him untill this Army took the field and not then; untill Colonel Cox had engaged Major Eyre to supply his place.

The preparations that were made at Easton, the place of rendezvous, was principally under the direction of Colonel Hooper,[4] and was as ample as the General's demands were extensive.

There is one subject of complaint which astonishes me: that is, a want of Pack saddles. The first estimate that was made was one thousand Pack Horses; a demand was soon after made for 1500; but before the Troops marched from Easton, three more drafts upon the Q. Master's department for upwards of 2200, as will appear by the inclosed Return. Colonel Hooper made 1500 Pack-Saddles; Colonel

Mitchell sent up to Easton 700; Colonel Cook[5] provided 300, and there were between 3 and 400 sent up the River, by way of the Susquahannah. At the time he complains of the want of Pack-Saddles, there were 240 returned on hand at Wyoming, and there were left behind upwards of 300 at Easton! I leave Congress to judge, therefore, with what propriety the complaint was made. I believe every body will agree the provision has been very great. And here I cannot help observing to Congress what I believe I have hinted before to the Board of War, and to the Committee for superintending the Staff, that the expences and oeconomy of the Quarter Master's Department depends infinitely more upon the Officer commanding, than the Agents conducting the business.

I am still more astonished at his representation respecting Batteau and Pack Horse men: there were actually inlisted between two and three hundred Batteau men, (and he says not an hundred,) and upwards of 200 still remain in the service as appears by a return from Colonel Sheriff, D.Q.M.G. with thirty.[6] But I am told there has a considerable number left the employ, from abuses they were subject to. There were also inlisted between 60 and 70 Pack Horse men. More might have been had, could we have obtained Money from the Treasury in season; but the preparations were so much more extensive than either His Excellency or myself had any Idea of, that the supplies of Cash did not keep pace with the demands of the General.

What advantage General Sullivan could propose from such an unfair representation, I cannot imagine; and his insinuations of neglects are the more surprising to me, as I have an acknowledgement, from under his own hand, that he believes there have been every possible exertion made in my Department to forward the business of his Expedition! It is not my business to arraign his conduct; neither am I disposed to censure without further knowledge; but his account betrays a want of Candour and Generosity which will do him no honor with the honest part of Mankind. I shall avoid commenting upon many things in his Letter, as my business is not to condemn, but to justify myself.

I was so anxious for the success of that expedition, and so sensible that His Excellency would submit to any inconvenience with this Army, which was necessary to give success and dispatch in the preparations for that, that I did not scruple to distress our Affairs here, to facilitate the operations there. In a word, I gave the preparations for that expedition the lead of every other consideration; and neither pains or expence were spared to make them ample and complete.

I have the honor to be, with great respect, Your Excellency's Most Obedient Servant

NATHL. GREENE QMG

ALS. DNA: PCC, 155, 171–81. Endorsed by Charles Thomson: ". . . Read 25. Referred to the board of war. 3 pages enclosed relative to Gen. Sullivan. 30th Septr. Ordered to be filed at the board of war until further orders." Enclosure: John Cox, "A Return of Stores ordered to be deposited at Estherton, for the Indian expedition, by the way of Susquehannah."

1 George Washington to Nathanael Greene, 2 March 1779, *GWF*, XIV, 176–78.

2 Major Benjamin G. Eyre of the Philadelphia County militia.

3 Estherton was a settlement on the Susquehannah a few miles north of Harrisburg.

4 Robert Lettis Hooper, Jr. (d. 1875), served as Deputy Quartermaster General, 1777–82.

5 These officers were probably Lieutenant Colonel David Mitchell of the Cumberland County, Pa., militia and Colonel Edward Cook (1738–1808) of the Westmorland County, Pa., militia.

6 Probably Cornelius Sheriff of York County, Pa.

To Edmund Pendleton

Philadelphia, 21 September 1779

Dear Sir

I had Yesterday the Pleasure of recieving your Favor of the 8th Inst. and am happy to find that my supplying our Friends absence in the Instance alluded to no less acceptable to You than agreable [to] me.[1]

In the Packet enclosed with this are two Copies of a circular Letter from Congress to their Constituents. We have good Intelligence of three Regiments having within a few Days embarked at and sailed from new York; their Destination is unknown, some supposing them bound for the W. Indies, others for Georgia.

There is Reason to believe Count DEstaing is on the american Coasts having lately been left by an Eastern Vessel on the Latitude of Bermudas.[2]

The Committees here are losing Ground.[3] I doubt their existing much longer. It is a Pity they were called into Being; Admitting the Rectitude of their Intentions, the Policy of their object and the wisdom of their Measures to attain it, will never be demonstrated.

Be pleased to present my best Respects to the Governor and Col. Harrison[4] both of whom I sincerely esteem and permit me to assure you that I am with great Truth and Regard, Your most obedient and most humble Servant

J. J.

Dft. Enclosures: 2 copies of a circular on finances, 13 Sept. 1779, written by JJ, printed in *JCC*, XV, 1052–62. Edmund Pendleton (1721–1803) of Virginia served in the Continental Congress, 1774–75, and thereafter held high positions in his native state.

[1] Letter in JP. Pendleton thanked JJ for the offer to send news of Continental affairs, for he had "Great anxiety to hear the progress of our important conflict." The friend Pendleton mentions is his kinsman, John Penn, a lawyer from Granville, N.C., and a delegate to Congress in 1778, to which he had been reelected the following year. Penn had served as Pendleton's correspondent in Philadelphia.

[2] More than 3,000 troops arrived in New York City on 25 August. However, their presence delayed rather than hastened a dispatch of British forces from the city since the fleet brought with it an epidemic of fever which hospitalized more than 6,000 British soldiers.

[3] JJ was perhaps a bit premature. The extralegal committees to which he refers had been set up by radical leaders in Philadelphia and elsewhere in Pennsylvania. They had increasingly taken the law into their own hands, and their example encouraged mob violence. Late in July they attacked the home of Whitehead Humphreys (1712–86), one of their critics, and forced entry at a time when Edward Langworthy (1738–1802), delegate-elect to Congress from Georgia, was rooming there. Langworthy protested to President JJ on 25 July that Continental troops had been improperly used in this proceeding, and indicated that others beside himself—notably Gouverneur Morris, Silas Deane, and William H. Drayton—were their prospective targets. Congress referred the facts concerning Continental troops to the Board of War on 26 July, as a result of which inquiry Colonel John Bull (1730–1824) and Captain Charles Willson Peale (1741–1827), the artist, addressed JJ, 17 Sept. 1779. Conceding that "a number of Respectable Citizens . . . were assembled," they nevertheless declared the reports "groundless" and claimed to have been cleared by a state inquiry. While the affair blew over, the radical activists' operation reached a climax on 4 Oct. 1779, less than a week after JJ had resigned the Presidency, when rioters attacked the home of James Wilson (1742–98), the noted lawyer and speculator, who had defended merchants before price-control committees. Langworthy to JJ, 25 July 1779, ALS in DNA: PCC, 78, XIV, 271–74; Bull and Peale to JJ, 17 Sept. 1779, LS in DNA: PCC, 78, III, 337–40; *JCC*, XIV, 888; XV, 1086. W. B. Reed, *Life and Correspondence of Joseph Reed* (2 vols., Philadelphia, 1847), II, 423–26; Robert L. Brunhouse, *The Counter-Revolution in Pennsylvania, 1776–1790* (New York, 1971), pp. 68–76.

[4] Thomas Jefferson, who succeeded Patrick Henry as governor of Virginia, 1 June 1779. Colonel Benjamin Harrison (1726?–91), Speaker of the Virginia House of Delegates in 1779.

Peter Jay to John Jay and Sir James Jay

Fish Kill, the 22d September 1779

Dear Jemmy and Johnny

Since the delivery of my Letter of the 20th Inst., I have received Jemmy's letter of the 14th.[1] It gives me pleasure that you were all Well; it also informs me of Johnny's intention to pass the Winter with me, wherewith I should be extremely happy if he could do it with safety to his Person. Gangs of Villains make frequent Excursions from our Neighbouring Mountains for Prey, which would make it very dangerous for him at my House; it's credibly said of 5 or 6 Active Wigs, they are determined to attempt to carry off at all Events to the Ennemy, by whom it's said they are imployed, so that I think Johnny's Person would be too tempting an Acquisition to be neglected by them. About 3 weeks ago as Plato[2] Was coming from Billy Van Wyck's between 9 and 10 oClock at Night, he was stoped by a parcel of armed fellows who rushed out from under the Bushes along the Fence; And he finding them determined to carry him off, he appeared very willing to go with them, and after a while they suffered him to go to Billy's house (which was not far off and where they thought he belonged) for a Shirt or two he was to fetch. He hastened round the house and Escaped through the Meadow till he got Home. He and old Plat have by uncommon hard Labour got 19 Bushels of wheat in the ground, they appear very sensible of the difficulty we labour under.

My Crop of Wheat is much blasted and I expect my Indian Corn will not exceed an half a Crop. Our love to Sally and to you both. I am your Affectionate Father

PETER JAY

ALS.

[1] Peter Jay to JJ and James Jay, 20 Sept. 1779, in JP; James Jay's letter of the 14th not located.

[2] One of the Jay slaves.

To Lafayette

Philadelphia, September 25, 1779

Sir

I have had the honor of recieving and communicating to Congress your Favor of the 12 June last.[1] The Sentiments of attachment and affection for these States expressed in it are highly agreable to Congress. It is with Pleasure they hear that your Royal Master entertains the same opinion of your Merit with which your good Conduct impressed the People <and Congress> of these States and tho your fellow Soldiers here regret your absence, they will sincerely rejoice in your acquiring Laurels <and Reputation> abroad.

Your Continued Attention to whatever may be interesting to America is a mark of your Zeal for her Cause and very pleasing to Congress.

Be <pleased> assured Sir <to accept the warmest> of our warmest Wishes for your Health, happiness and Glory, and that I have the Honor to be, with great Respect and Esteem Your most obedient and most humble Servant

Dft. Endorsed by JJ.

1 Lafayette to JJ, 12 June 1779, was read in Congress 13 September and "Ordered, That an answer thereto be prepared." The committee's report is not entered in the journals. *JCC*, XV, 1050.

To Benjamin Franklin

Philadelphia, 26 September 1779

Dear Sir

I have had the Pleasure of recieving your Favor of the 2d June last.[1] The act of Congress respecting Col. Diricks alluded to in it, mentioned no public Business committed to his Care, but in Compliance with his Request supported by Governor Trumbul simply recommended him to your Notice.[2]

As this will be delivered to you by Monsieur Gerard It will be unnecessary to enlarge on american Politics or Intelligence. This Gentleman has done essential Service to the Alliance, and by the Wisdom of his Conduct done much towards binding the two Nations to each other by Affection whose union at first resulted from motives of Interest. I am happy to assure you that similar Ideas of You prevail and extend in this Country as well as the one you are in.

The Chevalier De LaLuzerne has brought with him many recommendatory Letters. Few will be more useful to him than yours. If he treads in the Steps of his Predecessor, they will lead him to the Hearts of the Americans. My Endeavours shall not be wanting to render this Country agreable to him. <The aims of New York is a Rock in the midst of the ocean.>

You will oblige me by continuing this Correspondence and by believing that I am with great Esteem <Attachment> and Regard your most obedient and humble Servant

Dft. Tr in NN: Bancroft American Series, v. 31.

1 ALS in RAWC.

2 Diriks was granted a leave of absence in December 1778 but denied any official capacity to represent America in Holland, for Congress was "not yet prepared to adopt the scheme of a negotiation for the loan proposed." Diriks wrote from Amsterdam in July 1779 asking Congress to reconsider its position on obtaining a loan from Holland because he was confident that the mood of the country was very favorable for one. As a result, Congress committed Diriks's letter to a committee which recommended that Congress "authorize and instruct a proper person to negotiate that." On 18 October John Adams, Henry Laurens, and Woodbury Landon (1738–1805) of New Hampshire were nominated, and on

the twenty-first Laurens was elected. *JCC*, XII, 1106; XV, 1167, 1180, 1186, 1198; DNA: PCC, 78, VIII, 327–30. For the background of Dirik's proposal, including earlier efforts to secure a loan in the United Provinces, see P. J. van Winter's *Het aandeel van den Amsterdamschen handel aan den opbouw van het Amerikaansche gemeenebest* (The Hague, 1927–33), ch. 2.

FROM EDMUND PENDLETON

Edmundsburg, September 27, 1779

Dear Sir

I have had the Honor to acknowledge the receipt of each of your very obliging Favors by return of Post, neither of which I presume had reached you when your last of the 14th was written,[1] but will hereafter regularly find their way. I am just returned from attending our High Court of Chancary, where we found little business, people appearing more inclined to hunt the Sources of money, than of Equity. An express passing from Charles Town to Congress droped intelligence that Count D'Estaing had landed 5000 men in that or the Georgia State; if this be true, I suppose the british Army in that quarter must be Ours. It is said, probably on none other ground than conjecture, that a division of the Count's Fleet and Army is gone Northward to do something there at the same time. The preparation at New York may be for a General embarkation for Britain in consequence of the orders mentioned in my last; I hope at any rate they will not pay us another Visit, which would be unpolite as we have not returned their former. I am Dear Sir Your obliged and Obedient Servant

EDMD. PENDLETON

ALS. Endorsed.

1 Drafts of JJ to Pendleton, c. 1 Sept. and 21 Sept. 1779 in JP; that of the fourteenth has not been located.

VI

JAY'S MISSION TO SPAIN

Jay's Mission to Spain

The fall of 1779 witnessed a general overhaul by Congress of the diplomatic corps and a rigorous reexamination of peace objectives. These new initiatives came in response to both domestic and international pressures.

In large part, the impetus for extensive reform was a direct result of the Lee-Deane controversy. The partisans of those two commissioners had succeeded in creating such deep factional divisions in Congress that neither man was left with much claim to the public confidence. The debates on the conduct of the mission to France revealed, further, the ineffectiveness of using multiple commissioners at foreign courts. Late in March 1779 Congress voted that the commissioners be removed and "but one Plenipotentiary Minister or Commissioner" be appointed for each court.[1] Neither Lee nor Deane survived the reorganization, but Franklin proved more durable. A motion to recall him was defeated, and he now acted as America's sole minister to the Court of Versailles.[2]

Lee's partisans sought to have their man named minister to Spain to secure an alliance with that nation, and to have John Adams, a Lee backer, designated peace commissioner to deal with Great Britain. Though he failed to secure a majority on the first two ballots, Adams was elected on the third. JJ was chosen for the Spanish post, replacing Arthur Lee, who had earlier been named, and Henry Laurens was dispatched on a mission to the United Provinces.[3] JJ's election was regarded as a victory for the pro-French faction, and both the French foreign minister, Conrad Alexandre Gérard, and the Spanish observer, Juan de Miralles, were exultant.

More fundamental than the issue of personalities was the debate on peace terms, precipitated by Gérard's arrival early in 1779 and soon followed by Spain's secret alliance with France, committing Spain to war with Great Britain.

On 3 April 1779 Spain issued an ultimatum to Great Britain in which she offered to act as mediator in the war but, without even awaiting a reply, ratified the secret Convention of Aranjuez with France. Among other conditions, the treaty bound both courts to make no peace or enter into any truce until Gibralter was restored to Spain. France also promised that should she secure Newfoundland, Spain would be allowed to use the fisheries.[4]

Since Article VIII of the Franco-American alliance contained a pledge that neither party would conclude a truce or peace with England "without the formal consent of the other first obtained,"[5] this secret treaty of Aranjuez constituted a unilateral change in the terms of America's alliance with France, without the consent or knowledge of the United States Government. France's failure to make any provision for sharing the Newfoundland fisheries with the Americans might also be construed as violating the historic rights of the former colonists to fish off the Grand Bank. Spain formally declared war on Great Britain on 21 June 1779. This action prompted Congress to designate a minister plenipotentiary to Madrid to work out a treaty of alliance and obtain financial aid.

For virtually the entire year 1779 preceding JJ's appointment to Spain, Congress was engaged in a great foreign policy debate. As far back as February Gérard had given Congress an inkling of Spain's likely course and advised drawing up instructions and deciding upon ultimata.[6] At every point in the ensuing debates, the French minister intervened to moderate American expansionist claims.

A committee, formed to draw up peace terms, reported to Congress on 23 February. In addition to absolute and unlimited independence, it listed six stipulations to be considered as ultimata: (1) minimum boundaries from Canada to the Floridas and west to the Mississippi, (2) complete British evacuation of United States territory, (3) fishing rights on the banks and coast of Newfoundland, (4) "absolute and unlimited" navigation of the Mississippi to the southern boundary of the United States, (5) free commerce with some port or ports on the river below that boundary, and (6) the cession to the United States of Nova Scotia or the latter's independence.[7]

Most of these terms were soon approved by Congress, but those relating to the fisheries and the navigation of the Mississippi produced bitter controversy along sectional lines. The New Englanders continued through a good part of the summer to attempt to strengthen the fisheries articles, but their efforts proved futile. In the final instructions agreed upon by Congress on 14 August the fisheries claim was removed from the list of ultimata.[8]

Especially pertinent to JJ's mission was the lengthy debate over a stipulation regarding the free navigation of the Mississippi. On 17 September JJ was instructed to insist not only on the free navigation of that river, but also to obtain a free port on the lower Mississippi for American commerce. In its euphoric state Congress further instructed JJ to secure a loan of $5 million "upon the best terms in your power not exceeding 6 per cent., effectually to enable them to cooperate with the Allies against the Common Enemy."[9] Before borrowing, however, JJ was to try to get a subsidy in consideration of America's guaranteeing the Floridas to Spain if they were reconquered.[10]

As presiding officer of the sessions of Congress JJ had been a close observer of the drafting of his instructions. Now he was responsible for carrying them out. In late October JJ and his wife sailed for Europe in the Continental frigate *Confederacy* under the captaincy of Seth Harding of Massachusetts, who had already distinguished himself by his exploits as commander of the Connecticut brig *Defense*. Accompanying the Jays were JJ's official secretary, William Carmichael, his private secretary and brother-in-law, the twenty-two-year-old army veteran, Henry Brockholst Livingston, and his twelve-year-old nephew, Peter Jay Munro. The last named was in fact fatherless in view of the Reverend Harry Munro's defection to the British cause. The frigate also carried the party of the French minister, Gérard, who had been given leave to return home.[11]

1 *JCC*, XIII, 364.

2 *Ibid.*, 499–500.

3 The voting took place on 27 Sept. 1779. *Ibid.*, XV, 1113.

4 For the Convention of Aranjuez, see Henri Doniol, *Histoire de la Participation de la France à l'établissement des États-Unis d'Amérique* (5 vols., Paris, 1886–92), III, 803–10.

5 The spirit of that article was unanimously endorsed in a resolution of Congress, drawn up by JJ and Gouverneur Morris, which stated: "That as neither France or these United States may of right, so these United States will not conclude either truce or peace with the common enemy, without the formal consent of their ally first obtained, and that any matters or things which may be insinuated or asserted to the contrary thereof tend to the injury and dishonor of the said states." DNA: PCC, 25, p. 70; *JCC*, XIII, 63.

6 *RDC*, III, 39–40.

7 *JCC*, XIII, 239–44; PCC, 25: I, 71. The report is in Gouverneur Morris's hand.

8 *JCC*, XIV, 896, 897, 960.

9 *Ibid.*, XV, 1084; DNA: PCC, 25, I, 329.

10 *Ibid.*, 1119–20; *RDC*, III, 343–45.

11 For the transatlantic voyage of the Jays, see *Peacemakers*, ch. I.

TO ROBERT R. LIVINGSTON AND GOUVERNEUR MORRIS

Philadelphia, 29 September 1779

My dear Friends

I address this Letter to you both because I have not Time by this opportunity to write to each separately. In a few Days I shall write you both particularly. Mr. Gerards being about to sail happily prevailed upon Congress to proceed rapidly and unanimously in arranging their foreign Affairs. Young Colonel Laurens is going Secretary to Doctor Franklin, and had the general approbation of Congress for that office. Mr. Adams is appointed to manage the Business of Pacification with Britain, and Mr. Dana has been chosen his Secretary. I am going to Spain to treat with that Court on the Subject of

Alliance, amity, Commerce etc., and Mr. Carmichael is my Secretary.[1]

On all these Matters I wish to write particularly because the Knowledge of them will be useful especially to Morris. I exceedingly regret his not being sent to Europe where his abilities would have done Honor as well as Service to his Country, but it seems that Period is not yet arrived, and Congress must for some time longer remain his Field. I shall write a long Letter to the Governor on the Subject of the Delegation from New York and the Settlement of our New England and Vermont Disputes, which are now in a good Train, and if prudently managed must terminate to our Satisfaction. Of this I am certain. In my opinion Duane, Hobart and yourselves ought to be sent. The first is well acquainted with the minutiae of the Controversy and his Information from time to time on the different Points that may be the Subjects of Investigation will be useful. Hobart is very agreable to the People of New England and this Circumstance independent of his other Qualifications, merits Attention. Your Manners, Abilities and Address will give New York great Advantage in contested Matters, and if Morris governs his Imagination will conciliate Friends.

I won't bid you farewel in this Letter having much to say in the others which I shall certainly write. I shall conclude therefore with an Assurance which it gives me Pleasure to repeat that I am Your Friend

JOHN JAY

ALS. NHi: Robert R. Livingston Papers. Tr in NN: Bancroft-Livingston Papers. Addressed: "The Hon'ble Robt. R. Livingston Esqr. Chancellor of the State of New York, Kingston. John Jay." In George Clinton's hand: "Forwarded by your Humble Servt. Geo. Clinton," Endorsed.

[1] On 29 Sept. 1779 William Carmichael was elected secretary to the Spanish mission, Francis Dana to the English, and Colonel John Laurens (1754–82), son of Henry, to the French. *JCC*, XV, 1127–28.

To George Clinton

Philadelphia, 5 October 1779

Dear Sir

In a Conference with some of the Delegates of New Hampshire and Massachusets Bay it was agreed that I should draw the Draft of a Bill for carrying into Effect the Resolutions of Congress relative to our Disputes with Vermont and with each other.

The enclosed Draft has been perused and approved of by them, and they have promised tc transmit a Copy of it to their respective States and to press their immediate Attention to the Subject.[1]

It appeared to be expedient that the Acts to be passed for this Purpose by the three States should be nearly similar, lest variances which might be deemed important, should create Delay and Dispute. I also thought it most adviseable to be content with the Description of the Powers contained in the Resolutions, and not by new ones hazard Alterations or Deviations that might open other Fields for Discussion. For this Reason the Act in Question is made very general, granting in express Terms the Powers asked for by Congress and referring to the Resolutions for a Description of them.

With very sincere Regard and Esteem I am Dear Sir your most obedient Servant

J. J.

DftS. Enclosure printed below.

1 One of JJ's final acts as a New York delegate was to press Congress to make a final determination of the Vermont dispute and to draft a resolution for the New York legislature committing the state to abide by the decision of Congress. New York adopted the resolution on 21 Oct. 1779, but neither New Hampshire nor Massachusetts, the other parties to the controversy, followed suit. "An Act to empower the Congress of the United States of America, to determine all Controversies, relative to certain Lands in the Counties of Cumberland, Gloucester, Charlotte, and Albany, commonly called the New Hampshire Grants," *Laws of the State of New York* (Poughkeepsie, 1782), 3d sess., ch. XXIV, 91–92.

John Jay: Draft Act on Vermont

[*Philadelphia, 24 September–5 October*] 1779

An Act for complying with and carrying into Effect the Recommendations contained in certain Resolutions of the Congress of the united States of America of the Day of 1779

Whereas the Congress of the united States of America did on the Day of last past, *unanimously* enter into certain Resolutions in the Words following vizt (Here insert Resolutions Verbatim) and whereas the 1st Congress did on the Day of unanimously enter into a certain other Resolution in the Words following to wit (here insert reso[lutio]n repealing one and substituting another Clause)

And whereas the aforesaid Resolutions and Recommendation are founded on equal Justice and true Policy, and to have for their Object the Establishment of perpetual Harmony Friendship and mutual Confidence between the States therein named, which it is no less the Desire than the Interest of this State to promote

Be it enacted by the and it is hereby enacted by the Authority of the same, that all the Powers and Authorities which it is recommended to or requested of this State in and by the said Resolutions to vest in or grant to the said Congress shall be and hereby are vested in and granted there to as fully and amply as if the same were here again particularly enumerated and described. 2, And further that this Act shall be always construed in a Sense most advancive of the Design to the Intent and Meaning of the said Resolutions. 1st And that the Decisions and Determinations which shall be made in the Premisses in pursuance of the Powers and Authorities hereby granted shall be obligatory on this State and the People thereof so far as the said Decisions and Determinations or any other of them shall respect the same or any Part thereof.

And it is hereby further enacted by the Authority af[oresai]d That no Advantage shall be taken by this State of the non performance of the Conditions in any of the Grants of Land in the said Resolutions referred to, but that further Time be given to fulfil the same respectively to wit until the Expiration of six Years to be computed from the Publication of this Act.

Dft.

From George Clinton

Poukeepsie, 5th October 1779

Dear Sir

I received your Favour of the 29th Ultimo[1] on my Way from Kingston to this Place whither I was called Yesterday, by the Indisposition of my little Boy who is so extreamly Sick and low as to leave us but little Hopes of his Recovery. I congratulate you most sincerely on your late Appointment and be assured you have my warmest Wishes that your Embassy may be attended with Success equal to your Abillities and Integrity. I am persuaded it is of the utmost Importance to maintain a wise and respectable Representation in Congress; but tho we all agree in this as Elections are more frequently influenced by partial Considerations than the public good the Lott will not always fall on those best quallified to serve their Country in that Important Station.

The Members for the present year are yourself, Messers Duane,

Floyd, Scott and L'Homedieu. The latter and Mr. Morris had an equal Number of Votes in the first Instance but on the joint Ballot of both Houses it terminated in Favour of Mr. L'Homedieu by one or two only. Mr. Morris's Ellection was lost by several of his Friends including in their List Mr. L'Homedieu. I am however inclined to beleive he will now be ellected to fill the Vacancy which will be occassioned by your Absence.[2] Should this be the Case he must not decline serving as this would not only injure his own but the Interest of his best Friends.

The Resolutions of Congress for settling the Disputes with the Inhabitants of the New Hampshire Grants were received so short a Time before I left Kingston that I have not been able to collect the Sense of the Legislature respecting them. They appear to be agreable to such of the Members as I have had an Opportunity of conversing with and to those I have taken the Liberty of communicating your Letter on that Subject.[3] Altho it is almost two Months since the Meeting of the Legislature very few Bills and most of these of little Importance have as yet been enacted. The Confiscation and Tax Bills[4] are great Objects of Controversey and occassion the Delay of all other Business though there are some Matters which at this particular Juncture require the most immediate Dispatch if we are to expect the Arrival of the French Squadron in this Quarter.[5]

As I expect your Brother will hand you this I omit adding many Matters respecting the Affairs of the State of which he will be able to inform you. I cant expect the Pleasure of another Line from you before your Departure as your Time must be fully employed in the necessary Preparations for so long a Voyage. But if you should find a Moments Leisure when a Broad be assured you have not a Friend who will be more happy on hearing of your Wellfare. I conclude Mrs. Jay is to accompany you. Mrs. Clinton joins me in offering our best Respects to her and in wishing you a prosperous Passage, Health and Happiness. I am my Dear Sir Your Most Affectionate Friend and humble Servant

GEO. CLINTON

ALS. Addressed: "His Excellency John Jay Esquire, Philadelphia, Favoured by Fredk Jay esqr." Endorsed.

1 Printed in *GCP*, V, 288–91.

2 The Congressional delegation elected 9 Oct. 1779 consisted of JJ, James Duane, William Floyd, John Morin Scott, and Floyd's brother-in-law, Ezra L'Hommedieu (1734–1811), a Yale graduate and lawyer from Southold, L.I. Philip Schuyler, not Gouverneur Morris, was chosen 18 October to replace JJ.

3 JJ had sent Clinton a copy of the 24 Sept. 1779 Congressional resolutions, printed in *JCC*, XV, 1096–99. On that day Congress discharged the committee

appointed 1 June for failure to effect a solution to the New Hampshire Grants controversy, and resolved unanimously that New Hampshire, Massachusetts, and New York pass laws authorizing Congress to determine their boundaries. All parties were urged to observe a truce until an examination could be made of the evidence. In a covering letter to Clinton dated 25 September, dft in JP, JJ expressed satisfaction with this plan, as legitimacy of the New York claim would become obvious once the evidence was examined. Furthermore, he was convinced that Congress would not agree to interfere in Vermont in an arbitrary manner, because many delegates stated publicly that such action would be neither proper nor practical, and those from New England secretly favored the Vermont interest over that of New York. *JCC*, XIV, 673–76; XV, 1096–99.

[4] For the confiscation bill, see "An Act for the Forfeiture and Sale of the Estates of Persons who have adhered to the Enemies of this State, and for declaring the Sovereignty of the People of this State, in Respect to all Property within the Same," *Laws of the State of New York* (Poughkeepsie, 1782), 3d sess., XXV, 85–89, which passed 22 Oct. 1779. The tax bill, which passed on 23 October, providing a system of county quotas, was "An Act for raising the Sum of 2,500,000 Dollars by Tax, within this State," *Laws of the State of New York* (Poughkeepsie, 1782), 3d sess., XXVII, 93–96.

[5] A reference to rumors that the French fleet would sail to Rhode Island or New York.

George Washington to Sarah Livingston Jay

West-point, October 7th, 1779

General Washington presents his most respectful compliments to Mrs. Jay. Honoured in her request by General St. Clair he takes pleasure in presenting the inclosed,[1] with thanks for so polite a testimony of her approbation and esteem. He wishes most fervently, that prosperous gales, unruffled Sea, and every thing pleasing and desirable, may smooth the path she is about to walk in.

AL. Addressed: "Mrs. Jay. Philadelphia." Endorsed. Dft in DLC: Washington Papers, v. 118, 60.

[1] Written by SLJ at the bottom of the letter: "A lock of the General's hair."

From George Washington

West-point, October 7th, 1779

Dear Sir,

Permit me, amongst the number of your friends to congratulate you and my Country on your late honourable, and important appointment. Be assured Sir that my pleasure on this occasion though it may be equalled cant be exceeded by that of any other. I do most sincerely wish you a pleasant and an agreeable passage. The most perfect and honourable accomplishment of your ministry, and a safe return to the bosom of a grateful Country.

With the greatest regard and sincerest personal attachment I have the honour to be Dear Sir Your most Obedient and Affectionate Humble Servant,

G. WASHINGTON

Dft. DLC: Washington Papers, v. 118, 59.

FROM EDMUND PENDLETON

Edmundsbury, October 11, 1779

Dear Sir

As I conjectured so it happened, that your esteemed Favor of the 21st past made a Viset to Williamsburg and found me on its return; your next I suppose is now on the same route, as it is not yet come to hand.

I beleive Count D'Estang amongst the beneficial things he has done For America in General, has effected a most important purpose for Virginia, in stopping a large embarkation from York to pay us a Viset. We have not yet heard of his final success to the Southward,[1] a loose report is circulating that the enemy are endeavouring to steal a March by land to St. Augustine. It is however very loose.

The Committees in Philadelphia never appeared to me to be upon stable ground, nor can any thing of the sort produce public good which owes its rise to the Spirit of party, besides the objection to having an undirected, uncontrollable power acting within a state where regular Government is established. If regulations of prices are thought necessary and that they are not judged proper Subjects for direct laws, the only Secondary method seems to be an association to abide by the Regulations of a Committee and a law authorising the Committee to enforce the Articles of Association; the proceeding would then be legal and the Committee limited to some rule of determination. Though after all the policy of regulations will remain insufferable and experience only [to] produce a derision.

I congratulate you Sir, upon your appointment to represent the American States at the Court of Madrid, the just testimony of that confidence which the Honorable body you have presided over have in your Abilities and Integrity. May health, Success and every Felicity accompany you; but whilst I am sensible of the advantages we shall reap from your eminent Services there, I have my Fears that they will be missed importantly where you now are, and that the Spirit of party, almost laid to sleep, will revive upon your absence. I cordially wish you may be able to heal the new made breach between Spain and Britain, since France appears disposed to Peace and I am mistaken if the Court of London are not ready to make Up with us, if nothing respecting our Allies hinders it. Indeed we want an honorable peace, but I hope there lives not a wretch who wishes it upon terms of dishonor and Ingratitude to Our noble Allies. I am Sir with unfeigned regard Your most Obliged and Obedient Servant

EDMD. PENDLETON

ALS. Endorsed.
[1] There was no "final success."

To James Duane

Philadelphia, 14 October 1779

Dear Sir

Your obliging Favor by Mr. Phelps[1] has remained thus long unanswered because till very lately I promised myself the Pleasure of seeing you, but that has now become very improbable as we expect to sail in a few Days.

Your Reelection and Consent to Return to Congress are Circumstances which I consider as fortunate <in the present Situation of our State>. Your intimate acquaintance with our Controversies respecting Jurisdiction will not only enable you but your Colleagues to render the State very important Services. I hope the Train in which I shall leave these Matters meets with your approbation, and I assure you it will give me very sensible Pleasure to hear of their being drawn to a Conclusion satisfactory to New York. The sooner you take your Seat, in my opinion the better various Considerations, which will readily occur to you [to] point out the Propriety of this Measure. The State will be unrepresented after Tomorrow. Mr. Scot I am told will soon be here. I hope you will bring Floyd and L'Homedieu with you.

Morris it seems is not in the Delegation and I regret it. He would have been useful and particularly in the Vermont Business with Respect to which you are so circumstanced, as to be less serviceable on the Floor than on other occasions.

If there be any Services in my Power to render you abroad, be pleased to command them. A Line for you will accompany all my public Letters, and you will oblige me by a constant Correspondence.

With the best wishes for your Health and Happiness I am Dear Sir your most obedient Servant

My Respects to Mrs. Duane and all the Family.

Dft. Endorsed by JJ.
1 Not located.

RICHARD BACHE TO BENJAMIN FRANKLIN

Philadelphia, October 18, 1779

Dear and Honored Sir

Finding that Mr. Jay, who is appointed Minister Plenipotentiary to the Court of Madrid, goes with Mr. Gerard by way of France, and probably will stop at Paris a short time, I commit this, with the enclosed, and a packet of Magazines to his care. He carries his Lady with him, the Daughter of Governor Livingston. She is a fine sensible Woman, and will do honor to her native Country. I need not recommend them to your particular notice and regards, as I am confident they will a[lmost] certainly meet with them, as they meet with you.

I am ever Dear Sir Your affectionate Son

RICH. BACHE

ALS. PPAmP: Franklin Papers, Bache Collection. Addressed: "His Excellency Dr. Benjamin Franklin Minister Plenipotentiary from the United States of N. America of the Court of Versailles, Favored by his Excelly John Jay Esqr." Endorsed in an unidentified hand: ". . . recd June 12, 1780." Enclosure not located. Richard Bache (1737–1811), merchant of New York City and Philadelphia, was married to Franklin's daughter Sarah.

TO GEORGE CLINTON

On Board the Confederacy near Reedy Island, 25 October 1779

Dear Sir

Be pleased to keep the Letters herewith enclosed, until good opportunities of sending them offer.

Since the Successes of General Sullivan against the six Nations, some People have affected to speake of that Country as a conquered one, and I should not be surprized if they should next proceed to insist that it belongs to the united States, by whose Arms it was won from independent Nations in the Course and by the Fortune of War.

Would it not be proper for New York to establish Posts in that

Country, and in every respect treat it as their own.[1] In my opinion our State has had too much Forbearance about these matters. Virginia, who has Claims and Rights under much the same circumstances, manages differently.[2]

My best Respects to Mrs. Clinton.

I am Dear Sir with great Regard and Esteem Your most obedient Servant

JOHN JAY

ALS. PEL: Skillman Library. Enclosures not located.

[1] In the Congressional debates over the western lands, 1778–79, New York claimed the Iroquois territory by virtue of early English treaties with the Iroquois and the state's assumed sovereignty, generally voting with the landed states against ceding their claims to Congress. Barbara Graymont, *The Iroquois and the American Revolution* (Syracuse, 1972), pp. 27 *passim;* Thomas B. Abernethy, *Western Lands and the American Revolution* (New York, 1937), pp. 238, 242.

[2] Virginia, the largest claimant to western lands, not only contested the claim of the private land companies but also authorized George Rogers Clark to erect a fort at the mouth of the Ohio. Abernethy, *Western Lands,* pp. 217–29.

Jay's Use of Ciphers and Codes

Since JJ, as well as other notable contemporaries, found it expedient to employ ciphers and codes for confidential information in letters both public and private, consideration must be given to the art of cryptography as it had by then evolved.

Cryptography is the process of writing in such a way as to make messages unintelligible to people unacquainted with the method employed.[1] The two basic ways to accomplish this are called transposition and substitution. Transposition consists of scrambling the order in which the letters appear in each word. Substitution, the more important system, uses an alternate alphabet in which every letter is replaced by some other letter or by a number or symbol. Where there is only a single equivalent for each letter, the scheme is described as monalphabetic. When two or more substitute alphabets are used in a prearranged rotation, one speaks of it as being polyalphabetic.

Code and cipher are words often used interchangeably by those unfamiliar with secret writing, but they actually define different techniques. A cipher is a substitute alphabet or a set of alphabets used in prearranged rotation. A code, on the other hand, is a list of letters, syllables, words, and phrases, together with the codewords or codenumbers selected to represent them. Such a list may be described as a codebook. Examples of various kinds of ciphers and codes are explained below.

The nomenclator system of cryptology, in general use for almost four centuries prior to the Revolution, was a mixture of cipher and code. Many variations were possible, but there was usually both a cipher alphabet and a supplementary list of names, syllables, and words with numerical equivalents. The system derived its name from this list, which originally consisted only of names of people and places.

The simplest of all systems was a monalphabetic cipher used by itself. Any two correspondents who had exchanged grids on which were recorded the letters of the alphabet and their agreed-on equivalents could thereafter conceal the meaning of certain words or phrases in their communications with one another by rendering them in cipher. Even before his ship left the American coast, JJ wrote Robert R. Livingston on 25 October 1779 suggesting that they adopt a cipher with numbers representing the letters of the alphabet. He recommended the use of commas to separate numbers, and semicolons, colons, or hyphens to indicate the ends of words. The proposed cipher, when recorded on a grid, looked like this:

a	b	c	d	e	f	g	h	i	j	k	l	m	n	o	p	q	r	s	t	u	v	w	x	y	z
5	6	7	11	13	8	9	10	12	14	16	19	22	1	2	3	4	15	23	25	26	24	20	21	18	17

Possible alphabetical cipher combinations being literally unlimited, it was practical to exchange different ones with every friend and relative. JJ and Frederick Jay agreed on a cipher that utilized a combination of numerals and letters as equivalents.[2] JJ seemed to prefer grids that employed only letters as equivalents, because he used different versions in his correspondence with William Bingham,[3] Silas Deane,[4] Catharine W. Livingston,[5] and Henry Brockholst Livingston,[6] and he suggested still another one to Robert Morris, but apparently neither he nor Morris ever tried it.[7]

The very simplicity of the monalphabetic grid cipher was its great defect. In any language certain letters are used more often than others, and some commonly appear together in words. A skilled cryptanalyst can without too much difficulty solve a secret message utilizing a one-cipher alphabet, provided it is long enough to establish the normal letter frequencies.

Aware that monalphabetical ciphers furnished inadequate security, Robert R. Livingston declined to use the one JJ recommended. Instead, he urged the adoption of a polyalphabetical grid he devised and which he called the XZA cipher. His grid was twenty-four characters wide, and he compressed the alphabet into it by omitting the letters j and z. The grid's four-character depth provided for the alphabet and three sets of equivalents. His designation of the sets as X, Z, and A served no function except to give the cipher a name. The user was supposed to encipher by rotating among the three rows, using the equivalent from the X tier for the first letter of every word, and then moving to Z, to A, to X again, and so on until the word was completely reduced to cipher form. The grid appears below, and its use can be demonstrated by the word army, which in this cipher would be written as 1, 16, 12, 24:[8]

	a	b	c	d	e	f	g	h	i	k	l	m	n	o	p	q	r	s	t	u	v	w	x	y
X	1	2	3	4	5	6	7	8	9	10	11	12	13	14	15	16	17	18	19	20	21	22	23	24
Z	4	5	6	1	2	3	7	8	9	10	11	12	13	14	15	17	16	19	20	18	22	24	21	23
A	6	3	4	5	1	2	7	8	9	10	11	12	13	14	15	16	17	18	19	20	21	22	23	24

All during his residence in Spain JJ was aware that a good deal of correspondence never reached him and that many other letters arrived bearing evidence that they had been opened and examined. Suspecting that Livingston's communication enclosing the XZA cipher had been tampered with, he wrote back urging that he and Livingston use another and even more complicated polyalphabetic cipher. The grid he designed contained six rows, one for a conventional twenty-six-letter alphabet and the other five for equivalents. Like Livingston, he assigned non-functional letter designations to those five rows, thereby creating the name YESCA for his invention.[9] Livingston tried the system on 1 November 1781 in his first letter to JJ in his new capacity as Secretary for Foreign Affairs, but he made so many errors that it has never been completely deciphered.[10] JJ inserted passages of YESCA in his 14 March 1782[11] letter, but by that time both men were finding nomenclators more satisfactory, and neither of them attempted a cipher again.

The effort by Livingston and JJ to rely only on a grid cipher was unusual, because most people engaged in secret communication made at least partial use of codewords or codenumbers. Catharine W. Livingston's correspondence with JJ and his wife, for example, utilized a monalphabetic grid, but there were also roman codenumbers for specified people and arabic numerals to designate places. Thus XXIII stood for Frederick Jay and 89 for Philadelphia.[12]

A list of words with their code equivalents promised greater security than any grid cipher, because cryptanalysis was impossible unless somebody stole the list. Aware that this was true, JJ on 29 February 1780 sent a list of 138 words, each with a roman codenumber, to the Secretary of the Continental Congress, Charles Thomson. His list consisted of the Thirteen States, sixty-nine other locations, and the names of fifty-six public figures. For such additional vocabulary as might be needed, he proposed code designators representing words in the English-French section of Abel Boyer's *French Dictionary* (13th edition, London, 1771). Each word was to be encoded in three steps: first locate the word in the dictionary, add seven to the page number, and write down the sum; then place a line under one of the three numerals in that number to indicate that the word is in the first, second, or third column on the page; finally designate the word's position in the column by counting up from the bottom and adding ten.[13] Thomson acted on this proposal, and for over a year the two men depended on a combination of JJ's 138-word nomenclator and the dictionary-based nomenclator. The Committee for Foreign Affairs and Gouverneur Morris used it at least once apiece in letters to JJ, and he employed it in several communications addressed to the President of the Continental Congress, Samuel Huntington.[14]

JJ made an ill-fated attempt to exchange secret messages with Robert R. Livingston using a variation of the Boyer code. His instructions, forwarded to his friend on 19 February 1780, called for recording the actual page number, following that by a letter to indicate the column (C for the first column, A for the second, B for the third), and a number for the location of the word in the column (count down from the top and add seven). JJ tried this version at least once, on 6 October 1780,[15] but he had to abandon it when Livingston reported that he had been unable to acquire the dictionary.[16]

A more easily obtained dictionary and thus a more satisfactory one for the purposes of secret communication was *Entinck's New Spelling Dictionary* (London, 1777). William Carmichael used a code formula based on it that was understood by both Charles Thomson and JJ.[17] The latter relied on two variations of the same scheme in corresponding with William Bingham and Gouverneur Morris, and he tried unsuccessfully to get Robert Morris interested in still another version.[18] Ultimately the defects inherent in dictionary codes led to their abandonment by JJ and most of his correspondents. As Livingston learned, it was sometimes difficult to secure a particular edition of a dictionary. The arithmetic calculations introduced the possibility of errors. Finally, as JJ commented to Bingham, the dictionaries then available did not contain all the words that one might wish to include in a letter, so that grid ciphers or supplementary word lists were virtually a necessity.[19]

Large nomenclator lists eventually proved to be the best solution, because they did not have to be purchased in bookstores, there was minimum opportunity for errors in arithmetic, and a well-conceived list could include all the words that could possibly be needed. Silas Deane and JJ used this technique with satisfactory results, supplementing it, probably unnecessarily, with a monalphabetic grid cipher. Their list was made up of 889 words with arabic equivalents. Place names accounted for approximately one-fifth of the total, and there were about half that many names of public figures. The balance of the vocabulary was a mixture of commonly used words, such as "at," "enter," and "oblige," and words like "alliance" and "destroy" that would be particularly useful in time of war.[20]

James Lovell, who was spectacularly successful in deciphering several captured British dispatches, is recognized as the father of American cryptoanalysis, and he undoubtedly had a lot to do with creating fashions in cryptography during the Revolution. In 1777 he supported Arthur Lee's proposal that the Committee of Secret Correspondence use a dictionary as a codebook. Later he popularized complicated polyalphabetic grid systems of the type named for the sixteenth-century Frenchman Vigenère. This method defied contemporary cryptoanalysis but produced so many errors that it had to be abandoned.[21] Considering the influence Lovell exercised in Congress in matters pertaining to secret correspondence, it is not unlikely that he was behind the introduction in mid-1781 of printed word lists that were adopted promptly by government officials. These codesheets contained not only words but also parts of words, letters of the alphabet, and punctuation marks, and spaces were included where teams of users could enter their own code symbols. Although this 603-item nomenclator was shorter than the one shared by Deane and JJ, the inclusion of letters, punctuation marks, and approximately two hundred syllables made it much more versatile.

JJ recevied two versions of this nomenclator, one dated 7 July 1781 from Robert Morris[22] and the other sent to him four days later by Charles Thomson, both employing arabic numerals for code equivalents. From then on JJ availed himself of this innovation in his letters to both Robert and Gouverneur Morris, who as assistant to Robert Morris had access to the financier's codebook.[23] Deciding to take advantage of this improvement, Robert R. Livingston obtained a copy of Thomson's version and started using it in letters to JJ on 20 October 1781. Unfortunately Thomson gave Livingston the wrong codebook, and the latter sent off another undecipherable note on 28 November before he learned of his error and obtained the correct book.[24] He and JJ corresponded in that code thereafter, except for one last fling with the YESCA cipher, until Livingston abandoned the use of any secret writing in his 9 May 1782 communication. His frequent errors had made his letters difficult to decode, and JJ's complaints discouraged him from attempting any further secret communication. Livingston and JJ had tried most of the available schemes, but the end result of the majority of their experiments was confusion and imperfect communication. Significantly, Wharton in his publication of the diplomatic dispatches of the Revolution, including letters to and from JJ, omitted without notice to the reader the ciphered or coded portions of letters, which invariably contained the nub of the communication.

Deciphered or decoded words and passages in the documents that follow are identified by small and large capital letters.

1 David Kahn, *The Codebreakers: The Story of Secret Writing* (New York, 1967), is the best work on this subject.

2 A copy of this grid cipher, dated 2 March 1780, is in JP. It was apparently never used.

3 *WJ*, II, 88–91.

4 JJ to Dean, 2 Oct. 1780, dft in JP.

5 Catharine W. Livingston to SLJ, 10 July 1780, ALS in JP.

6 Henry Brockholst Livingston to JJ, 5 Feb. 1781, ALS in JP.

7 JJ to Robert Morris, 19 Nov. 1780, dft in JP.

8 Robert R. Livingston to JJ, 26 Aug. 1780, below. He had previously objected to JJ's monalphabetic cipher and had enclosed one that was never used and that has not been located. Livingston to JJ, 10 Feb. 1780, ALS in JP.

9 JJ to Robert R. Livingston, 25 April 1781, ALS in NHi: Robert R. Livingston Papers; dft in JP.

10 Robert R. Livingston to JJ, 1 Nov. 1781. RC in NHi: Robert R. Livingston

Papers; triplC in JP; LbkCs in DNA: PCC, 79, I, 302–09 and PCC, 118, 16–23; LS in NHi: Jay Papers; printed in *RDC*, IV, 814–16.

11 JJ to Robert R. Livingston, 14 March 1782, dft in JP.

12 Catharine W. Livingston to SLJ, 10 July 1780, ALS in JP.

13 JJ to Samuel Huntington, 29 Feb. 1780. LbkCs in DNA: PCC, 110, I and CSmH: JJ Lbk; printed in *RDC*, III, 526–27.

14 Resolution of Congress, in the hand of Charles Thomson, 19 May 1780, ADS in JP. Committee of Foreign Affairs to JJ, 16 June 1780; ALS in JP; C in JP; LbkC in DNA: PCC, 79, I, 128–29. JJ to Samuel Huntington, 6 Nov. 1780: LbkCs in CSmH: JJ Lbk and in DNA: PCC, 110, I; C in DLC: Madison Papers, I, 10429a–10461a. Gouverneur Morris to JJ, 17 June 1781, ALS in JP.

15 ALS in NHi: Robert R. Livingston Papers.

16 Livingston to JJ, 26 Aug. 1780, below.

17 Carmichael to JJ, 15 Feb. 1780: ALS in JP; LbkCs in DNA: PCC, 110, I, and CSmH: JJ Lbk. 18 Feb. 1780: ALS in JP; LbkC in DNA: Misc. PCC, roll 2; printed in *RDC*, III, 502–03. 26 Feb. 1780: ALS in JP. JJ to Huntington, 29 Feb. 1780: LbkCs in DNA: PCC, 110, I and CSmH: JJ Lbk.; printed in *RDC*, III, 526–27.

18 JJ to Bingham, 8 Sept. 1781, printed in *WJ*, II, 88–91 and *HPJ*, II, 66–69. JJ to Gouverneur Morris, 2 March 1780: dft in JP; 5 Nov. 1780: dft in JP; printed in *WJ*, I, 113–14 and *HPJ*, I, 444–45. Gouverneur Morris to JJ, 7 May 1781: ALS and duplALS in JP; dft in Gouverneur Morris Papers, NNC-SC. JJ to Robert Morris, 19 Nov. 1780: dft in JP; printed in *WJ*, II, 66–67 and *HPJ*, I, 445–47.

19 JJ to Bingham, 8 Sept. 1781, *WJ*, II, 88–91.

20 JJ to Deane, 2 Oct. 1780, dft in JP.

21 David Kahn, *The Codebreakers*, pp. 181–84.

22 ALS to VHi; LbkC in DLC: Robert Morris Papers, A 35–36.

23 JJ to Robert Morris, I Sept. 1781. RC in JP, ALS formerly in the possession of Charles Hamilton.

24 LbkCs in DNA: PCC, 79, I, 234–36 and in DNA: PCC, 118; LS in JP; dft in NHi: Robert R. Livingston Papers; TriplLS in JP; DuplLS in NHi: Jay Papers.

To Robert R. Livingston

On Board the Confederacy near Reedy Island, 25 *October* 1779

Dear Robert

Accept my Thanks for your very friendly Letter.[1] It recalled to my Mind many Circumstances on which it always dwells with Pleasure. I should have been happy in a personal Interview before my Departure, but since that has become impossible, let us endeavour to supply it by a regular and constant correspondence. To render this the more useful and satisfactory a Cypher will be necessary. There are twenty six Letters in our alphabet; take twenty six Numbers in Lieu of them thus.

a b c d e f g h i j k l m n o p q r s t u v w x y z
5-6-7-11-13-8-9-10-12-14-16-19-22 1-2-3-4-15-23-25-26-24-20-21-18-17

Remember in writing in this Way to place a , after each number, and a ; or : a - after each Word. This will prevent Confusion. It will be unnecessary to write a whole Letter in Cypher; so many words in Cypher as will blind the Sense will be sufficient, and more safe, as a Discovery will thereby be rendered more difficult.[2]

God bless you. I am your affectionate Friend

JOHN JAY

My best Wishes to all the Family.

ALS. NHi: Robert R. Livingston Papers. Addressed: "The Honble Robert R. Livingston Esqr. Chancellor of the State of New York Clearmont." Endorsed.

1 Robert R. Livingston to JJ, 6 Oct. 1779, ALS in JP.

2 This is a monalphabetic grid cipher.

Council of Commissioned Officers of the Confederacy

[*On board* Confederacy, 23 *November* 1779]

At a Council of the Commissioned Officers of the Confederacy called together this 23d November 1779 at the Request of Seth Harding[1] Esq. Commander in Consequence of loosing her, Boatsprit, Fore Mast, Main Mast, and Mizen Mast, on the 7th Inst. at half past 5 O'Clock A.M. in Lattitude 41:03 Longitude 50:39 Cape Henlopen bearing S. 83°W. Distance 1140 M. Corvo[2] S. 85°E. Distance 878 M. Steering. E B N. Wind at S.S.E. the above Boatsprit, and Masts together with allmost all of her Rigging were Carried away and lost likewise lost with the Rack, her Fore Sail, Fore top sail, Jibb Fore Stay Sail, Main top Mast Stay sail, Middle Stay Sail, Main top Gallant Stay Sail, Sprit Sail, Spirit Sail Top Sail, Fore top Gallant Steering Sail, and Royal Main Top Gallant Stay Sail and Royal Mizen top Sail, Mizen Stay Sail, Mizen top Gallant stay Sail, Mizen top Gallant Sail, Mizen top Gallant Royal, at 11 A.M. got Clear of our Rack. The Next day at 7 O'Clock A.M. found the Rudder Head to be gone, we immediately began to Refit it, and up Jury Masts, and have been Constantly imployed to this day, Endeavouring to get the Ship in Order to proceed on her passage, being in Lattitude 40:33 Longitude 48:28.[3] The following Questions were put to the following Officers:

Question 1st to Mr. Tanner, Master. Do You think it Proper to proceed to Europe with the Confederacy in her present Situation?

Answer. No I do not think it possible to make the Rudder so secure as to proceed with safety.

Question 2nd. Where do you think it would be most prudent to carry the Ship too [*sic*] in her present situation for the safety of the Ship and Crew?

Answer. As I do not think the Ship in a proper Situation to proceed on her intended Passage, I think it most prudent to proceed to the first safe Port in the West Indias.

Question 1st to Mr. Gregory, 3rd Lieutenant. Do You think it proper to proceed to Europe with the Confederacy in her present Situation?

Answer. No I do not think it Possible to secure the Rudder so as to proceed on her intended passage with safety; besides if we should meet with a Gale of Wind, and have Our Jury Mast or Sails Carried away we have none to Replace them.

Question 1st to Mr. Vaughan, 2nd Lieutenant. Do You think it proper to proceed to Europe with the Confederacy in her present situation?

Answer. Our Rudder I believe to be the greatest Obstacle to prevent the Ships proceeding to Europe which in my Opinion cannot possible survive a hard Gale of Wind without increasing the Leake very much, and should we be Necessitated to part with it the Ship would undoubtedly be thrown into Various difficultys in Consequence of which we might founder the Ship. I think it very imprudent to Approach the Coast of Europe, in Our present situation for this Reason should we have the misfortune to be Attacked by a gale of wind On shoar we must inevitably be Cast onshoar, and perhaps the greater part of us if not the whole fall a sacrifice to our own folly. I would by all means advise proceeding to the West Indias with the utmost expedition as our Water and provisions begin to Run Short.

Question To Mr. Gross, 1st Lieutenant. Do You think it prudent to proceed to Europe with the Confederacy in her present Situation?

Answer. I do not think it possible to secure the Rudder so as to proceed on her intended passage with safety, besides if we should meet with a Gale of Wind and have Our Jury Masts or Sails carried away we have none to Replace them.

Question. To Mr. Storer (Carpenter). Do You think it prudent to proceed to Europe with the Confederacy in her present Situation?

Answer. No the Rudder Can't be secured so as to proceed with Safety.

Question. To Mr. Hays (Boatswain). Do You think it prudent to proceed to Europe with the Confederacy in her present situation?

Answer. No. On Account of the Rudder being disabled and not a sufficient Quantity of Rigging and Blocks in Case we should meet with an Accident.

SIMON GROSS
THOMAS VAUGHAN
STEPHEN GREGORY
JOHN TANNER
EBENEZER STORER
JAMES HAYES

To Seth Harding

On board Confederacy, 26th November 1779

Sir

As Mr. Gerard declines giving any Opinion or direction On the subject of the within Report of a Council of Your Officers I can only inform You that their sentiments correspond with mine and that their advice ought in my Opinion to be followed.[4]

I am Sir Your Most Obedient Servant

JOHN JAY

Both are C's, in the hand of John Lawrence, "Clerk." Endorsed by JJ: "Minutes of Council of officers on board Confederacy in 1779."

[1] Seth Harding (1734–1814), a New England mariner, had commanded vessels trading with the West Indies during the French and Indian Wars. He was captain of several Connecticut ships at the beginning of the Revolution until being put in charge of the Continental *Confederacy*, which carried JJ on its first extended voyage.

[2] Corvo Island, northernmost island in the western archipelago of the Azores.

[3] For the mishap to the *Confederacy*, see *Peacemakers*, pp. 3–5, and SLJ to Susannah French Livingston, 12 Dec. 1779, below, in family correspondence.

[4] Anxious to get home to France, Gérard became temperamental when the officers recommended sailing to the West Indies. JJ found merit in their decision and gave it his support, but the Frenchman refused to do so and became sullen and uncoöperative. *Peacemakers*, pp. 4–5; JJ to Samuel Huntington, 24 Dec. 1779, LbkCs in DNA: PCC, 110, I and CSmH: JJ Lbk; printed in *RDC*, III, 436–45.

From James Lovell, Robert R. Livingston, and William Churchill Houston, Committee on Foreign Affairs

Philadelphia, December 11th, 1779

Sir

By the inclosed Resolves of Congress[1] you will find that we are become more dependent upon your vigorous Exertions for the Amelioration of our Currency than you perhaps expected when you left Philadelphia. We think it of so much Importance that you should be early apprized of the Measures determined upon respecting Bills of Exchange that we do not chuse to omit this good Opportunity of communicating them, though unattended with a full Explanation of the Reasons which urge Congress to draw more especially as you are so well enlightened by your late Presence in their Assembly.

We are with every Wish for your Prosperity Sir your humble Servants

JAMES LOVELL
ROBT. R. LIVINGSTON
WM. CH. HOUSTON

LS. The letter is in the hand of James Lovell. Enclosures: Resolutions of Congress, 23 and 29 Nov. 1779, printed in *JCC*, XV, 1299–1300, 1326–27. LbkCs in JP: JJ's Letterbook and DNA: PCC, 79, I, appendix; Tr in NN: Bancroft, American Series, V, 240.

James Lovell (1737–1814), a Harvard graduate and Boston schoolteacher, served as a Massachusetts delegate to the Continental Congress, 1777–82, where he became active in both the anti-Washington and the anti-Deane factions. William Churchill Houston (c. 1746–88) was also an educator, being a professor at the College of New Jersey, from which he had graduated in 1768. He was sent to Congress by New Jersey in 1779.

1 On 17 Nov. 1779 Congress passed resolutions calling for the emission of $10,050,540 in Continental currency, and a committee was named "to devise further ways and means for supplying the public treasury." Two days later the committee presented a report drafted by Gouverneur Morris, proposing that bills of exchange, at £100,000 each, payable at six months' sight, be drawn on JJ and Henry Laurens, the newly elected minister to the United Provinces. Morris's report also recommended a new domestic loan and an annuity office plan to aid in the repayment of the bills of exchange. On 23 November, however, Congress enacted only the bills themselves, and no provision was made for their redemption. Congress passed resolutions six days later describing how the Board of Treasury was to issue the bills and directing the Committee of Foreign Affairs to inform JJ and Laurens "of the drafts that will be made upon them, and explaining fully the reasons that urge Congress to draw, directing them to keep up a mutual correspondence and afford each other every assistance in procuring money to pay the bills." *JCC*, XV, 1285, 1288–89, 1299–1300, 1326–27.

FROM ROBERT R. LIVINGSTON

Philadelphia, 22d December 1779

Dear John

I am told there will be an opportunity of sending this to you; I wish therefore to embrace it tho as I know not how safe the conveyance may be, I shall only deal in generals. You who know the share that you have in a heart too susceptible of tender emotions will easily believe the pain it gave me to find no token of your friendship, no farewell line at this place, where I hastened immediately after my election with the pleasing, tho distant prospect of seeing you.[1] Here I discovered that a Letter that I had entrusted to Duer's care, did not reach you till after your embarkation, and took up another Letter which I had given to the Governor to forward to you, written immediately after the receipt of yours, which by a strange blunder of your brother, and the negligence of Benson was not till delivered in a week after it came to Kingston though I was there every day.[2] By this time I flatter myself that in conformity to the wishes of your friends, you and yours are arrived, settled, and recovered from the fatigues of your voyage. A new world is opened to you, and how gay and pleasing soever the prospects may be which it affords, you will meet with no mercy if you do not look back upon the friends you left in this; they have participated in the pains and dangers of your voyage, it is but just that they should share your pleasures.

Things here remain much in the state in which they were when you left us. The campaign has ended without any thing descisive, and our Army is at present in a better state as to numbers and discipline than it has been at any period during the war, And upon the whole the ballance has been greatly in our favor, if we except the unfortunate attempt upon Savannah of which I dare say you have particular accounts by the brave, but unfortunate, Count De Estang who has arrived before this time if his evil genious has not continued to persecute him.[3]

The enemy seem desirous of availing themselves of their success, and as we are informed, are about detatching from 8, to 10,000 troops which are already embarked as is supposed for that quarter. They have not yet sailed owing to their ignorance of the Station of Count De Grass, who was said to be in Chesapeek bay though he has, as the Chevalier informs me, arrived at Domenique, and the rest of his squadron at Martinique, some what injured by a storm.[4] We have a report in town, that Pesecala is taken by the Spanish troops.[5] I have not had leisure to inquire in to the truth of it tho from circumstances with which you are acquainted I give some credit to it. This is a wandring letter, but I wish to crowd every thing in it which I can trust to paper that may serve to amuse you.

Colonel Lawrance has resigned his secretaryship and tomorrow we are to have a new election, tho as I beleive none of the persons in nomination will be elected, at least not yet. They are Lovel, Morris, *Colonel Steward* put in nomination by *Mr. Plata* and Colonel Hamilton.[6] Floyd had very improperly named me, against my express declarations, both in publick and private that I would not accept it, and has obstinately refused to withdraw his nomination. I mention this that you may not be surprized if you see me stand upon the list without a vote (for I think I shall be able to carry the State against myself) nor argue from it, that I wish to have the place, or that I want interest to obtain it, one of which I know, and the other believe to be untrue. Duer is likewise a candidate tho he has not yet been named, nor will he venture upon it till he sees whether Morris fails which I believe he will. I shall endeavour to support him, but at present Lovels interest is the best, though I imagine not sufficient to bring him through. My plan would be considering all things and the characters of the two Ministers to send Mr. Carmichael to France and Morris to you, who best know his turn; how far this will succeed I know not. I could wish to settle a cypher with you that I might for the future write with more freedom than I can now dare to do. For want of which I must close after desiring you to remember me most affectionately to Mrs. Jay, the Colonel and Mr. Carmichael. I write nothing about your friends, as Caty will tell you by this conveyance that they are all well. I would copy this but for two reasons: 1st Because I am too Lazy, 2nd Because finding me unchanged in my negligence, you may argue from thence that I am equally unchanged, in the sentiments of affection, with which I always have, and hope ever to continue to subscribe myself Dear John Your friend

ROBT. R. LIVINGSTON

ALS. Endorsed: ". . . Recd. 16 May 1780."

1 Named a special delegate to Congress by the New York State Legislature, Livingston reached Philadelphia and took his seat 20 Nov. 1779. *JCC*, XV, 1293–94.

2 The only letter from Livingston to JJ during the period of JJ's embarkation for Europe that has been located is one dated 6 Oct. 1779, ALS in JP.

3 Comte d'Estaing did not reach Europe until early in 1780.

4 Admiral François Joseph Paul, comte de Grasse (1722–88), had commanded a squadron under d'Estaing during the siege of Savannah.

5 The Spanish did not take Pensacola until 9 July 1781.

6 Livingston's prophecy proved correct. John Laurens, who had been elected secretary to the minister to France in September, declined the office in a letter received by Congress on 10 Dec. 1779. On 17 December James Lovell, Gouverneur Morris, Walter Stewart (c. 1756–96), colonel of a Continental regiment from Pennsylvania, and Alexander Hamilton were nominated to succeed him. Stewart was proposed by George Plater (1735–92), a Maryland delegate, 1778–80. William Floyd later proposed Livingston, who declined. The letter mentions William Duer as another candidate, but his name was never put in nomination. The 27 December was assigned as the day for the election but,

Congress being deadlocked, agreement could not be reached on a candidate. *JCC*, XV, 1366, 1391, 1402–03; Max M. Mintz, *Gouverneur Morris and the American Revolution* (Norman, Okla., 1970), p. 138.

To Robert R. Livingston

Martinico, Fort Royal, 24 December 1779

Dear Robert

My Letters from St. Pierre a few Days ago will inform you of the Misfortunes which drove us here.[1]

Monsieur Le Mothe Piquet was yesterday so obliging as to order the Aurora a french Frigate of 36 Guns to carry us to France, and we are to sail on Tuesday next,[2] so that we hope before the Month of March to take Leave of the Ocean, to whose Civilities we are not half so much indebted as to the Politeness of the People of this Island.

The Cypher I sent you has I fear become useless. It is a Circumstance which I regret, as it deprives me of an opportunity of communicating some Things which I would not wish every body to know. If before our Departure a Leisure Hour should occur I will form and send You another. The Time allotted for our sailing is very short, but it seems particular Reasons render it proper and we must be the more industrious in preparing.

God bless You.

I am Dear Robert Your Friend

JOHN JAY

ALS. NHi: Robert R. Livingston Papers. Endorsed.

[1] JJ to Samuel Huntington, 20 Dec. 1779, LbkC in DNA: PCC, 110, App., printed in *RDC*, III, 432–33; 22 Dec. 1779, LbkC in DNA: PCC, 110, App., printed in *RDC*, III, 435–36; 24 Dec. 1779, LbkCs in DNA: PCC, 110, I and CSmH: JJ Lbk., printed in *RDC*, III, 436–45.

[2] The Jays and their party sailed on the *Aurora* on 28 December.

To Samuel Huntington

Martinico, St. Pierre's, 27th December 1779

Sir,

Agreeable to a Promise I made to Monsieur De Laiske of this Island, I transmit to your Excellency a Copy of his Letter to me (No. 1) and of my Answer (No. 2) from which Congress will perceive the Necessity of providing for the Payment of the public Debts in this Island.

I have also the Honor of inclosing a Copy of a Letter from

Captain Harding (No. 3) on the Subject of Instructions what to do after being ready for Sea, and my Answer (No. 4).

I have the Honor to be, etc.

(signed) JOHN JAY

From Terrier De Laiske

Original received at St. Pierre's, 26th December 1779

Sir,

In Quality of a Creditor and Bearer of a Bill of Exchange for 100,000 french Livres upon the United States of America I had the Honor of presenting myself before you to communicate my Claims.

The Answer which Mr. Bingham has made me on your part, and in your Presence, does not fulfil the Idea which I had formed upon the Assurance given to me by the Administrator, relative to the new Arrangements taken with Mr. Bingham.

I am unhappy, Sir, not to have received from you such an Answer as the Accident of your Appearance here seemed to authorize my demanding on the Score of the particular Circumstances and mutual Interests which connect our Nations.

Your Quality of President of Congress seemed to be a farther Reason for my addressing you, and founding the Security of Payment upon the Answer with which you honor me.

I am, with Respect, Sir, etc.

(signed) TERRIER DE LAISKE

To Terrier De Laiske

St. Pierre's, 26th December 1779

Sir,

In Answer to your Favor received this Moment I have the Honor to inform you, that I neither hold any Office, or have any Instructions from Congress, which authorize me to interfere in the Matter you allude to, or would justify my giving you any Assurances which may respect it, except, that you may be satisfied of the Integrity and Honor with which the United States will fulfil all their Engagements, and that I shall take the first Opportunity of transmitting a Copy of your Letter to his Excellency the President at Philadelphia.

I have the Honor to be, etc.

(signed) JOHN JAY

FROM CAPTAIN SETH HARDING

On Board Ship Confederacy Off Port Royal, December 27th, 1779

Sir,

I arrived within about three Miles of this Harbor, about Eight OClock last Evening when we were obliged to come to Anchor, where we lay till this Morning, weighed Anchor about Eight OClock, and stood in for the Harbor where we arrived about 9 OClock.

Have not had Time to make much inquiry about Spars, etc. for the Ship, but have Reason to think, from what I have heard, that I shall not be so well supplied as I expected, as I am informed the Masts are to be *made* Masts. I will write you more fully on the Subject Tomorrow; shall be as expeditious about *fixing out the Ship* as possible, and shall proceed agreeable to your Instructions, which you will please to send by Mr. Laurence,[1] who waits on you with this for the Purpose. As I am persuaded that we shall be but indifferently supplied in this Place I think it would be most prudent to give me Instructions to proceed to some part of the Continent of America where the Ship can be best supplied, which, I think, would be Boston, or Rhode Island, provided the Enemy does not leave New York Time enough for us to go there.

For further Particulars inquire, of Mr. Laurence.

I am, with Respect, etc.

(signed) SETH HARDING

TO CAPTAIN SETH HARDING

Martinico, St. Pierre's 27 December 1779

Sir

Your Favor of to day was this Moment delivered to me by Mr. Laurence. I am much of your Opinion that ample Supplies for your Ship will be difficult to obtain here, especially, of spare spars and Provisions, and, therefore, think with you, that as soon as she is reffitted, it will be best to run immediately to the Continent, but to what particular Part of it, I am unable to determine.

But, Sir, I do not conceive myself authorized to give you any Instructions whatever. Your present Situation was not foreseen, and, therefore, not provided for. I can advise, but not order you. Be pleased to attend to the Destinction. It is my Opinion, that after refitting the Frigate you proceed with her immediately to such Part of the United States as may be most advisable, provided you shall not in the mean Time receive other Orders from America, and I advise you to write immediately, and by every Opportunity for Orders.

Accept my Acknowledgments for your Politeness and Attention to myself and Family, and be assured that I am, with the best Wishes for your Health and Prosperity Your most obedient and humble Servant

LbkC. DNA: PCC, 110, App. Enclosures: all are LbkCs in DNA: PCC, 110, App.; JJ's dft to Harding is in JP.

Samuel Huntington (1731–96), a Connecticut delegate to the Continental Congress since 1775, was elected President, succeeding JJ, on 28 Sept. 1779.

1 John Lawrence was a member of the *Confederacy's* crew.

Family Correspondence

7 October 1779–28 August 1780

The letters that follow provide a vivid insight into the personal side of JJ's life during his first year abroad. This transatlantic correspondence among the members of the large but close-knit Jay and Livingston families testifies to their affection for one another, and it reveals what they were all thinking and experiencing. Of particular interest are JJ's and SLJ's fascinating descriptions of their ocean voyage, broken by near-disaster, and the interlude at Martinique, and then their arrival in Cádiz and their difficult overland journey to Madrid and the Spanish court.

William Livingston to Sarah Livingston Jay

Trenton, 7 October 1779

Dear Sally,

It is with great pain that I am obliged to part with you across a wide Ocean, and to a foreign Land. Considering the Mortality of Man, and my time of life, it is probable I may never see you again, and may God Almighty keep you in his holy Protection, and if it should please him to take you out of this World, receive you into a better. And pray my dear Child, suffer not the Gaities and Amusements of the World, and the particular Avocations of what is called *high Life,* to banish from your Mind an habitual sense of an all-present Deity, or to interrupt you in paying him the homage you owe Him. With my most ardent Wishes for your good Voyage and safe Return I am your affectionate Father

WIL. LIVINGSTON

ALS. Endorsed twice, once by SLJ.

SUSANNAH FRENCH LIVINGSTON TO SARAH LIVINGSTON JAY

Persipney, October 9 [*1779*]

My Dear Sally

Your letter[1] was Such a Check to the prospect I had of seeing you and Mr. Jay soon, and your Spending some time with me, that I hardly Supported under it. My Philosophy, my Religion was not Sufficent for three days and nights, to Comfort me. I Shall not trouble you With those train of Difficults that my affection for you, created in my mind. Let it Suffice to tell you that I am at last reconciled to your intended Voyag. Viewing you in the way of your duty and happiness to accompany your best Friend, your dear little boy I hope will be left with me to Comfort me in your absence.

I commend you to the care of Divine Providence and am your very affectionate mother

S. LIVINGSTON

ALS.

[1] Letter not located.

WILLIAM LIVINGSTON, JR. TO SARAH LIVINGSTON JAY

Persippeny, 16th October 1779

Permit me my dear Sister to mingle my Joy with yours, on the honorable Distinction which Congress have been pleased to confer on Mr. Jay.

It is not the Dignity of Embassadorship, nor the Lustre of high Office, considered in themselves, that did create, or that can authorize the uncommon Satisfaction, with which your Friends felt themselves impressed on that Occasion. But it is, the Benefit and Advantage your Country is likely to derive from the Appointment of one, who, having manifested every Testimony of his Zeal and Abilities in her Services here; is destined to carry abroad and raise her Reputation in foreign Countries. The Regret we feel in the temporary Loss of a firm and unshaken Patriot from a Community in which his Assistance is so necessary and useful, is silenced, when the Nature of his Mission is called in question; every Desire of his remaining among us, must be laid asleep when we consider the grand Object of his Embassy. But since you are no Partner in the Commission, can you Madam plead the same Apology with your Friends, for the Loss they are to sustain from your Absence? However sensibly they may feel themselves affected by this Seperation, they must all allow the Wisdom of your choice. To gratify a laudable Curiosity and to travel in the Pursuit of Knowledge under the Advantages that will attend you, through the Progress of your Journey, are motives, that appeal to your Friends and yourself with equal Force. With a Gentleman capable of directing your Enquiries, and a Judgment and Disposition to make the best Use of his Directions, you cannot fail attaining the greatest Improvements to yourself, and reflecting the brightest Honor on your Family and Country.

And so Madam, you are in good Earnest to become the *Castilian*. We have already been tracing your Rout on the Maps. What think you of the Pyrenean Mountains? But your Fortitude I suppose, has e'er this, levelled them with the Plains. But what think you of your inveterate Foe the *Flea*? *France* abounds with them. *Spain* too, is infested with that hostile Animal. But this say you shall not terrify the Mind of an American: very Right. And if neither *Mountains* nor *Fleas* can cool your Intrepidity nothing more formidable will I hope obtrude themselves. You are to travel we find through the most Southern and consequently the most fertile Provinces of France. But even there, one Object will present itself, that will at once call upon your Humanity and remind you of your native Country. The Poverty I mean of the Husbandman and his half-cultivated Fields. O happy America, will you say, thy Farms are better tilled, because thy Citizens are more free. But I find I am attempting the History of a Country, which you'll soon be perfectly acquainted with, from your own Observation.

When you get to the Land of the renowned *Don Quixote* you will not fail to select and give us an Account of every Piece of *Knight Errantry* that falls within your Notice; that is the fairy Land of Fancy, there Immagination frolicks in all her Wattonness. Many are the Romances she has given birth to. You will let us know, whether the ravishing Wit and Beauty of the Ladies and the valorous Gallantry of the Men reign in them only: And if the *Colonel*[1] turns *Cavilier*, enters the List and carries off some celebrated *fair-one* you will give us the earliest Intelligence.

And now my dear Sister I shall bid you Adieu. May the great

Ruler of the Universe make you his peculiar Care, shield you from every impending Danger and restore you in due Season to your Friends, Family and Country, enriched with every valuable Acquirement you wish to possess; these my dear Sister and many more are the most fervent Hope and Desire of

Your Affectionate Brother

WILLIAM LIVINGSTON JUNR.

ALS. Endorsed.

1 Henry Brockholst Livingston.

HENRY BROCKHOLST LIVINGSTON TO SUSANNAH FRENCH LIVINGSTON

On board the Confederacy, October 25th, 1779

My dear Mother

I am happy in having it in my power to bid You adieu once more before I lose sight of America. I wrote You a short letter and in great haste from Philadelphia, and sent you what little money I had left by Susan. We parted with the Girls at Chester last Wednesday. The next day we came on board. We have had good weather, but not a breath of fair wind 'till today so that we have been five tedious very tedious days sailing no more than forty miles. We are still in the Delaware and about seventy miles from the capes. At present, appearances are in our favor, and if the wind continues but a day longer where it now is, we shall be at sea to morrow night, and if we elude the vigilance of the British Cruizers, we have every prospect of a quick and safe passage. My next shall be from France when I shall have more to say than I have now, and when you will be more anxious to hear from us, than You are now. You cannot think how very commodiously we are settled in this Ship. Mr. and Mrs Jay have a very convenient and comfortable apartment to themselves, besides the Use of the Cabbin. I have swung my hammock in the cabbin, and notwithstanding the novelty of such a birth, or the unusual Noise of the sailors, I never slept better, or warmer in my life. Mrs. Jay if she writes, will tell you the same of herself. I cannot vouch for this part of her relation, but the effect the water has had on her appetite is too glaring to escape notice. Though few of the passengers are deficient in this point, there are none who do more justice to the good living we have than her. If her present health, and appetite continue the voyage cannot fail of being of infinite service to Mrs. Jay. She has now been five days on board, and has not had a moment's complaint. This leads her to hope that she will escape the Sea-sickness altogether. I am not so sanguine. I have a presentiment I shall be very sick and indeed, strange as you may think it, I wish I may be. Though I may suffer awhile, it will be of service in the end. Sick or well we shall want for nothing on board. We are largely supplyed with stores of every kind. Indeed one of my greatest mortifications, if we come to action, will be to see our Poultry of which we have a large flock, sacrificed to our own safety, as nothing in such a case can prevent their being thrown over board to clear ship as the sailors express it.

We are all very busy in learning french. We have a Law on board, (which is observed as well as Laws in general are) that not a word of english is to be spoken in the Cabbin, so that were you to pay us a visit on board you would not be permitted even to enquire after Mrs. Jay's health without first learning a few french phrases for the purpose. Sally is a very apt Scholar, and if we have a tolerable long passage she will appear at the Court of Versailles free from the embarrassment of those who neither understand or speak the tongue of those about them. Seriously I beleive she will soon speak french, and with fluency. Mr. Gerard is her Preceptor, and here I cannot omit informing you how very fortunate we are in having this Gentleman for a fellow passenger. He has a very strong attachment to Mr. Jay and will not only be of service as a companion on the Passage, but of still more on our arrival in Europe. The task I have allotted to myself during the voyage is the study of the Spanish. This will keep me closely and dully employed. I shall have no assistance from any one, there not being a single spaniard among near four hundred men we have on board. Perhaps the Sea sickness will save me the trouble of looking into any book.

Tell Billy, I have seen nothing wonderful yet, and therefore shall defer writing to him. He may rely on my writing from Europe, and though I will not promise him any entertainment from my Accounts, yet they shall be such as he may depend on. I wish him much happiness, and Success at the Bar. I have a thousand times wished Johny was a midshipman on Board the Frigate. 'Tis a good birth for a young fellow, and a very certain road to honor and preferment. I am sure he would like it, and in a little time be very fond of it. Mr. Clarkson's son is well pleased; he is active, healthy, and in fine heart. He bids fair to command a squadron soon. I will write to Pappa from France or Spain, and if the Confederacy returns to Philadelphia I may have it in my power to send you a few necessaries for the family.

I must again bid you farewell. Though I shall be at a great

distance from America I am in hopes I shall not always be without hearing from it, and from those friends I shall leave behind me; For beleive me when I assure You that one of the greatest pleasures I propose to myself in the long tour I am about to make is that of hearing from you and the family. God bless you all. May every happiness attend you. In a few years I trust we shall all meet again, happier for our separation. In the mean time be assured my dear Mother

Of the best wishes and most affectionate Regard of your dutiful Son,

HARRY BROCKHOLST LIVINGSTON

ALS. MHi: William Livingston Papers. Endorsed.

Sarah Livingston Jay to Susannah French Livingston

On board the Confederacy, 12th–26th December 1779

My dear mamma,

When at Philadelphia I was favored with your affectionate letter. I dared not trust myself to acknowledge it: the voyage I was then so soon to take, and which was to seperate me so long a time from my indulgent parents and other partial friends was a circumstance that engrossed my thoughts more than I chose to confess, and I was aware that to write either to papa or you would be the ready way to reveal a secret I wished to conceal even from myself.

How wise and tender in my dear papa and mamma to recommend their children to the care of that Being whose power is unlimitted and whose goodness and mercy are equal to His power. Nor has the prayers of my kind parents been disregarded: that Providence which they implored has kindly preserved us through uncommon dangers. May we never by our ingratitude forfeit its further protection!

We imbarked at Chester on the 20th of October, but did not lose sight of land 'till the 26th, when we launched out to sea with a brisk gale. The very first evening we were all seized with that most disagreeable sickness peculiar to our situation; my brother, Peter,[1] and myself soon recovered but my dear Mr. Jay suffered exceedingly at least five weeks and was surprisingly reduced; I imagine his health would have been much sooner restored had not our passage been so very unpleasant.

About 4 o'Clock in the morning of the 7th of November we were alarmed by an unusual noise upon deck, and what particularly surprised me, was the lamentations of persons in distress: I called upon the Captain to inform me the cause of this confusion that I imagined to prevail; but my brother desired me to remain perfectly composed, for that he had been upon deck but an half an hour before and left every thing in perfect security.

Perfect security! Vain words! don't you think so mamma? And so indeed they proved. For in that small space of time we had been deprived of nothing less than our bow-sprit, fore-mast, main-mast, and missen-mast; so that we were in an awkward situation rendered still more so by a pretty high south-east wind and a very rough sea that prevailed then; however our misfortunes were only began, the injury received by our rudder, the next morning, served to compleat them as we were ready to conclude. The groans that distressed me were uttered by two men who had suffered from the fall of the masts, one of them was much bruised, the other had his arm and hand broke: the former recovered, but the latter, poor fellow! survived not many days the amputation of his arm. Will it not be painful to my dear mamma to image to herself the situation of her children at that time? Her children did I say? Rather let my benevolent mamma imagine the dangerous situation of more than 300 souls tossed about in the midst of the ocean, in a vessel dismasted and under no command, at a season too that threatned approaching inclemency of weather. And would you for a moment suppose me capable of regretting that I had for a time bid adieu to my native land in order to accompany my beloved friend? Would you have dispaired of ever again embracing your affectionate children? Or would you have again recommended them to Him who appointed to the waters their bounds, Who saith unto the wave thus far shalt thou go. And to the winds, peace, be still? Mamma's known piety and fortitude sufficiently suggest the answer to the two latter queries: and to the former it becomes me to reply. I do, and assure you; that in no period of our distress, though ever so alarming did I once repine, but incited by his amiable example, I gave fear to the winds and chearfully resigned myself to the dispensations of the Almighty.

Your whole family love Mr. Jay, but you are not acquainted with half his worth, nor indeed are any of his friends, for his modesty is equal to his merit. It is the property of a diamond (I've been told) to appear most brilliant in the dark; and surely a good man never shines to greater advantage then in the gloomy hour of adversity; in sceenes of that kind I have lately beheld with pleasure, and even admiration, the firmness and serenity of mind that evidently shone out in the countenance of our invaluable friend. May he long, very long, be preserved a blessing to his connections and a *useful* as well as disinterested friend to his Country; pardon me! mamma, if I appear too prolix in the praises of the person we so highly love and esteem—am I not writing to a partial mother? And is it not a consolation to her, that the guardian of her children is worthy of her confidence? Besides, I've the pleasure to hope that none but friendly eyes will peruse this scrawl and I therefore indulge myself as though I were actually conversing with my dear family friends: I hope every letter I receive from them will be equally free from restraint. After our misfortunes on the 7th and 8th of November (the memorable aera from which we now date all events relative to ourselves) a council of the officers was held to consider where it was most expedient to bend our course and it was unanimously concluded by them that it would be impossible to reach Europe at this season, with a ship in the condition that ours was. They were likewise united in opinion that the southern direction was the only one that offered a prospect of safety, and of the Islands, Martinico was the most eligible, for its commodious harbour and the probability of being supplied with materials to refit: accordingly the first fair wind that offered (which was not 'till near three weeks from the above mentioned Aera) was embraced in pursuance of the advice given by the officers: and after having passed through very blustering, squally latitudes, we are now in smooth seas, having the advantage of trade-winds which blow directly for the Island; nor are we, if the calculations made are just, more than 220 miles distant from the destined port. Thus while our american friends are amusing themselves by a chearful fire-side, are we sitting under an awning, comforting ourselves with the expectation of being soon refreshed by some fine southern fruits. I expect in a few days to write to papa and the girls from Martinico, and if what I hear of crabs, fresh fish, and Oysters be true, I'll make papa's mouth water, and make him wish to forego the pleasure of pruning trees, speechifying Assemblies, and what not for the greater pleasure of messing with us. And now let me recollect—is there nothing that has occurred in the space of seven weeks worth mamma's attention? Why let me see—there's the celebration of Mrs. Gerard's birth-day. When we first came on board, Monsieur Gerard among other subjects mentioned that he hoped for the pleasure of our company at his house the 7th of December, as it was customary for his Lady to entertain her friends upon the aniversary of her birth day. The accidents I've already related account for our not arriving in France. Mr. Jay therefore surprised our Friend by inviting all the officers of the ship and gentlemen who were passengers to breakfast and spend the day with us, mentioning in the cards the occasion. Early in the morning we were amused by a small band of musick, and the discharge of a number of cannon, which led Mr. Gerard to enquire the reason that gave rise to the apparent joy; and when the gentlemen waited upon him to congratulate him upon the occasion, he received them very politely, and waited upon them into the Dining-room (alias Cabbin) where a very genteel breakfast was prepared. The vessel rolls so intollerably, and Mr. C——l and the Colonel who are playing drafts at the same table leave me no chance of writing legibly, so that I must lay aside my pen 'till some quieter opportunity offers. Thank fortune the gentlemen have thought fit to walk out and leave me at leisure to proceed with my narrative, and as to waiting for an easy motion of the ship, I believe it will be needless, for I begin to be of the Carpinter's opinion, that she would hardly lay still again were she put upon the stocks.

So much by way of digression, and now I think we'll return to the gentlemen in the Cabbin, and as they have had quite time enough to finish their breakfast, I'll conduct them up stairs, where the whole deck is covered with an awning for their reception. There they continued to amuse themselves with chess, cards, and drafts; musick still heightning their pleasure, 'till 4 o'Clock, when they were invited to (what in our situation might be called) an elegant dinner: after which a number of pertinent toasts were drank, to each of which was a discharge of cannon. I then withdrew, and the gentlemen had coffee, tea and cakes sent them, and then concluded the evening with dancing. That day happened to be a merry one to the sailors likewise, for crossing the tropick they insisted upon an ancient custom of shaving and ducking every person that had not crossed it before excepting only those who paid their fine. I could not forbear smiling at Peter's fate, who had been diverting himself with observing the operation performed on many of them, 'till they exclaimed at the injustice of exempting him, and insisted upon his being tarred at least, which by the by was their method of shaving. Peter, sobbing, declared that had not his new coat been spoilt, he would not have regretted so much the difficulty of getting rid of the tar. Apropos of Peter, his behaviour throughout this voyage has charmed me; I thought I could trace his grand-father's firmness in the equanimity of the child. May the resemblance be increased and perpetuated in every disposition and action of his life. Writing of one child but reminds me of the other; how I long to see the dear little varlet![2] I could ask a thousand questions about him, but to what purpose? When should I be answered? There was a diffidence in the dear child's disposition when I left him that I hope does not continue to distress him; do, my dear mamma, guard well his tender mind against such impressions, you know that honour and firmness are the parents of many virtues; how many inconveniencies, and even vices are young people frequently led into through a false shame; teach him therefore betimes to say no as well as yes. But to whom am I dictating? Pardon me mamma, I forbear. And may God Almighty bless you and your instruction's. God bless my child!

December 14th

Our calculation nearly expired, and no signs of land, so I'll e'en please myself with continuing my scrawl relying upon your indulgence. Shall I trouble you to assure Mrs. Ogden of my esteem and best wishes for Mrs. Ludlow and herself; you know mamma, since I've been acquainted with that lady, I've ever admired her, and though she is always amiable, yet she never engaged my affection so much, nor in my opinion ever appeared to so great advantage, as in the midst of her sweetly regulated domestic circle. Does Kitty still condescend to visit little P——. If Mr. and Mrs. Wickham are in your neighbourhood, let them know I value their friendship too much ever to forget them. Please to present my compliments to Mr. Courtland's Col. Ogden's, and Doctor Darby's familys.[3]

A land bird! A land bird! Oh! the pleasure of being near land! A pleasure I, more than once since I left Chester, had reason to fear never being sensible of.

Wednesday, 15th December

Early this morning we were awaked by a report that light was discerned a head of the ship, and the master of the vessel, concluding it to be from land as his reckoning was out the preceeding evening, hove the ship too, fearing to run aground; but the Captain arose to make preperations for an action, thinking it equally probable that the light proceeded from a sail: however, when day appeared no sign of sail or any thing else was visible, nor any further indication of land save only a small flock of birds that are known to deposit their eggs on shore.

And now to turn my thoughts again to my American friends. How is Uncle and Aunt Clarkson's family? I long to hear *of* them, for to hear *from* them is more than I can hope. Is cousin Sally married? If she is, congratulate her in my name. I wish her and cousin Peggy happiness equal to their merit. Aunt Van Horne and each of my cousins possess my sincere regard. May happiness attend them![4]

The recollection of a number of my friends press upon my memory for attention due to them, but they are so numerous that it would be imposing on your patience to particularize all whom I esteem; suffice it therefore, to request my dear mamma to remember me to all inquiring friends whom she knows I value.

Brother and sister Jay's[5] affectionate behaviour towards us at Philadelphia, encreased my attachment to them; in which however I was not deficient before. I hope the friendship already subsisting between our two families will not cease to be cultivated by either party. Next spring I think our little master is to pay his grandfather a visit. I had almost indulged a wish to make one of the party. What pleasure should I receive from a meeting with that worthy family!

Martinico, December 26th, 1779

Join with me, my dear mamma and sisters in grateful acknowledgements to that supreme Being whose indulgent care has preserved your friends through every danger, and permitted them to arrive in health in a most delightful Island, furnished with every thing necessary for health and almost every thing that can contribute to pleasure. On the 18th inst. early in the morning I was agreeably surprised to find that we were sailing [close] along the [most] verdant, romantic country I ever beheld. In that instant every disagreeable sensation arising from unpleasing circumstances during our voyage, gave place to the more mild and delightful emotions of gratitude.

At breakfast we were visited by some of the planters who live near the shore, and from them we learnt that Mr. Bingham was still at St. Pierre; when we arrived opposite to that City Mr. Jay wrote him a letter, and my brother waited upon him; upon which Mr. Bingham very politely returned with the Colonel and insisted upon our resideing with him during our stay at Martinique; and never was I more charmed with any thing of the kind than with the polite friendly reception we met with from that gentleman. The two families most dear to me would be delighted with this Island. The neatness that prevails here cannot be exceeded and I frankly confess I never saw it equaled. How mistaken was I as to the character of our allies! The Admiral Le Motte Piquet has granted to Mr. Gerard's request a Frigate to convey us to France, and we shall sail from this place the 28th inst. I regret exceedingly the perpetual hurry I have been involved in by the shortness of our stay in this place, but for nothing more than its preventing me from having the pleasure of writing to more of my friends, and to you, mamma, more explicitely about this Country. It's with pleasure I can inform you that Mr. Jay, Brockholst, and Peter never enjoyed better health than at present. As Peter was supposed to be my son upon my first arrival I had the pleasure of being complimented as the mother of a very lovely Boy; and indeed His engaging behaviour added to other circumstances attach me so much to him, that it would be difficult to convince me that he really was not my own child. The prices of every thing are so immensely high, that I think you will not be displeased if I defer sending to you at present those articles that I know would add to your convenience. Mr. Bingham expects to return to America 5 or 6 weeks hence and has promised to take charge of a few Boxes of sweetmeats to be divided between the two families. If you knew how many hundred times I've been interupted since I began the two last pages you would indeed make many allowances for me.

As I find it is impossible for me to write Mr. Jay, will you be so kind as to send this letter to him after your family have perused it; from his former indulgence, I have reason to expect his future partiallity and though I should dread the eye of an impartial person I fear nothing from that amiable family. When on board the Frigate I hope to pursue the subject; and flatter myself that the variety which has presented itself in the course of 10 days will furnish my friends with more entertainment.

And must I now bid adieu to my best beloved [frien]ds. Think not any more that I have forgotten you. Mamma's minature profile, and Kitty's picture with which she favored me, partake almost every day my most affectionate embraces, and though I've not the same memento to the rest of my friends in both families, yet are their memories impressed in my heart in indeliable characters.

May the Almighty guard, protect and bless, my ever dear, my ever valued friends. Embrace my little blessing. My heart is too sensibly affected to proceed, and to discontinue is like parting a new. Adieu!

SA. JAY

ALS. Endorsed. C in SLJ Lbk.

1 Peter Jay Munro.

2 Peter Augustus Jay remained in the care of his maternal grandparents while his parents were in Europe.

3 Mrs. Ogden is undoubtedly Hannah, the wife of Colonel Matthias Ogden.

Matthias's brother Aaron was referred to after the Revolution as "Colonel," but in 1779 he had only risen to the rank of major. Mrs. Wickham must have been the wife of William Wickham, who, as one of the two surveyors of the New York–New Jersey boundary in 1770, would have become known to JJ. Dr. John Darby was a Parsippany physician. Theodore Thayer, *As We Were: The Story of Old Elizabethtown* (Elizabeth, N.J., 1964), pp. 1, 106, 128, 143, 147; F. W. Ricord and William Nelson, eds., *Documents Relating to the Colonial History of the State of New Jersey* (Newark, 1886), X, 194–96; W. W. Munsell, *History of Morris County, N.J.* (New York, 1882), p. 220.

4 No record has been located of a Sally or Sarah Clarkson. Peggy was SLJ's cousin Ann Margaret Clarkson (1761–84).

5 Frederick Jay and Margaret Barclay Jay.

Sarah Livingston Jay to Peter Jay

Aurora frigate, sailing sweetly before the wind,
January the 9th, 1780

Little did I think when last I parted from my dear papa, that so many months, nay perhaps years would have elapsed before we should again have the pleasure of an interview. But the ways of Providence are mysterious! And though beyond our ken we know it to be an act of wisdom to submit with chearfulness to its dispensations. May you, sir still possess that amiable resignation which has heretofore sustained you under many severe tryals, and I hope we shall again rejoice together.

Our Voyage from America to Martinico was rather an unpleasant one, rendered so by several accidents and the degree of uncertainty naturally attending them; but the pleasure we received there would have amply compensated for the inconveniencies we sustained on our passage, had our own gratification been the sole motive that induced us to leave America. The variety, verdure, and fertility of the Island, afforded me not less pleasure than the hospitality, good breeding and cleanliness of the Inhabitants. The climate was not disagreeable at the time we were there, though we could have dispensed with a few rays of the Sun, had they been disposed to visit you in your retirement. I could not but reflect Sometimes upon the different manner in which my Fish kill friends were solacing themselves from that in which we found relief. On Christmas day I imagined that Peter[1] was calling for still more Wood, adding that the influence of a cheerful fire enlivened the company, and indeed, brother, I am of your opinion, for never at that season did I feel so languid as on the last, though in the midst of an agreeable circle of friends, not that I by any means suppose that more warmth had been requisite to animate my spirits but rather that they languished for want of that charming North West wind that renders a good fire so necessary in our Country.

Mr. Bingham, a young gentleman from Philadelphia, and Agent for Congress at St. Pierre's, favored us with every mark of politeness, and introduced us to many genteel families at here who likewise were very civil. The Viscount Damas[2] was so polite as to review his regiment in compliment to us, for which he chose a lovely piece of ground, Situated in a level Spot, (one of the rarest things to be met with in the Island, or at least near the town) between two rows of trees that were tall and very handsome, and on either hand fields, though somewhat hilly, covered with cane. The regiment made a very good appearance, to which their neat uniforms, their fine musick, and even the beauty of the adjacent country contributed. It was a satisfaction to me that in viewing such fine Troops, I recognized the friends of American Liberty, nor was it without emotion I heard that eight hundred men of that same division had already, since this contest, yielded to the too frequent fate of War. Justly may it be said that

"The paths of glory lead but to the grave."

Having mentioned the cane, perhaps peter may be curious to know the construction of the Mills for making sugar. Had Mr. Jay been sufficietly disengaged from writing to have seen one, he could have given a better description to his brother. I think it very like those we have for cyder, only that the rollers are of iron and the reservoirs for the juice directly under the rollers. The wheel is turned by another wheel, which receives its motion from a stream of water; the juice is conducted from the reservoir, that immediately receives it to a large bason by a gutter, and from thence by the same kind of conveyance into a large boiler, when it has considerably boiled away, it is then put into the next of a smaller size, and again when diminished to a certain quantity put into the third and last, to which they then pay a great attention, throwing it up continually with a large flat shovel to prevent it from burning, and when it attains a consistency the syrup is poured into large earthen pans in the form of sugar loaves with Holes in the bottom which they stop till the sugar begins to chrystalize, then unstopping them, they are set in jars and the syrup that contains no grain drains off, and is what we call molasses.

There is a convent at St. Pierre's, but I had not an opportunity of visiting it as our stay was short. I should regret it but that I expect to have the pleasure of seeing several before I return. There are very few carriages at that place, nor are they requisite for the town and country are so very hilly that it would be impossible to use them. It was at the risque of my neck that I ventured in one to visit a sugar plantation.[3]

We left Martinico on the 28th of December, in the Aurora frigate, commanded by the Marquis de la Flotte, and have been favored with fair winds ever since, so that there is a great probability that we shall reach Toulon sometime next week. The hurry we were in while at Martinico has cautioned me not to defer writing untill we make land again! As Toulon is pretty distant from Paris, I flatter myself with the expectation of a very agreeable ride, and when arrived at our Journey's end, hope for the pleasure of reassuring you of my constant regard. Will You be so obliging as to remember me affectionately to sister Jay, Nancy, Mrs. Munro, and Brother Peter and Sir James. Mrs. Munro may be perfectly easy about her son, he is in good health and fine spirits, and is quite the favorite among the Officers of the Frigate, some of whom he instructs in the English language, and receives lessons in French in return.

I have never known Mr. Jay enjoy his health more perfectly than at present: the rest of our family are likewise very well. Adieu, my dear sir, may tranquil days and peaceful slumbers soon succeed to those stormy and restless ones that unfortunately have disturbed your repose, and may no anxious cares invade your bosom for the safety of your children, in the number of whom its my pride and pleasure that you acknowledge your truly affectionate daughter

SA. JAY

Dft. LbkC with minor variations in JP.

1 Peter Jay.

2 Claude Charles, viscomte de Damas-Marçillac (1731–1800), an infantry brigadier. In 1782 he was made governor of Guadeloupe and in 1783 of Martinique as well.

3 This paragraph is much reduced in the LbkC.

Catharine W. Livingston to Sarah Livingston Jay

Philadelphia, 13 February 1780

Had I wrote a few days ago to my dear Friends I should have wrote in better spirits than at present. Congress having yesterday received Mr. Jays letter dated St. Pierres Martinique December 20th, the contents of which have afflicted me exceedingly.[1] Your situation in and after the Storm must have been truly distressing, and exposed you more to the dangers of another and to the Enemy. Very very anxious am I for the arrivel of those letters Mr. Jay promises to send by another opportunity. I hope the Vessel is not taken, many are apprehensive she is. How my dearsweet Sister was you supported in the hours of tryal and danger; the appearance of death in so terrible a manner must have awaken every fear. You have indeed seen the wonders of the deep, and experienced in a remarkable manner the goodness and mercy of an indulgent providence. Your Friends have all reason to bless and thank God for his interposition in your favor, and it ought to console and encourage us to trust in the Author of your *Salvation—For he spake and it was done. he commanded and it stood fast.*

I wrote this morning to Pappa, Mamma, and Mr. Jay. Col. Mitchel sends by express, as I wish them to be received before any reports reach them. Judge my dear Sister of my cruel disappointment when I inform you that a Gentleman of my acquaintance in his great zeal assured me there was good news, the Confederacy had arrived and Congress had a letter from Mr. Jay. It was just the time Mr. Morris had given me reason to expect intelligence. The sudden transition of my spirits together with your distresses, that my feelings led me to go over in imagination with you; and an indisposition at the time was indeed a severe tax on my sensibilities. In the mercies you have received and the hope that you are now beyond the dangers of that Element, is my releif. For a long time my friends had flattered me that you had had propiticious winds and favorable gales, and that you was in France the 4 of December (the night of which Miss West was married)[2] and we thought your situation enviable from the temperance of your Climate, whilst we were exposed to great severities from the Frigidness of ours. Our Winter set in earlier and with more severity than is remembered by the Oldest liver among us. The year thirty five, and forty, is agreed from circumstances not [to] be compared to this; in neither of those severe Seasons was the Chesepeak at twenty Miles below Anopolis a firm bridge as is and has been a long time the case. In Virginia it has impeded all Trade, several of there vessels have been cut to peices and sunk by the ice. The Merchants here think many of there Vessels that they expected in have perished on our coast, the last that got in was the Jay; and that was in November,[3] and she was much injured by the Ice and it was expected for several days that she and her cargo would be lost.

To the Eastward the Snow impeded all traveling in the State of New York—it cut of[f] Communication from Neighbour to Neighbour. The last accounts from Fish Kill it was four feet deep on a level. Numbers of Families in this City have suffered from its severity altho many among them made great exertions for their releif. In New York the want of fuel was never known like it, they cut down every stick of timber on Mr. Byards[4] place and would not permit me to keep any tho he offered to buy it. Several gentleman went upon long Island and felled the trees, and after bringing it to town with their own horses it was seized for the Kings Troops; its reported of two families that the want of wood obliged them to lay a bed a week for the [*sic*]. Through Mr. Elliots[5] interposition Uncle Clarkson has been paid six hundred pounds for his house in Smith Street.[6] I have not heard from his nor Aunt Van Hornes family this Winter.

Mrs. Livingston's situation becomes her exceedingly. She has been much admired this Winter. Lady Kitty does not look so well in the same way; she and Mr. Duer left Town last week. The Chanciller and his Lady return this week, Mr. and Mrs. Morris dont consent to my going till Spring, and as Mamma and Susan wished it, I complied.[7]

You shall hear from me by every opportunity; at least I will write by every one. This Letter is going to New London. I shall write tomorrow by a Vessel that is to sail from Boston—till then I bid you adieu

AL.

1 JJ's letter of 20 Dec. 1779 is in *RDC*, III, 432–33.

2 Mary West (d. 1820), the daughter of William West of Philadelphia, married David Hayfield Conyngham. "Reminiscences of David Hayfield Conyngham," Wyoming Historical and Geological Society, *Proceedings and Collections*, VIII, 195.

3 The *Jay* was a Pennsylvania ship of eighteen guns commanded by Harman Courter. Three other vessels, in the Continental service, were given the same name and saw service in the Revolution. Library of Congress, *Naval Records of the American Revolution* (Washington, D.C., 1906), pp. 357–58.

4 William Bayard (1729–1804), prominent New York merchant, served in the provincial legislature on its Committee of Correspondence and was originally sympathetic to the patriot cause. However, when the Revolution broke out, he became a firm Loyalist. Sabine, *Biographical Sketches*, I, 217.

5 Andrew Elliot served as the Crown's Collector of Customs in New York before and during the Revolution. Sabine, *Biographical Sketches*, I, 404.

6 Smith Street was the lower half of what is now William Street. Noah Webster, ed., *The New York Directory for 1786* (New York, 1889), frontispiece map.

7 Mary Stevens Livingston and "Lady" Catherine Alexander Duer were both expecting their first child during the winter of 1779–80. The Robert Morrises, close friends of Catharine Livingston, were frequently her hosts in Philadelphia.

Sarah Livingston Jay to Catharine W. and Susannah Livingston

Cadiz, 4th March 1780

But one Vessel has left this port for America since our arrival, and the Captain of that has letters from me for my father, Mr. Jay and Hannah Benjamin, and should likewise have written to my dear Sisters had not extreme indisposition prevented me.[1]

Two or three days before we made the Bay of Cadiz, we were chased by an English frigate and while a number of sailors were preparing the cabbin, for the expected engagement, I went upon deck and staid there till the chase was over, when it was already ten o'clock, and I had caught a severe cold, the effects of which did not leave me untill five weeks after: I am now, thank God! perfectly recovered but have by my confinement been prevented from Seeing any thing that can be entertaining to you.

We are now very agreeably accommodated, and I do assure you the view from my window reminds me of that dear spot that gave me birth.

There is an Irish brigade stationed in this City, officered by gentlemen who do honor to humanity, from whom we have received every mark of attention. Think how pleasing to me are the praises bestowed upon my worthy Countrymen by those as well as other gentlemen. Do you think, girls, that distance diminishes my affection for Americans, or my concern for their interest? Oh! no; it encreases my attachment even to enthusiasm. Where is the country (Switzerland excepted) where Justice is so impartially administered, industry encouraged, health and Smiling plenty so bounteous to all as in our much favored Country? And are not those blessings each of them resulting from, or matured by freedom, worth contending for? But whither, my pen, are you hurrying me? What have I to do with politicks? Am I not myself a woman, and writing to Ladies? Come then, ye fashions to my assistance! Alas! Sisters, it mortifies me exceedingly that the vessel which Sails to morrow is bound for Boston, and will therefore prevent me from sending you a specimen of them. The prevailing mode, however, is here the Same as it was in America last winter, with only a trifling variation. Every thing bears a most extravagant price here; only think of my being asked 60 Dollars for a table cloth only large enough to cover one table, and a dozen napkins, and every thing in proportion.

If, my dear sisters, you have any compassion for me, do let me hear from you soon and direct to me at Madrid, for next week we begin our Journey thither. This week I shall pay visits, and shall see all the rarer shows that this City affords, and then girls, prepare yourselves for a folio. Give my love to Mamma, and tell her that I often wish for her own Satisfaction She could now and then by looking into her mirrour behold our little circle, innocently happy, and most frequently conversing of our friends on the other Side the Atlantic. Mama must write me, indeed she must, and tell me that she confides in that Providence who has never ceased to bless me. My little lovely Son must not believe those insinuations which his uncle has interspersed in his letter to his Mama.[2] Kiss the dear little fellow for me, I know he deserves it, for I am Sure he is a good boy. Remember me to your neighbours, Mr. Caldwell's family and Mr. Randal's family.[3] Give my love to Papa, and request the favor of a letter for me from him. Tell William he has described the hosts of fleas in such terrific colours, that he has awakened my apprehensions at the thought of encountering them, more than when in hourly expectation of a naval engagement.[4]

Mr. Jay joins with me in love and best wishes to Papa, Mama, and the rest of the family—Adieu. God bless you all. When you write, be very particular, for you know how dear your welfare is to

Your affectionate Sister

SA. JAY

LbkC.

1 A LbkC of SLJ's letter to William Livingston, n.d. Jan. 1780 is in JP; letter to Hannah Benjamin has not been located.

2 SLJ was pregnant at that time. Brockholst Livingston wrote their mother on 20 Feb. 1780: "His [Peter Augustus Jay] Grand Mama may also tell him, if she does not think the news will be too disagreeable to him, that his Uncle believes and not without Reason, that his little nose will be disjointed in less than Nine months time." ALS in MHi: Wm. Livingston Papers.

3 The Reverend James Caldwell (1734–81), pastor of the Presbyterian church in Elizabethtown, N.J. He served as a chaplain in a New Jersey battalion during the Revolution. William B. Sprague, *Annals of the American Pulpit,* III, 222–28.

4 Brockholst Livingston gave this firsthand comment on Iberian insect life in a letter to his mother, 20 Feb. 1780: "Though we are told by every one of the millions of fleas, and other vermin we shall meet with, not one of them has yet told us of any remedy against their attacks—which from the specimen we have of those here are much to be dreaded. . . . the fleas are here so numerous, that I have frequently by walking once, or twice across my Chamber seen above six or seven at a time on my stockings, and in bed it is not uncommon to feel them at a dozen different places at once."

Sarah Livingston Jay to Susannah French Livingston

Madrid, 13 May 1780

Here my dear Mamma are we at last arrived after an absense of 6 months from our native country. The goodness of Providence has been exemplifyed to us in so many instances that I can neither recount them, nor without ingratitude pass it over in silence.

I think I promised William an account of our journey hither and therefore will not demand your attention to any circumstances that occured in our route, but rather proceed to tell you that I am pleased with Madrid, and expect that my satisfaction will be increased when I have acquired the language of the Country. As yet I've made but five acquaintances among the ladies and the chief amusement I have hitherto taken has been in the riding way.

Mr. Jay is at present at Aranjuez, where his Majesty has a very beautiful seat and which is at present the residence of the Court.[1] It is 7 leagues from this City and the road that leads to it is the finest I have ever seen, adorned on either side with handsome trees, that owe their flourishing state to the unremitted attention of persons appointed to water them, which they effect with more ease by means of small canalls that conveys the water from one tree to another. What a defect in this climate is the long droughts that prevail throughout this country and renders the produce of the finest soil extremely precarious. What do you think mamma of being nine months successively without any rain? We are not yet in the middle of may, and the fields already begin to fade and change their verdant appearance for one of an yellower hue.

The King is much fonder of his country palaces than being in Madrid, and therefore spends so little time here, that in the whole year it does not amount to more than 30 or 40 days. This may be very agreeable to his Majesty, but it is both inconvenient and expensive to the foreign Ambassadors and Ministers who are obliged to follow the Court; and I confess mortifying to me to part so frequently with Mr. Jay, whom Congress has scarecely ennabled to maintain a family in one place, much less to remove with him to half a dozen different ones in this expensive Country.

We have been so fortunate as to hire a very convenient house; which has the advantage of a fountain in the yard, a circumstance that but few of the inhabitants can boast as they are supplied with all the water they use from publick fountains. It has given me great concern that it has not been in my power to send you those articles that I know would be useful to yourself and family. My sisters have been disappointed and I fear have blamed me, but indeed they would not if they knew how we have been circumstanced.

Mr. Jay intends upon his return from Aranjuez to write to a gentleman in Holland[2] (from whom he has received offers of service) requesting him to send some things for both families to St. Eustatia with orders to be re-shiped on board an American vessel for Philadelphia, with proper directions.

I find by an american paper that the last winter has been extremely severe there. How I pity our soldiers for the sufferings they so much have sustained, and yet that pity is mingled with admiration of the magnanimity with which they supported every difficulty. The americans are highly esteemed by the Europeans, and in my opinion they greatly merit. May peace and tranquility soon succeed those scenes of war and toil that at present occupy my country-men and may they long enjoy the liberty for which they have so nobly struggled.

You can have no idea how anxious I am to hear from you; unless the same fatality that used to attend the letters intended for me, now follows mine, yourself and the rest of the family must have received several from me; but it has not been my good fortune to hear any thing directly or indirectly relative to persons so deservedly dear to me as are those that compose the family at Persipiney and Fishkill.

Pray mamma have you had any more appearances of the scurvy? If you have, let me entreat you to try the following prescription, which I was favored with by a very skilful Physician in this City.

To a pint of old madeira wine, add nine spoonsful of lemon juice and 5 spoonsful of loaf sugar, mixing them together in a bottle; provided you drink that quantity every day it is immaterial whether it is at meal-times or any other part of the day. The Doctor tells me, he never knew the most inveterate scurvy resist this remedy 8 days.

It is more than a year since I left mamma and my little son. When shall I have the pleasure to re-embrace them! Tell me my dear mamma will my beloved child answer the fond expectations of his partial mother? Is he amiable? Is he healthy? Does he still cultivate the acquaintance that had commenced between his little neighbors and himself while I had the pleasure of residing among you. There is no reflection from which I derive more satisfaction than the certainty I have of his imbibing with his earliest acquirements that probity and generosity that reigns throughout the family that has kindly taken charge of him. In short if in his mind and actions he as much resembles his father as he did in his Countenance when last I saw him I ask no more for him of heaven.

Please to remember me affectionately to Papa. I have ventured on a subject that unfits me for writing more at present; but to-morrow I'll resume my pen and devote an hour or two to my Sisters and William. If Jack has not assumed the government of Royal-town I presume he cannot be so much occupyed, but that I may expect the honor of a few lines from him.[3]

Adieu my dear mamma. May the great protector of virtue be ever near you! And may he inspire with goodness like you own

Yours etc.

LbkC in SLJ's hand. LbkC also in JP.

1 The Spanish court rotated among Madrid, the Pardo, Aranjuez, St. Ildefonso, and the Escorial. See JJ to Robert R. Livingston, 23 May 1780, n.3.

2 Jean de Neufville to JJ, 6 April 1780, ALS in JP; LbkCs in DNA: PCC, 110, I and CSmH: JJLbk; printed in *RDC*, III, 597.

3 SLJ's younger brother, John Lawrence Livingston.

Sarah Livingston Jay to Catharine W. Livingston

[Madrid], May 14th, 1780

If my dear sister could imagine how happy the receipt of her letter (of no date either of time or place)[1] has made me, the pleasure she would enjoy from that consideration would amply compensate for the favor she has bestowed; from some circumstances in your letter I have discovered that you was at Philadelphia and that the time you wrote must have been about the beginning of January. The variety of emotions that possessed my breast upon reading the first letter from America agitated me so much as to cause a slight fever; Joy to find that my dearest and most intimate friends were still happy and sympathy for the misfortunes that had fallen to the lot of others for some time divided my attention. I had been previously informed by a Pennsylvania Gazette that our favorite friend, Mrs. Peca, was no more. Ah! Kitty too lovely a flower to droop so soon! And what am I? Through what variety of dangers has providence preserved me! And shall not, ought not gratitude to be the prevailing passion of my mind? You distress me by your account of Walter Livingston's indisposition, he is too worthy a man to be dispensed with yet by his connections.[2]

Mr. Hews possessed my esteem; and it was not without regret that I perceived he had already paid the tribute which nature has imposed on all her children.[3] What ails the *insatiate archer*, that with malicious joy he is incessantly depriving my beloved country of many of its valuable ornaments. What additional pleasure must you have received from the company of Mrs. Livingston and Lady Kitty; thank them for their remembrance of me, and assure them of my sincere attachment to them. Though you know my great regard for Mrs. Morris you've not had the politeness to make her the subject of great part of your letter, but instead of chiding you, I'll make my complaint to her and if I can prevail upon Mrs. Morris to gratify me with her own pen, you'll acknowledge that what I lose by your silence is repaid by her generosity. And now I suppose your Ladyship is impatient for a word of Madrid; and a word may very well suffice, for as yet I know very little of it. At present there is not any public amusements; even bull fighting, the darling spectacle of the spaniards,[4] is suspended by an order from the King, who has substituted in its place directions for fasting as a means of deprecating the calamity that is feared from a drought.

This City has the advantage of very beautiful walks and publick gardens to which all the company of the place resort. The Court is now at Aranjuez, but it will be here a few weeks in the next month and then they remove to another seat of his Majesty's which is 14 leagues distant from hence. Please to give my Compliments to Don Juan, tell him his son is well, and that its my opinion that his expectations however flattering will not be disappointed in him. The young gentleman wishes much to visit America and to see his father.

Mr. Penn is returned to Philadelphia you say,[5] do pray assure him of my best wishes, and request the favor of him to transmit to me an account of what is transacting in your Quarter of the Globe. I am not a very punctual correspondent but Mr. Penn is disinterested and takes pleasure in pleasing. The warmth of the weather already makes me very indolent, what effect I may expect from it when the season is more advanced I know not; but if what I hear of this place be true, I think persons who set out from hence on their Journey to the other world in the summer might well be excused scorching in purgatory. I did not till this moment recollect that before you receive this you will most probably have left Philadelphia. Where-ever it finds you dispose of my respects, for I am sure that those whom Kitty regard are intitled to my esteem. If you receive this letter at Persipiney or Fishkill, assure the family we are all well. Adieu my dear sister; believe me to be most affectionately yours.

P.S. As I know not by what conveyance this letter will be sent it would not be prudent to venture too many articles, lest as your letters have miscarried the fate of this may be similar. I have sent through Madrid to try to get some black silk Handkerchiefs for Mamma, sister Nancy and Hannah but as those that were brought me were intollerably slight and winter at a distance I have deferred purchasing any at present and have only put up a Gauze handkerchief and pair of silk stockings for Susan and yourself, a Dozen pieces of tape and 5 Ounces of sewing silk for Mamma and sister Nancy and 2 Yards of Fustian for my little master and West and Small-Close. There is not any thing here of the first quality; everything is slight, tawdry and high priced.

Dft. LbkC with minor variations also in JP.

[1] Catharine W. Livingston's letter, undated but written c. 26 Dec. 1779, in JP.

[2] Catharine W. Livingston wrote SLJ on 26 December of the illness of Anne Harrison (Mrs. William) Paca, who "has been confined ever since you left us. . . . I pronounce her in a similar situation to my deceased friend Mrs. Lawrence and could not help cursing the worm that was gnawing the roots of so fair a flower." Of their cousin Walter Livingston she wrote: "Walter and Mrs. Livingston are gone on to the Southard, he is in search of health which the keen northern climate denies him, death is legible in all his features and he must shortly be a candidate for another world."

[3] Catharine also informed SLJ of the death on 10 November of Joseph Hewes (1730–79), North Carolina delegate to Congress, lamenting that "he had Poor Man amassed a great fortune in the Southern clime, but paid the price of his health and life without any enjoyment of it."

[4] For SLJ's brother's view of the sport, see Henry Brockholst Livingston to William Livingston, Madrid, 12 July 1780, *Magazine of American History* (1879), III, part 2, p. 512. Livingston relates a *torrida,* which he attended the previous day with JJ, and characterizes it as "inhuman." After describing how the horses were torn to pieces by the bulls and the bulls themselves tormented, he adds this comment: 'What surprised me most was the pleasure the Spanish Ladies received from the death of the poor animals."

[5] John Penn of North Carolina.

To Peter Jay

Madrid, 23 May 1780

Dear Sir

Various have been the Seenes thro which I have passed since <we parted> last we bid each other Farewel. Some of them have been dangerous, and many of them disagreable. Providence has however been pleased to bring me safe thro them all to the Place of my Destination, and I hope will restore me to my Country and friends as soon as the Business committed to me shall be compleated. Then I shall have the Pleasure of entertaining you with the Recital of many interesting matters which the Risque to which all my Letters <are in these times> exposed forbids me to commit to Paper. I will nevertheless give you some little account of our Journey from Cadiz to Madrid, because as the manner of travelling here differs entirely from that of our Country it may afford you some Amusement.

The Distance is between three and four hundred English Miles. We were told at Cadiz that it would be necessary to take with us beds, Hams, Tea, Sugar, Chocolate and other Articles of Provision as well as Kitchen utensils for dressing them, for that we should seldom find either on the Road. We were further <advised to hire a Carri> informed that these Journeys were usually performed in Carriages resembling a Coach and drawn by six mules the present hire of which was from a hundred and thirty to a hundred and fifty Dollars and that they would carry near a thousand weight of Baggage.

We accordingly <provided ourselves> made the necessary Provision for eating and sleeping comfortably by the way and set out the Day of March last. We crossed the Bay to Port St. <Mary>[1] in very pleasant weather, and a handsome Boat which the Brother of the Minister of Indes[2] was so kind as to lend us. <On our arrival at Port St. Mary we found> We staid a night at that place waiting for our Carriage, and were very hospitably entertained by Count Oreilly —the same who established the Spanish Government at New Orleans at the Conclusion of the last war. He is a Man of excellent abilities and great knowledge of men as well as things. He has risen <from an Ensign> to be Inspector and Lt. General of the armies of Spain, into which he has introduced a Degree of Discipline to which they had long been Strangers, and Captain Gen. of the Province of Andalusia etc.

The next Day we set out for Madrid. There are some peculiarities in these Carriages. The hind wheels are very high and heavy. The fore wheels are low and are made to play under the Carriage so that they turn very short. The Nails that fix the Tire have Heads as large almost as half a middle sized apple. They are driven thro the Fellow, and clinch. Over each axle Tree is Room for two large Trunks or Chests and Beds upon them. Under the Frame which supports the Trunks behind, there is a Netting of Rope capable of containing a large Hamper <of Provisions> and under the Floor of the Carriage there is a Place of about seven or Eight Inches Deep the whole Length and Width of the Floor in which many things may be stowed as well as under the Seats and some other lesser nettings about the Coach.

The hindermost mules were harnessed to a Bar run across by the Foot of the Pole and secured by Irons from each End to the fore axeltree, but the Traces of each of the other four were all laid in a Notch made in the hinder Part of the Pole and had no sort of Connection with each other. Instead of Collars they had Haims constructed with a Groove that admitted a Piece of wood exactly like our Hog Yokes strongly fastened in the Crotch by an Iron spike or Rivot that passed through it. The Ends of the Trace were tied <to a Hole> near the Points of this Yoke, which was run into the groove whenever the Mules were put to the Carriage and taken out again as often as they were turned into the Stable. As to the Harness they never were taken from the mules during the whole Journey, <and> each of their Necks was ornamented with six or Eight little Bells and made no little noise. A Driver setting over the foreaxle tree guided the two hindermost Mules with a pair of leading Lines. The other four went as they pleased in fair Roads, but in common a Man walked or ran by their Sides to take the foremost by the Head and guide them in Places where they could not safely be left to their own Discretion.

These Animals are fed entirely on cut Straw and Barley, <They make little or no Hay> and I am told are constantly going. We travelled at the Rate of between twenty and thirty Miles a Day and the same mules brought us to Madrid that we set out with from Cadiz, at which they had arrived from Madrid only a Day before we left it. We stopped but once in the Course of the Day. At the End of the Journey they appeared in as much flesh and Spirits as when we set out. The manner of driving them is in my opinion greatly to their Disadvantage, very fast up and down Hill, and slow on plain Ground. I had no Idea of there being animals of this Kind in the World so fine. I have seen some near sixteen Hands high. In common they are from 14 to 15, a great many 14 1/2, very active and well limbed. I am convinced that they are stronger as well as more durable than Horses tho <far from being> not so handsome. One Reason perhaps why the Mules of this Country <are finer than> exceed those of others is that the Generally of their Horses are better. The Andalusian Horses of which you have often heard are noble animals, handsome, sprightly, and well tempered. Many of them are rather too small and delicate, but it is not uncommon to meet with them <above fifteen Hand> strong and full sized. They are formed much like English Horses, and tho I have scarce ever seen any of the latter with so fine an air as many of the former, yet I have met with none of the Spanish so perfectly well made as some of those from England I have seen. They cannot be exported without special Licence from the King.

The asses are of two kinds very large and very small, they being of <different> distinct Breeds, as much so as our common Horses and Poneys. The little asses are by far the more common, because they live with less than the others, and are the chief Porters of this Country, Carts and waggons being very little used. The large ass is <a> very ugly <animal>—they call them fine, I suppose when compared with those of other Countries. I have seen none yet that exceeded fourteen Hands and I think them rather heavy limbed. <They certainly have a great deal of Bone.> It is more than probable that when I return I shall bring a couple of them with me. I am satisfied that for Labor two very good mules are at the least worth three very good Horses.

The Poradas or Inns were more tolerable then they had been represented to us. Many of them had very good Rooms, but swarming with Fleas and Buggs. The mules were generally lodged under the same Roof and my Bed Room has frequently been divided from them by only a common Partition. The Innkeepers give themselves little Trouble about their Guests further than to exact as much from them as possible. I found no Reason or Justice among them. They furnish scarce anything except food for the Mules and House Room for the Passengers, I may indeed add such Beds as nothing but necessity would induce one to use. Thoroughly Dirty. For all these they charge extravagently, and what you will hardly belief they have the Impudence to charge <you> for what they call the noise of the House, and this seldom costs us less at each Porada than from three to four Dollars. At one Tavern, which it seems keeps something to eat, we arrived and dined late, and excepting the Colonel, went to Bed without Supper. We took Breakfast in the Morning. Our Servants, 4 in number, except a little Bread and Milk, eat of the Provisions they brought. We all slept in our own Beds. When the Reckoning was called it amounted to 477 Reals—that is £9-10-9 York Money. They charged us for 14 Beds tho our Number, including Servants, amounted only to 8. (for as to the muleteers, we had nothing to do with them or their mules). On observing this to them we were told that there were many Beds in the Rooms in which we had slept and in other communicating with them, and that <it was our own fault we didn't use them> we might have used them all if we pleased. We remarked that it was impossible for Eight persons to use fourteen Beds; they replied that was not their Fault. There was no Remedy and

I paid it after taking an account of the particulars with a Receipt at the Foot of it which I Keep as a Curiosity.

I am told that these Impositions arise from this Circumstance: the Houses in which these Poradas are kept generally belong to <some> Great Men, who for Rent and License to keep Tavern demand from the poor wretches much more than they can honestly get by that Business and thence they are driven to make up the Deficiency by these inquitous Practices. The Landlords know this and to enjoy these high Rents support their Tenants against Travellers, and take Care that the latters be Loser by all Disputes with Innkeepers. Besides as Travellers cannot remain long enough at one Place to prosecute and abide the Event of such Litigations they generally put up with the first Loss.

My next will probably contain a Continuation of this Account which I hope will be confined to the Family.

On the Subject of politics I make it a Rule to write to none but Congress. We have no News except that the Dutch are grumbling and have half a mind to make War with England. I would send you News Papers if I had any besides Spanish, but as you dont understand that Language they would be useless.

My Brothers must consider this Letter as an apology for none to them. I have not at present Time to write to each of them separately. We are well. Peter had had the Fever and Ague but is recovered. He behaves well, but I find it difficult to make him apply.

I have ordered several little Articles for Family use. They will I hope arrive before cold weather. Dont however depend on them, for they may be taken.

Our Compliments to Dr. and Mrs. V. Wyck. Our Love to all the family.

I am Dear Sir Your Dutiful and Affectionate Son

P.S.

I bought a very fine negroe Boy of 15 years old at Martinico,[3] from whence as well as from Cadiz, I wrote you several Letters. No Letters from the Family since I left Philadelphia.

Dft.

1 Puerto de Santa Maria.

2 Matíias de Gálvez (1717–84), Commandant of the Bay, was the brother of José de Gálvez and the father of Bernardo de Gálvez, acting governor of Louisiana. *Diccionario de Historia de España* (Madrid, 1968), II, 160–61.

3 Benoit, the slave purchased in Martinique, remained a part of the Jay household during their entire stay in Europe. In March 1784 JJ executed an instrument of manumission to be effective three years later. *WJ*, I, 230.

To William Livingston

Madrid, 14 July 1780

Dear Sir

I give you Joy—there is a little Stranger here, who I hope will one Day have the Pleasure of calling you Grandfather. On the 9th Instant Sally was delivered of a Daughter as like her Brother as two Children can be. The Mother is in a fair Way and the Child thrives finely. It has as yet no Name nor am I certain what it will be. The old Goody has a great Mind to save it from *Limbo* (a Spanish Name for a Dark Receptacle for the Souls of Infants who die unbaptized). About Eight Days ago she presented Mrs. Jay with the Pictures of ——[1] who I presume have succeeded the ancient Goddesses in presiding over Births. If these Saints had any thing to do with it we are much obliged to them, for she had a fine time of it.

When the Child was born she proposed, as being customary here, to give it the Name of the Saint of that Day, for they are so happy as to have at least one Saint for every Day in the Year. But as the Saints are at War with us Heretics we shall name it after some Sinner that will probably have more affection for it. Besides on looking over the Almanack I found that the 9th July was the Day of St. Cirilo who was a pope, and as neither that Name or office except in the Case of pope Joan ever appertained to a Female I did not see how the old Ladys Advice could be followed in this Instance. I was nevertheless mistaken in supposing this Difficulty insuperable for in similar Cases it seems the Name of *Papa* which is Spanish for pope is taken, as being sufficently feminine for the most delicate Virgins.[2] However as the popes are as clever as the old Norman Lawyers were in drawing extensive Conclusions from weak premisses, and might possibly from such a Circumstance claim some Right to my little Girl, whom I wish not to embarrass with any Disputes with the See of Rome, I think it will be most prudent to let her take her Chance under the Name of Susanna who was a good Sort of a Woman and nobly resisted the lascivious Attacks of two Inquisitor Generals, whom the Latin Bible have in Compliment I suppose to the Presbyterians stiled *Presbyters*.

I am Dear Sir with sincere Regard Your most obedient Servant

P.S. Tell Deacon Ogden if you please that I have not forgot the promise I made <him> at Trenton to visit him on my Return to

Fish Kill.[3] We spent an agreable Evening together and I was much pleased with him.

Dft.

[1] Left blank in the ms.

[2] The reference is probably to St. Cyril, whose saint's day was celebrated on 7 July.

[3] Probably Robert Ogden, ruling elder of the Elizabethtown Presbyterian Church. Theodore Thayer, *As We Were: The Story of Old Elizabethtown* (Elizabeth, N.J., 1964), p. 94.

Sarah Livingston Jay to Susannah Livingston

Madrid, August 28th 1780

Your letter of the 29th of March I received this morning: and though I have just finished writing to Mama, and have wrote to Mr. Jay by the Servant who brought me the American pacquet, yet I cannot defer my thanks to my ever dear Sister.[1] Were words adequate to the emotions of my heart upon the receipt of your and Kitty's affectionate letters, I should spare no trouble to collect them, as I sincerely wish you to know what pleasure it is in your power to give me: you would not then require any other inducement to repeat the obligation, for to make another happy, or to be happy yourself my dear Sister knows no distinction. We have been fortunate in the arrival of seven or eight of Kitty's letters, though indeed the first has been last and the last first. I don't think any of our family have received three letters from America except those from our Sister.

I wish the letter (or rather pamphlet) I wrote to Mama from the Confederacy[2] as well as those since written may have come safe to hand, not from any value they possess, but merely to convince her there never was a time since our separation that she was absent from my mind.

I feel more for what my friends have suffered for me than ever I did for myself. It's true we have been in imminent dangers, and to be candid I did once think I never should have seen relations, friends, or country more, but to confess the whole truth (as if inspired by your example the preceding winter) I determined with Cornelia to fall with decency, or rather with submission to acquiesce in the dispensations of providence; our resignation was accepted and providence was pleased kindly to deliver us from every real and apprehended danger and conducted us in safety to Martinique, where we were much refreshed and hospitably entertained. Mr. Bingham's politeness deserves the warmest acknowledgments. Susan, how agreeable nay absolutely delightful to meet in a foreign climate a person whose native soil is that of one's own country!

The generous wishes of our friends for a safe passage from Martinique were not without effect. It was more than safe it was pleasant: the Marquis Le Flotte who commanded the Frigate we sailed in, is quite a gentleman and his whole suite of Officers well-bred men. We had very brisk gales all the way, as you may imagine by our performing a voyage of four thousand miles (increased to that length by the circuitous course we were obliged take to avoid encounters with our British friends) in twenty four days.

In one of my letters to Papa I have assigned the reasons that induced us to make the Port of Cadiz.[3] While we continued there I was constantly confined by indisposition, arising from two circumstances, one of them was the length of time we had been at sea and the other I leave you to conjecture.

Immediately after our arrival, Mr. Carmichael set out for Madrid with dispatches from Mr. Jay for that Court, and we remained at Cadiz until Mr. Jay received permission to proceed on his journey. How to give you a just idea of the inconveniences that occur in travelling through this country is somewhat puzzling, as our country is exempt from the like circumstances.

From Cadiz we went to Port St. Mary by water in a very handsome Barge, belonging to Mr. Galvez Commandant of the Bay, and brother to the Minister for Indian affairs.[4] It was ornamented by a crimson damask canopy handsomly fringed and the benches covered with cushions of the same, the rowers were 16 or 20 in number, in a uniform that was after a fanciful taste, and not unpleasing. The day was perfectly serene, and vastly different was the appearance of the sea from what I had lately beheld it! The regularity of the oars, the musick, the serenity of the weather, the mildness of the sea, and the beautiful prospect presented from the Bay conspired to render our passage extremely agreeable. Upon our arrival at the Port we found General Oreily's coach had been some time in readiness for us, and we were immediately conducted to his house, where we were received with great politeness by the Count and Countess,[5] and were introduced to a large circle of their acquaintances who had been invited in compliment to us. Port St. Mary is a pretty Town, greatly improved and much ornamented since Count O'Reily has made his residence there: and it was not without great regret that we left it the next day to pursue our journey.

Although we had been apprised of many inconveniences to be

expected in our route, my surprise was not less than if silence had been observed upon that subject, so greatly did the awkwardness and filth of every thing exceed description: the two carriages in which we were to travel were the first outre [*sic*] figures that caught my attention; they have the impudence to call them coaches, it's true they are made of wood and have four wheels, but there the resemblance ceases; and for a passage for ourselves and servants in two of these pretty vehicles we were obliged to pay seventy six doubloons, though the distance is short of three hundred miles. The coachmen do not differ less from the human species than the carriages they drive differ from those of other countries: in short drivers, mules, and carriages are admirably suited to each other, and not to be equaled elsewhere.

We had in consequence of the advice of some gentlemen provided every thing we thought would be necessary upon the road; but the very first evening we found that a broom was absolutely essential; was ever a broom deemed a part of travelling equipage before! With some little difficulty the servants purchased one in the village, and while we waited in the Court-yard, Abby and an irish Woman I brought with me from Cadiz cleared the room of some half dozen filthy beds and several loads of dirt in which were contained not that 2 or 3000 fleas, lice, buggs etc. if we may form any judgment by what still remained. We then had our catalonian bed opened which is the most complete of the kind I've seen: having in one trunk, bed, bedstead, musketto net etc. and indeed I would advise all persons who travel through this country by all means to provide something of this kind, for by that we were enabled to get some sound repose in spite of the many preventives that every where surrounded us; for the want of every thing convenient in our lodging place and the super-abundance of every thing we did not want was far from being the whole amount of the inconveniences that fell to our share. The adjoining apartment to ours was allotted to our Mules, and indeed they would have disturbed us less than any of the guests, had they been freed from the bells that the vanity of their drivers had encumbered them with, but unluckily for us they slept not much and we had the mortification of being serenaded with the tinkling.

After leaving Jeres we travelled on in the jog-trot way till we arrived at Cordova an ancient city, of which we had a most beautiful view from a height about a league this side of it: indeed I never saw any thing more enchanting than that prospect; its true it had an Advantage from the very time that we gained the Ascent, it being just before sunset, and then you know the shades by being lengthned vary the scene prettily; nothing can be imagined more luxuriant than the meadows which we beheld below us upon which were a great number of Cattle grazing and enjoying a respite from the toils and fatigues imposed upon them by restless and insatiate man: indeed I believe I received the greatest pleasure I felt upon that Occasion from the appearance of Innocence and ease that was visible in the whole scene; the flocks and herds peacefully contenting themselves with the provisions supplied for them by bounteous Nature, while the goats wantoning and frisking along the edge of the surrounding mountain seemed delighted with their elevation. The vineyards and groves of olive trees (oh! how I wish I could send you a branch from one of them) are here and there interspersed as if with matchless art, and appear as if intended to form a rural garden for the inhabitants of those piles of buildings that the City presents to view. We all by mutual consent requested the coachman to wait 'till we indulged ourselves with this attracting landscape; for now the Sun was retiring behind a dark and heavy cloud that was hanging over Cordova and now and then shot forth lightning like a trail of fire and the thunder was re-echoed from the mountains that terminated the view; but though the prospect was greatly improved by the alteration in the Atmosphere we could no longer enjoy it, our driver being absolutely averse to a wet skin.

Excuse me my dear Sister for staying so long near Cordova, the Coachman was perfectly right to be peremptory and we arrived at that City an hour after dark. The next day we continued there and received much civility from a number of irish Gentlemen who have retired from the Sea-ports and made that their residence. Mr. Moyland a brother of Col. Moyland was particularly polite,[6] he waited upon us when we visited the Bishop's palace gardens etc. and was one of the Gentlemen that went with us to see the Cathedral. I doubt whether it is exceded by anything in Spain, it was formerly a moorish Mosque and certainly gives us an high Idea of their proficiency in Architecture, but I am quite incapable of giving you an adequate Idea of it; leaving that for the Colonel. I'll only mention one circumstance that will convince you that it is a vast and splendid Edifice since it contains not less than nine hundred and ninety nine pillars of polished marble, elegantly wrought and of every kind that has been discovered. The spaniards have made great Additions to it equally magnificent and curious.

There are many things in Cordova worth seeing but as Mr. Jay's maxim is to prefer business to pleasure, we the next day proceeded on our Journey and I don't recollect any agreeable circumstances that occured after quitting the province of Andulusia. We very frequently passed little wooden crosses on the highway which had been placed there to denote the burying places of those who had been found murdered there, it being the custom to inter them on the same places they were found. When we came to La Mancha we naturally recollected the exploits that had been atchieved by the renowned Knight of the rueful countenance and looked but in vain, for those large trees that sometimes afforded a safe retreat for the affrighted squire. Few marks of cultivation after quitted Andalusia; there are to be sure some Vineyards and olive groves but the greatest Industry is visible in the Tiera Morena which is chiefly inhabited by Germans that have been invited there by his present Majesty and who by his encouragement have made the barren Wilderness to smile; for until his reign that large tract of country was perpetually infested by robbers and murderers.

But to what a length am I proceeding, surely your Patience is almost exhausted and as there is not the same necessity for you to travel through a country so barren of entertainment as there was for me to undergo that toil I think I'll un land you at Madrid without further Ceremony or even refreshing ourselves at Aranjuez. I am frightned to see how much Paper I have blotted and dare not begin to review it: if you find many words misplaced or misspelt and a whole train of blunders instead of criticising, consider if such a Journey is not sufficient to fatigue and distract such a feeble mortal as myself and don't conclude from your own perfect and beautiful manner of writing at all times and upon all Occasions that there should be no allowance made for others who have not arrived to such Improvements.

You tell me that our army still improve and mention an instance of generosity in some of the troops that charms me: nothing delights me more than the praises of my Countrymen. Tell me therefore in every letter some of their Actions, for but to mention them is a panegeric. May! Auspicious Heaven smile upon their noble efforts for liberty and crown their council and their Arms with success.

Although I have already encroached upon your time, indulge me while I request you to embrace my dearest son, thank him for those whishes he has expressed for our return, I do indeed most ardently long to see him: but he is ignorant of the excess of my love for him and grief for the loss of his lovely Sister—indeed my Susan she was a lovely babe.

Tell Hannah I've not forgot her but will write sometime this week, though I shall divide the Chances by sending some of my letters to Bilboa and others to Cadiz. Give my affectionate love to

Kitty, as soon as my fingers are a little supled I shall devote a large share of my Time to her. If it is convenient, you'll oblidge me by letting our friends at Fish Kill know that we are all well. Adieu my ever dear Sister.

C. Endorsed in an unidentified hand.

1 Neither Susannah Livingston's letter of 29 March 1780 nor SLJ's letter to JJ have been located.

2 See SLJ to Susannah French Livingston, 12 Dec. 1779.

3 A portion of SLJ's undated letter, January 1780, in JP.

4 Matiás de Gálvez's barge carried them to Puerta de Santa María, a small seacoast town at the mouth of the Guadalete River, across the bay from the peninsula on which Cádiz is located.

5 Count Alexander (Alejandro) O'Reilly (1722–94), an Irish-born general in the Spanish army who had seen service in the Austrian and French armies. He had also previously held appointments as governor of Havana and Madrid. In 1780 he was serving as governor of Cádiz and commander in chief of Andalusia. The Countess O'Reilly, the former Rosa de las Casas, was the sister of General de las Casas and of Luis de las Casas, governor of Oran, and she was the niece of Yranda. M. Seguí, ed., *Enciclopedia Ilustrada* (Barcelona, 1907).

6 Stephen Moylan (1737–1811), of Philadelphia, was a colonel in the Continental Dragoons and former quartermaster general. Born in Ireland, he had spent several years on the continent as a merchant before coming to America in 1768.

Sarah Livingston Jay to Susannah French Livingston

Madrid, August 28th, 1780

Had I wrote to my dear mamma a fortnight ago while my whole heart overflowed with joy and gratitude for the birth of a lovely daughter, I am sure every line must have conveyed pleasure to the best of parents, who well knows the affection of a mother. Every circumstance united in rendering that event delightful to us, excluded the society of our most intimate friends, behold us in a country, whose customs, language and religion are the very reverse of our own, without connections, without friends; judge then if Heaven could have bestowed a more acceptable present. Nor was the present deficient in any thing that was necessary to endear it to us: rather let me say that every wish of my heart was amply answered in the precious gift; in her charming countenance I beheld at once the softened resemblance of her father and absent brother, her little form was perfect symmetry; and nature, by warding off those disorders that generally attack infants, seemed to promise a healthy constitution added to those circumstances; her very name increased my pleasure; and I even flattered myself with a hope that Kitty and Nancy would be charmed with their little god-child. When I used to look at her every idea less pleasant vanished in a moment, scenes of continued and future bliss still rose to view, and while I clasped her to my bosom my happiness appeared compleat. Alas! mamma how frail are all sublumary enjoyments! But I must endeavor to recollect myself.

On monday the 22nd day after the birth of my little innocent, we perceived that she had a fever, but were not apprehensive of danger until the next day when it was attended with a fit. On wednesday the convulsions increased, and on thursday she was the whole day in one continued fit, nor could she close her little eye-lids untill fryday morning the 4th of August at 4 o'Clock, when wearied with pain, the little sufferer found rest in——.[1] Excuse my tears— you too mamma have wept on similar occasions. Maternal tenderness causes them to flow, and reason, though it moderates distress, cannot intirely restrain our grief, nor do I think it should be wished. For why should Heaven (in every purpose wise) have endowed it's lovely messenger with so many graces, but to captivate our hearts and excite them by a contemplation on the beloved object of our affection, to rise above those expectations that rather amuse than improve, and extend our views even to those regions of bliss where she has arrived before us. While my mind continues in its present frame: I look upon the tributes my child has paid to nature as the commencement of her immortality, and endeavor to acquiesce in the dispensations of the all-wise disposer of events; and if my heart continues in proper subjection to the divine will, then will she not have sickened, not have dyed in vain.

But let me not be so wrapt in my own feelings as to forget that you, mamma, are not without yours: doubtless you are solicitous to know the state of my own health; and I am happy that I can gratify your generous curiosity, and at the same time give you the pleasure which I know you'll receive from my assurances of my intire recovery. Never was any person more favored by providence than myself during my late confinement, for I not only escaped many disorders incidental to women in child bed, but was even free from the lightest fever, and indeed from all kind of pain: this climate is peculiarly favorable to women in that situation, of which I could tell you instances that are really surprising; but letters are no longer the free medium by which distant friends un-bosom themselves to each other; every thing therefore that prudence bids us suppress at present, we'll entertain ourselves with when sitting together by an American fire-side. You see mamma I don't dispair of the happiness of seeing you again.

The attention and proofs of fidelity which we have received from Abbe, demand, and ever shall have my acknowledgements; you can hardly imagine how useful she is to us, for indeed her place could not be supplyed, at least not here.[2]

I am so strangely bewildered when I attempt to write to any of my american friends that it's not to be wondered at if my letters are unconnected. Would you believe that this is the third time I have attempted to finish this; usually my thoughts make such rapid excursions toward my native country that it's with difficulty I can confine them within due limits, but at present I can scarcly detain them a single moment from the subject of the 1st part of this letter. Perhaps it engages my attention the more as Mr. Jay is at present absent, the Court being at St. Ildefonso between 13 and 14 leagues from hence: and I own I never feel so intirely myself as when in his company, for 'tis then that the silent encouragement I receive from his steady, modest virtue, operates most powerfully upon my mind: and I may add upon my conduct; for what can I fear, or how can I repine, when I behold him who is equally interested, composed in danger, resigned in affliction, and even possessing a chearful disposition in every circumstance. Excuse me my dear mamma, excuse my officious pen, perhaps too ready to obey the dictates of my heart, but he really is virtue's own self. I am interupted. A servant is arrived from Mr. Jay, who has rode all night to bring me a pacquet of letters from America, that were delivered to his master at St. Ildefonso—my emotions are so great that was not the Colonel to open the seals I should certainly tear them in my haste.

Thank God! my dear and ever worthy friends are well my child too is in perfect health; though I have been deprived of one the other is still preserved. Oh! mamma, I never fully comprehended the affection of parents for their children 'till I became a mother, and never even then was convinced how closely they were twisted with the fibrer of the heart until a late painful seperation. Kitty mentions a circumstance in one of her letters that greatly affects me; which is, that papa was disappointed in not receiving a letter from me before I left Philadelphia; it at the same time convinces me of his tenderness, and distresses me for having wounded it; but, Oh my dear papa! is it then an easy matter to write a farewell letter at such a time, under such circumstances, and where the heart is so deeply interested. Had I indulged my own feelings, must not those that were dearer to me than my own, been hurt; had I restrained them, might not I have been supposed insensible. I chose therefore to save us both, to let the idea of business prevail; but I was wrong: no affliction wounds so deeply, or lasts so long as neglect, or supposed neglect, from those we love and have obliged. My mistake was an error of the head, not the heart, for I would rather die than that papa and mamma should think me capable of ingratitude to them; on the contrary, I revere, admire and love them and wish to render myself worthy of such parents; and to justify by an amiable conduct the preference which Mr. Jay has honored me with: that is the sum of my ambition, that is indeed my heart's darling object.

Accept my sincere congratulation upon sister Judy's marriage, may the union prove agreeable to both families! Please to tell sister I have thought of an auspicious omen that did not occur to me while writing to her, and that is, that the month in which she was married is the same that I was myself and that though it was predicted from the fickleness of the season, that my happiness would not remain long unclouded, I have never known it eclipsed. May her fortune resemble mine. Difficult as it is to quit my pen, I must again bid mamma adieu. My love to Papa and the rest of the family. Numberless embraces to my dear boy, and affectionate remembrance to Hannah. Please to give my love to Mrs. Ogden and her mamma. I am with the sincerest affection, ever yours

SARAH JAY

ALS. Endorsed in an unidentified hand. LbkC in JP; Tr in NcD: Charles Campbell Papers.

1 Line drawn in ms.

2 Abigail, a black servant who had been in the Livingstons' service in America, accompanied the Jays to Europe.

FROM GOUVERNEUR MORRIS

Philadelphia, 3d January 1780

Dear Jay,

You will doubtless be glad to hear News from this Quarter. Your Friends are all well. Our Army are hutted in the Vicinity of Morris Town except a Detachment consisting of the North Carolina and Virginia Troops who are on their March to the Southward THREE THOUSAND. The DON[1] on the Part of the GOVERNOR OF HAVANNAH did lately PROPOSE to CONGRESS to assist in the REDUCTION OF FLORIDA. They have given every proper Assurance of their good Intentions, more they cannot do.[2]

You will be pleased to hear that the continental Money is on the mending Hand. This is the Case so much that Gold which a Fortnight ago was scarce at forty five is now plenty at Thirty five as I am told. Among other Causes this may partly be attributed to the LOQUACITY OF DRAWING ON YOU FOR ONE HUNDRED THOUSAND POUNDS STERLING AND LAWRENCE AS MUCH. I hope you are in Spain and doing well. Young Lawrence hath resigned his SecretaryShip. LOVELL in NOMI[NATIO]N WITH SIX VOTES. About a Week ago a british Fleet of Transports sailed from the Hook with about six thousand Troops. We have had since two tremendous Storms one of which now rages.

Rely on it that EUROPEAN MONEY IS ABSOLUTELY NECESSARY FOR US. We begin to economize which is a good Sign. I would advise to send a SQUADRON OF TWELVE OF SIXTY GUNS, SOME FRIGATES AND MEN DOWN TO NEW YORK TO ARRIVE THERE THE FIRST OF JUNE. THAT CITY WOULD FALL, AND OF CONSEQUENCE HALIFAX. ON THIS LAST DEPENDS NEW FOUND LAND, PERHAPS CANADA. THE SQUADRON MIGHT CAREEN AT HALIFAX, VICTUAL THEM TO CHESSAPEAKE AND TAKE in PROVISION BY THE FIRST OF OCTOBER. Whatever may be the Fate of the Floridas this Winter they would certainly fall the next and perhaps all the british Islands. The Destruction of Portsmouth would injure Great Britain but the Loss of her Islands would almost ruin her. Peace will, I beleive, soon be necessary for all Parties. Adieu.

Remember me to my Friends and beleive me most sincerely yours

GOUV MORRIS

ALS. Addressed: "Honle. Mr. Jay Minister plen: of the United States of North America at Madrid." Endorsed: ". . . Recd. 16 May 1780." The letter is partly in cipher with JJ's deciphering. ADftS in FU.

[1] Don Juan de Miralles (d. 1780), a Cuban merchant and slave trader, was commissioned by Spain in 1777 to proceed to the United States as an observer, but he did not hold a formal diplomatic appointment. Samuel Flagg Bemis, *The Diplomacy of the American Revolution* (Bloomington, Ind., 1957), p. 88.

[2] In a letter of 24 Nov. 1779 Miralles had offered Congress naval aid for the reduction of South Carolina, Georgia, and the two Floridas, if the Americans were prepared to supply the inhabitants of Havana with provisions. However, Congress could not promise this, for it was hard-pressed to provision even the American army. *JCC*, XV, 1301–02, 1331–32, 1369–70.

TO ARTHUR LEE

Cadiz, 26 January 1780[1]

Sir

As a Knowledge of the Measures you may have taken and the Information you may have <gained relative> acquired relative to the <in pursuance of your> objects of your Commission <ers plenipotentiary from the> from the united States of america to conclude Treaties with his most catholic Majesty <may> would probably enable me with greater Facility and Advantage to execute the Duties <imposed> of my Appointment. Permit me Sir to request the Favor of you to communicate the same to me in such manner as you may <be such and at the same Time most full in your opinion be> judge most prudent.[2]

<Major Scull <<sailed with me in the>> embarked with us at Ph[iladelphi]a in the Confederacy with Design to go to France for the Benefit of his Health but unfortunately died on the Passage.[3] After his Death and after it became certain that the Confederacy was not in Condition to prosecute her Voyage, Mr. Vaughan[4] the second Lieut. who had taken Charge of the Majors Effects, delivered me a Number of Letters found among them, among which were some for you. These with others that are large and to appearance contain many Enclosures, are now in my Possession. After the arrival of the Confederacy at Martinico it became certain that <<the Confederacy after being>> her Masts and injuring her Rudder was not in Condition to proceed to Europe>

I have in my Possession some Letters directed to you. They are voluminous and probably contain printed Papers. They may also be confidential and important to you. Under these Circumstances I can only judge of your Inclination by what would be my own in a similar Situation. <Hence I am led to> I should wish they might be detained till I could have an Opportunity of directing the Manner of their Conveyance. Upon this Principle they shall remain among my Papers till I recieve your order what to do with them.[5]

I am Sir your most obedient and very humble Servant.

Dft. 2 LbkCs in both CSmH: JJ Lbk and in DNA: PCC, 110, I. Printed in *RDC*, III, 471. None of these copies has the passage: "Maj. Scull imbarked with us . . . to proceed to Europe."

[1] The *Aurora* reached Cádiz 22 Jan. 1780.

[2] James Lovell had informed Lee of JJ's appointment as minister plenipotentiary to Spain in a letter of 13 Oct. 1779 and sent the former commissioner a copy of the Congressional resolve permitting him to return to the United States. *RDC*, III, 377–78.

[3] Major Peter Scull of Pennsylvania resigned as secretary to the Board of War 1 Sept. 1779 and had been an unsuccessful candidate for the post of minister plenipotentiary at Versailles. On Scull's death aboard ship, see Joseph Nourse to Horatio Gates, 20 Feb. 1780, ALS in NHi: Gates Papers.

[4] Thomas Vaughan was the second lieutenant on board the *Confederacy*.

[5] These papers have not been located.

The First Phase of the Spanish Mission

When JJ and his entourage arrived at Cádiz in the winter of 1779–80, he found himself entrusted with a mission of formidable dimensions and intricate complexities. What he sought was an alliance with Spain, the world power which controlled so large a part of the Western hemisphere. To accomplish this, it was necessary that JJ overcome two serious obstacles in the minds of the Spanish king and his principal minister for Foreign Affairs, José de Moñino y Redondo, Conde de Floridablanca. In the first place, JJ had the almost impossible task of convincing them that recognizing American independence would not provide Spanish colonies in the New World with an example of the fruits of revolt. Secondly, Spain had an equally strong apprehension of America's territorial ambitions in the lands west of the Alleghenies to the Mississippi River, territory which Spain felt free to claim, but which America considered rightfully hers, whether on the basis of charter rights of individual colonies or as succeeding to British acquisitions under the Treaty of Paris of 1763. The single most decisive issue concerned the navigation of the Mississippi River, then exclusively controlled by the Spaniards. Until the suspicions of the Spanish court could be laid to rest, or until some compromise regarding them could be reached with the American envoy, a treaty of alliance between the United States and Spain would remain an improbable event.

Even before JJ left for Spain, Floridablanca had begun to formulate his position towards the rebellious colonies. As he made clear to Montmorin, the French ambassador at Madrid, the most desirable outcome of this war, from Spain's point of interest, was a weak America locked in long-term quarreling with Great Britain, with Spain and France acting as "co-protectors" to the feeble thirteen states.[1] In addition, as a reward for entering the war against Great Britain, Floridablanca wanted to share the Newfoundland fisheries with the French, as well as Gibraltar, the cession of Minorca and Florida, and the elimination of English pockets of settlement in Central America.[2]

Since 1778 Spain had her observers in the thirteen states, notably Juan de Miralles, to sound out expansionist sentiment, at the same time bringing to bear such arguments as might be persuasive with personages considered moderates on this question, notably JJ and Gouverneur Morris.[3] However, once Spain entered the war for reasons unrelated to the American struggle, JJ concluded that the United States was ill-advised to "cede her any of our rights" or to do other than "insist upon our right to the navigation of the Mississippi."[4]

With Spain and the thirteen states pursuing largely inimical objectives, one might have anticipated that JJ would be treated with calculated coolness by the Spanish court. While he waited to be formally acknowledged, JJ set himself to the work of his commission. He remained in Cádiz, but dispatched William Carmichael, secretary of the mission, to Madrid.

This seemed the prudent course, for Carmichael possessed a fluency in the Spanish language that JJ lacked. Quite aware that Arthur Lee, his predecessor, had never been permitted to proceed as far as Madrid, JJ did not wish to risk another rebuff.

Despite the pair's caution, JJ and Carmichael made their first misstep when, on the advice of Gérard, JJ addressed a letter to Don José de Gálvez, Minister of the Indies, who handled American affairs, thus unintentionally circumventing the Conde de Floridablanca, who was to assume full command of the negotiations with America. What Floridablanca would do seemed evident from the refusal of Charles III to receive Gérard in his capacity of retiring French Minister to the United States on the ground that it would signify an implied recognition of the insurgents. Thus, when toward the end of February, Floridablanca sent word to JJ that he might come to Madrid but not in "a public character," it was more a disappointment than a shock to the American. Recognition, however, was to prove an elusive objective.

Congress was quite as concerned about securing financial aid from Spain as it was of winning official recognition, and JJ was frequently reminded that "we are become more dependent upon your vigorous Exertions for the Amelioration of our Currency than you had perhaps expected when you left Philadelphia."[5] His task would not have been easy at best, but it was greatly complicated by the disrepair into which American fiscal affairs had fallen and particularly by one of the expedients resorted to in an effort to effect improvements. Hoping to halt runaway inflation, Congress, on 18 March 1780, called in and burned $200 million, replacing it with a new issue of $10 million.[6] In order to avoid further inflation, Congress decided to start spending the money it hoped to obtain from abroad, and it therefore issued a total of £200,000 in bills drawn on JJ and Henry Laurens and payable in six months.[7] The Spanish officials understandably resented the naïve assumption that assistance to the United States would be granted cheerfully and automatically upon demand, and this annoyance added materially to JJ's difficulties.

Spain had, it is true, given some financial support to the United States before JJ arrived as minister plenipotentiary, but it had never done so either lavishly or with marked enthusiasm. In fact, the total of its monetary aid through 1779 was less then one-tenth the amount provided by France.[8] The earliest Spanish transactions remain necessarily obscure, because they were in the form of secret subsidies, but it is believed that gifts between 1776 and 1779 amounted to $397,230.[9] The first and largest grant, a sum of one million livres, was turned over to Beaumarchais in 1776 for the purchase of goods to be shipped to America.[10] The next year the House of Gardoqui of Bilbao was authorized to supply the United States with war goods, which were to be billed but for which no payments were expected. Acting on these instructions, Gardoqui paid 187,500 livres for two shipments that left in April.[11] The three American commissioners at Versailles reported home in December of 1777 that Spain had promised three million livres during the next year, but Spanish generosity was visibly waning, and only 170,000 livres were forthcoming.[12] Through a commercial house Arthur Lee did obtain 187,500 livres in 1778, a sum which the United States repaid quite soon without leaving a record to explain how the feat was accomplished.[13] One further loan that year which was not repaid rapidly was a sum of $66,961 furnished to Oliver Pollock, representing the United States, by the governor of Louisiana on behalf of Spain.[14]

JJ's loan negotiation started off on a reasonably optimistic note, with Floridablanca indicating to JJ at their initial meeting on 11 May that the king, acting as a private individual, would probably be willing to advance up to £40,000 at or soon after the end of the year, meanwhile pledging his credit toward payment of bills that were maturing.[15] Within a month, however, Floridablanca abandoned that tentative offer in favor of something much less acceptable to the American. Recognizing that JJ wanted more than the amount previously discussed but claiming that war expenses made a prompt loan impractical, the Spanish minister suggested that the bill holders might be satisfied if they were told that the King would make a £100,000 loan at the end of two years.[16] Such an arrangement would not have been at all practical, as Floridablanca must have known.

Encouraged to do so by the Spanish minister, JJ began accepting bills, but, with no money arriving from Philadelphia and with no progress toward a loan in Madrid, he rapidly found himself in a critical situation.[17] In a series of anxious letters, most of them unanswered, and in such occasional interviews as Floridablance permitted him, JJ pleaded for an immediate loan to meet the urgent need, but the only result he obtained was an occasional agreement to relieve him of a particularly troublesome small bill.[18] Events took a particularly ugly turn on 5 July when Floridablanca suspended loan discussions entirely, offering the excuse that a mysterious personage of great importance would arrive shortly to undertake discussions with JJ.[19] The reasons for this strategy of delay was Floridablanca's hope for a rapprochement with Great Britain, and it was only after Spain learned that there was no chance of obtaining Gibraltar by negotiation that the very important personage materialized suddenly as Don Diego de Gardoqui of Bilbao.[20]

Meeting with JJ on 3 September Gardoqui made it clear that a £100,000 loan would be contingent upon America's waiving her claims to the navigation of the Mississippi. This same condition was repeated in cavalier fashion the next day when the two men met at the offices of Bernardo del Campo, secretary to Floridablanca. Not only did del Campo insist that the loan should be requested from France rather than Spain, but he criticized the United States for having involved his country in a war from which it had nothing to gain. He bluntly reminded JJ that the latter was in no position to bargain, citing the flagging American military effort and reports of low morale.[21] This unsatisfactory interview caused JJ to write a strong letter to Floridablanca demanding to know what if any help the United States might expect.[22] Floridablanca returned an answer through Gardoqui, making an entirely new offer. The king, JJ was now told, could not lend any money himself, but he would be glad to guarantee a loan to the United States by somebody else for $150,000 spread over three years. This time, at least, the Mississippi was not mentioned.[23] Spain's increasingly niggardly stand can be partially explained by her own difficulties, having been refused a large loan by France's finance minister, Jacques Necker. JJ had to make do with what seemed available, and he therefore set about trying to schedule a conference with Floridablanca to determine how the king's name could be used to obtain a loan somewhere in Europe.[24]

In addition to seeking a solution to the embarrassing problem of the bills issued by Congress, the minister plenipotentiary also had to find ways to pay the day-to-day expenses of the mission. With no operating funds arriving from Philadelphia, JJ resorted early in 1780 to arranging credit in Paris.[25] He found it necessary thereafter to write periodic pleading letters to Benjamin Franklin and then to live through anxious days waiting to hear what, if anything, had been done to relieve his financial distress.[26] Franklin always did what he could, but the sums credited to JJ never lasted very long, and no serious progress was made toward putting the operation of the Spanish mission on a satisfactory basis.[27]

[1] Montmorin to Vergennes, 10 Jan. and 29 March 1780, MAE: CP: Espagne, v. 597, pp. 83–84 and v. 598, pp. 319–22.

[2] Samuel Flagg Bemis, *Pinckney's Treaty: America's Advantage From Europe's Distress, 1783–1800* (rev. ed., New Haven, 1960), p. 13.

[3] *Peacemakers*, pp. 13, 221.

[4] *WJ*, I, 99–101.

[5] Committee on Foreign Affairs to JJ, 11 Dec. 1779, above. See also Committee on Foreign Affairs to JJ, 7 Feb. 1780, William Bingham to JJ, 25 Feb. 1780, and Gouverneur Morris to JJ, 20 March 1780, all below.

[6] *JCC*, XVI, 262–66. A description of the preliminary moves leading to this decision can be found in Charles Thomson to JJ, 12 Oct. 1780. ALS in JP; LS in NHi: Jay Papers; C in Carmichael's hand in AHN: Estado, leg. 3884, exp. 8, doc. 25.

[7] William Bingham to JJ, 22 Oct. 1780, below. See also E. James Ferguson, *The Power of the Purse: A History of American Public Finance, 1776–1790* (Chapel Hill, 1961), p. 55; *Peacemakers*, p. 224.

[8] Samuel Flagg Bemis, *The Diplomacy of the American Revolution* (Bloomington, Ind., 1935), p. 93.

[9] *Ibid.*

[10] *Ibid.*, p. 28. This grant was worth approximately $185,000. Ferguson, *Power of the Purse*, p. 41.

[11] *RDC*, II, 290–91, 292–95, 308; III, 12–15.

[12] *Ibid.*, II, 453.

[13] *Ibid.*, III, 12–15; Ferguson, *Power of the Purse*, p. 41.

[14] Bemis, *Pinckney's Treaty*, pp. 333–34.

[15] JJ's Notes on Conference with Floridablanca, 11 May 1780, *HPJ*, I, 317–24; *RDC*, III, 722–25.

[16] Floridablanca to JJ, 7 June 1780, RCs in both Spanish and French, AHN,

Estado, leg. 3884, ex. 4, doc. 49; LbkC in French in MAE: CP: Espagne, v. 599, 231–33; LbkCs in French and Spanish in DNA: PCC, 110, I and CSmH: JJ Lbk; LbkC in French in DLC: Franklin Papers, III, 57–59.

17 At their 11 May meeting Floridablanca told JJ to accept the most pressing bills. *HPJ*, I, 317–24; *RDC*, III, 722–25.

18 For JJ's one-sided correspondence with Floridablanca in 1780 on the subject of loans, see JJ to Floridablanca: 9 June, 1780: LS and Spanish trans. in AHN, Estado, leg. 3884, exp. 4, doc. 50; Dft in JP; LbkC in French in MAE: CP: Espagne, v. 599, 261–69; LbkCs in DNA: PCC, 110, I, CSmH: JJ Lbk, and in DLC: Franklin Papers, III, 57–61. 19 June 1780: ALS and Spanish trans. in AHN, Estado, leg. 3884, exp. 4, doc. 53; LbkCs in DNA: PCC, 110, I, CSmH: JJ Lbk., and in DLC: Franklin Papers, III, 61–62. 22 June 1780: LS and Spanish trans. in AHN, Estado, leg. 3884, exp. 4, doc. 53; Dft in JP; LbkC in French in MAE: CP: Espagne, v. 599, 341–44; LbkCs in DNA: PCC, 110, I and DLC: Franklin Papers, III, 62–65; LbkC in French and English in CSmH: JJ Lbk; printed in *RDC*, IV, 119–21. 28 June 1780 (2 letters): AL and Spanish trans. in AHN, Estado, leg. 3884, exp. 4, doc. 54 and ALS and Spanish trans., docs. 55 and 56; one Dft in JP; LbkCs in DNA: PCC, 110, I and CSmH: JJ Lbk; printed in *RDC*, IV, 122. 4 July 1780: AL and Spanish trans. in AHN, Estado, leg. 3884, ex. 4, doc. 59. 11 July 1780: AL in AHN, Estado, leg. 3884, ex., 4, doc. 60; LbkCs in DNA: PCC, 110, I and CSmH: JJ Lbk. 11 Aug. 1780: AL and Spanish trans. in AHN, Estado, leg. 3884, ex. 4, doc. 66; LbkCs in DNA: PCC, 110, I and CSmH: JJ Lbk. 16 Aug. 1780: ALS and Spanish trans. in AHN, Estado, leg. 3884, ex. 4, doc. 67; LbkCs in DNA: PCC, 110, I and CSmH: JJ Lbk. 17 Aug. 1780: AL and Spanish trans. in AHN, Estado, leg. 3884, ex. 4, doc. 68. 18 Aug. 1780: ALS and Spanish trans. in AHN, Estado, leg. 3884, ex. 4, doc. 69; LbkCs in DNA: PCC, 110, I and CSmH: JJ Lbk; printed in *RDC*, IV, 127–28. 25 Aug. 1780: ALS and Spanish trans. in AHN, Estado, leg. 3884, ex. 4, doc. 70; LbkCs in DNA: PCC, 110, I and CSmH: JJ Lbk. Floridablanca to JJ: 20 June 1780: L in French, with JJ's trans. in JP; LbkCs in French and English, in DNA: PCC, 110, I and CSmH: JJ Lbk; LbkC in French in DLC: Franklin Papers, 62. 29 June 1780: Dft in French in AHN, Estado, leg. 3884, ex. 4, doc. 57; L in French, and English trans., in JP; LbkCs in French and English in DNA: PCC, 110, I and CSmH: JJ Lbk; printed in *RDC*, IV, 122–23. 3 July 1780: L in French, with English trans., in JP; Dft in French in AHN, Estado, leg. 3884, ex. 4, doc. 58; LbkCs in French and English in DNA: PCC, 110, I and CSmH: JJ Lbk. 12 July 1780: L in French, with English trans., in JP; Dft in French in AHN, Estado, leg. 3884, ex. 4, doc. 61; LbkCs in French and English in DNA: PCC, 110, I and CSmH: JJ Lbk. 29 July 1780: L in French, with English trans., in JP; LbkCs in French and English in DNA: PCC, 100, I and CSmH: JJ Lbk. 12 Aug. 1780: LbkCs in French and English in DNA: PCC, 110, I and CSmH: JJ Lbk. Information about the bills covered by Spain will be found in William Carmichael to Committee of Foreign Affairs, 9 Sept. 1780, DNA: PCC, 88, I, 87–90.

19 JJ to Vergennes, 22 Sept. 1780, ALS and French trans. in MAE: CP: États-Unis, v. 13; LbkCs in English and French in DNA: PCC, 110, I and in CSmH: JJ Lbk; LbkC in DLC: Franklin Papers, III, 68–72.

20 *Peacemakers*, p. 231; Floridablanca to JJ, 3 Sept. 1780, LbkCs in French and English in DNA: PCC, 110, I and CSmH: JJ Lbk. JJ to President of Congress, 6 Nov. 1780: LbkCs in DNA: PCC, 110, I and CSmH: JJ Lbk; C in DLC: Madison Papers, I, 10429a–10461a; printed in *RDC*, IV, 112–50.

21 JJ to Vergennes, 22 Sept. 1780; JJ to President of Congress, 6 Nov. 1780.

22 JJ to Floridablanca, 14 Sept. 1780, ALS and Spanish trans. in AHN: Estado, leg. 3884, exp. 8, doc. 24; LbkC in French in MAE: CP: Espagne, v. 601,

464–67; LbkCs in DNA: PCC, 110, I and in CSmH: JJ Lbk; printed in *RCD*, IV, 138.

23 Gardoqui to JJ, 15 Sept. 1780, ALS in JP; LbkCs in DNA: PCC, 110, I and CSmH: JJ Lbk; printed in *RDC*, IV, 139.

24 JJ to President of Congress, 6 Nov. 1780.

25 JJ to Robert R. Livingston, 23 May 1780, below.

26 JJ to Benjamin Franklin, 14 April and 17 July 1780, below.

27 Benjamin Franklin to JJ, 13 and 31 July 1780, below.

JJ: "Instructions For Mr. Carmichael"

Cadiz, 27 January 1780

Sir

You will proceed to Madrid with convenient Expedition, and if Mr. Gerard with whom you set out should travel too very deliberately I advise you to go on before him. The Propriety of this however will depend much on Circumstances, and must be determined by your own Discretion.

On delivering my Letter to Mr. Galvaise, it would be proper to intimate that I presumed it would be more agreable to him to recieve my Dispatch from you who would give him Information on many Matters about which he might choose to Inquire than in the ordinary Modes of Conveyance, and it may not be amiss to let him know that his not recieving Notice of our Arrival from me by Mr. Gerard's Courier was owing to a Mistake between that Gentleman and me.[1]

Treat the French Embassador[2] with great Attention, Candor and that Degree of Confidence only which Prudence and the Alliance between us may prescribe. <It may be proper to impress the Ministry.> In your Conversation with People about the Court impress them with an Idea of our strong Attachment to France, yet <cautiously> so as to avoid permitting them to imbibe an Opinion of our being under the *Direction* of any Counsels but our own. The former will induce them to think well of our Constancy and good Faith the latter of our Independence and self Respect.

Discover if possible whether the Courts of Madrid and Versailles <partake of> entertain in any Degree the same mutual Disgusts, which we are told prevail at present between the too Nations, and be cautious when you tread on that delicate Ground. It would also be useful to know who are the Kings principal Confidents and the Trains leading to each.

<The State of the public Revenues is of great Importance to be known.> To treat prudently with any Nation it is essential to know the State of its Revenues. Turn your Attention therefore to this Object

and endeavour to learn whether the public Expenditures consume their Annual Income or whether there be any and what overplus or Deficiency, and the Manner in which the former is disposed of or the latter supplied.

If an opportunity should offer inform yourself as to the Regulations of the Press at Madrid and indeed throughout the Kingdom; and the particular Character of the <Man> Person at the Head of the Department. Endeavour to find some Person of adequate abilities and Knowledge in the two Languages to translate English into Spanish with Propriety and if possible Elegance. I wish also to know which of the Religious Orders and the Individuals of <that order who have most Influence> it most esteemed and favored at Court.

Mention as matter of Intelligence rather than in the Way of argument the Cruelties of the Enemy, and the Influence of that Conduct on the Passions of the Americans. This will be the more necessary as it seems we are suspected of retaining our former Attachments to Britain.

In speaking of American Affairs remember to do <full> Justice to Virginia and the western Country near the Mississippi. Recount their <hardy> Achievements against the Savages, their growing numbers, extensive Settlements and aversion to Britain for attempting to involve them in the Horrors of an Indian War. Let it appear also from your Representations that Ages will be necessary to settle those extensive Regions.

Let it be inferred from your Conversation that the Expectations of America as to my Reception and Success are sanguine, that they have been rendered the more so by the Suggestions of Persons generally supposed to speake from Authority, and that a Disappointment would be no less unwelcome than unexpected.

I am persuaded that Pains will be taken to delay my recieving a decided answer as to my Reception until the Sentiments of France shall be known; Attempts will also be made to suspend the Acknowledgment of our Independence <be made only> on the Condition of our acceding to certain Terms of Treaty. Do nothing to cherish either of these Ideas, but without being explicit treat the latter in a Manner expressive of Regret and Apprehension, and <intimate the Propriety of immediate> seem to consider our Reception as a Measure which <may> we hoped would be immediately taken Although the Business of the Negotiation <may> might be postponed till France <can> could have an opportunity of taking the Steps she <may> might think proper on the Occasion.

You will offer to transmit to me any Dispatches which Mr.

Galvaise may think proper to confide to you, or to return with them yourself if more agreable to him. <You will be so obliging as to transmit to me regular and minute accounts of your Proceedings in Cypher as well as all other.> You will be attentive to all other objects of useful Information such as the Characters, Views and Connections of important Individuals, the Plan of Operations for the next Campaign; Whether any and what secret Overtures have been made by Britain to France or Spain or by either of them to her or each other; Whether any of the other Powers have manifested a Disposition to take a Part in the War; and whether it is probable that any and which of them will become Mediators for a general Peace and on what Plan. If the War should continue it would be advantageous to know whether Spain means to carry on any serious operations for possessing herself of the Floridas and Banks of the Mississippi, etc., etc.

<Throughout the whole of your> Altho I have <full> Confidence in your Prudence yet permit me to recommend to you the greatest Circumspection. Command yourself under every Circumstance; on the one Hand avoid being suspected of Servility, and on the other let your Temper be always even and your Attention unremitted.

You will oblige me by being very regular and circumstantial in your Correspondence, and *commit nothing of a private Nature* to Paper unless in Cypher.

Dft. Endorsed by JJ. LbkC in CSmH: JJ Lbk; 2 LbkCs in DNA: PCC, 110, I, 33–37, 76–81; printed in *RDC*, III, 472–74. Enclosure: JJ to Don José de Gálvez, 27 Jan. 1780: LS and Spanish trans. in AHN, Estado, leg. 3884, exp. 8, doc. 1; Dft in JP; Cs in MAE: CP: États-Unis, XI; LbkCs in CSmH: JJ Lbk and DLC: Franklin Papers, III, 5–7; 2 LbkCs in DNA: PCC, 110, I, 25–28, 72–76; printed in *RDC*, III, 476–78. Enclosed in this dispatch to Gálvez was a copy of JJ's letter of the same date to Vergennes, wherein he informed the French minister of foreign affairs that he was in Spain for the purpose of securing aid and an alliance with her. C in the hand of William Carmichael and Spanish trans. in AHN, Estado, leg. 3884, exp. 8, doc. 4; LS in MAE: CP: États-Unis, v. II; 2 LbkCs in both DNA: PCC, 110, I and CSmH: JJ Lbk; C in DLC: Franklin Papers, III, 7, 7x, 8.

[1] Acting upon normal procedures of diplomatic protocol, JJ addressed his letter to Don José de Gálvez (1720–86), the Minister of the Indies, who dealt with American affairs, thus unintentionally circumventing José Moñino y Redondo, Conde de Floridablanca (1728–1808), Minister of State, who was to take charge of the negotiations. In that letter JJ presented his credentials as U.S. minister plenipotentiary to Spain and indicated that it was the wish of Congress to comply with the secret article of the 1778 Treaty of Amity and Commerce with France, opening the door to a similar treaty with Spain and other powers. As regards writing Gálvez instead of appearing before him, JJ wrote the President of Congress: "being apprehensive that if present I should probably be amused with verbal answers capable of being explained away if necessary until the two courts

[France and Spain] could have time to consult and decide on their measures, I thought it more prudent that my first application should be by letter rather than in person." JJ to Samuel Huntington, 3 March 1780: 2 LbkCs in both CSmH: JJ Lbk and in DNA: PCC, 110, I; printed in *RDC*, III, 529–30.

2 Armand Marc, Comte de Montmorin-Saint-Hérem (1745–92).

To George Clinton

Cadiz, 1 February 1780

Dear Sir

Several Months have elapsed since we have heard from each other, and I imagine you will as little expect to recieve a Letter from me dated at this Place <will be as unexpected to you> as I did to write one. We arrived here in the Aurora a french Frigate the 22 Inst.[1] after a very <extraordinary> short Passage of *twenty six* Days from Martinico. The ship was bound to Toulon, but <having heard of> Admiral Rodneys Success in the Mediterranean, (of which we heard at this Place) (on touching for Intelligence) induced us to curtail our voyage.[2] There has not been a fair nor a dry Day since my arrival. I have therefore as the common Phrase is, seen little *to tell of*, nor has any Event happened in this Quarter worth mentioning, except that a Murderer was hanged here three Days ago, who had been in Close Custody twenty three Years after his apprehension for that Crime. I forbear Remarks on this Circumstance. I am sure we think alike; mention it to Hobart.

How long I may continue in this Town is uncertain as yet, and will depend on the Pleasure of his Catholic Majesty, which I expect or rather hope will be signified to me in about <four> Three Weeks Time.

I have some Reason to think the War unpopular in this City; the merchants have suffered. Some of the few Politicians with whom I have conversed, are puzzled in mazes and perplexed with Errors, while others are with us, and seem anxious for a Union. Among the Latter are the Officers of an Irish Brigade, who (to speake <Irish> in their Language) are as warm and zealous Americans as ever I have met with. Among them is a Col. Newgent a well informed sensible warm hearted man.[3] He has paid great Attention to our Affairs and considered them in a Point of Light in which few as yet (at least in America) have I believe accurately viewed them. I mean as they do or may affect the Interest and Objects of Spain. The famous General oReiley is daily expected in town. He is also an Irishman and from that Circumstance I presume friendly to us. His Countrymen here seem much attached to him, and speake highly of his Talents and

Merit. If I remember right, you sometimes feel yourself a little national.[4] I shall therefore in some future Letter tell you more of this General as well as of the generous Things done by some Irish Merchants here to distressed Americans.

But this latter Subject reminds me of a <very respectable> decent looking elderly man who introduced himself to me the other Day by the Title of the Consul of Ragusa and of Rome. Ragusa you know is a commercial Republic, but what Rome whose Trade consisted Chiefly in Bulls, Indulgences and the Souls of Men, should do with a Lay Consul, was less easy to concieve. But be this as it may, Mr. Carlos Maria Dodero, for that is his Name, told me he was then, and had been for some Time past, busily engaged in procuring the Enlargement of two unfortunate Americans who had been committed to Goal "for only breaking some of the Laws of Trade" to which they had been seduced by <some> one of the officers appointed to <keep> execute them, and so unremitted were his Endeavours that <three days ago> a day or two after he brought them to me in Triumph, having himself become bound for their Appearance when called for, and that without any other collateral Security than an american Loan Office Certificate for about four hundred Dollars, which is far from being thought of much Value here. Is it not a little extraordinary that a Man whom Rome and Regusa should think fit for a Consul, a Man, too, well advanced in fifty, should thus become bound for Men, of whose Characters he was ignorant, in whose Honor he had no Reason to confide and in whose Fate neither he nor his Country men were interested? Yet if he or they are to be believed, he not only became bound for them but has paid and engaged to pay for Meat, Cloaths etc. furnished them, one hundred and thirty Dollars. One of them is an English Surgeon, and a Tory, the other a Sail maker of the same Country who calls himself a Nephew of Major Gen. Lee. The Tory is about turning roman Catholic to qualify himself for a Place in the Hospital here, the other is following his Trade for the Present. Whatever Judgment may be passed on the Consul's Head we certainly must give him Credit for the Goodness of his Heart.

Mrs. Jay joins <with> me in requesting you to make our Compliments to Mrs. Clinton.

I am Dear Sir very sincerely Your Friend and Servant

Dft.

1 JJ intended ultimo.

2 Sir George Brydges Rodney (1719–92) successfully relieved the besieged

British garrison at Gibraltar in January 1780 at considerable expense to the Spanish fleet.

3 Probably Eduardo Nugent, an Irish-born lieutenant colonel in the Spanish service. Micheline Walsh, ed., *Spanish Knights of Irish Origin* (Dublin, 1960), p. 124.

4 Clinton's father had been born in County Longford, Ireland. *GCP*, I, 15.

FROM WILLIAM CHURCHILL HOUSTON

Philadelphia, 7 February 1780

Sir

It is not simply from being a Member of the Committee of Foreign Affairs that I take the Liberty of troubling you; my Curiosity to have Access to all the Sources of Knowledge in publick Affairs, is a further Apology. For this I confess I have a boundless Thirst and Eagerness.

A Vessel, lately arrived to the Eastward, reports to have spoken with the Confederacy on the Coast of France, and I indulge myself with the Confidence that you are safely arrived there, and have also reached the last Stage of your Destination: for your Success at which it must be the Inclination, Interest and Duty of every good American to pray.

The general Complection of Affairs here is favourable. The Subject of Finance constitutes our principal, if not only Embarrassment. To this, I know your early Attention will be turned, and, it is to be hoped, Strenuous Efforts at Home, with the Assistance of our Friends abroad, will in a little Time surmount it.

No military Event of much Notice has taken Place since the unsuccessful Attempt upon Savanna in Georgia by the allied Forces under Count D'Estaing and General Lincoln, in which we were so unfortunate as to lose the gallant Count Pulaski,[1] with other brave Officers and a Number of Men. From this however the Enemy have not derived any Advantage besides keeping Possession of the Town and a small Scope around it, for they have not occupied one other Post more interiour in that Country. I believe they suffered severely. By Dispatches, dated 23 December last, from Augusta, the present Capital of Georgia, and received the 3d inst. we are informed that the Government of the State, for some Time dormant or rather annihilated, is again organized and in Operation. George Walton, Esq. I think formerly known to you, is Governour; the Legislature and Executive are in plenary Exercise of their several Duties; and Delegates are appointed to Congress, although not yet arrived here. The Sentiments of the People are resolute and decided; Measures are taken to recruit their Troops, and the Conclusion of their Letter to Congress is, that "in the Fall and Wreck of the Union only, and Total Extirpation of their State, will they fall and perish."[2]

A large Embarkation took Place at New York about Christmas, said to be six or eight Thousand, confidently reported and believed to be destined to the Southward. Sir Henry Clinton and Lord Cornwallis have both sailed, and General Knyphausen commands in New-York.[3] This is the Intelligence, but whether Sir Henry is gone with the Troops or to Europe is not ascertained, nor have we heard any Thing of the Fleet since it sailed. Many suppose that the Weather which was uncommonly stormy for some Time after their Departure, must have altered their Course by the West-Indies. To put the Southern Army in Condition to oppose so formidable a Force, the whole North Carolina and Virginia Troops have been detached from hence, and Bodies of Militia called in the Southern Country. The Arrival of these Succours as soon as was calculated and as early as they may be wanted is a Matter of some Doubt from the extraordinary and continuing Rigour of the Winter.

It is clear the Enemy mean to bend a pointed Effort against the Southern States, and if possible to pare us down by trying this Extreme; but, I hope, they will find other use for their Time and Hardihood than plundering and desolating the Country, as in multiplied Instances they have heretofore done.

Accounts from the Floridas, which seem to wear every Mark of Credibility, except that they do not come through the official Line of Communication, say that the Forces of His Catholick Majesty are in Possession of the Town and Garrison of Pensacola, and that Operations against St. Augustine are well forward. Land-passage being at this Time extremely scarce, difficult and tedious, you will probably have pretty near as early authentick Intelligence in Europe, as we here. As to Navigation, the Delaware has been shut up since the 20th December last, and a Passage for loaded Waggons more than a Month. The News if true will draw deep in our Favour.

The Main Army is hutted for the Winter in the Vicinity of Morriston in New Jersy: a strong Garrison under the Orders of General MacDougall is at West point: General Heath comands the Posts at the Highlands; and a small Garrison occupies Rhode Island since it was evacuated by the Enemy. The Papers sent by the Comittee of foreign Affairs will give you the other current News.

Governour Livingston and Family are well by Letters lately from him.

The Vermont Business just come on.[4]

My best Compliments to Mrs. Jay and believe me Your Excellency's Most obedient Servant

WM. CH. HOUSTON

ALS. Endorsed: ". . . Recd 27 June 1780."

1 Count Casimir Pulaski was mortally wounded when he led a cavalry charge against the British lines at Savannah, 9 Oct. 1779.

2 Patriot government in Georgia ended in December 1778 with the British capture of Savannah. Sir James Wright returned as royal governor of Georgia in July 1779. The Whig government had fled to Augusta and attempted to reorganize itself. However, dissension soon broke out, and George Walton (1740–1804), a Congressional delegate from the state, and his supporters formed a constitutional assembly in opposition to the supreme executive council, electing Walton governor and thus creating a third civil government in Georgia. E. Merton Coulter, *A Short History of Georgia* (Chapel Hill, 1933), pp. 143–46.

3 Wilhelm, Baron von Knyphausen (1716–1800) commanded German troops in the British service in America after 1777. He was left in command of British forces in New York when Sir Henry Clinton and General Charles Cornwallis sailed south in December 1779 to open the British expedition against Charleston.

4 On 7 Feb. 1780 Congress received news that the New Hampshire legislature had implemented the Congressional resolutions of 24 Sept. and 2 Oct. 1779 concerning the Vermont dispute. *JCC*, XVI, 131–33.

From Robert R. Livingston

Philadelphia, 10th February 1780

Dear John

I have just steped out of Congress to let you hear by this opportunity that your friends in this part of the world are well and not unmindful of you and to acknowledge the receipt of yours from Reedy Island which after long and wearysome peregrinations reached me three days ago at this place.

The Cypher it contains is not sufficiently intricate to be in any wise relyed on if the conveyance by which this is to go should be delayed. I will inclose one that you may venture to express your most hidden thoughts in. If not we will continue the use of yours till a better is established.

The Winter has been so uncommonly severe here as to exclude all foreign intelligence, and for some time all commerce between the several States. Chesapeek, Delaware and New York bays, together with the Sound, are all frozen so as to bear loaded carts, and it is asserted that the Ice extends some miles into the sea. One hardly knows how to communicate information to a person so far removed from us, if we mention nothing but what is new in this part of the world we omit many things, which may possibly not have reached the other, And by writing transactions which have passed long since, we run the hazard of obliging you to read what some more punctual correspondent has communicated before. However as the last is the least evil, I will venture to inform you that Sir Henry Clinton sailed from New York with the light infantry and Granediers of the whole army together [with] most of the cavalry, and so many other troops as made the whole number about 7000 men. They left the Hook the 26th December, two days after which came on a most violent North East Storm accompanied with rain and snow. This was followed by North Westerly Winds, and the most extreme cold wheather that has been known in this climate. As several vessels foundered at their anchors within the Hook, we can not but promise ourselves that this fleet have suffered severely by it many of them being very probably lost and the remainder driven in a shattered condition to the West Indies. What gives weight to this conjecture is that neither the Enemy nor we have had the least intelligence of them since their departure, tho we have great reason to believe that they were designed for North and South Carolina, and had they arrived within the usual time I think we must have had intelligence from thence.[1]

You have doubtless received information of the operations of the Spanish Troops on the Missisipi where they have dispossessed the British of several posts and are as we are informed preparing a strong force at the Havanah to make an attempt upon St. Augustine, or Pensicola, which has very probably succeeded by this time, we having no accounts from Charlestown later than the 22d December at which times the enemies army under Provost still remained at Savannah. I am this particular because I concieve every information from that quarter of the world may be particularly useful to you in your present situation, and I am fearful that you do not get all you should from the committee for foreign Affairs of which I have at present the honor to be a member, and which I am labouring to get disolved in order to appoint a secretary for that department.

Though I know that our little differences of Sen[timent] can be of no great momment to you, yet I can not help telling you that Coll. Lawrance having refused to accept his appointment, we have been for some time endeavouring to supply his place. The Candidates Lovel, Morris, Hamilton and Coll. Steward. The first had six votes on three different ballotings, the second five. As both parties were fixed the matter rests till some other expedient can be fallen upon.

The Minister of france has done me the honor to express the warmest wish that I should go to his court, and as I am absolute in my determination not to fill the present vacantcy, he proposes to his friends to appoint a resident as my desire to go abroad is extreamly languid. I have done nothing to promote this design, and I am inclined to think that its novelty will be a good osstensible reason with many for not going into the measure tho' some embrace it very warmly. There is a method in which I could affect it, but then I should place LOV[EL] [IN A] SITUATION WHICH WILL GIVE HIM TOO MUCH INFLUENCE OVER FOREIGN NEGOTIATIONS, a thing by all means to be avoided.

We have determined to make the greatest exertions this campaign and have called upon respective States for their quotas of thirty five thousand men which is to be the number of our troops for the ensuing season and who may in a few days in the Northern States be increased to twice that number if required to act upon any sudden emergency.[2] While we anxiously wish for peace we see no other road to it but such as our arms account for us. This much for news and politicks. There is one other subject on which I might enter but it requires both more paper and more leisure than I have left. Let me then bid you adieu after requesting you to divide my best wishes with the partner of your heart and my other friends which you carried from hence and believe me to be Yours Most sincerely

ROB. R. LIVINGSTON

ALS. Endorsed: ". . . Recd 27 June 1780." Enclosure: a proposed cipher which has not been located. The ciphered sentence uses the monalphabetic grid described in JJ to Robert R. Livingston, 25 Oct. 1779.

1 Clinton's and Cornwallis's forces did indeed encounter difficulties on their voyage south. The expedition was nearly wrecked during the unusually harsh winter storms off Cape Hatteras; most of the cavalry and artillery horses were lost and the provisions were badly damaged. Thirty days after their departure from New York, the ships began to arrive off Tybee Island at the mouth of the Savannah River. After making repairs, they sailed for Charleston on 10 February, and on 11 February finally landed the troops.

2 On 1 February the Board of War submitted a report fixing quotas for the coming campaign. These quotas, designed to make up deficiencies from earlier drafts, amounted to 35,311 men. *JCC*, XVI, 117–21.

FROM WILLIAM CARMICHAEL

Madrid, 15 February [*1780*][1]

Dear Sir

I arrived in this city late in the Evening of the 11th after a tedious and Disagreable Journey. We had heavy rains for more than two thirds of the time, which rendered the roads so very bad that neither persuasion, threats or money could induce our Muleteers to proceed faster. My own State of health and the situation in which I left Cadiz would have prevented me from quitting THE COMPANY of my VOYAGE if other circumstances of a more DELICATE NATURE had not FORBID it.

Besides that the number of CURRIERS ON the ROAD made it impracticable for me to OBTAIN HORSES. The next day altho much indisposed I waited on the French Embassader, who had by a messuage overnight requested Mr. Girard to engage me to dinner.[2] I was received by Him and all his Family in the most friendly manner and was offered every service in his power to render us without those personal professions which give birth to many unmeaning words and MORE SUSPICIONS. Indeed I have neither expressions or time to represent the apparent candor and Liberality of his Sentiments. HE ENTER[ed] FULLY into THE GOOD DISPOSITION of his COURT and informed me that THE KING as a further proof OF his Friendship for US had agreed to pay us ANNUALLY the additional SUM OF THREE MILLIONS LIVRES during the Continuance OF THE [war] in order to enable us TO PROCURE[3] the necessaries for OUR ARMY etc. etc. and that his MAJESTY had also determined to send a considerable MARITIME and LAND FORCE EARLY in the YEAR TO America to be at the disposition and under the DIRECTION of OUR GENERAL 17 sail of the line and 4 THOUSAND TROOPS are also to be sent to the WEST Indies, if they have NOT ALREADY SAILED. Judge after this if ATTENTION, CANDOR and APPARENT UNRESERVIDNESS not the more NECESSARY on my PART. On inquiry I found that Monsieur De Galvez was at the Pardo about two leagues from Madrid where the King resides at present and in the course of conversation discovered that the PROPER CHANNEL of ADDRESS OUGHT to have BEEN THROUGH the Marquis de Florida Blanco. JEALOUSY it SEEMS PREVAILS BETWEEN THESE Ministers which renders our SITUATION more DELICATE and a little CAUTION NECESSARY. The EMBASSADOR OFFERED to INTRODUCE me, but as this could not BE DONE with PROPRIETY without previous APPLICATION HE undertook to make it the day following and to fix the TIME for my RECEPTION. THURSDAY is the day appointed when I am to be INTRODUCED to BOTH, and I think the MANNER will be the SOLE [difficulty].[4]

Among other Strong Circumstances which induce THIS CONCLUSION is the certain knowledge I have obtained THAT Monsieur Mirales RECIEVED INSTRUCTION SEVERAL MONTHS past to ENTER ENGAGEMENTS with CONGRESS to take into PAY a BODY to ASSIST in the CONQUEST OF Florida.

Your own good sense will point out the use which MAY BE MADE of this INTELLIGENCE and answers one point of the INSTRUCTIONS which I had the honor to receive from you. The Short time I have been in this City has not hitherto given me an opportunity of writing so circumstantially as I could wish in the matters above mentioned and much less to give a decided opinion on many objects Contained in YOUR INSTRUCTIONS. I find however hitherto no difficulty of acquiring in time a knowledge in most of the Subjects recommended to my Attention. I have reason to beleive that the same DISGUSTS do not subsist between the COURT as between the NATION but the most perfect HARMONY and good UNDERSTANDING. I have been positively assured and from good authority that no OVERTURE have BEEN made for PEACE.

The Dutch are arming, which is a circumstance in our favor as their preparations originate from their discontent with England on account of the late affair of the Convoy.[5] Mr. Harrison is here and proposes to proceed to Cadiz next week which will furnish me a good opportunity of writing to you.[6] I inclose you the last paper received from America. The People were in high Spirits and every thing in a good State in the beginning of January. I cannot conclude without mentioning the very polite manner in which the French Embassador offered his personal civilities in every thing that depended on Him to be useful to you in this place. Mr. Girard will write to you Himself, yet I must do him the Justice, to mention his personal Kindness to me and the Candid representations he has made in very public companies here of the prosperous situation of our Affairs. You will make use of the Method I proposed to decypher this, as time did not permit me to use the other. I beg you to make the proper Compliments for me to Mrs. Jay and Colonel Livingston.

I am with Much respect Your Most Obedient and most Humble Servant

WM. CARMICHAEL

ALS. Endorsed: ". . . rec'd 20 Feb. 1780." Another ALS, sent to Congress by William Carmichael, in DNA: PCC, 88, pp. 51–54, endorsed by Charles Thomson: ". . . Read May 12." Extracts from this letter, which JJ enclosed in his 29 Feb. 1780 dispatch to the President of Congress, appear in LbkCs in CSmH: JJ Lbk and DNA: PCC, 110, I, 39–44; printed in *RDC*, III, 496–97. There are minor variations in wording between the ALS and the copied extracts forwarded by JJ. A code based on *Entinck's New Spelling Dictionary* was used in this letter.

1 Carmichael misdated the letter 1779.

2 Conrad Gérard accompanied Carmichael on his journey to Madrid. *Peacemakers*, pp. 43–45.

3 "Purchase" in the copy sent to Congress.

4 In the ALS sent to Congress: "The manner of receiving you will be the *sole* difficulty."

5 In late December 1779 a Dutch merchant fleet, escorted by a small group of armed vessels, was stopped by a British party. After a short engagement, the

British overpowered the Dutch convoy and took the ships to port; there the prize courts confiscated both the ships and the goods they carried. The failure of diplomatic protests by the Dutch proved a blow to the pro-British party in the United Provinces. Samuel Flagg Bemis, *The Diplomacy of the American Revolution* (Bloomington, Ind., 1957), pp. 146–47.

6 Richard Harrison of Maryland represented a Virginia mercantile firm in Cádiz; he was later appointed American consul. Curtis Carrol Davis, *The King's Chevalier* (New York, 1961), pp. 42–43.

FROM WILLIAM CARMICHAEL

Madrid, 18th February 1780

Dear Sir

I did myself the honor of writing to you by a Courier whom the French Embassador dispatched to Cadiz yesterday morning since which I have been INTRODUCED BY Him TO THEIR EXCELLENCIES THE Marquis de Florida Blanca and Don Joseph de Galvez. I DELIVER[ED] YOUR LETTER to the LATTER and EXPLAIN[ED] to the FORMER the REASON which INDUCE[D] you [to] ADDRESS the OTHER with which HE APPEAR[ED] PERFECTLY SATISFY[ED]. Don Joseph de Galvez TOLD me HE SHOULD GIVE your LETTER TO THE Marquis de Florida Blanca whose BUSINESS IT WAS TO LAY it BEFORE the KING and receive his ORDER on the SUBJECT and that EITHER the Marquis OR Himself WOULD be DIRECTED to ANSWER it. I repeated the Substance of your INSTRUCTIONS to me as far as THEY RESPECT Him and was ANSWERED that he would take an OPPORTUNITY of conversing with Me on OUR AFFAIRS[S] and would inform me thro the FRENCH EMBASSADOR when it would be CONVENIENT for Him to RECEIVE me. Some COMPLIMENTS passed with respect to the Characters He had RECEIVED of US which it is unnecessary to repeat. The Marquis de Florida Blanca TOLD me that he would LAY your LETTER BEFORE the KING the same night for his consideration. I took this OPPORTUNITY of mentioning the pleasure it would give CONGRESS to hear of your RECEPTION at Madrid from the earnest desire they had to CULTIVATE the KINGS Friendship, that their Expectations were sanguine, having been led to beleive the DISPOSITION of the COURT WAS FAVORABLE by the suggestions of Persons supposed to be well acquainted with its INTENTIONS, that the hopes of the PEOPLE were also great and HINTED that there were several VESSELS about to SAIL FROM Bilboa and the PORT of France BY WHICH you would be happy to COMMUNICATE these NEWS to CONGRESS and to gratify the Expectations of the PEOPLE. He then told me that He had informed the KING of your ARRIVAL at Cadiz altho They had UNDERSTOOD your original DESTINATION was to France. That the KING had ordered Him to receive your OVERTURES and that I was at Liberty to give you this information and after a PAUSE ADDED that on Monday NEXT He hoped to have it in his power to RETURN an ANSWER to your LETTER. You will please to observe that it had not been READ by OTHER when this CONVERSATION PASSED.

He also told me that he would take an opportunity of CONVERSING with me, and would inform me when it would be convenient for Him to SEE me thro the same channel above mentioned. On MONDAY NEXT I GO TO THE Pardo by THEIR APPOINTMENT. HERE I see every day a PERSON whom I beleive to be sent BY THEM to CONVERSE with me altho I appear to know nothing of his CONNECTION with the COURT.[1] I think you may make the necessary preparations for your Journey on the receipt of this. Messrs. Adams and Dana were at Bordeaux on the 2d of February.[2] They MEAN to PROCEED TO Amsterdam FROM [there] so that the plan of our Friend Morris hath taken place. Mr. Lee CORRESPONDED with the Marquis de Florida Blanca, but if I am well informed the CORRESPONDENCE consisted of American NEWS on the one part and COMPLIMENT on the other. Mr. Girard leaves this tomorrow, he hath had CONVERSATIONS [with] the SPANISH MINISTER of about two HOURS at one TIME and three at ANOTHER. I am in a way of obtaining most of the INFORMATION you desired. I beg you to present the proper compliments for me to your Lady and the Colonel and to beleive me with much respect and esteem Your Most Obedient and most Humble Servant

WM. CARMICHAEL

ALS. The cipher sections in this letter, decoded by JJ and with minor corrections by the editors, are in the code based on *Entinck's New Spelling Dictionary*. C in DNA: PCC, Misc., roll 2; printed in *RDC*, III, 502–03.

1 Probably a reference to Don Diego de Gardoqui, of the Bilbao mercantile firm of Joseph (José) Gardoqui and Sons, which had been shipping goods to America for several years. He served as Floridablanca's emissary in negotiations with JJ concerning the financial aid the U.S. sought from Spain during the summer and fall of 1780. *Peacemakers*, pp. 228, 232–34; Bemis, *Diplomacy of the American Revolution*, pp. 57, 91.

2 Adams and Dana embarked for France in November 1779 but were forced instead to put to land on the Spanish coast. The Americans began the long overland journey from La Corunna to Paris on 26 December, finally arriving there on 9 Feb. 1780. John Adams, *Diary*, II, 440–34; IV, 191–240.

To PHILIP SCHUYLER

Cadiz, 19th February 1780

Dear Sir

Altho my Correspondents have necessarily become numerous I shall nevertheless think the Number too small, till your Name be added to the List. It has long been my Wish to cherish in private Life, the Connection which commenced between us when public Men; and to render that reciprocal Regard which attached us to each other in Times of Danger and Commotion, subservient to our mutual Satisfaction on the Return of Peace and Tranquility. I have often regretted the Suspension of our Correspondence. At the Time it happened, I had no Idea of being so long absent from You; and my omitting to answer your last Letter, arose from an opinion that the Subject of it could be more properly discussed by a Fireside than on Paper. Could I have supposed however that we should have been separated by some Years, instead of a few weeks or months, you should have had less Reason to think me negligent.

Your Attention is not I am persuaded so restrained to domestic objects, and the Pleasures or occupations of that Retreat which you have too much Reason to prize, as to prevent your turning your Eyes towards every Part of that great Circle of Politics, which envolves and affects us all. My Views are at present confined to a Segment of that Circle, but that Segment affords Field for many Inquiries, and yields Matter for Observations both interesting and entertaining. I will share them with you if you please, and to do it the more effectually, wish you would send me a Plan and Explanation of the Cypher you once shewed me at Rhynebeck, but which I do not now well recollect. Let the Key word be the name of the man who so long and regularly placed every Day a Tooth Pick by Mrs. Schuylers Plate, written backwards, that is the last Letter in the Place of the first, and so on.[1]

When at Madrid I shall recieve very few Letters but through the Post Offices of France or Spain, and I much doubt whether any Letters known or suspected to be for or from me, would pass through that Channel uninspected. I think it would be best for you to send your Letters to Philadelphia under Cover to our Friend Robert Morris, who will take proper Care to forward them; and they would probably come more directly to his Hands, if sent by the Post, inclosed to one of the New York Delegates. Soon after my arrival at Madrid I shall write to Mr. Morris on the Subject, and mention to him the name of some Gentleman there under cover to whom he may transmit Letters for me.

Unless the Vessel by which this Letter is to go, will sail sooner than I expect, you will probably recieve another enclosed with it. Make our Compliments, if you please, to Mrs. Schuyler, and believe me to be with sincere Regard Your obedient Servant

JOHN JAY

ALS. N: Schuyler Mansion Docs. #8. A duplicate ALS is in the same collection. Both endorsed. Endorsed DftS in JP.

1 Apparently this cipher was never used.

To Robert R. Livingston

Cadiz, 19th February 1780

Dear Robert

It cannot be necessary to give you a minute Detail of our having been driven to Martinico, or of our sailing from thence. Of those Events I am persuaded you are well informed. We staid only ten Days in that Island. Contrast them with those which preceded, and you will readily believe we enjoyed them. The Hospitality, Cleanliness and Cleverness of the Inhabitants pleased me greatly, so much so, that I assure You I should have been in less Haste to leave them, had I been actuated only by personal Considerations.

The Island has a romantic Appearance. The greatest *Rarity*, if I may use that Expression, which I saw in it, was here and there a piece of plain Ground, scarcely large enough for a bowling Green. The Country, or rather that Part of it which came within my View, consists of innumerable Hills, in the Form of Sugar Loaves, crouded together, and cultivated almost to their very Summits. How the Inhabitants can prevail upon the Earth to remain on them I cannot concieve. I was told however that in some Parts of the Island which I did not visit, there is a greater Proportion of plain ground.

The Town of St. Pierres is delightful, clean almost beyond Description, running Streams in every Street, convenient Baths of warm and cold Water in many; and Fountains in, I believe all the Houses.

'Till about nineteen months ago, there were no Bees in the Island. A Gentleman of the name of Pitault, then got a Hive from Marigalante and when I was there, forty odd Swarms, all originally proceeding from that single Hive, were then in the Island and in Mr. Pitault's Possession, except a few that had escaped to the Hills. As the Country is at no Season of the Year destitute of Food proper for them, they are not deprived of their Lives together with their Honey, as with us; and hence their Encrease becomes without Comparison greater. The Hives were all laid as it were on their Sides; what we should call the Bottom, fronted those who stood before the Beehouse, was entirely open, and afforded a full View of the Combs within. When full the Bees are removed to an empty Hive; and again proceed to lay up

Stores for a winter that will never approach them, a Circumstance thus, which shews that their much boasted Wisdom is confined to narrow Limits. Mr. Pitault was so obliging as to present us with several Flasks of the Honey and some Candles he had made of the Wax. The Honey was new from the Hive exceeding good, very white and limpid, but though collected chiefly from Orange Flowers, it was by no Means so fragrant as the Virgin Honey of our Country, made from White Clover, and untainted with Buckwheat. The Gentlemen at St. Pierres view this rapid Encrease of Bees in their Island with great Pleasure. Their Consumption of Wax Candles, in Churches as well as Dwelling Houses is great, and they expect in a few Years to find that Article among their Exports. It is certain that in Countries where the Earth is never without Flowers, the Propagation of Bees must be very easy, and the Proffits arising from them proportionably great. I have been told and from good Authority, that the Island of Cuba is a striking Instance of this. Its Inhabitants within these last fifteen Years were indebted to Europe for all the Wax Candles they used, and at present they export many hundred Tons of Wax every Year.

We left Martinico the 28th December in the Aurora a french Frigate commanded by the Marquis De La Flotte, a very genteel agreable Man. He went by the Way of St. Thomas to avoid Danger; and arrived here the 22d of last month. If when you have nothing else to do, you should consult your Map, you will percieve that we had a very uncommon short Passage. The Aurora is a dull Sailor, but we were favored with winds constantly fair, and I may add strong. The Marquis was bound to Toulon, from whence we expected to have gone to Paris, and from thence over the Pyrenees to Madrid. But on touching here for Intelligence, we learned that Admiral Rodney had saved us the necessity of going that round about Way to Madrid, he having gained an undoubted Superiority in the Mediterranean. This Point being settled, I immediately made the necessary Communications to the spanish ministry, from whom I am now in daily Expectation of recieving Dispatches.

The Cypher I sent you has become useless, and must be omitted. Take the following, vizt. the second part of Boyers Dictionary, in which the English is placed before the french. It is not paged. You will therefore number the Pages, marking the first page with no. 1, and so on. In each page there are three Columns, let *c* denote the first, *a* the second, and *b* the third, count the number of words from the Top, to the one you mean to use, inclusive, and add seven to it. Thus, for Instance, the word *Abject* is the *third* word, in the *third* Column, of the *second* Page; and is to be written in Cypher as follows, 2 - b - 10. The Dictionary I have was printed in London in the Year 1771 and is called the thirteenth Edition with large additions.

Enclose your Letters for me to our Friend Robert Morris who will with Pleasure forward them, and I think it would be well to send them so enclosed by the Post to him, under Cover to one of the New York Delegates in whose Care you may confide. Be particular in informing me whether this Letter comes to your Hands free from Marks of Inspection. I shall put a Wafer under the Seal; compare the Impression with those you have formerly recieved from me. If you should have Reason to suspect that all is not fair, I will on being informed of it send you another Cypher. Be cautious what you write in the common Way, as I am persuaded few Letters would reach me thro the Post offices of France or Spain uninspected.

Be so kind as to present our Regards and best Wishes to your Mama, Mrs. Livingston and the Rest of the Family.

I am Dear Robert Your Friend

JOHN JAY

ALS. NHi: Robert R. Livingston Papers. Dupl. ALS (endorsed) and tripl. ALS in the same collection with JJ's notation: "By the Brig Expedition Capt. Morgan bound to Boston." Endorsed dft in JP.

From Floridablanca

The Pardo, Madrid, 24 February 1780

To Don Juan de Jay, Minister of the American Provinces. In answering Sr. Jay's letter to Sr. Galvez, Minister, Bureau of the Indies and explaining to him the disposition of the King to his coming here in a public character, and proposing that he come without it.

Hand delivered by his secretary, who is here.[1]

Sir

Having received the letter Your Excellency sent by Mr. <Gerard> Carmichael, and after having informed the King of its particulars, His Majesty has commanded me to inform Your Excellency that His Majesty is most pleased and applauds Your Excellency's appointment by the American Congress to the charge stated in the letter, to express His Majesty's esteem for those members who named Your Excellency, as well as to acknowledge the repute held by His Majesty as to Your Excellency's <capabilities>, integrity, abilities, and station. Also His Majesty has heard with pleasure the desire of the Colonies to establish a liaison with Spain, of whose good will <or

without it>[2] they have already had sufficient proof. <But> Nevertheless, His Majesty believes first of all it is necessary to arrange the manner, the points, and the mutual understanding upon which ought to be based the <correct> union the <United> American States wish to undertake with this Kingdom. Therefore, <His Majesty would like for you to come> there is no difficulty in the way of Your Excellency's coming to this Court to explain your goals and those of the Congress, and to hear those of His Majesty, and by this means reaching an agreement, upon which can be built a perfect friendship <and alliance>, and mutually defining its extent and scope. <After which, and not before, Your Excellency will be able to carry out your duties in an official capacity.> The King believes <that Your Excellency will find his thoughts proper on this matter> that until the possibilities of an agreement become certain, as His Majesty expects it will, it is not fitting that Your Excellency be granted a public character, which must depend upon recognition and a future treaty. But Your Excellency can be assured of the earnest and sincere good will of His Majesty toward the United States and <of His Majesty's discretion with respect to these negotiations> of his wishes to remove any difficulty, whatsoever, preventing the mutual friendship between the United States and this Kingdom <to the beginnings of strong diplomatic ties, which should produce a mutual friendship>. The same has been <written> conveyed to Mr. Carmichael <and I expect that he>, who will inform Your Excellency. I, praying that the Lord may grant you a long life, <in hope that I have discharged these matters justly and discreetly, according to His Majesty's instructions> remain faithfully and respectfully, Sir, Your obedient servant

Translation, authenticated by Professor B. Bussell Thompson of Columbia University, of Dft in Spanish in AHN: Estado, leg. 3884, exp. 8, doc. 6. LS in Spanish and Trans. in hand of Brockholst Livingston in JP; LbkCs in Spanish in both DNA: PCC, 100, I and in CSmH: JJ Lbk; LbkCs in Spanish and English in DLC: Franklin Papers, III, 30–33; printed in *RDC*, III, 515–16.

1 Carmichael.

2 Apparently "*o sin ellas.*"

From William Bingham

St. Pierre, Martinique, February 25th, 1780

I have greatly Suffered from the Consideration of the Inconviencies that both you and Mrs. Jay must have been exposed to on your Passage from hence, arising from the scanty Accommodations of the French Frigate. I trembled at the thoughts of it before your Departure, but I was fearfull of mentioning it, least I might anticipate that Uneasiness of Mind which I am confident you must have experienced.

However, I hope this will find you Safe arrived and established at Madrid, with the Prospect of executing the important Business committed to your Care in Such a Manner as to give Satisfaction to yourself, and to justify the Hopes that are conceived of its success from your abilities in the Negotiation.

Notwithstanding the unfavorable Impressions that a *certain Gentleman*[1] maliciously insinuated in the Minds of the Government here in regard to Continental Affairs, and the Obstacles that thereby arose in procuring proper Assistance for the Reparation of the Frigate, I have the pleasure to inform you that I have surmounted all Such Difficulties, and that the Confederacy will take her Departure in a Fortnight,[2] fitted out in the best Manner that the exhausted State of the King's Magazines will permit. The Intendant, under whose Controul and at whose Disposal are the public Stores, persisted in refusing every Kind of Succor, but through the Influence of a spirited Remonstrance on the Subject, I procured an Order from the General[3] to have Such Articles as the Frigate had occasion for immediately delivered, and in Case of the Intendants obstinately persevering in a Refusal, to throw open the Doors of the Magazines by an armed Force, and take them out at pleasure.

I Shall soon return to America and shall endeavor to make my Stay there as short as possible. You are acquainted with the Object that attracts my Attention; will you be So obliging as to give me your opinion on the probability of my Succeeding.[4] I Shall write to Doctor Franklin and will endeavor to procure his Interposition in my Behalf. Can I flatter myself that you will do me the favor of Sounding him on the Subject and Know whether it will be agreeable to him and transmit me the Results of your Enquiries, which you will please to direct to me at Philadelphia, and forward by Triplicates, eventually to provide against the Accidents that your Letters may be exposed to.

The Success of a Detachment of 5000 Continental Troops under the Command of General Stirling in taking Possession of the Garrison and Stores on Staten Island, is the only Intelligence of any Importance from America. It consisted of 300 Men and a considerable Quantity of Provisions etc.[5] The Severity of the Winter far exceeding what has been Known in the Memory of Man gave an opportunity of executing this Expedition by forming a Bridge of Ice for our Troops to pass over.

A very large Reinforcement of 8 to 10,000 Men, under the Orders of General Lord Cornwallis took their Departure from New York bound for Georgia. Their Object, it is imagined, is the Conquest of So. Carolina. Altho General Washington has detached 5000 Men from the Virginia and No. Carolina Lines, to reinforce this important Garrison, I tremble for the Fate of it. Should the Arms of the Enemy prove Successfull in that Quarter, it will turn out a most brilliant Stroke for them; it will furnish them with great Pretensions and will enable them to assume a high and imposing Tone in the Conferences that may be expected to take place on the Subject of a Negotiation of Peace.

I was inclined to think, (but I find myself mistaken) that the formidable force stationed at the Havannah, would prevent the English from attempting any further Operations on the Southern States, as they are exposed to be greatly disconcerted in their Plans by an unexpected Attack of the Enemy. Should not the Defence of these States engage the peculiar Attention of the Spaniards, as by the local Situation of their Possessions, and the Strength they have collected there, they can easily and Speedily afford us Assistance. I cannot believe, as many do, that because they have not formally acknowledged and guarenteed our Independance, they esteem themselves under no Obligation to repel the Attacks made by the Enemy on any of the United States. However, Should this be the Case, I hope that through the good Effects arising from your Embassy, this desireable Event will Soon be brought about, altho Some political Reasons may hitherto have opposed it. Tuscro Duci, nil desperandum.[6]

The Continental Currency still continues depreciating. It is a Circumstance very alarming, and whose pernicious Effects must prove of fatal Consequence to the Interests of the United States. I am fully convinced that the only Method to arrest its Sinking Credit, is to redeem the greatest Part of it by calling it out of Circulation, which can only be effected by negotiating a Loan in Europe, and by the Application of it in the Manner and to the Purposes that I mentioned to you in a Conversation we had together on the Subject.

You have doubtless heard that Mr. Laurens is appointed Ambassador to the States General of the United Provinces. Mr. Lovell was to Sail for Europe, on Some important Mission, which was Kept a profound Secret.[7]

On my Arrival in America I shall frequently trouble you with my Reflections on public Affairs, though I cannot flatter myself with the

Hopes of being admitted into the Arcana of Business So as to be able to observe the various Springs and Movements that govern the political Machine, which are often no other than private Interest disguised under the fallacious Mark of public Virtue.

Do me the favor of making my most respectfull Compliments to Mrs. Jay, and tell her that I Sincerely wish her the greatest pleasure and Satisfaction during her Residence in Europe. A Number of her female Friends, amongst which are Madame Delhomme and Madam Pitault, who greatly regretted her speedy Departure, beg to be affectionately remembered to her.

Please to let Colonel Livingston Know that I am much interested in his Welfare and Shall be happy to hear from him. I Shall write him shortly by a Safe Opportunity.

I am with great Esteem and Regard Dear Sir Your Sincere Friend and obedient humble servant

WM. BINGHAM

P.S. Capt. Harding requests me to make his best Compliments to you and Mrs. Jay, and to inform you that he takes his Departure immediately for Philadelphia.

ALS.

1 Probably Gérard.

2 At Bingham's prodding the *Confederacy* was repaired in Martinique, and Bingham himself sailed for America on the vessel, embarking on 30 March 1780.

3 François-Claude Amour, Marquis de Bouillé (1739–1800), was governor of Martinique and the Windward Islands. *Dictionnaire de Biographie Française*, VI, 1315.

4 Bingham's motives for returning to America combined commercial interests, pending litigation, and the desire to be reimbursed by Congress for the sums he had advanced as agent in Martinique. Congress was in Bingham's debt 507,641 livres for these advances, and his unpaid salary plus expenses amounted to an additional 110,342 livres. Robert C. Alberts, *The Golden Voyage: The Life and Times of William Bingham* (Boston, 1969), pp. 70, 78, 87.

5 The reports of success were greatly exaggerated. The detachment of 3,000 under Sterling was repulsed.

6 Horace, *Odes*, Book I, no. 7, line 27. The full quotation is *Nil desperandum Teucro duce et auspice Teucro:* "Never despair under Teucro's leadership and Teucro's auspices."

7 Bingham had apparently gotten incorrect information that Lovell was the one selected as secretary to Benjamin Franklin in France, when in fact no decision had been reached.

FROM WILLIAM CARMICHAEL

Madrid, 26th February 1780

Dear Sir

I WAIT[ED] on his EXCELLENCY the Conde de Florida Blanca YESTERDAY AGREABLE to the APPOINTMENT of WHICH I had the HONOR to give you NOTICE the 18th instant. HE in a VERY POLITE AND GRACIOUS MANNER told me that YOUR LETTER[1] had been LAID BEFORE his MAJESTY and that HE WAS DIRECTED to ANSWER in the TERMS of the ENCLOSED LETTER. HE at the same TIME LEFT the CHOICE to me to COMMUNICATE this INFORMATION MYSELF or to RECIEVE a [reply] from Him to you on the SUBJECT. I without HESITATION PREFERRED the LATTER. I was FURTHER INFORMED that altho it did not order the KINGS DIGNITY or that of CONGRESS that you should (déployer)[2] APPEAR in a PUBLIC CHARACTER until the OBJECT of your MISSION and the INTERESTS of Spain had been FAIRLY DISCUSSED and DECIDE[D] on yet that we should be SU[E]D and TREATED as Strangers of DISTINCTION and that as we might appear at COURT an INTIMATION was GIVEN me at the same time that neither his MAJESTY or the PRINCE of Asturies[3] would be DISPLEASED to SEE me THERE. I had written thus far expecting to have the inclosed to send you by the Tuesdays post. In this however I was dissappointed, tho not intentionally as the delay was occasioned by the absence of a SERVANT INTRUSTED with YOUR LETTER. I WAITED again yesterday on the MINISTER who expressed his uneasiness for what had HAPPENED and promised me to send it this day. It has this moment been delivered to me UNSEALED and you will see that the REFUSAL is SOFTNED as much as possible by the manner in which it has been CONVEYED to you.

I was yesterday for the first time at COURT and received several GRACIOUS LOOKS and SMILES from his MAJESTY and the PRINCE De Asturies and CONSEQUENTLY many civilities from the COURTIERS. If in consequence of the ENCLOSED you should determine to come here immediately, I beg you to give me notice that I may provide proper apartments for your reception until you can accommodate yourself to your satisfaction and that I may meet you on the road either at Aranjuez or elsewhere to give you at large such information as I may be able to procure here and to escort you to Madrid. I have not heard from Dr. Franklin or any other American since my arrival, on which account and many others I am impatient to see you. I beg you to make the proper compliments for me to your Lady and the Colonel and to beleive me with great respect and esteem Your Most Obedient and Most Humble Servant

WM. CARMICHAEL

ALS. Endorsed. Letter employs a nomenclator based on *Entinck's New Spelling Dictionary.* JJ's partial decoding is written above the code symbols. The decoding process has been completed by the editors. Enclosure: Floridablanca to JJ, 24 Feb. 1780, in which the Spanish minister gave JJ permission to come to Madrid.

1 A reference to the letter JJ sent Gálvez on 27 Jan. 1780, which evidently was presented to Charles III, the king of Spain.

2 JJ wrote "display" above this word.

3 The prince of Asturias (1748–1819), heir to the Spanish throne.

To William Carmichael

Cadiz, 29 February 1780

Dear Sir,

I have had the Pleasure of recieving your Favor of the 18th Inst. The manner in which you mannaged the Matters mentioned in it perfectly corresponds with my Ideas of what would have been proper on that occasion. My next Letter to Congress shall enclose a Copy of that Part of yours which respects the Business in Question.

Mrs. Jay has been indisposed but is now better and with the Colonel desire me to make their Compliments to You. I am Dear Sir your most obedient and very humble Servant.

Dft.

To William Carmichael

Cadis, 8th March 1780

Dear Sir

<I have been honored with your Excellencys Favor of the 24th Instant> Your Favor of the 26th February with its Enclosure did not reach me till some Time after its arrival owing to an omission <for which Mr> which made the Subject of a Note I recieved with it from Monsieur Le Couteaut.[1]

As nothing now remains to <prevent> delay my leaving this City but the <Want of Carriages> necessary preparations for the Journey which I declined making till certain <of Remembering necessary> of having Occasion for them <requisite>, I hope soon to start for

Madrid. Your offer of meeting me at Aranjues is obliging and I accept it with Pleasure. I am exactly in your Situation respecting Intelligence from our Friends in France not having recieved a line from any of them.

It is impossible for me to ascertain precisely the Day when I shall leave this or be at Aranjues. You may expect therefore to hear further from me on that Subject.

When you deliver the enclosed be pleased to mention the omission which occasioned its being of so late a Date. I am very anxious to hear from America, especially as the English Accounts of the Dissipation of Sir Henry Clintons Fleet by a Storm are very interesting. If you have further Information on that head mention it in your next. I am told that so many weeks successively have not passed since the war without Arrivals at this Port from America.

You have omitted to tell me what is to be done with a Trunk you left with us, whether to send it to Monsieur L'Coutonts or <bring it with us> to Madrid with our Baggage.

Mrs. Jays Health is much mended and I hope will be perfectly restored by the <Exercise the> Journey provided the Fleas and other Inconveniences on the Road prove less formidable than they are represented to us, which I expect will be the case. The Col. is learning Spanish very fast. I suppose you are almost Master of it. They both desire their Compliments to you.

I am Dear Sir your most obedient Servant

Dft. Enclosure: JJ to Floridablanca, 6 March 1780. ALS and Spanish trans. in AHN: Estado, leg. 3884, exp. 8, docs. 7 and 8; LbkCs in DNA: PCC, 110, I, 83–85; in DLC: Franklin Papers, III, 33–34; and in CSmH: JJ Lbk.

[1] Jean-Barthélemy Le Couteulx de Cautaleu, a French financier.

From Arthur Lee

L'Orient, March 17th 1780

Sir

I had not the honor of receiving your Favor dated Cadiz, the 26th. of January 'till this day and at this place, where I am to embark as soon as the Alliance is ready. Your Letter had a double Seal upon it, the undermost seeming to be a head, and the one above a Coat of Arms, but what I cannot clearly make out. I mention this that you may judge whether these Seals were of your applying.

Give me leave, Sir, to take this opportunity of expressing my concern for the dangers and sufferings you and your Family experienced in your pasage; and to congratulate you and my Country on your safe arrival in Europe.

I waited some time in Paris, after I received notice of your appointment, in expectation of your arrival, that I might have communicated many things to you in a personal interview which cannot be commited to Paper. It would have given me very great pleasure to have obtained for you those recommendations to the confidence of some of the first persons at the Court of Madrid, that were promised me, and which I could have done by making you personally acquainted with those who were to give them.

The Copies of Memoires and the Letters which I wrote to Congress contained in general what you do me the honor of asking. I have reason to believe that you will find a favorable disposition where you wish. There is no Court in Europe at which Secrecy will so much recommend a Negociator as that to which you are destind. Insomuch that as far as you can keep the capital parts of your Negotiation entirely to your own breast, you will have reason to think it prudent. You are to negotiate with a people of honor and a Ministry of wisdom. They will propose fairly and perform faithfully. You will not be embarrassed by intrigue, at least none of Spanish origin, nor will it be advantageous to employ any.

These considerations together with the good sense and great abilities for which you are distinguished make me hope, Sir, that you will accomplish with facility the important purposes of your mission to the advantage of our Country and to your own honor.

The House of Gardoqui has executed what was entrusted to them with diligence, and as far as I can judge with fidelity. They therefore deserve your confidence. There is due to them from the Public 12000 Livres which they advanced for the freight of goods sent to Congress; and which, as it was done without my knowledge, I had made no provision for, and therefore coud not repay it. The part of the prise money due to the Public for the prises sent into the ports of Spain by Capt. Conyngham[1] was not remitted to me, nor have the Accounts been settled to my knowlege. Lagoanere a la Corogne,[2] and a House at Cadiz which, my Papers being packt up, I cannot recollect, had the sale of those Prises.

Accept my thanks, Sir, for your care of the Letters for me. As I shall certainly have quitted Europe, before they can reach me, I must beg the favor of you to enclose them to Mr. Lovell, with the first Dispatches that you send to Congress.

If an entire Stranger may be permitted to offer his homage to your Lady; permit me to request your making mine acceptable to Mrs. Jay.

I have the honor to be Sir, your most obedient and Humble Servant

ARTHUR LEE

ALS. Endorsed. LbkCs in CSmH: JJ Lbk and DNA: PCC, 110, I, 62–65; printed with minor variations in *RDC*, III, 554–55.

[1] See above, Anne Conyngham to JJ, 17 July 1779.

[2] Michel Lagoanère was described by John Adams as "a Gentleman who has acted for some time as an American Agent at Corunna". John Adams, *Diary*, II, 412n.

From Gouverneur Morris

Philadelphia, 20th March, 1780

Dear Jay

The Disaster you met with and the Delay occasioned by it will make all my Letters old before you see them. Your note from Martinique the Day after your arrival shuts my Mouth up to any Thing worth your knowing. This Letter will go by a circuitous rout but I trust a safe one. I shall therefore mention that Congress have anvilled out another new System of Finance the Plain English of which is a Breach of their Resolution to stop the Press.[1] After this the public Faith is to be pledged etc. on all which I shall make no Comments. In general I tell *you* that it wont do and Money must therefore be had in Europe for however there may be a Sufficiency in the Country that is of little Importance unless there could be ways and Means discovered to draw it out. I early foresaw what hath now happened and as early predicted it and as early labored to prevent it and according to Custom was answered with a Compliment to my *fine Imagination*. God help the knowning ones.

Adieu my Dear Friend. Remember me to yours.

GOUVR. MORRIS

ALS. PPInd. Addressed: "To Mr. Jay to be left chez Monsieure Manuel Grand Cauguiere. Paris." Endorsed: ". . . Recd 4 July 1780."

[1] This resolution provided for a revaluation of old Continental currency at the rate of forty paper dollars to one of specie and directed the states to tax this money out of existence. As the old money was brought in, new bills were to be issued and backed by state credit. These bills were to draw 5 percent interest, payable in bills of exchange. *JCC*, XVI, 262–66.

To Benjamin Franklin

Madrid, 14 April 1780

Sir,

On the 26th January last at Cadiz, I did myself the Honor of writing to your Excellency a Letter, by M. Gerard, enclosing one for the honorable Arthur Lee Esqr. and Copies of others I had written to the spanish and French ministers, and among other things informing you, that several Letters or rather large Pacquets directed to you were in my Possession, with which I was much at Loss what to do, and requesting your direction. I have also written to you other Letters of Later Date from the same Place, advising you of Bills I had drawn upon you viz. the 28th January, 3d March and 20th March.[1]

As the Receipt of other Letters carried by M. Gerard from hence to Paris has been acknowledged, there is no Room to Apprehend that mine to you by him, has miscarried. I find it therefore difficult to account for my not having been favored with a single Line from you since my arrival.

Your Letters should immediately on my arrival have been sent by the Post, but it being well known that all Letters whose Contents there is Reason to suppose interesting, are inspected in the Course of that Conveyance I would not prevail upon myself to expose yours to that Treatment especially as there are indorsements on some of them being Sunk in Case of Captance [*sic*]. Nor did it appear to me more prudent to send them by a Special Express, because being a stranger I knew not whom to trust or in whose Recommendation to confide.

But as between two and three months have already elapsed without my receiving any orders or advice from you on the Subject I should Expose myself to Censure were I longer to forbear transmitting them in such manner as appeared to me least hazardous. I shall therefore deliver them in a Bag Sealed and directed to M. Joshua Johnson[2] at Nantes this Evening, to Monsieur Henry Bouteiller a young French Gentleman, who will set out for that Please [*sic*] to morrow, and who travelled from Cadiz here in company with me. From the Character which I received of him there as well as my own observations of his Conduct since I am induced to confide both in this Honor and his Care. I shall enclose this Letter to Mr. Johnson and request the favor of him to send it to you together with the others by the first safe Conveyance and I shall apprise him of my Objections to their going by the Post. Among them are some directed to Persons of Suspicious Character in Britain, and were all delivered to me by the officers of the Confederacy at martinico, except the one directed to Mrs. Mary Brown at Trees Bank Scotland, which was committed to my Care by her Sister, a Daughter of Peter Van Brugh Livingston Esqr. of Baskindridge; the Contents of it are perfectly unexceptionable, and would give more Pleasure to an American than a Briton.[3]

As not only a good understanding but also a constant Interchange of Intelligence and attentions between the public Servants at the different Courts are necessary to procure to him Constituents all the advantages capable of being derived from this Appointment, it would give me very sensible regret in my Endeavours to cultivate the one and engage the other should prove abortive.

I this moment received a Note from the Marquis d'Yranda,[4] informing me that M. Grand of Paris[5] had desired him by his Letter of the 22d February to hold at my Disposition the Net Produce of Nineteen thousand nine hundred and twenty one Livres Tournois which I might receive when I thought proper; from the Particularity of the Sum I conjecture this to be in consequence of your order.

I have the Honour to be Your Excellency's most obedient and most humble Servant

(signed) JOHN JAY

P.S. I have just received from M. Lee an answer to the Letter I took the Liberty of sending inclosed to you by M. Gerard.

LbkC. DLC: Franklin Papers, III, 17–19.

1 LbkC of JJ's 26 Jan. 1780 letter is in DLC: Franklin Papers, III, 1–5; dft in JP; printed in *RDC*, III, 470–71. LbkCs of JJ's letters of 28 Jan., 3 and 20 March 1780, are in DLC: Franklin Papers. The 20 March letter is printed in *RDC*, III, 561–62; the dft of the 28 January letter is in JP.

2 Joshua Johnson (1742–1802), brother of Governor Thomas Johnson of Maryland, represented a U.S. mercantile firm in London until the outbreak of the Revolution, at which time he removed to France, settling at Nantes and executing various commissions for the Congress. After the war he served as the first U.S. consul in London, 1790–97. Edward S. Delaplaine, *The Life of Thomas Johnson* (N.Y., 1927), p. 14.

3 Mary Livingston (Mrs. John) Brown (b. 1746) was the second daughter of SLJ's uncle, Peter Van Brugh Livingston. Mary Brown's husband was a captain in the 60th Regiment of Royal Americans. She had two sisters living in America at this time, Susan (1759–1833) and Elizabeth (1761–1802) Livingston. Reynolds, *Family Hist. of So. N.Y.*, III, 1325–26.

4 Simón de Aragorri y Olavide, the Marquis d'Yranda, Spain's honorary minister of the Council of the Treasury, aided JJ occasionally during the latter's mission in Madrid.

5 Ferdinand Grand, the Paris representative of the famous Swiss banking family, was the unofficial American banker in Paris. John Adams, *Diary*, II, 303.

FROM TIMOTHY MATLACK

Philadelphia, April 21, 1780

Sir,

The American Philosophical Society for promoting useful knowledge etc. has the honor to enroll your name in the list of its members, of which you will receive official information through another channel; but the situation of the Society will not admit of your having a Diploma until a new one is [framed] agreable to the late change of circumstances. The Society applied to the late Sitting of General Assembly for an act to incorporate us, which was very readily granted. On this occassion the Reverend Dr. Ewing was requested to deliver the annual oration, to which duty he had been long since appointed; but having been lately chosen Provost of our University, and this Seminary of learning having been by the war thrown into great disorder, his immediate and whole attention became necessary to restore it to order again. He therefore declined the oration.[1]

You know the delay of business in publick bodies, and will therefore not wonder that too much time was spent before any other was appointed to that duty; so that some Gentlemen who might otherwise have done honor to the institution were, by this means, discouraged from undertaking the task. Seeing the opportunity likely to be lost, and my motto being "I can try" I determined to make the best use of the little time there was left, and threw together the thoughts enclosed herewith. When you read it pray remember, it was delivered in the presence of the Assembly of Pennsylvania, composed of pious good men, well read in Scripture.

The blush which I feel upon publishing so crude a performance would have restrained, effectually, the vanity of an author and prevented my troubling you with it, had I not known it would officially find its way to Paris, which renders some apology necessary, more on account of the Society than on my own.

The enclosing it to you affords me an opportunity of recommending to your notice the bearer, Doctor John Foulke, a young Gentleman of a good family in this city and whose abilities and industry will one day make him a useful and respectable character. The present contest has laid the doctor under very singular difficulties, which render the countenance and assistance of Gentlemen of Distinction abroad absolutely necessary to him. He has undergone a regular examination before the Trustees of the late College of this city; but the change in the institution taking place and the professors not being yet appointed, renders it impossible for him to obtain a diploma at present. Under these circumstances let me beg your interest in his favour, being firmly pursuaded that he will do honor to his country.[2]

The resolution of Congress of the 18th March, respecting the bills of credit, alarmed the holders of Loan office certificates, and occasioned several meetings of the citizens.[3] Great warmth appeared among them; but before the measures they proposed could be executed the resolve of the 18th instant was passed, which has put it in our power to reconcile the people to the measure with less difficulty than was expected. Something like this will probably happen in several of the States, and will, I hope, as happily subside.

I have the honour to be with great respect Your Excellencys Most obedient and very humble servant

T. MATLACK

ALS. Endorsed: ". . . Recd 27th Aug. 1780. anns. 17 Sept." Enclosure: Timothy Matlack's "An Oration, delivered March 16, 1780, before the patron, vice presidents and members of the American Philosophical Society held at Philadelphia for promoting useful knowledge." Evans, 16867.

Timothy Matlack (d. 1829), a Philadelphia merchant, was secretary of the Supreme Executive Council of Pennsylvania, and he had previously served as assistant to Charles Thomson. When the University of the State of Pennsylvania was granted a new charter in 1779, he was made a trustee.

1 The University of Pennsylvania traces its origins to a secondary school opened by Benjamin Franklin in Philadelphia in 1751, and it was formally chartered in 1753 as the Academy and Charitable School in the Province of Pennsylvania. A second charter (10 June 1755) conferred the right to grant degrees and created the College of Philadelphia. Provost William Smith was joined in England by James Jay in 1762 in a separate but related effort to raise funds for the College of Philadelphia and King's College respectively. The war caused the suspension of classes in Philadelphia in June 1777, but the institution was revived and reorganized in 1779. The legislature, dominated by the radical Constitution party, then issued a new charter confirming the old one but setting up a new Board of Trustees and changing the name to the University of the State of Pennsylvania. The Reverend John Ewing (1732–1802), pastor of the First Presbyterian Church of Philadelphia and professor of natural philosophy since 1762, was appointed provost. Thomas Harrison Montgomery, *A History of the University of Pennsylvania from Its Foundation to A.D. 1770* (Philadelphia, 1900), pp. 46, 112–13, 139, 178, 210–11, 337–38; Edward Potts Cheyney, *History of the University of Pennsylvania, 1740–1940* (Philadelphia, 1940), pp. 26, 37, 47–48, 63–66, 116–20, 123–25.

2 Dr. John Foulke (1757–96), a former army surgeon and protégé of Dr. Benjamin Rush, studied medicine at Paris and Leipzig and, on his return to America, served as demonstrator and lecturer in anatomy at the Medical College of Philadelphia. Dr. Foulke was similarly recommended to John Adams by Benjamin Franklin in a letter of 20 April 1780. *Pennsylvania Magazine,* XXIX, 22–23.

3 Holders of Loan Office certificates stood to lose most from this new emission. Although the certificates drew interest only in paper money after 1778, they

did maintain their value better than an equivalent amount of paper money. For this reason, both American and foreign merchants utilized them as a kind of mercantile currency. E. James Ferguson, *The Power of the Purse: A History of American Public Finance, 1776–1790* (Williamsburg, 1961), pp. 39–40.

TO JOHN ADAMS

Madrid, 26 April 1780

I have at Length had the Pleasure of recieving your very friendly Letter of the 22d February last.[1] It has been very long on the Road. Accept my Thanks for your kind Congratulations, and permit me to assure you that I sincerely rejoice in your having safely reached the Place of your Destination, on a Business which declares the Confidence of America, and for an object, in the Attainment of which, I am persuaded you will acquire Honor to yourself and Advantage to her.

The Circumstances you mention as Indications of the Disposition of Spain, undoubtedly <merit> bear the Construction you give them. <I found the same at Cadiz, altho there were Pains taken there and here, to prevent any conduct towards me, that might savour of an Admission or Knowledge of our Independence. Considering the Object of our Treaty with France, I thought this extraordinary. I do not however ascribe it to any Malevolence with Respect to us, but merely to a Design in that Gentleman or his Instructions, so to manage the proposed Treaties here, as that both Spain and America may hold themselves indebted for the Attainment of their respective Objects to the Influence and good Offices of their Common Ally, with the one and the other.

The acknowledged Integrity of his Catholic majesty, and the reputed Abilities and Candor of his minister, are very flattering Circumstances, and I have too much Confidence in our Friends the French, to believe that they wish to keep Spain and America longer assunder; Altho a Design of squeesing a little Reputation out of the Business, may embarrass the Measures for a Junction. Nor am I without Hopes, that> As the Count De Florida Blanca is I am told, a Man of Abilities <as well as Virtue,> he doubtless will see and <pursue> probably recommend the Policy of making a deep Impression on the Hearts of the Americans, by a seasonable <frank and generous> Acknowledgement of their Independence, and by affording them such immediate aids, as their Circumstances and the obvious Interest of Spain demand. Such measures, at this Period, would turn the Respect of America for Spain, into lasting Attachment, and in that way, give Strength to every Treaty they may form.

Sir John Dalrymple is here, he came from Portugal for the Benefit of his Lady's Health (as is said). He is now at Aranjues. He has seen the imperial Embassador, the Govenor of the City, Signor Campomanes, the Duke of Alva, and several others, named to him I suppose by Lord Grantham, who I find was much respected here. He will return through France to Britain. I shall go to Aranjues the Day after Morrow, and shall form some Judgment of that Gentlemans Success, by the Conduct of the Court towards America.[2]

I am much obliged by your Remarks on the most proper Route for Letters and Intelligence to and from America, and shall profit by them. You may rely on recieving the earliest Accounts of whatever interesting Information I may obtain, and that I shall be happy in every opportunity of evincing the Esteem with which I am Dear Sir Your most obedient Servant

JOHN JAY

Dft. ALS in MHi: Adams Papers; E in CSmH: JJ Lbk; DNA: PCC, 100, I, 149 and in NN: Bancroft American Series, 1780, I, 236.

[1] John Adams to JJ, 22 Feb. 1780, in JP; printed in *RDC*, III, 511–12.

[2] Sir John Dalrymple's trip to Spain was an apparently private and personal effort at Anglo-Spanish reconciliation. The imperial ambassador to Madrid was Count Joseph von Kaunitz-Rietberg (1746–85), son of the Austrian chancellor, Wenzel Anton Dominik, Prince von Kaunitz-Rietberg (1711–94). Thomas Robinson, second Baron Grantham (1738–86), had served as British ambassador to Madrid, 1771–79. *Peacemakers*, pp. 56, 60, 157.

To Vergennes

Aranjues, 9 May 1780

Sir

The Letter which your Excellency did me the Honor to write on the 13 March last, was delivered to me by the Count De Montmorin, on my arrival at Madrid.[1]

I should not have thus long <denied myself> delayed the Pleasure of replying to it, if I could have prevailed upon myself to have given your Excellency complimentary Professions, instead of sincere Assurances. Unreserved Confidence in an Embassador of our good and great Ally was just, as well as natural; and I am exceedingly happy to find that personal Considerations, instead of forbidding, prompt it. M. Gerard, whose Judgment I greatly respect, had given me a very favorable Impression of this Gentleman; and I am convinced from my own Observation, that he was not mistaken. His

Conduct towards me has been that of a wise Minister and a candid Gentleman. Your Excellency may therefore rely on his recieving all that Confidence from me, which these Considerations dictate. Permit me to add that I never indulge myself in contemplating the future Happiness and Independence of my Country, without feeling the warmest Attachment to the Prince and People who are making such glorious Exertions to establish them.

With the most lively Sentiments of Respect and Esteem I have the Honor to be Your Excellency's most obedient and most humble Servant

JOHN JAY

DftS. ALS in MAE: CP: États-Unis, v. 12; LbkCs in DLC: Franklin Papers, III, 35, in CSmH: JJ Lbk, and in DNA: PCC, 110, I, 71–72; printed with minor variations in *RDC*, III, 709.

1 In that letter Vergennes informed JJ that the king of France wished him well and that Montmorin had been requested to aid him. Dft in MAE: CP: États-Unis, v. 11; LbkCs in French in DNA: PCC, 110, I; in CSmH: JJ Lbk; and in DLC: Franklin Papers, III, 34–35.

To Mrs. Margaret Cadwalader Meredith

Aranjues, 12 May 1780

Dear Madam

It is a delightful evening, and I am just returned from a long solitary walk to pay my Respects to you. While the Court were enjoying a Bull Feast, I amused myself in the Gardens and ornamented Grounds which surround me, some of which are beautiful; but I forbear describing them or the Reveries they suggested. Mrs. Jay is at Madrid, and her absence makes me feel the force of the Reflection which concludes Milton's description of the charms of Paradize.

You will naturally suppose that the delicious Retreats to be found here, would give a romantic Complection to an Imagination less inclined to it than mine. Nor will it be difficult for you to believe, that the fairy scenes which present themselves in the Reveries I often indulge in these Retreats, are peopled from America, when I assure you, that the ocean has not been able to wash from my Remembrance, any of the many agreable Ideas impressed upon it in that country.

Could you perceive the direction of my thoughts, you would see them daily bending their course to the Hudson and the Delaware, sometimes sporting at the Hills, that seat of Hospitality, and at other Times admiring the Delicacy of sentiment and manners which created the esteem and friendship that prompt this letter. There are Recesses about this place that would please you, and to those who wish sometimes to enjoy Solitude, they afford it in Perfection. They are frequented by few except the Gardners who keep them in order.

The beau monde preferring a grand public walk, planted by Charles the fifth, where they see and are seen, where every evening they pass and repass each other, where the Courtier bows to his Patron, the Belle displays her charms, the pettit maitre his pretty Person, the Grandee his Equipage, and all have the Happiness of seeing the Princess of Asturies[1] take her evening Ride in a splendid carriage, drawn by six fine Horses, richly caparisoned, and surrounded by Guards well dressed and well mounted, and holding naked sabres in their Hands.

This Pageantry may be proper in Monarchies, and may entertain those who seldom entertain themselves. For my own Part I readily exchange it for the lonely devious walk, the water falls, the fountains, the Birds, and above all the ancient Elms bound to each other by innumerable vines of Ivy, and whose tops intermixing exclude the sun. But as much as I am in love with these, I would gladly leave them for less decorated scenes on your side of the water, and for the pleasure of spending the Remainder of my Days in that Peace Tranquility and Retirement, in which alone virtue and Liberty reward their Votaries for all their sacrifices; neither the whistling of a name, or the Fascination of ambition will be able to detain me from your shores, when the duties of a Citizen will permit me to return from this honorable Exile, for as such only can I consider it. Then Madam! I shall again have the Pleasure of seeing you shine in the Dance, at the Tea Table, and in those polite and proportioned attentions which bespeake Discernment as well as Grace.

But you may ask me how it happens that in thinking of Balls and Tea Tables I should forget the silks etc. we were to send you? If you understood Latin, or if I had an English Translation of Virgil I should exclaim in the words of Æneas, when the Queen desired him to relate his adventures. The winds and waves madam, have been cruel to us, and your Disappointment was involved in ours. Had we gone to France your orders should most punctually have been obeyed, or had we possessed more humble Ideas of your Taste, I should have employed some Person there to execute them. Unfortunately for these orders we were brought here, where fashionable People import handsome Things at a great expence and charged with very heavy Duties from abroad; unfortunately too, I knew no Person in France to whom I could trust the Task of choosing for you. If my Fellow Traveller's

Taste in Dress had been like yours, I should have requested the favor of him. Thus circumstanced, I was obliged to acquiesce in the mortification arising from your Disappointment, and I assure you nothing but the Reflection that to some Persons artificial ornaments are of little importance, can diminish it. As to this Country, believe me, it would be as difficult to find very elegant things manufactured in it, as Mrs. Merediths, and I have no reason to believe they are very often met with any where.

On reviewing what I have written, I find that this Letter is of tolerable length already for *a little Postcript,* but having fallen into Conversation with you, I am now in the same situation I often was at Philadelphia "loth to bid you good bye."

When next you see Don Juan,[2] tell him I have had the Pleasure of seeing his son, that he is a well looking polite young man, and that Mrs. Jay is much pleased with him. He lately returned from France, and expresses a Desire of visiting America. I offered to transmit his letters enclosed with mine, but have not as yet received any. You may tell him too, that in a conversation I had with his Patron Mr. Galvez, I took the Liberty of telling him all I knew about him, and that as I knew nothing to his disadvantage, the information was very agreable to his Friend. This will fill the little man's heart with Joy, and as you always derive Pleasure from communicating it, I am happy in giving you this opportunity of gratifying that Disposition.

Shortly before I left you, Mr. Meredith gave me a caution from Betsey[3] "not to return a new man." This was not very christian advice; however, I suppose the Bible was not then in her thoughts, and that she meant something else by it, which she would not believe me, if I should say I did not understand. The Caution was civil, and included a compliment, which from her good sense was flattering. I cannot prevail upon myself notwithstanding to return it; on the contrary I sincerely hope I may find her changed, though in nothing except, as some phrase it "in her condition."

I expect to hear that she is quite delighted with Trenton, and that she builds as many Castles on the Banks of the Delaware, as I do on the Banks of the Tagus. When I return, we will put all our Castles together; and be the founders of a visionary city, that will probably surpass Mr. Penn's real one. My only apprehension is, that Betsey will be for having too many Churches in it.

As the Atlantic is between us, and no great danger can attend the confession, General Dickinson may know that I endeavoured to persuade Mrs. Dickinson, whom we had the Pleasure of meeting at Chester the day before we embarked, to come with us, but unluckily she had been so frightned in a Rhode Island voyage, and was so attached to her husband and family, and Mrs. Bond threw so much cold water on the Proposal, that all my Rhetoric proved fruitless. She is a charming woman and has my esteem and best wishes.

Whether I shall be able to write to Mr. R. Morris by this vessel is uncertain. If I possibly can, I will, for I would not willingly forego the Pleasure of paying that mark of attention to a Gentleman who merits and shall have from me every proof of attachment. Be so obliging as to remember me affectionately to him and to Mrs. Morris; assure her how much Mrs. Jay and myself consider ourselves indebted to her Politeness and Civilities during our Residence at Philadelphia, and how happy we shall be in hearing of her welfare, and if possible of contributing to it.

I imagine you have had a very gay winter, and that the French minister has given you some little specimen of Paris. What has Hymen been doing? If he has been half as busy the last winter in making matches, as Mercury was the one before in making Lies and Mischief, you have had fine times.

Tell us something about these matters. You cant conceive how interesting every thing from America is, especially such as relate to our friends. I know I can give you in Return nothing equally so; but as I am sure you are disinterested I wont dwell on that circumstance. Adieu. Assure Mr. Meredith of my Regard and esteem, and believe me to be very sincerely, Your Friend and Servant

JOHN JAY

P.S. Mrs. Jay wrote to you from Cadiz.

Tr. NHi: Croaker. ALS, once owned by Edward Eberstadt and Sons, New York City, not located. Mrs. Meredith was born Margaret Cadwalader, daughter of Thomas Cadwalader, a prominent Philadelphia physician. In 1772 she married Samuel Meredith (1741–1817), a Philadelphia merchant. Meredith was an active patriot, serving three terms in the Pennsylvania Assembly and rising to the rank of brigadier general in the Pennsylvania militia. After the Revolution he served as a director of the Bank of North America and as the first U.S. Treasurer under the Constitution. Wharton Dickenson, "Brigadier-General Samuel Meredith," *The Magazine of American History,* III, No. 9 (Sept., 1879), 555–63.

1 Louise Marie of Parma, daughter-in-law of Charles III.

2 Don Juan de Miralles.

3 Probably Elizabeth Meredith Clymer (m. 1765), Samuel Meredith's sister, and the wife of George Clymer (1739–1813), a member of the Continental Congress and a partner in the Meredith family's mercantile firm. Walter H. Mohr, "George Clymer," *Pennsylvania History,* V, no. 4 (October, 1938); Jerry Grundfest, "George Clymer, Philadelphia Revolutionary, 1739–1813" (unpublished Ph.D. dissertation, Columbia Univ., 1973).

To Robert R. Livingston

Madrid, 23 May 1780

Dear Robert

Accept my Thanks, and cordial ones they are, for your friendly Letter of the 22d December last, which I had the Pleasure of recieving a few Days ago. It gives me no less Surprize than Regret to hear that the Letters I wrote you shortly before my Departure from Philadelphia (one of which contained a Cypher) have never reached you. I have been looking among my Papers for the Drafts, but find that I have brought no private Papers with me, that I either wrote or recieved prior to leaving Philadelphia. I nevertheless well remember the Contents. They were such as would have prevented those painful Emotions which Friendship always experiences from Appearances of Neglect. You will recieve herewith enclosed a Copy of the last I wrote you from Martinico, and a Duplicate of another from Cadiz. I should also send Copies of my others from Martinico, but I have really so much to write, and they are of so little Importance, further than as Marks of Attention, that I must at least postpone it.

I have often read over your Letter of the 6th October last.[1] It carried me through past Scenes and former Days, and gave occasion to a Train of Reflections not very dissimilar to those which I fancy passed in your Mind when you wrote it. Contrary to the common Remark, I think your Sensibility encreases with your Years. I am glad of it. You shall have no Reason to think mine declines. The Fact is, it does not. The only Change it has undergone is, that it has been rendered more manageable by that Experience which alone can convince us how liable we are to be mislead by it. But that Experience is in Favor of our Connection, and tho it restrains me from new ones, teaches me to adhere to the old. If I could write in Cypher I would tell you more on this Subject. You have the same Place in my Esteem and Affection which you have filled for near twenty Years, and neither has or will be diminished by Absence. In one Sense I percieve we are coming nearer to each other.

I am approaching the Age of Ambition without being influenced by its Allurements. Public Considerations induced me to leave the private Walk of Life; when they cease, I shall return to it. Believe me I shall not remain here a Moment longer than the Duties of a Citizen may detain me; and that I look forward with Pleasure to the Day when I shall again follow peaceably the Business of my Profession, and make some little Provision for my Family, whose Interests I have so long neglected for public Concerns. My Conduct moves on fixed Principles, from which I shall never deviate; and they will not permit me to leave the unfortunate part of my Family destitute of my Care and Attention longer than higher Duties call me from them.

As you are a Member of Congress and of Course will read my public Letters, it is unnecessary to say any Thing on the Subjects of them.

I wish to know the Success of the Nominations for France. I have no Objections to your Plan. Morris has my best Wishes; I admire his Abilities, and shall always be happy in seeing them useful to his Country. The Want of a Cypher prevents my saying some things further respecting your Plan, which do not affect him.[2]

I am here in a disagreable Situation. Congress have made me no Remittances. The small Credit I had on Doctor Franklin is expended. The Idea of being maintained by the Court of Spain is humiliating, and therefore not for the public Good. The Salary allowed me is greatly inadequate. No part of Europe is so expensive, nor did I ever live so Economically. The Court is never stationary, moving from Madrid to the Pardo, then to Aranjues, thence to St. El Defonso, thence to the Escurial, in perpetual Rotation.[3] To keep a House at each place is not within the Limits of my Finances. To take ready furnished Lodgings and keep my own Table at each, is beyond Belief expensive. I live at Aranjues, in a Posada, in one single Room, with but one Servant, and without a Carriage. When I left Philadelphia every thing was cheaper there than here.

Spain does not cloath its Inhabitants. Their Butter, Cheese, fine Linnen, fine Silks, and fine Cloths, come from France, Holland, etc. They have imposed an exorbitant Duty on all foreign Commodities, and a heavy Tax is laid on Eatables sold in the Market. The Sum allowed me will let me live, but not as I ought to do. A paltry post Chaise drawn by three Mules costs me every Time I go to or from here to Aranjues (7 Leagues) ten Dollars, all Things in that Proportion. To Day I am to try a pair of Mules for which I am asked 480 Dollars. They tell me they are very cheap. Yesterday I refused a pair, the Price of which was 640 Dollars. I cannot get a plain decent Carriage and Harness under 870 Dollars. Judge of my Situation, so circumstanced I cannot employ Couriers to carry my Dispatches to the Sea Side or to France. My Letters by the Post are all opened. Fortunately on this occasion Mr. Harrison now going to Cadiz will take my Letters. With whatever Allowance Congress may make, I shall be content. I know how and am determined to live agreable to my Circumstances. If Inconveniences result from their being too narrow, they will be public ones. They therefore merit the Consideration of Congress.

I wonder a little that Bingham is not thought of. He is a very deserving young Gentleman, and ought to be noticed. He has done us essential Services at Martinico.

Tell me what has become of the Confederacy.[4] I feel interested in her Fate. In Short tell me many Things of our State and of our Friends. By ceasing to be lazy, you will create in me no Suspicions of your having ceased to be my Friend.

Inform me of the Health of Mrs. Livingston your Mother and Family, to whom Mrs. Jay joins with me in desiring you to present our Compliments and best Wishes. Adieu my Dear Robert. I am your Friend

JOHN JAY

ALS. NHi: Robert R. Livingston Papers. "Copy" in JJ's hand, endorsed, in the same collection.

1 This ALS, congratulating JJ on his appointment but deploring his absence, is in JP.

2 See above, Livingston to JJ, 22 Dec. 1779.

3 The Pardo, nine miles from Madrid, was the winter home of Charles III; Aranjuez, 26 miles southeast of Madrid, was his summer palace. Escorial in the Guadarramas and San Ildefonso on the outskirts of Segovia were his two country residences.

4 Finally refitted in Philadelphia, the *Confederacy,* still under Captain Harding, was captured by a superior British naval force in April 1781 and taken into the British Navy as the *Confederate.* Gardner W. Allen, *A Naval History of the American Revolution* (2 vols., N.Y., 1940), II, 556.

FROM WILLIAM CARMICHAEL

Aranjues, 25th May 1780

Sir

I did myself the honor of writing to you the 18th and 23d instant inclosing in my first letter one from the Count de Florida Blanca and also a summary of news from America which the French Ambassador received via Cadiz.[1] In the last I gave you an account of the sailing of the Ferrol Squadron, and of Fleet under Monsieur Ternays[2] having doubled Cape Finister, with news of the departure of an expedition from the Havannah supposed to be destined against Florida. Last Night a courier arrived from Cadiz which brought letters from Monsieur Miralles of the 8th, 9th and 10th of April.[3] These confirm the Loss sustained by Clinton in his long passage to the Southward, and say that he had sent to N. York for a reinforcement of 2500 men, which sailed from the last mentioned City the fourth of April. This circumstance had determined General Washington to form the seige of N. York, to assist him in which He had applied to the Commander in cheif in the French Islands to send Him five or six sail of the Line. Congress had taken measures to send Strong reinforcements to the Southward. The paper money was in bad credit and the French Captain of the Polacre by which These advices are received declares publicly at Cadiz that Congress was bankrupt. I have not had the pleasure of hearing from you, which surprised me the more, as I am told you have written to his Excellency the Count de Florida Blanca and as I supposed that all communications from you to the Minister would have been made through me.

The King as I am told, appeared satisfied with the Advices abovementioned, as there is nothing which shows the least want of vigor or unanimity in the States. I was at court yesterday and this day there has been a grand procession at which the King assisted, which gave me an opportunity of observing his Majestys great piety and devotion.

I beg you to present compliments for me to Mrs. Jay, the Colonel and Harrison, and to believe me your Most Obedient and Most Humble Servent

WM. CARMICHAEL

P.S. Court will go into mourning for the Electress Dowager of Saxony in a day or two. I purpose to come to Town on Saturday for my suit of black and to take leave of M. Gardoqui If I do not hear from you to the Contrary. I put my letters for you in the Poste myself for fear of Accidents.

ALS.

1 Carmichael's letter of 18 May 1780 is in JP: that of 23 May has not been located. Floridablanca's letter to JJ of 18 May 1780 is also in JP.

2 Charles Louis d'Arsac, chevalier de Ternay (1722–80), commanded the fleet which escorted Rochambeau's forces to America in 1780. The expedition reached Newport, R.I., on 10 July 1780.

3 Not located.

To William Carmichael

Friday night, Madrid,[1] 26 *May* 1780

Sir

Your Favor of the 25 Inst. came to Hand about an Hour ago. I am much obliged to you for the <Information> Intelligence contained in it, as well as in your Letter of the 18th. That of the 23d I have not had the pleasure of recieving.

If any Thing interesting had occurred you should have heard from me. My Time has been wholly engrossed in preparing Letters for America.

I have written to His Ex[cellenc]y Count D'Florida Blanca, informing him of my Recovery and Intention of being at Aranjues next wednesday.[2] That Letter was not enclosed to you, because as I had nothing particular to communicate I would not send it under a Blank Cover, especially as the Channel of Conveyance to him was in that Instance of no Importance if certain of which I had no Reasons to doubt. Besides I dont recollect having laid myself under any Restrictions on this Subject. I can have no Objections to your coming to this Town; on the Contrary <I shall be gl> your Company will give me Pleasure.

I am Sir Your most obedient and most Humble Servant

Dft.

1 JJ had written Aranjuez but crossed it out.

2 JJ's draft to Floridablanca, 24 May 1780, is in JP.

To Samuel Huntington

Madrid, 28 May 1780

Dear Sir

You will readily believe from the Size of my public Letters that I have at present little Leizure for private ones.

I cannot however omit this opportunity of <declaring to you> expressing the Sense I <entertain> have of <the> Your delicate and polite Conduct towards me after I left the Chair and to assure you that it has <greatly> added to <that> the Esteem which <induced me> made me happy to see you in it.

Mrs. Jay <desires me to> presents you her best wishes <and Regar> and Compliments <and I am Dear Sir> and flatters herself that <yo> the Prints herewith enclosed will be agreable to Mrs. Huntington.

I am Dear Sir with sincere Regard your most obedient and humble Servant

Dft.

To Robert Morris

Madrid, 28 May 1780

My dear Sir

I have too much Reason to believe it will give you Pleasure to hear that we are safe and well here, to omit this opportunity of telling you.

The Messrs Joyces are said, and I believe, to be Anti Americans, so that the kind Intentions of your Letter will be frustrated.[1]

Inclosed with this is a Collection of spanish Dresses very accurately done. Mrs. Jay presents them with her affectionate Compliments to Mrs. Morris in which I cordially concur. My Memory is too good, and my Heart too susceptible not to remember the uniform series of friendly offices and Attentions for which we were your Debtors at Philadelphia, and which added to unequivocal Proofs of Merit and Abilities have produced the Esteem, attachment and Regard with which I am Dear Sir Your affectionate Friend and Servant

J. J.

P.S. Letters to Cadiz under Cover to Mr. Harrison there will be forwarded to me with care.

DftS.

[1] Gregorio Joyces, sometimes referred to as Joyez or Joyes, the head of Gregorio Joyces & Messrs. Joyces, was a prominent Spanish businessman who later served as a director of the Bank of Spain. Morris's letter to Joyces, which has not been located, had been enclosed in his letter of 18 Oct. 1779 to JJ, ALS in JP.

From Jan De Neufville & Zoon

[*Amsterdam, May 1780*]

Honored Sir,

We found ourselves infinitely obliged to what your Ex[cellen]cy did us the honor to write to us. That our Letters to Congress had come to hand, and that she had taken Notice of our zeal for the Interest of the United States.[1]

May we now beg leave to assure Your Ex[cellen]cy that this never will diminish, and that with the same Attention we shall always continue to promote the Interest and connection of the United States with our Republic. We hope to see our Endeavours strengthened by the Influence of Your Ex[cellen]cy and as it is probable that Mr. Henry Laurens, will likewise be prevented[2] in favor of our principle, we are able to flatter ourselves also with his Assistance, though we gott never a direct Notice of this Gentleman's coming over, some circumstances make it not improbable that he may arrive very soon, and even be designed in Character for our States, where we always wished that the American Independence soon might be openly acknowledged.

If we consider how matters stood sometime ago with us, we must confess we have largely gained, and the great point is the Russian Alliance with that of the Northern Powers.[3]

Most of our men of War are ordered to their Posts in our harbours in Expectation of the Russian Fleet, which must have sailed by this time, and to promote the Acceleration of the Equipment of our Navy, we have procured again an Address of Commerce to our States for the speediest and largest protection.

Our best Politicians wish to promote peace, these to every step seems tending, but very uncertain it is yet when it once may take place.

Clinton's fate in Carolina will have in England, as we learn from there, the greatest Influence in their politic System, and by Letters from Philadelphia dated the 6th of April, they had not the Least Apprehension there, that Charlestown would be taken and the approaching warm Season must certainly have injured very much the British Army.

We have the honor to be With all devoted Regard Honored Sir, Your Excellency's Most Obedient and most Humble Servants

Signed JOHN DE NEUFVILLE & SON

Honored Sir,

May it please Your Excellency that after having written her Yesterday, we should cause her a new trouble of reading us, but the subject must be our Apology.

By Vessels lately arrived from the Continent, and some from St. Eustatia, there appeared here some Bills drawn by the Treasurer of loans in America on Henry Laurens Esqr. Commissioner for the States in Amsterdam.[4] Every body hath been surprized with it, and we in particular, as we were directly applied to. We said to the first that we did expect Mr. Laurens should be in town very soon, begging from them to keep those Bills a fortnight, and that at all Events we should accept them. We have seen others since more willing to wait; but not knowing which Sums may have been drawn for already, we are in hopes to be soon released of this Anxiety by the arrival of our Minister, and we think Your Ex[cellen]cy may have some Intelligence about this Matter, and have it in her power at the same time to save the Credit of America. If Mr. Laurens by One or other Accident should not arrive We beg the favor to be informed how to conduct ourselves and to be sure we will do what lays in our power to prevent all Noise and trouble in the mean time about them, as much as possible. In case, we say, Mr. Laurens should not arrive, Your Ex[cellen]cy would have time left to make or provide for Remittances as the Bills are drawn at 6 Month sight.

We have the honor to be With all devoted Regard Honored Sir, Your Excellency's Most obedient and most humble Servants

(signed) JOHN DE NEUFVILLE & SON

C in hand of Henry Brockholst Livingston. 2 LbkCs in both CSmH: JJ Lbk. and in DNA: PCC, 110, I, 360–63. Second letter printed with variations in *RDC*, III, 741–42. Jan de Neufville (1729–96), the head of the Amsterdam mercantile house which bore his name, was an enthusiastic supporter of the American cause in the Netherlands. In 1778 de Neufville and William Lee had prepared a draft treaty of commerce between the two nations which the British later used as a pretext to declare war on the Netherlands. *Nieuw Nederlandsch Biografisch Woordenboek* (10 vols., Leiden, 1930), VIII, 1211–14.

[1] De Neufville addressed a letter to JJ in Philadelphia 28 July 1779, suggesting that his firm be named by Congress to act as "commissioner" and "Treasurer" for U.S. commercial affairs in the Netherlands. On 6 April 1780 he wrote JJ again, this time in Spain, congratulating him on his arrival in Europe and soliciting business. JJ acknowledged both letters in his communication to de Neufville 27 April 1780. De Neufville to JJ, 28 July 1779: 2 LS versions in DNA: PCC, 145, 5–9, 13–17; LbkC in DNA: PCC: Misc., roll 4; 6 April 1780: C in hand of Henry Brockholst Livingston in JP; LbkCs in DNA: PCC: 110, I, and CSmH: JJ Lbk; printed in *RDC*, III, 597. JJ to de Neufville, 27 April 1780, C in hand of Henry Brockholst Livingston in JP; LbkCs in DNA: PCC: 110, I and CSmH: JJ Lbk; printed in *RDC*, III, 634–35.

[2] Copyist erroneously misread "predisposed."

[3] The League of Armed Neutrality, proclaimed by the Empress Catherine 29 Feb. 1780, was designed to protect the commercial rights of such neutrals as Russia and the Scandinavian kingdoms from retaliation by Britain or the Allies. Isabel De Madariaga, *Britain, Russia, and the Armed Neutrality of 1780* (New Haven, 1962).

[4] These bills were drawn on Laurens under the Congressional resolutions of 23 and 29 Nov. 1779. See above, from James Lovell *et al.*, 11 Dec. 1779 and n.

To John Adams

Aranjues, 4 June 1780

Dear Sir

There is a Destinction between Ceremony and Attention which is not always observed tho often useful. Of the <latter> former I hope there will be little between us; of the latter much. Public as well as personal Considerations dictate this Conduct on my Part, and I am happy to find by your favor of the 15th <Inst> Ult. that you <approve it in the same Light> mean not to be punctilious.

The Hints contained in your Letter[1] correspond <very> much with my own Sentiments, and I shall endeavour to <render them more> diffuse them. This Court seems to have great Respect for the old adage "festina lente"[2]—at least as applied to our Independence.

The Count D Florida Blanca has hitherto pleased me. I have found in him a Degree of Frankness and Candor which indicates Probity. His reputation for Talents is high. The acknowledgment of Independence is <obstructed> retarded by Delays which in my opinion ought not to affect it. The Influence of that Measure on the Sentiments and Conduct of our Enemy, as well as the neutral Nations, makes it an object very important to the common Cause. I cannot think Its Suspension is <not> necessary to the Adjustment of the Articles of Treaty. They might with equal Facility be settled afterwards. As America is and will be independent in Fact, the being so in name can be of no great Moment to her individualy; but Britain derives Hopes <prejudice> from the Hesitation of Spain, very injurious to the common Cause, and I am a little suprized that the Policy of destroying these Hopes does not appear more evident <is of great consequence. America will never purchase <<such acknowledgement>> it of any Nation by Terms She would not otherwise accede to. Things not Names are her Objects.>

If the Delay proceeds from Expectation that they may affect the Terms of Treaty, it is not probable that they will be realized. America is to be attached by Candor, Generosity, Confidence and good Offices. A contrary Conduct will not conciliate or persuade. But whatever may by the Cause of the mistakes on these Subjects, I must do them the Justice to say that the general Assurances given me by the Count D F. B. argue a very friendly Disposition in the Court towards us, and I hope Facts will prove them to have been sincere. They certainly must be convinced that the Power of the united States added to that of Britain and under her Direction, would enable her to give Law to the western World, and that Spanish America and the Islands would then be at her mercy. Our Country is at present so well disposed to Spain, and such cordial Enemies to Britain, that it would be a Pity this Disposition should not be cherished. Now is the time for France and Spain to gain the Affections of that extensive Country. Such another opportunity may never offer.

France has acted wisely. I wish similar Counsels may prevail here. Would it not be a little extraordinary if Britain should be before Spain in acknowledging our Independence? If she had any wisdom left she would do it. She may yet have a lucid Interval, tho she has been very long out of her Senses. Spain will be our Neighbour. We both have Territory enough to prevent our coveting each others and I should be happy to see that perfect Amity and cordial Affection established between us, which would ensure perpetual Peace and Harmony to both. I cannot write you particulars, but nothing here appears to be certain as yet. I shall in all my Letters advise Congress to rely principally on themselves, to fight out their own Cause as they began it with Spirit, and not to rely too much on the Expectation of Events which may never happen.

Have you recieved any late Letters from America? Mrs. Jay recieved one from her Sister of the 10 April,[3] which mentions several having been sent home by the Way of France. I hear of many Letters but recieve scarce any.

I am Dear Sir Your most affectionate Servant

J.J.

P.S. My Compliments to Mr. Dana

DftS. Tr in NN: Bancroft American Series p. 11.

1 Adams to JJ, 15 May 1780, ALS in JP; printed in *RDC*, III, 678–79.

2 More haste, less speed; a Greek proverb quoted in Suetonius' *Augustus*, sec. 25.

3 No 10 April 1780 letter to SLJ from any of her sisters has been located.

FROM BENJAMIN FRANKLIN

Passy, 13 June 1780

Dear Sir,

It was a Mistake of a Figure in my Letter that occasioned you the Trouble of writing yours of the 28th April.[1] I find you charged only with 2564 Livres, 18.10. and not with £4564.18.10. That Bill is paid, as also another drawn since for £3596 livres, 13 Sols.o. dated March 20. In setting right these Money Matters, it is fit to mention a small Mistake that you have made. The Order of Congress required me to furnish you with 1000 Louis, or 2400 Livres. Your first Bill that came to my hands was for 4079 livres, which being paid and deducted left the sum of 19921 Livres, for which I lodged a Credit by means of M. Grand with M. d'Yranda, at your Disposal. But I have since paid the following Bills drawn on me by you, viz. One from Martinique, Livres 3379.8.0; One from Cadiz, March 3, Livres

2564.18.10; One from Ditto, March 20, Livres 3596.13.0; Amounting to Livres 9540.19.10. Which sum should also have been deducted from the 24000 but I lately understand from Mr. Grand that you had taken up the whole remaining 19921 Livres, by which means you are become indebted to me for those three Bills paid over and above the Order of Congress. Let us excuse one another.[2]

Yesterday, and not before, is come to hand your favours of April 14 with the Pacquets and Dispathes from Congress, etc. which you sent me by a french Gentleman to Nantes. Several of them appear to have been opened, the Paper round the Seals being smoked and burnt as with the flame of a Candle used to soften the Wax; and the Impression defaced. The Curiosity of People in this Time of War is unbounded; Some of them only want to see News, but others want to find (through interested Views) what Chance there is of a Speedy Peace. Mr. Ross[3] has undertaken to forward the Letters to England. I have not seen them; but he tells me they have all been opened. I am glad, however, to receive the Dispatches from Congress, as they communicate to me Mr. Adams's Instructions, and other Particulars of which I have been long ignorant.

I am at a Loss to conceive how it happened, that the Marquis d'Yranda, having received Orders from M. Grand to hold the sum of 19921. Livres at your Disposition, by his Letter of the 22d of February, should not acquaint you with so material a thing till the 14th of April. I have desired Mr. Grand to give me Copies of his Letters, and I Send them to you enclosed. He had represented the Marquis to me, as a Man who had much Acquaintance, and Influence in that Court, and who might be useful to you on many Occasions; and he tells me that the Marquis both formerly and lately complains that you are shy and reserved towards him.

I am very sensible of the Weight of your Observation "that a constant Interchange of Intelligence and Attentions between the public Servants at the different Courts are necessary to procure to their Constituents all the Advantages capable of being derived from their Appointment." I shall endeavour to perform my Part with you, as well to have the Pleasure of your Correspondence, as from a Sense of Duty. But my time is more taken up with Matters extraneous to the function of a Minister, than you can possibly imagine. I have written often to the Congress to Establish Consuls in the Ports and ease me of what relates to maritime and mercantile Affairs; but no Notice has yet been taken of my Request. Bills of Exchange and other Money Matters give me also a good deal of Trouble: And being kept in constant Expectation of a Secretary to be sent me, I have not furnished myself with the Help I Should otherwise have endeavoured to obtain. But I rub on, finding my Grandson daily more and more able to assist and ease me by supplying that Deficiency.[4]

A Number of Bills of Exchange said to be drawn by Order of Congress on Mr. Laurens, are arrived in Holland. A merchant there has desired to know of me whether if he accepts them I will engage to reimburse him. I have no Orders or Advice about them from Congress: do you know to what amount they have drawn? I doubt I cannot safely meddle with them.

In yours of April 27 you mention your Purpose of sending me some interesting Papers.[5] They are not yet come to hand. Inclosed I send you Copies of what has passed in writing, between the Danish Court and me. I have had also the Conference proposed to me with the Minister of that Court here. He said much of the Good Will of his Court and Nation towards the United States, with assurances of a kind Reception in their Ports to our Ships, provided they would only use the Precaution of coming in under french Colours, in which Case, no Enquiry would be made or Demand to see their Papers. But he made no Proposition of Restitution, alledging that the giving up the Prizes to the English, was what they were obliged to by Treaties. I do not however find any such Treaty. I see they are embarrassed and not well pleased with what they have done; but know not well how to rectify it. After my Memorial, our People at Berghen were treated handsomely, their Charges defrayed, and a Vessel provided to carry them to Dunkerque at the king's Expence. I shall continue to push them, but wish to know the Sentiments and receive the Orders of Congress.

Mrs. Jay does me much Honour in desiring to have one of the Prints that have been made here of her Countryman.[6] I send what is said to be the best of 5 or 6 engraved by different hands, from different Paintings. The Verses at the Bottom are truly exravagant. But you must know that the Desire of pleasing by a perpetual use of Compliments in this polite Nation, has so used up all the common Expressions of Approbation, that they are become flat and insipid, and to use them almost implies Censure. Hence Musick, that formerly might be sufficiently praised when it was called *bonne,* to go a little farther they called it *excellente,* then *Superbe, magnifique, exquise, celeste,* all which being in their turns worn out, there remained only *divine;* and when that is grown as insignificant as its Predecessors, I think they must return to common Speech, and Common Sense: as from vying with one another in fine and costly Paintings on their Coaches, Since I first knew the Country, not being able to go farther in that Way, they have returned lately to plain Carriages, painted without Arms or figures, in one uniform Colour.

The League of Neutral Nations to protect their Commerce is now established. Holland offended by fresh Insults from England is arming Vigorously. That Nation has madly brought itself into the greatest Distress, and has not a friend in the World.

With great and Sincere Esteem, I am Dear Sir, Your most obedient and most humble Servant

B. FRANKLIN

LS. Endorsed: ". . . Recd 27 June 1780." Enclosure: "Copy of a Letter from M. Behrnstorff a Minister of the King of Denmark for Foreign Affairs," 8 March 1780, in *RDC*, III, 540. LbkC in DLC: Franklin Papers; printed with deletions in *RDC*, III, 784–85.

1 In an earlier letter Franklin mentioned a bill drawn on him by JJ in the amount of 4564.18.10 livres. JJ denied writing such a bill but guessed correctly that Franklin had intended to make reference to one he had drawn for 2564.18.10 livres. Franklin to JJ, 7 April 1780, LS in JP. LbkCs in DLC: Franklin Papers, III, 15–16, DNA: PCC, 110, I, and CSmH: JJ Lbk; printed in *RDC*, III, 597–98. JJ to Franklin, 28 April 1780, LbkC in DLC: Franklin Papers, III, 25.

2 For the 15 Oct. 1779 Order of Congress authorizing JJ's draft on Franklin, see *JCC*, XV, 1179–80, 1183.

3 John Ross (1729–1800), a merchant, had commercial houses in Philadelphia and Nantes. John Adams, *Diary*, IV, 377.

4 William Temple Franklin (1760–1823), illegitimate son of Benjamin Franklin's illegitimate son, William, had accompanied his grandfather to France.

5 JJ to Franklin, 27 April 1780, dft in JP; LbkC in DLC: Franklin Papers, III, 22–23; Tr in NN: Bancroft American Series, I, 236-1/2; printed in *RDC*, III, 633–34.

6 In his letter of 27 April, JJ had written that SLJ "presents her respects to you, and begs that your next letters to me may enclose for her one of the prints of yourself, which we are told have been published in France, but are not yet to be had here. I believe that there is no man of your age in Europe so much a favorite with the ladies."

The Jay-Carmichael Relationship

Almost from the time they left America, JJ was dissatisfied with William Carmichael, the man Congress selected as secretary of the Spanish mission. There was a significant difference in their personalities, and the stiffly formal JJ was likely to have been made uneasy by Carmichael's almost compulsive gregariousness. Then, too, Carmichael invariably sided with the Chevalier Gérard, Henry Brockholst Livingston, and Lewis Littlepage[1] in their disputes with the minister. JJ might have overlooked his associate's manner and his disloyalty in what were essentially personal quarrels, but he also had serious reservations about the mission secretary's official conduct. Carmichael assumed more authority than was properly his, talked more freely than seemed prudent, and on at least one occasion handled funds in a way that appeared improper. Finally, JJ became convinced that the secretary was a spy.[2]

JJ's concern was understandable, because William Carmichael lacked some of the qualities demanded of a diplomat, and his record was not above suspicion. Raised in Maryland, he was living in London at the outbreak of the Revolution. He appeared mysteriously in France in the spring of 1776, offered his services to Silas Deane, and acted as secretary at the American legation until Arthur Lee and Vergennes, the French foreign minister, became skeptical about his loyalty. Unconvinced of Carmichael's guilt, Franklin and Deane extricated him from an awkward situation by sending him home as the bearer of official dispatches. He soon entered Congress as a representative from Maryland and resigned when he was added to the mission to Madrid in 1779. JJ formed such a poor impression of Carmichael's fidelity that he did not let him copy confidential reports, but lack of hard evidence of treason made it impractical to consider dismissing him. Carmichael became temporary chargé d'affaires at Madrid when JJ left for Paris, and he was appointed the first official representative to Spain in 1783. Recalled under suspicion in 1794, he died in Madrid before he could leave for home.[3]

JJ's final assessment of his secretary can be found in a note undated but written sometime soon after 9 February 1795, attached to a bundle of correspondence, reading as follows: "Care should be taken of these Papers. They include Letters to and from Wm. Carmichael—a man who mistook cunning for wisdom; and who in pursuing his Purposes, preferred the Guidance of artifice and Simulation, to that of Truth and Rectitude. He finally yielded to Intemperance, and died a Bankrupt."[4] JJ could make no more specific an accusation than this, but modern documentation has established that Carmichael had most probably been a secret agent employed by the British government.[5]

The strain that underlay the relationship between the two men is evident in the seven letters that follow. Detained in Madrid by his wife's illness, JJ encouraged Carmichael on 16 June 1780 to send him information about what was occurring at the Court in Aranjuez. Carmichael's reports provoked JJ's sharp rebuke dated 27 June, in which he accused his assistant of talking too much to other diplomats and presuming too much authority. The exchange of letters that followed reduced the tension between them while failing to remove the causes of their mutual coolness.

1 Lewis Littlepage (1762–1802) of Virginia, ambitious for a diplomatic career, arranged through his uncle, Colonel Benjamin Lewis, to become a guest in JJ's home in Madrid, which he reached in November 1780.

2 For Carmichael's involvement with Gérard, see *Peacemakers,* p. 4. SLJ to William Livingston, 24 June 1781, ALS in JP, describes his intrigue with Henry

Brockholst Livingston. ALS to William Livingston enclosed in SLJ to Catharine W. Livingston, not located. Duplicate ALS in JP: endorsed by JJ with the following notation: "N.B. The Letter of which this is a Copy, was enclosed to Miss C. Livingston with an Injunction not to Deliver it unless Brockholst's misrepresentations to his Father should be such as in her opinion to render it absolutely necessary. N.B. It never was delivered to him, his confidence in him remaining undiminished." For Carmichael's ambiguous meddling in the JJ-Littlepage relationship, see Curtis Carroll Davis, *The King's Chevalier: A Biography of Lewis Littlepage* (Indianapolis, 1961), pp. 58, 90–91. Evidence of JJ's mistrust of Carmichael will be found in Deane to JJ, 2 July and 26 Sept. 1781; JJ to Deane, 5 Dec. 1781, "Deane Papers," N.Y.H.S., *Colls.*, XXII, 444–46, 478–80, 549–50.

3 Cecil B. Currey, *Code Number 72/Ben Franklin: Patriot or Spy?* (Englewood Cliffs, N.J., 1972), pp. 111, 118–19, gives biographical information about Carmichael, as does *RDC*, I, 577, 578; II, 124, 551; III, 329, 343, 374; IV, 184. For proof that JJ kept Carmichael from seeing confidential correspondence, see JJ to Deane, 16 June 1781, "Deane Papers," N.Y.H.S., *Colls.*, XXII, 438–39.

4 Endorsement by JJ, n.d. after 9 Feb. 1795, in JP.

5 Samuel Flagg Bemis, "British Secret Service and the French-American Alliance," *AHR*, XXIX (April, 1924), 474–95, suggested that Carmichael "went to the verge, if not over the edge, of treason"; Cecil B. Currey, *Code Number 72/Ben Franklin: Patriot or Spy?* pp. 111, 118–19, 123, 127, offers evidence to establish the fact that Carmichael did in fact go "over the edge." See also *Peacemakers*, p. 510 n. 58.

To William Carmichael

Madrid, 16–17th June 1780

Dear Sir

On <coming to this Place last M> my Arrival here I unexpectedly found that Mrs. Jay had been and still was very much indisposed. The Col. had written for me, but neither his Letter, nor mine from Aranjues to Mrs. Jay, had ever come to Hand. She is now somewhat better tho far from well, having more Spirits than Strength, and rather an Exemption from Constant pain, than Health. In this Situation it would be cruel to leave her, especially as <my being at> my presence at aranjues is not immediately necessary, and the Court will so soon remove from thence here.

I am obliged by your Favor of Yesterday. The Intelligence you give me is very agreable.[1] <Be pleased to> Present my Compliments of Congratulations to Mr. Galvez on the Success and Honor acquired by his Brother. Inform Count Montmorin of the Reasons which induce me to deny myself the pleasure of dining with him on Sunday. Assure him of my Respect and best wishes.

The Gentleman you allude to will probably arrive soon.[2] Be pleased to keep for me and send when *proper* opportunities offer a regular Journal of such Intelligence and occurrences as may come to your Knowledge relative to the Objects and Business of the Legation <that when I right[*sic*] to Congress I may be the better enabled to inform them fully of their Affairs here. Should an opportunity offer I shall apprize you of it.> Should any thing happen which might render my being at Aranjues necessary, give me notice of it immediately, and I will at all Events set out the moment I recieve it.

I have told St. John to carry my Trunk with him. The enclosed Letters have been here some Days. Inform me when a Courier will set out for France. I shall write to you again on Monday or Tuesday. Mrs. Jay and the Col. present their Compliments to you.

I am Dear Sir Yours etc.

J. JAY

P.S. Remember the Notes of <your> Information in pursuance of the Instructions at Cadiz. Have everything ready for Audibert.[3] Not a Syllable yet from Dr. Franklin.

Madrid, 17th June 1780

Dear Sir

As I shall not return to aranjuez to Day, agreable to the Notice I gave the Count D F B, I think it best to inform him of it, and for that purpose enclosed a Letter to him, which be so kind as to <take care tha> <send it to him> Deliver this evening.

Yours etc.

J. JAY

P.S. I enclose a Letter directed to You.

DftS. Enclosures: letter for Carmichael not located; JJ to Floridablanca, 17 June 1780 enclosed in JJ to Franklin, 17 July 1780 in DLC: Franklin Papers, III, 57–61.

[1] Carmichael had reported the capture of Mobile by Spanish troops under Bernardo de Gálvez (1746–86), governor of Louisiana, the nephew of the minister of the Indies. Carmichael to JJ, 15 June 1780, ALS in JP.

[2] Like JJ, Carmichael did not refer by name to Richard Cumberland (1732–1811), a British playwright and minor government official, writing instead "A Person whom I need not name is not yet arrived." They had already learned of Cumberland's mission to Spain to try to negotiate a separate peace. Cumberland and his family reached Aranjuez on the morning of 18 June. *Peacemakers*, pp. 56–66.

[3] Étienne d'Audibert Caille, a French merchant in Morocco appointed by the emperor as consul for all foreign nations unrepresented there. The consul wrote the Continental Congress in September 1779 offering American traders the same privileges in Morocco they had enjoyed as British subjects. When he did not

receive a reply, he wrote JJ in Spain in April 1780, enclosing copies of his earlier letter to Congress and his credentials. D'Audibert Caille's letters and JJ's undated reply are in *RDC*, IV, 170–71, 173–74.

From William Carmichael

Aranjues, 19 June 1780

Dear Sir

Near 12 this night St. Jean brought me your favors of the 16th and 17th with their inclosures. As it was too late to carry your letter to the Count de Florida Blanca, I defer doing it until tomorrow morning. The Letters you sent me were from Mr. Lecouteux at Cadiz containing others for Mr. Harrison and two newspapers, the latter of which I now send you, Two letters also from London, one of the 14 April and the other of the same date in May. The one from a sensible young fellow from Maryland, a friend of your Brother Sir James, offering his services and correspondence, the other from a very pretty girl, also offering services. I have also received a letter from Mr. Carrol of Carlton,[1] who writes in good Spirits altho our Money was almost at its last gasp. Nothing can save us from all the ruinous effects of a Bankruptcy, but money in Europe.

My Journal will not be interesting this last week. I have formed new acquaintances and cultivated the old. I have seen our *Abby*[2] as you desired, and beleive him, what the Princess of Maserano[3] says he is, an intriguing enterprizing busy meddling Priest with a conscience as pliant as a Ladys kid Skin glove. He is mighty civil to me. At eight oclock this morning Mr. C—d and Family arrived. I sat up till two in the Morning in order to have sight of them, but dispairing of their arrival I went to Bed. I shall give you notice of his Motions. I find that *Our Abby* is as inquisitive about us, as we about him.

I am sorry that you could not be present at the Dinner given to the Corpes Diplomatis by the French Embassador. Your Absence will occasion much Speculation, as I find your not having been at Court doth. The papers you mention have long been ready. The information is not so complete as I could wish to send to Congress, as you can Judge who have had it in detail and as I received it. Audibert left Aranjues on Wednesday, promised me to wait on you at Madrid. I gave him all the papers with a note to you. He returned on Thursday, delivered me again the papers and the note saying that he could not find you, Set out yesterday morning for Seville, leaving me some Enveloppes for different houses in Cadiz, to whom he desired me to inclose your letter in answer to his. I had a great inclination to forward his papers to Harrison, to be sent to Congress, but Judging that you would chuse to write at the Same time, I declined doing it; and more particularly as he will be some time on the road.

I have delivered your letter without speaking to any one. I am inclined to think Mr. C—d will be heard before you receive an answer to your last while here. I paid my Compliments to Mr. Galvez the day after the news arrived. I was well received etc. I told him that I was going to communicate to you the news, which I knew would be particularly agreable to you and every other American both as contributing to the Public interest of Spain and the particular satisfaction of a family, which they ranked as their most powerful friends here.

I have been again seized with the colic and a lax and would most willingly excuse myself from dining with forty very Illustrious Spies, if I could well do it.

I beg you to present compliments for me to Mrs. Jay and wishes for her health and Strength. Pray write me now and then if it is only to inform me, how the family is, or prevail on the Colonel to do it.

I shall speak feelingly on the Subject of the Letters Stopped at the Parti [*sic*] to Monsieur Del Campo,[4] and even to the Count Himself Insinuating that I am afraid it is done by some one in the Post office, who betray them to the English Spies. All the Letters I received last night had been opened more than once. I am your Obliged and Humble Servant.

WM. CARMICHAEL

ALS. Enclosures not located.

[1] Charles Carroll (1737–1832) of Carrollton, a signer. At this time he was a member of the Maryland Senate, having resigned from the Continental Congress. Joseph Guin, *Charles Carroll of Carrollton* (New York, 1932), p. 105.

[2] Father Thomas Hussey (1741–1803), an Irish priest, had served as chaplain to the Spanish Embassy in London before diplomatic relations between Spain and England were broken. Hussey remained in London as a Spanish agent even after the ambassador had returned to Madrid. The priest accompanied Richard Cumberland on his mission to seek an end to the Anglo-Spanish hostilities. Samuel Flagg Bemis, *The Hussey-Cumberland Mission and American Independence: An Essay in the Diplomacy of the American Revolution* (Princeton, 1931), pp. 12, 15 *passim; Peacemakers*, pp. 51–52.

[3] The Princess Charlotte Louise Masserano, whom JJ described in a letter to Benjamin Franklin as "a Lady of much observation and Discernment," was the sister of Cardinal Louis René Eduourd de Rohan, who had been French ambassador to Vienna, 1772–74. Her husband was a member of an ancient Piedmontese family, but he lived in Madrid, commanded Spanish troops at the siege of Gibraltar in 1782, and was raised to the rank of brigadier general in that year by Charles III. "I am much indebted to the politeness of this Nobleman," JJ wrote,

"and except at his Table have eaten no Spanish Bread that I have not paid for since my arrival in this City." JJ to Franklin, 25 Oct. 1780, ALS in DLC: Franklin Papers, III, Dft in JP. Curtis Carroll Davis, *The King's Chevalier: A Biography of Lewis Littlepage* (Indianapolis, 1961), pp. 60, 69, 87.

4 Bernardo del Campo was Floridablanca's secretary. *Peacemakers*, p. 61.

From William Carmichael

Aranjues, 19 June 1780

Dear Sir

I wrote you this morning by St. Jean. I have since received the inclosed which I forward to you the Colonel Tenase.

I dined with the Embassador to day, where we had a great deal of Company, Not only the foreighn Minister but the Duke d'Arcos, the Duke de Ossada and others. The Count de Montmorin took great care to express publicly his regret at not having the pleasure of seeing you. I spoke with Mr. Del Campo who was of the Company; You will find that they will not be in a hurry to answer you, Not however until C—d hath been heard. I think he hath had his first audience Interview this night. I shall know more before I sleep. I just returned, as one of the Count's People brought me the inclosed Letter, from following Mr. C— or I am very much mistaken in my man. He is kennelld and La Guerre is my Terrier.

I had the pleasure of making a very pleasing acquaintance to day with the Abbe Casti,[1] An Italian, who hath travelled with The Imperial Ambassador and is a great favorite of his and his Fathers. The Omnipotent Minister of Vienna, He brought me a letter of Introduction from Paris.[2]

Several bills of exchange drawn by Congress on you are in circulation at Cadiz. I know not what to do on this Subject with my French Correspondent. Silence will rather be ominous. A Courier of the Cabinet accompanied these English folks from Lisbon. They have been ten days on the road. Mr. Ionace will take the Trouble of bringing any letters you may have for me.

I visited the Princess Maserano this afternoon who made many kind inquirries for Mrs. Jays health. I hope her Spirits will not leave her, and then she need not fear the heats of Madrid. I have no time to copy this Letter, as the Person who Carrys it is now at the door. I inquired to day when a Courier would set out from France and was told I Should have previous notice.

There hath been a flying report at Court today, that Clinton was beaten and taken Prisoner. I received many Compliments in the gardens on the Occasion, but did not incourage it, as it is but a report.

Please to make the proper Compliments for me to Mrs. Jay and the Colonel and take it for granted that almost all the Irish in this Country from highest to Lowest are friends to England,

I have the honor to be with respect Your Most obedient and Most Humble Servant

WM. CARMICHAEL

ALS. Enclosures not located.

[1] Giambattista Casti (1721–1803), a Catholic priest turned poet, was a favorite of the Russian, Austrian, and Prussian courts. *Dizionario Degli Scrittori D'Italia* (Milan), I, 93–94.

[2] Count Joseph von Kaunitz-Rietberg.

From William Carmichael

Aranjues, 23rd June 1780

Dear Sir

I write, cheifly to inform you that there is a report here, that the Spanish Consul at Bourdeaux hath advised his Court, that General Clinton has been repulsed at C. Town with considerable loss, that the Enemy have evacuated N. York, and that our Allies have taken St. Christopher's.[1]

I think I give you a paragraph as replete with good news as you could wish to hear in one day. But unhappily it wants confirmation. The English Gentleman of whom you heard so much at Madrid, is equally talked of here, and his name is as well known, as his business is supposed to be.[2] This however, after what we have heard cannot affect us personally, for we ought to have no apprehensions from this circumstance. But I am afraid its publicity will Make similar impressions, that those circulated by our Enemies did before our Alliance with France. This will more than compensate the Expence, to which This Gentleman puts his court, and so far answer their desighns. Proper compliments for me to your Lady and the Colonel and beleive me Your Most Obedient and Most humble Servant

WM. CARMICHAEL

ALS. Endorsed: ". . . Carmichael 23 June 1780."

[1] None of Carmichael's military intelligence proved accurate. Continental forces at Charleston, S.C., had surrendered to Clinton on 12 May 1780. The British did not evacuate New York City until November 1783. The island of St. Kitts remained in British control until February 1782.

[2] Richard Cumberland.

To William Carmichael

Madrid, 27 [*June* 1780]

Dear Sir

It is with <great> Reluctance that I can ever prevail upon myself to tell you that any thing you do is <not right> in my Opinion improper, and especially when my telling you so <may possibly be attributed as much> is capable of being imputed to Pride as well as to Prudence.

The Count de Montmorin informed me Yesterday that you had consulted him on the Subject of a Conference you proposed to have with the Spanish Minister relative to Mr. Cumberland <Errand> and he recapitulated the Advice he had given you <relative> on that Head.

As I consider the <exclusive Direction> Affairs of the American Legation at this Court to be committed to my exclusive Direction, and consequently that I alone am responsible for the Manner in which they may be conducted, I <cannot consent> must object to your taking any Measures respecting them but such as I <shall> may previously have approved of and assigned to your Management.

<Nor can I commend> I also think no Advantage can result from your having communicated to the Count Secretary the Chevalier DBurgoyne[1] all the Intelligence you had relative to Mr. Cumberland and his maneuvers as well as the Channels thro which it was <acquired> obtained. To <obtain> assist in gaining intelligence is doubtless within your Province as well as Duty but the Use to be made of such as may affect the Business <and Objects> of the Legation I concieve to belong solely to mine. <Besides> It would <I know> doubtless be rediculous to appear ignorant of what every Body knows, but it is not necessary nor always urgent to communicate what others do not know, and particularly the Means of acquiring it. <From ones knowledge>

I am a little suspicious that we entertain different Ideas as to the Extent of your Appointment. From your having urged your Commission of Charge Des Affairs as a Reason why you should countersign my Letters and from some other Circumstances I apprehend that you view it as being now in some Degree in Force, <and perhaps that my temporary Absences from the <<Habitations>> Seats of the King may in Virtue of that Commission devolve upon you on such occasions farther Powers than those annexed to your Office as Secretary.> On the other Hand I cannot look upon that Commission <as

contingent> in any other Light than as eventual and to take Effect only on the Death <or absence from Spain> of the American Minister here, and <that the only Powers you are now <<at present>> vested are those> therefore I think your Powers are confined to those which originate in your <office> appointment of Secretary <and that you have been led to take these measures merely from an opinion of their Expediency.>

<Perhaps these <<are only>> Conjectures may be ground less. I wish they may be; if they should not> If our Sentiments do really thus vary on these points, it will be best that they should be explained <and all Cause of Variance removed. Perfect Harmony between us is essential to the public Good, and I should regret exceedingly to> and <adjusted> the Difference removed. If you think my Construction of our respective Commissions right, I hope you will in future forbear taking any Steps in the Business of the Legation without the Line of Secretary <without previously> unless with my Approbation. As to Intelligence touching those Affairs you will continue with your usual Diligence and Address to obtain it, but avoid communicating more either of the Matter or the Means of acquiring it than may be already public to any Persons <except to Congress> without my Consent. If indeed you should chuse to transmit it yourself to Congress I have not the least Objection. But if on the other Hand you should be of Opinion that my Construction of our Commissions does you Injustice, In that Case <I must and> for the Sake of Harmony as well as to prevent <any> the Evils often resulting from interfering Measures I must request the Favor of you to <suspend> confine yourself to the Duties of Secretary until all Doubts can be removed by Congress.

<As on the one Hand> I assure you it will always give me Pleasure to be a Witness to your Services and to represent them in a true Light to Congress <so on the other I flatter myself you will ascribe this Letter to the true Motives> and nothing but <that Regard> the Consideration of public Good and that <Consideration> of being responsible for the Issue of Measures not my own, could <prompt> <prevail upon> induce me to write you this Letter.

<I acknowledge with Pleasure your Readiness to do your Duty, and <<think>> that you deserve Credit for the Attention and Address in gaining Intelligence.

It would give me Pain <<to be>> if the Restrictions I impose upon should be thought merely arbitrary and not founded in

Reason. I am persuaded you will not think they arise from Caprice when you Reflect.>

When you turn your Thoughts seriously on these Restrictions <on long> <upon> <agree> I am persuaded you will think them <found> reasonable and not <merely arbitrary and> capricious. I will not therefore pay so ill a Compliment to your good Sense as to suppose it necessary to assign the several Reasons which induce me to think them <proper> <indispensible> requisite.

<In a Word my dear Sir it is our Duty to harmonize and to avoid all occasion of Contentions and you have too much Experience not to know that it is.

I am Dear Sir Your obedient and humble Servant

J. J.>

I have given the Bearer an american newspaper for you, which <I have just recieved from France> arrived just after you left us. <Mr. D Neufville> A Dutch Merchant has made an Offer of accepting the Bills drawn on Mr. Laurens, on Terms very generous. <I have mentioned this to Count Montmorin.> I have seen Count O Dunne; I think you would do well to visit him. He may be very useful to our Affairs in Portugal which by a Letter I have just recieved appear to be in a very unpleasant Situation, Dohrman[2] having been ordered to cease attending to them.

The Count <appears> seems very well disposed, and has promised me to so extend his Care to such Americans as may unfortunately be carried to that Kingdom. As the Court will be here on Saturday, I think you had better not send the Journal I desired you to keep, by the Bearer but to retain it till you come yourself. There are various Speculations in this City respecting the Objects of Mr. Cumberlands Mission. Most People suppose he is charged with Offers for Peace, and as far as I can judge most People <appear> are very glad of it.

I had written thus far when a Number of Letters from Am. were delivered to me. We have later News than they contain. Among them was a Letter for you which you will find enclosed with this. <The Seals of my Letters have been barbarously toasted. They pass you know through hot Fires in France and in Spain.> I have recieved your Favor of the 23rd. Inst. The Report from Bordeaux you mention had reached us. God Grant it may be confirmed.

I am Dear Sir your most obedient and humble Servant

DftS.

[1] Jean François, baron de Bourgoing (1748–1811), served as secretary to the French ambassador in Madrid, 1777–1785.

[2] Arnold Henry Dohrman, a Lisbon merchant, was officially appointed agent for the U.S. in Portugal by Congress on 21 June 1780. *JCC*, XVII, 541–42.

From William Carmichael

Aranjues, 29th June 1780

Dear Sir

I know not whether I am more greived or hurt by yours of the 27th which St. John brought me about nine o'Clock last night. I impute it neither to Pride nor Prudence, because I am perswaded that if you had done me the Justice to wait my return to Town, the latter would have prevented you from giving me without cause the most uneasy sensations, I have felt, since I have been in Spain; and your own good sense, if not my conduct would have prevented you from being hurt in the former point.

The State of Facts will better remove your conclusions, which give me leave to say are hasty, than the present Situation of my mind will otherwise allow me to do. When In consequence of your directions, I showed to the Count de Montmorin your letter of the 22nd to the Count de Blanca,[1] He was pleased to give me his opinion on the Subject of it and advice how to conduct myself when I delivered it. I listened to him with that attention which is due to his character and Connection with us, and thanked Him in the manner, which his apparent good Intentions demanded. This is the manner in which I consulted Him. He at the same time told me he was going to Town, and He will do me the justice to say, that I requested him to see you and repeat the Sentiments he had just mentioned to me.

The Journal which I shall have the honor to deliver you in Madrid, will show whether I was guided by his advice or not. If that is not Evidence, your first Conference with the Count de F B may remove any doubts on that Subject.

You remember the proposition respecting the information to be communicated through the Channel of France to some one in England, respecting Mr. Cumberland and his supposed negociations, upon which you permitted me to consult the Embassador. This necessarily induced a conversation respecting him. With regard to the Chevalier and his knowledge of my attention in watching Cumberland, you will be pleased to recollect that I have more than once told you that, it was probable that the Same Person whom I particularly employed would communicate to the Embassador or Some one of his Family, in which He in a manner lives, not only all I gleaned through his means, but also most of what he knew respecting my Conduct in this business. I was led to form this Conclusion from many questions put me by the Chevalier and if not positively denying the truth of his Information, be to communicate Intelligence, I certainly communicated it, for I never will, if I can avoid it give, and that unncessarily, to Persons with whom our Interest and consequently my Duty obliges me to be on Intimate Terms, either a bad opinion of my heat or head. I have endeavored to procure all the Intelligence that the Small sphere of my knowledge or acquaintance in this Country would allow me to obtain, and This I have always communicated to you almost Instantaneously. The use of it hath been left hitherto entiraly to your discretion, and as long as I continue in Spain, I think, If I know myself, I shall not change my conduct.

I never had but one Idea of our Commissions, which is still the same, that you are Minister and I Secretary. The second time I had the honor of seeing the Count de Florida Blanca, I put the Copies of these commissions into his hands, of which circumstance I had the honor to inform you on our first Meeting at this Place, and when in Consequence of a reference in your Letter to Mr. Galvez to me for Information, The Count de F. Blanca sent me the quiries I also gave you on your arrival at Madrid, I declined answering them, not only in respect to your Commission, but to your superior knowledge of the past and actual Situation of America, and altho on account of your not ariving so soon as you was expected, I was more than once pressed on that Subject, I always declined answering them, alledging the Abovementioned Reasons.

When I hinted to you the propriety of Countersighning your letters, I thought it customary, and you may Judge whether I had it much at heart, Since I do not recollect having mentioned it more than once. To be frank with you the Idea Struck me, from Seeing Mr. Fergusons name countersighned to some of the Commissioners dispatches to Congress.[2] On Reflection you must Allow, that I could have no Idea but the proper one of my Commission, from the single Circumstance of being desirous to sighn Myself Secretary at the foot of your Public Letters. I am sorry that your opinion of my understanding or Prudence induced you to think the restrictions you have made necessary. I shall however profit by the Circumstance, as it shows me the necessity of Scrutinizing severaly my conduct, since it hath drawn upon me a censure, as unexpected as I hope it is unmerited.

I immediately delivered your Letters for the Count De F B to Monsieur Del Campo, His Excellency not being at the office, and told Him that I should set out for Madrid on Fryday evening and would charge myself with any answer to these or your former letter which his Excellency might Judge proper to make. I waited on the Count D Odunne on his arrival here and have seen him Several times Since. He has done me the honor to repeat the Same assurances which he made you in Madrid. I yesterday paid my respects to Mr. Galvez to take my leave of Him and was received with much Politness and many assurances of his disposition to be usefull to us. The Inclosed list of Delegates may be satisfactory to you. I beg you to make the proper Compliments for me to Mrs. Jay and the Colonel and to beleive me with much respect Your Most Obedient and Most Humble Servant

WM. CARMICHAEL

ALS. Enclosure not located.

[1] *RDC*, IV, 119–21.

[2] Dr. Adam Ferguson served as secretary to the Carlisle Commission of 1778. *JCC*, XI, 585.

To William Carmichael

Madrid, 29 June 1780

Dear Sir

Perhaps an opportunity may offer of sending you this before you leave aranjues. I wish it may. I assure you it was far from my Intention to give you Pain or Uneasiness by my Letter of the 27 Inst. It would have given me less Trouble and more pleasure to have talked the Matter over with you *after* your Return, but a Letter was necessary to suspend the Conference which I understood was to have been held *before* your Return.

Your speaking with Count DMontmorin about my Letter on Money Matters as well as about convoying thro him to England certain Matters respecting Mr. Cumberland was perfectly right, we having so agreed, but your proposing to have a Conference with Count D FloridaBlanca on the Objects and Influence of Mr. Cumberlands Journey hither and consulting Count Montmorin on that Subject as he told me I still think was not quite right, it not having been agreed to by or mentioned to me. Your declining to give Answers in my absence to Count D FB Queries had and has my approbation.

As to your having communicated to Chevalier DBurgoyne as much Information as you had Reason to think he possessed already on Mr. Cumberlands Affair was wise and I approve of it, but more was unnecessary. I mean the Names of the persons employed. Attention to our Allies is proper and I commend it.

I am pleased with the Correspondence of our Sentiments relative to our Conversation. I apprehended the contrary might be the Case. Your having urged your Commission of Charge des Affaires as a Reason for countersigning my Letters, together with your intended Conference led me principally to suspect you considered it as in some Degree in force. But your Letter removes that apprehension, and there is of Course an End of it. By marking our Lines of Action I had no Idea of impeaching your Understanding or Prudence, and I think you are mistaken in supposing it involves the Censure you think it does. I suspect that your pen has been guided on this occasion by your Feelings, which I would always much rather gratify than wound. Explanations are sometimes expedient tho often unpleasant. I shall always as a public Servant prefer the former but it shall always be my Study not to give avoidable Uneasiness to any Person especially those with whom it may be my Duty to cultivate Harmony and a Disposition to unite cordially in serving our Country.

I am obliged to you for the List of Delegates. There has it seems been little Change since we left Congress.

I am Dear Sir Your most obedient Servant

J. J.

DftS. Endorsed: ". . . proposed Conference with the minister."

To FLORIDABLANCA

Madrid, 20th June 1780

Mr. Jay has the Honor or representing to his Excellency the Count D'Florida Blanca that Thomas Shuker a Native of the State of New Hampshire, and Captain of an american armed vessel, was captured by the Enemy in September last, and finally carried to England.

That in January last he shipped himself on Board the Dover Cutter of London, then lying in Yarmouth Road. That on the 13th of April last, being at Madeira, he together with several other Americans on Board, made themselves Masters of the Cutter, and carried her into St. Crouz in the Island of Teneriff.

That the Governor of that Island hath taken the said Cutter from the Captors, who have not as yet been able to obtain that Justice on the Subject, which the Laws of Nations in such Cases prescribe.

Mr. Jay transmits herewith enclosed a Copy of the Petition sent by Captain Shuker to Congress, relative to this Transaction; in which his Excellency will find a plain and particular narrative of the Facts. And he flatters himself, that such orders will be given on the Subject, as that Justice may be done the Captors; and that the Citizens of the United States may not be deterred by such singular Embarrassments, from bringing their Prizes into the Ports of His Catholic Majesty.[1]

JOHN JAY

THE HUMBLE PETITION OF THOMAS SHUKER NATIVE OF NEW HAMPSHIRE.

Teneriff, 27th April 1780

Honourable Gentleman

Your Petitioner has been in the Continental Service, and in Private Ships of War belonging to the United States, from the first commencement of hostilities. In the year seventeen hundred and seventy eight I commanded the armed Sloop Snatch-Catcher mounting ten guns belonging to Boston, afterwards the Revenge mounting sixteen guns and was taken by the Venus frigate in September 1778 and carried into Rhode Island from whence I escaped, and went on board the Cumberland (a twenty Gun ship Commanded by Captn. Manly) in the capacity of a Lieutenant.

We sailed from Boston on the 1st of January 1779. On the 17th took a snow bound for Barbadoes which I went on board as Master, on the 23d. was taken under Fort Seline in Martinico by the Venus Frigate (being the second time by her). I had both legs in irons until the 15th of Septr. following when we arrived in England, my health being very much impaired by confinement. I was taken out of Irons, at the same time was informed, it was expected for me to be a true Subject of the King of England. Immediately I was sent on board the Alcide of seventy four Guns, after being on board about six weeks I made my escape from her, and after secreting myself sometime I found it impossible to get either to France or Holland, the little I had to subsist upon being expended, I was obliged to ship myself on board the Cutter Dover (belonging to London) on the 5th of January then lying in Yarmouth Roads off the Isle of White.

After being on board some time, finding several more Americans, I consulted with them about rising and taking the vessel from the English. My party being so much Inferior in number I was obliged to put it off from time to time. After Cruising some time about the Canary Islands, we went into Madeira to refit. Having got provision and water for a three Months cruise. The Captain, Second Lieutenant and Surgeon being on shore, likewise fourteen men upon pleasure, thinking I could not have a better opportunity, I acquainted my party with my intentions to seize the vessel that same night. At one oClock on Thursday morning the 13th Instant myself with three more went into the Cabin and Steerage, secured the first Lieutenant Master and Surgeons mate. We then made ourselves masters of the Arms and armed our Party, then secured twenty seven Englishmen. Immediately after we cut her cable and got under way, there was a brig mounting twenty guns belonging to London, within musket Shot. She was to have been our consort.

Finding it necessary to make the nearest port on account of our Prisoners being superior in number and we scarcely able to make sail, we arrived here the Saturday following. I immediately acquainted the Governor how I had taken the Vessel, that I was an American and under the protection of Congress. The Governor wanted the Cutter as a cruiser to protect the trade of the seven Islands. I told him I had much rather go home with the vessel. The Governor then told me as the King of Spain could not at this time assist them with a Cruiser to protect these Islands, he was under the necessity of detaining the Cutter, at the same time informing me he would write to the Court of Madrid to know how to act, as this is the first instance of such a capture coming into this Port. The Governor manned her a week ago with Officers and men and sent her on a cruise. My Officers and Part of my people are on shore. We are allowed out of the Treasury as follows, viz. Myself, three shillings and four pence Sterling per day, Lieutenant, Master and Mate one shilling and eight pence. Men ten pence.

The Governor without my being allowed to be present, sent Men on board to take an Inventory. What they valued her at, I cannot say. The cost of her in England, as I have been informed, was fourteen thousand Pounds Sterling. She is a fast sailing Cutter Sheathed with Copper, her sides are nine Inches thick, well stuffed with junk and ash, burden two hundred and twenty tons one year old, mounts 16 nine and four eighteen pounders and four swivels, Pistols and Cutlasses for seventy men. Nearly all her Powder and ball is on board, we not having had any engagement. I intended sending my Lieutenant and two or three of my men in the same scooner I shall send this, but the Governor refused to let them embark. I am at a loss, what His reason is for his proceedings, without it be that some of the Prisoners have sworn that I am an Englishman, and that we had only four or five Americans among us. Therefore I understand not an officer will be permitted to embark until the Governor receives his orders from Madrid. I hope your honours will take this into Consideration and act as you think proper. The Scooner is under Way.

I remain with the greatest respect Your honors Most Obedient and Most Devoted Servant

THOMAS SHUKER

ALS and enclosure in AHN: Estado, leg. 3884 bis, exp. 12, docs. 1 and 2. A Spanish translation of the enclosure is doc 3; C in hand of Henry Brockholst Livingston, JP.

1 Floridablanca replied that "he can say nothing until he has obtained some further information thereon." JJ wrote five months later, again requesting that "such Measures may be taken for deciding this Matter, as the Justice due to the United States, may give their Citizens a Right to expect from the Honor of Spain." Even that letter produced no resolution of the problem. Floridablanca to JJ, 29 June 1780, in JP and *RDC,* IV, 122. JJ to Floridablanca, 25 Nov. 1780, ALS in AHN: Estado, leg. 3884, exp. 12, doc. 4.

From Patrick Fitzmaurice

Cadiz, 27 June 1780

Dear Sir

Your most welcome favor I received conveyed to me by Mr. harrison who I assured that no recommendation could make a greater impression on me than yours, consequently that he might dispose on all occaisons both of my person and property, and since over he handed me the Letter wee are mostly togeither, he answers in every respect the caracter you give of him and hopes he will do well in this town being under such a satisfactory government as wee at present enjoy, under our good friend in command who is daily doing wonders in point of Justice and good dispositions in his new government.[1] Most of the inhabitants publickly says that he is an angel from heaven and that his equal never as in Cadiz. God almightly preserve him and prolong his days for the Satisfaction and Content of his friends and country to whom he does honour, and as I know his great regard and friendship for you I am fully convinced his Welfare and good Success will be always agreable to you.

I am proud to learn Mrs. Jay enjoys good health in Madrid tho I suppose she must have her little ups and downs untill she is delivered of a pritty Spaniard. God send it may be with all happyness. I must own I was a little jealous with you and still much more so with the Cornel who I know has less to do not to have favoured me with a few lines of your arrival for I was quiet unhappy since I was informed of the accidence of the Coach on the road, which misfortune I am affraid along with the court enchatments made the Cornel forget his friends in Cadiz which miss Valverda cannot pardon him for. She and family desires to be kindly remembered to you and Mrs. Jay, as well as Mrs. Jones who is inconsolable notwithstanding my sermons to her. She gives you many thanks for your kind offers.

Our news in the day here are reduced to our fleet composed of 27 Spaniard and eight frenchmen of war are to be ready to sail at first advice. Several other frenchmen of war are daily expected from Toulon and Brest that wee will be always able to oppose the English in all their undertakings. Our news from Charles town if true cannot be more agreable. Wee are anxious here to see Clinton Burgoyned. After what passes in London I suppose ireland to be by this in a general flame.

My best respects to Mrs. Jay and kind Compliments to the Cornel, and the young gentleman your nephew. Do conclude by being Dear Sir Your most affectionate and faithful humble Servant

PATRICK FITZMAURICE

ALS. Endorsed: ". . . ansd. 6 July. Recd. 4 July." Patrick Fitzmaurice was a Carmelite, born in County Clare, Ireland, who had lived in Spain for many years.

1 Count Alexander O'Reilly.

FROM ROBERT R. LIVINGSTON

Philadelphia, 6th July 1780

Dear John

Having just heard of an opportunity to write to you by way of France I relieve the fatigue of an uninteresting debate in which our Friends Fell and Holton take the lead to let you hear from me.[1] If I have not been unfortunate you must at your arrival have found several Letters from me, some of them written in our first cypher which you tell me has become useless so that they are probably unintelligible to you.[2]

I shall now confine myself to general subjects as my present cypher is not at hand. I have been here since the 4th of Novr. very much against my inclinations and know not how much longer I may be detained. Mr. D— is gone home,[3] and as he has views upon your old seat he will hurry back to be in time and he assures me that I shall have *leave to go* immediately upon his return, and as I do not look the same way I think I shall indulge him. You have I dare say heard of poor Morris misfortune in the loss of his leg.[4] He bears it with magnanimity and is in a fair way of recovery. I feel for him and yet am led to hope that it may turn out to his advantage and tend to fix his desultory genious to a point in which case it can not fail to go far.

As I know the interest you take in what may contribute to my happiness, I venture to inform you of a domestick occurence by which it is greatly increased, the birth of a daughter.[5] I saw your son at headquarters about two months ago. He is a fine healthy boy and the Idol of his grandmother. Now I am speaking of her, I must tell you that she was so imprudent as to remove with her family to Elizabeth town, where she was vissited by the enemies whole army, who treated her with civility as I learn by a letter to Mrs. Morris from Caty. But their troops being very hardly treated by the New Jersey Militia on a second vissit they made to Springfield, which they burnt, they called a second time at the Governors, and were with great difficulty prevented from burning the house by Mistress Livingston, Mrs. Livingston not being at home.[6]

You are happy in being so far from this scene of trouble. The enemy by the reduction of Charlestown have obliged us to make large detachments from the main army and by returning with the greater part of their force have kept us in a continual motion, tho fortunately they are now again by the aid of the militia shut up in New York. And we are waiting in anxious expectation the arrival of the French armament in order to attempt some thing important. In the mean while we shall need great assistance from the court at which you now are to enable us to make some arrangement of our finances, from the disorder of which our greatest evils flow. These however are by no means remediless; they want attention, and some support from our allies to put them upon the best and most stable footing.

I forgot to mention I have received within this few days your Letter from Cadiz.[7] I was mortified to such a degree at not hearing from you while at Martinique that I could not bring myself to continue writing as I had done till you Last convinced me that I was not forgotten. I have seen Mrs. Jays journal, feel her distress, admire her fortitude and offer her my congratulations upon her present agreeable situation. You will offer my compliments to the Colonel and Mr. Carmichael, and receive my best wishes for your happiness.

I am Dear John with the sincerest esteem Your friend and humble servant

ROBERT R. LIVINGSTON

Typescript.

1 On 6 July 1780 John Fell (1721–98), of New Jersey and Samuel Holton (1738–1816) of Massachusetts clashed over the provisions for the pay of the quartermaster general in the report of the committee on that department. *JCC*, XVII, 589.

2 See above, JJ to Robert Livingston, 25 Oct. 1779 and Robert R. Livingston to JJ, 22 Dec. 1779, 10 Feb. 1780.

3 James Duane.

4 Gouverneur Morris's leg was badly mutilated in a carriage accident in May 1780, and amputation was necessary. Max M. Mintz, *Gouverneur Morris and the American Revolution* (Norman, Okla., 1970), pp. 139–41.

5 The chancellor's elder daughter, Elizabeth Stevens Livingston (1780–1829), was born 5 May. Dangerfield, *Robert R. Livingston* (N.Y., 1960), p. 125.

6 Liberty Hall suffered at least two visitations resulting from the British incursions to nearby Springfield, one in February 1779 (see above, SLJ to JJ, 5 March 1779) and a second in June 1780. On the latter raid, Catharine Livingston, according to family legend, stood at the head of the hall stairs, and a sudden flash of lightning made her appear as an apparition. A drunken Hessian, mistaking her for the ghost of Mrs. James Caldwell, who had been killed by the British in a previous raid, made a hasty exit. The Livingston women, however, deemed it prudent to leave Liberty Hall temporarily. Theodore Thayer, *As We Were: The Story of Old Elizabethtown* (Elizabeth, N.J., 1964), pp. 128–29, 136–39; Theodore Sedgewick, Jr., *A Memoir of the Life of William Livingston* (N.Y., 1833), pp. 353–55; Thomas Fleming, *The Forgotten Victory: The Battle for New Jersey, 1780* (N.Y., 1973), pp. 177–78.

7 See above, JJ to Livingston, 19 Feb. 1780.

FROM JAMES LOVELL

[*Philadelphia*], *July 11, 1780*

Dear Sir

By a Letter from Messr. Gardoqui & Sons of May 3d received yesterday I have the Pleasure of knowing you were then well. In a Postscript to one of his former, of Feb. 24, the P S not dated, he says he hears of you *every Week*. This creates a *Chagrin* as we have none of your Favors later than March 3d.[1] You are not to suppose, however, that I dare to *complain*. I have read my Bible to better Purpose. I am not entitled to throw the "first stones." But I have as good a title as anybody to paliate my own faults, and to shift them upon others.

There is said to be a Committee of foreign Affairs, each member is loaded with a variety of business, two have amiable Wives near Pennsylvania. I miss the Gentlemen therefore frequently. Mr. Livingston is now absent but you have herewith a Letter he sent to my Care a few days ago. The weather is murderous hot and I cannot go up and down to the Offices in search of those authenticated Papers which ought to be regularly forwarded to you and other dignified Officers abroad.

You will be pleased therefore to know from me *individually* and by Way of a Resolve of Congress of June 21st certified by me, that Mr. Dohrman of Lisbon is appointed an Agent in Portugal.[2] The chief View at this time was that the lives of our poor sailers might not be lost in captivity in that Kingdom. Mr. Dohrman has done an infinitude of kind acts already to such as have been carried into Ports near Lisbon. He is a Gentleman of much Influence through his personal Character, his Riches and Relations. I have no doubt you will find Advantage from frequent Correspondence with him. He is not yet furnished with any authentic account of his appointment. He ought to have some Commission; perhaps beyond a certified Resolve, and he should have some regular instructions. I will endeavor to get Mr. Houston to join me in a Letter to the Gentleman to cover the Proof of his having been elected on the 21st of June. It was represented by Mr. Anderson of Virginia[3] who is his Agent, that Mr. Dohrman expected no other recompence then the repayment of his Advances, in the usual Way, and those Emoluments that will be naturally consequential upon his being known the public Agent of these States in Portugal. The Proofs of his Spirit in our Cause are unequivocal and his liberality to our suffering countrymen has abundant Proofs. I did give Mr. Anderson a Copy of the Resolve for his own satisfaction but I told him it would go with Authority through you and that Mr. Dohrman ought not to be deprived of the sole Judgement of making the appointment more or less a Thing of Notoriety according to the Politics of the Kingdom of Portugal.

Mr. Searle[4] is the Bearer of this Via France and Mr. Laurens will either go for Holland in the same Ship, the *Jay*, or will sail in a few days by another opportunity for Holland. The former Gentleman is on business for the State of Pennsylvania and perhaps for some mercantile Companies also. You already Know Mr. Laurens is to negotiate a Loan. Indeed an Instruction was given to a Committee to bring in a Draught of a Letter to the ministers Plenipotentiary of these States at Versailles and Madrid directing them to inform his most Christian and Catholic Majesty of the appointment of Mr. Laurens and to solicit the aid of their majesties respectively on this Occasion.

I am Sir your Friend and very humble Servant

JAMES LOVELL

ALS. Endorsed: ". . . ansd 27 Oct." Enclosure: Robert R. Livingston to JJ, 6 July 1780, above. Printed with deletions in *RDC*, III, 847–48.

[1] José de Gardoqui and Sons to Congress, 24 Feb. and 3 May 1780, were read in Congress 10 July 1780. *JCC*, XVII, 595. JJ to President of Congress, 3 March 1780, in *RDC*, III, 529–30.

[2] For the appointment of Arnold Henry Dohrman, see *JCC*, XVII, 541–42. Also see above, JJ to Carmichael, 27 June 1780.

[3] George Anderson. *JCC*, XVII, 541.

[4] James Searle (1730–97), Pennsylvania delegate to the Continental Congress, 1778–80, was appointed commissioner to France and Holland to negotiate a loan for his state. Although he remained in Europe until 1782, he was unsuccessful in his quest.

To George Clinton

Madrid, 14 July 1780

Dear Sir

My last Letter to you was dated the 20th June.[1] I have written many and hope you have already recieved several. None from you have as yet reached me.

By the Journals of Congress I percieve that your Disputes with your Neighbours are in a fair Way of being decided.[2] I think Mr. Duane might have been a useful Counsellor to your other Delegates on that occasion, but I dont find his name among those that then attended. It is also my opinion that the State would do well to maintain a post at their own Expence as far in the western Country as may be conveinent. My Reasons for this may be collected from a Letter I wrote you shortly before I sailed from the Delaware.[3] The Virginians have done a good Deal in this Way and probably from similar motives with those, which induce me to propose this measure.

A late Resolution of Congress recommends the Naturalization of French Subjects agreable to one of the articles of Treaty.[4] This strikes me as a Measure which requires some caution. I would have every article of the Treaty fully complied with, but I am not clear that american Protestants are intended to be *naturalized* in France, except as to certain purposes. These I think should be precisely known, and be made the Standard of Immunities to be granted by us to them.

Be pleased to present my Compliments to your neighbour Capt. Plat.[5] Mrs. Jay has a Daughter. Remember us affectionately to Mrs. Clinton. I am Dear Sir yours most sincerely

J.J.

DftS.

[1] JJ to George Clinton, 20 June 1780, Dft in JP.

[2] It is unlikely that JJ had before him the record of the most recent actions

of Congress concerning the Vermont dispute. On 2 June 1780, Congress agreed to hear and make final determination of the issue as soon as nine states, exclusive of the parties to the controversy (New Hampshire, Massachusetts, and New York), were represented. On 9 June the hearing was postponed until September. *JCC*, XVII, 484, 499.

[3] See above, JJ to George Clinton, 25 Oct. 1779.

[4] JJ was mistaken. Naturalization was not involved under Article XI of the Treaty of Amity and Commerce of 1778 with France, but rather rights to bequeath and inherit, which were to be reciprocally granted U.S. inhabitants in France and Frenchmen in America, thus distinguishing Americans in France from "Aubains in France" or unnaturalized aliens. Such rights, however, by the treaty were not to affect French laws against emigration. JJ's insistence on complete reciprocity and removal of bars to emigration were in later years to hold up ratification of the French Consular Treaty. *JCC*, XVI, 56–57.

[5] Jonathan Platt was captain of the 4th New York Regiment, 28 June 1775–Jan. 1776.

To John Adams

Madrid, 17 July 1780

Dear Sir

On the 4 June last I had the Pleasure of writing you a Letter acknowledging the reciept of yours of the 15 May,[1] since which none of your Favors have reached me.

I have just been reading the Capitulation of Charles Town. I suspect they wanted Provisions. The Reputation of the Garrison will suffer till the Reasons of their Conduct are explained. I wish a good one may be in their Power. They are severely censured here. What the Consequence of this Event may be, cannot easily be conjectured. I should not be surprized if they should eventually be in our Favor. It is difficult while invaded in the Center to defend Extremities which have little natural Strength.

I wish Ternays Squadron may touch at Halifax. The Capture of of that place would reduce the English Navy in the american Seas to extreme Difficulties. The Affair of Charles Town has an unfavorable Aspect on the Expedition against New York.

After the Conclusions of this Campaign, I think you will have something to do. In my opinion all the Powers at war wish for Peace. The Pride of the King of England will be the greatest Obstacle, and it may happen that in attempting to save his Dignity he may lose his Crown.

No News yet of Mr. Laurens. What is to become of his Bills? I have accepted to the Amount of between 10 and 12,000 Dollars of those drawn upon me. The Fate of the Residue is not fixed, but like many other Adventurers I imagine they will have good Luck.

On a Presumption that you are acquainted with Mrs. Izard[2] I take the Liberty of committing the enclosed Letter from her to your Care. It has been written some Time, and wanting only for the french Courier by whom you will recieve this.

My Family was increased last Week by the Birth of a Daughter. My Compliments to Mr. Dana.

I am Dear Sir With great Regard and Esteem Your most obedient Servant

JOHN JAY

ALS. MHi: Adams Papers. Endorsed: ". . . Recd. 27th." Enclosure: letter to Alice De Lancey Izard, dft in JP.

1 Adams's letter of 15 May 1780 is in Charles Francis Adams, ed., *The Works of John Adams, Second President of the United States* (10 vols., Freeport, N.Y., 1969), VII, 169–70 and *RDC*, III, 678–79.

2 Alice De Lancey (Mrs. Ralph) Izard (d. 1832), a native of New York City. Although her husband returned to the U.S. in 1780, she remained in Europe until 1783.

To Benjamin Franklin

Madrid, 17 July 1780

I have <been honored with> had the Pleasure of receiving your Favors of the 13th and 25th June last[1] <and am greatly obliged by the Communications they make. I refer>

After having recieved part of the Money lodged with Marquis D'Yranda I sent for another part not chusing to recieve the whole at once and intending to leave in his Hands the Ballance due to you. I recieved for answer that I might recieve the whole but not a Part. There was no Choice and I recieved it accordingly. The Remittances <I expected> from Congress have not arrived. I have written to them on the Subject,[2] and am now <in the mean Time> feeding on your Ballance, choosing rather to do this than humiliate my constituents by running them in Debt for my Bread here.

The Papers enclosed with this will make known to you the exact State of <our> Affairs <here> at this Court. I have been permitted <already> to accept Bills <drawn> to the amount of between ten and twelve Thousand Dollars and as the Court and particularly the Count D Florida Blanca seems well disposed towards us I hope the unpleasant Measure will terminate well. These Papers should have been sent you before but I have been long waiting for Count Montmorins Courier by whom I would rather transmit them than by the Post for Reasons which you will be at no Loss to conjecture.

From these Papers you will naturally conclude that it is very far from being in my Power to afford Mr. Ross the Aid mentioned in your Letter.[3] On the Contrary I find myself constrained to request the Favor of you to lodge here for Mr. Carmichael and myself a further Credit to enable us to recieve what may be due on Account of Salaries. <I cannot think of endeavoring> We shall otherwise be very soon in a very disagreable Situation. To take up Money from Individuals <for many Reasons> would not be eligible or reputable and it would not be prudent to trouble Government already a little sore about the Bills with further Requisitions at present.

<To you therefore I must recur, and that> I am also obliged to make this Request without being able to give you other assurances <of> respecting the Time of Repayment, than that the proceeds of the first Remittance I may recieve shall be applied to that in Preference to every other Purpose. <I have recieved no Information on this Subject since I left America and my principal Reason for expecting Remittances (next to the Faith of Congress) arises from the Facility with which they> I cannot however think the Time will be very distant as Remittances may now be made in Bills of Exchange. But if I should be decieved and if the servants of Congress here must live a while on the Credit they may seek and find with others, I think it more decent to recur to their Ally <than to others.> France I know has already done great things for us and is still making glorious Exertions. <I shall love the Nation as long as I live.> I am also sensible of your Difficulties and regret them, tho I am happy in reflecting that since they must exist, they have fallen into the Hands of one whose abilities and Influence enable him to sustain and surmount them at a Court which does not appear inclined to do things by Halves.

I should be surprized at the Treatment your Letters I sent to Nantz have met with, had I not experienced too many strange things to be much surprized at any. <It gives me pain to infer from a certain Gentlemans Reserve with Respect to you, that perfect and Cordial Confidence does not exist between you.>[4]

It is necessary you should be informed that the Papers inclosed with this are known to Count Montmorin and therefore are probably no Secrets to his Court. I am on <exceedingly> good Terms with the Count whom I esteem as a Man of abilities and am pleased with as a Friend to our Country. As France had interested herself so deeply in our Cause, had done us <such> essential Benefits, and had been requested to interpose her friendly offices for us here, I could not think of withholding from him all the Confidence which these considerations dictate, especially as <the Resolutions of Congress respecting their Legation here breathed that Spirit, and as> no personal objections forbid it. To have conducted the Negociation with <slyness> finesse, and unnecessary secrecy, and equivocating cunning was irreconciable with my Principles of Action and with every Idea I have of Wisdom and Policy—in a word France and America are and I hope will always be Allies. It is the Duty of each Party to cultivate mutual Confidence and Cordiality. For my own Part while their Conduct continues fair, firm and friendly, I shall remain thoroughly attached to their Interest and grateful for their Benefit.

Mrs. Jay is much pleased and thanks you for the print you was so kind as to send her. It is a striking Likeness. I find that in France great Men, like their Predecessors of old, have their Bards.[5] Your Strictures are very Just tho a little Severe, while there are young Telemachus's and fascinating Calypsos in the World, Fancies and pens and Hearts will sometimes run riot, in spite of the Mentors now and then to be met with.

Your Danish Correspondent was very civil as well as very much embarrassed. I am pleased with both Circumstances; they indicate more Caution in future, but I fear the present Case will continue without Remedy.

I recieve no Letters but what have passed through the Fire once and often twice, and that is not the Worst of it, for I am sure that some have been suppressed. I wish therefore that such as you may favor me with, be sent either by the Courier <or under Cover to some Person here from the House of Druillet Cabarrus> or in some other way that you may have Reason to confide in.

I am Dear Sir with very sincere Regard your most obedient Servant

P.S. <I had almost forgotten to tell you that> Mrs. Jay had a Daughter born the ninth Instant <and that> They are both well. Benevolent Minds enjoy <the> Events grateful to others. I can not therefore forbear telling you this little piece of news.

Dft. Enclosures: Floridablanca to JJ, 24 Feb. and 17 June 1780: LbkCs in DNA: PCC, I, and CsmH: JJ lbk; 2 Cs in Spanish in AHN: Estado, Leg. 3884, exp. 8. JJ to Floridablanca, 6 March 1780; LS in Spanish in AHN: Estado, Leg. 3884, exp. 8; LbkCs in DNA: PCC, 110, I and CSmH: JJ lbk; C in French in MAE: CP, Espagne, v. 579; 25 April: ALS in AHN: Estado, Leg. 3884, doc. 19; C in MAE: Espagne, v. 518; C in NHi: JJ Misc. Mss.; 31 April: ALS and C in

Spanish in AHN: Estado, Leg. 3884, exp. 8; C in French translation MAE: CP, Espagne, v. 599; 19 June 1780: AL and Spanish C in AHN: Estado, Leg. 3884, exp. 4, doc. 53; LbkCs in DNA: PCC, 110, I and CSmH: JJ Lbk; 20 June 1780: ALS in AHN: Estado, Leg. 3884, exp. 12, doc. 1; 22 June 1780: LS and Spanish Cs in AHN: Estado, Leg. 3884, exp. 4, doc. 53; C in French in MAE: CP: Espagne, v. 599, 341–44; LbkCs in DNA: PCC, 110, I and CSmH: JJ Lbk; dft in JP. Vergennes to JJ, 13 March 1780: ALS in French in DNA: PCC, 110, I; LbkC in French in CSmH: JJ Lbk; Dft in French in MAE: CP: États-Unis, II. JJ to Vergennes, 9 May 1780: a copy of Sir John Dalrymple's "Anecdote Historique," ALS in MAE: CP: États-Unis, XII; LbkCs in DNA: PCC, 110, I and CSmH: JJ Lbk; dftS in JP. These enclosures, plus JJ to Floridablanca, 9 March Franklin Papers, III, 34–35. E of the letter is in NN: in Bancroft American Series, II, 140.

1 Franklin's letter of 25 June, ALS in JP; LbkC in DLC: Franklin Papers, III, 27.

2 See JJ to the President of Congress, 10 July 1780, LbkCs in DNA: PCC, 110, I and CSmH: JJ Lbk; dft in JP; printed in *RDC*, III, 834–44.

3 In the 25 June letter Franklin asked JJ to assist John Ross, a merchant of Philadelphia and Nantes who had become involved in financial difficulties as a result of his employment by the Committee of Commerce. Franklin requested ". . . if you should be enabled by any Loan or Subsidy put into your hands, to extricate him, you would do it; as he has been a faithful Servant of the Publick."

4 Probably a reference to the Marquis d'Yranda.

5 The following passage, omitted from the Dft, is in LbkC in DLC: Franklin Papers: "Yours seem to have mounted high mettled Pegasus, and to have been inspired (if Bryden's Doctrine be right) and seem to have been by electwise muses."

To Floridablanca

Madrid, 22d. July 1780

Sir

I have just received a Letter, dated the 14th. Instant, from Mr. Richard Harrison,[1] an American Merchant who lately arrived at Cadiz; of which I take the Liberty of transmitting to your Excellency the following Paragraph—vizt.

"His Excellency General OReily sent for me this Morning to inform me that with every Disposition to serve the Americans, he could not without express Permission from the Minister, permit me to establish myself here, and that unless this Permission is soon obtained, he should be under the Necessity of ordering me out of the Kingdom, or twenty Leagues into the Country."

It is with Pleasure and with Confidence that I can assure your Excellency that this Gentleman is not only a Native of America, but a Friend to her Cause, in which some of his Family are now bearing arms, and that he is connected with some of the most opulent and respectable Merchants in that Country.

Permit me therefore to request that such Protection and Permission be granted to him, as may be necessary to enable him to remain at Cadiz, and to enjoy the Rights and Priviledges usually granted in such Cases to Merchants of other friendly Nations.

I have the Honor to be with great Respect and Esteem Your Excellencys Most obedient and humble Servant

JOHN JAY

ALS. AHN: Estado, leg. 3884, exp. 4, doc. 63.
1 No complete copy of this letter has been located.

From Benjamin Franklin

Passy, 31 July 1780

Dear Sir

I write this Line just to acknowledge the Receipt of your Favor the 17th and Mr. Carmichaels of the 18th with the Pacquet of Papers in good Order which I shall soon answer fully. At present I can only say that I have given Orders for a Credit to you of another 1000 £ sterling to be proportionally divided between you. I hope the Remittances will arrive before the Sum is expended. I find myself obliged to advance likewise to Messieurs Adams and Dana.

I congratulate you and Mrs. Jay sincerely on the Birth of your Daughter; being with sincere Esteem

Dear Sir, Your most obedient and most humble Servant

B. FRANKLIN

LS. PPAmP: Franklin Papers. Addressed: "Á son Excellence Monsieur Jay, etc. etc. Madrid." Endorsed: ". . . Recd. 18 Augt. 1780, mentioning his having ordered a Credit of 1000£ Ster." LbkC in DLC: Franklin Papers, III.

To Count Montmorin

[*Madrid, 1 August 1780*]

Dear Sir

<Mr. Jay presents his <<most>> Compliments to his Excellency Count D montmorin> We are told that Count D' Estaing is to be with you Tomorrow and will remain some Days at San Ildefonso. Altho Curiosity is not among my predominant Passions, I confess I have always a desire of seeing and conversing with those who have either done Things worthy to be written, or have written Things worthy to be read. Besides on this occasion, my Feelings will not permit me to omit paying the Count that Tribute of Gratitude and

Respect which every Am. owes to His generous Efforts in <her> our Cause. Permit me therefore to request the honor of you<r Excellency> to inform me whether the Count will pass thro Madrid, for if he should not, I will immediately set out for St. Idelfonso.

I have the Honor to be with great Respect and Esteem Your Excellencys most obedient and humble Servant

Dft.

From William Carmichael

St. Ildephonso, August 7th 1780

Dear Sir

I arrived here Yesterday much more fatigued with my Journey and want of Sleep, than I thought I should be when I set out from Madrid. I have also had a return of my bilious disorder, which depresses my spirits even more than it affects my health.

I waited on the Count D'Estaing, who received me as an old acquaintance. I made the proper apologies for you, and he expressed Strongly his regret for the unhappy circumstance that deprived him of the pleasure of seeing you. I dined with him that day, when he mentioned his concern that his Endeavors to serve America, had not been attended with the Success he wished. You may easily conceive my answer. He told me that he meant to visit Madrid, wehre he hoped to have the pleasure of seeing you. I do not think however that he will leave this place for 8 or 10 days at soonest. I had much conversation with him, in which he showed great regret and no dissatisfaction with respect to Us. Altho no one pretends to say with certainty what will be his destination, it is probable, it will be, what we conjectured.

The Count de Montmorin received me in his usual manner, that is with much friendship and politeness and desired me to mention to you his sensibility of Mrs. Jays and your Situation.[1] The Chevalier is so unwell as to prevent him from dining in Company. I waited on Their Excellencies the Count De Florida Blanca and the Minister of the Indies. They were both taking the Air, I therefore left my Name and a Messuage that I should do myself the honor of again paying my respects to them.

The Count de Montmorin received Letters from Philadelphia dated the 12 of May. I do not know their Contents for they were not entirely decyphered, but I have no reason to think they are dissatisfactory. The fleet from Brest had ordered to sail the 24th Ultimo and I think will join that from Cadiz. Every body is delighted by the Junction of Monsieur Guischen with that of —— Solano.[2] The papers from England are as late as the 21st July. They contain a list of the vessels taken by Admiral Geary,[3] viz. 11 St. Domingo men, and the Capture of a French Frigate after an auction of 4 hours by one of Superior Force. The former went to the Bottom immediately after Striking her colors.

A Courier arrived this day from Lisbon to the Ambassador of that Court here, But as yet nothing hath expired. I have been noticed civilly by those Foreighn Ministers that I have met with. The Russian[4] is much Indisposed, which is so much the case with myself at present, that I have been interrupted in writing this Letter by a bilious vomiting. This prevents me from enjoying the fine air and delightfull Gardens and fountains of this truly royal residence. I beg you to make the proper Compliments for me to Mrs. Jay and the Colonel and to beleive me with much Truth and respect

Your Excellencys Most Obedient and Most humble Servant

WM. CARMICHAEL

Mr. C—— ingaged a Lodging in the Same Inn, where I lodge, that of St. Sebastiens. My information with respect to the Letter from hence to him, was well founded. You will be so Obliging as not to mention the Count D'Estaings intended visit to Madrid.

ALS. Addressed: "His Excellency John Jay Esq. Calle St. Francisco Madrid." Endorsed.

1 This is an apparent reference to the fatal illness of the Jay's infant daughter, Susan, who died 4 August.

2 Left blank in original. Admiral Josef Solano commanded a Spanish fleet which sailed from Cádiz to rendezvous with the fleet of the Comte de Guichen (1712–90), French admiral commanding the West Indies fleet. Outwitting Britain's Adm. Rodney, they joined forces north of Guadaloupe 10 June 1780.

3 On 4 July Adm. Francis Geary captured thirteen prizes from a French convoy returning from Port-au-Prince.

4 S. S. Zinovyev was then the Russian ambassador to Spain.

From William Carmichael

St. Ildephonso, 10th August 1780

Dear Sir

I wrote you on the 7th instant, giving you an account of the friendly reception I met with from the Count D'Estaing and sundry other circumstances. I have since seen the Count De F B who informed me that the Person so long expected by us, was not yet arrived, and that when he did come, He would give me notice. I have not heard from him since, and of consequence have not waited upon him because I think the most respectfull mode of Conduct is that, which gives the least unecessary Trouble. I have reason to think however, that the Person alluded to arrived here yesterday at one o'Clock, under the Name of Dölba and is now lodged with the Minister.[1] This information will enable you to be ready to sett off, if circumstances will permit, as soon as you receive the Notice Abovementioned.

The Count D E——g appears to be in excellent spirits, and hath long and frequent conferences with the Minister. The French Ship of the Line which was obliged to put in at St Andre arrived at ferrol the 7th. Mr. Cumberland gives out that Admiral Geary is off the Coast of Galicia; a Copy of a Letter to this Gentleman with this News is in the hands of the Imperial Ambassador. The Jamaica fleet conveyed by the Lion and Carles hath got safe to England without the loss of a vessel. This event will give them a supply of Sailors. I find Myself much better these two days past by the help of Rhubarb and cream of Tartar. The Climate is quite different from that of Madrid, and I think if Mrs. Jay's health will permit, ten days residence here would greatly reestablish it. I beg you to send any letters for me to the Care of landlord Salaberry, who will forward them by a safe Conveyance.

I am, with the proper compliments to Mrs. Jay and the Colonel Your Excellencys Most obedient and Most Humble Servant

WM. CARMICHAEL

P.S. I have delayed sending this, in hopes of further Intelligence with respect to the Person expected, but have not received it. A Courier hath Just arrived from the Coast, but Nothing Hath transpired.

ALS.

[1] Carmichael was alluding to Diego de Gardoqui, whom both he and JJ mistakenly believed was about to be named by the Spanish government as official diplomatic representative to the U.S.

To William Carmichael

Madrid, 11 August 1780

Dear Sir

Your Favor of the 7th Inst. was delivered to me without any of those Marks of impertinent Curiosity which are impressed on almost all the Letters I recieve.

Be pleased to present my Respects to Count D Estaing and Count Montmorin. Assure them of the Regret with which I am obliged as yet to delay going to St. Ildefonso, and of the Pleasure I expect from an acquaintance with the former, and from brightning the Chain of Friendship with the other.

I have not recieved a Line from France since you left madrid. It is said Mr. C is soon to depart, and I have some Reason to think not perfectly satisfied. If France, Spain and America continue firm and United, all will be well. The Junction of the Fleet is a happy Circumstance. I expect much from it.

I am Dear Sir Yours etc.

JOHN JAY

ALS. CSmH. Addressed: "Monsieur Carmichael St. Sebastian St. Ildefonso. The DftS, endorsed by JJ, in JP, contains this postscript: "I have already written to you today. The Post is arrived, and I enclose a Letter for you just come to hand. As it came by the Post I send it thus. What would you have done with such others as may be brought here in your Absence? I have still no Letters from France."

From William Carmichael

St. Ildephonso, August 14th, 1780

Dear Sir

I wrote you on the 12th Instant since which I have had the honor to receive yours of the 11th. I yesterday dined with the French Ambassader at a grand entertainment given to 28 of the Nobility of both sexes and the Foreighn Ministers. The Ambassador and the Count D'Estaing took every opportunity of making their attention to me, and on the whole I was well received. The Count De F. B. came in after dinner and was polite.

This Afternoon the Ambassador and the Count D Estaing showed me part of their Letters from the Court of France by which the Junction of the two fleets in the West Indies is confirmed. This fortunate event happened on the 10th and not on the 19th of June, as the English have published. The King, as the Prince Masserano informed since dinner, appeared highly delighted with this Intelligence. The Count de Vergennes seems satisfied with the Situation of Affairs in America, and says that Charles Town surrendered for want of Provision and other necessaries. The Expected arrival of M. Ternay gave great Spirits and the Count de Vergennes remarks that this circumstance had a happy affect there in every respect except restoring the Credit of our paper, which was worse every day. These advices were brought by the Fier Roderique.

I have every reason to be satisfied, that the Count D Estaings former regard for me hath not diminished, as he converses with me with a frankness, which is remarked even by the Ambassadors Family. He dines with the Count de Lacey[1] on Wedneday at Segovia and will not I beleive quit this place this week at Soonest. Altho from some purchases of Post Saddles etc. and by the Count de Montmorins maitre De Hotel, I am induced to think he is preparing for a Journey. If I know him, he will not engage to serve, without Carte Blanche and this will be a mortal blow to Spanish hauteur.

The only child of Mr. Galvez, a daughter is ill, for which reason I enquire for her health every day, leaving my name with his Porter. The Person I mentioned[2] in my last letter is still here and lodges with Mr. Del Campo who overacts his part, if he sincerely espouses our Interest. It is whispered that Giusti will be replaced by the Abbe Casti. No Person in the Corps Diplomatique is more civil to me than the Count de Kaunitz. I walk with him now and then, and he appears to be convinced that our Independance will take place, in spite as he observes, of the wonderful Exertions of England and the Absurdity of this Court. With respect to the latter, you will readily beleive that I do not appear to concur with him in opinion. I have just heard that Spain hath a prospect of obtaining 8 millions of *hand* dollars by Loan. I shall endeaver to trace and ascertain the truth of this Intelligence.

Your *favorite* Mr. Tervase will put this into your hands. He is a way of succeeding here. The Plan for the seige of Gibraltar hath been approved, but the Expence, delays etc. I hope will delay the enterprize. I have this from the person who formed the plan.

The air is delightfull here, the trouts and the Walks are delicious and the Gardens as solitary as you can desire. I took the opportunity of a courier to write to Doctor Franklin, just informing him, that we were without remittances and without Intelligence from Him or any other Quarter. I hope this hint will not be dissapproved of by you. I beg you to present the proper Compliments for me to Mrs. Jay and the Colonel and to beleive me with much Respect Your Excellencys Most Obedient and Most Humble Servant

WM. CARMICHAEL

ALS.

[1] Francisco de Lacy, conde de Lacy, the son of Irish parents, was born in Barcelona in 1731. He was a member of the Spanish diplomatic corps, serving as ambassador to Russia.

[2] Diego de Gardoqui.

TO BENJAMIN FRANKLIN

Madrid, 16 August 1780

Dear Sir

On the 17th July I wrote you a Letter enclosing Copies of several interesting Papers, by Count Montmorins Courier. This conveyance appeared to me as direct and secure as any I could expect to meet with. I hope you have recieved this Letter. You will percieve from it my Situation, which is really such as to constrain me to repeat my Request for a further Credit. Pray let me hear from you by the Return of the Post. I ought now to be at St. Ildefonso, but I cannot go there and to Market too. Whatever Letters you may send me, should be under Cover to some Persen here. The House of Druillet are friendly and I believe would take Care of them.

The Fate of the Bills drawn on me is not yet decided. I cannot tell you why in this Letter. I hope for the best, and do my best. <I believe there is but little Corn in Egypt.>

M. De Neufville writes me that you have saved the Credit of Mr. Laurens Bills. I am very happy to hear it, and I am sure our Country are much obliged to you. It appears to me that M. De Neufville merits the thanks of America on this occasion, and if so he certainly ought to recieve them.[1]

Whether my Friends in America have forgot me, or whether their Letters cannot find the way here, I know not, but the fact is that I have recieved <very few> scarce any, and but one public one since I left the Delaware. We ought to have some other way of conveying Letters than the Post.

We have lost our little Girl. Adieu.

I am Dear Sir with very sincere Regard, Your most obedient Servant

Mr. Jay presents his Compliments to Mr. Grand and requests the Favor of him to forward the enclosed to His Excellency Dr. Franklin. Mr. Grands <attachment to America and the> polite recommendatory Letter <he was so obliging as to write> to the Marquis D Yranda in favor of Mr. Jay, (of which he has since recieved a Copy from Dr. Franklin,) demand his acknowledgement, and he requests Mr. Grand to be assured that he shall be happy in every opportunity of evincing the Sense he has of his polite Attentions.

Dft. Endorsed: "To Dr. Franklin 16 Aug. 1780. Ditto John Grand covering the former." E in Bancroft American Series, II, 206.

1 JJ himself wrote a note of appreciation to de Neufville on 16 Aug. 1780, in *RDC*, IV, 34.

To William Carmichael

Madrid, 17 August 1780

Dear Sir

I have had the Pleasure of recieving four Letters from you since you left us, vizt. one of the 7th, one dated the 10th at the Top and the 11th at the Bottom; the third is dated the 12th and the fourth the 14, Days of August. I have written to you two Letters, both dated the 11th August,[1] in one of them was inclosed a Letter which came by the Post from Paris. <and for that Reason was trusted to the> I am at a Loss to determine from your Letter whether you have recieved one only, or both.

The air of St. Ildefonso has I hope reestablished your Health. I am much obliged by your Inquiries respecting that of my little Family. Mrs. Jay gains Strength tho very gradually. Many Circumstances oppose her leaving Madrid. It would be only a Change of Hermitages. The Rest of the Family are well.

The Holders of the Bills here begin to be very impatient. The Delays which retard the Completion of this Business are disagreable, however <they may be> necessary <and I must have Patience>. I confide in the Ministers Honor, and cannot beleive he will permit his assurances to vanish into Air. When he said that "his Friendship for America should rise with her Distresses,"[2] he spoke like a great Man <and I presume he will>. If his Actions correspond with this Declaration, his Reputation in America will be high.

Your Letter to Dr. Franklin was <proper> seasonable. I have again written to him. I cannot account for recieving no Letters from America, not a Line by or from Dean. We are in every Respect singularly circumstanced. <Our Negociation here has no common Aspect, what its Issue may be is hard to predict. Let us do our Duty faithfully and prudently, and then whatever it may be, we shall be content, at least with ourselves.> But Difficulties should rather inspire Patience and Perserverance than Languor and useless Discontent. <I am sure> That America will remain Independent is an Article of my Creed, and I have not the least Doubt but that the Time will come, when the House of Bourbon will have Reason to rejoice in her friendship.

I am impatient to hear of Ternays safe arrival. <God speed

him success> If he maintains a Superiority at Sea, he <will probably> may succeed.

They have a great many wild Stories here about the two Carolinas having Revolted from the Confederacy etc. This I suppose is the Fruit of Mr. Cumberlands Labors. A licenced Spy (from an Enemy) in the Capital of an Empire is a Novelty in Politics.

I am Dear Sir Yours etc.

J.J.

DftS.

1 Carmichael to JJ, 12 Aug. ALS in JP. The second of JJ's letters to Carmichael, 11 Aug., appears in the draft version as a postscript.

2 This is apparently a direct quotation from remarks made by Floridablanca on 5 July 1780. JJ described the conversation in his letter to the President of Congress, 6 Nov. 1780: "By his whole conversation he endeavored to show how much he interested himself in the prosperity of our affairs, more than once desiring Mr. Jay not to be discouraged, for that with time and patience all would go well." LbkCs in DNA: PCC, 110, I and CSmH: JJ Lbk, printed in *RDC,* IV, 112–50.

From William Carmichael

St. Ildephonso, 18th August 1780

Dear Sir

I did myself the honor of writing to you yesterday, last night a courier dispatched by a merchant at Cadiz brought a letter from Mr. Galvez in that City, which announces that Mr. Cordova fell in with an out ward bound fleet for Jamaica the greater part of which it was probable would fall into his hands.[1] A French officer, Prize Master of one of the Captured vessels, had arrived with the prize and this news at Cadiz. It is supposed that 40 or 50 merchant vessels and transports are taken and also their Convoy which was chased by the Swiftest sailing Ships of the fleet when the prize left them. A 74 gun ship and 3 frigates compose the Convoy, one frigate was taken. I felicitate you on this agreable news, which cannot be more pleasing to any Spaniard than it will be to you.

There are various reports respecting Portugal, The news of the Siho hath been these two past, That that Kingdom hath shut its ports against all vessels of war belonging to the Belligerent powers. M. Ternay arrived on our Coast the 20th of June. The Count D Estaing was with me this morning agreable to his promise. I am sure you will be highly satisfied with his sentiments not only with respect to us but on other accounts. A courier with a detail of the news contained in the other page is hourly expected. I will not fail to give you particulars, altho I rather wish you to be on the Spot to receive them. This will be a bitter potion for Mr. Cd and will have more effect than a thousand lies circulated by his Irish Friends.

I received a letter from Mr. Queneal informing me that he had waited on you with other bills.[2] I hope you will not be left long in your present perplexed situation on this Account, for I am almost certain that the person, whose arrival was to finish this business hath been here 3 or 10 days.[3]

I beg you to present my respects to Mrs. Jay to whom this news will give a sensation that She hath not often experienced in Europe.

I am with much respect Your Excellencys Most Humble Servant

WM. CARMICHAEL

ALS.

1 Don Luis de Córdoba, commander of the Franco-Spanish fleet, captured a British squadron sailing from Portsmouth on 29 July. Cordova seized fifty-two ships with cargoes valued at approximately £1,500,000.

2 The bills presented by Queneau & Co. were those of Jean de Neufville. JJ was able to persuade Queneau to hold the bills until he had an opportunity to confer with Floridablanca at San Ildefonso. As he explained to de Neufville in a letter, 27 August, "Your Bills on me in the Hands of Messrs. Queneau & Co. have been presented for Acceptance, and the Term for Payment shall be computed from that Day. As the Necessary arrangements were not completed I was obliged to request from them a little Delay, and they have been so friendly as to forbear insisting on an Acceptance. In order to bring this matter to a speedy Conclusion I found it necessary to come here a few Days ago but other Matters (I presume of pressing Importance) have prevented my getting this Business done as yet. A little further Time therefore has become indispensable, and I know too well your distinguished Attachment to America, to Doubt of your Consent to its being granted. I cannot forbear expressing my Sense of Messrs. Queneau's friendly and delicate Conduct on this Occasion." Dft in JP.

3 Again, Don Diego de Gardoqui.

To Francis Dana

Madrid, 19 August 1780

Dear Sir

Your Favor of the 5th Inst. was delivered to me Yesterday Morning. I am happy to hear Mr. Adams is gone to Holland.[1] He will I am persuaded be very useful there. Accept my thanks for the Intelligence communicated in your Letter, and be so obliging as to continue the Correspondence you have begun. The Character I heard of you at Congress induced me to wish for an Occasion of commencing it, and our present Situation will enable us to render its Continuance not only agreable but useful.

Your Remarks on the Loss of Charles Town correspond with my Sentiments. After General Washington's Retreat from Long Island the Convention of New York unanimously advised him to abandon the City rather than risque his Army. Forts and Towns have too often proved Snares to us. I wait with Impatience for General Lincoln's Letters to Congress. I hope he will be able to rescue his own and the Honor of our Arms from the various Imputations they both suffer here from that Event. Ternay's Success is I think precarious, and for the Reasons you assign, but who knows what that Providence which has so often, and by such seemingly fortuitous Means interposed in our Behalf, may yet do for us? Captain Cooke who left Salem the 19 July informs us that Mr. Ternay had arrived safe and landed his Troops at Rhode Island.[2]

My Adventurers are in a most perillous Suspense.[3] God grant them a safe Deliverance.

As to Colonel Laurens I have heard nothing of him except as follows: Captain Bryan of the Schooner Peggy arrived at Cadiz this 18 July in 49 Days from Wilmington in North Carolina, freighted with 34 Hogsheads of Indigo by Colonel Laurens on Account of Congress. He says that Colonel Laurens had had his Stores on Board this Vessel upwards of ten Weeks, and was to have come with him to Europe, but was determined by the Fate of Charles Town to return to Philadelphia.

The Credulity of the English Nation has always afforded to Politicians an ample Field for playing of their Tricks and Squibs. You doubtless know that Mr. Cumberland one of L. George Germaines Secretaries, has been here sometime. His Mission as well as Admission has given Room to many Conjectures. I am not apprehensive that Spain will make a separate Peace, but I by no Means think it prudent to recieve the Spies of Britain into their Capital, and even into their Palaces. There are a great many Wheels in our Business, and the Machine wont move easily, unless the great Wheel be turned by the Waters of the Missisippi which I neither believe nor wish will be the Case. Successes in America would give it *Motion*.

The English pay more Attention to the Security of their Trade than any other Nation. France and Spain have that part of Policy yet to learn. The American Commerce would well bear the Expence of Convoys, and a fast Ship of War on that Coast would enable our Privateers to gain much Prey. France however has done, and is still doing, great Things for us, and we must not be extreme to mark what may be amiss.

Be pleased in your next to present my Compliments to Mr.

Adams. If he be near to Mrs. Izard, be so kind as to send the enclosed under Cover [to] him. If not, send it by such Conveyance and in such Manner as you may think best.

I am Dear Sir very sincerely Your most obedient and humble Servant

JOHN JAY

P.S. By Letters from Cadiz just arrived we hear, that a large Fleet from Britain bound to Jamaica, convoyed by a 74 and three Frigates, had fallen in with Admiral Cordova. That he had taken one Frigate and many Prizes (one of which had arrived at Cadiz) and was in pursuit of the others.

21 August

I have accidentally spilled so much Ink on Mrs. Izards Letter that I cannot now send it, it being too late at Night to copy it before the post goes.[4]

ALS. MHi: Dana Papers. Addressed: "The Honble Francis Dana Esqr. Paris." Endorsed: ". . . Received Sept. 3d."

[1] Dana's letter of 5 Aug. 1780 has not been located. John Adams left Paris for the United Provinces 27 July 1780.

[2] Ternay's fleet reached Newport 10 July 1780.

[3] JJ is refering to bills drawn on him.

[4] The letter to Mrs. Izard was finally sent as an enclosure in JJ to Francis Dana, 7 Sept. 1780, in MHi: Dana Papers.

From William Carmichael

St. Ildephonso, August 20th, 1780

Dear Sir

I received yours of the 18th this day.[1] Had you inclosed me your Letter for his Excellency the Count de F. B. I should have perhaps been in a situation to answer to its Contents. At all Events I do not think that He will let us be the only Persons in Spain chagrined, when every body besides hath the greatest reason to be pleased.

I communicated to the French Ambassador agreable to your desire, the information contained in your Letter. He, as I informed you, had received Notice of Mr. Ternays arrival.[2] I think that officer and the General of the Land Forces will put New Port in a good State of Defence Before they form any other enterprize.

Another Express hath arrived from Cadiz, which confirms what I mentioned to you last night. The fleet under the Command of Mr.

Corduba fell in with this Convoy about one o Clock in the morning and seeing its lights, conducted itself in such a manner, as at day break to be to windward of the whole fleet of the Enemy Except six, so that of course they whole will fall into the hands of our Friends. It is said that a thousand troops were embarked Aboard this fleet. When the frigate the Neried left it, they saw the Spanish flag hoisted aboard 30 vessels and the Convoy The *Invincible* and *Buffalo* chased by ships detached for that purpose. The Neried brought two prizes into Cadiz and when the last Express left that City an *Aviso* was in sight from Mr. Corduba. In short it is to be hoped that the Success hath been compleat and that our friends will be paid principal and Interest for what they lost last year.

The Count D Estaing and Monsieur Montmorin dine with Mr. Galvez this day. The Count De Lacy also gave a grand Entertainment to the Nobility at Segovia. The rumors with respect to Portugal still continue and I have reason to hope Capt. O Dun hath made proposals of a serious Nature to that Court. I wish we had declared against that Nation three years ago, we had much to gain and nothing to lose, and their conduct with respect to us, Justified such a measure.

I announced to you the Credit sent by Mr. Franklin.[3] I shall be glad to know whether you can consider it as common, because without receiving a due proportion of my Salary, I shall be constrained to have recourse to others, which doth not suit me in any manner in my present Situation.

I beg you to present my respects to Mrs. Jay and the Colonel and to believe me

Your Excellencys Most humble Servant

WM. CARMICHAEL

ALS.

[1] In JJ's brief note of 18 August, in JP, he wrote: "I am under the Necessity of deciding the Fate of the Bills drawn on me by Monday next. I have informed Count D Florida Blanca of this. Let Count Montmorin also know it . . ."

[2] JJ had forwarded the report of Ternay's arrival at Rhode Island.

[3] In a postscript JJ had noted: "I have recieved from the Doctor a Letter of Credit for £1000."

From Robert R. Livingston

Philadelphia, 26th August 1780

Dear John

I received yours of the 23d May from Madrid with Duplicates thereof and the Letters you wrote from Cadiz and Martinique. The original of the first of these came to hand shortly after I wrote my Letter of the 22d December. The last never. You have I flatter myself before this time received four Letters which I directed to the care of Doctor Frankling.[1] I should send you Duplicates of them were it not that having been home not long since I left all my papers there for which I had no immediate want, and the Drafts among them. Your remembrance of the pleasurable days of our youth and the scenes in which we mutualy bore our parts together with the attractions which this country still has for you afford me the most pleasing hope that neither time nor absence will weaken a friendship which has so long stood the test of both. <This indeed I hope and that the hour may yet arrive in which we may again> This indeed I expected from the steadiness of your temper but I must confess I had little hope that your speedy return would afford me a prospect of deriving that <same> consolation from it in the decline of life to which I looked even while it animated the pursuits and pleasures of youth.

You <fear> mistake your own heart when you say you are unambitious and without the assurance you have given me I should have believed that that ambition would have kept you continualy in the line in which you now are, more especially as the general satisfaction that your appointment and <particularly your> conduct since has given will render it the wish of every body less interested in your return than I am to keep you abroad. You tell me nothing of Mrs. Jay though I am the more interested in hearing of her health as I am told she is lik[l]ie soon to increase the Diplomatick body. Present my best compliments to her and tell her that on reading her letter to her mother from Martinique I partook both in the pain and pleasures of her voyage.[2] I believe I told you not long since that I had seen your son and Jersey friends who were all well since when I have heard nothing from them but that. They are still so. Your son is a very fine boy. We have already talked of a match between him and my girl and I have accordingly rejected many advantageous proposals. Mrs. Livingston about whom you are so obliging as to inquire is very well.

I have not been able to procure the means of using the cypher you direct me to;[3] besides which it is extremely troublesome and difficult. I shall therefore be obliged to confine what I have to say to meer common occurences and enclose a cypher which you will find very easy and utterly impossible to decypher while the key is concealed as the same figure serves to express a variety of Letters. In order that you may know whether it comes safely to hand I have in this letter used the precautions mentioned in yours.

Our advises from the Southward are far from being pleasing

after the loss of Charles town. The enemy extended themselves as far in to the country as Cambden which is about only 6 hours through a thin settled country. They took several other posts so as to secure the greater part of South Carolina. When the militia recovered their first panick and found themselves supported by a body of continental troops they collected under the command of General Gates and were extreamly successful in a variety of skirmishes with them surprizing and cuting off most of their posts when Gates advanced with his main body consisting of about 900 continental troops and 2000 militia to within 7 miles of Cambden, where he was attacked by Cornwallis with his whole force. The militia being surprized fled at the first fire and General Gates in order to raly them quited the ground while our regulars remained fighting nor did he stop till he reached Hilsborough which is near 200 miles from which place on the *fourth* day after the battle he writes to us, but as he knew nothing of what passed after he left the place and we had reason to conclude from his account that all the continentals were cut of[f]. But by later advices we learn that they maintained the battle with great spirit after the flight of the militia had enabled the enemy to turn their flank, that they retired in such order as totally to destroy the enemies horse which attacked them on their retreat, and it is even said they have brought up their cannon.

General D'Calb is dangerously (some say mortally) wounded.[4] No other officer of destinction as we have yet heard is missing. As we are in hourly expectation of some further information I hope to receive it before I am under a necessity of closing this.

We have long been flattering ourselves with a prospect of recovering New York and giving by the assistance of France a decisive blow to the enemy. For that purpose we took measures to augment our army under the command of General Washington to 30,000 men but our prospects grow more and more faint every day. The first division of the French fleet has been and still continues to be blocked up by a superior fleet at Rhode Island.[5] The second have not sailed that we can hear. The militia tired out are returning home. Our Magazines are exhausted and our finances before sufficiently deranged have been still more disordered thereby. Your Old friend the Confederacy is still here owing to our inability to procure the necessary means of fitting her for sea. However I believe that obstacle will be removed in a few days. Our privateers have been uncommonly successful. Every day sees new prizes enter our ports, among others no less than 27 of the Quebeck fleet richly laden have been brought in by the Boston and Salem privateers. <12 of them> Twelve more are said to have been taken by a French ship of the line and the remaining 8 fearful to proceed because of the privateers that were crusing in the gulph of St. Lawrance have put into Halifax. The combined fleets in the West Indies have separated and thereby lost a noble opportunity of taking Jamaica which is in a manner defenceless as Governor Dalling[6] with the greater part of the troops from that Island is said to be upon an expedition to the Spanish settlements on the main.

I write you <every thing> occurences without order just as they arise in my mind because I know that in your situation <things> facts are of more importance to you than <mere words> deductions from them. But not believe judging from myself that in proportion to a mans distance from home is his avidity to hear from it. I must not forget our poor little State. She has never rested a moment from her labours. The enemy still harass her on every side. Some of the finest settlements in Tryon County have been cut of[f] and the militia have been in the field the whole season. But her distress has not shaken her firmness; on the contrary toryysm declines among us every day. Our political system moves on much as usual without any great change either of men or measures.

Dear John I have a thousand things which I could wish to communicate but I dare not for want of a cypher. Acknowledge the receipt of this therefore as soon as possible as there are many things you should know that you will not be able to learn from our publick Letters. Nothing astonishes me more than the effrontery with which the Ministry and their friends assert that America sighs to return to their government since the fact that we never were more fixed in opposition. Nor if we except the derangement of our finances were we ever so capable of resistance.

Our friend Smith[7] is said to have imbibed the ministerial Madness so strongly as to have prevailed on General Kniphausen to march out of New York into the jersies before Clinton returned from Charlestown, hoping that discouraged by the loss of that place and weary of the war the militia would not oppose him.[8] And he should (as Mr. Smith is said emphatically to have predicted) have the whole honor of terminating the war before the return of his principal. The experiment proved the folly of the Idea. The militia flocked together on the 1st summons, some of them taking their horses from the plough, rode down full speed, hung them to the fences and engaged people of all ranks and ages collected, and all that was effected by an army of 5000 men unopposed except by militia and about 2000 continental troops was the destruction of 20 farm houses and the abuse and murder of some women, after which they retired with the loss of 200 killed wounded and taken—since which they have been much less sanguine.

Adieu. Remember me to the Colonel and Mr. Carmichael. I again offer my affectionate compliments to Mrs. Jay

Dft. NHi: Robert R. Livingston. Endorsed by Livingston. Enclosure: key to the XZA cipher, in JP.

1 The earlier letters referred to are JJ to Livingston, 24 Dec. 1779 and 19 Feb. 1780, above. The only letters from Livingston to JJ during the period in question that have been located are 22 Dec. 1779, 10 Feb. 1780 and 6 July 1780, all above.

2 SLJ to Susannah French Livingston, 12 Dec. 1779, above.

3 The cipher proposed in JJ's 19 Feb. letter required a specific edition of Boyer's *French Dictionary.*

4 Johann Kalb (1721–80), "Baron de Kalb," was a Bavarian-born officer in the French Army. He came to America with Lafayette in 1777, was commissioned a major general in the Continental Army, and was mortally wounded in the defeat at Camden, S.C., 16 August, dying three days later.

5 Ternay's fleet succeeded in reaching Rhode Island in July 1780, only to be bottled up by the superior British force under Admiral Thomas Graves (1725?–1802).

6 John Dalling (d. 1798), named governor of Jamaica in 1777, was severely criticized for sending expeditions to Honduras and Nicaragua in 1779 and 1780. While Dalling turned his attention to Central America, the Spanish captured the posts at Mobile and Pensacola.

7 William Smith, Jr., an early Whig and then a neutralist, leaned gradually toward the Loyalist position and acknowledged it officially 4 May 1779 by accepting appointment as Chief Justice of New York. He had taken up residence in the British-held city in 1778 and remained there until 1783. For an evaluation of his character and political convictions, see Richard J. Koke, *Accomplice in Treason: Joshua Hett Smith and the Arnold Conspiracy* (New York, 1973), pp. 17–20.

8 This is a reference to Baron von Knyphausen's Springfield raid, described previously in Robert R. Livingston to JJ, 6 July 1780. Smith confirms that he did indeed urge the general directly and through intermediaries to undertake this expedition into New Jersey. William Smith, *Memoirs,* II, 234, 240–41, 249–50, 253, 265, 266–67, 270, 271.

FROM JAMES SMITH

[*Bruxelles*], *September 12, 1780*

Dear Sir.

I am now at Bruxelles where I propose to reside untill I can have a convenient opportunity to remove my self and Family to America. In the mean time I think it a duty I owe my Country to contribute every assistance in my Power to aid you in the exicution of that great and important Bussiness in which you are employed and I trust my present situation and connections will afford many opportunities of rendering essential service to my Country. I have with this view setled a secret correspondence in England to give me the most early intelligence of the Sailing and destination of their Fleets that you may imbrace the most favorable opportunities of directing the Naval Armaments of our powerful Allies to their proper objects.

My long residence in England has put me in a condition of intimately knowing the political situation of that Country and can with truth aver by means of some connections with men formerly in power that I have as it were been behind the Curtain and seen the wheels and Pullies of the Machinery of its Government through every stage of this extraordinary and glorious revolution by which I have not been able to find among the Great except Lord Camden[1] one thorough friend to America who sees her Independence absolutely essential to the preservation of the Liberties of England. Among the body of the people there are many hundred thousands of the same complection and who most ardently wait for the first favorable opportunity to sacrifice on the same Altars of Liberty by a speedy removal to that Country. I have often lamented that bad health prevented me from giving more unequivocal proofs of my attachment to that Cause in which you have so honourably distinguished yourself. Not with standing which I trust it will appear that your friends in England have not been altogether useless and must have equally suffered in their persons and properties had The Tyrant ultimately prevailed against us.

Availing myself of my situation it has been my constant and unwearied endeavour through all the Conduits of public information to impede the progress of their arms by dividing the people from the Government and weakning their Strenght by making proselites to the Cause of America. With this view I projected the plan and carried into exicution the numerous Debating Societies not only in the Metropolis but in most of the capital Cities in England.[2] In these places the First Nobility as well as the body of the people attended every evening in immense numbers. It was here the measures of Government were freely discussed and their iniquitous Conduct toward America exposed to the minds of the populace who had been lulled into a fatal unsuspicious acquiescence in the measures of their System for want of properly understanding the true grounds of the controversy and ultimate tendency to enslave both Countries. By these means the flames of discontent spread to such a degree that administration after having endeavored to take me off in vain by personal contests and public abuse at lenght gave orders to seize me as a Traitor under the plausible pretext of my being employed by Congress at a Sallery of a thousand a year to sow sedition among the people. After every artifice to ensnare me had proved abortive a favorable opportunity at lenght happened to Gratify their Mallice. Accordingly taking advantage of the impression made by the late riots in their favor, and I beleive secretly encouraged for the purpose of throwing an odium on the measures of Opposition and the spirit of Association.

An Order of the privy council was issued to apprehend me as the Calatine of the consperecy and secret Agent of Doctor Franklin to Burn the City. Various rumors were propagated to colour these proceedings and justify their Conduct. Fortunately I was at a friends house when the Kings Messengers arrived to take me into Custody. Concluding I had taken Refuge under the jurisdiction of the City, Mr. Wilks[3] as a Majestrate in that district was applied to for to grant a warrent upon information who not only refused to comply with the request but sent Alderman Townhsand to advise me of my danger. By the advice of my freinds I took refuge in the Country but as from the suspension of the Habeas Corpus I could not avail myself of that Palladium of British Liberty to demand a Trial and apprehending least some of my letters to Congress might have been intercepted which would have been brought in evidence against me as corresponding with Rebells. After wandering a month upon the Sea Coasts of Suffolk and Norfolk I at last by means of my agents was secretly conveyed by a private ship to Holland and from thence to this City.

Many have been the conjectures concerning the Origin and foundation of the late riots. The Trial of Lord George Gordon will throw light on the subject.[4] I should not be surprised that it should appear to be an after game of Lord Bute[5] to over set opposition and that that Nobleman was in the Secret. Many signed the Protestant association from very different motives. The apprehension of danger to the cause of the protestant Religion from the late indulgences given to the Catholics brought many to sign the petition. But the more judicious part of the associators considering the late act in favor of the papists as a second arrow out of the same quiver with the Quebec Bills[6] to strenghten the Court party by Bringing over those people to their interest, opposed the late acts from principles of policy.

This you may be assured of that unless the System of affairs is speedily changed the whole of the business may be considered as the harbinger of another revolution. In short the mulitude who never reason but from their feelings begin to see through the Machiavelian Tricks of the Court, the Incapacity of their Rulers and the Wickedness of their adherents. They are convince of their danger from the avowed prostitution of Parliament and the effects of a rotten constitution which they are determined to remedy by the most salutary innovations. The reduced value of all the landed Estates, Immense encrease of Taxes, deminished revenue, together with a hopeless American War has seriously allarmed the Country Gentleman. The decay of Trade and manufactures, Prostitution of honours and offices, together with the loss of public Liberty from the acknowledged increasing influence of the Crown and prospect of National Bankruptcy has at last raked away the Ashes from the dying Embers of the antient spirit of the people and opened their eyes to the conviction of those Solemn truths which they formerly held in contempt and derision.

This sudden Change in the minds of the body of the Nation has been succeded by correspondent consequences. The Bedford faction[7] willing to make a merit of necessity have ceceded from the junto upon as they say principles of Honour and Concience and though first wavering have at last joined opposition. The most opulent families in the Kingdom and popular Whigs without doors have (immitating the example of America) formed themselves into County associations, Committees, and a Congress of Deputies, who meet under the very nose of parliament and publish their resolves in which they have expressed their abhorrence of the men and measures of the present System and amoung many other things the absolute Necessity of making peace with America upon her own terms to prevent impending ruin. This perminent Systematic Opposition joined to the democratical assendency of the armed Associations in Ireland[8] together with the Conduct and declerations of the Northern Maritime powers[9] have seriously Alarmed the Tyrant and Shook the obstinacy of Administration.

The severe blow given to their commerce by the late Captures joined to the daily expectation of more important Calamities from the superiority of the Fleets of our allies in the West Indies and armiments in North America has brought on a speedy dissolution of Parliament least the farther disgrace of their Arms operating upon the minds and influencing the Choice of the Electors should work such a change upon the democratical Branch of the Constitution as to restore the power of impeachment and the punishment of Ministers. Whether Administration will by this manouvre be able to obtain a majority in their favor I will not venture to affirm but from the temper and complection of the people when I left England I should imagine very considerable alterations would be made in the house of Commons from a conciensness of the evil tendency of trusting their Liberties and properties a second time into the hands of the late profligate members. If this is not accomplished I am sure the Godess of Liberty will forever take her flight from her once favorite Isle and prove what Rome experienced long before that the *Form* of a free and the *Ends* of an Arbitrary Government are not incompatible with each other when the People have lost those principles and Manners which make them great and Free.

But while we thus contemplate the fall of Britain an aweful monument of heavens vengence upon an oppressing people let us assiduously attend to the most speedy means of Elevating the Glory and securing the independancy of our own Country. Every days experience proves that the most effectual method to humble Britain into a compliance with our demands would be by directing the forces of the Allied powers to the intercepting of her Trade. By the capture of her seamen she will be unable to man her fleets and her Superiority being thus lost both at home and abroad her dependancys must fall to the more numerous armies of our Allies in every quarter of the Globe. This might be easily accomplished if proper means were established for carrying on a secret correspondence by the way of Holland and Flanders with our American friends in England and conveying speedy intelligence to the American Ministers in France and Spain. Such Vigilance would raise their credit with those respective Courts and make them more dependant upon their councils than I fear they have hitherto been in the prosecution of this War. A few such strokes as the late captures would disenable the merchants from Lending the Supplies and the landed Interest already too much burdened would abandon the Ministers in the continuance of the War. Had the Brest Squadron slipt out into the Chops of the Channel when the British fleet retired into their ports to refit the Libros Oporto and homeward bound Winward Island Trade would have fallen into their hands. So fortunate an event added to their other losses would not only have ruined the merchants but disenabled the Government from manning an additional number of Empty Ships to their grand fleet by which neglect a decided majority in favor of the house of Burbon may be lost in the most critical period of the War.

Is it not astonishing that so evident a piece of policy should not have engaged the attention of the French Court? Occasio Celeris. Too many of these opportunities have been lost during the course of the Struggle which had they been embraced would have convinced our Enemies long before this time of their incapacity to contend with success and put a period to the War. The house of Burbon would do wise to consider that her Enemy is annually growing stronger in her Navy. The vast sums granted by parliament for the support was expended by a profligate Minister upon the American War. It was by these means Her Dock Yards were ill supplied, her Ships Rotted in her harbours and she lost the Empire of the Seas. Impressed with a sense of her danger she is straining every nerve to retrieve her past errors by building a great number of ships and she will Ship her trade to man them untill she recovers the dominion she has lost. But if the plan I have the honour to suggest is vigorously persued these efforts will prove in vain. Destitute of Seamen her navy would be confined to her Docks. You would cut up her power by the roots. Wounded in her most tender Vital and accessable parts she would Stand immured within her own Isle and for want of a free circulation a mortification in her extremities would insue. America would no longer hear the Thunder of her Navy and her Armies destitute of sustinence and supplies must molder or perish by pestilence famine or the sword.

I submit it to your consideration whether the Southern Coasts of Ireland and the whole Tract of the East and West India fleets are not the places to which you should direct the operations of your combined fleets. While the Enemy might be amused with an appearance of invasion of their Coasts they would be obliged to keep a fleet in the Channel of sufficient Strenght to meet yours. In the mean time yours properly stationed would answer the double purpose of securing the safe convoy of your own trade and Carrying theirs into your ports before the plan could be known. To what purpose did the House of Burbon wave their Banners in Triumph in the Channel last year. Even that event if properly managed would contribute to this design. By discovering your intentions then it would throw them off their Guard and prevent them from discovering where you meant to Strick the Blow. If your Superior Combined fleets should once more enter the Channel what good consequence will it produce. If they are not strong enough to meet you there they will retire and defend themselves by Batteries under cover of their Guns. While you are wasting your revenues and exposing your Seamen to sickness and all the dangers of the Sea. An imbargo upon their outward bound Ships will secure their trade at home while that which was returning from abroad would find a safe retreat into the Irish Sea ports.

But I conceive it may be said having secured a safe passage to their Coast We will transport our Troops and attack them on their Shores. Would to God the Law of retribution might take place and that an Abandoned Nation might in her turn experience all the honors of that uncivillized War which to the disgrace of humanity she has been practising upon us. But if Invasion is your plan, I am very much affraid the favorable opportunity is irritrevably lost. Last summer it could be done with effect. Her dock yards might have been distroyed and a period put to the War. But experience has made even fools Wise. The conduct of America has given them lessons of instruction and taught them upon such an immergency how to act. Should the attempt be made I am convinced it would not only be attended with our disgrace but Strenghten the enemy by rousing the Martial spirit of the Nation and unite all contending parties into one a considerable source of their weakness and our Strenght. With an army of French and Spaniyards raging in the bowels of their Country party spirit would give way to National antipathy. Bewildred Councils would no longer prevail. The resentment of Ireland might subside. Compasionating her Sister Island and dreading her own safety with Eighty thousand Citizens armed in defence of their liberties she might give her effectual aid. A Gallant Nation thus driven to dispair by the extremity of distress would grow vigorous in her turn. The Weakness Inconsistancy and want of expedition in public measures would be suceeded by a Wise administration and a frenzy of Military prowess very difficult to subdue might procrastinate the War. On the other hand let any one take into contemplation the extent situation of the Sea Coasts of France and Spain and they will be convinced of the practicabily of this Scheme. A Blow may struck by expeditions from the Spanish ports before any intelligence of the design can arrive in England time enough to prevent the execution of the plan.

You will excuse the freedom I have taken in urging this matter so strenuously and flatter my self from the well known candor of your disposition that you will do me the justice to beleive that it proceeds from the strongest Conviction I have of its being the most Speedy method of finally obtaining the Independancy of our Country and a Glorious conclusion to the War which is the most fervent Wish and earnest desire of Your Excellencies Most Obedient, Most Devoted, Humble Servant

JAMES SMITH

ALS. Endorsed: ". . . rcd. 2 Dr. ans. 5 Dr." Dr. James Smith (1738–1812) was the younger brother of William Smith, Jr., the noted New York Loyalist and Chief Justice during the British military occupation. James graduated from the College of New Jersey in 1757, earned an M.D. degree at Leyden in 1764, and in 1767 became one of the two original members of the King's College faculty of medicine, serving as professor of chemistry and materia medica until 1770. Having married a wealthy widow from Jamaica, he resigned his position and settled in the Caribbean. He later moved to London "from whence he carried on a constant correspondence with the rebels in America . . . advising them never to submit, but to contend to the last; and upon every occasion haranguing the mobs in London in favor of the 'rights of mankind' and the 'liberties of the people.' "

The June riots of 1780 raised suspicions as to his part in these disturbances, causing Smith to leave England. Thomas Jones, *History of New York during the Revolutionary War,* Edward Floyd deLancey, ed. (2 vols., New York, 1879), I, 20–21; Richard J. Koke, *Accomplice in Treason: Joshua Hett Smith and the Arnold Conspiracy* (New York, 1973), pp. 6, 8, 13; Princeton University, *General Catalogue of Princeton University, 1746–1906* (Princeton, N.J., 1908), p. 85; Milton H. Thomas, *Columbia University Officers and Alumni, 1754–1857* (New York, 1936), p. 31.

1 Charles Pratt, Earl of Camden (1714–94).

2 The *Political Magazine* described Dr. Smith as "an intimate of Silas Deane and of John the Painter, who set fire to the Dock Yard at Portsmouth, for which he was executed; that he was known in all the debating clubs for arguing against Great Britain and in favor of America." Quoted in Jones, *History,* I, 20. For the strange case of John the Painter (John Aitken), allegedly paid by American agents to set fire to a number of English dockyards, see *Annual Register 1777,* pp. 28–31, 246–47; *Peacemakers,* p. 84.

3 John Wilkes (1727–97), the famous politician and champion of "the rights of Englishmen."

4 Lord George Gordon (1751–93), a Scot, led a Protestant association in the presentation of a petition to Parliament, 2 June 1780, protesting Savile's Roman Catholic Relief Act. The ensuing London riots, along with Gordon's trial for high treason, are described in *Peacemakers,* pp. 67–87.

5 John Stuart, Earl of Bute (1713–92), the former prime minister, had lost all influence over public affairs by 1765.

6 The Quebec Act, 20 May 1774, extended Canada's boundaries to the Ohio River, thereby invalidating the charter claims in the area asserted by Connecticut, Massachusetts, and Virginia, as well as the New York claims based on Indian treaties, while at the same time granting freedom of worship to French Catholics.

7 The Bedford faction, led by John Russell, fourth Duke of Bedford, stood for commerce with all countries on an equal basis. *Peacemakers,* p. 145.

8 In the course of the American Revolution, the patriotic and republican fervor of the colonists infected, among others, the Irish. Such groups as the Hearts of Oak Boys and the Hearts of Steel Boys had organizations both in America and in Ireland. Others, such as the Society of Free Citizens in Dublin and the Volunteers of Ireland, were indigenous to that country. The issues upon which such groups concentrated were both economic and political, with the Irish patriots identifying their plight with that of the American colonists, just as, in the 1790's, Irish and English radical societies identified themselves with the revolutionaries in France. On the Irish clubs, see Michael Kraus, "America and the Irish Revolutionary Movement in the Eighteenth Century," in Richard B. Morris, ed., *The Era of the American Revolution* (New York, 1939), pp. 332–48.

9 On 28 Feb. 1780 Catherine II of Russia issued a declaration announcing that the Russian navy would be used against all belligerents to protect neutral Russian trade. Russia's refusal to regard the naval stores required by the allies as contraband constituted a serious blow to the British attempts to blockade the French and Spanish coasts. In addition, Catherine issued an invitation to other European neutrals to form a League of Armed Neutrality. Denmark and Sweden accepted hastily, on 9 July and 1 August respectively, and within the next two years the Netherlands, Prussia, Austria, Portugal, and the Kingdom of Two Sicilies joined the League. Smith was perhaps too optimistic about the impact of the League. When Britain declared war on the Netherlands on 20 December, she succeeded in pinching off trade connections between the U.S. and the Dutch West Indian island of St. Eustatius, the principal center of contraband trade with the States. While the League was unsuccessful in aiding the

Dutch, it did hamper British naval measures against the allies. See Isabel de Madariaga, *Britain, Russia, and the Armed Neutrality of 1780* (New Haven, 1962). For the view of the Armed Neutrality as an "armed nullity," see *Peacemakers*, p. 167.

To Robert Morris

St. Ildefonso, 16 September 1780

Dear Sir

Had I been ever so much disposed to be out of Humour with the Silence of my Friends I assure you it would all have given Way to the Pleasure with which I recieved your Letter of the 6th July.[1]

Perhaps an opportunity may yet offer for settling a Cypher. I Shall attempt it within this Month in a Way I think will succeed.

Mrs. Jay has more Health than she has enjoyed this long time; she is <now> at Madrid, from whence I am sure Mrs. Morris may expect a Letter from her.[2] Kitty tells us she spent a very agreable winter, but as I intend this for a short Letter, I must omit repeating the many civil things she says of her Friends. I don't like Johns Situation; it can produce Nothing worth having, unless the Honor of broken Bones may be reckoned so.[3]

I am glad you told me what had become of Duer. He is an honest Man and I esteem him—the more perhaps, as the older I grow the more <scarce I find them> Reason I have to think them scarce. I have never known him do a mean thing or say a false one. If he is wise he <will stick to> wont readily quit his Farm.[4]

Gouverneurs Leg has been a Tax on my Heart.[5] I am almost tempted to wish he had lost *something* else. I have been able to hear very little of him. Many Letters for and from me Miscarry. I recieve very few.

I congratulate you on being so near *the Hills*:[6] theres nothing like them here in any Sense but Paper must not be trusted.

Your Bank etc. has a fine Effect here.[7] I think there are some Clever things in and about that Business. <America will be respectable and safe . . . Respectability . . . to your begging>[8] Indeed that is pretty much the Case with whatever you have a Hand in, unless when you are too civil to the Judgment of others.

By some less precarious Conveyance I shall have the pleasure of saying many things to you and Mrs. Morris. Adieu my dear Sir; nothing is more True than that I am Your affectionate Friend

Remember me to my old Friends—you know who they are.

Dft.

1 Robert Morris to JJ, 6 July 1780, ALS in JP.

2 SLJ to Mary White Morris, I Sept. 1780, ALS in JP.

3 "Mrs. Jays Brother John," Morris had written, "is now here a Midshipman on board the Saratoga, Capt. Young nearly ready to go out to a Cruize."

4 This comment was provoked by Morris's statement that "Mr. Duer and Lady Kitty are at their farm on the North River."

5 Morris had written: "Poor Governeur Morris you will have heard has lost his legg but is getting well again." See also, Robert R. Livingston to JJ, 6 July 1780, above.

6 "Mrs. Morris," her husband wrote, "is out at Springetsbury *next the Hills.*" The famed Morris estate, The Hills, on the east bank of the Schuylkill three miles beyond the limits of eighteenth-century Philadelphia, had been partially destroyed during the British occupation. Springetsbury, a "villa" near Philadelphia built by Thomas Penn, was another of the family's country homes. E. P. Oberholtzer, *Robert Morris* (New York, 1968), pp. 291, 295.

7 The Bank of Pennsylvania was an association formed in Philadelphia in 1780 to raise funds with which to underwrite the war effort.

8 A recurrent theme in JJ's correspondence at this time is his disinclination to beg or make "supplications," as revealed in his conversation with Montmorin, 30 Aug. 1780, reported to Congress, 6 Nov. 1780. LbkC in DNA: PCC, 110, I; LbkC in CSmH; *RDC*, IV, 112–50.

To Egbert Benson

St. Ildefonso, 18 September 1780

Dear Benson

I have written many Letters to my Friends in the State of New York since I left America, but have not yet recieved a single Line from any of them. Is not that a little hard? Am I to suppose that all your Letters have Miscarried, or that your Attention <so> has been too much engaged by Affairs at Home to extend to an old Friend abroad? Whatever is the Cause I assure you I regret it.

<Since> While America <has become> continues the theatre of the War, it is natural to desire Intelligence of what may be passing on it. This Satisfaction I seldom enjoy tho I often ought. Public Good Requires it, but individual Remissness procrastinates.

As few private opportunities offer of conveying Letters to the Sea Side, I frequently write by the Post. This Letter will <probably> go that Way. It must therefore be proportionably reserved. Indeed I make it a Rule to write on the Subject of Politics only to Congress, and tho various other Subjects present themselves yet as it is not the Fashion in this Country neither to let <either> ones Tongue or Penn run very freely, I think it best not to be singular.

Your Government ought by this Time to have recieved many of my Letters and I may add have answered some of them. <I am not

easy> Has your Legislature[1] thought of their Western Country. I incline to think it Time. By no Means <let Vermont> sleep over Vermont.[2] <You forget> Our people would not apply the Maxim obsta Principiis,[3] at first. Further delays will be equally unwise especially considering the Resolutions of Congress on that Subject.[4] I am told you have made R. Morris Ch. Justice.[5] This is well. I had my apprehensions about this Matter; in my opinion Duer should <be employed, because> not be forgotten; he is capable of serving the State, and it would be bad policy to let any useful Man <seek> leave <that State> it who can be retained with Advantage in it.

<Your> The State of New York is never out of my Mind nor Heart, and I am often <tempted> disposed to write much respecting its affairs but I have so little Information <respecting> of its present political objects and operations that I am affraid to attempt it. An excellent Law might be made out of the Pennsylvania one for the gradual Abolition of Slavery.[6] Till America comes into this Measure <our> her Prayers to Heaven for Liberty <are> will be impious. This is a strong Expression but it is <true> just. Were I in your Legislature I would prepare a Bill for the Purpose with great Care, and I would never cease moving it till it became a Law or I ceased to be a member. I believe God governs this World, and I believe it to be a Maxim in his as in our Court <of Equ> that those who ask for Equity <must> ought to do it.

Remember me to my old Friends. I am very much yours

J. J.

DftS. Endorsed.

1 The New York State legislature.

2 Sir Henry Clinton, Commander in Chief of the British armies in North America, was maneuvering to persuade the Allen brothers to discourage Vermonters from the Revolutionary effort and adopt the British cause.

3 Latin legal term: "Withstand beginnings; resist the first approaches or encroachments."

4 JJ was apparently referring to a resolution passed in Congress 2 June 1780 implementing his own efforts of the previous year, to the effect that: ". . . the acts and proceedings of the people inhabiting the said district [Vt.], and claiming to be an independent State as aforesaid, in contravening the good intentions of the said resolutions of the 24th September and the 2d October last, are highly unwarrantable, and subversive of the peace and welfare of the United States." The Vt. inhabitants were enjoined from exercising "authority, civil or military, over the inhabitants owing allegiance to any of the States claiming the jurisdiction of the said territory," until the issue was determined under the Congressional resolves. *JCC*, XVII, 482–83.

5 Richard Morris, JJ's successor.

6 JJ here alludes to the Pennsylvania law calling for the gradual abolition of slavery, passed 1 March 1780. 10 *Pennsylvania Statutes at Large*, 67.

The San Ildefonso Conference

23 September 1780

Little progress and much frustration characterized JJ's mission in Spain from January to September 1780. He had been able to get neither a treaty of alliance nor more than vague promises of aid from Floridablanca. By September the situation had become critical. With bills amounting to $50,000 coming due, JJ wrote to Vergennes and Franklin, "the honor of Congress, suspended on the fate of these bills, now hangs as it were by a hair . . ."[1] It became imperative for JJ to meet again with the Spanish minister. That meeting, which took place at San Ildefonso on 23 September, proved to be a climactic end to the first phase of the Spanish mission. The outcome of the conference only supported what had earlier seemed obvious: success was unlikely.

Of late Floridablanca had been receiving more optimistic reports of American affairs.[2] Accordingly, his mood at this meeting was markedly more cordial, but that alone could not produce substantive results. The conference did, however, clarify certain things for JJ, including the fact that it was going to be very difficult to get any sort of financial aid from Spain. Floridablanca announced that his government was not going to keep its promise of a £30–40,000 loan, and when asked how JJ could prove to prospective financial backers that the King of Spain would guarantee a $150,000 loan, Floridablanca claimed not to know.[3] He would, he said, discuss the problem with the minister of finance and convey the answer to the American minister shortly. JJ also learned, for the first time, that the Franco-American treaty had nearly caused the Spanish to break diplomatic relations with their Bourbon cousins.[4] If the Americans desired a treaty of alliance with Spain, they would simply have to draw up a new, independent one. At this point, Floridablanca candidly stated that no treaty of alliance would be possible unless JJ were able to obtain new instructions on the question of the Mississippi. Spain, JJ was informed, considered control of the Gulf of Mexico a principal object of the war.

The American minister left Floridablanca with a far more realistic awareness than before of European courts, politics, and diplomacy. If JJ arrived in Madrid with any idealism or naive trust, he had certainly discarded both by now. With new cynicism, he began to see how very little America could expect from Spain, and maybe even France. The war for independence was an American concern, and America would have to win without relying on the good will and moral commitments of others. JJ was becoming a seasoned diplomat.

[1] JJ to Vergennes, 22 Sept. 1780 LS and French trans. in MAE: CP: États-Unis, V. 13; LbkC in CSmH: JJ Lbk, dft in JP; printed in *RDC*, IV, 63–66. JJ to Franklin, 22 Sept. 1780, sent with a copy of JJ's letter to Vergennes, LbkCs in DLC: Franklin Papers, III, 68; DNA: PCC, 110, I; and in CSmH: JJ Lbk.

[2] In JJ to Huntington, 6 Nov. 1780, the American minister reported that on 14 September "some glorious reports from America arrived. It seemed as if she had risen like a giant refreshed with sleep and was doing wonders. I sent the news to the Count as usual, without appearing to be affected by his late conduct." LbkCs in DNA: PCC, 110, I; and in CSmH: JJ Lbk; printed in *RDC*, IV, 112–50.

[3] The £30–40,000 offer was made at the first JJ-Floridablanca meeting, 11 May. JJ to Vergennes, 22 Sept. 1780. On 15 September Floridablanca said that Spain would guarantee a $150,000 loan by someone else. Gardoqui to JJ, 15 Sept. 1780. LbkCs in DNA: PCC, 110, I and in CSmH: JJ Lbk; printed in *RDC*, IV, 139.

[4] Reported in cipher in JJ's notes of the 23 Sept. 1780 conference.

To Samuel Huntington

Madrid, 6 November 1780

Notes of a Conference between His Excellency the Count De Florida Blanca and Mr. Jay at St. Ildefonso, on Saturday Evening the 23d September 1780.

After the usual civilities, the Count began the Conference by informing Mr. Jay that the Court had received Intelligence from the Havannah of Congress having so far compiled with the request made them to permit the Exportation of Provisions for the use of his Majesty's fleets and Armies there, as to give Licence for shipping three thousand Barrels of Flour, circumstances not admitting a further supply at that Time. That this business was conducted by Mr. Robert Morris in a manner with which he was well pleased, That Congress had also, in order to promote the Success of the Spanish operations against Pensacola etc. agreed to make a diversion to the Southward, to detach a considerable Body of regular Troops and Militia to South Carolina under General Gates. That His Majesty was well pleased with, and highly sensible of these marks of their friendly disposition and had directed him to desire Mr. Jay to convey his Thanks to them on the occasion.

Mr. Jay expressed his Satisfaction at this Intelligence and promised to take the Earliest opportunity of Conveying to Congress the sense his Majesty entertained of their Friendship manifested by these Measures. He told the Count it gave him pleasure to hear the Business of the Spanish Supplies was committed to Mr. Robert Morris and assured him that the fullest Confidence might be reposed in that Gentleman's abilities and Integrity. He requested His Excellency again to assure His Majesty that he might rely on the good disposition of Congress, and of their evincing it in every way which the Situation of their Affairs and the Interest of the Common Cause might render practicable and expedient. The Count told Mr. Jay that he had proposed to the French Ambassador to send to Congress for the use of their Army, Clothing for Ten Regiments lately taken in the Convoy bound from Britain to Jamaica, and in which the two Crowns were equally interested; That the Ambassador approved the proposition, but had not yet given his final answer. He then observed that a Negotiation for a Peace between Britain and Spain appeared at present more distant than ever. That the former had offered his Majesty every thing he could desire, to induce him to a separate Peace; but the King, adhering to the same Resolutions in favor of America which had influenced his conduct in his Mediation for a general Peace, and since, had rejected them, and that Congress might rely on his Majesty's determination never to give up or forsake America, but on the contrary continue affording her all the Aids in his Power. He told Mr. Jay that the Court of London, disappointed in their expectations of Detaching Spain, had it in Contemplation again to send Commissioners to America, to treat with Congress on the Subject of an accommodation with them, That this Measure was at present under the consideration of the Privy Council, and that there was reason to suppose it would be adopted. He observed that the English had hitherto discovered much Finessee and little true Policy; That first they endeavored by their Intrigues in France to separate that Kingdom and America, but not succeeding there, they sent Commissioners to America; That the last Year they had attempted to detach France, and this Year Spain, and that being unsuccessful in both, they would now again attempt America; That the best way of defeating their designs was mutual Confidence in each other. He remarked that America could not rely on any promise of Britain, and asked; if she was once detached from France and Spain, who could compel an observance of them?

Mr. Jay thanked the Count for this Communication, and assured him that Congress would not only adhere to their engagements from Motives of Interest, but from a regard to their Honor, and the faith of Treaties; That the opinion of Congress on this Subject corresponded with that of his Excellency, and that their conduct with respect to the former English commissioners gave conclusive Evidence of their Sentiments on the Subject. Mr. Jay promised in case he received any intelligence relative to this matter, his Excellency might depend on its being communicated immediately to him. The Count appeared satisfied with this, and again repeated his former assurances of the King's good disposition towards America, etc. etc.

Mr. Jay informed his Excellency that the Subjects on which he was desirous of conferring with him arose from the Paper he had received from Mr. Gardoqui the 15th Instant, containing his Excellency's answer to Mr. Jay's letter of the 14th.[1]

Mr. Jay then requested the Count to communicate to His Majesty his thanks for the offer he had been pleased to make of his responsibility in order to facilitate a Loan in favor of America for one hundred and fifty thousand Dollars, and also for the promise of Clothing etc., etc. and to assure him that the gratitude of the States would always be proportionate to the Obligations conferred upon them. He observed to the Count that he intended to attempt this Loan in Spain, France, and Holland, and begged to be informed in what manner he should evidence the Responsibility of his Majesty to the Persons who might be disposed to lend the Money, for that in this and other similar cases he meant to be guided by his Excellency's Directions. The Count replied that as this matter fell within the Department of Mr. Musquiz,[2] the Minister of Finance, he would consult him upon it on Tuesday Evening next, and immediately thereafter inform Mr. Jay of the Result. He then apologized and expressed his regret for not being able to furnish the Money he had expected to Supply (alluding evidently to the *thirty or forty thousand pounds* which, in the Conference at Aranjuez the 11th Day of May last he said he expected to be able to Supply, the end of this or beginning of next Year). He said he had been disappointed in the Remittances expected from America, for he was advised that two Ships which he had expected would arrive from thence with Treasure in December or January next would not come, and that this, and other circumstances rendered it impossible for him to advance us any Money in Europe. But that he would nevertheless, agreeable to the King's intentions, give us all the Assistance in his power.

Mr. Jay desired to be informed whether any Steps were necessary for him to take for forwarding the Clothing at Cadiz to America. The Count answered that he waited the French Ambassador's Answer on the Subject, and that he had as yet no Inventory of them, but that he would again speak to the Ambassador, and make arrangements for sending them on to America as soon as possible.

Mr. Jay then proceeded to regret that the pleasure he derived from these instances of his Majesty's friendship to the United States, was mingled with pain from being informed by the above mentioned Paper, that the King conceived he might have just cause to be disgusted with them.

Because 1st—They had drawn the Bills of Exchange without his previous Consent, and 2ndly—Because they had not given any tokens of a recompense. Mr. Jay reminded his Excellency that these Bills were drawn upon himself, and not on Spain, and that although Congress might have hoped for reasons already assigned, to have been enabled to pay them by a Loan from His Majesty, yet that every other usual Measure was left open for that purpose. That an application to Spain for such a Loan could give no just Cause of Offence, for that if it had not been convenient to her to make it, all that she had to do, was to have told him so, and he was then at liberty to take such measures for procuring it Elsewhere as he might think proper. The count replied that what Mr. Jay observed was true, but that certainly the Bills were drawn with an Expectation of their being paid by Spain, and that this might probably have been done, if previous Notice of the Measure had been given. That he always intended to have done something towards their payment, but had been prevented by disappointments, and the Exigencies of the State. Mr. Jay continued to observe that the second Cause assigned for this disgust Vizt That Congress had given no tokens of a recompense, must have arisen from a mistake. He reminded his Excellency that he had never requested a *donation* from Spain, but that on the Contrary he had repeatedly offered to pledge the faith of the United States for the Repayment with Interest within a reasonable term after the War, of whatever Sum his Majesty might be so kind as to lend them. To these Remarks the Count said only that Interest for the Money would have been no object with them; That they would gladly have lent it to us without Interest, and repeated his regret at the Disappointment which had prevented them. He appeared rather uneasy and desirous of waving the Subject.

Mr. Jay then called the Count's attention to a part of the paper in question, which informed him "that there were hints (though no credit was given to it) of some understanding between America and the Court of London." He observed that this Subject was both delicate and important; That so far as this understanding related to Congress, or the Governments of either of the States, he was sure that this insinuation was entirely groundless; That there might possibly be intriguing Individuals who might have given cause to such suspicions; That if there were such Men or bodies of Men it would be for the good of the common cause that they should be detected, and their designs frustrated. He therefore requested that if his Excellency had any Evidence on this Subject he would be pleased to communicate it, and thereby enable Him to give congress an opportunity of taking such measures as Circumstances might render proper. The Count said he had nothing Specific or particular as yet to communicate.

That he was pursuing measures for further discoveries, and that he would mention to Mr. Jay whatever Information might result from them.

Mr. Jay resumed his animadversions on the Paper in question, by observing that it assured him it was necessary "That Congress should give sure and effective tokens of a good Correspondence, proposing reciprocal Measures of a compensation etc. In order that his Majesty might extend his further Dispositions towards them." That for his part, he could conceive of no higher tokens which one Nation could give to another of friendship and good will, than their Commissioning and sending a Person for the express purpose of requesting his Majesty to enter into Treaties of Amity and Alliance with them, and that on Terms of Reciprocity of Interest and mutual advantage. To this the count replied, that to this day he was ignorant of these Terms, and that no particular propositions had been made him. Mr. Jay then reminded him of his Letters from Cadiz and of the Conference on the Subject at Aranjuez on the 2d Day of June last, in the latter of which, after conferring on the Subject of Aids, and of the Treaty, his Excellency had promised to reduce his Sentiments on both to Writing and send him Notes on each; That, as to the first, Mr. Jay had received the Notes, but not on the *last;* That he had been in constant expectation of receiving them, and that Delicacy forbid pressing his Excellency on that matter, or offering any thing further till he should have leizure to compleat them. He said he thought he had given them to Mr. Jay or Mr. Carmichael, which both of them assured him he had not. Of this the Count appeared after a little time Satisfied, when Mr. Jay resumed the Subject by remarking that the Order of conducting that business appeared to him to be this, That as a right was reserved by the Secret Article to his Majesty to accede to the Treaty between France and America whenever he thought proper, and that the Latter would go into a discussion of any alterations the King might propose, that should be founded on reciprocity of Interest. The first question was whether his Majesty would accede to it as it was, or whether he would propose any and what alterations.

The Count here interrupted Mr. Jay by saying that the Interest of France and Spain with respect to America, were so distinct as necessarily different Treaties necessary. Mr. Jay answered that admitting this to be the case, the Treaty with France might be made the Basis, and they might go on Mutatis Mutandis; The Count replied THAT HIS MAJESTY WOULD NEVER CONSENT to MAKE that TREATY, THE BASIS OF ONE BETWEEN HIM AND the United States, that THAT TREATY had been CONCLUDED BY the FRENCH WITHOUT THE

KNOWLEDGE OF the King AND WITHOUT HAVING MADE HIM THE OFFER OF being a PARTY TO IT. THAT THE KINGS RESENTMENT had been so MUCH EXCITED BY THIS CONDUCT AS well NIGH TO HAVE OCCASIONED A RUPTURE BETWEEN the two Courts AND THAT ON THE SECRET ARTICLE BEING MADE KNOWN TO HIM HE had ANSWERED THAT WHEN HE found it convenient to ENTER INTO TREATY WITH THE COLONIES HE WOULD TAKE CARE OF HIS INTEREST WITHOUT CONSULTING ANY ONE. Hence he observed IT WOULD NOT BE PROPER TO MENTION ANY THING OF THE FRENCH TREATY BUT TO FORM ONE OF A NEW. Mr. Jay assured his Excellency that this was the FIRST TIME HE HAD EVER HEARD OF THIS ANECDOTE AND EXPRESSED SOME SURPRISE AT IT. The Count desired him to KEEP IT SECRET ADDING THAT THE FRENCH AMBASSADOR KNEW IT VERY WELL.[3]

The Count proceeded to say that it would not conduce to the general Pacification to hurry on the Treaty; That finding Congress were not disposed to Cessions without which the King would not make a Treaty, he thought it best by mutual services and Acts of Friendship, to continue making way for more condescensions on both sides and not excite Animosities and warmth by discussing Points which the King would never yield. That therefore Mr. Jay might take time to write to Congress on the Subject and obtain their Instructions. He said that previous to Mr. Jay's or Mr. Gerard's arrival at Madrid, Mr. Mirailles[4] had informed him that Congress would yield the Navigation of the Mississippi, but that Mr. Gerard informed him that Congress had changed their resolution on that Subject; That he had mentioned these obstacles to Mr. Jay and Mr. Carmichael, and it was probable that having done this, he had neglected or forgot to give Mr. Jay the Notes in question. Mr. Jay here reminded his Excellency that the Conference between them of the 2d Day of June last, turned among other points on these Obstacles and that they had then mutually expressed hopes that Regulations calculated to remove them in a manner satisfactory to both Parties might be adopted, and that the Conferences respecting them was concluded by his Excellency's promising to give Mr. Jay Notes of his sentiments on the proposed Treaty. The Count admitted this, and made several Observations tending to shew the Importance of this Object to Spain, and its determination to adhere to it, saying with some degree of warmth, that unless Spain could exclude all Nations from the Gulph of Mexico, they might as well admit all; That the King would never relinquish it; That the Minister regarded it as the principal Object to be obtained by the war, and *that obtained* he should be perfectly Easy whether or no Spain procured any other cession; That he considered it as far more important than the acquisition of Gibraltar, and that if they did not get it, it was a matter of Indifference to him whether the English possessed Mobile or not; That he chose always to speak his Sentiments plainly and candidly on those occasions, for which Reason he generally acted differently from other Politicians in always choosing to commit himself to paper, and appealing to the knowledge of the French Ambassador and others who had done business with him for the proofs of this being the principle of his conduct, He concluded by saying he would give his Sentiments in writing on this Subject to Mr. Jay.

Mr. Jay made no reply to the Counts remarks on the Navigation, but observing that being little acquainted with the Practice of Politicians he was happy in having to treat with a Minister of his Excellency's Principles; He added that there were many Points necessary to be adjusted in order to a Treaty; Thus they might proceed to agree upon as many as they could, and with respect to the others he should State them clearly to Congress and attend their further Instructions.

Mr. Jay then again turned the Conference to the Paper before mentioned by observing to the Count, that it appeared from it, that the King also expected from Congress equivalents to the Supplies formerly afforded, and also the Expenses of the War which it alledged had its origin from them. That as to the first he could only repeat what he had before said, that a general Account of them was necessary. That he neither knew the Amount of them, or the terms on which they were granted; That it was a Transaction previous to his Appointment; That on being furnished with the necessary information he would transmit it to Congress, and wait their Instructions; That an expectation of an Equivalent to the Expences sustained by Spain in the War was inadmissible on every principle; He read the passage in Question and remarked that America could no more be justly chargeable with the Expenses of the War sustained by Spain, than Spain could be justly chargeable with the Expenses of the War sustained by America. The Count replied that Mr. Jay had mistaken his meaning, and that he urged it merely to shew that as the States were deriving considerable advantages from very expensive operations on the part of Spain, that Consideration should incline them to more condescension towards the Latter.

Mr. Jay assured his Excellency that he knew it to be the disposition of Congress to contribute all in their power to the Success of the common Cause, and that they would on every occasion give proofs of it, and among others that he was confident that they would permit his Majesty to export from thence *during the war* Ship timber and Masts for the Royal Navy, and would readily consent to such Measures as might be proper and necessary for facilitating it. He further observed that having been informed by Mr. Gardoqui that his Majesty would like to take and finish a 74 Gun Ship now on the Stocks in one of the Eastern Ports, on which it was said no work was doing, he would with pleasure write to Congress and propose their Transferring her to his Majesty at prime Cost. That this previous Step was necessary as Congress might perhaps intend that Vessel for particular Services, but he was confident they would otherwise be happy in indulging his Majesty's inclinations. The Count appeared pleased with this. He said that with respect to Timber, they stood most in need at present of Yards, and should be glad to obtain a supply of them from Congress. That as to the Ship, he wished to be informed exactly of her present State, and the materials wanting to compleat and Equip her, which he observed might be sent from the Havannah, and whether a Crew of Americans could be had to navigate her there. Mr. Jay replied that though he was sure that Congress would readily give their aid in these and other matters interesting to Spain, yet he could not forbear reminding his Excellency as a friend that Public business, done under the direction of Public bodies was always more expensive than when done by Individuals. That therefore He would submit it to his Consideration whether it would not be more advisable to commit the Management of these Affairs to the Agent intended to succeed Mr. Mirailles, who, by being on the Spot would have opportunies of acting on exact information and in a manner more Consistent with the views of his Excellency. The Count agreed in this Opinion and promised to communicate to Mr. Jay his further Intentions on this Subject.

Mr. Jay informed the Minister that as his further Stay here would now be unnecessary and Business called him to Madrid he purposed to return there on Monday next. The Count concurred, and the Conference Ended.

Congress will permit me to observe that many things in this Conference are important, and demand Instructions. I forbear to point them out, because they are obvious, and I take the Liberty of giving this hint from a knowledge of the delays attending the Proceedings of large bodies.

I returned to Madrid on the Day appointed, and whether to accept, or not to accept the Bills, became a very serious question, which are numerous, and which Congress will readily perceive without a particular Enumeration; I determined to put a good Face on the business, and accept all that should be presented, which I have accordingly done, and am daily doing. What the Event will be I cannot pretend to decide. All that I can say, is that my Endeavors shall not be wanting to render it successful. The Responsibility of the King will not produce much, and the difficulty of borrowing Money has been encreased by the number of Agents sent to Europe for that purpose by several of the States, who I am told, have imprudently bidden on each other.

Mr. Gardoqui returned to Madrid a few days after I did, and brought me word from the Minister, that Instructions should be sent to their Ambassadors in Holland and France to assure in Due form the Responsibility of the King to such Persons as might there incline to lend us money on the credit of it, and that the Minister would do the same thing here. He told me further that the Minister hoped, I would not be discouraged nor consider things only on the dark side, for that it was still his Intention to afford America every Aid in his power.

All this I ascribe to the Exertions of America, and I am confident that it will always be necessary for the United States to be formidable at home, if they expect to be respectable any where. For my own Part I shall be disappointed, if I find Courts moving on any other Principle than Political ones, and indeed not always on those. Caprice, Whim, the Interests and Passions of Individuals, must and will always have greater, or lesser degrees of Influence. America stands very high here at present. I rejoice at it, though I must confess, I much fear that such violent Exertions may be followed by langor and relaxation.

What the Plan of this Court is with respect to us, or whether they have any is with me very doubtful. If they have rejected all the overtures of Britain, why is Mr. Cumberland still here: and why are Expresses passing between Madrid and London thro Portugal? If Spain is determined that we shall be Independent, why not openly declare so and thereby diminish the hopes and Endeavors of Britain to prevent it? She seems to be desirous of holding the Balance, of being in some sort of Mediatrix, and of courting the offers of each by her supposed Importance to both. The Bills drawn on me was considered as a desperate Measure, prompted by our Imbecility, and was a bad card to play at a time we were endeavoring to form a Treaty, and when Prudence demanded that the Importance of Spain to us, should not have been brought forward, or placed in such a glaring point of view.

One good consequence however has resulted from it. The Cordiality of Spain has been tried by it. For I know of a certainty that it was in her power easily to have made the Loan we asked: Indeed we shall always be deceived, if we believe that any Nation in the World, has or will have a disinterested Regard for us especially absolute Monarchies, where the temporary views, or passions of the Prince, his Ministers, his Women, or his Favorites, not the Voice of the People, direct the helm of State. Besides from the manner in which the War is carrying on, it would seem as if it was the design of France and Spain that the longest purse, not the longest Sword, should decide it. Whether such be really their Intention, or how far it may be politic, I cannot pretend to determine. This however is certain that it would be putting the Affair on a hard issue for us. It is also certain that some Respect is due to appearances, and probable Events, and we should be cautious how we spend our Money, our Men, or our public Spirit, uselessly. In my Opinion we should endeavor to be as Independent on the Charity of our friends, as on the Mercy of our Enemies. Jacob took advantage even of his Brother's hunger and extorted from him a higher price than the value of the Mississippi for a single Dinner. The way not to be in *Easau's* condition is to be prepared to meet with *Jacob's*.

From what I can learn of the King's character, I am persuaded that a present from Congress of a handsome fast sailing Packet boat, would be very acceptable, and consequently very useful.

I am informed, and believe that a Loan from Individuals in France is impracticable. Here nothing can be done in that way. What may be expected from the like attempts in Holland, I am unable to say.

I have received no answer to my Letter to Count de Vergennes.[5] The Ambassador informs me that the Count has written him on the Subject, and the following is an Extract from his Letter.

> I doubt whether I shall be able to render Mr. Jay the service he asks of me, beyond all that which My Ministry has furnished to the Americans in the course of this Year. Mr. Franklin is Urgent for a million Extra, to meet the drafts of Congress to the 31 of December. I understand how important it is to prevent them from being returned protested, but the difficulty is in finding the Means. I shall do my best in this exigency, without having any Certainty of Success; but it would be impossible for me to go beyond this.[6]

Dr. Franklin has obtained some more Money from his Court, and I am to have 25,000 Dollars of it, perhaps he may be able to advance more, but how much I cannot say.

LbkC. DNA: PCC, 110, I, 298–320. As was usual in his dispatches to the President of Congress, JJ enclosed several months' correspondence. Thus the report on the conference with Floridablanca of 23 Sept. 1780 was sent to Huntington on 6 Nov. 1780 with other material of earlier dates and JJ's comments of 6 November. LbkC in CSmH: JJ Lbk (in coded and decoded versions). C in hand of James Madison, DLC: Madison Papers, I, 10429a–10461a. Printed in *RDC*, omitting coded passage, *IV*, 112–50, at pp. 143–49.

1 Floridablanca had arranged to have Gardoqui deliver a letter in the king's name through del Campo. The nub of this document was that Spain would continue to underwrite the American efforts as long as the means to do so were available.

2 Miguel de Muzquiz, Marquez de Villar y Ladron, conde de García, and Minister of Finance.

3 The transliteration of this coded passage has never before been printed. The code was based on Boyer's *French Dictionary,* and it had been suggested in JJ to Charles Thomson, 29 Feb. 1780, dft. in JP.

4 Miralles.

5 22 Sept. 1780.

6 Translated from the French by the editors.

ACKNOWLEDGMENTS

Generous support from the National Endowment for the Humanities has made possible the preparation and editing of this manuscript, while the Avalon Foundation provided funds essential to the research and assembling of photocopies of documents in the Jay Collection, and the Rockefeller Foundation, by a special grant, underwrote the cost of calendaring the massive Xerox print collection of diplomatic sources which supplements the Jay archives proper.

The staff of the Jay Papers benefited immeasurably from the unstinted cooperation of a considerable company of librarians, archivists, and scholars in this country and abroad. First of all, this project would have been inconceivable had it not been for the acquisition of the original collection of the Jay Papers by the Trustees of Columbia University and by subsequent acquisitions out of special funds of the Columbia University Libraries, whose directors, Dr. Richard H. Logdson and Dr. Warren J. Haas, in turn, along with their dedicated staffs, provided essential services and facilities. A special acknowledgment must be made to Mr. Lino S. Lipinsky de Orlov, Curator of the Jay Homestead, Bedford, New York, who has generously contributed his time in support of our investigation.

Since its initiation the Jay Papers have been served by a dedicated, if revolving, staff of scholars. Dr. Mary-Jo Kline, now with the Adams Papers, served longest in time and her indefatigable efforts as scholar and sleuth are signally appreciated. Other talented scholars enlisted in the project include Professor Herbert A. Johnson, presently editor of the Papers of John Marshall, the late Professor Catherine S. Crary of Finch College, a valiant supporter and co-worker in the American Revolutionary Era, Dr. Eli Faber of the John Jay College, Professor Carol R. Berkin of Baruch College, Mrs. Marilyn Lavin Archdeacon, Mrs. Lois W. Banner, Miss Barbara Bennett, Professor Francis J. Bremer of Thomas More College, Mrs. Jantien Brinkhorst of Leyden, Mrs. Pamela Damman Budding, Dr. Norma de Candido, Professor Margaret Duggan, Miss Antoinette Fleur Empringham, Professor Rebecca Gruver, Hunter College, Mrs. Karen Humphrey, Dr. Barbara Weber Krüger of Karmstadt, Dr. Susan Previant Lee, Professor Jesse E. Lemisch, State University of New York at Buffalo, Miss Margaret Newcomer, Miss Jane I. Rosenthal, Miss Harriet Shorr, Professor Darline Gay Levy of Barnard College, Miss Roberta Tansman, Professor John J. Waters, Jr., University of Rochester, Miss Ilona Wells, Mrs. Marjolijn Werman, Mrs. Suzanne S. Williams, Mr. Chilton Williamson, Jr., and Mr. David Goldberg. In addition, the editors from time to time have benefited by the expert assistance of various members of the Columbia University family, including Professors Morton Smith and B. Bussell Thompson, Mr. Curtis Wolcott Church, and Mrs. Gloria-Gilda Deak.

Researches abroad were invariably facilitated in Great Britain by Mr. Roger Ellis, Secretary, Historical Manuscripts Commission and Miss W. D. Coates, Registrar, National Register of Archives; in Paris by M. Jean Baillou, Directeur du Services des Diplomatiques et de la Documentations, Archives, Ministères des Affaires Étrangères, who secured permission for extensive microcopying of the French diplomatic archives; in Spain by Professor Juan Pérez de Tudela, Instituto Oviedo, Madrid, Señor Tomás Pérez Sáenz, who was consulted on the records of the Archivo Histórico Nacional in Madrid and the Archivo General de Simancas, and to Señor Otto Pikaza for assistance in culling relevant items from the Archivo General de Indías at Seville.

The Jay Papers are especially indebted to the staffs of the National Archives and of the National Historical Publications Comission, notably to Miss F. Helen Beach, formerly Archivist of the Commission, and to the staff of the Library of Congress, including Dr. David C. Mearns and Dr. Roy P. Basler, chiefs in turn of its Manuscript Division, Dr. Paul H. Smith, Editor of the Letters of Members of the Continental Congress, and Dr. James H. Hutson, Coordinator, American Revolution Bicentennial Programs, also of the Library of Congress. We have repeatedly called upon Dr. Lyman H. Butterfield, editor of the Adams Papers and his staff, upon Dr. Leonard W. Labaree and Dr. William B. Willcox, editors of the Franklin Papers and their staffs; upon Dr. Julian P. Boyd, editor of the Papers of Thomas Jefferson; upon Dr. Harold C. Syrett, editor of the Papers of Alexander Hamilton and his staff; upon Drs. William E. Hutchinson, William M. E. Rachal, and Robert Rutland, editors of the Papers of James Madison, Miss Dorothy Twohig of the Washington Papers, and Dr. E. James Ferguson, editor of the Papers of Robert Morris, and his staff. Special courtesies have been extended by Dr. Howard H. Peckham, Director, and Mr. William S. Ewing, Curator of Manuscripts, William L. Clements Library, Dr. James J. Heslin, Director, New-York Historical Society; Mr. Robert W. Hill, formerly Chief, Manuscripts Division, New York Public Library; and the late Dr.

Allan Nevins and Dr. John E. Pomfret, Huntington Library and Art Gallery, among a host of special librarians and scholars, whose assistance and counsel contributed in so many essential ways to this editorial enterprise. Other libraries on whose services and resources the John Jay Papers have drawn extensively include the American Philosophical Society, Connecticut State Library, Yale University Library, Connecticut Historical Society, Historical Society of Delaware, Lilly Library, Indiana University, Hall of Records, Annapolis, Massachusetts Historical Society, American Antiquarian Society, Boston Public Library, Houghton Library, Harvard University, New Hampshire Historical Society, New Jersey State Library, Princeton University Library, Albany Institute of History and Art, Union College Library, Washington's Headquarters and Museum, Newburgh, Department of Archives and History, State of North Carolina, University of North Carolina Library, Historical Society of Pennsylvania, and the New York State Library.

The sources of all documents published herein which do not form a part of the Papers of John Jay in the Columbia University Libraries are indicated in the respective source notes and permission to publish these papers gratefully acknowledged.

INDEX

Abigail, the Jays' servant, 711, 712
Actaeon, 304, 305
Active, 509
Adams, Abigail Smith, 12
Adams, John, to, 751–52, 764–66, 792–93; mentioned, 3, 12, 16, 152, 164, 168, 197, 390, 391, 395, 450, 512, 630, 631, 644, 733, 746, 750, 797; in 2d Congress, 247, 248, 254, 265, 266, 276, 315; peace commissioner to England, 649, 651; in Netherlands, 806, 809
Adams, Samuel, 148, 197, 512, 587, 588
Addison, Joseph, 570, 571
"Address to the Electors of Great Britain" (Lord Mayor and Livery of London), 169, 171
"Address to the People of Great-Britain" (JJ), 12, 15, 23, 136–37, 147, 151, 171, 200
"Address to the Sun" (Ossian), 49, 50
"A Hint to the Legislature of New York" (JJ), 25, 461–63
Albany, N.Y., 103, 111, 143, 144, 159, 294, 297, 331, 332, 333, 389, 391, 404, 408, 420, 426, 438, 444, 452, 458, 459, 460, 479, 481, 589; county, 104, 105, 132, 143, 144, 295, 331, 333, 340, 344, 345, 405, 432, 465, 480, 481, 501, 653
Albert Edward, Prince of Wales (later King Edward VII), 4
Albouy, Leonard, 583
Alexander, Maj. Gen. William, Lord Stirling, 237, 238, 239, 243, 310, 312, 314, 373, 561, 739, 740, 741
Alfred, 244
Allen, Andrew, 364–65, 366
Allen, Ethan, 191, 192, 393, 396; and Vermont, 398, 399, 553, 554, 823
Allen, William, 448, 450
Alliance, 629, 630, 744
Alsop, John, 265; election to 1st Congress, 133, 134, 135; in 2d Congress, 213, 259, 269, 271, 280, 281
American Philosophical Society, JJ's election to, 26, 749, 750
Amherst, Lord Jeffery, 39, 40, 50, 51
Amphitrite, 530–31
Amsterdam, the Netherlands, 644, 733, 763, 764
"An Address of the Convention of the Representatives of the State of New-York, to their Constituents" (JJ), 14, 24, 359–62, 368, 374
Anderson, George, 790, 791
André, Maj. John, 346
Annin, Daniel, 591
Annin, Lavinia Van Wyck, 591
Anthony, Theophile, 297, 298
Apollo, 445, 447
Appius Claudius Crassus, 92–95
Aranjuez, Spain, 694, 697, 744, 752, 753, 754, 758, 759, 770, 827, 829. *See also* Treaties
Arbuthnot, Adm. Marriot, 600
Armstrong, Maj. John, Jr., 485, 486
Arnold, Benedict, 323, 346, 432, 439, 450, 548–49; and Canadian campaign, 183–84, 185, 220; accused of misconduct, 549, 562
Articles of Confederation, mentioned, 451, 454, 459, 460, 498, 592; debated in Congress, 275, 276, 280–81; ratification of, 460, 493, 508, 509
Asturias, Prince of, 742, 743
Atherton, Cornelius, 257, 258
Atlee, Samuel, 606
Atlee, William A., from, 619–20; mentioned, 620
Auchmuty, Rev. Samuel, 74, 85, 86
Audibert Caille, Étienne d', 772–73
Augusta, 445, 447
Augusta, Ga., 725

Aurora, 25, 672, 687, 689, 714, 736
Austria, 584, 820
Avery, Rev. Ephraim, 32, 85, 86

Bache, Richard, 659
Bache, Sarah Franklin, 659
Bache, Theophylact, 118
Baltimore, Md., 321, 364, 484
Bancker, Adrian, 226
Bancker, Gerardus, 121, 122, 483, 485
Bancker, Johannes (or John), 557, 558
Bancroft, Edward, 328, 330
Bancroft, George, 135, 149
Bank of North America, 756
Bank of Pennsylvania, 821, 822
Banks, Lt. Josiah, 104, 105
Banks-Lubeken tract, 104, 105
Banyar, Goldsbrow, 358, 359
Barclay, Andrew D., 125
Barclay, John, 481
Bard, Dr. Samuel, 113, 114, 229, 271, 305
Bascome, George, from, 581–82
Basden, Joseph, 583
Basking Ridge, N.J., 560, 564, 565, 567
Batten Kill River, N.Y., 104, 105
"Battle of the Kegs," 447
Bayard, Rev. Lazare, 30
Bayard, Nicholas, 30
Bayard, Rebecca, 485, 486
Bayard, William, 486, 691
Bayard & Co., 486
Bayley, Gen. Jacob, 539, 540
Bear Mountain, N.Y., 295
Beaumarchais, Pierre Augustin Caron de, to, 531–32; mentioned, 326, 507, 508, 716
Bedel, Brig. Gen. Timothy, 539, 540
Bedel's New Hampshire Rangers, 252
Bedford, John Russell, 4th Duke of, 816, 820
Bedlow, William, 202, 296, 297
Beekman, Henry, II, 96, 97, 220, 221
Beers v. *Hotchkiss*, 86, 87
Belvedere, N.Y., 160
Benedict, Maj. Joseph, 261, 262
Benezet, Anthony, to, 572; from, 544–45; mentioned, 545
Benjamin, Hannah, 414, 448, 450, 692, 698, 708
Bennington, Vt., mentioned, 342, 471, 498, 499, 554; Battle of, 436–37, 464
Benoit, the Jays' servant, 702
Benson, Egbert, from, 350–51, 514–15, 604–06, 632–33; mentioned, 49, 50,
Benson, Egbert (*cont'd*)
98, 99, 100, 113, 158, 160, 277, 346, 354, 411, 499, 527, 562, 563, 670; in debating society, 88, 92, 94–95; in N.Y. State government, 344, 347–48, 528, 584, 605; and Vermont lands, 605
Benson, Henry, 297
Benson, Robert, mentioned, 473, 474, 562, 563; in N.Y. State government, 393, 394, 401, 421, 606
Bermuda, 581–82
Beulah, 143, 144
Biddle, Lt. Col. Clement, 410
Bingham, William, from, 547–48, 558–59, 738–41; mentioned, 661, 663, 665, 718, 719; agent in Martinique, 548, 558–59, 673, 685, 686, 688, 704, 759
"Birch, Harvey," 333–37
Bishop, 258
Bishop of Landaff, 176
Blackwell's Island, N.Y., 312
Blaine, Ephraim, 597, 617
Bleecker, Anthony Lispenard, 99, 101
Bleecker, John N., 105
Bloomer v. *Hinchman*, 106, 107, 109
Bloomer, Rev. Joshua, 106, 107, 109
Bonhomme Richard, 631
Bonum Town, N.J., 417, 418
Boonton, N.J., 414
Bordeaux, France, 439
Boston, Mass., mentioned, 12, 132, 134, 332–33, 407, 408, 447, 490, 503, 539, 576–77, 674, 691, 784; tea party, 129, 137; Port Act, 129, 130, 132, 133, 137, 138; end of siege, 245, 246, 248
Bouillé, François-Claude Amour, Marquis de, 739, 741
Bourgoing, Jean François, Baron de, 777, 780, 781, 783
Bowen, Emanuel, 121, 122
Boyd, Robert, 245, 246, 257, 296, 297
Boyer, Abel, *French Dictionary*. *See* Ciphers and Codes
Braddock, Gen. James, 347
Bradford, Thomas, 198, 201
Bradford, William, 198, 201, 447
Bradstreet, Elizabeth, 573–74
Bradstreet, Gen. John, 573–74
Brandywine, Battle of, 448, 491, 512, 539
Brasher, Abraham, 208, 473, 474
Brattle, James, 231

Braxton, Carter, 256
Brest, France, 404, 489, 490–91, 502, 503
Brewer (or Brower), Nicholas, 340–41
Brinckerhoff, Dirck, 97
Bristol, 304
Bristol, England, 30, 34, 38, 44, 45
Bristol, Pa., 266, 267, 268, 271, 272
Brooklyn Heights, Battle of, 310–11, 314
Brooks, David, 49
Broome, John, 394, 528, 529
Brown, Capt. John, 748
Brown, Ensign John, 540–41, 577
Brown, Mary Livingston, 748
Browne, Mary Burnet, 564
Browne, Mary French, 563–64
Browne, Sarah, 563–64
Browne, William, 564
"Brutus," mentioned, 110; "To the Public," 111–12; "When Vice Prevails," 112
Bruyn, Capt. Jacobus, 293
Bull, John, 642
Burgoyne, Gen. John, mentioned, 422, 423, 432–33, 434–37, 438, 440, 490, 491, 593; invasion of N.Y., 416, 417, 418, 422, 423, 426–28, 433; proclamation to civilians, 423, 425, 426; and Battle of Saratoga, 446, 447, 449, 450, 452, 490, 491, 620
Burke, Thomas, 386, 514, 582, 628
Burlington, N.J., 372
Burton, David, 42
Bute, John Stuart, 3d Earl of, 815, 820
Byron, Vice Adm. John, 539, 540
Byvack, John, 236

Cádiz, Spain, 25, 692, 699, 705, 723, 796, 797
Cadwalader, Dr. Thomas, 756
Caldwell, Rev. James, 693
Cambridge, Mass., 613
Cambridge, N.Y., 436
Camden, 296–97
Camden, Battle of, 811, 813
Camden, Charles Pratt, Earl of, 814, 820
Campo, Bernardo del, 717, 774, 775, 782, 802
Canada, mentioned, 24, 147, 151, 160, 177, 207, 216, 228, 232, 233, 234, 235, 240, 248–52, 258, 259, 273, 274, 323, 325, 336, 442, 447, 453, 463, 464, 491, 511, 518, 539, 540, 554, 576–77; American campaign against, 176, 183–85, 190–91, 192, 219, 245; retreat of American forces from, 323; proposed 2d American campaign against, 453, 463, 464, 491, 511, 518, 539, 540, 554, 576–77; boundary with America, 650
Cape Ann, Mass., 410
Cape Breton Island, Canada, 328–29
Cape Charles, Md., 437
Carleton, Sir Guy, 183, 184, 185, 190, 207, 252, 324
Carlisle, William Eden, Earl of, 476, 487
Carlisle Peace Commission, 253–54, 264, 472, 473, 474, 475, 476, 477, 487, 826
Carman, Tom, 529
Carmel, N.Y., 334, 338
Carmichael, William, to, 720–22, 743–44, 760–61, 771–72, 777–79, 782–83, 800–01, 804–05; from, 729–31, 732–33, 742–43, 759–60, 773–74, 775–76, 780–82, 798–800, 801–02, 805–06, 808–09; mentioned, 326, 330, 651, 652, 662, 663, 665, 683, 705, 715, 716, 718, 719, 722, 737, 738, 772, 788, 797, 813, 829; relations with JJ, 15, 769–83; devious past, 16, 488, 770, 771
Carpenter, John, 300
Carpenters' Hall, Philadelphia, 136
Carroll, Charles, 232, 233, 773, 774
Carter, Edward, 538
Casti, Abbé Giambattista, 775, 776, 802
Castle, Robert, 296–98
Caswell, Richard, 386
Catherine II, Empress of Russia, 764
Cautaleu, Jean-Barthélemy Le Couteulx de, 743, 744
Chambers, Anne Van Cortlandt, mentioned, 31, 32, 33, 42, 43, 49, 53, 74; will of, 140, 141
Chambers, John, 31, 32, 33, 35, 36, 45, 49, 53, 74
Chambly, Canada, 187, 188, 189, 202, 204, 207
Chandler, Rev. Thomas Bradbury, 85, 86
Charles III, King of Spain, 716, 717, 718, 732, 733, 737, 738, 742, 743, 751, 760, 801, 825, 826, 827, 829, 830, 832, 834

Charles V, former King of Spain, 754
Charleston, S.C., mentioned, 372, 630, 645, 727, 728, 729, 763, 776, 787, 788, 801, 811, 812; British assault of, 304–05, 323; fall of, 776, 792, 807
Charlestown, Mass., 613
Charlotte County, N.Y., 331, 493, 653
Charlton, Rev. Richard, 467, 468
Chase, Samuel, 232, 233
Chatham, N.Y., 481
Chaumont, Jacques Donatien Le Roy de, 631
Cheesecock Patent, 140, 141
Chesapeake Bay, 434, 437, 562
Chesterfield, Philip Dormer Stanhope, Earl of, 442–43
Church, John Barker (alias John Carter in America), 499
Ciphers and Codes, explained, 660–64; discussed, 665–66, 734, 736–37, 787, 810; cipher letters, 712–13, 727–31, 732–33, 742–43, 825–34
"Circular Letter" on Finances (JJ), 15, 25, 592, 641, 642
Claas, JJ's servant, 166, 167, 172
Clajon, William, 552
Clark, George Rogers, 660
Clark, Capt. William, 340, 344, 345
Clarke, Dr. Thomas, 105
Clarkson, Ann Margaret, 563–64, 684
Clarkson, David, Sr., 684, 691
Clarkson, David, 443, 449, 450, 679
Clarkson, Elizabeth French, 450, 564
Clarkson, Matthew, 438, 449, 450, 518, 552
Claverack, N.Y., 345
Clements, Capt. Peter, 362, 363
Clinton, Cornelia Tappen, 625, 655, 660, 724, 791
Clinton, George, N.Y. colonial governor, 38
Clinton, George, to, 527, 561–62, 624–25, 635–36, 652–53, 659–60, 723–24, 791; to, from Judges of Oyer and Terminer, 480–81; to, from N.Y. delegation, 548–49; from, 473–74, 545–46, 654–55; mentioned, 259, 263, 265, 271, 273, 280, 470, 475, 479, 481, 492, 513; as general, 296, 297, 354, 373, 377, 468; as governor, 411, 451, 465, 469, 470, 471, 472, 491, 497, 498, 501, 511, 541, 551, 562, 563, 575, 606, 633, 652, 670; on Vermont, 655, 656
Clinton, Gen. Sir Henry, 260, 304, 449, 450, 468, 485, 564–65, 566, 604, 726, 727, 744, 759, 763, 775, 776, 787, 812, 823
Clinton, Brig. Gen. James, mentioned, 238, 239, 296; in Indian campaign, 616, 617, 619
Clymer, Elizabeth Meredith, 755, 756
Clymer, George, 364, 366, 370, 756
Cohoes, N.Y., 577
Colden, Cadwallader, 51
Colden, Cadwallader, Jr., from 355–57; mentioned, 356, 358, 359; imprisonment of, 354–55; notes of conference, 357, 358–59
Colden, Cadwallader, III, 355, 357
Columbia University, purchase of Jay Papers, 2–3, 6–10
Committee for Detecting Conspiracies (N.Y.), 14, 24, 288, 331–38, 340–59, 362–63, 373–74
Committee of Safety (N.Y.), 309, 310, 314, 356–58, 362, 368, 411, 416, 417, 420, 421
Committee of Secret Correspondence (later Committee of [for] Foreign Affairs), from, 668–69; mentioned, 13, 24, 195, 270, 316, 329, 330, 369–70, 371, 434, 508, 513–27, 530–32, 548, 559, 573–74, 662, 663, 665, 669, 718, 719, 720, 725, 789. *See also* 2d Continental Congress
Committee on the Defense of the Hudson (N.Y.), 13, 24, 288, 294–306, 389
Commonplace Book (JJ), 67
Common Sense (Thomas Paine), 197
Concklin, Nathaniel, 290, 293
Confederacy, Council of Commissioned Officers of, 666–68; mentioned, 25, 651, 690, 714, 739, 759, 811
Confederate, 759
Connecticut, colony, 103, 142; state, mentioned, 13, 197, 210, 312, 336, 347, 371, 444, 455, 604, 820; troops, 183, 252, 293, 312, 471; delegates to 2d Congress, 206, 208, 210; government of, 303, 401, 602–04
Continental Army, mentioned, 166, 175, 180, 181, 184, 194, 203, 221, 234–35, 238, 239, 240, 241–42, 247, 248–52, 258, 259, 273, 274, 278, 283, 314, 410, 468, 642; and N.Y. forces, 237–40; departments of, 462, 469, 533–35, 541, 542–43, 562; Wash-

Continental Army (*cont'd*)
ington's Headquarters, 302, 304, 371, 404, 415, 416, 425, 430, 431, 444, 468; Northern command, 160, 234–35; Northern theater, 258, 419, 460, 461, 465, 469, 471, 511, 535; and Schuyler-Gates rivalry, 323, 388, 404, 408, 418, 425, 433, 434–35, 444, 453; Southern theater, 234–35, 323, 561, 562, 630, 633–34, 645, 712, 725, 726, 727, 728, 729, 740, 759–60, 788, 810–11, 825

Continental Association, mentioned, 136, 137, 144, 157, 162, 163, 164, 165, 170, 171–72, 182; signed by JJ, 12, 136; enforcement in N.Y., 12, 164

Continental Congress, 1st, mentioned, 2, 133–34, 135–37, 141, 143, 150; N.Y. delegation at, 11, 23, 133, 134, 135–36, 204; JJ as penman in, 12, 23; secrecy, 137, 138; and Petition to the King, 147, 151, 152

———, 2d, mentioned, 12, 13, 23, 24, 25, 136, 143, 145–49, 151, 160–66, 170, 172, 174–76, 178–81, 185, 186, 188–89, 192, 195–201, 204, 208, 210–13, 216–18, 220, 221, 226, 229, 232, 233, 235–39, 241–47, 252–54, 256, 258, 259, 262–76, 279–83, 321, 360, 364–67, 370, 371, 374, 376, 386, 387, 388, 404, 427, 429, 450, 469, 470, 475, 482, 491, 494, 499, 509–10, 537, 538, 582, 615–18, 626, 643, 644, 654, 689, 690, 702, 712, 713, 732, 737, 743, 745, 758–60, 763, 766, 767, 772, 774, 781, 783, 790, 791, 793, 794, 815, 828; petitions to, 610, 614–15, 635–36, 784–86; foreign affairs, 275, 276, 280, 512; and England, 163, 164, 192, 204, 477–78, 482, 484, 486–87, 531–32; and France, 275, 475, 488, 651, 722, 826; and Spain, 25, 26, 650, 716–17, 718, 827, 831, 833; and peace terms, 649–51, 714, 722, 766, 767, 769, 830–31; finances, 15, 189, 376, 386, 448, 450, 465, 466, 499, 512, 548, 553, 554, 558–59, 566, 567, 590, 591, 592, 593, 604, 626, 644, 669, 673, 712, 713, 716–18, 740, 746, 747, 750–51, 760, 763, 766–68, 775, 779, 792, 794, 803, 804, 806, 809, 812, 827–28, 833; military affairs, 148–49, 194, 208, 289, 293, 322, 323,

Continental Congress (*cont'd*)
385, 386, 387, 388, 408, 409, 418, 428–29, 430–34, 437, 444, 453, 460, 461, 464, 471, 491, 496, 497, 498, 503, 510–12, 518, 519, 535, 541, 542–44, 562, 573, 574, 579–80, 591, 592, 595–96, 597, 616, 618, 633, 637–41, 712, 713, 832; New York delegation, 148, 150, 155, 156, 158, 172, 189, 196, 201, 202, 204, 206–08, 210, 211–13, 218, 239, 240, 255, 258–59, 264, 266, 280, 283, 370, 387, 388, 408, 434, 452, 496, 548–49, 551, 553, 554, 654–55; committees, 162, 163, 173, 189, 195, 196, 197, 226, 232, 233, 244, 270, 274, 283, 316, 364, 366, 370, 441–42, 458, 459, 548, 556, 559, 577, 587, 588, 589; resolutions, 173–74, 196, 204, 235, 236, 237, 241–44, 252, 256, 259, 264, 265, 270, 274, 346, 582, 592, 601, 602, 605, 609, 610, 613, 615, 620, 621, 623, 635, 636, 644, 649, 651, 653, 654–56, 665, 669, 714, 746, 750, 766, 767, 769; and establishment of state governments, 196, 254, 264, 265, 266, 268, 269; and independence, 195, 197, 256, 263, 265, 266, 267, 275, 276, 280, 287; boards, 408, 464, 485, 495, 496, 533–34, 539–40, 543, 566, 577, 591, 592, 617, 623, 642, 669, 729. *See also* Articles of Confederation, Committee of Secret Correspondence, Silas Deane, "Olive Branch Petition," Vermont lands

Continental Navy, mentioned, 211, 216, 226, 235, 236, 237, 239, 241, 242, 244, 270; privateering, 195, 241, 242, 245, 256, 328, 807, 811; flag, 235, 242–43, 244

Convention Troops, 620

Conway, Maj. Gen. Thomas, mentioned, 463, 464, 476

Conway Cabal, 498, 511, 513, 515–16

Conyngham, Anne Hockly, from, 614–15; mentioned, 615, 746

Conyngham, David Hayfield, 691

Conyngham, Capt. Gustavus, 615, 745

Conyngham, Mary West, 690, 691

Cook, Col. Edward, 640, 641

Cooke, Samuel, 290, 293

Cooper, James Fenimore, mentioned, 5; JJ's reminiscences and *The Spy*, 14, 335–37

Cooper, Myles, mentioned, 23, 60; King's College President, 55, 62–63, 85, 145; Loyalist, 145
Cooper, Susan, 334
Córdoba, Adm. Luis de, 805, 806, 808, 809
Cordova, Spain, 706–07
Corlear's Hook, N.Y., 312
Cornaro, Luigi, 232, 233
Cornwallis, Gen. Charles, 2d Earl of, 359, 451, 726, 727, 811
Coudray, Maj. Gen. Jean Baptiste Tronson du, 325–26, 329, 410
Council of Safety (N.Y.), 25, 421, 423, 424, 427, 430–31, 432, 434, 438, 451, 455, 500, 501
Cowperthwait, Joseph, 617, 619
Courter, Harman, 691
Cox, John, 607, 608, 609
Crisis Number 1, The, Thomas Paine, 359–61
Crosby, Enoch, 333–44, 345, 347
Croton River, N.Y., 324, 368, 380, 384
Crown Point, N.Y., 175, 176, 183
Cruger, Henry, 81, 101
Cruger, John, 97
Cruger, Tilemon (or Telemon), 99, 101
Cruikshank, Joseph, 545
Cuba, 40
Culper, Samuel, 335, 337
Cumberland, 784
Cumberland County, N.Y., 457–58, 633, 653
Cumberland, Richard, and Hussey-Cumberland mission, 771, 772, 773, 774, 775, 776, 777, 779, 780, 781, 782, 783, 799–801, 806, 807, 833
Cumming (or Cummins), John, 357
Curaçao, described, 97–98; mentioned, 99, 233
Curson, Richard, 208, 209
Curson, Samuel, 208, 209
Cuyler, Jacob, 476

Dalling, John, 812, 813
Dalrymple, Sir John, 752
Dalrymple, Col. William, 215, 218
Damas-Marçillac, Claude Charles, Viscomte de, 688, 689
Dana, Francis, to, 806–08; mentioned, 472, 473, 652, 733, 766, 793, 797
Dancing Assembly, 11, 116, 117
Darby, Dr. John, 446, 447, 561, 684
Dartmouth, William Legge, Earl of, petition to, 122; mentioned, 11, 120, 121, 123
Dean, James, 442
Deane, 558
Deane, Elizabeth Saltonstall, 410
Deane, Joseph, issued passport by JJ, 609–10; mentioned, 610
Deane, Silas, from, 325–29, mentioned, 136, 164, 180, 321, 366, 408, 474, 571, 572, 588, 642, 649, 661, 663, 664, 665, 770, 771, 820; Congressional agent to France, 195; delegate to 2d Congress, 223, 224, 226, 230; Commissioner to France, 315–16, 317, 330, 369, 371, 409–10, 434, 439, 475, 507; recall of, 460, 461, 507; Deane-Lee controversy, 487–88, 496–97, 507–08, 512, 514–16, 524–25, 530, 546, 556, 649
Deane, Capt. Simeon, 474, 475
Debating Society, 87–95
Deboe, Francis, 480, 481
Declaration of Independence, mentioned, 7, 13, 256, 287, 366, 509; debate in Congress, 275, 276, 280; presented to French Court, 327, 330
Defoe, Daniel, 545
De Lancey, James, N.Y. political leader, 38, 97, 101
De Lancey, James, 99–100, 101
De Lancey, John, 109
De Lancey, Oliver, 346, 347
De Lancey, Oliver, Jr., 102
De Lancey, Peter, 12, 123
De Lancey, Stephen, 88, 91, 92, 118
De Lancey Faction, 97, 111–12, 131
Delaware, 266, 267, 283, 366, 370–71, 549, 579, 581
Delaware Bay, 434, 562
Delaware River, 360, 437, 445, 447, 451, 452
Denmark, 768, 769, 820
De Noyelles, John, 110, 111–12
Denn (or Dean), Elizabeth, 141
De Peyster, Abraham, Jr., 31, 32, 33, 45, 52, 67, 68, 69, 70
De Peyster, James Abraham, 45, 46, 48, 98, 99, 102
De Peyster, Joanna, 67
De Peyster, Margaret Van Cortlandt, 31, 32, 33, 42, 43, 45, 68, 100, 101
De Peyster, Nicholas, 102
De Peyster, Pierre, 67
Despatch, 270

De Witt, Charles, from 367; mentioned, 331, 389
De Witt, John C., 367, 368
Dick, David, 480, 481
Dickinson, John, to, 581; in 2d Congress, 12, 196, 197, 276, 280; and Olive Branch Petition, 12–13, 148, 149, 150, 151; compromising conduct of, 364–65, 366–67; elected to Congress, 581
Dickinson, Brig. Gen. Philemon, 449, 450
Diriks (or Diricks), Jacob Gerhard, mentioned, 519, 520; and Dutch loan, 644, 645
Dodge, Henry, 290, 293
Dohrman, Arnold Henry, 779, 780, 790, 791
Dominica, 670
Donop, Col. Carl von, 447
Douw, Vokert P., 444–45
Drake, Gilbert, 144, 145
Drapens, Lady, 102
Drayton, William Henry, 472, 473, 642
Dred Scott v. *Sandford,* 137
Duane, James, to, 221, 269–70, 441–42, 454, 658–59; from, 264–67, 268–69, 386–88, 433, 451–52, 458–59, 491–95; from, *et al.*, to Clinton, 548–49; from, to McDougall, excerpt, 211; mentioned, 156, 191, 197, 209, 210, 230, 231, 263, 265, 266, 271, 365, 370, 374, 390, 434, 444, 491, 496, 561, 571, 584, 624, 654, 655, 788, 789, 791; and Vermont lands, 105, 493, 496, 510; lawyer, 106, 107, 109; on Committee of Fifty-One, 132; delegate to 1st Congress, 133, 135; delegate to 2d Congress, 148, 192, 386, 408, 494, 495, 496, 501; on Schuyler, 435, 496
Duane, Maria, 459, 460
Duane, Maria Livingston, 269, 454, 455, 459, 491, 495, 659
Dublin, Ireland, 820
Du Bois, Rev. Gaulterus, 31, 32
Du Bois, Henry, 289, 290, 292, 293
Du Bois, Lewis, 293
Duché, Rev. Jacob, 449, 450
Duer, Catherine Alexander, "Lady," 691, 822
Duer, William, from, 362–63, 406–08; mentioned, 367, 373, 381, 444, 469, 471, 484, 486, 492, 564, 583, 670, 671, 691, 821, 822; on Committee for Detecting Conspiracies, 331, 332, 340, 342, 407; advocates pardons for Loyalists, 362; on committee to draft N.Y. State constitution, 389; praises N.Y. government, 406; delegate to 2d Congress, 408, 485, 499
Dunlop, Lt. James, 445, 447, 594, 595
Dunmore, John Murray, Earl of, petition to, 104–05; mentioned, 105; and Vermont grants, 103, 104
Duportail, Brig. Gen. Louis Le Bégue de Presle, 576
Du Simitière, Pierre Eugène, 248
Dutchess County, N.Y., mentioned, 86, 132, 158, 160, 229, 231, 295, 314, 331, 340, 342–44, 346, 411, 434, 584, 634, 635; Beekman's Precinct, 96, 97
Dyckman, Samson, 305, 306, 378

Eagle, 295
Earnest, Matthew, 52, 53
East India Company, 129, 162
East River (N.Y.), 311
Easton, Pa., 616, 617, 622, 639
Ebenezer, Ga., 633, 634
Eden, William. *See* Carlisle, Earl of
Edinburgh, University of, Scotland, 35, 38, 40, 114
Edwards, Jonathan, 445
Edwards, Timothy, 445, 606
Egg Harbor, N.J., 237, 239, 243, 244, 257
L'Église des Refugiés, New York City, 29
Elizabeth II, Queen of England, 4–5, 264
Elizabethtown, N.J., 123, 144, 210, 212, 222, 281, 282, 294, 414–15, 417, 446, 447, 449, 534, 564, 568, 569, 572, 573, 579. *See also* Liberty Hall
Ellery, Wiliam, 582
Elliot, Andrew, 120, 370, 371, 691
Ellsworth, Oliver, 606
English Town, N.J., 485, 486
Entinck's New Spelling Dictionary. See Ciphers and Codes
Erkelens, Gosuinus, 519, 520
Escorial, 696, 758, 759
Esmond, James, 480
Esopus, N.Y., 354, 355, 412, 413, 421, 424

Estaing, Adm. Charles Hector Théodat, Comte d', 489, 490, 502, 503, 634, 645, 657, 670, 671, 725, 797–98, 799, 800, 801, 802, 804, 805, 809
Estherton, Pa., 639, 641
L'Estrange, Daniel, 70, 71
Eugene, Vt., 103, 104, 105
Ewing, Rev. John, 749, 750
Experiment, 304, 305
Eyre, Maj. Benjamin G., 638, 639, 641

Fanning, Col. Edmund, 379
"Farmer, A. W.," Samuel Seabury, 546, 547
Farrant, Henry, 104, 105
Faulkner v. *Rapalje*, 106, 107
Faulkner, William D., 107
The Federalist, mentioned, 2; JJ's No. 5, 3, 5; JJ's No. 64, 5
Fell, John, 582, 787, 789
Fellows v. *Bemus,* 110–11, 112
Ferguson, Dr. Adam, 781, 782
Ferguson, Robert, 480
Fishkill, N.Y., mentioned, 306, 314, 315, 320, 333, 337, 341–42, 344, 350, 352, 360, 393, 404, 431, 443, 448, 461, 465, 485–86, 490, 590, 691; JJ's father's wartime residence at, 7, 393, 453, 454; N.Y. Provincial Convention at, 287, 340
Fitch, Hezekiah, 297, 300, 301, 302, 303
Fitzmaurice, Patrick, from, 786–87
Flag (U.S.), 385, 386, 615, 628
Fleming, Col. Edward, 249, 252, 292, 293
Fleury, Donadieu de, from, 538–39; mentioned, 539
Fleury, Lt. Col. François Louis Teissèdre de, 538, 539
Fleury, François Teissèdre de, 539
Floridablanca, José de Moñino y Redondo, Conde de, to, 783–84, 796–97; mentioned, 722, 730, 732, 733, 742, 759, 760, 761, 772, 773, 775, 776, 780, 781, 782, 786, 798, 799, 801, 809; attitude toward U.S., 715, 716, 717–18, 738, 751, 765, 793, 804, 805, 829–30, 833–34; JJ's attitude toward, 717–18, 751, 753, 765, 804, 805, 833, 834; on navigation of Mississippi, 715, 717, 718, 824, 830–31; on Gibraltar, 649, 716, 717, 831; and loans to U.S., 716, 717, 718, 719, 732, 787, 793, 827,
Floridablanca (*cont'd*) 828, 833–34; at San Ildefonso Conference, 15, 16, 26, 825–34; and treaty with America, 829–31
Floridas, the, 314, 565–66, 650, 712, 713, 715, 759
Flotte, Marquis de la, 689, 736
Floyd, William, from, *et al.*, to George Clinton, 548–49; delegate to 2d Congress, 265, 280, 281, 387, 388, 501, 655, 658, 671
Folsom, Nathaniel, 510
Fort Albany, N.Y., 443
Fort Clinton, N.Y., mentioned, 322, 333; and loss of, 468, 486, 497, 498, 541
Fort Constitution, N.Y., 298
Fort Edward, N.Y., 419, 420, 423, 425, 426, 428–29, 434, 435
Fort Independence, N.Y., 383, 384, 385
Fort Mercer, N.J., 445, 447, 451, 452
Fort Mifflin, Pa., 448, 450, 451, 452
Fort Miller, N.Y., 440
Fort Montgomery, N.Y., mentioned, 13, 295, 296, 297, 298, 303, 322, 323, 354; loss of, 468, 486, 497, 498, 541
Fort Pitt, Pa., 172, 173
Fort Schuyler, N.Y., 589, 638
Fort Stanwix, N.Y., 439–40
Fort Ticonderoga, N.Y., mentioned, 160, 175, 176, 179, 181, 183, 185, 274, 316, 405, 409, 411, 436, 437, 443; American command at, 377, 404, 416, 418, 496; Gen. St. Clair evacuates, 418, 419, 420, 421–23, 425–31, 434; St. Clair relieved of command of, 433, 434; Congressional investigation of loss of, 472, 473, 483. *See also* Schuyler, Philip
Fort Washington, N.Y., 323, 362, 363
Fort William Henry (Fort George), N.Y., 183, 185, 408, 409, 422, 423
Foulke, Dr. John, 749, 750
Fowler, Capt. Jonathan, 338, 344
France, mentioned, 2, 12, 475, 626, 629, 649–50, 658, 765, 833, 834; American commissioners in, 270; treaties with U.S., 275, 276; Silas Deane in, 315, 316, 326, 507; aids and loans to U.S., 327, 369, 371, 385, 433–34, 507, 730, 732, 794, 827, 834; and Spain, 569–70; naval activities in America, 634, 645, 655, 656, 657, 670, 671, 725, 759, 760, 792, 799, 800, 801, 804–05, 807, 808,

France (*cont'd*)
809, 811, 813; JJ on alliance with, 651, 720, 794, 795, 826, 834. *See also* Treaties
Francies, Col. Turbot, 444–45
Franklin, Benjamin, to, 519, 644, 747–48, 793–95, 803; to, from Richard Bache, 659; from, 766–69, 797; mentioned, 3, 16, 173, 211, 232, 233, 330, 460, 519, 571; in 2d Congress, 149, 164, 276, 315; commissioner to France, 434, 476, 507, 558–59, 588, 598; and naval operations, 629–30, 767; minister to France, 649, 720, 739, 741, 742, 750, 770, 772, 774, 802, 804, 810, 815; financial aid to JJ, 718, 720, 766–67, 794, 797, 803, 809, 834
Franklin, William, governor of N.J., 11, 196, 197; and N.Y.–N.J. boundary, 119, 120
Franklin, William Temple, 768, 769
Fraunces, Samuel, 112
Fraunces Tavern, 112–13
Frederick II, King of Prussia, 326, 330
Fredericksburgh, N.Y., 338
Freehold Township, N.J., 485, 486
French, Charity, 362, 363
French, Philip, 123, 413, 414
French, Philip, Jr., 449
French and Indian War, 33, 40, 149, 185, 218, 464
Furman, Moore, 608, 609
Fyn, Frederick, 171, 172, 173

Gadsden, Christopher, 164, 244
Gage, Gen. Thomas, 62, 63, 218
Gaine, Hugh, publisher of *N.Y. Mercury*, 52, 62–63, 85, 182, 205, 275; printer to N.Y. colony, 96, 97
Galatea, 615
Galer, Christopher, 480
Galloway, Joseph, mentioned, 136; Plan of Union, 12, 136
Gálvez, Bernardo de, 702, 771, 772
Gálvez, Don José de, 716, 720, 722, 730, 732, 737, 742, 771, 774, 781, 782, 798, 802, 809
Gálvez, Matias de, 699, 702, 709
Gambier, Rear Adm. James, 539, 540
Gansevoort, Leonard, 331, 332, 337, 412–13
Gansevoort, Col. Peter, 383, 384, 440
Gardoqui, Don Diego de, 717, 718, 720, 760, 800, 802, 806, 827, 832, 833
Gardoqui, Joseph and Sons, 716, 733, 745, 789, 791
Gates, Elizabeth, 536, 537
Gates, Horatio, from, 539–40, 576–77; mentioned, 274, 293, 403, 404, 472, 474, 585, 587, 811, 825; and Schuyler, 388, 408–09, 418, 424, 425, 427, 437, 444, 496, 532, 533; and Saratoga, 435, 436, 437, 446, 447; in Northern theater, 460, 461, 471, 482, 485, 493, 576–77; and Conway Cabal, 476, 477, 498, 511, 512, 576–78; and Robert Troup, 404, 408, 409, 502, 503, 536–37, 552
General Gates, 558
Geary, Adm. Francis, 799, 800
George III, King of England, mentioned, 13, 24, 82, 150, 152, 153, 169, 171, 172, 192, 193–94, 196, 199, 200, 201, 438, 462, 792; reply to London Petition, 273, 275
Georgia, state, 276, 561, 725–26, 740
Gérard, Conrad Alexandre, to, 521, 527, 530; from 526–27, 531; mentioned, 513, 522, 659, 668, 679, 682, 683, 685, 716, 720, 730, 731, 733, 737, 739, 741, 747, 748, 752, 769, 770, 830; minister to America, 475, 488, 508, 512, 521, 525, 526–27, 530–31, 588, 644, 649, 650, 651; and Thomas Paine, 508, 512, 521, 525–27, 530–31
Germain, George Sackville, 1st Viscount Sackville, 426, 807
Germantown, Battle of, 491, 512
Gibraltar, 715, 717, 725, 774, 802, 831
Giles, Charles, 297, 298
Gillon, Alexander, from, 629–30; mentioned, 630
Glen, Cornelius, 232–33
Glentworth, Dr. George, 85, 86
Gloucester County, N.Y., 653
Goforth, William, from, 248–52; mentioned, 216, 218, 252, 291–92, 293
Goold, Edward, 114
Gordon, Lord George, 815, 820
Gordon, Patrick, 403, 405
Gordon Riots, 815, 819–20
Goshen, N.Y., 333
Governor's Island, N.Y., 311
Graham, Rev. Chauncey, 305, 306
Graham, Lewis, 347, 349
Graham, William, 167, 168

Grand, Ferdinand, 748, 766, 767, 803
Grant, Gen. James, 312, 314
Grant, Lt. Col. James, 312, 314
Grantham, Thomas Robinson, 2d Baron, 752
Grasse, Adm. François Joseph Paul, Comte de, 670, 671
Graves, Adm. Thomas, 813
Gray's Ferry, N.J., 445
Great Britain, mentioned, 2, 13, 133, 136, 138, 147, 150, 153, 154, 156, 158, 159, 162, 164, 168–71, 179, 198, 204, 242, 264, 266, 267, 268, 269, 273, 274, 275, 332, 346, 347, 356, 404, 439, 443, 447, 448, 450, 502, 545, 551, 565, 566–67, 600, 615, 626, 649, 650, 651, 765, 766, 769, 826; Empire, 2, 152, 154, 155, 156, 169; colonial policy, 11, 38, 103, 107, 118, 120, 131, 148, 169, 170, 194, 273, 274–75; JJ on, 14, 87, 136, 137, 143, 152–54, 172, 193, 198–99; forces in America, 175, 208, 215, 216, 260, 277, 278, 282, 363–64, 372, 378–464, *passim,* 572, 573, 579; and conciliation, 472, 473, 547. *See also* Carlisle Peace Commission, 2d Continental Congress, Parliament
Green Mountain Boys, 249, 273
Greene, Col. Christopher, 451, 452
Greene, Gen. Nathanael, to, from Washington, 279, to, from Thomas Chase, 613; from, 533–34, 542–43, 607–08, 611–13, 637–41, from, to Washington, 280; mentioned, 308, 309, 314, 360, 533–34, 542–43, 612
Gregory, 3d Lt. Stephen, 667, 668
Grenell, Thomas, 202
Greyhound, 410
Gross, 1st Lt. Simon, 667, 668
Guichen, Adm. Luc Urbain de Bouëxic, Comte de, 799
Gurney, Francis, 567, 569

Haddonfield, N.J., 372, 413
Hake, Helen Livingston, 551
Hake, Samuel, 550–51, 557–58
Halifax, Earl of, 38, 51
Halifax, Canada, 143, 295, 539, 540
Hallet, Joseph, 233, 234
Hamilton, Alexander, 3, 9, 145, 188, 189, 194, 379, 414, 415, 424, 537, 593, 670, 671, 728
Hamilton, Elizabeth De Peyster, will of, 67–70
Hancock, John, to, from N.Y. Provincial Convention, 289–92; President of Congress, 151, 209, 248, 293, 294, 321, 429
Hand, Edward, 616
Harding, Capt. Seth, to, 668, 674–75; from, 674; mentioned, 651, 741, 759
Haring, John, 272
Harison, Richard, 63, 85, 86, 113, 114
Harlem, N.Y., 310, 314, 421
Harlem Heights, Battle of, 323
Harnett, Cornelius, 514
Harpur, Robert, 431, 432
Harrington, James, 390, 391
Harris, Capt. Peter, 181, 182
Harrison, Benjamin, 151, 197, 369–70, 371, 641, 642
Harrison, Richard, 731, 732, 758, 762, 773, 786, 797
Harrison's Purchase, N.Y., 319
Hart, James, 480
Hartford, Conn., 119
Hartwig (or Hartwick), Rev. Johannes Christopher, 484, 485
Havana, Cuba, 712, 713, 740, 759, 825
Hawley, Maj. Joseph, 444–45
Hay, Col. A. Hawkes, 420
Hay, John, 113
Hayes, James, 667, 668
Hays, Judah, 43, 52
Hazard, Capt. John, 203, 204
Hazen, Col. Moses, 251, 252
Heath, Gen. William, 313, 314, 362, 363, 540–41, 577
Henry, Patrick, mentioned, 266, 267, 642; and JJ, 12, 136; in Congress, 136, 267
Hepburn v. *Griswold,* 137
Herkimer, Gen. Nicholas, 442
Hewes, Joseph, 697, 698
Hickey Plot, 277–80, 287
Hickey, Pvt. Thomas, 277–78
Hills, The, 460, 461, 821, 822
Hobart, John Sloss, mentioned, 395, 397, 401, 481; in N.Y. Provincial Congress, 204, 206, 208, 393, 394; justice of N.Y. Supreme Court, 411, 546, 547
Hoffman, Nicholas, 228, 229
Holland, Henry, 63
Holland. *See* Netherlands

Holt, John, mentioned, 498–99; publisher of *N.Y. Journal,* 428, 429, 430, 432, 434, 461
Holten, Samuel, 636, 787, 789
Honeywell, Gilial, 87
Hooghkirk, Lt. John, 532, 533
Hooper, Robert Lettis, Jr., 639, 641
Hooper, William, 212, 213, 369–70, 371
Hopkins, Commo. Esek, 244
Hopkins, Jonathan, 340
Hopkins, Stephen, 247
Hopkinson, Francis, 426, 447
Horace, 593, 594
Hortalez & Cie., 507
Hôtel Valentinois, Paris, 631
Houston, William Churchill, from 725–27; mentioned, 669, 790
Howe, Vice Adm. Viscount Richard, mentioned, 295, 315, 373, 451, 476; and naval engagements, 323, 489, 490; prescribes oath of allegiance, 354, 373
Howe, Gen. Sir William, mentioned, 215, 218, 295, 317, 347, 357, 375, 386, 447, 476; and military actions, 323, 360, 451; and prisoner exchanges, 325, 370; prescribes oath of allegiance, 354; proclamation of pardon, 373; and maneuvers, 415, 416, 425–26, 433, 434, 437
Hubbard, Elijah, 604
Hudson, 297
Hudson River, mentioned, 104, 105, 174, 175, 176, 179, 274, 287, 288, 346, 485; defense of, 13, 24, 295, 296, 298, 299, 300, 322, 324, 380, 417, 419, 426, 435, 452–53, 454, 460, 461, 469, 471, 472, 554
Hughes, Adm. Sir Richard, 539, 540
Hulbert, John, 372
Humphreys, Whitehead, 642
Hunt, Davis, 299
Hunter, Elijah, 578–79, 627
Huntington, Benjamin, 303
Huntington, Samuel, to, 672–73, 761, 825–34; mentioned, 636, 663, 665, 668; President of Congress, 15, 675, 719, 720, 722, 723, 761
Hurley, N.Y., 344, 354, 359
Hussey, Father Thomas, 773, 774
Hussey-Cumberland mission. *See* Cumberland, Richard

Imlay, William, 114
Indiana, 635–36
Indians, mentioned, 48, 50, 183, 250, 270–71, 422, 589–90; Continental Congress Indian Commission, 173, 211, 418, 441, 442, 444; Six Nations, 435, 436, 440, 441–42, 444, 532, 573, 574–75; and Sullivan campaign, 590, 615–19, 621–23, 637–41, 659; land claims of, 659–60, 820
Inglis, Rev. Charles, 85, 86
Ireland, mentioned, 111, 150, 162, 260, 327, 554, 787, 818, 819; American Revolutionary sentiment in, 816, 820
Iselin, Mrs. Arthur, 3, 5
Izard, Alice De Lancey, 793, 808
Izard, Ralph, 630, 631, 793

Jackson, Andrew, 2
Jackson, Dr. David, 376
Jamaica, Island of, 327, 565, 566
Jauncey, James, Jr., 370, 371, 372
Jay, 690, 691
Jay, Ann Margaret Barclay, 125, 233, 319, 443, 555, 556, 591, 610, 637, 685, 689
Jay, Anna Maria Bayard, 29, 30, 31, 32
Jay, Anna Maricka, JJ's sister, 31, 32, 33, 124–25, 529, 689, 698, 709
Jay, Augustus (or Auguste), JJ's grandfather, mentioned, 31, 32; background, 29–30
Jay, Augustus, JJ's brother, 31, 32, 33, 35, 36, 234, 635
Jay, Frederick, 5th son of Peter and Mary Van Cortlandt Jay, 31–32
Jay, Frederick, JJ's brother, from, 97–98, 99–100, 101–02, 144–45, 233–34, 309–10, 318, 528–29, 590, 610–11, 634–35, 637; mentioned, 35, 36, 42, 43, 47, 48, 53, 81, 115, 125, 146, 147, 205, 236, 257, 288, 380, 445, 527, 546, 555, 556, 624, 631, 636, 655, 661, 662, 670, 685, 702; birth and baptism, 32, 33; apprenticeship, 39, 40, 44, 45, 46; in N.Y. Assembly, 528
Jay, Jacobus, 2d son of Peter and Mary Van Cortlandt Jay, 31, 32
Jay, Sir James, to, from Peter Jay, 34–35, 44, 45, 631–32, 642; mentioned, 33–34, 36–37, 39, 43, 46, 47, 70, 100, 102, 138, 233, 234, 236, 326, 487, 497, 527, 528, 546, 590, 610,

Jay, Sir James (*cont'd*)
628, 635, 637, 688, 702, 773; birth and baptism, 31, 32; medical student in Britain, 34–35, 36–38, 40; medical practice in N.Y. City, 39, 40; returns to England, 39, 40; fund-raising for King's College and controversy, 48, 73, 74, 101, 106, 236, 750; and JJ's law apprenticeship, 45, 50; medical practice in London, 138; knighted, 48, 49, 73; invents invisible ink, 195, 316; and Gouverneur Morris, 488; tool of Lee faction, 507–08, 571, 572; in N.Y. State Senate, 528, 571, 572

Jay, John, papers of, 1–10; will of, 3; a biographical sketch of, 10–16; character of, 2, 8, 10–11, 46, 55, 106, 108–09, 113, 116, 117, 118, 120, 123, 124, 134, 135, 139; chronology, 23–26; parentage, 11, 15, 29–30, 34; childhood, 23, 32–37, 167; college career, 3, 10, 23, 39, 40, 41, 44, 45, 46, 48, 49, 51, 52, 53, 54, 55–61, 62–64, 85; and a church dispute, 41–42; law studies and clerkship, 23, 43, 44, 51–52, 53, 62, 67–70, 81–84; friendship with Robert R. Livingston, Jr., 71–72, 74–77, 77–79, 79–81, 138–39, 209, 219, 222, 223, 226, 227, 229–30, 231–33, 276–77, 556–58, 570–71, 757–59, 810; and Sir James, 73, 74, 138, 144, 195, 487–88, 497, 507–08, 571, 572; in Moot, 81, 86, 87, 111; in debating society, 87–95; law license, 23, 95; law practice, 8, 10, 86, 87, 106–09, 110–12, 118, 130–31, 136, 137, 145, 161, 167, 177, 178, 278; law papers, 7, 8; partnership, 8, 23, 71, 86, 132; judgeship bid, 11, 129, 130–31, 132–33; on law, 131, 136–37; confrontation with John Tabor Kempe, 106–09; in Social Club, 81, 112–14; in Dancing Assembly, 11, 116–18; petition for land in Vermont, 11, 25, 102, 103, 104–05; and N.Y.–N.J. Boundary Commission, 9, 10–11, 23, 118–22; marriage, 12, 23, 123–24; and early activism, 129–33; in 1st Congress, 11, 12, 23, 133, 134, 135–37; and N.Y. provisional government, 23, 24, 141–45; in 2d Congress, 12, 13, 23, 24, 25, 146–263; anti-Catholicism, 15, 147;

Jay, John (*cont'd*)
draft of "Olive Branch Petition," 12, 149, 150–51, 152–54; militia commission, 24, 180, 195; and continentalism, 13, 194–97; elected to N.Y. Provincial Congress, 227, 229, 263, 269; on taxes, 195, 213, 245, 257, 262; and state governments, 196, 254; attitude toward independence, 12–13, 14, 24, 196, 198–200, 263–64, 269–70, 281, 287; on popular sovereignty, 253; and Hickey Plot, 277–80, 287; supports Washington, 247–48, 287–88, 289, 511, 585–87; military activities, 288, 295–306, 362–63, 377, 511–12, 518, 532–43, 569, 576–77; detecting conspiracies, 14, 277, 287, 331–59, 362–63, 373–74; and Loyalists, 331–44, 347–59, 362–63, 373–74, 470, 478–79; and N.Y. State Constitution of 1777, 14–15, 24, 263, 272, 389–404, 406–08, 420–21; disavowed interest in governorship, 405, 411, 412–13; and Northern Command, 418, 419, 421–37, 439–40, 444–47, 460, 461, 463–65, 471; N.Y. State Chief Justice, 2, 14, 25, 394, 405, 475, 476, 478–81, 546, 624, 625, 636, 637; Presidency of Congress, 2, 15, 25, 113, 507–645; mission to Spain, 2, 15, 16, 25, 113, 649–52, 715–835; on U.S. expansionism, 721, 766; use of ciphers and codes, 15, 661–66, 734, 736–37, 787, 810, 812, 813, 821; on recognition of U.S., 765, 804; on U.S. self-reliance, 766, 824, 834; relations with Carmichael, 15, 16, 769–83; in San Ildefonso Conference, 10, 15, 16, 26, 824–35; later career, 2, 3, 6, 8, 14, 16, 113, 137; Homestead, 6, 8. *See also* Loyalists, Loyalty oaths

Jay, John, II, JJ's grandson, 4, 5

Jay, John, III, 7

Jay, Judith, 31, 32

Jay, Mary, 3d daughter of Peter and Mary Van Cortlandt Jay, 32, 33, 34, 36

Jay, Mary Anna Van Cortlandt, JJ's mother, mentioned, 11, 35, 39, 64, 145, 146, 205, 232, 233, 294, 318, 319, 320; marriage, 30, 31; family, 31–34; health of, 35, 38, 125, 263, 271, 380, 381; JJ concerned about

Jay, Mary (*cont'd*)
her welfare, 288, 382; death of, 383, 407
Jay, Pierre, JJ's great-grandfather, 29
Jay, Peter, JJ's father, to, 698–702, to, from Samuel Johnson, 40, to, from David Peloquin, 47–48, to, from SLJ, 687–89; from, 42–43, 48, 49, 51–52, 53, 64, 70, 74, 146–47, 205, 236, 259–60, 642–43; from, to JJ and James, 631–32; from, to James, 34–35, 44, 45; from, to David and John Peloquin, 36–37, to David Peloquin, 46–47, 50–51, 60, 62; mentioned, 11, 36, 38, 39, 40, 43, 46, 52, 53, 55, 62, 98, 99, 144, 145, 167, 236, 260, 294, 318, 443, 445, 490, 502, 528, 611, 636, 685, 686, 692, 704; background and training, 30; marriage, 30, 31; family, 31–34; move to Rye, N.Y., 33; on JJ, 35, 36–37, 46; and church dispute, 40–42; on JJ's legal studies, 43–44, 45, 46, 50; illnesses of his servants, 70; letters on behalf of Sir James, 73, 74; on JJ's marriage, 124; on reconciliation with England, 205; health of, 232, 233, 236, 263, 271, 319, 380, 465; JJ's concern for welfare of, 288, 382; residence in Fishkill, N.Y., 320, 453, 454
Jay, Peter, JJ's brother, 31, 32, 33, 42, 43, 124–25, 145, 205, 381, 382, 631, 637, 687, 689, 702
Jay, Peter Augustus, 1st child of JJ and SLJ, mentioned, 233, 234, 246, 294, 307, 319, 320, 375, 380, 381, 384, 413, 414, 438, 443, 467, 490, 502, 518, 521, 555, 560, 561, 563, 567, 683, 685, 693, 698, 709, 711, 712, 787, 810; birth of, 223, 226; inoculation of, 446, 447, 448; left in care of SLJ's family, 683–84, 686; and John Jay Papers, 3, 4, 5
Jay, Sarah Livingston, to, 145–46, 154, 166–68, 172–73, 187, 212–13, 246, 294, 305–07, 382–83, 414–15, 417, 534, 578; to, from Washington, 656–57; to, from family, 675–78, 689–91; from, 379–81, 413–14, 415–16, 442–43, 516–18, 520–21, 554–55, 560–61, 572–73; from, to family, 124–25, 437–38, 466–67 (with JJ), 680–86, 692–93, 694–98, 704–12; to Peter Jay, 687–89; mentioned, 129,
Jay, Sarah (*cont'd*)
139, 146–47, 156, 205, 211, 236, 239, 256, 265, 267, 272, 287, 318, 319, 320, 350, 372, 376, 378, 379, 384, 409, 415, 417, 421, 423, 425, 433, 458, 459, 473, 488, 490, 495, 497, 502, 517, 520–21, 529, 563–821 *passim;* Letterbook, 3, 7; marriage, 12, 23, 123, 124; character, 123; health of, 187, 228, 230, 231, 233, 246, 263, 264, 265, 270, 271, 273; birth of son, 223; trip to and stay in Spain, 680–86, 687–89, 692–93, 694–98, 704–05, 705–08, 709–12; birth and death of daughter, *see* Jay, Susan
Jay, Susan, 2d child of JJ and SLJ, birth of, 703, 709, 791, 793, 795, 797; death of, 710, 798, 799, 803
Jay, William, 2d son of JJ and SLJ, *The Life of John Jay*, 2, 4, 55; and John Jay Papers, 3, 4; on JJ and the Olive Branch Petition, 149; on JJ and the N.Y. State constitution of 1777, 389
Jay House, Rye, N.Y., 5, 6, 124, 212
Jay Treaty, 1794, 4, 8
Jefferson, Thomas, mentioned, 1, 3, 9, 137, 151, 390, 538, 641, 642; on JJ's "Address to the People of Great Britain," 136; in 2d Congress, 221, 276
John the Painter (James Aitken), 820
Johnson, Joshua, 747, 748
Johnson, Rev. Samuel, from, 49–50; from, to Peter Jay, 40; mentioned, 34, 42, 43, 48, 49, 55, 73; tutored Augustus Jay, 33; President of King's College, 40–41, 48; and church dispute, 41, 42; requests letter from JJ, 48
Johnson, Thomas, Jr., from, 374–75; mentioned, 370, 371; in 2d Congress, 149, 197, 369–70, 371, 748
Johnson, Sir William, 183, 195
Johnstone, George, 476, 487
Jones, John Paul, 600, 615, 630–31
Jones, Samuel, 161
Jones, Thomas, on JJ's marriage, 123
"Jones, Timothy," name used by Silas Deane, 369, 371
"Joyce, Junior," 407, 408
Joyces, Gregorio, 762

Kalb, Gen. Johann, Baron de, 811, 813
Katonah, N.Y., 6
Kaunitz-Rietberg, Joseph, Count von, 752, 775, 776, 802
Kaunitz-Rietberg, Wenzel Anton Dominick, Prince von, 752
Kelly, Henry, 114
Kempe, John Tabor, to, 106–07, 108–09; from, 107–08; confrontation with JJ, 11, 106–09; and *King* v. *Underhill*, 87; and Vermont lands, 104, 105; and King's College, 106
Kent, Conn., 447
Keppel, Viscount August, 489, 490, 502, 503
Ketchum, Isaac, 277, 278
Keteltas, Rev. Abraham, 228, 229
Kinderhook, N.Y., 332, 481
Kinderhook Patent, 122
King v. *Underhill*, 87
King George's War, 2, 33
King's Bridge, N.Y., 309, 313, 314, 318, 338, 489
King's College, mentioned, 3, 7, 10, 23, 39, 40, 41, 48, 49, 50, 52, 53, 55, 62, 71, 73, 74, 81, 84, 85, 86, 87, 99, 114, 118, 132, 144, 145, 147, 236, 240, 331, 819; demonstration at, 10, 23, 55; bill of fare, 54; statutes of, 55–60; salaries of instructors, 61; commencement, 1764, 23, 62–63, 64; 1767, 85–86; fundraising for, 48, 73, 750; governors and Sir James Jay, 48, 73, 74, 101, 106, 236, 750
King's County, N.Y., 214, 218
Kingston, N.Y., 25, 287, 297, 332, 354, 357, 411, 429, 443, 445, 454, 460, 478, 479
Kipp, Lt. James, 338, 344
Kirkland, Samuel, 440
Kissam, Benjamin, from, 81–82, 82–84; mentioned, 53, 62, 64, 67, 82, 99, 118; and JJ clerkship agreement, 51–52; law practice of, 67, 68, 83–84; opinion on will of Elizabeth Hamilton, 68–69; relationship with JJ, 81–84; in debating society, 88, 91, 92, 93
Kissam, Catherine Rutgers, 84
Kissam, Samuel, from, 114–15, 178–79; mentioned, 98, 99, 116; on JJ, 178
Knox, Gen. Henry, 555, 556, 563
Knyphausen, Wilhelm, Baron von, 726, 727, 812, 813
Korpinder, Jacob, 480

Lacy, Francisco, Conde de, 802, 809
Lafayette, Marie Joseph Paul Yves Roch Gilbert du Motier, Marquis de, to, 518, 643–44; from 597–600; mentioned, 3, 465, 598, 600, 601, 813; commissioned major general, 464; proposed invasion of Canada of, 463, 464, 511, 518; affection for America, 597–600
Lagoanère, Michel, 745, 746
Laight, William, from, 168–70; mentioned, 85, 86, 137, 138; on JJ, 141, 142; on English attitudes toward America, 168–70
Laiske, Terrier de, to, 673; from, 673
Lake Champlain, N.Y., 176, 177, 185, 323, 417, 422
Lake George, N.Y., 175, 185, 422
Lake Oneida, N.Y., 440
La Luzerne, Anne-César, Chevalier de, 598, 599, 600, 644, 670
Lamb, John, 190, 191, 591
La Motte Piquet, Adm. Touissant Guillaume, Comte de, 685, 689, 705
Lancaster, Pa., 619, 620
Landais, Capt. Pierre, 630–31
Landon, Woodbury, 644
Lane, Henry, Jr., 37, 38
Langdon, John, 185
Langworthy, Edward, 642
La Rochelle, France, 29
Lattouche, Isaac, 37, 38
Lattouche, Jeremiah, 38
Laurance, Elizabeth McDougall, 325
Laurance, John, 324, 325
Laurence, Augustine, 296
Laurens, Henry, mentioned, 470, 475, 507, 579, 580, 582, 644–45, 669, 716, 763, 764, 768, 779, 790, 792, 803, 807; President of Congress, 507; disclosures to Thomas Paine, 526; accuses Robert Morris, 556; commissioner to the Netherlands, 649, 740
Laurens, Col. John, 651, 652, 670, 671, 713, 728
Law, William, 545
Lawrence, John, 674, 675
Lawrence, Jonathan, 202, 501
Lawrence, Mary, 569

Lawrence, Mary Morris, 172, 173, 294, 295, 568–69
Lawrence, Richard, 226
Lawrence, Thomas, Jr., 173, 294, 295, 315
Lawrence, Thomas John, 295
League of Armed Neutrality, 763, 764, 769, 816, 820
Lebanon, Conn., 300, 301, 303
Lee, Arthur, to, 713–14; from, 744–46; mentioned, 150, 197, 475, 572, 588, 649, 663, 716, 717, 733, 745, 747, 748, 770; on prospects of French loan, 434; dispute with Silas Deane, 487–88, 507, 514, 515, 546; commissioner to France, 507
Lee, Gen. Charles, from, 564–66; mentioned, 184, 185, 234, 240, 313, 314, 325, 372, 469, 537; and loyalty oaths, 196, 236, 237; in Southern theater, 235; military engagements, 304, 305, 324, 485, 486; court-martial of, 486, 490, 491, 529; financial problems of, 564–66
Lee, Richard Henry, mentioned, 546, 587, 588; resolution in Congress affirming independence, 13, 263, 275, 276; in Continental Congress, 136, 163, 164, 197, 265, 369–70, 371, 407, 408; and Conway Cabal, 514, 515
Lee, Sidney, 566, 567
Lee, William, 572, 588, 628–29, 764
Legget, Isaac, 87
Leslie, Brig. Gen. Alexander, 565, 567
Lester, Mordecai, 158, 160
"Letter to the Oppressed Inhabitants of Canada (JJ), 12, 24
Lewis, Col. Benjamin, 770
Lewis, Francis, 114
Lewis, Francis, Jr., from (*et al*), 548–49; mentioned, 113, 114, 315, 606; member of Committee of Fifty-One, 129; in 2d Congress, 172, 173, 212, 226, 271, 280, 452, 501; quartermaster at Albany, N.Y., 484, 485
Lewis, Morgan, 113, 114, 584
Lexington and Concord, Battle of, 132, 145
Leyden University, the Netherlands, 819
L'Hommedieu, Ezra, 655, 658
Liberty Hall, Elizabethtown, N.J., mentioned, 123, 124, 265, 294, 306, 307, 318, 446, 447, 449, 568, 569;
Liberty Hall (*cont'd*)
British raids on, 572, 573, 579, 788, 789
Lincoln, Maj. Gen. Benjamin, from, 633–34; mentioned, 436, 437, 725, 807
Lisbon, Portugal, 790
Lispenard, Anthony, 113, 114
Lispenard, Leonard, 113, 114, 133
Litchfield, Conn., 41, 278
Littlepage, Lewis, 15–16, 769, 770, 771
Liverpool, England, 326, 439
Livingston, Abraham, 258, 259
Livingston, Catharine Wilhelmina, to, 320, 567–69; to, from SLJ, 692–93, 696–98; to, excerpt from Gouverneur Morris, 123–24; from, 448–50, 563–64; from, to SLJ, 689–91; mentioned, 124, 125, 167, 288, 305, 378, 379, 380–81, 382, 409, 414, 443, 447, 518, 520, 534, 555, 560, 561, 567, 573, 594, 628, 661, 662, 664, 665, 671, 686, 696, 704, 709, 711, 771, 788, 789, 821
Livingston, Catherine De Peyster, 32, 33, 53
Livingston, Edward, 558
Livingston, Elizabeth, 748
Livingston, Elizabeth Stevens, 788, 789, 810
Livingston, Gertrude, 584
Livingston, Gilbert, and committee on the defense of the Hudson, to, from JJ, 301–03; from, to Washington, 298–99; in N.Y. government, 202, 295, 296, 298, 299, 300
Livingston, Hendrick, 113, 114, 124
Livingston, Henry, 301
Livingston, Henry Beekman, from, 220–21; mentioned, 191, 192, 209, 210, 221, 223, 228, 230, 31; in military service, 159, 160, 184, 185, 240, 324, 325, 372, 377, 378, 379; resigns commission, 532, 533
Livingston, Henry Brockholst, to, from SLJ, 437–38; from, 421–23; from, to Susannah French Livingston, 678–80; mentioned, 15, 144, 145, 320, 449, 518, 519, 520, 521, 534, 537, 552, 555, 560, 563, 564, 567, 573, 578, 594, 628, 661, 664, 671, 677, 683, 685, 686, 711, 731, 733, 741, 742, 743, 744, 764, 769, 770, 771, 772, 774, 776, 782, 786, 787, 788, 799, 800, 802, 809, 813; in military

Livingston, Henry (*cont'd*) service, 321, 446, 447; in duel, 449, 450; accompanies Jays to Spain, 651, 678–80; on life in Spain, 693, 698
Livingston, Henry Gilbert, from, 373; mentioned, 373
Livingston, James, 277
Livingston, John, 32, 33, 53
Livingston, John, from Manor, 113, 114
Livingston, John Henry, 404, 405
Livingston, John Lawrence, 446, 447, 560, 561, 679, 696, 821, 822
Livingston, John R., mentioned, 219, 220, 221, 222, 228, 229, 230, 231, 551; in 4th N.Y. Regiment, 159, 160
Livingston, John William, 141
Livingston, Judith, 560, 561
Livingston, Margaret Beekman, 558, 737, 759
Livingston, Mary Stevens, 139, 140, 219, 229, 231, 232, 691, 737
Livingston, Peter Van Brugh, 155, 156, 748
Livingston Philip, 2d Lord of Manor, 71, 123
Livingston, Philip, Jr., mentioned, 95, 96, 112, 310; in 2d Congress, 133, 135, 158, 172, 173, 209, 210, 221, 386, 408; in N.Y. Provincial Congress, 277, 278, 279, 282; death of, 484, 485, 491, 496
Livingston, Robert I, 71
Livingston, Robert, of Clermont, 71, 81, 159, 160
Livingston, Robert, 3d Lord of Manor, mentioned, 114, 159, 160, 186, 454, 458, 459, 558; operator of ironworks and foundry, 300–01, 302
Livingston, Robert R., Jr., to, 71–72, 74–77, 77–79, 79–81, 96, 138–39, 209, 222–23, 229–33, 271, 276–77, 281–82, 397–402, 556–58, 575, 651–52, 665–66, 672, 735–37, 757–59; to, from Duane, 386–88; and committee to fortify the Hudson, to, from JJ, 301–03; from, to Washington, 298–99; from, 158–60, 182–84, 190–91, 218–19, 226–29, 282–83, 303–04, 395–96, 499, 549–51, 570–71, 583–84, 669–71, 787–89, 809–13; mentioned, 15, 72, 77, 81, 97, 98, 99, 113, 116, 131, 157, 220, 231, 264, 271, 272, 277, 278, 281, 288,
Livingston, Robert (*cont'd*) 370, 389, 402, 403, 433, 434, 464, 469, 471, 472, 477, 482, 484, 493, 494, 499, 500, 516, 527, 528, 557, 637, 691, 720, 789, 822; judgeship bid, 11, 130–31, 132–33; law partnership with JJ, 8, 23, 71, 86, 132; friendship with JJ, 71–72, 74–77, 77–79, 138–39, 219, 222, 223, 226, 227, 229–30, 231–33, 757–59, 810; in 2d Congress, 158, 160, 228, 265, 266, 267, 273, 274, 276, 668, 669; on Canada campaign, 182–84, 190–91, 192; death of his father, 218–19; health of, 227, 228, 229, 231–32, 499; in N.Y. government, 277, 283, 295, 296, 298, 299, 389, 390, 393, 394; N.Y. State Chancellor, 500, 501, 546, 547, 624, 634, 635; on politics, 550, 570; interest in diplomatic assignment, 550, 571, 572; personal characteristics, 500, 556–58, 570–71, 575; and ciphers and codes, 661, 662, 663, 664, 665, 666, 669, 736–37, 787, 810, 812
Livingston, Robert R., Sr., 110, 112, 125, 159, 160, 181, 182, 209, 210, 218–19, 220, 227, 228, 229, 277
Livingston, Susan, 748
Livingston, Susannah, to, 466–67; to, from SLJ, 692–93, 704–09; from, to SLJ, 445–47; mentioned, 167, 381, 414, 437, 443, 555, 560, 678, 691, 696, 787, 788; and raid on Liberty Hall, 572, 573
Livingston, Susannah French, to, from SLJ, 124–25, 680–86, 709–12; to, from Brockholst Livingston, 678–80; from, to SLJ, 676; mentioned, 123, 166, 167, 187, 346, 414, 415, 417, 443, 445, 446, 449, 450, 563, 690, 693, 704, 787, 788, 810; health of, 288, 560, 568
Livingston, Walter, to, from N.Y. Congressional delegation, 258–59; mentioned, 184–85, 186, 259, 696–98
Livingston, Gov. William, to, 703–04; from, 375; from, to SLJ, 675–76; mentioned, 11, 71, 123–24, 129, 166–67, 220, 229, 265, 288, 372, 378, 379, 413, 414, 443, 444, 445, 448, 467, 518, 520, 534, 560, 659, 689, 690, 692, 696, 705, 711, 712, 726; in N.Y. politics, 123; in 1st and 2d Con-

Livingston, Gov. (*cont'd*)
gresses, 135, 136, 167, 212; use of home for military purposes, 446, 447, 449; raid on home of, 572, 573
Livingston, William, Jr., from, to SLJ, 676–78; mentioned, 449, 560, 679, 693, 696
Livingston Manor, 13, 71, 112, 123, 186, 302, 455, 501
Locke, John, 390, 391
London, England, mentioned, 787, 814, 819, 820; attitudes toward America, 168–69; Lord Mayor and Livery of, 169, 171, 200; Address and Petition of the City of, 273, 274–75
Long Island, N.Y., mentioned, 114, 215, 218, 241, 318, 335, 347, 348, 354, 378, 489, 564, 594; Battle of, 295, 296, 310–13, 314, 315, 323, 373, 594, 807
Loockermans, Govert, 29
Loudon, Samuel, publisher of *New York Packet,* 430, 431, 446; mentioned, 360, 361, 445, 450, 514
Louis XVI, King of France, 328, 521, 530, 531, 753
Lovell, James, from, 789–90; mentioned, 609, 663–64, 669, 670, 671, 713, 714, 728, 729, 740, 741, 745; and ciphers, 469, 663–64
Low, Isaac, on N.Y. Committee of Fifty-One, 129, 132; election as Congressional delegate, 133, 134
Loyalists, mentioned, 158, 159, 192, 195, 196, 204, 206, 218, 241, 242, 243, 245, 251, 256, 260, 277, 346, 347, 363, 379, 424, 432, 475, 479, 481, 486, 594, 619, 642–43, 691, 812; view of JJ, 12, 141, 142, 241; investigation of alleged conspiracies by, 331–37, 338–44, 345–46, 347–48, 349–51, 352–59, 448, 450, 486; and forfeiture and confiscation, 593, 594, 605
Loyalty oaths, imposed by the military, 196, 235, 236, 237, 243; JJ on, 196, 235, 242; to the States and Congress, 332–33, 348, 349, 350, 351, 363, 373, 401; to the Crown, 353, 354, 373
Lubeken, Albert Minert, 104, 105
Ludington, Col. Henry, 343–44, 345
Ludlow, Daniel, 113, 114
Ludlow, George, 113, 114, 182
Ludlow, George Duncan, 114, 182
Ludlow, William, 113, 114, 181, 182
Lush, Maj. Stephen, 562, 563
Lynch, Michael, 277, 278
Lynch, Thomas, 148, 197, 220, 221, 232, 233, 265
Lynch, Thomas, Jr., 264, 265, 270

McCord, John, Jr., 249, 252
McDougall, Alexander, to, 171–72, 173, 188, 201–02, 210–11, 213, 235, 241–45, 253–54, 262–63, 581; to, from Duane, excerpt, 211; from, 174–76, 179–80, 181–82, 186–87, 193–94, 202–03, 205–08, 214–17, 224, 234–35, 237–39, 240, 256–57, 324–25, 377, 578–79; mentioned, 13, 15, 132, 163, 164, 182, 187, 193, 194, 195, 197, 202, 218, 236, 239, 244, 262, 277, 278, 293, 325, 373–74, 627, 726; early activism, 132–33, 142, 144; military appointments, 172, 314, 474, 475; on N.Y. warfront, 174, 175, 179, 180, 181, 182, 203, 207; on St. Johns' surrender, 186–87; in 2d Provincial Congress, N.Y., 204, 206, 218; on Canada, 207–08; on naval force, 216–17, 224, 225–26, 235; on military commissions, 237–39, 243–44; on taxation, 257, 262; JJ on, 262–63; in military engagements, 311, 381, 383–84
McDougall, 1st Lt. John, 203, 204, 324, 325
McDougall, Capt. Ronald, 324, 325
McKean, Thomas, 197, 609, 636
McKesson, John, from, 553–54; mentioned, 107, 395, 473, 474, 546; in N.Y. government, 393, 394, 421, 547
McPherson, James, 50
Maclean, Col. Allan, 185
Madison, James, 1, 9, 510, 835
Magaw, Col. Robert, 236
Magra, Dr. James, 35, 36
Malcolm, Col. William, 622, 623
Mamaroneck, N.Y., 324
Marie Antoinette, Queen of France, 327
Marr, John, 615
Martinique, 25, 503, 548, 558–59, 670, 672, 689, 704, 735–36, 784; Jays at St. Pierre, 685–86, 687, 688, 735–36
Maryland, colony, 152; state, mentioned, 283, 371, 374, 485, 509, 549, 774; Provincial Convention, 266, 267, 268, 269, 270; Congressional

Maryland (*cont'd*)
delegation, 268, 269, 370; and states' western lands, 508
Mason, George, 628–29
Mason, William, 555, 556
Massachusetts, colony, 111; state, mentioned, 147, 152, 199, 437, 444, 445, 471, 472, 477, 538, 556, 820; constitution of, 137; militia of, 362, 377, 576; General Court of, 613, 614; Convention troops at, 620; and Vermont, 652, 656, 792. *See also* Boston, Mass.
Masserano, Charlotte Louise, Princess de, 773, 774, 775
Masserano, Felípe Ferrero de Fiesco, Prince de, 774–75, 801
Matlack, Timothy, from, 749–50
Matthews, David, 141
Matthews, David, Mayor of N.Y. City, 278, 279, 280
Maxwell, Brig. Gen. William, 417, 418
Mease, James, 476, 477
Mercury, 530–31
Meredith, Margaret Cadwalader, to, 753–56; mentioned, 756
Meredith, Samuel, 756
Merkle, Johann Philip, 270, 275
Merlin, 447
Midagh, Jacob, 356
Middlebrook, N.J., 582, 593
Middlesex County, England, Freeholders of, 169, 171
Mifflin, Maj. Gen. Thomas, mentioned, 274, 283; and Conway Cabal, 512, 515–16
Miller, Thomas, 318
Milton, John, 390
Minisink Patent, 119
Miralles, Don Juan de, 649, 697, 712, 713, 730, 755, 759, 830, 832, 835
Mississippi River, mentioned, 549, 565–66; 728; navigation of, 650, 715, 717, 718, 830–31, 834
Mitchell, Lt. Col. David, 640, 641
Mobile, Ala., 772, 813, 831
Monaghan, Frank, and Jay Papers, 5, 6, 7; on JJ and Olive Branch Petition, 149
Monier, John, 105
Monmouth, Battle of, 485, 486, 491
Monmouth County, N.J., 486
Montagnie's Tavern, N.Y. City, 141
Montcalm, Gen. Louis Joseph de, 185
Montgomerie, 258
Montgomerie Charter, 43
Montgomery, Janet Livingston, 220, 221, 223
Montgomery, Brig. Gen. Richard, mentioned, 227, 229, 252, 293, 585; in Canadian campaign, 183, 184, 185, 186, 190, 191, 219, 220
Montmorin-Saint-Hérem, Armand-Marc, Comte de, to, 797–98; French ambassador to Spain, 715, 720, 723, 730, 731, 752, 753, 759, 771, 773, 775, 777, 779, 780, 782, 793, 794, 795, 798, 801, 802, 809, 826, 827, 830, 831, 834
Montreal, Canada, 185, 191, 192, 208, 248–52
Moore, Sir Henry, 85, 86, 95, 96, 97, 107
Moore, John, 113–114
Moore's Creek Bridge, Battle of, 260
Moot, the, 81, 86, 87, 111, 118
Morehouse, Col. Andrew, 343–44, 345
Morgan, Col. Daniel, 440
Morgan, George, 636
Morgan, Dr. John, from, 601–02; mentioned, 372, 511–12, 602
Morris, Gouverneur, to, 161–62, 386–88, 397–402, 423–24, 468–69, 475–76, 482–84, 496–98, 500–01, 651–52; from, 156–57, 161, 307, 395–96, 471–73, 477, 486–88, 712–13, 746; mentioned, 3, 124, 156, 173, 276, 281, 282, 304, 305, 309, 376, 397, 402, 403, 405, 414, 449, 469, 485, 499, 501, 531, 570, 571, 582, 584, 591, 597, 615, 624, 642, 655, 658, 662, 663, 664, 665, 670, 671, 718, 728, 758; background, 113, 114, 157, 161; describes SLJ, 123–24; on "plan of accommodation," 156–58; in N.Y. State government, 272, 273, 277, 278, 279, 281, 283, 308, 362, 389, 392, 393, 394; in 2d Congress, 408, 431, 432, 452, 468, 472, 473, 484, 501, 507, 557, 558, 669; on abolition of slavery, 402; and the Jays, 413, 414, 416, 484; and British peace proposals, 477–78, 482, 487; and Sir James Jay, 488; on French alliance, 651; on U. S. expansionism, 715; and loss of leg, 788, 789, 821, 822
Morris, Helena, 564
Morris, Maj. Jacob, 372, 468
Morris, Col. Lewis, from, 315, 371–

Morris, Col. (*cont'd*)
72, 376, 385–86; mentioned, 150, 191, 294, 304, 305, 318, 319, 403, 469, 514, 564; in 2d Congress, 172, 173, 192, 210, 211, 212, 220, 221, 224, 259, 265, 315, 371–72, 376, 385–86
Morris, Maj. Lewis, Jr., 37, 403, 487
Morris, Mary Philipse, 347
Morris, Mary Walton, 372, 564
Morris, Mary White, 762, 788, 821, 822
Morris, Richard, to, 402–03; from, 420–21; mentioned, 420–21, 487, 823
Morris, Robert, to, 140, 315–16, 321, 439, 460, 556, 762, 821; from, 317, 363–66, 369–71; mentioned, 3, 140, 197, 296, 370, 371, 372, 497, 528, 548, 588, 661, 663, 664, 665, 690, 691, 733, 734, 737, 756, 825; in 2d Congress, 315–16, 317, 321, 363–66, 369–71, 439, 460, 556; and Bank of Pennsylvania, 821, 822
Morris, Robert Hunter, 140
Morris, Roger, 346, 347
Morris, Thomas, 588
Morris-Jumel Mansion, N.Y. City, 347
Morristown, N.J., 371, 404, 413–14, 445, 516, 563, 726
Moses Creek, N.Y., 422, 423, 434–35
Mott, Capt. Edward, 190, 191
Mouchard, François, 36, 38
Mouchard, M. and Mme., 30
Mount Defiance, N.Y., 418, 420
Mount Ephraim, N.Y., 337
Mount Independence, N.Y., mentioned, 436, 472, 473; American evacuation of, 420, 422, 423, 427
Mount Washington, N.Y. *See* Fort Washington
Moylan, Col. Stephen, 707, 709
Mud Island, Pa., 450
Muller, Carel, 480
Munro, Eve Jay, mentioned, 31, 32, 33, 35, 36, 37, 48, 50, 62, 443, 635, 689; marriage of, 32
Munro, Rev. Dr. Harry, mentioned, 635, 651; background, 32, 33; and JJ's marriage, 124; Loyalist, 443
Munro, Peter Jay, mentioned, 32, 33, 635, 651, 683, 686, 688, 787
Munro, William, 105
Murray, George, 34
Murray, Brig. Gen. James, 216, 218
Murray, Lindley, law clerk, 52, 67; on JJ as clerk, 67; in debating society, 92, 93
Murray, Robert and John, 143, 144
Muzquiz, Miguel de, Marquez de Villar y Ladron, Conde de García, 827, 835

Nantes, France, 439, 588, 628
Nantes, Edict of, 29, 30
Nantucket, Mass., 456
Naturalization, and N.Y. State Constitution, 15
Necker, Jacques, 600, 718
Neil, Rev. Hugh, 85, 86
Nelson, Thomas, 221, 266, 267, 370
Netherlands, the, mentioned, 162, 163, 270, 275, 361, 820; and loans for U.S., 519, 520, 599, 600, 644, 645, 649, 827, 833, 834; and England, 598, 626, 731–32, 769, 820
Neufville, Jan de & Zoon, from, 762–64; mentioned, 695, 696, 768, 779, 803, 804, 806
Newark, N.J., 360
New Britain, N.Y., petition of inhabitants of, 122–23
New Brunswick, N.J., 375, 417, 450
New England, mentioned, 51; delegates in 2d Continental Congress, 276, 281; rivalry with New York, 418, 433, 434, 435, 444, 472, 507, 579
Newfoundland, mentioned, 326; fisheries of, 328–29, 649–50, 715
New Hampshire, state, 252, 314, 471, 510, 528, 540, 783; 792; and boundary dispute, 102–03, 511, 727. *See also* Vermont and Vermont Lands
New Hampshire Grants. *See* Vermont Lands
New Haven, Conn., mentioned, 496; correspondence with New York City committee, 12, 142, 143–44
New Jersey, College of, 86, 114, 819
New Jersey, colony, 135, 152; state, 11, 253, 257, 266, 318, 360, 361, 482, 536–37; government of, 120, 148, 196, 372, 413–14, 607–08; troops in, 194, 203, 204, 252, 375–76, 448, 450, 485, 549; and Congressional delegation, 283, 370–71; and military activity in, 324, 325, 359–60, 362, 415, 416, 425–26, 788–89. *See also* N.Y.–N.J. Boundary Commission

New London, Conn., 539, 691
Newport, R.I., 490, 808, 809
New Rochelle, N.Y., 23
New Windsor, N.Y., 297
New York City, mentioned, 7, 8, 43, 86, 106, 107, 114, 142, 144, 147, 161, 172, 188–89, 192, 229, 273, 278, 282, 295–97, 298, 308, 309, 310, 313, 315, 321, 323, 332, 333, 346, 347, 350, 353, 354, 355, 358, 359, 363, 365–66, 370, 371, 379, 391, 434, 450, 470, 473, 485, 490, 501, 502, 537–38, 539, 550–51, 562, 564–66, 567, 569, 573, 645, 691, 760, 776 807, 811, 813; Committees of, Fifteen, 23, 134; Fifty-One, 12, 23, 129, 130, 132, 133, 134, 135, 141; Mechanics, 133, 135, 253, 254; One Hundred, 23, 138, 145, 161, 182, 229; Sixty, 12, 23, 141–44, 145, 147
———, colony, 9, 10, 11, 12, 43, 44, 50, 51, 52, 62, 84, 86, 87, 96, 97, 102–03, 104, 105, 110, 111, 112, 113, 114, 119, 120, 129, 130, 131, 132–33;
———, county, 296, 309, 501
———, state, mentioned, 174–75, 176, 179, 180, 181, 182, 204, 211, 235, 236, 241, 242, 245, 246, 253, 256–58, 259, 262, 273, 274, 307, 309, 325, 336, 338, 368, 372, 373, 379, 385, 404, 437, 455, 457, 471, 501, 554, 584, 605, 606, 633, 635, 655, 660, 820, 823; Provincial Convention, 142, 143, 145, 173, 214; 1st Provincial Congress, from, 155, 165; mentioned, 13, 23, 24, 145, 147, 148–150, 151, 155, 156–57, 158, 160, 162–65, 172, 174, 175, 176, 180, 182, 214; 2d Provincial Congress, 181, 182, 186, 188, 189, 192, 193, 194, 195, 197, 201, 202, 203, 204, 205–07, 208, 210, 211, 212, 213, 214, 217, 218, 237, 239, 242, 246, 253, 254, 257, 258, 259, 265; 3d Provincial Congress, 262, 263, 264, 266, 267, 268, 269–70, 271, 272, 273, 274, 277, 278, 279, 281, 282; 4th Provincial Congress, 24, 277, 282, 287, 306, 346, 389, 403, 405, 421; Convention of the Representatives, to, 310; from, 289–92; mentioned, 24, 25, 287, 289–93, 307, 309, 310, 314, 318, 319–20, 325, 346, 351, 352, 356–58, 362, 363,
New York state (*cont'd*) 367–68, 371, 372, 373, 377–78, 379, 382, 384, 385, 411, 415, 416, 417, 420–24, 427, 430–31, 432, 438, 451, 454, 455, 458, 500, 501; Constitution of 1777, 14–15, 24, 389–404, 406–08, 420–21, 452, 454, 455, 549; Council of Revision, 14, 390, 420, 421, 465, 478, 500, 546, 547, 561, 562, 571, 605; Council of Appointment, 390, 397–99, 402, 420, 421, 469, 501; legislature, 25, 460, 461–63, 466, 469, 481, 482, 483, 510, 551, 553, 554, 571, 575, 605, 655, 656; judiciary, 25, 349, 411, 420–21, 465, 466, 474, 478. *See also* Committee for Detecting Conspiracies, Committee of Safety, Committee on the Defense of the Hudson, Council of Safety, N.Y.–N.J. Boundary Commission, Vermont lands
New York Hospital, 23
New York Journal (John Holt), 194, 429, 432, 461, 479, 481, 499
New York–New Jersey Boundary Commission, 9, 10–11, 23, 118–22
New York Packet, 361–62, 431, 461
Nicoll, Edward, 240, 502
Nicoll, Samuel, 502, 536
Nine Partners Patent, 467, 634
Nonimportation, 132, 133, 136, 141, 144, 169. *See also* Continental Association
North, Frederick, Lord, mentioned, 194, 475; reconciliation motion of, 148, 171, 192, 193, 204, 206, 210, 473, 474, 475, 477, 478, 482, 484, 487
North Carolina, state, 260, 726, 740
North Castle, N.Y., 362, 363
Norton, Lot, 300, 301
Norwalk, Conn., 455
Nova Scotia, Canada, 197, 650
Nugent, Eduardo, 723

O'Bryen, Christopher, 224, 226
Odell, James, 297, 298
Ogden, Aaron, 684
Ogden, David, 68, 69, 70
Ogden, Euphemia Morris, 413, 414
Ogden, Hannah Dayton, 684, 712
Ogden, Col. Matthias, 417, 418, 684
Ogden, Robert, 703, 704
Ogden, Samuel, 413, 414
Ogilvie, Rev. John, 85, 86

Ohio River, 549, 565–66
"Olive Branch" Petition (Dickinson), 12–13, 147, 148, 149, 150–51, 172, 194, 197, 199, 201; JJ supports, 12, 24, 147, 148, 149
"Olive Branch" Petition (JJ draft), 12, 149, 150–51, 152–54
Onondaga, N.Y., 589–90
Orange County, N.Y., 86, 111, 132, 141, 411, 571
O'Reilly, Alexander, Count, 699, 705, 709, 723, 786, 787, 796
O'Reilly, Rosa de las Casas, Countess, 705, 709
Oriskany, Battle of, 442
Orvilliers, Louis Guillouet, Comte d', 502, 503
Osborn, Dr. Cornelius, 342, 345
Osborne, Sir Danvers, 37, 38
Oyster Bay, N.Y., 334

Paca, Anne Harrison, 696, 698
Paca, William, 636, 698
Paine, Robert Treat, 184, 185, 186
Paine, Thomas, from 522–26; mentioned, 197, 508; *The Crisis Number 1*, 359–61; and disclosures about French aid, 508, 513, 521, 522, 526–27, 530; Congressional investigation of, 508, 522–26, 530–31
Palmer, Rev. Solomon, 41, 42
Palmer, Thomas, 208
Paoli, Battle of, 491
Pardo, Madrid, Spain, 696, 730, 733, 758, 759
Parker, Adm. Sir Peter, 304, 305
Parliament, mentioned, 12, 81, 129, 136, 147, 148, 150, 153, 157, 158, 164, 169, 170, 171, 192, 201, 204, 275, 312, 314, 490, 491, 814–16, acts of, 129, 148, 155, 157, 162, 163, 164, 254; JJ on trade regulation of, 150, 151, 153
Parr's Villa, Pa., 168
Parsippany, N.J., 448, 467, 521, 534, 568, 594
Parsons, Brig. Gen. Samuel Holden, 312, 314
Paulding, William, 295
Paulus Hook, Battle of, 511
Pawling, N.Y., 342
Peale, Charles Willson, 642
Pearsons, Edward, 46, 47
Peekskill, N.Y., mentioned, 325, 368, 377, 430; British raid on, 378, 380–81, 382–84, 404
Pell, Philip, Jr., 318
Pell, Samuel Treadwell, 292, 293–94
Peloquin, David and John, to, from Peter Jay, 36–37, 38–39, 46–47, 50–51, 60, 62; from, to Peter Jay, 47–48; mentioned, 34, 35, 36, 37, 38, 39, 40, 43, 44, 45, 47, 62; and assistance to James Jay, 36–38; on law apprenticeship in England, 47, 50, 62
Peloquin, Françoise, 39
Peloquin, Françoise Jay, 29, 30, 39
Peloquin, Marianne, 39
Peloquin, Stephen, 30, 39
Pendleton, Edmund, to, 641; from, 645, 657–58; mentioned, 628
Penn, John, from, 628; mentioned, 642
Penn, Thomas, 822
Pennsylvania, mentioned, 136, 197, 257, 268, 360, 361, 448, 450, 469, 477, 485, 486, 491, 509, 511, 790, 791; government of, 136, 196, 266, 267, 268, 269, 283, 387, 388, 618, 750, 756, 823; military affairs in, 241, 242, 252, 259, 371, 440, 448, 520, 562; Congressional delegation, 267, 283, 579; constitution of, 364, 366, and JJ on, 468, 562; and Continental Congress, 509–10
Pennsylvania Gazette, 475, 487
Pennsylvania Journal, 360, 361
Pennsylvania Packet, 198, 507, 508, 512, 530
Pennsylvania, University of, 749, 750
Penny, Timothy, 609–10
Pensacola, Fla., 670, 671, 726, 825
Perry, Lt. Mervin, 104, 105
Peters, Richard, 264, 265
Petersham, Charles Stanhope, Viscount, 449, 450
Petition to the King, 1774, 147, 151, 152
Pettit, Charles, 607, 608, 609
Phelps, Charles, 632, 633, 635, 658
Philadelphia, Pa., mentioned, 114, 133, 135, 152, 164, 176, 188–89, 287, 316, 318, 360, 387, 439, 444, 492, 493, 501, 502, 503, 509, 520–21, 534, 545, 568, 691, 749, 750, 755, 758, 790; committees of, 167, 176, 642, 657; fear of British attack on, 321, 360, 363–64, 366, 374, 375, 377, 379, 385,

Philadelphia (*cont'd*)
386; Continental Congress returns to, 374, 376; miliary events in, 385, 386, 541, 549; postal service of, 516
Philadelphia, College of, 73, 750
Philipse, Adolphus, 31, 32
Philipse, Frederick, 346, 347, 349
Philipse Manor, N.Y., 314
Phillips, Maj. Gen. William, to, 537–38
Phoenix, 295, 297
Pickering, Timothy, from, 621–23
Piquenit, Samuel, 46, 47, 50
Pitcairn, Capt. Thomas, from, 594–95; mentioned, 595
Pitts Town, N.J., 372
Plater, George, 670, 671
Plato, JJ's servant, 643
Platt, Jonathan, 791, 792
Platt, Zephaniah, mentioned, 385, 386, 433, 434, 527; in N.Y. State government, 331, 332, 337, 340, 341, 397–98, 402, 501, 528
Point Levis, Canada, 183, 185
Pollack, Oliver, 717
Pontiac's War, 47, 48
Poor, Brig. Gen. Enoch, 409
Porter, Joshua, 297–98, 300, 301–04
Portsmouth, England, 820
Portsmouth, N.H., 385
Portugal, mentioned, 326, 369, 371, 820; American affairs in, 626, 779, 780, 790, 805, 809
Post, David, 236
Potts, Dr. Jonathan, 252
Poughkeepsie, N.Y., 295, 297, 298, 299, 300, 301, 306, 344, 461, 467, 473, 481, 486, 499, 502, 548–49
Prescott, Maj. Gen. Richard, 191, 192, 312, 314
Price, James, 258, 259
Price, Michael, 182
Princeton, N.J., mentioned, 372; Battle of, 378–79
Prizes, JJ's draft resolution on, 254–56
"Proofs that the Colonies Do Not Aim at Independence" (JJ), 198–200; mentioned, 12, 194, 196–97, 201
Prudden, Nathaniel, 583
Prussia, 326, 330, 626, 631, 820
Puerto de Santa Maria, 699, 702, 705
Pulaski, Brig. Gen. Casimir, Count, 577, 578, 725, 727
Punderson, Rev. Ebenezer, from, 52–53; mentioned, 41, 42, 51, 53
Punderson, Hannah Miner, 52, 53
Putnam County, N.Y., 334, 338
Putnam, Maj. Gen. Israel, mentioned, 313, 314, 450, 485, 486; military service, 419, 460, 461, 475; and loss of Forts Montgomery and Clinton, 468, 469, 472, 473, 497, 498

Quackenbos, Capt. John, 175, 177
Quakers, 448, 450
Quebec Act, 137, 138, 250, 252, 815, 820
Quebec, Canada, 183, 184, 185, 190, 208, 218, 220, 234, 240, 248–52, 404, 417
Queens County, N.Y., mentioned, 86, 213, 218, 226; disaffection in, 195, 214–15, 218
Queneau & Co., 806

Randall, Robert Richard, to, 116–18; mentioned, 11, 117
Randall, Thomas, 117
Randolph, Edmund, 628
Ranger, 615
Rapalje, Garret, 107
Rapalje, Stephen, to, 166; mentioned, 114, 166
Read, George, 386
Reade, John, 114, 116
Redding, David, 493, 496
Reed, Joseph, 293, 562
Reemer, Frederick, 480
Reformed Dutch Church, N.Y. City, 32
Revenge, 614, 615, 784
Rhode Island, mentioned, 476, 539, 569, 674, 726, 807; Battle of, 489
Richard, Esther, 125
Richard (or Richards), Paul, 36, 38
Richelieu (or Sorel) River, Canada, 176, 177, 183, 185
Richmond County, N.Y., 132, 213, 214, 215, 218, 226, 241, 242
Riedesel, Frederike Charlotte Luise, Baroness von, 536, 537
Riesdesel, Maj. Gen. Friedrich Adolph, Baron von, 537
Riker, Capt. Abraham, 383, 384
Risberg, Gustavus, from, 591; mentioned, 592
Rittenhouse, David, 327, 330
Ritzema, Lt. Col. Rudolphus, 216, 218
Rivington, James, mentioned, 144, 145, 188, 189

Rivington's New York Gazeteer, mentioned, 145, 170; Sears' raid on, 188, 189, 201–02, 207, 210
Robertson, Capt. William, 630, 631
Robinson, Beverly, from, 349–50; mentioned, 354; active Loyalist, 345–46, 347, 384; committee examination of, 347–48; JJ on, 352–54
Robinson, Beverly, Jr., 341–42, 346, 347, 348
Robinson, Robert, 182
Robinson, Susanna Philipse, to, 352–54; mentioned, 125, 346, 349–50
Rochambeau, Jean-Baptiste-Donatien de Vimeur, Comte de, 760
Rodney, Adm. Sir George Brydges, 723, 736, 799
Rogers, Benjamin, 480
Rogers, Maj. Nicholas, from, 409–10; mentioned, 327, 330
Rogers, Maj. Robert, 362, 363, 464
Rogers, William, 480
Rohan, Cardinal Louis René Eduourd de, 774
Romans, Capt. Bernard, 240, 241
Rome, 88, 91–94
Rondout Creek, N.Y., 354
Roomes, Lawrence, 53
Roosevelt, I., 99, 101
Root, Jesse, 606
Rose, 295, 297, 312
Rose (or Roosa), Jacobus, 355–56, 357
Ross, John, 767, 769, 794
Rush, Dr. Benjamin, 511, 512, 750
Russell, Ebenezer, 501
Russell, John, 340–41
Russia, mentioned, 170, 626, 763, 764; offers mediation, 584
Rutherford, John, 564
Rutherford, Walter, 105
Rutledge, Edward, from, 275–76, 280–81, 304–05, 322–23, 515–16; in 2d Congress, 12, 220, 221, 263, 264, 265, 270, 275–76, 280–81, 304–05, 315, 322–23, 388
Rutledge, John, 149, 629, 630
Rye, N.Y., mentioned, 5, 23, 33, 86, 305, 318, 319; Anglican parish of, 40, 41, 42

Sackett, Nathaniel, 331, 337–38, 340, 342, 343, 345
Sailor's Snug Harbor, 117
St. Clair, Maj. Gen. Arthur, from, 428–29; mentioned, 423, 424, 440, 656; evacuates Ticonderoga, 418, 419, 422, 423, 426–29; on Schuyler, 428–31; relieved of command, 433, 434; court-martial of, 469, 470, 472, 473, 483
St. Cyril, 703, 704
St. Johns, Canada, mentioned, 324, 417; American campaign against, 175, 176, 177, 180, 185, 186, 189, 191, 192, 202, 204, 207, 245; Articles of Capitulation of, 185, 186–87, 188
St. Kitts, 776
St. Lawrence River, 177, 183, 185, 323, 404
St. Leger, Lt. Col. Barry, 417
St. Luc de la Corne, Pierre, 183, 185
St. Lucia, 561
St. Ours, Canada, 251, 252
St. Pierre, Martinique. *See* Martinique
Salisbury, Conn., ironworks at, 295–99, 302; JJ at, 300–03, 306–07
Sands, Comfort, 514, 515, 575
Sandy Hook, N.Y., 177, 489
San Ildefonso, mentioned, 696, 758, 759, 797, 798, 799, 802; Conference at, 825–34
Saratoga, 822
Saratoga, N.Y., mentioned, 420, 435, 436, 440, 535, 536, 619, 620; Battle of, 408, 409, 422, 432–33, 434–35, 438, 439, 440, 446, 447, 450, 491, 512, 538; Articles of Capitulation of, 446, 447
Savannah, Ga., mentioned, 725, 726, 727; siege and capture of, 634, 670, 671
Savile, Sir George, 815, 820
Schuyler, 235, 258
Schuyler, Arent, 118
Schuyler, Catherine Van Rensselaer, 734
Schuyler, Harmanus, 84
Schuyler, Hon Yost, 440
Schuyler, Maj. Peter B., 261, 262
Schuyler, Philip, to, 419, 429–31, 444, 452–53, 465, 466, 503, 532, 579–80, 733–34; from, 410–11, 416, 426–28, 432–33, 434–37, 463–64, 534–36, 573–74, 589; mentioned, 15, 175, 176, 185–87, 191, 197, 211, 228, 229, 231, 256, 258, 259, 261, 262, 303, 321, 395, 420, 423, 424, 427, 428, 429, 438, 440, 445, 453, 454,

Schuyler, Philip (*cont'd*)
476, 490, 499, 532, 533, 573–74; military career of, 160, 185, 322, 323, 408, 411, 416, 418, 419, 422, 425, 427, 429–31, 433, 434, 435, 463–65, 515, 532, 533, 534–36, 573, 574, 579–80, 589; political career of, 408, 411, 412–13, 417, 426, 435, 475, 476, 482, 483, 492, 496, 501, 511, 584, 589, 590, 655; Congressional investigations of, 387, 388, 406–08, 496, 503, 529, 534, 536; JJ supports, 412–13, 418, 429–31, 434, 444, 452–53, 466, 492–93, 503, 579–80; and Ticonderoga, 416, 419, 426–28, 429–31, 432, 434, 435, 444, 452–53, 491–93; Commissioner for Indian Affairs, 441, 442, 444, 589; court-martial of, 469, 470, 472, 473, 483
Scott, Capt. Alexander, 304, 305
Scott, John Morin, to, 134–35; from, to N.Y. Provincial Convention, 310–13; mentioned, 50, 134, 314, 380, 427, 428, 501, 655, 658; political career of, 97, 123, 135, 158, 204, 206, 272, 273, 275, 307–08, 393, 394, 416, 417, 483, 485, 501, 546, 547; lawyear, 107, 111, 123
Scudder, Nathaniel, 597
Scull, Maj. Peter, 714
Seabury, Samuel, 546, 547, 561
Seagrove, James, 113
Searle, James, 790, 791
Sears, Isaac, mentioned, 189, 236, 237, 244; raid of, 188, 189, 201–02, 207, 210
Secker, Thomas, Archbishop of Canterbury, 40, 41
Seine, 530–31
Serapis, 631
Seven Years' War. *See* French and Indian War
Shakespeare, William, 390
Shaver, Daniel, 480
Sheldon, Capt. Joseph, 343, 345
Sheriff, Cornelius, 640, 641
Sherman, Roger, in 2d Congress, 276, 387, 472, 473; on Vermont, 494, 496
Shippen, Dr. William, 511–12, 601, 602
Shuker, Thomas, petition of, 784–86
Sicilies, Kingdom of the Two, 820
Skene, Philip, 422, 423
Skenesboro, N.Y., 422, 423, 436, 440
Skinner, Ensign Abraham, 308, 309
Slavery, mentioned, 136, 137, 353, 402, 544, 545; JJ opposed to, 2, 401, 702, 823
Smallpox, 33, 252
Smart, George, 297, 298
Smith, James, from, 813–19; mentioned, 819, 820
Smith, Melancton, 158, 342, 344, 347, 351
Smith, Meriwether, 636
Smith, Richard, 197
Smith, Thomas, 158, 203, 204, 206
Smith, Rev. William, 73, 750
Smith, William, Jr., mentioned, 71, 123, 133, 152, 192, 193; and conciliation with England, 150, 204; Loyalist, 358, 359, 812, 813, 819
Social Club, The, 81, 112–14, 115
Socialborough Patent, 103
Society for the Propagation of the Gospel, 41, 42
Solano, Adm. Josef, 799
Somerset, 539–40
South Amboy, N.J., 362, 363, 485
South Carolina, 304, 305, 325, 561, 566, 567, 629, 630, 740, 825
Spain, JJ mission to, 2, 15, 16, 25, 113, 509, 547, 649–52, 714–835; and Congressional instructions, 650, 651, 722, 830–31; aids and loans to U.S., 327, 507, 650, 716–17, 718, 732, 787, 793, 826, 827, 828, 831, 834; treaties with France, 569–70, 649–50; mediation offers of, 626, 649; on Gibraltar, 649, 716, 717, 831; military activities in the Floridas, 670, 671, 712, 713, 726, 728, 730, 813, 825; Irish colony in, 692, 707, 723, 776; travel in, 693, 694, 699–702, 705–08; attitudes toward U.S., 715, 738, 751, 765, 793, 804, 805, 829–30, 833–34; secret negotiations with England, 717, 771, 772, 773, 774, 775, 776, 779, 780–81, 801, 807, 826; on American independence, 765, 766, 829, 830, 833; capture of Mobile, Ala., 772, 813; on French treaty with U.S., 829–30; peace objectives of, 649–50, 830–31
Sparks, Jared, 4
Spencer, Maj. Gen. Joseph, 313, 314, 324, 325
Spencer, Col. Oliver, 622, 623
Spencer, Thomas, 442

Springfield, N.J., 417, 788, 789, 812–13
Stamp Act, repeal of, 81, 82; Congress of, 136
Stanhope, Philip, 442–43
Stark, Brig. Gen. John, 463, 464, 474, 493
Staten Island, N.Y., 296, 314, 347, 354, 417; Battle of, 739, 741. *See also* Richmond County
Stevens, Lt. Col. Ebenezer, 476–77
Stevens, John, 114
Stevenson, John, 332–33
Stewart, Col. Charles, 476, 477, 591, 592
Stewart, Col. Walter, 670, 671, 728
Stillwater, N.Y., 420, 423, 435, 436
Stirling, Lord. *See* Alexander, William
Stony Point, Battle of, 511, 620, 621, 624
Storer, Ebenezer, 667, 668
Stouppe, Rev. Peter, 33–34
Strang, John, 145, 177, 178
Stuyvesant, Gerardus, 31, 32
Stuyvesant, Peter, 29
Suetonius, 765, 766
Suffolk, County, N.Y., 208, 215, 308, 314, 354, 394
Sugar Loaf Mountain, N.Y., 418
Sullivan, Brig. Gen. John, from, 615–18; mentioned, 626–27, 637, 640; military career, 310, 312, 314–15, 377, 489–90, 539; Indian campaign, 511, 615–18, 621, 622, 623
Swartwout, Capt. Abraham, 384, 385
Swartwout, Col. Jacobus, 338, 339, 340, 344, 347, 351
Sweden, 820
Switzerland, 326
Sykes, James, 386

Tallmadge, Benjamin, 335
Tallmadge, Mary Floyd, 335
Tanner, John, 666, 668
Tappen, Christopher, and committee to defend the Hudson, to, from JJ, 301–03; from, to Washington, 298–99; mentioned, 295, 296, 298, 299
Ten Broeck, Abraham, 360, 481
Ten Broeck, Cornelis, 84
Ten Broeck, Dirck Wessels, 501
Ten Broeck, John, to, 412; mentioned, 412
Ternay, Charles-Henri d'Arsac, Chevalier de, 759, 760, 792, 801, 804–05, 807, 808, 809, 811, 813
Tetard, John Peter, 584, 585
Texel, the Netherlands, 615
Thomas, John, Jr., 318, 319–20
Thomas, Col. Thomas, 318–20
Thompson, Col. William, 304, 305
Thomson, Benjamin, 197
Thomson, Charles, mentioned, 523–24, 526, 527, 530, 531, 532, 534, 540, 544, 577; secretary of Congress, 136, 248, 519, 589, 595, 596, 600, 602, 604, 608, 610, 613, 615, 618, 630, 634, 641, 662, 663, 664, 665, 718, 731, 835
Three Rivers, Canada, 249, 250, 252
Thurman, John, 141, 142
Ticonderoga, N.Y. *See* Fort Ticonderoga
Tilghman, Col. Tench, 564
Tobias, Thomas, 362, 363
"To the Oppressed Inhabitants of Canada" (JJ), 24, 147, 151
Tories. *See* Loyalists
Toulon, France, 490–91
Townsend, Capt. Micah, 338–40, 344
Townsend, Robert, 335–36
Townsend, Capt. Samuel, 310, 394
Townshend, Thomas, 129
Treason, 278, 279
Treaties, Alliance, 1778, 328–29, 330, 473, 474, 475, 477; Amity and Commerce, 1778, 474, 475, 722, 791, 792, 829, 830; Aranjuez, 570, 649, 650, 651; Kuchuk Kainarji, 626, 627; Paris, 1763, 121
Trecothick, Barlow, 73
Trent, William, 636
Trenton, N.J., mentioned, 283, 372, 561; Battle of, 14, 363, 378–79
Trinity Church, N.Y. City, 29, 32, 33, 34, 62, 63, 85, 86
Troup, John, 593, 594
Troup, Robert, from, 177–78, 378–79, 382–84, 403–04, 408–09, 424–25, 439–40, 485–86, 489–90, 502, 536–37, 551–52, 593; mentioned, 145, 166, 167, 529, 537; JJ's law clerk, 167, 177, 178; in military service, 404, 502, 536–37, 552
Trumbull, Gov. Jonathan, from, 602–04; mentioned, 202, 204, 207, 519, 520, 644; and defense of Hudson River, 298, 299, 300, 301–03
Trumbull, Joseph, 244, 258, 259, 368
Tryon, Gov. William, mentioned, 106, 123, 130, 131, 192, 193, 197, 203,

Tryon, Gov. (*cont'd*) 204, 206, 210, 228, 229, 230, 231, 237, 278, 282, 292, 354; and Vermont grants, 103, 104; and N.Y.–N.J. boundary, 119, 120–21; and JJ's and Livingston's proposal, 130–31, 132–33
Tryon County, N.Y., 132, 423, 424, 432
Tudor, Samuel, 296, 380
Tudor, William, 476, 477
Turner, Alexander, 104, 105
Tuscany, Italy, 327
Tyler, John, 85, 86

Ulster County, N.Y., 25, 86, 132, 295, 297, 298, 331, 341, 344, 354, 355–56, 368, 375, 389, 394, 411, 571
United Provinces. *See* Netherlands
Ushant, Battle of, 502, 503

Vallette, Augustus, 36
Vallette, Marie Jay, 30, 31, 32, 38, 39, 40
Vallette, Peter, 37, 38
Vallette, Peter (Pierre), 30, 31, 32, 35, 36
Valley Forge, Pa., 447, 468, 469, 472
Val Alstyne, Abraham, 481
Van Cortlandt, Augustus, from, 308–09; mentioned, 8, 42, 43, 309
Van Cortlandt, Eve Philipse, 30
Van Cortlandt, Françoise Jay, 30, 31, 32, 36, 43, 308
Van Cortlandt, Frederick, 30, 31, 32
Van Cortlandt, Jacobus, 30, 31, 32
Van Cortlandt, James, 32, 33, 34, 36
Van Cortlandt, Col., Philip, 238, 239–40, 292, 293, 383, 384
Van Cortlandt, Pierre, 67, 411, 419, 420, 421, 424, 430, 432
Vandalia, 635–36
Vandenburgh, Henry, 290, 293
Van Deusen, James, 297, 298
Van Deusen, Jan, 359
Van Dyck, Henry, 63
Van Gaasbeck, Peter, 345
Van Horne, Ann French, 449, 450, 685, 691
Van Horne, Augustus, 99, 101
Van Horne, Cornelius, 30, 31, 32, 33, 34, 36
Van Horne, David, 450
Van Horne, Garret, 205
Van Horne, Judith Jay, 30, 36, 101
Vanhorne's Lessee v. *Dorrance*, 137
Van Ness, Abraham, 480
Van Ness, John, 481
Van Ness, Col. Peter, 344, 345
Van Rensselaer, Col. John, 123
Van Schaack, David, 333
Van Schaack, Elizabeth Cruger, 80, 81
Van Schaack, Peter, to, 470; mentioned, 80, 81, 88, 92, 113; as Loyalist, 331–33
Van Schaick, Col. Goose, 243, 244, 589–90
Van Weissenfels, Lt. Col. Frederick, 239
Van Wyck, Dr. Theodorus, 319, 345, 380–81, 382, 421–22, 591, 634, 635, 702
Van Wyck, William, 591, 642
Van Zandt, Jacobus, 296
Vardill, John, to, 130–32, 137–38; mentioned, 129, 134, 138, 142; in debating society, 88, 91; in England, 132
Vaughan, Thomas, 667, 668, 714
Vaux, Noël de Jourda, Comte de, 600, 601
Venus, 784
Vergennes, Charles Gravier, Comte de, to, 752–53; mentioned, 330, 718, 719, 722, 770, 801, 834
Vermont, state, mentioned, 432, 478, 493, 540, 584, 624, 652–53, 658, 726, 823; declaration of statehood, 387–89, 510, 528
Vermont lands, controversy with New York, 25, 102, 103, 273, 387–89, 469, 470, 471, 472, 484, 494, 496, 498, 499, 510–11, 513, 527, 528, 545, 546, 553, 554, 605, 606, 624–25, 632, 633, 635, 636, 652, 653, 655, 792, 823; New Hampshire Grants petitioners, 274; and 2d Congress, 274, 494, 496, 498, 528, 553, 554, 605, 606, 624, 636, 652, 653–55, 656, 727, 791–92, 823; JJ on, 11, 102, 103, 104–05, 469, 470, 484, 498, 499, 510–11, 513, 527, 528, 625, 635–36, 652–53, 654, 656, 823
Ver Planck, Gulian, 31, 32, 232
Ver Planck, Gulian, Jr., 113, 114, 118
Ver Planck, Samuel, 118
Vesey, Rev. William, 31, 32
Viper, 175, 177
Virginia, mentioned, 234–35, 240, 253, 266, 267, 276, 509, 549, 645, 690,

Virginia (*cont'd*)
726, 740, 820; General Assembly of, 624, 625; and Western land claims, 635–36, 660, 791
Virginius, 92–95

Wadsworth, Jeremiah, to, 623–24; from, 595–96; mentioned, 632, 634, 637; and Commissary Department, 595–96, 597
Walker, Thomas, 191
Wallace, Hugh, 373
Walloomsac, N.Y., 342, 345
Walton, George, 364, 366, 370, 725, 727
Warner, Lt. Col. Seth, 249, 252
Washington, George, to, 247, 541, 569, 585, 620–21, 626–27; to, from N.Y. Committees, 279, 298; to, from Greene, 280; from, 656–57; from, to Greene, 279; from, to SLJ, 656; mentioned, 2, 3, 16, 288, 300, 313, 314, 347, 373, 404, 409, 419, 420, 427, 446, 448, 450, 465, 512, 562, 563, 568, 573, 576, 582, 585, 588, 589, 602, 616, 617, 637, 740, 760, 807, 811; and Hickey Plot, 14, 277, 278, 279; and N.Y. defense, 148, 282, 289, 296, 323; military service of, 185, 247–48, 259, 273, 274, 324, 325, 360, 362, 363, 377, 418, 425–26, 431, 432, 433, 434, 440, 447, 448, 450, 461, 464–65, 475, 477, 485, 486, 490, 491, 511, 539, 540, 541–42, 551, 562, 564, 576–78, 579; on Schuyler, 435, 444, 535, 579; and Conway Cabal, 498, 511, 513, 515–16; and Indians, 532, 618, 619, 622, 623
Washington, Martha, 563
Waterbury, Col. David, 191, 192
Watkins, Maj. John Watkyn, Jr., 560, 561
Watts, John, 185
Watts, John, Jr., 81, 102, 113, 118
Watts, Stephen, 183, 185
Wayne, Gen. Anthony, to, 621; mentioned, 626, 627; military career, 490, 491, 621
Webb, Col. Samuel Blatchley, 564, 568
Webster, Pelatiah, 624, 625
Wentworth, Gov. Benning, 103
West, William, 370, 372, 691
West, William, Jr., 370, 371, 372
Westchester County, N.Y., 86, 130,
Westchester County (*cont'd*)
132, 144, 145, 147, 157, 158, 161, 204, 207, 295, 296, 313, 314, 318–20, 323, 334, 338, 345, 349, 354, 498
West Indies, British, 121, 164, 173–74, 175, 176, 328, 561
West Point, N.Y., 174, 175, 176, 179, 591, 726
Western Lands, 508, 509, 511, 660. *See also* Virginia
Wetmore, Rev. James, 32, 33, 40, 41
Weyman, William, publisher of *New-York Gazette; or, The Weekly Post-Boy*, 52, 63
Wharton, Carpenter, 258, 259
Wharton, Francis, 664
Wharton, Thomas, 388, 447
Wheeler, Dr. Lemuel, 300
Wherry, Evans, 290, 293
Whipple, William, 588, 597, 615
Whitcomb, 2d Lt. Benjamin, 251, 252, 403–04, 405
Whitcomb, 1st Lt. Elisha, 251, 252
White, Eva Van Cortlandt, 101
White Eyes, Capt., 270–71
White, Henry, 99, 101
White Plains, N.Y., mentioned, 145, 147, 281, 282, 287, 292, 295, 305, 306, 310, 324, 339–40, 345, 485, 489, 497, 499; Battle of, 323, 325
Wickham, William, 684
Wilcox, Hazard, 342
Wilkes, John, 815
Wilkinson, Lt. Col. James, 498
Willett, Col. Marinus, from, 260–62, 440–41, 455–58; mentioned, 244–45, 262, 383, 384, 589, 590
Williams, Col. William, 321
Williamson, Hugh, 328, 330
Wilmington, Del., 440
Wilson, James, 173, 242, 276, 280, 642
Wirt, William, 137
Wirtz, Christian, 620
Wisner, Henry, 281, 389, 394
Witherspoon, Dr. John, 369–70, 371, 606
Wolcott, Oliver, 444–45
Wolfe, Brig. Gen. James, 218
Woodhull, Abraham, 335–36
Woodhull, Nathaniel, 160, 165, 189, 208, 313, 314
Wooster, Brig. Gen. David, 175, 176, 184, 248, 251, 252, 324, 325
Wright, Sir James, 727
Wright, Jotham, 70, 71

Wyncoop, Col. Cornelius, 240
Wythe, George, 196, 242, 256

Yale College, 50, 86, 330
Yates, Abraham, to, 405; on committee to draft N.Y. State Constitution, 14, 389, 391, 392, 394, 395, 405; in N.Y. government, 393, 405, 411, 431, 432, 464, 465, 482, 483
Yates, Peter W., to, 110–11; from, 412; mentioned, 110–11, 412
Yates, Robert, and committee to fortify the Hudson, to, from JJ, 301–03, from, to Washington, 298–99; to,
Yates, Robert (*cont'd*) 386–88; in N.Y. government, 295, 296, 297, 298, 299, 303, 389, 394, 478, 481, 545, 546, 547
Yates, William, Jr., 481
Young, Joseph, 338–39, 344
Young, Dr. Thomas, 387, 388–89
Yranda, Simón de Aragorri y Olavide, Marquis d', 709, 748, 766, 767, 793, 794, 796, 803

Zedwitz, Lt. Col. Herman, 240
Zinovyev, S. S., 799